ECONOMIC TRENDS IN COMMUNIST CHINA

Economic Trends in Communist China

Edited by
ALEXANDER ECKSTEIN, WALTER GALENSON
and TA-CHUNG LIU

★

EDINBURGH
at the University Press

Published 1968 by
EDINBURGH UNIVERSITY PRESS
22 George Square, Edinburgh 8
North America
Aldine Publishing Company
320 West Adams Street, Chicago
Australia and New Zealand
Hodder and Stoughton Ltd.
Africa, Oxford University Press
India, P. C. Manaktala & Sons
Far East, M. Graham Brash & Son
85224 043 0
*Printed in the
United States of America*

Contents

1.	Introduction, *Alexander Eckstein, Walter Galenson, Ta-Chung Liu*	1
2.	The Economic Heritage, *Alexander Eckstein*	33
3.	Quantitative Trends in the Economy, *Ta-Chung Liu*	87
4.	Population Growth, *John S. Aird*	183
5.	Manpower, Employment, and Unemployment, *Chi-ming Hou*	329
6.	Organization for Agricultural Production, *Kenneth R. Walker*	397
7.	Policy and Performance in Agriculture, *Anthony M. Tang*	459
8.	Capital Formation, *K. C. Yeh*	509
9.	Policies and Performance in Industry, *Kang Chao*	549
10.	Industrial Planning and Management, *Dwight H. Perkins*	597
11.	Labor Productivity in Industry, *Robert Michael Field*	637
12.	Foreign Trade, *Feng-Hwa Mah*	671
	Index	739

Preface

THE STUDIES IN this volume were prepared originally for a conference held at Carmel, California, in October, 1965, under the sponsorship of the Social Science Research Council Committee on the Economy of China; they have subsequently been considerably revised. The Committee was appointed by the Social Science Research Council in order to stimulate scholarly analysis of the contemporary economic scene in China. Support for the program was provided by the Ford Foundation.

Through the conference device the Committee hoped to take stock of some of the major current research in the field of Chinese economic studies. Many of the essays that appear as chapters in this book may eventually appear in expanded form as full-fledged monographs.

The Committee is greatly indebted to the scholars who participated in the conference and acted as discussants. Their suggestions were very helpful to the authors in revising the essays for publication. Those present, in addition to the authors, were: Abram Bergson, Joseph Berliner, J. Lossing Buck, Nai-Ruenn Chen, Chu-Yuan Cheng, Shun-Hsin Chou, M. Gardner Clark, Robert F. Dernberger, John D. Durand, George N. Ecklund, Oleg Hoeffding, Albert Feuerwerker, Gregory Grossman, John G. Gurley, Charles Hoffman, William W. Hollister, Ronald Hsia, Edwin F. Jones, Norman M. Kaplan, Anthony Koo, Simon Kuznets, Ching-Wen Kwang, Jung-Chao Liu, Richard Moorsteen, Peter Schran, Franz Schurmann, Shoh-Chieh Tsiang, and Yuan-Li Wu.

The Committee and the editors have endeavored to ensure that the essays contained in this volume are objective and accurate, but final responsibility for content must remain with the individual authors.

ALEXANDER ECKSTEIN
WALTER GALENSON
TA-CHUNG LIU

ECONOMIC TRENDS IN COMMUNIST CHINA

Introduction 1

ALEXANDER ECKSTEIN, WALTER GALENSON, TA-CHUNG LIU

THE ECONOMIC HERITAGE

WHEN THE CHINESE Communists came to power in 1949, they inherited a fragmented, disordered, war-torn economy. Traditionally, it had been fragmented because of an underdeveloped transportation and communications system. It had become only partially commercialized because of both transport and communications barriers and a whole host of market imperfections. In many respects it was not a single economic entity, but three separate economies more or less loosely linked, namely, the traditional sector, a relatively modern sector built around the treaty ports and nearby cities, and the economy of Manchuria, which had been under Japanese occupation since 1931.

The country's lack of industrial development can be illustrated by the fact that the share of modern industry in gross national product was quite small, about 5 per cent measured in 1933 prices, or 10 per cent in 1952 prices. Similarly, all "modern" sectors combined, *i.e.,* modern industry, transport, communications, trade, finance, and government, contributed no more than twice that share. Labor engaged in industry and all other modern sectors combined constituted an even smaller proportion of the total labor force. Furthermore, skilled labor was scarce, and scientific, technical, and managerial manpower was even scarcer in relation to the total size of the country and of the economy.

In absolute terms, however, fairly sizable industrial bases had been developed in Manchuria, in north China, in Chiang-Su province and in the Wu-Han area. By 1949 these bases were weakened by Soviet dismantling of industrial plants in Manchuria, by war-engendered shortages of raw materials, and by hyperinflation. However, although manufacturing facilities in these centers were disrupted, they were not crippled or destroyed. Moreover, for decades prior to the Communist capture of power, mainland China had experienced fairly continuous and sustained growth in the industrial sector. According to a recent study by John Chang, industrial production in China grew at an average rate of 5.5 per cent a year between 1912 and 1949. For shorter periods, such as 1923-36, the rate becomes 8.3 per cent, and for the 1931-36 period it rises to 9.3 per cent. In effect, what these figures show is that abstracting from the war years 1937 to 1949 and confining the period to the years between 1912 and 1936, mainland China's rate of industrial growth may have been as high as about 9 per cent a year. Although the data are imperfect and provide insufficient coverage, they nevertheless suggest a pattern of unusually rapid industrial growth in pre-Communist China. This rate would be substantially above the long-term historical average for most of the industrializing countries. However, it is lower than that for the Soviet Union during the period of its first two Five-Year Plans, and lower than the estimated rates for the First Five-Year Plan period in Communist China.

These findings indicate that the picture of industrial stagnation in pre-Communist China presented in most accounts of the period of the Republic are not valid. In effect, what seems to have occurred is very rapid growth of a very small sector in a preindustrial economy. After a long period of growth, this industrial sector still remained too small to bring about a significant transformation of the economy as a whole. Even in 1949 it remained only a thin peripheral overlay.

While total industrial growth between 1936 and 1949 was limited, there were significant war-induced changes in the structure of industry, which constituted an important element in the inheritance of the Communist regime. These transformations were largely a result of rapid development in the steel, electric power, coal, and engineering industries of Manchuria after the outbreak of the war until about 1942-43. It was accompanied by a decline in consumer goods production, concentrated largely in east China. As a result, the industrial production mix after World War II was different from that before the war, with mining, metallurgy and other heavy industries looming relatively larger. In effect, the Communists inherited an industrial plant in the process of being transformed in ways that were in accord with their scale of preferences.

The industrial developments outlined were almost exclusively confined to Manchuria, a few cities near the coast, and the Wu-Han area. Economic development in Manchuria prior to 1949 presents a sharp contrast to the rest of China. Manchuria in the nineteenth century was a sparsely populated frontier, the development of which can be roughly dated from around 1860, when the region was beginning to be opened to migration from north China. It developed quite rapidly under the interacting impact of land settlement, population growth, railroad development, agricultural production growth, and foreign trade.

Railroad development greatly facilitated the marketing of agricultural products, while the opening of ports stimulated the rise of foreign trade, and these two in combination fostered further expansion in agricultural production and marketing. The Manchurian experience in many ways duplicates the classic development pattern of newly settled areas with rich mineral and agricultural resources. This initial development spurt was followed by the beginnings of industrial development in the 1920's, particularly concentrated in mining. Rapid industrial development in Manchuria can really be dated from 1931 when the Japanese took over this region and created the puppet state of Manchukuo. Infusion of Japanese capital and management in combination with the mineral and agricultural resources of Manchuria provided the necessary conditions for the rapid expansion of a heavy industry base between the early 1930's and the early 1940's.

In the treaty ports, a different pattern of development occurred prior to 1927. Operating within a framework of extraterritoriality, they could provide the minimum conditions of law and order, freedom from tax pressure and exactions, and escape from the devastations of warlordism and civil war, all of which were necessary to permit a cumulative process of economic expansion. In this process, foreign trade in the early nineteenth century stimulated a demand for the development of financial facilities. Up to the middle of the century foreign trade had to be financed by the trading firms themselves. This necessarily limited the scope of the trade and the number of firms that could enter it. However, the rise of modern banking and insurance companies, particularly between 1858 and 1864, facilitated the entry of smaller merchants into foreign trade. We see here a sequence—the growth of foreign trade giving rise to a demand for banking facilities, which in turn furthered the expansion and widening of foreign trade, leading to the processing of export products, such as tea and silk, in the treaty ports and nearby cities, as well as to the processing of certain import products that were consumed in these regions. The latter involved the growth of such food-processing industries as flour milling, sugar refining, and brewing. In turn, this development, with a growth of foreign trade and allied industries, necessarily led to population growth in these areas. This stimulated the demand for public utilities, such as water, gas, electricity, and local transport. The development of public utilities and of shipping increased the demand for coal. At the same time, there was a need for engineering shops to service these enterprises. The expanding population demanded housing services. This stimulated housing construction, which gave rise to a growing demand for cement and other building materials. Meanwhile, as the market for imported textile manufactures widened, it became increasingly profitable for foreign firms to build and operate textile mills. A similar development occurred with respect to cigarettes and tobacco, canned goods, and other consumer products.

The development of manufactures, in contrast to foreign trade, gained momentum only after 1895 when, under the Treaty of Shimonoseki, foreign firms were permitted to build factories in the treaty ports. However, the question still remains as to why this self-generating process of economic growth remained largely bottled up in the treaty ports and nearby cities. On the basis of evidence presently available, one can only speculate on the types of factors that hindered the spread of economic stimuli from the treaty ports and nearby cities to the Chinese hinterland. There were undoubtedly institutional as well as physical (transport) barriers to the movement of goods and even more to the movement of productive factors. Enterprises in the ports enjoyed many privileges compared with business elsewhere, making it difficult for the latter to compete. The backwardness of the Manchu government, the almost continuous civil war from 1911 to 1927, the Japanese invasion, and the lack of tariff autonomy were undoubtedly the major factors. Moreover, leakages from the treaty ports to foreign countries through profit remittances must also have dampened economic expansion, since the multiplier effects of such investment upon income and employment may have been partially felt in the home countries of the foreign firms rather than in China alone. At the same time, the development of public utilities, banking facilities, and other overhead facilities raised the marginal productivity of investment and thus reinforced the economic advantages already enjoyed by the treaty ports and nearby cities over the economy of the Chinese hinterland.

Although politically and socially, the treaty ports were an undesirable feature of prewar China, they performed certain important historic functions in the long-run economic development of the country. First of all, they created external economies; second, as a result of the factory and business development that took place, they provided a training ground for Chinese technical and managerial personnel and for Chinese entrepreneurship. The Chinese *comprador* and his successor, the Chinese merchant and entrepreneur, built up the Chinese portion of the modern economy under the wing of the foreigners' privileges. In fact, the treaty ports became jointly administered centers of economic growth, from which the Chinese entrepreneurial class were by no means excluded. On the contrary, the ports attracted Chinese talent and capital. Moreover, through the Chinese merchant and official classes, the ports also served as a means of mobilizing Chinese savings and channeling them into either the modern banking system or direct investment in treaty port enterprises.

The "spread effects" of these developments in Manchuria and in the treaty ports spilled over into the traditional sector only to a very small extent. Change in the traditional sector was sluggish, and it is not possible to determine from the available data whether there was any net total growth, much less per capita growth, in the agricultural and handicraft economy of the hinterland. There is no doubt that handicrafts did undergo some transformation. Hand spinning of yarn was to a large extent displaced by yarn manufacture in the textile mills. However, hand weaving of textile cloth remained competitive for a long period of time. Moreover, the growth of foreign trade stimulated the rise and expansion of a number of handicraft industries such as carpet weaving, knitting, the processing of hog bristles, and the manufacturing of hairnets and a whole host of other so-called "native" products.

Among the causes of economic retardation in China's hinterland economy, a significant, if not major, factor may have been the negative influence of government. The Chinese imperial bureaucracy and the central government in Peking in the nineteenth century were essentially anti-development oriented; they resisted modernization and were too weak to prevent the fragmentation of political and economic power. Chinese government in the nineteenth century was characterized essentially by paralysis.

This was aggravated by political distintegration and warlordism after the 1911 revolution. There were two attempts to reverse this process. The first occurred after the Taiping rebellion, when, within the context of the self-strengthening movement, Chinese statesmen based in the provinces tried to develop some economic enterprises and launch a process of modernization. The other was during the National Government period of 1927 to 1936, which, while disrupted by civil war and world-wide depression and terminated by the Sino-Japanese war, witnessed restoration of tariff autonomy, a successful currency reform, progress in the railroad and highway systems, and fairly significant growth of industry and of a nucleus of technical and managerial manpower.

THE MAIN LINES OF ECONOMIC DEVELOPMENT SINCE 1949

The Chinese Communists inherited a profoundly disrupted economy in which both industrial and agricultural production had been drastically curtailed. Railroad lines had been blown up and the channels of distribution cut. Under the impact of deficit financing, military requirements, a narrowing tax base, and a decline in production, the economy was caught up in an accelerating process of hyperinflation.

The new regime restored the economy to working order within a relatively short period of time. By 1951, the process of inflation was arrested, fiscal and monetary stability was restored, and the foundations for the drive toward industrialization were being laid. According to official claims, by 1952 both industrial and agricultural output were restored to pre-1949 peak levels. On the basis of the studies in this volume, this claim seems to be pretty well validated as far as industry is concerned. However, there is some difference of opinion among scholars with respect to agriculture; some believe that agriculture had recovered by 1952, while others are doubtful.

During the initial recovery period (from 1949 to 1952), the Chinese Communists also went about transforming economic organization and institutions. They carried out a far-reaching program of land redistribution and introduced a series of measures designed to circumscribe the scope and operation of the private business sector, while at the same time expanding government enterprise. With the economy essentially restored, the Korean armistice negotiated, and a good 1952 harvest, the Chinese Communists felt ready to launch the First Five-Year Plan in 1953. However, in fact, long-term planning does not seem to have been initiated on any comprehensive scale until about mid-1955. The intervening period was used for preparing the plan, for creating the preconditions for long-term planning, for beginning the process of new plant expansion in industry and mining, and for expanding the government sector in industry, banking and trade. As soon as land redistribution was completed, campaigns were launched to push, induce, and cajole the peasantry into various forms of producer cooperatives.

With a favorable harvest outlook in 1955, the regime felt ready once more for significant new initiatives. State investment was raised by 60 per cent between 1955 and 1956, industrial output was increased very sharply, the process of collectivization was launched and consummated within a year and a half, and the remnants of private enterprise in industry and trade were eliminated and brought within the purview of the public sector. By the end of 1956, the process of nationalization and socialization of the economy was completed both in the countryside and in the cities. The big push of 1955-56 produced some acute supply bottlenecks, consumer goods shortages, and raw material scarcities throughout the economic system. Therefore, the regime was forced to cut back and retrench in 1957, as reflected in reduced investments and in a slowing down of the growth rate. Mediocre harvests in 1956 and 1957 aggravated this slowdown.

As the Chinese Communists approached the end of their First Five-Year Plan period in 1957, they could take considerable pride in the development of the industrial sector of the economy. Industry's rate of growth was unusually rapid, as indicated by the measurements developed in the studies by T. C. Liu (Ch. 3), Kang Chao (Ch. 9), Robert Field (Ch. 11), and K. C. Yeh (Ch. 8). However, the impressive record in industry was not matched by performance in agriculture. Although the output data for the agricultural sector are particularly unreliable, even official claims indicate that agriculture lagged very significantly behind industry. With the rapid rate of population growth, this lag began to create serious actual or potential problems of food supply for the urban population and the industrial labor force by late 1957. The problem facing the Chinese Communist regime as it approached the formulation of the Second Five-Year Plan was how to maintain the rate of industrial growth and at the same time improve the rate of agricultural performance.

Against this background the Great Leap Forward was devised. This strategy was based on mass mobilization of labor for irrigation, reclamation, and flood control tasks designed to raise agricultural yields and output with minimum input of capital. There was to be a dual approach to economic development, with simultaneous development of small- and large-scale industry, using highly labor-intensive methods in the first, and capital-intensive methods in the second. The inception of this strategy was in 1958, again a year of favorable harvest prospects.

The Great Leap was characterized by a high degree of politics in economic and administrative management. The statistical network, among other institutions, fell victim to the slogan of "politics takes command." Although the harvest in 1958 turned out to be favorable, the government and the party organs were not in a position to assess accurately how good it actually was. In the spirit of the times and the general mood of euphoria and optimism, the favorable harvest was interpreted as a consequence of the Great Leap strategy and a vindication of it. Thus the pattern of unrealistic expectations and of technical and planning errors was reinforced, leading to a marked downturn in agricultural production in 1959, amid continuing growth in the industrial sector.

The full dimensions of the agricultural disaster were not realised by the planners and policy makers until 1960. Following a very poor 1960 harvest, the winter of 1960-61 produced the worst food, agricultural, and economic crisis that had faced the Communist regime since it came to power. The agricultural crisis spilled over into the industrial and other nonagricultural sectors, so that by 1961 the whole economy was in the throes of an acute depression which lasted at least until the autumn harvest of 1962. The 1962 harvest showed the first signs of improvement, marking the beginnings of economic recovery.

Between 1949 and 1957, Communist China's economy experienced rapid recovery and significant growth. This process of rapid growth was led by the fast pace of expansion in the investment goods industries, in part helped by Soviet credits and technical assistance. As a result, industrial capacity expanded significantly, the economy became much more commercialized and money-oriented, and a far-reaching process of structural transformation began. However, the expansion was sharply interrupted by the great economic crisis of 1959-62. This crisis may have cost the regime a decade of economic growth, for gross national product in 1965 does not seem to have been above the 1958 level.

TRENDS IN AGGREGATE PRODUCT

The main purposes of T. C. Liu's study (Ch. 3) are (1) to compare and reconcile the several estimates of national product, including the Communists' own data, for the period with relatively reliable statistics,

1952-57 (Section II); (2) to appraise the performance of the economy during 1952-57 in comparison with those of other nations (Section III); and (3) to provide a rough estimate of the quantitative trends of the economy during the Great Leap Forward (1958-59) and its aftermath up to and including 1965 (Section V). A general discussion of Communist statistics precedes the analysis and serves as a background (Section I).

Perhaps the most encouraging result obtained in the comparative study of national product estimates for the period before the Leap is the almost complete reconciliation of the Eckstein [1] and the Liu-Yeh [2] estimates for 1952, the year immediately before the First Five-Year Plan began. The three authors have not reached agreement on a given figure for the total product of that year. But from an analytical point of view, it is important that practically all the sources of the discrepancy between the two estimates have been identified. The net unexplained difference amounts to only 0.32 billion *yuan,* out of a total product of 64.6 billion *yuan* at factor cost (Eckstein) and 74.7 billion *yuan* at market prices (Liu-Yeh). The Liu-Yeh estimate is higher by a margin (10.1 billion *yuan*) greater than the conceptual difference due to indirect taxes (6.6 billion *yuan*), which is due chiefly to Liu and Yeh's larger estimates of the outputs of agriculture and the other traditional sectors. Eckstein's estimates for these sectors are admittedly underestimates, even though he does not agree with Liu and Yeh on all the particular upward adjustments the latter have made. It remains true, however, that any upward adjustment of Eckstein's estimate for 1952 will bring the two very close together.

According to the estimates using official Communist data without adjustment for reliability (the Communists' own estimate and those of Hollister, Li, and the reconstructed Communist estimate by Liu and Yeh), the average annual rate of growth of the total product during 1952-57 is in the range of 8.6 to 9 per cent per year. All scholars in this area agree, however, that the Communist data on agricultural production for the earlier years in this period understated the actual output, which would result in an exaggeration of the average annual rate of growth for the period. There is also fairly general agreement that the Communist data understate the weight of the slow-growing traditional sectors in the total product, and hence overstate the overall rate of growth. Even without allowing for the tendency on the part of the local cadres to overstate their achievement in modern industrial production, the well-known "new product effect" alone would exaggerate the rate of growth of this sector.

1. Alexander Eckstein, 1961. *The National Income of Communist China.* Glencoe, Ill.: The Free Press.

2. T. C. Liu and K. C. Yeh, 1965. *The Economy of the Chinese Mainland.* Princeton: Princeton Univ. Press.

It is difficult to maintain that the overall rate of growth was as high as 8.6 to 9 per cent per year during 1952-57.

The Liu-Yeh estimate of the overall average annual rate of growth during 1952-57 is 6 per cent, 2.5 to 3 per cent lower than the Communist claim. Liu and Yeh, however, have made extensive adjustments in the Communist data, especially those on agricultural production, consumer goods output, and the traditional sectors of the economy. Such adjustments would have to be based on assumptions that are inevitably more or less arbitrary. In particular, their estimate of agricultural production crucially depends on assumptions that by 1952 the economy had recovered from the damage of World War II, that the per capita food consumption was constant during 1952-57, and that the Communist estimate of the rates of growth of population during this period was reliable. It should be noted, however, that according to Communist data, livestock production was higher in 1952 than in 1957, indicating that agriculture may have recovered from the damage of war by 1952. Moreover, when per capita consumption of food fell from the 1957 level during the years after the Great Leap, there was evidence of near starvation. Lack of such evidence for the early 1950's would tend to support the Liu-Yeh assumption of a per capita consumption level during those years not too far from the 1957 level.

However, changes in weather conditions during these six years were not taken into consideration in the Liu-Yeh estimate of agricultural output. Their estimates of year-to-year changes in the value added by agriculture are unlikely to be very accurate. A revision of their estimate will have to await the formulation of better assumptions, an admittedly difficult task.

In all likelihood, the adjustments made by Liu and Yeh have reduced the margins of biases in the Communist data. It is important to note that they have made no downward adjustment for the "new product effects" and other exaggerating factors in the Communist data on the output of producer goods. The Liu-Yeh estimate of the average annual rate of growth of the total product for the period 1952-57 as a whole is more reliable than their estimates of the annual changes within the period.[3]

The performance of the Chinese economy during 1952-57 is compared in Liu's paper with that of other nations in terms of both the Communists' own data on national product and its components (as reconstructed by Liu and Yeh without adjustments for the reliability of these data) and the independent Liu-Yeh estimate.

According to Communist data, all indicators of growth (the overall, the per-capita and the per-worker rates of increase of domestic product)

3. The estimate by Wu, Hoeber and Rockwell (1963) was modeled on the Liu-Yeh estimate. The few minor modifications made by Wu and his associates are discussed in Liu's paper.

are higher than those of practically all other nations compared during more or less the same period. The high overall rate of growth (9 per cent per year) is the result of a high savings ratio (24.4 per cent) and a rather low capital-output ratio (2.7 per cent). The proportion of total product invested was substantially higher than that in countries with comparable magnitudes of per capita product or similar industrial structure. At the same time, per capita consumption expanded at the high rate of 5.2 per cent per year. The rates of increase of labor and capital inputs were high, but the growth of "productivity" of combined labor and capital inputs (about 4 per cent per year) was higher than all other countries compared. The picture presented by the Communist data seems unprecedentedly successful.

On the basis of the Liu-Yeh estimate, the overall rate of growth (6 per cent per year), while much lower than the Communist claim, was still higher than those of two-thirds of the more than 40 countries compared during roughly the same period of time. Per capita consumption also rose at a much more modest rate (1.9 per cent per year) than that indicated by the Communist data (5.2 per cent per year); and at the end of the First Five-Year Plan period, the per capita consumption level had not regained the prewar 1933 level. The growth rate of "productivity" of combined labor and capital inputs was also high (2.9-3.4 per cent per year, depending upon the weights used for labor and capital inputs), but was substantially lower than the rates in West Germany and Japan. The proportion of total product invested (23.8 per cent) was high, but the capital-output ratio (3.9) was also higher than that implied in the Communist data. The very substantial investment made during this period was not sufficient to absorb all the new entrants into the labor force, and so employment was expanding far less rapidly (1.5 per cent per year) than population (2.3 per cent per year).

The Communist investment strategy during 1952-57 may thus be criticized as being excessively capital-intensive. The emphasis given to indigenous methods of production during the Great Leap Forward (1958-59) may indeed be ascribed in part to the regime's realization of this shortcoming in investment strategy. But the coercive measures taken during the Leap, and the unrealistic calculation of the technical possibilities of the indigenous methods, together with unfavorable weather conditions, first brought disaster to agriculture and then severely reduced the supply of agricultural raw material to industry. The economy took a serious leap backward during 1959-61.

Since the Communist data for the Great Leap years 1958-59 are untrustworthy, and since the regime has not published any systematic economic statistics since 1961, the estimates of domestic product and investment made by Liu for 1958-65 (Ch. 3, Section V) are necessarily very crude, and less reliable than the Liu-Yeh estimate for 1952-57. The estimates are based on output data for certain major products (staple food crops, cotton, and steel) which apparently are the consensus of qualified observers in Hong Kong. The product estimate also has an apparently reasonable relationship with the available information on exports, independently derived from the import statistics of countries having trade relationships with Communist China. Since exports are basically determined by domestic output, the reasonable relationship between them tends to support the plausibility of the output estimate. Moreover, the Liu-Yeh estimate of value added by the relatively modern sectors of the economy for the post-Leap years follows a trend similar to that pieced together by Chao on the basis of scattered Communist data on industrial production,[4] though it is lower for 1964-65. Omitting details about the year-to year change, which are unlikely to be as accurate as the estimate of the general trend, the overall development in the economy during 1952-65 may be summarized as follows:

	Net Domestic Product	Net Domestic Investment
	(in billions of 1952 yuan)	
1952	71	11
1957	95	18
1958	108	24
1959	104	20
1961	92	16
1962	94	16
1965	108	20

The domestic product fell by 15 per cent from the peak reached in 1958 (108 billion 1952 *yuan*) to a trough in 1961 (92 billion 1952 *yuan*). Recovery began after 1962, and the domestic product in 1965 returned to approximately the 1958 level. For a seven year period (1958-65) there was no overall growth in the economy. The rather impressive speed of growth (6 per cent per year) during the earlier period of the regime (1952-57) has been marred by the performance during more recent years. The Communist economy of mainland China has gone through a cycle of peak and trough, a phenomenon often alleged to be characteristic only of capitalist economies.

The aggregate figures presented in this introduction do not show an important element in the post-Leap picture. It is that the value added by the traditional sectors in 1964-65 was somewhat smaller than in 1957 and very substantially lower than in 1958, mainly because of the failure of agricultural output. In fact, agricultural production in 1965 was ap-

4. See p. 580, Ch. 9.

parently lower than in 1964, and the 1966 output may have been even smaller. Bad weather conditions may have been responsible for this unfavorable outcome, but the political struggle on the mainland could not have been beneficial to economic activities.

POPULATION

A knowledge of the size and structure of population is a basic prerequisite to any evaluation of the performance of an economy. Estimates of national income and product are hardly possible without it; nor can reliable growth rates be determined.

As John S. Aird points out (Ch. 4), pre-Communist Chinese population surveys and estimates were generally incomplete and unreliable. A series of natural and political catastrophes took a huge but indeterminate toll of human life, and rendered difficult the application of standard demographic estimating techniques. The most dreadful of all in modern times, the Taiping rebellion, which lasted from 1850 to 1866, resulted in a net population loss of somewhere between 20 and 50 million people. Aird estimates that 16 specific catastrophes from 1850 to 1953 cost China between 48 and 98 million lives.

Demograhers' intense interest in the population census of 1953 is understandable. For the first time in history, a strong central government attempted a comprehensive count of the nation's people, using techniques that were relatively modern by previous standards. The obstacles to accuracy were formidable: a central statistical office had just been established; local officials were given a great deal of leeway, with a consequent lack of uniformity in counting procedure; there were no trained enumerators; tabulation was haphazard; there were groups in society who had a stake in escaping enumeration. The mere size of the task, moreover, would have strained the capabilities of the most advanced of nations. Demographers are thus faced with a difficult quandary: can the results of the 1953 census be accepted as at least a rough index of the magnitude of the Chinese population, or must they be rejected as of little value in arriving at a true estimate?

Aird leans toward the former view, and in support of this conclusion, he has written a careful review of the background and procedure of the census. There are some who will disagree with his statement that

> with all its defects, which are undoubtedly many and serious, and despite the exaggerated official claims to accuracy on one side and the sometimes immoderate scepticism of foreign analysts and commentators on the other, it must be concluded that the reported 1953 census total of 583 million people is probably the nearest approach to a reliable population figure in the history of China.

Irene B. Taeuber and Nai-chi Wang are on record as considering the 1953 census to be so unreliable that it provides "no objective knowledge of the size of population of China and its rate of change over time." [5] However one may feel about this problem, there can be no question of the great value of Aird's work for its ultimate solution.

Aird by no means holds to the view that the 1953 census can be accepted uncritically as a starting point for population projections. It is his belief that the census understates the population total by between 5 and 15 per cent.[6] Moreover, he rejects the age-sex distribution given in the census as inconsistent with other evidence. To remedy this defect, he constructed six alternative population models for the period 1851-1953, each embodying a different set of assumptions with respect to fertility and mortality. This procedure can be challenged: there are those who believe that what we know of Chinese population history in the century before the census may not be at variance with the structure revealed by the census. But again it is necessary to work through Aird's argument as a means of helping resolve the issue.

Acceptance of the 1953 census as an adequate base for demographic analysis is just a first step in the process of estimating present and future Chinese population. What can be said with any degree of certainty about fertility and mortality rates since 1953? What were the effects of the crisis in agriculture after the failure of the Great Leap Forward? How have recent reported improvements in the food supply affected population trends? Aird attacks these and related problems by constructing four alternative models for the period 1953-65, each embodying a different set of birth and death rates to take into account various hypotheses about the impact of political and economic events. He arrived at a 1965 total of somewhere between the extremes of 714.6 million and 874.6 million people. This spread of 160 million people is a measure of our ignorance. Judged by what is known about the food supply and employment, however, the true magnitude is probably nearer the lower limit.

The public pronouncements of Chinese Communist leaders often contain inferential population totals—"in the name of *X* million Chinese people" and the like. Aird points out that prior to the 1953 census, the figure of 475 million was commonly cited, and that the higher census total may have come as an unwelcome surprise to the government. The state of demographic knowledge inside Communist China precludes giving too much weight to the totals contained in speeches.

As for the future, a number of unusual demographic factors render prediction hazardous. Because China is still an underdeveloped country, a certain pattern of change in population growth would normally be ex-

5. See Milbank Memorial Fund, *Population Trends in Eastern Europe, the USSR, and Mainland China,* New York, 1960, p. 302.

6. However, see T. C. Liu's study in this volume (Ch. 3, p. 91).

pected in light of the experience of other countries in a similar situation. But China is hardly a typical nation; its huge size and peculiar cultural characteristics render argument by analogy dangerous. The attitude of the regime toward birth control measures can have a decisive effect on fertility. The pattern of industrial development to be followed is another variable of great moment. The degree of success that will be attained in coping with the farm problem is a third element that can markedly affect population growth.

Aird attempts to allow for various future contingencies through the use of six projection models, ranging from one of "maximum development," which assumes political stability and a favorable rate of economic growth for the next 20 years, to one of "catastrophe," which allows for famine and a collapse of the social order. Anyone who objects to these models can use the Aird method to test the implications of his own assumptions. Aird's most "optimistic" model yields a 1986 total of 1.122 billion total population; his most "pessimistic" one pulls the total down to 925 million. This spread is not much greater than that for the estimated 1965 population, but of course this springs from the nature of the assumptions. Obviously, less confidence can be placed in the extreme limits for 1986 than in those for 1965. However, the exercise is extremely useful in providing us with possible orders of magnitude, present and future.

EMPLOYMENT

In the chapter on manpower and employment (Ch. 5), C. M. Hou builds upon Aird's population estimates as well as upon the published works of Emerson and Liu and Yeh.[7] His procedure is first to estimate the ratio of nonagricultural to total population, and then to determine the civilian nonagricultural labor force. Relying mainly on trends in employment garnered from official data, Hou obtains annual estimates of employment from 1949 to 1960. Unemployment is simply the difference between the labor force and estimated employment.

The data indicate that nonagricultural employment in China rose rapidly during the period covered. There is considerable doubt, however, about the economic significance of the huge increase during the Great Leap Forward, during which there were strenous efforts to establish new enterprises with exceedingly high labor-capital ratios; most of these enterprises collapsed after 1960.

Hou's estimates of nonagricultural employment differ substantially from

7. John Philip Emerson, 1965. *Non agricultural Employment in Mainland China: 1949-1958.* International Population Statistics Reports, Series P-90, No. 21. U.S. Department of Commerce, Bureau of the Census.

Liu and Yeh, *op. cit.*

others that have been made. For the year 1957, for example, his total is 47.7 million, compared with the 39.7 million secured by Emerson and the 64.2 million given by Liu and Yeh.[8] These discrepancies are due primarily to differences in coverage and definition. Liu and Yeh include in the non-agricultural labor force those farmers who worked part-time in nonfarm work (except that done without pay), while Hou does not. Farm workers who were also part-time handicraft workers were included in the Liu-Yeh estimate so that meaningful comparisons could be made with their estimate of handicraft output. On the other hand, Hou's estimates include workers in traditional transportation, rural peddlers, and domestic servants, while Emerson excludes these categories.

What is striking about all these estimates is the relatively small size of the nonagricultural labor force in China. The high rate of industrial development of the First Five-Year Plan did not result in the absorption of a great deal of manpower because much of the new industry was capital-intensive. However, even a more labor-intensive approach would probably not have changed the final distribution greatly, which may help to explain the frantic effort to use labor power during the Great Leap.

Hou estimates nonfarm unemployment among males at somewhere between 19.5 per cent and 29 per cent of the labor force in 1957; the estimates by Liu and Yeh are even higher. (It seems hopeless, at this stage, to make even a very rough estimate for women, because of the difficulty of separating true unemployment from domestic employment.) What an unemployment rate of this magnitude means for a country of China's level of economic development is questionable. Were the unemployed supported by a dole, or did they perform some work as a condition of receiving assistance? It is hard to believe that so large a portion of the labor force remained in idleness. More likely, both the Liu-Yeh and the Hou estimates implicitly or explicitly used the concept of full-time equivalent, so that the work actually done was distributed among more workers than the number estimated. In any event, the Chinese unemployment figure cannot be compared directly with unemployment data for more advanced countries.

Underemployment in agriculture is discussed, though this again is exceedingly difficult even to define, let alone measure. Buck's study of the pre-Communist agricultural scene indicated that while considerable idleness prevailed during the winter months, there was often a shortage of labor on the farms during the planting and harvest seasons. To judge by the policy of the Great Leap, the Communists evidently believed that there was a large surplus pool of labor hours that could be mobilized for capital creation. Miscalculation in this regard may have been a factor in their subsequent agricultural difficulties.

Because of the absence of data, very little can be said specifically about Chinese labor force developments since 1960. Hou argues that, at

8. Liu and Yeh, *op. cit.*, p. 69.

best, nonagricultural employment during 1961-64 was not higher than in 1960. During the worst years of the crisis following the Leap, many urban workers were apparently obliged to move to the country because of lack of food and employment in the cities.

If one were to take the lowest of Aird's population estimates for 1966, 728 million, and apply to it the age-sex distribution that minimizes the number of new entrants in the labor force, the resulting figure would be that about 86 million young people (less an appropriate allowance for mortality) will reach working age during the years 1966-70 inclusive. At the other end of the age range, only 23 million persons now in the 55-60-year age group will reach a retirement age of 60 years by 1970. Placing these huge new cohorts into useful employment will certainly tax the ingenuity of the Chinese Communist authorities, who are probably already faced with a larger pool of manpower than they can employ productively.

CAPITAL FORMATION AND DOMESTIC PRODUCT

K. C. Yeh in Chapter 8 deals with capital formation, while Liu (Ch. 3) and Chao (Ch. 9) also discuss certain problems relating to investment. Estimates of gross domestic capital formation are presented by Yeh for the prewar period 1931-36 and the postwar years 1952-57, in both 1933 and 1952 prices. For 1952-57, shares of fixed investment and changes in inventory in total gross investment have been estimated, together with the proportions of construction and producers' durable equipment in the former. Allocation of total fixed investment by economic sectors is also given for the same period. For the Great Leap Forward years (1958-59), only estimates of state fixed investment are provided. A rough estimate of the gross domestic product for these years has been derived on the basis of scattered data on the output of certain major agricultural and industrial products.

For 1952-57, both Yeh and Liu used Yeh's estimate of investment. The average proportion of total investment in domestic product is estimated at 23.8 per cent gross and 19.8 per cent net. Yeh's estimate was derived from Communist data with very minor adjustments, and he believes it to be somewhat exaggerated. Although it is difficult to evaluate the margin of overstatement, any reasonable correction of the Communist data would still lead to the conclusion that the proportion of total product invested in Communist China was significantly greater than that in most underdeveloped countries during the same period.

According to Yeh's estimate, 72 per cent of total gross investment during 1952-57 was in fixed capital formation, the rest in increases in inventories (Ch. 8, Table 3). Forty-six per cent of the gross fixed investment was in industry, and only 20 per cent in agriculture. This is roughly corroborated by the data given by Chao on "basic construction investment." The emphasis on heavy industry was unmistakable, with more than 80 per cent of the basic construction investment in industry going to this sector. Compared with seven Communist nations and six developing countries in Asia, Communist China had the smallest share of investment in agriculture. Moreover, the share of investment in industry in Communist China consistently rose during 1952-57, while that in agriculture declined almost uninterruptedly.

The low priority accorded to agriculture in the Chinese Communist investment strategy was not due only to the small volume of agricultural investment. Investment in industry adopted more advanced techniques, but investment projects in agriculture merely extended the use of traditional methods. The wisdom of this strategy is questionable. Through centuries of experience, Chinese agriculture had already achieved a high level of efficiency in the use of the traditional inputs. Further increases in agricultural productivity would have to come from the adoption of new technology in farming, such as the use of improved seeds and the heavy application of chemical fertilizers and insecticides. In the design and construction of irrigation and flood control works, antiquated schemes and inadequate equipment should have been replaced by more effective systems and carefully planned installations. The Communist regime failed to give proper emphasis to these important considerations in making investment in agriculture.

Both Yeh and Chao point out that the fairly rapid increase in industrial output during 1952-57 was only partly the result of the new investment made in this period, because of the long gestation period of much of the fixed investment in plant and equipment. It is, however, an open question how much of the increase in output can be attributed to increased capacity and how much to a fuller utilization of the capacity in existence before 1952. The Communist reports cited by Chao and Yeh on this point are not entirely consistent with one another. On the one hand, new investment was credited with contributing less than one-third of the *increase* in industrial output during 1952-57. On the other, one-third to one-fourth of the *total* industrial output was attributed to the expanded capacity. If the latter statement were valid, rather than the former, then the investment made during 1952-57 would have been a much more important factor in bringing about the rapid rise in industrial output during that period.

In view of the fact that the 1952 levels of practically all the major industrial products greatly exceed the respective prewar peak outputs, one wonders whether a great deal of unused capacity could have existed in 1952, as Yeh tends to believe. However, Field's work on productivity (Ch. 11) leads to the conclusion that the capacity factor might have been more important in light industry than in heavy industry. In any case, since a gestation period is required for fixed investment in all countries, the various capital-output ratios of Communist China can still be meaningfully compared with those of other countries during roughly the same period of time.

Through a reconstruction of the number of investment projects started, completed and discontinued, Chao gives a detailed account of the effort to curtail investment after 1961. A conjecture was advanced that the levels of construction activity in 1962 and 1964 were probably close to those in 1953 and 1954, respectively. As shown below, this roughly confirms a comparison of Liu's investment estimates for 1962 and 1964 with the Liu-Yeh estimates for 1953 and 1954:

ESTIMATES OF NET DOMESTIC INVESTMENT
(in billions of 1952 yuan)

	Liu's Estimate [9]	Liu-Yeh Estimate [10]	
1962	15.7	1953	15.5
1964	18.1	1954	16.7

Chao has also made tentative estimates of fixed investment in industry for 1960-64. The estimate for 1962 is only 1.5 billion *yuan,* much lower than his estimate of basic construction investment in industry for 1963, 2.8 billion *yuan.* It is difficult to reconcile such a large discrepancy with his view, cited earlier, that the level of basic construction investment in 1962 was comparable to that of 1953. It is likely that Chao's estimates of fixed investment in industry for 1961-63 understate the actual magnitudes.

As with other Communist statistics for the years 1958-59, the figures on state fixed investment for 1958-59 cited by Yeh appear extraordinarily large. If nonstate fixed investment and increase in inventory are added, the total gross investment would far exceed 30 per cent of the gross product during these years. As Yeh has pointed out, the quality of both the published statistics and the investment projects themselves was rather low during 1958-59.

Yeh has also made a rough estimate of gross domestic product for the years 1958-59. It compares with Liu's estimate of net domestic product for these years as shown in the table on page 19.

The net and gross figures for 1957 were estimated by Liu and Yeh in their joint study [11] and are consistent with each other. The percentage increase from 1957 to 1958 of Yeh's estimate of gross product, 16.8 per cent, is larger than Liu's estimate of the rate of increase of net product,

9. Ch. 3, p. 164.
10. Liu and Yeh, *op. cit.,* p. 68.
11. Liu and Yeh, *op. cit.,* p. 66.

	Liu's Estimate[12]		Yeh's Estimate[13]	
	Net Domestic Product (Billions of 1952 yuan)	Rate of increase over the Preceding Year (%)	Gross Domestic Product (Billions of 1952 yuan)	Rate of increase over the Preceding Year (%)
1957	95.3		100.8	
1958	108.0	+13.3	117.7	+16.8
1959	104.4	−3.3	128.0	+8.8

13.3 per cent. Both appear to be large. Whether a rate of increase in the range of 13 to 17 per cent in a single year is acceptable would depend upon the creditibility of the unusual stimulation of the Great Leap on production.

For 1959, the two estimates differ even in direction. In spite of a 9 per cent reduction in agricultural output, Yeh's estimate of gross product showed an increase of almost 9 per cent from 1958 to 1959; whereas a decline of 3 per cent occurred in Liu's estimate of net product. The rather high estimate by Yeh for 1959 reflects the extraordinarily large outputs reported for certain important industrial products in that year. Compared with the relatively reliable figures for 1957, the output data used by Yeh represents very great increases: 81 per cent for machinery, 83 per cent for cement, 166 per cent for coal, and 245 per cent for iron ore during a two-year period. Because of the confusion that occurred during the second year of the Leap, great caution must be exercised in using data of such unusual magnitudes.

Liu's estimate of the value added by the relatively modern sectors shows an increase of 11 per cent from 1958 to 1959. This increase, however, was not sufficient to counterbalance the decline in the traditional sectors; hence, the total product registered a small reduction of 3 per cent.

AGRICULTURAL DEVELOPMENT

The two chapters on agricultural development in mainland China since 1949, by Anthony Tang (Ch. 7) and Kenneth Walker (Ch. 6), complement one another. Tang's analysis is focused on the role and importance of agriculture in the industrial and economic development of the mainland. He shows what constraints agriculture has placed on industrial development and goes on to explore both the particular factors that have con-

12. Chapter 3, p. 164.
13. Chapter 8, p. 532.

tributed to increases in agricultural production and the elements that have tended to retard agricultural growth. Walker, on the other hand, investigates the technical, organizational, and incentive barriers to rapid growth in agricultural production.

Tang starts his analysis by pointing up the marked differences in the agricultural positions of the Soviet Union and Communist China. He shows that per capita food production and consumption in the Soviet Union before 1928 were significantly higher than in China in 1952. As a result, it was easier for the Soviet Union to develop an agricultural surplus and to impose a much higher extraction margin on agriculture. Reductions in agricultural output were absorbed in the Soviet Union either by the agricultural population in the form of reduced consumption or by the low-priority industrial sectors that produced consumer goods for both the urban and the rural population. Because of the much higher consumption standard in the Soviet Union, there was a margin over and above subsistence that could be squeezed; in China, the corresponding margin was much narrower.

As a result, agriculture did not seriously constrain industrial development in the Soviet Union during the period of the first two Five-Year Plans (1928-37). In spite of collectivization and consequent drastic reductions in farm output, agricultural marketings were maintained, and industrial growth proceeded unabated throughout the period except for a temporary slowing down in the rate of growth for one or two years. Tang points out that this interpretation is supported by the finding that the correlation between rates of agricultural growth and rates of industrial growth in the Soviet Union for the relevant period is low and statistically insignificant. Furthermore, while grain output declined from 82 million tons in 1913 to 63 million in 1932, total grain collected fell only from 21 million to 20 million tons. Thus, Soviet agricultural policy could afford to be primarily extractive rather than developmental, without seriously affecting the rate of growth in the high-priority heavy industry sectors.

Mainland China presents a sharply contrasting picture. Its per capita food availability in grain terms in 1952 was less than half the Soviet Union's in 1928. China, therefore, found it necessary to mount a developmental program for agriculture, even as concurrent steps were taken to enforce collections. The dependence of industrial growth in China on the fate of agriculture is shown by Tang's correlation analysis, which suggests that with a zero lag during 1949-58, the agricultural growth rate appears to have exerted statistically significant influences in China on the growth rate of all industry ($r = 0.67$), of the capital goods sector ($r = 0.75$), and of the "modern" sector ($r = 0.70$).

Since Chinese agriculture and the population in general were so close to the subsistence margin, fluctuations in agricultural output could not be absorbed by either the farm population or the low-priority consumer goods industrial sector. Instead they were reflected in fluctuations in farm marketings, state procurements, and total collections.

Agriculture in China can impose constraints on industrial development in several ways. Agriculture provides most of the raw material for consumer goods industries, *e.g.*, cotton for the cotton textile industry. At the same time, the farm sector supplies food to the growing labor force in the cities in both high and low-priority industrial sectors. Furthermore, agriculture directly or indirectly supplies the bulk of the exports that help to finance imports. Up to 1960 these imports were heavily concentrated on capital goods; *i.e.*, they were destined for the high-priority industries. Therefore a shortfall in agricultural production tended to be reflected in curtailed levels of production in the textile and food processing industries, all dependent on agriculture for raw materials. If an agricultural crisis was severe enough, as it was between 1960 and 1962, it could lead to acute nutritional deficiencies and disorders in the cities to the point that even the industrial labor force could not be adequately provisioned, with attendant negative consequences for labor morale, incentives, and productivity. Finally, reductions in farm output would almost immediately be reflected in declines in exports and attendant declines in imports, particularly of capital goods.

By the mid-1950's the Chinese Communist leadership became aware of the fact that if industrial growth were to proceed undisturbed, agricultural production must be raised. However, right up to and through the Great Leap, primary reliance for achieving increases in agricultural production was placed on increasing traditional inputs, rather than on introducing modern "hard" industrial inputs such as chemical fertilizer, or on new organizational devices.

Collectivization was designed not only to raise the extraction margin but also to improve the efficiency of agricultural production through hoped-for gains in economies of scale, through consolidation of land holdings, and through some extension of the cultivated land area by abolishing the strips that separated holdings. Through these means, some increased land inputs could in fact be supplied; more were added by extending the area that was double-cropped and in some cases even triple-cropped. Therefore, the sown acreage increased significantly more than the cultivated area. There was also a sizable rise in the labor force employed and in the intensity of labor utilization. Tang estimates that, as a result, total inputs increased by about 25 per cent between 1952 and 1957; that is, they grew at an average rate of roughly 5 per cent a year. However, because of overcentralization in planning and in the introduction of new techniques, and because of unfavorable incentives, the productivity of inputs declined over this period so that output grew at an average rate of only 3 per cent a year, barely keeping ahead of population growth.

It is to this last range of considerations that Walker primarily addresses himself. His central thesis is that most problems of agricultural organization in Communist China revolve around a continuing search by the planners and policy makers for the optimum degree of centralization—one that will assure the desired rate of extraction and technical innovation and at the same time provide appropriate material incentives to the farm cultivators. But the Communist leadership has from the outset tended to err in the direction of overcentralization at the expense of material incentives, and this tendency has been one of the principal factors in retarding technical innovation and efficiency of agricultural production. Unlike the agricultural sectors of other underdeveloped countries, the outstanding feature of agricultural organization in China has been its rapid and frequent transformation. The problem in Chinese agriculture was not one of too little, but of too much change, introduced too quickly, and without enough regard for local variations and conditions. Barely was land reform completed in 1952 when the focus of discussion shifted to an emphasis on collectivization as a precondition for "technical reform" and technical innovation. In the spring and summer of 1955, the government was anxiously preoccupied with the slow speed of socialist reorganization and the low rate of growth of agriculture. At the beginning of 1956, cadres were under intense pressure to effect a technological breakthrough in agriculture in the shortest possible time. Collectivization was believed to be the answer.

Chinese agricultural policy between 1954-55 and 1962 was characterized both by continuous and rapid transformation and by a combination of overcentralization in planning, unrealistic and ambitious plans for agricultural growth, and adverse incentives, with unfavorable results for agricultural production. This policy was changed radically in the early 1960's, and between about 1961-62 and 1965 there was some reversal in these tendencies, with less emphasis on centralization, less ambitious agricultural targets, and more favorable incentives. These years were also probably the longest period of organizational stability. Walker points out that perhaps the most important single reason for slow agricultural progress between 1955 and 1962 was the high degree of centralization in the planning system, to the point where collectives merely carried out orders from above in a mechanical manner. For most of the period, planning was not a genuine two-way process, with a downward flow of information and preliminary directives that were adjusted in the light of local realities before they were promulgated as formal directives.

This tendency toward overcentralization and "commandism" was aggravated by unrealistic and overambitious targets, which were imposed on the collectives, or sometimes initiated by them under pressure from the cadres who were responding in turn to pressures from above. Following collectivization, considerable pressure was exerted to extend the area that was double-cropped and triple-cropped.

In effecting changes from single- to double-crop patterns of cultivation, the most important organizational problem is to ensure that resources are available at exactly the right time and the right place. Dislocation of work at any one peak season will affect the entire agricultural yield. This means that double-cropping requires good organization and ample supplies of labor and draft animals. As it turned out, because of labor shortages, it was bound to be difficult, and in some areas impossible, to increase the double-cropped area without a remarkable rise in labor productivity. Moreover, in a number of provinces there was a scarcity of draft animals for double-cropping, and in quite a few other areas the livestock deficiency was so marked that it precluded double-cropping altogether. Yet such measures were in many cases introduced indiscriminately, without sufficient attention given to bottlenecks in the supply of labor and livestock or to the consequences of disrupting and even destroying the delicate sequence of agricultural work.

A concrete illustration of the consequences of overcentralization and indiscriminate application of new techniques is provided by attempts to introduce into paddy fields throughout China the heavy steel, double-wheeled, double-bladed plow. The plows were technically unsuitable for wet fields and they sank. The water buffaloes refused to work in pairs, but a single animal was not strong enough to pull the plow alone. As a result, most of these plows had to be discarded, with enormous attendant waste.

Agricultural development and the rise in the productivity of land, labor and other inputs were also seriously hampered by the unfavorable structure of incentives during the collectivization period. In the collective each task was assigned a norm. Every norm was rated in work points, ten of which constituted a labor day. The value of the labor day was equal to the value of the distributable product divided by the total number of labor days credited to all working peasants in the collective. Unless the harvest and the physical product were stable from year to year, and unless government purchases or collections of farms produce were similarly stable, it was impossible for the peasants to forecast either the value of the labor day, the level of wages that would be forthcoming, or their household income. There were strong inducements for the peasant to fall back on his private plot as a safety factor to provide him with the minimum necessary security. The private plot and the collective then severely competed for labor, organic manure, and other resources (a dilemma that was not unknown in Soviet agriculture during an earlier period).

The situation was aggravated by the fact that in 1956 many cadres regarded the physical production of grain as the overriding criterion of success, and allocated resources to achieve this goal regardless of financial and cost considerations. As a result, the net income of many collectives or the pool from which peasants received the bulk of their personal income failed to rise to the expected levels or, in many cases, actually declined. Even when this was not the case, the difficult process of defining the work norms, of evaluating the jobs, and assessing their value was beyond the capacity of many cadres in the collectives. The incentive to work was weakened either because norms and rewards were not fixed correctly, or because it was difficult to estimate accurately the value of the labor day, since it depended on the level of income to be distributed after the harvest.

As both Chapters 6 and 7 show, while Chinese Communist planners and policy makers recognized the importance of raising agricultural output, they were not prepared to channel the necessary modern industrial inputs into agriculture and to provide and fashion incentive systems that would motivate farmers to introduce innovations from below. Beyond this, to the extent that the state took initiative in introducing technical innovations, it did so in ways that were all too frequently counterproductive, because the changes were introduced too rapidly and without sufficient attention to local conditions. There was no careful coordination of increased fertilizer applications with suitable planned crop varieties, with appropriate conditions of soil moisture, with the right type of soil conditions. The experience of countries now developed and of a number of developing areas in which agricultural progress has been rapid suggests that advances in the farm sector require increases in the productivity of inputs; that is, output must grow more rapidly than inputs, which is just the reverse of what seems to have actually occurred in China thus far. It remains to be seen whether in the future the Chinese Communist leadership will be prepared to restructure incentives in the communes, to delegate technical innovation to lower level organs, and to lead the way in these innovations through careful preparation, programs of farm extension, and a comprehensive approach that takes into account most of the important variables affecting agricultural output and increases in farm productivity.

INDUSTRIAL PRODUCTION AND PRODUCTIVITY

There can be no doubt that a significant and rapid increase in industrial production was achieved during 1952-57. The Communist claim is that the gross value of modern industry rose by 152 per cent from 1952 to 1957.[14] Both Chao's estimate of factory production and the Liu-Yeh estimate of value added by manufacturing factories indicate lower rates of growth. A comparison of these two estimates is presented in Chapter 9. The two are practically the same for 1952-54. However, the Liu-Yeh index for 1955-57 is substantially higher than the Chao index. While the discrepancy is attributable to different weighting systems used and dif-

14. State Statistical Bureau, *Ten Great Years*, p. 91.

ferences in coverage for some subgroups of industries, it would be desirable to have a detailed comparison to track down the specific sources of difference.

In the absence of such an attempt, the relative plausibility of the two indices can be considered only superficially. The average annual rate of growth during 1952-54 is 24 per cent in both estimates. That for 1954-57 is 19.7 per cent according to Liu-Yeh estimate, but only 11.7 per cent in Chao's estimate. Thus, according to both estimates, the pace of industrial growth had slowed down from 1952-54 to 1954-57. The slackening in the rate of growth, however, was much more pronounced according to Chao's estimate, the average rate of growth during the second subperiod being only half that of the first. It is difficult to visualize this occurring when the share of the rapidly expanding heavy industries in total factory output increased substantially from the first to the second subperiod.

For the years 1958-59, both the Chao and Liu-Yeh estimates (given by Chao in Chapter 9) must be considered highly conjectural. They may be compared with the estimate of value added by the relatively modern sectors of the economy given by Liu in Chapter 3. The average annual rates of increase of the three estimates are as follows: Chao's estimate of factory production, 37.7 per cent; the Liu-Yeh conjectural estimate of value added by manufacturing factories, 25.2 per cent; and the Liu estimate of value added by the relatively modern sectors of the economy, 13.8 per cent.

Chao has pieced together some Communist data and tentatively reconstructed the Communists' own estimate of industrial production for the years following the Great Leap Forward. This may be compared with Liu's estimate, equally tentative, of value added by the relatively modern sectors of the economy. Both estimates are presented in index numbers (1957 = 100):

	Chao	Liu
1957	100	100
1962	101.8	104.7
1963	113.0	113.3
1964	130.0	124.8
1965	144.3	135.0

Liu's estimates for 1964-65 are lower than Chao's reconstructed Communist estimate, but the two trends are rather close.

Many would agree that, in view of the factor endowments of mainland China, a rational industrialization policy should have proceeded along a relatively labor-intensive path. In terms of statistical results, this would have meant a slow increase in the productivity of industrial labor and a high ratio of labor to capital. Robert M. Field's study (Ch. 11) enables us to make some initial judgment as to whether these were actually achieved during the First Five-Year Plan.

Because of the deficiencies of the official Chinese labor productivity index (deficiencies familiar to students of early Soviet industrial development), Field has constructed his own index. His index of industrial output, which is the numerator of the productivity ratio, differs somewhat from that of Kang Chao.[15] For example, the Chao index of factory production stands at 195.9 for 1957 (1952 = 100), compared with the Field estimate of 209.6 for the same year. Considering differences in coverage and weights, however, the divergence is not too great. The use of the Chao index would not materially alter Field's conclusions.

Field calculates indexes of labor productivity for ten branches of industry, as well as for industry as a whole. According to these calculations, there was a 42 per cent labor productivity increase for all industry from 1952 to 1957. The experience of individual industries varied considerably from the average; productivity in the paper and the iron and steel industries rose by more than double the average rate, while electric power productivity increased by only half the average.

A single year, 1956, accounted for almost half the productivity advance for the entire period, because of a 30 per cent increase in industrial output which must have been linked to the fruition of some of the large Soviet-aid projects. In the very next year, however, a large increment of labor together with a much smaller increase in output resulted in a productivity decline. In general, the average annual rate of productivity increase suggests that in the industrial sector, at least, Communist China was following a capital-intensive rather than a labor-intensive path to development. This conclusion is strengthened by estimates of per-worker availability of capital, which suggest that there was an increase of 55 per cent from 1952 to 1957 in this ratio.

As a by-product of his labor productivity estimates, Field derives a capital-output ratio series which rises about 10 per cent from 1952 to 1957. This rather modest increase may simply reflect a tendency frequently found in the course of economic development, but it indicates that, rightly or wrongly, the Chinese did not raise labor inputs sufficiently to offset the decline in capital productivity.

Field also examines capacity utilization as a source of productivity increase. It appears from his data that in the light industries, which had a low investment priority, more effective use of existing capacity was a relatively greater source of productivity growth than increases in productivity, while the reverse was true in heavy industry.

15. Chapter 11, p. 647.

INDUSTRIAL PLANNING, MANAGEMENT, AND POLICY

In Chapter 10, Dwight Perkins deals with planning in three aspects: (1) the determination of broad policy goals, (2) decisions on specific plan targets, for instance, for output, costs and investment, and (3) the implementation of those targets.

(1) Communist China's broad policy goals have been rapid economic growth in general, with particular emphasis on the heavy industrial sector. Growth of certain heavy industries would allow the country to reduce its dependence on foreign trade for military purposes and for future economic growth. In addition, industrial growth is desired for its own sake, as a part of the ideology of Soviet-type economic growth. As the unquestioning reliance of Communist China on the Soviet model began to wane, and the poor performance of agriculture made itself felt, the regime reallocated investment funds to industries supporting agriculture, but these generally were still heavy industries.

(2) The drawing up of plan targets involves two significantly different problems. One is deciding how to allocate current production among individual enterprises, given existing plant capacity. The other is determining the direction of investment, *i.e.,* where plant capacity is to be expanded and by how much. The general underdevelopment of Communist China's economy simplified the problems of drawing up allocation plans, particularly in the consumer goods sector, since there are not too many varieties of goods in the consumption basket. But this was not an unmixed blessing. The large number of small-scale firms using widely varying techniques considerably complicates the planning problem.

In drawing up the investment plan, the regime was limited in its choices by Communist China's emphasis on heavy industry and by its desire for autarchy. It has attempted to expand the range of choice by developing new small-scale labor-intensive enterprises while allowing the small-scale firms already in existence to continue to operate. To deal with these firms, Peking has instituted a variety of decentralization measures, some relying on the market, others being more administrative in nature.

Although crude, the investment criteria used by the Communist regime are probably adequate for present needs. The problem is that in the process of plan implementation, even those crude criteria sometimes are ignored.

(3) The key elements in plan implementation are the responsibility system, the centralized allocation of key materials, the various methods set up to ensure the timely flow of accurate information, and a variety of financial controls to back up the plan targets. Formally, this system, although still highly centralized, was more decentralized than its counterpart in the Soviet Union in the 1930's. This partial decentralization of control

was accomplished by such measures as a policy of high prices for the products of heavy industry, the constant upgrading of the profits target, and the transfer of authority (1957-58) over many kinds of activities to provincial and lower levels.

In actual practice, controls, particularly financial and market controls, were often ignored. This situation resulted in part from the inexperience of managerial and planning cadres, and partly from an ideological bias against such things as profits and finance. In 1958, a belief that the enthusiasm and drive of individual cadres could be substituted for controls of any sort led to general disorganization in the industrial sector. Many of these problems may be overcome in the future by training cadres in technical matters, but the basic problems caused by the paramount position given to politics cannot be so easily solved without changing the nature of the system itself (as has occurred in the USSR)—something the present leadership in Communist China fears and resists.

In the portion of Chapter 9 dealing with policy, Chao discussed four important problems. First, with respect to the direction of development, he agrees with Perkins that the guiding principle has been to develop a "comprehensive and independent industrial system," *i.e.,* to achieve economic autarky. Internally, the major problem encountered by the planners was to strengthen the weak links in the industrial system so that the industrial sector as a whole would become more or less autarkic. However, at times the Communist hierarchy miscalculated the relative strengths of the various sectors, and new bottlenecks and weak links were created. Consequently, the priority order had to be changed from time to time. Internationally, there are signs indicating that the desire of the Chinese Communist authorities to build up an "independent" economy was one of the causes behind the Sino-Soviet rift.

The second aspect analyzed by Chao is the geographic relocation of industry. Up to 1955, the principle was to build most new plants in the inland cities. This principle was criticized toward the end of the First Five-Year Plan period, and more attention was given to coastal areas. However, the changed attitude did not last long, and beginning in 1959, development of the interior was reemphasized. Another feature observable up to 1957 was the clustering of new plants in a small number of big cities. After 1958, the new policy was to disperse factories among a large number of smaller cities and towns.

Third, with respect to industrial administration and management, the goal of the regime prior to 1957 was to increase the degree of centralized control. Some efforts were made in 1958 and 1959 to decentralize the industrial system. The decentralized system worked so unsatisfactorily, however, that beginning in 1960 the central government had to take back most of the discretionary power given to local cadres and management during 1958-59.

Finally, Chao discusses changes in policy relating to technology. During the First Five-Year Plan period, stress was placed on modern industrial technology and large-sized plants. A drastic change took place in 1958 when the Communist leadership began to emphasize indigenous production methods and small plants under the slogan of "walking on two legs." This extreme dualism lasted only a short time. Most of the native production units, which turned out to be exceedingly uneconomical, were abandoned after 1960. There were also changes in policy regarding specialization in industry. The initial policy aimed at a high degree of specialization among industrial enterprises. During the Great Leap Forward, it was replaced by the new slogan of "multifarious operation." In more recent years, however, the importance of industrial specialization was again emphasized.

FOREIGN TRADE

The volume and value of international transactions on trade, service, and capital account combined is small in relation to the total transactions in the economy of Communist China as a whole. However, this small sector was strategic in terms of facilitating rapid industrialization in the 1950's, and in maintaining economic and political stability during the next decade.

According to Feng-Hwa Mah (Ch. 12), in terms of official Chinese Communist doctrine and policy, foreign trade has three objectives: to facilitate rapid industrial growth; to promote self-reliance; and to serve as an instrument for the implementation of foreign policy objectives. Foreign trade is designed to foster rapid industrial expansion primarily through the importation of capital goods. The most significant factor in this realm was the importing of complete plants from the Soviet Union. These plants made a sizable contribution to the growth of China's basic industrial production capacity.

Foreign trade is also designed to promote self-reliance in the sense that capital goods imports can extend China's industrial capacity and to this extent render China less dependent upon foreign manufactures. The hope is that this increase in manufacturing capacity might make China self-sufficient to the point that it could virtually dispense with all imports. In effect, it is based on the notion that imports now can obviate the need for imports in the future.

While the Chinese Communist regime clearly carries on trade primarily for economic reasons, foreign policy objectives do play a role in the conduct of the country's international economic relations. This seems to have been particularly the case whenever economic instruments could be applied with relatively little cost in order to attain a certain foreign policy objective. In particular cases and for a limited period, mainland China's resources seem to have been sufficient to put individual foreign firms or certain foreign markets into highly disadvantageous positions, thus using either economic coercion or economic inducements as a means of supporting foreign policy objectives.

In theory, at least, foreign trade planning is supposed to be integrated with overall economic planning. Material balances are constructed, and import requirements are derived from these, by identifying missing items of equipment, machinery, and raw materials that cannot be produced at home or can be produced only at prohibitive cost. The import requirements are then adjusted, taking into account the availability of supplies from abroad and the costs at which they can be imported; the identified sources of domestic supply for export goods; and the foreign exchange and trade situation and credit position. The most important single adjustment factor is export capacity. Up to 1954, government policy seems to have been based on the principle that imports should lead exports. This meant that, except for a few essential commodities such as food grains and edible oils, where an export quota was set, when export demand competed with domestic demand, exports were given higher priority. However, in 1957 this policy seems to have been changed by an order of the State Council indicating that export plans must be more realistically adjusted to domestic demand and that "exports should determine imports." In fact, there is considerable doubt as to how far foreign trade plans were integrated with domestic plans. Such unpredictable elements as harvest fluctuations seem constantly to have upset foreign trade as well as domestic economic planning, and to have led to rapid shifts in import orders and export deliveries.

In principle, Communist China's foreign trade with any one country was supposed to be based on a bilateral balance of imports and exports. This principle was to be followed particularly in trade with other Communist countries. However, deficits or surpluses were accumulated, and often these were unplanned. Most trade agreements between China and other Communist countries provided for small "swing limits" in the bilateral balance that could be carried over into the next year and then settled within a context of the following year's trade schedules. In cases where swing limits were exceeded, China would be contracting a short-term debt for which it would have to pay a two per cent rate of interest.

The trends in Communist China's total foreign trade turnover were closely correlated with the levels of domestic economic activity. There was a rapid expansion in foreign trade between 1950 and 1959, with the total value of imports and exports combined almost tripling. However, this trend was reversed with the onset of the agricultural and economic crisis in 1960, so that by 1962 trade values had declined by 40 per cent from those of 1949. They have been recovering since then; and in 1965 trade was beginning to approach 1960 levels, although it was still significantly below those for 1959. This would suggest that under present conditions, when we have very few indicators of domestic economic activity at our disposal, foreign trade may serve as at least a crude aggregate index of the state of China's economy.

Taking the period 1950 to 1964 as a whole, the international sector of the Communist Chinese economy represented a drain on Chinese resources. Another way of putting it is that cumulatively, for the period as a whole, the Chinese were capital exporters rather than capital importers. For the early part of the period (1950-54), they did incur a net cumulative trade deficit of about $500 million, indicating that at that time they were adding to their resources by being able to draw on Soviet credits. However, after 1955, the combination of repayment of Soviet debts and the extensions of foreign aid by China resulted in a situation in which China accumulated a trade surplus of over $2 billion for the 1950 to 1964 period as a whole.

China's economic development was considerably assisted by Soviet credits in the early 1950's and by Soviet supplies of complete plants and technical assistance. Part of the Soviet assistance to China was financial and part was technical, not only through direct technical assistance but also through provision of capital goods which could not have been produced in the country itself or obtained elsewhere because of the embargo and trade controls. However, in the 1960's neither of these forms of assistance was available to China. On the contrary, the country has had to carry a sizable financial burden at the time when its economy was least able to afford it.

This pattern of trade and payment mirrors fairly faithfully the state of Communist China's international relations, particularly the state of Sino-Soviet relations. As long as these relations were cordial, China obtained considerable assistance in various forms from the Soviet Union. During this period, China's trade orientation was preponderantly with Russia and eastern Europe; between 1952 and 1959 some 60 to 70 per cent of Communist China's foreign trade was carried on with these countries. This situation was radically reversed in the 1960's, and by 1964 only about 20 per cent of China's trade was with Russia and Eastern Europe, and about two-thirds was with the non-Communist world.

CONCLUDING COMMENTS

The complicated details that are unavoidable in treating a country the size of mainland China should not obscure the main lines of development since the Communists assumed power in 1949. Despite the divergence of estimates and the inevitable lack of precision, certain things are clear.

The Communists succeeded in bringing order out of a chaotic situation that was due to the prolonged Sino-Japanese war and the ensuing internal conflict. During the First Five-Year Plan period, they succeeded in achieving a fairly rapid rate of advance; but they had considerable assistance from the Soviet Union and the rest of the Communist bloc. This period came to an abrupt end with the Great Leap Forward, which was the culmination of a tendency toward constant organizational reform that came in part from a desire to maintain revolutionary fervor. There was, without doubt, overconfidence in the contribution of Maoist doctrine, as well as a distrust of strong neighbors, no matter how professedly Communist and how seemingly anxious to help.

One of the consequences of the deep economic depression that followed the failure of the Great Leap was the statistical blackout inaugurated in 1960. No matter how hard and careful the basic work, estimates of individual scholars must differ, since many assumptions are essential if any progress is to be made at all. The value of the work, which continues despite the scarcity of data, lies in presenting some notions of orders of magnitude; in preventing completely wrong conceptions; and in developing a group of scholars who can study, even if with great difficulty, an area that accounts for one-quarter of the world's population. The publication in detail of what are partly data, and partly conjecture based upon close study of scraps of information, much of it nonquantitative in character, is indispensable if the world outside China is to have some appreciation and understanding of events that affect directly so large a portion of mankind and that are indirectly of crucial importance to the rest of us.

The Economic Heritage 2

ALEXANDER ECKSTEIN

I. INTRODUCTION

COMPARATIVE VIEW OF CHINA AND JAPAN

AN INFORMED OBSERVER assessing from the vantage point of 1840 the prospects for economic development and modernization in Asia might have considered the vast Chinese empire as the most likely force to successfully repel the challenge from the West.[1] It was much larger and more populous than Japan. It was an independent and sovereign entity, while India was under foreign rule. Moreover, partly because of its vast size, it was much better endowed with mineral resources than Japan.

In terms of social and political institutions, too, China might have appeared in the better position. Unlike India, it had a long history as a unified empire. Feudalism in China had been displaced with the end of the Chou dynasty, in contrast both to Japan and to modern Europe, where the persistence of feudalism was associated with economic retardation. Moreover, as Professor Lockwood has reminded us,

> China alone among the peoples of Asia brought to the modern world a tradition of personal freedom and social mobility, of private property freely bought and sold. . . . If the Chinese remained imbued with the particularist loyalties of the family, and a certain contempt for commerce as a way of life, was this not true of all Asia? Was it not also true of the European elites of yesterday? (Lockwood, 1956, p. 40)[2]

Yet the historical record runs counter to what might have appeared as reasonable expectations a hundred years ago. Between 1840 and 1950 China was in the throes of dynastic decline, political disunity and partial dismemberment. At the same time it was subjected to continuing external pressure, oppression and penetration. All these factors in combination led to disturbance, disequilibrium, and slow and gradual change in the Chinese

In revising an earlier draft of this paper I have greatly benefited by the very helpful comments of Professors Walter Galenson, T. C. Liu, Rhoads Murphy, Dwight Perkins, and Richard Tilly.

1. This point was first developed by Professor W. W. Lockwood (1956, pp. 37-54).

2. For a good study of social mobility in traditional China, see P. T. Ho, 1964.

economy. The economic record of these hundred years is both uncertain and mixed. While the traditional economic order was disturbed and undermined, some growing points did develop in the treaty ports and in Manchuria.[3] However, *modern economic growth* remained confined and bottled up in these peripheral areas.[4] Consequently this was a century of considerable economic growth *in* China but not *of* China.

In retrospect, it would seem that external shocks and stimuli activated the already existing stirrings in Japan, so that within two to three decades these could be transplated into a national commitment to economic development (Rosovsky, 1966). In China, on the other hand, the internal stirrings, even under the impact of new influences, crystallized more slowly, taking about a hundred years to reach substantial segments of the society, polity and economy. Thus China's national commitment to industrialization and rising economic strength was correspondingly delayed.

THE SOURCES OF MODERNIZATION IN CHINA

Economic modernization was largely imposed upon China from abroad, principally by foreign enterprises and foreign institutions. This differs markedly from Japan, where modernization became a national undertaking soon after the Meiji Restoration. To cite just one example, a national bank as the sole bank of issue was established in Japan in 1885, while in China this was not seriously attempted until the 1930's (Rosovsky, 1966, p. 64; *Chinese Year Book,* 1935, pp. 1423-27; Tamagna, 1942). In the meantime a number of foreign banks, notably the Hong Kong and Shanghai Banking Corporation, issued banknotes that served as currency with wide circulation in many parts of China (Allen and Donnithorne, 1954, Ch. VI).

In a sense, China was thus caught in a vicious circle. With the commitment to traditionalism came naturally a strong resistance to modernization. Partly because of this resistance, the carriers of modernization had to be largely (though by no means solely) foreigners and foreign institutions. Consequently modernization became identified with foreignism and so was perceived as a threat not only to the traditional order but also to the very integrity of the Chinese state. This fact in turn reinforced the existing resistance to modernization and complicated its spread.

Two fundamental conditions for economic growth were absent in China: the emergence of a modern nation-state, and a technological and institutional transformation in agriculture. Both were delayed despite the efforts of the modernizers in the nineteenth century and the Nationalist government in the twentieth century.

3. For a discussion of the significance of growing points or nodes in economic development, see A. O. Hirschman, 1958.

4. For a definition of "modern economic growth," see Simon Kuznets, 1959.

Therefore the *central* government in China played virtually no role in the economic modernization of the mainland until the 1930's. The principal agents of economic change and innovation were: (1) foreign enterprises and their native followers based in the treaty ports; (2) foreign governments and their chosen instruments in Manchuria; (3) a few outstanding Chinese statesmen of the late nineteenth century, whose power base was preponderantly provincial; and (4) the Nationalist government in the 1930's. In this chapter, I intend to show that the efforts of the first, second, and fourth did yield substantial economic growth, while those of the third turned out to be largely abortive. As a result, modern economic growth—*i.e.,* sustained growth in per capita income accompanied by and interrelated with marked structural transformation and technological change—did indeed take place in some areas of the mainland economy. Since in Manchuria this process touched all segments of the economy, it led to economic growth not merely in some enclaves, but in the region as a whole. However, in China Proper, agriculture apparently remained more or less in its traditional state, so that economic growth was largely confined to the nonagricultural sectors in the treaty ports.

THE LAG IN CHINA'S MODERN ECONOMIC GROWTH

In the face of these contradictory tendencies, one of the questions that needs to be posed is whether one can legitimately speak of modern economic growth for China as a whole. In one superficial sense it could be regarded merely as a matter of averaging. That is, if there was a sustained rise in per capita income in Manchuria and in the nonagricultural sectors of China proper, while agriculture in China proper was stagnating, then in net terms there would be per capita growth in the economy as a whole. On the other hand, given the massive size of the farm sector in China proper and the comparatively large number of people dependent on it, even a small per capita decline in agriculture could more than outweigh a sizable rise in industry, transport and trade.

This whole problem is complicated by the fact that our knowledge concerning trends in agricultural development is at best extremely sketchy. Thanks to the surveys of the National Agricultural Research Bureau (*Crop Reports,* 1933-39) and of Buck (1930, 1937) we have a fairly reliable cross-section view of the state of Chinese agriculture in the 1930's (Chang, 1932; Shen, 1951). But we know very little about agricultural developments over time. It is uncertain whether yields per acre and product per person employed in agriculture declined, rose, or remained more or less stationary during these hundred years or even during shorter periods (such as 1890 to 1930). Similarly, there are no reliable data concerning trends in farm household income during these decades.

However, even some sustained rise in per capita agricultural income and the resultant net growth *in* the economy as a whole would not necessarily justify a finding of *modern economic growth* of the mainland economy as a whole. Several essential attributes of modern economic growth were missing; most notably, the industrial structure changed but little and the movement of factors out of agriculture and into manufacturing and services was very sluggish. Moreover, assuming that one could show economic growth in each of the three areas—Manchuria, the treaty ports, and the rural hinterland of China proper—one would still have to demonstrate that their developments were functionally and organically related. In more technical terms, one would have to demonstrate structural interdependence or linkages in the process of growth so that new stimuli to which one area might be exposed would reverberate through the national economy.

The fusion of the various parts of the country into one organic whole was seriously impeded both by transport and communications barriers and by political fragmentation. As a result, during certain periods parts of the country such as Shanghai or Manchuria were in some respects more closely integrated with foreign economies than with the Chinese mainland.

One might perhaps characterize this century of economic disturbance and change as one of gestation, during which many of the necessary preconditions for national development and modern economic growth were established.[5] One might also describe it as a very painful and costly century of "creative destruction" during which the traditional economic order was weakened and undermined, new economic institutions were created, an infrastructure was constructed, a modest industrial base was built, an industrial labor force—however limited—was trained and committed, and a small managerial and technical class was raised. Without these institutions, facilities and manpower, the industrialization drive following the Communist take-over would have been inconceivable.

Bearing these hypotheses in mind, in this chapter I will attempt to: (a) characterize briefly the traditional economic order prior to Western impact, (b) explore how this order was disturbed, (c) analyze the economic modernization efforts in nineteenth-century China, (d) contrast the experience of economic growth in Manchuria and China proper, and (e) present a cross-section view of the mainland economy inherited by the Chinese Communists. Since the focus of this whole essay is on the economy as inherited by the Chinese Communists, the analysis will be concerned with the mainland as a whole. For many purposes and from many points of view the economies of Manchuria and China Proper should be analyzed separately. However, both form part of the foundation on which the economy of People's Republic is built.

5. For an analysis of these economic changes approached within a somewhat different framework, see John K. Fairbank, A. Eckstein, and L. S. Yang, 1960.

II. THE TRADITIONAL ECONOMIC ORDER PRIOR TO WESTERN IMPACT

Our knowledge concerning the state of the Chinese economy around 1800 is hazy and imprecise. The understanding we have is largely qualitative, with quantitative indicators virtually absent. While there are some crude estimates for population size and cultivated land area (for instance, Ho, 1959), data on agricultural production, unit yields, and other systematic indicators of land productivity, on output per man, and on income levels are lacking. Of course this situation is not unique to the Chinese economy of that period. Nevertheless our degree of ignorance is undoubtedly significantly greater in this case than for early nineteenth-century Japan or India, not to mention Europe. The sources are scattered and difficult to use, and the data in the sources are fragmentary. Nevertheless, by building on foundations laid by some Chinese and Japanese scholars, it should be possible to reconstruct the situation and the trends in some specific areas. If a more or less representative sample of local data could be assembled, it might provide a more precise view of economic tendencies in the country as a whole.

EXPANSION OF THE TRADITIONAL ECONOMY

The late eighteenth century apparently marked the end of a long period of sustained expansion in the total size of the Chinese economy. Specific evidence for this is the more or less continuous growth in population and in the land area under cultivation. Expansion was also accompanied by an intensification in the patterns of land use. Whether the increases in food production and population also led to a sustained rise in per capita product cannot be determined on the basis of presently available evidence.

It seems, moreover, that expansion was not accompanied by a marked technical transformation in the methods of agricultural production. It rested principally on the introduction of new crops, which pushed the agricultural frontier from the low plains to the more hilly and mountainous regions (Ho, 1959, p. 169). Gradual dissemination of early ripening rice (soon after the year 1000) and the development of rice strains with short growing seasons facilitated the spread of double-cropping. A second aspect of agricultural expansion was the spread of dry-land crops such as sorghum, introduced after Mongol conquest, and maize, sweet potatoes, Irish potatoes and peanuts, adopted in the late Ming and early Ch'ing periods.

Finally, population growth was apparently stimulated not only by this expansion of the agricultural base but also by an extended period of peace and order during the seventeenth and eighteenth centuries. All indications thus point to a prolonged period of growth in total national product during the centuries preceding the Treaty of Nanking. This conclusion, based on more recent studies, contradicts the earlier prevalent image of an "unchanging China" with an economy subject to cyclical fluctuations around a more or less stable level, but without any rising trend. Furthermore, it suggests that the concept of a circular flow economy is not applicable to traditional China. The economy did not just reproduce itself; expansion in its total size could not have taken place without some net investment, even if this investment was perhaps not sufficient to permit a sustained growth in per capita product.

The whole pace of economic change in China was apparently accelerated between the eighth and the thirteenth centuries. This was evidenced by a significant increase in internal trade, which permitted a greater regional specialization in crops, with apparently some resultant gains in land productivity (Reischauer and Fairbank, 1960, p. 212). The economy as a whole became much more commercialized. Revenues from government monopolies—particularly those on trade in salt, tea, and wine—and from various commercial taxes increased so rapidly that they outweighed the land tax.

These developments were accompanied and reinforced by a marked rise in overseas trade, with oceanic commerce gradually outbalancing in importance the foreign trade carried on overland (Reischauer and Fairbank, 1960, pp. 214-215). China exported porcelain, fine handicraft products, silks, art objects, some gold, silver, lead and tin, and copper cash. Imports consisted largely of horses, hides, some fine woods and fine cotton textiles. Not unnaturally, this growth in domestic and foreign trade brought with it increasing monetization, marked in part by the increasing use of paper money (Yang, 1952).

This was a period during which China seems to have been developing much more rapidly than Europe. Because of this, it was also a time when China appeared much more advanced to European travelers. However, with the advent of the Renaissance, the Age of Discovery, and the beginnings of the scientific age, change in Europe began to accelerate just at a time when the general pace was slowing down in China.

China did not experience an agricultural revolution in the European sense of that concept. Although some changes in patterns of land use did take place beginning in the eleventh century, these did not lead to a disruption of existing agrarian institutions. To the extent that there was an identifiable commercial revolution in China, its force was largely spent by the fourteenth century. Quite apart from timing, it was much more modest in scope than any comparable European "revolution," and never as disruptive of the traditional order. It is doubtful whether one can find in Chinese history a counterpart to the age of mercantilism, either in the field of policy or theory. It is, of course, true that economic activity in

China was surrounded by a maze of regulations, restrictions, and government monopolies reminiscent of mercantilist practices in Europe. But European mercantilism was strongly infused with an economic nationalism coupled with an aggressive foreign trade orientation, which was absent in China. Sustained foreign trade expansion, commitment to a favorable balance of trade, and an active seeking of foreign treasure are mercantilist attributes uncommon in China.

To the contrary, the dominant world view of traditional China, as embodied in the orthodox line of Confucianism, conceived of economic welfare not in terms of economic growth but in terms of subsistence, of satisfaction of the basic minimum needs of the masses. The principal function of the state was the maintenance of social peace and harmony. In this view, a commitment to the pursuit of wealth and power by the state—in particular, the emperor as the embodiment of the state—would in no way differ from the behavior of an official pursuing his own selfish interests (Schwartz, 1964, pp. 10-11). Thus the dominant leitmotif of Chinese statecraft, from at least the fourteenth century up to the self-strengthening movement of the late nineteenth, was *maintenance* rather than *development:* maintenance of minimum subsistence for the peasantry, maintenance of a comfortable though frugal standard for the gentry, maintenance of law and order, maintenance of public works, and protection from barbarian incursions. The accent was on stability—social, political, and economic—rather than on growth. Closely related to this was a looking inward rather than an active seeking of foreign contacts, either friendly or hostile.

From this brief sketch of selected aspects of China's economic evolution prior to the nineteenth century, it is clear that at least two fundamental conditions for *modern economic growth* were missing: sustained foreign economic contacts on a significant scale, and the application of technological progress to production processes in agriculture and industry.

THE ECONOMY OF EARLY NINETEENTH-CENTURY CHINA

As a result, early nineteenth-century China exhibited the typical characteristics of a premodern, preindustrial economy. It was preponderantly agrarian, with the bulk of the population deriving their livelihood from crop production. Given the very high density of population per unit of cultivated area, a pattern of agricultural production had to be evolved to produce the greatest possible energy yield per acre. Consequently, except in the northwest, animal husbandry was purely supplementary and subsidiary to food production. Its high intensity of use probably made land in China, more than anywhere else, "an article manufactured by man." Farm husbandry was characterized by "economy of space, economy of materials, economy of implements, economy of fodder, economy of fuel, economy of waste products, economy of everything except forests and of the labor of human beings whom social habits have made abundant and abundance cheap" (Tawney, 1932, p. 48).

The prevailing system of landholding was based on freehold tenure with the peasant free to buy or sell land. There was no primogeniture, and inheritance was shared equally by all sons. But this system opened the way to fragmentation of landholding. Tenancy was subject to wide regional variation and generally tended to be more prevalent near cities and in the more densely settled farm areas where land values were high.

The peasant household was to a large extent self-sufficient, often processing its own food, spinning its own yarn and weaving its own cloth. At the same time, most households were at least to some extent involved in the local market (Skinner, 1964, 1965). As noted earlier, there was some regional specialization in agricultural production; cotton- or tea-producing households and regions had to purchase at least some foods, while grain-producing areas had to import some cotton, wool and tea. Virtually every farm household bought some salt, so that the processing and sale of salt under government license constituted one of the most lucrative trades of traditional China (Ho, 1954).

The peasant and his family lived close to the margin of subsistence, with their actual net income and standard of living subject to wide variations in different regions and periods. His fortunes depended, of course, not only on the physical environment in his own district, but also on annual fluctuations in rainfall, on the maintenance of public works (*i.e.,* irrigation and flood control), on the extent of tenancy, on tenure practices at any one time in any one area, on the terms on which he could obtain credit and, last but very important, the degree of tax pressure to which he was subjected. Many of these conditions depended on the strength of the imperial center, and the character of the local bureaucracy and the local gentry. Thoroughgoing studies of these variables and their interrelationship in the early nineteenth century are sorely lacking.

Manufacturing was carried on by handicraft and preindustrial methods in both rural and urban areas. There are no output data, and so the possibilities for economic analysis of this period are again limited. Some crude estimates might possibly be attempted through study of consumption patterns in peasant, gentry, and merchant households in the cities and the countryside, and in the imperial household.

The degree of commercialization in the economy also cannot be quantified on the basis of presently available data. But local gazetteers might perhaps be useful in an exploration of the volume of goods moving through local, intermediate, and central markets in different years. Data for even a scattering of years, provided it were for a certain minimum number of markets selected from different regions of the country or from one major region, might provide a suitable sample for analysis. Such an undertaking would be greatly facilitated now because of the availability of

Skinner's pathbreaking study (1964, 1965), which can in a sense provide the methodological framework for an investigation of this kind.

Despite the lack of data, there is no doubt that the volume of both local and interregional trade was considerable by the nineteenth century. Trade provided the basis for accumulating commercial wealth in traditional China. Although the merchant's status role was low, officially lower than that of the peasantry, his links with the gentry and with officialdom were in fact close (Ho, 1964, pp. 41-52). What the precise line of dependency was in these relationships is far from clear. Can one accept the rather widely held image of total subordination of merchants to officialdom, or is the relationship one of much greater subtlety and complexity, in which the wealthy merchant is in a position to influence the actions of officials? An equally important question from a long-run development point of view is why these occasional accumulations of merchant wealth did not become growing points for long-run capital accumulation. Why were they not embodied in the growth of reproducible tangible assets? Do the high prestige and security value assigned to investment in land, the traditional outlook and character of officialdom, and the character of traditional kinship obligations provide an adequate explanation?

There is no doubt that the long cycle of expansion outlined above had largely spent itself by about 1800. As the opportunities for extending the land frontier were more or less exhausted, population growth was slowing down and population was increasingly pressing against available land resources. This process was naturally aggravated by dynastic weakness and its consequences in the field of public administration, taxation, and public works.

In a sense the Chinese economy was now indeed beginning to fall into a more or less circular flow pattern, possibly into a period of decline. It was exhibiting the typical characteristics of a densely populated, underdeveloped economy in which land was limited, capital was short, and labor was abundant. Moreover, it was bound by a value system and based on a social structure that were not conducive to either the exercise of state initiative on behalf of economic development or the encouragement and rise of private entrepreneurship.

STAGE OF DEVELOPMENT IN EARLY NINETEENTH-CENTURY CHINA

Against this background, what stage of development did the Chinese economy attain by 1800-1840? Since there are no adequate quantitative indicators for these years, one possible approach is to contrast the state of the Chinese economy in a period for which data are readily available with the economy of early Meiji Japan; and then to use this as a basis for assessing what the mainland situation might have been earlier. This is attempted in Table 1.

TABLE 1

SELECTED INDICATORS OF STAGES OF ECONOMIC DEVELOPMENT IN EARLY MEIJI JAPAN AND REPUBLICAN CHINA

Item	Unit of Measure	Early Meiji	China, 1930's
Paddy rice yield	lb/acre	1623	2470 [a]-2930 [b]
Wheat yield	lb/acre	729	895 [b]- 960 [c]
Cultivated land per capita	acres	0.298 [d]	464
Degree of literacy:			
Male	per cent	43 [e]	30.3
Female	per cent	10 [e]	1.2
GNP Composition:			
Agriculture	per cent	65	65
Industry	per cent	9	11
Services	per cent	26	24
Share of agricultural produce sold off farms	per cent	25-31	18-34 [f]

Notes:

a. Liu and Yeh, 1965 (Tables 31 and A-4).

b. Buck as given in Liu-Yeh, 1965 (Table 30).

c. National Agricultural Research Bureau data as given in Liu-Yeh, 1965 (Table 30).

d. Based on a three-year average for 1880-1882.

e. These are estimates for "the proportion of each age-group who would ever have gotten some kind of schooling at 1868 rates of attendance" as derived by R. P. Dore, 1965 (p. 321).

f. The lower figure refers to the share of crop output sold off farms as given by Buck, 1937 (p. 236), while the higher figure adds to this the percentage used for rent. The percentage inclusive of rent overstates the share marketed since it is based on the implicit assumption that none of the rent was retained by the landlords for their own and their household's subsistence, and that therefore all of it is sold. On the other hand, the lower percentage understates the share marketed since it, in turn, is based on the opposite assumption; *i.e.,* that all the rent is retained in agriculture for self-consumption and none of it is sold.

Sources:

Early Meiji: Rice and wheat yields as given in Ogura, 1963 (p. 11); GNP composition and produce sold from Rosovsky, 1966; land per capita from cultivated acreage figures adapted from SCAP Report No. 143; population from Weda, 1934 (p. 163) and Ishii, 1937 (p. 53).

1930's China: Cultivated land from Buck, 1937 (p. 165); Liu and Yeh, 1965 (pp. 171-177); literacy from Buck, 1937 (p. 373); GNP composition from Liu-Yeh, 1965 (Table 8, p. 66).

Although these data and estimates are subject to sizable margins of error, they can serve as a fairly adequate basis for comparison. As indicated earlier, we have no long-term trend data for agricultural production or yield per acre in China. But there are no indications of advances in Chinese agriculture between 1800-1840 and 1930 that could have caused significant increases in rice and wheat yields. We know of no large-scale application of new inputs such as chemical fertilizer, or of greatly improved inputs such as better seeds used on a large scale, or of a technological breakthrough that would greatly increase the efficiency of existing inputs. Therefore we may be justified in concluding that land productivity in early or mid-nineteenth century China was definitely higher than in late Tokugawa or early Meiji Japan.

The problem of cultivated land area per capita is not quite so clear-cut. One cannot be certain whether China's population in relation to the cultivated land area has grown, declined, or remained more or less unchanged during this span of approximately 100 years. On balance, however, even allowing for the devastation of the Taiping rebellion (1850-64) and of the civil wars, the presupposition of some rise in density seems reasonable. Even if this conclusion were not borne out by subsequent research, a significant decrease in population pressure during this period is improbable. Therefore the quite large differential that Table 1 shows for this indicator would strongly suggest that the degree of population pressure was more acute in Meiji Japan than in early nineteenth-century China.

This fact combined with the yield differentials indicates that the average Chinese had more domestically produced food staples at his disposal than the average Japanese. To some extent the data in Table I exaggerate the land productivity differentials, since China's greatest yield advantage is in rice, which is relatively much less important in China's crop production basket and diet than in Japan's. Moreover, given the fact that the overwhelming bulk of the population in both countries lived and worked on the land, one might deduce that the productivity of both land and labor was probably higher in nineteenth-century China than in Meiji Japan.

However, a rather different picture emerges if one examines the "structural" rather than the "absolute level" indicators. In respect to the stock and flow of general basic education, as indicated by the degree of literacy or the share of school age population enrolled (the latter is not given in Table 1), Meiji Japan is well ahead of mainland China in the 1930's, and so must have been even further advanced in relation to nineteenth-century China. The nineteenth-century gap must have been so large that it could not be closed even by allowing for possible margins of error caused by the basic character of the data or possible differences in definition.

Roughly similar conclusions emerge from a comparison of the degree of commercialization in agriculture. One would expect a significant rise in market involvement between 1800-1840 and 1930's for a number of reasons. With the introduction of steamships on the inland waterways and the construction of railways that reached many major market centers, distribution costs were lowered and farm marketing was facilitated and encouraged. This is explicitly confirmed by Skinner's work (1964, 1965) and by Buck's findings (1937, p. 357). Therefore one may be justified in concluding that Chinese agriculture of the mid-nineteenth century was almost certainly less involved in the market nexus than its early Meiji counterpart in Japan.

The structure of the two economies seems to have been rather similar, as indicated by the interindustry composition of GNP as shown in Table 1. As one would expect, by the 1930's China was more industrialized than Meiji Japan, but the differences are not very great. On this basis it might be safe to surmise that the Chinese economy at mid-nineteenth century was at least as dependent on agriculture, if not more so, as that of Meiji Japan. On the other hand, the service sector was probably much more important in Japan. Given the differential in the commercialization of agriculture, one would expect transport and trade, and other associated services to make a larger contribution to GNP in Meiji Japan.

What conclusions can one draw from this analysis of the data in Table 1? Bearing in mind the tentativeness of the data and the limited number of comparative indicators available, it would seem that agricultural product per capita and (given the overwhelming weight of agriculture in the economy) perhaps even GNP per capita was higher in nineteenth-century China than in Meiji Japan. However, despite that, one might suggest that the Chinese economy was in a sense less "developed." That is, it was perhaps less prepared for modernization and less capable of absorbing and digesting new influences and external stimuli. This would be the case at least to the extent that one might expect a positive association between modernization and the degree of literacy and commercialization.

The data in Table 1 suggest yet another conclusion. It would seem that the Japanese peasant was even closer to the margin of subsistence than his Chinese counterpart, yet this did not prevent him from making a significant contribution to financing the economic development of the country through taxation and voluntary saving (Ohkawa and Rosovsky, 1960). This comparison confirms once more the absence of any necessary or automatic relationship between average per capita product or average agricultural product and the capacity to save.

III. DISTURBANCE, SELF-STRENGTHENING AND THE ABORTIVE BREAKTHROUGH

China's traditional economic order was disturbed, and eventually permanently displaced, by the interaction of internal weaknesses in a period of dynastic decline and external pressure. There is no need here to repeat the well-documented story of the growth of China's overseas trade in the eighteenth century, the expansion of the triangular trade between Britain, India and China, the increasing opium trade, and the collapse of the Canton system (Fairbank, 1953; Greenberg, 1951). Nor is this the place to restate the origins of the Taiping rebellion and to trace its course. Both China's defeat in the Opium War and the serious challenge to dynastic survival made by the Taipings were symptoms of internal weakness and of its contributing causes. As such they had a far-reaching effect on the course of economic change in nineteenth-century China.

They affected that course both directly and indirectly. The most direct and immediate effect was on the foreign trade sector which then, through the operation of demand and supply forces, gradually affected internal trade and domestic production as well. The rise of the treaty ports and the associated institutions provided an institutional and geographic base for the development of foreign enterprise and, later, of Chinese enterprise. The Taiping rebellion, on the other hand, wrought great devastation, led to marked depopulation of a number of areas, and contributed greatly to economic decline, particularly in agriculture. At the same time it further undermined and weakened the traditional Chinese state, reducing its capacity for a positive response to the external challenge.

The indirect economic effects flowed from a reactive or defensive nationalism embodied in the self-strengthening movement; led by regional and provincial leaders, rather than by the central government, the movement was a series of more or less abortive modernization efforts and public investment projects. It was clearly an attempt at a creative response to the Western challenge, and coincided roughly in timing with the Meiji Restoration. Bearing these cataclysmic events in mind, in this section I will first outline briefly the immediate trade effects of the Treaty of Nanking, then examine the economic consequences of the rebellion, and finally analyze the economic program of the self-strengtheners.

CHINA'S FOREIGN TRADE IN THE EARLY NINETEENTH CENTURY

The pattern of foreign trade that emerged in the course of the eighteenth century was based on the rapidly growing demand for Chinese tea, primarily in Britain, and to a lesser extent in other parts of Europe. There was at first no corresponding demand for foreign goods in China, so that the balance of trade was consistently unfavorable from a British point of view. By the nineteenth century this situation was "corrected" by the export of opium and raw cotton from India to Canton. As a result, in the first decades of the nineteenth century the trade balance was reversed, as illustrated by the data in Table 2. Although total Canton imports did not rise very rapidly during this period, opium purchases more than doubled in value between 1817 and 1821, and almost quadrupled between 1817 and 1830. As a result, the share of opium in total imports increased from a little over 20 per cent to nearly 60 per cent. This in turn stimulated the expansion of domestic opium production (Remer, 1926, p. 27).

On the export side, tea remained the major export item throughout this period, with silk products in second, and raw silk in third place. The first constituted about 55-65 per cent of total sales, while the latter two were about 15 and 10 per cent respectively.

These trading patterns changed gradually after the opening of the ports. Imports of cotton goods were gaining, and in the 1840's they began to exceed the imports of woolens as well as the exports of cotton goods. Silk exports started to rise rapidly after the "opening" of Shanghai in 1843. Thus until about the 1870's, China's exports were virtually confined to tea and silk, while imports were dominated by opium and cotton goods. The total volume of trade, however, was still quite small.

As already noted, opium production grew because of rising demand stimulated by imports. One may assume that tea and silk production also rose in response to increasing export demand. It is doubtful that imports of cotton goods had a depressing effect on the handicraft textile industry at the time. Data for the late nineteenth and early twentieth century indicate that handicraft weaving continued to be competitive with imported and domestically manufactured cloth for a long time in mainland China, just as in other countries in the process of industrialization (Hou, 1965, Ch. 7). There are a number of reasons for this, not the least of which is that imported and domestic cloth tended to supply different markets. If this was true in the late nineteenth century when more cotton goods were imported, the resilience of native handicrafts must have been even greater earlier in the century when imports of manufactured cloth were smaller.

For all of these reasons, one might surmise that the initial income effects of foreign trade were positive for the domestic economy. But while foreign trade did stimulate possible increases in production, it also turned the internal terms of trade against agriculture and thus depressed the real income of the peasantry. Which of these effects—the positive or the negative—was more important is impossible to judge from the available evidence. The adverse shift in the internal terms of trade was induced by the rising price of silver. As the foreign trade balance became unfavorable (see Table 2, A), silver flowed out of the country. According to one

TABLE 2

CANTON TRADE, 1817-1830

A. Exports, Imports and Trade Balance
(in millions of Spanish silver dollars)

Year	Exports	Imports [a]	Balance [a]
1817	15.57	18.69	−3.12
1821	20.52	21.43	−0.91
1825	22.23	23.27	−1.04
1830	17.60	26.81	−9.21

B. Commodity Composition of Canton Exports
(in per cent)

Year	Tea	Raw Silk	Silk Goods	Other	Total
1817	69	4	6	21	100
1821	57	10	15	18	100
1825	61	10	13	16	100
1830	60	10	13	17	100

C. Commodity Composition of Imports
(in per cent)

Year	Woolen Goods	Metals	Furs	Cotton	Opium [a]	Other	Total
1817	17	3	1	44	22	13	100
1821	15	2	2	24	44	13	100
1825	17	3	2	27	42	9	100
1830	11	3	0.3	21	56	9	100

Note:
a. Opium import data are incomplete since they do not include the quantities smuggled in, and it is not certain whether they fully encompass the legally imported amounts.

Source:
Computed by author on the basis of data in Y. K. Cheng, 1956, Tables 1A and 1B (p. 6), which are in turn from Morse, 1926-29.

estimate the flow of specie increased to 11.2 million Chinese dollars by 1841 (C. M. Li, 1946, p. 501).[6] Since taxes and other contributions were computed in silver, and silver bullion also served as a store of value, an outflow of specie tended to raise its price. Therefore, as the price of silver increased, the speculative demand for it increased as well. However, a rise in the price of silver meant a decline in the value of copper cash expressed in silver. Yet the peasant sold his rice for copper cash while silver remained the standard by which his taxes were computed. Therefore, unless the copper-cash price of rice was adjusted correspondingly, the peasants' real tax burden was bound to increase considerably (Wright, 1957, pp. 150-153).

ECONOMIC CONSEQUENCES OF THE TAIPING REBELLION

Whatever the net economic effects of foreign trade expansion may have been, they were overwhelmed by the devastation of the Taiping rebellion (1850-64). It greatly accelerated the process of economic decline which had started in the late eighteenth century. The rebellion reduced the land area under cultivation, thus compressing the tax base at a time when government expenditures were rising. In a sense the economy was caught up in a vicious downward spiral, starting with a decline in farm production because of war devastation, and leading to a decline in government revenues at a time of rising military outlays. As a result, public works and other government services deteriorated while tax pressure on the peasantry increased. These factors in combination contributed to a further curtailment in agricultural production. To finance the constantly rising deficits, the government resorted to the printing of paper notes on the one hand and the introduction of a new tax, *likin,* on the other.

Initially conceived as an ad hoc emergency tax, *likin* became a permanent institution, not abolished until 1931, which had deleterious effects on China's long-term development. It was an ad valorem tax levied either as a transit tax on goods as they passed a *likin* barrier or as a sales tax on the shops where the goods were sold (Beal, 1958). It was collected by local and provincial officials and was for the most part spent locally. Moreover, unlike the land tax, it was not systematically reported. Because of its very character and the method of administration, *likin* was even more subject to abuses than the traditional taxes. Since a product on its way to final markets might pass by several *likin* stations, it could be subject to multiple taxation. The principal economic effect of this tax was to raise the cost of distribution and erect new economic and institutional barriers to the flow of goods.

In one sense one can view the Taiping rebellion as a symptom of deep-

6. According to Li, citing Sargent, merchandise imports amounted to 25 million Chinese dollars in 1841 and exports to 13.3 million Chinese dollars, with the difference covered by silver exports.

seated peasant unrest engendered by the growing population pressure on land resources which by this time were more or less fixed. Chinese agriculture, operating within a context of unchanging technology, was increasingly subject to the law of diminishing returns. A decline in per capita product resulted, which, in the absence of positive policy measures to reverse it, could only be arrested by the Malthusian checks of war and pestilence. Whether or not one takes this view, there is no doubt that one of the consequences of the rebellion was far-reaching depopulation of the lower Yangtze. The following quotation from a statement by a local official of Chekiang (cited in Ho, 1959, p. 154) may serve to illustrate the extent of the problem.

> After the Taiping wars vast areas of agricultural land were laid waste and various cities and towns reduced to a shambles. Villages far and near are very sparsely populated and ridges and furrows are all covered with thorns and weeds. . . . To rehabilitate this area it is vital that immigrants be attracted.

Therefore it is not surprising that the efforts of the T'ung-chih Restoration were concentrated on rehabilitating agriculture, which in turn provided the fiscal foundations for the traditional Chinese state. Restoration leaders undertook an ambitious colonization program to settle millions of refugees and demobilized soldiers (Wright, 1957, p. 158). At the same time, tenant farmers from the mountainous and congested areas were encouraged to settle in some of the best agricultural areas of the country. The Restoration program incorporated all the traditional farm improvement measures, such as repair of old and badly deteriorated waterworks, construction of new water conservation projects, land tax reduction, and more efficient collection arrangements for the land tax levied.

As already indicated, the Taiping rebellion had certain long-run political consequences that had important economic implications. In the course of defeating the rebellion, political power had become much more fragmented. As Peking was cut off from central China, mobilizing armies and carrying on the war effort became increasingly a regional and provincial responsibility. As a result, the Restoration also became, to a considerable extent, a provincially based effort. Fragmentation of the polity, the rise of quasi-fiefs, and the crystallization of local satrapies became a hallmark of the Chinese political scene virtually until the advent of the Chinese Communist regime.

Thus at roughly the same time as Japan was doing away with feudalism and moving in the direction of a unified nation-state, China was moving in an opposite direction. Its lack of political unity not only reinforced economic fragmentation due to transport, communications, and various institutional barriers, but prevented the formulation of comprehensive programs of modernization that could be made effectively applicable to the country as a whole. It precluded the formulation of a national development program based on measures designed both to remove impediments to economic growth and to actively foster it.

SELF-STRENGTHENING AND THE ABORTIVE INDUSTRIALIZATION PROGRAM

This does not mean that such measures were not attempted. In fact, closely linked to the T'ung-chih Restoration was the "self-strengthening" (*tzu-ch'iang*) movement, which signaled a recognition of China's need for industrialization and the inauguration of projects designed to launch it on that path.[7] The recognition by some came early as evidenced by the following excerpt from a letter by Lin Tse-hsü in 1842 (Teng and Fairbank, 1954, p. 28):

> . . . Ships, guns and a water force are absolutely indispensable. Even if the rebellious barbarians had fled and returned beyond the seas, these things would still have to be urgently planned for, in order to work out the permanent defense of our sea frontiers. Moreover unless we have weapons, what other help can we get now to drive away the crocodile and to get rid of the whales?

However, nothing was done about this need for about twenty years, until Tseng Kuo-fan and Li Hung-chang assumed the leadership of the movement. An 1862 entry in Tseng's diary will serve to illustrate his approach to the problem (Teng and Fairbank, p. 62):

> If we wish to find a method of self-strengthening, we should begin by considering the reform of government service and the securing of men of ability as urgent tasks and then regard learning to make explosive shells and steamships and other instruments as the work of first importance. If only we could possess all their superior techniques, then we would have the means to return their favor when they are obedient, and we would also have the means to avenge our grievances when they are disloyal.

This revealing passage illustrates simultaneously the traditional view of China as the universal empire that expects obedience and loyalty from the barbarians; the feeling of deep humiliation produced by the defeats of this empire; and the recognition of the need for acquiring modern techniques of production if the challenge posed by external threats is to be met. These elements of thought and attitude were to run like a leitmotiv through much of China's subsequent history. In effect they represent a crucial element of inheritance that has become a very important part of Chinese Communist cosmology and as such has played a major role in shaping Communist China's economic policy. They also epitomize strivings that were evident in Japan at roughly the same time; these are perhaps most vividly and most succinctly stated by the slogan that played such a

7. The term *tzu-ch'iang* was first used by Feng Kuei-fen in 1860 (Teng and Fairbank, 1954, pp. 50-53).

major role in the Meiji Restoration—*fukoku kyohei* ("a rich country and a strong army"). Probably Japan perceived the connection between these two elements more clearly than did China; certainly the translation into actual programs and projects was more effective there.

In China, economic modernization efforts in the late nineteenth century proceeded along three parallel paths, government projects; joint public-private undertakings under the aegis of the *kuan-tu-shang-pan* (official supervision–merchant management) system; and private enterprise—Chinese and foreign—mostly operating in the treaty ports. The first two were closely linked to the self-strengthening movement while the last was preponderantly foreign-led.

As Feuerwerker clearly demonstrates, the distribution between the *kuan-pan* and *kuan-tu-shang-pan* forms of organization is an artificial one (1958, p. 16); partly because some enterprises started in one form and then were converted into the other and vice versa, and more importantly, because both forms had more or less similar practices and methods of operation. Nevertheless there is some point in making a distinction, inasmuch as the strictly government projects were virtually confined to "military industries," *i.e.,* arsenals and shipyards, although an ironworks and railroads fell into this category too.

Several points need to be made about this total effort. First, it marked the beginnings, the first halting steps, of modern industry in China. Second, the total size of the effort was quite modest. It entailed altogether (including both the *kuan-pan* and the *kuan-tu-shang-pan*) about 15 to 20 major undertakings over a thirty year period, starting roughly with the establishment of the Kiangnan arsenal in 1865 and ending with the Treaty of Shimonoseki in 1895.

Third, the different projects in combination do represent a more or less rational economic design, even if that design was not blueprinted in advance. The initial stimulus for the whole undertaking came from the urge to produce weapons and strengthen the defense establishment—thus the arsenals and the Foochow shipyard. It was soon realized that modern transport and communications are essential ingredients of defense, and this led to the organization of the China Merchants' Steam Navigation Company and, somewhat later, the Imperial Telegraph Administration. Then a coal mine was opened to supply fuel for the arsenals and the steamships. This, in turn, made it necessary to provide transportation from the pithead to a suitable port, and so the first railroad line was built. Military requirements also induced the construction of several textile mills to manufacture cloth for the army. Iron and steel works were established to provide the necessary raw materials for the arsenals and to manufacture rails for the new railroads.

Fourth, most of these projects could be regarded as social overhead investments that, because of large initial capital requirements, long gestation periods, and their external economy effects, logically belong within the purview of public or semipublic investments. Moreover, one could argue that precisely because of their social overhead character, they should be established in the early phases of a development program when they can make an important contribution to decreasing costs of manufacturing.

Fifth, this industrialization effort was sponsored by high provincial officials, notably Tseng Kuo fan, Li Hung-Chang and their followers and allies, in the face of either indifference (at best) or active resistance (at worst) by the imperial center. Officials such as Tseng, Li and Chang Chih-tung perceived the need for at least limited modernization and industrialization, although they wished to keep the changes within the bounds of tradition. Their motives were mixed. In part they were anxious to strengthen the defensive capabilities of the country. At the same time these provincial leaders wanted to utilize the new projects as a means of strengthening their own power base. They saw in them an opportunity to tap new sources of potential revenue and political patronage, while at the same time providing a more or less independent industrial base for their armies. Precisely for these reasons, the court and their political rivals both in the central government and in the provinces perceived this industrialization effort as a threat. Moreover, the court apparently showed very little understanding of the need for, and the potential benefits of, industrialization but viewed the new enterprises as prime object for despoliation (Feuerwerker, 1958, p. 174).

Sixth, this first attempt at modern industrial development in China must be adjudged a failure in several terms. Some projects failed, but this in itself would not have been decisive since the economic history of industrialization in every country is strewn with a record of bankruptcies and unsuccessful experiments. More important despite its superficial economic logic in terms of projects selected and their interdependence, the effort as a whole had very little cumulative impact on China's modern economic growth. As we will see further below, to the extent that China experienced such growth, it came from another quarter.

The reasons for this apparent failure are manyfold and complex. One must bear in mind first of all that the total scope and size of the program was quite small in relation to the size of the country and the deadweight of tradition. Furthermore, each project experienced acute difficulties, due to shortages of capital, particularistic business and government practices, and the fact that the risks of such pioneering efforts were so high that to attract private capital, high rates of return had to be guaranteed even if the fortunes of the enterprise did not warrant the payment of large dividends. While all of these enterprises depended to a greater or lesser extent on provincial and central government support in the form of government loans, subsidies, and guaranteed market arrangements, they were constantly exposed to fiscal pressures from these public authorities.[8] Of course, there were other contributing factors closely associated with the country's economic backwardness, such as lack of technical, managerial and organizational skill and the constant scarcity of capital. However, one might venture the view that the more fundamental problems were not economic but ideological and institutional.

Perhaps the fate and character of this early industrialization program is most clearly illustrated by the fortunes of the China Merchants' Steamship Navigation Company (see Feuerwerker, 1958, Chs. 4 and 5; K. C. Liu, 1962). The company did very well by its managers and shareholders, so much so that in 1882 the managers could report that during the nine years of the company's life the shareholders had earned an average rate of annual return of 20 per cent on their investment in the form of guaranteed dividends, special stock dividends and bonuses. In contrast, the company as a steamship enterprise did not prosper. After 1887, at a time when the industry as a whole was expanding, it virtually stopped growing, and in 1914 the size of its fleet, both in number of ships and total tonnage, was almost the same as at the earlier date; and this in spite of rapid expansion in foreign and domestic trade and in the total volume of shipping.

Seventh, despite its apparent failure in one sense, the experiment did in the long run have a lasting impact on the modernization of China. The different projects singly and in combination chipped at the traditional order and helped to weaken and undermine it. Put in a different way, although the institutional, ideological, political and economic impediments were too strong to permit a breakthrough, the mere attempt—even though not too successful—served to weaken the barriers to modernization and thus open the way for later and more successful attempts. In more positive terms it also served as a training ground for modern entrepreneurship, for the development of modern forms of business organization, and for the training of technical cadres.

Although these different points have been stated rather categorically, they must in many ways still be treated as subject to further verification and validation. For instance, the relationship between this early industrialization effort and other subsequent efforts requires much closer study. Did these projects indeed have virtually no impact on stimulating the development of other enterprises? Did the *kuan-tu shang-pan* enterprises have any external economy or market stimulating effects? Did they have any learning effects and; if so, what kind and to what extent?

8. For a detailed, well-documented, and most sophisticated analysis of this attempt at early industrialization, see the study by Feuerwerker, 1958.

THE EMERGING PATTERN OF TRADE IN THE LATE NINETEENTH CENTURY

While these developments were taking place in the traditional economy, the treaty ports sector was growing very gradually under the impact of foreign trade expansion and closely associated economic activities. Several factors combined to stimulate foreign trade growth. A number of new ports were "opened" to trade. The Suez Canal was opened in 1869, and the trade route to Europe was markedly shortened. Telegraph communication between London and Shanghai was established in 1871 (Remer, 1926, pp. 38-45). At the same time, the demand for foreign goods was slowly increasing in China, while demand for China's products was rising abroad, with both of these developments actively promoted by the foreign trading enterprises in the treaty ports.

As a result, in terms of quantity indices both imports and exports roughly doubled between 1870 and 1895 (Cheng, 1956, Appendix I, p. 258). Nevertheless, by 1895, imports amounted to no more than U.S. $140 million and exports to U.S. $115 million (Remer, 1926, Tables 2, 3, 6). As exports and imports were rising, trade deficits were also increasing. Between 1868 and 1871 the average annual deficit was about U.S. $7 million. In the following five-year period this was converted into an average annual surplus of about the same amount. But after 1877 there was a consistent trade deficit, which by 1890-94 averaged around U.S. $35 million.[9]

During this period there began a secular decline in the gold value of silver, amounting in effect to a continuing devaluation of China's foreign exchange. This is illustrated by the fact that the U.S. dollar value of a Haikwan *tael* was just about halved, falling from 1.58 in 1871 to 0.80 in 1895. Other things being equal, one would have expected this to encourage exports and discourage imports. In fact the opposite happened, with imports rising more rapidly than exports, both in terms of current and constant (1913) prices. The precise reasons for this are not entirely clear. However, the sustained and rapid rise in the demand for imported goods, combined with supply inelasticities, must certainly have played an important role. These supply inelasticities in turn were rooted in the difficulties of organizing the silk and tea trade, improving the quality, standardization and internal distribution of these products.

This conclusion is borne out by a closer study of the changing structure of China's exports during this period. In general, Chinese exports became more diversified as the tea trade declined and new products began to be sold. Both India and Japan had begun to compete with China for the world tea trade, with India gaining ascendancy in the United Kingdom

9. Computed by the author on the basis of trade figures given by Y. K. Cheng, 1956 (p. 258).

market and Japan in trade with the United States. As a result China's tea exports in the 1880's and 1890's began to decline.

Silk and silk exports, on the other hand, continued to increase throughout the period in spite of growing Japanese competition. However, they lost ground in relation both to total world silk exports and to China's total export trade.

Under the impact of these developments the combined export share of tea and silk declined from more than 90 per cent in 1868 to no more than 60 per cent in 1890. By 1890, silk displaced tea as China's leading export product. To these traditional items new export products were now added, such as raw cotton, vegetable oils, hog bristles, skins and hides, eggs and their products, and other agricultural commodities. (See Table 3, A.)

Marked changes took place in the structure of imports as well, as shown in Table 3, B. By 1885 cotton goods displaced opium as China's leading import, marking the beginning of a continuing decline in the import of this drug. At first this was due largely to the spread of opium cultivation in China; later on there was also a gradual decline in domestic opium consumption. This decline is illustrated by the fact that while in 1888, 82,00 *piculs* of opium were imported, by 1893 the figure was reduced to 68,000 *piculs,* and by 1898 to 50,000 (Remer, 1926, pp. 48, 89-90). In the meantime cotton textile imports were gaining steadily in volume and relative importance. This was particularly true for cotton yarn imports, which doubled every few years. The growth in yarn imports was so rapid that by 1898 yarn exceeded in value the manufactured cotton textiles purchased from abroad. We can see here the emergence of a significant industrialization pattern: Imports of manufactured cotton goods find their way into Chinese markets, tapping new sources of demand without displacing handicraft weaving of cloth. To the contrary, handicraft weavers begin to use imported cotton yarn which is cheaper than the yarn produced domestically.

Another significant change characteristic of this period is the rise in imports of kerosene after the 1880's. In 1887, 12 million gallons were imported, and this amount jumped to 100 million gallons within the next decade (Cheng, 1956, p. 17). The oil was mostly used for household illumination; its use spread quickly because it gave a better light and yet was cheaper than bean, tea or other vegetable oils. These latter products could now be exported instead of being used for lighting, a case of economic adaptation based on gains from foreign trade.

TABLE 3

TREND AND COMMODITY COMPOSITION OF CHINA'S EXPORTS AND IMPORTS, 1868-1890

(in per cent)

A. Exports

Year	Tea	Silk and Silk Goods	Vegetable Seeds and Oils	Beans	Hides and Skins	Raw Cotton	Wool	Other	Total	Quantum Index (1913=100)
1868	53.8	39.7	......	1.0	......	0.9	......	4.6	100	33.7
1880	45.9	38.0	0.1	0.2	0.5	0.2	0.4	14.7	100	47.2
1890	30.6	33.9	0.6	0.4	1.4	3.4	1.6	28.1	100	42.0

B. Imports

Year	Opium	Cotton Goods	Cotton Yarn	Cereals and Wheat Flour	Sugar	Coal	Kerosene	Metals	Ma-chinery	Other	Total	Quantum Index (1913=100)
1868	33.1	29.0	2.5	0.8	0.8	2.1	......	4.8	......	26.9	100	25.4
1880	39.3	24.9	4.6	0.1	0.4	1.2	......	5.5	......	24.0	100	36.2
1890	19.5	20.2	15.3	9.6	0.9	1.6	3.2	5.7	0.3	23.7	100	54.8

Source:
Y. K. Cheng, 1956 (Tables 3 and 4, pp. 18-19; Appendix I, p. 258).

FOREIGN TRADE GROWTH AND DOMESTIC ECONOMIC DEVELOPMENT

What was the impact of these changes in foreign trade composition on economic development in the treaty ports and in the domestic economy? In the treaty ports we can see the beginnings of a cumulative development pattern. Foreign trade expansion generated a demand for modern banking services, and so in 1864 the Hongkong and Shanghai Banking Corporation was founded (Allen and Donnithorne, 1954, p. 107). In turn, the establishment of modern banking facilities contributed to a further growth in foreign trade in a number of ways, not the least of which was that it lowered the capital requirements for a foreign trading firm and thus eased freedom of entry into this business branch. Foreign trade growth stimulated the increase in shipping, which in turn led to the construction of ship repair and shipbuilding yards. Moreover, as foreign trade and its auxiliary services expanded, the number of foreigners resident in the treaty ports grew as well. This foreign population was estimated by Remer to be around 17,000 in 1899.[10]

The demand for urban facilities and public utilities increased rapidly as the total population, particularly the foreign population, of the treaty ports grew. The first electric power generating plant went into operation in Shanghai in 1882 and the first waterworks in 1880. The Shanghai Gas Company was founded in 1863 (Allen and Donnithorne, 1954, pp. 145-147). The provision of social overhead facilities combined with the prospects of profitable business opportunities encouraged the further growth of both the Chinese and the foreign populations in the treaty ports. As a result, the ports themselves became an increasingly important source of import demand.

Foreign trade and other economic activities in the treaty ports were largely dominated by foreign firms. However, by 1895 Chinese merchants were sharing more in this business, either directly through the establishment of Chinese firms or indirectly through the evolution of the comprador system. Not surprisingly, large accumulations of commercial wealth came into the hands of Chinese merchants operating out of the treaty ports. Some of this merchant wealth went into financing the *kuan-tu shang-pan* enterprises discussed above. However, prior to 1895 the bulk of it was apparently channeled into speculative activities in the treaty ports, *e.g.,* in real estate and in inventories, into investment in land, and into usury.

The impact of foreign trade expansion on the domestic economy is

10. Actual number computed by author on the basis of the number of American residents and their share in the foreign population as given by Remer, 1926 (Table 25, p. 338). Treaty ports were not only open to foreign trade but were subject to extraterritoriality, under which foreigners and their activities in China were subject to foreign and not Chinese law.

much more difficult to assess. Export growth of silk and silk products more than compensated for the decline in tea shipments. Moreover, exports of other farm products rose so that one would expect positive income effects from exports for the farm economy. (This finding may need to be qualified for districts in which tea production was of great importance.)

The situation is much more complicated on the import side. We have already noted the marked rise in cotton yarn imports, and this factory yarn was undoubtedly displacing handspun yarn with quite destructive effects on the position of rural handicrafts in a number of areas. However, it was at the same time augmenting the competitive strength of handicraft weaving against imported piece goods, inasmuch as domestic cloth manufactures could now use the cheaper imported yarn. The import of kerosene probably represented an immediate and direct economic gain, while the wide miscellany of other imports went mostly to the expanding urban market where they were tapping new sources of demand.

IV. THE BEGINNINGS OF MODERN ECONOMIC GROWTH, 1895-1949

On the eve of the Sino-Japanese war there was virtually no modern industry in China. There were fewer than ten cotton textile mills with a total spindlage of about 320,000 (Lieu, 1936, pp. 421-22). In comparison, India had a textile manufacturing establishment of one million spindles by 1876 and Japan attained that size by 1898 (Remer, 1926, p. 93). As a matter of fact, China was by then importing the largest share of its cotton yarn from India (Remer, 1933, p. 54). As noted above, there were a few arsenals and shipyards, some silk filatures laboring under great difficulties, and a small number of shops in various other branches of manufacture.

At the same time, construction of the first railway lines had just begun on the Chinese mainland, with no more than about 200 miles actually completed (Chang Kia-ngau, 1943, pp. 23-24; Morse, Vol. III, 1918). Shipping, on the other hand, was more highly developed. Chinese enterprises were running 35 or 40 vessels with a total tonnage of 35- to 40,000 (Feuerwerker, 1958, Table 17 and p. 290; U.K., 1945, p. 585). Nevertheless, foreign firms, which had over three-quarters of the carrying capacity, dominated overseas and even coastwise shipping.[11] With foreign trade expansion, the growth of shipping, banking and other services associated with it, the treaty ports, particularly Shanghai, were becoming

11. The foreign share in total modern shipping was 77 per cent in 1897 on the basis of tonnage of steamers entered and cleared through maritime customs. See C. M. Hou, 1965 (Table 28).

small islands of economic modernity on the periphery of the Chinese land and population mass.

However, the turning point in China's modern economic growth can be clearly traced back to the Treaty of Shimonoseki (1895) by which the Japanese secured the right to own and operate industrial establishments in the treaty ports. Then all the other powers having "most-favored nation" treaty arrangements with China took advantage of this right, and as a result industrial capacity, railroad mileage, shipping, and foreign trade grew quite rapidly.

In a sense it is surprising that such expansion could take place amid China's political weakness and later chaos. Imperial rule in the last decade or two of its existence was even more debilitated than in the latter half of the nineteenth century. The capacity of the public polity to play a positive role in promoting economic development was further undermined by the reparation burdens and indemnities the Chinese government had to assume, first after their defeat in the Sino-Japanese War, and then following the Boxer Rebellion. The situation was further aggravated by a number of uneconomic foreign loan obligations incurred by the governmental authorities. Between 1911 and 1928, China had no single government that could claim to rule all the country. With the Japanese conquest in 1931, the continuing civil war in the 1930's, the wartime Japanese occupation of north and east China, and the heightened civil war between 1945 and 1949, it would be fair to say that not even the Nationalist government effectively controlled all of the country's provinces.

China's record contrasts sharply with the history of government and of government's role in the economy in Japan. The contrast is so marked that by itself it could account for the different fates of modern economic growth in the two countries. Of course, government itself is not an autonomous factor but a product of a variety of forces and variables, among which the economy undoubtedly played a very significant role.

Whatever economic growth took place in China was accomplished despite, rather than because of, the government's role in the economy. This certainly applies to the Empire which was at best a passive bystander (in regard to modern economic growth) and at worst a seriously retarding influence. During the period of warlordism and civil war (1911-28), government (largely provincial) must have imposed tremendous burdens on the economy. Financing of large military expenditures during the Nanking government period (1928-37) and during the war undoubtedly represented additional heavy burdens. Whether the burdens imposed by the Nanking government were lesser or greater than its direct or indirect contributions to economic growth requires much more study. In fact, the public sector's role in the Chinese economy needs to be explored much more systematically and rigorously than has been done heretofore.

On the basis of presently available evidence it would seem that the bulk of this economic burden was borne by the traditional, rural sector. The government's failure to reform land tenure effectively, organize an agricultural extension service, or institute an effective farm credit system, combined with direct and indirect tax pressure, must have played a crucial role in preventing the technical transformation of agriculture and in perpetuating agricultural stagnation.

The treaty ports, on the other hand, operating within a framework of extraterritoriality, could escape the tax pressure, the exactions, and the devastations of warlordism and civil war. Moreover, they could substitute those attributes of law and order that were lacking in the traditional sector during most of this period. Once the governmental barriers were removed, a number of factors combined to foster modern economic growth in the treaty ports.

The ports as points of entry and exit for the mainland became natural foci for the concentration of foreign trading and shipping activities and all the associated economic services. Extraterritoriality and the foreign concessions attracted foreign residents and foreign firms as well as Chinese firms. This in turn created a demand for modern urban facilities. Once these facilities were installed, they reinforced the attraction of treaty ports as places of residence for both business establishments and households. The presence of social overhead facilities, *e.g.*, electric power, relatively good transportation, communications, and banking services, attracted modern industry after 1895, the first year in which foreign manufacturing firms were permitted to locate in the treaty ports. In addition to these external economies, certain demand factors reinforced the locational advantages of treaty ports as industrial centers. As the population of these ports grew, they necessarily became major market outlets for the manufactured products. These locational advantages are not so clear-cut in the case of raw material supplies for the modern industries. The ports in China proper were in most cases not well situated in relation to the best coal and iron ore reserves. On the other hand, they were close to the sources of agricultural raw material for the consumer goods industries. But it would seem that the external economy effects, broadly interpreted, provided such overwhelming locational advantages as to outweigh any possible increases in costs due to distance from raw material supplies.

These relationships can perhaps best be illustrated by the case of Shanghai, the largest of the ports. Before the opening of China to foreign trade, Hangchow, Soochow and Nanking were larger than Shanghai, but it quickly outstripped them. Though all three were also treaty ports and remained important commercial centers, Shanghai's location at the apex of the Yangtze basin turned out to be decisive. The Yangtze watershed encompasses about half of the land area of China proper, with about 40 per cent of the country's prewar population. The total of inland waterways navigable from Shanghai by junks at all seasons is nearly 30,000 miles. To this must be added an estimated half million miles of canalized or artificial waterways in the delta area. It is not surprising, therefore, that between 1865 and 1936, Shanghai handled 45 to 65 per cent of China's total foreign trade (Murphy, 1953, pp. 47-49).

However, development in the treaty ports was undoubtedly bought at a high social cost, both locally in the ports themselves; and nationally because of the psychological and political impact of the ports as a symbol of imperialism and because of the effect on economic growth in the hinterland. Economic development was based on a foreign-trade orientation that was in part a function of political, institutional and transport barriers within China and in part a function of the circumstances under which foreigners forced open China's door. The treaty ports were naturally favored. At the same time, and perhaps for the same reasons, provinces such as Szechwan remained underdeveloped in spite of their great natural wealth, and the coal resources of Shansi and Shensi were poorly exploited. The inability to develop inland industrial centers of prime importance in China proper may also have contributed to agricultural retardation. Such centers could have undoubtedly served as growing points for modern economic growth, from which modernizing influences could have been transmitted to the surrounding countryside more easily than from the distant treaty ports.

ECONOMIC DEVELOPMENT IN MANCHURIA

An entirely different set of advantages favored Manchuria as a locus of economic development on the Chinese mainland. Manchuria was an undeveloped frontier, rich in resources but very sparsely settled until the twentieth century. It was legally thrown open to Chinese immigration in 1860, Newchwang was opened as a port for foreign trade in 1861, and by 1903 the Russians had completed the construction of both the main and branch lines of the Chinese Eastern Railway (Ho, 1959, p. 160; Jones, 1949, p. 101; Allen and Donnithorne, 1954, p. 267). These developments, combined with the political instability and apparent economic decline in the rural sector of China proper, attracted large-scale immigration, particularly from north China. There must have been sizable movement in the late nineteenth century and again in the 1920's.

Population growth, railroad and harbor development, and land settlement produced a vigorous pattern of cumulative growth. Population growth and land settlement brought with them rapid expansion in farm production, as may be seen from the data in Table 4. Railroad and harbor development encouraged the rise of domestic and foreign trade. Kaoliang emerged as the principal food staple and soybeans as the main commercial crop. Manchurian agriculture became much more market-oriented and more readily responsive to market stimuli than the farm sector in China proper. Foreign trade grew very rapidly. In terms of current prices, ex-

TABLE 4

SELECTED INDICATORS OF ECONOMIC DEVELOPMENT IN MANCHURIA, 1900-1940

Year	Population (in millions)	Railroad Mileage (in miles)	Total Cereal Production (in thousands of metric tons)	Soybean Production (in thousands of metric tons)
1900	14	1,500	n.a.	(600) [f]
1907-1915 [a]	15-17 [b]	2,150 [c]	5,700 [d]	2,645 [e]
1930	34.3	3,700	18,810	5,360
1940	44.5	6,250	21,150	4,390

Notes:

a. This is not an average, but merely indicates that the different figures in this row refer to individual years within this eight-year interval.
b. For 1907.
c. For 1912.
d. For 1914.
e. For 1915.
f. Figures in parentheses are estimates.

Sources:

P. T. Ho, 1959 (pp. 160-163).
F. C. Jones, 1949 (pp. 4-7 and 101-106).
Grover Clarke, 1932 (p. 18).
Manshikai, 1964, Vol. I.

pressed in Haikwan *taels,* it increased tenfold in 20 years (1907-27), while for the mainland as a whole it took 56 years (1864-1920) to achieve the same percentage increase.[12]

Agricultural development led to the rise of farm processing industries, *i.e.,* bean-oil pressing, bean-cake milling, flour milling and tobacco manufacture. Population growth combined with railroad and harbor development fostered urbanization, with ports and railroad junctions serving as urban nuclei. Urbanization was further reinforced by industrial development.

During the first few decades of Manchurian development, economic growth was based on the interrelated expansion of population, agriculture, and foreign trade. Only in the 1930's do we witness the beginnings of mining and some heavy industry. However, as may be seen from the data in Table 5, industrial development (other than agricultural processing) gathered momentum only after the complete Japanese takeover in 1931. By this time most of the better farm lands were occupied and the force of agricultural expansion was largely spent. In the 1930's and early

12. Based on data in the South Manchurian Railroad *Report on Progress* (p. 48) and Y. K. Cheng, 1956 (Appendix I, pp. 258-259).

TABLE 5

SELECTED INDICATORS OF INDUSTRIAL DEVELOPMENT IN MANCHURIA, 1925-1944

Year	Iron Ore	Pig Iron	Steel Ingots	Coal	Cement	Pulp	Paper (in thousand lbs.)	Electric Power Generation (in million kwh.)
			(production in thousand metric tons)					
1925		137		6,948				239
1927	959	244		9,910	112			341
1928	710	285		9,510	151	6		403
1930	832	349		9,020	194	8		504
1932	993	368		8,830	109	12	22	593
1935	1,362	608	137	12,166	378	14	33	1,084
1940	2,978	1,069	532	21,200	1,035	76	83	2,998
1941	3,703	1,236	561	23,800	1,164	80	117	3,520
1942	4,413	1,341	716	24,169	1,532	95	162	4,086
1943	5,408	1,710	862	25,320	1,503	67	168	4,475
1944	3,758	1,159	439	25,627	1,141	59	101	4,481

Sources:

Iron ore: for 1927-32, SMR, *Manshu Sangyo Tokei,* various years; for 1935, SMR, 1938 (Table 1); for 1940-41, SMR, 1942; for 1942-44, E. W. Pauley, 1946 (pp. 90-92).

Pig iron: for 1925-35, *The Orient Year Book, 1942* (pp. 603, 607); for 1940-41, SMR, 1942; for 1942-44, Pauley, 1946.

Steel: for 1935, Wang Chen-Ching, 1947 (p. 101); for 1940-44, Manshikai, 1964, Vol. II. (p. 196).

Coal: for 1925-28, *Japan-Manchuokuo Year Book, 1934* (p. 599); for 1930-44, Pauley, 1946 (p. 74).

Cement: for 1927-35, *The Orient Year Book, 1942* (p. 686); for 1940, SMR, 1942; for 1941-44, Chang Chen-ta, 1954 (p. 196).

Pulp: for 1928-44, Chang Chen-ta, 1954 (pp. 230-231).

Paper: for 1932-44, *Chi Chi Chih Chiang,* 1946 (Table 13).

Electric power: for 1925-35, Manshikai, 1964, Vol. II. (p. 537); for 1940-44, State Statistical Bureau, 1958 (p. 40).

1940's, mining and producer goods industries took the place of agriculture as the "leading" sector in the region's economic growth.

The contrast between the course of twentieth-century economic change in Manchuria and in China Proper is marked. At the turn of the century, Manchuria had relatively abundant land and mineral resources and a sparse population. It benefited greatly from sizable injections of Russian and later Japanese capital and entrepreneurship. Capital imports per capita were undoubtedly much higher than in China Proper. Finally, Manchuria was much less affected by the vicissitudes of civil strife.

INDUSTRIAL DEVELOPMENT ON THE CHINESE MAINLAND

According to a study by John K. Chang (1965), industrial growth in pre-Communist China was quite rapid. His index, based on 15 series including mining and manufacturing products and electric power (which in 1933 encompassed 40-60 percent of industrial output value), indicates that industrial production grew between 1912 and 1949 at an average annual rate of 5.5 per cent.[13] As noted earlier, this period was disrupted by civil strife and by the Japanese occupation of east and north China during World War II. The record of industrial performance revealed by the findings of Chang's study (Table 6) therefore seems particularly remarkable.

According to this index, value added in industry grew more or less continuously until 1936 and then declined; but as Manchurian industrialization gained momentum it started expanding again in 1939, exceeding the earlier (1936) record by 1940, and attaining a peak level in 1942. Gross industrial output value followed a similar course with one important exception, that even after its growth was resumed in 1939 it never again exceeded the 1936 level. These differences in the trends of the two value series reflect the rapidly changing composition of industrial product after 1936, with the textile industry declining in China Proper, and the iron and steel, electric power, cement and some other branches of manufacture expanding in Manchuria.

These results must be interpreted with caution. The reliability of the physical production data on which Chang's index is based requires further scrutiny, particularly for the earlier years. As the investigation progresses, specific figures will undoubtedly be revised, so that the rates of growth presented in Table 6 may need to be changed. Nevertheless, it is doubtful whether these changes will markedly alter the general impression of a preindustrial economy in which a small industrial sector is rapidly growing.

These trends are the product of a number of mutually contradictory

13. The selection of commodities for inclusion was governed by the availability of data. The following are included in the index: coal, iron or pig iron, steel, antimony, copper, gold, mercury, tin, tungsten, cotton or cotton cloth, flour, cement, crude petroleum, and electric power.

TABLE 6

AVERAGE ANNUAL RATES OF INDUSTRIAL GROWTH IN MAINLAND CHINA, 1912-1949 AND SUBPERIODS [a]

Period	Average Growth Rate per Year
1912-1949	5.5
1912-1920	13.8
1912-1936	9.2
1912-1942	8.2
1923-1936	8.3
1923-1942	7.1
1928-1936	8.4
1928-1942	6.7
1931-1936	9.3
1931-1942	6.7
1936-1942	4.5

Note:
a. Based on value added in terms of 1933 prices.

Source:
John K. Chang, 1965.

tendencies. The earliest period shows unsually rapid rates of expansion for two principal reasons. First, China's industrial base in 1912 was very small so that any substantial increment would yield rapid rates of increase. Then mainland industry experienced a boom during World War I, when it enjoyed many of the benefits of infant industry protection without a tariff, due to the marked decline of imports as Western nations diverted shipping to military uses.

Not too surprisingly, except in this early period, industrial output increased most rapidly between 1931 and 1936, the period when civil strife was at a minimum, when government policies both in China Proper and in Manchuria were conducive to economic growth, and when the country's tariff autonomy was restored. The reality of a quickly expanding industrial sector is confirmed even if we extend the period so as to encompass the chaotic years of the early 1920's; the average annual rate of growth appears as 8 per cent a year for the 1923 to 1936 period.

It is possible that the result would have been quite different if the omitted industries could have been included in the index. Yet even if we assume that the excluded branches expanded only half as rapidly as those covered, the average annual growth rates for 1923-36 would be reduced from 8 per cent only to 5.6 per cent, depending on whether the index encompasses 40 or 60 per cent of the industrial product.

Other indicators tend to validate this view of rapid industrial growth in mainland China. The pace of expansion for Manchurian industry was noted above and a few selected series are shown in Table 5. The number of cotton yarn spindles in China increased from about 740,000 in 1912 to approximately 2.5 million in 1923 and 5.1 million in 1936, *i.e.,* trebling in the first 11 years and doubling in the next 13 (Yen Chung-p'ing, 1955b, pp. 134-136). The same impression of expansion is conveyed by the growth in railroad traffic. Total freight miles nearly doubled between 1912 and 1921, and then increased by another 40 per cent between that year and 1936 (Yen Chung-p'ing, 1955b, Tables 21 and 30).

What was the composition of this industrial expansion? Growth in industrial output was based first of all on the rather rapid development of the textile industry, which became by far the most important single branch of manufacture in China. It also entailed the growth of food processing (*e.g.,* flour milling and tobacco manufacture) and mining, particularly coal mining. Except for the last, these were preponderantly concentrated in China Proper, especially in the treaty ports. On the other hand, Manchuria dominated iron and steel, electric power generation, oil shale, and cement production. Moreover, as industrial production declined in China proper under the impact of World War II and the Japanese occupation, it continued to rise in Manchuria at least until 1942 and possibly until 1944. As a result, mainland industrial output as a whole did not fall as drastically after the outbreak of Sino-Japanese hostilities as one might have expected. In certain areas, both in Free China and in Japanese-held regions, the war led to an expansion of industrial capacity.

As indicated earlier, foreign enterprise led the way in industrial development, but it was gradually displaced by Chinese enterprise. This is most clearly illustrated by the fact that according to the Liu-Yeh estimates, about 67 per cent of industrial gross ouptut value was produced in Chinese-owned factories in 1933, with these factories employing 73 per cent of the industrial labor force (Liu and Yeh, 1965, Table F-1). According to Yen Chung-p'ing's compilation, by 1936, Chinese firms produced 71 per cent of the cotton yarn, 36 per cent of the cotton cloth, 42 per cent of the cigarettes, 89 per cent of the matches, 96 per cent of the edible vegetable oils (refers to 1933), 34 per cent of the coal, and 45 per cent of the electric power (1955b; pp. 124, 130-131). Whatever the indicator used, Chinese business firms played a significant role in this process of industrial growth and carried a major share of it. This must mean that an industrial labor force was trained and a Chinese managerial and business class was formed. But how large was this industrial sector and how important a role did it play in the economy as a whole?

According to Liu and Yeh, total employment in factory industry, mining and public utilities was no more than 2 million in 1933, or about 4 per cent of the total nonagricultural labor force. At the same time these sectors contributed only 3.4 per cent to national product in terms of 1933 prices, or 6.4 per cent in terms of 1952 prices. If to these industries we add construction, modern transport and communications, and modern trade and finance, we find that the modern sectors generated about 13 per cent of the national product in 1933 prices, or over 20 per cent in 1952 prices (Liu and Yeh, 1965, Tables 8, 11, 21).

Therefore, on the basis of a number of different measures it would seem that the modernized sectors of the economy, and most particularly industry, were small in the 1930's despite a fairly long period of quite rapid growth. How can this apparent paradox be reconciled? If GNP in China was growing very slowly between 1912 and 1936, while the industrial output increased tenfold, at the end of the period the share of industry in national income would still be quite small if this rapid growth had started from a tiny base.

It is fundamental to realize that industrial growth remained confined within narrow limits. Within these confines it expanded rapidly but it did not spread and it did not really lead to a structural transformation of the economy as a whole during the pre-Communist period. This conclusion applies only to China proper, not to Manchuria, but because of the relative size of the two it can legitimately be applied to the mainland economy as a whole.

The small size of modern industry necessarily meant that even in the 1930's most of the demand for manufactures continued to be supplied by handicrafts. In fact, all the available studies find that, in terms of aggregate output, handicrafts outweigh modern industry by a sizable margin.[14] The question still unanswered is whether the handicrafts output increased, declined or remained more or less stationary between 1895 and 1936, or between 1912 and 1936. Unfortunately, information on trends in this sector is so poor that one must proceed on the basis of highly fragmentary data. This is a case where a priori reasoning is inclusive and direct evidence is mixed. It should first be noted that there must have been a relative displacement in handicrafts in relation to the manufacturing sector as a whole. Since before 1895 virtually all manufacturing was done by handicrafts establishments, any growth in modern industry would automatically reduce the former's share to some degree.

14. This conclusion emerges from Ou Pao-san's and Liu-Yeh's (1965) national income studies for 1933; it is confirmed by the author's own national income study for 1952, and by some other more specialized monographic studies as well.

However, the more significant question is whether the handicrafts sector grew, and if so at what rate.

One can almost be certain that if handicrafts expanded, they did so much more slowly than modern industry. It is much less certain whether they expanded faster or more slowly than national product as a whole. At the present state of our knowledge, and for this period, the rate of growth cannot be ascertained.

Disregarding the question of rate, a sifting of at least some of the evidence suggests that there was probably a rise, not a decline, in handicrafts output between 1895 and 1936, or 1912 and 1936. A priori, it is probable, though by no means certain, that there was some population growth in the rural sector of China Proper. This increase may have been more than canceled out by a decline in per capita income and a resulting decline in the aggregate demand of the traditional sector. Moreover, if aggregate demand rose only by, say, 20-30 per cent, such an increase could have been met by the expansion that took place in modern industry. Modern industry would thus have captured a certain share of the traditional market. There is no doubt that in some branches of manufacture this actually happened, the most outstanding case being the displacement of handicraft yarn by manufactured yarn.

In addition to cotton-yarn spinning, at least two other handicrafts branches declined, silk reeling and tea processing. Filature silk gradually displaced hand-reeled silk, while tea production and processing decreased under the impact of shrinking export demand for Chinese tea. On the other hand, the export demand for a wide range of Chinese handicraft products increased continuously, and a number of handicraft branches held their own in the domestic market. According to a recent study published in Communist China, the total export value of 67 handicraft products deflated for price changes increased at an average annual rate of 1.1 per cent between 1912 and 1931 (P'eng Tse-i, 1957, Appendix 3).

In indigenous mining, pig iron and iron ore production based on native methods did not decline until 1928-30. Native coal production increased quite rapidly between 1912 and 1923 but decreased thereafter (Yen Chung-p'ing, 1955b; Hou, 1965, Ch. 7). Reference has been made to the fact that hand weaving was expanding while hand spinning was being displaced. As a matter of fact, some new hand-weaving centers developed using manufactured cotton yarn. This growth in handicraft cloth production continued until at least about 1930. Again, this cloth was principally sold in the rural hinterland, so that it was catering to a more or less different market than imported or domestically manufactured piece goods.

Present indications, some of them sketched above, would suggest that on balance the handicraft sector grew in absolute size between 1895 and 1936 as well as between 1912 and 1936. Within this expansion some branches undoubtedly declined in response to changes in the character of export or domestic demand, and under the impact of increasing competitive pressure from the industrial sector and from imports.

Most of the discussions of Chinese handicrafts have focused on their "ruin," decline, or slow growth. But one could perhaps argue with greater justification that it is surprising that they have grown at all and changed so little. One certainly tends to associate rapid industrialization with marked transformation in the character of handicrafts and small-scale industries. They do not need to disappear, as the experience of Japan amply illustrates, but they do have to change in terms of their techniques, the character of their products and the kind of economic activities they perform in the interstices of modern industry. Seen in this light, the absence of such marked changes in the handicrafts sector is still another indication of the marginal and superficial character of modern economic growth in pre-Communist China.

This, then, brings us back to a question posed earlier. How can one explain the confining character of modern industrial and economic growth in China? What have been the barriers to the diffusion of modern technology, modern economic institutions and practices? Obviously this is only in part an economic problem.

CHANGES IN THE COMPOSITION OF FOREIGN TRADE

As an intrinsic part of the rapid growth in the modern sectors of the economy, foreign trade expanded markedly during the years following the Treaty of Shimonoseki. As may be seen from the data in Table 7, foreign trade in terms of current prices approximately trebled between 1895 and 1913, with imports rising somewhat faster than exports. In terms of quantity, imports doubled while exports rose by a third. The pace of trade expansion slowed down with the outbreak of World War I, and in general the rate of growth of foreign trade—both imports and exports—was considerably slower after 1913. Exports reached their highest level in 1929 while imports attained their peak in 1931. During the whole period between 1895 and 1936, China maintained an unfavorable balance of trade financed by capital imports in the form of foreign loans and foreign investments.

During World War I, imports valued in constant (1913) prices declined by about a third, largely due to the diversion of Allied shipping to the war zones (Cheng, 1956, Appendix 1, pp. 258-59). The positive impact of this decline on domestic industrial development was noted above. At the same time, wartime shortages in a number of commodity markets raised the demand for Chinese products. Put in another way, shortages, rising prices, and sellers' markets reduced the competitive pressures, and it was easier to find outlets for China's products. As a result, while imports declined, exports (in quantity terms) rose by 40 per cent

TABLE 7

CHINA'S FOREIGN TRADE, 1895-1936

Year	Imports	Exports	Quantum Indices Imports	Quantum Indices Exports
	(in million Haikwan *taels*)			
1895	171.7	143.3	45.8	66.3
1913	570.2	403.3	100.0	100.0
1928	1,196.0	991.3	131.5	156.1
1929	1,265.8	1,015.7	139.9	149.2
1930	1,309.8	894.8	131.0	131.1
1931	1,443.5	909.5	129.9	136.5
1936	880.7 [a]	930.5 [a]		

Note:

a. Includes Manchuria. Manchurian data are given by Y. K. Cheng in U. S. dollar terms; these were then converted into Haikwan *taels* on the basis of the implicit exchange rates given by Y. K. Cheng in his Appendix I.

Source:

Y. K. Cheng, 1956 (Appendix I, pp. 258-259, and Appendix VIII, p. 269).

between 1913 and 1919. They then fell quite rapidly in the postwar years, not exceeding these levels again until 1926.

The slowing down of the rate of foreign trade expansion that accompanied the beginnings of modern industrial development was probably due to both the import-displacing character of Chinese industrialization, and the marked supply inelasticities in Chinese agriculture. As will be shown below, import displacement was particularly marked in the textile industry. At the same time, with limited growth and little transformation in the economy as a whole, the range and variety of products demanded and the level of that demand remained quite limited. Though imports rose rapidly in the first few decades after China was opened, their total value and volume was small. This rate of expansion was then slowed down in the twentieth century as it bumped against the ceiling imposed by the limited effective demand of an economy caught up in the vicious circle of backwardness.

Serious transport and communications barriers, as well as political disunity, contributed to a fragmentation of markets. The resulting imperfections were then reinforced by institutional factors rooted in the character of marketing and farm credit in agrarian China. As already noted earlier, without government encouragement and active support, it was difficult to introduce the quality controls and standardization necessary to maintain and improve the competitive position of China's exports in world markets. The same types of barriers also slowed producers' responses to changing world market conditions, thereby reinforcing supply inelasticities rooted in a traditional peasant society.[15]

However, foreign trade was not unaffected by growth in the modern economic sectors or by increasing commercialization under the impact of railroad development and the expansion of inland shipping. The most apparent change in China's foreign trade in the twentieth century has been growing diversification. While silk and tea accounted for nearly 95 per cent of total exports in 1868 and for 65 per cent in 1890, their share fell to about 25 per cent by 1920, and to 17 per cent by 1930. The most precipitate drop occurred in tea, which declined both in relative and absolute terms. Silk, on the other hand, held its own much longer, declining as a share of total Chinese exports, but maintaining or even somewhat increasing its absolute level of sales until the 1920's. At the same time, however, it was being more and more displaced in world markets by Japanese silk and later by synthetic fibers.

As these two traditional exports shrank in importance, their place was taken by soybeans, soybean oil and bean cake, mostly from Manchuria. Other export products that began to assume some importance after 1900 were vegetable oils, hides and skins, coal, ores, and a wide variety of minor products. The bulk of these exports were agricultural, with mining products also assuming some importance.

The interrelationship between foreign trade and industrial development is shown most clearly in the development of the Chinese textile industry. In the late nineteenth century China was a net exporter of raw cotton while it was importing increasing amounts of piece goods. The volume of net raw cotton exports increased until about 1910, paralleled by rising imports of cotton yarn, which reached record volumes in the first decade of the twentieth century. Then the situation was reversed. By 1920, China was a net importer of raw cotton; imports of cotton yarn were halved, and yarn exports on a modest scale were started. By 1928, China had become a net exporter of cotton yarn, with yarn imports shrinking to negligible proportions by the 1930's.

Before the establishment of a textile industry (*i.e.*, before 1895 or 1900), China exported raw cotton and imported manufactured cloth. Yarn imports were rising in importance in the late 1800's and were displacing handicraft spinning of yarn; they continued to rise as long as the textile industry was small. As the industry grew rapidly during World War I, yarn imports shrank, but raw cotton requirements increased, so that cotton exports had to be curtailed and imports stepped up until

15. To avoid misunderstanding, my argument is not intended to imply a zero elasticity of supply, but merely that it may be assumed to be well below unity. Thus I am not saying that the traditional peasantry does not respond, or is not capable of responding to price changes and changing market conditions; the point is merely that such responses tend to be delayed and slow.

TABLE 8

COMMODITY COMPOSITION OF CHINA'S EXPORTS AND IMPORTS, 1900-1931

(in per cent)

A. Imports

Commodity Category	1900	1905	1913	1920	1925	1928	1931
Cotton goods	21.5	25.6	19.3	21.8	16.3	14.2	7.6
Cotton yarn	14.3	15.0	12.7	12.4	4.4	1.6	0.3
Raw cotton			0.5	2.4	7.4	5.7	12.6
Cereals and flour	7.0	2.9	5.2	1.1	8.4	8.3	12.6
Sugar	3.0	5.1	6.4	5.2	9.5	8.3	6.0
Tobacco	0.5	1.4	2.9	4.7	4.1	5.1	4.4
Paper			1.3	1.9	2.0	2.4	3.2
Kerosene	6.6	4.5	4.5	7.1	7.0	5.2	4.5
Liquid fuel				0.4	0.9	1.4	1.8
Transport materials		1.8	0.8	2.6	1.9	2.3	2.3
Chemicals, dyes and pigments			5.6	6.4	5.6	7.5	8.0
Metals	4.7	10.4	5.3	8.3	4.7	5.4	6.2
Machinery	0.7	1.2	1.4	3.2	1.8	1.8	3.1
Coal	3.1	1.6	1.7				
Opium	14.8	7.7	7.4				
Others	23.8	22.8	25.0	24.3	26.0	30.8	27.4
	100.0	100.0	100.0	100.0	100.0	100.0	100.0

Source:
Y. K. Cheng, [10] 1956 (Table 4, p. 19 and Table 10, p. 32).

TABLE 8 (Cont'd)

B. Exports

Commodity Category	1900	1905	1913	1920	1925	1928	1931
Silk and silk goods	30.4	30.1	25.3	18.6	22.5	18.4	13.3
Tea	16.0	11.2	8.4	8.4	1.6	2.9	3.7
Beans	1.9	3.0					
Beans and bean cake			12.0	13.0	15.9	20.5	21.4
Seeds and oil	2.5	3.4	7.8	9.1	7.9	5.8	8.4
Eggs and egg products		0.9	1.4	4.0	4.3	4.4	4.1
Hides and skins	4.3	6.6	6.0	4.3	4.0	5.4	4.1
Ores and metals			3.3	3.2	2.9	2.1	1.6
Coal			1.6	2.3	2.6	2.9	3.0
Cotton yarn and cotton goods			0.6	1.4	2.0	3.8	4.9
Raw cotton	6.2	5.3	4.1	1.7	3.8	3.4	2.9
Wool	1.9	3.7	2.4				
Other	36.8	35.8	27.1	40.8	31.2	29.6	32.7
	100.0	100.0	100.0	100.0	100.0	100.0	100.0

Source:
Y. K. Cheng, 1956 (Table 12, p. 34 and Table 3, p. 19).

China became a net importer of raw cotton. Rising raw cotton consumption then encouraged an expansion in domestic cotton production, and by the 1930's, the exports and imports of the raw material were more or less in balance.

This first sequence was followed by a second. As the demand for cotton cloth increased, it was filled in part by an expansion of the hand-weaving industry, which relied on domestically manufactured yarn, and in part by the growth of mechanical weaving. As a result, cotton piece goods, which had dominated China's imports since the 1890's, began to decline in relative importance after 1920 and then shrank considerably in absolute terms after 1930. Continuing this long-term historical trend, China became a sizable net exporter of finished cotton textiles in the 1950's.

One could trace yet a third, almost parallel, sequence. As the cotton textile industry grew in China, it relied on imported machinery. However, at a later stage the domestic demand for such machinery encouraged the rise of a textile machinery industry that gradually displaced imports. By the late 1950's and early 1960's, China became a net exporter of textile machinery.

Such neat patterns of backward and forward linkage, at least on this scale, do not appear in the case of other industries and other imports. From the standpoint of China's industrialization, one of the interesting aspects shown by the data in Table 8, A is the very modest scale of machinery imports. If one were to carry the series beyond 1931, the importance of machinery and metals would undoubtedly rise under the impact of Manchurian industrialization.

V. THE INHERITED ECONOMY

In 1949 the Chinese Communists took over a war-torn and devastated economy suffering from acute and prolonged inflation. However, from the vantage point of this discussion, it might be quite misleading to consider this as the inherited economy. Production capacities in different branches of the pre-1949 economy may provide us with a more appropriate basis for appraising the level and character of Chinese Communist economic performance against the background of a long-term historical perspective. These production capacities, in turn, might perhaps be best approximated by comparing performance since 1949 with peak performance before that year. However, this approach, too, presents certain difficulties since there is no denying that the production capacities themselves were reduced by war, civil war and the Soviet dismantling of plants in Manchuria. The pre-Communist peak production levels overstate the capacity of the interited economy, while the 1949 output understates it.

Agriculture was probably less affected by these vicissitudes. Therefore one might surmise that the farm sector inherited by the Chinese Communists was not too different from that found by J. L. Buck in the course of his survey (1937). In outlining the principal features of Communist China's agricultural inheritance, I will draw on this body of data relating to 1929-31. For industry we will compare the output of some of the principal products in 1933, in the pre-Communist peak year, in 1949 and in 1952. At the same time, we will examine briefly the structural changes experienced by the economy as a whole between 1933 and 1952.

According to the Liu-Yeh estimates (1965) national product increased by 10 to 15 per cent (in terms of 1933 and 1952 prices respectively) between 1933 and 1952. Unfortunately, no really usable estimates are available for any intervening year. Moreover, given the character of the basic data, it would be very difficult indeed to construct meaningful estimates for the period between 1937 and 1952. Therefore we can not be certain whether this growth occurred mostly before or after the advent of the new regime. However, there is no doubt that there was some growth between 1933 and 1936, and very rapid recovery (from a low point) between 1949 and 1952. It is, however, far from clear what path the mainland economy as a whole followed after the start of the Sino-Japanese war. Finally, even the 1933 and 1952 estimates are subject to sizable margins of error, so that the rise in national product may have in fact been more or less than the 10 to 15 per cent indicated. In any case it is almost certain that there was no significant growth in per capita terms, and probably not in total terms, during these two decades.

On the other hand, there is no doubt that the economy experienced some structural change as shown by the estimates in Table 9. Stated most broadly, the importance of agriculture declined, while there was a rise in the national product share of the modern nonagricultural sectors, including government services. Although some of the expansion in government undoubtedly occurred after 1949, a good part of it must have been a product of war in all areas of the mainland, *i.e.,* in Free China, in occupied China, and in Manchuria.

The share of modern industry in the national product almost doubled in 1952 as compared with 1933. As noted earlier, it would seem that total industrial output increased until 1942. It then declined, recovered somewhat after the war, and then declined again quite markedly by 1949. As Table 10 shows, except for textiles, industrial production in the early 1940's tended to be much higher than in the early 1930's. Clearly, then, a goodly share of the industrial expansion in this 1933-52 period must have taken place before the Communists came to power. Some of this increased productive capacity was dismantled during the Soviet occupation of Manchuria, but the new investment necessary to restore this capacity was less than would have been required for entirely new plants.

TABLE 9

COMPOSITION OF NATIONAL PRODUCT BY INDUSTRIAL ORIGIN, 1933 AND 1952
(in per cent)

Economic Branch	1933 National Product 1933 prices	1933 National Product 1952 prices	1952 National Product Liu-Yeh [a] 1933 prices	1952 National Product Liu-Yeh [a] 1952 prices	1952 National Product Eckstein [b] 1952 prices
Agriculture	65.0	56.9	56.6	47.9	47.1
Industry:					
Large-Scale	3.4	6.6	6.2	11.5	9.2
Handicrafts	7.1	7.4	6.6	6.6	13.6 [c]
Construction	1.2	1.7	1.9	2.6	2.9
Transport & Communication:					
Modern	1.5	1.8	2.5	2.9	3.0
Traditional	4.1	4.4	3.7	3.7	1.7
Trade	9.4	13.8	8.9	13.5	8.3
Government Administration	2.8	2.4	5.7	4.6	4.9
Other	5.6	4.9	8.0	6.7	9.3

Notes:
a. Net domestic product at market prices.
b. Gross domestic product at factor cost.
c. Includes farm processing of products consumed within the peasant household.

Sources:
Liu-Yeh, 1965 (Table 8, p. 66; Table 20, p. 88).
Eckstein, 1961 (Table 10, p. 74).

This process of expansion was accompanied by changes in the composition of industrial output. After 1936 textile production declined, while electric power generation, iron and steel, and cement producing facilities and output rose. These marked changes in industrial structure antedate the Communist advent to power. They constitute an element of inheritance forced upon the mainland economy by the exigencies of Japanese occupation and war.

In all these respects agriculture presents a sharp contrast. There is no indication of agricultural growth during the years between 1933 and 1952. According to the Liu-Yeh estimates net agricultural product in these two years was about the same. Allowing for the possibility that this finding is due to the assumptions on which their agricultural estimates are based, all other evidence as well points to agricultural stagnation as a

TABLE 10

SELECTED INDUSTRIAL PRODUCTION INDICATORS, 1933-1952

Product	Unit of Measurement	1933	1949	1952	Pre-Communist Peak Output	Year
Electric power	billion kwh	2.07	4.31	7.26	5.95	1943
Coal	million MT	28.38	32.43	66.49	64.86	1942
Crude oil	thousand MT	89.00	n.a.	871.00	842.00	1942
Pig iron	thousand MT	609.00	252.00	1,929.00	1,889.00	1943
Steel	thousand MT	negl.	158.00	1,349.00	923.00	1943
Cement	thousand MT	784.00	660.00	2,860.00	2,300.00	1942
Cotton yarn	million bales	2.45	1.80	3.62	2.45	1933
Machine-made paper	thousand MT	45.00	108.00	372.00	165.00	1943

Sources:
Chao Kang, 1965 (Table C-1)
State Statistical Bureau, 1956 (p. 28)
Additional Sources:
Coal: Ching Chi-pu, 1943; and Yen Chung-p'ing, 1955 (p. 143).
Crude oil: Geological Survey of China, 1945 (p. 85).
Pig iron: Yen Chung-p'ing, 1955b (p. 143); and *Chung-hua Nien-chien,* 1948, Volume II (p. 1569).

reality. As a result, the situation that prevailed in the early 1930's may provide a fairly good basis for asserting the Chinese Communist inheritance in this sector.

Mainland agriculture was characterized by high population density on the land as evidenced by the fact that an average-sized farm had to support 6.2 persons on about 4.2 acres (Buck, 1937, pp. 173-174).[16] However, about 60 per cent of the farms had a median size of 2.8 acres or less. Population pressure on arable land resources was greatly aggravated by the pattern of land-holding and tenure. Land fragmentation was a widespread phenomenon with an average of 5.6 parcels per farm. Each of these parcels was less than an acre, the furthest ones being, on the average, 0.7 miles from the farmstead. This naturally led to considerable waste of time and energy, producing a very inefficient pattern of factor use, not only of labor but of livestock and equipment as well.

The situation was aggravated in south China in particular by tenancy combined in some instances with quite adverse terms of tenure. Tenancy data are far from satisfactory and have been the subject of considerable controversy. According to the National Agricultural Research Bureau, nearly one-third of China's farms were tenant-operated in the early 1930's. Buck's data, in contrast, show a tenancy ratio of only 17 per cent. There is a strong probability that in this case sampling errors produced a downward bias in Buck's data.

However the most serious and intractable problem facing Chinese agriculture was not distribution of the product and income inequality, but technological backwardness and resultant low labor productivity. There is no doubt that the Chinese peasant utilized the factors of production at his disposal most intensively at the existing level of technology. Yet according to Buck's estimates, at this level he could produce the equivalent of only 1,400 kilograms of grain per man, compared with the United States, where the corresponding figure was 20,000 kilograms. Another illustration of low labor productivity in agriculture is provided by the Liu-Yeh national income estimates, which show that product per man in farming in 1933 was less than one-fifth of the level prevailing in modern industry (Liu-Yeh, 1965, Table 21).

Acute population pressure was also reflected in the pattern of land use and was in turn partly a function of that pattern. Only 27 per cent of the land area was cultivated, with most of the remainder uncultivable. Of the land in farms, 90 per cent was in crops; of these, close to 70 per cent was in grains. Through a long process of adaptation the Chinese peasant had developed a pattern of farm production to give high energy yields per unit of land. This left very little room for pasture and for livestock raising.

16. All the quantitative data, unless otherwise indicated, cited in this section dealing with agriculture are drawn from Buck's monumental study.

Under the combined impact of all these circumstances, the Chinese peasantry traditionally lived quite close to the margin of subsistence, highly vulnerable to natural or man-made disaster. It is not surprising to find that China's farmers have encountered periodic famines and frequent crop failures short of famine proportions. According to Buck, there had been on the average three famines per *hsien* within the memory of his informants from 146 *hsien*. The causes of the different famines (*e.g.,* floods and droughts) had lasted from ten days to three years, but averaged over ten months in the wheat region and less than four months in the rice region. In addition, there was an average of 16 calamities per locality that resulted in the loss of nearly half of the crop.

Crop failures were most often caused by droughts and floods, with droughts being more common. The effects of adverse harvests were greatly aggravated by the backward state of transport and communications, by grossly inadequate storage and warehousing facilities, and by the poorly developed marketing and credit system. While certain parts of China, particularly in the Yangtze valley, were fairly well provided with inland waterways, the country's total railroad mileage at the end of World War II was only about 15,500, of which approximately 6,500 miles were in Manchuria. For large areas inaccessible by water, the cost of transporting farm products was very high, four to six times the railroad charge if carried by animals, and three to eight times as high if transported by men (Buck, 1937, p. 354).

This, combined with the institutional impediments cited above and the acute population pressure on farms, necessarily restricted the scope of commercialization. Therefore, depending on whether one includes rent in the marketed potion, only about 15 to 36 per cent of the rice, 25 to 30 per cent of the kaoliang, 29 to 33 per cent of the wheat, and 30 to 34 per cent of the soybeans was sold off farms. As noted in Table 1 of this chapter, an estimated 28 per cent of the total farm output was sold in 1952. One might surmise that this marketed share was probably no higher, and possibly lower, in the 1930's. This would suggest then that the Chinese Communists inherited an agricultural sector that was adapted to sell about 25 to 30 per cent of its output and so was to a limited degree involved in a market and money nexus.

VI. CONCLUDING COMMENTS

When the Chinese Communists came to power in 1949, they inherited an economy which by practically all available measures was near the bottom of the world development scale. GNP per capita was possibly in the neighborhood of $50 as compared with two to three times that level in late seventeenth-century England.[17] As shown in Table 9, about half the GNP was produced in agriculture; all of the modern sectors combined contributed only about 20 per cent.[18] The same pattern is evident in labor force composition, with at most three million workers engaged in modern industry (including mining and public utilities).

Labor productivity was very low in agriculture, which was still operating largely within a traditional technological and institutional framework. This, in turn, was a function of a number of interrelated factors rooted in and epitomized by acute population pressure and a lack of employment opportunities in the nonagricultural sectors.

Modern industrial production was still quite small (contributing about 10 per cent to national product) despite apparently rapid rates of growth in the quarter century preceding the Sino-Japanese war. As indicated in Table 6, the impression of rapid rates of advance remains basically unaltered even if we disregard the early period for which the data are least reliable. However, as pointed out by Deane and Cole, "an index of industrial production for a preindustrial economy is an indicator of developments in a small sector. It tells us nothing about the growth of output as a whole or its relation to changes in the size of the population" (Deane and Cole, 1962, p. 41). In effect, modern industry in mainland China was merely a shallow overlay on a preindustrial agrarian economy.

Yet as an element of inheritance it was of crucial importance for Communist China. Although narrowly based, both in an economic and geographic sense, it provided the new regime with at least a modicum of plant capacity, trained manpower, and management, without which the industrialization drive of the First Five-Year Plan and the Great Leap Forward could not have been launched. This vast outpouring of effort apparently led to an acceleration in the rate of industrial growth from possibly 9 per cent per annum in the Nanking Government era (1931-36) to about 14 per cent during the First Five-Year Plan period (Table 6 above; Chao, 1965, Table 21). However, just as in Republican China,

17. The errors and estimated biases incurred by converting China's per capita product into dollars are shared by similar conversions for other low income countries. Therefore, while the particular GNP figure thus obtained is undoubtedly subject to a large margin of error, this need not affect the relative standing of a country on a comparative per capita scale. Conversion of early national income estimates for currently developed countries is subject to similar kinds of biases. Of course, conversion of late seventeenth-century product estimates into current prices is fraught with a host of additional hazards. Nevertheless, given a 100 to 200 per cent differential, it is improbable that the margins of error would be so large as to nullify the point made; namely that in 1949 China's GNP per capita was lower than that of preindustrial England. These early British figures are from Phyllis Deane and W. A. Cole, 1962 (p. 3); they represent a revised and adjusted version of Gregory King's original estimates.

18. For comparative data on interindustry composition of GNP and labor force, see Simon Kuznets, 1957.

this industrial expansion seems to have been accompanied by agricultural stagnation, which in time arrested industrial growth as well.

Viewed from the vantage point of the mid-1960's, it would seem that at least in a limited sense the pattern of economic development in Communist China bears certain elements of similarity to and continuity with pre-Communist China; *i.e.,* rapid development of a small modern industrial sector in a preindustrial economy without perceptible growth in agriculture. The development drive mounted in the 1950's left the technological base of Chinese agriculture largely untouched, at least up to 1960-61. The Chinese Communists apparently contented themselves with a massive assault on rural institutions and agricultural organization, hoping that institutional transformation might serve as a substitute for technical transformation. It is quite possible that these organizational changes rendered the farm population more receptive to the introduction of innovations and technological change. However, many of these same changes had strong counterincentive effects. If there was any increased receptivity to innovations, it was merely a facilitating or passive factor that only the introduction of a more favorable incentive structure and additional investment in agriculture could transfer into an active force.

In analyzing elements of Communist China's economic heritage, its agricultural backwardness, population pressure, and "space friction" stand out as the most critical long-run problems. From a development point of view, population pressure is at least a two-dimensional problem with both the initial stock and the flow playing a very significant role. The Chinese Communists inherited an initial population mass of perhaps 500 to 550 million people. This presented problems not only in terms of population pressure on arable land resources, but in terms of food supply, distribution, and provisioning with other consumer goods as well. However, perhaps even more important are the general scale effects and the sheer implications of size of such a large population. Without dealing with the complex range of factors relating demographic and size variables to economic development, some of the possible effects are outlined below to illustrate their importance in the case of China.

On *ceteris paribus* assumptions concerning per capita income and other variables, the foreign aid requirements per unit of output increment of a large country such as China would be of an entirely different order of magnitude than for, say, Ceylon. This proposition would probably be valid even if one granted that the relationship is not likely to be proportional, and that counteracting factors might tend to reduce the foreign aid requirements of a large country. More generally, the most important consequences of size revolve around barriers to innovation and the introduction of new influences through aid, trade and all other forms of contact. The task of diffusion is rendered much more difficult in a territorially large national unit, preponderantly continental, with a large population and poor transport and communication. The transport requirements themselves are in part conditioned by population size and territorial scope. These factors have undoubtedly been of great importance in mainland China's economic retardation before and since 1949.

For Communist China these handicaps arising from a large initial population stock were seriously aggravated by changes in flow. According to a number of sample investigations conducted in the interwar period, crude death rates in China may have been around 40± per thousand and crude death rates around 30± per thousand, thus yielding rates of natural increase of 10± per thousand (Buck, 1937, pp. 383-387). The advent of the new regime marked the end of a long period of war and civil strife and restoration of law and order on the mainland as a whole. This in itself was bound to lead to a decline in the death rates. However, the new regime instituted a whole series of public health measures that served to reduce infant mortality and led to better control of epidemics, with resultant reductions in deaths of all age groups. Moreover, improvements in distribution have apparently contributed to better control of famines and thus to reduction in the death rate. As a result, rates of natural increase were at least doubled. Such a spurt in the rate of population growth superimposed on a large initial stock has created a host of new problems which have seriously complicated Communist China's development task.

REFERENCES

ALLEN, G. C., and A. G. DONNITHORNE, 1954. *Western Enterprise in Far Eastern Economic Development*. New York.

BEAL, E. G., 1958. *The Origin of Likin*. Cambridge, Mass.

BUCK, J. L., 1930. *Chinese Farm Economy*. Chicago.

BUCK, J. L., 1937. *Land Utilization in China*. Nanking.

CHANG, C. C., 1932. *An Estimate of China's Farms and Crops*. Nanking.

CHANG CHEN-TA, 1954. *Tung-pei Ching-chi* (*Economy of the North East*). Taipei.

CHANG, JOHN K., 1965. *Indexes of Industrial Production of Mainland China, 1912–1949*. (Ph.D. dissertation, University of Michigan).

CHANG KIA-NGAU, 1943. *China's Struggle for Railroad Development*. New York.

CHAO, KANG, 1965. *The Rate and Pattern of Industrial Growth in Communist China*. Ann Arbor, Mich.

CHENG, Y. K., 1956. *Foreign Trade and Industrial Development of China*. Washington, D.C.

Chih Chi Chih Chiang (*Paper and Pulp*), 1946. Economic Handbook Series on Manchuria, No. 13. Shenyang.

Chung-hua Nien-chien (*Chung-hua Year Book*), 1948. Vol. II. Shanghai.

The Chinese Year Book, 1935–36. Premier Issue, 1935. Shanghai.

CHING CHI-PU, 1943. *Hou-fang Chung-yao Kung-k'uang ch'an-p'ing t'ung-chi,* No. 2. Chungking.

CLARK, GROVER, 1932. *Economic Rivalries in China.* New Haven, Conn.

DEANE, PHYLLIS, and W. A. COLE, 1962. *British Economic Growth, 1668–1959.* Cambridge, England.

DORE, R. P., 1965. *Education in Takugawa Japan.* Berkeley.

ECKSTEIN, A., 1961. *The National Income of Communist China.* New York.

FAIRBANK, J. K., 1953. *Trade and Diplomacy on the China Coast: The Opening of the Treaty Ports, 1842–1854.* Cambridge, Mass.

FAIRBANK, JOHN, K., A. ECKSTEIN, and L. S. YANG, 1960. "Economic Change in Early Modern China, An Analytic Framework," *Economic Development and Cultural Change,* October, 1960, Part I, pp. 2–26.

FEUERWERKER, A., 1958. *China's Early Industrialization.* Cambridge, Mass.

Geological Survey of China, 1945. *General Statement on the Mining Industry,* No. 7. Chungking.

GREENBERG, MICHAEL, 1951. *British Trade and the Opening of China, 1800–42.* Cambridge, England.

HIRSCHMAN, A. O., 1958. *The Strategy of Economic Development.* New Haven, Conn.

HO, P. T., 1954. "The Salt Merchants of Yang-chou: A Study of Commercial Capitalism in Eighteenth-Century China," *Harvard Journal of Asiatic Studies,* XVII, Nos. 1–2, June.

HO, P. T., 1959. *Studies on the Population of China, 1368–1953.* Cambridge, Mass.

HO, P. T., 1964. *The Ladder of Success in Imperial China.* New York: Science Editions.

HOU, C. M., 1965. *Foreign Investment and Economic Development of China, 1840–1937.* Cambridge, Mass.

ISHII, RYOICHI, 1937. *Population Pressure and Economic Life in Japan.* London.

Japan-Manchuoko Year Book, 1934. Tokyo: The Asia Statistics Co.

JONES, F. C., 1949. *Manchuria Since 1931.* London.

KUZNETS, SIMON, 1957. "Quantitative Aspects of the Economic Growth of Nations: Industrial Distribution of National Product and Labor Force," *EDCC,* Supplement to Volume V, July, 1957

KUZNETS, SIMON, 1959. *Six Lectures on Economic Growth.* Glencoe, Ill.

LI, C. M., 1946. "International Trade," in H. F. McNair (ed.), *China.* Berkeley.

LIEU, D K., 1936. *The Growth and Industrialization of Shanghai.* Shanghai.

LIU, K. C., 1962. *Anglo-American Steamship Rivalry in China, 1862–1874.* Cambridge, Mass.

LIU, T. C., and K. C. YEH, 1965. *The Economy of the Chinese Mainland: National Income and Economic Development 1933–1959.* Princeton.

LOCKWOOD, W. W., 1956. "Japan's Response to the West, the Contrast with China," *World Politics,* Vol. IX, No. 1 (October, 1956).

MANSHIKAI, 1964. *Manshü Kaihatsu Yonjünenshi,* Vols. I and II. Tokyo.

MORSE, H. B., 1918. *The International Relations of the Chinese Empire,* Vol. III. London and New York: Longmans, Green.

MORSE, H. B., 1926–29. *The Chronicles of East India Company: Trading to China 1635–1834,* Vols. III and IV. Oxford.
MURPHEY, RHOADS, 1953. *Shanghai, Key to Modern China.* Cambridge, Mass.
National Agricultural Research Bureau (National Government), 1933–39. *Nung-ch'ing Pao-kao* (*Crop Reports*). Nanking.
OGURA, TAKEKAZU, 1963. (Ed.) *Agricultural Development in Modern Japan.* Tokyo.
OHKAWA, K. and H. ROSOVSKY, 1960. "The Role of Agriculture in Modern Japanese Economic Development," *EDCC,* Vol. IX, No. 1, Part II (October, 1960).
OU PAO-SAN *et al.,* 1947. *Chung-kuo-kuo-min so-te* (*China's National Income*), 2 vols. Shanghai.
The Orient Year Book, 1942. Tokyo: The Asia Statistics Co.
PAULEY, E. W., 1946. *Report on Japanese Assets in Manchuria.* Washington, D.C.
P'ENG TSE-I, 1957. (Ed.) *Chung-kuo chin-tai shou-kung-yeh shih tzu-liao, 1840–1949.* (*Some materials on the modern history of Chinese handicrafts*), Vol. 3. Peking.
REISCHAUER, E. O., and J. K. FAIRBANK, 1960. *East Asia, The Great Tradition,* Vol. I. Boston.
REMER, C. F., 1926. *The Foreign Trade of China.* Shanghai.
REMER, C. F., 1933. *Foreign Investment in China.* New York.
ROSOVSKY, HENRY, 1966. "Japan's Transition to Modern Economic Growth, 1868–1885," in *Industrialization in Two Systems,* Essays in Honor of Alexander Gerschenkron by a Group of His Students. New York: Wiley.
Supreme Command Allied Powers (SCAP). SCAP Report No. 143, "Japanese Crop and Livestock Statistics, 1878–1950."
SCHWARTZ, BENJAMIN I., 1964. *In Search of Wealth and Power, Yen Fu and the West.* Cambridge, Mass.
SHEN, T. H., 1951. *The Agricultural Resources of China.* Ithaca, N.Y.
SKINNER, G. WILLIAM, 1964. "Marketing and Social Structure in Rural China," Part I, *JAS,* Vol. XXIV, No. 1 (November, 1964).
SKINNER, G. W., 1965. "Marketing and Social Structure in Rural China," Part II, *JAS,* Vol. XXIV, No. 2 (February, 1965).
(SMR.) South Manchurian Railroad Co. *Report on Progress in Manchuria, 1907–1928.* Dairen.
SMR, 1938. *Manshu Keizai Nenpo.* Dairen.
SMR, 1942. *Manshu Keizai Tokei Kiho,* No. 2.
SMR, various years. *Manshu Sangyo Tokei.*
(SSB.) State Statistical Bureau, 1956. *Report on National Economic Development and Fulfillment of State Plan.* Peking: Foreign Laguage Press.
SSB, 1958. *Wo-kuo kang-t'ieh, tien-li, mei-t'an, chi-chieh, fang-chih, tsao-chih, kung-yeh ti chin-hsi.* Peking.
TAMAGNA, FRANK, 1942. *Banking and Finance in China.* New York.
TAWNEY, R. H. 1932. *Land and Labor in China.* London.
TENG, S. Y., and J. K. FAIRBANK, 1954. *China's Response to the West.* Cambridge, Mass.

United Kingdom, Naval Intelligence Division, 1945. *China Proper,* Vol. III (July, 1945).

WANG CHEN-CHING, 1947. *Tung-pei Chih Ching-chi Tzu-yuan* (*Economic Resources of Manchuria*). Shanghai: Commercial Press.

WEDA, SADAJIRO, 1934. (Ed.) *Nihon Jinko Mondai Kenkyu,* Vol. I.

WRIGHT, MARY C., 1957. *The Last Stand of Chinese Conservatism.* Stanford, Calif.

YANG, L. S., 1952. *Money and Credit in China.* Cambridge, Mass.

YEN CHUNG-P'ING, 1955(a). *Chung-kuo mien-fang-chih shih-kao* (*Draft history of Chinese cotton spinning and weaving*). Peking.

YEN CHUNG-P'ING, 1955(b). *Chung-kuo chin-tai ching-chi shih t'ung-chi tzu-liao hsuan-chi* (*Selected statistics in China's modern economic history*). Peking.

Quantitative Trends in the Economy 3

TA-CHUNG LIU

ANY STUDY OF the quantitative trends in an economy as a whole and in its major sectors must resort to the data on national product and its components. For a study of the Chinese mainland, two reservations must be made immediately concerning such an attempt. First, the basic Communist data are inadequate and inaccurate. In fact, an important reason for making an independent estimate of the national product is to evaluate the reliability of these data and of the Communist estimate of national income. Some independent estimates of national income by scholars in the United States differ substantially, and it is probably too early in the development of research on Communist China to expect general agreement among experts in this area. One way to deal with this difficulty is to present and compare all the available estimates, and then analyze the quantitative trends in the Communist Chinese economy on the basis of several of them. The findings will then vary within a range that reflects different degrees of trust of the Communist data. The reader can draw his own conclusion about the plausibility of the different estimates.

The second reservation is of a different nature. It has to do with the inadequacy of national product estimates as indicators of human welfare, even if they are reasonably accurate in the conventional sense.[1] A great many sources of human satisfaction find no expression in national product; nor are all the costs incurred in producing monetary and imputed incomes recognized in national income accounting. All the difficulties discussed by Kuznets (1963, pp. 368-372) with regard to this problem in his comparative appraisal of the Soviet economy are relevant to our study. During the period under study, there has been a reduction of personal liberty on the Chinese mainland, both outside and within the family, for all classes of people, including the peasants. Other radical changes in the social and political environment have also taken place. All these have a definite and profound bearing on the welfare of the people. The analysis in this chapter will be restricted to the conventional national product framework, in

1. The index number problems involved in drawing inference on welfare from time series data on national income are well known, but these are not our concern in this connection.

the belief that a study of such limited scope is necessary, even though far from sufficient, for an understanding of the Communist society on the Chinese mainland.

The Communist regime was set up on the mainland in October, 1949, but this chapter deals only with the quantitative trends during 1952-65. Communist data for the rehabilitation period 1950-51 are much less reliable than those for 1952-57. There is general agreement among scholars in the United States that Communist data on agricultural production during 1950-51 underestimated the actual output (Hollister, 1958, p. 23; Liu and Yeh, 1965, pp. 43-45). Since it cannot be assumed that agriculture had completely recovered from war damage during these early years, it is difficult to correct the downward bias in these data on the basis of what little is known about the normal productivity of agriculture in China. Similar difficulty exists with regard to statistics on industry and trade for these early years. The Communists did not attempt to make a more or less comprehensive canvass of private industry and trade until 1954 and 1955, and the revision of the earlier data for these sectors was carried back only to 1952, on the basis of private records that became available during 1954-55 (Li, 1962, p. 27). Private industry and trade, however, were very important during 1950-51; but such data as are available in Communist sources for those years are even more inadequate and unreliable than those for 1952-57. With basic data on agriculture, industry and trade poor in both quality and quantity, and without a reasonable method to supplement and correct them, it seems to be wisest not to attempt a quantitative evaluation of the economy during this early period. This omission is regrettable but not serious, as what happened in 1950-51 was of only transitional importance.

Data for 1958 and 1959 are again very poor, and statistics for 1960-65 are scarce to the point of being nonexistent. Some conjectural estimates however, have been made here to give a crude image of the quantitative trends during these recent years, only because it is important to have at least an impression of the development in the recent past. Inevitably, all such estimates will have to be thoroughly revised when more information becomes available.

There are, then, two separate tasks to pursue in this chapter. The first is to evaluate the quantitative trends during 1952-57 on the basis of the fair amount of statistics released by the Communists and the independent studies by scholars in the United States. The second is to provide a crude picture of the performance of the economy during 1958-65, a task that would be impossible to tackle were it not for the knowledge, however scanty, that we have gained of the relationships between agriculture and industry during 1952-57.

I. THE COMMUNIST STATISTICAL SYSTEM

To understand the nature and the quality of the Communist data, it is important to know how the Communist statistical system developed. This task is greatly facilitated by the contributions of Li (1962), Aird (1961), and Emerson (1958).[2]

Statistics were generally poor before the Communists took over the control of the mainland. Exceptions are the good data on modern transportation and communications and on tariff revenue. Several population censuses, poorly taken and recorded, are available. There was an annual crop reporting system that consistently underestimated production because of the downward bias in the recorded acreage under cultivation. Scholarly studies by Buck (1930, 1937), however, present an alternative estimate of agricultural production. There were a general survey of modern factories for the single year 1933 and some very rough annual estimates of the output of industrial products, mostly for the 1920's and 1930's. Relatively good statistics are available for industries in Manchuria under Japanese occupation during the 1930's and early 1940's. Scattered data on handicraft, trade and personal services were collected by Ou (1945) in his national income study. In a recent contribution, Yeh (1964) estimated national product and capital formation for 1931-36, probably the only prewar period for which a reasonably acceptable estimate can be attempted.[3]

The Sino-Japanese war (1937-45) and the internal strife afterwards (1945-48) made it practically impossible to collect reliable statistics. There are indications that after the Communist regime was set up in October, 1949, the old crop reporting system was kept in use for some time. First, there was simply no immediate alternative. Second, the Communist data on crop production for 1949 equal almost exactly the pre-Communist estimate for 1947 (Liu and Yeh, 1965, pp. 43-44).

Prior to 1952, Communist efforts to improve statistics were largely limited to the state sector. The only major statistical undertaking was the 1950 national survey of state and joint state-private industrial and mining enterprises. Regular reporting on uniform statistical schedules was initiated first for major state and joint enterprises in industry and construction, and then extended to agricultural and trading enterprises; but the main emphasis was on state and joint industrial enterprises.

A national statistical system began only with the establishment of the

2. Except for the discussion of prewar statistics in the next paragraph, this section is entirely based on these three sources, even though the author is in disagreement with some of Aird's analysis. Detailed citations of sources of information will therefore be omitted.

3. For sources of prewar statistics, see reference given in Liu and Yeh (1965) as well as Yeh (1964).

State Statistical Bureau on August 8, 1952. It was the responsibility of the bureau to organize all the statistical work in the country, to standardize methods of checking accuracy and computation, and to centralize the distribution of all basic statistical schedules. The actual collection of statistics remained in the hand of the governmental and business organs that were in charge of the economic and other activities concerned; but during 1952-57 local offices of the bureau were gradually established to supervise the organization and the operation of local statistical services.

The actual improvement of statistics can best be measured by the work done in filling gaps in the data supply, rather than by the increasingly elaborate organization charts. Progress by local government and industrial units in collecting reliable statistics was understandably slow, especially in agriculture, for they lacked competent personnel for this kind of work and often had motives in conflict with faithful reporting. Apart from the large and modern state-operated enterprises, accurate reporting could not be expected. Routine reporting had to be checked and supplemented by national and regional surveys and censuses, designed and executed independently of the routine reporting. More than any other indications, the timing and nature of these investigations reflect the true situation of statistical progress. A brief enumeration of them is central to our understanding of Communist statistics. This summary is limited to 1952-57, when a serious effort to improve statistics was made by the Communist regime.

1. POPULATION

The basic source of information on the postwar population of the Chinese mainland is the Communist population census of June 30, 1953. This census has been criticized by scholars both inside and outside Communist China. It was not obtained by house-to-house canvassing, but heads of households were required to report to registration stations set up for this purpose. Since the census was taken primarily for registering voters for the national election of 1953-54, it is questionable whether political undesirables would have come to register. Inadequate preparation and insufficient pilot surveys, a prolonged period of enumeration, the highly inaccurate "pencil stroke" system of tallying, the troublesome problem of temporary residents (supposedly to be reported by families or neighbors at place of permanent residence), and the traditions of under-reporting of females must have resulted in substantial inaccuracy. The high degree of social control in Communist China, the one factor favorable to an accurate count, was not sufficient to counterbalance all the unfavorable factors.

Doubts were further cast on the accuracy of the census on the basis of demographic analysis. Aird (1961, pp. 68-69) found a marked deficiency of persons aged 5 to 14 years old and an excess of persons aged 45 and over in comparison with other countries with perhaps similarly high fertility and mortality rates. But as Aird admitted, international comparisons would be inconclusive to start with, especially if it involved an unusual period for China. It appears that the marked deficiency of children (ages 5 to 14) relative to the numbers in other countries could, contrary to Aird's belief, be reasonably explained by the Sino-Japanese war (1937-45) and the ensuing internal conflict (1945-48). During 1937-48, there were mass migrations, heavy conscriptions, general disturbances, food shortages and severe deterioration in living standards and sanitary conditions all over China.[4] In addition to higher mortality, the fertility rate must have been sharply affected, a factor that Aird discounted as unimportant.[5] As to the excess of persons aged 45 and over, it must be recalled that the last two or three decades of the Manchurian dynasty saw some brief wars with foreign powers, quickly settled to China's disadvantage, but were otherwise more peaceful and orderly than the first 17 years or so of the Republic, when large-scale civil wars were continuously being fought. Thus, it would seem that the reported 1953 population may not be as inconsistent with China's demographical history as Aird believed.

Using certain scattered data on the Chinese vital rates, Aird could not derive the reported 1953 population. Although this has been considered another reason for believing the 1953 population count to be unreliable, it is likely that these scattered vital rates, being the result of less systematic surveys than the 1953 population count, are even more unreliable than the population count itself, and so cannot be used to invalidate it.

Aird has made a further, and very elaborate, analysis of the Chinese population data in Chapter 4 of this volume.[6] He reiterates the position taken in his earlier work that the margin of undercount was substantial and that the margin "should be set both wider and higher than the range of 3 per cent to 11 per cent suggested in the earlier study—how much wider and higher is impossible to say with any assurance" (Aird, Ch. 4). It is possible to take strong exception to this position. The uncertain bias introduced by the "pencil stroke" system of tallying alone would

4. It is quite unreasonable to assume, as Aird did, that this period (1937-48) "probably coincided with a gradual reduction in mortality due to the slow diffusion of Western health and medical practices, at least in urban areas, so that the effects of the war may have been partly masked by the long-term trend toward lower death rates." (See Aird, 1961, p. 71.)

5. A rather small reduction of the crude birth rate, say, from 35 to 32 per thousand, would account for a loss of very roughly 1.5 million infants per year, or 18 million for the 12 years. Changes of such magnitudes in the crude birth rate would have been possible even during more peaceful periods in China. As to the greater shortage of female infants, a 10 per cent differential infanticide for females does not seem to be impossible. (See Aird, 1961, p. 70, footnote 17.)

6. In analyzing the Chinese population data, the task of making plausible assumptions is not easier than when dealing with other economic data. It is difficult to accept, for instance, that the loss of population on account of the local wars in Szechwan, 1933-35, was twice as great as the war deaths during the campaigns against the Communists in 1934. The reverse would seem more correct.

make it impossible to make any quantitative evaluation of the net effect of the various factors leading to overcount and undercount. An undercount in the neighborhood of 10 per cent would probably have reduced the 1956-57 per capita calorie intake from food crops to a level too low for these relatively normal years. While there is some discussion in Aird's paper of the effects of food supply on population, the quantitative implications of a large undercount with respect to per capita food requirements have not been analyzed.

It seems that further analysis of the population statistics on the basis of the population data alone, whether by checking the internal consistency or resorting to models constructed on model life-tables, would not yield fruitful results for such a turbulent period in China, when vital rates were most probably changing from year to year because of wars and disturbances. More light can perhaps be thrown on the problem by studying the population data together with data for food production and consumption. The latter data are admittedly even weaker than the population count of 1953. The three sets of data together, however, constitute constraints for one another; and consistency among them is a first requirement for an intelligent understanding of these most fundamental aspects of the economy.

The 1953 census is certainly not comparable in accuracy to those of the more developed countries. Nevertheless, it was collected by a systematic and comprehensive effort, however poorly designed. Comparable efforts have never been made for the small producing units in the underdeveloped sectors in agriculture, industry, transportation and trade, or for the incomes and expenditures of households. These other statistics must be considered inferior to the population data for 1953.

2. AGRICULTURE

Numerous attempts were made to standardize report schedules and to improve the agricultural data collecting organization.[7] However, as preliminary reports went from the local level to the central government, adjustments and modifications were made at each intermediate stage. In terms of statistical standards, the quality, while improving, and much better than it would become after 1958, was low up to the very end of 1957. So-called "model surveys" were employed in collecting the data. It is significant that in 1953 and 1954, model surveys were centered only on food crops and cotton, indicating that information on other items was obtained without even the benefit of such surveys. In a "model survey," the investi-

7. It was reported that nationwide surveys on the gross value of output of industry and agriculture and on employment were undertaken by the State Statistical Bureau in October, 1952, only two months after its founding. The reliability of these surveys cannot be taken too seriously. Nothing is known about either the coverage or the procedure.

gator chose a small number of samples considered by him to be "typical" of the situation. There was obviously no serious statistical design involved in the procedure.

The first of a series of sample studies of rural income and expenditures for 1954 was carried out early in 1955; studies were repeated in subsequent years. Some sample studies of agricultural cooperatives were initiated in 1956, but these were later judged to be too complicated. A much smaller sample of "typical" cooperatives was studied in 1957. An investigation of land utilization other than for crops was initiated in 1956.

In Li (1962, p. 33), the following remark by the director of the State Statistical Bureau as late as in April, 1958, was quoted: "Strictly speaking, agricultural statistical services and statistical organization at the *hsien* level have not been installed in the great majority of areas up to the present. The *hsien* government still does not have any experience in handling statistical work."

3. PRIVATE INDUSTRY AND TRADE

A census of individual handicraftsmen and private industrial enterprises was taken in 1954, and one of private trade and restaurants (food and drink establishments) in 1955. In 1956, local government units were asked to revise their statistics on industry and trade since 1952 on the basis of the private records now available. Even less is known (outside China) about the procedures used in these surveys than the scanty knowledge of the population census. Nothing was said about the way in which the 1956 revision of the earlier data was carried out.

An important point should be noted in this connection. In 1952, private industry and trade were still important, accounting for about 39 and 57 per cent, respectively, of total industry and commerce according to Communist estimate (Liu and Yeh, 1965, pp. 38, 40). There could have been no reason for private enterprises to exaggerate the volume of their business at that time. During the socialist transformation, private business vanished rapidly after 1952, and the drive to achieve quotas was intensified. The statistics collecting system probably did improve during the later years, but so did the tendency to exaggerate performance, as was inevitable in such a compulsive system. It is an open question whether the net result of the opposing influences is an improvement in the data.

4. EMPLOYMENT AND STANDARD OF LIVING

In October, 1955, the State Statistical Bureau took the first serious census of workers and employees in state and cooperative establishments. Another survey of workers and employees in all industrial, construction, transportation and communications enterprises was conducted as of February 28, 1957.

A series of surveys on incomes and family budgets of workers and employees was initiated in 1956. (Surveys of rural income and expenditures had begun in 1955, as mentioned before.)

To conclude this brief summary, the following observation by Emerson (1965, p. 69) is worth quoting:

> In 1955, Hsüeh Mu-Ch'iao (the Director of the State Statistical Bureau) said that state sector economic data were better than the others, capitalist sector data were defective, and data on self-employed persons (including both handicraftsmen and tradesmen) were still more defective. However, even state sector worker and employee data collected through the periodic reporting system were continuously underreported throughout the First Five-Year Plan period, and industrial workers and employees for 1956 were underreported by several hundred thousand early in 1957. If industry employment data were in fact the best in the Bureau and were still underreported in 1957, when Bureau reporting reached its peak level of performance, it seems likely that among the millions of scattered, tiny workshops, family businesses, and stalls in the private sector, substantial numbers were omitted both before, during, and after the censuses of handicraft and private industry in 1954 and the census of private trade in 1955.

The effort toward improving the statistical system was abruptly shattered by the Great Leap Forward in 1958. The collection and reporting of statistics were in effect taken over by the Communist Party mechanism, and were integrated into emulative drives to increase production. This led to an unprecedented statistical fiasco in 1958.[8] In this fiasco, the Communist regime learned a sober lesson. A serious effort was made in 1960 to rehabilitate and strengthen the statistical system. With this effort, however, the publication of national economic statistics practically stopped.[9]

8. When the *Communiqué on Economic Development* for 1958 was issued in April, 1959 the regime announced that the output of such important products as food crops, cotton, iron, and steel had more than doubled during 1958, and that the gross value of agriculture and industry had increased about 65 per cent. A drastic downward revision of the claims was announced in August, 1959, reducing the estimated production of food crops and cotton in 1958 by one-third. The claimed increase in iron and steel production was scaled down in a more subtle way. It was admitted that roughly 30 per cent of the iron and steel produced in 1958 was "native" and not really usable for modern industrial purposes. The increase in agricultural production announced for 1959 was more restrained, but the increase claimed for steel and industrial production in general was high.

9. For a detailed discussion of the development of the Communist statistical system after 1958, see Li, 1962.

II. NATIONAL PRODUCT, 1952-1957: COMPARISON OF AVAILABLE ESTIMATES

The Communist regime started to estimate national income on a regular basis in 1955, but extended their estimates back to 1950. From the basic data on agriculture, industry, trade, employment, wage rates, government accounts and other items published by the Communists, scholars in the West have attempted to make independent estimates. Table 1 presents the different results [10] for 1952-57, expressed in constant 1952 *yuan,* together with the estimated rates of growth. (The estimates for 1958 and thereafter are discussed in Section V.)

1. THE COMMUNIST ESTIMATE

Two concepts of national income are commonly used in the Communist literature. The first, *kuo-min shou-ju* ("national income"), or *kuo-min shou-ju sheng-chan* ("national product"), is defined as the net material product, *i.e.,* the net value produced by agriculture, industry, construction, freight transportation, the part of communications that serves other productive sectors, and trade and restaurants. In principle, only that part of trade in the service of other material sectors is counted as material production; however, for practical purposes the Communists have included the entire value. This definition of national income follows the Marxian concept of "productive" and "nonproductive" economic activities. The following sectors are considered nonproductive, and therefore their services are excluded from the calculation of national income: government administration; military and police forces; cultural, educational, and social organizations; and people rendering personal services.

Apart from its rather restrictive scope, there are several other noteworthy features of the Communist definition. First, national income is apparently measured at market prices instead of factor cost; there are indications that indirect taxes are included in national income. No information can be found on how government subsidies to business enterprises are handled, but it is probable that the Soviet practice is followed, and subsidies are treated as negative indirect taxes. Second, national income is apparently net of depreciation allowances, for depreciation charges are listed among the costs deducted from gross value to arrive at value added. However, depreciation includes only the depreciation charges in the material sectors. Third, it is not clear how factor payments from abroad are treated in the national income accounting, nor are there any statistical data available on whether their inclusion or exclusion would fit better with

10. Including only those which were derived from basic Communist data with fairly elaborate procedures.

TABLE 1

NATIONAL INCOME ESTIMATES OF THE CHINESE MAINLAND, 1952-1957
(billions of 1952 yuan)

	Communist (Net material product) (1)	Eckstein (Gross national product) (2)	Hollister (Gross national product) (3)	Li (Net national product, recon-structed Communist estimate) (4)	Liu-Yeh [a] (Net domestic product) Recon-structed Communist estimate (5)	Liu-Yeh [a] (Net domestic product) Authors' own (6)	Wu [b] (Net national product) (7)
1952	61.13	71.26	67.86	72.9	68.55	71.41	72.4
1953	70.04		77.06	80.2	73.27	75.33	75.4
1954	73.88		81.92	86.6	77.81	79.28	78.3
1955	78.80		85.41	93.8	83.34	82.30	82.0
1956	88.75		97.21	107.3	96.41	92.08	91.7
1957	93.53		102.42	111.8	104.22	95.34	94.8
Average annual growth rate [c]	9.0		8.6	8.8	8.8	6.0	5.6

Sources:
Column 1: Liu-Yeh, 1965 (p. 220).
Column 2: Eckstein, 1961 (p. 56).
Column 3: Hollister, 1958 (p. 2).
Column 4: Li, 1959 (p. 106).

Column 5: Liu-Yeh, 1965 (p. 213), the "adjusted estimates." This estimate was reconstructed from basic Communist data without corrections for reliability, but was computed on standard Western concept of net domestic product. It will be called the "reconstructed estimate," instead of "adjusted estimate" as in Liu-Yeh.

Column 6: Liu-Yeh, 1965 (p. 66).

Column 7: Wu et al., 1963, Vol. I (p. 241).

Notes:

a. Estimate of gross domestic product is also available in Liu-Yeh, 1965 (p. 66).

b. Estimate of gross national product is also available in Wu et al., 1963, Vol. 1 (p. 241).

c. These are the simple arithmetic averages of the annual rates of change. The geometric means differ insignificantly from the respective arithmetic averages. Projected total product for 1952-57 as a whole, with 1952 as the base and on either the arithmetic or the geometric mean, is close to the actual total product. Take the estimate in column 6 as an example. The arithmetic and the geometric means are respectively 5.99 and 5.95 per cent per year, and the projected total products are 497.99 billion and 497.47 billion *yuan* respectively, both being close to the actual total product of 495.74 billion for 1952-57. In certain cases, the two average rates may differ not insignificantly, and the projected output may not approximate the actual output too closely. This is not the case with the estimates given in his table, because the estimates increase quite consistently throughout the period.

the Communist estimates. It is therefore uncertain whether "national income" in Communist terminology refers to national product or domestic product. However, the amount of factor payments from abroad during the period under study is likely to be rather small relative to total national income, so that interpreting the Communist figures as those of domestic product would not involve large errors. To sum up, the Communist concept of national income appears to be essentially the same as that of net domestic product at market prices as defined by the U.S. Department of Commerce, except for the narrower scope of economic activities covered in the Communist definition.

The second Communist concept of national income is *kuo-min shou-ju shih-yung* ("domestic expenditures"), which refers to the sum of personal, government, and communal consumption, along with net domestic investment. This definition approximates that of net domestic expenditure as used in standard international practice, except that the Communist definition includes only expenditures on material product; and depreciation charges for the use of capital goods in service industries and on residential housing are included as part of social and personal consumption expenditures.

Among the various methods of estimating national income, the basic approach adopted by the Communist State Statistical Bureau appears to be that of value added. They have also computed national income by the distributive shares method, that is, by summing up the income received by, or accruing to, the individuals and enterprises in the productive sectors. These results, however, have not been released.

According to the Communist estimate, the average annual rate of growth of the net material product during 1952-57 was 9 per cent per year (in terms of constant 1952 *yuan*). In all likelihood, it is an overestimate of the overall growth rate of the economy for several reasons. First, the concept of "net material product" excludes many so-called "nonproductive sectors" that apparently expanded less rapidly than the sectors that were included. This is reflected in the growth rate of 8.8 per cent per year in the estimate (Table 1, column 5) reconstructed by Liu and Yeh on Communist basic data, without correction for reliability but on the standard Western concept of domestic product, which includes incomes originating in the nonproductive sectors.[11] Second, and most important, there is general agreement among scholars in the United States that the Communist data on agricultural production during the early years of the period underestimated the actual output, resulting in an overstatement of the rate of growth of this sector. (See Eckstein, 1961, p. 32; Hollister,

11. While the growth rate of the estimate reconstructed by Li (Table 1, column 4) is also 8.8 per cent per year, the difference between the Communist rate of 9 per cent and Li's 8.8 per cent cannot be attributed to the slower growth of the "nonproductive" sectors, because Li assumed the material product to be 84 per cent of the domestic product throughout 1952-57.

1958, pp. 19, 29; Li, 1959, p. 65; Liu and Yeh, 1965, pp. 43-46; and Wu *et al.,* 1963, p. 185.)

The third source of upward bias in the growth rate lies in the way the value of industrial production was computed by the Communists. Prices for 1952 (third quarter) were used as weights in computing the official gross values of production for years prior to 1957. Consumer goods prices were depressed in the fall of 1952 because of the "Five Anti" campaign against private enterprises but prices of producer goods were little affected. Thus, producer goods were "overvalued" relative to consumer goods. Since producer goods increased faster than consumer goods after 1952, the official rates of growth of industrial production were therefore upward-biased. The valuation of new products at trial-manufacturing expenses, the so-called "new product effect," also exaggerated the increasing trend.

Another important source of upward bias is the omission from the employment estimate of workers in many small, traditional, and scattered production units in handicrafts, trade and transportation (Emerson, 1965, p. 69). Since the output of these workers during 1952-57 hardly increased, and may have actually declined, their omission would result in an exaggerated overall rate of growth.

Finally, there are the reports by the Communists themselves that local units deliberately falsified reports and overstated output in order to seem to be fulfilling and overfulfilling quotas.[12] It is reasonable to assume that the pressure to expand output intensified during 1952-57, and that attempts to falsify reports may also have increased.

2. ECKSTEIN

Eckstein used the value added approach to derive agricultural product and income, and the distributive shares approach to estimate the wage bill (on the basis of data on employment and wage rates) and enterprise earnings. Incomes of farm households, the total wage bill and enterprise earnings, together with estimates of rental incomes and indirect taxes, complete the income side of the gross product at market prices. Estimates of expenditures were also made, but Eckstein considered them less complete and reliable, the most important item missing being investment in inventories, which was intentionally left out because of the lack of reliable basic data. The statistical discrepancy therefore includes, among unavoidably irreconcilable residuals, an implicit estimate of investment in inventory. An excellent discussion of the reliability of his estimate (Eckstein, 1961, pp. 59-64) dealt with both its strong and weaker components.

An estimate of the industrial composition of the national product has been derived from a systematic marshaling of the relevant components in the basic income account. This version of Eckstein's estimate, together with his estimate of nonagricultural employment, presents the data in a

12. See, for instance, *People's Daily,* September 12, 1953.

way most convenient for comparing and reconciling it with the Liu and Yeh estimate. This comparison will deal only with major differences, referring to data in Table 3 (comparison of gross domestic product) and Table 4 (comparison of nonagricultural employment). A more intensive effort to cover the less important aspects would bring the two estimates still closer, but is not essential to our purpose.

To start with agriculture, Eckstein's estimate of gross value added is 30.43 billion *yuan,* or 4.56 billion *yuan* lower than the Liu and Yeh estimate of 34.99 billion (Table 3). This discrepancy is almost entirely explained by the difference in the estimate of the physical volume of output and in classification. It could not have come from the valuation of the products because, as shown in Table 2, the two estimates of the prices

TABLE 2

TWO ESTIMATES OF FARM PRICES
(yuan per metric ton)

	Eckstein	Liu-Yeh
Rice	108	106
Wheat	166	160
Miscellaneous food crops	111	120
Potatoes	160	160
Soybeans	144	140
Cotton	1,600	1,698

Sources:
Eckstein, 1961 (pp. 101-106).
Liu-Yeh, 1965 (pp. 374-379). Prices in Liu-Yeh are given in *yuan* per *picul;* they have been converted to *yuan* per ton in this table.

of major crops, independently obtained and often from very different sources, are extremely close.

Eckstein used the Communist data on agricultural output, recognizing the likelihood that they are underestimates, but not attempting to correct them (1961, pp. 32, 60). If the Liu-Yeh adjustment of this downward bias (2.4 billion *yuan*) is added to Eckstein's estimates, the latter would come to 32.83 billion *yuan.* Eckstein omitted forest products from his estimate and did not include lumbering in agriculture, whereas Liu and Yeh did. The inclusion of these two items (1.2 billion *yuan*) in Eckstein's estimate would raise the latter to 34.03 billion *yuan.* After these adjustments, the two estimates are so close that further reconciliation seems unimportant.

To compare the Eckstein and the Liu-Yeh estimates of employment in industry (manufacturing, mining and utilitics), the number of workers employed in handicraft workshops and lumbering must be subtracted from Eckstein's figure, and the number engaged in urban utilities added.[13] The results are rather close, as shown in Table 4. When the same adjustments are made for the value added in these sectors (Table 3), however, the discrepancy between these two estimates is very large—4.77 billion *yuan*. A large part of this difference is certainly accounted for by indirect taxes,[14] as the respective bases of the two estimates are factor cost (Eckstein) and market prices (Liu-Yeh). A sizable unexplained discrepancy would still remain. The Liu-Yeh estimate of the value added by factory, mining and utilities in 1952 was derived from the Communist statistics on industrial production, with adjustments made for concept and classification but no adjustment in the data for inaccuracy. The procedure is fairly straightforward. On the other hand, it is admittedly difficult to estimate the average wage rate and business earnings in these sectors. Possibly the Eckstein figure is on the low side.

A substantial difference exists between the two estimates for handicrafts. It is more convenient to start with the value added estimates (Table 3). The estimates of value added by handicraft workshops, cooperatives and individual craftsmen, covered in the Communist data, were not derived in the two estimates from exactly the same source in Communist statistics; and the two results are also different. But the main difference occurs in the treatment of farm handicrafts and in the lack of an estimated "controlling total" in Eckstein's estimate. He included the entire value added by farm handicrafts, as estimated from the Communist data, in the national product. A part of this represents incomes from "collecting, fishing and hunting" by farmers. Since both Eckstein and Liu-Yeh estimated agricultural product "from the ground up" (*i.e.,* through item-by-item estimation without using the Communist figure of the aggregate value of agricultural production), and since both of them included a catch-all "others" or "miscellaneous" group in their estimates of agricultural production, it is doubtful that this item of "collecting, fishing and hunting" should be included again.

Another large portion of farm handicrafts was in the nature of unpaid household services (*i.e.,* making clothing, shoes and stockings, salting vegetables, etc., for household consumption). These are not included in national product according to the usual Western concept, but though Eckstein recognized this, he included it in his estimate. Although it has merits of its own, this practice would make it difficult to make comparisons with the income estimates of other countries, industrial or underdevel-

13. See the discussion of the Communist concept of "industry" in Liu and Yeh (1965, pp. 147, 193).

14. Data on indirect taxes are available only in the aggregate. No attempt will be made here to allocate them to the different sectors. Eckstein's estimate of total indirect taxes will be used to reconcile the two estimates of total product. See the last two lines of Table 3.

TABLE 3

ESTIMATES OF GROSS DOMESTIC PRODUCT: ECKSTEIN AND LIU-YEH
(billions of 1952 yuan)

	Eckstein [a] (at factor cost)	Adjustment because of difference in: Classification	Concept, assumption, method, and source data		Unexplained difference	Liu-Yeh [b] (at market prices)
Agriculture			2.40 [c]			
			1.13 [d]			
	30.43	0.07 [d]	3.53		0.96	34.99
Industry:		−1.42 [e]				
Modern factories,		−0.07 [d]				
mining and utilities)		0.19 [f]				
	5.98	−1.30		(4.77) [g]		9.45
Handicrafts:						
Workshops, cooperatives and individual craftsmen	1.68	1.42 [e]			−0.86	2.24
Farm handicrafts	7.08		−5.66			1.42
Others			1.48 [h]			1.48
	8.76	1.42	−4.18		−0.86	5.14
Construction	1.85		0.21			2.06
Modern transportation and communications	1.90		0.33			2.23
Traditional transportation	1.13		1.55			2.68
Trade	5.38			(4.38) [i]		9.76

Government:						
Administration	1.68	−0.19 [f]	0.78			2.27
Defense	1.50				−0.47	1.03
	3.18	−0.19	0.78		−0.47	3.30
Finance	0.42		0.90			1.32
Residential rents	2.80			−0.22		2.58
Personal services	2.79			−2.24		0.55
Work brigades	0.0		0.62			0.62
Indirect taxes			6.64 [j]			
Gross Domestic Product	64.62		10.38 [k]	−0.32 [l]		74.68

Notes:

a. All Eckstein's estimates are from 1961, Table 9 (p. 71). The total gross domestic product (64.62 billion *yuan*) is slightly larger than Eckstein's figure because of rounding of the component items.

b. Figures in this column are from Liu-Yeh, 1965: agriculture, p. 140; modern factories, p. 150; mining and utilities, p. 157; the first two categories of handicrafts, pp. 647, 655; the "others" category of handicrafts is the difference between the total gross value added by handicrafts (5.14 billion *yuan,* p. 153) and the sum of the first two categories; construction, p. 157; modern transportation and communications, p. 592; traditional transportation, p. 161; the net value added given for trade (p. 167), government (p. 602) and finance (p. 603) should be increased by 1 per cent to account for depreciation (see p. 606); residential rents, p. 612; personal services, p. 610; and work brigades, p. 171.

c. See text about underestimation of crop production. Eckstein's estimate of the value of cereal and tubers production is 18.3 billion *yuan*. When raised by the ratio of the Liu-Yeh estimate (177 million tons) to the Communist estimate (154 million tons), it becomes 21 billion *yuan*. The difference is 2.7 billion. Gross value added by this difference is roughly estimated at 90 per cent of the gross value, or 2.4 billion *yuan*.

d. The Liu-Yeh estimate of gross value added by forest products is 1.2 billion *yuan,* of which value added by modern lumbering is 0.07.

e. Handicraft workshops. Liu-Yeh, 1965 (Table 58, p. 196, footnote for "others").

f. Water and gas utilities, Liu-Yeh, 1965 (p. 578).

g. A large portion of this is accounted for by indirect taxes. Also see note l below.

h. The Liu-Yeh estimate of the "others" group of handicraft production. See note b above.

i. A large portion of this is accounted for by indirect taxes.

j. Eckstein, 1961 (p. 56).

k. The sum of all the figures in this column, except the bracketed figures for industry (4.77) and trade (4.38). See text.

l. The sum of all the figures in this column, except the bracketed figures for industry (4.77) and trade (4.38), is —2.83. To this we add the difference between the sum of 4.77 and 4.38 and the amount of indirect taxes (6.64). The result is $-2.83 + 2.51 = -0.32$. This procedure implicitly assumes that indirect taxes were imposed only on the industry and the trade sectors. This assumption is, of course, not exactly valid. A more refined procedure would require an allocation of indirect taxes to the different sectors, a task which has not been attempted here.

oped, as their estimates do not include these services. In any case, if unpaid farm household services were to be included, the same procedure should be followed for urban families also, and, to push the argument to its logical conclusion, the estimates for the different countries should be adjusted for the different marketing structures. It is doubtful that all these adjustments are feasible in the near future. As the Liu-Yeh estimate included only the portion of farm handicraft production customarily included in national income estimates, a large discrepancy (5.66 billion *yuan*) appeared between the two estimates (Table 3).

It is quite certain that the Communist data on handicraft workers, and therefore on output, fall short of the actual amount (Emerson, 1965, p. 69). An estimate of the total value added by handicraft production on the basis of agricultural and mining raw materials was used by Liu-Yeh as a "controlling total." Although this estimate of the total value added is admittedly rough, the inclusion of the difference between the total and those accounted for in the Communist data, given as "others" in Table 3 (1.48 billion *yuan* compared with a total of 5.14 billion), is unlikely to lead to greater errors than its omission. This item is absent from Eckstein's estimate.

The two estimates of employment in handicrafts are compared and reconciled in Table 4 parallel to the adjustments in value added made in Table 3.

The Eckstein and the Liu-Yeh estimates of the value added in construction (Table 3) came from the same Communist source, except that Eckstein did not add an estimate of depreciation. He did not make a firm estimate of employment in construction because of the seasonal nature of this industry, though he did give the Communist figure of 1.02 million workers in public construction. It is smaller than the Liu-Yeh estimate of 1.29 million (Table 4).

The Liu-Yeh estimate of the value added in modern transportation and communications was derived from the Communist data for 1952; Eckstein had to extrapolate business earnings from 1955 back to 1952. Both estimates of employment in this sector were based on Communist data (Table 4). The difference between the two estimates is attributable to Eckstein's much larger estimate of employees engaged in private modern transportation. However, it is extremely doubtful that private employment in modern transport could have accounted for 0.4 million workers out of a total of 1.1 million in 1952. There was no private modern transport to speak about even before the Communists took over, and there must have been even less after the Communist regime was established. The 0.4 million figure appears to be of very doubtful validity. However, since both estimates were based on Communist data, the reasons for this discrepancy remain to be found.

As in the case of the handicraftsmen, the Communist data on traditional transport are grossly underestimated (Emerson, 1965, p. 69). The Liu-Yeh estimate (1965, pp. 596-99) covered a wider scope of activities than those included in the scattered Communist data, even though the 1952 estimate was derived by extrapolation from the data for 1957. This explains why the Liu-Yeh estimates of value added and employment in this sector are much larger than the Eckstein estimates.

Eckstein and Liu and Yeh give roughly the same estimates of employment in trading stores and restaurants. Evidences in the Communist data indicate that Eckstein's estimates of peddlers is a substantial underestimate.[15] The Liu-Yeh estimate of value added by trade was derived from the Communist national income data, which were estimated by the Communists much later than 1952 and which, it is believed, took their own larger estimate of the number of peddlers into consideration. Eckstein's estimate of value added by this sector is smaller partly because of his smaller estimate of peddlers and partly because indirect taxes are not included in his estimate at factor cost.

The larger Liu-Yeh estimate of the value added by government services is due to two reasons. First, Eckstein apparently did not include employees in agricultural, forestry, water conservation and meteorological services, while Liu and Yeh further added an estimate of the number of people engaged in mass organizations. Second, the average wage rate (430 *yuan*) used by Eckstein (1961, p. 37) is smaller than that used by Liu and Yeh (490 *yuan*) (1965, p. 602). Urban utilities are classified under industry in this comparison. The defense expenditure is roughly estimated in both cases.

Eckstein's estimate of employment in finance did not include those in the purely private sector,[16] and is therefore smaller than the Liu-Yeh estimate. This omission presumably also explains Eckstein's smaller estimate of value added by this sector.

The two estimates of residential rents are both rough approximations, but are not far different. Eckstein assumed that the incomes of "various services and occupations" constituted 5 per cent of the wage bill in the economy, a great deal higher than the Liu-Yeh estimate of personal services. The Liu-Yeh figure was obtained by rough itemized estimates on the basis of prewar data. Eckstein did not give an estimate of the employment in this sector. A figure of 1.62 million would be obtained by taking 5 per cent[17] of the total nonagricultural employment as given by him, which is 32.42 million (1961, Table 2, p. 37). This is smaller than the Liu-Yeh estimate of employment in this sector because of the smaller wage

15. See the detailed analysis of this point given in Liu and Yeh (1965, pp. 199-202).

16. See Liu and Yeh, 1965, Table 63 (footnote for "Finance").

17. Corresponding to the assumption Eckstein made for the wage bill of this sector.

TABLE 4

ESTIMATES OF NONAGRICULTURAL EMPLOYMENT: ECKSTEIN AND LIU
(in million workers)

	Eckstein [a]	Adjustment because of difference in: Classification	Adjustment because of difference in: Concept, assumption, method, and source data	Unexplained difference	Liu-Yeh [b]
Industry:					
Modern factories, mining, and utilities		−1.98 [c]			
		−0.20 [d]			
		0.04 [e]			
	5.20	−2.14		0.48	3.54
Handicrafts:					
Workshops,		1.98 [c]			1.98
cooperatives, and individual craftsmen	7.23			0.13	7.36
Farm	(30.47) [f]		−26.29		4.18
	37.70	1.98	−26.29	0.13	13.52
Construction	(1.02)		0.27		1.29
Modern transportation and communications	1.13		−0.40		0.73
Traditional transportation	4.17		6.73		10.90
Trade					
Stores and restaurants	6.71			−0.12	6.59
Peddlers	2.76		4.24		7.00
	9.47		4.24	−0.12	13.59

rates used by Liu and Yeh; they also included an item on work brigades which is absent from Eckstein's estimate.

In comparing the two estimates of gross domestic product (Table 3), adjustments for difference in classification cancel out. The net sum of the adjustments for difference in concept, method, assumption and source

		Adjustment because of difference in			
	Eckstein [a]	Classification	Concept, assumption, method, and source data	Unexplained difference	Liu-Yeh [b]
Government:					
Administration	1.57		0.73		2.30
Social and cultural services	2.32	−0.04 [e]			2.28
Defense	(3.00) [g]				3.00
	6.89	−0.04	0.73		7.58
Finance	0.31		0.23		0.54
Personal services	(1.62		2.01		3.63
Work brigades	–		4.08		4.08
Total	32.42 (35.09) [i]				
	67.51	−0.20 [j]	−8.40	0.49	59.40

Notes:

a. All Eckstein's estimates are from Eckstein, 1961 (Table 2, p. 37), except otherwise noted.

b. The Liu-Yeh figures are from Liu and Yeh, 1965 (p. 69), except the following: handicraft workshops, p. 194; handicraft cooperatives and individual craftsmen, p. 196; other handicrafts, p. 196; and the three figures for government, p. 204.

c. Handicraft workshops, Liu-Yeh (p. 194).

d. Lumbering, Liu-Yeh (p. 194).

e. Water and gas utilities, Liu-Yeh, (p. 194).

f. Agricultural handicraftsmen. Eckstein did not give this estimate explicitly, but he gave an estimate of value added 6.368 billion *yuan* (imputed, p. 71). At the average wage rate of 209 *yuan* (p. 130) for members of handicraft cooperatives, the employment estimate is easily obtained as given.

g. The Liu-Yeh estimate.

h. The total given in Eckstein (p. 37) is 32.42, which is equal to the sum of the unbracketed components plus employment in construction.

i. The sum of bracketed components except construction.

j. Lumbering (see note d above) which is classified under agriculture by Liu and Yeh.

data, excluding the bracketed figures 4.77 billion *yuan* for industry and 4.38 billion *yuan* for trade, but including 6.64 billion *yuan* for indirect taxes as estimated by Eckstein, comes to 10.38 billion *yuan*.[18] Although

18. The sum of the positive items is 16.04 billion *yuan*, and there is a negative entry of 5.66 billion.

this discrepancy is not small, the sources of the difference are now clear; indirect taxes alone amounted to 6.64 billion. The "unexplained difference" is only 0.32 billion *yuan*. The reconciliation of the two estimates of total nonagricultural employment is similar to that of the product estimates.

3. HOLLISTER

Hollister's estimate (1958) is undergoing extensive revision. Hence, it may not be fair or necessary to comment in detail on his estimate as it appears here. A detailed comparison of Hollister's estimate with the others is also difficult because his basic estimates of the components of national income and product are in terms of current prices,[19] whereas the others are in constant 1952 and 1957 prices. A further difficulty is the brief explanation given of the basic data and his estimating procedure. An important example of the lack of full documentation is his estimate of agricultural production, the most important single item in the national product. While recognizing that the Communist data on agricultural output for 1952 probably understate the actual production (1958, p. 19), he nevertheless used the Communist statistics on the value of output on the grounds that since the Communist data on prices were overstated, they would compensate for the underestimation of physical volume (p. 22). His estimate of the volume of production of basic food crops and animal products (*i.e.*, the value of production in constant 1952 prices) was derived from the 1952 figure by extrapolation on an index. How this index was compiled, however, was not discussed in any detail. The only mention was: "Official figures for the production of basic food crops and animal products were adjusted for probable overstatements in trend for 1950, 1951 and 1953-1954 resulting from changes in statistical coverage" (p. 23). The adjustment process was not described. It was explained only that the 1955 Communist output figure was accepted and that the 1955 output was estimated to be 5 per cent higher than that of 1952 (p. 19). These relative levels were decided "on the basis of what is known about weather conditions in the years 1952 through 1955 and the probable effect of the serious floods in 1954, together with estimates of increases in fertilizer and irrigated land." No further details are given. The index mentioned above reveals a roughly steady rate of increase of 5 per cent per year from 1954 to 1957.[20] There seems to be no evidence that there was also a roughly 2.5 per cent per year increase in per capita food consumption during this period. The rationing schedule was unchanged from 1955 to 1957.

19. The expenditure components were converted to 1952 prices (Hollister, 1958, pp. 130-137). But conversion of the income and product components is lacking, except for the agricultural sector.

20. 1954:99; 1955:105; 1956:110; and 1957:114 (Hollister, 1958, p. 24).

A discussion of Hollister's estimates of nonagricultural employment and wage bill is necessary, as both estimates contributed greatly to the high rate of growth in his estimate of gross national income (Table 1). Two observations can be made. First, his estimate of nonagricultural employment in 1952 is far too low, resulting in a low estimate of compensation of employees for that year. His estimate of nonagricultural employment is only 21.02 million, as compared with 32.42 million given by Eckstein (1961, p. 37), 36.75 million given by Emerson, (1965, p. 128) and 59.4 million given by Liu and Yeh (1965, p. 69). Hollister's estimate was obtained by using a few aggregates given in the Communist data, without filling the gaps with scattered Communist data as Eckstein and Emerson did.

Second, as shown in Table 5, Hollister estimated an increase in nonagricultural employment of 43 per cent, from 21.02 million workers in 1952 to 30.05 million in 1957. This is an excessively high rate compared with the 8 per cent increase in both the Emerson and the Liu-Yeh estimates,[21] and is due to the fact that he failed to include in his estimate the more slowly growing components of employment. This of course also results in an excessive high rate of increase in Hollister's estimate of compensation of employees.

What are the implications of these two weaknesses? Much, of course, depends upon the accuracy of Hollister's estimates of the other items in the national product. Other things being equal, however, it is rather certain that the downward bias of his estimate of compensation of employees for 1952 indicates that his estimate of private consumption for that year is also too low; at least part of that downward bias is "canceled" in the national income account by the low estimates of private consumption. Further, the upward bias in the rate of increase in Hollister's estimate of compensation of nonagricultural employees from 1952 to 1957 is at least partially reflected in the excessively high rate of growth he gives for private consumption—35 per cent.[22] The Liu-Yeh estimate for the same period is 23 per cent. (See Section II. 5.) Since Hollister's estimate of consumption was based on the Communist series on retail sales, one may infer that the rate of increase of the Communist data on retail sales is also too high.

21. Emerson's estimates for 1952 and 1957 are respectively 36.75 and 39.67 million, and the corresponding Liu-Yeh estimates are 59.39 and 64.19 million. The apparently large difference between the Emerson and the Liu-Yeh estimates is largely accounted for by the larger Liu-Yeh estimates of employment in the handicraft, traditional transportation and the trading sectors. Emerson admitted that the Communist data on these sectors are underestimates (1965, p. 69).

22. In 1952 *yuan,* computed from data in Hollister, 1958 (p. 133).

TABLE 5

ESTIMATES OF NONAGRICULTURAL EMPLOYMENT:
HOLLISTER, EMERSON AND LIU-YEH
(in million workers)

	Hollister	Emerson	Liu-Yeh
1952	21.02	36.75	59.39
1953	23.22	39.12	59.57
1954	23.14	39.75	59.39
1955	23.60	38.86	60.41
1956	28.36	39.37	61.83
1957	30.05	39.67	64.19

Sources:

Hollister: 1958, Table 7, p. 75. Although employment in individual handicrafts and carrier services is not given for 1953-57, Hollister mentions in a footnote on p. 76, that the 1952 number was used also for 1953-57. Employment in private personal services is given only for 1952. The numbers for 1953-57 are estimated by the present writer as follows:

1953	643,000
1954	665,000
1955	689,000
1956	807,000
1957	833,000

from information given by Hollister (p. 78) on wage bill for this sector and the index of money wage rate (p. 72). Hollister's estimates of temporary workers are not included in the total figures given here; these estimates are very small and would not affect the comparison in any way.

Emerson: 1958, p. 128.

Liu-Yeh: 1965, p. 69.

4. LI

The overall rate of growth given in Li's estimate of the national product during 1952-57 is high (Table 1). But it must be remembered that Li's work was completed earlier than most of the other estimates, and he could use only the data published before August, 1957. His purpose was not to derive an independent estimate of the national income of Communist China, but rather to reconstruct the national account on the basis of the Communist data then available and to study the plausibility of the result (Li, 1959, p. 84). As such, it was a pioneering work that threw a great deal of light on the Communist concepts and methods of estimating national income. Through the process of reconstruction, Li found much inconsistency among the fragmentary Communist data (1959, pp. 97-100). Since these data were used essentially without adjustment, it is not surprising that the average overall rate of growth in Li's estimate approximately equals the Communist estimate.

The value of Li's work, besides its help in clarifying Communist concepts and methods, lies in the observations he has made on the reliability of the Communist data and the reconstructed estimate. Li definitely believed the reconstructed overall rate of growth to be unrealistically high. He gave several important reasons for this conclusion. First, the well-known "new product" effect exaggerated the rate of growth of the net industrial product. Second, the depressed pricing of agricultural products at the biased period (3rd quarter of 1952) assigned too small a weight to the more slowly growing agricultural sector. Third, agricultural product was understated for the earlier years during 1952-57. (Li was among the first to point out this factor.)

5. LIU AND YEH

The Liu-Yeh estimate given in column 5 of Table 1 was reconstructed from the basic Communist statistics without correcting the apparently unreliable Communist data on food crops and consumer goods production. The reconstruction, however, followed the standard Western concept of net domestic product.[23] Estimates of the nonproductive sectors (see Section II. 1 above) were derived and added to those of the productive sectors. In addition, the insufficient Communist data on traditional transportation were supplemented by our own estimates. Table 1, column 5, shows that the average annual rate of growth in the Liu-Yeh reconstructed estimate is 8.8 per cent, only slightly lower than the 9 per cent rate given in the Communist estimate (Table 1, column 1). The effect of the conceptual change is very small.

Attempts to correct the apparent defects in the Communist data on food crops and consumer goods were made in deriving the Liu-Yeh estimate given in column 6 of Table 1.

Practically all Western scholars now agree that the Communist figures on the production of food crops for the early years of the 1952-57 period are underestimates of the actual output. (See Eckstein, 1961, p. 32; Hollister, 1958, pp. 19, 29; Li, 1959, p. 65; Liu-Yeh, 1965, pp. 43-46; and Wu et al., 1963, p. 185). The difficult problem is to correct this bias.

In the Liu-Yeh estimate the Communist figure for the per capita consumption of food crops in 1957 was accepted as roughly correct.

The Communist figures for output in 1956 and 1957 are probably not clear-cut underestimates, because the per capita consumption figures

23. The detailed computations are given in Liu-Yeh, 1965 (Tablc 70, pp. 221-224 and Appendix J). The terminology used in this chapter has been changed from that in Liu-Yeh. The "reconstructed Communist figures" in Liu-Yeh (Table 70) are simply the Communist estimate (by "reconstructed" was meant the reconstruction of the product by industrial orgin); and the "adjusted estimate" in Liu-Yeh (Table 70) is the "reconstructed estimate" given in column 5, Table 1, of this chapter. The word "adjusted" was used originally simply to denote the adjustments in concept from the Communist net material product to the standard Western concept of net domestic product.

implied in the data for these years are as much as 14 per cent higher than the estimated average ration allowed by the regime. It is reasonable to assume that the Communists, knowing that rationing and control regulations could not be completely enforced, would fix the ration at a lower level than the actual amount of consumption; but the rationing and control systems were probably effective enough to keep actual consumption from being more than 10 to 15 per cent above the ration amounts allowed (Liu and Yeh, 1965, pp. 47-51). On the other hand, it seems unlikely that the 1957 per capita figure overestimates the actual output, for the calorie intake implied in that 1957 figure is 5 to 6 per cent lower than the estimated 1933 level; and there is no evidence that the per capita food consumption in 1957 was much less than in 1933.

It is exceedingly difficult to estimate the amount of production during 1952-56; at best, we can give no more than an educated guess. There is no reason to assume that per capita consumption of food crops had been increasing during 1952-57. In fact, the control of food consumption had been gradually tightened throughout the period, which would have been unlikely had there been increases in per capita supply of food crops, a point elaborated on by Liu and Yeh (1965, pp. 53-54). On the other hand, there is no evidence that per capita consumption was reduced during this period; it seems that the only reasonable assumption one can make is that consumption stayed more or less constant.

Such an assumption enabled us to estimate the production of food crops for all the years 1952-57. Crops were increasingly used for food, and data are available on the annual percentage of total food crop production that was used for food, including quantities exported. If we assume that the importation of food crops during this period was negligible, and that there had been no change in the amount in storage, the output can be easily computed for 1952-57 on the basis of the population data. The increase in total production therefore reflects the growth of population, modified only by the increasing percentage of crops used for food.[24]

An adjustment was made also in the Communist figure of hog production in 1957. It was reported by the Communists that the number of hogs increased by as much as 47 per cent during 1957, a claim which is not only improbable, but was contradicted by a number of events discussed in Liu-Yeh (1965, pp. 54-55). Not only is there no evidence of increases in exports and consumption of pork subsequent to 1957, but food crops

24. A number of possible criticisms of this assumption have been discussed and answered in Liu-Yeh (1965, pp. 53-54). They include such questions as whether the recovery from war damages could have been largely completed by 1952; whether the effects of increasing use of fertilizers and mechanized implements and of the completion of certain irrigation and flood control projects have been taken into consideration; and whether the rationing controls were not imposed to prevent higher consumption of food crops in response to higher income, implying that per capita consumption of food crops may have been higher during 1952-57 than in 1933.

used for animal feed actually declined in 1957 (Liu and Yeh, 1965, p. 55). It seems reasonable to assume a percentage increase in the number of hogs equal to the rate of growth of population in 1957.

Although it is clear that the particular price weights used, the "new product effect" and the tendency to exaggerate performance all point to an upward bias in the Communist data on the output of producer goods (Section II. 1 above), no adjustments were made in the Liu-Yeh estimate because of the lack of a reasonable procedure to do so. There is, however, a reported increase of 200 per cent for an aggregate group of unidentified consumer goods produced in modern factories from 1952 to 1957, as compared with the 45 per cent increase in the identified essential consumer goods during the same period (Liu and Yeh, 1965, p. 60). The latter increase is already fast, as it reflected not really an increase in the actual consumption volume but, to a large extent, a shift from handicrafts and home-produced consumption goods to modern factory production. Such a fast rate of increase (200 per cent over five years) of goods of unknown identity cannot be accepted at face value without making a further effort to examine what commodities they could have been.

From 1952 to 1956 the Communists published some aggregate data on daily consumption items including china and earthenware; consumers' metal products; leather and fur products; glass products; furniture; soaps and cosmetic products; cultural, educational, and "technical" products; and an unnamed "others" category that varied in size from one-fifth to one-third of the total. The gross value of output of this aggregate group of consumer goods increased 44 per cent from 3.7 billion *yuan* in 1952 to 5.3 billion *yuan* in 1956. This is about equal to the rate of increase of the identified portion of total consumer goods, but is a great deal less than the 200 per cent increase reported for the unidentified portion from 1952 to 1956, and so fails to support the claim made for the rate of increase of the overall total of consumer goods output. At the risk of duplicating some of the items already covered in the daily consumption items mentioned above, we also put together some fragmentary data on such "luxuries" as fountain pens, radios, clocks, hot-water bottles, pencils, bicycles, and antibiotics. The total value of these goods (in 1952 *yuan*) could not have exceeded about 1.1 billion in 1957, but the total value of unidentified consumer goods (again in 1952 *yuan*) was 9.6 billion. However fast the rate of increase of the "luxury" items may have been, their increased production could not possibly explain these figures.

The 200 per cent increase in the unidentified portion of consumers' goods from 1952 to 1957 is therefore inexplicable. Actually, even the 45 per cent increase in the identified portion of consumers' goods from 1952 to 1957 is probably too high in view of the fact that resources were increasingly channeled to investment. The nature of the identified consumer goods is largely known, though, and we have no reasonable basis on which to make an adjustment in the data; but there can be no doubt that the rapid rate of increase reported for the unidentified portion is exaggerated. To use the data on the value of production of consumer goods without adjustment would result in overestimating the rate of growth of the national product. We have recomputed the total annual value of consumer goods production from 1953 to 1957 by assuming that the unidentified portion increased at the same rate as the identified portion. If that assumption is wrong, it overstates the increase in unidentified goods and our estimate errs in the upward direction.

The Liu-Yeh estimate given in column 6 of Table 1 was derived after adjustments were made in Communist data on agricultural output and consumer goods production, as well as the consequent modifications in the other sectors of the economy.[25] The average annual rate of growth, according to this estimate, is 6 per cent per year. Though substantially lower than the Communist estimate of 9 per cent, it is by no means a low overall rate of growth compared with those of many other nations (see Section III. 1 below).

It is of interest to see what separate effects these different adjustments had on the overall rate of growth. As shown in Table 6, the overall rate of growth of the net domestic product would be reduced from 8.8 per cent (the Liu-Yeh "reconstructed estimate," Table 1, column 5) to 7.36 per cent (= 8.80 — 1.44), if the correction were made *only* for the Communist data on agricultural product. The effect of adjustment in consumer goods data *alone* would be even smaller. But the "multiplier" effect of the two adjustments on the total product [26] is rather large.

The Liu-Yeh estimate (Table 1, column 6) is subject to the following criticisms. First, since the estimate of food crop production was derived from a constant per capita consumption of food crops throughout 1952-57, the substantial changes caused by floods and drought from year to year are not reflected in the estimate. An attempt should be made to use the data available on natural calamity to adjust the estimate of output. The estimate is, in any case, subject to a large margin of uncertainty due to the underlying assumptions regarding population and the stock of inventory. Second, the use of Communist data on producer goods without adjustment for the "new product" effect, for the unsatisfactory price weights and for the exaggerated achievement reports by local units is unsatisfactory. This criticism, however, is partially met by the estimates of domestic product in constant 1957 *yuan* given in Liu-Yeh (1965, p. 67).

Third, while the Communist data on the traditional sectors of handi-

25. A smaller amount of production of agricultural products and consumer goods would reduce the incomes of the trading, transportation and finance sectors, and would reduce the flow of raw materials to the handicraft sector.

26. See footnote 25.

TABLE 6

EFFECTS OF ADJUSTMENTS ON GROWTH RATE

	Per cent
Rate of growth computed on the Liu-Yeh reconstructed Communist estimate [a]	8.80
Rate of growth computed on the Liu-Yeh estimate [b]	6.00
Difference	2.80
Accounted for by the adjustment in the Communist data on agricultural production	1.44 [c]
Accounted for by the adjustment in the Communist data on consumer goods production	0.28 [d]
Accounted for by the "multiplier effect" of the two adjustments through the other sectors in the economy	1.08 [e]

Notes:

a. Table 1, column 5.

b. Table 1, column 6.

c. First, compute the average rate of growth of a new series of net domestic product obtained by substituting the figures on agriculture given as "our estimate" for the "adjusted" figures in Liu-Yeh, 1965 (Table 68, p. 213) with the other components remaining the same as the "adjusted" estimate. (For the meaning of "adjusted" estimate, see footnote 23.) This rate is 7.36 per cent. Then, find the difference between 8.8 and 7.36.

d. Apply the procedure given in the preceding note to "factories" in Liu-Yeh, Table 68, p. 213.

e. $1.08 = 8.80 - 1.44 - 0.28 - 6.00$.

craft, trade and transport were clearly underestimates (see, for instance, Emerson, 1965, p. 69), the attempt made by Liu and Yeh to supplement these statistics was based on fragmentary prewar and postwar data and is unlikely to be accurate. The Liu-Yeh estimate of the traditional sector is admittedly crude, but it is exceedingly difficult to evaluate its margin of error. Since the Liu-Yeh estimate of employment in the traditional sectors is larger than the more recent estimate by Emerson for all the years 1952-57,[27] it may appear that the former is an overestimate.

It should be borne in mind, however, that even on the basis of the rather high Liu-Yeh estimate of nonagricultural employment, the number of unemployed nonagricultural male workers increased from 25-27 million in 1952-53 to approximately 31 million during 1955-57 (Liu and Yeh, 1965, p. 105). An unemployment figure of 31 million out of a total non-agricultural male labor force of roughly 80 million appears to be quite

27. This is reflected in the larger Liu-Yeh estimate of total nonagricultural employment given in Table 5.

high. The implied percentage of unemployment would be even higher if the nonagricultural labor force were smaller. [28] It is also interesting to observe that the percentage increase in Emerson's estimate of nonagricultural employment from 1952 to 1957 (7.9 per cent) is close to the Liu-Yeh estimate (8.1 per cent).

6. WU

Using the Liu-Yeh (1965) framework for estimating value added by industrial origin, Wu, Hoeber and Rockwell have made another estimate of the domestic product for 1952-1962 (Wu *et al.,* 1963). In this section, the discussion of this contribution will be limited to the estimates for 1952-1957.

For the following nine industrial sectors, which accounted for roughly 34 and 38 per cent of the gross product in 1952 and 1957 respectively, the Liu-Yeh estimate was used without modification: construction, modern transportation and communications, traditional transportation, trade, finance, government service, personal services, residential rents, and work brigades. Modifications were introduced in the estimate for value added by agriculture, handicrafts, and modern factories. These will be discussed separately.

Agriculture

Although Wu and his colleagues prepared a rather elaborate set of food balance sheets containing interesting information, such an exercise was not really essential to their estimate of production or consumption. The starting point is practically the same as in the Liu-Yeh estimate: Liu-Yeh accepted the Communist output data for 1957 (1965, Table 32, p. 132); and Wu accepted both the 1956 and the 1957 figures (1963, Vol. 1, p. 94). Both estimates relied heavily upon estimated calorie intake from food crops to evaluate the reliability of the Communist data and to estimate consumption of grains for food purposes. Both paid attention to the Communist rationing schedules as an important check. The Liu-Yeh estimate of per capita calorie intake per day was 1,940 (1965, p. 28); the Wu estimate was 2,020.[29] But because of the somewhat different estimates of the calorie yields of food crops, the amount of consumption of food crops for food purposes turned out to be practically the same (see Table 7), except for 1957. Wu's 1957 figure is substantially lower, because the national consumption figure was adjusted downward by 14 per cent on the basis of a reported reduction of rations in one prov-

28. This is also an argument against Aird's position that there was a substantial undercount in the population census.

29. The per adult figure 2,350 (Wu, 1963, Vol. 2, p. 17) multiplied by the adult-population ratio of 0.86 (given on the same page).

ince (Shantung) alone (Wu et al., 1963, Vol. 2, p. 17). This adjustment does not appear to be warranted.

TABLE 7

CONSUMPTION OF GRAINS FOR FOOD PURPOSES
(in million tons)

	Liu-Yeh [a]	Wu [b]
1952	138	139
1953	141	142
1954	145	146
1955	148	149
1956	151	152
1957	155	142

Notes:
a. 1965, Table 32, p. 132. Data given there are in *piculs.*
b. Wu et al., Vol. 1, Table 36, p. 188.

Liu and Yeh derived their estimate of grain production for 1952-56 on the assumption of a constant per capita consumption, the population data, and the Communist estimate of the proportion of food crops used for food purposes. Wu and his coauthors derived their estimates for 1952-55 by allocating the portion underestimated by Communists (*i.e.*, the difference between estimated consumption adjusted by export balance [30] and the Communist data on output) on the basis of estimated underreporting of cultivated acreage (Wu et al., 1963, p. 181). Wu's procedure is interesting, except that the estimated cultivated acreages would not really reflect the actual output because of the varying severity of natural calamities in the different years. The different methods of extrapolation used in the two estimates, however, did not turn out to be very important insofar as the total output of food crops during 1952-57 is concerned.[31] The difference between the two totals amounts to 0.2 per cent of the Liu-Yeh estimate, as shown in Table 8. Only Wu's estimates for 1952 and 1954 are roughly equal respectively to those of Liu-Yeh for 1954 and 1952. These differences, as we have seen, were not reflected in the two estimates of the consumption of food crops.

Wu used the Liu-Yeh estimate of other agricultural outputs and the cost structure. Since the two estimates of total agricultural production are

30. Wu's estimates of inventory changes can be omitted from both the reasoning and the computation without significantly affecting the result.

31. Before a method is developed to take into consideration the effects of floods and droughts, it does not seem possible to make very accurate estimates of the year-to-year change of grain production during this period.

TABLE 8

OUTPUT OF FOOD CROPS
(in million tons)

	Liu-Yeh [a]	Wu [b]
1952	177	184
1953	180	180
1954	185	177
1955	186	184
1956	184	182.5
1957	185	185.0
	1095	1092.5

Notes:
a. 1965, Table 32, p. 132.
b. 1963, Table 35, p. 185.

TABLE 9

NET VALUE ADDED BY AGRICULTURE
(billions of 1952 yuan)

	Liu-Yeh [a]	Wu [b]
1952	34.2	35.1
1953	34.8	34.8
1954	35.5	34.6
1955	35.9	35.5
1956	37.0	36.8
1957	37.2	37.2

Notes:
a. 1965, Table 8, p. 66.
b. (20) 1963, Table 38, p. 193.

not significantly different, the two estimates of net value added in agriculture, shown in Table 9, are also very close.

Handicrafts and Modern Factories

Wu's estimate of the net value added by handicrafts during 1952-57 (Wu et al., 1963, Table 39, p. 200) is practically identical with the Liu-Yeh estimate (1965, Table 8, p. 66), and was derived by the same procedure.

The Liu-Yeh framework for converting the Communist data on industrial production to those of the output of modern factories (1965,

Table 40, p. 148) was also used in Wu's estimate (1963, Table 46, p. 224). But in the method of correcting the upward bias in the Communist data on industrial production, the two estimates are basically different. Liu-Yeh's adjustment was made only for the output of consumer goods. The overall rate of growth of the aggregate value of consumer goods output was adjusted downward on the basis of the rate of that portion that was identifiable in terms of concrete commodities (Liu-Yeh, 1965, pp. 56-63, pp. 151-152). The "new product" and certain other biases were recognized by Liu and Yeh (pp. 57-58), but instead of making direct correction for the "new product" effect, they recomputed the domestic product and the industrial value added in terms of 1957 prices; and the upward bias of the "new product" effect on the overall rate of growth was thus eliminated to some extent.

Wu and his coauthors did not make adjustments in the Communist data on consumer goods, but made an interesting attempt to eliminate the upward bias of the "new product" effects. Believing that the new product effect occurred mainly in the metal-processing sector, they removed the effect by assigning a rate of growth to this sector equal to the rate of growth of the other sectors in modern industry (Wu et al., 1963, Vol. 1, pp. 132-135). Wu may have "over-eliminated" this effect, as the metal-processing sector may (and is likely to) have expanded at a faster rate than most of the other sectors. On the other hand, the "new product" effect certainly must have exerted influences on some of the other sectors also, notably the chemical industry, which expanded 400 per cent during 1952-57, compared with the 270 per cent expansion in metal processing (Wu, 1963, p. 131). These opposite influences may or may not cancel out.

The two estimates are compared in Table 10. (There is not much difference between the two estimates of value added by mining and utilities.)

III. A COMPARATIVE APPRAISAL, 1952-1957

Data on national income, employment and population in China for 1952-57 are sufficiently detailed with respect to industrial origin and end use to enable us to attempt an analysis of the economy as a whole in terms of five components: (1) overall, the per capita, and the per worker growth rates; (2) the industrial structure in terms of the shares of major sectors in total product and in total employment, and the relative product per worker; (3) the investment proportions in total product; (4) the various incremental capital output ratios, the rate of "combined input" of capital and labor and the increase in "productivity"; and (5) the characteristics of consumption.

TABLE 10

NET VALUE ADDED BY MODERN FACTORIES
(billions of 1952 yuan)

	Consumer goods		Producer goods		Total	
	Liu-Yeh	Wu	Liu-Yeh	Wu	Liu-Yeh	Wu
1952	3.3	3.3	3.2	3.1	6.5	6.4
1953	3.9	4.2	4.4	4.3	8.3	8.5
1954	4.3	4.8	5.3	5.0	9.6	9.8
1955	4.1	4.6	6.3	5.8	10.4	10.4
1956	5.1	5.7	9.4	8.5	14.5	14.2
1957	4.9	5.5	11.1	9.9	16.0	15.4

Sources:
Liu-Yeh, 1965, Table 8, p. 66.
Wu et al., 1963, Vol. 1, p. 225.

This analysis will be made on the format used by Kuznets (1963) for his appraisal of the USSR in comparison with other countries.[32] He compiled data on the USSR from Bergson (1961) and other sources, together with the statistics of a large number of industrial and underdeveloped countries, both for long periods and for the early postwar years 1950-58. The early postwar data are especially relevant for a comparative appraisal of the Communist economy on the Chinese mainland during 1952-57. Because of the internal conflict in China (1945-48) after World War II, recovery from war damage was completed in China later than in other countries; hence, with respect to the state of rehabilitation from the war, the late starting year 1952 for China roughly corresponds to 1950 for other nations. Even the comparison of the short-period performance in Communist China with the long-term records of other countries is of some interest, as it may throw light on the relative potential and durability of quick, forced industrialization and the more "natural" process of long-term growth.

Two questions immediately arise. First, some of the estimates of national income for Communist China (Table 1) differ substantially. Which should be used as a basis of the comparative appraisal? It can be readily observed that the various estimates fall into two groups, which can be distinguished by the rates of growth estimated. One group (the Communist estimate, Hollister's estimate, Li's reconstruction of the Communist estimate, the Liu-Yeh reconstruction) has average annual rates of growth of 8.8 to 9 per cent for 1952-57; the four estimates do not differ signifi-

32. Supplemented by data from Kuznets, 1957, 1960, 1961.

cantly. In the other group (Liu-Yeh and Wu) the growth rate is about 6 per cent, and these two estimates are also rather similar. The comparative analysis will be made using Liu and Yeh's reconstructed Communist estimate and the Liu-Yeh estimate itself. These two estimates are selected because they have both the gross and the net versions of the domestic product, together with the required employment data by sector. The different growth rates implied in the two estimates should satisfy readers with different degrees of belief in the reliability of the Communist data. They also facilitate a comparison with the prewar estimate (Section IV).

The second question concerns the familiar argument against premature international comparison. Reservations about comparative studies were stated at the beginning of the chapter, and the tentative, preliminary and incomplete nature of the analysis presented here cannot be overemphasized. The author, however, agrees with Kuznets that if it is desirable to have quantitative evaluations of the economic development of a given country, then "there is surely more justification for comparing them with those for other countries" (Kuznets, 1963, pp. 333-34). Very little can be learned from isolated statistical measurements of the development of one country in one short period. The reader looking at the record of one nation for one period is, in any case, making international and inter-temporal comparisons implicitly in his mind. Of course, comparative appraisal should be revised as better data became available; but the poor quality of the existing information should not rule out getting some knowledge from preliminary comparisons, especially when estimates covering a range of possibilities are presented. In fact, international comparisons can also throw some light on the relative plausibility of the different estimates and point out directions for possible revision. Finally, those who are not interested in tentative comparisons can focus on just the analysis of the data for the Chinese mainland.

1. GROWTH OF TOTAL, PER CAPITA, AND PER WORKER PRODUCTS

The reconstructed Communist estimate and the Liu-Yeh estimate of the rates of growth of the total product, and the per capita and per worker products, are presented in Table 11.

According to the reconstructed Communist estimate, the overall rate of growth during 1952-57 is 9 per cent per year on a gross basis and 8.8 per cent on net basis. These rates substantially exceed all the estimates for the USSR in any period, except those computed in 1928 (pre-industrialization) prices for 1928-37 or 1928-40 (Kuznets, 1963, Table VIII. 1). They are also much higher than the long-term growth rates of 12 nations given by Kuznets (1963, Table VIII. 3). Comparing them with the postwar records of 44 non-Communist countries, only Israel (12.8 per

TABLE 11

RATES OF GROWTH PER YEAR IN POPULATION, EMPLOYMENT AND PRODUCT 1952-57
(in per cent)

<table>
<tr><th></th><th>Communist Data reconstructed on Western concept
(1)</th><th>Liu-Yeh estimate
(2)</th></tr>
<tr><td>1. Population</td><td colspan="2">2.3</td></tr>
<tr><td>2 Workers (total employment)</td><td>4.0</td><td>1.5</td></tr>
<tr><td>GDP, 1952 yuan</td><td></td><td></td></tr>
<tr><td>3. Total</td><td>9.0</td><td>6.2</td></tr>
<tr><td>4. Per capita</td><td>6.6</td><td>3.9</td></tr>
<tr><td>5. Per worker</td><td>4.9</td><td>4.6</td></tr>
<tr><td>NDP, 1952 yuan</td><td></td><td></td></tr>
<tr><td>6. Total</td><td>8.8</td><td>6.0</td></tr>
<tr><td>7. Per capita</td><td>6.5</td><td>3.6</td></tr>
<tr><td>8. Per worker</td><td>4.7</td><td>4.4</td></tr>
</table>

Source:
Appendix.

cent) and Jamaica (10.7 per cent) had higher rates.[32] If the Communist estimate were reliable, the growth performance of Communist China during 1952-57 would have been almost unprecedented. Given the rather limited endowments in technical knowledge and material resources of Communist China, however, it would seem unlikely that its growth could have been more rapid than postwar West Germany (8 per cent), Japan (8 per cent), or the USSR (7.6-6.8 per cent) (Kuznets, 1963, Table VIII. 2). It is also difficult to attribute the high rate of growth given by the reconstructed Communist estimate to the effect of postwar recovery, as the war damages in the largely rural economy of China were probably much smaller than those in the three countries cited above, in both absolute and proportionate terms.

The Liu-Yeh estimated rates for Communist China (6.2 per cent gross and 6.0 per cent net) have been exceeded in the postwar years by Germany, Japan, the USSR, Israel, Greece (6.7 per cent), Turkey (6.9 per cent), the Republic of China in Taiwan (8.8 per cent), and five other small nations. The Communist Chinese rates are roughly the same

32. Kuznets, 1963, Table VIII. 4. These 44 nations are fairly evenly distributed among the seven groups of countries ranked by Kuznets on the basis of per capita product.

as those of Austria and Burma. The other 30 nations included in Kuznets (1963, Table VIII. 4) all have lower rates of growth. Thus, the performance of the Chinese Communist economy during this period, judged on the basis of the growth rate of total product without regard to the relative cost of development, ranked far above the average of 44 nations.

The reconstructed Communist estimate of the growth rate of per capita product (about 6.6 per cent gross or net) again greatly outstripped the Soviet rate for all periods (Kuznets, 1963, Table VIII. 2). Of the 44 non-Communist nations, only West Germany (6.8 per cent), Israel (6.5 per cent), Japan (6.6 per cent), and Jamaica (8.7 per cent) had faster or roughly equal growth (Kuznets, 1963, Table VIII. 4).

The Liu-Yeh estimate of per capita growth (3.9 per cent gross and 3.6 per cent net) ranks the Chinese mainland above 32 non-Communist nations, but far below 11 others; these rates are somewhat higher than for the USSR during 1928-40 (3.2 and 3.0 per cent) (Kuznets, 1963, Table VIII. 2). The per capita growth rate of Communist China ranks in the relative scale of nations roughly the same as the total rate.

For the rate of growth per worker, the two estimates are close (4.4 to 4.9 per cent per year).[33] Their implications, however, are very different. According to the reconstructed Communist data, there was an accelerated use of labor relative to population, so that the per worker rate of growth is lower than the per capita rate. The Liu-Yeh estimate, on the other hand, shows that employment expanded more slowly than population, so that per worker growth was greater than per capita growth.

The estimated 4.4 to 4.9 per cent growth rates of per worker product are much higher than the USSR rates (0.5-0.7 per cent) during 1928-40, but substantially lower than the USSR rates (5.5-5.9 per cent) during 1950-58. When compared with the rates given by Kuznets for 12 non-Communist nations (1963, Table VIII. 3), they are roughly equal to those of Germany and Japan and are exceeded by Italy (5.5 per cent). But they are higher than the rates of the other 9 nations for either long or short periods.

2. INDUSTRIAL STRUCTURE

To facilitate the comparison with the analysis of industrial structure in Kuznets (1963), we have divided the economy of the Chinese mainland in a more or less similar way, into the A, M+ and S— sectors,[34] as shown in Table 12.

33. The higher Communist estimate of the rate of growth of total product is more or less compensated for by the higher growth rate of employment.

34. For the data on the Chinese mainland, the A (agriculture) sector includes the small components of fishing and forestry which are excluded from this sector for the USSR; and the M+ sector includes a small component of utilities in addition to manufacturing, mining, construction, transport and communications (all included in the case of the USSR). The S— sector covers the rest of the economy.

TABLE 12

COMMUNIST CHINA AND USSR: COMPARISONS OF SHARES OF MAJOR SECTORS IN NET PRODUCT AND LABOR FORCE, PRODUCT PER WORKER BY SECTORS, AND TOTAL SECTOR INEQUALITY IN PRODUCT PER WORKER

	Communist China				USSR	
	Communist data reconstructed on Western concept		Liu-Yeh estimate			
	1952	1957	1952	1957	1928	1940
Share in NP (per cent)						
A sector	46.1	38.6	47.9	39.0	49.2	28.9
M+ sector	29.0	37.9	28.2	38.7	27.9	44.8
S− sector	24.9	23.5	23.9	22.3	22.9	26.3
Share in labor force (per cent)						
A sector	69.9	73.1	72.9	72.9	70.9	50.9
M+ sector	17.1	16.4	15.5	16.6	17.6	29.4
S− sector	13.0	10.5	11.6	10.5	11.5	19.7
Relative product per worker						
A sector	0.66	0.53	0.66	0.53	0.69	0.57
M+ sector	1.70	2.31	1.82	2.33	1.59	1.52
S− sector	1.92	2.24	2.06	2.12	1.99	1.34
Total inequality among sectors	47.0	69.0	50.0	67.8	43.4	44.0

Source:
Appendix.

According to either the reconstructed Communist data or the Liu-Yeh estimate, the industrial structure of the economy on the Chinese mainland in 1952 was strikingly similar to that of the USSR in 1928.[35] This is true in all aspects of the comparison: the shares of the A, the M+ and the S— sectors in the net product; the shares of the different sectors in the labor force; relative product per worker; and the total inequality among sectors. The striking similarity in the proportions of the three sectors in both the total product and the labor force implies that the output per worker varies among the different sectors in roughly the same proportions in the two countries.

Both countries started their respective First Five-Year Plans with about half of their total product originating in agriculture, a little more than a quarter in the M+ sector, and slightly less than a quarter in the S— sector; and with roughly 70 per cent of their labor force engaged in agriculture, 16 to 18 per cent in the M+ sector and about 12 per cent in the S— sector.

Industrialization brought, of course, a reduction in the share of the total product originating in agriculture and an increase of the share of the M+ sector. It is interesting to observe that the decline in the share of agriculture occurred at roughly the same speed in Communist China during 1952-57 and in the USSR during 1928-40: about 17 percentage points per decade.[36] The expansion of the M+ sector was more rapid in China: 21 per centage points per decade against 14 for the USSR. The S— sector declined slightly in Communist China, but it expanded a little in the USSR.

As Kuznets (1963) has pointed out, the share of agriculture in the total product of the USSR during 1928-40 declined much faster than in other industrial countries during their early stages of development. What occurred in the USSR in twelve years took 30 to 50 years in countries such as France, Denmark, Sweden, Italy and Japan in its earlier period. Only Japan during more recent years has approached the speed of Russia (Kuznets, 1963, Table VII. 7 and p. 347). The same comparison holds true for Communist China, with the important qualification that its record is only for a five-year period.

A basically different pattern emerged in the allocation of the labor force in the two countries. In the USSR, as the shares of the three sectors in the total product changed, the labor force shifted as it had in the early

35. This striking similarity may be reduced if the traditional manufacturing and transport units are separated out from the M+ sector for both countries. The author, however, is not able to adjust the USSR data for this comparison.

36. Since this calculation was made on the basis of a five-year change for Communist China and a twelve-year change for the USSR, it must be received with caution. If the speed of change had declined through time, it would mean that in the first five years of 1928-40, the USSR moved faster than the rate of 17 percentage points per decade.

experience of other industrial countries: a reduction in agriculture and an increase of the proportion engaged in the M+ sector. However, in Communist China the distribution of the labor force was practically the same in 1957 as in 1952, especially according to the Liu-Yeh estimates. The Communist estimates even reveal a slight increase in the shares of employment in agriculture and a small reduction in the M+ sector. The change in the S— sector is very minor. The implication is clear: The increase in per worker product reported in Section III. 1 was due entirely to the increase in output per worker in the different sectors; it was not at all the result of a shift of the labor force from a low yield sector to a high yield one. The increase in product per worker took place entirely in the M+ and the S— sectors, in both of which there was a substantial shift from traditional enterprises to more modern establishments.

The almost unchanged distribution of the labor force in Communist China from 1952 to 1957 appears somewhat unusual. To check it, the data on nonagricultural employment in Emerson (1965) and our data on agricultural employment were put together and examined. The distribution for the two years is as follows: [37]

	1952 (percentage)	1957 (percentage)
A	79.3	81.9
M+	11.1	10.3
S—	9.6	7.8

The directions of the shifts are very similar to those of the Communist estimates given in Table 12; but the magnitudes of the shifts are very small, indicating more or less unchanged industrial structure of the labor force from 1952 to 1957.

As expected, the relative product per worker in agriculture was extremely low in 1952, and those in the M+ and the S— sectors were very high (Table 12). What distinguished the Chinese mainland from the USSR, and even more from many other countries, is that the gaps widened noticeably from 1952 to 1957, with the relative product of agriculture lowered and those of the other two increased. The measure of total inequality increased substantially from 1952 to 1957. This is indicated by both the Communist and the Liu-Yeh estimates.

Kuznets (1963, p. 351) was puzzled by the distinctive contrast in the USSR between the rather low product per worker in agriculture and the high product per worker in the M+ sector, even allowing for the different capital yields. But in the case of Communist China, the even greater dif-

37. Computed on data from the following sources. Agriculture: Appendix. Notes to Table 11, of this paper. M+ and S— sectors: Emerson 1965 (p. 128).

ference between the agriculture sector and the M+ and the S— sectors does not appear to be surprising. Much greater knowledge and training are required of workers in the M+ and the S— sectors than in the primitive agricultural sector in Communist China, even allowing for the fact that there were traditional enterprises in both the M+ and the S— sectors.

TABLE 13

COMPARISON OF INDUSTRIAL STRUCTURE: COMMUNIST CHINA (1952-57) AND OTHER NATIONS (EARLY POSTWAR YEARS)

Share in product	A Sector	M+ Sector (per cent)	S— Sector
Communist China	43.5	33.5	23.1
Groups I and II	15.2	49.5	35.3
Groups III and IV	24.6	34.3	41.1
Groups V and VI	39.0	27.4	33.5
Groups VI and VII	48.6	19.6	32.4
Share in labor force			
Communist China	72.9	16.1	11.1
Groups I and II	18.9	45.7	35.4
Groups III and IV	39.5	30.7	29.8
Groups V and VI	53.6	23.0	23.4
Groups VI and VII	59.3	18.8	21.9
Relative product per worker			
Communist China	0.60	2.08	2.09
Groups I and II	0.80	1.08	1.00
Groups III and IV	0.62	1.12	1.38
Groups V and VI	0.73	1.19	1.43
Groups VI and VII	0.82	1.04	1.48
Total inequality among sectors			Inequality
Communist China			58.9
Groups I and II			7.6
Groups III and IV			29.8
Groups V and VI			29.1
Groups VI and VII			22.0

Source:

Communist China: Figures are the average of the Liu-Yeh estimates for 1952 and 1957 given in Table 12. The reconstructed Communist estimates (also given in Table 12) are not very different from the Liu-Yeh estimates.

Groups of Nations: Kuznets, 1963 (Table VIII. 9). Per capita product decreases from Group I to Group VII.

Compared with the industrial structure of other countries during the postwar years (Table 13), the share of the M+ sector in Communist China's total product ranks it with country groups III and IV (countries having a fairly high per capita product). But the large share in agriculture puts Communist China into the lowest groups, VI and VII; this is explained by the fact that the share of its S— sector is smaller than the average of any group. For the labor force, China's share in agriculture is greater, and that in the M+ sector is smaller, than the averages of even the lowest groups, VI and VII. This explains why the relative product per worker is exceedingly low in agriculture and unusually high in the M+ sector. The relative product per worker of the S— sector is higher than the average of any group. As a result of the exceedingly large discrepancy between the products per worker in the A and M+ sectors, the measure of total inequality for Communist China is higher than the average of any country group, much greater than even the high measure (41.4) for India (Kuznets, 1963, Table VIII. 9).

3. CAPITAL FORMATION PROPORTIONS

The reconstructed Communist estimate and the Liu-Yeh estimate of the proportions of capital formation in total product are very close, the more rapid increase in the reconstructed Communist estimate of capital formation being more or less compensated by the greater rate of growth of total product, as shown in Table 14.

The proportion of investment in total product increased substantially and uninterruptedly from 1952 to 1956, and then dropped significantly in 1957. This remains true whether investment and product are measured gross or net and whether total or fixed investment is concerned. The rapidity of the increase in the proportions from 1952 to 1956 is quite impressive, but this accelerated rate of investment apparently could not be maintained. It was admitted in Communist sources that investment was excessive in 1956, causing shortages of raw materials and inflationary pressure (Liu and Yeh, 1965, p. 113). The smaller 1957 proportions are rather close to the averages for the whole period, especially as given in the Liu-Yeh estimate of the gross and net total proportions.

The price weights used in computing the proportions make a noticeable difference in the results. If computed on constant 1957 prices, the proportions are roughly nine-tenths of those computed on constant 1952 prices.

The average gross total proportion during 1952-57 (21 per cent, 1957 prices) roughly equals the Bergson estimates for the USSR for 1937, 1950 and 1955 (22 per cent, 1937 prevailing prices), but is significantly higher than the Bergson estimate for 1928 (10 per cent, 1937 prevailing

Table 14

PROPORTIONS OF INVESTMENT IN DOMESTIC PRODUCT
(per cent)

	1952 prices				1957 prices			
	Gross		Net		Gross		Net	
	Total	Fixed	Total	Fixed	Total	Fixed	Total	Fixed
A. Communist Data Recomputed on Western Concept								
1952	20.8	11.1	17.0	6.9	17.8	9.5	14.4	5.9
1956	26.9	24.8	23.0	20.8	23.3	21.5	19.8	17.9
1957	22.6	19.0	18.7	14.9	19.6	16.5	16.1	12.8
Average 1952-57	24.4	17.4	20.6	13.2	21.1	15.1	17.7	11.4
B. Liu-Yeh Estimate								
1952	19.5	10.2	15.8	6.1	16.7	8.8	13.5	5.2
1956	26.8	24.6	22.6	20.4	23.2	21.4	19.5	17.5
1957	23.5	19.6	19.1	15.0	20.4	17.0	16.5	12.9
Average 1952-57	23.8	16.9	19.8	12.6	20.6	14.6	17.1	10.8

Source:
Appendix.

prices).[38] The average gross fixed proportion (15 per cent, 1957 prices) is significantly higher than the Bergson estimates for all prewar years (6 to 12.5 per cent, 1957 prevailing prices), but is lower than the postwar Soviet proportions (16 to 18 per cent). It appears that, during the First Five-Year Plan period, the Communist Chinese regime made a greater effort to invest, in terms of the gross proportion in total product, than the Russians did in the early years of their planning; but in 1957 and in the postwar years their efforts were roughly comparable.

The Chinese proportions, while high, are roughly equaled or exceeded by the long-term records of Germany, Norway, the United States, Canada, Argentina and the Union of South Africa (Kuznets, 1963, Table VIII. 13). For net fixed proportions, the situation is similar. The Chinese Communist record (11 per cent) has been substantially exceeded in more recent long periods (since the 1890's or 1900's) by Germany (12.7 per cent), Norway (14.4 per cent), Australia (14.1 per cent), Japan (14.1 per cent), Argentina (14.0 per cent) and the Union of South Africa (17.8 per cent). Italy, Sweden and Canada have also approached or equaled the Chinese record.

It should be pointed out that the Chinese Communist data are more accurate for fixed investment than for inventories. If the comparison is limited to gross fixed capital formation in postwar years, the Chinese record (15 per cent) is bettered (in most cases by substantial margins) by 11 of the 13 industrial countries included by Kuznets, and approached by the other two nations (1963, Table VIII. 14).

The above comparisons of capital formation proportions are made on the basis of Kuznets' data (1963), which are mostly for industrial nations. The reason why most of these countries have equaled or exceeded the Chinese Communist record may be that, being wealthier and more developed, they were in a better position to put resources aside for investment. A comparison with poorer and less developed nations should reveal a different picture. This is confirmed by the figures in Table 15, comparing the Chinese Communist proportions with a large number of non-Communist countries ranked by per capita product and by the share of the M+ sector in total product for the postwar years (Kuznets, 1960). Since the proportions given by Kuznets are mostly computed on current prices, the Liu-Yeh proportions in constant 1952 and 1957 *yuan* given in Table 14 are averaged for this comparison.

Communist China belongs to Group VII, countries with the lowest per capital product. Countries in the low groups (VI and VII) invested on the average 14.6 and 12.7 per cent respectively (gross total ratios). The

38. In 1928 prices, however, the proportion for 1928, as estimated by Bergson, is 22.7 per cent. The change from the 1928 price weights to the post-industrialization price weights of 1937 has a much greater effect in the case of the USSR than the change of price weights from 1952 to 1957 in the case of Communist China. (See Kuznets, 1963, Table VIII. 11).

TABLE 15

COMPARISON OF PROPORTIONS OF GROSS INVESTMENT IN GROSS PRODUCT: COMMUNIST CHINA AND OTHER COUNTRIES

(per cent)

I. Countries grouped by per capita product

Communist China (1952-57)	Groups of countries (mostly 1951-57)						
	I	II	III	IV	V	VI	VII
22.2	21.4	23.4	17.2	17.6	17.8	14.6	12.7

II. Countries grouped by the M+ share in total product

Communist China	Groups of countries						
	A	B	C	D	E	F	G
22.2	21.4	23.5	18.9	19.9	17.8	13.2	15.6

Sources:

I. Communist China: Mean of the averages of the Liu-Yeh estimates for 1952-57 in 1952 prices (23.8 per cent) and in 1957 prices (20.6 per cent) given in Table 14.

Groups of countries: Kuznets, 1960 (Table 1, panel D, line 20).

II. Communist China: Same as in I.

Groups of countries: Kuznets, 1960 (Table 2, panel B, column 3).

corresponding investment proportion for Communist China is 22.2 per cent, which is comparable to the average of the highest groups, I and II (21.4 and 23.4 per cent respectively). Although, as Kuznets has noted, the dispersions of the proportions within groups are wide and the range of the averages for the groups is narrow, it is nevertheless clear that Communist China was making a much greater effort toward savings than the equally poor non-Communist countries. On a net total basis, the Chinese ratio of 18.5 per cent [39] exceeds the averages of even groups I and II (Kuznets, 1960, Table 4).

On the second criterion of comparison, the share of the total product in the M+ sector, Communist China also appears to have made a proportionally larger effort toward investment. Communist China's gross total proportion, 22.2 per cent, is in the range of the proportions for groups A and B (the high M+ groups); but its M+ share, 33.5 per cent (Table 13, ranks it in the E group, which has an average M+ share of 31 per cent (Kuznets, 1960, Table 2).

4. THE INCREMENTAL CAPITAL OUTPUT RATIOS, COMBINED INPUT AND PRODUCTIVITY

While the reconstructed Communist data and the Liu-Yeh estimate of the proportions of capital formation in total product are roughly the same (Table 14), the reconstructed Communist estimate of the growth rate of total product is significantly higher than the Liu-Yeh estimate (Table 11). Therefore, the incremental capital output ratios derived [40] from the Communist data are correspondingly lower than those derived from the Liu-Yeh estimates (see Table 16). The ratios computed on constant 1952 prices are roughly 10 per cent higher than those computed on constant 1957 prices.

On the basis of Bergson's data on national income and Powell and Moorstein's data on capital formation, Kuznets found that the capital output ratios for the USSR were about the same during the two periods 1928-40 and 1950-58. The ratios are about 3.5 to 3.7 on a gross total basis, 2.6 to 2.8 on a net total basis. For fixed capital, the ratios are 3.1 to 3.2 for gross and 2.3 and 2.1 for net (Kuznets, 1963, Table VIII. 12). The Liu-Yeh estimates do not differ greatly from these USSR estimates, whereas the reconstructed Communist ratios are substantially lower. Since, during the First Five-Year Plan period, Communist China pursued a development program modeled on the USSR and in fact used Russian designs for her major plants, these lower estimates of the ratios seem less plausible.

Table 17 shows the comparison between the ratios for Communist

39. Average of Liu-Yeh estimates of 19.8 and 17.1, given in Table 8.

40. The incremental capital output ratio can be derived by dividing the capital formation proportion by the rate of growth of product.

TABLE 16

INCREMENTAL CAPITAL OUTPUT RATIOS, 1952-57

Computed in 1952 yuan	Communist Data Reconstructed on Western Concept	Liu-Yeh Estimate
Gross		
Total	2.7	3.9
Fixed	2.0	2.8
Net		
Total	2.3	3.3
Fixed	1.6	2.2
Computed in 1957 yuan		
Gross		
Total	2.4	3.5
Fixed	1.8	2.5
Net		
Total	2.1	3.0
Fixed	1.4	1.9

Source:
Appendix.

China and the non-Communist countries during the postwar years. In terms of the gross total ratios, the Liu-Yeh estimate puts Communist China in the group where it belongs (the lowest per capita groups, VI and VII), while the reconstructed Communist ratio ranks it with the higher groups IV and V. On the other hand, in terms of the net total ratios, the reconstructed Communist figure is comparable with those of the lower groups; the Liu-Yeh ratio would place Communist China above group II, the second highest. Such a comparison fails to throw light on the relative plausibility of the two estimates.

To give a picture of the relative magnitude of the incremental ratio of fixed capital to output, Table 18 shows a comparison with 12 industrial countries on the basis of the data given by Kuznets (1963). On a gross basis, both the estimates for Communist China are the smallest, even though the Liu-Yeh estimate is very close to those for Japan and West Germany. On a net basis, the ratios for West Germany and France are slightly lower than the Liu-Yeh estimate for Communist China, but the reconstructed Communist estimate remains the smallest. (It has al-

TABLE 17

INCREMENTAL CAPITAL OUTPUT RATIO: COMMUNIST CHINA AND NON-COMMUNIST COUNTRIES EARLY POSTWAR YEARS

	Non-Communist Countries by Per-capita Product Groups				Communist China	
	I	II & III	IV & V	VI & VII	Communist Data Recon-structed on Western Concept	Liu-Yeh Estimate
A. Gross total	7.30	4.33 (4.41) [a]	2.49 (2.61)	3.33 (3.01)	2.55	3.7
B. Net total	5.27	2.88 (2.95)	1.80 (1.89)	2.30 (2.06)	2.2	3.15

Sources:
Non-Communist Countries:
A: Kuznets, 1960 (Table 10, Calculation B, line 15).
B: Kuznets, 1960 (Table 13, line 5).
Communist China: Average of the Liu-Yeh estimates in 1952 *yuan* and 1957 *yuan* (given in Table 16).

Note:
a. Figures in parentheses exclude politically and financially dependent countries.

TABLE 18

INCREMENTAL FIXED-CAPITAL OUTPUT RATIOS: COMMUNIST CHINA (1952-57) AND 12 INDUSTRIAL NATIONS (1950-58)

	Incremental Gross Capital Output Ratio	Incremental Net Capital Output Ratio
Communist China		
Reconstructed		
Communist data	1.9	1.5
Liu-Yeh	2.65	2.05
USSR	3.2	2.0
Japan	2.8	2.2
West Germany	2.8	1.7
Italy	3.6	2.2
Netherlands	4.9	3.0
France	4.0	1.9
Canada	5.45	3.4
United States (1950-59)	5.0	3.0
Norway	9.8	7.7
Belgium	5.0	2.2
Sweden	6.9	4.5
Denmark	7.3	5.5
United Kingdom	6.5	3.1

Sources:

Communist China: Averages of the estimates in 1952 *yuan* and in 1957 *yuan* (given in Table 16).

Other countries: Kuznets, 1963 (Table VIII. 14).

ready been mentioned that the Liu-Yeh estimates are closer to the USSR ratios than are the reconstructed Communist estimates.)

In spite of its popularity, the capital output ratio leaves much to be desired as a measure of the input-output relationship underlying growth. It does not explicitly show the role of labor, nor does it give any indication of the contributions of improvement in knowledge, technology and organization, and the scale effect. The combined capital and labor input approach, while far from ideal, does throw some light on these other factors. It, however, requires data on capital stock which can be only very roughly approximated. (The derivation of this rough estimate of the 1952 and 1957 capital stock is presented in the Appendix.)

The computation of inputs is limited to labor and reproducible fixed capital. Alternative weights of 8:2 and 7:3 are assigned to labor and capital, and the results obtained for the Chinese mainland can be readily compared with the similar computations done by Kuznets (1963) for ten industrial nations.

In Table 19, the nations are arranged in the order of the growth rate of "productivity,"[41] which may be attributed to the combined effect of improvement in knowledge, technology, and organization, and of larger scale operation. On the basis of the 7:3 weights and the reconstructed Communist estimate of growth rate of productivity, Communist China (3.9 per cent per year) would outrank all the other nations, coming ahead of West Germany (3.8 per cent). France (3.3 per cent), Japan (3.1 per cent), the Netherlands (2.6 per cent), the USSR (2.5 per cent), and the other countries with still lower rates. One can seriously doubt the plausibility of this outcome.

On the basis of the Liu-Yeh estimate, however, Communist China (2.9 per cent) occupies the fourth place, after West Germany, France and Japan, but still slightly ahead of the USSR. On the 8:2 weights the reconstructed Communist estimate would place the Chinese mainland second (4.1 per cent) after West Germany (4.3 per cent); but on the Liu-Yeh estimate (3.4 per cent), Communist China would take fifth place after the USSR (3.5 per cent). Since all the other nations in Table 19 are developed countries, Communist China did rather well in terms of increase in "productivity."

It is interesting to observe that, among these nations, the USSR had the largest rate of growth of capital (11.2 per cent). On either the Communist or the Liu-Yeh estimate, Communist China, Japan, and West Germany make up the next group of countries that augmented their capital at high rates (6 to 8 per cent). These four countries also increased their combined labor and capital input at much higher rates than the others.

5. CONSUMPTION

The Communist and the Liu-Yeh estimates of the shares of the various categories of expenditure in total gross expenditure are fairly close, as shown in Table 20. The share of consumption (including communal services) was somewhat above 70 per cent in 1952 in both estimates. It dropped by a few percentage points from 1952 to 1957, the decline being larger in the Liu-Yeh estimate (3.6 percentage points) than in the reconstructed Communist data (1 percentage point). The share of Government expenditure declined slightly from 7 per cent in 1952 to about 6 per cent in 1957; this reduction may be attributed to higher military and related expenditures during the Korean war in 1952 than in later years. The proportion of gross investment in total expenditure increased by 4.7 percentage points, from 19.1 per cent in 1952 to 23.8 per cent in 1957

41. On the basis of the 7:3 weighting, with Communist China ranked by the Liu-Yeh estimate.

Table 19

RATES OF GROWTH IN INPUT AND IN PRODUCTIVITY PER YEAR: COMMUNIST CHINA (1952-57) AND OTHER NATIONS (1950-58)

				Weight 1 (L at 7, K at 3)		Weight 2 (L at 8, K at 2)	
	Labor	Net fixed capital	NDP	Combined input	Productivity	Combined input	Productivity
West Germany	2.1	7	7.5	3.6	3.8	3.1	4.3
France	0.6	3	4.6	1.3	3.3	1.1	3.5
Japan	2.4	8	7.3	4.1	3.1	3.5	3.7
Communist China							
Reconstructed							
Communist estimate	4.0	6.8	8.8	4.8	3.9	4.6	4.1
Liu-Yeh	1.5	6.5	6.0	3.0	2.9	2.5	3.4
Netherlands	1.2	4	4.7	2.0	2.6	1.8	2.0
USSR	1.2	11.2	6.8	4.2	2.5	3.2	3.5
Belgium	0.3	3	2.6	1.1	1.5	0.8	1.8
USA	1.0	4	2.9	1.9	1.0	1.6	1.3
Norway	0.4	5	2.8	1.8	1.0	1.3	1.5
UK	0.9	3	2.2	1.5	0.7	1.3	0.9

Sources:
Communist China: Appendix.
Others: Kuznets 1963 (Table VIII. 14).

TABLE 20

HOUSEHOLD CONSUMPTION OUTLAYS AND OTHER COMPONENTS OF GROSS DOMESTIC EXPENDITURE PER CAPITA: SHARES IN THE TOTAL, RATES OF GROWTH, AND SHARES OF ADDITIONS TO THEM IN ADDITIONS TO THE TOTAL, 1952-57 [a]

	Shares in Gross Expenditure		Rates of Growth Per Year Per Capita	Shares of Additions to Component Per Capita in Additions to Gross Expenditures Per Capita
	1952	1957		
Household consumption:				
Reconstructed Communist estimate	70.2	68.7	5.2	64.1
Liu-Yeh	71.4	67.0	1.9	40.7
Communal services:				
Reconstructed Communist estimate	2.6	3.0	10.0	4.3
Liu-Yeh	2.5	3.3	10.0	7.8
Household consumption plus communal services:				
Reconstructed Communist estimate	72.8	71.8	5.3	68.4
Liu-Yeh	73.9	70.3	2.1	48.5
Government consumption:				
Reconstructed Communist estimate	7.2	5.4	1.1	−0.2
Liu-Yeh	7.0	5.9	1.1	−0.4
Gross investment:				
Reconstructed Communist estimate	20.0	22.8	9.2	31.8
Liu-Yeh	19.1	23.8	8.6	51.9

Gross expenditure:				
Reconstructed Communist estimate	100.0	100.0	5.7	100.0
Liu-Yeh	100.0	100.0	3.2	100.0

Note:
a. Based on totals in 1952 *yuan.*

Source:
Appendix.

according to the Liu-Yeh estimate; the corresponding increment is smaller (2.8 percentage points) on the reconstructed Communist estimate.

The changes in the shares of the various categories of expenditure in the total are very minor compared to those for the USSR from 1928 to 1937 or to 1940 (Kuznets, 1963, Table VIII. 16). As will be shown, from the prewar years to 1952 in Communist China, there were substantial reductions in the share of consumption and great increases in the shares of government expenditure and of investment. Most of these changes must have occurred during the earlier years of the Communist regime, 1949-52. If we assume that in 1949 consumption accounted for a share not much below 89 per cent (the share in 1933; see Table 23 in Section IV)—say, slightly over 85 per cent—then the drop in the consumption share from 1949 to 1952 (74 per cent in the latter years) was very drastic indeed, considering the short span of time involved. A roughly comparable decline of the consumption share, from somewhat below 80 per cent to between 60 and 70 per cent, occurred in other countries over a period ranging from three or four to eight decades (Kuznets, 1963, p. 360)—not a drop of some 10 percentage points in four years.

Consumption in Communist China, even in 1952, was much nearer to the bare subsistence level than that in the USSR in 1928. The USSR was able to reduce the consumption proportion from about 84 per cent in 1928 to 63 per cent in 1937; to 60 per cent in 1940 and to still lower proportions in the 1950's. Despite the rationing of staple consumer goods and the substantial efforts to increase investment, the Chinese Communists were not able to reduce the share of consumption much below 70 per cent during 1952-57.

While the two estimates of the share of the various categories of expenditure in total are roughly the same, the implied growth rates of per capita expenditures are very different indeed. According to the reconstructed Communist estimate, per capita total expenditure increased at an average annual rate of 5.7 per cent per year, and the rate of growth of per capita consumption was only slightly lower, 5.3 per cent. As a consequence, addition to consumption per capita amounted to 68.4 per cent of the addition to total expenditure per capita from 1952-1957; not much lower than the average percentage for consumption as part of total expenditure during this period. This means that, during this period of rapid industrialization, consumption shared in the the total increase about equally with all the other categories of expenditure together.

This, however, appears to be a overly rosy picture. According to the Liu-Yeh estimates, per capita total expenditure and consumption increased at the rate of 3.2 and 2.1 per cent respectively. Hence, the share of the addition to per capita consumption amounts to only 48.5 per cent of the additions to the per capita total expenditure from 1952 to 1957, much lower than the average proportion of total expenditure given to consumption (roughly 72 per cent).

The high reconstructed Communist estimate of the growth rate of per capita consumption (5.3 per cent per year) is far above the rate prevailing in the USSR during 1928-40 (0.45 per cent), almost approaching its 1950-58 rate of 6 per cent (Kuznets, 1963, Table VIII. 2). Comparing this estimate with the 44 non-Communist countries during 1950-58 shows that only West Germany and Japan had higher rates (Kuznets, 1963, Table VIII. 4). Even the Liu-Yeh estimates (2.1 per cent) [42] would rank Communist China above the USSR during 1928-40 and above 19 non-Communist nations during 1950-58.

Table 21 compares the average shares of the various categories of expenditure in the Communist Chinese economy during 1952-57 with the non-Communist countries grouped by per capita product. The proportion of gross investment in the total expenditure of Communist China (23 per cent) ranks it in the high groups I and II (Kuznets, 1963, Table VIII. 17). The proportionate consumption of the different country groups falls within a very narrow range; Communist China's proportion (67.6 per cent excluding communal services) is within that of the low groups III-VII.

The share of government expenditure, with communal services included, averages to 9 per cent, slightly lower than in the groups with low per capita products (11 to 12 per cent). When communal services are excluded, the share of government expenditure is only 6.4 per cent, among the lowest for any country. This is less strange than it may appear at first. A three-million man army is large for any country, but it is proportionately small for a large country like Communist China. The expenditure for maintaining armed forces of such size is also relatively smaller in Communist China, where the subsistence provisions for the men in uniform are far below the standards of the industrial nations.

Table 22 shows that the change in the structure of consumption from 1952 to 1957 was not very marked. The share of food consumption de-

42. The rate of growth of per capita consumption excluding communal services is 1.9 per cent (Table 20).

TABLE 21

COMMUNIST CHINA AND GROUPS OF COUNTRIES: SHARES IN TOTAL DOMESTIC USES OF PRIVATE CONSUMPTION EXPENDITURES, GOVERNMENT CONSUMPTION, AND GROSS DOMESTIC CAPITAL FORMATION, EARLY POSTWAR YEARS
(per cent)

	Shares in total domestic uses		
	Private Consumption [a]	Government Consumption [b]	Gross Domestic Capital Formation
Communist China [c]			
Reconstructed			
Communist estimate	67.6	9.2	23.2
Liu-Yeh	67.6	9.4	23.0
Groups of countries	(classified by per capita product): [d]		
I	64.9	13.0	21.2
II	61.8	13.6	24.5
III	69.8	12.8	17.4
IV	72.7	10.7	16.6
V	69.3	12.2	18.5
VI	73.0	11.2	15.9
VII	71.5	11.7	16.8

Notes:
a. Excluding communal services.
b. Including communal services.
c. Average, 1952-57, computed in 1952 *yuan.*
d. Based on totals in current prices.

Sources:
Communist China: Appendix.
Groups of countries: Kuznets, 1963 (Table VII. 17).

clined by two or three percentage points, accompanied by gains in the shares of communal services and other consumption categories. The high proportion of food consumption expenditure in the total is somewhat higher than the average share (53.4 per cent) of countries in groups VI and VII, the low per capita product countries (Kuznets, 1963, VIII. 20). The reconstructed Communist estimate of increases in food and other consumption from 1952 to 1957 (Table 22, lower part) is much larger than the estimates by Liu and Yeh.

TABLE 22

PER CAPITA CONSUMPTION AND STRUCTURE OF CONSUMPTION
(in 1952 yuan)

	1952		1957	
	Amount	Percentage of total	Amount	Percentage of total
1. Consumption per capita				
Food				
Reconstructed Communist	53.4	56.2	66.5	54.1
Liu-Yeh	58.1	58.5	60.3	54.8
Communal services				
Reconstructed Communist	3.4	3.6	5.2	4.2
Liu-Yeh	3.4	3.4	5.2	4.7
Others				
Reconstructed Communist	38.3	40.2	51.3	41.7
Liu-Yeh	37.8	38.1	44.6	40.5
Total				
Reconstructed Communist	95.1	100.0	123.0	100.0
Liu-Yeh	99.3	100.0	110.1	100.0
2. Index, 1952 = 100				
Food				
Reconstructed Communist			124.5	
Liu-Yeh			103.8	
Communal services				
Reconstructed Communist			152.9	
Liu-Yeh			152.9	
Others				
Reconstructed Communist			133.9	
Liu-Yeh			118.0	
Total				
Reconstructed Communist			129.3	
Liu-Yeh			110.8	

Source:
Appendix.

6. SUMMARY REMARKS

If one accepts the reconstructed Communist estimates as reliable, the performance of the Communist economy on the Chinese mainland during 1952-57 must be considered as an outstanding success. The overall growth rate (8.8 per cent net, or 9 per cent gross) is higher than those of nearly all the nations compared, including the USSR, West Germany and Japan (Table 11); the only exceptions being Israel and Jamaica, two small countries where circumstances are perhaps very unusual.[43] The growth rates per capita (6.5-6.6 per cent) and per worker (4.7-4.9 per cent) were also most impressive compared with those of other nations. The change in industrial structure from 1952-57, in terms of the shift from agriculture to the M+ sector, was at least as rapid, on a per decade basis, as that which occurred in the USSR from 1928 to 1940 (Table 12). Employment (Table 11) expanded at a much faster rate (4 per cent) than population (2.3 per cent); but because of the existing amount of unemployment (including disguised; Liu and Yeh, 1965, pp. 101-105), this relative change would be a blessing for quite some time to come.

Still according to the Communist estimate, the proportion of total product invested (24.4 per cent at 1952 prices; or 21.1 per cent at 1957 prices, as in Table 14) though equaled or bettered by many industrial nations, was considerably higher than that in countries with an equally low per capita product or with a similar industrial structure in terms of the M+ sectors share in the economy (Table 15). Yet, in spite of the high rate of savings, consumption expanded at 5.2 per cent per year on a per capita basis and shared almost equally with other expenditures in the increase in total expenditure (Table 20). The various incremental capital output ratios were very low, substantially smaller than those of the USSR and most other nations, industrialized or not. On the basis of the 1952 *yuan,* a gross total capital output ratio of 2.7 (Table 16), coupled with a corresponding capital formation proportion of 24.4 per cent, resulted the outstanding overall rate of growth of 9 per cent per year. The rates of increase of labor and capital inputs, separate or combined, were high; but so was the growth rate of "productivity," at 3.9 per cent per year, higher than any other nation during roughly comparable postwar years (Table 19).

This would be the history of economic growth in Communist China during 1952-57 if the Communist data were to be believed. The performance would approach a miracle, considering the very limited technical knowledge and personnel to start with; the virtual nonexistence of uncultivated land; the gradual disappearance of private incentives for the peasants; the severe tightening of control of economic activities by cadres

43. In the case of Israel, for instance, heavy immigration of skilled population.

lacking training in such spheres; and the rather short period of time in which the people and the economy had to be conditioned to the rather unfamiliar industrial organizations and operations that were to produce a growth record greater than in West Germany and Japan.

But strong reservations must be expressed concerning the credibility of such a picture. One wonders why the Communist leadership, however ambitious they were, were so anxious to institute as radical a change in their economic policies as the Great Leap Forward in 1958 if everything was indeed making such amazing and unprecedented progress.

The growth history represented by the Liu-Yeh estimate seems more in accordance with reality. The overall growth rate (6.2 per cent gross or 6.0 per cent net) is by no means slow; in fact, it was higher than roughly two-thirds of the nations used for comparison. But population (Table 1) was expanding much faster (2.3 per cent) than employment (1.5 per cent). The rate of investment (23.8 per cent at 1952 prices; 20.6 per cent at 1957 prices) while high, was not sufficient to absorb the fast-growing population into the employed labor force (Table 14). Attempts to increase the proportion of investment to still higher levels failed in 1956 (Table 14). Per capita consumption was rising at a much more modest rate (1.9 per cent, excluding communal services; see Table 20) than indicated by the reconstructed Communist estimate (5.2 per cent); and as will be shown in the next section, the prewar 1933 level had not been regained even by the end of the period (1957). The capital output ratios were reasonably low. But a gross total capital output ratio of 3.9 (at 1952 prices; see Table 16), coupled with a corresponding investment proportion of 23.8 per cent (Table 14), yielded the overall growth rate of 6 per cent per year. This rate, in combination with the industrial structure consistent with the program and policies then in effect, could not bring about a faster increase in employment and consumption.

Though this picture based on the Liu-Yeh estimate is not really poor at all, to leaders with extraordinary ambitions, both domestic and international, and unusual confidence in their ability to put through a radical reorganization of the economy, it may have seemed unsatisfactory. A radically different program under which they could hope to utilize fully the increasingly underemployed human resources without having to divert capital resources from large-scale modern projects, would have been attractive to the Communist leadership. Thus the motivation underlying the Great Leap Forward seems more understandable.

IV. COMPARISON OF 1952 AND 1957 WITH THE PREWAR YEAR 1933

It is of interest to compare the total and the per capita products, consumption, capital formation, government expenditure, and the industrial structure at both the beginning (1952) and the end (1957) of the First Five-Year Plan period, with those prevailing during the 1930's. The Liu-Yeh estimate for 1933 is taken as the basis of comparison.[44]

Rehabilitation from war damages had evidently been completed by 1952, as the level of output was higher in 1952 than in 1933. This is true whether the total, the per capita, or the per worker product is considered, or whether the reconstructed Communist estimate or the Liu-Yeh estimate is accepted for 1952, as can be seen in Table 23. Since growth during 1952-57 was very significant according to either estimate, the 1957 output exceeded the prewar level by a substantial margin; only the reconstructed Communist estimate appears to have exaggerated the achievement (as shown by the analysis in the preceding sections).

In the case of consumption, the comparative situation is radically different. Both estimates indicate that per capita consumption was lower in 1952 than in 1933. According to Liu and Yeh, the 1933 per capita consumption level had not been regained even by as late as 1957; but the reconstructed Communist estimate shows an increase of 8 per cent. As pointed out in Section III. 5 ("Consumption"), however, the rapid increase in the Communist estimate of consumption implies a marginal consumption-output ratio during 1952-57 that was not much below the initial average ratio in 1952 (Table 20), a rather unlikely situation during a period of forced industrialization.

The higher levels of investment and government expenditure in 1952 than in 1933 point to the fact that the Communist effort toward industrialization and centralization actually started before the First Five-Year Plan. This effort resulted in a smaller proportion of consumption and in

44. In a recent study, Yeh (1964) has estimated the domestic product and expenditure for the prewar years 1931-36. Unfortunately, a severe depression occurred in 1934; the net domestic product declined by 8 per cent from 1933 to 1934. In addition, Japan invaded Manchuria in 1931 and Shanghai in 1934, and the Chinese government was unable to carry out its functions in North China in any regular manner because of Japanese interference throughout 1931-36. The National Government also launched four military campaigns against the Communists during this period. It is therefore rather misleading to compare the average annual rate of growth during 1931-36 with the uninterrupted development during the postwar years 1952-57. Because of the depression, it would also be difficult to get any meaningful estimates of the capital output ratios and the growth rate of productivity per unit of combined input for 1931-36.

The analysis in this section is in terms of the product and expenditure estimates in constant 1952 prices for all three years 1933, 1952 and 1957. For an analysis in terms of the 1933 *yuan*, see Liu-Yeh, 1965, Chapter III.

TABLE 23

TOTAL AND PER CAPITA PRODUCT, CONSUMPTION, CAPITAL FORMATION, AND GOVERNMENT EXPENDITURE IN 1952 PRICE, 1933, 1952, AND 1957
(Index: 1933 = 100)

	1952 Communist data reconstructed on Western concept	1952	1952 Liu-Yeh estimate	1957 Communist data reconstructed on Western concept	1957	1957 Liu Yeh estimate
Population		113.8			127.4	
Workers	89.0		100.5	108.2		108.5
NDP						
Total	115.2		120.0	175.2		160.3
Per capita	100.8		105.9	137.8		126.1
Per worker	129.3		119.4	161.5		147.6
Consumption (including communal services)						
Total	95.2		99.4	137.8		123.4
Per capita	83.7		87.3	108.2		96.9
Net domestic capital formation						
Total	456.1		443.5	762.7		715.3
Per capita	400.0		390.2	598.0		560.8
Government expenditure						
Total		226.3			250.8	
Per capita		198.7			196.8	

Source:
Data for 1952 and 1957 are from the same sources explained in notes to Tables 11, 14, and 20. Data for 1933 are Liu-Yeh, 1965 (Table 8, p. 66; Table 10, p. 68; and Table 11, p. 69).

greatly increased proportions for investment and government expenditure in total domestic expenditure (see Table 24).

It has been noted (Section III. 5) that, during 1952-57, there was a shift in industrial structure from agriculture to the M+ sector, in terms of the shares of value added of the major sectors in the total product. A comparison of the data in Table 25 and in Table 12 shows that there

TABLE 24

SHARES IN GROSS EXPENDITURE IN 1952 PRICES
(per cent)

	1933	1952		1957	
		Communist data reconstructed on Western concept	Liu-Yeh estimate	Communist data reconstructed on Western concept	Liu-Yeh estimate
Consumption (including communal services)	88.90	72.79	73.94	71.75	70.30
Gross capital formation	7.41	20.02	19.07	22.83	23.77
Government expenditure	3.69	7.18	66.99	5.42	5.93

Source:
Data for 1933: Liu-Yeh, 1965 (Table 10, p. 68).
Data for 1952 and 1957: See note to Table 20.

TABLE 25

SHARES OF MAJOR SECTORS IN NET PRODUCT AND LABOR FORCE, PRODUCT PER WORKER BY SECTOR, AND TOTAL SECTOR INEQUALITY IN PRODUCT PER WORKER: 1933 IN 1952 PRICES

	A Sector	M+ Sector	S— Sector
Share in NP (per cent)	56.9	22.0	21.1
Share in labor force (per cent)	75.1	14.0	10.9
Relative product per worker	0.76	1.57	2.55
Total inequality among sectors:		36.0	

Source:
Computed from data in Li-Yeh, 1965 (Table 8, p. 66, and Table 11, p. 69).

had been a very substantial similar shift from 1933 to 1952. Much of this shift must have occurred from 1949 to 1952. In terms of proportionate labor force, however, the shift from 1933 to 1952 was not so significant; but it was more pronounced than the corresponding shift in labor during 1952-1957.[45] There was a widening of the gap between the relative products per worker from 1933 to 1952, resulting in a greater measurement of total sector inequality in 1952 than in 1933. It is recalled that the same widening tendency continued during 1952-57 according to both the reconstructed Communist and the Liu-Yeh estimates (Table 12).

V. TRENDS IN THE ECONOMY, 1958-63

Since the "statistical fiasco" brought about by the Great Leap Forward in 1958 (see Section I. 4), it has become practically impossible to estimate Communist China's national income and its components with any reasonable degree of confidence. There is general agreement that the Communist data for 1958 and 1959 are greatly inflated, so that the methods employed by different scholars to correct the much more modest biases of the relatively "normal" years of 1952-57 are no longer adequate. Starting in 1960, the flow of economic statistics from Communist China practically stopped. Not only were people in the West left in the dark about the situation on the Chinese mainland, but it is doubtful whether, in the chaos accompanying the Leap and the ensuing crises in agriculture, the Communists themselves had any unpublished reliable data for those years.

1. AVAILABLE ESTIMATES

Existing estimates of the post-1957 total product are presented in Table 26, together with the estimates for 1957.

The Communist estimate and the estimate reconstructed by Liu and Yeh (1965) for 1958 and 1959 were both based on the extravagant Communist claims of increase of agricultural and industrial output.[46] An

45. See the Liu-Yeh estimate in Table 12. It will be recalled that the reconstructed Communist estimate of the shift in labor force is "perverse" in nature. See also the discussion in Section III. 3 ("Industrial Structure").

46. When the *Communiqué on Economic Development in 1958* was issued in April, 1959, the regime announced that the output of such important products as food crops, cotton, iron, and steel had more than doubled during 1958, and that the gross value of agriculture and industry had increased about 65 per cent. A drastic downward revision of the claims was announced in August, 1959, reducing the estimated production of food crops and cotton in 1958 by one-third. The claimed increase in iron and steel production was scaled down in a more subtle way. It was admitted that roughly 30 per cent of the iron and steel production in 1958 was "native" and not really usable for modern industrial purposes. The increase in agricultural production announced for 1959 was more restrained, but the increase claimed for steel and industrial production in general was high. These claims are summarized in Liu-Yeh, 1965, Table 26.

overall rate of growth as high as 34 per cent in a single year from 1957 to 1958 does not seem to be in the realm of possibility. Hollister's estimate of a 23 per cent increase from 1957 to 1958, though lower than the Communist claim, also appears to be quite unprecedented.

After the dusts of the Leap have settled, it is certain that all the estimates for 1959 (including the exploratory estimates by Liu and Yeh and the Wu estimate of a modest 7 per cent increase from 1958 to 1959) are overestimates. A basic reason for this conclusion is that agricultural production not only did not increase from 1958 to 1959, but actually declined substantially.[47] Two estimates of food crop production after 1957 are given in Table 27 (Wu's estimate will be discussed later).

TABLE 27

TWO ESTIMATES OF OUTPUT OF FOOD CROPS, 1958-65
(in million tons)

	U.S. Agricultural Officer (Consul General's Office), Hong Kong [a]	Jones-Poleman [b]
1958	194	210
1959	168	192
1960	160	185
1961	167	185
1962	178	
1963	179	
1964	183	
1965	180	

Notes:

a. Reported in Emery, 1966. Identical figures for 1958-63 have been reported in *Current Scene,* Jan. 15, 1964, and *Far Eastern Economic Review,* March 12, 1964 (p. 556), and October 1, 1964 (p. 25).

b. Jones and Poleman, 1962 (p. 4).

Both indicate a reduction in production from 1958 to 1959.

The Jones and Poleman (1952) estimate for 1958-61 is higher than that made by the U.S. Consul General in Hong Kong (Emery, 1966). The latter was derived from estimated cultivated area and unit yields by different crops. The method by which the Jones-Poleman estimate was made is not known; however, there is some apparent implausibility in it.

47. The exploratory estimate by Liu and Yeh (1965) was completed in 1961, before any independent estimate of agricultural production in 1959, other than the Communist claim itself, became available. It was assumed there that agricultural production increased at the same rate as population.

TABLE 26

NATIONAL INCOME ESTIMATES OF THE CHINESE MAINLAND, 1957-63
(in billions of 1952 yuan; preceding year = 100)

	1957	1958	1959	1960	1961	1962
Communist (net material product)						
Magnitude	93.53	125.33	152.90			
Rate of increase		34.0	22.0			
Hollister (gross national product)						
Magnitude	102.42	126.23	142.57	158.11		
Rate of increase		23.2	12.9	10.9		
Liu-Yeh (net domestic product)						
Reconstructed Communist estimate:						
Magnitude	104.22	144.97	176.75			
Rate of increase		39.1	21.9			
Authors' own exploratory estimate:						
Magnitude	95.34	108	125			
Rate of increase		13.0	15.7			

	1957	1958	1959	1960	1961	1962
Wu (net domestic product)						
Magnitude	94.8	104.8	112.0	112.5	73.2	
Rate of increase		10.5	6.9	0.4	−34.9	
Wu (gross domestic product)						
Magnitude					82.1	109.0 [a] (101.4) [b]
Rate of increase						32.8 [a] (23.5) [b]

Notes:

a. Without taking into consideration possible "investment limitations and waste."
b. Taking into consideration possible "investment limitations and waste."

Sources:

Communist: Liu-Yeh, 1965, p. 220 (1957) and p. 116 (1958 and 1959).
Hollister: Li, 1964, pp. 5-6.
Liu-Yeh: Reconstructed Communist: 1965, p. 213 (1957) and p. 660 (1958 and 1959).
Authors' own: 1965, p. 66.
Wu: 1963, p. 241, and 1964, pp. 120-122.

The Communists imported roughly 6 million tons of grains in 1961;[48] adding the Jones-Poleman estimate of 185 million tons would make the sum of imports and domestic output 191 million tons. This is 3.2 per cent higher than the total supply in 1957.[49] But the population growth must have slowed down substantially after 1958 as a result of the havoc during the Leap—unprecedented mass mobilization for public works; disruption of family life; overwork, fatigue and undernourishment, and diseases accompanying floods and drought during and after 1959.

Assuming an average 1.5 per cent growth per year from 1958 to 1961, the population would have been about 682 million in 1961.[50] The 1961 per capita food supply, then, would be about 280 kilograms, or only 3.6 per cent lower than the 1957 figure of 290 kilograms.[51] Such a small reduction does not appear to be consistent with the severe food shortage that existed in 1961, a situation serious enough to be considered famine. The series on food crops production given by the U.S. Consul General in Hong Kong (Emery, 1966) will be used later in deriving our estimate of post-1958 total product.

One may question whether the production of food crops could decline by 13.4 per cent from 1958 to 1959, as indicated by the first estimate given in Table 27, since the common impression is that the Leap did not collapse until 1960. There are strong reasons for believing that it could. First and most important were the natural calamities in 1959, reported by the Communists to be extraordinarily great. It is well-known that the Communists claimed that, in 1960, natural disasters hit 9 million out of a total of 16 million *mou* of cultivated area, a disaster unprecedented even in China.[52] But Western scholars have seldom mentioned that, in the same source, the Communists say that 6 million *mou*—more than one-third of the total cultivated area—were affected by natural disaster in 1959. The 1959 calamity, if real, was also quite unprecedented in China. Whether the Communist report was true or not, the regime was obviously trying to explain to the people of Communist China why the grain supply was so scarce in both 1959 and 1960.

Second, the severe overexertion and lack of reward during the Great Leap in 1958 must have had very unfavorable effects on the peasants'

48. U.S. Department of Agriculture, *Foreign Agriculture,* May 6, 1963, p. 3.

49. Jones and Poleman accepted the Communist estimate of 185 million tons for 1957.

50. Population at the end of 1957 is given in *Ten Great Years,* p. 11, as 646 million (Taiwan excluded). Population at the end of 1958 may be approximately estimated at 659 million (total minus Taiwan, the former being given in Hu Kang, "Making a Success of Wage Statistical Work in 1959," *HYTC,* February 23, 1959). The mid-year population in 1958 was therefore roughly 652 million. The 1961 population estimate can then be easily computed.

51. 185 million tons divided by 637 million people, the mid-year population for 1957 (Liu-Yeh, 1965, p. 132).

52. *People's Daily,* December 29, 1960.

incentive to produce in 1959. Finally, the statistics on exports also tend to support this reported decline. A change in the volume of agricultural exports would lag behind causative change in farm output by roughly a year. China's exports of agricultural products to the Soviet Union and the free world increased from 1958 to 1959 in response to the initial spur of the Leap in 1958, but they dropped sharply from 1959 to 1960.[53] In fact, total exports also declined significantly from 1959 to 1960, indicating that the economy as a whole did less well in 1959 than in 1958.

One more estimate remains to be analyzed—Wu's estimate for post-1957 (see Table 26).

Take the important agricultural sector first. Value added by agriculture was determined mainly by the output of food crops. Wu's estimate of the 1958-60 output was based on the "redistribution of apparent surplus" of the output, as reported in the official Communist data, over estimated consumption and other outlets. The essential steps leading to the estimated "surplus" are the following:

(1) During 1958, "average grain consumption returned to the pre-1957 level of 245 kg. per adult per year" (Wu et al., 1963, Vol. 2, p. 17).

(2) A sharp drop in the estimate of per capita consumption occurred in 1959 because of information that "An author in Grain Weekly, house organ of the Ministry of Food, estimated an available supply of only 166 kg. of milled grain per adult per year as of the latter part of 1959. To represent the entire year of 1959, however, an average may be taken between 166 kg. and 245 kg., the assumed 1958 consumption, yielding an estimated mean consumption of approximately 205 kg. of milled grain per year per adult in 1959" (p. 18). No detailed issue or page reference is given for the information taken from the *Grain Weekly.*

(3) For 1960-1962, the per capita consumption figures were estimated from "extensive data" gathered on "ration allowances for various types of workers in various urban and rural areas" (p. 18). An evaluation of these data is not possible, as the basic figures and their sources were not given by Wu and his coauthors.

In Wu (1964), the total 1962 output of food grains was raised upward to 160 million tons from the 150 million tons, given in the earlier estimate (Wu et al., 1963, Vol. 1, Table 35).

This upward adjustment is based on the estimated gross value added by the grain crop, for which the relationship between tons of grain produced and gross value added is obtained from the 1958 figures in Table 37, Volume 1. These data show a gross value added of 19.6 billion *yuan* corresponding to a grain output of 175 million metric tons. or 112 *yuan* gross value added per ton of grain. Applying this figure to the revised estimate of 160 million tons

53. See F. H. Mah, Ch. 12 in this volume, Table 11 and Table 13.

of grain output in 1962, the gross value added by food grains in 1962 amounts to 17.9 billion yuan. (Wu *et al.,* 1964, pp. 103-104.)

The quoted passage, though, seems to explain how the total value added figure was obtained from the total output figure, rather than how the upward revision was made.[54]

The Wu estimate of total food crops production (in millions of metric tons) is as follows (Wu et al., 1963, Vol. 1, Table 35; 1964, p. 103):

1957	185
1958	175
1959	154
1960	130
1961	140
1962	160

Wu's estimates for 1958-62 are smaller in absolute magnitudes than those by the U.S. Consul General in Hong Kong (Table 27; Emery, 1966), but show more clearly the increasing trend during 1960-62. But Wu considered this estimate to be the barn yield, and hence not inconsistent with the higher estimate given by the U.S. Department of Agriculure (the same as in Table 27), which Wu interpreted as an estimate of biological yield.[55]

Although Wu's analysis of agriculture contains much interesting information on the effects of technology on output, it was difficult to utilize it in improving the estimate of output for 1958-62. A more detailed evaluation of Wu's estimate of agriculture can only be made if the scattered source data used in it became available.

Serious reservations exist concerning Wu's estimate of industrial value added after 1957. For 1958-60, the estimate of industrial value added was derived from regression relationships during 1952-57 between industrial output and production of steel and electric power (Wu et al., 1963, Vol. 1, pp. 207-222). However, one important and rather noncontroversial development in the Chinese Communist economy during 1958-60 was the severe decline of agricultural production, resulting in a reduction of the flow of agricultural raw materials to the industrial sectors. So to estimate industrial production for 1958-60 on the regression relationships

54. A more direct explanation of the upward adjustment was the impression given in Wu (1964, p. 17) that "the 1962 harvest apparently aggregated 10 to 15 per cent more than in 1961."

55. Because of the intensive harvesting methods practiced by the Chinese peasants over centuries, it is unlikely that there were significant differences between the so-called biological and barn yields before the Great Leap in 1958 (see Li, 1962, p. 96). Significant differences between the two yields most probably existed during the Great Leap years 1958-59. It is doubtful whether they persisted to 1962.

mentioned above would seem to have completely neglected the effect of the agricultural crises on industry, especially the consumer goods industries. The increasing trend so obtained for industrial output during 1958-60 (Wu et al., 1963, Vol. 1, Table 45) would appear to be invalid.

Going on to 1961, the Wu estimate states: "The gross value output of producers' goods for 1961 (line 3, Table 46) was estimated at one-third the value for the producers' goods in 1960. This estimate was based on information obtained from personal interviews in the Far East in May 1962" (1963, Vol. 1, p. 223). Consumer goods output in 1961 was scaled down from the 1960 level by a formula (p. 226). It would be of interest to know how the formula was derived.

The 1962 industrial output was first estimated "on the basis of the latest information obtainable during personal visits to the Far East in August 1962 and in January 1963" (p. 227). In a later revision, Wu again used estimated output of steel and electricity and the 1952-57 regression relationships to estimate total industrial production (1964, pp. 103-113).

There is an interesting discussion of the balance of payments constraint on investment (1963, Ch. 5). The difference between "investment calculations with and without the balance-of-payments constraint" is defined to represent "waste" in the economy (1964, p. 97). The estimated GNP (see Table 26) was scaled down to take "into account possible waste" (1964, p. 122). The concept of "waste" would probably have been made clearer if the effect of agricultural crises on the economy had been dealt with more explicitly in quantitative terms, and if the possibly excessive accumulation of inventories had been discussed.

2. A SIMPLE STRUCTURAL MODEL FOR ESTIMATING DOMESTIC PRODUCT WITH UNDERUTILIZATION OF CAPACITY

As shown in Table 27, there was a sharp decline in agricultural production from 1958 to 1960. A reduction in agricultural production would cut down the flow of raw materials to the other producing sectors of the economy and, through the multiplier process, slow down the entire economy. The methods used by scholars in the United States to derive national income estimates of Communist China for the earlier years do not provide a scheme for analyzing inter-industrial relationships, especially those that demonstrate the effects of agricultural production on the rest of the economy.[56] Time and resources do not permit an attempt to make a detailed inter-industrial analysis; a very simple, crude model is constructed here to study the effects of changes in agricultural production on the economy, especially its relatively modern sectors.

56. Neither those who used adjusted Communist data on output by sector to calculate value added (Liu-Yeh and Wu) or those using primarily Communist data on employment, incomes and sales (Eckstein and Hollister).

Some such simple models are necessary to make even a rough guess about the post-1958 total product. First, because of the shortage of agricultural raw materials, there was a great deal of unused capacity in the manufacturing sector during 1959-63. Thus the usual capital-output relationships (such as the marginal capital-output ratios or the more sophisticated production functions) cannot be used in this model to estimate the output. When capacity is not fully utilized, the constraint on production is the supply of raw materials. There was no shortage in the supply of common labor in Communist China, but the under-utilization of capacity was so serious during 1959-63 that even the limited supply of skilled labor was not a bottleneck. Second, the fragmentary pieces of information we have about the post-1958 economy are the few educated guesses of the output of food crops (Table 27) and a few industrial goods. The model must be constructed in such a way that rough approximations of the total product can be obtained from these fragmentary data.

The model consists of a few simple relationships built on the data for 1952-57, the period of relatively reliable statistics. It is idle to say that the number of observations is too small to develop firm relationships; we have only the data that are available, and the problem is to extract from them as much information as we can. Only those relationships helpful in estimating the post-1958 total product will be constructed.

The variables included in the model are listed below. Basic data used in constructing the model are given in Table 29. The value figures (including value added, value of raw materials consumed, consumption, imports, exports, net product and savings) are in billions of 1952 *yuan*.

- VA: Net value added by 20 commodity groups produced by modern factories.
- R_A: Value of agricultural raw materials produced in the current year and consumed by modern factories in producing VA.
- R'_A: Value of agricultural raw materials produced in the preceding year for consumption by modern factories in the current year in producing VA.
- R_M: Value of raw materials produced by the mining sector for consumption by modern factories in producing VA.
- F: Net value added by modern factories as a whole.
- A: Net value added by agriculture.
- A'_{-1} Value of cotton production and one half of the value of crop production during the preceding year.
- M: Net value added by the mining sector.
- M': Value of coal and iron ore produced by modern mines.
- V_m: Net value added by all the modern sectors except government. (Modern factories, mining, utilities, construction, modern transportation and communications, trading stores, restaurants, finance, and urban rental incomes.)

V_o:	Net value added by the traditional sectors (handicrafts, traditional transportation, peddlers, rural rental incomes, work brigades and personal services).
NDP:	Net domestic product.
G:	Value added by government.
E_m:	Employment in the modern sectors (corresponding to V_m above), in millions of workers.
C_u:	Consumption of urban population.
C_r:	Consumption of rural population.
P_u:	Urban population in million persons.
P_r:	Rural population in million persons.
P:	Total population in million persons.
I_m:	Value of imports.
X:	Value of exports.
I_d:	Net domestic investment.
C_g:	Government consumption.

The relationships in the model are as follows. (The figures given below for r^2 have not been adjusted for the degree of freedom.)

(1) $VA = -0.87\,(R_A + R'_A) + 5.83\,R_M$

(2) $F = -1.89 + \underset{(0.06)}{1.57}\,VA$ $\qquad r^2 = 0.99$

(3) $R_A = -8.89 + \underset{(0.03)}{0.30}\,A$ $\qquad 0.97$

(4) $R'_A = -5.29 + \underset{(0.10)}{0.23}\,A_{-1}$ $\qquad 0.63$

(4_a) $R'_A = -5.25 + \underset{(0.11)}{0.61}\,A'_{-1}$ $\qquad 0.91$

(5) $R_M = -0.22 + \underset{(0.06)}{0.45}\,M$ $\qquad 0.93$

(5_a) $R_M = -0.20 + \underset{(0.03)}{0.71}\,M'$ $\qquad 0.99$

(6) $V_m = 8.62 + \underset{(0.06)}{2.02}\,F$ $\qquad 0.99$

(7) $V_o = 8.65 + \underset{(0.10)}{1.10}\,A$ $\qquad 0.97$

(8) $NDP = V_m + V_o + G$

(9) $E_m = 8.91 + \underset{(0.03)}{0.17}\,V_m$ $\qquad 0.90$

(10) $P_u = 6.39 + \underset{(1.20)}{5.21}\,E_m$ $\qquad 0.83$

(11) $\frac{C_u}{P_u} = 116.33 + \underset{(0.08)}{0.20}\,\frac{V_m + G}{P_u}$ $\qquad 0.63$

(12)[56]	C_r	=	$86.39\ P_r$	
(13)	P_r	=	$P - P_u$	
(14)	I_m	=	$1.47 + 0.02\ NDP_{-1}$ (0.01)	0.55
(15)	X	=	$1.96 + 0.96\ NDP_{-1}$ (0.02)	0.76
(16)	I_d	=	$NDP - C_u - C_r - C_g - (X - I_m)$	

Equation (1) represents the relationship between value added (VA) by 20 modern factory product groups and the value of the raw materials consumed in producing them. The coefficients in equation (1) are derived from the data for 1957, the last year in the sample period.[57] The agricultural raw materials consumed came partly from the output of the current year (R_A) and partly from the output of the preceding year (R'_A). One *yuan* of agricultural raw materials consumed[58] generated directly 0.87 *yuan* of net value added. The ratio of net value added to the value of the raw materials was much higher (5.83) for products[59] using mining resources (R_M).

The products included in VA accounted for 46 per cent of the total net value added by modern factories (F) in 1957. The regression relationship between F and VA during 1952-57 is given in equation (2).

The value of agricultural raw materials produced and used in manufacturing[60] in the same year (R_A) had a good regression relationship with the net value added by agriculture (A), as given in equation (3). The relationship between the preceding year's agricultural raw materials (R'_A) and the net value added by agriculture in the preceding year (A_{-1}), however, is less close (equation 4). In using this model for estimating the total product for 1959-63, an alternative variable A'_{-1} (the value of cotton production plus half of the value of crop production, both from the preceding year) is used as the determining variable for R'_A in equation (4a).

56. Per capita annual rural consumption for 1957 was 86.39.
57. For the derivation, see the Appendix note to Table 29.
58. Including the raw materials for manufactured food products, textiles, clothing, gunny sacks, paper and some chemical products.
59. The products were pig iron, steel, rolled steel, machinery, cement, coke, and some chemicals. The ratio is very much higher than for products using agricultural raw materials because of the many more stages of fabrication involved and the higher cost of the fabrication processes. For example, iron ore would generate successively the net value added by pig iron, steel, rolled steel and machinery.
60. Because of the lack of detailed data, it has not been possible to estimate imports and exports of agricultural raw materials for manufacturing production. A rough estimate of the imports and exports of textile raw materials indicates that the value of net imports is negligible compared with the total value of agricultural raw materials produced domestically.

The value of raw materials from the mining sector[61] consumed by modern factories (R_M) is related to net value added by the mining sector (M) in equation (5); and, alternatively, to the value of output of coal and iron ore produced in modern mines (M′) in equation (5a). Since M′ can be estimated roughly for 1959-63 (as will be discussed), equation (5a) will enable us to estimate R_M.

Net value added by all the modern sectors (except government administration) of the economy (V_m) moved closely with F during 1952-57. The relationship is given in equation (6). Similarly, the net product of the traditional sectors (V_o) followed that of agriculture (A) closely (equation 7).

Equation (8) is the definition of net domestic product.

Employment in the modern sectors (E_m) had a good linear relationship with value added by the modern sectors (equation 9). The size of the urban population (P_u) was, in turn, closely correlated (equation 10) with employment in the modern sectors (E_m).

In a totalitarian economy, consumption cannot be expected to change with production in any systematic manner. Consumption in Communist China was controlled through rationing and other more subtle schemes. Nevertheless, a discernible relationship did exist between the per capita consumption of the urban population $\frac{C_u}{p_u}$ and the per capita product of the modern sectors ($\frac{V_m + G}{P_u}$, G being income originated in government). (Equation 11). On the other hand, rural per capital consumption hardly changed during 1953-54, and then was slightly higher during 1956-57. The Communist regime was quite successful in keeping down rural consumption; and it seems best to consider it (C_r) as a function of rural population (P_r), with the per capita amount decided by government policies (equation 12).

Total population is defined in identity (13).

Imports (I_m) and exports (X) are both related to lagged net domestic product in equations (14) and (15).

Equation (16) is the definition of net domestic investment.

Thus the model consists of 16 equations, determining the 16 jointly dependent variables VA, F, R_A, R'_A, R_M, V_m, V_o, NDP, E_m, P_u, C_u, C_r, P_r, I_m, X, and I_d. The predetermined variables are A, A_{-1} (or A'_{-1}), M (or M′), G, P, NDP_{-1}, and C_g.

The system of equations can be solved for the jointly dependent variables in terms of the predetermined variables; the result is, of course, the

61. As with agricultural raw materials, detailed data are not readily available on the value of net imports of mining raw materials. The net balance is believed to be small.

reduced form equations.[62] We used the reduced form equations to compute the values of domestic product for 1957 (the last sample year), and compare them with the Liu-Yeh estimate, as shown in Table 28. The result shows that the model yields good estimated values for 1957.

TABLE 28

ESTIMATES OF NET DOMESTIC PRODUCT AND SAVINGS, 1957
(billions of 1952 yuan)

	1957
Net domestic product (NDP)	
Liu-Yeh estimate [a]	95.34
Computed from model	95.72
Net domestic savings (NDS = I_d)	
Liu-Yeh estimate [a]	18.88
Computed from model	18.24

Notes:
a. Liu and Yeh, 1965, pp. 66, 68.

The coefficients in the reduced form equations represent the impact multipliers of the predetermined variables on the jointly dependent variables. We are particularly interested in the impact multipliers of A and A_{-1} on net domestic product and savings:

IMPACT MULTIPLIERS OF A AND A_{-1}
(1952 yuan per 1952 yuan)

	NDP	NDS
A	1.91	1.66
A_{-1}	0.64	0.44

A decrease of one *yuan* in agricultural net value added would reduce net domestic product by 1.91 *yuan* and savings by 1.66 *yuan*. Agricultural net value added in the preceding year also would have a substantial effect on the economy; a one *yuan* reduction would decrease domestic product by 0.64 *yuan* and savings by 0.44 *yuan*. These impact multipliers clearly indicate the importance of agriculture in the economy of Communist China.

62. The first eight equations form a self-determining submodel with only A, A_{-1} (or A'_{-1}), M (or M′) and G as predetermined variables.

3. CONJECTURAL ESTIMATE OF THE PRODUCT FOR 1958-1965

Although there has been a practically total blackout of economic statistics from Communist China since 1959, there has emerged a set of conjectural but educated estimates of the output of food crops, cotton and a few major industrial products for 1959-65. These data appear to be the most generally accepted estimates of recent trends of production by qualified sources in Hong Kong.[63] On the basis of these data, the first eight equations of the model (with equations [4] and [5] replaced respectively by [4a] and [5a]) can be used to make a rough estimate of the domestic product for 1959-65.

First, solving equations (1), (2), (3), (4a), (5a) and (6) for V_m (value added by all modern sectors except government administration) in terms of A, A'_{-1}, and M′, we obtain:

$$V_m = -37.87 + 0.81A + 1.68A'_{-1} + 13.06M' \qquad (17)$$

Equation (7) enables us to estimate V_o (value added by all traditional sectors) in terms of A. On the assumptions that value added by government administration (G) increased after 1958 in proportion to population, and that population increased by 1.5 per cent per year after 1958,[64] domestic product for 1959-65 can be derived from equation (8) on the data given in Table 30. The result is presented in Table 31.

Equations (9) to (16) can be used to derive an estimate of net domestic investment during 1958-65. With V_m obtained in Table 31, E_m, P_u, C_u and P_r can in turn be computed from equations (9) to (11) and equation (13). On the assumption that per capita rural consumption varied from 1957 to 1958-63 in proportion to per capita product, C_r can then be calculated from equation (12). Given $(X - I_m)$ and assuming that C_g changed in proportion to population, net domestic investment can be estimated from equation (16). The estimated net domestic investment for 1958-65, together with the 1957 figure, is given in Table 32. Since additional assumptions are involved in deriving the investment estimate from

63. See the recent issues of the *Far Eastern Economic Review, Current Scene* and *Asian Survey* cited in the Appendix, Notes to Table 30, in particular, Emery, 1966.

64. See Section V. 1. The rate of increase of population affects the estimate of the domestic product only through value added by government, which accounts for only a minor portion of the domestic product (see Table 31). Assumptions other than this more or less arbitrary one would change the estimate of domestic product very little. For instance, if we use the census-based series in the 4 different models presented in Chapter 4 (Aird), Table 5, the 1965 magnitudes for G in our Table 31 would be in the range of 5.6 to 5.7 billion *yuan* (as compared with our estimate of 5.5 billion *yuan*). There would be no perceptible effect on the estimate of total product.

TABLE 29

DATA FOR ESTIMATING THE

	R_A (1)	R'_A (2)	R_M (3)	VA (4)	F (5)	A (6)	A'_{-1} (7)	M (8)	M′ (9)
1952	1.22	2.23	0.39	5.27	6.45	34.19		1.47	0.87
1953	1.38	2.58	0.48	6.25	8.28	34.82	13.04	1.46	0.94
1954	1.54	2.84	0.62	7.42	9.58	35.50	13.05	1.82	1.14
1955	1.74	2.81	0.73	8.22	10.36	35.84	13.22	2.32	1.36
1956	1.94	3.35	0.98	10.31	14.51	36.97	14.07	2.38	1.63
1957	2.15	3.18	1.15	11.34	15.99	37.16	13.86	3.07	1.93

For meanings of symbols, see text.
Columns (1)-(13) and (18)-(19): billions of 1952 *yuan.*
Columns (14-(15): millions of persons.

TABLE 30

ESTIMATE OF A, A'_{-1}, and M′
(billions of 1952 yuan)

	Value of cotton output (1)	Value of food crops output (2)	Net value added in agri-culture A (3)	Value of cotton output plus one-half value of food crops, both of the pre-ceding year A′ (4)	Value of steel output (5)	Value of iron ore and coal produced by modern mines M′ (6)
1959	3.06	20.71	34.51	14.83	5.36	2.88
1960	2.38	19.73	32.10	13.42	5.04	2.76
1961	1.53	20.60	32.13	12.25	4.74	2.64
1962	1.53	21.94	34.08	11.83	4.50	2.52
1963	1.70	22.08	34.53	12.50	4.80	2.67
1964	2.04	22.56	35.72	12.78	5.40	2.92
1965	2.21	22.19	35.43	13.32	6.00	3.19

Source:
Appendix.

the product estimate, the result presented in Table 32 is subject to a greater margin of uncertainty.

The decline of the domestic product from 1958 to 1961 confirms the

EQUATIONS IN THE MODEL

V_m (10)	V_o (11)	NDP (12)	G (13)	E_m (14)	P_u (15)	C_u/P_u (16)	$(V_m+G)/P_u$ (17)	I_m (18)	X (19)
21.65	46.49	71.41	3.27	12.65	69.0	179.7	361.2		
24.76	46.87	75.33	3.70	13.76	74.6	188.7	381.5	2.80	2.59
28.01	47.32	79.28	3.95	13.47	79.6	214.6	401.5	3.06	2.82
30.27	47.96	82.30	4.07	13.74	82.2	201.3	417.8	3.08	3.36
38.00	49.32	92.08	4.76	15.13	86.0	212.2	497.2	3.41	3.98
40.65	49.66	95.34	5.03	16.44	90.6	216.9	504.2	3.31	3.89

Columns (16)-(17): 1952 *yuan.*

Source:
See Appendix.

deepening difficulty encountered by the economy during these years. The domestic product in 1961, 92.2 billion (1952) *yuan,* was 15 per cent lower than the 1958 peak of 108 billion (1952) *yuan.* In 1962, the economy began to recover. The annual rate of recovery, as measured by the percentage growth in domestic product, increased from 2 per cent in 1961-62 to 6.2 per cent in 1963-64. The speed, however, slackened to 3.7 per cent during 1964-65, mainly because of the drought in northern China.

Domestic product regained the 1957 level during 1962-63, and the 1965 product was about the same as in 1958. The economy in 1965 stood where it was in 1958, a "loss" of seven years without growth.

Net domestic investment decreased by 34 per cent from 1958 to 1961, from 23.6 billion (1952) *yuan* to 15.6 billion (1952) *yuan.* The proportion of investment in total product declined fairly consistently from 21.9 per cent in 1958 to 16.7 per cent in 1962. By 1965, however, investment exceeded the magnitude reached in 1957, though the proportion of investment in domestic product in 1957 had not yet been fully regained.

The plausibility of the post-1958 estimate must be investigated. Sources of data independent of those used in deriving the estimate are practically nonexistent. The product estimate, however, can be checked against the data on exports, and the investment estimate examined in the light of certain Communist policy pronouncements.

Although the Communist regime has assigned a high priority to the allocation of resources to exports, the export level is basically constrained by domestic output. As shown in Table 33, the ratio of exports to domestic product lagged by one year rose fairly consistently from 1952 to 1959, within a range of 3.6 to 4.9 per cent. This proportion fell from 4.9 per cent in 1959 to 3.7 per cent in 1961, reflecting the economy's increasing

TABLE 31

ESTIMATE OF NET DOMESTIC PRODUCT, 1957-65
(billions of 1952 yuan)

	Value added by government G	Value added by all modern sectors, except G V_m	Value added by all traditional sectors V_o	Net domestic product NDP	Rate of change of net domestic product from the preceding year (per cent)
1957	5.0	40.7	49.6	95.3	
1958	5.0	47.3	55.7	108.0	+13.3
1959	5.1	52.7	46.6	104.4	−3.3
1960	5.2	46.8	43.9	95.9	−8.1
1961	5.2	43.0	44.0	92.2	−3.9
1962	5.3	42.6	46.1	94.0	+2.0
1963	5.4	46.1	46.6	98.1	+4.3
1964	5.5	50.8	47.9	104.2	+6.2
1965	5.5	55.0	47.6	108.1	+3.7

Source:
1957-58: Liu-Yeh, 1965, p. 66.
1959-65: See text.

TABLE 32

ESTIMATE OF NET DOMESTIC INVESTMENT, 1957-65

	Net Domestic Investment (billions of 1952 yuan)	Proportion of Net Domestic Investment in Net Domestic Product (per cent)
1957	18.2	19.1
1958	23.6	21.9
1959	20.0	19.2
1960	17.1	17.8
1961	15.6	16.9
1962	15.7	16.7
1963	16.7	17.0
1964	18.1	17.4
1965	19.5	18.0

Sources:
1957: See Table 14.
1958-65: See text.

TABLE 33

EXPORTS AND NET DOMESTIC PRODUCT LAGGED BY ONE YEAR

	Exports	Net Domestic Product Lagged by One Year	Percentage of Exports in Net Domestic Product (per cent)
	(billions of 1952 yuan)		
1953	2.59	71.4	3.6
1954	2.82	75.3	3.8
1955	3.36	79.3	4.2
1956	3.98	82.3	4.8
1957	3.89	92.1	4.2
1958	4.65	95.3	4.9
1959	5.31	108.0	4.9
1960	4.74	104.4	4.5
1961	3.59	95.9	3.7
1962	3.59	92.2	3.9
1963	3.67	94.1	3.9
1964	4.55	100.8	4.5
1965	4.91	104.2	4.7

Sources:
Exports: 1953-64: supplied by F. H. Mah.
1965: *Current Scene,* February 1, 1966, p. 2. The exchange rate used in converting the U.S. dollar value to *yuan* is 1 U.S. $ = 2.355 *yuan.*
Net Domestic Products: 1952-57: Liu-Yeh, 1965 (p. 66).
1958-64: Table 31.

difficulty; thereafter it recovered quite consistently, reaching 4.7 per cent in 1965. The post-1960 range of this proportion, 3.7 to 4.7 per cent, is close to the one observed during 1952-57; but the ratios for the most difficult years, 1961-63 (3.7 to 3.9 per cent), are lower than those for the best year before the Leap (1956-57) and those attained in 1958-60 under the initial impetus of the Leap. The picture reflected by these data appears plausible. Although the foreign trade data are also subject to a substantial margin of error, they are derived from the statistics of the countries with trade relations with Communist China, and are more reliable than our conjectural estimate of the domestic product. That a reasonable relationship exists between the export data and the product estimate would lend credibility to the latter.

Our estimate of net domestic investment (Table 32) indicates a very substantial decline from 1958 to 1961-62. Investment in 1963-65 was still low in its ratio to the total product as compared with 1957 and the Great Leap years 1958-59. The magnitudes of investment during 1962-65

(15.7 to 19.5 billion [1952] *yuan*), however, remained substantial. This may seem to contradict certain policy pronouncements of the Communist regime.

When the agricultural crisis continued into 1960, the Eighth Plenum of the Central Committee decided early in 1961 that "since there had been tremendous development in heavy industry in the last three years, its output of major products already far in excess of the planned level for 1961 and 1962, the scale of basic construction should therefore be appropriately reduced" (Li, 1964, p. 10). Moreover, it is known that in December, 1961, the Communist Party issued a secret document to cadres in the field directing that "all basic construction should be suspended, all those enterprises that had been operating regularly at a loss be shut down, and the practice of recruiting labour from rural areas be abandoned for at least three years." (Li, 1964, p. 11). Then on March 27, 1962, Chou En-Lai again reported the decision to reduce basic construction (Li, 1964, p. 11).

In view of the apparently firm decision to cut down basic construction after 1961, it may be questioned whether investment in 1961-65 could have been as high as our estimate indicates. It is, of course, possible that the model constructed in Section V. 2 is unsatisfactory; and that the derived estimates of domestic product and investment (especially the latter) are therefore unreliable. Yet there are three major reasons for believing that investment may not have been significantly below our estimate.

(1) According to our estimate, the average level of investment during 1961-63 (16 billion [1952] *yuan*) was 4.6 billion *yuan* lower than that during 1957-59 (20.6 billion [1952] *yuan*). In view of the large number of construction projects known to be under way at the end of 1959, the momentum might have been such that a more drastic curtailment was unenforceable, in spite of the announced retrenchment policy. By 1964 the domestic product exceeded the 1957 level (Table 31), and the policy of curtailing investment may have been relaxed. Moreover, although the 1965 product was virtually the same as in 1958, the investment we estimated for 1965 is substantially smaller than that for 1958.

(2) While basic construction in general may have been reduced, it is known that the Communist regime increased investment in the petroleum and fertilizer industries, and significantly expanded the production of tractors and other farm equipment. Investment relating to the production of atomic weapons must have been very substantial. It is not possible, however, to make a quantitative estimate of the investment in these areas at the present.

(3) Another possible explanation for the substantial amount of investment during 1961-65 is an excessive increase in the stock of inventory. Steel, machinery, and other producer goods were perhaps actually produced in quantities compatible with the investment estimate, but they were merely being stockpiled. They had not been installed and put to use.

A degree of confusion in the management of economic affairs may have existed after the agricultural crises of 1959-61. Orders were issued to curtail basic construction; but there was no corresponding reduction in the production of those producer goods that did not rely upon agriculture as the major source of raw materials. In fact, the regime may have been more anxious to avoid the difficult problem of excessive unemployment, already serious because of the slowing down of activities in such industries as textiles and food processing, than the problem of excessive stockpiling.

4. SUMMARY REMARKS

Tentative estimates of the domestic product and investment during 1958-65 have been derived from a model of structural equations, focusing on the relationship of agriculture to the relatively modern sectors of the economy (tables 31 and 32). Because of the very low quality of the Communist data for the Great Leap Forward years, 1958-60, and the almost complete blackout of economic statistics during 1961-65, our estimates can be considered no more than an educated guess about the post-1958 trends. A degree of plausibility of this product estimate, however, is indicated by the apparently reasonable relationship it has with the more reliable export data. The investment estimate may perhaps err on the high side, but it is difficult to evaluate the margin of overestimation. The disastrous Great Leap brought the domestic product down from the 1959 peak of 108 billion (1952) *yuan* to 92.2 billion in 1961. The subsequent recovery probably restored the total product in 1965 to somewhere around the 1958 level. During the seven-year period from 1958 to 1965, when every other country in the world experienced at least a measure of growth and development, the economy of Communist China first plunged and then recovered merely to where it started.

The Great Leap Forward was based on a sound diagnosis of the basic weakness of the Chinese economy but on a serious misconception of the proper way to deal with it. As late as 1957, there was a tremendous amount of surplus labor and a serious shortage of capital and highly trained manpower, despite the significant degree of industrialization achieved during 1952-57. The emphasis put on labor intensive undertakings during 1958-59 was correct. But the unprecedentedly strict regimentation through the organization of the communes; the complete denial of work incentives through the abolition of private plots; the total miscalculation of technical possibilities in introducing the backyard furnaces and unworkable agricultural techniques (*e.g.*, deep plowing, close planting and the poorly designed irrigation and flood control systems); and the exhausting pace imposed on the population would have been sufficient to break the back of any economy, even if there had been no natural calamities.

Under the initial stimulus of the Great Leap Forward, there was perhaps a 13 per cent increase in the total product from 1957 to 1958 (table

31). This is, however, quite misleading. There is no way of estimating the proper depreciation charges for such wasted resources as the bricks and other materials used to construct the backyard furnaces, let alone the deterioration in the health of the people and the quality of the land, which must have followed the abuses inflicted upon them. A long period of idle industrial capacities must also have resulted in a more rapid depreciation of industrial plants. The conventional method of calculation is seriously inadequate for estimating the national product for the years 1958-60, and perhaps for the next two or three years.

The relaxation of the worst features of the Leap (*e.g.,* the abolition of such unworkable schemes as the commune mess halls and the "miracle techniques of cultivation," with the limited restoration of private plots and incentive payment schemes) probably led to a recovery of the economy to the 1957-58 level. However, in spite of the great emphasis given to agriculture since 1961-62, all qualified observers are agreed that the 1964-65 level of food crops production was no higher than what may be considered as the normal output of the Good Earth, attained in 1957. While the 1965 total product may have regained the 1958 level, the portion contributed by the modern sectors increased at the cost of an *absolute* reduction of the value added by the traditional sectors (Table 31).[65]

The years 1958-65 can be described as a period of further industrialization without growth. It is doubtful that, with such a low agricultural base, this apparent supplanting of the traditional sectors by the relatively modern ones will be conducive to sustained growth in the future. In the meantime, population must have increased significantly. The economy of Communist China in 1966 was hardly in a strong condition to absorb the effects of the current political unrest which in all likelihood would again hinder an orderly development of the economy for some time to come.

APPENDIX
NOTES TO TABLES

(All references to "Liu-Yeh" refer to *The Economy of the Chinese Mainland,* 1965.)

Table 11: Rates of Growth per Year in Population, Employment, Product

All rates given are simple arithmetic averages of the annual rates of change during 1952-57. Different ways of computing the mean rates do

65. During 1952-57, a much more satisfactory period of growth, the relative share of the agricultural sector declined (Table 12) as it should have during industrialization, but the absolute magnitude of the value added by the traditional sectors did not.

not give significant different results for 1952-57, because all variables increased fairly steadily throughout the period. (See footnote c to Table 1.)
Population: Computed from data in Liu-Yeh (Table 24, p. 102).
Workers:

(a) Reconstructed Communist data: Computed from the sum of the following: (1) Nonagricultural employment: the "adjusted estimate" in Liu-Yeh (Table 65, p. 208). The "adjusted estimate" is the reconstructed Communist estimate used in this paper. (See footnote 23.) (2) Agricultural employment: 80 per cent of the data on agricultural employment in Liu-Yeh (Table 11, p. 69). According to Buck (1937, p. 294), idleness and sickness averaged 1.9 months per man per year in agriculture; employment in agriculture is therefore reduced by the rounded figure of 20 per cent to represent a rough estimate of full-time equivalent.

(b) Liu-Yeh estimate: Computed from the sum of the following: (1) Nonagricultural employment: Given in Liu-Yeh, Table 11, p. 69. (2) Agricultural employment: Same as in (a) above.
GDP and NDP

Both the reconstructed Communist estimate (the "adjusted estimate" in Liu-Yeh (see footnote 23) and the Liu-Yeh estimate are given in Liu-Yeh, Table 68, p. 213.

Table 12: Comparisons of Shares of Major Sectors (Communist China and USSR)
Communist China

Share in NP: Both the reconstructed Communist estimate and the Liu-Yeh estimates are computed from data given in Liu-Yeh, Table 68, p. 213. The reconstructed Communist estimate is the "adjusted estimate" given in Liu-Yeh (see footnote 23 in text).

Share in labor force:

(a) Liu-Yeh estimate: Computed from data by sector given in Liu-Yeh, Table 11, p. 69. Agricultural employment is reduced by 20 per cent. (See explanation of "workers" in the note to Table 11.)

(b) Reconstructed Communist estimate: For the A sector, see note to Table 11. For the nonagricultural sector, same as the Liu-Yeh estimate, except that the data on old-fashioned transportation are replaced by the "adjusted estimates" given in Liu-Yeh (p. 199), and the figures on handicrafts are replaced by the "adjusted estimates" derived from Liu-Yeh, Table 58 (p. 196) by replacing the data on the "others" category by the adjusted estimate for "others" given on p. 195.

Relative product and total inequality: Computed from the figures given in this table by the same method explained in Kuznets, 1957.
USSR

Kuznets, 1963 (Table VIII. 6).

Table 14: Proportions of Investment in Domestic Product

The proportions are computed from the various versions of investment and domestic products given in the following sources.

Both the reconstructed Communist estimate and the Liu-Yeh estimate of gross and net domestic product in 1952 are in Liu-Yeh (Table 68, p. 213). The Liu-Yeh estimate in 1957 prices are in Liu-Yeh, Table 9 (p. 67). The reconstructed Communist estimates in 1957 prices are derived from the reconstructed Communist estimates in 1952 prices by multiplying the latter by the ratio of the Liu-Yeh estimate in 1957 prices to that in 1952 prices for the respective years.

The investment figures in 1952 prices used in the Liu-Yeh estimate are the revised estimates of investment in Yeh (1964) as follows:

Gross and net totals: Yeh, Table C-1 (p. 329).

Gross fixed: Sum of construction and equipment, Yeh, Table C-3 (p. 337).

Net fixed: The above minus the depreciation figures given in Yeh, Table C-1 (p. 329).

The various versions of the reconstructed Communist estimate of investment in 1952 prices are derived from the corresponding Yeh estimates given above by adding to the latter the data on "understatement of depreciation" given in Yeh, Table C-1 (p. 329).

All the investment figures in 1957 prices are obtained by multiplying the corresponding data in 1952 prices by the price deflator for basic construction given in Liu-Yeh, (Table 74, p. 235).

Table 16: Incremental Capital Output Ratios, 1952-57

The various versions of the incremental capital ratios given in this table are obtained by dividing the various proportions (gross or net, and total or fixed) of investment in domestic product during 1952-57 with the rate of growth of the corresponding versions of the domestic product. The sources of data are the same as those of Table 14.

Table 19: Rates of Growth in Input and in Productivity per Year

A rough estimate of fixed reproducible capital stock in 1952 and 1957 (in 1952 prices) is obtained as follows:

According to Buck (1937), the average values of buildings used per farm in the late 1920's and early 1930's were 328, 140 and 116 *yuan* respectively for residence, for farm business, and for the two purposes combined. Allocating the last on the ratio of the first two and summing, the average values of buildings used for residence and for farm were 409 and 175 *yuan* respectively. The average values of livestock, trees and equipment per farm are given in Buck (1930) at 65.8, 38.4 and 45.9 *yuan* respectively. Total fixed reproducible capital per farm for business purposes was therefore 325 *yuan* before the Sino-Japanese war. There were

62 million farms (Liu-Yeh, p. 129), and the total farm capital was therefore 20.14 million *yuan,* or 36.86 million *yuan* in 1952 prices (the price index for agricultural value added for 1952 being 183, with 1933 = 100; see Liu-Yeh, p. 629). Value added by agriculture increased from 33.86 to 34.19 billion *yuan* from 1933 to 1952 (see Liu-Yeh, p. 66). Assuming equal percentage increase of capital and value added, farm capital amounted to 37.23 billion *yuan.* The value of public work on irrigation, conservation, etc., is roughly estimated at 10 per cent of 37.23 billion *yuan.* Total farm capital was therefore 40.95 billion *yuan* in 1952.

The value of rural residential housing is then estimated. The value of residential housing per farm has been estimated above at 409 *yuan* per farm before the Sino-Japanese war. Multiplying by the number of farms and by the price index number used above, and further increasing the magnitudes by the ratio of rural population (499.9 million, Liu-Yeh, p. 212) to agricultural population (433 million, p. 184), the value of rural residential housing in 1952 is estimated at 53.62 billion 1952 *yuan.*

An estimate of the value of residential housing in urban areas is obtained by multiplying the value of per capita rural housing (53.62/499.9 = 107 *yuan*) by the urban population (69 million, Liu-Yeh, p. 212); and the ratio of gross annual rent per person in urban areas to that in rural areas (4.5 to 2.1 *yuan,* Liu-Yeh, p. 170). The result is 15.80 billion *yuan* in 1952.

Value of public building is roughly estimated at 10 per cent of the total value of rural and urban housing (53.62 + 15.80 = 69.42 billion *yuan*), or 6.94 billion *yuan.*

A crude estimate of the value of capital stock in the old-fashioned sectors is then made. The *Industrial Handbooks* of Kiangsu, Chekiang, Hunan, Shantung and Shansi gave scattered data on capital-output ratios in the handicraft industries. They ranged from 0.35 to 1 for the important food-processing industries to 0.17 to 1 for some others. We made the arbitrary assumption that the capital-value added ratio in all the traditional sectors (handicraft, old-fashioned transportation and trade) is 0.25. The total value added in these sectors was 9.37 billion *yuan* in 1952 prices (Liu-Yeh, p. 66). The total capital stock is therefore 2.34 billion *yuan.* Since capital stock in these sectors must have been small relative to the total stock, different assumptions would not lead to very different results in the analysis of productivity.

The reproducible capital stock in the four modern sectors of (1) factories, mining, and utilities, (2) modern transportation and communications, (3) trade and (4) construction at the end of 1952 are given in Liu-Yeh (Table 77, p. 240) at 8.74, 5.94, 1.02 and 0.68 billion 1952 *yuan* respectively, totaling 16.38 billion yuan.

Summing up the different categories, the total value of reproducible capital stock in 1952 is estimated at 136.03 billion 1952 *yuan.*

According to Yeh (1964), net fixed investment during 1953-57 totaled 59.89 billion 1952 *yuan*.[1] The Liu-Yeh estimate of the value of the capital stock in 1957 is therefore 195.92 billion 152 *yuan*.[2]

The reconstructed Communist estimate of the 1957 capital stock is obtained by adding to the Liu-Yeh estimate of 195.92 billion *yuan* the "understatement of depreciation" during 1953-57.[3] The result is 200.40 billion 1952 *yuan*.

The Liu-Yeh and the reconstructed Communist estimates of average annual rates of growth of net fixed capital during 1952-57 can then be easily calculated. With the average rates of increase of labor and net domestic product obtained in Table 11, the rates of growth of the combined input and productivity are then obtained in the table.

Table 20: Household Consumption Outlays and Other Components of Gross Domestic Expenditure per Capita

Because of the revision in Yeh (1964) of the investment estimate in Liu-Yeh, the miscellaneous component of the Liu-Yeh consumption estimate has to be revised.[4] For convenience of reference, the revised Yeh estimate of investment is given in Table A. 1.

TABLE A.1

GROSS TOTAL DOMESTIC INVESTMENT
(billions of 1952 yuan)

	Yeh's estimate [a]	Reconstructed Communist estimate [b]
1952	14.57	14.89
1953	18.81	19.33
1954	20.31	20.95
1955	21.46	22.23
1956	26.04	27.38
1957	23.72	24.93

Notes:

a. Yeh, 1964, Table C-1 (p. 329).

b. Yeh's estimate plus the estimate of "understatement of depreciation" given in the table cited in the preceding note.

1. Sum of the data on construction and equipment in Yeh, 1964, Table C-3 (p. 337) minus the data on depreciation in Table C-1 (p. 329).

2. 136.03 + 59.89 = 195.92.

3. Given in Yeh 1964, Table C-1 (p. 329). This understated amount was originally deducted to get Yeh's estimate.

4. In Liu-Yeh, the miscellaneous component of consumption was obtained by subtracting all expenditures other than miscellaneous consumption from total expenditure. Estimate of total expenditure was obtained from that of total product by adding to the latter the balance of trade.

Reconstructed Communist Estimate

First, preliminary estimate of total household consumption is obtained by subtracting from gross domestic expenditure the sum of all expenditures[5] other than consumption. The result is given in the first column of Table A.2. Consumption components other than the "miscellaneous" category were independently estimated in Liu-Yeh, Table 93 (p. 269). Subtracting the other components from total household consumption, we obtain a preliminary estimate of miscellaneous consumption given in the second column of Table A.2.

TABLE A.2

RECONSTRUCTED COMMUNIST ESTIMATE OF CONSUMPTION[a]
(billions of 1952 yuan)

	Preliminary Estimate of Household Consumption	Preliminary Estimate of Miscellaneous Consumption	Revised Estimate of Miscellaneous Consumption	Revised Estimate of Household Consumption
1952	52.19	5.68	5.68	52.19
1953	49.57	1.44	7.15	55.28
1954	53.35	2.45	8.71	59.61
1955	58.21	5.86	10.32	62.67
1956	65.47	7.16	11.98	70.29
1957	75.06	13.78	13.78	75.06

Note:
a. For derivation, see text.

An implausible sharp reduction of miscellaneous consumption from 1952 to 1953 can be seen. The 1954 figure is also implausibly low. The revised estimate of miscellaneous consumption is obtained by linear extrapolation on the 1952 and the 1957 preliminary estimates of miscellaneous consumption on a per capita basis.[6] The difference between the revised and the preliminary estimates of miscellaneous consumption represents statistical discrepancy between the product and the expenditure estimates.[7] The revised estimate of miscellaneous consumption is then added to the other categories of consumption (unchanged from the original Liu-

5. Data on the reconstructed Communist estimate of gross domestic expenditure and its components are in Liu-Yeh, Table 93 (p. 269), except that the data on gross domestic investment are replaced by the revised figures of reconstructed Communist estimate given in Table A.1.

6. The population data are in Liu-Yeh, Table 24 (p. 102).

7. Because of the method of making the estimate (see footnote 4 in this Appendix), there is no statistical discrepancy in the original estimate in Liu-Yeh.

Yeh estimate) to get the revised estimate of household consumption.

The Liu-Yeh Estimate

The revision of the Liu-Yeh estimate of household consumption, as a result of the revision of the investment estimate in Yeh (1964), is explained here. As the Liu-Yeh estimate is used in constructing the model in Section V. 2, miscellaneous consumption is separated into urban and rural components.

Subtracting the sum of Yeh's revised estimate of gross total domestic investment (Table A. 1, column 1) and the Liu-Yeh estimates of all other expenditure items other than consumption from the gross domestic expenditure (Liu-Yeh, Table 93, p. 269), we get a preliminary estimate of household consumption. A preliminary estimate of miscellaneous consumption is then obtained by subtracting all other components of household consumption from the total. The result is presented in Table A. 3.

TABLE A.3

THE LIU-YEH ESTIMATE OF CONSUMPTION
(billions of 1952 yuan)

	Preliminary Estimate of Household Consumption	Preliminary Estimate of Miscellaneous Consumption	Revised Estimate of Miscellaneous Consumption	Revised Estimate of Household Consumption
1952	54.55	5.43	5.43	54.55
1953	52.14	1.44	6.23	56.92
1954	55.42	2.04	7.08	60.47
1955	57.84	4.96	7.89	60.77
1956	62.15	6.22	8.77	64.70
1957	66.87	9.74	9.74	66.87

As with the reconstructed Communist estimate, the sharp decline of miscellaneous consumption for 1952 to 1953 and the small magnitudes for 1953-56 do not appear to be plausible. The revised estimate of miscellaneous consumption is obtained from linear extrapolation on the 1952 and the 1957 data on a per capita basis. For later use in constructing the model in Section V. 2, this extrapolation is carried out for the urban and rural sectors separately.

According to Ou Pao-san (1945), the ratio of per capita miscellaneous consumption in rural areas to that in urban districts is 6.90 to 30.11.[8]

8. Ou's estimates of rural and urban miscellaneous consumption are given on pp. 160 and 169 respectively (Ou Pao-san, 1945). Ou's data on rural and urban population are on p. 151. It should be emphasized that we have used here only Ou's estimate of the ratio of rural to urban miscellaneous consumption; we have not used his estimates of the absolute magnitudes.

This ratio, together with our data on rural and urban population (Liu-Yeh, p. 212) is sufficient to apportion the estimate of 1952 and 1957 miscellaneous consumption to rural and urban sectors. Per capita miscellaneous consumption can then be separately computed for these sectors for 1952 and 1957, and linear extrapolation for 1953-56 can be obtained. The per capita and total figures for the two sectors are given in Table A. 4. The revised estimates of miscellaneous and total consumption are presented in Table A. 3.

TABLE A.4

MISCELLANEOUS CONSUMPTION
(1952 yuan)

	Rural		Urban	
	Per Capita (yuan)	Total (billions of yuan)	Per Capita (yuan)	Total (billions of yuan)
1952	6.84	3.42	29.14	2.01
1953	7.56	3.83	32.21	2.40
1954	8.28	4.27	35.28	2.81
1955	9.01	4.74	38.34	3.15
1956	9.73	5.21	41.41	3.56
1957	10.45	5.71	44.48	4.03

As in the case of the reconstructed Communist estimate, the difference between the preliminary and the revised estimates of miscellaneous consumption represents the statistical discrepancy between the product and the expenditure estimates.

Both the reconstructed Communist and the Liu-Yeh estimates of communal services, government consumption, and gross expenditure are in Liu-Yeh, Table 93 (p. 269). Sources of data on investment have been given in note to Table 14.

Table 21: Shares in Total Domestic Uses of Private Consumption, Government Consumption, Gross, Domestic Capital Formation

For Communist China, the sources of data are the same as for Table 20.

Table 22: Per Capita Consumption and Structure of Consumption

Both the reconstructed Communist and the Liu-Yeh estimates of food and other expenditures are in Liu-Yeh, Table 93 (p. 269).

Table 29: Data for Estimating the Equations in the Model

Column (1), R_A: Value of agricultural raw materials produced in the current year and consumed by modern factories in producing VA.

To take into account the lag in time between harvest and the processing of the produce by modern factory mills, it is assumed that one-half the raw materials consumed by modern factories for producing the following products in a given year comes from the agricultural output of the preceding year: [9] sugar, milled rice, wheat flour, edible vegetable oils, and cigarettes. It is also assumed that raw materials for making gunny sacks, paper and one-third [10] of chemicals during a given year originated in agriculture during the same year. The percentage of gross value of output accounted for by raw materials for the products mentioned above are given in Liu-Yeh (p. 480). The gross values of output of these products for 1952-57 are given in Liu-Yeh (p. 146). The series on R_A is obtained by multiplying the gross values by the respective percentages and then summing.

Column (2), R_A: Value of agricultural raw materials produced in the preceding year for consumption by modern factories in the current year in producing VA.

In addition to one-half the raw materials used by modern factories for producing sugar, milled rice, wheat flour, edible vegetable oils and cigarettes (see note for column (1)), raw materials consumed by modern mills for making the following products belong to this category: cotton yarn, silk and woolens. The shares of raw materials in total gross values of output and the data on the gross values are in Liu-Yeh, p. 480 and p. 146, respectively.

Column (3), R_M: Value of raw materials produced by the mining sector for consumption by modern factories in producing VA.

Belonging to this category are the raw materials for producing pig iron, cement, coke and one-third of chemicals. The percentages of gross value of output accounted for by raw materials and the data on gross values of these products are given in Liu-Yeh, p. 480 and p. 146 respectively.

Column (4), VA: Net value added by 20 commodity groups produced by modern factories.

The 20 commodity groups are: (a) gunny sacks, paper, chemicals, cotton yarn, cotton cloth, silk, silk piece goods, woolen textiles, clothing, sugar, milled rice, wheat flour, vegetable oils and cigarettes; and (b) pig iron, steel, rolled steel, machinery, cement, and coke.

The coefficients 0.87 and 5.83 in equation (1) are obtained as follows. The gross value added by the twenty commodities in 1957 are given in Liu-Yeh (p. 146). The gross value added by category (a) in 1957 was

9. The other half is assumed to come from the harvest of the preceding year.
10. This proportion is arbitrarily assumed.

5.248 billion 1952 *yuan*. Net value added amounted to 4.664 billion, with depreciation assumed at 4 per cent of gross value of output. The sum of R_A and R'_A was 5.332 billion *yuan* in 1957 (Table 27). The ratio is 4.664/5.332 = 0.87. Similarly, the net value added by category (b) in 1957 is estimated at 6.736 billion *yuan* (Liu-Yeh, p. 146). M amounted to 1.155 billion *yuan* in 1957. (Table 27). The ratio is 6.736/1.155 = 5.83.

Column (*5*), F: Net value added by modern factories as a whole.

Liu-Yeh, p. 66.

Column (*6*), A: Net value added by agriculture.

Liu-Yeh, p. 66.

Column (*7*), A'_{-1}: Value of cotton production and one half of the value of crop production during the preceding year.

Liu-Yeh, p. 397.

Column (*8*), M: Net value added by the mining sector.

Liu-Yeh, p. 66.

Column (*9*), M′: Value of coal and iron ore produced by modern mines.

Liu-Yeh, p. 573.

Column (*10*), V_m: Net value added by all the modern sectors except government administration. (Modern factories, mining, utilities, construction, modern transportation and communications, trading stores, restaurants, finance and urban rental incomes.)

Net value added by all these sectors are given in Liu-Yeh (p. 66). Total value added by residential rents are distributed to urban and rural sectors on the ratio of these two types of gross rents explained in note to column (17) below.

Column 11, V_o: Net value added by the traditional sectors (handicrafts, traditional transportation, peddlers, rural rental incomes, work brigades, and personal services.)

Liu-Yeh (p. 66). For rural rental income, see note to column (10) above.

Column (*12*). NDP, and *Column* (*13*), G: Net domestic product and value added by government administration.

Liu-Yeh, p. 66.

Column (*14*), E_m: Employment in the modern sectors (corresponding to V_m above).

Liu-Yeh, p. 69.

Column (*15*), P_u: Urban population.

Liu-Yeh, p. 212.

Column (*16*), C_u/P_u: Per capita urban consumption.

For P_u, see note to Column (15).

The revised Liu-Yeh estimate of total consumption and the distribution of the revised estimate of miscellaneous consumption to the urban and rural sectors have been explained in note to Table 20. The allocation of the Liu-Yeh estimate of consumption expenditures on food, clothing, fuel and light, and housing [11] to the urban and rural sectors will now be explained.

For the expenditure on food, consumption of the rural population is calculated first and that of the urban sectors is obtained as a residual. It will be recalled that the Communist concept of rural population is broader than that of the agricultural population. (See Liu-Yeh, pp. 210-211.) Food consumption by the rural population during 1952-57 is approximated by adding to food consumption at producers prices (representing consumption by the farm population, the data being given in Liu-Yeh, p. 246) an estimate of food consumption by people in the other traditional sectors (handicrafts, traditional transportation, peddlers, personal services and work brigades). The latter is obtained on the assumption that the per capita consumption of the other traditional sectors was the same as that of the farm population, except that trade and transportation margin should be added to the consumption in the other traditional sectors. The calculation can be easily done, given the data on agricultural population and those in the other traditional sectors (Liu-Yeh, p. 69) and the estimated trade and transportation margin (Liu-Yeh, p. 259).

The allocation of total clothing expenditure to the urban and rural sectors is made on the ratio of urban to rural per capita consumption given in Ou (1945). This ratio, 13.34 to 2.44,[12] together with the data on rural and urban population (Liu-Yeh, p. 212), enables us to apportion total expenditure on clothing (Liu-Yeh, p. 68) to urban and rural sectors.

The estimated total housing rent (Liu-Yeh, p. 68) is distributed to the urban and rural sectors on the basis of the ratio of per capita urban to rural rent (Liu-Yeh, p. 610) and the urban and rural population (Liu-Yeh, p. 212). The same method is used to apportion the total expenditure on fuel and light, except that the urban to rural per capita ratio is taken from Ou's estimate (1945, pp. 160, p. 169).

Column (17), $(V_m + G)/P_u$

See notes to columns (10), (13), and (15).

Column (18) and (19), I_m (imports) and X (exports).

Supplied by F. H. Mah.

Table 30: Estimate of A, A'_{-1} and M'

Column 1: Value of cotton output.

The data on the quantities of cotton production for 1959-65 are the

11. Estimates of these expenditures are in Liu-Yeh, p. 68. The revision of the estimate of miscellaneous consumption does not affect these figures.

12. Ou's data on rural and urban clothing consumption are in (1945), pp. 160, 169; those on rural and urban population are in the same source, p. 151. We have used only Ou's estimate of the urban to rural ratio; his estimates of the absolute magnitudes are not used.

estimate of the Agricultural Officer of the U. S. Consulate General in Hong Kong.[13]

	Million bales
1959	1.8
1960	1.4
1961	0.9
1962	0.9
1963	1.0
1964	1.2
1965	1.3

These output figures are then converted into *piculs* and multiplied by the price of 84.9 *yuan/picul* (Liu-Yeh, p. 381) to get the series presented in column 1.

Column (*2*): Value of food crops production.

The data on the physical output of crops for 1959-65 are given in Table 27, column 1, together with the sources of data. The output of crops in 1957, 185 million tons, had a total value of 22.81 billion 1952 *yuan* (Liu-Yeh, p. 397). The value figures given in column 2 for 1959-65 are obtained by multiplying the quantity figures by the value per ton in 1957.

Column (*3*), A: Net value added by agriculture.

The value of cotton and food crops produced during 1959-65 has been estimated (column (1) and (2)). In 1957, the ratio of net value added by agriculture (37.16 billion 1952 *yuan;* see Liu-Yeh, p. 66) to the value of cotton and food crops (25.59 billion 1952 *yuan;* see Liu-Yeh, p. 397) is 1.452. Value added by agriculture during 1959-65 is then estimated by applying this ratio to the value of cotton and food crops produced during these years.

Column (*4*), A'_{-1}: Value of cotton output plus one-half of that of food crops, both of the preceding year.

Computed from the same data explained in notes to columns (1) and (2).

Column (*5*): Value of Steel Output

Recent data on steel production are presented below (in million metric tons).

All sources are in agreement that the Communist figures for the Great

13. As reported in Emery, 1966. These data are very close to those reported in *Current Scene,* April 15, 1965, *Far Eastern Economic Review,* February 18, 1966, and the various issues of *World Agricultural Production and Trade,* U.S. Department of Agriculture.

	Current Scene [a]	Emery [b]	Far Eastern Economic Review [c]	Liu-Yeh [d]
1957	5.35	5.2	5.25	5.35
1958	8.00 [e]	8.0 [e]	11.08 [e]	6.3
1959		13.4 [e]	13.35 [e]	8.9
1960	18.45 [e]	18.5 [e]	18.45 [e]	
1961			11-12	
1962	7-8		7-8	
1963	7-9	7.0	8-9	
1964	8-10		10	
1965		10.0	12	

Notes:

a. April 15, 1965, p. 9.
b. 1966, p. 307.
c. March 31, 1966, p. 623.
d. P. 454 and pp. 681-683. The 1958 and 1959 figures are obtained by dividing the value figures of 3.8 and 5.36 billion *yuan* by the price (600 *yuan* per ton).
e. Communist claimed figures.

Leap years 1958-61 are highly inflated. The Liu-Yeh estimate for 1957-59 is used for these years. Starting with 1962, the scattered data shown in the table begin to converge to a fairly uniform pattern. The figures used in our estimate are 7.5, 8, 9 and 10 million tons respectively for 1962, 1963, 1964 and 1965. For 1960 and 1961, the linearly extropolated figures (respectively 8.4 and 7.9 million tons respectively) from the 1959 and 1962 observations are used. The value figures for all the years are obtained by multiplying the output figures by the price of 600 *yuan* per ton (see Liu-Yeh, p. 462).

The only set of data on steel production which differs sharply from those given in the table above is the estimate by the U.S. Bureau of Mines as follows (supplied by the Bureau of Mines to the author):

	Million metric tons
1960	18.45
1961	9.5
1962	10.0
1963	12.0
1964	14.0

It is explained, however, by the Bureau of Mines that these are the Communist "claimed figures" which "appear to be grossly exaggerated by perhaps one-fifth or more." No opinion is expressed on how much "more" than one-fifth. If the exaggeration were from one-fourth to one-third, the 1961-64 data would be quite close to the data we used.

Column (6): Value of iron ore and coal produced by modern mines.

During and after the Great Leap years 1958 and 1959, there were large reported increases in the production of coal and iron ore from native mines. The quality of coal from native mines may or may not have been much inferior to that from modern mines, but the reliability of the statistics on coal and iron certainly had deteriorated. In this conjectural estimate, the value production of coal during 1960-65 was obtained by extrapolation on the linear relationship between steel and coal produced by modern mines during 1957-59.[14] In 1957, the ratio of the value of iron ore to that of steel is estimated at 0.39 to 3.21 (Liu-Yeh, p. 146, p. 573). On the basis of this ratio, the value of iron ore produced during 1959-63 is then derived from the estimated value of steel production, given in the note to column (5).

REFERENCES

AIRD, J. S., 1961. *The Size, Composition and Growth of the Population of Mainland China.* Washington, D.C.

BERGSON, A., 1961. *The Real National Income of Soviet Russia since 1928.* Cambridge, Mass.

BUCK, J. L., 1930. *Chinese Farm Economy.* Chicago.

BUCK, J. L., 1937. *Land Utilization in China.* Chicago.

CHAO, K., 1965. *The Rate and Pattern of Industrial Growth in Communist China.* Ann Arbor, Mich.

ECKSTEIN, A., 1961. *The National Income of Communist China.* Glencoe, Ill.

EMERSON, J. P., 1965. *Nonagricultural Employment in Mainland China: 1949–58.* Washington, D.C.

EMERY, R. F., 1966. "Recent Economic Development in Communist China." *Asian Survey* (June, 1966), p. 303.

HOLLISTER, W. W., 1958. *China's Gross National Product and Social Accounts, 1950–57.* Glencoe, Ill.

JONES, P. P. and T. T. POLEMAN, 1962. "Communes and the Agricultural Crises in China," Stanford Research Institute Studies, Vol. III, No. 1 (February, 1962).

KUZNETS, S., 1957. "Quantitative Aspects of the Economic Growth of Nations: II. Industrial Distribution of National Product and Labor Force," *Economic Development and Cultural Change* (July, 1957).

KUZNETS, S., 1960. "Quantitative Aspects of the Economic Growth of Nations: V. Capital Formation Proportions: International Comparisons for Recent Years," *Economic Development and Cultural Change* (July, 1960).

14. The data for 1957-59 are given in Liu-Yeh, p. 146, p. 573, p. 682, and p. 686. The data on steel for 1960-65 are given in the note to column (5).

KUZNETS, S., 1961. "Quantitative Aspects of the Economic Growth of Nations: VI. Long-Term Trends in Capital Formation Proportions," *Economic Development and Cultural Change* (July, 1961).

KUZNETS, S., 1963. *Economic Trends in the Soviet Union. A Comparative Appraisal.* Cambridge, Mass.

LI, C. M., 1959. *Economic Development of Communist China.* Berkeley and Los Angeles.

LI, C. M., 1962. *The Statistical System of Communist China.* Berkeley and Los Angeles.

LI, C. M., 1964. *Industrial Development in Communist China.* New York and London.

LIU, T. C., and YEH, K. C., 1965. *The Economy of the Chinese Mainland: National Income and Economic Development, 1933–1959.* Princeton.

ORLEANS, L. A., 1960. *Professional Manpower and Education in Communist China.* Washington, D.C.

OU PAO-SAN, 1946, *National Income of China, 1945.* (*In Chinese*)

Ten Great Years. State Statistical Bureau of Communist China, Peking, 1960.

ULLMAN, M. B., 1961. *Cities of Mainland China: 1953 and 1958.* Washington, D.C. (August).

WU, Y. L., F. P. HOEBER, and M. M. ROCKWELL, 1963. *The Economic Potential of Communist China,* Vols. 1 and 2. Menlo Park, Calif.

WU, Y. L., F. P. HOEBER, and M. M. ROCKWELL, 1964. *The Economic Potential of Communist China,* Vol. 3. Menlo Park, Calif.

YEH, K. C., 1964. *Capital Formation in Mainland China 1931–36 and 1952–57.* (Unpublished thesis, Columbia University.)

Population Growth 4

JOHN S. AIRD

I. PROBLEMS OF SOURCES, METHODS, AND PROFESSIONAL COMMUNICATIONS

NO WORLDWIDE GENERALIZATIONS about human affairs are complete without appropriate allowance for conditions among the considerable portion of humanity that resides in mainland China. Few valid generalizations can be made about present and prospective social, economic, and political developments in China without reference to population, the universal denominator of human experience. Yet information on the essential demographic parameters for China is limited in quantity and reliability, and the few demographers who study China are not agreed on what may safely be asserted about the size, structure, and future growth of its population. The uncertainty about population compounds the uncertainties already inherent in any assessment of China's gross potential and further vexes the already vexed questions about China's current and future place in the world.

Between the urgent need for demographic data and the difficulties of preparing reliable estimates, the demographer who studies China is enveloped in what the Chinese Communists would call a "contradiction." How is he to meet the legitimate demands of his colleagues in other disciplines for working figures without exceeding the warrant of his information and of whatever generalized demographic knowledge may be relevant to China? If he yields to the importunings of those who would rely on his

The analysis of sources and the calculations presented here were carried out at the Foreign Demographic Analysis Division of the Bureau of the Census, U.S. Department of Commerce, as part of a continuing analysis of the population of mainland China. However, the views and opinions expressed in this paper are those of the author and do not necessarily coincide with the official views of the Unted States government.

In the preparation of the source materials, statistical analyses, computer runs, and the writing and review of the text, a great deal of invaluable advice and assistance was given by Paul F. Myers, Chief of the Foreign Demographic Analysis Division, and by my colleagues, James W. Brackett, John Philip Emerson, Florence L. Yuan, James L. Scott, and Frances T. Manning. Their help is deeply appreciated. Responsibility for the judgments set forth in these pages and the manner in which they are stated remains exclusively my own.

expertise, he may inadvertently assert more than he believes and thus betray a trust he never meant to invite. But if, in a strenuous effort to avoid letting others lean on him, he exaggerates the magnitude of doubt or withholds judgments he actually feels competent to render, those he disappoints may resort by default to the official figures from mainland China, or to uncircumspect evaluations and estimates of their own, or to the advice of others less inhibited by scruple. One way or another, his caution may lead others to incaution, a consequence opposite to that he intended. Moreover, both the anomalies and the pressures of this situation may cause the demographer to commit himself too strongly to whatever position he assumes, whether it be categorical assertion or categorical disbelief. Once he has succumbed to punditry, an occupational disease among China specialists, it is very difficult for him to disengage and reconsider his position in the light of new evidence or new perspective without suffering some loss of face.

Probably no course open to the demographer guarantees immunity from all forms of professional risk, but the happiest resolution of his dilemma would be one that permits him to set forth his best judgments tentatively, with their limitations and uncertainties duly noted, but expressly reserves for him the option of changing his mind subsequently whenever he deems it necessary. In this way he would be able to maintain his professional standards while rendering maximum service to the larger community. If the issues waiting for demographic enlightenment about China are as important as they seem, it is essential that he do both to the best of his ability.

If this course is to be pursued, there are three major problems to be solved. First, there is the problem of assembling the mass of fragmentary evidence, both quantitative and descriptive, on the population of China. Second, there is the problem of how to adapt and apply the experience and techniques accumulated in the study of other peoples to the particularities of the Chinese situation. Third, there is the tactical problem of how to present the results of the analysis in such a way that even persons who may know little about demography or about China will be able to make intelligent use of them. The choice of solutions to these problems depends in part on how the problems themselves are conceived; hence some further elaboration of all three is useful as a perspective for what is discussed in subsequent sections of the chapter.

THE NATURE OF THE EVIDENCE

The source materials for the study of the population of contemporary China are of three types: the figures themselves, information on how they were obtained, and background information on conditions, trends, and events that affect population. The relevant record covers three periods: the latter part of the Ch'ing dynasty (from 1741 to 1911), the Republic of China period, and the Communist period. The materials from the earlier periods are significant for the study of the present because the demographic trends of the last century will have left their mark on subsequent generations, and because traditional attitudes and methods in public administration, including population investigations and record-keeping, may still influence current practice.

The stock of information from the Ch'ing period includes an extensive collection of annual population totals for the empire as a whole, some shorter series for the provinces, and a few *hsien* (county) figures. Local reports give some information on numbers of households, numbers of males and females, numbers of children and adults, and a few other scattered bits. There are almost no figures on births, deaths, or natural increase, and no systematic information on in- and out-migration. In accordance with imperial decrees, the annual population totals were compiled and reported to Peking along with other information on local affairs and administration. The system of public records and reports greatly impressed some foreign visitors in China, who supposed that under such firm and efficient administration statistical reliability was bound to be high; but local officals knew better, and some of them said so in official reports, at considerable peril to their careers. Their critical observations provide invaluable insights into the malfunctions of the system.

The origin of many of the difficulties was the fact that the imperial decrees governing the *pao-chia* organization, which was the basis of rural organization and accounting after its establishment in 1741 and hence the ultimate source of population data, failed to include detailed directions on how the local records were to initiate and maintain contact with demographic realities. Since the *pao-chia* system was also used for taxation and police purposes (which all levels clearly recognized as having higher priority than population record-keeping) its functionaries were bound to be unpopular, and discrepancies were likely to exist between the information on door placards and the actual composition of households. Nevertheless, without adequate organization, personnel, or funds for the task, local officials were expected to furnish accurate population data each year at the appointed time. All derelictions of duty were threatened with severe punishment, but, as local officials apparently realized, there was no central inspection apparatus capable of detecting deviations so long as plausible figures reached Peking on schedule, and their resourcefulness certainly included the devising of simple and practical accommodations. These undoubtedly varied from place to place, with the result that there could have been little uniformity in whatever local expedients produced the numbers sent to Peking.

As for the Ch'ing figures themselves, even the summary totals are frequently guilty of obviously undemographic behavior, including sudden, acute changes of level due to changes in concept or coverage. The provincial totals also leap and plunge irregularly or advance by increments that are too regular to represent the instabilities of life in an agrarian society. The fragmentary age and sex data are sometimes too far from the normal balance and proportion to be believed. More will be said on this subject hereafter, but, taken as a whole, the collection cannot be regarded as a body of reliable data or as even an approximation of the actual trend of population growth. On the other hand, the fact that information about the system of data collection and reporting is incomplete, not wholly consistent, and sometimes ambiguous does not justify the conclusion that the numbers are worthless for all time. The question needs more exploration than it has yet received.

The last half century of Ch'ing rule was tormented by famines, plagues, and rebellions, during which civil administration deteriorated and population reporting either ceased altogether or was reduced to clerical ritual. When its authority had crumbled beyond hope of restoration, the faltering government of the Dowager Empress attempted to rally popular support with the promise of a representative government, in preparation for which a new count of the population was ordered. Unlike previous counts, this was to have been an actual field investigation independent of the old records, consisting of an enumeration of households in 1909, to be reported to Peking during 1910, and a count of individuals during 1911, to be reported in 1912. What actually happened in the field is not known in detail, but even the scholars of that time thought that the work was badly done and distrusted the figures. Reports from the provinces were still incomplete when the regime was overthrown in 1911, yet the early returns were used as the basis for several attempts to estimate the total population of China, adding fuel to an already raging controversy over the size of that total.

The so-called "census" of 1910 was the forerunner of a series of national and provincial population investigations during the period of the Republic of China that show the influence of Western census concepts. Few of these were actually carried out according to plan, and some of the best laid plans were never carried out at all. Execution remained, as in earlier periods, the weak link in the administration of data-collecting activities; Chinese officialdom tended to assume that once orders were given to accomplish a task, the only remaining problem was local compliance, and that the key to local compliance was the vigor of the edict. Planning usually stopped short of specifying the procedures for field work, organization and training of personnel, and the system of supervision; and no provision was ever made for checking the accuracy of the results. Hence, the records of these investigations do not contain an adequate account of the methods actually employed during fieldwork, the most essential information for evaluation of the figures. This is a critical point, especially since in many areas the traditional population records still survived after the end of the Ch'ing dynasty, and in others they had been revived from time to time, providing a convenient and economical supply of numbers for unsupervised local officials anxious to avoid the burden of field operations.

Simultaneous with the new influences in official population investigations, modern demographic ideas and interests were being imported into China through the universities, where foreign and Western-trained Chinese scholars and social scientists engaged jointly in special surveys and studies from the 1920's onward. Among these were some promising initial explorations on a small scale into questions of population structure and vital rates. Meanwhile, monographs and articles in scholarly journals pressed past the technical aspects of demography into the broader implications of population growth for the manifold economic and social ills of Chinese society. Malthusian views of China's predicament began to take root in Chinese intellectual circles, and the general ferment aroused further interest in population both in and out of the government.

Throughout this period, both the official and the private investigations produced a great harvest of population figures, which opened up many new questions about China's demographic characteristics without resolving the old questions about size and rate of growth of the total population. Although many of the data collected were visibly defective, realization of this fact was not universal, and much effort was expended in devising plausible explanations for what should have been recognized as distortions. Given the status of demographic knowledge at that time, even those scholars who expressed critical reservations were unable to pursue the technical analysis of the figures to the point where reality and artifact could be distinguished. Hence, there was no way of knowing whether similarities in the findings of two or more investigations confirmed empirical phenomena or demonstrated the pervasiveness of methodological and cultural biases; or of determining whether differences in the findings signified local variation in demographic characteristics or simply the local variation of investigative biases. However, analytical techniques have advanced somewhat since the last pre-Communist population studies in the late 1940's, and there is reason to believe that even these studies have not yet given all the testimony that can be extracted from them before they are returned to the archives for the last time.

Enter at mid-century the Chinese Communists, bringing with them a new discipline, a new organization, a new passion for data gathering, a self-conscious determination to sever certain connections with the past, and a vast, unconscious heritage of old cultural compulsions with attachments too strong and deep for facile ideology to sever. Could they succeed where previous governments had failed in ending once and for all the debate about the size of the Chinese population?

From the start there could be little doubt but that the new regime would want a system of population records as soon as possible; the Chinese Communist conception of national planning required both population data and population control. Immediately after the new government was established in Peking in 1949, work was begun on the restoration of population registration in the major cities. Population records were also compiled in connection with the "land reform" drive, which had begun prior to 1949 in some areas and continued until it was completed in the Han majority areas and most of the minority areas in 1953. During 1953-54 the Chinese Communists took their first (and so far their only) population census, the records from which were used to strengthen urban registration and extend the registration system into rural areas during 1954-57. During the Great Leap Forward of 1958, and the acute food shortages of 1959-62, the system seems to have lapsed, but one more attempt, apparently not very successful, was made to revive it during the summer of 1964. Certainly these efforts, carried out at considerable cost and despite many obstacles, indicate that the new regime attached some importance to population accounting.

Were the Chinese Communists more successful than their predecessors in taking the measure of the population of China? The answer to this question depends, as before, on the internal evidence of the data and the inferential evidence based on what is known of field methods and circumstances. Here, in contrast to earlier periods, relatively fewer data actually collected have been released in a form that permits analysis, but a somewhat more complete collection of evidence is available on the methods actually employed during fieldwork.

Why have so few figures been released by Peking? There are probably four principal reasons. The first and most important is that the statistical operations of the regime have not produced much data, and so there are few data to release. The second is that the data collected have often been so incomplete, unstandardized, and contradictory that local reports and survey results could not be assembled in summary tables for use at provincial and national levels. A third is that the regime is acutely sensitive to the embarrassment which could result from exposing to criticism by Chinese and foreign scholars data that might turn out to have defects not recognized by the official statisticians. The fourth is that "security" considerations require the suppression of information which might supply arguments to the opponents of the regime or draw attention to policies and trends that the leaders prefer to keep from domestic or international notice.

Whatever the relative significance of these four explanations, all of which are supported by evidence in mainland China publications, the fact remains that very little of the at least hypothetically possible statistical yield from the various investigations and reporting systems that have gathered population data in Communist China has been published or made available to either mainland or foreign analysts. *Hsien* data from the census of 1953 were compiled and used in mapmaking in China but are not obtainable elsewhere. Population totals for all provinces are available for only three years: census data for midyear 1953, and registration data as of year-end 1954 and year-end 1957. Total, urban, and rural population figures for the years 1949 through 1957 were released by the State Statistical Bureau, but some of these are admittedly estimates, and it seems quite likely that others are partly estimates or required adjustment before they could be assembled. Complete age data are available in two series of percentage figures for 10-year age groups, and data by age and sex in percentage values for 5-year age groups that had to be read from a rather crudely drawn age-sex pyramid, all from the 1953 census. Year-end totals by sex in millions have been published for 1949, 1953, and 1957, but the 1949 figures could only have been rough estimates by reverse extrapolation of both totals and sex ratios. There are figures by sex for the "directly enumerated" population of the 1953 census which are specific down to the last of nine digits, but these figures were apparently not taken from the census returns; instead they were obtained by applying to the total "directly enumerated" population the per cent male or female in the population as officially reported (given to four significant digits). There are some survey figures on vital rates and a series of "national" vital rates for the years 1952-1957.

In addition to these national figures, there are a number of figures for particular municipalities, provinces, *hsien,* and smaller units; most are population totals, but there are a few figures on age, sex, permanent and temporary residents, crude vital rates, infant mortality rates, and so on. These figures are too fragmentary to be of much use, and some of them appear in the customary disguise of Communist official data—percentage rates of change devoid of their base absolutes. All in all, by international standards, the collection of population figures from Communist China is very modest for a country with such pretensions to statistical modernity.

The collection of descriptive materials on the establishment and operation of reporting systems and on the plans and execution of special investigations and surveys is also incomplete by the standards of other countries, but, at least, prior to 1957, it is far more abundant than many people suppose. In the early years, mass investigations were usually planned in Peking and carried out in local areas by a process of trial and error. The central plans were reworked and adapted to local conditions in meetings at provincial and local levels, tested in "experimental" applications, reviewed and further revised in meetings called to "exchange experiences," and then carried out in full scale. The plans, adaptations, achievements, errors, lessons learned, and derelictions detected were described in detail in the national and local press, often in purely propagandistic terms, but not infrequently in a remarkably candid fashion. The careful assembly and perusal of these materials provides considerable insight into the nature of the reporting systems and investigations, as well as much valuable material on the effectiveness of central and local supervision and the extent to which local cadres understood and complied with the directives handed down to them.

However, extracting information from such sources as these requires major efforts in collection, interpretation, and generalization. It cannot be done quickly and superficially and still done well. If the collection process is short-changed, there will be gaps in the materials that can easily be mistaken for gaps in coverage or even purposeful omissions in the original sources. There is no more dangerous statement on the basis of a casual perusal of sources than one that begins "There is no evidence that. . . ."

Interpretation also takes time. A first prerequisite is to note the source of the original item. A New China News Agency dispatch or a Chinese Communist foreign language periodical is not generally entitled to the same consideration as an item in the *People's Daily* (*Jen-min jih-pao*). In the latter, an entry in a "letters" column, an article signed by a nongovernment academician, a domestic news dispatch, and an editorial are by no means all equally authoritative. A different kind of significance may be attached to an article in a professional statistical journal, signed or unsigned, a speech by a director of the State Statistical Bureau, or a technical critique by a statistical specialist reviewing a particular type of statistics. What is published in a period in which self-examination was the mode may deserve more attention than supposedly evaluative items issued during times in which Marxist apologetics were the order of the day.

Among the items themselves, there are some that claim too much or deny too much, and others that have an unmistakable ring of verisimilitude. Some local press items are obviously nothing more than an echolalia of slogans and clichés designed to convey the impression that the local agency is faithfully following its instructions to the last character. Others display a completely undogmatic seriousness of purpose or describe specific actions and circumstances. Some items bow first to the Party stereotypes and then get down to business; with these it is easy to determine where to begin reading. But often the text is a mixture of idioms, including Party jargon, Chinese folk expressions, and literary conventions, which can impart some news if they are read in the appropriate situational context, including characteristic modes of expression, the internal peculiarities of the administrative system, and the main political currents of the time. Acquiring the necessary understanding calls for a heavy investment of time and patience in the sifting and sorting of grubby details, but there is no easier access to the kind of judgment that makes interpretation possible.

When all the bits and pieces of descriptive information have been interpreted, consolidated, and assembled into a meaningful composite, a fairly clear picture emerges of the way in which the major population data-collecting activities in China since 1949 have been conducted. There are a number of interesting, though not very surprising, resemblances between the procedures used by the Communist authorities and those of their antecedents back to Ch'ing times. Once again there are indications of a failure to anticipate field problems, to test specific field procedures, and to define all essential concepts operationally. Where so much was left to local ingenuity, some lack of uniformity of methods was bound to develop; the central authorities recognized this but made little attempt to standardize local procedures, either in the establishment and maintenance of population registers or during the 1953 census. As in the past, both registration and census work were linked with other goals, including population control, police investigation, and fulfillment of production targets, with little apparent recognition of how these connections might affect the accuracy of population data. Basically, the central authorities, even the professionals in charge of statistical reporting and investigation, seem to have had little real interest in or understanding of demographic statistics. They were content, especially in registration work, to leave the management of record-keeping to relatively untrained clerks and to rely upon voluntary reporting by a people who had never before shown much inclination to volunteer information to government officials. The problems that arose from these miscalculations were exactly what could have been predicted on the basis of past experience, and the Chinese Communist officials were no less surprised and chagrined when what might have been predicted promptly began to happen.

On the other hand, there are also some significant differences between the Chinese Communist population investigations and their antecedents. Although registration work was an extra burden on security police and other local officials, and its costs had to be borne locally, the census costs came out of the central budget, and a very substantial field staff was allocated for the work. Moreover, the Chinese Communist authorities applied to land reform, registration, and census work their standard formula of combining personnel training with the testing and modification of field procedures in a series of "key point" experimental operations, a kind of pragmatism that has no very close precedent in the past. Registration work was subjected at various times to press criticism designed to make it accountable to "the people"; and in land reform and census work there were instances of field supervision by traveling inspectors from higher administrative levels, intended to prevent if possible the ancient practice of local evasion of central directives. The requirements implicit in the registration as outlined in the central directives were, as before, quite unrealistic, but those of the census were deliberately kept simple so that execution would not be impossible. For these reasons, it may be concluded that while many of the old defects have persisted in the Chinese Communist population investigations, the present regime has been able to improve upon the traditional methods and implement them much more effectively than its predecessors.

This does not mean that all the data collected by the Communist Chinese can be assumed to be fairly reliable or that they are necessarily superior to all previous data of the same type. Some investigations conducted by the new regime were more successful than others, and some types of official figures have been improved upon more than others. To know what can be said about each type, it is necessary to put specific questions, both quantitative and descriptive, to the evidence. However, certain simplistic preconceptions and assumptions commonly advanced in connection with population data and other official figures from mainland China never had a substantial foundation and are contradicted even by a general survey of the record. One of these is the view that the Chinese Communist control system is absolute, that the street committees and activists know and report everything, and that official information is therefore complete and accurate. Another is that data are falsified and fabricated on a large scale at local or at central levels, and that official figures may therefore be regarded as fraudulent. Some activists probably do know their charges well and some may report in full; some local officials may invent or adjust data at their desks when filling out reports. Such instances do not, however, sustain sweeping conclusions, which may only be asserted in contempt of the evidence.

A review of the source materials on the population of China shows most clearly that, demographically, China is a great swamp—tantalizing for speculative exploration but offering little solid foundation for constructive analysis. For an analyst in quest of certainties, it is a veritable Slough of Despond; but if tentative results are sufficient reward for the patience and persistence that the study of China's population demands, a demographer can find no greater challenge.

CONSTRUCTING POPULATION ESTIMATES FOR MAINLAND CHINA

With such limited source materials, how is it possible to trace the development of the population of mainland China in recent years and project it into the future? The answer depends in part on what purpose is to be served and how much uncertainty can be tolerated in the positing of basic assumptions necessary for the analysis of the evidence. If the aim is to extract as much information from the available source materials as they can be made to yield by relating circumstances in China to the relevant worldwide demographic experience, demography can tell us something about China. Certain demographic syndromes are characteristically found in peasant societies in which initial stages of medical and public health development have lowered mortality but fertility remains high, thus releasing a sudden surge of population growth; these can certainly be applied to China without confirmation by any of the standard demographic measurements, sample soundings, or precise descriptive accounts. Standard analytical techniques can be applied to fragmentary data to determine whether they have anything useful to reveal, and model populations can be constructed to represent limiting and intermediary assumptions that appear to be warranted by the analysis. Embodiment in a set of models tends to systematize judgments by pressing them into mutually contingent relationships that demand congruence and may sometimes narrow tolerance limits. It also forces the demographer to assign mathematical quantities to his abstract assessments, thus converting them to a form on which further research or future events can pass a definitive sentence.

The models themselves should incorporate internally consistent combinations of assumptions representing the reasonable limits of the essential demographic parameters for mainland China. For each model it is necessary to have a base population total, an age-sex distribution, and a set of values for fertility, mortality, and migration that covers the period to which the estimates and projections apply. Establishing all these prerequisites calls for a considerable exercise of interpretation, judgment, and assumption, but this does not mean that the essential ingredients, and therefore the end products, are wholly arbitrary. If the source materials have been subjected to a thorough and circumspect evaluation, and the derivations made from them are explicitly systematic and logical, there is no need to apologize for the use of round figures or graphically interpolated trends simply because they came from no empirical data-collection process. Demographic judgment has much experience to draw upon, and many techniques can be applied to the analysis of quantitative records and to the representation of phenomena and trends known only in descriptive terms.

Among the most useful devices for analyzing data and making projections are the model life-table and its derivative, the stable population model, which is in essence an age-sex structure determined by a particular set of life-table mortality rates and a given constant rate of natural increase. Stable population models can be modified to provide a hypothetical age-sex structure against which the reported age-sex structure of an actual population can be measured for possible omissions, age misreporting, and other forms of distortion; or they may be applied in reverse to generate retrospectively the past trends in vital rates implied by the reported age-sex structure. The stable population model offers a way of relating systematically a number of different assumptions about various parameters in a single profile, so that the reciprocal effects of one parameter are brought to bear on another and their implications traced over a period of time. The one major drawback, however, is that a great deal of research and calculation is required to assemble the evidence of mortality patterns by age and sex and the trends of such patterns, to adjust and homogenize the collected life-tables, and to construct model life-tables representing gradients in the process of mortality change. Once such models are available, a great deal of calculation is also necessary in their application, particularly in the case of single-year projections over a long term of years.

Both the construction of model life-tables and the application of stable population models to analysis and projections of population have been greatly facilitated in very recent years by the development of the computer and the programming of population projections. The projection program developed by James Brackett at the Foreign Demographic Analysis Division of the Bureau of the Census has made it possible to project a larger number of models over a longer period, with greater flexibility in the manipulation of components of change and more detailed results than was conceivable before computerization. The potential of electronic devices for model construction and for analysis is probably far beyond anything yet imagined. In the future, the population of China may well be projected as part of a total socioeconomic model in which alternate assumptions about food production, nutrition, capital accumulation, levels of living and other elements of the total complex are explored in contingency with each other, and the demographic and economic implications for each model read off at any point in time.

In a very limited sense the construction and projection of population models for mainland China is a preliminary exercise of the type just envisioned, inasmuch as it does involve some decisions about the current and prospective development of the economy and social structure, and certain assumptions as to the effects of these developments on the course of fertility and mortality. In some respects China may be viewed as the perfect case for the exploration of such broadly conceived contingencies, since precise demographic data are lacking and demographic parameters must be estimated with the fullest possible use of correlative information on food, health, and the status of the economy. Moreover, one cannot simply assume for China, as one can for many other underdeveloped countries, that fertility and mortality will most probably follow relatively stable downward trends that may be represented mechanically without reference to other aspects of the total situation. This has not been true for mortality in the recent past in China, and it may not apply to either fertility or mortality in the future.

Contingency models might make it possible to narrow somewhat the range of parameters that need be posited for the basic socioeconomic dimensions of Chinese society, but they are not now available. Hence, there are few guidelines as to what limits of assumption may be set on the essential demographic inputs. These limits depend partly on the purposes for which the projections are made. If the object is to explore the fullest range of possibilities that can be hypothetically entertained, or to be able to say with assurance that actuality must lie within the broad swath cut by the alternative models, all limits should be deliberately pushed to extremes. For example, there is virtually no likelihood that the birth rate of China at the present time exceeds 55 per thousand per year or falls below 25 per thousand. However, models incorporating such wide limits would probably find few users. Most would want to know what alternative models represented the maximum *probable* limits of assumption, and they would expect the demographer to make the decision about probability with its implicit definitions and judgments, for he should, after all, be in a better position to render that decision than they. There is therefore little point in the production of extreme models, and, as will be seen later in the chapter, they have generally been avoided.

PROBLEMS OF COMMUNICATION

Differences are inevitable both in evaluations of the demographic evidence from mainland China and in the choice of assumptions for reconstructions, estimates, and projections, and they pose communication problems of two kinds. Some problems involve the exchange of views between scholars who study the population of China, while others concern how best to convey to users of population figures the information they need to select the appropriate data from those offered them and then to make an appropriate use of the figures selected. The problems of the first type are of somewhat narrower concern and will not be elaborated upon here, except for a few comments at the close of this section. The problems of the second type are of critical importance for all users of population figures for mainland China, whether they prefer to accept the official figures and make their own extrapolations if necessary or whether they elect to rely on estimates and projections instead.

One major problem demographers have in communicating with their colleagues in other disciplines about the population of China is how to convey the proper measure of doubt about the reliability of the official figures. Even though they differ as to how much doubt is justified, they are generally agreed that greater caution is needed than is usually exercised in citing and using the official figures. On this issue the demographers who study China have found common cause as apostles of unbelief in a land of believers. The basic difficulty is that fragmentary official data often present no very obvious clues to their inherent limitations. It is difficult to gain much of an impression of their reliability without knowing how they were originally collected or compiled, including both the methods of investigation as worked out by the statistical agencies and the way in which these methods were actually carried out. Usually the information available on both counts is insufficient for definitive judgments; often it is published separately from the data and difficult to locate. If methodological information is lacking, there are few criteria for judging a series of official numbers that have escaped from mainland China like refugees, devoid of statistical credentials. Plausibility has been urged in some cases where other indications are lacking, but though plausibility has some value as a negative test—implausible data are not to be trusted—it affords no basis of affirmation, especially when the definition of what is plausible is loose or overgenerous.

Another criterion sometimes used is the credence lent to the official figures by persons of authority or eminence who issued, cited, endorsed, or used them without reservation. However, even if the official spokesman is a highly placed administrator in one of the technical ministries, it is not safe to assume without other proof that the figures cited were based on compilations or estimates by his ministry or by the State Statistical Bureau, that they refer to the area discussed in the context, or that the reference date was either the immediate present or the previous midyear or year-end, whichever was closer. There are instances on record in which figures are cited without regard to dating or coverage, and the error does not always favor the point being argued. Some figures are repeated year after year as if by force of habit, without any sign of awareness that they may be out of date. Obviously the figures used in speeches cannot be strung together and taken as components of a single official series merely because they have been quoted by a series of officials. There is no reason to assume that official population data are still being compiled in Peking since the Great Leap Forward years; if they are, they are probably only crude estimates and without value as an indication of current population changes.

The conscientious researcher should not be content to use a series of figures simply because no conspicuous defect or obtrusive counterargument stands in his way, and he will not readily give his confidence to peripheral indicators which may not be indicative. If the study of official statistics from China teaches anything, it is that no use should ever be made of them without prior study in depth of the systems that produced them and without allowance for their inherent limitations and biases. If the demographers working on China could succeed in carrying this message, negative as it is, to all whom it may concern, they would have made a major contribution to research on China without advancing a single population estimate.

So far as estimates and projections are concerned, though they may not inspire as much gratuitous trust as official figures do, they too are subject to misuse by analysts who ignore the accompanying caveats and apply the figures in ways contradictory to their inherent assumptions. The demographer is obliged to take whatever steps he can within reason to discourage unwarranted uses of his product. He must state clearly what his methods and assumptions are. He should indicate as frankly as he can the limits of confidence that apply to his results. He may also try to anticipate some of the commoner mistakes in using demographic data and offer specific cautions against them. But beyond a certain point, precautionary text reaches a surfeit that is self-defeating; one glimpse of a long screed of dire warnings in the introduction, and the incautious user will probably head for the tables without a backward glance. In the last analysis, the users of population estimates and projections must accept the obligation to read carefully all of the discussion of sources, assumptions, and methods accompanying the figures before they select the series best suited to their purposes. They must also accept the responsibility for carrying over into their own analyses and conclusions the qualifications and limitations attached to the population figures by the person or persons who prepared them. If they find the background text ambiguous, or if it seems not to answer the questions they need to ask, or if for any other reason they are in doubt as to what choice of models or applications they ought to make, it may be well worth their while to consult directly with the demographer who has published the figures before proceeding.

So far as communication within the small circle of demographers studying China is concerned, the scope for individual judgment is large, in view of the ambiguities of the materials with which they work; and there are bound to be divergences of opinion not only in the evaluation of source materials but also as to what kinds of estimates and projections, if any, should be attempted and how the results of demographic studies should be presented to a larger audience. Within certain limits, such divergences have a salutary effect on the quality of research. They stimulate the flow of ideas, sharpen the focus on unresolved questions, and lead to more thorough research and more circumspect statements of findings. But beyond these limits there is always some danger that the differences may generate tensions that cause a breakdown in scholarly communication, to the disadvantage of all concerned. If an excess of either professional courtesy or professional rivalry is permitted to isolate the divergent viewpoints from one another, the valuable opportunities for a constructive interchange of critical appraisal will be restricted. Ultimately the test of any piece of research is whether or not competent colleagues working with the same materials arrive independently at the same conclusions. This is not an infallible test, inasmuch as the collections of source materials are never quite identical and the replications are never wholly independent, but it is the only kind of test available. It is especially important that such testing be continuous in a field where research workers are few, where there is a natural tendency to avoid overlapping of individual research domains, and where, as a result, the replication of particular pieces of research is infrequent.

Consistent with the views just expressed, the following sections of this chapter contain some direct criticism of the work of other analysts; and alternative hypotheses and conclusions are presented in detail to facilitate further review. Obviously the last word has not yet been said on any of the subjects treated here. The criticism of colleagues is therefore invited.

In Section II, the choice of a base population is discussed, with particular attention to the methods and results of the 1953 census of Communist China and its relations to some of its antecedents. In Section III, the methods and assumptions used in the construction of alternate age-sex structures as of 1953 are presented, together with a discussion of interpretations and uses of Ch'ing dynasty population reports; and these model age-sex structures are compared with that for the 1953 census. Section IV gives the assumptions and methods employed in projecting various model populations through 1985, some comparisons of the resulting projections with those prepared by the staff of the United Nations population branch, and some suggestions for the appropriate use of the projections. In this paper, emphasis is on source materials and arguments that the author has not previously presented in other publications; there is no attempt to repeat here the details of analyses given elsewhere unless the conclusions arrived at earlier must now be modified or withdrawn.

II. THE BASE POPULATION TOTAL

CIRCUMSTANCES OF THE 1953 CENSUS OPERATIONS

The leading contender as the base population total for mainland China is without question the figure announced by the Ministry of Interior in Peking on November 1, 1954: 582,603,417. This figure, representing the areas under control of the regime as of June 30, 1953, was said to be the result of a full field enumeration undertaken within a period of about one year, from the spring of 1953 to the spring of 1954. The fact that the Chinese mainland was under a strong central administration for the first time in more than a century was a uniquely favorable circumstance for a successful head count. The power of the new regime was transmitted from Peking through both the governmental organization, including a sizable police network, and the Party organization, and behind them stood the recently victorious People's Liberation Army. Moreover, the leaders of the regime, after rather mild beginnings, had just demonstrated their ability and their disposition to deal ruthlessly with domestic noncooperation in the course of the land reform and "five-anti" campaigns.[1] Party and government personnel had also been subjected to the first of many reform drives and, despite some misadventures with unfortunate domestic consequences, the regime appeared confident of its ability to manage the country while transforming it from a subsistence level agrarian society to a socialist industrial society and a major world power. The same confi-

1. The "five-anti" campaign was directed against businessmen and factory owners who were accused of bribery, tax evasion, theft of state secrets, fraud in government contracts, and disclosure of state economic secrets. It began in October, 1951, and concluded in the summer of 1952.

dence was evident in the energetic and ambitious planning and execution of the census, the voter registration, and the general elections of 1953-54.

However, there were also some unfavorable cricumstances, of which the leaders of the regime and most of the administrators and technicians in charge of the census and elections campaign were not fully aware. Senior statistical cadres and local officials lacked the capacity to plan and direct such a major statistical effort as the census required. These limitations became increasingly apparent in the course of the census work, as supplementary instructions were issued to cover problems not anticipated in the original plans, as the schedule for fieldwork and reporting had to be extended, and as impossible claims of accuracy were accepted and improbable data configurations released for publication. Some of the cadres charged with technical guidance and supervision of the work at local levels did not understand their directions, some failed to secure the cooperation of the population, some did not know how to summarize and report the results of the investigation, and some did not do a conscientious job. It may be argued that, despite these defects, the work was on the whole well done and the results generally valid, but it can also be argued that evasions of census directives and deception of higher authorities introduced serious distortions in the data that were never fully apprehended and corrected. There are, therefore, reasonable doubts about the quality of the census which must be examined before limits of confidence may be suggested.

THE CREDIBILITY OF THE CENSUS

After the census results were announced with a great show of pride, some skeptics outside China surmised that the census total was fabricated for political purposes and bore no relationship to demographic reality. Most of these opinions were based on prejudices not supported by analysis of evidence or by logically cohesive arguments. However, one treatment of the subject arrives at essentially the same conclusion after reviewing part of the circumstantial record and comparing census provincial totals with previous official figures dating back to the Ch'ing dynasty population reports for 1850. This is the paper presented by Irene B. Taeuber and Naichi Wang at the conference of the Milbank Memorial Fund in November, 1959; its authorship alone would command serious attention. The paper is entitled "Questions on Population Growth in China," but as its final summation makes clear, it does not merely raise questions, but dismisses the Chinese Communist census, along with all its predecessors, as without value for demographic purposes:

> The conclusion is inescapable. There has never been either a field enumeration or a controlled registration of the population of all China. There has never been a record or reporting system that yielded accurate data on births, deaths, and migrations in all China. Hence there can be no objective knowl-

edge of the size of the population of China and its rate of change over time. China remains "the country without statistics." (Taeuber and Wang, 1960b, p. 302.)

Putting aside for the moment questions about the registration of births and deaths, the part of the statement that refers to field enumerations is literally true, and applicable to the 1953-54 enumeration by virtue of its inclusion of the word "all," for as the Chinese Communist census authorities made clear, administrative estimates had to be substituted for field enumeration in some of the territories occupied mainly by minority populations, and Taiwan was not under Communist control. However, since the mainland areas not directly enumerated accounted for only 8.4 million people, a fraction of the total population, it would be caviling to insist that because of their exclusion the country had not had a field enumeration or that there could be no "objective knowledge" of the size of the population; and it is certainly an exaggeration to say on these grounds that China is "without statistics" on its population. Hence, Taeuber and Wang's conclusion must rest on inferences developed earlier in their paper that a substantial portion of the rest of the population was not, in fact, enumerated, but that the reported numbers were derived instead from *pao-chia* figures reported for earlier years. As Dr. Frank Notestein said in the ensuing discussion, Taeuber and Wang had challenged the credibility of the census, and unless this challenge could be dismissed, the census data could not be used (1960b, p. 309). Since that time, this challenge has neither been answered nor withdrawn.[2] Let us now examine its essential points in relation to the evidence.

METHODS AND FIELD WORK

The argument of Taeuber and Wang with respect to the census methods and field work is essentially that (1) supervision of local activities by the central authorities was not close enough to assure faithful observance of directives; (2) the work was done carelessly throughout the country; (3) failure to make much progress during 1953 induced the regime to relax its specifications and order a speed-up of the work in January, 1954; (4) 70 per cent of the population was enumerated, according to official figures, after the relaxation of requirements; and (5) local authorities were given, for guidance, population figures for their areas based on figures compiled from local "administrative" reports, adding

2. In an article in June, 1964, Mrs. Taeuber stated that "In Communist China there was a simple census registration in 1953-54, four years after the revolution." This may be taken as granting that a field investigation of some sort was carried out, and, if so, it may signify some modification of the position represented in Mrs. Taeuber's Milbank paper. However, a little later in the same article, the Milbank paper's summation is partly reiterated in a statement that "There are not now, nor have there ever been, age distributions, birth rates, death rates, or rates of population change for all China" (Taeuber, 1964, pp. 15, 17).

to a total some 100 million higher than the last Republic of China figure. The crucial inference toward which this argument is pointed is not stated explicitly, but it is implicit in its general direction, in the argument subsequently developed about earlier provincial populaton figures, and in the final summation of the article already quoted: Under pressures to speed the count by loosening the technical requirements, the census workers and officials at one level or another simply returned the figures already given them without actually completing an independent field count (Taeuber and Wang, 1960b, pp. 283-289).

This conclusion is not, however, consistent with the evidence. Whether or not supervision was close enough to prevent local authorities from substituting available figures for fieldwork cannot be determined directly from source materials. There are ample indications that local authorities were required to make regular reports on the progress of work, that they did so in considerable detail, and that central, regional, and provincial inspection teams circulated in local areas to check on the quality of the work.[3] The inferences that carelessness was general, that omissions and double counting were "prevalent," that erroneous answers were "common," that "residence definitions were neither understood nor followed," and that "rechecking was done in meetings," were arrived at by selecting out and generalizing from instances of defective work cited in the press as bad examples, mainly during the experimental period.[4] Such inferences take

3. The statement of Taeuber and Wang that "there were no requirements for reports on progress prior to the submission of final reports" is attributed to a source reporting supplemental instructions issued in the spring of 1954, among which is a stipulation that "provincial and municipal population investigation and registration offices should establish a system for reporting to the Central Population Investigation and Registration Office at all times" (*JMJP,* March 11, 1954b). Even if this stipulation is taken to mean that there were no such arrangements previously, it would not support the assertion that no progress reports were required. In fact, the 1954 directives were merely repeating instructions given in the original census directions of April 6, 1953, that census offices at *hsien, ch'ü,* and municipal levels should report their progress to the next higher levels for forwarding (Article 15). In conformity with this requirement, one region required all its provinces and municipalities to submit weekly summary reports to the regional administrative council and the Central Election Committee (*JMJP,* May 7, 1953). The hundreds of local and summary progress reports appearing in local and national newspapers and in NCNA dispatches throughout the period of census and election activities attest to the fact that the requirement for progress reports was generally met.

4. Taeuber and Wang state that these complaints were made "by local party officials from Szechwan to Heilungkiang" in September, 1953 (1960b, p. 285). The sources are two editions of a regular column devoted to letters from readers which was carried in *People's Daily* (*JMJP*) at that time. The first (September 21) discusses a letter from a reader in Szechwan reporting serious defects in leadership and field work; the second (September 28) cites two letters from two different *hsien* in Heilungkiang. The first of the Heilungkiang letter writers describes a number of errors found during what was apparently a fairly careful recheck; the second Heilungkiang writer reveals that the original recheck in some villages in his *hsien* consisted simply of calling mass meetings and asking the views of those attending, with the result that no errors were found. One of the three letter writers was a member

very little account of the careful field supervision and conscientious recheck (described in the same sources) without which the derelictions would not have been discovered. Obviously, if the reports of derelictions are accepted as true, the investigations that exposed them cannot be dismissed altogether.[5]

The observation that the census, instead of being completed by November 15, 1953, as originally scheduled, reached only 29 per cent of the population by the end of December, then covered 30 per cent in January and February of 1954 and 40 per cent "in the single month of March 1954,"[6] is subject to misconstruction when two relevant facts are left out of the account. These are, first, that early in June, 1953, the central authorities ordered a delay in census and elections work to avoid interfering with agricultural production and, second, that an acceleration of coverage during the latter phases of the work was inherent in the census procedures.

The original census directive had specified that rural areas should utilize slack periods in agricultural activities for census-taking and that "agricultural production should not be hindered" (NCNA, April 6, 1953a, p. 30). Yet on June 6, 1953, three weeks before the critical date of the census, the *People's Daily* complained editorially that cadres in some areas had misunderstood the order that elections were to be combined with production and had allowed elections to work to interfere with production:

> By "combination" we do not mean that "the two things are given equal importance" but that elections must be subordinated to production, which must be considered the pivotal work taking precedence over all other things, according to instructions by the Central Committee of the Chinese Communist Party. When serious contradictions develop between the elections and the

---

of his *hsien* election committee, but none were described as Party officials. None complained that omissions and double counting were "prevalent" or attempted to generalize beyond the limits of their own localities (*JMJP*, Sept. 21 and 28, 1953).

5. The critical question is how far one may legitimately extrapolate from instances of deviation from regulations reported in the mainland press. It is certainly reasonable to assume that the reported instances stand for a much greater number that were neither detected nor reported. Yet assumptions as to the prevalence of what was not reported clearly go beyond the conclusions that may be supported simply by citing sources.

6. Taeuber and Wang, 1960b, pp. 286-287. The acceleration of census work as indicated in mainland sources was not quite as rapid as these figures imply. The attainment of 60 per cent coverage was not precisely dated but was reported only on March 10. A subsequent news item on the Peking radio on March 29 stated that the census had reached 64.7 per cent of the population as of March 18. But by the end of March the work was still incomplete in some provinces, notably in the central south. A news item from the Kwangtung provincial census office stated that as of April 20 the census in Kwangtung had been completed in 64.4 per cent of the basic-level units in the province. Several other provinces also apparently did not complete census work until well into April (*JMJP,* Mar. 11, 1954b; Kwangtung Prov. Pop. . . . Office, 1954).

production demands of the masses, we would rather postpone slightly the election work than adversely affect production and delay the farming season. (*JMJP*, June 6, 1953, p. 15.)

The editorial warned against doing election work "independently and subjectively" and involving the people in too many, too long, and nonessential meetings during propaganda work, in violation of the "five things too many" campaign.[7] It advised local cadres to solve local production problems, especially in areas affected by natural calamities, before proceeding with census and election work.

The new priorities were immediately evident in the progress reports and news items from local areas throughout the country. Many areas began to report success in "straightening out the cadres," in eliminating "bureaucratism, commandism, and violations of law and discipline" on the part of cadres involved in elections work, and the elimination of "hasty" methods and competitive achievement standards. The North China bureau of the Central Committee instructed areas under its jurisdiction to "examine and rearrange the work of rural villages" to ease the pressure of too many tasks for peasants:

The rural work for 1953 shall make agricultural production the task of prime importance, with the demarcation of *hsiang* and the ensuing *hsiang* elections coming next. (NCNA, June 21, 1953, p. 15.)

In Szechwan, local authorities in all areas reportedly had "criticized and corrected" the practice of carrying out election work "in one big splash," which had alienated peasants, and adopted instead the method of "gradual penetration" (*JMJP,* June 19, 1953). The Kansu provincial election committee passed a resolution "changing the time and procedures for basic level elections in order to safeguard production and calamity relief" (*JMJP,* June 22, 1953). Other jurisdictions also ordered delays, and shortly after midsummer the declining frequency of press reports reflected the general slowdown in census and elections work. After hearing an explanation of the situation by Teng Hsiao-p'ing, the Central People's Government Council passed a resolution on September 18 calling for the postponement of the date of completion of basic level elections until the end of January, 1954, with further extensions for areas having special difficulties (NCNA, Sept. 18, 1953, p. 4). By the time January arrived, it was obvious that even this schedule would not be met, and a new priority was assigned to census and elections work to bring it to completion before another round of agricultural activities began in the spring of 1954.

During February and March, 1954, a considerable acceleration oc-

7. An aspect of the antibureaucratism drive calling for avoidance of too many tasks, too many meetings, too many government documents and forms, too many organizations, and too many simultaneous assignments for activists.

curred in the tempo of census work, as was shown by the rapid rise in the reported proportion of the population in the areas covered, but this was to be expected. The experimental phases of the work, which included sample investigations in selected villages and urban districts, were intended to test procedures, to develop measures appropriate to local situations, and to train supervisory staff and cadres, all of which took considerable time and effort without adding much to the percentage of the population in areas where census and election work had been completed. Once the full-scale census work got under way, it was usually carried out simultaneously in as many as one-third to one-half of the *hsien* in any given province; the transition from experimental to full-scale work inevitably involved a change of pace. Thus, the delay in census work during 1953 may not be construed as evidence of local negligence or loss of central control over local operations, nor should the acceleration of the effort in the spring of 1954 be taken as support for the view that, on orders from Peking, the census work was being hastily and heedlessly rushed to completion.

Taeuber and Wang's conclusions that new orders were given at the start of 1954 to speed registration by "loosening the technical requirements of the original directions," and that 70 per cent of the total census figure was compiled under the new, "relaxed" regulations are based on a surmise as to when the new directives were issued and a misunderstanding of some of their provisions. The New China News Agency (NCNA) release of March 10, 1954, which gives the only available information on the contents of the new directives, does not specify their date of promulgation but merely states that they were issued "recently." In Communist China, directives for mass campaigns are usually given prompt and complete press coverage, so that local authorities, cadres, activists, and the population at large can begin at once to comply with their provisions, but the present case is ambiguous. Taeuber and Wang apparently assume that, since the directives observe that census work had covered 29 per cent of the population by the end of 1953, and should cover the remaining 70-some per cent during the spring of 1954, the directives must have been issued "early in January 1954" (1960b, p. 285).

But even if the new directives had been issued promptly upon the compilation of progress reports as of the end of 1953, they could have been issued no earlier than the latter part of January, if the interval between reference date and time of issuance of other progress reports is any guide. For example, a report that basic level elections had been carried out in areas with about 18 per cent of the total population as of the middle of December, 1953, did not appear until January 2, 1954 (*TKP,* Jan. 3, 1954). A figure indicating that elections had been completed in areas with about 24 per cent of the population as of the end of January, 1954, was released only on February 19 (*JMJP,* Feb. 20, 1954). Apparently, compilation of progress reports required from two to three weeks.[8] If such lapses were common for press releases where coverage figures were the main feature and timeliness was important, longer intervals may have been involved in the case of the supplementary census directives, in which coverage figures were incidental.

Another approach to the question of the timing of the new directives is to examine other news items on census work both before and after the March 10th (1954) NCNA release to see whether or at what point the instructions and slogans in the directives began to influence the wording of local progress reports. Ordinarily when such directives are issued, their particulars are immediately and widely echoed in other press dispatches, since local authorities are eager to show prompt compliance. In the case of these directives, however, this approach yields no positive clues. One reason is that most of their instructions and slogans were not new; they had already appeared either in the original census directives or in other press reports in April, May, or June of 1953.[9] But even those recommendations in the new directives for which no previous mention can be found—making the registration areas smaller, increasing the number of mobile registration stations, registering the particulars of migrants as of the time of registration, and letting the office clerks adjust Chinese ages—are rarely repeated in other press items, even after March 10, 1954. Some were apparently disregarded.

From the latter part of January through early April, 1954, numerous local meetings and conferences were held throughout China, in the course of which supplementary local directives and instructions were issued, the high points of which were sometimes discussed in the press. The local regulations published by the Canton municipal census office on January 23 do not specifically refer to the new directives or contain any provisions that are clearly based on them (*KCJP,* Jan. 23, 1954 b). A central census office release of March 21, 1954, states that the provincial census office of Hopei had issued a directive on February 20, but its five principal points as summarized in the release include none of the unique recommendations of the new directives (Central Population . . . Office, 1954). Reports of meetings held by Kwangtung provincial census office on April 4-7, 1954, which were attended by "comrades" from the central office, repeat some of the key phrases in the new directives and were obviously

8. In another instance, toward the end of March, the interval was 11 days for a progress report on the census work and 9 days for one on election work.

9. The injunctions to "do a good job," transfer more cadres, perfect organization, strengthen leadership, carry out supervision and inspection, adopt simple methods for convenience of the masses, prevent carelessness, coordinate with production, coordinate with election work, take account of local conditions, and stress importance of census work for national economic development had all appeared for the first time early in 1953.

influenced by them, but do not repeat the optional shortcuts for registering migrants and correcting ages (Kwangtung Prov. Pop. . . . Office, 1954). Nevertheless, the old themes revived by the new directives appeared with increasing frequency in other news items from about the last week in February, 1954, which may indicate approximately when the directives were circulated.

The significance of precisely dating the new regulations derives largely from the presumption that they were intended as a call for haste at the expense of quality; if this were the case, it would be important to know what proportion of the census-taking was carried out under their influence. However, there is nothing in the published summary of their contents to indicate that they would have had much effect on the quality of the census fieldwork. They did call for greater speed in completing the tasks of population enumeration and registration, but this was to be accomplished mainly by administrative expediting and the assignment of additional personnel to the work.

The new regulations did not call for much loosening of requirements. The principal concession involving a possible sacrifice of the standards required by the original directives was the suggestion (somewhat ambiguous as worded in the NCNA release) that the "mobile" population might be registered according to its "circumstances" at the time of registration, without referring back to the critical date. Presumably the term "mobile" refers to those members of the migrant population who had no permanent residence or were constantly on the move.[10] The original census regulations of April 6, 1953 stated:

> When a person has moved out of his original domicile and has not yet found a new domicile, or has no definite domicile, he shall be registered as a permanent resident of the place where he is at the time of the registration, with his certificate of removal, or any other such identity paper, marked to that effect. (NCNA, April 6, 1953b, p. 33 [Article 8, Section 4].)

What is meant by "circumstances" is not clear, but presumably it refers to place of residence and household composition, both of which would have been extremely difficult to adjust back to the status on the critical date in the case of persons with unstable spatial and social connections. The suggested simplification probably did not apply to age, which, as the very next instruction makes clear, was still to be given as of the critical date, by a calculation no more difficult for migrants than for nonmigrants. The new provision on computation of ages was designed to allow for the lapse of time since the preparation of the original age-conversion table, which, if used without adjustment, would put ages off by one year. It

10. The same Chinese expression (*liu-tung*) is used elsewhere in the release in the phrase "mobile registration stations."

also allowed harassed population registration personnel who found it difficult to apply the conversion system at the time of registration to record the date of birth according to the Chinese calendar in the "remarks" column for subsequent editing, a provision that probably would, if anything, have increased the accuracy of age recording.[11]

Aside from asking that more cadres be assigned to the job and that closer supervision of the work be instituted, one of the main suggestions made in the directives was that a "simple method of registration should be adopted for the convenience of the masses." The principal simplification was that instead of heads of household being required to report to the single fixed registration center in each electoral district, substations should be established and mobile registration stations should visit the people at their place of work so that spring plowing and production need not be interrupted. This point is not made clear in the quotations and interpretations of the source provided by Taeuber and Wang, from which it would be inferred that all simplifications involved less, rather than more, procedural elaboration and were for the convenience of the officials rather than that of the "masses." [12]

On the whole, the provisions described in the NCNA news release would not have affected adversely the quality of the census work but would probably have improved it if carried out literally. Whether they were in fact carried out carefully and with positive results, and whether the directives themselves contained other less positive provisions not mentioned in the release, are, of course, not ascertainable, but at least there is no warrant in the NCNA article for the supposition that local authorities had been told to sacrifice quality of work for the sake of speed.

No source is cited by Taeuber and Wang in support of their claim that local census workers and officials were given population totals for the areas they were to enumerate. This inference may have been drawn from the fact that, according to the election law, local election committees were to subdivide their areas into election districts on the basis of administrative convenience and the ratio of population per delegate to the local people's congress (NCNA, April 7, 1953, p. 11). They also seem to have

11. Taeuber and Wang say that "there were also relaxations of the requirements for computing and entering age" (1960b, p. 286). Though not literally incorrect, this would seem to imply that age was not henceforth to be determined with as much care as before, which is not the case.

12. For example, Taeuber and Wang say that "in rural areas, publicity, registration, and verification were to be done simultaneously" (1960b, p. 286), but the original source may more completely and accurately be rendered: "Rural villages where spring plowing and production work are heavy may adopt the method of setting up small registration units, increasing the number of mobile registration stations and carrying out propaganda, registration, and recheck simultaneously with production. Cities not affected by spring plowing and production work may carry out registration according to the specifications laid down in the original regulations" (*JMJP*, March 11, 1954b).

concluded from the mention in a second NCNA release of March 10, 1954, of a *Simplified Handbook on Population Statistics of the Nation,* compiled by the Ministry of Interior in January, 1953, that this item must have been in possession of local authorities prior to the start of census fieldwork (1960b, p. 284).[13]

To sustain the Taeuber and Wang argument at this point, it is not enough merely to show that the Ministry of Interior had issued a handbook of local population figures giving a national total only a little below the census figure, and that this handbook was used by authorities in Peking for comparisons with local census reports in March, 1954. It must also be shown that these figures were provided (presumably by authorities in Peking, or else local authorities would not uniformly have used them) to local census offices, and that they were either used as guides or controls in the course of the fieldwork or were reported back to Peking, perhaps with some adjustment to allow for interim increase, in lieu of actual fieldwork.

The most convincing proof of the first demonstration would consist of showing that the figures from the handbook were used in defining election districts or in compiling the census returns locally, but this is impossible with the evidence available. The next best proof would be to show that early progress reports used the new, higher population figures rather than the lower figures from the Republic of China Ministry of Interior, which were current in the early years of the Chinese Communist regime. Here the proof is difficult, because census progress reports did not cite many population figures until after the experimental work was completed and full-scale census work had begun. The populations covered during the experimental phases were generally too small to be reported as a measure of progress. The population figures cited during the full-scale census work, which got under way in some areas in the fall of 1953, often covered only parts of a province or of several provinces and municipalities, and were not accompanied by estimates as to what percentage of the unit total the population covered so far was supposed to represent.

Only two references have been found that indicate clearly what magnitudes were being used prior to the start of full scale census work; both are NCNA items released in September, 1953, referring to regional populations. The first is an item from Peking which predicts that within that month elections will be held among "one-fifth of Southwest China's popu-

13. The NCNA release noted that census returns for parts of seven provinces and the Inner Mongolia Autonomous Region averaged 4.1 per cent higher than the figures given in the handbook (*JMJP,* March 11, 1954a). The Soviet census adviser, S. K. Krotevich, who was in China during the census-taking, refers to a compilation of data as of January 1, 1953, by the Ministry of Interior which yielded a mainland population total of just under 570 million. Presumably the two sources refer to the same item (Krotevich, 1957, pp. 93-94).

lation, or some 15 million" (NCNA, Sept. 8, 1953, p. 26). This would imply a total population of about 75 million for the region, which is much closer to the 1947 Republic of China total of 70 million than it is to either the 1953 census total of 98 million or to the total of 90 million given in the December, 1953, edition of the *Provincial Atlas of the People's Republic of China.*[14] Probably 70 million was the base figure used. The second reference is an item from Shanghai giving the population of East China as 140 million, which is the 1947 Republic of China total (NCNA, Sept. 21, 1953).

News items from about February, 1954, onward seem generally to have used higher population figures. For example, an item of March 13 (*JMJP,* March 13, 1954b) giving figures as of the end of February puts the population of Szechwan at "over 56 million," well below the census total of 62 million but close to the *Atlas* figure of 57 million, which may have approximated the Ministry of Interior figure. An item from Kaifeng on March 29 says that elections in Honan had reached 20 million people by March 23 and would reach another 20 million by mid-April (NCNA, March 29, 1954); the implied total of 40 million is the same as given in the *Atlas,* though still below the census figure of 44 million. An item from Peking on March 29 gives absolute figures as specific percentages of the total population of the country, implying a figure of just under 570 million in one instance and about 575 million in another (Peking radio, March 29, 1954). An item from Wuhan on March 30 gives a population figure for about a third of the basic-level units in the central south region that implies a total close to that of the census (NCNA, March 30, p. 23).

On the other hand, the southwest region, for which the 1947 population figures were still being used in September, 1953, was reported to have completed election work in 96.8 per cent of its basic-level units by the end of February, 1954, though the population of these units was given only as "over 71 million" (*JMJP,* March 13, 1954b). By March 20, when the census and registration in the southwest were said to be "almost completed," a population of 76,500,000 had been enumerated (NCNA, April 5, 1954, p. 32). By April 20, the elections were said to have reached areas in the southwest with a population of 90 million, which was "99.2 per cent" of the total population of the region (NCNA, April 27, 1954, p. 26), implying a figure still well below the final census total of 98 million. The percentage increases over 1952 figures that are indicated by census results in the northeast, in a dispatch of March 25 from Mukden, are so high as to raise some doubt about whether the 1952 figures were actually recent compilations, and serious doubt that they would have been

14. *Atlas,* 6th ed., Dec. 1953. The overall mainland total given in this source is 543 million, somewhat less than the figure given by Krotevich for the Ministry of Interior compilation (see footnote 12).

of any use as controls, let alone for purposes of borrowing instead of enumerating.[15] Most of the national, regional, and provincial progress reports gave only the populations counted in the areas covered, or population figures and numbers of basic level units, or numbers of basic level units and the percentages of the total number of such units within the area reporting.[16]

The infrequent use of control population totals in progress reports, along with the fact that 1952 and 1948 figures were used as often as those for January, 1953, casts doubt on the surmise that the Ministry of Interior's 1953 handbook was in the possession of many of the local units or was used by them, with or without central direction, to establish target figures for local enumeration efforts. It is doubtful whether enough copies of the handbook were published to allow for distribution to the *hsien* level. The handbook is never mentioned among the numerous reports of published materials issued to local level census and elections cadres by the provincial census offices during the experimental work in 1953. In any case, it is apparent that the higher population figures in the compilations of 1952 and 1953 were not used even by the regional and central offices until the trend of local census reports had given them definite confirmation, in about March, 1954. This is wholly consistent with statements made subsequently by census official Pai Chien-hua, Soviet adviser Krotevich, and other writers, to the effect that, though the central authorities were aware of higher local figures prior to the census, they tended to distrust them until the census results were available. This does not mean, of course, that local officials would have been dissuaded from using their own previous figures in the course of census work; the question of when and how these figures originated and what relation they may have had to the census must be taken up later. But the evidence just presented does contradict inferences that local officials had been directed by Peking to return high population figures, or that officials at any level were implicated in a general conspiracy to produce fraudulent census results.

RESEMBLANCE TO EARLIER FIGURES

The statistical part of the Taeuber and Wang argument purports to confirm the inference that the 1953 census figures were actually based on figures available before the census, by showing that their antecedents were

15. Parts of Jehol (now divided between Hopei, Liaoning, and Inner Mongolia), Sungkiang (now part of Heilungkiang); and Kirin provinces reported figures 6.99 per cent higher than those for 1952, those in Sungkiang alone being 11.78 per cent higher; and figures for various cities ranged from 10.54 per cent higher for Tsitsihar to 71.49 per cent higher for Fou-hsin. The dispatch indicates that part of the increase is due to better data collection (NCNA, March 25, 1954).

16. *Hsin-hua jih-pao,* April 1, 1954; *JMJP,* Feb. 20, April 26, and April 27, 1954; *NFJP,* April 3 and April 20, 1954; NCNA, March 13 and April 9, 1954; *TKP,* Jan. 3, March 18, and March 23, 1954.

historical provincial totals going back as far as 1850. The essential evidence given is putative resemblances between some of the 1953 census provincial totals and those reported in former times; and the argument is that since these involve too many cases to be dismissed as coincidence and since no circumstantial explanation will account for them, it must be concluded that the relationships are artifact. Since it is argued earlier in the article that all previous population figures are without empirical basis, the demonstration of a connection between them and the 1953 census also discredits the latter, leading directly to the verdict that "China remains 'the country without statistics' " (Taeuber and Wang, 1960b, pp. 290-301).

The data consist of six sets of population figures for the 18 provinces of "China Proper" and Taiwan—the Ch'ing figures for 1850 and the investigation of 1909-1911, the Republic of China figures for 1928 and 1947, the figures from the December, 1953, edition of the *Atlas,* and the census figures. Setting aside for the moment the discussion of relationships between the *Atlas* figures and the census, which involves some special problems, the important comparisons are those between the 1953 census figures and the first four sets of totals. The underlying assumption is that, since the historical figures have been shown to have little connection with empirical fact, there should be no congruence between them and an actual count except by accident.

This is, in effect, a kind of null hypothesis, to test in this instance the significance of similarities rather than differences. But the test has two conspicuous defects. In the first place, even if the historical figures and the census of 1953 were subject to varying and considerable margins of error and artifact, there would be no reason to assume that either set is absolutely unrelated to reality. Therefore, one cannot assume that, except for "design of estimation" (Taeuber and Wang, 1960b, p. 298), they should bear only a random resemblance to each other. In the second place, the earlier of the Ch'ing figures is presumably separated from the census figures by 50 years of catastrophe and another 50 years of limited population growth, while the earlier of the Republic of China figures preceded 25 years of limited growth for the country as a whole, held back in some areas by prolonged periods of war and revolution. These circumstances might have placed the 1953 census figures in the proximity of earlier ones even if all of them were subject to considerable and unequal degrees of systematic error. If this is granted, the null hypothesis is not appropriate to the point at issue.

If factors other than chance or borrowing may account for some degree of similarity in magnitude between provincial figures for different years, the essential question is what degree or type of resemblance is required to prove that borrowing is the *only* acceptable explanation? Unfortunately, the Taeuber and Wang analysis does not include a definition, statistical or otherwise, of what is to be regarded as a "similarity," "relation," "bridge," or "linkage."[17] The choice of terms adds to the ambiguity, for none of them clearly denotes suspicion of borrowing, yet without such an implication the argument would be irrelevant to the final conclusion. From context, it appears that what is actually intended by these terms is a relationship between an earlier and a later provincial figure sufficiently close to suggest that the second was based on the first and not produced by an independent field operation. Moreover, these cases must be prevalent enough to attach doubt to a major portion of the 1953 census results.

One kind of resemblance, not uncommon in Chinese population figures, is simple identity of the digits. Such identities sometimes reach to the last digit, but more often they extend only as far as the thousands or ten thousands, with the remaining digits at variance or rounded off. Sometimes the identity is interrupted at the ten-thousands or hundred-thousands digit, suggesting that the original total has been adjusted by addition or subtraction of a round figure. How much identity is required for reasonable suspicion? Taeuber and Wang give several examples of borrowing of the 1850 figures in the compilation of the figures for 1909-11: for Szechwan the respective totals are 44,164,000 and 44,140,000; for Kwangtung they are 28,182,000 and 28,011,000. In these cases the identity reaches only to the hundred thousands in the first case and the millions in the second. But the percentage differences are so small in both cases—0.05 per cent for Szechwan and 0.6 per cent for Kwangtung—that under the circumstances the inference of borrowing is beyond doubt.

However, in comparing the 1953 census figures with earlier figures, Taeuber and Wang find "similarities" where identity involves only the ten-millions digit, and in one instance a percentage difference in excess of 10 per cent.[18] With such generous criteria, the proof could hardly be said to err on the side of caution. Even so, relatively few resemblances are found. Still leaving aside the *Atlas* figures, the 1953 census provincial figures fall within plus or minus 10 per cent of those in the four sets from the Ch'ing and Republic of China periods in only 11 out of a possible 73 instances. If, following Taeuber and Wang, we count only positive differences, there are eight cases involving six provinces (see Table 1). If all 73 percentage difference figures are arrayed in a frequency distribution with 10 per cent class intervals, something roughly approximating a normal curve appears, with modal values at plus 20 to 30 per cent and with, at most, about two instances more than might be expected by chance in the interval for 0 to plus 10 per cent (see Table 2).

Nevertheless, Taeuber and Wang claim to find connections with

17. This point was noted by Prof. Frank Lorimer in the discussion at the Milbank meeting. (Taeuber and Wang, 1960b, pp. 307-308)

18. The 1953 total for Chekiang province exceeded the 1928 total by 10.8 per cent.

TABLE 1

PERCENTAGE DIFFERENCES BETWEEN 1953 CENSUS FIGURES AND PREVIOUS OFFICIAL FIGURES FOR 18 PROVINCES OF "CHINA PROPER" AND TAIWAN

Region and province	Ch'ing Dynasty 1850	1909-11	Republic of China 1928	1947
North				
Shantung	47.5	65.4	70.5	22.0
Hopei	77.1	55.1	32.7	29.4
Shansi	−5.4	41.7	17.1	−6.0
Northwest				
Shensi	31.2	96.7	34.6	51.7
Kansu	−16.3	175.1	105.8	85.3
East				
Kiangsu	7.5	83.3	39.1	14.5
Anhwei	−19.3	87.0	39.7	36.1
Chekiang	−23.8	26.5	10.8	16.5
Central				
Honan	84.8	69.3	44.7	51.1
Hupei	−17.6	0.5	4.1	28.3
Kiangsi	−31.5	−0.1	−17.5	34.5
Hunan	61.2	42.0	5.5	28.0
South				
Fukien	3.7 (Fukien and Taiwan combined)	5.1	30.5	18.3
Taiwan		......	......	18.9
Kwangtung	23.4	24.1	7.2	19.3
Kwangsi	150.0	153.1	43.3	34.0
Southwest				
Szechwan	41.1	41.2	29.8	29.5
Kweichow	176.7	72.8	2.0	43.3
Yünnan	136.9	142.3	26.4	93.5

Source:
(Taeuber and Wang, 1960b, Table 1, p. 292) except for Kiangsi (see text).

former figures for all but 4 of the 18 provinces, mainly by what they call "multiple similarities," which are obtained by combining the figures for provinces that had both higher and lower totals in 1850; by combining those for provinces whose 1850 and 1953 figures differ by more than

TABLE 2

FREQUENCY DISTRIBUTION OF PERCENTAGE DIFFERENCES FROM TABLE 1

Per cent difference	Number of cases
Total cases	73
−40 to −30	......
−30 to −20	2
−20 to −10	4
−10 to 0	3
0 to 10	8
10 to 20	7
20 to 30	10
30 to 40	9
40 to 50	8
50 to 60	3
60 to 70	3
70 to 80	3
80 to 90	4
90 to 100	2
100 to 110	1
110 to 120	......
120 to 130	......
130 to 140	1
140 to 150	1
Over 150	4

Source:
Table 1.

10 per cent with those for which the differences are less than 10 per cent; and by showing that the increase rate implied by the 1850 and 1928 combined population totals for several provinces was almost the same as that for the same combination between 1928 and 1953.[19] Though not clearly stated, these methods implicitly assume that although the 1953 figures were actually based on the 1850 figures or subsequent increase rates indicated in official figures, either changes in the provincial boundaries or manipulations of the 1953 figures by central census personnel

19. Details of the three "multiple similarities" are as follows: The sum of the 1953 census provincial totals for Kansu, Shensi, and Shansi was only 1 per cent above the corresponding sum for 1850; the corresponding sums for Kiangsu, Kiangsi, and "Fukien-Taiwan" differ by "less than 10 per cent"; the sum for Kwangtung, Kwangsi, Yünnan, and Szechwan in 1928 was 23 per cent above that for 1850, and the sum for 1953 was 24 per cent above that for 1928 (Taeuber and Wang, 1960b, p. 299).

have masked these connections, which can be revealed only when figures for several provinces are combined.

If boundary changes are to be part of the explanation, the provinces must be contiguous, and the populations involved in the adjustments would presumably be small. However, in the one "multiple similarity" in which the adjustments would be small enough to be reasonable, the provinces involved are not contiguous.[20] In another case, the differences are too large, requiring a reallocation of about one-quarter of the 1850 population of Shensi betwen Kansu and Shansi. None of the "multiple similarities" involves only provinces from a single region according to the regional administrative system in effect at the time of the 1953 census; hence all manipulations would have had to take place at the central office.[21] Here the implication is that responsible officials reapportioned part of the figures for groups of provinces without regard to regional organization, in order to conceal resemblances to the 1850 figures. This hypothesis supposes that the manipulators exercised great cunning and recklessness in reallocating the combined provincial totals but lacked the wit and originality to depart from the 1850 figures or the 1850-1928 increase rate in order to prevent detection of their artifice.

Moreover, the broad criteria for "multiple similarities" allow considerable scope for ingenuity in assembling fortuitous—and suspicious—combinations. The adventitious quality of this method is apparent in the fact that one of the Taeuber and Wang "multiple similarities" resulted from a clerical error in their tabulation of the 1953 census figures.[22] It can also be demonstrated by the ease with which other "multiple similarities" can be devised. For example, if the six provinces that had larger population figures in 1850 than in 1953 are combined with a careful selection of provinces having larger figures in 1953 than in 1850, it is possible to devise a "multiple similarity" involving 10 contiguous provinces and nearly half the total population count for 1953, with a combined

20. The provinces in this case are Kiangsi, Kiangsu, and "Fukien-Taiwan," but Kiangsi and Kiangsu are not contiguous.

21. Yet a directly contrary implication is implicit in the observation by Taeuber and Wang that three of the four provinces for which they could find "no specific patterns of differences" had received "specific assistance from Peiping in 1954." The unspecified implication here is that the provinces listed were the only ones under central inspection during census-taking and that they tended to report figures for which no suspicious antecedents could be found. Presumably, then, falsification took place at the provincial level wherever central inspection was lacking. (1960b, pp. 299-300)

22. The 1953 population of Shanghai (6,204,000), which, like that for Peking and Tientsin, was given separately in the source, had to be added to its appropriate province, but was inadvertently included both in Kiangsu, where it belongs, and in Kiangsi. Since both provinces were included in the comparison, the population of Shanghai is counted twice. Without the extra Shanghai, the difference changes from +3 per cent to —4 per cent. No other similarities involving negative percentages are cited, apparently because the hypothesis does not suppose the Peking authorities would let a 1953 census figure slip *below* the corresponding 1850 total.

percentage difference 1850-1953 of only 0.13 per cent.[23] One can also show that the figures for the contiguous provinces of Kiangsu, Anhwei, and Chekiang declined by 31.6 per cent between 1850 and 1928, and increased by 31.6 per cent between 1928 and 1953. Before concluding that such relationships are "striking," however, one would want to see whether similar combinations could not be obtained from a table of random numbers having the same range of magnitudes.

Having established what they call "consistent patterns of similarities and differences" between the provincial figures from the 1953 census and those for 1850 and 1928 (1960b, pp. 300-301), Taeuber and Wang first reject the hypothesis that all of the alternate series are accurate counts (one that few analysts of the population of China today would seriously entertain), then reject the hypothesis that the resemblances are a matter of coincidence, since coincidence could hardly apply to "the total picture in all China and the provinces." The latter argument would have to be accepted if the resemblances were as numerous as Taeuber and Wang claim, or as close as they seem to regard them. But as has already been indicated, the operational definition of "similarities," though broad enough to embrace large differences, falls far short of engulfing "all China" or even the majority of the provinces. It is the "multiple similarities" that broaden the coverage of the argument to the point where coincidence may be excluded, so that the whole case rests upon the validity of that device. Without "multiple similarities," Taeuber and Wang would have to confront the one hypothesis that would have occurred first to most analysts: That both similarities and differences between provincial figures from the 1953 census and those from earlier records were due to varying degrees of error in all the figures and to the vicissitudes of population increase and decline during the intervening years. This is, in effect, an affirmative and somewhat amplified statement of the null hypothesis mentioned earlier. It should not be rejected without an adequate test.

In conclusion, the challenge posed by Taeuber and Wang to the credibility of the 1953 census rests in part on interpretations and inferences that are contradicted by a full review of the relevant sources, and in part on statistical improvisations that do not constitute statistical proof. Their challenge cannot be sustained upon closer examination of the evidence.

However, the rejection of the challenge in its total form must not be mistaken for a vindication of the accuracy of the 1953 census figures.

23. The 10 provinces are Shansi, Kansu, Anhwei, Chekiang, Hupei, Kiangsi, Shensi, Kiangsu, Kwangtung, and Szechwan, which had a reported population of 285,067,000 in 1850 and 285,426,000 in 1953. The latter figure is 49 per cent of the 1953 census total. If geographical contiguity is no object, the combined populations of Hupei, Kiangsi, Anhwei, Kansu, Kweichow, Shensi, and Yünnan total 136,218,000 for 1850 and 136,226,000 for 1953, giving identity of digits to the hundred thousands, and a net difference of only 8,000, or 0.006 per cent, between the totals.

Limiting the choice to two alternatives—the census was either accurate or fraudulent—is a false antithesis. Accuracy of field investigations and estimation alike is never an all-or-nothing affair. Similarly, one need not conclude either that the census figures were entirely or largely borrowed from previous counts or that there was no borrowing or deception in the compilation and reporting of figures. Deception of higher authorities, adjustment of reported figures, concealment of implausible results found in investigation are not unheard of elsewhere in the world, and the central census officials in Peking in 1953-54 were probably incapable of detecting evidence of such activities among the *hsien* and provincial figures pouring into their offices in late 1953 and early 1954. The essential questions are matters of degree, and to these we must return a little later on.

So far as the 1953 census is concerned, the most valuable contribution of the Taeuber and Wang analysis is the fact that it calls attention to the upward revisions of provincial figures just prior to the census activities, and raises questions as to what connection the census work in local areas may have had with previous population investigations conducted during the 1949-53 period. It is to these questions that we turn next.

PRE-CENSUS POPULATION INVESTIGATIONS

What was the basis of the upward revision of provincial figures? Taeuber and Wang, following an ambiguous attribution by Krotevich, surmised that they were "administration revisions" by *hsien* and provincial officials, possibly based on traditional *pao-chia* population records from the Republic of China period "with appropriate estimates of omissions" (1960b, pp. 296, 298).[24] The official explanation was that they were based on field investigations conducted in connection with land reform and other activities.[25] The most explicit statement available was contained in a news release by the propaganda section of the Ministry of Interior in April, 1953:

24. Krotevich said that the State Statistical Bureau had "collected and correlated data from current administrative records of population from all parts of the country," which may have been literally correct as far as it went, but Krotevich fails to indicate what types of activities produced the sharp upward revisions in these records. Since he was trying to give a complete picture of the background of the census, it seems likely that he was unaware of the official explanations given in the Chinese press at the time, or he would have been careful to repeat them. (1957, p. 93).

25. Taueber and Wang give no indication of having noted this explanation, though it was given by census official Pai Chien-hua at the time of the final census announcement in a source that Taeuber and Wang cite in another connection (Pai, 1954, p. 32). Taeuber and Wang usually refer to the source of revisions as "administrative reports," "administrative records," or "administrative officials," describe the changes in the local figures as "administrative revisions," and the results as "administrative figures." In one place (1960b, p. 296) they say of these revisions that "Experience elsewhere indicates that operations such as those in China between 1950 and 1954 are not likely to yield accurate counts," but a little later they admit that they do not know the basis for the revisions (p. 300).

. . . In the past three years preliminary population investigation work has been done by the people's governments at all levels during the land reform and other mass movements. In addition to these, other specific government policies, such as distribution of land and agricultural tax exemption according to the number of persons in a household, encouraged the people to report the correct numbers of persons without concealment. These measures enabled us to obtain a figure which was closer to the truth year after year and which exceeded the traditional figure of 475 million persons. However, these population data and figures are still incomplete and inaccurate. Therefore, it is necessary to make a unified and scientific population investigation and registration throughout the whole country. (*JMJP*, April 30, 1953.)

The same explanation in abreviated form was given by Pai Chien-hua at the time of the release of final census results, with the added information that the Ministry of Interior had worked over the local population reports six times between the beginning of 1950 and the end of 1952, but that the results of these compilation efforts were never released because there had been no scientific general census (Pai, 1954, p. 32).

The first questions that must be answered are those raised by the official explanations: What was the nature of the various field investigations conducted prior to the census of 1953? Were the upward revisions of provincial figures made locally in connection with these activities? Is there any evidence to corroborate the official implications that these figures were not wholly trusted by the central authorities?

The pre-census population investigations were mainly of three types: (1) the security police investigations in connection with the establishment of urban population registers; (2) the rural population investigations conducted during or in preparation for the "land reform" movement; and (3) investigations conducted in connection with the revision and refinement of rates of agricultural taxation.

Urban Population Registers, 1949-1953.

When the Chinese Communists took over the control of the mainland in 1949, the remains of a system of police control, including forms, procedures, and records, were still to be found in many of the major cities. These were promptly abolished by the new regime and replaced by a new system, which differed from the old mainly in that household "books" were substituted for the old household lists, and oral reporting was to replace the large number of forms formerly required for reporting changes in household composition. The new system was instituted gradually, beginning with Peking, Shanghai, and possibly Tientsin in the fall of 1949, and was extended to other cities and towns during 1950 and 1951. In Peking some investigations were carried out during June, July, and August of 1949, the old regulations were abolished in July, old forms were declared invalid as of November 18, new regulations were published about the same time, and, after a week of propaganda, the installation of the new system of household books was carried out between November 24 and December 23, 1949 (*JMJP,* Nov. 17, Dec. 4 [a, b], 1949; K'o Fu, 1950). The people were required to purchase their own blank copies of the new household books, which were then filled out on a door-to-door basis by the security police registration teams, collected, stamped, and returned to them later. The stated purposes of the new system were threefold: (1) to ascertain the "place of origin" of the people, (2) to obtain household statistics for purposes of planning urban development and services, and (3) "to further strengthen the revolutionary order of the People's Capital" (*JMJP,* Dec. 4, 1949a). The authorities were well aware that despite the extremely ambitious propaganda program many people would continue to avoid registration; reassurances that all was for the best were accompanied by notices of penalties for failure to report, for making false reports, and for illegal use of the household books and other documents. But the authorities were generally pleased with the results. Not only did many persons not previously registered come forward, but a number of "Nationalist agents," military deserters, "dangerous elements," persons who had made false reports, and persons who had tried to avoid registering were discovered in the course of the investigation, suggesting that it was conducted with some thoroughness.[26]

Comparable reports are not available for other cities, probably because locally published press accounts were not picked up by national news channels and have not found their way into research files outside China. But from fragmentary accounts of the time, and retrospective accounts in subsequent years, it appears that similar efforts were made in Shanghai, Canton, Hangchow, Wuhan, Chungking, Harbin, Antung, Soochow, Tihwa (Urumchi), and Liuchow; and this list is doubtless far from complete. In November, 1951, the Kwangtung provincial administration issued orders for the strengthening of control over population movements in all *hsien* cities and towns and in rural market towns. The press release noted that the new regulations had been enforced for a time early in 1950 but had been suspended; now they were to be reinstated and observed more strictly, with a new registration of population and a rechecking of public accounts. Sixteen towns were mentioned as having begun the new effort in October, 1951 (*Hsing-tao jih-pao,* Nov. 2, 1951). From these indications, it may be inferred that the new registration system was probably installed in most large urban centers and may have penetrated to the

26. There were 208 "Nationalist agents," 1,603 military deserters, 12,676 "dangerous elements," 15,338 would-be evaders of the present system, and 99,829 persons who had made false reports or avoided registration under the old system (K'o Fu, 1950; *JMJP,* Feb. 4, 1950).

smaller towns in at least some provinces. If so, many city and town administrations were probably compiling and reporting new population figures during these years.

The quality of the new figures would certainly have been questionable. Though varying in completeness with the effectiveness of the local police, they presumably bore a much closer relationship to the actual numbers of the population than did the figures from the Nationalist records dating back to 1947 and 1948. But few cities would have been able to mount as strict a police registration sweep as Peking, and if there were efforts to evade the new registration system in Peking, in spite of the elaborate propaganda to win popular confidence, there may have been similar and perhaps more successful efforts in other cities. All persons having any connection with the previous government and all whose incomes or occupations classified them as "bourgeois" would have had ample reason to fear investigation by the security police. They would have been slow to credit the propaganda claim that the new system was not for oppression and extortion, but to bring political and economic benefits to the people.

Those who did put their trust in these promises were shortly disappointed, for throughout 1951 there were signs of a general tightening of controls in both urban and rural areas.[27] In rural areas the pace of land reform was accelerated during 1951; and in the first six months of 1952 the urban areas were plunged into the throes of the "three-anti" [28] and "five-anti" movements, with their tribunals, investigations of social backgrounds and private property, and "tiger hunts." Thus, before the new system was a year old, it was being used as a control device in some of the harshest repression campaigns in the history of the regime, which would certainly not have enhanced its dependability as a source of population data.

The utility of the system for either purpose may have been limited by the fact that, initially at least, regulations and the formats of household

27. In May, 1951, regulations were issued on the inspection of train and airplane crews and passengers entering or leaving the country. In August, new regulations were issued regarding entry and departure of overseas Chinese, registration of patrons of hotels and lodging houses, and registration of people who had been members of "reactionary parties and corps, secret service organizations, and other counterrevolutionary elements." In November, new regulations were issued governing exit, entry, and residence of foreign nationals (*Ch'ang-chiang jih-pao,* Aug. 13, 1951; NCNA, May 26, Aug. 2, Aug. 4, Nov. 30, 1951.)

On August 18, 1951, the Kwangtung provincial government was reported to have ordered the *hsien* of the province to redemarcate areas of districts, *hsiang,* and villages, to name previously unnamed streets, and to placard houses throughout rural areas. The purpose was frankly to increase the degree of political control. The dispatch says: "In the past, the roads in rural areas of Kwangtung were not named and the houses not placarded. The *pao-chia* system was really not strict enough. The household system now enforced by the authorities is ten thousand times more strict." See *Hsing-tao jih-pao,* Aug. 19, 1951.

28. The "three-anti" movement of 1952 was a drive intended to wipe out corruption, waste, and bureaucratism among government personnel. See also fn. 1.

books differed from one city to another; some cities required identity cards while others did not. In July, 1951, the central Ministry of Public Security issued general regulations on urban registration for the purpose of "maintaining civil peace and order, safeguarding the security of the people, and protecting their freedom of residence and movement" (NCNA, July 16, 1951). But standardization according to the general regulations would have required some time, and local variation was still permitted under the terms of Article II of the general regulations. It was July, 1953, before the public security bureau of Chungking announced suspension of the provisional regulations for household registration that had been passed in November, 1950, and issued new regulations consistent with the directive of July, 1951 (*Hsin-hua jih-pao,* July 21, 1953). Shanghai apparently did not conform to the new regulations until June, 1955 (*Hsin-wen jih-pao,* June 5, 1955). These delays in implementation of central regulations suggest that, whatever the energy devoted to the original installation of the system in each locality, not much priority was attached to keeping it up-to-date.

Even if the people had been completely beguiled by the assurances of the regime that if they told the truth they need not fear "settling of accounts," or if they had been uniformly intimidated by warnings to the effect that whatever they tried to conceal would eventually be found out and punished anyway (Liu Yü-ju, 1953), compliance with the regulations would not have been easy. There was a bewildering number of different time limits within which the various types of household changes had to be reported. For example, in Peking, whose regulations probably served as a national model prior to the issuance of general regulations, persons moving out were to report to the security police branch station three days before departure, in-migrants were to report within three days of arrival, births were to be reported within 15 days, deaths on the day of occurrence, marriages on the second day of the marriage, divorces on the second day after the divorce, divisions of one household into two households within three days of the division, mergers of two households into one three days prior to merging, persons lost on the same day on which they were lost, children adopted within two days of the adoption, new hirings on the first day of the new job, firings three days prior to discharge, changes of head of household three days prior to the change, and temporary visitors on the day of arrival (*JMJP,* Nov. 17, 1949). It is doubtful that the heads of household, upon whose initiative the system of reporting depended, could keep all these provisions in mind. Many would surely have found themselves in default by the time they reported.

Moreover, there were indications in later years that the security police registrars were sometimes lax, inept, and arrogant in dealing with those who attempted to report in observance of the system. In Urumchi the cadres failed to "pay serious attention" to the work (*Hsin-chiang jih-pao,*

Dec. 22, 1954), in Shanghai those who reported to the branch stations found them crowded and had to wait (Ch'eng Chou, 1955), and in Canton some police registration personnel were found guilty of "using pressure, giving orders, violating the law, and disobeying discipline, which alienated the masses from them" (*KCJP,* Aug. 6, 1956). Letters complaining of specific instances of bureaucracy and incompetence were published in the newspapers of Foochow, Canton, Heng-yang, Shenyang, Shanghai, Hangchow, Kirin, Sining, and Soochow.[29] Many of the foibles lampooned in these complains had to do with mistakes in recording name, occupation, place of origin, marital status, sex, and age, which would not have affected the number of persons listed in the registers, but they also attest to a general laxity on the part of the security police that surely would have discouraged the people from taking household reporting seriously.

In fact, public noncooperation seems to have been widespread, ranging from obstructing the efforts of the security police and falsifying the records to simply ignoring the system. Some people thought it was too bothersome, others thought household control was for bad people but not for law-abiding citizens, and many others simply failed to report births, deaths, visitors, and other changes. There were official admissions that the accuracy of population data was affected and population control impaired (*Ch'ang-chiang jih pao,* May 23, 1956; *Ch'ung-ch'ing jih-pao,* Aug. 11, 1956; *Hsin-chiang jih-pao,* Dec. 22, 1954. Major cities like Canton, which had started fairly early and developed a complex system of regulations to deal with special problems, repeatedly found it necessary to reorganize the system. Even after the 1953 census, during which special copies of the census form were prepared for retention by the local security police station in cities where the household system was "not yet well implemented" (NCNA, April 6, 1953b, p. 35), police were still being ordered out to do field checks.[30]

From the fragmentary information available, it is apparent that the registration system lapsed after each effort at resuscitation. Despite the claims that it was gradually being perfected, it is obvious that the ambitious and costly efforts to recheck household records and issue new books would not have been made unless the system was failing to meet the requirements of population control and statistical data. This was what might have been expected when a system requiring a fairly high level of sophisti-

29. Ch'en Hsüeh-ming, 1956; *Chi-lin jih-pao,* Nov. 1, 1956; *Ch'ing-hai jih-pao,* Dec. 6, 1956; *Fu-chien jih-pao,* Aug. 20, 1956; *Hang-chou jih-pao,* Oct. 28, 1956; *Heng-yang hsin-wen,* Aug. 29, 1956; *KCJP,* Aug. 26 and Nov. 28, 1956; *Lao-tung pao,* Oct. 5, 1956; *NFJP,* Sept. 4, 1956. The concentration of these letters in the latter half of 1956 suggests they were in the established tradition of sponsored spontaneity, but there is no reason to suppose that the negligence and incompetence they disclosed were not real or had made their first appearance during that year.

30. *An-tung jih-pao,* Aug. 7, 1956; *Ha-erh pin jih-pao,* Nov. 14, 1956; *Hsin Su-chou pao,* July 31, Aug. 9, 1956; *Kung-jen sheng-huo,* Dec. 13, 1956; *Liu-chou jih-pao,* Nov. 30, 1956; *NFJP,* July 11 and 14, 1955.

cation and willing cooperation on the part of the people was imposed by security police upon a population who could not have understood its technical aspects and who had both traditional and current reasons for regarding the police with distrust. In any case, what was supposed to have been a system of continuous population registers seems to have amounted to little more than a series of one-time police censuses separated by lapses in record-keeping.

Such a system could hardly have produced good figures, though they would certainly have been better than no figures and probably came much closer to actuality, even in their periods of neglect, than the Republic of China figures for the late 1940's. Also, it should be pointed out that economic planning as practiced by city administrations in China at this time required much less accuracy in data on numbers, age, and sex of the population than police surveillance required in the listing of names and addresses. The dissatisfaction with the system expressed by the authorities may not signify that it was equally useless for both purposes. The numbers it produced probably were well below the actual numbers of permanent residents in each case and even further below the numbers of de facto residents. Nonreporting after the registers were established and evasion during subsequent field checks would have resulted in underestimation of the levels of vital rates among the resident population, while failure to comply with regulations for reporting movement would have caused even greater underreporting of migrants, particularly those fugitives from land reform who took part in the "blind drift" into the cities that began to alarm the authorities in 1952. Some overcounting would have resulted from the failure to record deaths and the avoidance of moving-out procedures by intercity migrants who had been caught in previous sweeps and were anxious to disappear once more from the police files. But the net effect was probably heavily weighted on the side of an undercount. The authorities, though admitting that the figures were defective, used them out of necessity as the only data available, published them in local papers, and probably incorporated them in reports to provincial and central authorities. They are, therefore, the most likely basis for the revisions of urban population figures during the years 1949-53.

The "Land Reform" Population Investigations.

The land reform "movement" was the first major effort to reorganize Chinese rural society made by the Communist regime after it came to power. Actually, land reform was not new, having been carried out in the Communist-occupied areas long before 1949. Land reform methods included the drafting of central directives; their adaptation to local conditions in specific local procedures; the training of field teams of cadres, activists, and other personnel; the selection of certain units as experimental areas for preliminary training exercises; the summing up of experiences and modification of procedures; the general application of the program to large areas a parcel at a time; the ordering of recheck work in some areas; the dispatching of central investigation teams to review the work of local authorities; and the requirement of progress reports at every stage by local authorities. These procedures became standard for many later drives and programs, including the urban registration work of 1949-56, the census and elections work of 1953-54, and the rural registration work of 1954-57.

Despite all the efforts that went into the program, little is known of what actually happened in the various rural areas. This lack of information about the conduct of land reform may be due partly to the suppression of information on its more brutal aspects and perhaps partly to local cadres' efforts to avoid revealing to the central authorities how far their plans had miscarried. But there may also have been basic defects in the system of records and reporting, so that the central authorities could not know what actually was happening at the time or get a reliable summary after the event.[31]

The Agrarian Reform Law of 1950 contained no instructions on carrying out surveys of land and population, though it seems to have intended both, since confiscated land was to be allocated to landless peasants or peasants with small holdings within each *hsiang* according to the average holding in that unit (Agrarian Reform Law, pp. 5-6). This would have required figures on population and land within each *hsiang*. Moreover, some of the stipulations of the law called for detailed subclassification of types of land and crops, while others required investigation of the social and political backgrounds of the whole population, not only to determine Marxist "class" identities, but also to gather information on other details of personal life that would be considered in applying the law.

Despite the fact that the Agrarian Reform Law in its English version makes several references to landholdings in per capita terms, the context suggests that the framers were thinking of land allocations per *household*. That this may have been the measure used in the field in some areas is indicated by a complaint from Honan in 1950 that some landlords and peasants, in order to receive more land during the redistribution, had forced their young children to marry early in defiance of the new marriage law. In one instance, a 5-year-old boy was married to a 12-year-old

31. Years later a prominent official of the State Statistical Bureau commented in retrospect: ". . . After liberation, in the course of the heaven-and-earth-shaking land reform movement, in which 500 million peasants participated, Party committees at all levels and in all areas conducted many statistical investigations and collected a great deal of valuable data on subjects ranging from class status to population and from politics to economics. Yet, when the First National Peoples' Representatives Congress was convened in 1954, and we were about to prepare a resumé of this great land reform movement with its worldwide historical implications, we were unable to assemble comprehensive national statistical data that would give a complete picture of this great movement." See *Chia Ch'i-yün,* 1958 (p. 6).

girl (*TKP,* July 7, 1950b). Evidently early marriage qualified the young couple as a separate household to receive an allocation of land, in effect an addition to the landholdings of the boy's father.

However, available evidence indicates that at least in some areas there were detailed investigations of the population within households as well, and it is a reasonable presumption that this was in fact the rule. Many of the reports of population covered during land reform investigations give totals to the last digit, and local figures frequently give the breakdown by sex. In experimental work in 106 *hsiang* of Kansu province early in 1952, the total population, as well as males and females separately, were subclassified as landlords, rich peasants of semi-landlord status, other rich peasants, persons renting small parcels of land, middle peasants, poor peasants, hired farm laborers, workers and merchants, and others. There were also elaborate tabulations by social class of holdings of land, livestock, and other assets, as well as the all-important tables of confiscations and redistributions. The article presenting these tables also discussed the difficulties of assembling summary tables from the defective statistics submitted by local authorities and warned the cadres being trained in these experimental investigations of the importance of attaching priority to statistical work and avoiding discrepancies between tables.[32] In all this, what is most impressive is not the fact that there were errors in the statistical work, but that such elaborate demands were met as well as the tables suggest, and that they were not being modified. In fact, the presence of errors and anomalies in the tables is further evidence that the data were the result of actual fieldwork. Had the entries been fabricated or estimated on the basis of fragmentary information, or at least adjusted to conceal obvious defects before being sent to Lanchow, the discrepancies probably would have been eliminated prior to transmission.

32. In its summation, the report said: "The problems discovered in these statistical tables showed that attention was not being paid to statistical work in all areas. The importance of statistical work was not fully recognized, Statistical work was not considered as an important and specific task in summarizing the job. It was not taken seriously, but was carried out superficially and hastily. Some places did not even make reports. This is obviously not proper. We must understand that the way in which statistical work is carried out has great significance and a great effect on the accurate evaluation of the entire land reform movement, and on knowledge of the actual conditions for purposes of giving accurate guidance to large-scale production this coming spring and to various types of construction in the future. . . . For these reasons, we request that the leadership comrades in land reform committees at all levels treat statistical work seriously and conscientiously and organize the cadres for study so that they thoroughly understand the meaning of every form, every column, and every item and fill out the forms accurately and in detail without the slightest haste, and without leaving blank spaces (some were found in statistical tables that were submitted). Furthermore, they should not procrastinate in filling out the forms. After the forms are filled out they should be carefully examined by the leadership comrades in order to catch mistakes and correct errors so that they represent the actual conditions. Finally, we hope all areas will fill out the forms and submit reports to the provincial government in good time so that the data will not be scattered and lost" (Kansu Provincial Govt., 1952).

Although the procedures for investigation of population, land, and agricultural assets were not spelled out in the original provisions of the land reform law, many details of which had been left to local administrations to standardize within their own jurisdictions, there apparently were some supplementary directives from the central authorities during 1950, providing more explicit directions on various aspects of the program. In August, 1950, further instructions were issued on the differentiation of Marxist "class status," which would have required considerable investigation into the economic resources of individual households. Other requirements seemed to call for the determination of job status, family relationships, and the ages of at least some individuals (Govt. Admin. Council, 1950). To follow these instructions to the letter would have necessitated a complete economic and social survey of every rural household. There is little doubt that the central authorities thought the importance of land reform justified such ambitious efforts, but they seemed to have little idea of the actual work involved in carrying out some of their instructions. They were impatient with delays and unsympathetic to the complaints of cadres that the burdens of statistical work only increased the already considerable burdens of land reform administration.

In few, if any, areas were there figures on population and land that could be used in lieu of new investigations. When in July, 1950, *hsien* boundaries were being redrawn and *hsiang* limits established to provide administrative units of a size convenient for land reform work in the central south region, the only available figures were those of the Republic of China Ministry of Internal Affairs for 1947 and some provincial compilations for 1948 (*TKP,* July 7, 1950a). These figures were used to estimate roughly the numbers of persons in the areas affected by land reform and other activities during these years, particularly in reports prepared at the provincial and higher levels; but for work in the field at local levels, the old data were not adequate.

In midsummer of 1950, the Central-South Military-Administrative Committee ordered the five provinces under its jurisdiction to conduct rural investigations to supply needed data on land, population, and the condition of the whole rural economy (*TKP,* Aug. 8, 1950). Available sources give no information about how these orders were carried out in other provinces, but a news item from Canton indicates that the provincial authorities issued a number of directives and supplementary instructions and that workers in Kwangtung were given to understand that the investigations were nationwide. The Kwangtung directive also recognizes the difficulties encountered by local authorities in trying to administer economic affairs without up-to-date statistics:

> Our province was liberated later than others. In addition, our duties were numerous. Investigation and research work was unable to unfold fully, and

in particular the investigation of the rural economy was not started due to lack of leadership, lack of organization, and lack of system. For this reason, when we make a specific policy and draft a plan, we have to use the old statistical data. It is very difficult to accommodate to the actual conditions. (*NFJP,* Aug. 12, 1950.)

The investigation in Kwangtung was planned to include a complete survey of cultivated area, rural population, types of crops and output, labor force and animal power, and acreage of wasteland and forests; and these data were to be supplemented by more intensive sample surveys in a few "representative" villages in each of the economic subregions in the province. The work was to be carried out, along with the summer grain levy and rent reduction work, by local cadres and activists supervised by inspection and leadership teams from higher levels. Experimental investigations were to be conducted by college students from various local universities, who were to receive prior training under the provincial government's agriculture and forestry department. Forms had apparently been prepared, and training and mobilization begun in July, and the field teams dispatched by the beginning of August. The investigation was to be completed by the end of August, and the compilations were to reach the provincial authorities during the first ten days of September (*NFJP,* Aug. 12, 1950).

However, all did not proceed as planned. The local cadres rebelled at being told to conduct another investigation in the midst of summer grain levy work. This was, they complained, "already the fifth investigation; investigations one after another are really meaningless." They predicted that the end result would be the same as with previous investigations: "A great many forms will be distributed and then nothing further will be heard of it." When, after much "explanation" from higher levels, they were constrained to proceed in spite of their objections, they worked slowly and without enthusiasm. The few forms that were sent in by August 22 contained omissions and visibly wrong figures. More explanations were provided at a meeting on August 25, and the cadres took back their incorrect forms to try again (*NFJP,* Sept. 24, 1950). What happened on the second attempt is not described in available sources, but in August, 1951, Kwangtung provincial authorities ordered the installation of door placards on rural houses in order to tighten administrative control.[33] In October, 1951, the provincial civil affairs department and the Land Reform Committee issued a joint directive for another rural investigation to serve the purposes of land reform and government administration. The fate of the previous year's efforts was revealed in a few brief comments in a report from Canton:

According to what we found out, in the past a few individual *hsiang* and

33. See footnote 27.

villages had already obtained such investigation data. But the majority did not pay any attention to it and there was confusion. In order to implement thoroughly democratic political work and carry out land reform work, the authorities stipulated again that all places throughout the province must without exception observe the above mentioned directive to carry out the investigation on a large scale and quickly. (*Hsing-tao jih-pao,* Oct. 27, 1951.)

The prophesies of the *hsiang* cadres a year earlier had evidently been fulfilled; but, of course, they were themselves in a position to see to this by simply not taking action. When the land reform movement finally reached Kwangtung late in 1951, a different order of priorities prevailed, and the pressures on local cadres were much increased.

The requirements of the later land reform population investigations in Kwangtung still seem rather ambitious; obviously they were intended to provide much information besides that needed for land reform. Data were to include the total population classified by age, sex, occupation, level of educational attainment, work experience, "personal history," and class status. Details on landholdings and assets were also elaborate, and there were miscellaneous other questions about weapons, absent family members, and so on, answers to which were to be "listed in detail." The work was to be completed by March, 1952 (*Hsing-tao jih-pao,* Oct. 27, 1951). But in August, 1952, more than two years after the first orders were issued for rural surveys, instructions were still being sent out on how to do land reform statistical work, based on the experience of a supposedly successful *hsiang*. By this time, the provincial authorities, after fighting an uphill battle against the indifference or outright resistance of local cadres for two years, had come to the conclusion that leadership cadres must be held accountable for the work, that it was best to designate a specific person to take charge of the work, and that the cadres should "rely on the masses" to the extent of calling upon educated peasants to assist in conducting statistical investigations, a concession to the complaints of overworked local cadres (Kwangtung Prov. Land Reform Office, 1952).[34]

The situation in Kwangtung was evidently not unique. In August, 1951, the *People's Daily* described the travails of *hsiang* cadres in an area of west Szechwan, who had received 60 different forms to fill out in June and July alone, 12 of which arrived on July 16 and were to be completed in 5 days. Of these, the most difficult was one calling for a tabulation of "unlawful landlords," including a detailed tabulation of all their "unlawful actions" in the past by type and by the numbers of households involved. The cadres were understandably flattened by these demands; they

34. Some cadres still complained that statistical work hindered land reform work, or that it was not essential, or that they did not have the time and the staff to complete their statistical assignments. Officials complained that reports were not submitted on time and contained unexplained discrepancies and mistakes.

stayed up until late at night, or even all night in some cases, trying to meet deadlines. When, after the completion of its land reform surveys, which had only collected data on confiscations in absolute terms, one *hsiang* received a form calling for their cash value, the cadre in charge, noting that there was no time for another field investigation, declared: "We'll just have to fudge!" (*JMJP,* Aug. 24, 1951.) In February, 1952, the Hupei Party Committee issued a bulletin against making false reports and suppressing "bad news," a defect also noted among "a few cadres" in Kwangtung.[35] Instances of concealment of land and false population figures were reported from Sinkiang in 1951 and 1953,[36] and more complete source collections probably would have turned up many other instances.

Under these circumstances, the quality of statistical work could not have been high. Nevertheless, figures on the total population probably were more reliable than figures on age, sex, occupation, and other details involving more complex determinations and perhaps more incentives for evasion. In areas where the cadres were conscientious in compiling figures and the peasants were fairly cooperative, whether voluntarily or through fear of the cadres, new figures for the total population would have been a considerable improvement over the old. In all areas, the biases would generally have tended toward undercount because of the concealment and temporary flight of landlords, wealthy peasant families, and any other persons who had reason to avoid the cadre-sponsored denunciations of the "anti-tyranny" movement. In areas where the work was less conscientious, enumerations were probably less complete, and if estimates were substituted, those based on old figures were probably serious underestimates.

There is, of course, no way of quantifying the margin of error, or even of surmising the extent to which estimating was used in lieu of fieldwork. But the evidence indicates that field inspection teams were conducting rechecks in many areas, some of which were required to repeat the whole process of land distribution when their work was found defective. Given the danger of discovery, the strength of the central authorities' determination, which was evident in the severity of penalties for obstructing land reform, and the general tension and anxiety that infected cadres and peasants alike, it would be difficult to make a case for the presumption

35. *Ch'ang chiang jih-pao,* Feb. 20, 1952. The examples suggest that the mistake referred to had more to do with political achievements of local land reform efforts than with economic and demographic data; some of the "false reports" consisted in generalizing from a few exceptional cases to give a false impression of conformity to directives.

36. *Hsin-chiang jih-pao,* Nov. 20, 1951; Feb. 11, 1953 (a, b). The latter source warns against treating statistical work as a matter of making estimates, since such practices cause statistical figures to "lose their reality." However, it should be remembered that Sinkiang province was largely inhabited by minority peoples, some of whom could not be enumerated directly during the census of 1953.

that deception was the rule. Hence, the rural population figures produced during land reform, despite inaccuracies, were probably much closer to the mark than those obtainable from previous records.

Agricultural Tax Reform and Other Central Tasks.

Population investigations conducted in connection with agricultural taxation work probably were less significant as sources of new rural population figures than the land reform population investigations, except in those areas where tax reform work antedated land reform. Where land reform had already been carried out or was in process of being carried out, no independent investigation of taxable land by grade was necessary unless the existing records were thought to be inadequate; presumably the same applied to household records. But in areas where there had been no recent investigation, agricultural tax investigators were required to compile new data on their own. So far as the official instructions indicate, the unit for both landholding investigations and tax records was the household, and there is nothing to suggest that household composition was also recorded (NCNA, July 5, 1951). However, this work probably yielded new figures on numbers of rural households in some areas. There are no sources available to indicate how it was carried out or what problems it may have encountered, but the purpose of the work would not have been such as to inspire the eager cooperation of the population, particularly those persons whose landholdings exceeded the amount for which they were taxed or who had thus far escaped the tax rolls.

Other central tasks during this period included an emergency rent reduction drive, the "anti-tyranny" movement directed against landlords, the "five-anti" movement against merchants and industrialists, the mutual aid movement among peasants, and the beginnings of the cooperative movement. All of these movements involved some record-keeping, and would probably have increased the numbers of households listed in the local administrative records in rural and urban areas to the extent that they succeeded in enveloping families who had previously been able to stay out of whatever registers were being kept by local authorities. However, it is unlikely that any of these sources of information were of much significance in adding to locally compiled population figures.

REVISION OF LOCAL POPULATION FIGURES

In view of the variety and extent of population investigations that took place during the years 1949-53, there is nothing very mysterious about the upward revision of provincial and local population figures. However, tracing the revisions directly to these investigations is not as easy as might be supposed, mainly because of gaps in the evidence.

What is principally missing at this point is a clear indication of what sort of compilation work was going on during these years in the central government agencies. In February, 1950, the People's Liberation Army headquarters announced a population total of 471,763,000 "as of the end of 1949." [37] But at about the same time the statistical office of the Government Administrative Council's Financial and Economic Committee was said to have compiled a new series of figures for the population and cultivated acreage of China with the help of the Ministry of Agriculture, Ministry of Internal Affairs, Ministry of Finance, Ministry of Foreign Trade, and Ministry of Forestry, in which the populatiton totalled 483,-687,862 for the country as a whole; in March, 1950, it was recommended that these figures be used throughout China (*Hsin wan-pao,* Dec. 7, 1952). Whatever prompted such broad-based cooperation, it was not the magnitude of the statistical effort involved, for the provincial and regional population figures were admittedly Republic of China figures for 1948, and the agricultural population figures, were mainly estimates assembled at a national agricultural conference in December, 1949.[38] Despite high-level endorsement, the newly authorized figures were quickly contradicted. In May, 1950, the Ministry of Internal Affairs in its bulletin on administrative divisions gave an overall population total of 483,869,687 (*Atlas,* 4th ed., June 1951.); in June, 1950 Chou En-lai, in an address to the Political Consultative Conference, said that the population of the country now totaled 487,690,000, not including Taiwan and Tibet (Li Hsü-tan, 1951, p. 130); and in July, 1950, the People's Liberation Army Headquarters issued a new total of 492,530,000.[39]

The differences in these totals are minor and seem to have resulted mainly from adding different estimates for Tibet and the Inner Mongolia Autonomous Region (IMAR) to the Republic of China figures for all other areas. Nevertheless, the discrepancies troubled the compilers of the *Atlas* and the *People's Handbook* (*Jen-min Shou-ts'e*). The *People's Handbook* edition of April, 1950, gave the February (1950) People's Liberation Army total along with two not wholly consistent sets of regional and provincial figures, both of which add to totals larger than the Army figure. The provincial figures were compiled from a variety of administrative listings and newspaper items, including speeches of officials, descriptive articles, and correspondents' reports (*JMST,* April 1950). An edition of the *Handbook* dated February 5, 1951, gave the new Army total released in July, 1950, and a somewhat altered series of regional and provincial totals adding to a figure smaller than the Army figure (*JMST,* Feb. 1951). The edition of August 20, 1952, abandoned both provincial figures and the Army total, giving instead the regional figures for total

37. *Atlas,* 4th edition, June 1951, Map 19, citing the People's Liberation Army, "Communiqué Summarizing Three and a Half Years of the Liberation War."

38. *TKP,* July 19, 1950. The original item had appeared in *JMJP.*

39. *Atlas,* 2nd edition, June 1953, Map 19, citing the People's Liberation Army "Communiqué Summarizing the Military Achievements of Four Years of Battle, July 1, 1946-June 30, 1950."

and agricultural population from the joint compilation of March, 1950, except that larger figures were added for the total population of Tibet and the IMAR, and the agricultural populations for these areas were simply dropped; with the overall result that the total population was slightly above and the agricultural population slightly below the March, 1950, totals. All figures were attributed to newspaper and journal sources.[40] The July 1, 1953, edition repeated the figures in the 1952 edition except for the addition of 100,000 to the total for the IMAR. However, on the same page it gave figures by region on the agricultural populations in areas affected by land reform during three time periods; for all but one region, these substantially exceeded the other agricultural population figures. The sources of these figures were newspaper accounts of the progress of land reform. No notice was given to the discrepancies between the two sets of agricultural population figures (JMST, July 1953, p. 149).[41] No new edition of the *People's Handbook* was published for 1954, but the 1955 edition contained the provincial and municipal figures from the 1953 census (*JMST*, Jan. 1955).

The compilers of several series of atlases were bolder than the compilers of the *People's Handbook* in incorporating not only the new urban data, but also the land reform figures for rural areas. However, they were less explicit in identifying their sources, and so it is not possible to account for all the changes that appeared in these compilations from one edition to another.[42] The June, 1951, edition of the *Atlas* gives the Ministry of Interior compilation of May, 1950. The September, 1952, edition repeats most of these figures, but for a few provinces, notably Anhwei, Szechwan, and Yünnan, markedly higher totals are given. The March, 1953, edition showed marked upward revisions for nearly all provinces except Hupei and the three provinces listed above. Most of the new totals were attributed to newspaper sources, as were the previously raised totals for Anhwei, Szechwan, and Yünnan, but some were obtained from 1951 issues of *Ti-li chih-shih* (*Geographical Knowledge*) and others from a

40. *JMST*, Aug. 1952. The joint compilation figures were attributed to *Chieh-fang jih-pao, (Liberation Daily)*, Shanghai, April 23, 1950; the figure for Tibet to *JMJP*, November 23, 1950; and the figure for the IMAR to *Nei-meng-ku chien-she (Inner Mongolia Construction)*, Huhehot, May 1, 1951. The figures were referred to 1950.

41. The new IMAR figure was attributed to an article by an IMAR government official in the *Nei-meng-ku jih-pao (Inner Mongolia Daily)*, Huhehot, January 1, 1953.

42. The collection of atlases for the years 1950-53 on which this discussion is based is obviously incomplete. It includes eight editions of the *Atlas (Chung-hua jen-min kung-ho-kuo fen-sheng ti-t'u)* and twelve editions of the *Detailed Provincial Atlas of the People's Republic of China (Chung-hua jen-min kung-ho-kuo fen-sheng ching-t'u)*. Only one edition each is available for the 1948 *Provincial Atlas of China (Chung-kuo fen-sheng t'u)*, the *Atlas of New China*, 1950 *(Hsin Chung-kuo ti-t'u)*, and the *New China Provincial Atlas*, 1953 *(Hsin Chung-kuo fen-sheng t'u)*.

junior middle school geography textbook of August, 1951. The June, 1953, edition made further increases in the figures for Kansu and Sinkiang and a second sharp increase in that for Yünnan. The July edition showed no further changes, and the August and December editions included relatively minor changes in the populations of five provinces. Only the population of Hupei remained unchanged at the level of the Republic of China figure for 1947.

The various editions of the *Detailed Provincial Atlas of the People's Republic of China* give figures generally similar, with minor variations, to those given in the *Atlas* editions of about the same time. In a few cases the *Detailed Atlas* seems to have picked up higher figures somewhat sooner, but there are many unexplained variations in the figures from one edition to another. Some provincial totals given in the editions of January, 1950, and February, 1951, are higher than the corresponding figures in 1952 editions. For example, the January, 1950, edition gives higher totals for Chekiang and Hupei than appear in any subsequent edition of either the *Detailed Atlas* or the *Atlas* until after the 1953 census. The major upward revisions of provincial populations in both atlases occurred at about the same time in editions of the spring of 1953; new urban population totals seem to have been introduced much earlier and were already included in editions of 1950 and 1951.

From the changes in the figures and from the sources and explanatory notes in both the handbooks and atlases, it is apparent that the compilations were made without guidance by any official agency. The appropriate authorities seem to have been uncertain as to what to do and in no position to establish a single set of official figures. The compilers were therefore left with a dilemma: whether to hold to the Republic of China figures as issued by the Ministry of Interior in 1950, or to try to incorporate the new totals for cities and rural areas appearing in local press items in the course of registration and land reform. The *People's Handbook* opted for the former course, only to be scooped by the atlases, which took a chance on the local population reports lated vindicated by the census results.

Meanwhile, if Krotevich is to be believed, the State Statistical Bureau had made its own compilation in 1952, and the Ministry of Interior followed with another as of January 1, 1953. Both efforts yielded total populations exceeding by 14 to 25 million the highest that the atlas compilers could assemble, but apparently neither was made generally available prior to the publication of the *Atlas* edition of December, 1953, or they would certainly have been the prime sources. Though it cannot be shown conclusively that the State Statistical Bureau and the Ministry of Interior figures were assembled in the same manner as those in the atlases (perhaps with more complete local reports), this would seem to be a safe presumption in the absence of any contrary evidence. There is therefore no reason to reject the official explanation of the upward revision of local population totals prior to the census quoted earlier.

OFFICIAL ATTITUDES TOWARD HIGHER POPULATION FIGURES

Assuming that the upward revision of local population figures during the 1949-53 period occurred in the manner indicated above, there remain important questions as to what influence these figures might have exerted on the census fieldwork and how such influences would have affected the accuracy of the census results. The answers depend partly on the attitudes of local cadres toward the pre-census figures and partly on what inclinations, if any, were conveyed to them by the central authorities. Did the local cadres feel obligated to confirm the results of earlier population investigations for reasons associated with their own security and careers? Did the central authorities expect or want these figures to be confirmed or did they distrust them?

The evidence bearing on these questions is fragmentary and oblique. The central authorities seem to have been critical of the early figures on several counts: they were incomplete, inaccurate in detail, and did not include information on age and sex needed for administrative purposes. The criticism about incomplete coverage would imply that the actual totals were still higher, yet there is no indication in available sources that this inference was ever made explicit. The expectation of higher census totals would have been plausible, in view of the facts that the urban registers were not adequately maintained and that the one-time rural surveys yielded only a static record. But there is no indication whatsoever that the regime was eager to have a high population total confirmed by the census. On the contrary, despite a public show of conventional Marxist optimism, there are numerous suggestions that the size of China's population was a cause of anxiety to at least some persons in high places. As has been noted elsewhere, the expressions of pride in the size of the census total were accompanied by anti-Malthusian arguments that sound as though they may have been addressed to this anxiety (Aird, 1962).

There may even have been some senior leaders who felt that the population totals reported during the land reform movement were unreasonably high and not to be trusted. No direct evidence for this suspicion can be found, but it would help to explain the caution of the regime in not permitting general release of the later compilations of the State Statistical Bureau and the Ministry of Interior, despite the fact that no such caution had been shown in 1950 in releasing much lower figures based on the Republic of China records of 1947 and 1948. Revised rural population figures were freely used in discussing the achievements of land reform by rural work director Teng Tzu-hui and various officials of the Ministry of Agriculture, whose reputations and careers may have been at stake in the corroboration of land reform statistical work. But not even these officials ventured to use revised overall population totals, though their rural population figure had climbed to 470 million by the end of 1952.

Throughout the early years the preferred population total for speech-making purposes was 475 million. In 1951, a writer in a geographical journal argued that if an allowance for the overseas Chinese were added to the then-current slightly revised Republic of China totals, it would be quite reasonable to talk of 500 million as the population of China (Li Hsü-tan, 1951). Subsequent editions of the *Detailed Atlas* followed his suggestion, but very few officials did so. On several occasions when Mao and others used the total of 475 million, they added that the actual population was probably larger, but they seem to have had little idea that it might be very much larger (Feng Wen-lan, 1950; *JMJP,* June 24, 1950). If it was the consensus of the Central Committee of the Chinese Communist Party that a large figure was desirable, it was a remarkably well-kept secret. The more plausible view is that larger figures were not welcome, that they were received tentatively and with skepticism during land reform, and that their confirmation by the census may have been a not altogether pleasant surprise.

Certainly there is no hint in the plans and directives prepared in the spring of 1953 or in the supplementary instructions issued during experimental work in the summer and fall of 1953 that the central authorities wanted the land reform figures confirmed, or even that they wanted these records consulted during the census work. Such consultations did take place, as we shall see, but apparently without the encouragement of the central authorities. There is no indication in any available source that the intent of the central census office or the Central Committee was different from that expressed by Chou En-lai when he announced the slogan for the census work in April 1953: "No omissions, no double-counting, complete coverage, and accuracy" (NCNA, April 6, 1953 [a]).

What matters in the last analysis is, of course, not what the central authorities intended but what actually happened during the fieldwork. What use was actually made of the existing population records during the census-taking?

RELATION OF EXISTING POPULATION RECORDS TO CENSUS WORK

Neither the original census directives nor the supplementary instructions issued by the central office seem to have anticipated any use, proper or improper, of the existing population records during the census-taking. Consistent with the expectation that the census results would take precedence over all previous efforts, they specified, as was mentioned earlier, that in those cities where the household registration system was not complete, an extra copy of the census records should be prepared and turned over to the local administration. The idea of using the census records as the foundation for a rural registration system does not seem to have taken hold before the end of 1953, but it is curious that no suggestions were made about checking census against registration records in those cities where the registration was thought to be well maintained, even though such cross-checking could have led to the improvement of both efforts. Nor were there any warnings, so far as available sources show, against the use of old population records in lieu of fieldwork, though some of the census planners must have known that in the past this had been a not uncommon practice of local authorities from the provincial level down. Although no one in authority seems to have thought of such a connection during the planning work, local reports on the progress of experimental census work during the spring and summer of 1953 had quite a bit to say about how the old records could be used, and a variety of applications persisted into the final stages of census fieldwork. By all indications, the central authorities neither objected to, nor approved and encouraged, these procedures.

In some cities at least, special efforts were made to put the household registers in order just before census fieldwork began, ostensibly for the purpose of facilitating census work. In Tientsin, what was represented as a full field check of households was conducted by the security police during April and May, 1953, in the course of which many recording errors and omissions were found (*T'ien-ching jih-pao,* May 27, 1953). Various cities in the northeast strengthened their street organizations and set up residents' committees, and Mukden, Luta, and Harbin made unspecified improvements in their household registration systems (*JMJP,* Aug. 7, 1953). Canton issued a notice warning residents to report changes and errors in their registration, or, if unregistered, to get themselves on the registers and apply for their residents' permits at once. They were promised they would not be prosecuted for "past mistakes" (*NFJP,* Nov. 18, 1953).

In most cases it is apparent that the local municipal officials were using public anxiety about the forthcoming census investigation as a stimulant to lagging public cooperation in maintaining the registers. The officials may also have had some anxieties of their own lest the census should disclose major deficiencies in the local registers. But in Canton, Tsinan, Shanghai, and Tientsin the registers were also used as an aid in census-taking. In Canton, a checklist of households was to be obtained from the household registration records for use by census registrars (*KCJP,* Jan. 23, 1954a). During experimental work in Tsinan, checklists based on household registers were used as a check against omissions during the census, the police registration records were checked against census records to detect errors in names, and the census records were then checked against household books on a door-to-door basis (Central Political . . . Organ, Tsinan, 1953). In Shanghai, election work cadres studied the household records during April and May, 1953, as part of the preparatory work prior to experimental investigations (*JMJP,* June 10, 1953). In Tientsin, where the security police registers had just been checked, the preparatory work for experimental investigations in June, 1953, included use of these records to prepare a complete advance listing of households and to obtain preliminary counts of de jure population, absent population, and nonresident population, and of the population of voting age, on the basis of which the electoral districts were demarcated, the number of representatives allocated, and registration stations located. The lists were rechecked with the records of the security branch stations and with the actual households to make sure that no households were omitted (*T'ien-ching jih-pao,* June 11, 1953).[43]

Similar uses of household books were reported in several rural areas. In some areas census records were apparently expected to be superior, and the comparisons resulted mainly in the correction of the old household records. In Kirin, the number of households was first obtained from the residence group head, then registration was completed, and finally the new records were compared with the original household records. Numerous errors and omissions were found in the old records (Kirin Prov. Election Comm., 1953). During full-scale census work in Kiangsu and Shantung, heads of residence groups and local activists were asked to assist registration personnel in checking the census records against the old records (Central Population . . . Office, 1954). However, during the experimental work in Kiangsi and Chekiang the household records were sought out first, before any registration work was done. In Chekiang these records were compared with the preliminary drafts of census information that the peasants had been mobilized to prepare before coming to the registration centers (*JMJP,* June 4, 1953). In Kiangsi the old records were apparently used in the course of census interviews, after which the information recorded on the census form was read back to the peasant as a check (*JMJP,* June 11, 1953). These procedures could very easily have degenerated in practice into superficial census work. In some villages of Liaotung during the experimental work, several technical cadres were apprehended in the ultimate dereliction: they had merely copied data out of the household books (Liaotung Prov. Election Comm., 1953). Except for the fact that they were caught, their case was probably far from unique.

Having the heads of household prepare in advance a draft of the information required for registration would undoubtedly have speeded up the process a good deal, as was claimed, but it may also have compromised the accuracy of the data. Sometimes the drafts were prepared by the peasants alone, sometimes under the supervision of residence group

43. This method was appropriate in Tientsin because the police household records had just been brought up to date. In other cities, where record-keeping had lapsed, the registration records would have been less helpful for census work.

heads and activists. The lack of outside supervision would have made it easier for heads of household to continue whatever deliberate omissions or misstatements of information they had been able to preserve in the local household records. Unintentional errors would also have been more likely to escape detection. The convenience of the drafts would have increased the temptation for the registrars to copy into the census records whatever was set before them. Hence, the use of drafts probably introduced in many places a covert connection between the existing household records and the census.

What effect would the use of household records have had in general upon the accuracy of the census results? Conscientiously carried out, the compiling of household checklists and the comparison of census and household records, even if both sets of records were seriously deficient, would undoubtedly have contributed to their mutual improvement, in both coverage and accuracy of details. However, cross-checking two sets of records arranged in different sequence is an extremely tedious job that cannot be done in a hurry and done well. Careful cross-checking may have been possible during the experimental investigations, which were comparatively well staffed and supervised, but the tempo of full-scale census work would probably have precluded the use of such elaborate procedures. In general, since most household records would have been incomplete at best, and out-of-date by the time census work had begun in most areas, any use of these records that led to less thorough census field investigations would have resulted in less complete and less accurate census records and a larger net undercount in the census population figures.

How prevalent the influence of the old records was and how much allowance should be made for undercount cannot be determined from the materials available. The census total was only about 2.5 per cent above the total compiled by the Ministry of Interior as of January 1, 1953, but of course there were two provinces, Sinkiang and Kiangsi, for which the census totals were smaller than those in the *Atlas* compilation of December, 1953. For some of the areas inhabited largely by minority populations, where census work was not undertaken, the census figures were only slightly above the estimates given in the *Atlas*. Aside from these areas, the *Atlas* provincial figures were substantially below the census figures except for Anhwei province, for which the census figure was only 1.1 per cent higher. Probably the Ministry of Interior provincial figures for January 1, 1953, if available, would show other close approximations. Certainly the census results were, as Taeuber and Wang pointed out (1960b, p. 282), not much different in the total from the results of the compilations made during 1953.

But this fact is subject to several interpretations. If it is assumed that the census was to a considerable degree based on local population records instead of an independent field investigation, the reliability of the census figures depends upon the quality of the earlier investigations. One might even go so far as to assume that neither the earlier figures nor the census figures were based on fieldwork, but this assumes two instances of massive deception of the central authorities, in one of which the local perpetrators with singular uniformity sharply increased the totals above those in previous records, and in the other, with equal unanimity, elected not to make further substantial increases. Without supporting evidence, no such explanation is creditable.

If it is assumed instead that the census and the previous investigations were, despite some degree of borrowing, essentially independent head counts, or that their connections consisted more in improving than in short-circuiting the process of investigation, then the census results must be regarded as confirming in general the findings of the earlier investigations. If it is also assumed that the margin of undercount in the census remains large, then the slight difference between the census total figure and that shown by the previous compilations would suggest that the quality of the census work was not much above that of the earlier investigations. If the census figure is assumed to be a fairly close approximation of the actual population total for midyear 1953, the slight difference between it and previous totals suggests a respectable improvement in accuracy over earlier efforts, which were already a remarkable achievement in population counting. But this conclusion also is difficult to credit. A more cautious view, and one that does a minimum of violence to the evidence, would hold that though there was in general a marked improvement in population record-keeping after the Communist regime came to power in China (due more to the effectiveness of the Communist systems of civil control than to methodological sophistication), probably neither the results of the urban registration and land reform investigations nor those of the 1953 census were accurate by the standards of registration and census-taking in more developed countries.

THE CENSUS ACCURACY CHECKS

What then are we to make of the claims of accuracy based on the records of "recheck" operations after the census work? Probably their greatest significance is as a measure of the naiveté both of the local cadres and officials who compiled and reported the recheck figures, and of the central officials who assembled them and publicized the claim.

In requiring that accuracy checks be made and the errors promptly corrected, the central census officials were following an administrative tradition already well established during previous mass data-collecting and reorganization programs, including the land reform movement. Yet in spite of past experience, they failed to specify clearly what sort of operation they wanted carried out. Once again, as in previous mass operations, the nature of the checking was left to the ingenuity of the local cadres. The result was that the local efforts varied widely in method, coverage, and conscientiousness. During experimental registration in Kirin province, three methods were employed: (1) checking the already completed census forms against the original household records; (2) checking with heads of residence groups or with other persons; and (3) individual interviews with persons whose ages were given incorrectly (Kirin Prov. Election Comm., 1953). This combination of methods not only disclosed many errors but provided the only available information on the types of persons found to have been frequently omitted during registration. During full-scale census work in Kwangtung, a reinvestigation of sample areas in two municipalities again found numerous errors (Kwangtung Prov. Pop. . . . Office, 1954). On the other hand, in Shantung province only a few households were checked directly; for the rest, residence group heads were called together to go over each other's records (Central Population . . . Office, 1954). In Tsinan during the experimental work, recheck consisted simply of comparing census records with voter registration records and the household registration records kept in the public security stations (Central Political . . . Organ, Tsinan, 1953). It is not reported whether this method disclosed many errors. In Heilungkiang, during the experimental work, one recheck conducted at the village level was found to have consisted merely in calling mass meetings and asking for the views of the people, as a result of which, of course, no errors were found.[44]

The quality of recheck work also depended to a considerable degree on who was made responsible for it, and here again local practice varied. In Kiangsu, during the full-scale investigation, it was left to the head of the residence group and a local activist to compare the census forms with the household registration records. In one district of Shantung, the "*hsiang* intellectuals" (probably mostly primary school teachers) were responsible for making the prepartory drafts of census information, conducting propaganda, and doing recheck work (Central Population . . . Office, 1954). In Canton during experimental work, "a few technical personnel" were to carry out the recheck along with the examination of voter qualifications (*KCJP,* Aug. 14, 1953). However, during full-scale census work in Fukien, statistical personnel of one district were divided into two investigating teams, following a district conference, to conduct the recheck in all the *hsien* in the district (*JMJP,* March 13, 1954a). In Kwangtung, rechecking was considered a leadership function, and the work was to be conducted by trained statistical cadres. An indication of the seriousness and level of sophistication with which leaders and technicians approached

44. *JMJP,* Sept. 28, 1953. But it should be noted that the *hsien* election committee officials whose check uncovered this instance of local negligence were doing a more careful job. See footnote 3.

their task is given in their instructions to field units, which are worth quoting at length:

> Do a good job of rechecking the population. It should be understood that rechecking is one of the important keys to achieving completeness and accuracy in population investigation and registration. It is a step which is indispensable to populaton and registration work. At present there are still some places where the importance and the complexity of population investigation and registration work are not sufficiently recognized. They think that recheck work is not essential. Some are full of self-satisfaction. They believe that their investigation and registration work was carried out meticulously, and therefore there is no need to have a recheck. Some are reluctant to do recheck work because they are afraid of the trouble and are rushed for time. Some consider that carrying out registration and checking at the same time is equivalent to recheck. Some even take sample checking at keypoints and proofreading of forms as recheck. All these (methods) are unsuitable. . . .
>
> The leadership of *hsien* and cities must carry out keypoint sample checks. Basic units which have made too many mistakes and omissions must carry out over-all recheck. Kwangtung Prov. Pop. . . . Office, 1954.)
>
> . . . All basic level units of all areas must conduct a complete and accurate recheck in all electoral districts from house to house according to the filled-out population investigation and registration forms after preliminary population investigation and registration has been carried out. After recheck is done and all mistakes are corrected, tallying of population statistics should be carried out. This work should be under the direction of statistical cadres who have undergone training. (*NFJP,* April 20, 1954.)

These directions, calling for what amounted to a double investigation of all areas in which the sample checks found numerous errors, would certainly have improved the quality of the census results if carried out to the letter. But if the same authorities who made the sample checks were responsible for the full recheck wherever it seemed necessary, as was probably the case, they may have tended to find few mistakes during the sample checks.

At any rate, the fragmentary reports on the results of the rechecking suggest that errors were found to be numerous wherever it was done conscientiously. They also suggest that the central authorities, who failed initially to specify and thus to standardize the recheck procedures, did not issue any subsequent instructions on the basis of the findings of recheck work during the experimental period. As a result, until the end of the period of full-scale census work, some areas tried to inspire conscientious work in their field personnel while others seemed to be content with perfunctory gestures.

So far as available evidence shows, when the data on recheck investigations were reported to the central offices in Peking, those representing actual field investigations were not distinguished from those resulting from comparisons of records or other short-cut procedures. If the census officials were aware that numerous errors signified a conscientious job of field rechecking, this did not prevent them from lumping all reports together indiscriminately so that extravagant claims could be made for the accuracy of the work. In March, 1954, a New China News Agency dispatch said that in some areas the check had found the statistics "99.5 per cent accurate" (NCNA, March 10, 1954). A report from Chungking in April also claimed "over 99 per cent accuracy" (*JMJP,* April 7, 1954). No further details were given on these accomplishments, but a report of sample checks in 41 villages in Sungkiang and Liaohsi provinces stated that in 39 of the villages "100 per cent accuracy" was achieved, while in the remaining 2 villages omissions and double counting together amounted to 0.25 per cent (*JMJP,* March 25, 1954). This report suggests that in the compilation of recheck statistics at regional as well as central levels, the errors reported by a few areas were submerged by other areas' meaningless claims of total accuracy. In this manner, presumably, the summary recheck figures showing net omissions of 0.116 per cent in a population of 52,950,000 were assembled. If there were statisticians in the central census office or in local units who knew better than to believe such claims, they must also have known better than to dispute them, for by the end of the census operations "politics" had taken command.

MAGNITUDE AND DIRECTION OF ERROR IN THE CENSUS TOTAL

If the official accuracy check statistics are of no value as a measure of the magnitude of error in the reported census total, then how are the census figures to be assessed? Only two approaches are possible. One is an independent evaluation of the biases inherent in the methods used in census-taking, with whatever inferences may be drawn from census-taking experience elsewhere in the world. The other is an examination of the credibility of the census results themselves. Both efforts are hampered by lack of information. If we had access to the files of official correspondence passing in both directions between the central, regional, provincial, and local census offices, or even a complete file of the newspaper accounts, probably a much more penetrating methodological analysis could be undertaken. But those records are inaccessible if, indeed, they still exist. The statistical records of census work, including the population totals and the distributions by age and sex for units of the *hsien* and *hsiang* levels in rural areas and for the district level in urban areas, probably still survive, but they have never been, and may never be, published in full. Almost certainly their release would provide the material for further criticism of the quality of census work, and the statisticians of the Ministry of Interior and State Statistical Bureau may be aware of this.[45] There is therefore little likelihood that the supply of source materials, statistical or descriptive, will be greatly augmented in the future.

In a previous work the writer attempted to assess the direction and magnitude of net error in the census total by inferring the probable biases introduced by defective methodology and by analyzing the age-sex distribution as reconstructed from various sources. My conclusion at that time was that factors making for undercount outweighed those making for overcount, and I have seen no substantial evidence or argument since, either in Chinese or non-Chinese sources, to contradict that conclusion. However, the methods used in that study to estimate the possible maximum and minimum undercount in the 1953 census were based on only one assumption as to the level of the crude birth rate in prior years and one assumed trend of past natural increase; no allowance was made for male war casualties during the military actions of the proceding 15 years (Aird, 1961, especially pp. 22-25, 65-78).

The first two limitations were criticized by John Durand in reviewing an earlier report of the analysis given at the Milbank Memorial Fund meetings in November, 1959; he also pointed out that the use of lower fertility rates and a lower increase trend would reduce the estimate of undercount and yield an age-sex distribution more similar to that found by the 1953 census (Aird, 1960, pp. 93-133).[46] Whether the use of lower fertility rates is appropriate for this purpose, and if so, how much lower, are questions which will be discussed further in Section IV, but the essential point of Durand's criticism is valid: that the methods used in the earlier analysis failed to test the limits of alternative assumptions. The current effort goes beyond the previous one in exploring a wider range of alternatives, but the results suggest that reconstructions do not provide a basis for estimating the effects of undercounting by age and sex on the official age-sex structure of the 1953 census.

This leaves the question of the credible margin of undercount open without even a mechanical measure as a guide. In view of the circumstances of the census-taking, the margin probably should be set both wider and higher than the range of 3 per cent to 11 per cent suggested in the earlier study—how much wider and higher is impossible to say with any assurance. Even in countries with many years of census experience,

45. An official publication by the State Statistical Bureau entitled *Chung-hua jen-min kung-ho-kuo 1953-nien jen-k'ou tiao-ch'a tzu-liao (Results of the 1953 Population Census of the Chinese People's Republic)*, containing 1953 census data on age, sex, and ethnic status for the country as a whole and *hsien* population totals was advertised in *T'ung-chi yen-chiu*, 1958, p. 30, but, so far as is known, no copy of this publication has turned up outside China and no reference to it has been found in any other Chinese source.

46. Durand's discussion is summarized on pp. 134-137 of this reference.

well-trained census supervisory and field staffs, well-tested methods for assuring completeness of enumeration, and neither past traditions nor current political conditions that favor large-scale evasion of census-taking, the estimates of net omissions are sometimes more than 2 or 3 per cent. The planners of the mainland China census of 1953 seem to have had little conception of the seriousness of the problem of omissions. They developed no specific, uniform methods for securing complete coverage, relying instead on the ingenuity of local census cadres and on the voluntary cooperation of the people. Under these circumstances it is unlikely that net omissions could have been less than 5 per cent.

There are absolutely no guidelines for establishing an upper limit for the range of net undercount. If the magnitude of the 1953 census figures is taken as generally correct, the Republic of China total for 1947 would have represented an undercount of not less than 13 to 15 per cent of the total population; if the 1953 figure undercounted the population by 5 per cent, the 1947 total must have understated the total as of that date by nearly 20 per cent. Yet nothing about the methods and circumstances of either of these enumerations would have precluded still larger errors, nor would anything in the administrative records and operations in 1947 or 1953 have made even much larger errors apparent. It is therefore not impossible that the 1953 census total understated the actual population of mainland China as of June 30, 1953, by as much as 10 or even 15 per cent. For many of the purposes for which Mainland China population estimates are needed, it may be advisable to explore the implications of an assumed undercut of this magnitude in the 1953 census.

In concluding this discussion of the census, which has been rather critical of the quality of the work, it is necessary to place this remarkable undertaking in a somewhat larger historical perspective, lest the evaluation appear unduly negative. With all its defects, which are undoubtedly many and serious, and despite the exaggerated official claims to accuracy on one side and the sometimes immoderate skepticism of foreign analysts and commentators on the other, it must be conceded that the reported 1953 census total of 583 million people is probably the nearest approach to a reliable population figure in the history of China. Both for the magnitude of the task and the magnitude of the achievement, the 1953 census is entitled to some respect. It may be a long time before any comparable effort is undertaken.

III. THE AGE-SEX STRUCTURE

If, all things considered, the 1953 census did a fairly good job of counting heads, the same cannot be assumed to be true of the data it produced on age and sex. Here the problems are much greater. Recording age data by sex for single years of age is elaborate, subject to errors of recall or estimate, liable to misrepresentation, and difficult to compile. Moreover, the errors and biases introduced by these factors tend to be cumulative rather than compensatory. It must be admitted that the 1953 census age-sex distribution is less unbelievable than those produced by many of the enumerations in the first half of the twentieth century, but it is still improbable. No reasonable assumptions about varying patterns of fertility and mortality in the century prior to 1953 could produce such an age-sex structure. If it is used for projections of the population, its anomalies will be discernible as they age out of the picture with the passing years and are replaced at the lower end of the age-sex pyramid by more reasonable configurations. Some of the anomalies will influence the size of the newer cohorts and thus produce an echo of their own distortions on succeeding generations. Hence it is preferable to substitute new age-sex distributions representing the limits of plausibility in the reconstruction of past demographic history.[47] Even when these limits are set rather wide to accommodate the considerable degree of uncertainty about that history, the alternate structures exhibit more overall similarity to each other than to the 1953 census age-sex structure.

In the earlier study cited at the end of the last section (Aird, 1961), a single model of demographic trends during the century prior to 1953 was constructed on the assumptions that fertility, with allowance for infanticide, was equivalent to a constant crude birth rate of 42.5 per thousand population per year prior to 1948, after which, without infanticide, it rose to 45.0 per thousand; and that the crude death rate fell by stages such that the natural increase rates were as follows:

Prior to 1898	2.5 per thousand
1898 to 1918	5.0 per thousand
1918 to 1933	7.5 per thousand
1933 to 1948	10.0 per thousand
1948 to 1953	19.1 per thousand

The limitation to a single model and the use of mechanically graduated assumptions in its computation were necessitated by the amount of time required for successive trial-and-error approximations with a desk calculator to control to the assumed crude rates. However, as noted earlier, that study has been criticized for (1) failing to utilize assumptions more in line with what would be the assumed past demographic history of China

47. The demographic staff of the United Nations Department of Economic and Social Affairs, though they find less to object to in the 1953 census age-sex structure, have nevertheless preferred to substitute a model age-sex distribution in both their previous and their current projections for mainland China. See United Nations, 1959 (pp. 84-85); 1966 (p. 56).

if the Ch'ing population figures for the mid-nineteenth century were any measure of the size of China's population at that time,[48] and (2) failing to encompass a wider range of assumptions about birth rates throughout the subsequent century.[49] But using the electronic computer for population projections makes possible the projection of alternate population models over long periods of time, using intrinsic rather than crude rates and allowing year-to-year variations in the components of change to reflect assumptions about changing social and economic conditions. Hence a much more ambitious effort at reconstruction of the 1953 age-sex structure for mainland China has now been undertaken.

If the new reconstructions are to reflect the range of reasonable assumptions about historical demographic trends in China, it is necessary to enter a subject area which, though remote in time, has been kept very much alive by scholarly dispute, particularly about the size and rate of growth of the population during the Ch'ing dynasty. The discussion opened by earlier contestants in this field, such as H. P. Howard, W. W. Rockhill, and W. F. Willcox, has recently been considered enlightened by the extensive historical studies of Ho Ping-ti and the demographic evaluations of Irene Taeuber and John Durand. But contemporary scholars still differ significantly regarding not only the reliability of the official Ch'ing figures as a record of population development, but even the appropriate modes and levels of analysis that should be applied to them. This chapter can do little more than review, mainly at second hand, the information and evaluations they have made available.

Even to do no more than that involves some crucial choices. The first question which must be answered is similar to the one already dealt with in respect to the 1953 census total. Were the Ch'ing figures actually the result of some kind of continuous population reporting activity, or were they merely numbers conjured up for the convenience of local officials in submitting reports to higher authorities? If the Ch'ing figures, despite some systematic errors, had a consistent relationship with actual demographic realities, then perhaps they can be used with appropriate allowances as an indication of the size and rate of growth of the population. If they were entirely or largely clerical productions, related to reality only by accident or not at all, they are not demographic information and must be discarded

48. In his critique of the version of the model presented at the Milbank Memorial Fund conference in November, 1959, John Durand noted that the implied population obtained by reverse projection at the indicated rates of natural increase would have been about 300 million in 1850, far below the official Ch'ing dynasty population total of about 430 million in 1851. This discrepancy indicated to him that the rates of increase allowed in the intervening century were much too high. Roland Pressat made the same criticism in a subsequent review of the final report in which this model reconstruction was retained. See Aird, 1960 (pp. 134-137) and Pressat, 1961 (p. 658).

49. This point was also made by Prof. Frank Notestein at the Milbank conference in 1959. See Aird, 1960 (p. 138).

for present purposes. In examining these questions there is no a priori reason why the conclusion about the Ch'ing figures should be the same as that reached in the case of the 1953 census. The times, circumstances, and methods were different in each case and must be analyzed independently.

THE CH'ING POPULATION FIGURES

The analysis of the Ch'ing figures, as of all other historical population figures, divides into two parts: the examination of the figures themselves, and the study of the investigative and administrative procedures and processes that produced them. The criteria of judgment in respect to the systems of data production involve the effectiveness of the arrangements, their susceptibility to systematic biases, the degree of competence they required and with which they were served, and the amount of conscientiousness and energy applied. On all these counts recent scholars show a fair amount of agreement: The system of reporting through the *pao-chia* channels could not have produced accurate reports of population (Ho, 1959, Chs. III and IV; Durand, 1960, pp. 214-215; Taeuber and Wang, 1960a, pp. 404-408).

But the views of these analysts apparently diverge as to the amount of error, and whether it renders the Ch'ing figures unusable. Ho thinks that, with careful attention to the historical context and a further analysis of the local figures, particularly the implied sex ratios and average size of household, it is possible to derive useful information from the Ch'ing figures. For the period 1741-75, he believes the coverage of the system was incomplete, and suspects that the actual population may be at least 20 per cent higher than the reported figures indicate. However, he believes that the quality of the *pao-chia* registration improved considerably during the years from 1776 through 1850; underregistration was presumably declining and was perhaps partially offset by a certain amount of double counting, due to the inclusion of persons absent from their traditional residence. Ho feels that the figures still understated the total size of the population in 1850 (1959, pp. 46-55), but he regards the increase rates he obtains for two subperiods as being, despite their limited reliability, at least consistent with what is known of the economic conditions of the time (1959, p. 64).[50]

Durand also believes that the Ch'ing figures, despite limitations that render them useless for exact measurement of either the size of the population or its year-to-year changes, may nevertheless be fairly valid as rough approximations of the magnitude of the population at a given time and of its rate of increase over long periods (1960, pp. 239-240). The

50. The average annual rates of growth are 0.63 per cent for the whole period, 0.87 for 1779-94 and 0.51 for 1822-50. Ho stresses the importance of correct periodization and a knowledge of Chinese institutional history.

basis for his conclusion is the plausibility of the reported general and regional trends of population growth.

Taeuber and Wang take a much more skeptical view. The main burden of their criticism rests on the analysis of the figures themselves. This is indeed the proper place to begin with historical population figures, for if it turns out that the reported figures are demographically implausible, it matters little what inferences may be drawn from descriptive information about the nature of the reporting system. Taeuber and Wang also point out that if the annual changes in provincial figures are not possible, there is little point in arguing the plausibility of changes in the overall totals (1960a, p. 408). In fact, it can be shown by hypothetical models that when a series of "annual" component population totals, some of which advance or retreat irregularly by unbelievable proportions while others progress by moderate and obviously mechanical increments, are added together, the overall totals may exhibit a fairly "reasonable" trend and convincingly irregular year-to-year changes. Hence the plausibility of overall totals should not be taken as assurance that the data collection system on which they were based was functioning properly.

If this argument is relevant for the relationship between the Ch'ing provincial figures and the totals for all China, it may also apply to the relationships between *hsien* figures and provincial totals, and so on down to the smallest inclusive unit and its components. But since relatively few series for these smaller units have survived in the available records, the search for artifact in the Ch'ing figures cannot be pursued to its roots, and the ultimate question of plausibility resolved. For this reason, Taeuber and Wang are correct in stating that "provincial evaluations may permit firm negative answers, but they cannot yield firm positive answers" (1960a, p. 408).

The answers that Taeuber and Wang derive in the course of their analysis are both negative and firm enough to preclude further use of the Ch'ing figures for demographic purposes. In reference to the period 1741-80, when the *pao-chia* system was being extended and developed, they say:

> The evidence on the statistical credibility of the *pao-chia* figures in the first four decades of reporting is conclusively negative. The changes in provincial populations and hence in the population of all China included additions to the reporting areas, additions to the populations of areas already reporting, and additions associated with altered definitions. Under these circumstances, the figures cannot be used as a basis for computing rates of population growth in China or in its component parts.
>
> Even in the initial decades, the *pao-chia* mechanism was partially separated from the facts it presumably reported. Despite the domination of growth by a high mortality that must have fluctuated greatly from year to year, provinces were characterized increasingly by persistent rates of change, interrupted

occasionally by sharp upward movements. Neither famine, epidemic, nor flight produced decreases in provincial populations. (1960a, p. 411.)

A similar verdict is rendered for the period 1852-1911, when the system was disrupted by the Taiping, Miao, Nien, and other disturbances, and was obviously no longer functioning in many areas. But the crucial questions arise in connection with the middle period, 1780-1851, when the system was presumably at its best; if it were ever to provide a measure of the actual size and rate of growth of the population, it should have done so during these years. Here again Taeuber and Wang reached sweepingly negative conclusions. They find "regularities in the amount or the percentage of change year by year for all provinces except Hopeh, Shensi, Shantung, and Fukien" during the years from 1786 through 1791, and they say that "patterned regularities were even more prevalent in the years from 1830 to 1851." A number of examples are cited to illustrate the use of standard absolute or percentage increments during both periods (1960a, p. 413).

Unfortunately, however, the argument here, like their argument in connection with the 1953 census, suffers from several serious defects: (1) failure to establish clearly the criteria for determining that artificial regularities are present;[51] (2) ambiguity or inaccuracy in describing the regularities found; and (3) overgeneralization. The question of criteria is not a simple one in this case, for the source data are given only in thousands, which means that where the increments are small, only one significant digit is available, and so the test for artifice based on the identity of digits of successive increments is not applicable. Where the digits are not identical, the essential question is whether the size of the annual increments for any particular province over a period of years shows insufficient year-to-year variation to allow for the fluctuations in mortality that may reasonably be expected to have occurred given the conditions of the time and place. Establishing the criteria for this judgment calls for at least some historical and statistical analysis to establish the limits of permissible variation. Only in extreme cases can the assertion that regularity is excessive be made simply on inspection. Moreover, the significance of the evidence based on identity of digits and variability of increments depends somewhat on the number of years for which data are available. In the period 1786 through 1791, for example, only five increments are

51. Taeuber and Wang point out that "there are objective standards that permit the evaluation of the possibility or the probability that given series of figures are records of existing populations and their changes." They then list four such "standards" in abstract form but do not provide the quantitative tolerance limits without which the standards cannot be operationalized (1960a, p. 408). In the case of gross anomalies in the population figures, precise specifications are obviously unnecessary, but the failure to indicate statistical criteria for marginal cases leaves a hiatus between generalized standards for evaluation and generalized statements of findings, which makes replication difficult.

available for each province. On the one hand, this means that some regularities may escape detection because their pattern is not discernible within so few years, but on the other hand, the span is so short that any coincidence of numbers must involve not less than two-fifths of the available instances, which may result in exaggeration of the prevalence of the phenomenon. Without the rigorous application of explicit and reasonable criteria, the identification of "regularities" is susceptible to unsuspected biases in one direction or another on the part of the observer. More precise analysis, while it would undoubtedly eliminate some supposed regularities, might turn up others not apparent to the unaided eye.

When reporting evidence of this type, it is important to make sure that the findings are set forth clearly. In presenting their evidence, Taeuber and Wang cite some instances in which the yearly increments in the provincial figures for one period or the other are said to vary from "2,000 to 3,000" or from "3,000 to 4,000," while for other provinces or years the increments are stated as "2,000 or 3,000" and "19,000 or 20,000" (1960a, p. 413), from which the reader would infer that in the first examples the increments were unrounded figures falling within the indicated ranges, while in the latter cases either one or the other figure was used in rounded form. Since, as was indicated, the source data were all rounded to thousands,[52] this distinction could not have been found. Unless the unrounded provincial totals are examined, there is no way of knowing whether or not round figures were used in the original compilations. Similarly, some provinces are said to have increased by "0.1 or 0.2 per cent" or by "0.6 or 0.7 per cent," and others are said to have increased by a single percentage figure (1960a, p. 413), from which the reader might infer that percentage figures in the exact amounts given had actually been used in manufacturing the figures. Actually, the source materials give no evidence that percentage increments were used in computing the figures for these years, for the percentage values vary within the ranges indicated by Taeuber and Wang and around the single figures, and sometimes depart from them. Obviously such inferences are not justified, but the ambiguity that gives rise to them leads to an impression of greater regularity than in fact exists in the source figures.

The same criticism applies to a statement in reference to the period 1830 to 1851 that "Anhwei added 19,000 or 20,000 each year, while Szechwan added 610,000 to 620,000" (1960a, p. 413). In fact, alternate additions of 19,000 or 20,000 were made to the population of Anhwei only during the years 1846-1852, and the range of increments for Szechwan during the 21 years from 1830 to 1851 is from 446,000 to 775,000, with only 8 increments in the range 610,000 to 620,000. There is still a

52. The Ch'ing figures for this part of the analysis were taken from Yen Chung-p'ing et al., 1955.

strong suggestion of artifact in both instances, but the case for it is less impressive when precisely stated.

Moreover, the statement quoted earlier that all but four provinces show regularities in their increments during the years 1786-91 is not clearly sustained by the figures. In the case of Chili, Anhwei, Hunan, and Shansi there are identities of digits in two- or three-digit numbers in two years out of the five, which might or might not be confirmed if unrounded figures were available. For five other provinces where the increments are determinable only in one-digit numbers, there are, naturally, other identities, but without the unrounded figures it cannot be shown whether any of these are significant for the point in question. In the case of Chekiang, Szechwan, and Yünnan, as Taeuber and Wang note, each of the four succeeding increments is larger than its predecessor, and in Kwangsi a reverse progression is shown, but the increments do not change at a constant rate. The assumption that such successively increasing or decreasing increments, involving only four changes each and appearing in only 4 provinces out of a total of 21 provinces examined, lie outside the range of chance in all respects would seem to be questionable. Even if all the 13 provinces mentioned above showed unquestionable evidence of artifact, there would still be 8, not 4, that did not.

Turning to the question of overgeneralization, it is not at all certain that the discovery of a few instances of identical increments justifies the conclusion that the taint attaches not only to those figures but to all their lineal antecedents and descendants as well. It would at least have to be shown that the periods of identical repetition, during which the errors of artifice would almost certainly be cumulative (in whatever direction), were not merely due to arbitrary estimates caused by temporary lapses in reporting, the effects of which were eliminated when the local records were reported again at a later date. In view of the intermixture of regularities with marked irregularities, this hypothesis would have to be tested and proved false before the figures could be definitely and finally rejected on the basis of short intervals of obvious artificiality. If the more intensive research proposed by Taeuber and Wang at the end of their article is conducted with more rigorous criteria of evidence, the findings, though they may not sustain unequivocal statements, might permit a more definitive answer as to what value the Ch'ing figures have for demographic purposes.

Nevertheless, even if their conclusions are somewhat premature, the review of the Ch'ing figures by Taeuber and Wang has raised serious doubt as to their usefulness for measuring the overall size or rate of growth of the population at any time during the eighteenth or nineteenth centuries. Moreover, it is likely that further research would turn up more evidence in support of their case. For reasons already stated, the examination of figures for smaller components may be expected to disclose artificialities not apparent in the provincial figures, where the latter were actually obtained by summing local reports. The study of specific local trends in economic and social conditions will probably disclose further discrepancies between the trends of increase shown in the population figures and the probable trends in mortality, challenging the credibility not only of series that show constant increases, but also of some that show fluctuating changes not consistent with the record of local conditions. Comparing the population figures for adjacent small areas with similar economic and social conditions may turn up other discrepancies. If, when all the work is done, there are still many areas and periods for which the population figures have escaped serious challenge, an indeterminate margin of doubt must be allowed for further improbabilities not identifiable because of lack of information.

Assuming that this is the ultimate verdict, what use may be made of the Ch'ing figures? Taeuber and Wang say that, since they are not "statistical" in the modern sense of the term, "abstract statistical manipulation of the figures may be as naive as uncritical acceptance of them in their crude form" (1960a, p. 416). Durand, reviewing their case, agrees that the figures are useless for tracing year-to-year changes, but he asks whether they may not still be valid as approximations both of the size of the population at a given time and of its increase over a long period. A positive answer depends, he notes, on the degree of realism with which the initial figures were established; the degree to which the increments for subsequent years, whether arbitrary or not, coincided with actual growth trends over the long run; or the degree to which major revisions and adjustments overcame whatever cumulative error had occurred in previous years. The answer he gives is that, in the light of what is known about general economic development and regional population distribution at the time, the long-range average annual increase rates for the provinces are reasonable enough to justify a certain amount of confidence in their representation of demographic trends. Despite their defects, Durand concludes, "the evidence does not . . . warrant dismissing them as entirely unrealistic and useless for study of the major features of population history of the period" (1960, pp. 239-244).

Durand's criterion is essentially one of historical plausibility,[53] but the

53. A similar argument for the credibility of the Ch'ing figures was advanced in 1950 by K. W. Taylor, who argued that "these records, properly interpreted, are substantially correct and consistent with the known history of this period." What he meant by the seemingly contradictory phrase "properly interpreted" is not clear even in the full context, for he seems to accept not only the trends of increase of the official figures for China before, during, and after Ch'ing times but also their absolute levels, on the grounds that the increase rates indicated are "not extraordinary," and the patterns of growth and stability agreed generally with the historical record of economic and social conditions. However, the unreliability of the criterion of plausibility as a basis of judgment may be illustrated by the fact that three years

plausibility of a long-term trend of increase in a set of population totals adds little to their credibility if it is possible that they were originally artificially constructed to look plausible to the higher officials to whom they were to be submitted. It adds even less if there is also the possibility that the mechanics of reporting and coverage, including extension of the system in periods of prosperity and omissions of reports in time of distress, may have lent the figures an accidental plausibility, as the investigations of Ho Ping-ti and Taeuber and Wang suggest.

So far as the trend of vital rates and natural increase is concerned, if it were possible to determine a plausible demographic pattern from historical information on general and local economic trends, there would seem to be no particular reason not to base demographic assumptions directly on what is considered plausible without becoming involved in the kind of statistical manipulations of the Ch'ing figures that Taeuber and Wang oppose. The figures are of little use as sources of information if their credibility is contingent on their plausibility, for plausibility in this case sets rather broad limits for both natural increase and population size. The fact that the long-range trend of the official figures falls within these limits does not recommend that trend over others that must be accepted as equally plausible; it constitutes no endorsement of the total population figures for any year or period. Alternate assumptions about vital rates differing only slightly in their implied annual increase rates will over long periods of time generate vastly different population totals.

---

after Taylor had reached his conclusion that "Since 1850 the population of China appears to have come up against a new ceiling in the neighborhood of 425 to 450 million," the Chinese Communists came up with a figure definitely in a new neighborhood (Taylor, 1950, pp. 310-312).

Half a century earlier W. W. Rockhill also attempted to apply a criterion of plausibility to the Ch'ing figures, but he came out with a very different conclusion. Rockhill compared the increase rates implied by the Ch'ing figures for various periods with information on mortality conditions from the historical records to see whether "the annual rates of increase were at all reasonable," and found that as a reflection of what was known historically "nothing less satisfactory could be conceived." The implied rates varied sharply from one period to another without regard to whether conditions for population growth were favorable or not. Moreover, he noted, the average yearly increase for the whole period from 1743 through 1783, the most prosperous years under the Ch'ing, was 1.83 per cent, whereas "in Japan, where much more favorable conditions exist than in China, the average yearly increase of the population from 1872 to 1899 has been only 1.04 per cent." For this reason he rejected the official series except for the figure for 1741, which he regarded as "closer to the truth than some subsequent ones" because at that time the government was "in strong, intelligent hands [and] its mandates [were] executed with more faithfulness and precision than at any other subsequent period." Rockhill supported his view with a generalization the plausibility of which would not be widely accepted today: "In China all statements of population are largely guess-work, and where numbers are guessed they are always magnified . . ." (Rockhill, 1904, pp. 303-321). These are only a few of many statements that could be cited to show the great plasticity of the criterion of plausibility as it has been applied to the population of China.

Even if we were to accept Durand's contention that the figure for 1749 had some ties to reality (1960, p. 240), or Ho's view that the figure for 1779 was a better one (1959, p. 63), a large margin or error would have to be applied to either figure. If the upper and lower limits of these margins were carried forward to 1851, with a rather modest allowance for the range of possible increase rate trends, the overall difference between the upper and lower estimates of the total population by 1851 would be immense. A spread of only 2.5 per thousand (0.25 per cent) in the increase rates applied to the 1749 figure can yield a difference of about 80 million in the population total by 1851, without allowing for a range of error in the starting figures, and using lower increase rates than those implied by the Ch'ing figures. If the 1779 figure is employed in the same series, the difference by 1851 is more than 65 million. If we start instead with the 1953 census total and move backward to 1851, the possible range of error in the 1851 population total, again without allowance for a range of error in 1953, is larger still, probably not less than 150 million, because of the uncertainty about population increase rates during the tormented century between. Under the circumstances there would seem to be little basis for statements that the 1851 Ch'ing figure is "consistent" with the 1953 census figure, and even less basis for inferring that doubt about the 1851 figure may thereby be attached to the figure for 1953.[54] Hence plausibility, an ambiguous criterion at best, and only loosely applicable in this context, does not justify the derivation of increase rates from the Ch'ing figures.

It is still more difficult to define what would constitute plausibility in respect to the size of the total population under the Ch'ing dynasty. How does one posit a reasonable figure for the total population of China in 1775 or 1851? How does one know when the outer limits of an increasing series of hypothetical ranges of error begin to touch the limits of credulity? What, in this case, is the basis for incredulity? It must be something more than a vague sense of discomfort as the expanding limits depart further from the familiar magnitude of the official figures.

Perhaps a review of the historical information on the administrative uses of population data under the Ch'ing might indicate what margin of error the system could tolerate without dysfunction. How far could the official population figures for a unit of a given level depart from actuality before the discrepancy became inconvenient? What would be the minimum discrepancy that the local officials would be capable of detecting? Would the limits for different administrative purposes vary? Would the limits for figures greater than the true number be different from those for figures below it? Presumably the limits of perception, and perhaps also the limits

54. The estimates of difference given here were based on assumed alternative increase trends for 1750-1851 and 1851-1953 employed hereafter in the construction of model populations.

of toleration, would be narrower for smaller units than for larger, and there would also be differences by type of community, pattern of habitation, economic base, and so on. For example, would a *pao* chief in a rural area where rice is grown in irrigated fields be able to detect an error in his population figures as small as 10 per cent? Would he be able to overlook or ignore an error as large as 25 per cent? Would a provincial official be able to recognize an error of 25 per cent? Would provincial taxation, military levies, and other activities be seriously inconvenienced by a 50 per cent error?

All these questions depend upon precise knowledge as to how population figures and administrative activities were operationally related. If there were definite functional ties, on the basis of which approximate limits of tolerable error could be determined, the next question is what local officials would have done when confronted with discrepancies exceeding these limits. Would they attempt to correct the population reports, convey their concern to the next higher official, or devise expedient solutions and keep silent until the accumulation of discrepancies across the country became visible from the imperial palace?

While historical research is examining these questions, it might also deal with the question of the probable direction of net error for any particular time and place. A number of known or suspected biases, some pointing in one direction, some in the other, have already been noted by Ho, Durand, and Taeuber and Wang. Some were inherent in the organization and operation of the *pao-chia* reporting system. Others may be suspected because of administrative practices and attitudes that might have influenced population reporting. The significance of particular biases and the direction of net bias may have varied in time and place.

Even if historical research were able to answer these questions, and the magnitude and direction of error in the Ch'ing figures could be estimated, the reasonable expectation is that the limits would remain far too broad for many analytical purposes. In view of this tentative conclusion and the likelihood that the critical judgments of Taeuber and Wang would be further corroborated, it would seem advisable to invert Durand's conclusion about the utility of the Ch'ing figures: the evidence thus far does not warrant using them to study China's population history during this period. For present purposes it seems more appropriate to use hypothetical alternate assumptions about vital rates and magnitudes rather than to place an unjustifiable reliance on the single series of Ch'ing totals.

DEMOGRAPHIC MODELS FOR 1750-1850

The period of critical importance in determining what alternate age-sex structures should be assumed for 1953 is, of course, the century immediately preceding, not only because the 1953 population were the survivors of its vicissitudes but also because its catastrophes and holocausts were so extreme as to obscure the structural traces of the more moderate demographic conditions during the century before it. Probably any stable population model with high mortality and a low increase rate would have sufficed to start the reconstructions as of 1851;[55] the choice of an initial model would not have had a significant effect on the resulting age-sex structures as of 1953. Nevertheless, for present purposes generalized historical models were designed to reflect demographic trends during the period 1750-1850, partly in order to study the relationships of fertility, mortality, and natural increase rates in a population with changing growth patterns so that this experience could be applied in planning the historically specific inputs for 1851-1953.

A specific historical base population total is not necessary for the century 1750-1850. All that is needed are a set of alternative trends in natural increase, corresponding alternate birth and death parameters, and a reasonable age-sex structure for 1750. Reasonable patterns must first be established for the trend of natural increase during the years to be covered by the reconstructions; then values must be assigned to the high and low points of the curve; and finally the intervening values may be obtained by a convenient interpolative process. For this purpose, the basic source material is the relevant historical information on developments in the Chinese economy, agriculture, food production, food prices, settlement patterns, and general living conditions collected and evaluated by Ho, along with the general implications for population growth set forth in the final chapter of his book (1959, pp. 266-275).

According to Ho's review of the records, a period of civil disturbances, rebellions, local wars, famines, pestilences, and severe economic conditions occupied much of the seventeenth century, until about 1683. The conquest of Formosa in that year, which marked the end of organized resistance to Manchu rule, was followed by an era of peace and prosperity, during which favorable economic conditions began slowly but progressively to increase the rate of population growth. In the first half of the eighteenth century, there was apparently a definite rise in living standards and population growth rates. The price of rice also rose during this period, but apparently this was more a reflection of the general prosperity than a cause of distress. Optimum conditions were reached, Ho believes, between 1750 and 1775, but from then on, the pressure of population began to make itself felt. Most arable land was already under cultivation, and the expansion of the farming population under pressure onto more marginal lands caused increasing soil erosion and diminishing agricultural returns by the end of the century.

55. A stable population is one having constant age-specific birth and death rates and an unchanging age-sex structure. Its size may be increasing or decreasing, depending upon the relative levels of birth and death rates. If births and deaths balance, it is called a stationary population.

As rice surpluses dwindled, prices continued upward, and a noticeable deterioration of living standards set in. Scholars and officials, reflecting the general awareness of the nature of the problem, no longer spoke of a rapidly increasing population as a cause for optimism. This was the period in which the "Chinese Malthus," Hung Liang-chi, set forth his theories about the economic consequences of overpopulation. Throughout the first half of the nineteenth century the population continued to grow, though presumably at a decreasing rate. Economic conditions became more and more stringent, until by 1850 the population was back to subsistence level and on the threshhold of a major cataclysm.

The natural increase trend that this account implies would begin at a low point during the third quarter of the seventeenth century, rise to its highest point in the third quarter of the eighteenth century, and return to another low point by 1850. Probably the two low points would be adequately represented by assuming a zero increase rate or one not much above it. The high point is more of a problem, involving assumptions about birth and death rates as well.

What is the maximum believable increase rate for the Chinese population during the perior of optimum conditions, the third quarter of the eighteenth century? Chen Chang-heng constructed total population estimates using an increase rate of 10 per thousand population per year for the whole period from 1741 to 1750 (1931, pp. 48-51). This increase rate is well below the trend of the official figures, which Chen rejects because he suspects that the earlier figures were understated and the later ones exaggerated. Durand allows an average increase rate of 15 per thousand for the period 1749-1775, 9 per thousand for 1775-1794, and 7 per thousand for the period 1794-1851 (1960, pp. 243-244). These increase rates correspond to those implicit in the official total population figures. But the case for such high increase rates must be judged on its own merits: the official figures, as has been argued earlier, offer no substantial support.

The rate of 7 per thousand as an average for the period 1794-1851, even though it represents a marked decline from a high of 15 per thousand, would seem much too high to describe the demographic conditions of a population being reduced by increasing population pressures, general food shortages, and local famines to a perilous margin of survival. If the deterioration of conditions after 1775 was anywhere near as severe as Ho suggests, neither this rate nor the rate of 9 per thousand for 1775-94 would seem adequate to fit the historical materials. But this judgment depends in part on how realistic it is to assume an average rate of 15 per thousand for the peak years 1749-75. Durand points out that this rate could be achieved with a crude birth rate of 45 and a crude death rate of 30 per thousand (1960, p. 243), but what was possible arithmetically may not have been possible demographically. The essential question is whether an increase rate of 15 per thousand is a reasonable one. There is no evidence of a demographic nature bearing directly on this question. The traditional view of demography has always been that long-range average population increase rates prior to the modern era could not have been much above replacement level through most of human existence, but the implicit time reference for such a generalization is a much longer period than the segment of history we are here considering. The rise and fall of empires over centuries and millennia may have produced long-term average increase rates close to zero, while the actual trend consisted of relatively long periods of stationary or slightly increasing population, somewhat shorter periods of fairly rapid growth, and relatively brief periods of brutal depopulation. But these presumptions do not help resolve the question.

Perhaps a better basis for judgment can be obtained by considering what a 25-year average increase rate of 15 per thousand in a large and populous country might imply for its temporal and spatial components. The figure is an average, which means that it is made up of higher and lower country-wide averages for any given year, with still more deviant rates for the component provinces and *hsien*. If there were one or more peak years in the period 1749-75, representing the attainment of optimum living conditions and the maximum rate of population growth, the increase rates for those years would have to have risen well above the rate of 15 per thousand; how far above would depend on the sharpness of the slope of the trend line in approaching the maximum and departing from it afterward. The sharper the peak, the more it must exceed the assumed period average.

Simple hypothetical models can demonstrate this proposition, but it is obvious that if there was gradual improvement in the early years of the period of recovery that began in 1683, as Ho says, the rate of improvement must have accelerated nearer the peak years. If deterioration was also fairly sharp, the trend line for 1750-75 and the adjacent quarter-century periods would have assumed more of a leptokurtic (peaked) pattern than a sine curve. In that case, Durand's period average of 15 per thousand would mean that the peak years witnessed an increase rate of at least 20 per thousand and perhaps higher. If we allow for year-by-year fluctuations in both directions from a mean trend line at 20 per thousand during the peak years, the rates for some individual years would have to go higher yet to counterpoise those falling below the trend. Are we willing to credit an increase rate as high as 20 per thousand or higher as the country-wide average during any single year in China, or in any other premodern agrarian country in which social and economic conditions approximate those in the Ch'ing dominions of the late eighteenth century?

If the answer is yes, then we must consider the implications of such a country-wide average for a vast territory and population living under varying local conditions. The provincial rates cannot all fall in line like soldiers at exactly 20 per thousand; some must fall below, while others, to maintain the average, must exceed that figure. If some provinces fall to 10 or 15 per thousand or below, others must reach a rate of 25 per thousand or thereabouts, and the populations involved and the degrees of deviation from the mean must balance. Is it conceivable that the increase rates for provinces of China during the eighteenth century, many with larger populations than most European countries, could have exceeded by ten points or more the highest rates recorded for any Western European country during the rapid growth period of the nineteenth century? Even allowing for higher fertility rates in China than in Europe, this is hard to credit. Moreover, if we accept this proposition and assume that the birth rate in these Chinese provinces was 45 per thousand, the necessarily resulting death rates of 25 per thousand or below were less than those recorded in the early nineteenth century for France, Sweden, and Finland, for example. Is this credible? If the answer is still affirmative, the argument proceeds to the province with the highest increase rate and from there to its *hsien*.

Actually, the logic here may not be as compelling as it can be made to sound. It must be borne in mind that the maximum dispersion of component unit averages around the overall mean may not be equidistant in both directions and is probably more constricted at the upper end. Even so, viewed from these perspectives, a country-wide average increase rate of 15 per thousand would seem excessive even for the peak years, let alone the whole quarter century 1750-75, for a population living under the social and economic conditions of Ch'ing China. The claim that such a rate is reasonable requires more supporting argument.

The lower the peak of the increase trend, the less the implied increase rates for particular times and localities, but a much lower increase trend means the end of any hope of accommodating the Ch'ing population totals. Despite what has been said about them, many people will feel a certain uneasiness at being asked to lay the Ch'ing totals aside once and for all. Some may still cling to the remote expectation that further research just might accord them a measure of confirmation or at least suggest some way of rehabilitating them with a minimum of adjustments. Reluctance to abandon the official totals altogether is quite understandable, since scarcity and antiquity combine to make them seem more precious than they are. However, it is better to be resolute in rejecting bad data, even if the alternative is to use purely hypothetical parameters.

For the period 1750-1850, two increase trends were constructed, one of which began its rise from zero in the last quarter of the seventeenth century, reached a peak of 10.0 per thousand in 1762-63, declined rapidly thereafter, and was still falling at 2.5 per thousand in 1850. The other began its rise only in 1700, peaked at 7.5 per thousand in 1762-63, and declined to zero again by 1850. The initial age-sex structures for 1750 and the subsequent growth patterns for both models were based on these trends. A third model with a peak at 12.5 per thousand was contemplated but was not constructed, since, as was to be expected, the two increase trends used yielded very little difference in age-sex structure compared with that which resulted from alternate assumptions about birth and death rates.

In premodern agrarian societies, changes in increase rates are due mainly to changing mortality rates. Birth rates probably are not actually constant, but since they are intimately bound up with some of the most stable elements of traditional culture, such as age at marriage, marital and family relationships, and specific values and behavior in respect to procreation, which are relatively immune to cyclical economic conditions, changes in the intrinsic fertility rates are presumably slight. Death rates, on the other hand, are immediately and directly responsive to pandemics, famines, and social upheavals, which often occur simultaneously. Hence, under premodern conditions, the death rate is likely to be the principal adjuster of the increase rate and subject to sudden as well as gradual changes.

For this reason, the simplest procedure, once increase rates have been chosen, is to select alternate fertility levels and let mortality trends follow the changes required by the trend of the increase rates. The only major decision remaining, then, is what levels of fertility to use. So far as Ch'ing China is concerned, there is little to go on at present except generalized demographic experience and whatever inferences can be drawn from the local population investigations of the twentieth century. Demographic experience in other countries with high fertility, but with more adequate measurement, suggests that an agrarian society characterized by a fairly early age for marriage and a high proportion of people married during the childbearing years is likely to have a crude birth rate somewhere in the range of 40 to 50 per thousand population per year. Local population studies from the second quarter of the twentieth century sometimes indicated birth rates below 40 per thousand, but the quality of these investigations was not above reproach. What was undoubtedly one of the better ones, an experiment in vital registration reported by Ch'iao, Thompson, and Chen, found a crude birth rate of 45.1; and the authors specifically cautioned that a higher rate would probably have been found if registration had been complete (1938, pp. 40-48). (Section IV will discuss this further in connection with the fertility assumptions for 1953, and further development of the rationale underlying the choice of birth rates will be deferred until then.) For the period 1750-1850, crude birth rates of 40 and 45 per thousand, compounded with the two increase trends discussed above, were projected in four separate models. From these models, the two that gave the most divergent age-sex structures—the high fertility, high increase model and the low fertility, low increase model—were selected as the alternate base populations for 1851.

PROJECTIONS FOR 1851-1953

For the period 1851-1953, more complex demographic inputs are appropriate. Not only is this the period in which the population of 1953 was born and raised, but it was one marked by crises that would have deeply scarred and distorted the age-sex structure. Because the severity of the crises and their demographic impact is not determinable with any degree of precision, it is necessary to incorporate a wider range of assumptions about population growth trends during this period. The assumptions in regard to some factors, particularly those about catastrophic population losses, remain crude and mechanical; for some other factors, it did not seem appropriate, for various reasons, to test the extreme limits of alternative values.

In the models for this period, fertility levels were again assumed to remain constant, and mortality levels were varied to conform to the assumed patterns of population growth and decline. But fertility in this case was controlled not to constant crude birth rates but to constant gross reproduction rates[56] equivalent to crude birth rates of 40 or 45 per thousand as of 1953. This was done to permit crude birth rates and the size of the birth cohorts to change year-by-year in response to changes in the age-sex structure caused by erratic mortality in a century of recurrent catastrophe. There must surely have been fluctuations in fertility levels, apart from those due to changing age composition, that are not taken into account in these models. Changes in intrinsic fertility levels may have resulted from long-term changes in economic conditions and from sustained periods of civil disturbance and large-scale distress migrations. To make appropriate allowances for the effects of these events on fertility, it would be necessary to decide on the degree of fertility reduction likely to have been caused by each one; the amount of reduction would vary not only with the severity and extent of the crisis but also with the type of crisis. At present there is no information on which to base such estimates, and even if there were, it is doubtful whether long-term crises have had much impact on fertility in a society in which the resilience of domestic institutions has been tested by thousands of years of recurrent crises.

In the case of acute short-term crises, a more marked impact may be possible, perhaps sufficient to leave a permanent and noticeable imprint on the age-sex structure of the population. Here again, however, there may be some question as to how significant these effects could be.

56. The gross reproduction rate is the number of female infants who would be born to 1,000 women surviving through the childbearing years according to current or assumed age-specific fertility rates.

Take, for example, a catastrophe severe enough to raise the level of the crude death rate by 15 points in a single year, the sharpest short-term rise in mortality registered by any of the models developed hereafter; would the corresponding drop in the crude birth rate be as much as one-tenth as great? If so, in the particular model in which this occurs, which happens to have almost identical crude birth and death rates for the year prior to the crisis, the birth rate would have dropped 1.5 points from a figure just over 40 per thousand, resulting in a reduction of the birth cohort for that year of less than 4 per cent. If a ratio of one-fifth is used instead, the birth cohort reduction would be about 7 per cent. However, at the levels of mortality being used here, the sudden rise in mortality necessarily includes a very sharp upturn in infant mortality, which by itself would leave a mark on the birth cohorts for the year in question. Would an additional depression of 7 per cent, three-fourths of which would have to be allocated to the year following the year of crisis to allow for the term of pregnancy, add enough "realism" to the model to justify the effort involved in making small adjustments in the gross reproduction rate? Probably not, especially since the survivors of this particular crisis, which occurred in 1877-78, would have been over age 75 by 1953 and thus lumped together in the residual age group where their singular deficit is not discernible. All in all, in view of the inaccuracy of all assumptions about the severity of historical catastrophes, delicate adjustments of intrinsic fertility rates are probably unjustifiable.[57]

Assumptions about mortality were also greatly complicated in the models for the period 1851-1953, partly by the necessity of accommodating to a more irregular trend of natural increase and some variability in the crude birth rates, and partly by the necessity of taking into account the special mortality patterns introduced by periodic and sometimes overlapping catastrophic events. For present purposes, major catastrophes were thought of as interruptions of a general trend in mortality, which would tetnd to return to "normal" when they were over. In actual fact, of course, any major catastrophe that afflicts a considerable part of the country is likely to alter the basic living conditions and thus contribute to some deviation from the "normal" trend line, and this was taken into account

57. Scholars whose work does not afford them a close familiarity with demographic processes and their socioeconomic concomitants may wonder why a demographer cannot simply throw into the hopper an arbitrary allowance for fertility reduction during crisis, say 10 per cent or 20 per cent for all historic catastrophes, and consider the matter taken care of. Such a gesture would probably satisfy the objections of casual users of statistics who suppose that it is more important to have made some kind of mathematical allowance for every factor in the situation than to worry about scale and proportion in the adjustments they apply. However, excessive adjustments for trivial factors are worse than none, and trivial adjustments are usually more trouble than they are worth. In constructing hypothetical models, sooner or later a point is reached where it is best to stop tinkering and get on to the next stage.

in establishing the line itself. But some catastrophes, such as locally severe famines in otherwise stable periods, military deaths in Korea, and the killing of landlords, may have rather little to do with general living conditions, and can therefore be regarded as outside the general trend line. Hence the treatment of "normal" and "special" mortality as semi-independent inputs seemed justifiable.

Choosing which catastrophes to include in the schedule of "special" mortality posed a complex problem that could only be solved (within the time that could be allotted to it) by extremely arbitrary decisions. The criterion for selection was that "special" catastrophes were those that promised to leave a perceptible trace on the age-sex structure of the population. All other catastrophes were assumed to have merged with the general mortality trend without individually visible traces. However, to apply even this ambiguous criterion with any thoroughness would have called for the assembling of a prodigious mass of historical detail and a major effort of evaluation. This was a practical impossibility. Instead, it was necessary to limit the effort to a reliance on secondary sources, especially Ho Ping-ti's valuable chapter on "Catastrophic Deterrents" (1959, pp. 227-256), and to employ bold assumptions and freehand estimates as needed. The resulting estimates are arbitrary and unreliable, and will probably be extensively revised in the future.

For that matter, the descriptions and figures given in the original sources could hardly be called reliable either. If it is difficult for demographers to set retrospectively the limits of plausibility on "normal" demographic events in historical times, it must be much more difficult for local observers or administrators, without demographic training, who are immersed in circumstances of acute disaster or social upheaval. Besides, local officials may have their own purposes to serve either by understating bad news that reflects on their administration or by exaggerating it to secure a larger share of central relief or tax remission. The reports of independent observers have their own biases. Death on a massive scale is shocking not only to Western observers but also to conscientious Chinese officials, who may involuntarily exaggerate the toll. On the other hand, the most severely affected rural areas are not likely to be accessible to outside observers in a period of crisis; hence there may be some tendency to underestimate the loss of human life in the unvisited hinterlands.

Even if we decide there is no choice but to rely on what has been reported, many reports give no figures, or give a single figure rather than a range, or give figures in such a way that it is hard to tell what they mean, if indeed the original reporter knew what *he* meant. Were the figures on "losses" to be taken as deaths in excess of "normal" mortality, or deaths from all causes, including "normal" mortality? Do they apply to the whole population or only to adults? Are the losses limited to deaths, or do they include persons who have sought refuge in other areas?

Usually these questions cannot be answered definitely. Sometimes it may be suspected that the figures given were not conceived in strictly statistical terms at all, but were merely a way of saying vividly that conditions were terrible.

Similar problems arise in connection with reports of population losses in connection with military actions. Military losses may be deliberately understated to enhance the impression of success, or overstated to conceal the extent of desertions. Sometimes the figures refer only to "casualties," without distinguishing killed, wounded, and missing in action. Civilian casualties during military action are usually less accurately recorded or estimated than military deaths, and the estimates may not distinguish between deaths due directly to the fighting and those resulting from war-caused accidents and epidemics.

For the reasons indicated, the list of catastrophes probably contains some that might have been omitted and neglects some that should have been included, and the relative force of particular catastrophes, determined by the estimated losses attributed to them, is probably out of balance at many points. Moreover, some artificial smoothing effects were introduced by the arbitrary methods used here to fit the "special" mortality schedule into the various projection models. For catastrophes that lasted for a period of years, such as the Taiping rebellion, the total loss estimate was arbitrarily allocated in equal portions among the years; this assumption is obviously contrary to fact, yet there seemed little point in constructing special trend lines for these catastrophes unless the trends could be based on detailed historical information, which was not practical under present limitations. However, so far as the end product in 1953 is concerned, the difference which would result from substituting a more "realistic" trend would probably be so slight that it would scarcely justify the considerable additional effort involved.

Another element of methodological arbitrariness was added by the fact that, in preparing inputs for the projections, the estimates of catastrophic losses were retained in absolute form until the final stages in all models, instead of being controlled to the population totals implied by the alternate base population totals and rates of growth. The reason here was that such control would have been justifiable only on the assumption that the original estimates had been made with a specific total population figure in mind, which was almost certainly not the usual case. Hence, in addition to the differential produced by the arbitrarily assigned maximal and minimal values for most of the catastrophes, some variation in the weighting of catastrophic losses was introduced by the differences in total population size that resulted from different assumed increase ratios. Generally speaking, the higher catastrophic loss schedule was applied to models having lower increase ratios and vice versa; but since low increase ratios imply large initial populations and high increase ratios imply smaller initial populations, the effect of this uncontrolled factor is to reduce somewhat the rather ample range of catastrophic population losses, particularly in the earlier years.

The 16 catastrophes and estimated net population losses used in the models for 1851-1953 are as follows:

Taiping rebellion	20,000,000-50,000,000
Nien wars	2,000,000- 3,500,000
Great drought famine of 1877-1878	9,000,000-13,000,000
Yellow River flood of 1888	1,000,000- 2,000,000
Famine in the loess provinces, 1892-1894	500,000- 1,000,000
Mohammedan rebellion of 1894-1895	150,000- 225,000
Great North China famine of 1920-1921	250,000- 500,000
Famine in Shensi, Honan, and Kansu of 1928	2,500,000- 5,000,000
Local wars in Szechwan, 1933-1935	550,000- 1,000,000
Nationalist and Communist war deaths as of 1934	250,000- 500,000
Yangtse flood of 1935	250,000- 500,000
Civil and anti-Japanese Wars, 1937-1945	6,500,000-13,000,000
Yellow River flood of 1938	750,000- 1,500,000
Civil War, 1946-1949	1,250,000- 2,500,000
Korean War, military deaths	500,000 [58]
Political liquidation programs, 1950-1952	3,000,000 [58]

The total range and catastrophic losses implied by these figures is between 48,450,000 and 98,075,000.

The one remaining adjustment made in the inputs for the century from 1851 to 1953 was the inclusion of an allowance for infanticide. The occurrence of infanticide is widely attested in the historical records for China even down to Communist times, when an effort was made to stamp it out once and for all. It apparently was not a constant factor in all times and places. Though it persisted in good years as well as bad, and among rich families as well as poor, the incidence of infanticide evidently rose in times of adversity. Most accounts indicate that both girl and boy infants were destroyed, but the destruction of girls was evidently more extensive.[59] How important a factor infanticide may have been on a country-wide scale, or how much female infanticide exceeded male, is impossible to say.

58. Though supporting evidence is insubstantial, these loss figures are believed to be moderate to conservative. Single figures were preferred to extreme ranges here, sinc the use of extreme values for catastrophes selective of males so close to 1953, while they would have constituted a better test of the range of assumptions, might have caused considerable distortion in the age-sex structures needed from 1953 onward.

59. Infanticide is usually found in association with child neglect, a kind of infanticide by inadvertence, which may be more or less deliberate and which exhibits the same sex-selectivity. It is not treated separately from infanticide here, though in fact its effects may be more protracted, causing some increase in mortality levels through the early years of childhood.

No data were ever collected on the frequency of infanticide, and efforts to estimate its incidence, both by Western observers and Chinese officials, were probably subject to considerable exaggeration. It is difficult to accept as face value some of the reports cited by Ho which claim that in some localities up to 80 or 90 per cent of all female infants were put to death (1959, pp. 58-62). Long before the practice could have approached that degree of prevalence, customs devaluating women would have been overturned by the economics of scarcity. Furthermore, in a high mortality situation, even a far lower incidence of female infanticide would depopulate a community within a generation, causing the practice in its extreme form literally to die out. The assumed prevalence of infanticide has often served as a too-convenient explanation of impossibly high sex ratios found in defective local population counts during the 1930's and 1940's, for which the major causes were probably sex-selective biases in enumeration or other systematic errors.

Compared with the sex ratios reported for some of the earlier population counts in China, the 1953 census ratio of 107.6 males per 100 females is not extremely high. Figures for 30 provinces as of 1946, published by the Republic of China in 1947, show a range from 96 to 128 with an overall average of 110; all but 8 of the 30 provinces had sex ratios above that reported for 1953 (Directorate General of Budgets, 1947, p. 2). The sex ratios reported in various other provincial counts and in *hsien* censuses and surveys during the three decades prior to 1949 reported sex ratios in a somewhat wider range, but generally higher than the 1953 census figure. Taking the results of all these censuses, surveys, and official reports at face value, one might assume that sex ratios in China were tending downward over the first half of the century in response to the gradual suppression of infanticide and improved chances of survival for females. However, this explanation does not take account of the obvious defectiveness of most of these population counts, and of the possibility that the drift toward lower sex ratios may have been due in part to decreasing sex-selective biases in reports and enumerations.

The actual sex ratio of a population is the result of (1) the sex ratio at birth, (2) past and present mortality levels by age and sex, including infanticide and the special mortality situations caused by famine, plague, war, and civil unrest, (3) sex-selective migration, and (4) the distribution of the population by age. Sex ratio at birth is generally believed to be 105-106 males per 100 females throughout the world, and therefore is a minor variable. Mortality levels by age and sex seem to show considerable variability in various parts of the world, and those for any particular country have varied over time. Generally speaking, however, all life-tables seem to show markedly higher death rates for males during the first year of life (unless female infanticide and neglect are practiced), more equal rates for both sexes during childhood, and an increasingly unfavorable balance for males during the adult years, except in times and places where maternal mortality is high enough to give males a temporary advantage during the childbearing ages for females. Even in the latter cases, the overall trend of mortality is sufficiently unfavorable to males to reduce the sex ratio of the total population from 2 to 9 points below the initial 105 to 106.

War may further reduce the sex ratio, but its role in a country like China is easily exaggerated. War casualties are selective of males in very few age groups, and in agrarian societies, where much of the male population must continue to work at food production even during periods of peak military action, the proportions of males in the young adult ages involved in battle are necessarily limited. Unless the ravages of war include a systematic extermination of males in captured areas, the change in overall sex ratios caused by war is probably slight.

Migration is usually selective of males, particularly if it spans long distances or if it represents the rural-to-urban movement of surplus rural labor. In China, rural-to-urban movement, frontier settlement, and other forms of internal migration have doubtless affected the sex ratios of some provinces, but not, of course, the sex ratio of the country as a whole. Overseas migration, though it may represent a substantial accumulation in the receiving areas over a period of years, is probably too small a proportion of the population of China to have any significant effect on the sex ratios. The age distribution of the population has only a slight effect on the sex ratio of the total population; an increasing population is more heavily concentrated in the younger years, in which the age-specific sex ratios tend to be relatively high, but the difference in overall sex ratio between an unchanging population and one growing at 2 per cent is probably less than 2 points.

So far as reported sex ratios are concerned, the misreporting of ages may affect sex ratios by age but not the sex ratios of the total population. However, sex-selective omissions and sex-selective double counting may together affect the overall sex ratio rather sharply. None of the local accounts of accuracy checks during the 1953 census give any indication of sex-selective biases in omissions or double counting, but some patterns may be surmised from tendencies observed elsewhere and certain peculiarities of the 1953 census methods. Infants and young children, persons without permanent residence, persons in transit at the time of census-taking, servants living in, resident nonfamily members, aged persons, and invalids are often involuntarily omitted by respondents and not discovered by census investigators. In some of these groups, particularly persons without permanent residence and persons in transit, males usually predominate; in others, such as servants, the balance would depend on local customs. In countries where women are traditionally accorded less social importance, females are often undercounted at all ages, and this may apply especially to infants, young children, and young married women, who are believed to have been frequently omitted in the past in Chinese population counts. During the 1953 census, any failure on the part of census registrars to maintain the statistical distinction between resident and nonresident family members could have led to double counting of persons absent more than six months, who would probably have been reported both at their place of employment and at their family home. The presumption would be that males are more likely to be double counted than females. The higher omission rates for females combined with the double counting of males would have tended to increase the sex ratios of the population as reported. On the other hand, the political investigations that accompanied voter registrations would probably have given former members of the Kuomintang, ex-soldiers in the armies of the Republic of China, fugitives from "land reform," and other persons whose anxieties were aroused by these inquisitions ample reason to avoid the census and registration stations if possible. No matter how conscientious the registrars, the nonsimultaneous conduct of census work within provinces would have increased the chances that those who wished to remain uncounted could do so simply by moving from areas where the work had not begun to areas where it was already completed. It is impossible to weigh all these influences with precision, but presumably the net effect would be a higher rate of omissions for females than for males, and therefore the sex ratios as reported would be higher than the actual.

There is no way of ascertaining how much allowance should be made for sex-selective biases in reporting. However, since infanticide and differential omissions of females operate in the same direction, whatever latitude is allowed for one diminishes the potential scope of the other. This can be illustrated simply by an arbitrary example. A stable population model based on the United Nations level 20 life-table (U.N., 1956) with a sex ratio at birth of 105 males per 100 females and an annual increase rate of 1 per cent, will have an overall sex ratio of 102.6. The implied crude birth rate of this population is about 43 per thousand population per year and the implied crude death rate is about 33. If we now assume that sex-selective infanticide equivalent to 5 per cent of all births was a constant factor in this population, but that the previously given crude birth and death rates failed to take account of it, the actual birth rate of the population would rise to just over 45 per thousand and the crude death rate to just over 35. If the 5 per cent infanticide allowance is allocated by sex in the proportion of 2 female infanticides to 1 male infanticide, the sex ratio of the total population would rise to about 106.5; if the ratio of infanticides is 4 females to 1 male, the sex ratio would be about 108.4. Under these assumptions, age-specific fertility rates must rise by an even greater proportion, because the larger cohorts of infants must be born to smaller cohorts of females in childbearing years. For these reasons, there are some rather stringent limits on the size of infanticide allowances that can be tolerated without driving other parameters to unrealistic extremes.

A similar test can be made of the implications of differential under-reporting by sex. Assuming that the stable population described above (without allowance for infanticide) is an actual population that has been counted by a census with a net omission of 5 per cent, if twice as many females as males have been omitted, the sex ratio of the population as recorded in the census will be about 105.3, and if the ratio of omissions is 4 females to 1 male the recorded sex ratio will be about 106.6. Taking both sex-selective infanticide and sex-selective undercounting together, it is obvious that either the magnitude or the ratio for each factor must be reduced somewhat if allowances for both are to be kept within a limit as low as the sex ratio of 107.6 reported for the 1953 census.

It can be argued, of course, that the differences between the sex ratio in the 1953 census and the hypothetical ones have been narrowed somewhat by the fact that the stable populations used in these calculations were based on the high mortality levels of the United Nations model life-tables. The mortality patterns at these levels were strongly influenced by the use of several Indian life-tables, and they therefore tend toward relatively high mortality rates for females, with resultant high sex ratios. Perhaps the actual age-specific death rates for China during the past century, exclusive of infanticide, would have been less favorable to males and so, except for infanticide, would have yielded much lower sex ratios. Unfortunately there is no evidence on age-specific mortality levels by sex in China that is not derived from and influenced by the peculiarities of the enumerated age-sex distributions. Probably the best information on mortality by age and sex for a Chinese population with high mortality levels is that calculated by Barclay from the registration data of Taiwan during the early years under Japanese occupation. These life tables show distinctly higher ratios of male to female mortality rates at all ages than are found in the high mortality model life-tables prepared by the United Nations. Though female mortality exceeds male mortality during childhood and early adulthood in both the Taiwanese and the United Nations life-tables, the Taiwanese pattern is much less favorable to males. The point at which male mortality again exceeds female occurs about in age group 20-24 for the earlier Taiwanese life-tables and only at age group 40-44 in the United Nations high mortality life-tables (Barclay, 1954, pp. 153-160).[60]

60. Barclay notes that there was considerable talk about infanticide in Taiwan in the early years, just as there was on the mainland, but he observes that the reported sex ratio of registered births in the early years was only 109, which, if one assumes that the births of infants destroyed in this way were not registered, would imply a differential loss of female infants due to infanticide of not more than 2 per cent.

However, it is doubtful whether mortality patterns on Taiwan can be taken as typical of China as a whole. The sex ratios in the registered population of Taiwan were lower than those reported for most mainland provinces, whatever such differences may mean. Even if it is assumed that the sex ratios appropriate for the mainland population apart from infanticide were as low as those reported for Taiwan *with* some degree of infanticide, the use of the United Nations life-tables, with their higher female infant mortality rates and generally high female death rates at later ages, may be regarded as equivalent to an implicit additional allowance for infanticide and female neglect on the mainland beyond that separately applied in the reconstructions of the 1953 mainland China population described in this paper. For lack of a better solution, the present reconstructions assume a constant infanticide rate for all years from 1851 through 1948 equivalent to 2.5 per cent of all male births and 5.0 per cent of all female births.

When decisions had been made concerning the appropriate levels of fertility and mortality, the special allowances for crisis mortality and for infanticide, and the trends of natural increase for the period 1851-1953, the major problem remaining was to select the levels of population increase during the century. These levels, together with given assumptions about fertility and catastrophic mortality, would then constitute the alternate models of the reconstructed hypothetical demographic history of mainland China. Since the assumptions about components of change were subject to great uncertainty, it was necessary to impose some control on their combined effects by specifying net allowable growth, but the margin of allowable growth was not easily defined. The method ultimately adopted was to establish a range of values representing extremes and intermediate points for both the initial and terminal populations, select those combinations that were not inherently self-contradictory on historical or demographic grounds, and express them as ratios of terminal to initial populations. From the range of these ratios, a certain number could be selected to represent the outside limits, along with as many intermediate stages as necessary either to trace significant differences in assumptions or to represent combinations likely to be preferred for historical or demographic reasons. These ratios could then be associated with the corresponding sets of assumptions about fertility and mortality, and the models would be ready for conversion to computer inputs.

But what limits could be placed on the range of growth ratios with so much in doubt about both ends of the century? For 1953, the problem was more limited; here at least a case had been developed that the census total was an undercount, hence the allowable figures must all fall above the level of the census total itself. Using graduated margins of error in multiples of 5 per cent, alternate totals of 613 million, 647 million, or 685 million as of 1953 take the place of the census figure for ratio calculations. However, the same approach cannot be used for 1851, since there is no reason for taking the Ch'ing figure of 432 million as the midpoint of the hypothetical range in which the true figure falls.

One way of setting the range limits independently of the 1851 Ch'ing figure is to quantify some of the judgments ventured in descriptive terms by various scholars as to the patterns of growth during the century following, and then work backward from 1953. According to one view, population losses during the latter half of the nineteenth century were little more than made up by modest increase rates in the first half of the twentieth century, so that net growth was slight. Another view assumes little or no growth between 1850 and 1900, but a moderate growth pattern for 1900-1953 and a substantial net population increment for the century as a whole. If no growth is allowed for the period, the 1851 population figures are the same as those already suggested for 1953 and the ratio of 1953 to 1851 is 1.00. On the other hand, Rockhill's generally discredited estimate of 250 million as of 1842 (1904, p. 318) would imply more than a doubling of the population during this troubled century.

But a growth ratio as low as 1.00 seems unlikely, and a ratio of 2.00 or more impossible. Even a ratio of 1.50 would require an extremely high increase trend throughout the century and minimum estimates of catastrophe; the implied totals as of 1851 would be around 410 to 460 million, depending upon what figure is assumed for 1953, and the total increment during the century would be some 200 to 225 million. At the other end of the scale, an increase ratio as low as 1.10 implies totals of from 550 to 620 million for 1851, with net increments of 55 to 70 million. This low net increase would mean that the increase rates during the century must be set very low and catastrophic losses must be high. Thus, at one end of the scale of ratios, the implied 1851 population total is in the vicinity of the official Ch'ing figure, but the high rates of increase during the century following do not agree with the severity of living conditions during much of the period; at the other end of the scale, the low increase rates imply population totals for 1851 far in excess of any that officials, scholars, or social scientists have been willing to entertain up to now. Though no firm quantitative limits can be set on what is credible, the latitude for alternate assumptions is evidently not wholly unlimited. A range of increase ratios from 1.10 to 1.50 may be judged wide enough to serve for present purposes.[61]

For the period 1851-1953, six models were constructed, approximating growth ratios of 1.10, 1.15, 1.25, 1.35 (two models), and 1.50. The first three models and one of those with the ratio of 1.35 began with the low

61. It may be noted in passing that increase ratios as low as 1.10 produce such high figures for earlier years that the implied undercounts in the Ch'ing figures for 1779 or 1749, by any reasonable assumptions about intervening increase rates, would be in excess of 30 per cent and perhaps above 50 per cent. This would be tantamount to a final rejection of the Ch'ing figures as population data. On the other hand, any assumption that the Ch'ing figure for 1851 was exaggerated by as much

fertility, low increase age-sex structure in 1851 and were carried forward using the low fertility, high catastrophic mortality assumptions through 1953. The two remaining models began with the high fertility, high increase age-sex structure in 1851 and continued with the high fertility, low catastrophic mortality assumptions through 1953. Two models were permitted to overlap at the increase ratio 1.35 to take a measure of the significance for age-sex structure of alternate levels of fertility and mortality when net increase was held constant.[62]

The results of these reconstructions showed that the rate of increase was less significant for age-sex structure than were the levels of the vital rates, including the levels of catastrophic losses. In view of the arbitrary assumptions underlying the reconstructions, there seemed little point in carrying a multiplicity of slightly varying age-sex structures forward in projections beyond 1953; hence at this point all but two of the six models were eliminated. The two retained were the high fertility, low catastrophic mortality model with the increase ratio of 1.35, and the low fertility, high catastrophic mortality model with an increase ratio of 1.15. Table 3 gives the age-sex composition of these models and, for comparison, the age-sex structure of the 1953 census and that produced in the previous attempt at historical reconstruction described at the beginning of Section III. Sex ratios by age for the four populations are given in Table 4.

Comparing the age structure of the census with those of the high increase and low increase ratio models, it is apparent that the census population is somewhat older than either of the two reconstruction models; though the difference between it and the low increase model is less than that between the low and the high increase models. Nearly half of the census population (46.8 per cent) is 25 years old or older, compared with 42.2 per cent in the high and 44.4 per cent in the low increase ratio models. However, for the age group 0-4 years, the census proportion is about midway between those of the high and low increase ratio models. All models exceed the proportions given for the census at ages 5 through 24.

---

as 10 per cent or more would require acceptance of increase ratios of 1.50 or above to get to even the official census total by 1953. These examples suggest that there may be contingencies between the historical and demographic assumptions for the period 1851-1953 that would further limit the believable ranges for at least some parameters.

62. The asymmetry of the distribution of increase ratios resulted from (1) some changes in assumptions and methods during the preparation of computer inputs for the period 1851-1953; (2) generation of some extra models in the course of successive approximation by computer of other increase ratios; and (3) difficulties encountered in fitting even the lower catastrophic population losses to a high increase ratio without implausibly high increase rates during "normal" years. The latter problem chiefly determined the selection of the ratio of 1.35 as the one on which the two sets of assumptions about vital rates and catastrophic losses should be made to overlap.

TABLE 3

DISTRIBUTIONS OF THE POPULATION OF MAINLAND CHINA BY AGE AND SEX CENSUS DATA AND VARIOUS MODELS: 1953
(midyear figures in per cent of the total population)

	Census data			Previous reconstruction model			High increase ratio model			Low increase ratio model		
Age	Both sexes	Males	Females	Both sexes	Males	Females	Both sexes	Males	Females	Both sexes	Males	Females
All ages	100.0	51.8	48.2	100.0	50.9	49.1	100.0	50.6	49.4	100.0	50.2	49.8
0 to 4 years	15.6	8.0	7.6	16.6	8.4	8.2	16.3	8.2	8.0	15.1	7.7	7.4
5 to 14 years	20.3	10.9	9.5	23.1	11.7	11.4	22.4	11.5	10.9	21.4	11.0	10.5
15 to 24 years	17.3	9.1	8.2	18.5	9.5	9.1	19.1	9.8	9.4	19.1	9.7	9.3
25 to 34 years	14.6	7.8	6.8	14.5	7.5	7.0	14.7	7.4	7.4	14.2	7.0	7.3
35 to 44 years	12.0	6.2	5.8	11.0	5.7	5.3	11.1	5.6	5.5	11.1	5.4	5.7
45 years and over	20.2	9.8	10.3	16.3	8.1	8.1	16.4	8.1	8.2	19.1	9.4	9.6
45 to 54 years	9.3	4.7	4.5	8.0	4.1	3.9	8.2	4.2	4.0	9.0	4.5	4.4
55 to 64 years	6.5	3.2	3.3	5.1	2.5	2.5	5.2	2.5	2.6	6.1	3.0	3.1
65 to 74 years	3.4	1.5	1.9	2.5	1.2	1.3	2.4	1.1	1.3	3.1	1.5	1.6
75 years and over	1.0	0.4	0.6	0.7	0.3	0.4	0.6	0.3	0.3	0.9	0.4	0.5
0 to 14 years	35.9	18.9	17.0	39.7	20.2	19.5	38.7	19.7	18.9	36.5	18.6	17.9
15 to 59 years	56.8	29.6	27.3	54.9	28.1	26.8	56.1	28.5	27.8	56.8	28.4	28.4
60 years and over	7.3	3.3	3.9	5.4	2.6	2.8	5.2	2.4	2.7	6.7	3.2	3.5

Note:
a. Row totals independently rounded.

Source:
Census data: Based on sources and methods described in Aird, 1961 (pp. 65-68).
Previous reconstruction model: Aird, 1961 (p. 82).
Other two models: See text.

TABLE 4

SEX RATIOS BY AGE IN MAINLAND CHINA
CENSUS DATA AND VARIOUS MODELS: 1953
(males per 100 females)

Age	Census data	Previous recon-struction model	High increase ratio model	Low increase ratio model
All ages	107.6	103.7	102.3	100.6
0 to 4 years	105.9	103.1	102.7	102.8
5 to 9 years	112.2	102.9	105.0	104.5
10 to 14 years	117.1	103.3	105.4	104.9
15 to 19 years	111.6	103.9	105.7	105.4
20 to 24 years	108.4	104.6	103.2	103.1
25 to 29 years	113.7	105.5	101.0	98.4
30 to 34 years	114.0	106.5	99.1	93.2
35 to 39 years	108.6	107.3	100.1	93.4
40 to 44 years	106.4	107.6	103.0	97.6
45 to 49 years	104.6	106.5	104.1	100.4
50 to 54 years	103.9	104.1	102.6	101.2
55 to 59 years	102.2	100.6	99.1	100.0
60 to 64 years	95.2	96.8	94.4	97.3
65 to 69 years	88.1	92.3	89.3	93.2
70 to 74 years	72.0	87.5	83.9	88.3
75 years and over	64.5	80.1	76.4	80.5

Source:
Same as for Table 3.

Various interpretations of these differences are possible, though they are admittedly little better than rationalizations after the fact. For example, it can be surmised that the higher average age of the census population was due to some exaggeration of age by both sexes, such as is commonly found in traditional peasant societies in which old age is accorded special status. So far as the proportions in age group 0-4 are concerned, if the census proportion is assumed to be too low, it could be argued on the basis of census experience elsewhere that the omission rates for young children were probably higher than the overall omission rates, and that children were seldom counted twice. If the census proportions for children are assumed to be too high, explanation becomes more difficult. It could be argued that the age conversion charts given to census registrars to aid in converting Chinese lunar and animal-year ages were indiscriminately applied to young children whose ages had actually been given according to the Western method or reckoning; but this explanation would have to assume that no lunar ages were recorded in unconverted form, or that such cases and the effects of differential undernumeration of children were more than compensated for by excessive use of the conversion table, which is scarcely plausible. It would be more plausible to suppose that the low increase ratio model is based on too low a level of fertility, and that the census proportion is closer to actuality than that shown by this model. (In general, however, interpretations of the type adduced here to explain the differences between census and model populations should not inspire much confidence. Whether they are designed to rationalize official data or to rationalize a preference for models over official data, all that they are capable of demonstrating beyond doubt is the ingenuity of the rationalizer.)

It is in the sex ratios that the model populations differ most sharply from the census. As Table 4 shows, the overall sex ratios of all three models are well below that of the census, and the two newer models, because of their allowances for war mortality among males, differ even more than the old model, which contained no such allowance. When sex ratios by age are examined, the new models bear a somewhat greater resemblance to the census in several respects; like the census, they both show rising sex ratios after ages 0-4, reach a high point in early youth, and have a subsequent decline followed by a secondary peak (see Figure 1). But the bottom of the dip in the model population sex ratios occurs 10 years later than that in the census sex ratios, and the secondary peak 15 or 20 years later. The second peak of the census sex ratios almost coincides with the dip in the model sex ratios. The similarity between model and census sex ratio trends would be rather pronounced if the census sex ratio peak involving ages 25 through 39 were replaced by a dip, in which case the two peaks and the dip would be common to all three trends, appearing about 5 years earlier in the census data than in the models. Once again, rationalizations could easily be devised to defend the change and explain away the 5-year offset, but in the absence of strong corroborating evidence such rationalizations cannot be trusted and so will not be proposed.

To summarize, the age-sex structure of the 1953 census population and those of the two models produced by historical reconstruction, though similar in some respects, contain some pronounced differences. There is no way of using the census age-sex distribution as a guide in further modifying the assumptions underlying the reconstructions, nor can the reconstructions give any definite clues as to the nature, extent, or causes of the anomalies in the census age-sex distribution. If the assumptions used in constructing the new models are generally valid, the comparison of the models with the census data suggests that, apart from some deficiencies

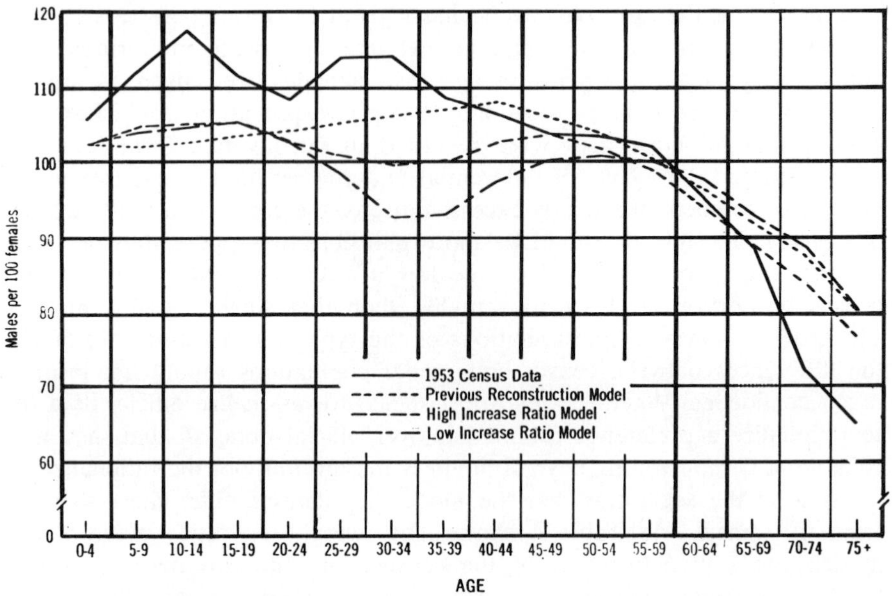

Source: Table 4

FIGURE 1. SEX RATIOS BY AGE. CENSUS DATA AND VARIOUS MODELS: 1953

in the youngest age group and some surplus in the older groups, the combination of whatever age-selective omissions, double counting, and age misreporting may have occurred in the census-taking does not seem to have caused major distortions in the reported age distribution of population. The census sex ratios show some marked deviations, particularly an excess of males in the age groups that should have been most depleted by recent military actions; however, the sex ratio, being a ratio between two proportions of the same totality, is inherently a highly sensitive measure and tends to give an exaggerated impression of imbalances, especially where males exceed females.

IV. ESTIMATES AND PROJECTIONS: 1953-1985

The review of evidence on the credibility and limitations of the 1953 census and its antecedents given in Section II concluded with the opinion that the census total of 583 million was too low by an indeterminate amount, perhaps by as much as 5 to 15 per cent of the actual population. Nevertheless, for projections beyond 1953 the census total was retained as one of the base figures, together with the totals implied by assuming census undercounts of 5, 10, and 15 per cent, because projections using the census total as a base may have some uses in studies of the First Five-Year Plan period, in which other official data are used in unadjusted form.

The age-sex distributions produced by the reconstructions of China's past demographic history described in Section III differ in varying degrees, but all differ significantly from the age-sex structure given for the 1953 census. The census age-sex structure is not used in any of the present projections.[63] Only the two model age-sex structures described at the end of Section III have been used as a basis for the projections discussed in the following pages.

THE FIRST PERIOD: 1953-65

Despite ambiguities and gaps in the relevant sources, the principal demographic parameters for the period 1953-65, and especially for the years 1953-57, may be set within relatively narrower limits than those for any prior period. The efforts of the Chinese Communists at population investigations and record-keeping during these years were defective in methods and coverage, as has already been noted, but they yielded results that can be evaluated, adjusted, and extrapolated on the basis of descriptive materials on health, nutrition, and other relevant conditions in accordance with general demographic experience. The further we go beyond 1957, the greater the margin of uncertainty; only descriptive indicators are available for the later years of the period, and the events of the crisis years of 1959-62 are hard to evaluate. Nevertheless, the 12-year-period from the census to 1965 is short, and even divergent assumptions about increase rates have not much time to accumulate effects; thus they are less significant for estimates of the size of the population by 1965 than is the choice among alternate base populations as of 1953.

The principal sources of statistical information on the birth, death, and natural increase rates for mainland China are (1) several combinations of surveys of selected rural and urban areas covering periods from 1951 through 1954, supposedly representing populations totaling over 30 million people; (2) official national birth, death, and increase rates for 1954-57; and (3) vital rates for several large cities for various years through 1957. Some further information on overall population increase rates is provided by official population reports and estimates, results of which for the years 1949-56 were issued by the State Statistical Bureau in 1957 (*TCKT,* June 14, 1957).

All of these sources are evidently defective in some degree. The vital rates surveys were apparently a combination of actual experimental registrations conducted by the Ministry of Health (until it was ordered to cease

63. One such projection covering the period 1953-58 is already available in the "official data model" given in a previous publication of the Foreign Demographic Analysis Division of the U.S. Bureau of the Census (Aird, 1961, pp. 79-84).

in 1954), and reported births, deaths, and populations for various cities, probably based on the population registers, together with some figures from rural areas, including, for no stated reason, "the whole province of Ninghsia" (Pai Chien-hua, 1954, p. 33). The apparent concentration of urban population and the unlikely selection of the Hui majority province of Ninghsia exemplify the usual Chinese Communist approach to sampling, which is to put together as large a base population as possible, using whatever is handy without regard to the representativeness or quality of the components. Probably the data obtained from the vital registration experimental program of the Ministry of Health are more complete than those from the always defective urban population registers. What sort of data sources were used in the case of other areas can only be surmised, but they were almost certainly subject to far greater defects than those of the Ministry of Health.

In his paper for the 1957 meetings of the International Statistical Institute, Ch'en Ta cites surveys of vital rates in parts of 16 different *hsien,* which, he implies, were selected from among a much larger number of studies because they were "of fairly high accuracy" (Ch'en Ta, 1957, p. 14, Table 6). The inference is that others in the total collection were more obviously defective than these. But some of these are quite defective too; they show curiously low birth and death rates and a positive correlation between them that is best explained as due to acute underregistration. The range of the rates given by Ch'en is: birth rates, 26.1 to 52.8; death rates, 13.4 to 24.0; natural increase rates, 12.7 to 28.8.[64] For the population of 1.8 million covered by the 16 surveys, the birth rate was 41.6, the death rate 21.0, and the natural increase rate 20.6.

The national vital rates published for 1954-57 probably also were based on selected registration data, though not necessarily from the same areas as were covered in the surveys of 1951-54.[65] The increase rates from these surveys do not conform to the increase rates implied in the total population figures for 1954-56 published by the State Statistical Bureau, but, of course, there is no reason to expect them to if the populations covered were not the same. Yet they are close enough to be regarded as being in general agreement.

Assuming that the State Statistical Bureau figures for 1954-56 are, despite some supplementation by estimates, essentially a representation of national population growth insofar as the population registers were capable of recording it, the increase rates indicated by the vital rates

64. These upper and lower limits, as Ch'en notes, were set by the two extreme cases among his collection of 16 surveys.

65. Since the Ministry of Health experiments had been terminated, and since the local population registers were admittedly unstable during these years, the later vital rates figures were probably based on different component area figures each year. Hence there is no reason to attach much significance to small year-to-year variations in these figures.

surveys may not be too far wrong. Since the same type of records was used to produce both sets of figures, the inherent net biases were probably in the same direction. Both the descriptive materials on the operation of the system and the figures themselves suggest that the net increase that they recorded was conservative. The system was apparently widely evaded, largely because of the urban exclusion policies, which reached their peak in 1955. Some evasions would probably have taken place anyway, since the population registers were used primarily as a means of population control by the security police, whom the people, by most accounts, feared and distrusted. The implication is that the actual increase in the population may have been higher in most years than the official figures indicate.

The one exception is 1954, in which both vital rates and population increase rates show the largest increase for any single year in the series. This was the year when rationing was installed as part of the policy of "planned purchasing and supply" of food grains. In urban areas, at least, registration was necessary to claim food rations. Both the national vital rates and the individual city vital rates show generally higher birth and death rates for 1954 than for either 1953 or 1955. This, though, was apparently no more than a temporary deviation from the general trend toward increasingly incomplete registration, which probably introduced a downward bias in the official figures for births and deaths.

How is it possible that a system of population records that undercounts births and deaths may nevertheless come fairly close to representing the actual increase rate of the population? The answer is that the errors in the birth and death rates caused by underregistration tend to be compensatory. The omission of both the births and deaths of infants who die shortly after they are born has, of course, no effect on increase rates. Unreported births of infants who survive, and of deaths at all other ages, are not likely to be exactly compensatory, but the balance may be rather close, even though the proportions of all births and deaths that are unreported may be by no means equal. For example, suppose that the official 1953 vital rates (birth rate, 37; death rate, 17; natural increase rate, 20 per thousand population) represented the rates derived from nationwide registration. Suppose further that unreported births and deaths of infants dying soon after birth represented 3 per thousand of the total population; correcting for this omission would raise the birth rate to 40 and the death rate to 20. Then suppose that other omissions amounted to 5 per thousand for both births and deaths; the actual vital rates would then have been a birth rate of 45 and a death rate of 25, while the natural increase rate would still be 20 per thousand. The corrections just made would have meant that the registration system had omitted 18 per cent of all births and 32 per cent of all deaths. However, if the proportion of all deaths omitted had been the same as the proportion of births, 18 per cent, the corrected death rate would only have risen to 21, while the natural increase rate would have gone up to 25, implying that the recorded natural increase rate had been too low by about 13 per cent. Of course, in actual cases of underregistration, it is not likely that the proportion of both births and deaths unregistered would be exactly equal, nor is it likely that they would be unequal in such proportions as to require the addition of exactly the same number of points to both rates, leaving the natural increase rate unchanged.

Underregistration is usually the net effect of a number of factors in the statistical record-keeping and administrative system, not all of which affect birth and death registration in the same degree or in the same direction. Rationing, for example, tends to favor more complete birth registration and less complete death registration, but this effect is influenced by the degree of strictness with which rationing is enforced. Where burial certificates are required and obtainable only after the death has been registered, concealment of deaths may be more difficult than concealment of births, since it is easier to keep an unregistered infant than to hide a corpse without attracting official notice. But if both ration and burial certificates are required, the interplay between these two factors depends on differential enforcement. If neither requirement is strictly enforced, the use of population registers by the police may cause people to avoid going to the registration stations for any purpose, whether to report birth, death, migration, marriage, divorce, or any other change in family composition. As a result, all recorded rates may fall well below actuality. If migrants who wish to escape from the records can obtain permits needed for relocation without having to report when they reach their destination, the disappearance of migrants from the registers may cause further understatement of the rate of growth of the population.

Whatever the prevailing public attitudes toward conforming to or evading registration regulations, the effectiveness of the system may also depend upon how much care and attention are paid to it by the responsible agencies. In mainland China, the security police were given full responsibility for both rural and urban registration in February, 1956, but it became immediately apparent that they lacked the manpower and the skill to maintain the elaborate record-keeping that the system required. Defeated by the complexity of their task, they lapsed into indifference, as indicated by the newspaper complaints against them cited earlier,[66] and were neither able nor inclined to accommodate those persons who came voluntarily to the registration centers to report. All evidence suggests that the system disintegrated and after 1957 was unable to supply usable national figures.[67]

From what has just been said, it should be apparent that, except in

66. See earlier section "Urban Population Registers," and footnote 27.
67. Further discussion of the registration system is given in Chapter IV of the previously cited Census Bureau monograph (Aird, 1961).

special circumstances, a defective registration system will tend to omit births and deaths in varying proportions, and since in a rapidly growing population births are more numerous than deaths, the actual increase rate of the population may be somewhat higher than that shown by the registration figures.

The judgments set forth here explicitly contradict those presented in a recent report by the population branch of the United Nations Department of Economic and Social Affairs in connection with its newest projections of the population of mainland China (U.N., 1966, pp. 51-58). The United Nations demographic staff estimated a birth rate for China by applying assumed mortality levels to age distributions obtained in a number of local surveys and provincial censuses taken in China over the years from 1929 through 1947, so that the implied birth cohorts are derived and crude birth rates obtained. The resulting crude rates ranged from 45 per thousand down to 36 per thousand for males, with the average at about 40 per thousand; and from 41 to 36 per thousand for females, with the average at about 37 per thousand. From these calculations, the United Nations staff concluded that the crude birth rate in China in past decades was "more likely than not" between 37 and 40 per thousand. For their projections they set the figure at 38 per thousand. Noting that this corresponds closely with the official figure of 37 per thousand for 1953, they observed that "although the agreement may be fortuitous, it lends strength to a tentative conclusion" that their estimates are correct.

But, for reasons already indicated, the official crude birth rate of 37 per thousand has little strength to lend, and its proximity should instead have been cause for concern, or at least for a reexamination of the basis of the estimate. In their analysis of the data from the surveys and censuses of 1929-33 and 1942-47, the United Nations staff were well aware that they were working with defective data. They noted that all the sets of figures show incomplete counting of females, both children and adults, and they found deficits among the males of the young adult ages; but they regarded the deficits among females as partly compensatory, and assumed that those among males would tend to exaggerate the male birth rates. Hence, they made no adjustments in the estimated birth rates.

In this case, the assumption of compensating errors is improbable, and the methods and conclusions based on it are questionable on a number of counts. In the first place, the surveys and censuses of 1929-47 are not all of equal quality, and there is no advantage in following the Chinese Communist example of adding good, bad, and indifferent results together to get a larger base population. Certainly the experimental vital registration work carried out in 1931-35 by Ch'iao, Thompson, and Chen in Hsiao Chi *hsiang,* Kiangyin *hsien,* Kiangsu province, which was conducted with relatively sophisticated methods and analyzed with a proper regard for the limits of the data, deserves more serious consideration, for its implications at least, than do the provincial censuses of the 1940's. Despite their efforts to secure completeness of registration, Ch'iao, Thompson, and Chen felt that their investigation probably undercounted births, especially female births, and that the actual birth rate was probably higher than the figure of 45.1 per thousand that was their overall average for 1932-35 in the area studied (1938, pp. 40-41). A figure for a single *hsiang* cannot, of course, be generalized to all the rest of China. On the other hand, neither can the varying results of a number of local investigations carried out with varying methods be assumed to represent local variations in vital rates, even if there is some consistency in the reported levels by region over time, so long as the possibility remains that this apparent consistency of findings was due to a consistency of regional biases, in methods of collecting or compiling data or in the habits of the investigating officials and the respondent populations. The one observation that can safely be extrapolated to all China on the basis of limited intensive study is the nearly universal tendency to underreport the number of births in vital registration and the number of young children in population counts.

Second, it is not easy to determine the extent of omissions by age and sex in a defective enumeration, particularly if there is also the likelihood of considerable distortion due to misreporting of ages, since the two effects become interlocked, at some points masking and at others reinforcing each other. To adjust a badly distorted age-sex distribution, one must have a fair degree of confidence as to what the past birth, death, and natural increase rates of the population may have been, but if past increase rates are unknown, death rates uncertain, and birth rates what one hopes to determine, there are already too many unknowns in the equation to permit a narrow range of solutions. Certainly, to apply reverse survival techniques to defective age-sex distributions without allowing for differential underenumeration of children by sex is a dubious method of estimating actual birth rates.

Third, no allowance was made, so far as the United Nations report indicates, for the possible effects either of general or of differential infanticide. The United Nations model life-tables do not contain any specific allowance for this factor, though it is possible that the effects of infanticide and differential care of young females have affected mortality levels by sex and age in some of the early Indian life-tables used in the preparation of the models. In Hsiao Chi *hsiang,* the recorded female infant mortality rate was some 38 per cent higher than that for males, the death rate at ages 0 to 4 years was 55 per cent higher, and that for ages 5 to 9 years was 27 per cent higher. The Hsiao Chi rates may also have been defective, as their erratic variations from year to year and the high sex ratios at birth for some years suggest. Female mortality rates in the early years for Hsiao Chi may also have been inflated by gross underenumeration of females in the younger age groups, as the peculiarities of the sex ratios by age strongly suggest (Ch'iao, Thompson, Chen, 1938, p. 28). However, some allowance must be made for infanticide in the mortality rate used in estimating birth rates by reverse survival, or the estimated rates will probably be too low.[68]

Fourth, although the United Nations demographers rejected the level of mortality indicated by the official death rates for 1952-57 on the reasonable grounds that the recording of deaths in a household registration system is bound to be incomplete, they say of the birth rates derived from

68. The United Nations estimates of birth rates by sex from old population censuses and surveys assume that undercounting of females in the very young age groups, which are used to estimate the original birth cohorts by the reverse survival method, was matched in part by undercounting of females at older ages, which are used as the base population in calculating the rates. However, it is unlikely that the compensation was complete, since undercounting was almost certainly much higher in the younger group. If the omission rate for young females was 10 per cent and that for older females only 5 per cent, the estimated birth rates would have a downward bias of over 5 per cent; if the omission rates were 20 per cent and 10 per cent respectively, the downward bias would amount to over 11 per cent. If this range is applied to the United Nations estimated female birth rate range of 37 to 38 per thousand, the range becomes 39 to 43 per thousand. This is merely by way of showing that allowances of this type can be significant. The United Nations discussion of the male rates notes visible deficits in the labor conscription and military service ages, which would tend to lower the base population for males and thus cause some upward bias in the male birth rates, if no other factors were operating. However, it is questionable whether the omissions in some age groups among males could cause overall omission rates for the adult male population to exceed the omission rates for male children in the ages used to calculate the birth cohorts of males. Here, indeed, there might have been almost equal compensation if the omission rates for young adult males were large enough to sustain high omission rates for all adult males. To examine this question further, one would need to make a detailed analysis of the original age distributions for both sexes. There is undoubtedly much more analytical work to be done on these materials.

The United Nations demographic staff make it clear in their commentary (1966, pp. 52-53) that they do not regard the age-sex distributions with which they are working as the equivalent of stable populations which have been generated by the mortality patterns of the model life-table used for their calculations. That this assumption is invalid is apparent from the excessively high ratios of male to female birth rates which they obtained. A stationary population based on the United Nations model 20 life-table would have a male birth rate 2.8 per cent higher than its female birth rate; a stable population based on the model 20 life-table and increasing at 1 per cent per year would have a male birth rate about 2.4 per cent above the female birth rate. The United Nations estimates, which employed the level 20 life-table with an increase rate of about 0.5 per cent per year, obtained male birth rates that exceeded the female birth rates by about 5 per cent on the average in the case of the 1929-33 data, and 11 per cent in the case of the 1942-47 data. The United Nations staff do not accept the relationships between these rates as real; instead they assume that the estimated male and female rates may be taken as alternate indications of the level of the overall crude birth rate in China both before and after 1949. However, if the assumption that the reported age structure corresponds to that of a level 20 stable population does not hold for one sex, it is not very likely to hold for the other. Moreover, there is no indication of how much uncontrolled factors may have affected the results of the calculations. Hence it may be doubted whether either the males or the female rates as estimated by this procedure may be taken to represent the level of the actual birth rates, even during the period before 1929.

the same registers that "a sufficient basis for evaluating the accuracy of these data is lacking" (U.N., 1966, p. 52) and that "in general, it seems that the risk of omissions in reporting is greater in the case of deaths than of births" (p. 54). It would seem that if a priori assumptions of under-registration provide a basis for evaluating death rates, similar assumptions might be applied to the birth rates; or, if more basis is needed for the evaluation of the latter, it can be found in the source materials from mainland China, which indicate that birth registration and death registration were both neglected, despite the existence of rationing after 1954. It may be true that, a defective registration system is likely to omit a higher proportion of deaths than of births, but, as has already been shown, if the birth rate is roughly twice the death rate, the omission rate for births could be half that for deaths, and yet the adjustment for omissions would require the addition of the same number of points to both rates. Moreover, a significant proportion of the deaths omitted would have been deaths of infants whose births were also unregistered. Hence to adjust the official death rates without adjusting the official birth rates is inconsistent, and the inconsistency cannot be defended on the basis of estimates drawn from defective population counts of the 1930's and 1940's. The effects of this decision are difficult to trace from the data given in the United Nations monograph, but it seems to have resulted in projection of the population during the First Five-Year Plan period at an annual increase rate less than 1.5 per cent per year. This rate is so far below the official figures as to imply a year-end 1957 population total of nearly 25 million less than that given by the State Statistical Bureau.[69]

The United Nations staff do not claim that their estimates for mainland China are more accurate than those published elsewhere, but they say that they prefer their method of estimating the Chinese birth rate because they have used the same method for other countries for which adequate statistics on births are lacking (1966, p. 51). However, to purchase methodological consistency at the expense of appropriateness is to pay a high price for a small virtue.

For the projections given here, the constant gross reproduction rates equivalent to crude birth rates of 40 or 45 per thousand in 1953, which were assumed for 1851-1953, were continued in the models for 1953-65. The use of constant gross reproduction rates permits the crude birth rates to vary over time in response to varying age-sex composition. It does not allow for changes in gross reproduction rates in response to changing social conditions. For reasons presented elsewhere (Aird, 1961, p. 81), it may be assumed that the fertility control efforts of 1954-58 did not have a perceptible effect on the overall fertility rates. Changes in social, polit-

69. The United Nations staff also prepared a "high variant" series consistent with the increase rates in the official totals, which is presented in Table 10.2 of their monograph (1966, p. 57) as "variant combination V."

ical, and economic conditions may have introduced some slight variations, either by their influence on marriage rates or by the separation of husbands and wives during the mass labor campaigns, but they cannot be estimated on the basis of available information.

Even with constant gross reproduction rates, the crude birth rates of a population passing through a period of sudden change in rates of mortality and population growth will exhibit a noticeable change because of changing age composition. Prior to 1953, the crude birth rates were generally higher than those assumed for 1953; after 1953 the rates declined until around 1965, after which they would have risen again if gross reproduction rates remained unchanged as the post-1949 birth cohorts entered the reproductive ages. The total variation in crude birth rates for the years from 1851 through 1965, was as much as seven points in some models.

Four models were constructed for 1953-65. Mortality levels for these models were set initially by combining the assumed 1953 crude birth rates with assumed natural increase rates as follows:

Model	Natural increase rate	Crude birth rate	Crude death rate
I	22.5	45.0	22.5
II	20.0	45.0	25.0
III	20.0	40.0	20.0
IV	17.5	40.0	22.5

The spread of increase rates assumed for 1953 was intended to make some allowance for the possible understatement of the actual level of increase in the official vital rates, and for the possibility that a more representative sample might have shown lower rates. The average life expectancy at birth implied by the mortality levels required to produce these 1953 crude rates ranges between 38 and 44 years.

In the reconstructions of the 1953 age-sex distribution, mortality was allowed to drop rapidly after 1949 on the assumption that peace on the mainland and the new regime's policies on food distribution and welfare would have removed rather quickly those causes of mortality that were directly related to war, civil unrest, and large-scale malnutrition. Sanitation and health policies would have taken perhaps a little longer to affect the death rate. But at some hypothetical point the maximum mortality reduction possible under these measures would have been approximated, and as this point was approached, mortality would decline more slowly. It is assumed here that the deceleration of the rate of reduction in mortality took place during 1953-58, and that by 1958 not much additional mortality reduction could have taken place without a significant advance in nutrition, medical care, and the general easement of life, none of which was possible with the limited economic means then available in mainland China.

In the current models, mortality was permitted to reach its lowest point in 1958. In model I this is sufficient to allow natural increase to reach 25.0 per thousand; in the other models the same relative mortality differences assumed for 1953 were preserved. After this point, without even defective official vital rates to use as a basis of assumptions, all assumed trends until the end of the period in 1965 are based on descriptive information with implications for the level of mortality.

The unique feature of this period is the subsistence crisis of 1959-62. Opinions vary as to the relative contribution of various factors to the crisis. Certainly the weather was unfavorable for maximum crop production. However, some analysts have suspected that the weather was by no means as bad as the regime claimed, but served as a convenient explanation for the ill effects of bad management by the Party from the Central Committee on down. The commune movement, which was evidently forced through by sheer exercise of political "persuasion" in 1958, and the mass activities promoted by similar means, under the inspiration of Great Leap Forward thinking in high places, undoubtedly contributed to the same kind of peasant noncooperation that had been precipitated several times before when agricultural policy exceeded the peasants' "level of political consciousness." Whether the leaders were able to acknowledge privately that their own policies had played a part in bringing the country to the brink of a major food crisis, they clearly recognized the need to ease political pressures and restore peasant incentive for agricultural production. During the depths of the crisis and recovery years, socialism retreated in rural areas; private plots, private ownership of livestock, and "free" marketing of private produce were partially revived. These backward steps suggest that socialist "transformation" of agriculture was regarded in Peking as at least a complicating factor in the crisis. They also signify that the crisis was considered severe, for there would have been no retreat along these lines unless the need seemed urgent.

Another sign of the seriousness of food shortages was the expenditure of a large part of Communist China's limited foreign exchange reserves to buy millions of tons of grain from Canada, Australia, and other countries. The general economic stringencies of the period were also reflected in sharp declines in industrial production. The Chinese Communists later tried to place much of the blame for industrial cutbacks on the withdrawal of Russian technicians, but this could hardly have accounted for all the idled factories whose uncrowded gates and smokeless chimneys were remarked by foreign observers during 1960 and 1961. In the early 1960's, another massive transfer of city dwellers to rural areas was planned, which was expected to reduce the total urban population of the country by 20 million people (NCNA, April 16, 1962; Strong, 1964, p. 7). Finally, there were signs of an increased proportion of national investment in agriculture, particularly in the production of more chemical fertilizers. These measures, some of which involved a sacrifice of the regime's preferred order of priorities, provide further proof of the exigencies of China's domestic situation at the time.

The most direct indications of acute food shortages were also the most fragmentary and the hardest to assess and extrapolate. These were the reports of local famines, food riots, use of wild plants and animals as dietary supplements, reduced work loads and hours, stories about workers collapsing at their jobs from hunger, and the general preoccupation of the people with the subject of food. There were indications of morale problems in the People's Liberation Army among soldiers who were receiving letters and visits from hungry relatives. Cases of night-blindness, famine edema, famine diarrhea, amenorrhea, and other symptoms of vitamin deficiencies and low caloric intake were also reported. How prevalent acute undernutrition was cannot be determined from scattered reports, even though they come from many different areas in China. Individual refugee reports may have been somewhat exaggerated, perhaps to cater to the suspected prejudices of the interrogators. Some observers noted that few persons among the flood of refugees that began to cross the Hong Kong border in May, 1962, seemed to be suffering from serious malnutrition; from this they concluded that conditions on the mainland must not be as bad as was generally supposed. However, other famine experience suggests that generally it is the still healthy people driven by fear of impending starvation who take to flight; those who are actually starving tend to succumb to lassitude and remain where they are. Whether or not there were local areas of acute famine in parts of mainland China during the crisis, the widespread reports of nutritional diseases are probably sufficient to warrant the conclusion that general mortality was on the rise. If it can be assumed that the food distribution system, though it was not intended to achieve equality in the level of food consumption across the country, was able to prevent, for the most part, extremely wide variations at least within provinces and regions, then the appearance of signs of undernutrition in many areas may signify that most of the rest of the population was not a great deal better off.

If the distress was widespread, the effects would have been general, and these would certainly have included higher overall mortality. Lower caloric intake and the absence of important elements in the diet would have meant less resistence to disease, more widespread illness, more severe cases, slower recovery, and higher fatality rates than would normally have prevailed. Still, there is no way to convert the information available first into estimates of the extent and kinds of undernutrition, and then into estimates of the level of the death rate. Although the food shortages and local famines of the years 1953-56 were much more openly discussed in the press than was the crisis of 1959-62, the information available suggests that food shortages during this later crisis were more severe than at any other time since 1949. This could well have been the case even if the level of food production in 1960 or 1961 was no worse than in any previous year, since there was a much larger population to be fed. One approach to the problem of estimating mortality levels during the years 1959-62 is to assume that, at the depths of the crisis, mortality returned to the level of 1949; the mortality assumptions for alternate projection models can represent a range consistent with the range of levels of mortality assumed for each model as of 1953. This approach is, of course, no more than an argument by analogy, which shifts the problem of determining mortality levels to the equally uncertain guesses already made for 1949. It is no substitute for a method of estimating mortality levels for 1959-62 directly from contemporary evidence, but in the absence of such a method it will have to serve.

From 1962 through 1965 a fairly rapid recovery seems to have taken place, though there is some doubt whether by 1965 per capita food consumption had been restored to the 1958 level. There is also some doubt whether medical care and the general health of the population made any significant net gains between 1958 and 1965. Once again it is important to distinguish between open-heart and hand-graft surgery in Peking and the campaigns against dysentery and schistosomiasis in the rural hinterlands; only the latter are relevant to an estimation of mortality levels for 750 million people of whom 85 per cent are still peasants. Lacking more reliable evidence and analysis than is now available, it is assumed here that no additional advances in general health need be allowed for in estimating mortality levels as of 1965. Such trends are not automatic and inevitable. They presuppose substantial investment in personnel, facilities, and technologies for disease control and modern medical care, which are not to be expected in a marginal economy without substantial outside material and financial help. Given the scale of the Chinese problem, this would probably have been out of the question even if the regime had wanted it. In the four models for 1953-65, mortality is permitted to return by 1965 to the level attained in 1958; however, changing age structure causes the crude birth rate to fall steadily from 1953 through 1965, and so in all four models the natural increase rate in 1965 is below that for 1958.

THE SECOND PERIOD: 1965-1985

Even for a country with such dubious demographic antecedents as China, the transition from estimates of past demographic trends to the projections of future demographic developments involves a perceptible increase in uncertainty. Neither the simple extrapolation of past trends nor the use of analogy to past demographic experience in other countries will do much to reduce the uncertainty, for there is no reason to suppose that China's population development in the next several decades will repeat previous experience in the West or in Japan, or that it will necessarily parallel the experience of other Asian countries that seem to be facing many of the same problems. In a country where radical shifts in domestic policy have been frequent, in which complex and obscure interrelationships exist between the implementers of national policy at local levels and those who are the ultimate recipients of the official edicts and directives, and in which even the continuity of leadership and ideology is incalculable, international analogies may be totally irrelevant.

Moreover, this is an age of rapid technological changes, which have recently much altered the potential prospects for agricultural production, fertility control, and mortality. What may develop within the next year or two in any of these fields cannot be foreseen. The speed with which new methods of fertility control have been appearing, and the sudden increase in awareness by world leaders of the advantages of fertility control in national development, could hardly have been predicted a few years ago. The increasing attention to research in fields related to food production, fertility, and health almost certainly means that the pace of technological development will accelerate in the next few years. The outlook for the basic demographic parameters throughout the world may be entirely different by the end of the present decade. Hence population projections have probably never had a shorter life expectancy than they have today.

However, it may be advisable to avoid haste in extrapolating the apparent implications of the latest laboratory product to the peasant villages in underdeveloped countries. The rate of invention usually outpaces the rate of application on a mass scale, and there are some promising discoveries that never live up to their promises, because of unforeseen side effects or consequences. If the purpose of a set of population projections is to express the limits of possibility as of the moment, and if it is recognized that even the greatest circumspection in the choice of assumptions probably cannot save them from being outmoded in a very few years, there is little point in trying to anticipate technological developments that probably cannot be anticipated anyway. Whatever we say about China today we shall probably have to revise tomorrow or the day after. It is probably best to extrapolate what appear to be the immediate limits of the demographic situation in China and not try to outguess history.

There can be no doubt that the population of China at present, whatever its actual size and rate of increase, continues to strain the food resources, and that, as long as this condition exists, economic development will, at best, operate under major inhibitions, and may suffer further setbacks as in the very recent past. Escape from this condition depends upon increasing productivity in agriculture, or reducing the rate of population growth, or a combination of the two sufficient to provide a large enough margin of safety so that the normal cycles of agricultural productivity become less threatening. There is apparently plenty of room for improvement in productivity if the applications of available technologies can be made quickly enough and on a large enough scale to have a significant effect within whatever period of time remains until the next serious food crisis. Much higher levels of productivity have been attained in other countries, including Taiwan and Japan, in the production of the food crops upon which the mainland Chinese depend. Yet not all the techniques that have worked well elsewhere can be successful in China. The obstacles include cost of development and application, climate, soils, terrain, and the diffuse and imponderable problems relating to culture, organization, and motivation. The barrier these constitute is not wholly impenetrable; some technologies cross it and disseminate quickly. Others spread more slowly, and some not at all. It remains to be seen whether the Chinese Communists, who have not until now been able to escape from chronic and recurrent food difficulties, can break into the open and outrun the problem within the near future. For whatever it may be worth, recent mainland China press statements on the subject of food still emphasize the need to economize in order to build up reserves for bad years to come.

Some similar obstacles seem to stand in the way of success in the control of fertility in mainland China. If the lowering of fertility depended only on the existence of effective techniques for contraception and abortion, and if there were no problems in respect to national policy, cost, dissemination, acceptability, or popular motivation, then the new intrauterine and abortifacient devices would already have begun to change China's demographic prospects. In actual fact, however, it is not clear at the moment whether the present authorities in Peking view the fertility control problem as an urgent matter or are able to express that urgency in effective propaganda or programs without arousing popular anxieties to complicate their problems of civil control. Moreover, it has yet to be demonstrated that significant long-term progress can be made in promoting birth limitation programs among a peasant population in the absence of a marked rise in living standards.

In a country of China's size, rising living standards depend upon domestic economic development, which must be financed largely out of domestically generated capital resources, but capital accumulation is not likely to be rapid under the best of circumstances. Moreover, the regime has not, up to now, been inclined to accord consumer goods a very high priority among competing uses for its limited supply of capital. The values and ideals promoted in the press for public adoption still emphasize frugality, self-denial, and the indefinite deferment of material rewards for the sake of future generations. Without the "positive" incentive of rising living standards to provide popular motivation for smaller families, the regime must find ways of developing "negative" incentives by calling attention to the burden that excess childbearing imposes on both the family and the state. The possibilities in this direction are limited somewhat by the relative security of income, food, and health and other services, which are basic elements in the Chinese Communist ideological commitment toward the welfare of the masses, but which tend to limit the significance of economic anxiety as a source of motivation. In some parts of China there have recently been attempts to introduce an element of practical urgency in support of the official position on family limitation by refusing further ration allotments and maternity benefits after the third or fourth child. However, in other parts of the world, special economic benefits and privileges to couples with many children have met with little success in encouraging large families; it is by no means clear whether the Chinese Communists can be more successful in applying opposite measures toward an opposite goal.

In general, the regime has never accomplished much in previous mass campaigns that required voluntary cooperation from the people, particularly those, like the Marriage Law reforms and the birth control drive of 1955-58, that lie in the area of intimate relations. The first birth control campaign seems to have encountered considerable popular resistance, some of which expressly opposed government meddling in what were thought to be personal affairs. There is no reason to suppose that such resistance would not continue so long as the basic social and economic conditions under which the majority of the Chinese people live remain as they are now. For the time being, it must be assumed that the immediate prospects for lowering fertility levels for mainland China as a whole are still contingent upon socioeconomic changes that are not likely to occur suddenly.

As long as the pressure of population on food resources continues to be a central feature of the economy of Communist China, mortality cannot be expected to approach Western levels. Even under the best of circumstances that can realistically be foreseen, only limited gradual reduction in mortality is possible in the next 20 years. Under more ordinary circumstances, mortality may be expected to maintain its present level, or perhaps rise and fall irregularly in response to variations in general nutritional levels and in the degree of control maintained over communicable diseases. No limits can be set on more pessimistic expectations. As long as the threat of food crisis remains imminent, the possibility of a major catastrophe, which could result in the depopulation of large areas of the mainland and the emergence of a new set of economic, political, and demographic conditions, is not to be excluded. Such a catastrophe could occur if a single year of agricultural disaster or a series of crisis years with cumulative effect should strike with enough severity to disrupt civil control over a significant part of rural China, with a consequent collapse of the systems for production, distribution, and emergency allocation of food.

The demonstrated capacity of mainland China to sustain today a population far larger than those that pressed the limits of subsistence in the past probably owes as much to a relatively effective control of food distribution and consumption as it does to improvements in agricultural technology and increases in the area under cultivation. A strong civil control system is required to take possession of surplus grain and provide for its storage and allocation on a country-wide basis. The success of the Chinese Communists in food management should not be exaggerated; they have compiled a long record of trial and error since 1949, in which the errors are both numerous and grave. Nevertheless, the record suggests a marked general improvement in the security of the food supply in China. The continuing food shortages, though probably more severe than the authorities have been willing to admit, are doubtless less severe than they would have been without any such arrangements. At least it is apparent that since 1949 there have been no major famines of the type common in China in former times. The fact that local areas are no longer solely dependent on their own resources in times of crop failure has doubtless eased somewhat the effect of such crises on general mortality, and correspondingly increased the population. However, these changes may have resulted in a more delicate balance between population and food resources throughout the country and a much greater dependence on the surplus production of other areas and on the system of collection, storage, and distribution that maintains the balance. If this is so, then any social upheaval, whatever its cause, that disrupted the system in any considerable area of China could precipitate a famine on a scale never before witnessed in human experience.

A collapse of the system could be caused by failures in agriculture or by political causes if they entailed a demoralization of the authority structure or a loss of public confidence in the ability of the regime to provide the necessities of life. History affords numerous examples of how quickly a population normally docile and submissive to authority can turn to violence if its rulers seem to have lost their power or resolve. A collapse need not affect the entire country to bring about a massive disaster; it need only reach extremes in one densely populated region. If the onset of acute famine conditions were sudden, or if the early warning signs were concealed or discounted, or if the regime waited too long to call for assistance from other countries, there probably would be little the outside world could do to help, even if there were no limits to world food reserves and no problem of procurement costs. Logistics alone would impose very narrow restrictions on international aid, and problems of distribution in areas where civil control had disintegrated would impose still others. It is not inconceivable that the death toll could exceed 100 million.

The range of possibilities for mortality in mainland China is wide, and no upper limit can be set.

Taking fertility and mortality together, it seems likely that the favorable economic conditions prerequisite for a successful family limitation program would also lead to further declines in mortality, in which case success in reducing birth rates might not immediately bring much reduction in the rate of natural increase. This means that the pressure of population on food resources and the threat of further food crises might linger for some time even under favorable conditions. On the other side, chronic food shortages and recurrent crises of the type that have persisted to the present time would probably mean that the regime could not maintain propaganda and economic pressures for delay of marriage and smaller families. As a rule, in times of general distress the Chinese Communists have found it necessary to abandon demands for conformity, particularly those which have encountered popular resistance. Whether the higher mortality levels which go with short-term crises might reverse tendencies toward lower fertility levels initiated by a successful birth control campaign remains to be seen. There are no current examples of a society in which mortality, after having been reduced by modern medicine and sanitation, once again resumes its former level; hence there is no experience upon which to base expectations as to what such circumstances could mean for fertility. If crises in China are severe enough, of course, not only would birth rates be directly affected through general health impairment, infertility, and loss of libido, but there could also be a recurrence of high mortality among infants and children. In that event, the traditional problem of replacement of numbers and continuity of generations, which has been supposed to constitute the inherent rationality behind high fertility in peasant societies, would also reappear. In any case, under recurrent crisis conditions it will probably be mortality rather than fertility which is the prime determinant of the rate of population growth. Hence the total range of prospects for the future growth of the population of China is wide.

Representing these prospects in model projections involves some unique choices not usually encountered in making population projections. Most projections assume fairly steady future trends in fertility and mortality. Models may differ in the time of onset or rate of change assigned to these parameters but seldom in the direction of the trend, and rarely if ever do trend lines reverse direction or fluctuate within the projection period. In the case of mainland China, however, assumptions of steady and unbroken trends, however gradual, bear no relationship to recent actualities and are therefore somewhat unreal. How can an expectation of recurrent crises or of a major catastrophe be projected without assuming at least cyclical variations in vital rates? Yet if cycles are assumed in lieu of linear trends or are superimposed on long-term trends, the resulting projections are bound to appear less abstract than more conventional projections in which the changes in basic parameters are more in the nature of continuous mathematical functions.

The six models presented below include some that assume steady progress in economic development for China and a similar steady progression of demographic trends. Others, based on less favorable economic expectations, involve more elaborate and more specific assumptions about fertility and mortality. There is, however, no more historical inevitability about one projection than about another. These models do not represent the full range of possibilities, nor do they exemplify all possible combinations of circumstance within the range which they cover.

MODEL A: MAXIMUM DEVELOPMENT

Model A assumes that the economy of mainland China, though it has its problems, is basically sound, and that the regime, though it has made mistakes in its management of the economy, has learned enough from these experiences to pursue a more rational course hereafter. This coincides essentially with the public assessment that the leaders of the regime have put forward since the recovery from the last period of crisis. Specifically, the model assumes that enough changes have been made in the basic resources and management of agriculture so that it can henceforth withstand bad years without serious mishap. The model assumes that general economic development and policies for the next 20 years show a degree of stability not evident before. In short, this is the prospect for an agrarian society that has rounded the corner and is now on the road to steady progress.

This model assumes that encouragements to fertility control and delay of marriage, supported by prospects of rising living standards, begin to have a perceptible impact immediately on the level of fertility, while improvements in general medical care permit new achievements in mortality control. Since both these trends are dependent upon indigenous resources, the pace is not sudden, but the accomplishments by the end of the next 20 years are considerable. By 1985, the gross reproduction rate has been reduced by one-third from its 1965 level, and life expectancy at birth has increased from 50 to 60 years. The base population in 1965 is taken from model III for the previous period.

MODEL B: MODERATE DEVELOPMENT

Model B represents a moderately optimistic prospect for Communist China compared with the trend of recent Chinese experience. It assumes that there are no major crises in the economic or political life of China during the next 20 years but that chronic economic problems prove somewhat recalcitrant and are overcome only very gradually. It also assumes that health programs and a fertility reduction policy make perceptible but not spectacular progress. It allows for fluctuations in the rate of economic development but no periods of severe crisis. Social and political conditions are, by implication, remarkably stable despite only a modest rate of improvement in living conditions. The trends in fertility and mortality are essentially the same as those for model A, except that the pace is slower and the trend in mortality less uniform. This model assumes half the rate of decline in fertility assumed for model A. Expectation of life at birth rises irregularly from 50 years in 1965 to 55 years by 1985. The base population is the same as that used for model A.

MODEL C: LIMITED DEVELOPMENT

Model C assumes that China still has about 10 years to go before the pressures of population growth usher in a serious time of troubles. For the first half of the period some economic gains are registered, and along with this advance, fertility and mortality register a slight decline. During the last 10 years of the period, the forward motion of the economy is reversed, fertility control is unable to gain further ground, and mortality is once again on the rise. Nevertheless, despite the worsening economic conditions, it is assumed that the control apparatus is still functioning well enough to prevent any serious deterioration of civil order through 1985. In model C the gross reproduction rate follows the same trend as for model B except that it levels off at 1975 and remains constant thereafter. Life expectancy at birth rises from about 45 years in 1965 to 47.5 years in 1975, but falls irregularly to 42.5 years by 1985. The base population in 1965 is taken from model IV for the previous period.

MODEL D: STAGNATION

Model D assumes that the economy of China is not able to cope with the rate of population increase after 1965, and that for the next 20 years economic conditions are unsteady, with alternate periods of adversity and temporary respite. It is assumed that in its efforts to deal with recurrent economic difficulties, the regime has recourse, as in the past, to a number of desperate expedients, with frequent changes in domestic policy. Because the level of public morale and confidence in the leadership have been undermined, programs requiring voluntary cooperation have little success, and coercive programs succeed only as long as the coercion can be sustained. Efforts at fertility control do not accomplish much during the periods of respite and have to be abandoned altogether during periods of adversity. However, deteriorating general living standards, periodic food shortages, and the disruption of family life in emergency mass labor projects lead to a decline of 10 per cent in the original gross reproduction rate by 1985 and cause mortality to move irregularly upward. Life expectancy falls, in several stages, from about 45 years in 1965 to 40 years in 1985. The base population in 1965 is taken from model I for the previous period.

MODEL E: RECURRENT CRISIS

Model E assumes what amounts to a continuation of recent trends: the halting of net overall economic development because of economic crises of increasing frequency, duration, and severity resulting from population pressures, alternating with periods of economic recovery. The time schedule for this progression is based on the crisis of 1959-62 and proceeds as follows:

1963-1967	(five years)—Period of recovery
1968-1972	(five years)—Crisis II
1973-1976	(four years)—Period of recovery
1977-1982	(six years)—Crisis III
1983-1985	(three years)—Period of recovery

Each period of crisis is accompanied, as in the past, by a setback in economic growth in general, including retrenchment in the nonagricultural sector, and preoccupation with short-run maximization of agricultural output, especially food. During these periods, other types of political pressures on the population must be suspended, including efforts at fertility reduction. Fertility control programs achieve no direct success, but the overall decline in living standards and the effects of undernutrition and local famine during the periods of crisis bring about an irregular decline in fertility, reaching a maximum of 15 per cent below the initial gross reproduction rate during the bottom of crisis III (1979). Mortality rises acutely during the crisis periods and fails to rebound fully during the recovery periods. Life expectancy at birth is about 45 years in 1965 but drops to 35 years by 1985, just before the onset of crisis IV. The base population in 1965 is the same as that used for model D.

MODEL F: CATASTROPHE

Model F assumes that a succession of agricultural failures at the end of the 1960's brings about a collapse of social order and a major famine in large areas of China beginning in 1970, reaching the maximum extremity in 1971, and tapering off in 1972 and 1973. Gradual recovery begins in 1974 with the slow restoration of social order under a new balance of economic and demographic forces that continues through 1985. The net loss of population during the four years of acute catastrophe is set at 100 million, allocated as follows:

1970	15 million
1971	60 million
1972	20 million
1973	5 million

The assumption underlying this protracted catastrophe, which is about twice the duration of other major depopulations on record, is that, unlike the famines in self-sufficient peasant economies in which the crisis ends with the return of normal harvests, this catastrophe is associated with the deterioration of a social order and a reversion to a less organized form of society. Its effects are therefore both more profound and more extensive in time. For the same reason, fertility and mortality return after the catastrophe to levels consistent with a much earlier stage in the evolution of Chinese society and begin an accelerated recapitulation of China's previous demographic history. By 1985, mortality and fertility are again approaching the levels of 1965. The mortality levels used in this model are equivalent to a life expectancy at birth of 42.5 years in 1965, 30.0 years in 1975, and 40.0 years in 1985. The base population is taken from model II for the previous period.

RESULTS OF THE PROJECTIONS, 1953-1985

The estimated total populations for the four models for 1953-65 and the six models for 1966-85 are given in Tables 5 and 6, respectively, in four series for each model, a census-based series and three alternate series representing different percentages of undercount in the 1953 census. Within the short period from 1953 through 1965, the corresponding series for the four models differ by less than 5 per cent; for these years the choice of series is more important to the size of the total than the choice of model. By the middle 1970's however, there is a spread of 28 per cent between corresponding series, which increases to over 30 per cent in the 1980's, before it begins to decline. The main cause of the divergence is the depopulation assumed in model F; after the recovery of model F its increase rate exceeds those of all other models, so that by 1985, the percentage differences between model F and the other models are lessening.

The crude birth, death, and natural increase rates for the various models for 1953-65 and 1966-85 are presented in Tables 7 and 8, respectively. As Table 7 shows, a marked decline in the crude birth rate occurs in all four models despite the fact that the gross reproduction rate was constant throughout the 1953-65 period. The movement of the death rate in all four cases reflects the assumption of general improvement in control of mortality through 1958, its rapid deterioration through 1962, and recovery by 1965 to approximately the conditions prevailing in 1958. As

TABLE 5

ESTIMATED POPULATION OF MAINLAND CHINA, FOUR ALTERNATE MODELS: 1953-1965
(January 1 figures in millions)

	Model I				Model II			
Year	Census-based series	5 per cent under-count series	10 per cent under-count series	15 per cent under-count series	Census-based series	5 per cent under-count series	10 per cent under-count series	15 per cent under-count series
1953	576.0	606.4	640.1	677.7	576.8	607.1	640.9	678.6
1954	589.2	620.2	654.6	693.1	588.4	619.4	653.8	692.3
1955	603.5	635.2	670.5	709.9	601.1	632.8	667.9	707.2
1956	618.6	651.2	687.4	727.8	614.6	647.0	682.9	723.1
1957	634.3	667.7	704.8	746.2	628.6	661.7	698.5	739.6
1958	650.4	684.6	722.6	765.2	642.9	676.8	714.4	756.4
1959	666.6	701.7	740.7	784.3	657.5	692.1	730.5	773.5
1960	682.1	718.0	757.9	802.5	671.2	706.5	745.8	789.7
1961	695.7	732.3	773.0	818.5	682.3	718.3	758.2	802.8
1962	705.6	742.7	784.0	830.1	688.7	725.0	765.3	810.3
1963	714.9	752.5	794.3	841.0	694.5	731.0	771.7	817.0
1964	727.8	766.1	808.7	856.3	704.2	741.2	782.4	828.4
1965	743.4	782.6	826.0	874.6	717.6	755.4	797.4	844.3

	Model III				Model IV			
Year	Census-based series	5 per cent under-count series	10 per cent under-count series	15 per cent under-count series	Census-based series	5 per cent under-count series	10 per cent under-count series	15 per cent under-count series
1953	576.8	607.1	640.9	678.6	577.5	607.9	641.7	679.4
1954	588.4	619.4	653.8	692.3	587.7	618.6	653.0	691.4
1955	601.2	632.8	668.0	707.3	599.0	630.6	656.6	704.8
1956	614.7	647.1	683.0	723.2	611.2	643.3	679.1	719.0
1957	628.8	661.9	698.7	739.8	623.8	656.6	693.1	733.9
1958	643.3	677.2	714.8	756.8	636.7	670.2	707.5	749.1
1959	658.1	692.7	731.2	774.2	649.8	684.0	722.0	764.5
1960	672.3	707.7	747.0	791.0	662.4	697.2	736.0	779.3
1961	685.1	721.1	761.2	806.0	673.5	708.9	748.3	792.4
1962	695.7	732.3	773.0	818.5	682.4	718.3	758.3	802.9
1963	706.2	743.4	784.7	830.9	691.1	727.5	767.9	813.1
1964	719.1	757.0	799.0	846.0	702.1	739.0	780.1	826.0
1965	733.6	772.3	815.2	863.1	714.6	752.2	794.0	840.7

TABLE 6

PROJECTED POPULATION OF MAINLAND CHINA, SIX ALTERNATE MODELS: 1966-1986

(January 1 figures in millions)

Year	Model A: Census-based series	Model A: 5 per cent under-count series	Model A: 10 per cent under-count series	Model A: 15 per cent under-count series	Model B: Census-based series	Model B: 5 per cent under-count series	Model B: 10 per cent under-count series	Model B: 15 per cent under-count series
1966	749.1	788.5	832.3	881.2	749.1	788.5	832.3	881.2
1967	764.7	804.9	849.6	899.6	764.2	804.4	849.1	899.1
1968	780.7	821.8	867.4	918.4	779.3	820.3	865.9	916.8
1969	797.1	839.0	885.6	937.7	794.8	836.6	883.1	935.1
1970	813.8	856.6	904.2	957.4	810.8	853.5	900.9	953.9
1971	831.0	874.7	923.3	977.6	827.3	870.8	919.2	973.3
1972	848.5	893.2	942.8	998.2	844.3	888.7	938.1	993.3
1973	866.5	912.1	962.7	1,019.4	861.9	907.3	957.7	1,014.0
1974	884.8	931.4	983.2	1.041.0	880.1	926.5	977.9	1,035.5
1975	903.6	951.2	1,004.0	1,063.1	899.0	946.3	998.8	1,057.6
1976	922.8	971.4	1,025.4	1,085.7	917.8	966.2	1,019.8	1,079.8
1977	942.4	992.0	1,047.1	1,108.7	936.8	986.1	1,040.9	1,102.1
1978	962.3	1,012.9	1,069.2	1,132.1	955.8	1,006.1	1,062.0	1,124.4
1979	982.4	1,034.1	1,091.6	1,155.8	975.3	1,026.6	1,083.6	1,147.4
1980	1,002.8	1,055.5	1,114.2	1,179.7	995.3	1,047.7	1,105.9	1,171.0
1981	1,023.2	1,077.1	1,136.9	1,203.8	1,015.9	1,069.3	1,128.7	1,195.1
1982	1,043.7	1,098.6	1,159.6	1,227.8	1,036.8	1,091.4	1,152.0	1,219.8
1983	1,064.0	1,120.0	1,182.2	1,251.8	1,058.2	1,113.8	1,175.7	1,244.9
1984	1,084.1	1,141.1	1,204.5	1,275.4	1,079.8	1,136.6	1,199.8	1,270.3
1985	1,103.5	1,161.6	1,226.2	1,298.3	1,101.6	1,159.5	1,224.0	1,296.0
1986	1,122.1	1,181.2	1,246.8	1,320.1	1,123.4	1,182.5	1,248.2	1,321.6

Year	Model C				Model D			
Year	Census-based series	5 per cent under-count series	10 per cent under-count series	15 per cent under-count series	Census-based series	5 per cent under-count series	10 per cent under-count series	15 per cent under-count series
1966	728.1	766.4	809.0	856.6	760.3	800.3	844.8	894.5
1967	741.0	780.0	823.3	871.8	776.7	817.6	863.0	913.8
1968	753.8	793.5	837.5	886.8	793.3	835.1	881.5	933.4
1969	766.4	806.8	851.6	901.7	810.3	852.9	900.3	953.2
1970	779.5	820.5	866.1	917.1	827.5	871.0	919.4	973.5
1971	793.0	834.8	881.1	933.0	844.7	889.2	938.6	993.8
1972	807.0	849.5	896.7	949.5	862.1	907.4	957.9	1,014.2
1973	821.6	864.8	912.9	966.6	879.5	925.7	977.2	1,034.6
1974	836.7	880.8	929.7	984.4	896.9	944.1	996.5	1,055.2
1975	852.5	897.4	947.3	1,003.0	914.4	962.5	1,016.0	1,075.7
1976	869.0	914.8	965.6	1,022.4	932.2	981.3	1,035.8	1,096.7
1977	886.0	932.6	984.4	1,042.3	950.4	1,000.5	1,056.0	1,118.2
1978	903.4	950.9	1,003.7	1,062.8	969.1	1,020.1	1,076.8	1,140.1
1979	920.8	969.3	1,023.2	1,083.4	988.2	1,040.2	1,098.0	1,162.5
1980	938.1	987.5	1,042.3	1,103.7	1,007.7	1,060.7	1,119.6	1,185.5
1981	955.1	1,005.4	1,061.3	1,123.7	1,027.1	1,081.2	1,141.2	1,208.4
1982	972.6	1,023.8	1,080.6	1,144.2	1,046.5	1,101.6	1,162.8	1,231.2
1983	990.4	1,042.5	1,100.4	1,165.2	1,065.7	1,121.8	1,184.1	1,253.7
1984	1,008.2	1,061.3	1,120.2	1,186.1	1,084.6	1,141.7	1,205.1	1,276.0
1985	1,025.7	1,079.6	1,139.6	1,206.7	1,103.2	1,161.3	1,225.8	1,297.9
1986	1,042.7	1,097.6	1,158.5	1,226.7	1,121.8	1,180.9	1,246.5	1,319.8

Table 6 (Cont'd)

Year	Model E				Model F			
Year	Census-based series	5 per cent under-count series	10 per cent under-count series	15 per cent under-count series	Census-based series	5 per cent under-count series	10 per cent under-count series	15 per cent under-count series
1966	760.3	800.3	844.8	894.5	732.6	771.1	813.9	861.8
1967	776.7	817.6	863.0	913.7	747.1	786.4	830.1	879.0
1968	793.2	834.9	881.3	933.1	761.4	801.4	846.0	895.7
1969	808.1	850.6	897.9	950.7	775.1	815.9	861.2	911.9
1970	817.4	860.5	908.3	961.7	788.1	829.6	875.7	927.2
1971	816.3	859.2	907.0	960.3	773.2	813.8	859.1	909.6
1972	823.9	867.2	915.4	969.3	713.2	750.8	792.5	839.1
1973	836.1	880.1	929.0	983.7	693.4	729.9	770.4	815.7
1974	850.9	895.6	945.4	1,001.0	688.6	724.8	765.1	810.1
1975	867.9	913.6	964.3	1,021.1	696.2	732.8	773.5	819.0
1976	885.5	932.1	983.9	1,041.8	706.2	743.3	784.6	830.8
1977	901.7	949.1	1,001.9	1,060.8	718.4	756.2	798.2	845.1
1978	916.1	964.3	1,017.9	1,077.8	732.7	771.2	814.1	862.0
1979	925.8	974.5	1,028.7	1,089.2	748.2	787.5	831.3	880.2
1980	926.1	974.8	1,029.0	1,089.5	765.0	805.2	849.9	899.9
1981	917.8	966.1	1,019.8	1,079.8	782.4	823.6	869.4	920.5
1982	921.8	970.3	1,024.2	1,084.5	800.6	842.8	889.6	941.9
1983	931.9	980.9	1,035.4	1,096.3	819.5	862.6	910.5	964.1
1984	944.9	994.6	1,049.9	1,111.6	839.0	883.2	932.2	987.1
1985	960.5	1,011.0	1,067.2	1,130.0	859.1	904.3	954.6	1,010.7
1986	974.0	1,025.2	1,082.2	1,145.9	879.2	925.5	976.9	1,034.3

TABLE 7

ESTIMATED CRUDE BIRTH, DEATH, AND NATURAL INCREASE RATES FOR MAINLAND CHINA, FOUR ALTERNATE MODELS: 1953-1965

	Model I			Model II			Model III			Model IV		
Year	Birth rate	Death rate	Natural increase rate	Birth rate	Death rate	Natural increase rate	Birth rate	Death rate	Natural increase rate	Birth rate	Death rate	Natural increase rate
1953	45.0	22.5	22.5	45.0	25.0	20.0	40.0	20.0	20.0	40.0	22.5	17.5
1954	44.7	20.7	24.0	44.7	23.3	21.4	39.8	18.4	21.4	39.8	20.7	19.1
1955	44.3	19.5	24.8	44.4	22.2	22.2	39.6	17.3	22.3	39.7	19.6	20.1
1956	43.9	18.8	25.0	44.0	21.5	22.5	39.3	16.6	22.7	39.4	19.0	20.5
1957	43.5	18.4	25.0	43.6	21.1	22.5	39.0	16.2	22.8	39.2	18.7	20.5
1958	43.0	18.3	24.7	43.2	20.9	22.4	38.7	16.0	22.7	38.9	18.6	20.3
1959	42.6	19.7	22.9	42.9	22.2	20.7	38.4	17.0	21.4	38.7	19.5	19.1
1960	42.3	22.5	19.7	42.6	26.1	16.4	38.1	19.3	18.8	38.4	21.8	16.7
1961	42.0	27.9	14.1	42.4	33.1	9.3	37.9	22.5	15.4	38.2	25.1	13.2
1962	41.8	28.7	13.1	42.3	33.9	8.3	37.7	22.7	15.0	38.0	25.4	12.7
1963	41.4	23.5	18.0	42.0	28.2	13.8	37.4	19.3	18.1	37.8	22.1	15.7
1964	41.1	19.9	21.2	41.7	22.7	19.0	37.1	17.1	20.0	37.5	19.8	17.7
1965	40.8	18.4	22.4	41.5	20.9	20.6	36.8	16.1	20.8	37.3	18.6	18.7

TABLE 8

PROJECTED CRUDE BIRTH, DEATH, AND NATURAL INCREASE RATES FOR MAINLAND CHINA, SIX ALTERNATE MODELS: 1966-1985

	Model A			Model B			Model C		
Year	Birth rate	Death rate	Natural increase rate	Birth rate	Death rate	Natural increase rate	Birth rate	Death rate	Natural increase rate
1966	36.6	15.9	20.6	36.6	16.6	20.0	37.1	19.5	17.6
1967	36.3	15.6	20.7	36.4	16.9	19.5	37.0	19.9	17.1
1968	36.1	15.3	20.8	36.3	16.6	19.7	36.9	20.2	16.6
1969	35.8	15.0	20.8	36.1	16.2	19.9	36.8	19.8	16.9
1970	35.5	14.6	20.9	36.0	15.9	20.1	36.7	19.4	17.2
1971	35.2	14.3	20.9	36.0	15.6	20.4	36.6	19.1	17.5
1972	35.0	14.1	20.9	35.9	15.3	20.6	36.6	18.8	17.9
1973	34.8	13.8	21.0	35.9	15.0	20.9	36.7	18.4	18.3
1974	34.5	13.5	21.0	35.9	14.7	21.2	36.8	18.1	18.7
1975	34.2	13.2	21.0	35.8	15.0	20.8	37.0	17.8	19.2
1976	33.9	12.9	21.0	35.8	15.3	20.4	37.2	17.9	19.3
1977	33.5	12.6	20.9	35.7	15.6	20.0	37.3	17.9	19.4
1978	33.0	12.3	20.7	35.5	15.3	20.2	37.4	18.3	19.2
1979	32.5	12.0	20.5	35.3	15.0	20.4	37.5	19.0	18.6
1980	31.8	11.6	20.2	35.0	14.6	20.4	37.6	19.6	18.0
1981	31.1	11.3	19.8	34.7	14.3	20.4	37.7	19.6	18.1
1982	30.3	10.9	19.3	34.3	14.0	20.4	37.8	19.6	18.2
1983	29.3	10.6	18.7	33.9	13.7	20.2	37.8	20.0	17.8
1984	28.0	10.2	17.8	33.3	13.3	20.0	37.9	20.7	17.2
1985	26.5	9.8	16.7	32.6	13.0	19.6	37.9	21.5	16.5

Year	Model D Birth rate	Model D Death rate	Model D Natural increase rate	Model E Birth rate	Model E Death rate	Model E Natural increase rate	Model F Birth rate	Model F Death rate	Model F Natural increase rate
1966	40.6	19.2	21.4	40.5	19.2	21.3	41.2	21.5	19.7
1967	40.4	19.2	21.2	40.2	19.2	21.0	40.8	21.9	18.9
1968	40.3	19.2	21.1	39.7	21.0	18.7	40.1	22.2	17.9
1969	40.3	19.2	21.0	39.1	27.6	11.5	39.1	22.5	16.6
1970	40.3	19.6	20.6	38.2	39.7	–1.4	36.0	55.2	–19.2
1971	40.3	20.0	20.3	38.8	29.6	9.3	31.4	112.0	–80.6
1972	40.4	20.4	20.0	39.5	24.7	14.8	35.5	63.8	–28.3
1973	40.5	20.8	19.6	40.2	22.8	17.5	38.9	45.8	–6.9
1974	40.5	21.2	19.3	40.7	20.9	19.8	44.0	33.0	11.0
1975	40.5	21.2	19.3	41.1	21.1	20.1	45.9	31.8	14.3
1976	40.6	21.2	19.4	41.4	23.3	18.1	47.0	29.9	17.1
1977	40.7	21.2	19.4	41.4	25.5	15.9	47.8	28.0	19.7
1978	40.7	21.2	19.5	41.1	30.6	10.5	48.3	27.4	20.9
1979	40.8	21.2	19.5	40.4	40.1	.3	48.6	26.4	22.2
1980	40.8	21.7	19.1	39.1	48.1	–9.0	48.8	26.2	22.6
1981	40.7	22.1	18.7	39.8	35.5	4.3	48.9	25.9	23.0
1982	40.6	22.4	18.2	40.4	29.6	10.9	48.9	25.6	23.3
1983	40.4	22.8	17.6	41.0	27.2	13.8	48.7	25.1	23.6
1984	40.2	23.1	17.0	41.3	25.0	16.4	48.3	24.6	23.6
1985	40.8	23.1	16.8	41.5	27.5	14.0	47.7	24.6	23.1

it happens, the net change in the crude birth and death rates for all models between 1953 and 1965 is about the same number of points; hence the natural increase rate for each model in 1965 is about the same as in 1953.

In the period 1966-85, covered in Table 8, both the gross reproduction rates and the life expectancies at birth vary by different patterns for each model. In models A and B, in which the gross reproduction rate declined by one-third and one-sixth, respectively, the crude birth rates also decline, but less markedly, because toward the end of the period, age composition, a cause of falling birth rates in the preceding period, begins to exert its influence in the other direction, as the larger cohorts of young females surviving since 1949 move into the childbearing years. Because the death rate is also falling steadily in model A, the natural increase rate does not turn definitely downward until the late 1970's. In model B, where the decline in the death rate is unsteady and the decline in the birth rate extremely slow, natural increase rates do not change significantly throughout the 20-year period. In model C, the effects of age composition wipe out by 1975 the early decline in the crude birth rate caused by declining gross reproduction rates; mortality is also rising in the second half of the period, however, and the trend of the natural increase rate is fairly constant throughout the period.

In model D, a slight reduction in the gross reproduction rate is almost exactly matched by the effects of changing age composition, so that the crude birth rate is held within a range of six-tenths of one point throughout the 20 years. The rising trend in mortality is matched by a falling trend in natural increase. In model E, the depression of the gross reproduction rate during the crisis periods, 1958-72 and 1977-82, causes dips in the trend of the crude birth rates, which tends to move slightly upward in response to age composition changes. Mortality takes a marked toll during both crises, causing net losses to the population in 1970 and 1980, as the natural increase rates indicate. In model F, the effects of the catastrophic mortality pattern, with its heavy toll of young children and aged persons, are apparent in the crude birth rates, which reach the high 40's during the last 10 years of the projection period because of the concentration of the surviving population in the young adult years, including the ages of childbearing. The crude death rates in model F remain higher after the catastrophe than before it, even though life expectancy at birth is the same in 1985 as in 1965. Age composition is again the reason, since the loss of young children, for whom age-specific death rates are low, more than compensates for the loss of aged persons for whom the age-specific death rates are high. Nevertheless, the high crude birth rates cause natural increase to remain high after completion of the recovery period in the late 1970's.

Table 9 gives the age composition of the four models for the period 1953-65 as of January 1, 1966. At a glance it can be seen that models I

TABLE 9

ESTIMATED DISTRIBUTIONS OF THE POPULATION OF MAINLAND CHINA BY AGE AND SEX
FOUR ALTERNATE MODELS: 1966
(in per cent of the total January 1 population)

Age	Model I			Model II			Model III			Model IV		
	Both sexes	Male	Female	Both sexes	Male	Female	Both sexes	Male	Female	Both sexes	Male	Female
All ages	100.00	50.52	49.48	100.00	50.54	49.46	100.00	50.18	49.82	100.00	50.20	49.80
0 to 4 years	15.59	7.89	7.70	15.33	7.76	7.57	14.72	7.46	7.26	14.53	7.36	7.17
5 to 9 years	13.73	6.95	6.78	13.39	6.78	6.61	13.13	6.65	6.48	12.89	6.53	6.36
10 to 14 years	12.46	6.31	6.15	12.41	6.29	6.12	11.81	5.98	5.83	11.75	5.95	5.80
15 to 19 years	9.74	4.97	4.77	9.97	5.09	4.88	9.46	4.82	4.64	9.61	4.90	4.71
20 to 24 years	7.80	4.01	3.79	8.00	4.12	3.88	7.74	3.96	3.78	7.89	4.04	3.85
25 to 29 years	7.12	3.67	3.45	7.27	3.75	3.52	7.23	3.71	3.52	7.34	3.77	3.57
30 to 34 years	6.63	3.40	3.23	6.73	3.46	3.27	6.88	3.52	3.36	6.97	3.57	3.40
35 to 39 years	5.75	2.91	2.84	5.82	2.95	2.87	5.87	2.95	2.92	5.94	2.99	2.95
40 to 44 years	4.92	2.46	2.46	4.96	2.48	2.48	4.98	2.43	2.55	5.03	2.46	2.57
45 to 49 years	4.15	2.05	2.10	4.17	2.06	2.11	4.20	2.00	2.20	4.22	2.01	2.21
50 to 54 years	3.51	1.74	1.77	3.52	1.74	1.78	3.70	1.78	1.92	3.71	1.78	1.93
55 to 59 years	2.91	1.45	1.46	2.89	1.43	1.46	3.23	1.57	1.66	3.22	1.56	1.66
60 to 64 years	2.26	1.11	1.15	2.23	1.09	1.14	2.64	1.28	1.36	2.62	1.27	1.35
65 to 69 years	1.63	.78	.85	1.59	.76	.83	1.98	.95	1.03	1.94	.93	1.01
70 to 74 years	1.03	.48	.55	.99	.46	.53	1.32	.62	.70	1.28	.60	.68
75 years and over	.77	.34	.43	.73	.32	.41	1.11	.50	.61	1.06	.48	.58
0 to 14 years	41.77	21.15	20.62	41.13	20.83	20.30	39.67	20.09	19.58	39.17	19.84	19.33
15 to 59 years	52.54	26.66	25.88	53.33	27.08	26.25	53.28	26.73	26.55	53.93	27.08	26.85
60 years and over	5.69	2.71	2.98	5.54	2.63	2.91	7.05	3.36	3.69	6.90	3.28	3.62

TABLE 10

PROJECTED DISTRIBUTIONS OF THE POPULATION OF MAINLAND CHINA BY AGE AND SEX
SIX ALTERNATE MODELS: 1986
(in per cent of the total January 1 population)

Age	Model A			Model B			Model C		
	Both sexes	Male	Female	Both sexes	Male	Female	Both sexes	Male	Female
All ages	100.00	50.26	49.74	100.00	50.27	49.73	100.00	50.34	49.66
0 to 4 years	12.55	6.38	6.17	14.01	7.10	6.91	14.67	7.43	7.24
5 to 9 years	12.27	6.22	6.05	12.52	6.34	6.18	12.56	6.36	6.20
10 to 14 years	11.30	5.72	5.58	11.24	5.69	5.55	11.11	5.63	5.48
15 to 19 years	10.19	5.16	5.03	9.96	5.04	4.92	9.81	4.97	4.84
20 to 24 years	8.97	4.54	4.43	8.83	4.47	4.36	8.75	4.44	4.31
25 to 29 years	8.21	4.15	4.06	8.08	4.09	3.99	8.03	4.08	3.95
30 to 34 years	7.29	3.69	3.60	7.15	3.62	3.53	7.17	3.64	3.53
35 to 39 years	5.75	2.92	2.83	5.62	2.86	2.76	5.73	2.93	2.80
40 to 44 years	4.65	2.37	2.28	4.54	2.32	2.22	4.61	2.36	2.25
45 to 49 years	4.28	2.18	2.10	4.17	2.13	2.04	4.20	2.14	2.06
50 to 54 years	3.96	2.00	1.96	3.85	1.94	1.91	3.84	1.94	1.90
55 to 59 years	3.24	1.59	1.65	3.14	1.54	1.60	3.09	1.51	1.58
60 to 64 years	2.55	1.20	1.35	2.45	1.15	1.30	2.38	1.11	1.27
65 to 69 years	1.91	.86	1.05	1.82	.82	1.00	1.72	.77	.95
70 to 74 years	1.39	.62	.77	1.30	.58	.72	1.19	.53	.66
75 years and over	1.49	.66	.83	1.32	.58	.74	1.14	.50	.64
0 to 14 years	36.14	18.33	17.81	37.78	19.14	18.64	38.33	19.41	18.92
15 to 59 years	56.56	28.61	27.95	55.32	28.00	27.32	55.23	28.01	27.22
60 years and over	7.30	3.32	3.98	6.90	3.13	3.77	6.44	2.92	3.52

	Model D			Model E			Model F		
All ages	100.00	50.50	49.50	100.00	50.56	49.44	100.00	50.95	49.05
0 to 4 years	15.20	7.70	7.50	14.70	7.44	7.26	17.87	9.05	8.82
5 to 9 years	13.02	6.59	6.43	11.43	5.78	5.65	14.01	7.09	6.92
10 to 14 years	11.57	5.86	5.71	11.56	5.86	5.70	7.62	3.91	3.71
15 to 19 years	10.35	5.25	5.10	10.10	5.13	4.97	6.95	3.71	3.24
20 to 24 years	9.00	4.57	4.43	9.80	4.99	4.81	9.69	4.96	4.73
25 to 29 years	8.16	4.15	4.01	8.91	4.55	4.36	9.07	4.65	4.42
30 to 34 years	7.22	3.67	3.55	7.80	3.99	3.81	8.11	4.17	3.94
35 to 39 years	5.51	2.82	2.69	5.85	3.02	2.83	6.26	3.25	3.01
40 to 44 years	4.32	2.22	2.10	4.51	2.33	2.18	4.82	2.51	2.31
45 to 49 years	3.83	1.96	1.87	3.93	2.01	1.92	4.16	2.16	2.00
50 to 54 years	3.43	1.73	1.70	3.45	1.73	1.72	3.61	1.83	1.78
55 to 59 years	2.79	1.37	1.42	2.74	1.33	1.41	2.83	1.38	1.45
60 to 64 years	2.15	1.03	1.12	2.08	.98	1.10	2.11	.99	1.12
65 to 69 years	1.55	.72	.83	1.46	.67	.79	1.45	.66	.79
70 to 74 years	1.02	.47	.55	.93	.42	.51	.88	.39	.49
75 years and over	.88	.39	.49	.75	.33	.42	.56	.24	.32
0 to 14 years	39.78	20.14	19.64	37.68	19.08	18.60	39.49	20.04	19.45
15 to 59 years	54.61	27.74	26.87	57.10	29.08	28.02	55.50	28.63	26.87
60 years and over	5.61	2.62	2.99	5.22	2.40	2.82	5.01	2.28	2.73

and II, the higher fertility models, have more youthful populations than the two low fertility models, III and IV. The proportion at ages under 15 in model I is about 2.6 percentage points higher than in model IV; the proportions at ages 60 and over in models I and II are lower than in models III and IV. In the middle years there is not much difference between the four models; the total range is less than 1.5 percentage points.

By the end of the projection period (January 1, 1986), the differences in age composition between models are greater, as Table 10 shows. Comparing all six models, models A and B, with their declining birth rates, have smaller proportions of children under 15 years of age and larger proportions of aged persons. Models C and D have larger proportions under 15 and smaller proportions in both the intermediate and advanced years than do models A and B. Models E and F exhibit some peculiarities resulting from their special mortality experiences in the past. Both models have low proportions at ages 60 and over because of past high mortality rates, but model E also shows the marks of crisis in its relatively small cohort at ages 5 to 9; while model F has even more marked deficits at ages 10 to 19, and the largest proportions found in any of the models at ages 0 to 9, both reflections of the catastrophe of the 1970's and the 10 years of high birth rates thereafter. Taken altogether, however, despite the extreme circumstances assumed for models E and F, the differences between them and models A through D are not very great when the broad age groups at the bottom of the table are compared. All six models show smaller proportions at ages 0 to 14 than do their base populations as of January 1, 1966.

SELECTION AND USES OF ALTERNATE ESTIMATES AND PROJECTIONS

Most uses of population estimates and projections for Communist China fall into either of two categories: (1) analyses of domestic trends and prospects for mainland China, in which population data are related to other kinds of data or estimates, especially in per capita rates and trends; or (2) comparative studies relating data for China to those for other countries or regions. Studies of the first type tend to focus on the First Five-Year Plan period, because of the lack of official data and difficulties of making estimates for other years. International comparisons, particularly those involving many countries and many other aspects of national development, usually have a longer time span and may plunge onward to the year 2000 or beyond. These two uses of population data are quite different, and the selection of models and figures may therefore observe different criteria.

In analytical studies of the society and economy of mainland China during the First Five-Year Plan period, it is important to distinguish between analyses that are specifically aimed at testing the congruency of official data, and those that attempt to escape the quantitative and qualitative limitations of the official data by substituting estimates that, it is hoped, come closer to actuality. If the purpose of a given study is to test official data, none of the population series presented in this paper should be used. Instead, the official population figures issues by the State Statistical Bureau should be employed, either in the form in which they were originally released, with an unexplained change in level between the 1957 year-end figures and those for earlier years, or in a smoothed series based on the official totals for 1953 and 1957. However, analyses based on official data should not assume that congruities between population and other data are proof of reliability and therefore warrant the drawing of empirical conclusions.

If the analysis is oriented instead to the exploration of possible empirical relationships between population and other parameters, it may be better to make use of estimated figures and to take full account of the differences in trends and magnitudes represented by alternate series. As was noted in the previous section, estimates and projections that take the 1953 census figure as their base total do not differ very significantly in the totals they produce by 1965, even if the assumed increase rates are quite different. If, however, alternate assumptions about the size of the base population are also allowed, as they must be in short-run projections, the differences can be much greater. In the estimates prepared for this study, the range as of 1953 exceeds 100 million, and by 1965 it exceeds 150 million. For some uses of population estimates, such as the calculation of estimated daily caloric intake per capita, especially where the intake rates fall close to the physiological minimum, differences in the population estimates can be critical. Analyses in which the conclusions depend upon relatively small differences in the trend of per capita rates may be affected one way or the other by the increase rates implicit in the population estimates.

It is extremely important, as noted earlier, that all statistical analyses involving estimated population figures be tested using alternate series, especially series that tend to weaken the conclusions to be drawn from the analysis. If the case cannot be made with the least favorable series of population figures, a serious reexamination of the whole analytical framework may be advisable. If the least favorable series is one based on the census total, the conclusions may not necessarily be in danger, since there are reasons for believing that the census total was too low. If the least favorable series is one assuming a 15 per cent undercount, it must be conceded that this assumption is wholly arbitrary and may be too large. However, other things equal, a study which can sustain its conclusions with any population series is on firmer ground than one in which the conclusions cannot be reached when the more extreme population figures are utilized.

What has been said regarding total population figures applies also to uses of component totals by age and sex and to estimates of births, deaths, and increase rates. In fact, if proper allowance is to be made for the margin of uncertainty inherent in all reported or estimated figures for mainland China, alternate series should be tested for every parameter in the study. Under no circumstances should the case for an empirical conclusion be considered proved on the basis of a single series of values for each variable.

In relating population estimates and projections to other kinds of data or estimates, it is important to make sure that the underlying assumptions for each type are not mutually contradictory. Population estimates that imply maximum economic development should not be combined with estimates for other social or economic variables that represent distress conditions or stagnation in economic development (and vice versa). It should be noted that the relative size of a projected population total is not necessarily a clue as to whether the projection assumes favorable or unfavorable socioeconomic conditions; a large population may reflect the failure of the economy to supply incentive for control of fertility, while a small one may reflect the economy's failure to insure control of mortality.

In the case of long-range projections of the population of mainland China, many of the same strictures discussed above are again relevant, but there are others as well. Here, of course, everything is a matter of assumption, and the hazard of assumptions about the future in an age of change is far greater than the risk in assumptions about the past or the present. Barring radical changes in mortality levels, the survivors of existing cohorts can be projected with fair assurance for several decades, assuming that the estimates at the start of the projection period were not unreasonable. However, the size of new cohorts can be greatly affected by changes in both fertility and mortality levels, and if these cohorts differ much from those in prior years, the vital rates, structure, and size of the population as a whole can also be affected. It is no exaggeration to say that projections for more than 15 or 20 years are probably meaningless except as abstract hypothecations. Most makers of long-range projections are careful to include cautions to this effect in their advice to users, and users in their turn should be careful not to place more confidence in the figures than the person who prepared them did.

If the projections for mainland China are to be used with projections for other countries in comparative analyses, it is particularly important that the evaluations underlying the assumptions in each case represent the application of consistent criteria or a common perspective. For example, hopeful projections for one country should not be compared with "realistic" projections for another. On the other hand, projections involving the extrapolation of past demographic experience or an assumption of analogous development, without considering basic differences in demographically relevant conditions between mainland China and other countries, though they seem to be methodologically consistent, are actually quite inconsistent, for they assume the universal relevance of expectations that are not equally applicable to all countries. There are serious unresolved problems inherent in any attempt to devise a comparable standard for evaluating demographic data and prospects for two countries for which accurate or complete data are lacking; such problems are most acute when mainland China is one of the countries involved. Not only the lack of information but the aura of political feeling that may pervade even scholarly approaches to China can lead an analyst unwittingly to grant or grudge more toward China than toward other countries, and the operation of such biases is by no means peculiar to demographic analysis. Although, unfortunately, there is little that the user of population projections can do about problems the makers of the projections cannot resolve, it is important to recognize the dangers and their implications for international studies.

The estimates and projections of the population of mainland China presented here, and those given in the United Nations monograph on world population prospects (U.N., 1966) provide altogether about five or six different estimates for the First Five-Year Plan period and 12 projections for 1965 and beyond,[70] but the two sets of models were designed for different purposes and employ somewhat different methods and assumptions. For particular uses some models are more suitable than others, and for some purposes none of the estimates and projections in this collection may be entirely satisfactory.

For domestic studies of Communist China during the First Five-Year Plan period, it should be noted that all but one of the United Nations models as well as model IV of the estimates presented here assume increase rates below those in the official population data for 1953-57. By midyear 1955, one of two alternate base years used for the United Nations models, the base total common to all but one of their models is 8.5 million below the corresponding official figure; by midyear 1960, the other base year, the base total assumed is 650 million, which coincides with the round figure commonly used for speechmaking purposes in Communist China since 1958, apparently based on the State Statistical Bureau's figure of 646,530,000 as of year-end 1957. In model IV of the series given here, the increase rates employed are intermediate between the official rates and those in the United Nations models. By midyear 1955 model IV is about 3 million below the official figure.

For the years 1958 through 1965, for which there are no official population figures, the differences between the United Nations models and those

70. The numbers vary for different periods and depending upon what is counted as a separate alternative.

presented in this chapter mainly concern the assumptions about the effects of the food crisis of 1959-62 on general mortality levels and the resulting effects on population growth rates during those years. The United Nations models do not vary their basic pattern of assumptions to take account of the crisis. For all years and for all models in their series, mortality declines at a rate equivalent to a gain of 2.5 years of life expectancy at birth for every five-year period. The high mortality variants begin their decline with a higher starting level than do the lower mortality variants, but the rate of decline in both cases is that represented in the United Nations model life-tables, which in turn are designed to represent a kind of recorded world average experience in mortality reduction (U.N., 1959, especially pp. 27-30). All four of the models presented in this paper include a rising mortality trend during the crisis years. Though none of them permits mortality to force the natural increase rate below 10 per thousand even during the worst year, their lower increase rates allow the United Nations models to do some catching up, partially compensating for their lower growth rates during the First Five-Year Plan period. However, analyses that require year-to-year figures reflecting the trends of the crisis period probably should not use the United Nations models. Interpolations would necessarily be involved, since the United Nations models advance by five-year intervals, and these interpolations would have to be linear to be consistent with the assumptions implicit in the method.

The bases of choice are somewhat different for applications of long-range projections of the population of mainland China. Many such uses do not require year-to-year figures, and only a few involve components of change or age-sex structures. The analysis is often broad in scope and pointed toward generalities, and the conclusions are usually posed in conditional terms. Hence the tolerance limits for the various measures that serve as inputs are sometimes regarded as matters of no great concern. There may be some reluctance, therefore, to consider the possibility of entertaining alternate values for the demographic and other parameters, on the grounds that this procedure would introduce needless complication into an already complex statistical operation, the results of which are not meant to be definitive anyway. However, in view of the size of mainland China's population and the uncertainty about its prospective growth, there is always some danger that reliance on a single projection for China could swing the whole analysis toward one conclusion or another, depending upon which model was selected. For example, the United Nations models, which start from a common base total in 1960, attain a range of about 500 million by the year 2000 (from 868 to 1,366 million) (U.N., 1966, p. 57). It would be difficult to imagine any analytical purpose, whether it involves the economic development of mainland China alone or compares the prospects of different countries or regions of the world, that would not be affected in some degree by a difference of such magnitude.

Moreover, the United Nations models do not include any that are particularly "pessimistic" about prospects for the future control of either fertility or mortality in mainland China. In all the United Nations models, fertility declines to one-half the initial rate in the space of 30 years, a rate very close to that assumed for model A, the most "optimistic" of the models presented in this chapter. In some of the United Nations models, the decline begins in 1955, about a year before the official birth control campaign in China began to intensify. In others, fertility declines in several of the models described in this paper. The early fertility decline models do not assume any slowing of the rate of decline during the years 1958-62, when the official birth control campaign was in eclipse. None of these models implies a failure of the efforts at fertility and mortality reduction, such as might result from economic stagnation or recurrent crises. The consideration of such eventualities was excluded partly because pessimistic expectations were inconsistent with the stated purpose of all projections in the United Nations monograph, which is "to provide a basis for assessing the magnitude of efforts required to attain future goals in economic and social development" (U.N., 1966, p. 7). They are evidently intended primarily for use in long-range planning by government officials and administrators rather than for analytical use by social scientists and scholars. Moreover, the United Nations staff felt it advisable to keep the general pattern of assumptions and models similar for all countries for the sake of comparability. Obviously there would have been problems in rationalizing a unique or a particularly pessimistic treatment for mainland China as long as the treatment of other countries followed a uniform and more optimistic pattern.

Even where no such problems are involved there are certain difficulties in constructing pessimistic models for population projections and then using the resulting figures for analyses and comparisons. In the first place, although generalized trends are not particularly unrealistic in representing expectations of steady progress in control of mortality and fertility, the same cannot be said for representations of loss of control of fertility and mortality. Both past experience and logic suggest that a collapsing social system is not likely to wither away slowly according to a monotonic trend line; it is more likely to pass through a series of ups and downs of varying severity, with perhaps one or more very marked periods of disintegration. There is a certain unreality about assumptions of unchanging or gradually rising mortality. Yet more specific models of the type developed here to represent conditions of economic stagnation, recurrent crisis, and catastrophe also seem highly arbitrary in that they assign cycles of recession to specified future time periods. Even if the general expectations represented by one or another of these sets of assumptions should coincide with the course of events in China in the next 20 years, there is virtually no chance that actual experience would happen to conform to the trends and cycles shown by these projections. The year-to-year changes in the models therefore have little utility except as illustrations of some of the many possible forms which pessimistic eventualities might take. The size of the population at the end of the projection period may be taken as one indication of the possible cumulative effects of these eventualities on population growth, but the age-sex structures bear the imprint of the particular timing, sequence, and severity of the crisis or crises assumed and are therefore again merely illustrative. Such models cannot easily be related to models at the other end of the range or to the United Nations models. Hence their practical applications may be somewhat limited. They serve mainly to correct whatever bias might be implicit in a perspective that excluded from the range of projections any representation of the more somber, but still possible, prospects. It is especially important to guard against any such bias at a time when officials of international aid organizations and government leaders in many countries are deeply concerned about the economic and social consequences of uncontrolled population growth, lest someone suppose that in mainland China these problems are less urgent.

In general terms, both the United Nations projections and those presented here indicate a considerable margin of uncertainty about the future growth of the population of mainland China, yet both anticipate a very substantial increase during the immediate future. In the short run, at least, their implications for China's domestic development and relations with other countries, insofar as these are influenced by demographic factors, are much the same. Under any set of assumptions, the leaders of mainland China must cope with the problems of accommodating large increments to an already large population.

REFERENCES

The Agrarian Reform Law of the People's Republic of China, 2nd ed. Peking, 1951.

AIRD, JOHN S., 1960. "The Present and Prospective Population of Mainland China," in Milbank Memorial Fund, *Population Trends in Eastern Europe, the USSR and Mainland China,* pp. 93–137. New York.

AIRD, JOHN S., 1961. *The Size, Composition, and Growth of the Population of Mainland China,* International Population Statistics Reports, Series P–90, No. 15. Washington, D.C.: U.S. Bureau of the Census.

AIRD, JOHN S., 1962. "Population Policy in Mainland China," *Population Studies,* July, 1962, 16, pp. 38–57.

BARCLAY, GEORGE W., 1954. *Colonial Development and Population in Taiwan.* Princeton.

An-tung jih-pao, Aug. 7, 1956. "Wei-shen-ma yao chin-hsing hu-k'ou pu-ch'a" ("Why Must We Carry Out a Household Investigation?"). An-tung.

Central Political and Legislative Organ, Tsinan, 1953. (Tsinan Municipality Political Work Team.) "Chi-nan-shih ti-erh-ch'ü p'u-hsüan chung-tien shih-pan kung-tso shih tsen-yang chin-hsing jen-k'ou tiao-ch'a ho hsüan-min teng-chi te" ("How Did the Second District of Tsinan Municipality Carry Out Population Investigation and Registration of Voters During Keypoint Experimental Election Work?"), *JMJP,* May 26, 1953.

Central Population Investigation and Registration Office, 1954. "Ke-ti chia-ch-iang tui jen-k'ou tiao-ch'a teng-chi kung-tso te ling-tao ch'uang-tsao ch'u hsü-to pien-li ch'ün-chung te chien-i pan-fa" ("Various Areas Strengthen Their Guidance over Population Investigation and Registration Work and Devise Many Simplified Methods for the Convenience of the Masses"), *JMJP,* March 21, 1954.

Ch'ang-chiang jih-pao, May 23, 1956. "Jen-jen tou ying tsun-shou ru-k'ou huan-li chih-tu" ("Everybody Should Observe the Household Control System"). Wuhan.

Ch'ang-chiang jih-pao, Feb. 20, 1952. "T'i-ch'ang lao-shih jen-chen fan-tui tso chia-pao-kao" ("Advocate Honesty and Conscientiousness, Oppose the Making of False Reports"). Wuhan.

Ch'ang-chiang jih-pao, Aug. 13, 1951. "Regulations for Registration of Personnel of Reactionary Parties and Corps, Secret Service Organizations, and Other Counter-Revolutionary Elements in the Central-South Region." Hankow. (Translated in *SCMP,* No. 158, August 21, 1951, pp. 12–14.)

CHANG-HENG CHEN, 1931. "Some Phases of China's Population Problem," *Bulletin de l'Institut International de Statistique.* Tome 25, 2ème Livraison, pp. 18*-54*. Tokyo.

CH'EN HSÜEH-MING, 1956. "Ni-shuo hao-hsiao pu-hao-hsiao hu-k' ou-pu pien-ch'eng yen-yüan-piao" ("Don't You Think It Funny that a Household Book Should Be Transformed into a Cast of Characters?"), *Hsin Su-chou pao,* Dec. 28, 1956. Soochow.

CH'EN TA, 1957. "New China's Population Census of 1953 and Its Relations to National Reconstruction and Demographic Research." International Statistical Institute, Stockholm, Aug. 8–15, 1957. (mimeo)

CH'ENG CHOU, 1955. *"T'an-t'an hu-k'ou wen-t'i"* (Lets Talk About the Problems of Household Registration"), *Hsin-wen jih-pao,* June 5, 1955, Shanghai.

CHIA CH'I-YUN, 1958. "Tang-chien t'ung-chi kung-tso kai-ke yün-tung-chung te chi-ke wen-t'i" ("Several Problems in the Current Statistical Reform Movement"), *TCKT,* No. 15 (Aug. 1958), pp. 5–10.

CH'IAO, C. M., W. S. THOMPSON, and D. T. CHEN, 1938. *An Experiment in the Registration of Vital Statistics in China.* Oxford, Ohio.

Chi-lin jih-pao, Nov. 1, 1956. "Yao pien-li ch'ün-chung chuan hu-k'ou" ("Serve the Convenience of the Masses in Transferring Household Registration"). Ch'ang-ch'un.

Ch'ing-hai jih-pao, Dec. 6, 1956. "Wei-shen-ma pu kei wo ch'ien-i-cheng" ("Why Refuse Me a Moving Permit?"). Sining.

Ch'ung-ch'ing jih-pao, Aug. 11, 1956. "Ying-chieh hsüan-chü tso-hao hu-k'ou chiao-tui kung-tso" ("Welcome the Elections; Do a Good Job of Household Checking"). Chungking.

Chung-hua jen-min kung-ho-kuo fen-sheng ching-t'u (*Detailed Provincial Atlas of the People's Republic of China*). Shanghai.
Jan. 1950, 1st ed. (pocket size ed.)
Oct. 1950, 1st ed. (popular ed.)
Feb. 1951, 3rd ed. (popular ed.)
May 1951, 23rd ed. (pocket size popular ed.)
Aug. 1952, 4th ed. (pocket size ed.)
Aug. 1952, 2nd ed. (deluxe ed.)
Oct. 1952, 7th ed. (pocket size popular ed.)
April 1953, 1st ed. (popular ed.)
April 1953, 3rd ed. (deluxe ed.)
Aug. 1953, 8th ed. (deluxe ed.)
Aug. 1953, 9th ed. (popular ed.)
Nov. 1953, 13th ed. (deluxe ed.)

Chung-hua jen-min kung-ho-kuo fen-sheng ti-t'u (*Provincial Atlas of the People's Republic of China*). Shanghai.
Sept. 1950, 1st ed.
June 1951, 4th ed.
Sept. 1952, 6th ed.
March 1953, 1st ed.
June 1953, 2nd ed.
July 1953, 3rd ed.
Aug. 1953, 5th ed.
Dec. 1953, 6th ed.

Chung-kuo fen-sheng t'u, 1948. (*Provincial Atlas of China*).
July 1948, 1st ed. Ta-lien.

Directorate General of Budgets, Accounts, and Statistics, 1947. *Chung-hua min-kuo t'ung-chi t'i-yao, 1947* (*Statistical Abstract of the Republic of China, 1947*). Nanking.

DURAND, JOHN D., 1960. "The Population Statistics of China, A.D. 2–1953," *Population Studies*, March 1960, 13, pp. 209–256.

FENG WEN-LAN, 1950. "Chung-kuo te jen-k'ou chi Chung-kuo te t'ung-i" ("The Population and the Unification of China"), *Kuang-ming jih-pao*, June 21, 1950. Peking.

Fu-chien jih-pao, Aug. 20, 1956. "P'ai-ch'u-so t'ien-hsieh hu-k'ou-pu pu-kai ts'o-wu pai-ch'u" ("There Should Not Be All Sorts of Mistakes When the Public Security Station Fills Out the Household Book"). Foochow.

Government Administrative Council, 1950. "Decisions Concerning the Differentiation of Class Status in the Countryside," *People's China*. Oct. 1950, 2 (Supplement), pp. 1–14.

Ha-erh-pin jih-pao, Nov. 14, 1956. "Keng-huan hu-k'ou chü-min man-i" ("Exchange of Household Books Is Satisfactory to the Residents"). Harbin.

Heng-yang hsin-wen, Aug. 29, 1956. "Ying-kai chi-shih chuan-i hu-chi kuanhsi" ("Change of Residence Should Be Made at the Proper Time"). Heng-yang.

Hang-chou jih-pao, Oct. 28, 1956. "Ch'ing-nien pien-ch'eng erh-t'ung" ("A Young Man Became a Child"). Hangchow.

HO PING-TI, 1959. *Studies on the Population of China, 1368-1953.* Cambridge, Massachusetts.

Hsin-chiang jih-pao, Urumchi:

Hsin-chiang jih-pao, Nov. 20, 1951. "T'u-lu-fan-hsien erh-ch'ü Po-szu-t'ang-hsiang chao-k'ai szu-tzu nung-tai-hui tsung-chieh chien-tsu fan-pa t'ao-lun ch'iu-cheng tai-piao-men ming-ch'üeh-le cheng-ts'e tzu-tung pao-lu ping p'i-p'an ch'ü-nien yin-man t'u-ti yü hsü-pao jen-k'ou teng ts'o-wu" ("Po-szu-t'ang *Hsiang,* in the Second District of T'u-lu-fan *Hsien,* Held a Fourth Farmers' Representatives Conference; It Summarized the Rent Reduction and Anti-Tyranny Movements and Discussed the Fall Levy; the Representatives, after They Understood the Policy, Exposed and Criticized on Their Own Initiative Their Mistakes in Concealing Land and Making False Population Reports").

Hsin-chiang jih-pao, Feb. 11, 1953 (a). "Chien-i chung-shih t'u-kai te t'ung-chi kung-tso" ("A Suggestion That Attention Be Paid to Statistical Work During Land Reform").

Hsin-chiang jih-pao, Feb. 11, 1953 (b). "Tui t'u-kai chung kao-hao t'ung-chi kung-tso te chi-tien i-chien" (Several Opinions on Doing Land Reform Statistical Work Well").

Hsin-chiang jih-jao, Dec. 22, 1954. "Wu-lu-mu-ch'i-shih tung-fang chih-an kung-tso p'u-p'ien chan-k'ai" ("Winter Public Security Work Carried Out Throughout Urumchi Municipality").

Hsin Chungkuo fen-sheng t'u, 1953. (*New China Provincial Atlas*). Nov. 1953, 21st ed. Shanghai.

Hsin Chung-Kuo ti't'u, 1950. (*Atlas of New China*). Sept. 1950, 1st ed. Shanghai.

Hsin Su-chou pao, July 31, 1956. "Ho-tui hu-k'ou huan-fa hu-k'ou-pu" ("Check the Households and Distribute New Household Books"). Soochow.

Hsin Su-chou pao, Aug. 9, 1956. "Tso-hao hu-k'ou ho-tui ho huan-fa hu-k'ou-pu kung-tso" ("Do a Good Job of Checking Households and Distributing New Household Books"). Soochow.

Hsin wan-pao, Dec. 7, 1952. "Wo-kuo jen-k'ou tsui-hsin t'ung-chi szu-i-pa-chien-san-pai-to-wan" ("The Latest Population Figure for Our Country Is Over 483 Million"). Hong Kong.

Hsin-wen jih-pao, June 5, 1955. "Shih kung-an-chü wei chia-ch'iang ch'eng-shih kuan-li chi-hsü chin-hsing ho ta chu-min hu-k'ou pu te kung-tso" ("The Municipal Public Security Bureau Continues to Carry Out Checking and Distribution of Household Books for Residents in Order to Strengthen Control of the City.") Shanghai.

Hsing-tao jih-pao, Hong Kong:

Hsing-tao jih-pao, Aug. 19, 1951. "Kuang-tung ch'üan-sheng hsiang-ts'un hu-k'ou chüeh-ting pien-lieh men-p'ai hao-shu" ("Kwangtung Decided to Assign Door Placards in Rural Areas Throughout the Province"). (Dispatch from Canton, Aug. 18, 1951.)

Hsing-tao jih-pao, Oct. 27, 1951. "Yüeh tang-chü chih-shih ke-chi cheng-fu ch'üan-sheng nung-ts'un chu-hu tiao-ch'a tso-wei shih-cheng chien-she ken-chü" ("Kwangtung Provincial Authorities Direct Government Agencies at All Levels to Carry Out Rural Household Investigations for Use as a Basis for Government Administration and Construction").

Hsing-tao jih-pao, Nov. 2, 1951. "Ch'üan-sheng hsien-shih hsiang-ts'un hsü-chen jen-k'ou i-tung hsü ching ho-chun" ("Population Movements in *Hsien* Cities and Towns in Kwangtung Must be Approved").

Hsin-hua jih-pao, July 9, 1953. "Ch'ung-ch'ing-shih jen-min cheng-fu pu-kao" ("Public Notice of the Chungking Municipal People's Government"). Chungking.

Hsin-hua jih-pao, July 21, 1953. "Ch'ung-ch'ing-shih jen-min cheng-fu kung-an-chü pu-kao ("Public Notice of the Public Security Bureau of the Chungking Municipal People's Government"). Chungking.

H'sin-hua jih-pao, April 1, 1954. "Ch'uan-shen chi-ts'eng hsüan-chü chi-chiang chi-pen wan-ch'eng" ("Basic Level Elections Will Soon Be Completed in the Whole Province"). Nanking.

JMJP. Jen-min jih-pao (*People's Daily*), Peking:

JMJP, Nov. 17, 1949. "Pei-ching-shih jen-min cheng-fu pu-kao" ("Public Notice of the Peking Municipal People's Government").

JMJP, Dec. 4, 1949 (a). "Ching-shih hsin hu-k'ou kuei-tse shun-li t'ui-hsing shih-min tzu-tun ch'üeh-shih sheng-pao lou-pao hsü-pao to fen-fen sheng-ch'ing keng-chen" ("The New Houshold Regulations Are Being Carried Out Smoothly in Peking Municipality; People of the Municipality Report the Truth Voluntarily; Numerous Requests for Correction of Underreporting and False Reporting").

JMJP, Dec. 4, 1949 (b). "Yung-hu hsin-te hu-k'ou chih-tu" ("Support the New Household System").

JMJP, Feb. 4, 1950. "Ching chien hsin hu-k'ou kung-tso wan-ch'eng" ("Work of Establishing the New Household System in Peking Completed").

JMJP, June 24, 1950. "Mao chu-hsi chih pi-mu tz'u" ("Chairman Mao's Closing Speech").

JMJP, Aug. 24, 1951. "Ch'uan-hsi hen-to pu-men ch'ao-yüeh tsu-chih lan-fa t'ung-chi piao-ke tsao-ch'eng hsiang-ts'un cheng-ch'üan kung-tso yen-ch'ung mang-luan hsien-hsiang" ("Many Agencies in West Szechwan Exceeded Their Authority by Distributing Too Many Statistical Forms and Created Serious Confusion in *Hsiang* Administrative Work").

JMJP, April 30, 1953. "Jen-chen tso-hao ch'üan-kuo jen-k'ou tiao-ch'a teng-chi kung-tso" ("Conscientiously Do a Good Job in the Nationwide Population Investigation and Registration Work").

JMJP, May 7, 1953. "Tung-pei hsing-cheng wei-yüan-hui k'ai-hui pu-chih chi-ts'eng hsüan-chü kung-tso" ("Northeast Administrative Council Held Meeting to Make Arrangements for Basic Level Election Work").

JMJP, June 4, 1953. "Che-chiang chi-ts'eng hsüan-chü tien-hsing shih-pan kung-tso chan-k'ai" ("Model Experimental Election Work Unfolds at the Basic Level in Chekiang").

JMJP, June 6, 1953. "Create and Promote the Experience of Combining Election with Production." (Translated in *SCMP*, No. 592, June 18, 1953, pp. 14–16.)

JMJP, June 10, 1953. "Shang-hai-shih p'u-hsüan shih-pan kung-tso cheng-shih chan-k'ai" ("Experimental Election Work Started in Shanghai").

JMJP, June 11, 1953. "Chiang-hsi-sheng wu-ke chung-tien shih-yen hsiang wan-ch'eng p'u-hsüan kung-tso" ("Five Keypoint Experimental *Hsiang* in Kiangsi Province Complete Election Work").

JMJP, June 19, 1953. "Szu-ch'uan-sheng p'u-hsüan tien-hsing shih-pan kung-tso chung i ch'ü-te fa-tung ch'ün-chung te ch'u-pu ching-yen" ("Preliminary Experiences in Mobilizing the Masses Gained from Model Experimental Election Work in Szechwan Province").

JMJP, June 22, 1953. "Kan-su-sheng hsüan-chu wei-yüan-hui chüeh-ting pien-keng chi-ts'eng hsüan-chü shih-chien" ("Kansu Provincial Election Committee Decides to Change the Time of Basic Level Elections").

JMJP, Aug. 7, 1953. "Tung-pei hsi-nan wan-ch'eng tien-hsing shih-pan hou chan-k'ai ti-i-ch'i chi-ts'eng hsüan-chü kung-tso" ("First Stage Basic Level Election Work Started in the Northeast and Southwest after Completion of Model Experiments").

JMJP, Sept. 21, 1953. "Chao-hua-hsien hu-shih p'u-hsüan chung-te jen-k'ou tiao-ch'a teng-chi kung-tso" ("Chao-hua *Hsien* Neglected Population Investigation and Registration During General Election Work").

JMJP, Sept. 28, 1953. "Ying-kai jen-chen tso-hao jen-k'ou tiao-ch'a teng-chi te fu-ch'a kung-tso" ("We Must Do the Work of Rechecking Population Investigation and Registration Well").

JMJP, Feb. 20, 1954. "Wo-kuo chi-ts'eng hsüan-chü kung-tso i ch'üan-mien chan-k'ai i-i-ssu-ch'ien-wan jen-k'ou ti-ch'ü wan-ch'eng hsüan-chü" ("Basic Level Election Work Has Started Throughout the Country; Areas with One Hundred Forty Million Population Have Completed Elections").

JMJP, March 11, 1954 (a). "Ch'üan-kuo kuo-pan-shu jen-k'ou tiao-ch'a wan-pi; ch'üan-kuo jen-k'ou shu-mu cheng-tsai chu-pu tseng-chia" ("Population Investigation and Registration Completed Among Over Half of the Population; the Number of People in China Is Increasing").

JMJP, March 11, 1954 (b). "Chung-yang hsüan-chü wei-yuan-hui pan-kung-shih ho chung-yang jen-k'ou tiao-ch'a teng-chi pan-kung-shih teng chi-kuan t'ung-chih ke-ti tso-hao jen-k'ou tiao-ch'a teng-chi kung-tso" ("The Office of the Central Election Committee, the Central Population Investigation and Registration Office, and Other Organs Instructed All Areas to Do Population Investigation and Registration Work Well").

JMJP, March 13, 1954(a). "Fu-chien-sheng Lung-yen-chuan-ch'ü pu-chih jen-k'ou fu-ch'a ho-shih kungtso" ("Lung-yen Administrative District, Fukien Province, Made Arrangements for Population Recheck")

JMJP, March 13, 1954(b). "Hsi-nan-ch'ü i-tsai ch'i-ch'ien-to-wan jen-k'ou ti-ch'ü wan-ch'eng hsüan-chü (General Election Completed in Areas with Over 70,000,000 Population in the Southwest Region").

JMJP, March 25, 1954. "Tung-pei-ch'ü jen-k'ou tiao-ch'a teng-chi kung-tso sheng-li wan-ch'eng ch'üan-ch'ü kuang-ta ch'eng hsiang jen-k'ou yu hsien-chu tseng-chia" ("Population Investigation and Registration Victoriously Completed in Northeast Region; Populations in Rural and Urban Areas Show a Significant Increase").

JMJP, April 7, 1954. "Hsi-nan-ch'ü wan-ch'eng ch'i-ch'ien-to-wan jen-k'ou te tiao-ch'a teng-chi kung-tso" ("Southwest Region Completes Population Investigation and Registration Among Over 70 Million People").

JMJP, April 26, 1954. "Hu-pei-sheng chi-ts'eng hsüan-chü chi-pen chieh-shu" ("Basic Level Elections Basically Concluded in Hupei Province").

JMJP, April 27, 1954. "Ho-pei-sheng wan-ch'eng chi-ts'eng hsüan-chü kung-tso" ("Basic Level Election Work Completed in Hopei Province").

JMST. Jen-min shou-ts'e (*People's Handbook*).
April 1950, suppl. ed. Shanghai.
Feb. 1951, 1st ed. Shanghai.
Aug. 1952, 3rd ed. Shanghai.
July 1953, 1st ed. Tientsin.
Jan. 1955, 1st ed. Tientsin.

Kansu Provincial People's Government, Rural Investigation and Research Section, Land Reform Committee, 1952. "Chung-shih t'u-ti kai-ke chung-te tiao-ch'a t'ung-chi kung-tso" (Pay Attention to Investigation and Statistical Work During Land Reform"). *Kan-su jih-pao,* Jan. 24, 1952. Lanchow.

Kirin Provincial Election Committee Officie, 1953. "Chi-lin-sheng Yü-shu-hsien Yung-fu teng ts'un chin-hsing jen-k'ou tiao-ch'a ho hsüan-min teng-chi te tso-fa" ("Method of Population Investigation and Registration of Voters in Yung-fu and Other Villages in Yü-shu Hsien, Kirin Province"), *JMJP,* June 28, 1953.

K'o Fu, 1950. "Chien-li ch'i jen-min te hu-k'ou chih-tu" ("Establish a People's Household System"), *JMJP,* Feb. 4, 1950.

Krotevich, S. K., 1957. "Vsekitayskaya perepis' *naseleniya* 1953 g." ("The All-China Population Census of 1953"), in Moscow Institute of Economics and Statistics, *Poslevoenniye perepisi naseleniya* (*Postwar Population Census*), pp. 80-122.

KCJP. Kuang-chou jih-pao, Canton:

KCJP, Aug. 14, 1953. "Kuang-chou-shih hsüan-chü wei-yüan-hui Chu Kuang chu-hsi tui chiao-ch'ü p'u-hsüan hsiang-chen ti-erh-tuan kung-tso tso chung-yao chih-shih" ("Chairman of the Canton Municipal Election Committee, Chu Kuang, Gives Important Instructions Concerning Second Election Work in Surburban *Hsiang* and *Chen*").

KCJP, Jan. 23, 1954 (a). "Ju-ho tso-hao jen-k'ou tiao-ch'a no hsüan-min teng-chi kung-tso" ("How to Do Population Investigation and Registration Work Well").

KCJP, Jan. 23, 1954 (b). "Kuang-chou-shih jen-k'ou tiao-ch'a teng-chi pan-kung-shih ting-ch'u kuan-yü jen-k'ou tiao-ch'a teng-chi jo-kan chü-t'i wen-t'i te kuei-ting" ("The Office of Population Investigation and Registration of Canton Municipality Drafts Regulations Concerning Several Specific Questions on Population Investigation and Registration").

KCJP, Aug. 6, 1956. "Shih kung-an-chü chao-k'ai hu-k'ou kung-tso hui-i" ("The Municipal Public Security Bureau Holds a Household Work Meeting").

KCJP, Aug. 26, 1956. "Ch'ing-kuei chiai-lü ("The Commandment").

KCJP, Nov. 28, 1956. "Wo-te hu-chi ch'ien-i pan-le i-nien-to" ("My Moving Arrangements Took Over One Year").

Kwangtung Provincial Land Reform Committee Office, 1954. "Jen-chen tso-hao t'u-ti kai-ke t'ung-chi kung-tso" ("Do Land Reform Statistical Work Conscientiously and Well"). *Nan-fang jih-pao,* Aug. 7, 1952. Canton.

Kwangtung Provincial Population Investigation and Registration Office 1954. "Pi-hsü tso-hao jen-k'ou tiao-ch'a teng-chi ho fu-ch'a kung-tso" ("Population Investigation and Registration and Recheck Work Must Be Done Well"). *Nan-fang jih-pao,* April 20, 1954. Canton.

Kung-jen sheng-huo, Dec. 13, 1956. "Wei-shen-ma hsien-tsai yu yao ho-tui hu-k'ou" ("Why Must the Household System Be Checked Once Again?") Wuhsi.

Lao-tung pao, Oct. 5, 1956. *Shanghai.*

LI HSÜ-TAN, 1951. "Kuan-yü tsu-kuo mien-chi ho jen-k'ou te shu-tzu wen-t'i" ("Problems Concerning the Area and Population Figures of the Fatherland"), in *Ti-li chih-shih* (*Geographical Knowledge*), June 1951, 2, pp. 130–131.

Liaotun Provincial Election Committee, 1953. "Liao-tung-sheng Feng-ch'eng hsien Pien-men-ch'ü chin-hsing jen-k'ou tiao-ch'a ho hsüan-min teng-chi te fang-fa" ("Method of Population Investigation and Registration of Voters in Pein-men District, Feng-ch'eng *Hsien,* Liaotung Province"), *JMJP,* June 30, 1953.

Liu-chou jih-pao, Nov. 30, 1956. "Liu-chou-shih kung-an-chü t'ung-kao" ("Notice of the Liuchow Municipal Public Security Bureau"). Liuchow.

LIU YU-JU, 1953. "Tung-yüan ch'i-lai tso-hao hu-k'ou pu-ch'a teng-chi kung-tso" ("Get Mobilized and Do Household Census and Registration Well"), *Hsin-chiang jih-pao,* Jan. 10, 1953. Tihwa (Urumchi).

NFJP, Nan-fang jih-jao, Canton.

NFJP, Aug. 12, 1950. "Ch'üan-sheng nung-yeh chi-pen ch'ing-k'uang chung-tiao-ch'a Kuang-tung-sheng jen-min cheng-fu fa-ch'u chih-shih" ("A General Investigation of Basic Agricultural Conditions in the Whole Province; the Kwangtung Provincial People's Government Issues a Directive").

NFJP, Sept. 24, 1950. "Hui-yang tsen-yang chan-k'ai nung-yeh tiao-ch'a kung-tso" ("How Hui-yang Carried Out Its Agricultural Investigation Work").

NFJP, Aug. 7, 1952. "Chung-shan Chang-chia-pien-hsiang tso-hao t'u-kai t'ung-chi kung-tso te ching-yen" ("Experiences of Chang-chi-pien *Hsiang* of Chung-shan *Hsien* in Doing Land Reform Statistical Work Well").

NFJP, Nov. 18, 1953. "Kuang-chou-shih jen-min cheng-fu kung-an-chü t'ung-kao" ("Notice of the Public Security Bureau of the Canton Municipal People's Government").

NFJP, April 13, 1954. "Pi-hsü tso-hao chi-ts'eng hsuan-chu kung tso" ("Basic Level Election Work Must Be Done Well").

NFJP, April 20, 1954. "Kuang-tung-sheng hsüan-chü wei-yuan-hui jen-k'ou tiao-ch'a teng-chi pan-kung shih chao-k'ai Kuang-tung-sheng ti-i-tz'u jen-k'ou tiao-ch'a t'ung-chi hui-i" ("Kwangtung Provincial Election Committee and the Population Investigation and Registration Office Convene Kwangtung Province's First Population Investigation Statistics Meeting").

NFJP. July 11, 1955. "Kuang-chou-shih kung-an-chü t'ung-kao" ("Notice of the Canton Municipal Security Bureau").

NFJP, July 14, 1955. "Kuang-chou-shih chieh-ho cheng-tun liang-shih t'ung-hsiao k'ai-chan ho-tui hu-k'ou kung-tso" ("Canton Municipality Is Carrying Out Household Checking Work in Conjunction with the Reorganization of State Food-Grain Sales").

NFJP, Sept. 4, 1956. "Wei-shen-ma chei ya-yao hsieh pao-kao" ("Why Should a Report Be Written for This?").

NCNA. New China News Agency. Peking. (unless otherwise noted)

NCNA, May 26, 1951. "Provisional Regulations Governing Inspection of Trains, Crew, and Passengers Entering end Leaving the Country." (Translated in *SCMP*, No. 110, June 1–5, 1951, pp. 47–48.)

NCNA, July 5, 1951. "Central Ministry of Finance Announces Program for Land Investigation and Production Evaluation in Connection with Agricultural Tax." (Translated in *SCMP*, No. 130, July 8–9, 1951, pp. 14–17.)

NCNA, July 16, 1951. "Ministry of Public Security Promulgates Regulations Governing Urban Population." (Translated in *SCMP*, No. 137, July 18, 1951, pp. 7–9.)

NCNA, Aug. 2, 1951. "Ministry of Public Security Promulgates Provisional Measure Governing Entry and Exit of Overseas Chinese." (Translated in *SCMP*, No. 148, Aug. 3–5, 1951, p. 28.)

NCNA, Aug. 4, 1951. "Ministry of Public Security Proclaims Provisional Rules for Control of Hotels and Lodging Houses." (Translated in *SCMP*, No. 149, Aug. 6–9, 1951, pp. 25–27.)

NCNA, Nov. 30, 1951. "Provisional Rules Governing Entry, Exit, and Residence of Foreign Nationals Promulgated by Government Administrative Council." (Translated in *SCMP*, No. 227, Dec. 2–3, 1951, pp. 1–2.)

NCNA, April 6, 1953 (a). "Directive on National Census and Registration." (Translated in *CB*, No. 241, May 5, 1953, pp. 29–30.)

NCNA, April 6, 1953 (b). "Measures for National Census and Registration of Population." (Translated in *CB*, No. 241, May 5, 1953, pp. 31–35.)

NCNA, April 7, 1953. "Directive on Election Work at Basic Levels" (issued by the Central Election Committee on April 3, 1953). (Translated in *CB*, No. 241, May 5, 1953, pp. 8–14.)

NCNA, June 20, 1953. "CCP North China Bureau To Improve Leadership Work in Rural Villages." (Translated in *SCMP*, No. 596, June 24, 1953, pp. 14–17.)

NCNA, Sept. 8, 1953. "Local Elections in Different Parts of China." (Translated in *SCMP*, No. 646, Sept. 9, 1953, pp. 26-27).

NCNA, Sept. 18, 1953. "The 27th and 28th Meetings of thc Central People's Government Council: Reports on Political, Legal, Cultural and Educational Work Given by Peng Chen and Kuo Mo-jo; General Election Postponement Approved." (Translated in *SCMP*, No. 654, Sept. 19–21, 1953, pp. 1–4.)

NCNA, Sept. 21, 1953. "Elections at Lowest Level in East China." Shanghai. (In *SCMP*, No. 655, Sept. 22-23, 1953, p. 39.) Original was in English. Everything in the SCMP is in English.

NCNA, March 10, 1954. "Census and Registration Work Completed in Areas with 60 Percent of the Population in China." (Translated in *SCMP*, No. 766, March 13–15, 1954, p. 27.)

NCNA, March 13, 1954. "Elections Almost Concluded in Northeast." Mukden (in English) (In *SCMP*, No. 766, March 13–15, 1954, p. 34.)

NCNA, March 25, 1954. "Population Census and Registration Completed in Northeast." Mukden. (Translated in *SCMP*, No. 778, March 31, 1954, p. 24.)

NCNA, March 29, 1954. "Population Census and Statistical Work Strengthened in Honan." Kaifeng. (Translated in *SCMP*, No. 782, April 6, 1954, p. 24.)

NCNA, March 30, 1954. "Basic Level Elections Carried Out in Central-South." Wuhan. (Translated in *SCMP*, No. 782, April 6, 1954, pp. 23–24.)

NCNA, April 5, 1954. "Population Census Completed in Areas in Southwest with Population of 76,500,000." Chungking. (Translated in *SCMP*, No. 785, April 9, 1954, pp. 32–33.)

NCNA, April 9, 1954. "Elections Concluded by Three Hundred Million." (in English) (In *SCMP*, No. 786, April 10–11, 1954, p. 33.)

NCNA, April 27, 1954. "Basic Level Elections Victoriously Concluded in Southwest." Chungking. (Translated in *SCMP*, No. 803, May 7, 1954, pp. 26–27.)

NCNA, April 16, 1962. "Press Communiqué of the 3rd Session of the 2nd National People's Congress of China." (in English) (In *CB*, No. 681, April 18, 1962, pp. 1–4.)

PAI CHIEN-HUA, 1954 "600 Million—A Great Sterngth for Socialist Construction of China," *JMJP*, Nov. 1, 1954. (Translated in *SCMP*, No. 926, Nov. 11–12, 1954, pp. 32–34.)

Peking Radio, March 29, 1954. "Over 50 Percent of Elections Finished."

PRESSAT, ROLAND, 1961. "La Population de la Chine: Structure et Évolution Récente," *Population*, Oct.–Dec. 1961, 16, pp. 649–664.

ROCKHILL, W. W., 1904. "Inquiry into the Population of China," *Smithsonian Miscellaneous Collections (Quarterly Issue)*, Dec. 1904, 47, pp. 303–321.

STRONG, ANNA LOUISE, 1964. "Interview with Po I-po on Economic Readjustment," *Ta-kung pao*, Jan. 15, 1964. Hong Kong. (Translated in *SCMP*, No. 3152, Feb. 3, 1964, pp. 5–9.)

TAEUBER, IRENE B., 1963. "The Conundrum of the Chinese Birth Rate," International Statistical Institute, Ottawa, Aug. 1963. (mimeo)

TAEUBER, IRENE B., 1964. "China's Population: an Approach to Research," *Items*, June 1964, 18, pp. 13–19.

TAEUBER, IRENE B., and NAI-CHI WANG, 1960 (a). "Population Reports in the Ch'ing Dynasty," *The Journal of Asian Studies,* Aug. 1960, 19, pp. 403–417.

TAEUBER, IRENE B., and NAI-CHI WANG, 1960 (b). "Questions on Population Growth in China," in Milbank Memorial Fund, *Population Trends in Eastern Europe, the U.S.S.R., and Mainland China,* pp. 263–310. New York.

TAYLOR, K. W., 1950. "Some Aspects of Population History," *The Canadian Journal of Economics and Political Science,* Aug. 1950, 16, pp. 301–313.

TKP. Ta-kung pao (Impartial Daily), Hong Kong:

TKP, July 7, 1950 (a). "Chung-nan-ch'ü chi-chi chun-pei t'u-kai" ("The Central-South Region Actively Prepares for Land Reform").

TKP, July 7, 1950 (b). "Yü t'u-kai-ch'ü ch'i-shih" ("Strange Goings-On in the Land Reform Areas of Honan").

TKP, July 19, 1950. "Ch'üan-kuo jen-k'ou ho keng-ti mien-chi chiu-ching yu to-shao" ("What Is the Population and the Cultivated Area of the Whole Country?").

TKP, Aug. 8, 1950. "Chung-nan chün-cheng-hui t'ung-ling ke-sheng chü-pan nung-ts'un p'u-ch'a" ("Central-South Military-Administrative Committee Orders All Provinces to Carry Out Rural Censuses").

TKP, Jan. 3, 1954. "Ch'ü-nien shih-erh-yüeh chung-hsün wei-chih i-i jen-k'ou ti-ch'ü wan-ch'eng p'u-hsüan" ("As of the Middle of December of Last Year Areas with One Hundred Million Population Had Completed General Elections").

TKP, March 18, 1954. "Pu-hsüan hsin-su chin-chan-chung" ("The General Election is Progressing Rapidly").

TKP, March 23, 1954. "Chung-nan p'u-hsüan ch'üan-mien chan-k'ai yüeh san-ch'ien-wan jen-k'ou ti-ch'ü i wan-ch'eng p'u-hsüan Chan-chiang p'u-hsüan chin cheih-shu Ch'ao-chou hsia-yüeh k'ai-shih" ("Elections Unfold Throughout Central-South; Area with Approximately 30 Million Population Completes Elections, General Elections Near Completion in Chan-chiang; Ch'ao-chou Will Start Next Month").

T'ien-ching jih-pao, May 27, 1953. "Ying-chieh p'u-süan wei jen-k'ou tiao-ch'a teng-chi tso-hao chun-pei Ching-shih chin-hsing hu-k'ou ch'a-tui kung-tso" ("To Welcome the General Election, Tientsin Is Checking Households in Order to Do Population Investigation and Registration of Voters Well"). Tientsin.

T'ien-ching jih-pao, June 11, 1953. "Liu-ch'ü Nan-hua-li Ma-ch'ang liang-ko chung-tien-chieh k'ai-shih shih-pan jen-k'ou tiao-ch'ah ho hsüan-min teng-chi" ("Two Keypoint Streets, Nan-hua-li and Ma-ch'ang, in the Sixth District, Start Experimental Population Investigation and Registration of Voters"). Tientsin.

TCKT, June 14, 1957. "Data on China's Population from 1949 to 1956." (Translated in *ECMM,* No. 91, July 22, 1957, pp. 22–25.)

T'ung-chi yen-chiu, 1958. (*Statistical Research*), No. 2, Feb. 1958.

United Nations, 1956. Department of Economic and Social Affairs. *Manual III: Methods for Population Projects by Sex and Age.* New York.

United Nations, 1959. Department of Economic and Social Affairs. *Future Population Estimates by Sex and Age, Report IV: The Population of Asia and the Far East, 1950–1980.* New York.

United Nations, 1966. Department of Economic and Social Affairs. *World Population Prospects as Assessed in 1963. Population Studies* No. 41. New York.

YEN CHUNG-P'ING, *et al.*, 1955. (Ed.) *Chung-kuo chin-tai ching-chi-shih t'ung-chi tzu-liao hsüan-chi (Selected Statistical Materials on the Modern Economic History of China).* Peking.

Manpower, Employment, and Unemployment 5

CHI-MING HOU

CHINA IS AMONG the most densely populated developing countries in the world. A recurrent question concerning these countries is whether they are victims of the Malthusian trap. The purpose of this chapter is to examine certain elements which are necessary to provide an answer to this question for China. The focus will be on whether China has been able to keep her growing population gainfully employed. The paper is divided into three parts. Part I provides an estimate of labor force, and Part II, an estimate of nonagricultural employment and unemployment. In Part III certain aspects of manpower utilization and policy will be discussed.

I. LABOR FORCE

By generally accepted Western practice, the term "labor force" usually includes all persons above a specified age who are either employed or unemployed, defined in various ways. Figures for the labor force of Communist China cannot be obtained in this manner, however, for there are no published data on unemployment at the national level. The labor force has to be estimated from population data. By Western concept and practice, the size of the labor force may be derived, in general, by deducting from total population the following categories: children below a specified age, housewives, students, the permanently disabled (physically or mentally), retired persons, the voluntarily idle, and people in institutions.

The reliability of labor force data so estimated depends very much upon the reliability of the population data: the size, the rate of growth, the age composition, and the sex ratio. Since the official Chinese population data are used in this paper, a brief evaluation of them is called for.

I should like to express my thanks to Professors J. D. Durant, Walter Galenson, and Simon Kuznets for their comments on an earlier draft of this paper. I have also benefited from discussions on certain points of this paper with Dr. John Aird and Dr. K. C. Yeh. John Philip Emerson, whose work I have relied upon very heavily in this paper, read the entire manuscript and provided me with very detailed and useful comments. I wish to express my sincere thanks to him.

TOTAL POPULATION, 1953

The 1953 census is an important base for official population data. The procedures and methods of conducting the 1953 census have been carefully examined and evaluated by Aird (1961; and Ch. 4 of this volume) and need not be dealt with here.[1] Unquestionably, many criticisms may be made of the census, but they should not be exaggerated. In the first place, the information sought by the census was rather simple: only the number, sex, age, and nationality of the population. This information is probably always known to the people at the village level. There are about 1,250,000 villages in China, with an average size of about 400 persons (UN, 1959, p. 17). These villagers have, in most cases, lived their entire lives in their own village and, because of a number of traditions (such as mutual visiting during the New Year), they know their fellow villagers well. Thus, the real question is not so much one of accurate counting as of how to collect information from the villagers and transmit it to the central government.[2] Judging from the way the land reform was conducted (the distribution of land was theoretically on a per capita basis); the manner in which the agricultural tax was computed (per capita agricultural income of agricultural population); how the agricultural mutual aid teams were organized, and how other programs were carried out, it appears reasonable to assume that by the time the census was taken, the Communist regime had developed a very effective control mechanism. This mechanism was evidently mobilized to achieve the stated purposes of the census. In urban populations, the people were subject to registration by the police long before the

1. The procedures and methods of conducting the 1953 census have been criticized both from within and outside China. The main points of criticism are: (1) the mobilization of some 2,600,000 cadres and an uncounted number of "activists" for census taking, without training them adequately for the job; (2) too short a period of planning the census (only six months), and no sufficient pilot surveys; (3) too long a period of enumeration; the census was to count the number of people as of June 30, 1953, but the enumeration was not finished until about a year later, thus giving rise to the problems of eliminating the births and including the deaths after the census date, and of dealing with the changes in household composition; (4) insufficient attention to problems relating to residencey and urban-rural population movements during the period of enumeration; (5) too much reliance on registration rather than house-to-house canvassing; (6) the use of the pencil-stroke system of tallying with all its possibilities for error; (7) the political purposes of the census (to register voters for elections and to determine political fitness to participate in the election, especially of those identified as landlords and counter revolutionaries), which may have motivated some persons to avoid enumeration. (For an evaluation of these points, see Aird, Chapter 4 in this book.)

2. This is not to say that census taking was simple; all that is suggested here is that the social organization in China was such that the villagers knew each other well. Events such as birth, death, marriage, and migration were usually known to the residents of villages that had, on the average, less than 80 households. It is, therefore, not surprising that in the census accuracy check fewer omissions and repetitions were found for the villages than for the cities. For the reliability of census-taking in the rural areas, see Chen Ta, 1957, p. 12.

Communists came into power. Residents' teams and committees, among other devices used by the Communist regime, would have made it even easier to know the size and movement of the urban population.

Admittedly, there is no proof that the 1953 census was fully reliable, and it is difficult to give credence to the official claim that the census, on the basis of a sample check, had a net omission of only 0.116 per cent. But circumstantial evidence suggests that the official census figure is a plausible one and should be used at least as a comparison with any other alternative estimate.[3] One such estimate is made by Aird, who maintains that factors making for undercount outweighed those making for overcount. He suggests that a range of undercount of 5 per cent to 15 per cent would not be excessive. His estimates are presented in Table 1, together with the official data.

TOTAL POPULATION, 1949-1964

If we are not entirely sure of the size of the Chinese population for the census year (1953), we are even less sure of the population totals for other years. The official population data, as shown in Table 1, are available only for 1949-57. The official explanation is that the figures for 1949-51 were estimated on the basis of the growth trend of the population. The 1952 figure was obtained from reports of provinces and municipalities. The 1953 figure was from the census. The figures for 1954 and 1955 were the annual report figures by provinces and municipalities. The 1956 figure was based partly on estimates (it is not indicated how the

3. It might be of interest to compare the 1953 census figure with earlier population estimates. In a recent study, after carefully examining the key population terms and institutions under which population data were collected, Professor Ho reached the conclusion that of the official Chinese population data of the past five centuries, the most useful come from the years 1368-98 and 1776-1850; those for 1741-75 may be of some help, and they are most defective for 1851-1949 (Ping-ti Ho, 1959, p. 97). He ventures to suggest or "guess" (this is his own word) that the Chinese population may have reached 65 million in 1400; 150 million in 1600 (Ho, 1959, pp. 277-278). He is of the opinion that these population changes tally well with the changing social, political and economic conditions. These figures imply that the Chinese population increased at 0.42 per cent a year from 1400 to 1600, remained unchanged from 1600 to 1700, grew at 0.79 per cent a year from 1700 to 1794, and at 0.57 per cent a year from 1794 to 1850.

If one takes the Chinese population to be 430 million in 1850 and 582.6 million in 1953, the annual rate of growth during the entire period would be 0.30 per cent—a rate that is not entirely out of line with the historical rates, nor entirely unexplainable by the political and economic conditions during the period. The greatest civil war in human history—the Taiping rebellion—was fought between 1851 and 1865, affecting nearly all provinces of China proper, and probably killing many more than the commonly suggested figure of twenty or thirty million people. It was followed by the Nien Wars, and the Moslem rebellion, not to mention the wars with foreign powers before the Republic was founded in 1912. The civil wars between 1912 and 1927 are well known; and during the Nationalist rule, hardly a year went by without a war. Thus a low rate of population growth is to be expected.

TABLE 1

POPULATION OF MAINLAND CHINA 1949-1964
(Year-end, in millions)

	Official Data		Aird			
			Lowest Estimate		Highest Estimate	
	Total	Rate of growth (per cent)	Total	Rate of growth (per cent)	Total	Rate of growth (per cent)
1949	541.67					
1950	551.96	1.90				
1951	563.00	2.00				
1952	574.82	2.10	608		678	
1953	587.96	2.29		1.75		2.25
1954	601.72	2.34	631		710	
1955	614.65	2.14		2.01		2.48
1956	627.80	2.14				
1957	646.53	2.98				
1958	662.60	2.49				
1959	679.07	2.49	697		802	
1960	692.65	2.00		1.67		1.97
1961	706.50	2.00				
1962	720.63	2.00				
1963	737.17	2.30				
1964	754.12	2.30	752	1.87 [a]	875	2.24 [a]

Note:
a. 1965 figures.

Sources:
For official data, 1949-56, *TCKT,* 1957 (p. 4); for 1957, *Ten Great Years* (p. 6). (Taiwan is excluded according to figure given on p. 9); for 1958-64, see text.
For Aird, see Ch. 4 of this book, Table 2.

estimates were made). As for the 1957 figure, no explanation is given as to how it was estimated, though presumably it was also from the annual reports of the provinces and municipalities. Whether these provincial and municipal annual reports were based on population registration data (such as births, deaths and migration) or on estimates of total population cannot be ascertained. A system of urban registration was formalized in 1951; for rural areas, formal registration was widely adopted by 1955. It is doubtful, however, that registration was ever strictly enforced or satisfactorily carried out (Aird, 1961, Ch. IV).

In evaluating the population figures in Table 1 by examining the implied growth rates, one is troubled by the high rate for 1957. This increase of nearly 3 per cent is not consistent with other reported growth rates. Both Pressat and Chandrasekhar obtained from the State Statistical Bureau the following vital rates for 1957: birth rate, 3.4 per cent; death rate, 1.1 per cent; natural rate of increase, 2.3 per cent (Aird, 1961, p. 41). These rates were also reported by the Ministry of Health. The vital rates are themselves subject to serious doubt, but a rate of growth in the neighborhood of 2 per cent is more compatible with the available estimates than the 3 per cent figure.

Of course, it is possible that the 1957 figure is accurate while the figures for previous years are underestimated. This possibility may be advanced on the strength of an article published by Hu Huan-yung in September, 1957, in which he gave 604.7 million for year-end 1954 (Hu, 1957) (as compared with the 601.7 million for 1954 as shown in Table 1). If Hu's figure is acceptable, and if the pre-1957 figures are adjusted on the basis of his figure, then a population of 646.5 million in 1957 seems compatible with an annual growth rate of about 2.2 per cent. But no official upward revision has ever been published for the 1953 census year or for any pre-1957 year.

How reliable are the implied growth rates (before 1957) as shown in Table 1? An official sample study of the 1953 census, covering about 5 per cent of the total population, records a birth rate of 3.7 per cent and a death rate of 1.7 per cent for 1953 (Pai, 1954). In a paper presented at Stockholm, Chen Ta gave the results of 16 local investigations conducted during 1951-54, covering a total of 1.8 million people mostly in rural areas (Chen, 1957, Table 6). On the average, the birth rate was 4.16 per cent and the death rate 2.1 per cent, with a net growth rate of 2.06 per cent. But Chen's samples reveal marked regional differences, especially in birth rate. Four areas in Szechwan, covering almost one-half of the population sampled, had an average birth rate of 4.84 per cent and a death rate of 2.29 per cent. For the remaining 12 areas, the average birth rate was 3.59 per cent and the average death rate was 1.94 per cent.

It is not easy to explain why regional differences prevailed, but population data for pre-Communist years tend to support their existence. Regional variation in birth rates also prevail elsewhere, as in Japan and Europe (both before and after modern methods of birth control became widely used) (UN, 1959, p. 87). In the Chinese case, the regional variation makes it extremely difficult to estimate the national vital rates from only sample data, simply because no sound basis of weighting is available. If one arbitrarily assigns a weight of 0.107 to the four areas of Szechwan as against 0.893 for the other 12 areas (on the grounds that in 1953 the population of Szechwan was about 10.7 per cent of the population of China), the national birth rate would be 3.72 per cent and the death rate 1.98 per cent (UN, 1959, p. 77).

It is interesting to note that on the basis of local studies from 1917 to 1944 (most of them in the 1930's) Chen Ta estimated a birth rate of 3.8 per cent and a death rate of 3.3 per cent for all China in 1934 (Chen, 1946, pp. 28, 32). (The birth rates ranged from 1.65 per cent to 5.84 per cent.) In an extensive survey of the rural economy of China (1929-31), Buck reported a birth rate of 3.83 per cent and a death rate of 2.71 per cent (1937, pp. 383, 387). This birth rate seems compatible with age composition data from local investigations during the same period (UN, 1959, p. 81). For the 1940's, Chen Ta has made the following estimates: birth rate, 3.6 per cent; death rate 2.9 per cent; national increase, 0.7 per cent (1957, p. 23).

Thus, in terms of data for the pre-1949 years, a birth rate of 3.7 per cent for 1953 does not seem to be out of line. Whether or not a death rate of 1.7 per cent for 1953 is too low as compared with pre-1949 data cannot be ascertained. Improvements have been claimed since 1949 in sanitation and health protection, especially in control over epidemic and infectious diseases, but it is difficult to measure their results. It may not be too far off to assume that the death rate began to decline when peace and order was restored in 1949. Thus the growth rates as implied by the official population figures (at least for 1953-56) seem to be consistent with a constant birth rate of 3.7 per cent and a 1953 death rate of 1.7 per cent. Obviously, if the death rate is regarded as too low, then the official population figures for the post-1953 years are high.

However, the vital rates mentioned above may be seriously questioned principally on the ground that both the pre-1949 and the post-1949 data represent gross underenumeration of births and deaths. In his projections of China's population, Aird assumes a birth rate ranging from 4.50 per of 2.50 per cent to 1.61 per cent (Ch. 4, this volume, Table 2). His fig-cent to 3.68 per cent for 1953-65. For the death rate, he gives a range ures for natural rate of increase thus vary from 2.48 per cent to 1.64 per cent. In Table 1, two of his estimates are given, one representing the lowest, and the other the highest, population figures. These two extremes are given to indicate the limits with which the official figures may be compared.

As already noted, official data on population end with the year 1957; but both Chandrasekhar and Hsu Kang reported a figure of 673 million for 1958 (Chandrasekhar, 1959, p. 55; Hsu, 1959). This would mean an increase of about 4 per cent over 1957, hardly compatible with the growth rates from 1949 to 1957. It is probable that the reported figure includes Taiwan, for if we exclude the latter (assumed to be 10.4 million) the growth rate over 1957 would be nearly 2.5 per cent, which appears more plausible. The same rate is assumed for 1959 in Table 1. The population figures for 1960-62 are estimated on the basis of a growth rate of 2 per cent reported by Chou En-lai (*JMJP,* Dec. 26, 1963). Chou also reported a 2.5 per cent rate of growth for 1963 and 1964,[4] but we have arbitrarily used 2.3 per cent (about the average for pre-1957 years) for these two years. Chou attributed the changes in the growth rate to altered economic conditions.

AGE COMPOSITION

Limited data on age composition of the population in 1953 have been published in a few sources; they seem to be mutually consistent and hence must have been derived from the official results of the 1953 census (UN, 1959, p. 78; Aird, 1961, pp. 65-66). The percentage distributions as presented by Chen Ta (1957, Table 3) and T'ien Feng't'ao (Aird, 1961, p. 66) are given in Table 2. Serious doubts have been cast on the reliability

TABLE 2

SEX RATIOS AND AGE COMPOSITION, MAINLAND CHINA,[a] 1953 (June 30)

Age	Sex Ratio	Male	Female
All Ages	107.7	100.0	100.0
0-4	106.2	15.5	15.7
5-9	112.7	11.2	10.7
10-14	117.3	9.8	9.0
15-19	112.1	9.3	8.9
20-24	108.2	8.3	8.2
25-29	114.0	8.0	7.5
30-34	113.9	7.1	6.7
35-39	108.6	6.4	6.4
40-44	106.6	5.5	5.6
45-49	104.4	4.9	5.1
50-54	104.6	4.2	4.3
55-59	102.5	3.5	3.7
60-64	94.8	2.7	3.1
65-69	86.8	1.8	2.3
70-74	73.1	1.1	1.6
75-79	68.4	0.7	1.2
80-84	58.7		
85 & over	45.3		

Note:

a. Derived from an age-sex pyramid given in T'ien Feng-t'ao (Aird, 1961, p. 66) with extrapolation for ages 80 years and over. Age distribution for both sexes is the same as given by Chen Ta, 1957 (Table 3).

Sources:

Computed from Aird, 1961 (pp. 81, 82).

4. Cited in *Fei-ch'ing Yen-chiu,* Vol. 7, Number 7 (July 31, 1964), p. 51.

of these data, however. It is pointed out that in terms of the United Nations model life tables, the percentage distribution for ages 5 years and over is not consistent with the birth rates in China in the past. It would be consistent only with a nearly constant birth rate as low as 3.15 per cent for a period of at least six decades before 1948 (UN, 1959, p. 97; Aird, 1961, pp. 71-72). Available evidence suggest that this rate is much too low for China in the stated period. Furthermore, there is a marked deficit of persons aged 5 to 14 years and an excess of persons aged 45 and over, as compared with age distributions in other countries that might be expected to resemble China in vital rates (Aird, 1961, p. 68).

These evaluations of the age composition data notwithstanding, it may be that China is unique demographically, and that the United Nations model life tables or the experience of other countries may not be entirely applicable. For example, as pointed out by Professor Liu (Ch. 3, this volume), the small number of children (aged 5 to 14) may be explained by the war years 1937-48, while the excess of persons aged 45 and over may be due to the relatively peaceful period from the 1880's to 1910. Furthermore, as Buck reported in his survey of China's rural economy (1937, p. 381), in China the average age at marriage (1929-31) was very low compared with other countries. The high mortality rate of women of childbearing age would certainly have an effect on age distribution of the population. Buck also reported that in 1929-31, the Chinese mortality rates at different ages for both males and females were considerably different from those in countries such as India (1931) or Japan (1921-25) (1937, pp. 390-392). It is difficult to account for these differences but, to the extent that Buck's data are reliable, they would make the age distribution of the Chinese population different from that of other countries.

Age composition obviously has an important bearing on the supply of labor. Fortunately, as shown in Table 3, the various estimates do not differ significantly for the particular age group (15-64) in which we are interested.

THE SEX RATIO

A chronic source of trouble for the demographers of China has been the high sex ratio (number of males per 100 females) recorded in Chinese population data. The population registration of Yung-chou in 1381-82, for instance, yielded a sex ratio of 125.9 (Ping-ti Ho, 1959, p. 8). Other ratios may be obtained from local histories for 23 localities at various times during the period 1771 to 1845. They range from 156.4 (for Ning-shan-t'ing county, Shensi, in 1829) to 101.1 (for Ch'iung-chou county, Szechwan, in 1814). The simple mean of the highest five was 142.4, while that of the lowest five was 107.4 (the median was 118.8) (Ping-ti Ho, 1959, pp. 58-59). A dozen censuses at the *hsien* level were

TABLE 3

PROPORTION OF AGE GROUPS 15-64 IN TOTAL POPULATION, JUNE 30, 1953
(in per cent)

	Total	Male	Female
Official data			
United Nations	59.7	31.1	28.6
(A)[a]	60.4	......	......
(B)[b]	59.2	......	......
Aird			
Models I & II	58.3	29.4	28.9
Models III & IV	59.5	29.7	29.8

Notes:

...... not available.

a. Assuming a constant birth rate of 3.7 per cent before 1943, 3.6 per cent in 1943-48 and 3.7 per cent in 1948-53. Expectation of life at birth assumed to be 30 years (or a death rate of 3.34 per cent) before 1943, 35 (or a death rate of 2.9 per cent) in 1943-48 and 40 (or a death rate of 2.1 per cent) in 1948-53.

b. Same assumptions as (*a*) except that a birth rate of 4.16 per cent is assumed in 1948-53.

Sources:

Official data: see Table 2.
United Nations, 1959 (p. 85).
Aird, Ch. 4, this book (Table 3).

taken in the 1930's and early 1940's; they yielded sex ratios from 129.4 (in Chang, Fukien province) to 90.7 (in Cheng Kung, Yunnan province) with a median of about 110 (Chen Ta, 1957, Table 1). The Buck study reported a ratio of 108 for all rural China in 1929-31 (1937, p. 376). Finally, the 1953 census yielded a ratio of 107.7.

A few factors may be suggested to account for this long history of high reported sex ratios: a high sex ratio at birth; the practice of female infanticide; a higher female mortality rate in general, largely because of the low status and resultant neglect of females; underenumeration of females, especially children, in population registration or census. In a survey conducted in the 1930's covering 54,743 infants born in 227 hospitals, it was found that there were 108.5 male per 100 female births (Buck, 1937, p. 382). Buck's survey for 1929-31 reported that there were 112 male births in north China and 113 male births in south China per 100 female births (1937, p. 376).[5]

5. Buck suspected that his ratios, though well below those often reported in Chinese sample studies, were probably high because of underreporting of female births.

The practice of female infanticide has often been described in local histories, especially from the southern provinces. Its existence in the past, particularly among the poor, cannot be doubted, although it was prohibited officially at least in certain provinces. But no quantitative estimate can be made of its extent. To what extent this practice has continued in modern times cannot be determined.

Evidence on the relative mortality rates of males and females is not clear. For example, the infant mortality rate in Hsiao Chi (1931-35) was 2.84 per cent for males and 3.92 per cent for females (Ch'iao, Thompson, Chen, 1938, p. 52). At Cheng Kung, Yunnan province (1940-44), the infant mortality rate was 2.12 per cent for males and 2.11 per cent for females (Chen Ta, 1946, p. 103). For the Chinese rural population as a whole in 1929-31, Buck reported a death rate of 2.76 per cent for all females and 2.67 for all males. But he also reported a sharp regional difference: the death rate was lower for females (2.62 per cent) in north China, but higher (2.89 per cent) in South China. (The respective rates for males were 2.21 per cent and 3.10 per cent.) (Buck, 1937, p. 388).

The data above should make it clear that the factors contributing to the high ratio of males to females in China in the past were complex, and available evidence is not sufficient to ascertain the importance of each one. Whether the historical pattern was still present in 1953 is an open question. It is possible that the high sex ratios have been a result of certain persistent biases in population enumeration; it is also possible that they are a result of certain historical forces unique to China. Thus, in the absence of better evidence, it is as hard to reject the 107.7 ratio for 1953 as to accept it.[6] At any rate, for the age group we are interested in, the Aird estimates do not differ greatly from the official ratio, as noted in Table 3.

To sum up our discussion of Chinese population data, it is clear that there is room for disagreement on almost every aspect of Chinese population: the size, vital rates, age composition, and sex ratio. But in terms of available evidence, the Chinese Communist official data do not appear

6. When the 1953 data on sex ratios by age groups are examined, it is found that the ratio rises sharply before the age group 10-14 years, then declines until the ages of 20-24. It rises again until the ages of 25-29, then declines continuously afterwards. It is not easy to explain why the sex ratio rises during early childhood, but similar trends appear in some other countries with high fertility and mortality, such as Egypt (1947), India (1951), and Thailand (1947) (Aird, 1961, p. 75). The Chinese county and provincial censuses taken in the 1930's and 1940's also reported the same phenomenon, although the peak was not reached at the same age. The decline of the sex ratio after 10-14 years is again hard to explain, but here again, the same feature occurs in other countries and in the same earlier Chinese censuses. The rising phase before ages 25-29 and the virtual stability at the high level before ages 30-34 may be accounted for by higher childbirth mortality, but in the other three countries cited, this rising phase lasts considerably longer than in China.

entirely unreasonable; at least, convincing evidence is still needed to establish that alternative estimates are necessarily so much better than official data that the latter should be discarded. In our estimate of labor force, the official population data will be used; then the result will be checked by Aird's estimates.

POPULATION OF WORKING AGE

The concept of "working age" is not easy to define, especially for the agricultural sector, where children may be expected to begin to work at an early age (say 10 years) and older persons never retire so long as they are physically capable of doing some work. In his rural study cited earlier, Buck regarded those who were between 15 and 60 years old as "able-bodied" men (1937, p. 292); but he also reported that in terms of work accomplished, children performed 7 per cent of all the farm labor in China (1929-33). To some degree, the same may also be said of the industrial sector, where apprenticeship has long been a tradition and children begin work early.

In some Communist literature, the age ranges 16-60 years for men and 16-55 years for women are often suggested in dealing with employment or unemployment (Chi Ch'eng, 1960), though students 16 years old or over are not included in the social labor force (Ch'en Chih-ho, 1959). For agricultural work, a male between 18 and 50 years of age, or a female between 18 and 45 years of age is considered a full labor unit. A male between 51 and 60, or a female between 46 and 55, or a 17- to 18-year-old youth, either male or female is considered a half labor unit (Huang Meng-fan, 1956).

How "working age" is defined depends on the purpose for which the category is to be used. If one wants to estimate national product by the use of labor force data, the age range should perhaps be larger than that for the measurement of employment or unemployment. If the purpose is to measure unemployment from labor force and employment data, the working age should certainly be defined in terms of how employment data are collected. In the case of China there is no information on what age groups are included in employment in various fields, but according to a labor census in 1955, only 1 per cent of all the workers and employees in industry and basic construction were under 18 years of age, while 0.9 per cent were between 56 and 60 years of age, and 0.3 per cent were over 61 years of age (*TCKT* Data Section, 1956). According to official regulations, apprenticeship in all enterprises should not, except in rare cases, begin before the age of 16 (*HHPYK,* 1958, p. 144); and the retirement age is set at 60 years for men, and 50 (workers) or 55 (employees) years for women (*HHPYK,* 1958b, p. 142). Thus, in our estimate of the non-agricultural male labor force we use the age group 15-59 years in order to be more or less consistent with the Chinese usage. At the same time, we also use the age group 14-64 years as an alternative estimate to guard against the possibility that the younger (under 15) and the older (over 59) workers may be quite numerous in fields outside industry and basic construction. In all probability, workers in the traditional sectors begin when they are very young and do not retire as long as they are physically capable of working.

AGRICULTURAL VERSUS NONAGRICULTURAL POPULATION

"Agricultural population" is defined to include all those solely engaged in agricultural pursuits and those engaged both in agriculture and in subsidiary occupations. Several Communist estimates of agricultural population are available (Table 4). It may be assummed that they were collected

TABLE 4

AGRICULTURAL POPULATION, 1949-1956

	Communist Estimates			Adjusted	
	Millions (1)	Sources (2)	As per cent of total population (3)	Millions (4)	As per cent of total population (5)
1949	470	Tan Chen-lin	88	414	77
1952	492	Li Shu-teh	87	433	76
1953	485	Ma Yin-chu	84	427	73
1956	417	Ma Yin-chu	83	455	73
	528	Tan Chen-lin	85	465	75
	532	Li Shu-teh	86	468	75

Source:
Liu and Yeh, 1965 (p. 184).

in connection with the agricultural tax which until 1958 was levied on the basis of per capita income of agricultural population in each farm household (State Council, 1951, p. 302). Only those who lived primarily on agricultural income were counted as agricultural population. Although the tax regulations did not define the term *agricultural income,* it is evident that it also included income from subsidiary occupations. The agricultural tax was levied on subsidiary income in at least some Communist-controlled areas during the war against Japan; this was discontinued because of the difficulties of calculating subsidiary income (Li Cheng-jui, 1959, p. 80).

Thus, in Communist terminology, the agricultural population includes: (a) those engaged in agricultural occupations only; (b) those engaged in agricultural and subsidiary occupations jointly; and (c) those engaged in subsidiary occupations only (Liu and Yeh, 1965, p. 183). According to Buck's study of employment of farm population (1937, p. 290), groups (a) and (b) amounted to 88 per cent of the total. Assuming the same percentage for the post-war years, the ratio of agricultural population to the total (in terms of our definition given above) is given in Table 4.

The Communist figures of agricultural population (Table 4, Column 1) appear to be on the high side. On the basis of reports of local governments in 25 provinces, C. C. Chang estimated that the farm households (and agricultural population) constituted 73 per cent of total households (and total population) in the early 1930's. Accepting Chang's data but including more provinces, Buck arrived at 74.5 per cent and Ou Pao-san 75.5 per cent (Liu and Yeh, 1965, pp. 182-183). Chang suspected that his figure of 73 per cent was probably on the low side (1932, p. 8). Buck's own survey data indicated a figure of 79.4 per cent (1937, p. 363) which Buck now regards as more reasonable (1966, p. 39).

The Communist estimates, though, are all higher than 80 per cent. According to the 1950 agricultural tax regulations, farm households were allowed to include in the agricultural population those family members who were in the armed forces; and the 1951 and 1952 revisions permitted the "poor"peasants with one or two persons in each household to double-count the actual number of persons in each household for tax purposes (Li Cheng-jui, 1959, p. 149). But it is doubtful that this would account entirely for the high Communist figures; and so when the official data on agricultural population are used to derive nonagricultural population, it is likely that the latter is understated.

The original Communist agricultural population data (Table 4) are all given by authoritative persons; it is not possible to reconcile the difference between Ma's and Tan's figures for 1956. Nor can the accuracy of these estimates be ascertained. There is no question, however, that serious efforts were made by the Communists to estimate the agricultural population as accurately as possible. The data were reported from the villages to the higher authorities annually and evidently were also checked. According to Yueh Wei of the State Statistical Bureau, when the reported agricultural population was deducted from total population to obtain the nonagricultural population, the latter was found to be too small in relation to nonagricultural employment data. Upon investigation it was discovered that when the agricultural population data were passed upward from the village level, some nonagricultural population in rural areas had been included. Yueh further reports that corrections were made when the data were used (1956, p. 26). Yueh's remarks were published in 1956, while Tan's article was published in 1957, Ma's in 1958, and Li's in 1957 (Tan, 1957; Ma. 1958; Li, 1957). It is not possible to tell whether the data given by the three later articles reflect Yueh's corrections. It may be noted, however, that in 1951 and 1952 there was a nationwide investigation or survey of agricultural population; according to this survey there was in 1952 a total of 502,310,000 agricultural population (Li Cheng-jui, 1959, p. 134). This may be compared with the figure of 492 million reported by Li (Table 4).

In our estimate of nonagricultural population (Table 5), two sets of

TABLE 5

URBAN POPULATION AND RATIO OF NONAGRICULTURAL TO TOTAL POPULATION 1949-1960

	Urban Population		Urban in Total Population (per cent)	Ratio of Nonagricultural to Total Population (per cent)	
	Millions at year end (1)	Rate of increase (per cent)	(2)	Estimate I (3)	Estimate II (4)
1949	57.65		10.6	25.5	23.0
1950	61.69	7.0	11.1	26.0	23.5
1951	66.32	7.5	11.8	26.7	24.2
1952	71.63	8.0	12.5	27.4	24.9
1953	77.67	8.4	13.2	28.1	25.6
1954	81.55	5.0	13.6	28.5	26.0
1955	82.85	1.6	13.5	28.4	25.9
1956	89.15	7.6	14.2	29.1	26.6
1957	92.00	3.2	14.3	29.2	26.7
1958	107.64	17.0	16.2 [a]	31.1	28.6
1959	118.82	10.4	17.5 [a]	32.4	29.9
1960	130.00	10.9	18.8 [a]	33.7	31.2

Note:

a. Based on official total population data given in Table 1.

Sources:

For (1) and (2), 1949-1956, see *TCKT,* 1957. 1957, see Wang Kuang-wei, 1957 (p. 7).

For (1), 1960, see Cheng Shih-wu, 1962.

For the rest, see text.

figures are given, one assuming that at the end of 1949 the proportion of nonagricultural to total population was the same as Buck's estimate for the early 1930's (namely, 25.5 per cent);[7] while the other assumes that the proportion in 1949 was 23 per cent, as given by Tan Chen-lin (after adjustment). For later years both sets of estimates reflect urban growth.

It should be noted that in Communist terminology, the distinction between agricultural and nonagricultural population is not equivalent to that between rural and urban. Rural population includes all rural residents in the "urban areas" as well as all residents in nonurban areas (Ullman, 1961). But an "urban" area is defined so as to exclude all villages and small towns with a population below 2,000 (or 1,000) unless the majority (or 75 per cent) of their population are engaged in other than agriculture. In fact, a number of the people living in such small towns or villages are engaged in nonagricultural activities.

As shown in Table 5, there has been a rapid increase in urban population in Communist China, despite the repeated attempts by the government to send people to the countryside. The figures for 1949-57 and for 1960 are reported figures. The 1958 figure represents a 17 per cent increase over 1957 (Emerson, 1965, p. 170). The 1959 figure is the average of 1958 and 1960.

The 1958-60 figures may be on the high side as compared with other information. Both Liu Hsiu-feng (1959, p. 207) and Sha Ch'ien-li (1959, p. 382) have reported an urban population of about 100 million, presumably for late 1958 and early 1959. An editorial in the *People's Daily* (*Jen-min yih-pao*), of August 25, 1960, reported that there was an increase of 20 million people in the cities in the "recent three years." It was not indicated whether the increase represented migration only or total urban growth. Assuming that it was migration only and that the entire migration took place in 1958, total urban population would still be 6.6 million less than what was reported for 1960 (assuming that the natural rate of increase of urban population was 3.5 per cent a year). If the reported 1957 and 1960 figures are correct, there must have been more than 25 million people who migrated from the rural to urban areas in 1958-60.[8]

7. As noted later, this is about the same ratio that Liu and Yeh (1965, p. 102) use for 1933. To what extent the economic situation in 1949 resembled that in the early 1930's cannot be determined. Ou Pao-san has estimated that national income in 1946 was about 94 per cent of that in 1933, while the share of agriculture in national income declined slightly from 61.5 per cent in 1933 to 59.4 per cent in 1946 (1947, p. 20). But on the basis of some limited data, the degree of urbanization appears to have increased, and this must have affected the ratio of nonagricultural population in the total. The total population of some 65 cities in twelve provinces increased about 18 per cent from 1938 to 1948, suggesting urban population grew faster than rural population (Ullman, 1961, p. 36).

8. Note, however that in an article published in *Kuang-ming jih-pao* (October 7, 1963, p. 4), Hsüeh Cheng-hsiu reported that between 1953 and the end of 1957 the urban population increased by 38.9 per cent. Such a percentage increase would yield an urban population total of 99.5 million for the end of 1957, based on the 1953 urban population total given in Table 5. But this figure would mean a sizable

The size of the nonagricultural population must be closely associated with that of the urban population. The growth of the latter, whether due to natural increase or migration, will increase the labor supply for nonagricultural economic activities. Since migrants usually include more men of working age, migration will increase the labor supply more than natural increase. As noted above, there was a very rapid increase in urban population in China in 1949-1960; since the natural rate of increase was probably between 3.5 and 4 per cent (Aird, 1961, p. 40; Choh-ming Li, 1959, p. 203), migration must have been substantial in 1949-53. In 1954 urban population grew slightly more than natural increase could account for; in 1955 and 1957 there was an outflow of people from urban to rural areas. But in 1958-60 migration to the urban areas was again substantial.

The estimated ratios of nonagricultural population to the total (given in Table 5) reflect urban growth, as noted above. We take the ratios in 1949 as a base and then add to them the yearly percentage point changes in the ratio of urban to total population (Column 2 in Table 5). This adjustment assumes that the natural rate of increase is the same for urban and rural population and that the migrants were agricultural population in the rural areas who became nonagricultural population after they went to the cities. To the extent that the natural rate of increase was higher in urban than in rural areas, the adjustment understates the nonagricultural population. On the other hand, to the extent that some migrants were nonagricultural to begin with, it overstates the nonagricultural population. Since the rural residents in the urban areas are included in rural population by official definition, we need not be concerned with those migrants who remained in agriculture after moving into cities.

The estimates of the agricultural and nonagricultural population for the age groups 14-64 years are given in Table 6; and those for the age groups 15-59 years are presented in Table 7. In each case it is assumed that for all the years covered, the respective age group constitutes the same proportion of total population as in the midyear of 1953, for which official data on age composition are available. This assumption probably overstates the growth rates of both agricultural and nonagricultural population in the age group 15-59 years. In Aird's estimates (Ch. 4, this vol-

migration in 1957, if one accepts the 1956 urban population figure as published in *TCKT* (cited in Table 5). No available information suggests migration of such magnitude in 1957. The 99.5 million figure would also indicate a much smaller amount of migration from rural to urban areas in 1958 than is generally believed. As noted in the text, both Liu Hsiu-feng (1959, p. 207) and Sha Ch'ien-li (1959, p. 382) reported an urban population of about 100 million for late 1958. Ullman (1961, p. 13) suggests that part of the population growth of certain cities (especially in 1958) was due to the extension of the boundaries to include additional territory. But this should not have had much effect on total urban population, for the change of boundaries was probably a matter of regrouping of administrative areas.

TABLE 6

AGRICULTURAL AND NONAGRICULTURAL POPULATION, AGES 14-64 (Year-end 1949-1960)
(in millions)

	Agricultural Population				Nonagricultural Population			
	Estimate I [a]		Estimate II [b]		Estimate I [a]		Estimate II [b]	
	Male	Female	Male	Female	Male	Female	Male	Female
1949	129.6	118.9	133.9	122.9	44.4	40.7	40.0	36.7
1950	131.2	120.3	135.6	124.4	46.1	42.3	41.7	38.2
1951	132.5	121.6	137.0	125.7	48.3	44.3	43.8	40.1
1952	134.0	123.0	138.6	127.2	50.6	46.4	46.0	42.2
1953	135.7	124.6	140.5	128.9	53.1	48.7	48.3	44.3
1954	138.2	126.7	143.0	131.2	55.1	50.5	50.2	46.1
1955	141.3	129.7	146.2	134.2	56.1	51.4	51.1	46.9
1956	142.9	131.1	148.0	135.8	58.7	53.8	53.6	49.2
1957	147.0	134.9	152.2	139.6	60.6	55.6	55.4	50.9
1958	146.7	134.6	152.0	139.5	66.2	60.7	60.9	55.9
1959	147.4	135.2	152.8	140.2	70.6	64.8	65.2	59.8
1960	147.4	135.3	153.0	140.4	74.9	68.8	69.4	63.7

Notes:

a. Based on the ratio of agricultural to total population as given in Table 5, Estimate I.

b. Based on Table 5, Estimate II.

Sources:

Table 1 and Table 2.

TABLE 7

AGRICULTURAL AND NONAGRICULTURAL POPULATION, AGES 15-59 (Year-end 1949-1960)
(in millions)

	Agricultural Population				Nonagricultural Population			
	Estimate I [a]		Estimate II [b]		Estimate I [a]		Estimate II [b]	
	Male	Female	Male	Female	Male	Female	Male	Female
1949	119.7	109.6	123.7	113.3	41.0	37.5	36.9	33.8
1950	121.1	110.9	125.2	114.7	42.6	39.0	38.5	35.2
1951	122.2	111.9	126.3	115.7	44.5	40.8	40.3	36.9
1952	123.7	113.3	128.0	117.3	46.7	42.8	42.4	38.9
1953	125.3	114.8	129.7	118.8	49.0	44.9	44.6	40.9
1954	127.6	116.9	132.0	120.9	50.8	46.6	46.4	42.5
1955	130.5	119.5	135.0	123.7	51.8	47.4	47.2	43.2
1956	132.0	120.9	136.6	125.2	54.2	49.6	49.5	45.4
1957	135.7	124.3	140.5	128.7	56.0	51.3	51.2	46.9
1958	135.4	124.0	140.3	128.5	61.1	56.0	56.2	51.5
1959	136.1	124.7	141.1	129.3	65.2	59.8	60.2	55.1
1960	136.2	124.7	141.3	129.4	69.2	63.4	64.1	58.7

Notes:
a. Based on Table 5, Estimate I.
b. Based on Table 5, Estimate II.

Sources:
See Table 6.

ume, Tables 3, 4) the proportion of this age group (both sexes) in the total population declines from 56.1 per cent in 1953 to 53.0 per cent in 1966 for his model I and model II. For models III and IV, it declines from 56.8 per cent to 53.6 per cent. Thus, over a period of 13 years the proportion declines by some 3.1 or 3.2 percentage points (or roughly 0.24 percentage points a year).

On the other hand, the figures in Tables 6 and 7 may understate the proportion of nonagricultural males. As noted above, a considerable part of urban growth was due to migration; it is likely that the sex ratio of the migrants was higher than that for the entire population. (The official sex ratio for 1953 is used in Tables 6 and 7. It is assumed to be the same for both the agricultural and nonagricultural populations).[9] Similarly, the number of nonagricultural males may also be underestimated because of the likelihood that there was a higher proportion of adults among the migrants than in the total population.

THE NONAGRICULTURAL LABOR FORCE: CIVILIAN MALE

No official estimate of the total labor force in China has ever been published. In fact, it was not until 1959 that the equivalent of the term "labor force" was introduced, when the term "social laborers" was explicitly defined and discussed by Ch'en Chih-ho (1959). Ch'en's "social laborers" include the able-bodied population minus those who do not participate in "social work," such as students, housewives, those in religious orders, and those in prisons or labor camps.

For our purposes, only the male nonagricultural labor force is estimated; it is not possible to determine the number of housewives who unsuccessfully seek employment. The starting point is the nonagricultural male population data given in Tables 6 and 7. We allow one per cent for those permanently disabled, those in religious orders, and those in prisons

9. This was certainly the case in the 1930's in the Manchurian cities, whose populations had grown, for the most part, from migration. The nature of migration since 1949 is not so clear, however. Traditionally there were always many male workers and employees who went alone to live in the cities, leaving their dependents behind in the villages. It is conceivable that, during the land reform in 1949-52, some of the dependents moved to the cities to avoid the disturbance in the countryside. It has been reported that in fifteen large cities the "basic population" (persons who worked in various political, economic, and cultural fields) increased by one million, or 28 per cent, from 1953 to 1956. "Service population" had increased by only 5 per cent, while the "dependent population" increased by 2.48 million, or 70 per cent. The dependents constituted 60 per cent of total population (1956). Of the increased dependents, 1.2 million immigrated from the rural areas (*Jen-min shout-t'se,* 1958, p. 650). Here the term "dependents" does not seem to include women, children, and elderly people only. Usually only those rural people who had personal ties in the cities would go there to look for a job; the term "dependents" most probably includes all those, whether of working age or not, who went to stay with their urban relatives.

or labor camps. This is arbitrary; it may be noted, however, that in the United States, about one per cent of the total population was in the custody of institutions in 1950, primarily because of mental illness (accounting for 50 per cent of this group), crime and delinquency, and old age (Bogue, 1959, p. 671). In an advanced industrial society, of course, there are probably more persons permanently disabled due to mental illness and industrial accidents than in an underdeveloped society. But there is no comparable information on the number of the permanently disabled in China. Presumably the number of such persons (relative to total population) has increased as a result of rapid industrialization. As for those in religious orders, there are estimated to have been one million in the 1930's (Chang Chi-hung, 1947, p. 78). There is no reliable information on the number of persons in prisons or labor camps. (These persons have to do hard work, and though their products are included in official production figures, they themselves are not included in official employment figures.) Since many religious orders and prisons and labor camps are located in rural areas, their occupants may have been included in official rural or agricultural population data.

The armed forces are not deducted from the nonagricultural male population on the grounds that most of them (generally estimated to be 3 million) are from rural areas. As noted above, for tax purposes farm households may count as agricultural population those family members who are in the military services. A system was introduced in 1955 according to which all males who reached 18 years of age were subject to the draft. But it was also indicated that, for the sake of economy, the armed forces would not expand beyond what was necessary for national defense (*JMJP,* Aug. 1, 1955). Thus, it may be assumed that the number of urban males who went into the military services after 1955 was small. At any rate, it is not possible to determine whether, or how many, of the armed forces are regarded as urban or rural residents. They are not included in the population of the place where they are stationed; their number is reported directly to military authorities (*JMST,* 1955, p. 27).

Male students are deducted in estimating the male labor force. The total enrollments for secondary schools and higher education are given in Table 8. From these figures the number of students aged 14 and over (and 15 and over) can be calculated, as is done in the table. Assuming further that 50 per cent of all students are nonagricultural,[10] and that male students constitute 75 per cent of the total,[11] the number of nonagricul-

10. Based on the information that in 1955 about 50 per cent of the middle school students and 25 per cent of college and graduate students were from rural families. (Fung Chi-hsi, 1957, p. 30).

11. Based on information given in *Ten Great Years,* (p. 178).

TABLE 8

ENROLLMENT OF STUDENTS, 1949-1960
(in thousands)

	Graduate Schools (1)	Higher Education (2)	Secondary Professional Schools (3)	Secondary General Schools Total (4)	Senior (5)	Junior (6)	Students aged 14 & over (7)	Students aged 15 & over (8)
1949	0.6	117	229	1,039	207	832	1,108	831
1950	1.3	137	257	1,305	238	1,067	1,187	910
1951	2.2	153	383	1,568	184	1,384	1,452	939
1952	3.5	191	636	2,491	260	2,231	2,198	1,604
1953	4.2	212	668	2,931	360	2,572	2,962	1,838
1954	4.8	253	608	3,587	478	3,109	3,322	2,468
1955	4.8	288	537	3,902	582	3,320	3,397	2,266
1956	5.0 [a]	403	812	5,165	779	4,386	4,465	3,130
1957	5.0 [a]	441	778	6,281	957	5,324	5,436	3,516
1958	5.0 [a]	660	1,470	8,520	1,180	7,340	7,304	5,235
1959		810	1,052 (3)+(4)				7,979	4,628
1960							8,000 [a]	4,649

Notes:
a. Assumed figures. The reported 1960 figures for (2) to (4) appear to be too high and hence are not used.

Sources:
(1). Orleans, 1961b (p. 78).
(2). 1949-1958, see *Ten Great Years* (p. 170). 1959, *Shin Chugoku nenkau* (p. 383).
(3). 1949-1958, see *Ten Great Years* (p. 170). 1959, see *Shin Chugoku nenkau* (p. 383).
(4), (5), and (6). For 1949-1955 and 1958, Orleans, 1961b (p. 35). For 1956 and 1957, the totals are from *TGY* (p. 170), and they are distributed between Junior and Senior at the same ratio as given in Orleans (1961b, p. 35) for 1957, and at the average of the 1955 and 1957 ratios as given there for 1956.
(7) and (8). Computed on the assumption that school age for secondary general schools runs from 13 to 18. The enrollment is assumed the same for the first, second and third year students in junior secondary schools in 1949. The distribution among these students is then computed for later years. (The number of the first year students in 1950 is the difference between the 1950 junior total and the sum of the first and second year students in 1949; the first year students in 1949 became the second year students in 1950, etc.) The number of the first year students in 1959 is assumed to be the same as in 1958.

tural males in the student population aged 14 and over (and 15 and over) can be computed.[12]

The final figure for the nonagricultural male labor force is computed by deducting from the total male nonagricultural population (Tables 6, 7) the 1 per cent allowance for the disabled, etc., and the nonagricultural male students. The result is given in Table 9. Although the absolute size of the labor force depends on the different estimates, the rate of growth is essentially the same. From 1949 to 1960 the nonagricultural male labor force increased from 64 per cent to 70 per cent, giving a rate of 5.8 to 6.4 per cent a year.

II. NONAGRICULTURAL EMPLOYMENT AND UNEMPLOYMENT

The key term of the official employment data is *chih-kung*. *Chih* is the abbreviation of *chih-yuan* which means "white-collar workers"; *kung* is the abbreviation of *kung-jen* meaning "blue-collar workers." The compound *chih-kung* may be translated here as "workers and employees," corresponding to the Russian term *rabochiye i sluzhashchiye* (Emerson, 1965a, p. 42). The best and perhaps the only comprehensive discussion of the definition and scope of workers and employees before 1957 was given by Ch'en Chih-ho in an article published in the official journal of the State Statistical Bureau in January, 1957 (Ch'en, 1957).

According to Ch'en, the term "workers and employees" must be defined in terms of the socioeconomic status of the members of society, which in turn is determined basically by ownership of the means of production. "Workers and employees" are only those who are engaged, manually or mentally, in the production of material goods or services, who have no investment of any form in enterprises, and who are completely or chiefly dependent on wage income for their livelihood. Thus, the category includes all personnel of the government as well as wage earners em-

12. The calculation is as follows (in 1,000's):

	Age 14 and over	Age 15 and over
1949	416	312
1950	446	341
1951	545	353
1952	824	602
1953	1,111	689
1954	1,246	926
1955	1,274	850
1956	1,675	1,174
1957	2,039	1,319
1958	2,739	1,964
1959	2,992	1,736
1960	3,000	1,744

TABLE 9

NONAGRICULTURAL MALE LABOR FORCE [a]
(millions at year-end)

	Ages 14-64				Ages 15-59			
	Estimate 1[b]		Estimate II [c]		Estimate 1[b]		Estimate II [c]	
	Total	1949=100	Total	1949=100	Total	1949=100	Total	1949=100
1949	43.49	100.0	39.18	100.0	40.23	100.0	36.26	100.0
1950	45.17	103.9	40.78	104.1	41.78	103.9	37.74	104.1
1951	47.24	108.6	42.76	109.1	43.71	108.7	39.58	109.2
1952	49.24	113.2	44.68	114.0	45.63	113.4	41.41	114.2
1953	51.41	118.2	46.74	119.3	47.80	118.8	43.49	119.9
1954	53.26	122.5	48.48	123.7	49.40	122.8	44.99	124.1
1955	54.22	124.7	49.34	125.9	50.38	125.2	45.88	126.5
1956	56.40	129.7	51.40	131.2	52.45	130.4	47.84	131.9
1957	57.98	133.3	52.84	134.9	54.09	134.5	49.35	136.1
1958	62.81	144.4	57.54	146.9	58.53	145.5	53.66	148.0
1959	66.93	153.9	61.54	157.1	62.84	156.2	57.86	159.6
1960	71.19	163.7	65.69	167.7	66.78	166.0	61.69	170.1

Notes:

a. Obtained by deducting from nonagricultural male population the following: (1) per cent allowance for the permanently disabled, etc., and (2) nonagricultural male students.

b. Based on Estimate I (Tables 6 and 7).

c. Based on Estimate II (Tables 6 and 7).

Sources:

Tables 6, 7 and 8.

ployed in enterprises (state-managed, joint state-private operations, and privately owned) and in cooperatives. Members of cooperatives, private proprietors, students and persons in religious orders are not included.[13]

The workers and employees as defined above constituted the main subject of Communist labor statistics before 1959; starting in 1959, the scope of labor statistics was broadened, at least in theory, to include all "social laborers." The definition and scope of this term were again given by Ch'en Chih-ho in an article published in the official journal *Planning and Statistics* of the State Planning Commission and the State Statistical Bureau (Ch'en, 1959). "Social laborers" comprised all persons engaged in social labor; that is, workers and employees, as well as laborers in the rural people's communes, in cooperatives, in civilian-run urban street enterprises, and in privately managed enterprises.[14]

Excluded from the category were those who had not participated in social labor or had engaged in nonsocial labor, such as: (1) students 16 years old and over; (2) those engaged in household work; (3) those in religious orders or practitioners of superstitions; (4) landlords, rich peasants, reactionaries, and rightist elements and other criminals who were undergoing labor reform or labor education in special institutions or who had been transferred to prisons; (5) military forces.

As Ch'en points out, the above classification of social laborers was largely based on type of ownership; the wage income criterion, used in his 1957 article, was no longer used for classifying workers and employees. This change was made because of the introduction of a wage system in 1958 in all the major sectors of the economy. Under this new classification, the wage earners of the cooperatives, the privately-owned enterprises, and the state-private joint enterprises who were not covered by the regulations on fixed share and fixed interest were no longer included in the category of "workers and employees." But persons in these three groups were few.

It may be noted that the concept of social laborer as used by Ch'en is essentially equivalent to total civilian employment, or gainfully employed. It is the same as total civilian labor force if unemployment is regarded as nonexistent (as it was regarded by Ch'en in 1959).

There have been no published figures based on Ch'en's classification of social laborers, except the estimate that there were about 360 million *lao-tung-li* (laborers) in the latter part of 1958 (Chang Fo-chien, 1958, p. 30). It is not known how this figure was estimated, though probably it was based on population data.

Published data on workers and employees are relatively more plentiful. The national total is given for the years 1949-58; subtotals for various branches of the economy are also available for various years. The basic

13. For detailed classification, see Ch'en Chin-ho, 1957.
14. For detailed classification, see Ch'en Chin-ho, 1959.

source of official labor statistics is the regular reports of enterprises. Additional data are also provided by various surveys. It was reported that a survey of workers and employees was made in February, 1957, covering all industrial, construction, and communications and transport enterprises (Emerson, 1965a, p. 18). Information on age and sex, number of years employed, level of skill, and cultural and educational level was included. Apparently no summary of this survey was ever published.

A similar survey or census was taken in 1955 covering workers and employees in all state (national and local), state-private and cooperative enterprises, and in all government organizations. (Not included were political parties, the military, private enterprises and civilian organizations.) The result was published in 1956 (*TCKT* Data Section, 1956). It included data on the proportion of the Marxian "productive" vs. "non-productive" workers, the age distribution, the levels of skill, the educational level, and both industrial and geographical distribution of the workers. Prior to this census, an attempt to collect employment data on a nationwide basis was made by the State Statistical Bureau in 1952; probably the employment data in the First Five-Year Plan (published in 1955) were taken from this survey (Emerson, 1965a, p. 13).

In addition to these surveys of employment, the State Statistical Bureau also conducted other surveys, notably the 1954 survey of private industry, the 1954 census of handicrafts, and the 1955 census of private trade and the food and drink industry. All these surveys yielded information on employment. But, as the Chinese Communists admit, the official data on employment were poor (Hsieh Mu-ch'iao, 1955).[15]

NONAGRICULTURAL EMPLOYMENT: AN ESTIMATE, 1949-1960

Nonagricultural employment is defined to include all those persons who make a living solely from nonagricultural activities. Persons who are engaged in both agricultural and subsidiary activities are not included in nonagricultural employment. Both Emerson (1965a) and Liu and Yeh (1965) have made estimates of nonagricultural employment in China. Though both basically relying on official data, their estimates differ substantially. We will try to compare their estimates and explain the sources of the differences in an Appendix. New estimates will be made when necessary.

One way to estimate nonagricultural employment is to start with the official Communist figures for workers and employees. From these figures must be subtracted the number of persons engaged in state farms and forestry, who are by definition included in agricultural employment. To

15. But this should not be exaggerated. Hsüeh's remarks were published in May, 1955, probably before the results of the 1954 surveys had been completely summarized, before the 1955 surveys had been taken, and before the periodic reporting systems on state sector employment were functioning satisfactorily.

"workers and employees" must be added the categories that should be included in nonagricultural employment: handicrafts, salt extraction, fishing, traditional transport and communications, traditional trading stores, restaurants, and peddlers, native banking, personal and professional services. (An explanation as to how these items are estimated is given in the Appendix.)

Table 10 presents our estimates of nonagricultural employment from 1949 to 1960. It should be noted that the total for 1958-60 does not include workers on such mass-labor projects as irrigation, road building, and backyard blast furnaces. They were drawn from the agricultural labor force and worked for short periods or on a part-time basis. Nor does it include workers in the "street industries," the great majority of whom were women or housewives probably working largely on a part-time basis.

The total of "workers and employees" for 1959 (year end) is based on a reported increase of 19.65 million over the year-end total of 1957. There is no information, however, on any changes in the various additional categories. The figure for workers and employees for 1960 is a planned figure and might be on the low side. According to Ma Wen-jui, the Minister of Labor, the total number of workers and employees more than doubled in the three years of the Great Leap (Ma, 1961, p. 12). Presumably he was referring to 1958-60 as the three Great Leap years and using 1957 as the base year. If so, the total workers and employees would be about 49 million in 1960. But Ma (p. 12) also reported in 1961 that after the autumn of 1960 some 20 million persons were transferred to agricultural production. The transfer was primarily a reallocation of manpower within the rural communes, as Ma indicated, but it must also have included some people who had previously been employed in nonagricultural branches. Furthermore, nonagricultural employment must also have been adversely affected by the shrinking supplies of agricultural raw material, due to poor harvests. Thus is is highly questionable whether the number of workers and employees in 1960 was as high as 49 million, or about 5 million more than in 1959.

No reported figure for workers and employees is available for 1961 and the years afterward. It may have declined in 1961, when industrial production was probably at its lowest point since 1958, partly because of the agricultural setback and partly because of the Soviet withdrawal of technical personnel in 1960. In the same article, Ma (1961) suggested that there was already a surplus of manpower in many industrial branches and that there should be no further increase in industrial employment. He cited the directives of the Communist Party ordering a curtailment in basic construction in 1961 in order to release some manpower for agricultural production. He urged appropriate reallocation of manpower in all industries so that production could be increased without increasing labor input, but he also suggested that adequate manpower be maintained in mining and the newly established small-scale labor-intensive industries.

The situation was probably worse in 1962. In March, 1962, a 10-point program was officially adopted for the adjustment of the economy, one of the points being that urban population and industrial workers be further reduced to an appropriate level (*JMJP,* April 17, 1962). In 1963 and 1964 industrial production appeared to be going up (*JMJP*, Dec. 31, 1964), but this may have been accomplished by a fuller utilization of the existing labor force. It remained a theme of many Communist writers that there was a labor surplus in the industrial sector and that more manpower should be mobilized and transferred to help agricultural production. Transfer of labor from urban to rural areas has also been reported. Thus, nonagricultural employment in 1961-64 was, at the most, at the same level as in 1960. In all probability it was lower, but it is not possible to ascertain the extent of the decline quantitatively. To the extent that industrial production and employment are a function of agricultural output, it may be noted that the 1957 level of agricultural production was apparently not restored until 1964, even according to official estimates. In 1965, food grain production was reported to be only 8 per cent higher than in 1957 (China News Summary, 1966).

NONAGRICULTURAL EMPLOYMENT: AN EVALUATION OF DATA

How accurate or meaningful are the estimates presented in Table 10? A glance at it will reveal that there are a number of items for which we assume a constant figure for several years (for example: animal-drawn carts from 1949 to 1954, or domestic servants for the entire period). Estimates could be made for these items on the basis of population change or the rate of change of an item for which information is relatively more complete, such as handicrafts; but the result would not be materially different. We have used constant figures to emphasize the degree to which data are lacking. Figures might be omitted entirely for these items, but if we wish to observe the trend of development in employment or unemployment, a grand total of employment should be estimated. From this point of view, omitting the items for which we have no data would be even less desirable. All these items are in the traditional sector where the rate of increase in employment was much slower than in the modern sector. Furthermore, as in the case of boats and junks, the practice of using the employment figure of 1954 for the preceding years (1949-53) may not be entirely out of line with reality, for changes in the traditional sector over a short period tend to be small.[16]

16. For example, based on total output and production data, Liu and Yeh's estimate of total employment in traditional transport shows little change for all the years during the First Five-Year Plan period. See Liu and Yeh, 1965, p. 198.

TABLE 10

NONAGRICULTURAL EMPLOYMENT IN MAINLAND CHINA

(thousands at year-end) [a]

	1949	1950	1951	1952	1953	1954	1955	1956	1957	1958	1959	1960
1. "Workers and employees"	8,004	10,239	12,815	15,804	18,256	18,809	19,076	24,230	24,506	45,323	44,156	45,960 [b]
2. State farms	4	43	70	97	111	137	134	206	500	990	1,310	2,800
3. Forestry	23	30	40	51	74	80	75	85	85	110	110	110
4. Nonagricultural "workers and employees',	7,977	10,166	12,705	15,656	18,071	18,592	18,867	23,939	23,921	44,223	42,736	43,050
5. Individual and cooperative handicraftsmen	5,855	7,229	7,258	7,364	7,789	8,910	8,202	7,300	8,000	2,900		
6. Salt extraction	(270)	(270)	(270)	270	270	270	420	440	470	700		
7. Fishing	800	1,200	1,268	1,336	1,404	1,472	1,540	1,500	1,500	2,000		
8. Traditional transport	(5,348)	(5,348)	(5,362)	(5,362)	(5,362)	(5,362)	5,362	4,826	4,826	4,863		
a. Boats and junks	(911)	(911)	(911)	(911)	(911)	911	911	859	859	896		
b. Animal-drawn carts	(982)	(982)	(982)	(982)	(982)	(9982)	982	826	826	826		
c. Hand-drawn carts	(2,069)	(2,069)	(2,069)	(2,069)	(2,069)	(2,069)	2,069	1,741	1,741	1,741		
d. Rickshas, pedicabs and sedans	(700)	(700)	(700)	(700)	(700)	(700)	(700)	(700)	(700)	(700)		
e. Coolies and longshoremen	(686)	(686)	(700)	(700)	(700)	(700)	(700)	(700)	(700)	(700)		
9. Trade, food and drink industry	10,868	10,944	12,625	11,416	11,063	8,701	7,384	6,086	5,374	5,465		
10. Financial institutions: nonstate sector	(230)	(230)	(230)	230	230	248	320	260	221			
11. Personal and professional services	3,204	3,212	3,221	3,230	3,239	3,248	3,257	3,279	3,339	3,339		
a. "Services"	417	425	434	443	452	361	470	479	489	489		
b. Traditional medical doctors	(487)	(487)	(487)	(487)	(487)	(487)	487	500	550	550		
c. Domestic servants	(2,300)	(2,300)	(2,300)	(2,300)	(2,300)	(2,300)	(2,300)	(2,300)	(2,300)	(2,300)		

12. Total nonworkers and employees	26,575	28,433	30,234	29,208	29,357	28,211	26,485	23,691	23,730	19,367	(19,367)	(19,367)
13. Total nonagricultural employment	34,552	38,599	42,939	44,864	47,428	46,803	45,352	47,630	47,651	63,590	62,103	62,417
14. (12) as per cent of (13)	76.9	73.7	70.4	65.1	61.9	60.3	58.4	49.7	49.8	30.5	31.2	31.0
15. Total tentative estimates	(8,635)	(7,949)	(8,649)	(8,149)	(8,149)	(7,238)	(3,700)	(3,700)	(3,700)	(3,700)	(19,317)	(19,317)
16. (15) as per cent of (13)	25.0	20.6	20.1	18.2	17.2	15.5	8.2	7.8	7.8	5.8	31.2	31.0

Notes:

a. Figures in parentheses are very tentative estimates; see text.

b. Planned figure.

Sources:

Line 1. 1949-1958, *Ten Great Years* (p. 159). 1959, Hsu Hsin-hsueh, 1960 (p. 7). 1960, Li Fu-ch'un, 1960 (p. 13).

Line 2. Emerson, 1965a (pp. 148. 94).

Line 3. 1949-1958, Emerson 1965a (p. 148). 1959-1960, assumed the same as in 1958.

Line 4. Difference between (1) and the sum of (2) and (3).

Line 5. 1949-1955, Emerson, 1965a (p. 133). 1956-1957, Liu and Yeh, 1965 (p. 196). 1958, see Appendix.

Line 6. 1952-1957, based on Liu and Yeh, 1965 (pp. 194-195, 573-576); see Appendix. 1958, Emerson, 1965a (p. 133). 1949-1951, assumed the same as in 1952.

Line 7. Emerson, 1965a (p. 133).

Line 8. a. 1954-1958, see Appendix. 1949-1953 assumed the same as in 1954.

b, c. 1955-1958, see Appendix. 1949-1954 assumed the same as in 1955.

d. 1957, Liu and Yeh, 1965 (p. 597) based on 1933 data; other years assumed the same as in 1957.

Line 9. Sum of Emerson's "traditional" components of trade, and the food and drink industry (1965a, p. 133) and Liu and Yeh's (1965, p. 200) rural peddlers. Liu and Yeh covers 1952-1957 only; the number of rural peddlers for 1949-1951 is assumed the same as that in 1952, and that in 1958 the same as in 1957.

Line 10. 1954-1958, Emerson, 1965a, (p. 133). 1952-1953, Liu and Yeh, 1965 (p. 206). 1949-1951, assumed to the be the same in 1952.

Line 11. a. Emerson, 1965a (p. 133).

b. 1955-57, Emerson 1965a (p. 142). 1958, assumed the same as in 1957. 1949-1954, assumed the same as in 1955.

c. 1952-1957, Liu and Yeh, 1965 (p. 206). Other years assumed the same.

Line 12. Sum of line 5 through line 11.

Line 13. Sum of line 4 and line 12.

Actually, there are only two categories (8d and 11d in Table 10) for which there are no reported figures for any year, and for which the estimates must be based on prewar data. For all other years, to the extent that the reported figures are reliable, our assumed figures cannot be too far wrong. In Table 10, the proportion of what we call "tentative estimates" in total employment is shown. If we include rural peddlers (1949-51) as a tentatively estimated group, the proportion would be 37 per cent in 1949, 32 per cent in 1950 and 30 per cent in 1951. The proportion of weak estimates declines gradually, being about 8 per cent in 1957 and 6 per cent in 1958. It is higher for 1959 and 1960 simply because of the fact that all the figures for the categories added to workers and employees are assumed for these two years.

For nonagricultural employment as a whole, the estimates for the years before 1952 and after 1957 are less reliable. This is not only because of the higher proportion of tentative estimates in these years, but also because of the lower quality of Communist statistics in general. Furthermore, the estimates for all years (except post-1957 years) are probably understated, with the degree of understatement decreasing through time.

Two factors may be adduced to explain why understatement may have occurred. The first is underreporting. As Emerson (1965a, p. 68) has pointed out, the revised official figures on employment, with the exception of private trade (p. 58), are a great deal higher than the figures released first.[17] This is true even for the 1956 employment data for industry [18]—supposedly the best employment data collected by the State Statistical Bureau. There is also evidence that the discrepancies between original and revised figures on employment are much greater for the years before 1955,[19] than for 1956-58 (Emerson, 1965). It is doubtful that the revised figures have completely eliminated the element of error due to underreporting, especially for the years before 1955 for which data are more incomplete.

The second factor is the omission of certain items in the official employment records—such as self-employed proprietors ("capitalists"); drivers of pack animals (camels, yaks, etc.); private tutors; persons engaged in black market trade; unpaid family workers in handicrafts and trade (Emerson, 1965a, pp. 69-70). Since the reported figures are used for many of the categories to which the above items belong, our estimates (Table 9) also suffer from the omission.

17. The 1955 worker and employee total published in June, 1956, was more than half a million fewer than the revised total published in 1959 (Emerson, 1965a, p. 68).

18. The originally published figure for workers and employees in industry in 1956 was said to have been in error by several hundred thousands (*ibid.*, p. 68).

19. The revised state sector worker and employee total for 1953 was 1.4 million more than originally published (*ibid.*, p. 69).

Underestimation is suggested by other data as well. Using estimates of employment (by Liu and Yeh) for 1933, of output (net value added, 1933 and 1952) and of 1952 employment, it appears that labor productivity in the nonagricultural sectors increased 39 per cent (in 1952 prices) or 34 per cent (in 1933 prices) from 1933 to 1952.[20] This cannot be easily accounted for. There is no information on capital stock for all nonagricultural sectors in 1933 or 1952. It is doubtful, however, that capital stock in 1952 was so much greater than in 1933, or that other factors in 1952 were so much more favorable than in 1933, that an increase of productivity of such an order was possible. The Communist economic achievements in 1949-52 were, on the whole, more an accomplishment in recovering than in making a broad advance. Thus, on the basis of Liu and Yeh's estimates, there seems to be a strong possibility that the 1952 employment figure is understated, though the degree of understatemnt cannot be ascertained.

By comparing Ou Pao-san's estimate of nonagricultural employment for 1933 and his own estimate for 1949, Emerson (1965a, p. 73) comes to the conclusion that the net understatement of actual nonagricultural employment in 1949 is probably about 27 per cent. He further suggests that because of the progressive extension of data reporting systems and the gradual improvement in reporting after the founding of the State Statistical Bureau in 1952, understatement may have been reduced to 5 per cent of the actual level by 1957. But, as Emerson would probably agree, any quantification of the degree of the understatement is a risky affair, to say the least. Aside from the reliability of the 1933 data, an unknown margin of error is involved when the economy in 1933 is compared with that in 1949. However, Emerson's judgment for 1957 may not be far from reality; at least the official employment data seem consistent with other data, such as the reported number of persons each worker supported.[21]

20. The data are as follows (nonagricultural sectors)*:

	Employment (millions)	Net value added (billions)		Productivity	
		1933 yuan	1952 yuan	1933 yuan	1952 yuan
1933	54.30	10.10	25.63	186(100)	472(100)
1952	56.56**	14.11	37.22	249(134)	658(139)

* Liu and Yeh (1965, pp. 66, 232, 239).

** Our employment total (Table 10) plus the full-time equivalent of part-time workers (in handicrafts, transportation and work brigades) and military service, as estimated by Liu and Yeh. Our year-end figure has also been converted into an annual average in order to make our employment estimate comparable with the Liu and Yeh data.

21. Ma Wen-jui (1959, p. 51) has reported that, according to a sample survey of 30 cities including Peking and Shanghai, the average worker in industry supported 3.3 persons (including himself) in 1957 and 2.9 persons in 1958. Hsu Hsin-hsueh (1960, p. 7) reports that on the average, every 10 laborers supported 32

To conclude, it may be said that our total employment estimates, at least for 1955 to 1957, are probably as accurate as the available evidence permits. For other years, there remain reservations in view of the lack of data for certain traditional sectors. Therefore, the estimates of nonagricultural employment for the period covered should not be regarded as a time series in the ordinary sense, with any high degree of precision. Defective as they are, the yearly estimates do serve the purpose of pointing up the trend of development for; as noted below, no plausible adjustment of probable biases (upward or downward) would change the general picture. The trend of development seems clear: the rate of increase was much faster for "workers and employees" than for non-"workers and employees" (Table 11). This reflects not only the lower growth rate of the traditional sector of the economy (as compared with the modern sector where "workers and employees" are hired), but also the fact that non-"workers and employees" were reclassified to the category of workers and employees.[22] But the rate of growth in total nonagricultural employment was still not so high as Table 11 shows, because of the increasing degree of understatement in the earlier years.

Table 12 presents our estimate together with those of Emerson and Liu and Yeh. The Liu and Yeh estimates exceed ours by as much as 12.3 million (1954) to 16.5 million (1957); whereas our estimates are from 6.5 million (1955) to 8.3 million more than Emerson's. The differences between our estimates of yearly changes and Emerson's are also smaller than those between ours and Liu and Yeh's.

Large as they are, the differences between the three sets of estimates can be accounted for. They are mainly the result of differences in coverage; the basic data for the three estimates are largely the same, all relying heavily upon official data. A reconciliation is made in Table 13 between our data and the Liu and Yeh estimates for 1957, the year that shows the greatest discrepancy. Substantial differences are found for handicrafts, fishing, traditional transport, military service, and work brigades. For the other categories, our estimates are generally larger than Liu and Yeh's, largely because of the use of different sources (see the Appendix).

In the handicrafts category, in addition to individual handicraftsmen and those in handicraft workshops and cooperatives, Liu and Yeh also

---

persons in 1957 and 28 persons in 1959. Dividing the urban population figure in 1957 by Ma's 3.3, we get 28 million, as compared with 25 million, which was the total of workers and employees in 1957. The discrepancy may be explained by differences between industry and other branches as regards the number of persons each worker supports: there were wokers and employees who did not reside in the cities; and in the cities there may have been workers who were not classified as "workers and employees."

22. It is reported that out of the increase of workers and employees of some 16.2 million from 1949 to 1956, some 13.0 million represented new employment, the remaining 3.2 million representing reclassification (*TCKT,* 1957, p. 13).

TABLE 11

GROWTH RATES OF NONAGRICULTURAL EMPLOYMENT

	Modern Sector		Traditional Sector		Total	
	1949= 100	Annual Increase (per cent)	1949= 100	Annual Increase (per cent)	1949= 100	Annual Increase (per cent)
1949	100.0		100.0		100.0	
1950	127.4	+27.4	107.0	+7.0	111.7	+11.7
1951	159.3	+25.0	113.8	+6.3	124.3	+11.1
1952	196.3	+23.2	109.9	−3.4	129.8	+4.7
1953	226.5	+15.4	110.5	+0.5	137.3	+5.6
1954	233.1	+2.9	106.2	−3.9	135.5	−1.3
1955	236.5	+1.5	99.7	−6.2	131.3	−3.0
1956	300.1	+26.9	89.1	−10.5	137.9	+4.8
1957	299.9	−0.1	89.3	+1.6	137.9	+0.2
1958	554.4	+84.9	72.9	−17.4	184.0	+33.3
1959	535.7	−3.4	72.9	0.0	179.7	−2.3
1960	539.7	+0.7	72.9	0.0	180.6	+0.5

Source:
Table 10.

include "such others as the full-time equivalent of housewives and farmers engaged in part-time handicrafts" (Liu and Yeh, 1965, pp. 193-194). This "others" category numbered 4.51 million in 1957, accounting for the entire difference between our estimates and those of Liu and Yeh for this category. By our definition, those who are engaged in part-time nonagricultural work are not included in nonagricultural employment; no conversion to full-time equivalents is made.

The Appendix largely explains the difference in estimates for traditional transport, which is due mainly to different assumptions made regarding the number of workers in junks, animal-drawn carts, and hand-drawn carts. In addition, Liu and Yeh also include 1.4 million "farmers working in transportation" and 0.9 million "others," such as "full-time coolies in rural areas" (Liu and Yeh, 1965, p. 597). The differences in estimates for fishing, military service, and work brigades are the easiest to explain. Liu and Yeh do not include the first, while we do not include the last two categories. Our estimate is of civilian employment, and we regard those who constituted work brigades as being basically farmers who were drafted to do construction work (road building, water conservation work, etc.) during farming off-seasons.

Thus, the difference between our estimate and Liu and Yeh's is largely due to the inclusion or exclusion of part-time work in nonagricultural

TABLE 12

COMPARISON OF ESTIMATES OF NONAGRICULTURAL EMPLOYMENT, 1949-1958
(in millions)

	Author's Estimate		Emerson		Liu and Yeh	
	Total [a]	Yearly Change (per cent)	Total [a]	Yearly Change (per cent)	Total [b]	Yearly Change (per cent)
1949	34.6		26.3			
1950	38.6	+11.6	30.3	+15.4		
1951	42.9	+11.1	34.7	+14.6		
1952	44.9	+4.7	36.8	+5.8	59.4	
1953	47.4	+5.6	39.1	+6.4	59.6	+0.3
1954	46.8	−1.3	39.8	+1.6	59.4	−0.3
1955	45.4	−3.0	38.9	−2.2	60.4	+1.7
1956	47.6	+4.8	39.4	+1.3	61.8	+2.4
1957	47.7	+0.2	39.7	+0.8	64.2	+3.8
1958	63.6	+33.3	56.9	+43.3		

Notes:

a. Year-end.

b. Annual average.

Sources:

Table 10; Emerson. (1965a, p. 128); Liu and Yeh (1965, p. 69).

categories. This conceptual difference has important implications for the measurement of unemployment. For example, suppose there are four farmers who spend 75 per cent of their time in farming and 25 per cent in handicraft work or building roads. By Liu and Yeh's definition, there are three workers in agricultural employment and one in nonagricultural employment, while by our definition all four are agricultural employees. Suppose for some reason they stop working in handicrafts or road building. By Liu and Yeh's definition, there would be one person unemployed in the nonagricultural sector, while by ours there would be no change in nonagricultural employment. The four farmers remain employed in agriculture, although obviously there is an increase in agricultural underemployment.

The difference between our estimates and Emerson's can also be explained; the framework of the two is essentially the same. The difference between the estimates for individual and cooperative handicraftsmen is indicated in the Appendix. For traditional transport, in addition to the difference for junks and carts, which has also been explained in the Appendix, we include rickshas, pedicabs, sedans, coolies and longshoremen,

TABLE 13

RECONCILIATION OF AUTHOR'S AND LIU AND YEH'S ESTIMATES OF NONAGRICULTURAL EMPLOYMENT, 1957
(in millions)

Sector	Author's estimate [a]	Difference in coverage	Difference in sources, assumptions	Liu & Yeh's estimate [b]
1. Industry				
a. Factories, mining & utilities	(6.29) [c]	−0.36 [d]	−0.43	5.50
b. Handicrafts	10.00	+4.51		14.51
2. Basic construction	(2.43)		−.03	2.40
3. Fishing	1.50	−1.50		0.00
4. Transportation & communications				
a. Modern	(1.72)		−0.29	1.43
b. Traditional	4.83		+5.17	10.00
5. Trade, food and drink	(10.75)		+0.65	11.40
6. Finance, banking and insurance	(0.65)		+0.10	0.75
7. Personal & professional services	3.34		−0.01	3.33
8. Government				
a. Administration	1.70		−0.06	1.64
b. Social and cultural services	3.20		−0.16	3.04 [f]
c. Agriculture, forestry, water conservation & meteorology	0.35 [e]	+0.04		0.39
d. Mass organizations	(1.20)		+0.04	1.24 [g]
e. Military service	0.00	+3.00		3.00
9. Work brigades	0.00	+5.56		5.56
Total	47.96	+11.25	+4.98	64.19

Notes:

a. Figures in parentheses are annual averages. Others are year-end figures that seem comparable with Liu and Yeh's estimates.

b. Annual averages.

c. Includes salt extraction and timbering.

d. Timbering.

e. Water conservation and meteorology only.

f. Includes communal services.

g. Party and other organizations.

Sources:

Table 15 and Liu and Yeh (1965, pp. 194-206).

while Emerson does not. The difference in the trade, food and drink industry lies entirely in our inclusion of rural peddlers. For traditional medicine, Emerson includes midwives and we do not. Finally, we include domestic servants and Emerson does not. (See Table 14.)

TABLE 14

RECONCILIATION OF AUTHOR'S AND EMERSON'S ESTIMATES OF NONAGRICULTURAL EMPLOYMENT, 1957
(in millions)

Sector	Author's estimate	Difference in coverage	Difference in sources, assumptions	Emerson's estimate
1. "Workers and employees"	23.92			23.92
2. Individual and cooperative handicraftsmen	8.00		−1.44	6.56
3. Salt extraction	0.47		+0.03	0.50
4. Fishing	1.50			1.50
5. Traditional transport	4.83	−1.40	−0.89	2.54
6. Trade, and food and drink	5.37	−2.80		2.57
7. Finance	0.22			0.22
8. Personal and professional services				
a. "Services"	0.49			0.49
b. Traditional medicine	0.55	+0.81		1.36
c. Domestic servants	2.30	−.230		0.00
Total	47.65	−5.69	−2.30	39.66

Sources:
Table 10 and Emerson (1965a, p. 133).

INDUSTRIAL DISTRIBUTION OF NONAGRICULTURAL EMPLOYEES

The industrial distribution of nonagricultural employees may be estimated by allocating "workers and employees" (as shown in Table 10) among the various branches of the economy, and then adding to each branch the non-"workers and employees." "Workers and employees" are classified officially into productive branches and nonproductive branches. Included in productive branches are, principally, industry, basic construction, trade (including the food and drink industry), and transportation and communications. The nonproductive branches include mainly finance, banking and insurance, education, health and cultural affairs, government, mass organizations, and urban public utilities. Since the distribution of "workers and employees" between "productive" and "nonproductive" branches is given, and since the numbers of workers and employees for most fields within each branch are also given, it is possible to estimate the occupational distribution of "workers and employees."

The figures for the modern component of each category as given in Table 15 are basically those gathered or estimated by Emerson (1965a, p. 129).[23] They differ, but not significantly, from those given by Liu and Yeh (1965, p. 194). Emerson's figures are used here because they are from sources published later.[24]

23. In Communst terminology, "industry" includes manufacturing (factories and handicraft workshops), mining, electric power, timbering, and state-managed fishing operations (prior to 1958). The total number of workers and employees in industry is reported for 1949, and 1952-57. "Basic construction," in official usage, includes building and installation, survey and design, and geological survey. Employment data for workers and employees in basic construction are given for all the years from 1949 to 1957, though it is not clear whether they are all comparable. The numbers of workers and employees in transport, posts, and telecommunications are reported for 1949, 1952, 1956 and 1957. The numbers for the other years are estimated by interpolations.

Reported figures for "workers and employees" in trade and the food and drink industry are basically available for 1949, 1950, 1952, 1955, and 1956. For 1951, 1953, 1954 and 1957, the numbers of "workers and employees" are derived as the difference between the reported total number of "workers and employees" in productive branches and those in productive branches other than trade and the food and drink industry. For th numbers of workers and employees in banking, finance, and insurance, reported figures are available for only 1952, 1953 and 1955. Estimates for other years are made either by interpolations or, as for 1956, by the method used for the trade and food and drink industry (in this case, the "nonproductive" category is relevant).

For government administration, reported figures of "workers and employees" are available for 1952 and 1955. For education, health and cultural affairs, reported figures of workers and employees are available for 1949, 1952 and 1956. No reported figures (except for 1956) are available for the numbers of workers and employees in mass organizations (political parties and other organizations); they are derived as the difference between the reported total number of workers and employees in nonproductive branches and the sum of the reported or estimated totals of workers and employees in all other nonproductive branches. (For 1956, it is basically a reported figure.)

24. In Table 15 the number of persons employed in basic construction in 1953 is different from that given by Emerson. It may be noted that the English version of the original Chinese source as rendered in *People's China* (No. 22, November 16, 1954, Supplement, p. 7) to which Emerson referred, reads as follows:

> . . . The number of workers and employees in state-owned and joint state-and privately owned enterprises in the capital construction category grew to 2,170,000, of whom 1,540,000 were engaged in building and installing equipment.

This translation or interpretation differs from ours as given in Table 15. It is true that building and installation work is only one of the three major subdivisions of basic construction (the other two being survey and design, and geological survey), but the number of persons engaged in survey and design was only 39,000 in 1953

TABLE 15

INDUSTRIAL DISTRIBUTION OF NONAGRICULTURAL EMPLOYEES, 1949-1958
(thousands, at year-end)

Sector	1949	1950	1951	1952	1953	1954	1955	1956	1957	1958
1. Manufacturing and mining	9,206	10,916	11,943	12,938	14,249	15,646	14,866	15,353	16,510	26,734
a. Factories and mining	1,079	1,406	2,399	3,283	4,121	4,370	4,121	5,480	5,907	20,984
b. Urban utilities	22	31	36	41	69	96	123	133	133	150
c. Handicrafts	7,835	9,209	9,238	9,344	9,789	10,910	10,202	9,300	10,000	4,900
d. Salt extraction	270	270	270	270	270	270	420	440	470	700
2. Basic construction	200	400	600	1,048	1,540	2,100	1,935	2,951	1,910	5,336
3. Water conservation	61	80	108	134	198	266	261	409	340	1,360
4. Fishing	800	1,200	1,268	1,336	1,404	1,472	1,540	1,500	1,500	2,000
5. Transportation and communications	5,982	6,147	6,326	6,491	6,600	6,709	6,788	6,390	6,704	7,818
Modern	634	799	964	1,129	1,238	1,347	1,426	1,564	1,878	2,955
Traditional	5,348	5,348	5,362	5,362	5,362	5,362	5,362	4,826	4,826	4,863
6. Trade and food and drink industry	12,090	12,442	14,640	14,140	14,140	11,323	10,499	10,885	10,619	10,300
Modern	1,222	1,498	2,015	2,724	3,077	2,622	3,115	4,799	5,245	4,835
Traditional	10,868	10,944	12,625	11,416	11,063	8,701	7,384	6,086	5,374	5,465
7. Finance, banking and insurance	411	489	530	576	607	632	704	677	621	400
Modern	181	259	300	346	377	384	384	417	400	300
Traditional	230	230	230	230	230	248	320	260	221	100
8. Personal and Professional services	3,204	3,212	3,221	3,230	3,239	3,248	3,257	3,279	3,339	3,339
9. Government	2,598	3,713	4,303	4,971						
Administration	796	1,138	1,318	1,523	5,451	5,407	5,502	6,186	6,108	6,303
Education, health and					1,698	1,598	1,576	1,748	1,698	1,183
cultural affairs	1,176	1,787	2,071	2,392	2,607	2,715	2,824	3,211	3,211	3,811
Mass organizations	625	787	912	1,053	1,143	1,090	1,096	1,215	1,184	1,281
Meteorology	1	1	2	3	3	4	6	12	15	28
Total	34,552	38,599	42,939	44,864	47,428	46,803	45,352	47,630	47,651	63,590

Sources:

Line 1: a. Difference between industry as given in Emerson (1965a, p. 129) and handicraft workshops, as given in Liu and Yeh (1956, p. 194. For the latter, the figure for 1952 is used for 1949-51, and the figure for 1957 is used for 1958. Thus factories and mining include timbering and state-managed fishing operations. But employment in these two categories was small.

b. Emerson (1965a, p. 128).

c. Sum of individual, cooperative and workshop handicraftsmen.

d. Table 10.

Line 2: Emerson (1965a, p. 128) except 1953, for which 1.54 million is used. Emerson's 2.17 million figure, according to the source he cited, was the total number of workers and employees of the enterprises for which construction was undertaken. Of this total, only 1.54 million were workers and employees in basic construction.

Line 3: Emerson (1965a, p. 128).

Line 4: Table 10.

Line 5: *Modern,* Emerson (1965a, p. 129). *Traditional,* Table 10.

Line 6: *Modern,* Emerson (1965a, p. 129). 2,000, 4,000, and 6,000 are added to Emerson's figures for 1953, 1954, and 1955 respectively. Emerson apparently overstates the figures for state farms, forestry and water conservation (p. 129) by the respective amounts; they are added to trade, and the food and drink industry of 1953 and 1954 in accordance with Emerson's own method of estimation. For the year 1955, the addition is made somewhat arbitrarily. Also, to Emerson's 1953 figure is added 0.63 million to reflect the correction of his 1953 base construction figure.

Traditional, Table 10.

Line 7: *Modern,* for 1952-1958, (1965a, p. 129). The figures for 1949-1951 are estimated on the assumption that the proportion of finance in nonproductive branch is the same as that in 1952.

Traditional, Table 10.

Line 8: Table 10.

Line 9: *Meteorology,* Emerson (1965a, p. 129).

Others: for 1952-1958, Emerson (1965a, p. 129); for 1950-1951 and the 1949 government administration, the figures are estimated on the assumption that the proportions of the sub-categories in nonproductive branch (Emerson, 1965a, p. 129) are the same as that in 1952. The 1949 figure for education, health and cultural affairs is also given in Emerson. The 1949 figure for mass organizations is the difference between the total of nonproductive branch and the sum of all nonproductive branches other than mass organizations.

The classification of nonagricultural employment in Table 15 is not entirely that of the Communists. In fact, in Chinese Communist usage, the term nonagricultural employment is not used, and water conservation and meteorology are classified as agricultural. The percentage distribution of nonagricultural employment by major groups for 1952 and 1957 is given in Table 16, together with that for the Soviet Union in 1928. In Communist China, the share of industry and construction increased from 1952 to 1957, but in 1957 it was still less than in the Soviet Union in 1928. The share of "tertiary industries" was still a great deal larger in Communist China in 1957 than in the Soviet Union in 1928.

TABLE 16

NONAGRICULTURAL EMPLOYMENT BY MAJOR SECTORS
(in per cent)

	Communist China		Soviet Union
Sector	1952	1957	1928
1. Industry	32 [a]	38 [a]	45
2. Construction	2 [b]	4 [b]	8
3. Transportation	14	14	12
4. Commerce	33 [c]	24 [c]	9
5. Government and other services	19 [d]	20 [d]	26
Total	100	100	100

Notes:
a. Includes manufacturing and mining and fishing.
b. Basic construction.
c. Includes trade and food and drink, and finance, banking and insurance.
d. Includes personal and professional services, government and water conservation.

Sources:
Communist China, Table 15.
Soviet Union, Eason, 1963 (p. 80).

(Emerson, 1965a, p. 139). The number of persons engaged in geological survey in 1953 is not known, but judging from other years, it could not be large. It was 30,000 in 1953 and 166,000 in 1955 *(ibid.)*. Therefore, the total number of persons engaged in basic construction in 1953 could hardly have been as many as 2.17 million. The original Chinese source which Emerson cited was the State Statistical Bureau's "Communiqué on National Economic Development and Fulfillment of the State Plan in 1953," which may be found in *Jen-min Jih-pao* (*JMJP,* September 28, 1954, p. 1).

TABLE 17

NONAGRICULTURAL UNEMPLOYMENT: MALE
(in millions)

	Ages 14-64				Ages 15-59			
	Estimate I [a]		Estimate II [b]		Estimate III [a]		Estimate IV [b]	
	Total unemployed	As percentage of labor force %	Total unemployed	As percentage of labor force %	Total unemployed	As percentage of labor force %	Total unemployed	As percentage of labor force %
1949	13.8	31.7	9.5	24.2	11.2	27.4	6.6	18.2
1950	12.5	27.6	8.1	19.8	9.8	23.1	5.0	13.2
1951	10.3	21.8	5.8	13.6	7.6	17.0	2.7	6.8
1952	11.0	22.3	6.4	14.3	8.4	18.0	3.1	7.5
1953	10.9	21.3	6.3	13.4	8.5	17.4	3.0	6.9
1954	13.9	26.2	9.2	18.9	11.5	22.7	5.7	12.7
1955	16.1	29.6	11.2	22.7	13.6	26.3	7.7	16.8
1956	16.5	29.2	11.5	22.4	14.3	26.3	7.9	16.5
1957	18.3	31.6	13.1	24.8	16.2	29.0	9.6	19.5
1958	9.3	14.9	4.1	7.1	7.6	12.5	0.2	0.3
1959	16.2	24.2	10.8	17.6	14.5	22.3	7.2	12.4
1960	20.2	28.3	14.7	22.3	18.2	26.3	10.7	17.3

Notes:

a. Nonagricultural population assumed to be 25.5 per cent of total population in 1949 (Table 5, Estimate I).

b. Nonagricultural population assumed to be 23.0 per cent of total population in 1949 (Table 5, Estimate II).

Sources:

See text.

NONAGRICULTURAL UNEMPLOYMENT

Estimates of male nonagricultural unemployment are presented in Table 17. No attempt is made to estimate female unemployment, because there is no way to estimate the number of the female population who seek employment. In an economy like China's, housewives have to do a considerable amount of work, and hence may be regarded as self-employed.

The procedure involved in estimating nonagricultural male unemployment is rather simple. Female nonagricultural employment (roughly estimated in Table 18) is deducted from total nonagricultural employment to obtain male employment. The male nonagricultural labor force has been estimated in Table 9. Unemployment is derived as the residual between labor force and employment. Thus it includes both involuntary and voluntary unemployment. Since yearly data are used, seasonal unemployment is not measured. Needless to say, the unemployment figures themselves tell nothing about the nature or causes of unemployment—whether it is frictional, structural, due to fluctuations in production, or due to planning errors or unforeseen developments (witness the presumably unexpected rapid urban growth).

Alternative estimates of unemployment have been made, reflecting the uncertainty of the reliability of basic data. Estimate I of Table 17 has the largest number of unemployed, because it is based on a larger nonagricultural labor force. Estimate IV has the smallest unemployment because of the smaller labor force figure used. For all four estimates, the employment data are the same; it may also be noted that all four estimates are based on official population data. If Aird's estimates of population are used, the amount of unemployment would be considerably more in each of the four estimates. (It may be recalled that Aird estimated the official census figure in 1953 to have been undercounted by 5 to 15 per cent.)

It is difficult to say which of the four estimates is closer to reality, except to note that Estimate IV is essentially based on official concepts and data. To the extent that the official agricultural population data are on the high side, Estimate IV may be regarded as a conservative estimate of nonagricultural unemployment. Unfortunately, no unemployment data for comparable underdeveloped countries are available to check against the figures as shown in Table 17. However, in Ceylon it was estimated that in 1959-60 the unemployed constituted a little over 10 per cent of the labor force. The rates in the rural and urban areas were, respectively, a little under 10 per cent and a little over 14 per cent. In East Pakistan in 1955 the rate of unemployment was 10 per cent in large towns and 6 per cent in smaller urban areas. The urban rate of unemployment in Indonesia was 7 per cent in 1958. There were high levels of unemployment, of the order of some 10-20 per cent of the labor force, in British Guiana, Trinidad, Jamaica and some other islands of the Caribbean region during the 1950's.

TABLE 18

NONAGRICULTURAL EMPLOYMENT: FEMALE
(thousands, at year-end)

	1949	1950	1951	1952	1953	1954	1955	1956	1957	1958	1959
1. Workers and employees	600	1,224	1,224	1,848	2,132	2,435	2,473	3,266	3,286	7,000	8,286
2. State farms and forestry	—[a]	—	—	—	—	—	74	87	99	700	700
3. Nonagricultural workers and employees	600	1,224	1,224	1,848	2,132	2,435	2,399	3,179	3,187	6,300	7,586
4. Handicrafts	1,604	1,981	1,989	2,018	2,134	2,441	2,247	2,000	2,192	795	
5. Salt extraction	130	130	130	130	130	130	200	200	200	350	
6. Fishing	80	120	127	134	140	147	154	150	150	650	
7. Transportation: junks	91	91	91	91	91	91	91	86	86	90	
8. Trade, food and drink	831	836	945	866	827	738	606	608	609	430	
9. Personal and professional services	1,500	1,500	1,500	1,500	1,500	1,500	1,500	1,500	1,500	1,500	
10. Total nonworkers and employees	4,236	4,658	4,782	4,739	4,822	5,047	4,798	4,544	4,737	3,815	3,815
11. Total	4,836	5,882	6,006	6.587	6,954	7,482	7,197	7,723	7,924	10,115	11,401

Notes:

a. Assumed to be negligible.

Sources:

Line 1: 1949, 1952-1958, *Ten Great Years* (p. 161). 1959, *JMJP,* March 8, 1960, cited in Emerson (1965b, p. 25). 1950-51, average of 1949 and 1952.

Line 2: Emerson (1965b, p. 25). 1956 assumed to be the average of 1955 and 1957.

Line 3: Difference between Line 1 and Line 2.

Line 4: Assumed to be 27.4 per cent of individual and cooperative handicraftsmen as given in Table 10. The proportion is the same as given in Teng Ying-ch'ao, 1956.

Line 5: For 1955, 1957 and 1958, Emerson (1965b, p. 25). 1949-1954, assumed to be same proportion of total employment in salt extraction (Table 15) as in 1955. 1956, assumed the same as in 1955.

Line 6: 1955, 1957 & 1958, Emerson (1965b, p. 25). 1949-1954, assumed to be same proportion of total employment in fishing as in 1955. 1956, assumed to be the same as 1957.

Line 7: Assumed to be 10 per cent of total employment in junks (Table 10), same assumption is made by Emerson (1965b, p. 25). The assumption is made in view of the information given by Buck 1937, p. 372) for 1929-1933.

Line 8: Sum of (a) peddlers as given in Liu and Yeh (1965, p. 207) and (b) Emerson's trade, food and drink industry as given in Emerson (1965b, p. 25). For (b) Emerson gives estimates only for 1955, 1957 and 1958. For 1949-1954, assumed to be same proportion in total employment in the traditional sector of the industry as in 1955. (Total employment figures taken from Emerson (1965a, p. 133). For 1956, average of 1955 and 1957.

Line 9: 1952-1957, Liu and Yeh (1965, p. 207); for other years, assumed.

In Chile, an unemployment rate of about 6 to 8 per cent of the labor force has prevailed in recent years. In Egypt the unemployment rate in large cities was about 7 per cent in 1957-58 (ILO, 1964, pp. 22-24).

Obviously, when unemployment is estimated as a residual, there is an enormous risk of error. Even a small margin of error in labor force or employment data may have a substantial effect on unemployment figures. Our labor force and employment data are far from being firm. However, the estimates in Table 17 suggest two broad generalizations: (1) there was considerable amount of unemployment in every year, and (2) unemployment declined in the recovery years (1949-51) and then went up increasingly until 1958 when the problem was temporarily solved. Thereafter it resumed an upward course.

Scattered information indicates that the Communists recognized the existence of unemployment. It has often been reported that the new regime inherited a total of four million unemployed persons in 1949, presumably in the urban areas (*Ten Great Years,* p. 157). From 1950 to the end of 1953, a total of 2.07 million of the unemployed are said to have found jobs through government assistance (Hsing Yu-hung, 1954). It is also reported that during the first six years of the regime, the government found jobs for some 2.58 million formerly unemployed persons in the urban areas (*Shih-shih shou-tse,* 1956, p. 32). By 1957, it is further reported, only 70,000 persons remained unemployed out of the original four million (Hsu Kang, 1958). In his report on the First Five-Year Plan in 1955, Li Fu-ch'un (1956, p. 50) recognized the problem of unemployment inherited from the past and suggested that it might not be entirely solved until the second or third five-year plan.

From these reports it can be inferred that the problem of unemployment was not a matter of inheritance from the past; after 1949 there was an enormous increase in employment outside agriculture, and it is difficult to believe that it would take a number of years to find employment for the four million unemployed in 1949. In fact, in the original version of the *Draft Outlines of Agricultural Development,* the problem of unemployment was also recognized, but no reference was made to the past. It was merely stated that the unemployment problem in the urban areas would be solved in five or seven years beginning with 1956 (Chang Kai-fan, 1956).

No official figure for total unemployment has ever been published, but the following report is revealing. According to a survey in the spring of 1956, covering 74 cities in the province of Anhwei (Chang Kai-fan, 1956), it was found that there was a total of 93,183 unemployed persons. In this total there were, it was indicated, 30,377 women who should not have been regarded as unemployed but should be on social relief, and 9,755 who had lost their ability to work. Thus, the truly unemployed, according to the report, were only 53,051, constituting 2.6 per cent of the urban population. Based on the same sex ratio and age composition as given in Table 2, the total unemployed would be about 9 per cent of the male population (aged 15-59).[25] Probably the figure for the unemployed included a small number of females, but there is little doubt that male unemployment was considerable in the urban areas in the province of Anhwei. (If we include the reported number of disabled persons in unemployment, the total unemployed would be almost 11 per cent of total male population, aged 15-59. The percentage would be even higher if male labor force, rather than male population, were used as the denominator.) Unfortunately, no such reported figures have been found for other provinces.

The reported rate of urban unemployment in Anhwei in 1956 is lower than our lowest estimate (IV), but it should be remembered that our non-agricultural unemployment includes both urban and rural areas. Furthermore, whether Anhwei is representative of the entire country cannot be ascertained.

That the rate of unemployment became increasingly higher after the initial recovery years can also be explained. But it can hardly be explained purely as a result of statistical biases. It is likely that our male labor force is underestimated through time, largely because of the probability that the migrants to the cities included a higher proportion of adult males than in the total population. As for employment estimates, the degree of underestimation was higher in earlier years. Thus, the biases due to these two sources would understate the rising unemployment trend. Also, we held constant the employment figures for certain years for some traditional sectors; if employment in these sectors actually declined, then we would again understate the rates of unemployment through time. If it grew, then we would overstate the trend; but to nullify the increasing tendency of unemployment (as shown in Table 17) would require improbable growth rates in employment in the traditional sectors. For most of these traditional sectors, there are reported figures on employment for later years. High growth rates would imply that employment in the initial years had been improbably low.

Thus, there must be factors other than statistical bias to explain the course of unemployment. Since a full explanation cannot be given here, it may suffice to note that the trend of unemployment was essentially a result of the interplay of supply and demand. According to official statistics, the rate of economic growth in 1949-52 was higher than for any other years before 1958; rapid increase in employment should be expected, since much of the increased economic activity was the result of applying more labor to existing capacities. During the First Five-Year Plan period, the rate of increase in national income slowed down, and so did the rate

25. Total urban population, 2.04 million; male population (aged 15-59), 29.5 per cent of total population.

of increase in nonagricultural employment. The latter averaged only 1.3 per cent by our estimate and 1.5 per cent by those of Emerson and of Liu and Yeh. This slow increase may be explained by the overall economic development strategy which gave high priority to modern, capital-intensive industrial projects. At the same time, there was a large increase in the supply of nonagricultural labor because of the unexpectedly rapid increase in urban population, which grew at an average rate of 5.2 per cent during the First Five-Year Plan period. Since in 1952 there was already considerable unemployment, the higher rate of growth in labor supply than in employment would naturally result in greater unemployment. The Great Leap in 1958 cut down unemployment considerably, but the economic slump afterward put it back on an upward course, because industrial production was slowed down while labor force continued to grow.

Emerson (1961, p. 73) has tried, on the basis of some reported information, to divide nonagricultural employment into urban and rural components. He then compares urban employment with urban population (thus avoiding the problem of determining the size of the nonagricultural population) and concludes that "the rate of growth of the urban population exceeded that of nonagricultural employment throughout the First Five-Year Plan" (1961, p. 75). His conclusion confirms our observation on the trend of nonagricultural unemployment.

The Liu and Yeh estimate of nonagricultural unemployment, though conceptually different from ours, also supports the two generalizations mentioned above. According to their estimate (1965, p. 102), male nonagricultural unemployment for the age group 12-64 years grew from 25 million in 1952 to 32 million in 1957, or from 34 per cent of labor force in 1952 to 38 per cent in 1957. Of the 25 million males unemployed in 1952, 18 million were in rural areas; only 7 million were in urban areas. For 1957, 21 million were in rural areas, while 11 million were in urban areas.

The difference between our estimate and that of Liu and Yeh's can be reconciled. Aside from the difference in employment estimates (which have been explained above), there is a major difference in the estimate of the nonagricultural labor force. We both use official population data, but Liu and Yeh regard 12-64 years as the working age. More important, the relative size of nonagricultural population which Liu and Yeh imply for 1952-57 differs greatly from what we use. According to their estimate, nonagricultural population constituted about 38.5 per cent (in 1952) and 40.1 per cent (in 1957) of the total population. This high proportion for nonagricultural population follows from their concept of agricultural population and their estimate of agricultural production. They derive agricultural population by deducting "the number of man-labor units engaged in farm subsidiary work" from the total of those both in agricultural pursuits only and in subsidiary work. Thus, their agricultural population constituted about 69.4 per cent of the total population in 1933 (Liu and Yeh, 1965, p. 102). By our concept, agricultural population included the total of those in agricultural pursuits only as well as those who also had subsidiary work. Calculated in this way, Liu and Yeh's agricultural population would be 73.1 per cent of total population in 1933 (1965, p. 102), the proportion given by C. C. Chang, as noted above.

Liu and Yeh obtain nonagricultural population by deducting agricultural population from the total. For 1952, they estimate agricultural population on the assumption that it increased from 1933 to 1952 at the same rate as agricultural output over the same period (101 per cent for 1952, with 1933 = 100). For 1953-57, agricultural population is derived on the same basis. Taking Liu and Yeh's assumption, our estimates of agricultural population and nonagricultural unemployment thus would seem to imply either a decline in productivity or substantial underemployment in agriculture, for our agricultural population increased much faster than agricultural production from the 1930's to the 1950's.

III. UTILIZATION AND POLICY

STRUCTURAL SHIFT AND DISGUISED UNEMPLOYMENT

In the years of Communist rule it has been claimed that China has undergone drastic economic changes and has experienced extraordinarily rapid economic development. Official statistics show that national income increased at an average annual rate of 9 per cent in 1952-57 and industrial production (in terms of gross value) at nearly 25 per cent in 1949-57 (*Ten Great Years,* pp. 16, 18). These claims may be questioned, but independent estimates by scholars in the West also show rather rapid development. For example, Liu and Yeh (1965, p. 87) have estimated that the national income of China increased at 6 per cent a year in 1952-57 (in 1952 prices) and that factory production increased by 21 per cent a year from 1952 to 1957. Such rapid development is usually associated with a shift in the composition of output as well as employment; that is, the share of industry (vs. agriculture) rises both in total output and in total employment.

In the Chinese case, the shift in output is clear; according to official data, the share of industrial production increased from 30 per cent of total industrial and agricultural production in 1949 to 57 per cent in 1957 (*Ten Great Years,* p. 15). Liu and Yeh's estimates show that the share of the modern nonagricultural sectors in net domestic product (in 1952 prices) increased from 28.8 per cent in 1952 to 41.2 per cent in

1957 (1965, p. 89).[26] But no significant shift in employment has taken place. What Colin Clark used to call "Sir William Petty's Law of Economic Progress" was evidently not applicable. The proportion of nonagricultural employment in the labor force showed a modest increase during the early, largely recovery, years from 1949 to 1953, then became stable at a level somewhat lower than in 1953. It was not until the Great Leap in 1958 that the proportion rose very sharply, but also very briefly. It declined in 1959 and 1960 and probably declined even further in 1961-64, for nonagricultural employment was, at best, perhaps the same as in 1960, while the labor force continued to increase. The share of nonagricultural employment in the total labor force is given in Table 19.

TABLE 19

PROPORTION OF NONAGRICULTURAL EMPLOYMENT TO TOTAL CIVILIAN LABOR FORCE, 1949-1960 (per cent)

	Male (ages 15-59) [a]	Both sexes (ages 15-59) [b]
1949	19.1	14.9
1950	20.7	12.9
1951	22.6	13.8
1952	23.3	14.1
1953	24.1	14.6
1954	22.9	14.1
1955	21.7	13.3
1956	22.3	13.7
1957	21.6	13.4
1958	28.5	17.5
1959	26.4	16.6
1960	25.9	16.3

Notes:

a. Male nonagricultural employment in total male civilian labor force, ages 15-59. The latter is obtained by deducting from total male population (15-59) the following: 3 million in armed forces, 1 per cent as disabled, and male students (age 15 and over).

b. Total nonagricultural employment in total civilian labor force, ages 15-59. The latter is obtained in the same manner as in a, except both sexes (age 15 and over) are included.

Sources:

Tables 7, 8, 10, and 18.

The lack of a structural shift in manpower allocation is not difficult

26. Modern nonagricultural sectors include factories, mining, utilities, construction, modern transportation and communications, trading stores, restaurants, and modern financial institutions.

to explain. Although the rate of capital formation has been exceedingly high—about 20 per cent of domestic product in net terms and in 1952 prices in 1952-57 (Liu and Yeh, 1965, p. 74)—the choice of technique and scale was such that investment was put mainly into large and highly capital-intensive projects. The result was an increasing amount of investment per worker and a rising productivity of labor. But given this investment criterion, the rate of capital formation, high as it was, was not high enough to absorb even the nonagricultural labor force.

The choice of technique was probably dictated by the fact that the backbone of industrial development was the 156 projects designed and built with the help of the Russians—projects that were modern, large-scale and capital-intensive. We need not consider here why Communist China adopted such projects or whether there were other alternatives available (given the objectives of the regime). The fact remains that China did not have enough resources to build ultramodern industries and, at the same time, create enough jobs for the labor force.[27]

The implications of the Chinese pattern of development (that is, rapid development without a shift from agricultural to nonagricultural employment) are fairly obvious. Given fixed land area and growing population, the land-population ratio must decline; this presents serious difficulties for agricultural development, especially in an already crowded country.

It is often suggested that the land-population ratio in China was already so low in the 1930's that there was a considerable amount of disguised unemployment in the agricultural sector. (Disguised unemployment is usually defined as existing when, other things being equal, output can be maintained or even increased with a lesser amount of labor; in other words, when the marginal productivity of labor is zero or negative.) Although this assertion cannot be easily substantiated, it is safe to say that agricultural labor, at least on a year-round basis, was considerably underutilized.

According to Buck's study for 1929-33, crop acres per man-equivalent for "very large" farms were 4.0, whereas for "medium farms" it was 2.1, and for "small farms" only 1.5; yet there was no significant difference in crop yields per acre in the various size-groups of farms (Buck, 1937, p. 279). It is tempting to infer from this that there was under-utilization of labor or even disguised underemployment in small- and medium-sized farms, but Buck's data also show that there were factors that at least partly contributed to the greater efficiency of labor in large farms: the larger average size of parcels and fields, the greater percentage of farm area in productive use, and the use of more fertilizer per unit of land. It should also be noted that although crop yields were about the same for various sizes of farms, the percentage of net income from other than farm

27. For an interesting discussion of the investment strategy of Communist China, see K. C. Yeh (1965).

sources was larger for small and medium farms than for large ones. (For small farms it was 21 per cent, whereas for "very large farms" it was only 9 per cent.)

At any rate, the fact that labor was less efficient in small farms does not necessarily mean that its marginal productivity was zero.[28] In fact, Buck's data on labor shortages in busy seasons strongly suggest that output could not very well have been maintained if some labor had been removed from the farms. According to Buck, nearly two-thirds of the 260 localities that were surveyed reported insufficient labor at harvest time, over one-fourth too little labor at planting time, and one-eighth a shortage of workers for irrigation (1937, p. 299).

On a year-round basis, however, there was considerable idleness among farm workers. According to Buck, the average was 1.7 months of idleness per able-bodied man (over 15 and under 60 years of age). The winter months of November, December, January and February were responsible for 80 per cent of the idle time. (Note also that idleness among able-bodied men was only slightly greater on the small farms than on the large) (Buck, 1937, p. 295). Seasonal idleness was also reported by another, probably less reliable, source; in north China the idle time of farmers who did not have outside employment was said to have lasted from five to six months a year, and for the whole country the idle time of farmers in the age group 15 to 54 years was equivalent to the full-time unemployment of 55 million farmers.[29] As Buck noted, the Chinese farmers only partially met the problem of seasonal idleness by finding subsidiary work either on the farm or in cities.

Was there rural disguised unemployment in the early 1950's when population had been increasing by nearly one per cent a year since 1930?[30] Again no conclusive evidence is available. It has been reported that there was considerable "surplus" labor in the mid-1950's: farmers spent only two-thirds of their time directly on farms; and there was a 26 per cent surplus of labor in six agricultural cooperatives in Hopei; 30 per cent in 18 agricultural coperatives in Shensi; 17 per cent in 497 agricultural cooperatives in Kiangsi; and 35 per cent in 18 agricultural cooperatives in Szechwan (Li Yuan-chen, 1957, p. 17). ("Surplus" is apparently defined in terms of time not used on farm work). According to a larger survey of 26,000 agricultural cooperatives in 1955, a "labor unit"

28. Commenting on Buck's data, Viner (1957, p. 20) has noted that "Buck's data do not suffice to show that the marginal productivity of labor was less on the smaller farms than on the larger ones, and certainly do not suffice to show that there is zero marginal productivity of labor anywhere in the Chinese economy."

29. These estimates were made in an unpublished memorandum, "Proposals for Industrial Research and Training: A Phase of Rural Reconstruction," prepared in 1933 by the Industrial Association of North China. See Fang Hsien-ting and Wu Chih (1933).

30. Assuming Chinese population had reached 500 million by 1933. See Liu and Yeh (1965, p. 171).

only worked 96 "labor days" a year, with half of a year's time being "unproductive" (Li, 1957, p. 17). It was also reported, however, that for the "full labor units" idleness was seasonal, whereas there was a year-round surplus of "half labor" and "subsidiary labor" (Li, 1957, p. 20). Since a "full labor unit" refers to a male between 18 and 50 years of age or a female between 18 and 45 years of age (Huang Meng-fan, 1956) it is doubtful that there was much disguised unemployment as defined above. In fact, a shortage of labor in busy seasons has also been reported, although the shortage was sometimes blamed on regional immobility of labor due to the elimination of labor markets.[31]

Whether or not there was rural *disguised* unemployment in the strict sense, there is little doubt that *seasonal* unemployment had reached such proportions that a fuller utilization of manpower was necessary. It is reported that the peasants asked for more work (in order to increase their income), but the agricultural cooperatives were not able to meet their demands (*JMJP,* 1959). When no opportunities for employment were available in the nonagricultural sector, because of considerable unemployment there too, new measures had to be adopted.

THE STRATEGY OF GRAND SUBSTITUTION

The Great Leap Forward, which was launched at the end of 1957 and gained full momentum in 1958 and 1959, was, according to the Chinese expression, a large-scale attempt to "walk on two legs" to speed up economic development at a rate of 20 to 30 per cent a year in industrial growth (Chou En-lai, 1959, p. 22). The "two legs" were simultaneous development in industry and agriculture; in heavy and light industries; in centrally and locally managed enterprises; in large, medium and small enterprises; in modern and native technologies; in centralized leadership and mass participation (Hsu Li-ch-un, 1959, p. 2). Simultaneous development did not mean development at the same rate, however, for industry was still given priority over agriculture, heavy industries over light, large enterprises over medium and small ones, modern techniques over native, central enterprises over local ones.[32]

But it was pointed out the simultaneity was necessary for rapid development because of the complementary nature of different kinds of development. For instance, agriculture provides raw materials, markets and a source of capital for industry; heavy industry makes possible the mech-

31. It is reported that in the past, farmers were able in peak season to obtain help from other areas where the peak season might be at a different time. But such "labor markets" were eliminated as a result of agricultural cooperativization. See Li Yuan-chen (1957, p. 17).

32. The share of state investment in industry in 1958-1959 was larger than ever before, while that in agriculture increased only slightly. Total investment in light industry in 1958 doubled over 1957, but investment in heavy industry in creased even more sharply. See K. C. Yeh (1965, pp. 33, 35).

anization of agriculture; light industry is necessary to improve living standards and hence incentives to work. Large and modern industries are essential for products that require advanced technology, high quality and large quantity; small and native industries require less capital and can be established in large number in a short time, satisfying many needs of the people and training skilled labor in the process.[33]

How was this simultaneous development on a broad front possible in view of the scarcity of capital? The answer is that the capital was still to be used primarily for the development of heavy industry, while labor was to be the main input for other development. The strategy was one of large-scale substitution of labor for capital, a massive mobilization of the under-utilized manpower, or what Nurkse called "hidden rural savings." Thus, in industry the establishment of small, highly labor-intensive indigenous plants was an outstanding feature of the Great Leap, while in agriculture, intensive farming and multiple operations were the guiding principle. Intensive farming was simply intensive use of labor as required by the "eight principles" of increasing agricultural production.[34] Multiple operations meant that the peasants were urged, especially in off seasons, to engage in fields of production other than farming, such as forestry, animal-raising, fishing, subsidiary work and rural basic construction (irrigation projects, road building, etc.). Such intensive use of labor was the very essence of the Great Leap; it was designed for the dual purposes of solving the problem of unemployment (especially seasonal) and at the same time accelerating economic development. All this had been attempted before, but the grand scale and manner in which the Great Leap was launched made it unique.

It is not necessary here to examine the details of how labor was used in the Great Leap; the following reported statistics should suffice to show the general picture:[35]

1. In 1958, there were founded some 300,00 small, indigenous industrial establishments (in manufacturing and mining); 90,000 of them were administered at the *hsien* level or above, 210,000 at the *hsiang* level (or rural communes). An estimated total of 4.4 million workers were newly recruited to staff these establishments. (This may be compared with about 6 million workers newly recruited in 1958 to staff the modern sector of industry) (Emerson, 1965a, p. 86). In addition, by the end of 1959 some 10 million peasants had participated in temporary industrial work during the off seasons (*Kuang-ming jih-pao,* July, 1960).

33. For an exposition of this argument, see, for example, Hsu Li-chun (1959, pp. 3-6).

34. The "eight principles" are: improve soil; increase fertilizer; irrigate; improve seeds; practice close-planting; protect plants (insecticides); provide better farm management; and improve implements and tools.

35. For a discussion of utilization of labor, see, for example, Orleans (1961) and Emerson (1961).

2. There was an increase of 3.4 million construction workers in 1958, most of whom went into local building enterprises (Emerson, 1965a, p. 88).

3. "Street" and urban commune industry employed in 1959 and 1960 a total of 2 million workers, of whom 85 per cent were women (Emerson, 1965b, p. 9).

4. Some 60 million persons were reportedly involved, at the end of 1958, in the movement of smelting iron and steel in backyard furnaces (Chang Fo-chien, 1958, p. 30); presumably this fantastic figure includes all persons who participated in all phases of the movement: searching for coal, iron and other material, transportation, constructing furnaces, etc.[36]

5. There was a reported total of more than 100 million persons engaged in water conservation work in the winter of 1957-58 (*JMJP,* May 3, 1958), of whom 73 million were women. More than 67 million women reportedly worked on afforestation projects in 1958; they probably constituted more than half of all participants (Emerson, 1965b, p. 20).

6. In the winter of 1959-60, some 70 million persons were reportedly engaged in water conservation work; 30 million in forestry, animal raising, fisheries and subsidiary work; and 15 million in public welfare services (T'an Chen-lin, 1960, p. 4).

7. More than 7 million persons were mobilized in the fall of 1959 for road building and short-distance transportation (Emerson, 1965a, p. 94).

Although the accuracy of the above statistics is highly questionable, there is little doubt that in 1958 and 1959 a great number of persons, especially women, were mobilized, the primary strategy being to utilize rural labor in both agricultural and nonagricultural activities, especially those off-season. Apparently the peasants were asked to do too much nonfarming work; only 50 per cent of the manpower was actually engaged in farm production (T'an Chen-lin, 1960, p. 4). As was indicated later, at least 80 per cent of rural labor was necessary for farm work in the busy seasons (Ma Wen-jui, 1961, p. 11). Thus, in the Great Leap years a severe labor shortage was widely reported. The peasants were worked so hard that it was necessary for the highest authorities to issue directives that they should work no more than 12 hours a day.

How successful was the strategy of "walking on two legs"? Any attempt to evaluate the result of the intensive utilization of labor in the Great Leap years is complicated by the fact that many other things also happened at the same time. The people's communes which were introduced in 1958 probably facilitated the efforts to mobilize rural labor, but must also have dampened the peasants' incentive to work by the confiscation of private plots, the more or less egalitarian distribution system, and the drastic change in family life. The Great Leap years also saw the down-

36. For a description of the movement, see Academy of Sciences (1958).

grading of technical expertise; the party cadres gained control of production in the name of mass participation and "politics takes command," and pushed the campaign so ambitiously or fanatically that many basic technical constraints were neglected.

The effects of labor intensification were further blurred by the natural calamities in three consecutive years 1959-61, and by the Soviet withdrawal of technical personnel in 1960. Agricultural production in 1959 was also in part affected by a planned reduction of sown area, a mistake in planning caused by false reports of production increases in 1958.

Thus the efforts to use labor intensively were made at a time when many other events also took place—events not necessarily related to labor intensification. The economic slump following the Great Leap offers no proof that the strategy of intensive utilization of labor was wrong. But the technical mistakes associated with party control over production seem to suggest that a massive mobilization of under-utilized labor without the guidance of trained personnel is likely to result in a waste of resources.

A quantitative measurement of the result of the Great Leap is made particularly difficult by the poor quality of official statistics; the statistical system disintegrated as the Leap began. But if one regards the statistics for the industrial sector as reliable enough to indicate at least the rough trend of development, the basic strategy of the Great Leap did yield some positive results. The gross value of industrial production is officially reported to have increased sharply in 1958, and to a lesser degree in 1959. On the basis of the sharp increase in the incremental output-capital ratio in 1958,[37] it is reasonable to assume that the increase in production was partly brought about by intensive use of labor, although both labor productivity and the quality of output sharply declined. If net value added in industry as estimated by Liu and Yeh is used rather than the official gross value, the incremental output-capital ratio also rose in 1958, though to a much lesser degree.[38]

MANPOWER AND POPULATION POLICY: SOME CONCLUDING REMARKS

Our estimates of employment and labor force suggest that the problem of unemployment and underemployment became increasingly serious after the initial recovery years. Despite the high rate of capital formation and

37. To compute incremental output-capital ratio, fixed investment is used for total investment in industry (*Ten Great Years,* p. 57) after deflation by the price index for basic construction given in Liu and Yeh (1965, p. 235). The index for 1957 is used for 1958. For gross value of industrial output, see *Ten Great Years,* (p. 76). Thus the incremental output-capital ratio was 8.02 for 1958, as compared with 1.64 for 1957. For previous years: 9.18 (1953); 3.11 (1954); 1.03 (1955) and 4.39 (1956). It does not make material difference if a one-year lag is allowed for investment to take effect.

38. Based on data given in Liu and Yeh (1965, p. 66).

industrial growth, there were not enough jobs to provide the increasing labor force with adequate employment. This factor may be regarded as an important explanation, not only of the strategy of the Great Leap, which was basically a massive utilization of labor, but also of the population policy.

The debate on the need for birth control began, at the latest, in 1954. A determined birth control campaign was launched in 1957 and lasted until May, 1959, when it was called off (Chandrasekhar, 1961, p. 143). No official explanation was given for the change in policy. It may be that the grossly exaggerated achievements of the Great Leap, as reported by local cadres, were an important factor. After all, the Malthusian trap is primarily based on the law of diminishing returns, but if labor can be used to create capital and to increase land (in terms of sown area), the very foundation of the law of diminishing returns is invalidated. There were numerous local reports on how output was increased by intensive use of labor, and on how much labor shortage there was. A worker was not just a consumer but also a producer; and he could produce a lot more than he could consume. Thus, "a large population is a good thing."

But the actual performance of the economy began to deteriorate in 1959 or 1960, and a serious economic slump set in. The factors were many (the commune system, the weather, the withdrawal of Soviet personnel, the extremism of the cadres).

It is not clear whether the Communists have since lost faith in the use of labor as a source of wealth. In fact, despite the change in basic development policy (shift from industry to agriculture), the call for labor intensification has continued. Population control was renewed in 1962, but it has not been carried out as vigorously as in 1957-58.[39] Regardless of population policy, the enormous size of the labor force makes it certain that the Communist regime will not be able to equip it with modern means of production in a short period and will have to continue to "walk on two legs"—as China had for decades before the Communists came.[40] It will be a long walk.

39. According to a *New York Times* report (April 27, 1966), strict measures have been recently adopted to control the birth rate. For instance, food and cloth allowances usually granted at the birth of a child were reported to be withheld in the case of a fourth child, and even for the third child in some areas. Abortion, sterilization, the use of contraceptives, and late marriage (30 years of age for men and 25 for women) were reported to be encouraged by government officials.

40. For economic dualism in pre-Communist China, see the author's *Foreign Investment and Economic Development in China, 1840-1937* (Cambridge, Mass.: Harvard University Press, 1965), Chapter 7.

APPENDIX TO CHAPTER 5

This appendix indicates how the items for non-"workers and employees" given in Table 10 were estimated.

In handicrafts, there are included handicraft workships, handicraft cooperatives and individual handicraftsmen. Workers in handicraft workshops are included in "workers and employees" by official definition. In addition, there are also housewives and farmers who are engaged in part-time handicrafts. It has been estimated that the full-time equivalent of these part-time handicraft workers numbered 4.18 million in 1952, 4.26 million in 1953, 4.30 million in 1954, 4.39 million in 1955, 4.51 million in 1956, and 4.56 million in 1957 (Liu and Yeh, 1965, p. 196). Although Liu and Yeh include these full-time equivalents in the total of handicrafts, they are not included in nonagricultural employment as presented in Table 10; they would be included in agricultural employment according to our definition. It may be noted that according to official statistics on handicrafts, handicraft work for one's household use as well as for other consumers who supplied raw materials was, until 1957, included in farm subsidiary production which, in turn was a part of agricultural production (Wang Keng-chin, 1957). Since 1958, however, handicraft work for one's own use was no longer included in agricultural output; presumably it was then regarded as a part of output of commune-industries.

The figures on individual and cooperative handicraftsmen for 1949 and 1952-55, as presented in Table 10, are all reported figures and are used by Emerson and Liu and Yeh (1952-55). The figures for 1956 and 1957 call for explanation. During the peak of the socialization drive in 1956, a large number of individual handicraftsmen were organized into members of handicraft cooperatives; some joined factories and hence were classified as "workers and employees"; some remained as individual handicraftsmen; and a considerable number were absorbed by agricultural producers cooperatives. According to one account (*TCKTTH,* 1956), by the end of March, 1956, a total of 4,300,000 handicraftsmen had joined cooperatives, accounting for 88 per cent of all the handicraftsmen who would be made members of cooperatives by the Central Handicraft Administration Bureau. (Thus, the total number of handicraftsmen to be organized by the bureau was 4,890,000.) In addition, there were 2,400,000 handicraftsmen who were to be organized by the Ministries of Agriculture, Commerce, and Local Industry. Thus, the total handicraftsmen organized (or to be organized) as of the end of March, 1956, was 7.3 million. This is the figure used by Liu and Yeh as the total of individual and cooperative handicraftsmen in 1956.

But what happened to the above-noted 2.4 million handicraftsmen?

Those whose work was closely connected with commerce and industry were transferred to private or state-private joint enterprises, and hence classified as workers and employees. They were small in number, however. The largest part of the 2.4 million joined the agricultural producers cooperatives. The question arises as to whether they should still be classified as handicraftsmen. Reported figures (Emerson, 1965a, p. 146) show that there were 5.2 million cooperative handicraftsmen and 597,000 individual handicraftsmen (a total of 5.8 million) in 1956, and 5.9 million cooperative handicraftsmen and 670,000 individual handicraftsmen (a total of 6.6 million) in 1957. Thus, the reported figures for handicraftsmen do not seem to include those who had joined the agricultural producers cooperatives. These reported figures on cooperative and individual handicraftsmen are consistent with the reported gross output per handicraftsman and the total gross handicrafts output for 1957.[1] Emerson uses these reported figures.[2]

It was also reported, however, that there were 8 million professional handicraftsmen in 1957 (*TKP,* 1957). Apparently this figure included those who had joined the agricultural producer cooperatives in 1956. Liu and Yeh use this figure for 1957.

The crucial point is whether these handicraftsmen, after having joined the agricultural producers cooperatives, were still engaged primarily in

1. It was reported by Teng Chieh (1959) that in 1957 the output per worker of handicraft cooperatives was 2,194 *yuan,* whereas that per individual handicraftsman was 1,086 *yuan.* Multiplying these figures by the respective reported numbers of cooperative and individual handicraftsmen, the total gross value output would be 13.7 billion *yuan,* very close to the 13.4 billion *yuan* which was the reported gross value output of handicrafts in 1957 (*TGY,* p. 14).

2. In correspondence with the author, Emerson has stated very clearly why he used the reported figures. It was reported that 2.89 million persons were classified for the first time as "workers and employees" in 1956 but not considered as newly employed (*CHCC,* No. 3, March 9, 1957, p. 14). These persons were either previously employed in individual handicrafts, petty trade and peddling, and private business, or were capitalists in industry and commerce. Thus, there must be a reduction of about 3 million persons in these categories in order to avoid double counting. Since handicrafts and private trade were listed first among the occupations, they probably can be regarded as more important in terms of number of persons reclassified. Thus, Emerson's figures show a decline of 2.4 million handicraftsmen in the private sector in 1956 (individual and cooperative) (1965a, p. 134). Persons engaged in traditional forms of trade are estimated by Emerson to have declined by 700,000 in the same year (1965a, p. 130).

According to our account of the development of handicrafts, however, the number of individual handicraftsmen who were reclassified as workers and employees in 1956 was rather small, about 900,000 (Table 10, line 5). But the number of persons engaged in private trade declined by 1.3 million in the same year (Table 10, line 9).

Apparently the crucial difference between our estimate and Emerson's in this case lies largely in the treatment of the 2.4 million handicraftsmen who were to be organized by the Ministries of Agriculture, Commerce, and Local Industry, as noted in the Appendix. For reasons stated in the text, we believe that most of them joined the agricultural producers cooperatives; Emerson's figure implies that they were reclassified as workers and employees.

handicraft production. We assume that they were, and so should still be regarded as individual handicraftsmen. Thus we use (after Liu and Yeh) 7.3 million for 1956 and 8 million for 1957 as the total of individual and cooperative handicraftsmen. The figure for 1957 may be a little on the high side inasmuch as it may include some of the handicraftsmen who had joined factories and were classified as workers and employees.[3]

The reported total handicraft output increased by 16 per cent in 1956 and by 14 per cent in 1957; it would be difficult to account for such an increase (even after allowing for the reported increase in efficiency due to cooperativization) if one is to exclude (as the official definition apparently does) the output of those handicraftsmen who had joined agricultural producers cooperatives. At any rate, there is descriptive material indicating that these handicraftsmen continued to work at their crafts even after being absorbed by the agricultural producers cooperatives, though it is likely that they also participated in farm work during busy farm seasons (Teng Chieh, 1958, p. 28).

By the end of 1958 only 795,000 were still members of handicraft cooperatives (Teng Chieh, 1959a), the rest having been transferred to local factories (state-owned), cooperative factories, and commune industries. Assuming that the number of individual handicraftsmen remained the same as in 1957, that is, 2.1 million, the total number of individual and cooperative handicraftsmen would be 2.9 million at the end of 1958. The transfer of cooperative handicraftsmen to local factories, cooperative factories, and commune-run industries continued in 1959; by May of 1959, only about 700,000 remained in handicraft cooperatives (Teng Chieh, 1959b).

The number of persons engaged in salt extraction for 1952-57 is estimated from information given by Liu and Yeh (1965, pp. 194-195, 573-576).[4] It is found by taking the difference between the number of workers in native mining and the number in native coal mining, the latter being estimated on the basis of total output and output per worker. The number of workers so estimated for 1957 is about the same as that estimated by Emerson (1965a, p. 133). For earlier years, Emerson assumes that it was the same as in 1957. For fishing, all the figures are taken from Emerson; Liu and Yeh do not include this item in their estimates.

Information on the number of persons engaged in traditional transport is extremely scarce. The number of junks is reported for 1954-58, but the reported figures are not entirely consistent. For 1954 and 1955, the number of junks is given as 294,000 (Wang Ming-hsien and Yuan Hsing-

3. It was reported that in 1954 there were 8 million individual handicraftsmen (Teng Chieh, 1958, p. 8). As noted before, some of these were transferred to factories during socialization.

4. Workers in salt cooperatives were included as handicraftsmen for 1956 in data published in *Ten Great Years* (p. 30). They are not included in our estimates of individual and cooperative handicraftsmen as given in Table 9.

nan, 1955; Wang Shou-tao, 1955), which is the figure that Liu and Yeh (1965, p. 597) use for 1957. The reported number for 1956 (Yuan Hsing-nan, 1957) is 240,000 and that for 1957 (*KJJP,* 1958) is 250,000. Emerson (1965a, p. 151) uses the 1954 and 1957 reported figures for the respective years and makes an estimate for 1955 on the basis of the 1954 figure, allowing for a reported decline in junk tonnage from 3.1 million tons in 1954 to 2.9 million at some unspecified time before 1957. He uses the 1957 reported figure for 1956, and a reported figure (289,000) for 1958 (*JMJP,* Dec. 3, 1958).

In Table 10 we have used all the reported figures except 1956 and 1957. For these two years the figure 277,000 is used, representing a decline of about 6 per cent from 1954, in accordance with the reported decline in junk tonnage as noted above. During the socialization drive in 1956, a number of junks were transferred to agricultural producers cooperatives and apparently were not included in the reported number of junks. The reported junk tonnage seems to indicate, however, that these junks continued to be used for transportation, although some junk operators may have had to do farm work during peak farm seasons.

To estimate the number of operators of junks, Emerson uses a ratio of 4 persons per vessel, a ratio derived from the reported number of vessels and operators for 1958. The ratio used by Liu and Yeh is 3 per vessel, estimated from reported figures for 1955 on total number of junks and total number of operators and their dependents. However, another source (*KJJP,* 1958) which also gives the number of junks and operators, suggests a ratio of 3.1 workers per boat, a ratio we use for all years in Table 9. It may be noted that a ratio of 3 was used for the early 1930's by Ou Pao-san (1947, Vol. II, p. 184).

In order to estimate the net value added by old-fashioned transportation, Liu and Yeh assume that only 60 per cent of the reported junks were in use. This assumption is not used for our purpose on the belief that the idleness was seasonal. (Emerson also does not make any allowance for under-utilization). It should be noted here that the figures for junk operators as given in Table 10 are most probably underestimates. The reported figures for the number of junks are given as "based on incomplete statistics" and usually refer to wooden sailing vessels that navigate in inland waters. Whether vessels navigating in coastal waters are included is not clear. Besides, there must be other vessels than wooden sailing vessels. According to Ou Pao-san's estimate (1947, Vol. II, p. 181), which admittedly was based on incomplete and not very reliable data, there were in the 1930's as many as 988,000 boats and junks in all. Probably this figure included boats for fishing and for part-time home use; but it does seem to suggest that the reported figures we use for Table 9 are most likely underestimated, though the degree of underestimation cannot be ascertained.

Information on the number of persons employed as carters is also very incomplete. It was reported by Wang Shou-tao in 1957 (*Ta-kung pao*, Sept. 2) that there were 140,000 animal-drawn and 300,000 man-drawn carts in professional use. In addition, in the rural area there were 5 million animal-drawn carts and 10 million man-drawn carts of various types. It is assumed by Emerson (1965a, p. 150) that those who were engaged in carting in rural districts did so as a secondary occupation in slack farming seasons, and so he does not include them in his estimate on nonagricultural employment. He takes 10 per cent of carts in rural areas (both animal-drawn and man-drawn) as the basis for estimating the number of carters included in nonagricultural employment. The 10 per cent figure is based on a reported estimate that 90 per cent of all animal-drawn carts were absorbed by agricultural producers cooperatives in 1956. He makes no mention of the reported number of carts in professional use, as noted above.

Liu and Yeh (1965, p. 597), on the other hand, take the number of carts in professional use as those used in urban areas, and assume that in rural areas one-half of the animal-drawn carts and one-third of the man-drawn carts (or wheelbarrows, as they call them) were for hire. The number of carters per animal-drawn cart is taken to be 1.7 both by Emerson and Liu and Yeh, in accordance with reported figures. But for man-drawn carts, Emerson uses 1.5, whereas Liu and Yeh use 1.7. Furthermore, Liu and Yeh assume (on the basis of a reported figure) that only 71 per cent of all the carts were in use, whereas Emerson makes no such allowance.

In another source (Huang Hsiu-chuan, 1957, p. 11), it was reported that the number of animal-drawn carts participating in highway transportation declined by 21 per cent from the end of 1955 to the end of 1956. Since this 21 per cent is given to represent 91,900 carts, it may be calculated that the total number of such carts was 437,620 in 1955. The reason given for the decline was that as a result of agricultural cooperativization, there was more work in intensive farming, water conservation, and collection of fertilizer, and so there was more demand for the use of animals and carts. A great number of animal-drawn carts that had been used either for part-time or full-time transportation purposes were now used for agricultural production. In addition, some agricultural producers cooperatives did not give adequate pay to those who participated in transportation as a side occupation; in some other cases, the cadres did not permit the agricultural producers cooperatives to participate in transportation work, presumably because of a desire to increase agricultural production.

It was further suggested that participation in transportation, could increase the income of the agricultural producers cooperatives. Thus, it seems clear that the above-mentioned number (437,620) referred to the number of animal-drawn carts contributed to highway transportation in 1955 by the agricultural producers cooperatives. If our interpretation is correct, then the total number of animal-drawn carts may be obtained by adding up the number from the agricultural producers cooperatives and the number of professional animal-drawn carts. In Table 10, the number of professional animal-drawn carts is taken to be 140,000 (as given above) for 1955-58; the number of animal-drawn carts from the agricultural producers' cooperatives is taken to be 437,620 for 1955 and 345,720 for 1956-58 (reflecting a decline of 21 per cent from 1955). The number of carters per cart is taken to be 1.7 (Wang Shou-tao, 1955).

For the man-drawn carts, it may be calculated from the information that there were 1,070,000 animal-drawn and man-drawn carts used for highway transportation in 1958 (*JMJP,* 1958). Most probably, this figure refers to the carts from the agricultural producers cooperatives. Deducting the number of animal-drawn carts (345,720) from the total, the resultant number of man-drawn carts is 724,280 for 1958. This figure is also used for 1957 and 1956. For 1955, the figure 917,000 is used to reflect the same percentage increase as in the case of animal-drawn carts. The number of professional mandrawn carts is taken to be 300,000 for 1955-58. The number of carters per cart is assumed to be 1.7.

Our estimate (2.6 million in 1957) for the total number of carters (for both animal-drawn and man-drawn carts) is higher than Emerson's (1.7 million in 1957), largely because we include the professional carters. On the other hand, our estimate is lower than that of Liu and Yeh (5.8 million in 1957), largely because we only include a small portion of the carts that the agricultural producers cooperatives had—the portion they provided for highway transportation. It is possible that there were persons who worked as full-time carters within the agricultural producers cooperatives, but their number cannot be ascertained. It may be noted, however, that according to Buck's study (1937, p. 372) only 0.4 per cent of the rural male population (aged 7 and over) took up transportation as a full-time occupation. Applying this proportion to official data for 1957 (rural population constituted 86 per cent, and males in the age group 7-64 years were 40 per cent of the total), there would be only 0.88 million males as full-time transportation workers in the rural area.

According to our estimate, in 1957 1.7 million carters were provided by agricultural producers cooperatives to participate in highway transportation. Since the traditional form of transport was still dominant in short distance transportation in 1957, it seems plausible that more of the male population was in transportation than in the 1930's.

For trade and the food and drink industries, two groups make up the total number of workers who should be added to the "workers and employees" category. One is the difference between what might be called the reported total of employment in trade and the food and drink industry and the number of "workers and employees." The reported total of employment may be gathered together from various sources, as is done by Emerson (1965a, pp. 151-152).

The other component to be added to "workers and employees" is the number of rural peddlers. As Liu and Yeh (1965, pp. 199-202) have convincingly argued, the Communist-reported totals of peddlers actually do not include rural peddlers.[5] The figures for rural peddlers in 1952-57 as included in Table 10 are those estimated by Liu and Yeh, based primarily on official data. They declined from 4.2 million in 1952 to 2.8 million in 1957. When rural peddlers are added to the total employment figures as given by Emerson, the difference between Emerson's (adjusted) and Liu and Yeh's estimate of total employment in trade and the food and drink industry becomes insignificant except for 1957. For that year Liu and Yeh's total is 1.2 million more than Emerson's (adjusted). The difference lies largely in the interpretation of a reported total of employment of 8.5 million in the "financial and trade system." Liu and Yeh's interpretation is that this total did not include restaurants, whereas Emerson's did. In terms of Communist classification, restaurants are included in trade, but whether all statistical data are in accord with the standard classification is not clear.

5. In correspondence, Emerson has called my attention to the following: The census of private trade and of the food and drink industry taken in the fall of 1955 was to include rural trade as well as urban, according to Hsueh Mu-ch'iao (*TCKTTH* #8, August 7, 1955, pp. 16-18). The State Statistical Bureau summary of the development of the trade network in China (published in *TCKTTH* #18, September 29, 1956, pp. 7-10) reported that in 1955 there were 1.43 million trade "establishments" (*chi-k'ou*) in rural areas, employing a total of 2.42 million persons. There was no mention as to whether these 2.42 million persons included rural peddlers. The same summary, however, reported that there were 1.1 million persons employed in trading cooperatives. Even assuming these cooperatives were all in the rural areas, there would still be 1.3 million persons to be accounted for. It might, therefore, be assumed that these 1.3 million persons were, for the most part, rural peddlers.

Such speculation is interesting, but all the reported figures for rural peddlers as given by Liu and Yeh (1965, p. 200) exceed 2.67 million. This suggests that the 1.3 million figure is probably too small to be regarded as representing rural peddlers. There are no data on the number of rural traders who were neither peddlers nor employees of the cooperatives.

The two reasons that Liu and Yeh give to support their contention that the rural peddlers are not included in the State Statistical Bureau's totals are rather convincing. They have noted that in one Communist source (Chien Hua *et al., Chi-nien-lai wu-quo sze-ying kung-shang-yeh ti pien-hua,* Peking, 1957), the number of peddlers and private trading stores given is roughly the same as the State Statistical Bureau's figure but represents only a part of the national total. This source deals primarily with private industry and trade but includes only part of the small merchants and peddlers. It is not stated which part was included (p. 3). The second piece of evidence Li and Yeh cite is a statement by Hsu Ti-hsin, Director of the Central Administration of Industry and Commerce, indicating that in 1952 the number of workers in the private trading sector in the urban areas totaled 6.7 million, which comes very close to the State Statistical Bureau's total of 6.768 million (Liu and Yeh, 1965, p. 199).

It may be noted that the total number of persons engaged in trade and the food and drink industry in 1933 as estimated by Liu and Yeh (1965, p. 202) was 15 million, suggesting that the estimates in Table 10 are probably underestimates because of incomplete statistical coverage.

Statistical data on the number of employees in state and state-private joint financial institutions are available only for 1952, 1953 and 1955. Based on these data, the number of "workers and employees" is estimated by Emerson for 1952-1957 (1965a, p. 133). Added to "workers and employees" are the employees in the nonstate sector, which may be taken, as is done by Emerson, to mean rural credit cooperatives. The personnel of rural credit cooperatives may be estimated by multiplying the reported number of such cooperatives by the average number of personnel per cooperative (available for 1955 and 1956). The figures for the nonstate sector for 1954-57 as given in Table 9 are the figures so derived by Emerson. The total personnel in the nonstate sector for 1949-53 is assumed to be the same as that in 1952, namely, 230,000—an estimate derived from data reported by Liu and Yeh (1965, p. 206). Since total employment in the financial sector is rather small, the difference between Liu and Yeh's and Emerson's estimates is not significant.

The number of persons engaged in personal and professional services who should be added to the "workers and employees" category cannot be estimated with any high degree of accuracy. Official estimates of employment in "services" (as presented in Tabie 10) cover only hotels, bath houses, barbershops, photographic studios, and cleaning and dyeing establishments, with a large number of other service occupations being omitted, though these occupations are officially recognized.[6]

The estimate for traditional medical doctors is a rough official one. Midwives, who numbered over half a million in 1956, are included in Emerson's estimate on employment in traditional medicine; they are not included here on the ground that they are found primarily in rural areas and that they practice as a side occupation. The estimate for domestic servants is that for 1933 (Liu and Yeh, 1965, p. 206); it is pretty close to an estimate for 1949 based on some limited information.[7]

6. The following services are included in the 1954 SSB list of private sector services but are not included in employment data: (1) buses, trolley cars, and ferries; (2) tourist services, public hotels, and wagon stations; (3) places of amusement (such as theatres and places renting pleasure boats); (4) seal-cutting and letterwriting; (5) job typing and mimeographing; (6) publishing; (7) advertising; (8) rental of carts, boats, tools, and furniture; (9) portrait painting; (10) scroll mounting; (11) providing fresh and boiled water; (12) traditional repair of teeth and making of glass eyes; and (13) catering and undertaking (Emerson, 1965a, p. 43).

7. Based on an estimate for Peking, Emerson suggests there were 2.9 million domestic servants in 1949 (1965a, p. 71). Emerson does not include domestic servants in his estimate of total nonagricultural employment.

REFERENCES

Academy of Sciences, 1958. *Kang-tieh sheng-chan ta-yao-chin lun-wen hsuan-chi (Essays on the Great Leap Forward of Iron and Steel Production).* Peking.

AIRD, JOHN S., 1961. *The Size, Composition, and Growth of the Population of Mainland China.* International Population Statistics Reports Series, p. 90, No. 15. Washington, D.C.: U.S. Department of Commerce, Bureau of the Census.

BOGUE, D. J., 1959. *The Population of the United States.* Glencoe, Ill.: Free Press.

BUCK, JOHN L., 1937. *Land Utilization in China.* Nanking.

BUCK, J. L., O. L. DAWSON, and YUAN-LI WU, 1966. *Food and Agriculture in Communist China.* New York.

CHANDRASEKHAR, S., 1959. *China's Population: Census and Vital Statistics.* Hong Kong: Hong Kong Univ. Press.

CHANDRASEKHAR, S. 1961. *Red China, An Asian View.* New York.

CHANG, C. C., 1932. *An Estimate of China's Farms and Crops.* Nanking.

CHANG CHI-HUNG (Djang Gee-hung), 1947. "An Estimate of the Working Population of China," *She-huit ko-hsueh tsa-chih* (*Quarterly Review of Social Sciences*), Vol. IV, No. 2 (Dec.). Shanghai.

CHANG FO-CHIEN, 1958. "Some Suggestions on Solving the Problem of Labor Shortage," *CHCC,* No. 12 (Dec. 9, 1958).

CHANG KAI-FAN, 1956. "Allocate Properly the Subsidiary Labor in the Families of Small Merchants and Peddlers," *HHYPK,* No. 21, p. 194.

CH'EN CHIH-HO, 1957. "The Problems of the Statistical Scope of Workers and Employees in Our Country at Present," *TCKT,* No. 1 (Jan. 14, 1957), pp. 19–20.

CH'EN CHIH-HO, 1959. "The Question of Subjects in Labor Force Statistics," *CHYTC,* No. 11 (Aug. 23, 1959), pp. 27–30.

CHEN TA, 1946. *Population in Modern China.* Chicago.

CHEN TA, 1957. *New China's Population Census of 1953 and Its Relations to National Reconstruction and Demographic Research.* Stockholm: International Statistical Institute, August 8-15, 1957.

CHENG SHIH-WU *et al.,* 1962. "A Discussion on the Problems of Division and Designing of Residential Districts," *Chien-chu hsueh-pao,* No. 3, pp. 1–3.

CHI CH'ENG, 1960. "Viewing the Excellence of Urban Communities from the Standpoint of Labor Work," *Lao-tung (Labor),* No. 9 (May 3, 1960), pp. 7–10.

CH'IAO, C. M., W. S. THOMPSON, and D. T. CHEN, 1938. *An Experiment in the Registration of Vital Statistics in China.* Oxford, Ohio.

China News Summary, 1966. No. 117, April 28, 1966.

CHOU EN-LAI, 1959. "Report on the Adjustment of Major Targets in the National Economic Plan for 1959 and Further Development of the Campaign for Increasing Production and Practising Economy," *HHPYK,* No. 17.

EASTON, WARREN W., 1963. "Labor Force," in A. Bergson and S. Kuznets (eds.), *Economic Trends in the Soviet Union*. Cambridge, Mass.

EMERSON, JOHN PHILIP, 1961. "Manpower Absorption in the Non-Agricultural Branches of the Economy of Communist China," *The China Quarterly* (July-September, 1961).

EMERSON, JOHN PHILIP, 1965a. *Nonagricultural Employment in Mainland China: 1949–1958*. International Population Statistics Reports, Series P–90, No. 21. Washington, D.C.: U.S. Department of Commerce, Bureau of the Census.

EMERSON, JOHN PHILIP, 1965b. *Sex, Age, and Level of Skill of Nonagricultural Labor Force of Mainland China*. Washington, D.C.: Foreign Demographic Analysis Division, Bureau of the Census (June 1965).

FANG HSIEN-TING and WU CHIH, 1953. "Rural Industries of China," *Ching-chi t'ung-chi chi-k'an (Quarterly Journal of Economics and Statistics)*, 2.3:617 (Sept., 1933).

FUNG CHI-HSI, 1957. "Growth of China's Economy as Viewed from the State Budget," *TCKT*, No. 2 (June, 1957).

HO, PING-TI, 1959. *Studies on the Population of China, 1368–1953*. Cambridge, Mass.: Harvard Univ. Press.

HSIEH MU-CH'IAO, 1955. "Summary Report to the Fourth Conference on Statistical Work," *HHYP*, No. 6 (June, 1955), p. 148.

HSING YU-HUNG, 1954. "Struggle for Continuously Carrying out the New Employment Policy," *HHYP*, No. 7, p. 141.

HHPYK, 1958a. (*Hsin-hua pan-yueh-kan.*) "Provincial Regulations Concerning the Period of Apprenticeship and Living Allowances in State, Joint, Cooperative and Private Enterprises," No. 5, pp. 144–145.

HHPYK, 1958b. "Provincial Regulations Concerning Retirement of Workers and Employees," No. 5, pp. 142–143.

HSU HSIN-HSUEH, 1960. "Highspeed and Proportionate Development of the National Economy," *HC*, No. 3 (Feb. 1, 1960), pp. 6–9.

HSU KANG, 1958. "Labor Wage Work Must Be Guided by the Policy of Developing the Nation Through Comprehensive Planning, Industry, and Frugality," *CCYC*, No. 2, p. 21.

HSU KANG, 1959. "Make a Success of Wage Statistical Work in 1959," *CHYTC*, No. 4 (Feb. 23, 1959).

HSU LI-CH'UN, 1959. "On 'the Policies of Walking on Two Legs'," *HHPYK*, No. 9.

HU HUAN-YUNG, 1957. "Graph of Area and Population of China by Provinces and Regions," *Ti-li chih-shih*, No. 9 (Sept. 14, 1957), pp. 390-391.

HUANG HSIU-CHUAN, 1957. "Increase the Efficiency of Local Highway Transportation," *CHCC*, No. 3.

HUANG MENG-FAN, 1956. "An Opinion Regarding Statistics on Labor in Rural People's Communes," *CHYTC*, No. 11 (Aug. 23, 1956), pp. 30–32.

International Labour Office, 1964. *Employment and Economic Growth*, Geneva.

JMJP, various dates. (*Jen-min jih-pao: People's Daily.*) Peking.

JMJP, Dec. 3, 1958. "Transport Cooperatives Should Be Further Transformed."

JMJP, Dec. 19, 1958. "Resolutions on the Problems of People's Communes."

JMJP, April 18, 1959. "A Preliminary Survey of the Labor Problem in Hung-Kuang Commune." Reprinted in *HHPYK,* No. 11, 1959, p. 105.

JMST (*Jen-min shou-tse*), 1955. "Registration Methods of the Census," p. 26.

Kuang-ming jih-pao (*Kuang-ming Daily*), July 18, 1960; Oct. 7, 1963.

KJJP (*Kung-jen jih-pao*: *Workers' Daily*), Sept. 18, 1958 (p. 2).

LI CHENG-JUI, 1959. *Chung-hua jen-min kung-ho-kuo nung-yeh-hui shih kao* (*A Draft History of the Agricultural Tax in the People's Republic of China*). Peking.

LI, CHOH-MING, 1959. *Economic Development of Communist China.* Berkeley: Univ. of California Press.

LI, CHOH-MING, 1962. *The Statistical System of Communist China.* Berkeley: Univ. of California Press.

LI FU-CH'UN, 1956. "A Report on the First Five-Year Plan of Developing the National Economy," reprinted in *JMST,* pp. 52–77.

LI FU-CH'UN, 1960. "A Report on the Draft Plan of the National Economy in 1960," *CHYTC,* No. 4.

LI SHU-TEH, 1957. "Peasant's Burden in 1956: Conditions and Problems," in *Ts'ai Cheng* ("Public Finance"), No. 8 (August, 1957).

LI YUAN-CHEN, 1957. "The Problem of Surplus Labor in Present-Stage Agriculture in Our Country," *Chiao-hsueh yu yen-chiu,* No. 2 (Feb. 4, 1957), p. 17.

LIU HSUI-FENG, 1959. "Accelerating Construction at High Speed," *Hui-huang ti shih-nien* (*Ten Glorious Years*). Peking

LIU, T. C., and K. C. YEH, 1965. *The Economy of the Chinese Mainland: National Income and Economic Development, 1933–1959.* Princeton: Princeton Univ. Press.

MA WEN-JUI, 1959. "Ten Years of Struggle of Increasing Productivity and Living Standards of Workers and Employees," *KJJP,* Sept. 25, 1959. Reprinted in *HHPYK,* No. 20, 1959, pp. 50–53.

MA WEN-JUI, 1961. "The Problem of Labor in Building Socialism in Our Country," *HC,* No. 5 (March 1, 1961).

MA YIN-CHU, 1957. "A New Theory of Population," *HHPYK,* No. 15, pp. 34–41.

ORLEANS, LEO A. 1961a. "Problems of Manpower Absorption in Rural China," The China Quarterly (July–Sept. 1961).

ORLEANS, LEO A., 1961b. *Professional Manpower and Education in Communist China.* Washington, D.C.: National Science Foundation.

OU PAO-SAN, 1947. "The National Income of China, 1933, 1936 and 1946," in *She-hui k'o-hsüeh tsa chih* (*Quarterly Journal of Social Sciences*), Vol. 9, No. 2 (December, 1947), pp. 12–30.

Ou Pao-san *et al.,* 1947. *Chung-kuo kuo-min so-te 1933* (*The National Income of China, 1933*), two volumes. Shanghai.

PAI CHIEN-HUA, 1954. "600 Million People—A Great Strength for Socialist Construction in China," *JMJP,* Nov. 1, 1954.

SHA CH'IEN-LI, 1959. "Glorious Achievements on Food," *Hui-huang ti shih-nien.* Peking.

Shih-shih shou-tse, 1956. (*Current Events Handbook.*) "How to Solve the Unemployment Problem," No. 16 (Aug. 25, 1956), 32.

Shin Chugoku nenkan 1965 (*New China Yearbook 1965*). Tokyo: Chugoku Kenkyujo.

State Council, 1951. Financial and Economic Commission, "Tentative Regulations on Agricultural Tax for Newly Liberated Areas," *Chung-yang t'sai-ching cheng-tse fa-ling hui-pien,* Vol. II, June, 1951.

TKP (*Ta-kung pao*), Sept. 2, 1957 (p. 1).

TKP, Dec. 17, 1957 (p. 1).

T'AN CHEN-LIN, 1957. "A Preliminary Analysis of the Income and Living Standards of the Chinese Peasants," *HHPYK,* No. 11 (June, 1957).

T'AN CHEN-LIN, 1960. "Questions Concerning the Mechanization of Agriculture of our Country," *HC,* No. 6 (March 16, 1960).

(TGY) Ten Great Years, 1959. (*Wei-ta ti shih-nien.*) State Statistical Bureau, Peking.

TENG CHIEH, 1958. *Chung-kuo shou-kung-yeh she-hui-chu-i kai-tsao ti chu-pu tsung-chieh* (*A Preliminary Summary of the Socialist Transformation of China's Handicrafts*). Peking.

TENG CHIEH, 1959a. "The Great Victory of the Socialist Transformation of Handicrafts in Our Country," *JMJP,* Sept. 17, 1959, p. 4.

TENG CHIEH, 1959b. "The Historical Task of Transforming the Handicraft Cooperatives into the System of Ownership by the Whole People Has Been Basically Completed," *JMJP,* May 8, 1959, p. 13.

TENG YING-CH'AO, 1956. "Remarks" in *HHPYK,* No. 21 (Nov., 1956), p. 82.

TCKT, June 14, 1957. (*T'ung-chi kung-tso.*) "China's Population, 1949–1956," No. 11.

TCKT Data Section, 1956. "China's Workers and Employees in 1955: Their Number, Composition and Distribution," *TCKT,* No. 23 (Dec. 4, 1956), p. 29.

TCKT Data Section, 1957. "Data on the Improvement of Living Standards of Workers and Employees," *TCKT,* No. 14, pp. 13–14.

TCKTTH, 1956. "Great Victory Achieved in Socialist Transformation in the First Quatrer of 1956; National Economy Began a New High Level of Development," No. 9, pp. 1–3.

ULLMAN, MORRIS B., 1961. *Cities of Mainland China: 1953 and 1958.* International Population Reports, Series P-95, No. 59 (August, 1961). Washington D.C.: U.S. Department of Commerce, Bureau of the Census.

United Nations, 1959. *The Population of Asia and the Far East 1950–1980, Future Population Estimates by Sex and Age,* Report IV. New York.

VINER, JACOB, 1957. "Some Reflections on the Concept of Disguised Unemployment," *Indian Journal of Economics,* XXXVIII (July, 1957).

WANG KUANG-WEI, 1957. "Views on Allocating Agricultural Labor," *CHCC,* No. 8, pp. 6–9.

WANG KENG-CHIN, 1957. "My Views on Methods of Calculating the Gross Agricultural Value Output," *TCKT,* No. 4 (Feb. 28, 1957), pp. 3–4.

WANG MING-HSIEN and YUAN HSING-NAN, 1955. "Transforming the Wooden Sailing Junk Transport Industry Through Mutual Assistance," *JMJP,* Nov. 4, 1955, p. 2.

WANG SHOU-TAO, 1955. "Do a Good Job on Transportation, Support the Agricultural Cooperative Movement," *JMJP,* Nov. 10, 1955, p. 2.

Yeh, K. C., 1965. *Soviet and Communist Chinese Industrialization Strategies.* The RAND Corporation (May, 1965).

Yuan Hsing-nan, 1957. "Fully Utilize the Wooden Sailing Junks," *JMJP* March 11, 1957, p. 3.

Yueh Wei, 1956. "Some Reflections on the Methods of Estimation and Interpolation," *TCKTTH,* No. 18, pp. 25–27.

Yueh Wei, 1958. "Further Expand the National Economy and Balance the Statistical Work," *TCKT,* No. 20.

Organization of Agricultural Production 6

KENNETH R. WALKER

INTRODUCTION

PERHAPS THE MOST outstanding feature of agricultural organization in China during the first fifteen years of Communist government was its rapid and frequent transformation. In the first ten years there were five radical changes, and in no single year was there real stability in organization. Between 1950 and 1952 the land reform and private small-scale farming dominated the countryside, followed in 1953 and 1954 by mutual aid teams and semi-socialist cooperatives. The nationwide cooperativization campaign initiated in the summer of 1955 by Mao's speech "On Cooperativization," led to the "high tide of socialism" during that autumn, so that fully socialist collective farms were established in most areas of China by autumn, 1956. Long before the economic problems arising from these changes had been solved, the Great Leap Forward of 1958 produced the rural people's communes, which replaced the collectives as the unit of agricultural organization. The establishment of the communes was followed quickly by yearly reorganizations of agriculture in 1959, 1960, 1961, and 1962, restoring a modified form of the collectives that had been displaced. The years 1962-65 were the longest—indeed, the only—period of stability in the entire span of fifteen years.

The aim of this chapter is to examine the most important of these changes in the economic organization of agriculture, the main problems arising from them, and some of the effects they had on production and income.

The Communist period has been so packed with activity that it is impossible to discuss all the changes in organization. Inevitably, some important aspects have been ignored. For example, neither the land reform nor the mutual aid teams are covered, and the cooperatives (as opposed to collectives) are only mentioned briefly. Instead the organization of the collective—or "higher stage cooperative"—is analyzed in some detail (but not exhaustively), followed by a brief discussion of the creation and reorganization of the communes. This focus is justified because it was under the collectives that the basic problems of socialized agriculture that have dominated the years since 1955 were fully revealed. When the communes proved to be unworkable, it was a version of the collective that the government restored and retained. Although the communes did create some new problems, in general they merely underlined and exacerbated those already in existence. Furthermore, despite severe limitations, the most satisfactory economic analysis of China's agricultural organization can be done in terms of the collectives. The years when they dominated the scene constitute the only period for which Chinese data are extensive and reliable enough for a fairly detailed examination to be made.

The discussion in this chapter is further restricted to one or two themes. The main one is the nature of decision-making and its effect on agricultural plans, on techniques adopted, and on production. This chapter is not primarily about *national* agricultural policy but about how the local unit of production was actually organized, in relation to theoretical organization as revealed by the government regulations and directives. Supporting evidence has been presented from individual units of production and from different counties and provinces. Most frequently this evidence has not been scientifically selected but is just what happens to exist; and this inevitably raises the whole question of bias. For example, how uniform are policies and problems throughout China? If evidence is drawn only from a few provinces, counties or collectives, it is difficult to refute the charge that the picture may be grossly distorted. In addition, much of the data has been drawn from a single province, Kwangtung, which may have been atypically successful or unsuccessful in its agricultural organization. It is hoped, however, that enough data are presented from other areas to show that Kwangtung was by no means unique in China but that, on the contrary, China's agrarian problems were remarkably similar throughout the entire countryside. And it is hoped that the material on Kwangtung will be of interest in itself.

Finally, in the light of the historical survey, the chapter tries to draw some general conclusions about organization and its relation to production in Chinese agriculture.

I. BACKGROUND TO THE COLLECTIVIZATION OF AGRICULTURE

The Chinese leaders never made any secret of their long-term aim to collectivize agriculture. As Marxists who closely followed the Soviet model, they emphasized the relationship between institutional change and productivity. Without appropriate institutional reform, it was held, technical advance and the resulting increased production were impossible. Until 1954 technical progress was to a large extent, though not exclusively, identified with mechanization; and it was believed that collectivization was possible only when mechanization had been introduced to agriculture (Teng Tzu-hui, 1953). This, in turn, involved waiting until China's industry was in a position to supply the necessary machines. Large-scale, mechanized, *collective farms,* it was argued, would be able to use resources more efficiently, raise the level of investment, introduce better agricultural methods and so raise output greatly. All this had been shown by the example of the Soviet Union, according to the Chinese leaders.

However, the leadership recognized that to prepare the way for a fully collective agriculture, reorganization must be done slowly in distinct stages: land reform, mutual aid teams, cooperatives of a semi-socialist type and, finally, cooperatives of a socialist type—*i.e.,* collectives. In 1954 an important shift in the discussion about the relationship between collectivization and mechanization took place (Chao Tzu-yang, 1954; Teng Tzu-hui, 1955). Collectivization was now seen as a precondition of mechanization, and not vice versa. At the same time, attention was focused on a wider conception of "technical reform" of agriculture, one that included more than mechanization. For China, it was argued, the high man-to-land ratio and low level of savings demanded technical innovations of a "labor-intensive" kind, such as double cropping of rice, close planting, deeper plowing, and the introduction of improved but traditional types of implements. These technical improvements were considered to be dependent upon the prior cooperativization and collectivization of agriculture; small-scale private agriculture could not supply the necessary conditions, such as savings, management or farm layout. Despite the shift in the argument concerning mechanization and collectivization, the basic point remained: only large-scale *collective* agriculture could achieve a growth rate adequate to sustain the kind of industrialization drive envisaged by China's leaders.

Between 1949 and the summer of 1955, land reform and the introduction of mutual aid teams were accomplished, but remarkably little progress was made in collectivizing agriculture; that is, in effecting any truly socialist transformation. The land reform was completed around the beginning of 1953 in south China (and earlier in other areas). It was accompanied by a rise in incentives for the new land-owning peasants and a swift restoration of peacetime production levels of some crops. At the same time it created many problems. For example, it reduced farm size, in many cases below the minimum required to provide subsistence output for a family. Resources such as draft animals and farm tools were inevitably distributed unequally, and this impeded production. Credit and seed were scarce. The class policy implemented by many cadres had an adverse effect on the incentive to produce: when rich peasants, wrongly classified as landlords, lost their property, middle-class peasants tended to reduce their output to mere subsistence, fearing the consequences of upward social and economic mobility.

The government's plan was, in any case, to move immediately after the land reform to the creation of mutual aid teams, primarily to bring about a more even allocation of scarce factors (such as draft animals and labor) at seasons of peak demand. These temporary teams were gradually to become permanent, and "socialist elements" such as a collectively owned stock of implements and draft animals were to be introduced, financed by voluntary levies on members. The move to mutual aid teams occurred throughout China during 1952 and 1953.[1]

The first campaign [2] to bridge the narrow gap between permanent (*i.e.*, "advanced") teams and cooperatives was initiated in 1954, but was temporarily suspended in February, 1955, to allow for a period of stock-taking and consolidation. By the spring of 1955 only 14 per cent of all peasant households in China had joined semi-socialist cooperatives (SSB, 1957), and most of these were situated in north, northeast and east China. Many central and southern provinces had very few. The remaining 86 per cent of households were either loosely associated in mutual aid teams or completely independent; all 86 per cent were still engaged in private farming. Cooperativization, let alone collectivization, had barely begun.

There is adequate evidence (Walker, 1966) that in the spring and summer of 1955 the government was anxiously preoccupied with the entire question of the slow speed of socialist reorganization and the low current rate of growth of agriculture. The performance of agriculture, according to official figures (*Ten Great Years*) was poor in both 1953 and 1954. Cotton output fell by 9.9 per cent in 1953 and 9.4 per cent in 1954, while grain production increased only by 1.5 per cent and 2.3 per cent. Generally speaking the weather was normal in 1953, but in 1954 some central and southern provinces had severe rains resulting in widespread floods. In 1955 the spring crop was very bad in south China, where grave food shortages were reported.

The overall agricultural situation was by no means satisfactory. On the one hand it could be argued that the low growth rate reflected the inherent weaknesses of small-scale private agriculture (still 86 per cent of all households). At the same time, it could equally well be argued that it reflected the declining incentives of the middle and upper peasant classes (engaged in private farming), who viewed with alarm the coercive methods adopted by cadres (despite official directives banning them) to establish and organize cooperatives in 1954. Violations of the principles of

1. A great deal of information on the 1952 campaign to establish mutual aid teams and on the economic conditions in rural China immediately after the land reform had been completed is contained in Chinese Academy of Sciences Economics Research Institute, *Compendium of Materials on Agricultural Producers' Cooperatives during the Reconstruction Period of the National Economy, 1949-1952* (2 volumes, Peking, 1957).

2. Details of the campaign are given in State Council, 1955.

"voluntariness" and "mutual benefit" (between members), which were to be the cornerstones of the cooperative movement, were widespread in 1954 (Walker, 1966).

Among the top leaders of China, some almost certainly favored a cautious policy of slow advance toward cooperativization and, untimately, collectivization, while others advocated a much speedier transformation to retrieve a rapidly deteriorating situation. It must be remembered that the summer of 1955 marked the halfway stage in the First Five-Year Plan. Its targets had already been scaled down and now it seemed that unless agricultural growth could be radically increased those for industrial expansion would have to be reduced further.

In a powerful speech in July, 1955, however, Mao Tse-tung ended whatever debate existed regarding the strategy for agricultural reorganization (Mao, 1955). He called upon the leadership to respond to the "high tide of socialism" already sweeping through the countryside. The undoubted support of the poorer peasants, who considered they had much to gain from socialization, together with Mao's personal directive, combined to make the "high tide" an established fact. By June, 1956, no less than 63 per cent of peasant households had joined fully socialist collectives (as opposed to a mere 4 per cent at the end of 1955), and 92 per cent of households were in some kind of cooperative (SSB, 1957). These figures must be contrasted with the relatively cautious targets advocated by Mao, who still insisted that socialization should be attained by the gradual process of first creating teams, then cooperatives and, finally, collectives. In fact, many collectives were formed directly from private independent farms and teams, and *not* from cooperatives (Ch'en and Kan, 1956).

It would not be appropriate to discuss in any detail here why Mao's strategy of the "stages" of reform was abandoned, but the two main reasons must be mentioned (Walker, 1966). (1) Cadres had not assessed rent payable to land shareholders in the cooperatives to the satisfaction of either those heavily dependent on rent in their standard of living or the poorer peasant members, who owned little land but relied overwhelmingly on the wages of labor for their income. (2) At the beginning of 1956, cadres were under intense pressure to effect a technical breakthrough in agriculture in the shortest possible time. This was associated with the publication of the Twelve-Year Plan for Agriculture (*HHPYK,* Vol. 78, 1956) and the directive to attain First Five-Year Plan (1957) targets a year earlier, in 1956 (Chou En-lai, 1956). The move to collectives was believed to be the answer, especially since the land rent payments, which would be abolished with the collectivization of land, could be diverted (at least partly) to investment (Hwang and Wang, 1956). The larger scale of collectives and the stricter government control possible over their affairs were central arguments determining the speedy transformation. Before examining how the collectives functioned in practice during their brief period of existence (1956-58), their theoretical organization, as revealed by government regulations and directives, is first outlined.

II. ORGANIZATION OF THE COLLECTIVE ACCORDING TO GOVERNMENT REGULATIONS

The regulations for collectives (*HHPYK,* Vol. 88, 1956) were accepted by the National People's Congress in June, 1956. They stipulated that a collective was to be a voluntary association of peasants, managed democratically by an elected management committee that carried out the policies of a member's conference. Each collective was required to draw up plans for increasing production, but it is surprising to find that the regulations indicated virtually nothing about the process of plan formation or the relations between the collective, the party and the government. For example, Article 1 stated that a collective was a socialist economic organization formed ". . . with the direction and help of the Communist Party and the People's Government." Article 5 ruled that the collective "must properly integrate its own interests with those of the state. The cooperative should independently manage production under the direction of the national economic plan." Article 27 referred to the collective's plans for increasing output "in accordance with the state plan and local conditions." There were no other references to the powers of the collective in formulating its plans. The clear implication was that a collective would be obliged to follow the state plan but that it would have powers to adapt it to local conditions. The collective's main obligation to the state was to fulfill its tax and sales quotas.

The main feature of a collective, as opposed to a semi-socialist cooperative, was that all the land, except small private ("retained") plots, graves, and building sites, was collectively owned. Land was to be collectivized without compensation because, it was argued, the owners would share fully in the benefits accruing from collectivization. Land rent was thus abolished. A private plot of arable land would be allocated to members for their own use, free of rent. Its maximum area must not exceed 5 per cent of the average arable area per head in the collective. All draft animals and large farm implements (such as plows) became collective property at agreed prices, while irrigation works, large groups of trees, and fishponds were to be collectivized on terms that took into account the extent to which owners had already obtained a fair return on their investment. The rules promised that members might still leave collectives, taking with them their land (or its equivalent) and money invested. They were to retain in private ownership pigs, poultry, domestic utensils and small numbers of trees.

A collective was divided into production brigades, each of which was a permanent unit with its own labor, land, draft animals and implements. The creation of brigades gave the collective the opportunity to reallocate resources in such a way as to create viable economic units. It was envisaged that brigades would contract with the collective authority to fulfill given tasks for agreed rewards, thus combining the advantages of centralization with local initiative. The regulations did not state how large (measured by the number of households or villages) the average collective should be, but this was specified later in many government directives. The collective was undoubtedly to be a larger unit than the cooperative, and its subdivision (the brigade) was in fact generally equivalent in size to the former cooperative. In 1956, collectives had between 100 and 300 households, as opposed to the 30 or 40 households in the average cooperatives of 1955. In many cases it is likely that the cooperative became a brigade in a collective without changing its boundaries or resources significantly.

The success or failure of the collective depended very considerably on its ability to safeguard the economic interests of all its members despite their differences in class status, skills and capital. It was particularly important to devise an incentives and payments system that would satisfy and unite the poor and middle peasants, who together were the majority of peasants. The income of a collective available for distribution to the members consisted of the value of production after deductions were made for taxes, costs of production, and reserve and welfare funds. In the cooperative, which preceded the collective, personal income from the cooperative sector consisted of income from capital (land, draft animals, tools) as well as from labor; and, as has already been mentioned, the assessment of the rewards of capital and labor was one of the chief problems of the cooperatives and a major source of dissension among the peasants.

In the collective, by contrast, personal income from the collective sector was entirely derived from labor. The reward for labor was the product of the number of "labor days" worked multiplied by the value of the labor day. Where possible, each job was given a norm, which was the quantity and quality of work done in a working day under certain physical conditions. Every norm was rated in work points, ten of which usually constituted "one labor day." On fulfilling a norm, therefore, each peasant was credited with the rated number of work points. Tasks important for production, requiring great skill and strength, earned the most points. The value of the labor day was calculated by dividing the value of the distributable product by the total number of labor days credited to all working peasants in the collective. Two points must be made about this system:

(1) Under conditions of decreasing marginal returns to labor, the value of the labor day (*i.e.*, the wage rate per day) would de-

cline with increasing labor input (given no change in the distributed proportion of output), but total wages received per head would still increase as the number of labor days accomplished increased. Peasants for whom the value of the labor day (or wage *rate*) was the most important incentive, therefore, would not readily support plans for a great increase in the use of labor for relatively nonproductive work or work with deferred returns because it would reduce the value of the labor day, even though the decline in the wage rate might be more than offset by the greater number of days worked, which would give them a higher total wage. However, to the extent that peasants focused on the total wage they received, they would welcome the opportunity to do more work, regardless of the decline in the daily wage rate. This relationship confused both cadres and peasants.

(2) Unless both the physical product of the collective and the government's distribution policy were very stable over time, it was impossible for peasants to forecast either the value of the labor day or the level of wages forthcoming. The private sector was, therefore, important not only for the absolute level of income it provided but also for the security it gave.

The government stressed that collectives must be created and organized according to the principles of "voluntariness" and "mutual benefit." They were to pursue policies that both benefited production and guaranteed 90 per cent of members an increase in income during 1956. These managerial tasks required cadres with intelligence, political skill and a profound knowledge of traditional and modern agricultural techniques, who also had enough time to do the careful preparatory work necessary for the smooth transition to collective farming. Good relations between cadres and peasants, and between cadres of different levels, were essential. Clear and realistic orders from above had to be combined with freedom for local cadres to judge the situation and adapt plans if necessary.

In practice, many of the collective cadres owed their position to the fact that they were poor peasants who had demonstrated their political reliability, especially during the land reform. Some were illiterate, inexperienced in organizational work and unskilled in farming. Others had considerable experience in cooperatives of the old liberated areas and knew the difficulties involved in changing the traditional organization of agriculture. Although this made them wiser than the inexperienced cadres, it may also have taught them that persuasion by argument was not as effective as coercion in obtaining quick results. In the minds of the cadres time was short, despite Mao Tse-tung's insistence on a slow transformation of agriculture lasting ten to fifteen years. The cadres at all levels were working in an atmosphere of campaigns and targets. They were inevitably preoccupied with their own performance in the eyes of their superiors, realizing the importance of proving themselves active in building socialism, while steering a fine course between any action that could be criticized as conservative or rightist on one hand, adventurist or leftist on the other, and at the same time avoiding the errors of dogmatism, formalism, localism and bureaucratism. Every cadre knew he must aim to be regarded as a "progressive."

III. ECONOMIC ORGANIZATION IN THE COLLECTIVES DURING 1956

THE QUESTION OF DOUBLE CROPPING: SOME BASIC DATA

The Twelve-Year Plan for agricultural development focused upon raising total crop output by increasing yields per unit area per year, rather than by extending the arable area. Particularly in south and central China, this involved changing the cropping system to obtain two or even three crops a year from the same area of land (for example, two rice crops, or one rice crop followed by wheat, or two rice crops and a winter crop of wheat). It was believed that the collectives could achieve such a change both by using existing resources more effectively and by securing a higher level of investment.

This section examines some of the fragmentary evidence concerning the extent to which the collectives actually succeeded in achieving this important change from single to double cropping, and how they dealt with the problems involved. It will be argued that although they did prove themselves capable of introducing double cropping, often in the face of local opposition, and did achieve some successes in raising crop yields, they did not display adequate skill in planning with care—balancing available resources against those required in the proposed change. As a result, unrealistic, overambitious plans to extend double cropping met with shortages of labor, draft animals, seed, fertilizer and water, in some cases resulting in lower crop production. It will also be shown that collectives did not by any means succeed in providing the kind of financial incentives that were needed to call forth the required quantity and quality of farm labor.

Before examining actual plans adopted by collectives in 1956, it will be helpful to present some data relating to the major conditions governing the success of double cropping and to the approximate state of these conditions in 1956. The economist is not so much concerned with the agronomical problems involved in double cropping as with its claims on resources, compared with the supply. Here only two necessary resources are discussed: labor and draft animal power, with the emphasis on how the collective as an institution organized these two factors to secure higher production through double cropping. The discussion is in three parts: (a) the problem of phasing the necessary farm work; (b) the demand and supply conditions of farm labor; (c) the demand and supply conditions of draft animals (both in relation to double cropping).

The Problem of Phasing Farm Work

In the change from single to double cropping and, even more, from double to treble cropping in China, one of the most important organizational problems is to ensure that resources are available at exactly the right time. The time available for certain crucial work is severely limited, especially in the summer when the first crop is harvested and the second crop is sown. Consider an annual cropping pattern found in parts of Kwangtung province, with three crops a year—early rice, late rice and winter wheat. Table I shows the timing of the agricultural year for this system.

The table shows that with this treble-cropping system, there are three periods of intense farming activity in the year: spring, summer and autumn. In the spring the seed for the first rice crop is sown in the nursery, the wheat planted during the previous autumn is harvested, rice fields now vacated are flooded, plowed, harrowed, and flattened, and base fertilizer is applied. The wheat must be planted early enough in the autumn to produce a spring harvest that does not encroach on the time needed for preparing the paddy fields. The date on which the rice is transplanted has a decisive effect on the final rice yield and is itself set by the date the rice seed is sown, for transplanting must be done only when the seedlings have reached a certain age and height. In Kwangtung this is usually after 30 days for the first crop. The seed cannot be sown until the low winter temperatures have gone; before transplanting can take place, the paddy fields must be prepared. This can only be done if water is available, and so involves waiting for the spring rain if there is no irrigation water. If the rain arrives unusually late, the seedlings grow past their optimum age and, to ensure even a moderate crop, transplanting must be done extremely quickly. In parts of Kwangtung, if the first rice crop is not transplanted before May 6th, there will not be enough time in the remaining months to grow and harvest two rice crops.

Throughout many centuries Chinese farmers have evolved an agricultural year by assigning each agricultural task to one of the 24 seasons in the Chinese calendar. In the 1950's peasants still adhered to this traditional agricultural working year,[3] doing jobs on the same date as their ancestors had done them for centuries before. At the spring season, for

3. An interesting collection of Chinese proverbs concerning the importance of the traditional seasons in agriculture is found in Chu Hsien-li *et al.*, *Agricultural Proverbs and Explanatory Notes* (Peking, 1957).

TABLE 1

THE PHASING OF AGRICULTURAL WORK IN A TREBLE-CROPPING SYSTEM OF KWANGTUNG PROVINCE

		Traditional Date		Latest Time Possible	
Crop	Agricultural Work	Chinese calendar	Western calendar	Chinese calendar	Western calendar
First Rice	Sowing seed in nursery	Ching Chi [a] (excited insects)	March 5-6		
	Transplanting seedlings	Ch'ing Ming [b] (calm and bright days)	April 5-6	Li Hsia [b] (setting of summer)	May 5-6
	Harvesting rice		End June-Mid-July [a]		
Second Rice	Sowing seed in nursery	Mang Chung [a] (grain in ear) to Hsia Chi (summer solstice	June 6-7 to June 21-23		
	Transplanting seedlings	Ta Shu[a] (great heat) to Li Ch'iu (setting of autumn)	July 23-24 to August 7-8	Li Ch'iu [c]	August 7-8
	Harvesting rice	....	End Sept. [a] to Nov.[d]		
Winter Wheat	Sowing seed	Li Tung [e] (setting of winter)	Nov. 7-8	Hsiao Hsieh [e] (lesser snow-fall)	Nov. 22-23
	Harvesting wheat	around Ch'un Fen [e] (vernal equinox)	March 21-22		

Sources:

a. *Agricultural Practical Knowledge* (4 vols) Shanghai 1935, vol. 2, pp. 68-69.

b. "A method of retrieving dead transplant seedlings following delayed transplanting of the Early Rice," *NFJP*, April 26, 1955. Note, however, that in the North Kwangtung Special District of Shaokwan the limit for transplanting the first rice is Ku Yü (grain rains): April 21-22. *See* Kwangtung *District and Township Cadres News,* April 8, 1956: "The Current Situation and Problems in Production Throughout the Province."

c. T'ao Chu, "On All Sides Develop Agricultural Production to Ensure that Peasants Increase Their Income." *NFJP,* June 9, 1956.

d. *Economic Geography of Kwangtung* by Liang Jen-ts'ai. Peking, 1956 (p. 26).

e. "How to Organize the Sowing of Winter Crops Rationally," *NFJP,* October 27, 1961. Also *Agricultural Knowledge Instruction Book. The Method of Sowing Wheat.* Shanghai, 1951 (pp. 16 and 25). (One of a series of handbooks compiled by Chekiang University.)

many areas in Kwangtung, a maximum of 30 days is available for preparing rice fields and transplanting the seedlings. Some areas only have 20-25 days, because water is not available, or it is too rainy to work, or cold weather has delayed the sowing of the rice seed.

The second rice crop cannot be transplanted until the land has been vacated by the first crop and then prepared in the same way. It must be transplanted early enough to ensure time for it to ripen before the onset of winter. This, in turn, involves guaranteeing the timely planting of the first crop. Time is very short at this summer "turnover" period. For the second crop to produce good yields, transplanting must be completed in Kwangtung by about August 8th, and experiments have shown [4] that yields are remarkably higher if it is brought forward by several days. The maximum time available for harvesting the first rice, preparing the land, and transplanting the second rice is about 37 days in many parts of Kwangtung. Again, in practice, it is often appreciably less because of the heavy rainfall in July and August. For planning purposes, a realistic figure is 25-30 days.

In autumn the second rice crop is gathered, the land is plowed, harrowed, supplied with fertilizer and sowed directly with wheat. The earlier the winter wheat is sown the less risk there is of damage from low temperatures or of the spring wheat harvest's affecting the preparations for the first rice crop. In Kwangtung there may be six weeks available for the autumn work.

Where two rice crops are grown there are, therefore, two periods of intense activity, while if a third (winter) grain crop is added, the pressure, especially in the spring, is increased. Dislocation of work at any one peak season will affect the entire agricultural year. Even in Kwangtung, which has the most favorable climatic conditions in China for double cropping, not many days are available at the busy seasons.

Other south Chinese provinces have the climatic conditions required to grow two rice crops, but their time is more limited because the winters are longer and cooler. Very good organization is thus needed for successful double cropping. With allowance for regional variations (Mechani-

4. For example, experiments in Chekiang provided the following data:

Date of transplanting rice	Yield of rice obtained (catties per *mou*)
July 20	500
July 30	400
August 5	300
August 10	200

These and other data are published in *Problems of Agricultural Mechanization in China,* compiled by the Mechanization Bureau of the Ministry of Agriculture (Paoting, 1958, p. 132 *et passim*). Much information about rice culture in China is found in Ting Ying *et al.,* 1961.

zation Bureau, 1958, pp. 124-159), the provinces of Anhwei, Chekiang, Kiangsi, Kiangsu, and Honan generally have about 210 days, from the end of March to the end of October, when the climate is appropriate for the cultivation of rice. However, the time *required* to grow two rice crops is 190-215 days. In these provinces the spring comes later than in Kwangtung, so that the first rice has to be sown and transplanted later. Since the growing season is shorter, the time available for the summer turnover is very limited indeed. In Kiangsu, Chekiang and Anhwei only 5-15 days are available; in Honan and Kiangsi, 10-15 days (Mechanization Bureau, 1958, pp. 124-159).

The Demand and Supply Conditions of Labor

With so little time available at certain seasons, the feasibility of double cropping depends on whether the supply of labor and draft animals is adequate to fulfill the tasks within the given period (assuming that water, fertilizer and good seed are also available in required quantities). How much labor is "required" in reality at the busy summer turnover period? No single figure can be cited, since it depends so much on the physical conditions of the land, the standard of husbandry adopted and the skill of the peasants. A few figures, however, have been presented in Table 2. They refer only to individual *hsiang* (townships) and collectives in seven south Chinese provinces, and this should be remembered when using them to draw any general conclusions. Moreover, these figures for labor requirements refer to standard units of labor, namely those workers who in a Chinese collective would be considered strong and skilled enough to be given the maximum rating of ten work points per day. No figures were available for labor required to carry irrigation water. In some places this would increase the total markedly.

In order to obtain even a rough idea of how such labor requirements compare with actual labor supplies in south China, the figures in Table 2 must be restated in a form showing the maximum area of land on which one labor unit can fulfill all the necessary tasks in the number of days available. For example, the total labor required in one Hunan collective is shown in the table as 8.82 man days per *mou,* which is equivalent to stating that, if 15 days are available to carry out the work, then $1 \div 8.82 \times 15 = 1.701$ *mou* is the maximum area of land one standard labor unit can tend. This area may then be compared with the *actual* burden of land per unit of total farm labor in that area. Ideally, for the comparison, figures for labor supplies should be given in standard labor units; these data should be for the same collectives and *hsiang* as those for which labor requirements have been recorded. Neither of these is available. Instead, figures have been collected for 1956 of the average area of arable land in each *province,* per *unweighted* unit of agricultural labor in the province. They have been given alongside the figures of labor requirements

TABLE 2

STANDARD UNITS OF LABOR [a] REQUIRED PER *MOU* OF ARABLE LAND USED FOR DOUBLE CROP RICE, AT PEAK SUMMER SEASON

(in man days per *mou*) [b]

	Hunan	Chekiang	Kwangtung	Kwangsi	Kiangsi	Anhwei	Kiangsu
I HARVESTING FIRST RICE CROP							
Cutting and gathering	1.500	1.015	2.145	1.400	1.380	1.260	1.200
Threshing	0.800	0.460	0.305	0.455	0.210	0.300	1.000
Carting the crop	0.075	0.135 [c]	0.105 [c]	0.105 [c]	0.105 [c]	0.105	0.830
Drying	0.725	0.380	0.270 [d]	0.416	0.290 [d]	0.416	
Total I	3.100	1.990	2.825	2.376	1.985	2.081	3.030
II PLANTING SECOND RICE CROP							
Collecting and applying base fertilizer	1.865	2.025	2.450	1.815	2.350	2.165	1.590
Plowing and harrowing	1.635	1.475	0.830	2.080	3.080	3.195	1.330
Lifting and carrying seedlings	0.370	0.665 [e]	0.500	0.500 [e]	0.500	0.265	0.700
Planting seedlings	1.850	1.600	1.910	1.440	1.200	1.005	1.200
Total II	5.720	5.765	5.690	5.835	7.100	6.630	4.820
Total I plus II	8.820	7.755	8.515	8.211	9.085	8.711	7.850
∴ Area serviced per man per day (*mou*)	0.1134	0.1290	0.1174	0.1217	0.1101	0.1148	0.1274

Notes:

a. For each province the data refer to a single collective, except in the case of Kiangsi, where they are drawn from a *hsiang*.

b. A standard unit of labor is that which has such skill and strength as to warrant the maximum rating of 10 work points per day in a collective; it is a labor unit of the maximum quality.

c. The average of figures for Hunan and Chekiang has been used since figures for Kwangtung, Kwangsi, Kiangsi and Anhwei are not given.

d. The average of figures for Hunan, Chekiang, Kwangtung and Kwangsi has been used.

e. The average of figures for Hunan, Chekiang, Kwangsi, Anhwei and Kiangsu.

Source:

Figures in "Report of a Survey Concerning Problems of Agricultural Mechanization in Paddy-Fields of South China" published in *Problems of Agricultural Mechanization in China* (Mechanization Bureau, 1958).

in Table 3. The main issue raised in this table is whether or not the figures suggest the continued existence of the traditional labor gap at the peak season, great enough to impede the extension of double cropping.

The figures in Table 3, taken at their face value for the moment, clearly do suggest that a wide gap exists except in Kwangtung and Kwangsi. But can the figures really be interpreted thus? Two objections may be raised: (1) the figures for labor demand and supply are not com-

TABLE 3

THE SUPPLY AND DEMAND CONDITIONS OF LABOR IN DOUBLE CROP RICE AREAS AT THE SUMMER SEASON

	Area serviced per standard labor unit per day (in mou) (i)	Number of days available for fulfillment of work (ii)	Maximum possible burden of land per labor unit (in mou) (iii) = (i) x (ii)	Average area of land per *unweighted* unit of agricultural labor in province, 1956 (*i.e.*, total arable area in province ÷ agricultural labor force (in mou) (iv)	Given current farm labor supply, number of days required to complete work of harvesting first rice and planting second crop (v) = (iv) ÷ (i)
Hunan	0.1134	15	1.70	4.94	43.6
Chekiang	0.1290	15	1.93	3.07	23.8
Kwangtung	0.1174	30	3.52	3.89	33.1
Kwangsi	0.1217	30	3.65	4.29	35.2
Kiangsi	0.1101	15	1.65	5.51	50.0
Anhwci	0.1148	15	1.72	7.19	62.6
Kiangsu	0.1274	15	1.91	5.10	40.0

Sources:

Col. (i) from Table 2. Figures relate to a single *hsiang* or collective.

Col. (ii) Kwangtung figure from Table 1; others from Mechanization Bureau, 1958 (pp. 124-159).

Col. (iv) Mechanization Bureau, 1958, p. 135. Evidence that these relate to unweighted labor supply is provided by figures on p. 281 compared with data on p. 135.

parable: the former refer to single *hsiang* or to collectives, and to standard labor, while the latter refer to the entire province and nonstandard labor; (2) the supply figures do not indicate the *potential* labor force or, in other words, the number of farm people who, though not engaged in agricultural work, could be induced to be, given the attempt to introduce double cropping.

There are reasons, however, why the data in Table 3 can, indeed, be taken as a very strong indication of a labor gap:

(1) The time available for the work, assumed in the exercise in Table 3, may be regarded as the maximum in general, and more than that actually available in some places.

(2) The fact that the labor supply figures relate to nonstandard labor (for example, male, female, skilled, and unskilled workers are all counted alike) strengthens the case that a large labor deficit exists. If the actual labor force of 1956 were expressed in standard units, it would, of course, be smaller, and the burden of arable land would be higher. For example, in three Chekiang collectives (Mechanization Bureau, 1958, p. 281) the agricultural labor force, converted to standard units of labor (a worker who could be rated at ten work points per day), was found to be 52.2 per cent, 45.5 per cent and 48.8 per cent of the total unweighted agricultural labor force.

(3) Although it is true that the labor supply figures do not indicate the *potential* supply, they do, nevertheless, overstate the actual supply available *for rice cultivation* during the summer season in 1956. This is because some labor would also be engaged in such work as livestock rearing, horticulture, fishing, and repairing farm implements.

To argue that the labor gap is likely to be unimportant it would be necessary to show *either* that in double crop areas, or in areas contemplating its introduction, the burden of land per unit of labor is considerably below the average for the province (or that the labor force is much greater than the average); *or* that labor requirements for the summer turnover period are generally below those listed in Table 2.

The conclusion drawn here is that, in planning the extension of double cropping in 1956, the collectives should have been concerned primarily with the labor gap. Without a remarkable rise in labor productivity it was bound to be difficult and, in some areas, impossible to increase the double-cropped area, because of the labor shortage alone. It should also have been obvious that in some areas it would be difficult to maintain traditional standards of cultivation on the existing area and quite impossible to raise standards where this involved (as it usually did) applying more labor.

Attempts to increase the double-cropped area or the standard of cultivation were likely to destroy the delicate sequence of agricultural work. The extent to which collective cadres and the planners above them were, in fact, aware of these matters, and how they reacted to them, will be discussed later.

The Demand and Supply Conditions of Draft Animals

In the 1950's almost all the arable land of China was plowed and harrowed with implements pulled by animals. Animals also provided most of the power needed to turn water wheels for irrigation and to transport much of the fertilizer used (although a great deal of it was carried by the workers themselves). In planning the double-cropped area of any collective it was as important to estimate the requirements and supply of draft animals as carefully as those of labor. The question is the same for animals as for labor: given the time available to do certain work, what is the maximum area of land one draft animal can service? This area may then be compared with the supply of beasts per arable *mou*. Like the figures for labor, those for animals must be regarded as a very broad indication of the magnitudes involved. The performance of animals in plowing, for example, varies widely with the age and strength of the animal, the condition of the land worked, the kind of plow used and the standard of plowing required. Table 4 presents data for the areas that draft animals have been observed to plow, harrow or irrigate in a day.

For the rice-growing areas of south China in general, a liberal assumption may be that one water buffalo can plow 4 *mou,* or harrow 7 *mou,* or water 5 *mou* per day. Using these figures, one can say that 1 *mou* requires 0.593 beast days for all three items of work, or that in one day one buffalo can service 1.686 *mou.* If in the spring season there are 20 days available for the preparation of the land, and at the summer turnover period 10 days, then in spring one beast can support 33.7 *mou* and in summer 16.8 *mou.* Only minor changes in these assumptions alter significantly the maximum area one beast can service. For example, if—as must be the case in some places—a beast can plow only 3 *mou,* harrow 6 *mou* or water 3 *mou* in a day, then given 20 days in the spring and 10 days in summer, it can support only 24 *mou* in spring and 12 *mou* in summer. The supply of draft animals should, therefore, be considered in terms of the fairly wide range of 24-34 *mou* per beast as the maximum burden for the spring season, and 12-17 *mou* for the summer. Incomplete figures of the actual arable area per draft animal during the period 1952-58, in eleven provinces, are presented in Table 5.

Comparing the 1956 and 1957 areas of land in Table 5 with the maximum burden per beast postulated (24-34 *mou* for spring and 12-17 *mou* for summer), it would appear that only in Kwangtung, Yunnan and Szechwan did a generally adequate supply of animals exist for both

TABLE 4

THE PRODUCTIVITY OF DRAFT ANIMALS IN CHINA

	Type of Beast	Area of China and Type of Land	Area Worked per Day (in mou)	Source
I *Plowing with native plow*	1 medium quality ox	medium dry land	10-11	*1*
	1 very good water buffalo	shallow mud	8.0-9.0	*2*
	1 very good water buffalo	deep mud	2.0	*3*
	1 10-yr. old female water buffalo	sticky land, Chekiang and Hunan	3.6	*4*
	1 10-yr. old male water buffalo	sticky land, Chekiang and Hunan	3.75	*5*
	1 ox	tidal flats, Kwangtung	2.5	*6*
	1 water buffalo	Yangtse valley	4.2	*7*
	1 ox	Yangtse valley	3.1	*8*
	1 water buffalo	Szechwan	3.9	*9*
	2 oxen	Yellow River valley	4.1	*10*
	1 ox and 1 horse	Yellow River valley	4.6	*11*
	2 oxen and 1 mule	Yellow River valley	6.2	*12*
	2 horses	Yellow River valley	5.9	*13*
	2 mules	Yellow River valley	5.8	*14*
II *Harrowing*				
	1 water buffalo	Yangtse valley	6.5	*15*
	1 ox	Yangtse valley	6.2	*16*
	1 water buffalo	Szechwan	7.3	*17*
	2 oxen	Yellow River valley	15.6	*18*
	1 ox and 1 horse	Yellow River valley	20.7	*19*
	2 oxen and 1 mule	Yellow River valley	33.2	*20*

	Type of Beast	Area of China and Type of Land	Area Worked per Day (in mou)	Source
	2 horses	Yellow River valley	22.0	*21*
	2 mules	Yellow River valley	27.6	*22*
III *Irrigating land by turning water wheel*				
	1 water buffalo	Yangtse valley	5.3	*23*
	1 ox	Hopei	3.0	*24*

Sources:

1-5 are from *Livestock Rearing* by Ch'iu Huai. (Nanking 1957, *passim.*) Where only hourly figures are given they have been converted into daily rates by assuming a 9 hour day. *4* and *5* are based on experiments carried out on a fine day after heavy rain, in sticky fields.

6 T'ao Chu, April, 1956.

7-23 "The Use of Farm Implements Before the Liberation in 12 Provincial Districts of the Yellow & Yangtse Valleys" by Shen Hung-sheng, in *Collected Research Papers on Agricultural History,* vol. II (Peking, 1960, pp. 186-206). These figures were collected by the author 1920-1946, during which time he both farmed and conducted agricultural surveys.

24 Mechanization Bureau, 1958 (p. 194).

seasons. By contrast, in areas of Hunan, Honan, Shantung and Shensi, where the summer turnover is particularly short, the figures suggest a shortage of draft animals for double cropping; while in Liaoning, Kiangsu, Chekiang and Hopei, even assuming a fairly long spring plowing season, the livestock deficiency was likely to prevent double cropping in many places.

It is true that the figures for draft animal supply, expressed in *mou* of arable land per beast, are for all arable land in the province and not specifically for either rice land in general or double-cropped rice land. It could be argued, therefore, that an expansion of the double-cropped area might be accomplished by diverting draft animals from places where the natural environment precluded double cropping. In some cases this could undoubtedly be done, perhaps on a temporary basis, within relatively limited areas. It might also be argued that the livestock supply position is understated because in considering the arable area to be served, no account has been taken of the areas worked by tractors. However, that would affect the figures for north China only a little and would have virtually no effect on those for south China.

On the other hand, since the figures for the area of land per beast relate to area per head of *total* draft animals, not just those used for agri-

TABLE 5

THE ARABLE AREA PER HEAD OF TOTAL DRAFT ANIMALS IN ELEVEN PROVINCES OF CHINA
(in mou)

	Kwang-tung [a]	Yunnan [b]	Hunan [c]	Szech-wan [d]	Kiangsu [e]	Chekiang [f]	Honan		Hopei [j]	Shan-tung [k]	Shensi [l]
1952	12.7			16.5					37.6		
1953				25.2							
1954	12.6						21.6 [g]	24.7 [i]			
1955	12.0		20.8	22.8			22.5 [g]	25.5 [i]			
1956	13.2		20.0			41.3	23.7 [g]	27.0 [i]			
1957	12.7	11.0		15.8	67.0		19.3 [h]		41.9	27.8	25.7
1958											

Sources:

a. *Kwangtung:* Arable areas assumed: 1952: 49.5 million *mou* (*Hong Kong Ta-kung pao,* Dec. 6, 1957. 1954: 52.0 million *mou* (assumed). 1955: 55.0 million *mou* (*NFJP,* Aug. 18, 1951). 1956: 56.79 million *mou.* (Mechanization Bureau 1958, p. 126).

No. of animals assumed: 1952-56 from *NFJP.* 1952: April 8, 1956. 1954: Dec. 31, 1955. 1955: April 8, 1956. 1956: June 9, 1956. (This figure is for June 1956, the rest for end of year). 1957: *Hong Kong Ta-kung pao,* April 7, 1958.

b. *Yunnan:* Given in *Rural Work Bulletin,* 1957, No. 8 (p. 22-23). This was said to be the lowest burden in China.

c. *Hunan:* Arable area assumed: 1957: 14 million *mou* (Mechanization Bureau, 1958, p. 126).

No. of animals: 1955 and 1956; *JMJP,* June 2, 1957.

d. *Szechwan:* Arable area assumed: 114 million *mou* (CHCC, 1957, No. 3, pp. 2-3).

No. of animals: 1952 and 1957: *Economic Geography of Szhecwan* (Peking, 1960). 1953: *Szechwan jih-pao,* Oct. 5, 1954. 1955: *Szechwan jih-pao,* Dec. 5, 1957.

e. *Kiangsu:* Given in *Rural Work Bulletin,* 1957, no. 8, (p. 22-23). This was said to be the highest burden in China.

f. *Chekiang:* Given in Mechanization Bureau, 1958 (p. 282). The number of draft animals did not increase throughout the entire period of the First Five-Year Plan, according to this source.

g. *Honan:* Given in *HHPYK,* Vol. 99, pp. 88-90.

h. *Honan:* Given in Mechanization Bureau, 1958 (p. 169).

i. *Honan:* Arable area assumed: 136 million *mou* (*Mechanization Bureau,* 1958, p. 189).

j. *Hopei:* Given by Teng Tzu-hui, 1958.

k. *Shantung:* Given in Mechanization Bureau, 1958 (p. 169).

l. *Shensi: ibid.*

m. *Liaoning:* Given in *CHCC,* 1958, no. 11 (pp. 25-26).

cultural work, they *overstate* the supply position. The situation would look even worse if the numbers of working animals could be converted into standard units on a basis of working capacity. A little evidence for 1957 suggests that the difference between total and working animals was enough to turn what appeared to be a relatively sufficient supply into a deficiency. Table 6 illustrates this point. If the figures in Table 6 for area

TABLE 6

A COMPARISON BETWEEN THE BURDEN OF ARABLE LAND PER HEAD OF TOTAL DRAFT ANIMALS (I) AND PER HEAD OF WORKING DRAFT ANIMALS (II) IN 1957
(in mou)

	I	II
Kwangtung	12.7	21.3 [a]
Hopei	41.9	64.3 [b]
Honan	19.3	24.5 [c]
Shantung	27.8	32.9 [c]
Szechwan	15.8	25.6 [d]

Sources:

Column (I) given by Table 4.

Column (II): a. *Kwangtung:* Based on the assumption that 62% of total animals are used. This is the national average percentage derived from figures cited by Teng Tzu-hui, 1958 and by *pn-min show-tse* (*People's Handbook*) for 1957, p. 487.

b. *Hopei:* given by Mechanization Bureau, 1958 (p. 44). This does not explicitly state that the figure is for area per working beast but all other evidence signifies that this is so.

c. *Honan and Shantung:* Given in *Mechanization Bureau,* 1958 (p. 169).

d. *Szechwan:* Estimated as for Kwangtung, by assuming that 62% of beasts work.

of arable land per head of *working* beasts are matched against the burden of double-cropped land a draft animal can bear, even Kwangtung and Szechwan have a livestock deficit at the summer season, while the spring, though still manageable, becomes tighter. The livestock gap in Hopei now becomes very acute, and Honan and Shantung approach deficit point.

The conclusion is that the data, despite their inadequacies, strongly suggest that over a very wide area of south and central China, the lack of draft animals was likely to be a serious bottleneck in any attempt to extend greatly the area of double-cropped rice. Of course, in some areas the supply would be adequate or could be made so by reallocating livestock, but in others it would certainly be inadequate. How much was this problem considered in the plans of the collectives?

COLLECTIVES AND THE REFORM OF FARM PRACTICE IN 1956

One of the main arguments for collectivization was that it would allow the implementation of technical improvements necessary for raising crop yields. The substitution of collective for private ownership of the major means of production, it was argued, would give the Government greater control over resource utilization. At the same time it would set free considerable funds (hitherto paid to peasants as rent on land, implements and animals) for investment purposes. It was also believed that the benefits of large-scale production would be considerable. For example, since the basic production and organization unit of a collective (the brigade) was to be the size of the former cooperative, the authorities could allocate resources more easily and over a wider area; and the greater supply of resources at the disposal of the brigade cadres would enable the introduction of new practices that had not been possible before.

Before analyzing the ambitious attempt to effect a technical revolution almost overnight, it must be stated that China, unlike so many poor agricultural countries, did succeed in getting reforms that had been conceived in Peking implemented in the villages. Collectives did prove that they were capable of introducing changes. The extension of double cropping alone increased the sown area of rice throughout China by 55 million *mou,* equal to a 12.6 per cent rise over 1955 (Liao Lu-yen, 1957). According to official Peking figures (*Ten Great Years*), total rice output rose in 1956 by 5.7 per cent, although rice yield per sown *mou* fell by 7.5 per cent. Reporting on the year's achievements, the Minister of Agriculture, Liao Lu-yen, did not conceal the facts that this extension of double cropping had not been an unqualified success, and that in some areas where it had been newly introduced, total rice production had fallen *below* the level produced by the former single crop (Liao, 1957).

It would seem that although output was successfully raised in many places in 1956, agricultural problems were created by attempts to bring about too much, not too little, change in traditional farming methods. Targets adopted both for total grain production and for the area to be double cropped frequently did not reflect adequately the limiting conditions (short time available, and supply of labor, draft animals and other resources) outlined in the previous section. The unrealistically high targets set were more the result of the anti-conservative campaign waged in the villages by the government, than of careful surveys of local conditions and possibilities. In May, 1956, a national campaign [5] was already underway to secure within the year yields of 100 catties of cotton, 1,000

5. Central Broadcasting Station, 1956, *Speeches on the Draft Outline of the Plan for the Development of Chinese Agriculture* (p. 20). Even allowing for the multiple cropping index, the discrepancy between attained and planned yields is very great.

catties of grain and 10,000 catties of potatoes per arable *mou,* as compared with the national average yields actually attained—35 catties for cotton, 197 catties for grain and 1,004 catties for potatoes per sown *mou* (*Ten Great Years*). The provinces of Chekiang (Chi Nong, 1956) and Fukien (Yeh Fei, 1956) planned to attain self-sufficiency in grain during 1956, while in the same year 1957 grain production targets were to be overfulfilled in Kwangtung.[6] Shantung province, having achieved an average rate of growth of 3 per cent a year in grain output during the previous three years, planned to achieve a rise of 13 per cent in 1956 (Chao Chien, 1956).

As plans proceeded down the administrative line, targets were often raised. For example, the grain target adopted by the Kwangtung special districts authority (below the provincial level) was 14 per cent higher than the central government's target (T'ao Chu, April, 1956). To achieve their goals, provinces planned to extend the winter sown area, improve water conservation and irrigation facilities, increase the use of natural fertilizers, introduce double cropping, sow better seed and generally raise the standard of intensive cultivation by applying more labor per *mou.* Labor productivity was also to be raised through the use of improved implements. All these measures would have been very sound if applied in places where conditions were favorable. In 1956 they were too often introduced indiscriminately.

In south China, an important method of raising production was to extend the winter sown area. Thus, Kwangtung province added 4 million *mou* to the sown area in winter 1955-56, bringing the total to 17.5 million *mou,* of which 13.9 million *mou* were planted with grains (*NFJP,* June 14, 1956). Since many areas previously had no tradition of winter sowing, both the peasants and some of the cadres lacked confidence in their ability to secure a winter crop (*NFJP,* Dec. 26, 1955). The 1955 autumn harvest in Kwangtung was later than usual, (T'ao Chu, 1956), and the land to be cropped in winter had to be prepared very quickly to ensure that the winter wheat harvest would not affect the spring plowing. Despite the fact that there were insufficient draft animals to do the work in the time available, cadres *compelled* peasants to sow wheat after the advent of the season known as "lesser heat"—traditionally the latest possible time for sowing winter wheat. Many collectives, though, were able to substitute labor for draft animals to accomplish the work. However, in their concern to plant as much land as possible, collectives failed to leave

6. "Kwangtung's Plan to Increase Grain Production this Year by 4,000 Million Catties Will Bring Forward the Attainment of Next Year's Target for Increased Output" (*NFJP,* Jan. 23, 1956). The plan was to increase grain production by 18.2 per cent in 1956, compared with the following attained increases: 1952-53: +10%; 1953-54: +5.5%; 1954-55: +0.0%.

sufficient land vacant to serve as the nurseries for rice seedlings in spring 1956, so that when the time to sow the spring rice arrived, the winter wheat crop had to be plowed under to release the required area.[7]

Kwangtung in 1956 extended (T'ao Chu, Jan. 1956) its area of double-cropped rice by 4 million *mou* (the total arable area devoted to rice was 44.77 million *mou* in 1956). Since this expansion involved increasing the amount of work to be done in a short time, orders were given to sow the rice seed for the first spring crop earlier than usual, to reduce the pressure on the summer season, even if this meant sowing it onto dry fields. Although this meant that the first crop could also be transplanted earlier than usual,[8] it could not reduce the pressure on the spring season, and time was saved only by reducing the standard of land preparation. In Lokchong county, Kwangtung, the land was plowed and harrowed only three times, rather than the usual plowing three times and harrowing nine; even this necessitated the peasants' working night and day (*Chü, Hsiang Kan-pu-pao,* 1956). In the Hwangpu district of Kwangtung, where there were, on an average, no less than 177 *mou* per draft animal (including many too weak to pull a plow or harrow) the *hsiang* Party branch organized fifty-one labor teams as substitutes for animals, consisting of 5 men per plow and 2 men per harrow (*Chungshan nung-min-pao,* 1956). They plowed 4 *mou* each per day. If the district had relied solely on the available draft animal power, land preparation alone would have taken until the end of April. Plowing was further dislocated in spring 1956, by the misguided attempts to introduce into paddy fields throughout China the heavy, double-wheeled, double bladed steel plow. Experiments had already shown that in their existing form these plows were technically unsuitable for the wet fields, into which they sank. The water buffaloes, lacking a collective spirit, remained true to their tradition by refusing to work in pairs, while a single animal was not usually strong enough to pull the plow. As a result, thousands of these expensive plows were discarded by the collectives, at incalculable cost.

When the time came to transplant the first rice crop in Kwangtung, there were further organizational problems. Sowing the seed on dry land and departing from the traditional sowing date had combined to kill many seedlings or reduce their quality. Although winter wheat planted the previous autumn had not yet ripened, peasants were commanded to cut it (in Fa county 10 days before it was ready; *Rural Work Bulletin,* 1956,b) or to plow it under. At the same time as the standards of land preparation

7. Kwangtung Provincial and People's Committees, Oct. 1956. Generally 1 *mou* of nursery is required per 10 *mou* of rice land.

8. "Oppose Blindness" (*NFJP,* March 14, 1956). This revealed that dry sowing had been carried out indiscriminately on 50 per cent of the entire rice area. See also editorial, "Production in Cooperatives Must Strengthen its Planned Nature and Overcome Blindness" (*NFJP*, March 15, 1956).

were lowered, those for transplanting were raised by government decree, initiating a general drive to transplant seedlings either in small groups very close together (*hsiao-k'o mi-chi*), or singly, one seedling at a time (*tan-chu mi-chi*). This greatly increased the demand for labor despite its existing scarcity.

The issue of close planting can not be examined here. The voluminous scientific literature published in China on the subject emphasizes that optimum spacing and the number of seedlings per group varies according to conditions of soil fertility, sunlight, water, type of seed used and several other factors. The relationship between yield and planting density is certainly not a straight line indicating that the denser the planting, the higher the yield. Apparently, though, some cadres believed this to be the case. Entire administrative districts were ordered to adopt the same planting density, irrespective of the varying conditions within that district. Mencheong county authority in Kwangtung sent cadres to direct a collective to adopt a density known by the local peasants to be technically disastrous (*NFJP,* June 26, 1956). Again, in Hunan, *all* collectives were ordered to adopt one of two densities at the first rice transplanting (*HHPYK,* Vol. 96, 1956).

Acute shortages of draft animals, labor, seed and fertilizer similarly dislocated farm work at the summer turnover period, but by then there was less commandism in the collectives because the government had realized the seriousness of its effects during the earlier months and had made a genuine attempt to stop it. Under the existing conditions of grain scarcity, there was pressure from peasants to use much of the grain crop for human consumption, each collective erroneously believing that it would be able to buy grain from government agencies to use as seed and livestock fodder rather than setting enough aside out of its own harvest. The resulting decline in fodder supplies, the collectivization of draft animals, the low level of collective livestock management, and the excessive burden of work placed on animals all accounted for the continuing decline recorded in their number and strength.

It was conceded (Mech. Bureau, 1958, p. 134) that the standard of husbandry applied to the second rice crop in 1956, compared with the first, was generally lower in south China, primarily because of the shortages of labor and animals. Although the second crop usually requires closer planting than the first, the labor supply was frequently inadequate to meet this standard, given the unrealistic targets for some areas. Some land was neither plowed nor harrowed after the first harvest. In Yanfa county,[9] Kwangtung, 30,000 *mou,* out of the existing 40,000 *mou* of double-

9. Assuming a modest yield of 200 catties per *mou,* this loss would be 6 million catties. Assuming further a food consumption level of 400 catties per person per year, the loss would have provided grains for 15,000 people in a year.

cropped rice land, could not be cultivated because of the labor deficiency. In Anhwei province (Mech. Bureau, 1958, p. 132) [10] the crop failed on 2 million *mou* (20 per cent of the entire double-cropped area) because labor and animal shortages had delayed transplanting; in addition, there was neither sufficient water nor fertilizer. In general, the yields obtained from the second crop were considerably below those of the first, although the total annual yields on double-cropped land were still higher than those of single-crop land, as figures in Table 7 show.

Apart from Chekiang and Kwangtung (figures for which are not given in Table 7), the areas of double cropping, as a percentage of total arable land devoted to rice cultivation, appear surprisingly small in view of the relatively favorable climatic conditions. It would be most interesting to acquire figures for the double-cropped areas and yields obtained in earlier years, but so far they have not been sifted from local Chinese records. The main point illustrated by the figures in Table 7 is that only in Kwangsi was the rice yield of the second crop above that of the first. In Kiangsu, Hunan and Kiangsi it was about 50 per cent, and in Anhwei and Chekiang under 80 per cent. It is worth noticing how modest the rice yields from double-cropped land were in relation to both the target yield of 1,000 catties set by the campaign already mentioned, and the much higher targets set in 1958.

Although we have discussed only rice cultivation, the adoption of new farm practices was also attempted in collectives growing other crops, especially maize and wheat. The same excessively high production targets were set for these crops, and collectives similarly enforced the adoption of techniques unknown to peasants. Seed was introduced to areas from other provinces without prior experimentation; crops were sown on land known locally to be ecologically unsuitable. These technical errors undoubtedly caused many local crop failures but they must not be exaggerated, for there is no evidence of *widespread* crop failure or hunger in China during 1956. There were certainly some areas where grain was so scarce that only effective relief work by the government retrieved the situation, and others where the government's grain distribution plans had to be revised. The poor harvest in Kwangtung, for example, compared with expectations, led the government to cancel the planned shipment of grain out of the province (T'ao Chu, 1956). However, it is not possible yet to draw a firm conclusion concerning the net effect of the agricultural reforms introduced by collectives in 1956. There is much evidence that, as forecast by government officials, collectives did mobilize more resources for agricultural work than had ever been possible before. For example, they organized labor during the slack winter season, and increased the number of work-

10. Using the same assumptions as in footnote 9, this loss was equivalent to a year's grain requirements for 1 million people.

TABLE 7

ARABLE AREAS DEVOTED TO RICE AND RICE YIELDS OBTAINED IN SIX PROVINCES OF CHINA, 1956

Province	Percentage of total arable area devoted to rice	Percentage of rice arable under double cropping	Rice yields obtained in 1956 (in catties per mou)		Second crop yield as a percentage of first	Total rice yield for 1956 from double-cropped land (in catties per mou)	Rice yield in 1956 from single-cropped land (in catties per mou)	Yield of single-cropped land as a percentage of yield of double-cropped land
			1st crop	2nd crop				
Kiangsu	37.7	1.7	466	224	50.1	690	410	59.4
Chekiang	72.9	25.3	388	302	77.8	690	513	74.3
Kwangsi	67.5	60.9	300	350	116.5	650	450	69.2
Hunan	81.4	23.9	367	185	50.4	552	363	65.8
Kiangsi	87.0	16.9	322	151	46.9	473	350	74.0
Anhwei	35.3	32.8	301	186	61.8	487	371	76.2

Source:
From figures in *Problems of Agricultural Mechanization in China* (Mechanization Bureau, 1958, pp. 126-128).

ing women.[11] In the winter of 1955-56 this enlarged labor force built new water conservation works and collected vast quantities of natural fertilizer. On the other hand, they were generally unsuccessful in raising (or even maintaining) the quality and number of draft animals; though the dire consequences of the decline in animals were mitigated by the substitution of labor, which has tended to obscure this failure.

In considering the 1956 decisions of collectives concerning steps to raise production, one must view them in the context of the entire planning and control system, about which too little is known so far. Why did collectives attempt to implement such unwise and unrealistic plans? Perhaps the most important single reason was that the planning system was overcentralized to the point where collectives merely mechanically carried out orders from above, especially those received from the *hsien* (county) authority, which was the level of planning at which the lower and higher administrative layers met. The *hsien* cadres might legitimately argue that they, in turn, had no alternative but to carry out orders received from the provincial authorities. Was planning, therefore, not a genuine two-way process? It would appear that, at least until the autumn of 1956, it was not.

The consequences of disobeying plans could be serious for cadres at all levels. The main punishment feared came under the broad term "discipline and punishment" (*chi-lü ch'u-fen*) which could involve public criticism, long hours of questioning by government officials in private, the writing of confessions which were published and circulated throughout a wide area, fines, dismissal from one's post and expulsion from the Communist Party. Cadres were anxious to avoid even the mildest loss of face, such as being criticized publicly or classified as a conservative. The most serious punishments, of course, were to be avoided at all costs. During the public inquest on the "bureaucratism, subjectivism, and adventurism" in agricultural planning, held toward the end of 1956, considerable evidence came to light about these controls. The following typical examples illustrate the fact that, contrary to the government's own rulings that collectives must be democratically managed, considerable coercion was used to ensure the implementation of plans.

Collectives, it would appear, had no powers to object to any plan they were given. In Kwangtung, it was "emphasized that they [orders] must be fulfilled" without question (*NFJP,* Nov. 14, 1956). One report went so far as to state (*JMJP,* Jan. 1, 1957), in connection with the implementation of technical reforms, that "he who did not adopt the reform was, therefore,

11. The Chinese authorities admitted that these efforts had a deleterious effect on health, particularly that of peasant women. Cases were recorded of women dying, of high rates of abortion and infant mortality, all as a result of excessively hard work: Editorial, "Protect the Health of Rural Women and Children (*JMJP,* May 16, 1956).

a counter-revolutionary." Collectives dared not (*NFJP,* Nov. 28, 1956) "question the State plan" which, in Kwangsi at least, had the force of laws and decrees (Ch'en Man-yuan, 1956) Thus, as cadres of Suikai *hsien* (Kwangtung) complained (*NFJP,* Oct. 30, 1956), although they knew that both the targets and farm practices handed down were unrealistic, they adhered to them closely, "fearing punishment." The same was true in Wusiang *hsien,* Shansi, where the *hsien* Party committee ordered peasants to plant maize in a way that not only was unknown to them, but also raised the demand for labor at a time when it was already in short supply. In this case, the *hsien* authority sent cadres into the collectives to supervise the system's introduction. A cadre later stated: "Not a single person could disobey; anyone who would not implement the directive of a higher level of the Party, if a Party member, would receive punishment; if a member of a collective, he would be compelled to write 'essays of self-examination' (*fansheng shu*)." However, supervision was not strict enough to prevent two production brigades from retaining the old planting method while the deputy director of the collective was away from the district. But this, and a similar act of disobedience in a collective of the same *hsien,* were discovered by the authorities. The brigade captains were arrested and confined for two days and the deputy director of the entire collective, though away at the time, was also detained for questioning. All three men were required to write *fansheng shu,* which received wide publicity. The guilty team captain was demoted to the status of probationary Party member for a year. (It is noteworthy that on 30 per cent of the land where the new farming technique was used, there was considerable crop failure.)

It would be incorrect, therefore, to view these planning errors simply as examples of the "failure of collective farming," for they appear to reflect more the weaknesses of the overcentralized planning system. Collective cadres were fairly effectively controlled from above, and they in turn were obliged to use coercive methods to induce peasants to carry out the orders they had inherited. Some cadres stated explicitly that they used such methods reluctantly: [12] "We know coercion is bad but the tasks are urgent and time is short; there are few alternative methods; you are anxious and, therefore, cannot avoid using a little coercion."

COLLECTIVES AND INCENTIVES IN 1956

The government always recognized that financial incentives must play a crucial role both in securing the support of the peasants for collective farming and in raising the supply and productivity of farm labor. We have seen how the formation of most collectives in China took place at a

12. Chiang Wei-ch'ing, 1956. Chiang was First Secretary of the Kiangsu Party Committee.

time when the government was urgently attempting to raise crop yields mainly by labor intensive methods. How successful were the collectives in implementing a system of incentives and payments that did, in fact, induce peasants to work on the collectively owned land?

As background, it will be recalled that the regulations for collectives allowed for the existence of a small private sector, consisting of a private plot of land, domestic animals such as pigs and poultry, and scattered trees. An important function of the collective system of financial rewards, therefore, would be to ensure that the collective sector competed successfully with the private sector for such resources as labor and natural fertilizer. There were two central aspects to the incentives question: the level of income to be shared out, and the method of allocation. In 1956, serious problems arose concerning both. Low revenue from collectively organized activities, excessively high costs, and problems of job evaluation all affected the level of income available from the collective sector, while income from the private sector fell drastically during the first half of the year because of the restrictions placed upon private enterprise by the cadres.

Incentives in the Collective Sector

Collectives were not free to allocate resources in such a way as to maximize net income. For example, they could not allocate land between alternative crops according to relative costs and returns. Allocation, instead, was determined theoretically by the state plan, which was not drawn up with the specific purpose of providing collectives with maximum income. There was a marked difference in the gross revenues and costs involved in growing various crops. Because the government had set and maintained a particularly low purchase price for grain, the gross revenue a collective could obtain per *mou* of grain was considerably below what it could get from economic crops such as sugar and tea. In Fatshan *hsien,* Kwangtung (Cheng Hsing-yen, 1956), the *net* value of output (gross revenue minus production costs) per *mou* of economic crops was generally 5-10 times that of rice, even assuming the high rice yield of 1,000 catties per *mou.* The difference in relative net returns from grain and economic crops was reflected in the varying value of the labor day that collectives could afford to pay peasants for growing different crops. In Chankiang special district of Kwangtung (*NFJP,* Nov. 15, 1956), the average value of the labor day per *mou* of rice land was 1.4 *yuan,* compared with 3.0 *yuan* per *mou* of sugar cane. In South China particularly, the cost, in income foregone, of transferring land and labor to rice from sugar cane, lotus, water chestnuts, mulberry, mushrooms, tropical fruits, tea, tung oil and timber production was very high.

In 1956, approximately 33 million *mou* of land throughout China were transferred to grain, excluding the rise in the sown area of grain due to an extension of double cropping. This reflected the central government's preoccupation with the need to produce more food for the growing population and was, in part, a planned transfer. But it is also highly probable that pressure from within the collectives themselves led to transfers of land exceeding those planned, with a corresponding reduction in the area under other crops. Such pressures are understandable in a situation where food supplies were more important to people than money income. From the Chinese sources it is clear that in 1956 many collective cadres who were responsible for land utilization regarded the actual production of grain as the overriding criterion of success, and allocated resources to achieve this aim, regardless of cost, either direct or indirect. Although collectives were required to balance income and expenditure, financial work was given a very low status,[13] not only by collectives but also by *hsiang, chü* and *hsien* authorities. Regarding it as "technical," as opposed to "political," work, and as far less important than maximizing physical output, they transferred financial cadres to work of "greater importance," with the result that there was both financial chaos and corruption.

At the same time that collectives, for whatever reason, were failing to maximize revenue, they were allowing expenditure to soar (State Council, 1956). With a rapid increase in government credit available, they were able to spend lavishly on nonproductive buildings such as schools, offices and village halls, believing that "socialism demanded this" (T'ao Chu, April, 1956). They neither planned capital expenditures with reference to the rate of financial return nor phased it. Large, collectively owned pig-sties were built to accommodate collectivized pigs, leaving private sties unused; during the winter of 1955-56 brigades of labor were set to work on overambitious, long-term, high-cost water conservation schemes; collectives purchased (sometimes compulsorily) expensive agricultural implements such as modern plows, donkey boilers, coal-gas engines, and water wheels, many of which were never used.

Managerial costs were also allowed to increase in collectives. The number of administrative cadres rose, frequently above the level recommended (or required); and the organizational problems of large collectives proved to be so time-consuming that cadres were unable to participate frequently in "productive work," and thus became a burden on the "producers." Since some cadres were paid entirely out of collective income, this led to dissension, which in some cases resulted in the payment to cadres of such low wages that they had little incentive to work effi-

13. Editorial, "Do Not Neglect Financial Tasks and Accounting Work in Cooperatives" (*JMJP*, June 6, 1956). According to the editorial, a common attitude was "provided that production is well organized, everything is well managed, financial tasks and accounting work are insignificant."

ciently (for example, Ch'ang Ch'ing, 1956; Chi Shih-hsun, 1956). Administrative costs were at times inflated because, where the boundaries of the *hsiang* and collectives coincided, the duties of the two became blurred; and the collectives were made to administer and finance such work as the grain and militia levies, social relief, education, road repairs, household and marriage registration, medical services, posts and telegraphs—all of which were really the responsibility of the *hsiang* government (*Rural Work Bulletin,* 1956a).

Thus, with physical achievements such as the volume of grain produced, the amount of fertilizer collected and the number of wells dug taking precedence over financial considerations, the net income of many collectives, or the pool out of which peasants received the bulk of their personal income, failed to rise to the expected levels or actually declined (*HHPYK,* Vol. 98, 1956; *JMJP,* Mar. 25, 1957). As has been explained previously, workers' labor done in the collective sector was rewarded according to the system of work points, or labor days. Theoretically, it was a good system in that it rewarded skill and physically hard work, but it could only succeed if great care was exercised in fixing the norms and reward standards. Trials and experiments should be held for each agricultural task, as well as democratic meetings to revise norms in the light of experience and achieve full agreement between peasants and cadres. It was, in fact, a task of considerable magnitude requiring time and care.

An account of the process (*HHPYK,* Vol. 81, 1956) from Wuan *hsien,* Hopei, illustrates this. It pointed out that the first task was to make a detailed production plan that listed all agricultural jobs to be undertaken, classified according to season and type of work (for example, skill and strength required, degree of unpleasantness). In Wuan *hsien,* 23 items of work had been classified as grade I (including cutting wheat and plowing), 47 items as grade II (including pulling a cart and harvesting maize), 24 items as grade III, 26 items as grade IV and 3 items as grade V, making a total of 123 tasks in all. Then norms had to be established for each of these 123 tasks. This entailed setting the technical standard for each job, which in turn involved examining in detail the condition of available tools, draft animals, land, etc., as a basis for judging what standard of performance could reasonably be expected. Finally, the reward standards, in work points, were set for the norms of each grade of work.

If the norms and rewards were fixed correctly, the peasants would not be reluctant to undertake heavy, dirty work, since the rewards would reflect adequately all aspects of each job. There is evidence to show that, in 1956, this detailed and difficult process of job evaluation and assessment was beyond the capacity of many collective cadres who, in any case, were too busy creating collectives, mobilizing manpower or attending numerous meetings at the *hsien* level, to do the necessary preparatory work. There were many disputes [14] over norms and rewards; peasants competed for jobs they considered were liberally valued and became intensely preoccupied with the number of work points obtainable from different tasks. If the collective managers were not economically rational, the peasants undoubtedly were.

Even if the norms and reward standards were fixed correctly, the incentive to work was weakened by the fact that the *value* of the labor day (10 work points) could not be estimated with the utmost certainty until the end of the financial year, since it depended on the level of income to be distributed. Grain and cash were, of course, distributed monthly to peasants on a basis of work done (measured in points) and *forecasts* of the value of distributable product (forecasted value divided by the number of work points recorded equals the value of the work point). But peasants could not be sure that the forecasts would turn out to be correct. The monthly payments, in grain or *yuan,* might suddenly be reduced in the light of more realistic (and sober) estimates. In 1956, when collectives were striving to reach unattainable targets, they tended to make overoptimistic forecasts of distributable income, and hence overvalued the labor day (Kwangtung Party Committee, May 1956; *HHPYK,* Vol. 93, 1956). As they revised their estimates of final output downwards, they devalued the labor day; and this devaluation must have affected the incentive to work in the collective sector.

Incentive was further diminished in 1956 by a devaluation of the labor day that resulted from the winter employment of labor on long-term and often nonproductive construction works. Collectives allowed the number of labor days accomplished to increase without paying sufficient attention either to the future rise in the value of production likely to stem from this work or to when such a rise would materialize. It soon became clear that if the labor days registered were *all* to be included in the collectives' budget for 1956, the value of the labor day would drop so steeply that peasants would be inclined to press for the dissolution of collectives or at least to devote more time to the private sector.

The government, by its directive (*HHPYK,* Vol. 83, 1956) on economical and frugal management in cooperatives (collectives) of April 3, 1956, showed that it was aware of this problem. It ordered cadres to suspend work on unproductive activities which the collectives could not afford, and to concentrate on projects yielding high financial returns in the short-

14. The preoccupation with work points led to the coining of the new phrase "work point-ism" (Yen Ling, 1956). See also "On the Distribution System which Coordinates A Wages and Supply System," *Chiao-hsüeh yü yen-chiu (Teaching and Research),* 1959, No. 2, pp. 28-36; Hwang Chün, *JMJP,* Feb. 14, 1956; and *JMJP,* June 10, 1956, which revealed that in spring, 1956, many cooperatives of North China had set no norms; there was chaos in labor allocation and work registration.

est time. Secondly, instead of including all work points registered for work done during 1956 in the annual budget for 1956, collectives were to include them in the accounts for the year (or years) in which the work resulted in extra income for the collective. This would prevent the value of the labor day from being depressed in the year when no returns accrued, but it also meant that peasants might fear that they would never be paid for their arduous labor. Third, the directive proposed that peasants should do some types of work voluntarily, in the interests of the collective (claimed to coincide with their own interests), and receive only food rations as a reward. In Kwangtung, road making, afforestation and bridge repairs were included in this category (Kwangtung Party Committee, Oct. 1956).

As so often happened in China when weaknesses in the economic system were being eradicated, some cadres implemented the directive in an extreme form. Just as the level of the daily wage rate was an important incentive, so was the total amount of wages received, but cadres reacted (Yen Ling, 1956) to the directive by concentrating on raising the daily wage to the extent that they reduced the level of employment excessively. They suspended essential work, reduced the standard of intensive cultivation even where labor was available, canceled orders for pesticides and chemical fertilizers (which were some of the most profitable outlays), classified too many jobs as "voluntary," raised work norms and reduced the number of points registered for their fulfillment.

Finally, for peasants in the richer villages, the incentive to work was reduced by the effect that the merger of many villages into collectives had on both the distribution of resources and income. The actual creation of collectives and their main subdivision, production brigades, was accompanied by friction [15] between brigades (often made up of a village) competing for good factors of production. Well-endowed brigades resisted attempts to dissipate their resources among other areas of the newly formed collective, emphasizing the adverse effect such a move would have on their hitherto high level of production. By contrast, these same brigades, when discussing with the collective authorities the terms of the contract betwen themselves and the collective, stressed the low productive capacity of their resources (Rural Work Bulletin, 1956a). The adoption of a contract system did not alter the fact that, since the value of the labor day in a collective was determined centrally by the collective authority (not by the brigade), on a basis of the collective's total disposable income, the relatively productive brigades subsidized the poorer ones. In 1956 a contract system, which ensured that differences in productivity be-

15. Since this was one of the major problems in the collectives during 1956, the Chinese literature on the subject is extensive. The following few articles cover all the points raised: Hwang Chün, 1956; Kwangtung Provincial Party Committee, 1956; *HHPYK,* Vol. 93 (1956), No. 19, pp. 52-59.

tween brigades would be adequately rewarded, had not been widely implemented; and rich brigades demanded (*JMJP,* Dec. 15, 1956) the right to secede in order to become independent collectives in their own right. This, together with the managerial problems that were found to be characteristic of large collectives, led the government in September, 1956, to direct (*HHPYK,* Vol. 93, 1956) a reduction in the size of collectives and brigades. In June, 1957, it finally allowed (*HHPYK,* Vol. 111, 1957) brigades, under certain circumstances, to become separate units of accounting and distribution.

Treatment of the Private Sector

With so many problems to be solved concerning the incentives structure in the collective sector, the importance of the private sector to the peasants increased because of the security it offered. Theoretically the two were not to compete for resources. The private sector was to provide the peasants with only a small part of their food and income. Its main function was to satisfy their desire to indulge in private enterprise.

In the first half of 1956, private activity within collectives was severely curtailed (Walker, 1965) for two reasons: first, because resources were channeled so completely into the collective sector that little remained for private work; second, because cadres, viewing the private sector as a threat to the collective sector, restricted it. This was accomplished by applying political and economic sanctions that violated the published regulations governing the organization of collectives. Cadres ordered the compulsory collectivization of privately owned pigs, poultry, handicraft tools and trees, in the face of regulations stipulating that they must be collectivized only on a voluntary basis. They further disregarded the regulations concerning the financial terms by which draft animals, trees and fishponds (legitimately subject to collectivization) were collectivized, giving them a low valuation and fixing excessively long periods within which the collective would pay for them. Some collectives allocated no private plots, others less than the official minimum. Natural fertilizer owned by peasants was compulsorily acquired by collectives at low prices, payable at a future date. Peasants who did more private work than cadres considered appropriate were illegally fined, the fine being paid in work points acquired; or they were barred from working in the collective sector for a given period. Political oppression, in the form of public ridicule or classification as "capitalist" or "rightist," was also used.

As a result, peasants suffered marginally important reductions in food and cash. Although income per household from private sources varied widely from place to place, it generally accounted for 20-30 per cent of the total. Although the suppression of private activity did, at first, allow cadres to divert much labour into the collective sector, nevertheless, it created great resentment among certain sections of the peasantry and a decline in their support for collectivization. This must have been particularly true where the kind of mismanagement already outlined had resulted in the collective sector's paying lower day wage rates than the earnings to be had from a day's private work—if it were available. For example, in Kükong *hsien,*[16] Kwangtung, a day's private work was generally worth 1.3 *yuan* to a peasant, whereas the value of the labor day during the period of the first 1956 rice crop was only 0.56 *yuan.*

Summing up, this survey of some features of collective organization in 1956 has shown how collectives, under orders from higher authorities, made very ambitious attempts to increase grain production, mainly by extending the area of double cropping and introducing other new farm practices. Most underdeveloped agrarian countries have little success in implementing their plans for transforming traditional agriculture, but this could not be said about China. The creation of collective farms, combined with a highly centralized planning system, ensured that plans drawn up in Peking would affect the organization of agriculture in the remotest villages. Indeed, the problem was not one of too little, but too much change, introduced too quickly and without enough regard for the local situation. The area of double cropping was greatly increased; rice was planted closer than ever before; improved seeds were introduced from other provinces; new farm implements were employed; labor was organized in constructing earthworks and collecting fertilizer. The picture was certainly one of immense activity. We have seen how most of the agricultural innovations envisaged by the government raised the demand for resources, especially farm labor and draft animals. Evidence has been presented indicating that the extension of double cropping was impeded in some places by shortages of these factors. Were collectives successful in devising ways of reducing the shortages, or did they make them worse?

COLLECTIVES AND LABOR

Collectives were successful in increasing rural employment in both winter 1955-56 and spring 1956. However, they were less successful in using this increased labor supply efficiently, and a great deal of human energy was wasted. Nor did they balance their demand for labor with the available supply. This, it has been argued, was not so much a fault of collective organization as of the entire planning system and the high targets imposed on collectives. A weakness in collective organization was that the incentives system adopted by collectives did not directly result in

16. "Record of a Visit to Tunghsia Cooperative," *Kükong Nung-min-pao (Kukong Peasants' News),* October 23, 1956. The financial attraction of private, as opposed to collective, activity is further illustrated by the low price paid by the state to collectives for grain, compared with prices obtained for privately produced items. For example, in Fatshan special district, Kwangtung, the state paid 0.0732 *yuan* per catty for grain, while peasants sold pork at 0.5 *yuan* and poultry at 0.4 *yuan* per catty, and eggs at 0.05 *yuan* each. See *NFJP,* Oct. 13, 1956.

an increase in labor supply. The method of rewarding work, although theoretically attractive, had many drawbacks and was extremely difficult to implement. Cadres too often resorted to nonfinancial inducements, such as persuasion, appeals to patriotism and coercion in various forms. But these could only increase the labor supply in the short run, as showed by reports of the dissolution of collectives [17] coming in during summer and autumn 1956. Finally, the incentive to work in the collectives was diminished by the fact that, for many peasants, especially those belonging to the skilled middle class, collectivization brought little increase in real income. For some it brought a reduction in income and, for most peasants it meant a marked increase in physically hard work as well as tighter control by cadres of their daily life.

COLLECTIVES AND DRAFT ANIMALS

There is abundant evidence (though it has yet to be put together in a systematic way) that not only did collectives fail to increase the supply of draft animals to meet the increased demand they had induced, but they in fact adopted policies that diminished the supply. It must not be thought that when the movement toward socialization of agriculture began around 1952, there was a sufficient supply of draft animals, for there had been a shortage for a long time. In transforming agricultural institutions, however, the government did not ensure that steps were taken to preserve and expand the supply of this essential factor of production in Chinese agriculture. Especially in its early days, the Communist regime issued so much propaganda linking the advent of mechanized farming with socialization that some cadres came to believe that as soon as cooperatives or collectives had been established, draft animals would be replaced by tractors.

But the main reason for the declining number of draft animals was the failure of mutual aid teams, cooperatives and collectives to provide peasants with the financial inducement to preserve them. In mutual aid teams and cooperatives, animals were overworked and their services undervalued. Independent peasants, viewing the way cooperatives and collectives treated privately owned animals, saw little point in raising draft animals only to have them taken into collective ownership by compulsory order, at low prices (or none at all) payable over several years without interest. Many, therefore, reacted by selling their animals as quickly as possible, or by neglecting or slaughtering them.

Animals taken into collective ownership were not, generally, managed with care. They were frequently kept in large groups, thus increasing the risk of infectious disease, and livestock management was too often given a low priority by collectives; unskilled and poorly paid peasants were

17. The NCNA (English language), March 25, 1957, reported that 80,000 households left cooperatives in Kwangtung during autumn, 1956. See also editorial, *JMJP*, Nov. 22, 1956.

considered appropriate for the task. The burden of work rose, but supplies of animal fodder declined.

IV. ECONOMIC ORGANIZATION IN THE COLLECTIVES DURING 1957

The flexibility of the Chinese government is illustrated by the speed with which it reacted to the agricultural problems already outlined. In the autumn of 1956 it called for two important changes in agricultural organization:

(a) Agricultural planning and management were to be decentralized. State plans, containing fewer targets than in 1956, were now to be formulated after genuine consultation between the basic producing units of agriculture and the various levels of government. Collectives and production brigades were to become smaller and to be given wide powers over day-to-day organization. The old, experienced peasants were reinstated as the experts on agricultural technique.

(b) Along with decentralization, more material incentives were to be provided for the peasants. In the first place, collectives were directed to pay more attention to "profit" (revenue minus costs) in organizing their affairs. Provided it was consistent with the state plans, the allocation of land to different crops was to be made with regard to relative costs and returns. Second, the place of the private sector within the collective framework was reaffirmed. The government stressed the importance of giving peasants private plots of useful size as well as more freedom to market their products. Collectives were to refrain from collectivizing pigs and draft animals compulsorily and, when acquiring them by agreement, were to pay fair prices. In order to induce peasants to deliver natural fertilizer for use on collective land, instead of applying it to their private plots, collectives were instructed to pay the market price.

Several of these reforms appear to have been implemented to a greater extent than the central government intended, with the result that its control of agricultural planning declined drastically in 1957, with serious consequences. The momentum of 1956 was lost, the private agricultural economy expanded and, partly because of this, the collective economy stagnated.

THE COLLECTIVE SECTOR IN 1957

The government's condemnation of the errors of 1956 and its directives calling for a slower pace of change, with more liberalization and decentralization of planning, quickly led to a decline in collective activity and government control of agricultural organization. This was evident at the beginning of winter 1956-57. In contrast to the previous year, as far as collective work was concerned, the winter season once again assumed its traditional slow tempo. In Kwangtung, where the winter sown area was reduced, collectives handed over (Kwangtung Party & People's Comm., 1957) a great deal of land to peasants for their private use throughout the winter. The Kwangtung authorities did not organize a fertilizer-collecting campaign as they had done the previous winter, partly because it was widely believed that additional fertilizer applications would have no effect—the maximum output having already been attained—and partly because it would have been incompatible with the growth of the private agricultural sector.

The decline in activity also followed the substitution of "profits" for physical production targets as the main driving force in collectives. Some collectives were reluctant to formulate any plans, while others were unwilling to set targets as high as the level of production attained in 1956. As a report from Szechwan stated (*Szechwan jihpao,* Dec. 22, 1956), this was because cadres had lost confidence as a result of the planning problems of 1956, associated with such high targets. In February, 1957, when the agricultural work of the spring season was about to commence throughout south China, a *People's Daily* editorial (*JMJP,* Feb. 24, 1957) admitted that disregard for the state's annual plan was widespread. Furthermore, the collectives' implementation of the new directives on agricultural organization was not always exactly as the government had intended. For example, having been instructed to pay more attention to costs and returns in allocating resources, some collectives transferred too much land out of grain into economic crop production. In Kwangtung, for example, 2 million *mou* of land devoted to grain production in 1956 were either reallocated (*NFJP,* July 23, 1957) to more valuable economic crops or used as private plots in 1957. Collectives believed that any grain deficits resulting from the transfer would be made good by the central government. By spring 1957, in Kwangtung at least, the loss of control was so serious that the provincial government sent cadres to the villages to enforce the adoption of higher targets and the correct implementation of government policies (*Hong Kong Wen-hui pao,* March 1957).

The transfer of land from grain to other uses was not offset by an appropriate expansion of double cropping. In fact, the official index of multiple cropping (*Ten Great Years*) for 1957 showed a decline from 1956, from 142.3 to 140.6. The total sown area of grain fell by 51 million *mou,* or 2.7 per cent; grain output, it was claimed, rose by only 1.4 per cent. The output of wheat fell by 4.6 per cent, that of coarse grain by 2.9 per cent (*Ten Great Years*). Although the weather conditions and natural disasters of 1957 were reported as very severe, and must therefore partly account for these unimpressive achievements, growth in the collective economy was also retarded by the continued shortages of necessary resources. The double-cropped area was not reduced to the point at which labor and animal supplies were adequate, nor were collectives able to solve the shortages through better organization.

Both the total number of draft animals and the supply available for agricultural work continued to decline. The death rate among animals was high during winter 1956-57. At the beginning of winter, Kirin provincial authorities had warned that many of the province's 0.3 million weak animals would not survive until spring (*Kirin jih-pao,* Dec. 1956), while in Kiangsu more than 60,000 animals died. By spring 1957, more than 40 per cent of all draft animals in Kiangsu and 30 per cent in Shantung were classified as weak. Shensi province claimed to have a shortage of 0.4 million animals (*JMJP,* April 19, 1957). Collectives could no longer count on importing animals from traditional sources such as Heilungkiang. For example, at the end of 1956, Noho *hsien* (one of the biggest exporters of draft animals in Heilungkiang) notified the government that it no longer had an export surplus (*Heilungkiang jih-pao,* Dec. 1956).

The supply of animals available for agricultural work was affected by the increase in competition between the enlarged private sector and the collectives. Following the opening of the free market for certain produce (especially from the private sector) and the adoption by the government of a more liberal policy toward private commerce, many peasants took their animals out of collectives and used them for the more lucrative business of transport (Central Committee, 1957). No evidence has yet been discovered to show whether some collectives managed to obtain the services of animals returned to private ownership by paying higher rents for their use. There is no doubt that, in general, the shortage of animals was serious. At the spring plowing, 58,000 men had to pull plows in three *hsien* of Hopei (Mechanization Bureau, 1958, p. 4).

In the summer of 1957, the government drew attention to the situation by publishing the results of a comprehensive survey (Ch'iao Pei-kuo, 1957) of the supply of draft animals in the Party's journal, *Rural Work Bulletin* (*Nung-ts'un Kung-tso t'ung-hsün*). This revealed that the breeding stock was already declining towards the point beyond which it would be biologically impossible to maintain the current animal population. Existing horses, donkeys and oxen of medium to good quality constituted only about 40 per cent of the total, while the remaining 60 per cent were both small and weak. Between 30 per cent and 50 per cent of all animals were old and useless for farm work. In September, 1957, the northern provinces of Hopei, Shansi, Liaoning, Kirin, Shantung and Heilungkiang estimated their shortage of draft animals at 8 million (Hsiao Yü, 1957), and although the position of the southern provinces was better, it was by no means good. According to a survey (Hsiao, 1957) of 50,000 animals in 305 Kwangtung collectives, for example, 54.7 per cent of the oxen were weak. Throughout China the birth rate of animals in 1957 was extremely low, and the death rate high. The government made no secret of its conclusion, stating that "the present situation is that the supply of livestock is seriously affecting agricultural production and will continue to do so" (Ch'iao Pei-kuo, 1957). How far it was affecting production is indicated by a report from Hopei, where in August, 1957, 16.81 million *mou* were planted, without having been plowed "for several years" (Mechanization Bureau, 1958, p. 44). Land once producing crop yields of 200-300 catties per *mou* now produced 50 catties. Pregnant livestock were used for plowing, thus increasing the risk of spontaneous abortion, while substitution of men for animals was a common phenomenon. It was also reported (*Szechwan jih-pao,* Dec. 1957) that in Szechwan, despite the shortages, many beasts capable of plowing were being slaughtered for meat and hides.

THE PRIVATE SECTOR IN 1957

There is no doubt that the government's policy of expanding the private agricultural sector, as an incentive measure, was implemented in 1957. Collectives returned pigs, poultry, trees, fishponds and draft animals to private hands and increased the size of private plots. The evidence leads to the conclusion that these measures, together with the loss of control over local affairs by the central government and with the liberalization of commerce, resulted in an intensification of the competition for labor and fertilizer between the collective and private sectors that was enough to damage the collective economy and the very foundations of socialism in the countryside. Although it is fairly certain that few areas increased the area of private plots up to the permitted 10 per cent of the arable area per head, the expansion that did take place affected the balance between the two sectors.[18]

Absenteeism from collective work was common. It affected crop production in some collectives enough to turn what had been a grain surplus into a deficit. The directive to collectives to pay more to peasants for

18. It is possible that the increase in the private plot area in Kwangtung was considerable, but the reports are too vague to draw a firm conclusion. For example, *NFJP,* January 15, 1957, stated that the area of private plots was 3 million *mou,* or approximately 5.2 per cent of the arable area of the province. The Hong Kong *Ta-kung pao (Impartial Daily)* Sept. 20, 1957, however, stated that 2.67 million *mou* had been allocated for private production of vegetables, miscellaneous grains, and fodder crops. It is not clear whether this was in addition to the 3 million *mou* above. If so, the area would be 9.9 per cent of the arable area. There is no doubt that the existence of the private plot adversely affected collective agriculture in Kwangtung. In the rich Canton delta, competition between the two sectors was described as "an acute contradiciton": *Chung-kuo Ch'ing-nien pao (Peking Chinese Youth News),* June 10, 1957. In autumn 1957 it was argued that not only was the area of private plot too great, but much of it was not being used to grow fodder crops—theoretically its main use (*Hong Kong Ta-kung pao,* Oct. 19, 1957).

domestically produced fertilizer does not appear to have had the desired effect. Peasants applied much of it to their enlarged private plots, and this again must have affected the yields of the collectively owned land. By emphasizing private livestock rearing, the government made it more difficult for itself to control the use of animal fertilizer; and since chemical fertilizer supplies were minute (and not expanding rapidly), it was essential that the bulk of animal fertilizer be applied to the collective land.

The extent to which the enlarged private sector reduced the peasants' dependence on the collective for food and cash varied widely over the countryside. The output of the private sector was greatest in south China, where very high yields of vegetables and fruit could be obtained. The larger the yield of vegetables from the private plot, the greater the number of pigs that could be reared. The expansion of private enterprise increased most peasants' cash incomes more than their food supplies, of which the overwhelming part still derived from the collective sector. Nevertheless, moderately sized plots, less than the 10 per cent maximum, could produce enough vegetables and pork to supply marginally significant calories and nutrients [19] in a diet that was otherwise unbalanced. The number of calories supplied would be considerably higher if, as is likely for 1957, peasants grew grains on their plots. In some collectives, particularly in south China, cash income from private sources *exceeded* that from the collective, and cases were recorded of collusion between cadres and peasants, resulting in the rapid development of lucrative private activities.

The spread of black markets in grain, and the serious difficulties facing the government in controlling grain supplies during summer 1957, were partly the result of this rise in effective demand associated with the expansion of the private agricultural sector (*JMJP,* Aug. 30, 1957; *Rural Work Bulletin,* 1957). But although the high black market price of grain reflected this increase in personal income, it also reflected the grain shortage.[20] Some peasants demanded (and got) increases in grain rations (*JMJP,* Editorials, Aug. 1957), and this affected both the supplies available for the towns and the rate of investment in collectives. It would appear, however, that the rise in income from private sources and the concessions relating to grain rations did not lead to a general revival of confidence in collectives. The standard of living and the employment opportunities in the towns still far exceeded those of the countryside, although grain supplies in the towns were declining. Apart from the realities of the situation, the prospects for economic advancement in the towns seemed immense to the peasants, and toward the end of the year more and more joined the

19. Some evidence of possible magnitudes is given in Kenneth R. Walker, *Planning in Chinese Agriculture,* 1965.

20. According to *Ten Great Years,* total grain output in China rose by only 1.4 per cent; wheat production fell by 4.6 per cent and coarse grains by 2.9 per cent.

exodus from the countryside,[21] with obvious implications for the future labor supply in agriculture.

This sketch of economic organization in collectives during 1957 has stressed the contrast with 1956. The "big push" of 1956, accompanied by high targets, tight government control of planning, and a certain amount of coercion, gave way to a year of reduced activity. Agricultural planning was decentralized, and more financial incentives were provided for the peasants, especially in the form of an expanded private agricultural sector. There is a great deal to be discovered about the changes that took place in the collectives during this momentous year of China's post-war history, but it is clear that from the government's point of view the experiment in liberalization misfired, for the consequent decline in collective activity was greater than the government can have anticipated. The collective sector of agriculture suffered from competition for resources with the private sector, the size of which began to constitute a serious threat to the future development of the collective sector. It cannot be said that in 1957 collectives solved their outstanding organizational problems of 1956. The number of healthy draft animals continued to decline, and although the number of pigs almost certainly increased (as private ownership increased), much of the valuable fertilizer produced was applied to private land. It is impossible to judge how far the problems relating to incentives and distribution in collectives were solved. The widespread transfer of land from grain to more valuable crops was designed to raise the level of collective income, but it helped to produce the grain shortage.

Now the government had to regain control and consolidate collective agriculture, without reverting to the excesses of 1956. In directives that were almost identical to those of September, 1956 (*HHPYK,* Vol. 117, 1957), it reaffirmed the importance of small collectives, a decentralized management, a private sector, a class policy that recognized the upper peasants' contribution to production, and the need for stability in organization.[22] At the same time, however, the government also launched the

21. (i) Central Committee of C.C.P. and State Council, 1957. (ii) Editorial, *JMJP,* December 19, 1957. This source stated that between the end of the autumn harvest of 1956 and the summer harvest of 1957, 0.57 million people went to the towns; during the autumn of 1957, Shantung, Honan, Anhwei and Kiangsu provinces lost 0.11 million people from the rural population. It was admitted that the drift was seriously affecting agricultural production. In Kwangtung there were reports of rural cadres striking in support of their demands to be transferred to the towns because of the low living standard in the countryside (*NFJP,* Aug. 17, 1957). Rural depopulation was especially causing the abandonment of arable land in hill and mountain areas. As Teng Tzu-hui pointed out, this land accounted for 35.8 per cent of the Chinese total; its grain output was 30 per cent of the national total. See Teng Tzu-hui, 1957a.

22. It is interesting to record that at the end of 1957, so near the Great Leap Forward and the formation of the larger communes, T'ao Chu, First Secretary of Kwangtung, called for smaller collectives and brigades and concluded that, once the adjustments in size had been made, these units should remain fixed for 10 years (T'ao Chu, 1957).

"socialist education" and "rectification" campaigns to win back control lost during the "Hundred Flowers" period, to consolidate socialism in the countryside, to expose peasants with "rightist, capitalist" leanings as enemies of the people, and to bring the private agricultural economy within acceptable limits. Once again, therefore, the cadres directly responsible for agricultural organization were faced with policy directives that were a very imprecise guide to action: government control was to be reimposed but decentralized management maintained; a private sector was to be maintained but restricted; capitalists and rightists were to be exposed but the interests of the upper peasant classes closely guarded. As in 1956, the political situation led the cadres to err on the side of socialism.

V. THE GREAT LEAP FORWARD AND THE PEOPLE'S COMMUNE

The stability in agricultural organization called for by the government was not achieved in 1958. On the contrary, it was in 1958 that the most radical reorganization of agriculture yet attempted by the government was carried out, beginning with the Great Leap Forward and ending in the creation of the "people's communes." The Great Leap grew out of several factors. It could, no doubt, be argued that one of them was the regime's *optimism* about conditions being favorable to a second, and more elaborate, big push on all fronts, but it is argued here that the Leap was the government's response to a *serious* economic and political situation which provided little freedom of maneuver. Despite the slow rate of growth of agriculture in 1957, local surveys showed that the lower levels of government and collectives were, once again, planning for insignificant increases in construction and production during 1958. In Kwangtung, for example, the targets for the area to be sown in winter were "shrinking as they went down from layer to layer" (*JMJP,* Oct. 21, 1957). One of the main features of meetings organized in villages as part of the campaigns in socialist education, rectification, water conservation and fertilizer collection—all of which became inextricably merged—was the call by cadres sent from higher authorities to raise targets and revive productive activity.

Reading reports of these meetings, it is possible to discern how the Leap gathered momentum. Collectives were urged to discover "new production potentialities"; as in 1956, the height of the targets adopted became an important index of political reliability. The Party now rejected the use of the historical trend of output as a planning criterion, considering it irrelevant to possible future attainments; the correct *attitude* was now considered to be the key to raising production to new levels. Local Party cadres were given very wide powers not only to ensure that high targets were in fact set, but also to guarantee that every resource was strained to the utmost to fulfill them. Within a few weeks, targets were raised to astronomical heights: plans to raise production by 70-100 per cent were common. Collectives attempted to mobilize every person in rural China who was capable of working, and succeeded in expanding the labor force to a level surpassing that of winter 1955-56. They organized large scale water conservation projects which crossed the boundaries of districts (ch'ü) and even counties (*hsien*). To finance them, they raised the rate of investment.[23] As in 1956, further impetus was given by the publication of another 12-year plan for agriculture, a revised version of that issued in 1956.

The amount of work done in rural China during 1958, measured in man hours of physical labor, was truly remarkable, quite apart from the results of the work. More women were induced to join the labor force and all peasants worked longer hours than ever before. As the collective sector revived, the private sector declined.[24] Private plots, family graves, shrines, (Luo T'ien, 1958), trees and even dwelling houses were eliminated in order to expand and reorganize the arable area (*Ch'engtu jih-pao,* March 1958). Pigs were once again collectivized.[25] Advanced agricultural tech-

23. The rate of investment in many collectives had fallen in 1957 as a result of the emphasis on private activity and high percentage of output distributed to members (Liao Lu-yen, 1958. Although the directive raising the level of investment in collectives was published Jan. 6, 1958, Teng Tzu-hui had already announced that the rate could be raised to 10-12 per cent of net output, instead of 5-8 per cent. The article "We Must Have Strength to Welcome a New High Tide for Increased Agricultural Production" (*Szechwan jih-pao,* Nov. 6, 1957). criticizing the low rate of investment in 1957, pointed out that if members were required to increase their investment in the collectives to a level of around 200-300 *yuan* per family, there could then be no talk of leaving the collectives, concluding ". . . this has great political significance."

24. A call to strengthen the collective economy was accompanied by an attack on the private sector (*HHPYK,* Vol. 127, 1958). Many articles revealed that collectives at this time reduced the area of private plot as part of the socialist education and rectification campaigns. Teng Hsiao-p'ing (1957) called for "appropriate restriction of the private plot and individual reclamation of land." A report from Szechwan revealed that one of the important issues under discussion was "how appropriately to reduce members' private plots and restrict the growing on private plots of vegetables for sale" ("Achieve a Great Leap Forward in Agricultural Production This Year," *Chungking jih-pao* [*Chungking Daily*], January 10, 1958). The poor performance of agriculture in Kwangtung during 1957 was blamed partly upon the allocation of "excess" area of private plot (T'ao Chu, 1957).

25. As late as November and December, 1957, Teng Tzu-hui had affirmed his belief that the best way to develop the livestock industry was to emphasize private rearing. Pointing out that over 90 per cent of all pigs in China at that time were in private hands, he attributed the rapid growth in the number of livestock during 1957 to (1) higher prices for pigs and pig manure; (2) the policy of expanding private ownership; (3) the increase in the area of private plots. In November he attacked cadres who were restricting private livestock early during the socialist education campaign. (See Teng Tzui-hui, 1957 "On Extended Reproduction.") However, during winter, 1957-58, many reports confirmed that Teng Tzu-hui's criticisms had been ignored. For example, see *HHPYK,* Vol. 127, 1958; *Szechwan jih-pao,* April 20, 1958.

niques such as deep plowing and close planting were adopted over a very wide area.[26] To increase labor productivity, collectives were directed to organize communal canteens in the fields.

It is impossible, in the present state of research, to give any indication of how much the 1958 rural labor force had increased over that in 1956. Two general points are relevant, however. In the first place, the outflow of labor from the countryside to the towns increased as the Great Leap in industry and commerce raised the demand of urban centers for labor. At a time when the demand for skilled, strong agricultural workers was also rising rapidly, then, possibly many workers in this category were leaving for the towns. Second, although precise figures are not available, it is certain that the supply of draft animals was smaller in the spring of 1958 than it had been the previous year and, with the extraordinary rise in demand for draft power, more labor than ever had to be substituted. It can be assumed, therefore, that the increase in the agricultural labor force that did take place was not enough to make such innovations as the extension of double cropping very much more feasible than in 1956. Perhaps future research on the history of particular communes will indicate just how much new agricultural labor was added during the Leap.

The orders of autumn 1957 that collectives were to become smaller—and remain so—had been forgotten by the spring of 1958, when the large-scale communes were already in sight. There were frequent reports of collectives merging to reap the advantages of pooling resources in construction schemes (for example, *Ch'engtu jih-pao,* May, 1958). When provinces began to report achievements in production commensurate with their unattainable targets, it seems that the central government, for a short time at least, believed that the figures were correct. The apparent success of the construction campaign, together with these claims of unprecedented spring and summer harvests, led the government to conclude that a new stage in the revolution had been reached, and that the time was ripe to move to a system of agriculture with communist elements.

During the few months of summer, the large, highly centralized, almost entirely socialist people's commune replaced the relatively small, decentralized, mixed economy of the collective. The commune, as described in government regulations (*HHPYK,* Vol. 139, 1958) and in regional reports, had three main features:

(i) It was an administrative unit of government, as well as a comprehensive planning authority, combining the duties of the *hsiang* (township) and, in some cases, the *hsien,* with the task of

26. A report from Kwangtung, commenting on the opposition to new techniques from peasants, stated that securing a technical revolution was a task in ideological work; that peasants' experience was limited, and that they must abandon "old superstitions handed down from their ancestors" and adopt new methods (Chao Tzu-yang, 1958).

organizing all production and services, including defense and education. It was therefore very much larger than the collective.[27] Since each commune enjoyed a considerable amount of autonomy, the new system, in effect, reimposed a centralized system of control at the commune level.

(ii) Although the commune was highly centralized, it was generally divided into three tiers—the commune itself, the "organization district" (or large production brigade), and the production brigade, or production team. It is useful to consider the tiers below the commune level as equivalent to the former collective and cooperative. From the point of view of agricultural organization, perhaps the most notable aspect of the commune was that the commune authority itself became the main unit of ownership and distribution, with the power to move labor and other resources anywhere within its vast area. The collective, it will be recalled, had been unsuccessful in bringing resource allocation and income distribution under its more limited control, because of pressures from its constituent brigades (villages). The commune system now introduced a far more egalitarian income distribution than that attempted by the collectives. In addition to this, the incentives system was changed. "Distribution according to labor" gave way to distribution based partly on need and partly on work accomplished. Each commune member received a free supply of grain, allocated according to need, on a per head basis, and if he worked, a wage payment. Time wage rates replaced the intricate system of work points which had been so laboriously evolved by the collectives. The latter was now condemned as "bourgeois" because it penalized families weak in labor and productive power (*Chiao-hsüeh yü yen-chiu,* 1959a); it was individualistic, encouraging a capitalist mentality. The government must have believed that food production had reached such heights that it was no longer necessary to relate the income of peasants entirely to productivity in order to maintain and increase their effort.

(iii) The commune regulations allowed for almost no private sector, and in practice it was often totally abolished. The private plots, houses and their sites, most domestic animals, trees, fishponds, all became the property of the commune, either immediately or within a short time.

Most communes were created during August, September and October, 1958, at a time when the mass campaign for "backyard" iron and

27. For information on the size of communes, see "All the Villages of China Have Already Basically Carried Out Communization." *TCKT* (*Statistical Work*), 1958, No. 20, p. 23.

steel production was at its height. Both activities dislocated agricultural work so severely that the autumn harvest was not entirely gathered. With reports coming in from major agricultural provinces that grain production had risen by over 100 per cent, communes inflated the proportion of food they distributed as the free supply, and much of the country indulged in a short-lived food consumption boom. Claiming that the grain problem had been "fundamentally solved" but that still higher production could be achieved, the government set even higher targets for 1959 (Liao Lu-yen, 1959), which were to be attained by raising yields. Over a ten-year period communes were to reduce the area sown in grain by as much as 30 per cent. One of the main reasons for the grain shortage in 1959 was that there was such a state of euphoria that many communes implemented this directive *immediately*.[28]

Before the end of 1958 the government began to appreciate the real nature of the economic situation in agriculture, especially the critical decline in incentives that had followed the establishment of the communes. The incentive to work had been destroyed by the excessive allocation of food on a basis of need, and also by the communization of almost everything the peasants possessed, even their domestic cooking utensils and furniture. When the government also realized that food output in 1958 had been grossly overestimated, it faced the double task of reducing consumption to a realistic level and raising incentives to ensure that 1959 production would increase. The December resolution on the communes (Central Committee, 1958), designed to fulfill these aims, marked the beginning of the return to reality and the end of the commune in its pure form. It ordered a decentralization of powers and ownership, more distribution "according to labor," and freedom for peasants to rear small numbers of domestic animals.

28. A county in Shensi planned to increase grain output in 1959 by 400 per cent on a reduced area, on the assumption that it could raise yields from 668 catties to 2,464 catties per *mou:* Changan county's plan for the "Three Three System," *HHPYK,* Vol. 146, 1958, No. 24 (pp. 89-91). A similar plan was put forward by Ningtsing county, Hopei: "We Must Follow the Way of Sowing a Small Area of High Yielding Crops and Obtaining a Bigger Harvest," *HHPYK,* Vol. 147, 1959, No. 1 (pp. 89-91). Kwangtung province reduced its winter sown area of grains from 14 million *mou* in 1957-58 to under 6 million *mou* in 1958-59: "The Spring Grain Output in Kwangtung This Year Will be Much Greater than That of Last Year," NCNA, April 15, 1960. In May, 1959, the authorities admitted that the policy of reducing the sown area had wrongly been implemented in Kwangtung, both in the winter and in the first rice sown area—which was less than that of 1958: "Kwangtung Provincial Committee Resolves To Promote Immediately a Campaign for Yields of 1,000 Catties of Rice and 10,000 Catties of Potatoes," *JMJP,* May 31, 1959. A *People's Daily* editorial of July, 1959, stated that "a great many areas had reduced the sown area of wheat" (*JMJP,* July 12, 1959). The *People's Daily* of June 11, 1959, directed communes to sow *more* not less, as "an urgent requirement," indicating that the policy of reducing the sown area would not be implemented for at least 10 years.

VI. AGRICULTURAL ORGANIZATION, 1959-1964

By the spring of 1959 four factors dominated the formulation of agricultural policy:

(1) The fact that no economic miracle had taken place in 1958 but that, instead, food consumption had greatly exceeded the level appropriate to actual production.

(2) The winter sown area had been reduced, so that the spring harvest would be poor.

(3) The short supply of resources and the low morale would inevitably restrict the spring sown area, which meant that the government could not count on a good summer harvest.

(4) Grain stocks and higher food imports would have to be used to prevent the first serious famine since the Communist government had assumed power.

The ills of agricultural organization under the communes were merely an acute form of those encountered during 1956; and so it was easier for the government to diagnose them than to decide on the treatment. The task was to restore adequate material incentives without losing control. The situation in the spring of 1959 was the most serious since 1949—first, because food was scarcer than before; second, because the low-level cadres must certainly have been so bewildered, demoralized and disillusioned that they were incapable of making decisions; and third, because the government must have lost the support of many peasants who had been activists in the cooperativization and collectivization drives. The solution adopted between 1959 and 1962 was to restore, in turn, the large production brigade (former collective) and the smaller production brigade, or team (former cooperative in size), as the units of ownership, accounting, distribution, and control over the choice of agricultural practices.

THE FIRST REORGANIZATION, 1959-1961

Although the government clearly directed, in many policy statements during 1959 and 1960, that the large production brigade was to be the basic unit of ownership and distribution, it is apparent that these were years of considerable uncertainty among the local cadres as to the kind of organization the government desired. While there is evidence that some areas reorganized the communes quickly, elsewhere there was a long time lag. Policy toward the private plot, the private ownership of pigs, and the management of mess halls was ambiguous. No detailed official figures of sown areas or agricultural production were published for 1959 or 1960, but there is enough evidence that the shortage of farm labor was acute and must have impeded production. During 1958, 1959 and 1960, it was estimated (*JMJP,* March 31, 1960) that the town and mining populations rose by 20 million through migration. In 1960, as a result of government efforts and the high level of urban unemployment (due to the shortage of food and raw materials), the population drift to the towns was reversed. (*JMJP,* July 27, 1960). Nevertheless, in Kwangtung, where one million workers returned to agricultural work, there were reports (Chao Tzu-yang, 1960) throughout the summer that an acute labor shortage was impeding agricultural work connected with the second rice crop.

Any ambiguity remaining in agricultural policy was eliminated at the end of 1960 when the government sent to the communes the secret orders [29] known as the "12 rules," which directed the immediate implementation of policies already advocated in 1958, 1959 and 1960. These covered the old issues of egalitarian distribution, the payments system, size of organization unit, ownership of resources by subdivisions of the commune, decentralization of powers, commandism, blind instructions regarding technical matters, and corruption among cadres. The incentive to work was raised by the rehabilitation [30] of the norms and work point system of "distribution according to labor," in place of time wages and free supply, and by the allocation of private plots,[31] once again, on the 5 per cent criterion. The produce of the plots could be sold on the newly opened free markets. In May, 1961, the government sent to all communes the "60 articles" (*Hong Kong Union Research,* 1962) which were, in fact, a detailed statement of the regulations for communes and the rights of peasants. There is much evidence that in 1961 these policies were indeed implemented. During the spring of 1961, the government, for the second time, turned to private enterprise as the main future supplier of pigs, acknowledging (*JMJP,* June 14, 1962) that collective rearing had been unsuccessful and very costly.

THE SECOND REORGANIZATION, 1961-1962

In 1961, preparations were made to decentralize the communes even further, by replacing the large production brigade with the smaller brigade, or team, as the level of accounting and distribution. In Kwangtung the

29. These were not published in China but their content has been revealed by refugees. See "The Twelve Rules, the Sixty Articles, and the Campaign Against the Prejudicial Conduct of the Cadres," *Hong Kong Union Research Service,* 1962.

30. It is interesting to note that neither Chiang Hsüeh-mo (1962) nor T'ao Chu, in a recent statement on the development of the communes, made reference to even a temporary existence of free supply (T'ao Chu, 1964).

31. Sources are given in Kenneth R. Walker, 1965.

change was accomplished during the second half of 1961 and the beginning of 1962 (*NFJP*, June 12, 1961; Oct. 26, 1961; March 14, 1962). The government now argued that organization by the larger brigade was too rigid; agricultural management, unlike industry, required a detailed knowledge of every local situation that was to be found only in the smaller brigade.

When the small brigade became the basic planning unit in 1961-62, the organization of agriculture was the same as it had been under the collectives during the summer of 1967. Kwangtung cadres at the large brigade level actively resisted this change on the grounds that it made them redundant and reduced government control over agriculture. Their arguments—that government policies were "going into the pockets" of the small brigade cadres, and that peasants were doing as they pleased (*NFJP*, Aug. 5, 1962)—were particularly reminiscent of those voiced during the rectification campaign that had preceded the Great Leap in autumn 1957. According to one report (*NFJP*, Oct. 28, 1961), the return of the private plot and free market had already led to speculation, absenteeism and demands that work contracts be made between the small brigade and individual households, rather than the brigade subdivision (the former mutual aid team). Against these arguments it was claimed that the few cadres remaining at the large brigade level still had important work to perform. For example, it was their job to persuade lower levels to carry out "correct policies," to train inexperienced cadres and to settle disputes. Cases were cited in which such cadres successfully solved problems concerning the use of water, the registration of work points, the sharing of sickles among small brigades, and absenteeism. This discussion especially gave clear evidence of demoralization among cadres (*NFJP*, April 6, April 8, April 18, June 3, 1962).

In what must be regarded as an official policy statement (T'ao Chu, 1964), T'ao Chu, first secretary of Kwangtung (and in spring 1965 made a deputy Prime Minister), revealed in 1964 that no further changes had been made in agricultural organization, which meant that for the first time since 1949 there had been relative stability for two years and, in some areas, perhaps for three years. T'ao Chu explicitly confirmed that the commune of 1964 was like the former collective, particularly in its system of responsibility and distribution. He insisted, however, that it was more efficient, having a larger and more securely based collective economy, the organization of which had benefited from the experience accumulated in the previous years. Official communiqués during the years 1961-64 gave no details of agricultural production, but claimed that it increased in each successive year. Indirect evidence suggests that both the collective and the private sectors of agriculture recovered significantly from their depressed state during the years 1959-61. How the new organization of the communes has affected the supply of agricultural labor, draft animals,[32] farm implements and fertilizer and, above all, the productivity of land, has not yet been revealed; it would be difficult to draw any precise conclusions on a basis of the evidence available at present.

SUMMARY AND CONCLUDING REMARKS

Among the problems of agricultural organization encountered during the period covered by this chapter, many were associated with two fundamental issues: (1) the optimum degree of centralization; (2) the provision of appropriate material incentives for the peasants.

THE OPTIMUM DEGREE OF CENTRALIZATION

In China, one of the arguments advanced for collectivization was that it would enable the government to bring agriculture on to the "path of planning" and force the pace of modernization. But the history of collectivized agriculture has shown how difficult it is to attain the degree of centralization that both ensures the implementation of the national plan and yet guarantees enough local autonomy to allow for the flexibility in implementation that is so important in agriculture. In 1956, agricultural organization was highly centralized: most of the crucial decisions, including what to produce and what agricultural methods to adopt, were taken by government and party cadres who were far removed from the place of production, in *hsien* administrative offices and higher levels. This chapter has shown how this led to the imposition of targets that were unrealistically high in relation to the available resources, to rigidity in planning, and to the indiscriminate adoption of new farm practices.

On the other hand, it did result in the implementation of the policies laid down by the central plan. A remarkable amount of activity was organized, especially during the first eight months of 1956, through a mixture of exhortation, promises of future financial reward and a certain amount of outright coercion. The results, however, were far from spectacular. The net effect on output cannot yet be estimated; undoubtedly some areas raised grain output significantly, for example, by extending the double-cropped area, while elsewhere bad planning led to local crop failures. Excessive strain was placed on labor and draft animals, with serious long-term implications. Neither the intensity of effort nor the heavy reliance on nonfinancial inducements could be kept up for long.

32. Li Wen-ch'ao, in "The Status and Role of the Livestock Industry in the National Economy" (*JMJP,* December 10, 1963), stated: "At present, the basic situation in China is that throughout all areas there is widespread experience of livestock deficiency; in particular, horses, oxen, donkeys and mules—the animals used as 'manpower'—are distinctly more scarce." Li admitted that the shortage was impeding agricultural development.

In 1957 agricultural organization was decentralized. "Commandism" ceased, the experienced peasants in collectives regained their control over day-to-day decisions pertaining to farm management, and an expansion of private agricultural enterprise was permitted. This, too, involved costs to the nation. The central government lost control to such an extent that in some places even appropriate technical reforms made in 1956 were abandoned; the private economy competed successfully with the collective for resources, and the collective economy suffered as a result. There is no evidence that the liberal economic policies of 1957 gave rise to a faster growth of output of those products which were most important to the national economy—cereals, fiber and oil crops. It was small consolation to the government that an increase in the private sector had led to larger supplies of pigs, vegetables, poultry and fruit.

It has been shown how the government's response was to make a partial return to the type of control system of 1956. Agricultural planning became centralized once again, in that the enlarged *hsiang* level of government (soon to become the commune authority) was given wide powers to allocate resources within its wide area. Planning remained decentralized, though, in that the *hsiang* authority was not (as in 1956) controlled rigidly from above. The main parallel with 1956 was the use of political campaigns. These were now used by the government to reassert its control over resource allocation, to revive collective (as opposed to private) activity and to restore all the tensions of the "target economy." Coercion and exhortation again took precedence over financial inducements, as the largest rural labor force ever recruited was mobilized in construction works and in the adoption of all manner of "advanced" farm practices. Production targets bore no relation to reality. One may well ask, therefore, why the government, having tried in 1956, without a great deal of success, to achieve a quick breakthrough in agricultural production by using most of these very same methods, adopted them again during 1958, only to see them implemented in an exaggerated form, with serious, yet predictable consequences. Had the government failed to learn from experience?

The answer depends on how one views the origin and nature of the Great Leap of 1958. This is a big subject which cannot be explored in any detail here. A few comments must suffice. If it is true, as has been argued earlier, that the measures promoting the Leap represented the government's attempt to regain control over an economy that was heading for economic and political disaster, then they are understandable. It must be remembered that the government was well aware of the errors committed in 1956 and the consequences of their continuing, as was fully shown by the public inquest it conducted during the autumn of 1956. The liberalization of 1957 was a genuine attempt to remedy the mistakes. As we have seen, this was carried too far: the goverment discovered that, once control was relaxed, it was difficult to maintain any control at all. By the autumn of 1957 socialism could not be considered securely established in the countryside and, indeed, it is possible that much ground had already been lost. The growing imbalance between industrial and agricultural production had not been corrected, despite the advent of collectivization. Population growth was impeding the rate of investment and hence the pace of industrialization. Furthermore, foreign aid was no longer available. The most important task was to mobilize all available resources in a vast production drive, to get the economy moving once more.

From the government's point of view, therefore, the policies of 1956 had much to commend them; they had effected an impressive rise in the level of activity, injected some technical progress into agriculture, and increased capital formation and, in some places, output. The government could argue that the serious problems of 1956 were due to the inexperience of cadres and to the fact that it was the first year of collectivization. Perhaps it believed that it would be able to regain the dynamism of 1956 by tightening its control over local affairs again, while at the same time avoiding the excesses of 1956; hence the partial recentralization of planning and the political pressure to step up activity, investment and production. These measures got out of hand because, although the lower levels of government did restore control over rural China, their actions were inadequately controlled by the central government. The political atmosphere created by the rectification, anti-rightist and several other campaigns, led the local cadres to carry the government's measures to extremes and to depart from reality in their claims about production. How the central government came to believe in the validity of such claims, and thus decide to establish the communes, defies explanation. Only a year after the beginning of the Great Leap, the movement toward central planning and the introduction of another round of liberal economic reforms began.

THE PROVISION OF MATERIAL INCENTIVES FOR THE PEASANTS

The subject of incentives and their relation to agricultural production in China covers many important issues, ranging from the income level of the peasants to the methods of distribution adopted by collectives. Four main points have been made here:

(i) The egalitarian income distribution in the large collectives (1956) and the communes (1958) reduced the incentive for relatively productive villages to raise their production. Egalitarian allocation resulted from making the collective authority (and later the commune) the unit of distribution for the entire area. This policy appealed to the central government because it made for tighter control over grain disposal and enabled collectives to set a higher rate of investment. Furthermore, as the events of 1957 showed, when distribution was handed over to the subdivisions of collectives, cadres found it difficult to resist local demands for increased consumption, and thus grain deliveries to the central government were threatened.

(ii) The work-point system used by collectives for rewarding collective labor proved to be very difficult to implement. It required detailed experiments in job evaluation, accurate financial accounting and, to avoid great uncertainty regarding the daily *value* of the work point, reasonable stability in production. None of these conditions was fulfilled in 1956. Collective cadres had neither the time nor the ability to make a detailed assessment of work norms and their appropriate reward standards; cost accounting was often nonexistent. Peasants could not forecast with any accuracy what fulfilling a given number of work points would mean in cash and grain.

(iii) How far the initial problems relating to the work-point system had been solved by the summer of 1958 cannot be assessed. The communes, however, discarded it as "bourgeois." In the new distribution system, a part of the income distributed to peasants was made on the basis of need, not work. The allocation of free food, although short-lived, reduced the incentive to work in the fields, at a time when competing demands for rural labor had already so depleted the agricultural labor force that it would be difficult to gather all the autumn harvest.

(iv) The existence of a private agricultural sector within the collective framework was an important incentive for peasants, but it had serious implications for the growth of the collective sector. If the private sector was to serve as a meaningful incentive to peasants to accept collectivization, it had to be large enough to produce a significant amount of income and food. The government conceded that to allow a private sector to concentrate on the production of pigs, vegetables, poultry and fruit, while the collective focused on important cereals and industrial crops, seemed a rational division of labor. Moreover, a crucial by-product of the private sector was animal fertilizer which, in the absence of chemical fertilizers, was needed by the collective if yields were to be raised. The real problem arising from the existence of such a private sector was that it was difficult to stop the peasants from excessively diverting labor, fertilizer, draft animals and water away from collective land and on to the private plots. In 1956 a common reaction of local cadres was to curtail the private sector and even suppress it entirely. In 1957, on the other hand, the tendency was to allow it to grow so big that the collective sector suffered.

We have seen how the regulations for collectives published in 1956, with their emphasis on decentralized control, democratic management, a mixed economy and distribution according to labor, were not implemented for any significant period of time during the 1950's and in some places, probably not at all. The mid-1960's constituted the only period of any real stability in agricultural organization since 1950, and perhaps the government, for the first time, succeeded in organizing collective agriculture according to its regulations of 1956. Unfortunately there is insufficient evidence available to indicate the extent to which the problems outlined here have been solved since 1961.

An important factor determining the performance of Chinese agriculture in the future will be the government's view of time: whether it is prepared to accept the fact that the economic gains from institutional reform alone are quickly exhausted and that agricultural development on the scale required to feed the growing population (let alone finance rapid industrialization) will take a long time. It will depend on the efficient use of greater supplies of water, fertilizer, draft animals, farm implements (including tractors), superior seed strains and skilled manpower—including managers and farmworkers. To provide some of these resources will require considerable investment in appropriate sectors of industry. The supply of other items, such as animal fertilizer, draft animals, skilled workers and to some extent, water, can be increased without this, however, by providing the right kind of financial incentives to peasants—itself a matter of considerable difficulty.

The government appears to have drawn these conclusions and has acted upon them. For example, it stepped up domestic output of chemical fertilizers, pesticides, irrigation machinery and tractors. In the countryside, apart from decentralizing agricultural planning and increasing incentives for the peasants, it launched a national campaign for the scientific modernization of agriculture, apparently attempting to secure collaboration between peasants and scientists. But if, as the events of 1956-62 suggest, the preservation of a highly decentralized system of organization with its emphasis on material incentives and a flourishing private sector, weakens the central government's control, one can expect periodic campaigns designed to curb private enterprise ("spontaneous capitalism") and promote the collective economy, accompanied by coercive measures of the type used in the 1950's. It seems likely, however, that in view of the experience now accumulated by the Chinese government, agricultural organization will be more stable and successful in the next decade than in the last.

REFERENCES

Central Broadcasting Station, 1956. *Speeches on the Draft Outline of the Plan for the Development of Chinese Agriculture*, compiled and edited by the Central Broadcasting Station, Peking.

Central Committee of C.C.P. and State Council, March 1957. "Directive on Doing the Spring Arable Work Well and Striving to Attain an Abundant Harvest in Agriculture during 1957," *HHPYK*, Vol. 106, No. 8 (March 19, 1957), pp. 70–73.

on Stopping the Blind Exodus of the Rural Population" (Dec. 18, 197); Editorial, "Stop the Blind Exodus of the Rural Populatin,"

Central Committee of C.C.P. and State Council, December 1957. "Directive *JMJP*, Dec. 19, 1957.

Central Committee of C.C.P., 1958. "Resolution Concerning Certain Questions in the People's Communes," *HHPYK*, Vol. 146, No. 24 (Dec. 10, 1958), pp. 3–11.

Ch'ang Ch'ing, 1956. "Rationally Determine the Wages of Administrative Personnel in Cooperatives," *HHPYK*, Vol. 86, No. 12, pp. 59–60.

Chao Chien, 1956. "Industrial and Agricultural Production in Shantung," *HHPYK*, Vol. 86, No. 12, pp. 136–137.

Chao Tzu-yang, 1954. "On a Basis of Greatly Promoting Cooperativization, Strengthen the Technical Reform of Agriculture and Develop Agricultural Production on All Sides," *NFJP*, Aug. 12, 1954.

Chao Tzu-yang, 1958. "The Rate of Growth of Grain Production Can Be Speeded-up," *HHPYK*, Vol. 133, No. 11, pp. 86–88.

Chao Tzu-yang, 1960. Speech to Kwangtung Telephone Conference, "Each Area Must Firmly Introduce Four Measures to Grasp an Abundant Harvest from the Late Crop," *NFJP*, Aug. 3, 1960.

Cheng Hsing-yen, 1956. "A Typical Example of Consolidating A Cooperative," *NFJP*, Dec. 21, 1956.

Ch'engtu jih-pao, March 24, 1958. (*Ch'engtu Daily*). "Fa Hsuan Collective Amalgamates the Area of Dwelling Houses and Opens up the Ground for Operations."

Ch'engtu jih-pao, May 13, 1958. "Two Hundred and Fifty-Three Cooperatives Amalgamate to Become One Hundred and Thirty-Seven."

Ch'en Ko-chien and Kan Min-chung, 1956. *The Objective Basis of the Rapid Attainment by China of Higher Stage Agricultural Cooperativization*. Shanghai: Shanghai People's Publishing Company.

Ch'en Man-yuan, 1956. "Promote Many Kinds of Economic Activity, Comprehensively Develop Agricultural Production," *HHPYK*, Vol. 95, No. 21, pp. 168–169.

Chiang Hsüeh-mo, 1962. *The Distribution Ssystem of Socialism*. Shanghai: Shanghai People's Publishing Company.

Chiang Wei-ch'ing, 1956. "Only by Following the Mass Line Can the Cooperatives Be Run Well," *HHPYK*, Vol. 95, No. 21, pp. 174–176.

Ch'iao Pei-kuo, 1957."Research into Problems Concerning the Development and Protection of Draft Animals," *Nung-ts'un kung-tso tung-hsün* (*Rural Work Bulletin*), No. 8, pp. 22–23.

Chiao-hsüeh yü yen-chiu, 1959a (*Teaching and Research*). "From Min Sheng Commune View the Change in the Distribution System," No. 2, pp. 37–42.

Chiao-hsüeh yü yen-chiu, 1959b. "On the Distribution System which Coordinates A Wages and Supply System," No. 2, pp. 28–36.

CHI NONG, 1956. "Why the Restoration of Mulberry Production in Kiangsu and Chekiang is Slow," *JMJP,* June 6, 1956.

CHI SHIH-HSÜN, 1956. "Several Problems at Present Requiring a Solution in the Cooperatives," *Szechwan jih-pao* (*Szechwan Daily*), April 17, 1956.

CHOU EN-LAI, 1956, "Political Report," Jan. 14, 1956. *HHPYK,* Vol. 79, No. 5, pp. 1–10.

Chü, Hsiang Kan-pu-pao, 1956 (*District and Township Cadres' News*). "To Bring Forward the Completion of Rice Transplanting Work We Must Have Concrete Measures," April 8, 1956.

CHI HSIEN-LI *et al.,* 1957. *Agricultural Proverbs and Explanatory Notes.* Peking.

Chungking jih-pao, 1958 (*Chungking Daily*). "Achieve A Great Leap Forward in Agricultural Production This Year," Jan. 10, 1958.

Chungshan nung-min-pao, 1956 (*Chungshan Peasants' News*). "*Niu Chüeh* Township Substitutes Manpower for Bullock Power," April 7, 1956.

Heilungkiang jih-pao, 1956 (*Heilungkiang Daily*). "Examine the Future of Cattle Rearing Closely," Dec. 16, 1956.

Hong Kong Union Research Service, 1962. "The Twelve Rules, the Sixty Articles, and the Campaign Against the Prejudicial Conduct of the Cadres," Vol. 28, No. 12, Aug. 10, 1962.

Hong Kong Wen-hui pao, 1957 (*Hong Kong Cultural News*). "Kwangtung Raises its Plan for Grain Production," March 26, 1957.

HSIAO YÜ, 1957. "How to Allocate Agricultural Investment," *Chi-hua ching-chi* (*Planned Economy*), No. 9, pp. 5–8.

HHPYK. Hsin-hua pan-yueh-kan (*New China Semi-monthly*).

HWANG NAN-SEN and WANG CH'ING-SHU, 1956. *On the Objective Foundation of the Cooperativization High Tide in China.* Shanghai: Shanghai Peoples Publishing Company.

HWANG CHUN, 1956. "Several Problems Urgently Awaiting Solution in Established Collectives," *JMJP,* Feb. 14, 1956.

HHPYK, Vol. 78, 1956. "Draft Outline of the Plan for the Development of Chinese Agriculture, 1956–1967," No. 4, pp. 2–5.

HHPYK, Vol. 81, 1956. "How to Fix Norms and Reward Standards," No. 7, pp. 107–108.

HHPYK, Vol. 83, 1956. Directive "On Economical and Frugal Management of Cooperatives." No. 9 (April 3, 1956), pp. 40–41.

HHPYK, Vol. 88, 1956. "Model Regulations for Advanced Stage Agricultural Producers' Cooperatives," No. 14 (June 30, 1956), pp. 19–25.

HHPYK, Vol. 93, 1956a. Directive "On Strengthening the Building of Organization and Control over Production in the Cooperatives," No. 19 (September 12, 1956), pp. 52–59.

HHPYK, Vol. 93, 1956b. "With Much Activity in Subsidiary Activity, Why Aren't There Better Real Benefits?" No. 19, pp. 63–64.

HHPYK, Vol. 96, 1956. "Accept the Lesson of Extending 'Ch'ingsen number 5," [seed]. No. 22, pp. 82–83.

HHPYK, Vol. 98, 1956. Directive "On Certain Concrete Problems in Distributing the Autumn Harvest in Cooperatives," No. 24 (Nov. 24, 1956), pp. 56–58.

HHPYK, Vol. 111, 1957. Directive "On Doing the Work of Distributing the Summer Harvest Well," No. 13, pp. 139–140.

HHPYK, Vol. 117, 1957. (a) "On Rectification in the Agricultural Producers' Cooperatives"; (b) "On Making a Good Job of the Work of Production Management in Agricultural Producers' Cooperatives"; (c) "On Thoroughly Carrying Out a Policy of Mutual Benefit inside Agricultural Producers' Cooperatives," No. 19, pp. 135–138.

HHPYK, Vol. 127, 1958. "Actively Develop the Collective Economy," No. 5, pp. 140–141.

HHPYK, Vol. 39, 1958. "Draft Regulations of the Weihsing People's Commune," No. 17, pp. 59–62.

JMJP. Jen-min jih-pao (People's Daily). Peking.

JMJP, May 16, 1956. Editorial, "Protect the Health of Rural Women and Children."

JMJP, June 6, 1956. Editorial, "Do Not Neglect Financial Tasks and Accounting Work in Cooperatives."

JMJP, Nov. 22, 1956. Editorial, "Strongly Develop Peasant Trade."

JMJP, Dec. 15, 1956. "Kwangtung Adopts Active Measures to Strengthen the Cooperatives."

JMJP, Jan. 1, 1957. "Great Achievements in Kwangtung in the Grain Production Front."

JMJP, Feb. 24, 1957. Editorial, "The Spring Sowing Plan Must Be Both Progressive and Reliable."

JMJP, March 25, 1957. Editorial, "Use the Large Agricultural Implements Already Owned Properly."

JMJP, April 19, 1957. Editorial, "Improve Management in Livestock Rearing."

JMJP, Aug. 1957. Editorials of August 5, 7, 12, 15 and 30, 1957.

JMJP, Aug. 30, 1957. Editorial, "In Areas with an Abundant Harvest Buy Some More Grain."

JMJP, Oct. 21, 1957. "Kwangtung Provincial Committee Implements the Spirit of the Party Congress."

JMJP, March 31, 1960. Editorial, "The Whole Party and Every Person Is To Be Occupied with Agriculture and Grain."

JMJP, July 27, 1960. Editorial, "Use the Majority of Manpower in the Fields."

JMJP, June 14, 1962. "Again Talking About the Way to Rear Pigs."

Kirin jih-pao, Dec. 1956 *(Kirin Daily).* "The Provincial Agricultural Office Calls a Livestock Work Conference," Dec. 10, 1956.

Kükong Nung-min-pao, 1956 *(Kukong Peasants' News).* "Record of a Visit to Tunghsia Cooperative," Oct. 23, 1956.

Kwangtung Provincial Party Committee, Sept. 1956. Directive "On the Work of Rectifying the Cooperatives in Elevating them to Collectives and Amalgamating them." *NFJP,* Sept. 23, 1956.

Kwangtung Provincial Party Committee, Oct. 1956. "Views on Certain Concrete Policy Problems in Elevating Coops to Collectives and Amalgamating Coops," *NFJP*, Oct. 10, 1956.

Kwangtung Provincial Party and People's Committees, Oct. 1956. "Directive Concerning Opening the Work of Agricultural Production for the Winter Season," *NFJP*, Oct. 26, 1956.

Kwangtung Provincial Party and People's Committees, Jan. 1957. Joint Directive, "Draft Measures to Develop Agricultural Production in 1957," *NFJP*, Jan. 15, 1957.

LIAO LU-YEN, 1957. "A Summary of the Work of Agricultural Production in 1956 and the Tasks for 1957," *HHPYK*, Vol. 106, No. 8, pp. 81–88.

LIAO LU-YEN, 1958. "An Explanation Regarding the Question of Appropriately Increasing the Reserve Fund Proportion in Collectives," *HHPYK*, Vol. 125, No. 3 (Jan. 9, 1958), pp. 79–80.

LIAO LU-YEN, 1959. "The Tasks of the Agricultural Front in 1959," *Hung-ch'i* (*Red Flag*), No. 1, pp. 11–18.

LUO T'IEN, 1958. "Carry Out a Great Levelling and Adjustment of the Land; Guarantee a Further High Output of Agriculture," *HHPYK*, Vol. 133, No. 11, pp. 71–73.

MAO TSE-TUNG, 1955. "On The Question of Agricultural Cooperativization," *Hsin-hua yüeh-pao* (*New China Monthly*), Vol. 73, No. 11, pp. 1–8.

Mechanization Bureau, 1958. *Problems of Agricultural Mechanization in China*, compiled by the Mechanization Bureau of the Ministry of Agriculture. Pages 124–159: "Report of a Survey Concerning Problems of Agricultural Mechanization in Paddy Fields of South China" (March, 1957). Paoting, 1958.

NFJP. *Nan-fang jih-pao* (*Southern Daily*). Canton.

NFJP, Dec. 26, 1955. Editorial, "A Year's Plan Hinges on the Winter."

NFJP, Jan. 23, 1956. "Kwangtung's Plan to Increase Grain Production This Year by 4,000 Million Catties Will Bring Forward the Attainment of Next Year's Target for Increased Output."

NFJP, March 14, 1956. "Oppose Blindness."

NFJP, March 15, 1956. Editorial, "Production in Cooperatives Must Strengthen its Planned Nature and Overcome Blindness."

NFJP, May 29, 1956. "Developing Subsidiary Production and Promoting a Many-Sided Economy."

NFJP, June 14, 1956. "The Spring Grain Harvest in Kwangtung This Year Increased by Over 900 Million Catties."

NFJP, June 26, 1956. "Subjectivism Has Hampered Work. Uniform 6 x 6 [planting] Yields a Good Deal Less Grain."

NFJP, Oct. 13, 1956. "Problems of Principle in the Development of Agricultural Production in Fatshan Special District."

NFJP, Oct. 30, 1956. "The Lesson of Blindly Reforming the Methods of Arable Work."

NFJP, Nov. 14, 1956. "Views on Implementing Production Plans in Cooperatives."

NFJP, Nov. 15, 1956. "According to Reality Implement the Principle of Comprehensively Developing Agricultural Production."

NFJP, Nov. 28, 1956. "The Bad Effects of Blindly Carrying Out the Policy 'Taros to the Hills.' Taro Production in Yingtak County This Year Has Fallen by 60–70%."

NFJP, July 23, 1957. Editorial (no title).

NFJP, Aug. 17, 1957. "How Can Overfulfillment of the Planned Increase in the Late Crop Be Achieved?"

NFJP, June 12, 1961. "Are There Any Advantages in Developing the Economy of the Production Brigade?"

NFJP, Oct. 26, 1961. "Develop Still Further the Activeness of the Production Brigade."

NFJP, Oct. 28, 1961. Editorial, "Teach the Peasants Simultaneously to Consider Public and Private [Interests]: Public First, Private Afterwards."

NFJP, March 14, 1962. "Strengthen Production Brigade Construction."

NFJP, April 6, 1962. "Large Production Brigade Cadres are not Merely 'Propaganda Personnel' and 'Personnel for Exacting Donations'."

NFJP, April 8, 1962. "How the Large Production Brigade Cadres Ought to Recognize their Tasks and Responsibilities."

NFJP, April 18, 1962. "How the Large Production Brigade Cadres Ought to Recognize their Tasks and Responsibilities."

NFJP, June 3, 1962. "The Key Is a Question of Work Method."

Rural Work Bulletin, 1957. (i) "Through Ideological Education Solve the 'Grain Disturbance' Problem," No. 8, pp. 9–10; (ii) "Correctly Recognize and Solve Present Problems of Grain Supply," No. 8, pp. 11–12; (iii) "Let the Rural Free Market Develop on a Correct Basis," No. 8, pp. 13–14, 15.

Rural Work Bulletin, 1956a. (*Nung-ts'un kung-tso-hsün*). "A Discussion on the Question of the Scope and Size of Cooperatives." 1956 No. 8, pp. 18–21.

Rural Work Bulletin, 1956b. "Draw Out the Lessons from the Mistakes of Subjectivism and Commandism," No. 8, pp. 8–9.

State Council, 1955. "Resolution on the Spring Arable Production," March 3, 1955. In *Compendium of Laws and Regulations of the Chinese People's Republic*, Vol. I (Sept. 1954-June 1955), pp. 368–376. Peking: Legal Publishing Company, 1956.

State Council, 1956. "Directive on Diligent and Frugal Management in Cooperatives," *HHPYK*, Vol. 83, No. 9 (April 3, 1956), pp. 40–41.

SSB. State Statistical Bureau, 1957. *Statistical Materials on Agricultural Cooperativisation and the Distribution of the Product in Cooperatives during 1955*. Peking: Statistical Publishing Company.

Szechwan jih-pao (*Szechwan Daily*), Dec. 22, 1956. "Why Are This Year's Achievements in Agricultural Production So Great Compared with Other Years?"

Szechwan jih-pao, Dec. 5, 1957. "Amended Draft Plan for the Development of Agriculture in Szechwan, 1956–1967."

Szechwan jih-pao, April 20, 1958. "To Extend Public Accumulation and Assist Agriculture's Leap Forward the Democratic Socialization of Pigs is Increasing Quickly."

T'AO CHU, 1956. "More Comprehensively and Efficiently Carry Out the Principle of Taking Agriculture as the Point of Emphasis." *HHPYK*, Vol. 95, No. 21, pp. 68–70.

T'AO CHU, Jan. 1956. "Provided that Cadres Fully Estimate the Successes and Promote Courageous and Active Work, Agricultural Cooperatives and Production Can Definitely Be Even Better This Year," *NFJP*, Jan. 9, 1956.

T'AO CHU, April 1956. "How to Carry Out Kwangtung's 7-year plan for Agricultural Construction," *NFJP*, April 8, 1956.

T'AO CHU, Nov. 1957. "Views on Reforming and Raising Production Management Work in Cooperatives." *NFJP*, Nov. 19, 1957.

T'AO CHU, Dec. 1957. "Kwantung Strives to Become a Province of Thousand Catty Grain Yield in Ten Years Time," *JMJP*, Dec. 14, 1957.

T'AO CHU, 1964. "The People's Communes Go Forward," *Hung-ch'i*, 1964, No. 4, pp. 1–12.

Ten Great Years. State Statistical Bureau, 1959. Peking: People's Publishing Company.

TENG HSIAO-P'ING, 1957. "Report on the Rectification Campaign," *HHPYK*, Vol. 120, No. 22, pp. 49–59.

TENG TZU-HUI, 1953. "Basic Tasks and Policy Principles in Village Work," *HHYP*, No. 8 (July 2, 1953), pp. 49–52.

TENG TZU-HUI, 1955. "Questions Regarding Rural Work and the Socialist Reconstruction of Agriculture," in *Financial and Economic Work During the Past Five Years*. Peking: Financial and Economic Publishing Company.

TENG TZU-HUI, 1957a. "Summary Report at Forum on Production in Mountain District." *HHPYK*, Vol. 122, No. 24, pp. 67–70.

TENG TZU-HUI, 1957b. "Concerning Extended Reproduction in Cooperatives and Several Other Problems." *HHPYK*, Vol. 121, pp. 155–159.

TENG TZU-HUI, 1958. "Summary Report at Forum on Livestock Production in Livestock Areas," *HHPYK*, Vol. 124, No. 2, pp. 101–103.

TING YING *et al.*, 1961. *Rice Cultivation in China*. Peking: Agricultural Publishing Company.

WALKER, KENNETH R., 1965. *Planning in Chinese Agriculture. Socialisation and the Private Sector 1956-1962*. London: Frank Cass, 1965.

WALKER, KENNETH R., 1966. "Collectivisation in Retrospect: The 'Soccialist High Tide' of Autumn 1955–Spring 1956." *The China Quarterly*, April–June 1956 pp. 1–43.

YEH FEI, 1956. "Comprehensively Develop Agricultural Production and a Many-Sided Mountain Economy," *HHPYK*, Vol. 95, No. 21, pp. 201–203.

YEN LING, 1956. "What Virtue Is there in Economizing on Labor Days?" *HHPYK*, Vol. 84, No. 10, 59–60.

Policy and Performance in Agriculture 7

ANTHONY M. TANG

INTRODUCTION

WRITING IN 1961, Professor Eckstein argued that during the period of the First Five-Year Plan Communist China followed "a Stalinist strategy of economic development with local adaptations" (Eckstein, 1961, p. 508).[1] Both official pronouncements and the course of action taken by the Party attest to the soundness of this judgment. Starting from this proposition, this chapter intends to (1) bring out the crucial elements of the Stalinist model; (2) outline the role or performance criteria in agriculture in the light of the model's requirements; (3) deduce from such a framework empirically testable propositions in terms of which agricultural performance may be appraised via indirect inferences; (4) specify the nature and consequences of the "local adaptations" as imposed by the reality of the Chinese economy at that time; and (5) evaluate the particular agricultural policy employed in China, as well as future prospects, by analyzing input-output relations and sources of growth.

With these purposes in mind, the chapter is organized into five sections. In the first, we take up the analytical framework. The second is devoted to an appraisal of agriculture's performance in relation to the sector's role in the model. We shall make extensive comparisons between Communist China and Stalinist Russia in terms of initial conditions, broad agricultural policy, and the sector's performance. The third section considers production relations in Chinese agriculture and the productivity trend. This is followed by a section on sources of agricultural growth and future prospects for China, in which the focus is on evaluating specific policy measures through which the state sought to tap and develop sources of output growth. The chapter ends with a brief section on the conclusions that have been reached. For data reasons, the study deals

The author wishes to express his appreciation to Professors A. Eckstein, T. W. Schultz, A. Koo, K. Ohkawa, S. Ishikawa, and Dr. J. L. Buck for their helpful comments. To Professors Eckstein and Schultz he owes a special debt. Any errors that remain in this contribution are his.

1. For a more comprehensive treatment of the Stalinist model, see also Oleg Hoeffding, 1959.

mainly with the period 1952-58 in China, and with the comparable period, the early 1930's, for the Soviet Union.

To gauge economic efficiency is a difficult task under any circumstances. It is doubly difficult in situations where lack of consumer sovereignty renders market tests invalid. It is true that scarcity relationships and rational prices can be inferred in principle from an economic plan so long as the plan itself reflects the planned's values and preferences. The departure of actual prices—to the extent that these prices serve an allocative function—from the rational would then give us a measure of how close the economy comes to satisfying the planner. Where prices are used for accounting and market-clearing purposes rather than as allocative signals, as is essentially the case in the Soviet Union and China, efficiency can be gauged only by establishing the plan's rationality against the planner's welfare function, together with given technological and economic factors in the setting. Here, there is no operational procedure to cope with the staggering range of problems involved. About all that one can say is that Soviet-type economies are growth-oriented in values, that their realized growth rates attest to the general success of their economic policies, and that to raise the issue of comparative performance among "competing" systems is to enter the realm of ethics.[2]

Fortunately, in considering a sector such as agriculture within the framework of the Stalinist model, it is possible to state explicit performance criteria. The task of specifying criteria and comparing performance against them turns out to be relatively straightforward both in the Chinese and Soviet cases because of the simplicity of the underlying model.

I. ROLE OF AGRICULTURE: PRINCIPLE

A FRAMEWORK

The outstanding feature of the Stalinist model is the primacy of its concern with growth or, more specifically, with industrial growth.[3] To be sure, even with Stalin, consumption must remain the ultimate goal of production. But the long-range view implicit in the model supports the general validity of Bergson's epigrammatic statement that, for any relevant planning period under consideration, "steel was a final good to Stalin, and bread an intermediate one." [4]

2. Stanislaw Wellisz aptly distinguishes between the analytical approach and the pathological approach. The latter tends to stress gross "inefficiencies" of an alien system using our own normative concepts as the vantage point while ignoring differences in goals among systems. For a sample of good analytical works on command economies, see Wellisz (1964), Grossman (1960), and Campbell (1960).

3. The important elements of the model are well known. But for a detailed exposition, see Alexander Erlich (1955).

4. As quoted in P. J. D. Wiles, 1962 (p. 283).

As for the determinants of growth, one might begin, as a good Marxist would, with Marx's Department I—the sector that produces the means of production. As a limiting case, one might say that investment (hence, growth) is governed by the capacity of Department I rather than by the more familiar propensity to save. This constitutes the crucial element of an initially obscure model developed in 1928 by the Soviet economist, G. A. Fel'dman. The model, later popularized by Domar (1957) and rediscovered by Mahalanobis, is highly abstract and entails several restrictive assumptions. Yet, for our purposes, it serves as a useful point of departure in inferring agriculture's role from the general context of a Stalinist framework. Fel'dman assumes a closed economy and complete absence of bottlenecks, not to mention fixed or exogenously changing capital coefficients.

Marx's Department I is not an operational entity; nor is his Department II, the consumer goods sector. No economy is organized according to his two departments. Neither industries nor individual commodities fall neatly in his mutually exclusive categories. There is no physical distinction between seed potatoes and table potatoes, for example. Moreover, Stalinist growth is selective growth. The production and reproduction of seed potatoes is not the same in Stalinist terms as the production and reproduction of steel. For our purposes here, and for the sake of relevance, it is well to adopt the agriculture-industry dichotomy instead.[5] In this context, Stalinist strategy views industrialization as the object to maximize, and agriculture as an accommodating agent.

Fel'dman's framework would have us believe that industrialization is limited by the capacity of the industrial sector itself. A relaxation of some of his assumptions will quickly show that industrialization may just as easily be constrained by agricultural performance. Without trying to be exhaustive, we offer the following considerations:

(1) The plausibility of Fel'dman's conclusion is most readily appreciated in a closed economy. However, even there industrial growth may be restrained by bottlenecks arising from agriculture. This would be the case if the latter fails to release enough workers, raw materials, or wage goods

5. This dichotomy need not require us to ignore different priorities attached to various branches of the industrial sector. In Section II, we shall examine the manner in which the growth of the component branches may be differentially affected by agriculture as a limiting factor. The priority sector is variously called basic, heavy, modern, or large-scale. Li Hiu-hung and coworkers in an article in *T'ung-chi kung-tso* (1957) define heavy industry as "modern industry that provides a material basis for the technical transformation of the national economy in the process of industrialization and for the modernization of national defense." As Wiles (1962, p. 282) points out, there can be no doubt that this is the sector that is foremost in the mind of the Communist party leadership both in China and Russia in their development effort. Li's list of industries falling in the priority sector comes close to including elements crucial to growth and to the determination of the power base viewed from a military and political standpoint. For discussions of the taxonomic problems, see Wiles (1962, ch. 14) and Domar (1957, ch. IX).

(food) to permit capacity production in industry, and thereby limits investment.

(2) In a completely open economy—where trade is assumed to take place in a frictionless manner, unlimited by elasticities of foreign demand and supply—industrial expansion would be constrained by agricultural production. Since agricultural output is exportable without limit in exchange for capital goods, the exhaustion of the agricultural surplus (which is analogous to limited savings) ultimately restrains industrializaion by failing to sustain imports of capital goods. Even in such an improbable setting, industrial expansion may be constrained in the first instance by industry's capacity for absorbing capital. At any rate, in the real world trade opportunities are limited. And this probably applies with even greater force to China during the 1950's and to the Soviet Union in the 1930's.

(3) Thus far, we have approached the two-sector model only unidirectionally—through resource transfer from agriculture to industry, either directly or indirectly via foreign trade. Two-way transformation between sectors can be easily introduced, however. Thus, if the planner finds that agricultural production is effectively constraining production and investment in industry, one way to permit a higher industrial performance would be to make a part of the industrial output available as inputs in agriculture. So long as, say, an electric motor that has been transferred to agriculture affects agricultural output and leads to an incremental flow of labor, materials, and/or food to industry to the extent that more than one electric motor or its equivalent is subsequently added to industrial output, such transformation between sectors is consistent with maximization of the rate of industrialization. The process would continue until either capacity production is obtained in the industrial sector or diminishing returns in agriculture render further transformation unprofitable. (Here, also, trade may be introduced as a link.) If production capacity is reached, the effective constraint on industrialization passes from agriculture to industry itself. With diminishing returns the constraint would continue to lie in agriculture. However, industrial output and investment will now proceed at a higher level.

The import of these remarks is that (1) the number of potential constraints on industrialization is legion; (2) the identity of the effective constraint and whether it lies in the agricultural or industrial sector can be established only by appealing to the data; and (3) our consideration of intersectoral transformation shows that "modernization" of agriculture through transfer of industrial output to agriculture as inputs is not necessarily precluded under a logical interpretation of the Stalinist model. In fact, such a use of industrial output by agriculture, if warranted by the calculation of appropriate returns, is fully consistent with the Stalinist goal of maximizing investment and growth of industry. What must be equally clear is that modernization of agriculture enters into the policy realm of Stalin only when agriculture becomes the effective constraint on industrialization and when the alternative of raising agricultural output by means of low social value is unavailable. The manner in which the agricultural problems were approached and solved in China and the Soviet Union is, of course, a question of utmost importance. To this question we shall turn in a later section.

We will not attempt to arrive at a hierarchic ordering of the potential bottlenecks confronting industrialization or to establish the specific identity of the effective constraint (which may vary from one year to the next). Consistent with our two-sector approach, it will be sufficient to identify the sector in which the effective constraint belongs. With this in mind, we classify the bottlenecks (including capacity limitations) under two headings: those internal to the industrial and trade sectors, and those belonging to agriculture. If one supposes, first, that agriculture has an unlimited capacity to satisfy industry's requirements for its resources (labor, materials, wage goods, and commodity exports in exchange for capital goods imports), then the rate of industrialization must be governed by internal limitations in the industrial and trade sectors. Let us call this rate of industrialization the *maximum endogenous rate*. Suppose, on the other hand, that trade opportunities as well as industry's capital and labor absorptive capacity are unlimited, then the rate of industrialization must be limited by agricultural performance. Let us call this rate the *maximum exogenous rate* of industrialization. If the endogenous rate is the higher of the two, agriculture is the effective constraint on industrialization. If the exogenous rate is higher, the constraint lies outside the agricultural sector. We shall take it to be true, as is plausible under the Stalinist model, that industrialization has been pushed in China and the Soviet Union until limited by one or the other of the two maximum rates.[6]

In evaluating agricultural performance, it is important to know which of the two rates has been operative in the period under consideration. If the endogenous rate prevailed, then agriculture imposed no constraint on industrialization, and the underlying agricultural policy must be regarded as successful. This would be true even if agricultural output fell as a result of that policy, as it did in the Soviet Union during the first plan period. The converse holds if the exogenous rate prevailed. While such a criterion for performance may appear unacceptable from a Western viewpoint, it is fully consistent with the design that has governed the development of China and the Soviet Union and with the planner's values implicit in it. This chapter will try to discover how the Communist Party, which regards itself as the sole repository of truth, would go about "grading" its own handiwork. It is hoped that the framework proposed here will enable

6. If it were possible to determine empirically the two maximum rates, a simple comparison locates the constraint's sectoral affiliation. Since this is not feasible, in what follows we shall develop an indirect inference approach.

us to acquire a firmer basis for predicting future course of events than that afforded by merely supplying ad hoc explanations to vacillating past events and policies.

A TESTABLE HYPOTHESIS

We shall take it to be true that the Communist Party leadership regards agriculture as an instrument to accommodate planned industrialization, and that agriculture's intended function is to permit industrial growth to proceed at the maximum rate set by the internal constraints of the trade and industrial sectors. The requirements for agricultural resources that this maximum industrial growth rate implies may be called *maximum requirements*. Whether agriculture can discharge such a role depends mainly on the size of the agricultural surplus that can be siphoned off in relation to the maximum requirements. "Agricultural surplus" is defined as the difference between output and consumption by farm households. We suppose that there is a minimum consumption standard that places a ceiling on the volume and rate of compulsory deliveries, beyond which the Party would not wish to go. How this minimum is arrived at need not concern us. The extractive urge of the Party may, of course, be tempered by its recognition that food is a productive input that affects labor productivity and incentive.[7] Nor is it necessary to postulate an unchanging minimum. The agricultural surplus given by the consumption minimum may be called the *maximum AS*. We are now prepared to distinguish between three hypothetical cases.

Case I: The maximum requirements imposed on agriculture are equal to the maximum AS under *normal* crop conditions. This balance would have permitted investment and industrial growth to proceed at the maximum rate, unconstrained by agriculture. The state, however, will have to alter its compulsory delivery plan in accordance with fluctuations in yield, and operate and control a storage program to balance supply and requirements over time. The farm population in any given year enjoys only the minimum consumption standard.

Case II: The maximum requirements are substantially below the maximum AS. The excess is so great that it holds even in years of adverse weather. Not only does agriculture fully discharge its expected function, but it relieves the state of other problems of control. The state no longer is burdened with the troublesome task of instituting a storage program. It simply exacts from agriculture a steady delivery each year without regard to output fluctuations. If the collective farms and their peasant workers are interested in an efficient allocation of consumption over time, they can

7. For a theoretical exposition of the influence of the above relationship on state consumption policy under conditions of austerity and "maximum speed development," see John Fei and Alpha Chiang (1965) and the author's forthcoming discussion of the paper.

of course have their own storage facilities. At any rate, farm consumption in all years exceeds the minimum implicit in the mind of the Party leadership.

Case III: The maximum requirements *normally* exceed the maximum AS. Here, agriculture effectively constrains industrial growth. In an excellent crop year, the requirements may be more or less met; in average or poor years, industrial retrenchment becomes necessary. Deliveries exacted by the state fluctuate. But state storage is established only if the maximum AS in good crop years exceeds requirements. In any event, any excesses are still (by definition of this case) insufficient to make up for the deficits of poor years. Farm consumption is held to the minimum in all years. Whereas in Case II the collectives are the true residual claimants and the state the prior claimant that freely collects amounts as determined by the maximum industrial requirements, in Case III the shoe is on the other foot. The peasant claims his share first—even though a minimum share—and the state becomes the residual claimant. However paradoxical (or even ironical) it may appear in the light of the Communist Party's monolithic devotion to industrialization, there can be little doubt about the validity of the proposition. The only question about Case III is its empirical relevance.

We are now in a position to summarize the essential elements of these cases. In Case I, industrialization is not constrained by agricultural performance. A testable consequence is that there ought not to be any association between the annual rates of industrial and agricultural growth. Another empirically meaningful aspect is that state procurement does fluctuate. In Case II, industrialization is also independent of agricultural performance, but state procurement is nonfluctuating. Nonfluctuating procurement is consistent with either steady deliveries or those with a trend increment. In Case III, with agriculture limiting industrial growth, one would expect an association between industrial and agricultural growth rates. In fact, the greater the agricultural constraint, the stronger the association. One would also expect greater variability in industrial growth rates in Case III as compared with the dispersion in the first two cases. One might also anticipate a difference in the average industrial growth rate between Case III, on the one hand, and Cases I and II, on the other, although these a priori expectations rest on less secure ground because of the effect of the initial base on growth rates. More assuredly, one would expect to find quite different agricultural policies, especially between Case II and Case III. In Case II, agricultural policy is likely to be mainly extractive rather than developmental. In case III, it would stress both aspects, with development effort relying in the first instance on resources with little or no opportunity cost.

Our hypothesis, then, is this: The Soviet Union, because of its initially sizable agricultural surplus, belongs to either Case I or Case II. Communist

China, because of its initially small agricultural surplus, belongs to Case III. Whether Case I or Case II affords a better approximation to Soviet reality is subject to the type of empirical checks outlined above.

II. ROLE OF AGRICULTURE: PERFORMANCE

BACKGROUND: CHINA AND THE USSR

In 1913, a good crop year in Russia, total grain production amounted to 82 million tons, or 580 kilograms per capita. Even in the absence of the Soviet apparatus of forced collection, 21 million tons, or nearly 26 per cent of the total output, were marketed outside the villages in that year.[8] Of this amount, some 9 million tons were exported (Hodgman, 1954, p. 41). In 1928, Soviet grain output totaled 73.3 million tons, or about 480 kilograms per capita (Hoeffding, 1959, p. 539). In contrast, even in a year such as 1957, when the balance between food supply and population in China was relatively favorable, a total grain output of 163 million tons yielded a per capita availability of only 256 kilograms. The 1952 Chinese per capita figure was even lower, 220 kilograms.[9] Thus, when each of the countries entered its respective First Five-Year Plan period, in which socialization of agriculture and forced industrialization were to take place, Communist China's per capita food availability in grain terms was less than half that of the Soviet Union.

It is true that the above grain statistics exclude potatoes, an important crop in any consideration of subsistence margins. But since potatoes bulked larger in the Soviet production in 1928 than in the Chinese output of 1952, their inclusion would further reduce China's relative position. It is also true that in China a substantially larger fraction of the grain output was used for direct human consumption than in the Soviet Union. But this merely reflects the intended import of the above figures for comparative availability.

More specifically, the Soviet 1928 statistics for grain and population suggest the existence of a substantial initial "cushion" in the subsistence margin. This cushion gave the Soviet people considerable access to indirect forms of grain consumption (for example, vodka and meats). The outstanding characteristic of these forms of consumption is that, from a subsistence standpoint, they represent highly inefficient conversion processes. It takes several calories worth of grains to produce one calorie worth of

8. This percentage should be interpreted with caution since the data are gross. Much of the grain was for indirect human consumption; and the proportion represented by the latter use varies between the marketed and farm retained portions.

9. Grain output is from *TGY* (p. 119); population statistics from Liu and Yeh, 1965 (p. 102).

meat. The greater the relative importance of indirect consumption, therefore, the more extensive are the substitution possibilities in times of food shortage or austerity planning, when subsistence becomes important. To a Stalinist planner, then, the value of the initial cushion lies in the maneuvering room that it affords. Technically, the argument amounts to saying that the demand for food *in caloric terms* had been substantially more elastic in the Soviet Union than in China.

This background helps us understand how in spite of the drastic output decline in the Soviet Union during the first plan period (25-30 per cent during 1928-32) the proportion and the amount of farm output marketed rose. In grain terms, the agricultural surplus exacted by Stalin increased from 8 million tons in 1928 to 20 million tons in 1932, or nearly the 1913 level of 21 million tons. It will be recalled that grain output amounted to 82 and 63 million tons in 1913 and 1932, respectively. Agricultural exports also were maintained during the collectivization drive and, in fact, increased between 1928 and 1932 (Jasny, 1949, pp. 78-79, 682, 751). It was not surprising, therefore, that Jasny should have been moved to comment that "Soviet officials acted as if they expected the peasants to market on the same scale as before the war" despite output declines and rural population increases (1949, p. 223). Yet, in the calamitous year of 1932, per capita grain availability on farms, net of forced collection, still amounted to some 375 kilograms. At the same time, grain availability per person, urban and rural, stood at 415 kilograms—as compared with the corresponding Chinese figures of 220 and 256 kilograms in 1952 and 1957, respectively. In these terms, it appears plausible to suggest that, because of the initial Soviet cushion, Stalin would have declared his intended role for agriculture as feasible even if he had fully anticipated collectivization's disastrous consequences for output. It is a matter of record that, as a grain pump, the collective farm mechanism did free the Soviet planner from the "scissors crisis" of the 1920's and cause marketings to rise almost exactly as planned. It is also to be noted that nothing in the generally accepted magnitudes shown earlier suggests that the mass starvation which actually took place in the Soviet countryside in 1931-32 was inevitable.[10]

In brief, we conclude that the Soviet agricultural policy could well have been extractive rather than developmental. And the near equality between the planned and realized marketings suggests that the forced industrialization program might well have proceeded at a pace unrestrained by the agricultural production "crisis" of the early 1930's. Communist China, on the other hand, confronted by an initially meager margin, found it necessary to mount a development program for agriculture, even while

10. For planned and actual marketings, see Jasny, 1949, (pp. 78-79). Jasny puts the number of people starved at 5.5 million, mostly in the rural areas (p. 553).

steps were being taken to enforce collection. And learning from past Soviet mistakes, China was able to increase agricultural output steadily during its collectivization drive.

The agricultural policies of the two countries, though vastly different, nonetheless share a common goal: To free investment and growth in industry from restraints by agriculture. It is the purpose of the next section to ascertain how fully this goal has been realized in the two countries. Implicit in the question is the inference that under the Stalinist design for economic development, the success or failure of an agricultural policy must not be judged by the resulting agricultural growth or decline as such, but by the ultimate effect of the policy on industrialization.

COMPARATIVE PERFORMANCE: CHINA AND THE USSR

Table 1 presents data on agricultural and industrial output for China during 1949-58, together with annual growth rates and certain category breakdowns. The data used are from official sources. This choice grows out of several considerations. First, we are interested here in a behavioral proposition having to do with the planner's actions in industrialization in the light of agricultural realities. Second, as suggested by the Soviet Union's 1941 Gosplan (which eventually came into Western hands during

TABLE 1

AGRICULTURAL AND INDUSTRIAL OUTPUT, GROWTH RATES CHINA, 1949-1958

Year	Gross Agricultural Output			Total Gross Industrial Output		
	X_t=value (in million yuan)[a]	X_t/X_{t-1}	$\frac{1}{2}\left(\frac{X_t}{X_{t-1}}+\frac{X_{t-1}}{X_{t-2}}\right)$	$Y_{1,t}$=value (in million yuan)[b]	$Y_{1,t}/Y_{1,t-1}$ (n=9)	$Y_{1,t}/Y_{1,t-1}$ (n=8)
1949	32,590	......	......	14,020	......	......
1950	38,360	117.7 *(2)*	......	19,120	136.4 *(3)*	......
1951	41,970	109.4 *(4)*	113.6 *(2)*	26,350	137.8 *(2)*	137.8 *(2)*
1952	48,390	115.3 *(3)*	112.4 *(3)*	34,330	130.3 *(4)*	130.3 *(3)*
1953	49,910	103.1 *(9)*	109.2 *(4)*	44,700	130.2 *(5)*	130.2 *(4)*
1954	51,570	103.3 *(8)*	103.2 *(8)*	51,970	116.3 *(7)*	116.3 *(6)*
1955	55,540	107.7 *(5)*	105.5 *(6)*	54,870	105.6 *(9)*	105.6 *(8)*
1956	58,290	105.0 *(6)*	106.4 *(5)*	70,360	128.2 *(6)*	128.2 *(5)*
1957	60,350	103.5 *(7)*	104.3 *(7)*	78,390	111.4 *(8)*	111.4 *(7)*
(1957)	53,700			70,400		
1958	67,100	124.9 *(1)*	114.2 *(1)*	117,000	166.2 *(1)*	166.2 *(1)*

Year	Gross Capital Goods Output [d]		Gross Modern Sector Output [e]		Gross Consumer Goods Output	
	$Y_{2,t}$=value (in million yuan) [b]	$Y_{2,t}/Y_{2,t-1}$	$Y_{3,t}$=value (in million yuan) [c]	$Y_{3,t}/Y_{3,t-1}$	$Y_{4,t}$=value (in million yuan) [b]	$Y_{4,t}/Y_{4,t-1}$
1949	3,730	......	7,910	......	10,290	......
1950	5,650	151.5 (*2*)	10,890	137.7 (*4*)	13,470	130.9 (*3*)
1951	8,500	150.4 (*3*)	15,910	146.1 (*2*)	17,850	132.5 (*2*)
1952	12,220	143.7 (*4*)	22,050	138.6 (*3*)	22,110	123.9 (*5*)
1953	16,680	136.5 (*6*)	28,810	130.7 (*6*)	28,020	126.7 (*4*)
1954	19,990	119.8 (*7*)	33,980	117.9 (*7*)	31,980	114.1 (*7*)
1955	22,890	114.5 (*9*)	37,080	109.1 (*9*)	31,980	100.0 (*9*)
1956	32,040	140.0 (*5*)	50,340	135.8 (*5*)	38,320	119.8 (*6*)
1957	37,940	118.4 (*8*)	55,630	110.5 (*8*)	40,450	105.5 (*8*)
(1957)	33,000		49,670		37,400	
1958	67,000	203.0 (*1*)	87,270	175.7 (*1*)	50,000	133.7 (*1*)

Notes:

a. From *Ten Great Years (TGY),* p. 118. Data in 1952 prices except for the smaller 1957 figure and the 1958 value, which are in 1957 prices and exclude value of subsidiary output. The exclusion of subsidiary output in 1957 and 1958 does not create any real problem of comparability since for the focal year, 1957, output was reported both on the old and new bases. Net output data are superior for our purposes; however, it is well known that growth rates do not differ appreciably between the gross and the net. See, for example, D. Gale Johnson and Arcadius Kahan, "Soviet Agriculture: Structure and Growth," in *Comparisons of the United States and Soviet Economics,* Joint Economic Committee, U.S. Congress, 1959, Part I (pp. 204-205). The disparities are somewhat more noticeable for China as between the official gross series and Liu and Yeh's adjusted value added series (*op. cit.,* p. 213). However, the latter series is too short for meaningful statistical manipulations.

b. From *TGY,* p. 87. Data in 1952 prices except for the smaller 1957 and the 1958 values, which are in 1957 prices.

c. From *TGY,* p. 91. Data in 1952 prices except for the smaller 1957 and the 1958 values, which are in 1957 prices.

d. Category called "means of production" sector in Communist publications.

e. Precise definition not given. The "modern sector" presumably encompasses all establishments of the factory type.

World War II), the planner acts on the basis of the information, faulty or otherwise, available to him; and this is the information contained in official releases. In other words, it appears that only one set of books is kept. Of course, the released data may well diverge from those confronting the planner when he makes decisions, because of the time lag and the differing degree of comprehensiveness.

The argument for using official industrial statistics is less cogent, since the actual industrial growth is to be our basis for gauging agriculture's restraining effect—an effect transmitted to industrial production by the planner's effort to modify the annual industrial plan in accordance with the agricultural conditions conveyed to him by the official compilations. For this reason, in Table 2, which contains similar data for the USSR for 1928-37, Hodgman's revised industrial output series is used in place of the highly unreliable official series. For China, however, the official industrial releases are used because statistical manipulations in this section require longer time series than independent estimates provide.

In Section I above, we have distinguished between three cases in which certain theoretical relationships between agriculture and industry are specified. From such relationships we have further deduced consequences that are empirically refutable. We have also hypothesized that China belongs to Case III and the Soviet Union to Case I, Case II, or a mixture of the two. For China, if the hypothesis is to be consistent with the data, we would expect to find (a) a significant correlation between annual rates of agricultural and industrial growth, with the relationship plausibly subject to some form of distributed lag; (b) a coefficient of variation in industrial growth rates that is large compared with that of a country falling under Case I or Case II; and (c) relatively steady per capita farm consumption of agricultural output, with varying amounts of state procurement. For the Soviet Union, we would expect noncorrelation between industrial and agricultural growths, a small coefficient of variation in industrial growth rates, and farm consumption fluctuating relative to state procurement.[11]

Rank (Spearman's) correlation coefficients calculated from Tables 1 and 2 show that the data are consistent with the predicted relationships between agricultural and industrial growth rates for the two countries. With zero lag, the agricultural growth rate appears to have exerted statistically significant influences in China, during 1949-58, upon the growth rates of industry as a whole ($r = 0.67^*$), of the capital goods sector ($r = 0.75^*$), and of the "modern" sector ($r = 0.70^*$).[12] By contrast, in the Soviet Union of 1928-37, variations in the agricultural growth rate apparently had exerted no influence upon the growth rate of either Hodgman's large-scale industry ($r = 0.10$) or Nutter's consumer goods industry ($r = 0.15$).

Given the seasonality of agricultural production and the possible role

11. This assumes that forces internal to industry and trade that cause fluctuations in industrial growth rates are similar in kind and magnitude between the various cases distinguished above and that the amplitude of fluctuations as given by agricultural constraints is greater than that by the endogenous restraints.

12. Starred values indicate statistically significant coefficients—(*) for 5 per cent significance level and (**) for 1 per cent. One-tail test is applied since the direction of the correlation is specified by our hypothesis.

TABLE 2

AGRICULTURAL AND INDUSTRIAL OUTPUT, GROWTH RATES USSR, 1928-1937

	Gross Agricultural Output			Industrial Output: Large-Scale (Hodgman)			Industrial Output: Consumer Goods (Nutter)		
Year	X = Index [a]	$\frac{X_t}{X_{t-1}}$	$\frac{1}{2}\left(\frac{X_t}{X_{t-1}}+\frac{X_{t-1}}{X_{t-2}}\right)$	Y_t = Index	$\frac{Y_t}{Y_{t-1}}$ (n=9)	$\frac{Y_t}{Y_{t-1}}$ (n=8)	Index	$\frac{Y_t}{Y_{t-1}}$	$\frac{Y_t}{Y_{t-1}}$
1928	100.0	......	......	100	......	......	100	......	......
1929	101.0	101.0 (*5*)	......	120	120 (*2*)	......	106	106 (*6*)	......
1930	104.2	103.2 (*4*)	102.1 (*4½*)	139	116 (*6*)	116 (*5*)	107	101 (*7*)	101 (*6*)
1931	92.4	88.7 (*8*)	95.9 (*7*)	164	118 (*4*)	118 (*3*)	114	107 (*5*)	107 (*5*)
1932	81.7	88.4 (*9*)	88.5 (*8*)	172	105 (*9*)	105 (*8*)	103	90 (*9*)	90 (*8*)
1933	84.7	103.7 (*3*)	96.1 (*6*)	192	112 (*7*)	112 (*6*)	101	98 (*8*)	98 (*7*)
1934	85.1	100.5 (*6*)	102.1 (*4½*)	229	119 (*3*)	119 (*2*)	113	112 (*2½*)	112 (*2½*)
1935	95.6	112.3 (*2*)	106.4 (*2*)	295	129 (*1*)	129 (*1*)	127	112 (*2½*)	112 (*2½*)
1936	89.9	94.0 (*7*)	103.2 (*3*)	344	117 (*5*)	117 (*4*)	148	117 (*1*)	117 (*1*)
1937	112.8	125.5 (*1*)	109.8 (*1*)	371	108 (*8*)	108 (*7*)	162	109 (*4*)	109 (*4*)

Sources:

Agricultural index: from Johnson and Kahan, 1959, p. 204.

Large-scale industry: from Donald R. Hodgman, *Soviet Industrial Production, 1928-51* (Harvard University Press, 1954) p. 89. Hodgman's index for years through 1937 refers to "large-scale industry."

Consumer goods: from Warren Nutter, *The Growth of Industrial Production in the Soviet Union* (Princeton University Press, 1962) p. 198.

Notes:

a. In 1926-27 price weights.

of inventories, it is undoubtedly preferable to employ statistical associations that incorporate some suitable form of distributed lag. Under a lag formulation giving equal weight to the independent variable (the agricultural growth rate) of the current and previous periods (Table 1, Col. 3), the correlation coefficient for all industry rises to 0.91** for China. The coefficients for the subsectors—capital goods, "modern," and consumer goods—also show general increases, all rising to 0.88**. Under the same lag formulation, the correlation for the Soviet Union between the agricultural growth rate and that of large-scale industry remains low and insignificant (r = 0.28). However, the correlation for the consumer goods industry increases to 0.71* and becomes statistically significant. Despite data limitations and the brief time period considered, these findings nonetheless are quite consistent with the hypothesis put forth in Section I: that because of the great disparity in their initial conditions, China—unlike the Soviet Union—was not able to industrialize in a manner unrestricted by variations in agricultural output, despite both countries' adherence to the Stalinist model of forced industrialization.[13] The findings also seem to make clear the dilemma that is implicit in the Stalinist program when the country implementing it begins with a setting that leaves little room at the subsistence margin.

The argument requires elaboration. One of the characteristics of Soviet-type planning is that, when shortages develop, the planned targets for the priority industrial sector can be protected to an extent by lowering the targets for the low-priority sector. The loose technical input-output relations between these sectors allow such retrenchment to be made without compromising the integrity and consistency of the priority sector plans to any significant extent. It is clear from the finding that both China and the USSR adjusted annually the plan for the low-priority consumer goods sector to meet fluctuations in the agricultural sector. However, contrary to the Soviet experience, and in spite of flexible annual plans for the low-priority industrial sector, the effect of agricultural disturbances in China spilled over into the priority sector as well.

Whether the low-priority industrial sector is capable of absorbing the full impact of a given agricultural disturbance depends on (1) the extent to which the disturbance affects the extracted agricultural surplus; and (2) the degree of freedom that the planner has in adjusting his plan for this

13. We recognize that rank correlation coefficient is no substitute for the regression coefficients which are needed to show, say, the percentage effect on industrialization from a given change in agricultural growth rate. Rank procedure is used for obvious reasons: the smallness of the time sample and the crudeness of the data. However, taking (as a purely approximation statement) the equivalence between the rank and Pearsonian correlation coefficients, we note that the Pearsonian r is in fact the regression coefficient with all variables expressed in standard unit. For certain purposes, such regression form is highly useful.

sector to the changing agricultural surplus. On both scores, it would appear that the Chinese planner finds himself confronted with a far more difficult task than his Soviet counterpart. As we shall see below, the Soviet Union, because of its initially favorable per capita agricultural product, was able to extract a more or less steady agricultural surplus in spite of the pronounced fluctuations in output. Thus, in sharp contrast with the Chinese experience, minor variations in the agricultural surplus could be easily absorbed by flexible planning for the consumer goods sector.

In what ways are the fluctuations and disturbances in agriculture transmitted to the industrial sectors? Without attempting to be exhaustive, we shall outline several ways in which the mechanisms of transmission may work. Let us take an unplanned shortfall in agricultural production as the disturbance. Its first result may be a reduction in the number of workers to be transferred out of agriculture. The low-priority consumer goods sector takes an improvised cut in its planned increase in employment; the priority heavy industrial sector accepts the residual revision, if any, in employment. Second, the reduction in food and industrial crop output from the farms leads to lowered production targets for such industrial consumer goods as textiles and wines destined for domestic consumption. Such revisions in the plan for the low-priority sector may be intended to maintain exports of primary agricultural commodities for which external markets exist. The maintenance of such exports then permits planned importation of capital goods for the priority industrial sector. (On the other hand, failure to maintain exports at planned levels brings about some retrenchment in the priority sector.)

The expedient of squeezing the low-priority industrial sector can be carried out in yet another way. Assume that a portion of the output of the priority sector is designated as inputs for the consumer goods sector. Assume further that some of this output is subject to alternative use as inputs by the agricultural sector. What the planner may do is to divert the delivery from the consumer goods industry to the agricultural sector. If the consumer goods sector contains an ample initial "cushion," the process can go on until agricultural output is raised to the level consistent with the requirements of the planned maximum growth for the priority sector.

It is also of interest to note that, consistent with the predicted consequences of the relationships found earlier between industry and agriculture in the two countries, the relative variability of the Chinese industrial growth rates (coefficient of variation or CV = 16.7 per cent for all industry, and 17.3 per cent for the capital goods sector) is more than twice that for the Soviet Union (CV = 6.7 per cent for the large-scale sector.) This is true in spite of China's relatively greater stability in agricultural growth rates. For grains alone, the coefficient of variation in growth rates comes to 10.1 per cent for China as compared with 20.1 per cent for the

USSR.[14] For all agriculture, the coefficients for the two countries are 6.6 per cent and 10.8 per cent, respectively.[15]

Available data are also consistent with the implications of our hypothesis concerning the distribution of the agricultural output between the farm and nonfarm claimants. Table 3 shows that in China the amounts

TABLE 3

DISTRIBUTION OF AGRICULTURAL OUTPUT, CHINA, 1952-57

Year	Marketed Value (millions of yuan) [a]	Retained Value (millions of yuan) [b]	Retained Per Farm Population (in yuan)	Farm Population (millions) [c]
1952	12.970	35.420	91.5	387
1953	15.320	34.590	88.2	392
1954	17.360	34.210	86.0	398
1955	17.800	37.470	92.7	407
1956	18.400	39.890	96.4	414
1957	20.280	40.070	94.7	423
Total	102.130	221.920	549.4	2421
X	17.021	36.987	91.6	404
s	2.334	2.390	3.16	
s/X	13.71%	6.46%	3.46%	

Notes:

a. From *TGY*, p. 168. Marketings include "products of agricultural side occupations."

b. Value of gross output less marketings.

c. Calculated as follows: Chang's 1933 ratio (0.73) of agricultural population (AP) to total population (Liu and Yeh, 1965, p. 182) is assumed to apply to 1949. The ratio of the estimated 1949 AP (= 391.5 or TP of 536.3 [Liu and Yeh, p. 212] times .73) to rural population (RP) is then assumed to apply to the official RP for 1952-57 (Liu and Yeh, p. 212) to obtain the estimated AP., Finally to allow for the number engaged in nonagricultural subsidiary work, the latter estimates are adjusted downward by a factor of .9493 (established for 1933 by Liu and Yeh, p. 102).

marketed were far more variable (CV = 14 per cent) than either output (CV = 7 per cent) or the value of the product retained in the agricultural sector; this is particularly true if, as is preferable, farm retentions are

14. To anticipate possible questions about the use of the Chinese coefficients calculated, as they are from the official data widely taken to be highly unreliable, we offer the fact that the coefficients based on prewar output statistics, 1931-40, exhibit similar magnitudes. Prewar data are from Ladejinsky and Rossiter, 1942 (pp. 155-56) and show a CV = 8%.

15. Actually, variability measures are calculated from the data expressed as one plus the growth rate. These data are from Cols. 2, 5, 7, Table 1; Cols. 2, 5, Table 2. Grain statistics are from *TGY* (p. 119) and Johnson and Kahan (1959, p. 231).

placed on a per person basis for the farm population (CV = 3 per cent). Because of the trend increment noticeable in the data, part of the variation so measured does not represent fluctuations in a meaningful sense. However, the coefficients of variation computed from the deviations about the trend lines do not alter the conclusions.[16]

In contrast, farm deliveries to the state (including those to tractor stations) were amazingly stable in the Soviet Union (CV = 9 per cent), relative either to total output (15 per cent), to *kolkhoz* residuals (21 per cent), to distribution to *kolkhozniki* (28 per cent), or to the value of *trudoden* (labor days) (29 per cent). Although the Soviet data (Table 4) pertain to grains only, there can be little doubt that they are indicative of the more comprehensive data. It may be of interest to note that even after the abnormally good crop of 1937 (nearly 25 per cent above Jasny's average for 1935-39, or 61 per cent over the 1936 total yield) there was virtually no change in deliveries to the state, compared with 1936, a notoriously bad year. At the same time, however, total distribution to collective farm members rose 136 per cent in 1937, while the value of the workpoint went up by 150 per cent.

(In all these Soviet data, no attempt is made to apply a farm population deflator or to adjust for trend increment because of the stability of both these factors.)

CONCLUSIONS

The three sets of findings—on associations between agricultural and industrial growth rates, on fluctuations in industrial growth areas, and on the distribution of the agricultural output—appear to hang together, as it were, very well indeed. Taken together, they are quite consistent with our hypothesis suggesting that, within the framework of the model presented earlier, China would appear to belong to Case III and the USSR to Case II. Insofar as Soviet deliveries to the state did undergo fluctuations, the affluence of agriculture as compared with China may not have been such as to take the country completely beyond the purview of Case I. At any rate, it is clear that the minor Soviet fluctuations in procurement were easily absorbed by the consumer goods industry, so that the growth of the priority industrial sector remained unconstrained by agriculture.

Thus, in spite of their common adherence to the Stalinist model of development, the two countries during their respective first periods of planning were forced by their disparate initial conditions to employ quite different policies for both agriculture and industry. The Chinese variant in this regard falls under the heading of Eckstein's "local adaptations." For

16. Physical crop data may well be preferable to the value data because of the valuation problem implicit in the latter and because global value data may gloss over significant details. Unfortunately, crop distribution data between the farm and nonfarm claimants are not available.

TABLE 4

DISTRIBUTION OF GRAIN OUTPUT
USSR, 1932-39

Year	Deliveries to State and MTS (millions of tons) [a]	Distribution to Kolkhozniki (millions of tons) [b]	Value Per Trudoden (in kilograms) [c]	Output [d] (millions of tons)	Kolkhoz Residual [e] (millions of tons)
1932	19.9	n.a.	2.3	n.a.	n.a.
1933	17.8	14.2	2.9	n.a.	n.a.
1934	21.1	16.3	2.8	n.a.	n.a.
1935	23.9	16.5	2.4	75.2	51.3
1936	21.2	12.4	1.6	59.8	38.6
1937	22.1	29.3	4.0	96.0	73.9
1938	20.7	18.0	2.2	75.9	55.2
1939	23.9	16.4	1.9	82.2	58.3
Total	170.6	123.1	20.1	389.1	277.3
X	21.3	17.6	2.5	77.8	55.5
s	2.0	5.0	0.73	11.8	11.4
s/X	9.4%	28.4%	29.2%	15.2%	20.6%

Notes:

a. Data not completely comparable as between 1932, 1933-36, and 1937-39. However, crude adjustments to remove noncomparability do not change the essential conclusions shown in the text as drawn from these data. The 1932 figure is from Jasny, 1949, p. 78; those for 1933-36 are from p. 745 and entitled "all deliveries to the government;" those for 1937-39 are from p. 738 and include obligatory deliveries and payments to MTS.

b. From Jasny, 1949, pp. 738, 745. Jasny puts the decline in gainfully employed in agriculture at 10% during 1928-39 (p. 714). Probably fully half the decline took place during 1928-32. Given the stability in numbers for 1933-39, the application of a population deflator changes the relative values but a little (cf. the case for China, Table 3). At any rate, it reinforces the conclusions in the text.

c. From Jasny, 1949, p. 695 (official data).

d. From Jasny, 1949, p. 744 (Jasny's estimates).

e. Output minus State and MTS deliveries.

China, the adaptation has meant an industrial investment policy (even for the priority sector) that recognizes external constraints and the need for flexibility. Effective constraints from agriculture not only held industrial growth below the endogenously feasible maximum rate but tended to subject it to wider fluctuations. These were due to the characteristics of agricultural production and to still greater fluctuations in the residual claimant's share of an unstable product. While in the USSR *kolkhoz* members were the residual claimant, in China the unpleasant burden fell on the state despite its awesome power and its intent to extract from agriculture. The resulting need for flexibility in planning and for periodical retrenchment in the priority sector obviously entails costs and frustrations.[17] To have their priority sector subjected to such afflictions is undoubtedly something that the Chinese planners would want to correct as speedily as possible. Their development-oriented agricultural policy was intended to accomplish this. An analysis of that policy is considered in a later section.

At this juncture, we simply note that in relation to its objective the Chinese policy was not successful. Industrial growth was still restrained by the vagaries of agricultural production and unstable state procurement. Even more telling is the evidence from the end of the First Five-Year Plan period, and still more so from the Great Leap debacle. The year of 1957 turned out to be a year of retrenchment and reappraisal. Grain output showed virtually no increase over the previous year—itself a mediocre crop year despite the massive injection of inputs. That apparently was enough to bring about an industrial growth rate for 1957 that ranked as the second lowest since 1950. It must have occurred to the planner, then, that agriculture was acting as a drag on industrialization toward the end of the "Ten Great Years" much as it had at the beginning.

Agriculture in the Soviet Union, coerced and neglected as it was, did manage to discharge the role reserved for it under the Stalinist model. Industrialization (in the priority sector) developed unaffected by production shortfalls and other assorted woes that beset the agricultural sector. This, of course, was a short-run success but it gave the Soviet Union the opportunity it sought to enlarge its industrial base at a maximum speed unrestricted by agriculture. How soon the day of reckoning is likely to come or whether it will come depends on many things. It is significant to note that during the 1950's Soviet agriculture showed impressive increases both in total output and in productivity per unit of resources. Output grew at an average rate of about 5 per cent per year and the ratio of output to input rose by perhaps 20 per cent between 1950 and 1959.[18] Yet, one comes up with a startling finding: The growth rate of the machinery sector, the *sanctum sanctorum* of Soviet industrialization, began to fluctuate along with the agricultural sector. A distributed lag relationship similar to the one used earlier yields for the growth rates of the two sectors a rank correlation coefficient of 0.66.[19] At the same time, the consumer goods industry, oddly enough, displayed no such tendency.

17. These costs and frustrations would have been all the more serious if the Chinese planner had failed to anticipate the need for flexibility and found it necessary to make adjustments later.

18. Output growth rate is calculated for 1950-58 from Johnson and Kahan (1959, p. 203); productivity increase is taken from D. Gale Johnson (1963, p. 219).

19. The coefficient is not quite significant but highly suggestive nevertheless. The period covered is 1952-58. Had a longer period been documented by data, a significant result may well be obtained. Industrial data are from N. M. Kaplan and R. H. Moorsteen, 1960 (p. 296).

Could it be that Khrushchev, in relaxing Stalin's harsh consumption policy, raised both the minimum farm share and the urban requirements of food to the extent of causing the agricultural surplus to impinge upon industrialization efforts? Could it also be that, consistent with the same policy, he hesitated to allow the impact of agricultural bottlenecks to fall on the familiar consumer goods industry? That per capita consumption of food did rise substantially under Khrushchev is clear. As Chapman (1963) indicates, the Soviet per capita real consumption roughly doubled between 1928 and 1958, with the bulk of the increase occurring during the 1950's. Her estimates of commodity consumption suggest that by 1950 per capita food consumption had probably only regained the level of 1928, so that the gains during the 1950's were impressive indeed compared with the Stalinist era. If one takes a crude average from Chapman's data, the increase in the per capita consumption of principal food items turns out to be roughly 50 per cent during 1950-58.[20] This increase, together with population growth, appears to outstrip decisively the output growth shown earlier.

In this light Khrushchev's unusual concern with agriculture is perhaps only natural. But this also points up a contradiction. Having cast aside (or at least relaxed) one important element of the Stalinist model—the harsh consumption policy—Khrushchev nevertheless wanted to cling to another element, *i.e.,* agriculture as a mere instrument to industrialization. When agriculture appeared to hamper the development of the priority sector, the erstwhile Party leader fretted. Once bread has been elevated to the status of a "final good" (to return to Bergson's analogy), there is no longer any internal logic to the Stalinist role for agriculture. Logic aside, the bind in which Khrushchev, and presumably his successors, found themselves appears to be a real one, especially in the short run. Meanwhile, in terms of Fel'dman's analytical elements, the propensity to save is beginning to assert itself over the productive capacity of the capital goods sector as the limiting factor to Soviet growth. As this happens, the Fel'dman model loses its relevance in the Soviet Union just as it did from the very beginning in Communist China.

Before closing this section, it may be well to recall that this chapter is an attempt to advance our understanding of the nature of agricultural problems that confront Communist countries bent on rapid industrialization. Although volumes have been written on the subject, much of the work is institutional in character and some appears to be "pathological," to use Wellisz's apt word. Gross "inefficiencies" no doubt existed and still do. But to a Stalinist planner, the more fundamental question is whether

20. The average is computed from the physical quantities consumed in 1950 and 1958 for 11 commodities shown in Chapman, 1963 (Table VI-1). Arbitrary weights of 5 for flour and 1 for all others are used in computing the average increase. Also two of the listed commodities, vodka and beer, are excluded.

agriculture is discharging its intended role, "inefficiencies" aside. It is hoped that our framework permits an explicit answer to this question. The findings of this section, though no doubt tentative, are offered in that spirit.

It may also be well to point out another Chinese "local adaptation," which also results from their extremely low initial position in per capita food production.[21] A significant aspect of the early Soviet development policy was the massive injection of labor into the economy, particularly into the nonfarm sector. This was accomplished through wage (money) incentives operating within the framework of a relatively "free" labor market. The resulting increases in total wage income led to rapid inflation as Stalin held the supply of consumer goods more or less constant in real terms. This was a convenient expedient—one that also benefited to an extent from the effects of "money illusion." It was feasible because of the initial Soviet margin in per capita consumption, which made tolerable the redistributive effects of inflation.

China also relied heavily upon labor mobilization as a source of growth. But its initial consumption level was probably judged to be too low to absorb the effects of a similar redistribution of income. As a "local adaptation," the planner resorted to "planned supply" of the key consumer goods, principally food items. The Party's decision to commit considerable personnel to the administration of an elaborate rationing system can be understood only against the background of such a need. However, the effect of rationing is also relevant to our framework in yet another sense. Based on the official rationing schedule, complete with sophisticated differentiation between age, sex, occupation, etc., there can be little doubt that the effect of the system was to raise the efficiency of consumption, not necessarily from the standpoint of Western welfare but from that of Marxist reproduction. The relevance to our model is that rationing reduced the requirements for agricultural output for any level of industrialization.

Finally, attributing "success" to the Soviet agricultural policy and "failure" to the Chinese policy does not imply in any way greater effort or more astute planning on the part of the Soviets. It should be clear that the Soviet policy had been almost exclusively extractive. And this statement stands despite the sizable agricultural investment made at the time, largely in the form of machine tractors. This investment took place for two main reasons: to replace the working livestock slaughtered during the ill-conceived collectivization drive—a mistake that the Chinese avoided—and to institute a coercive collection mechanism in the form of machine tractor stations (MTS). Of course, implementation of a policy that is either extractive or developmental need not present insurmountable problems. To implement one that tries to be both is a very different proposi-

21. For a couple of excellent treatments of the importance of an initial agricultural surplus and its maintenance, see William H. Nicholls, 1963, 1964.

tion. An evaluation of the Chinese agricultural policy should be tempered by this consideration; the goals of that policy are inherently conflicting. Peking did not unwittingly choose the conflicting goals but was forced to embrace them by the Stalinist model and by the economic realities in China. Two additional considerations are worth bearing in mind. The concommittant large-scale mechanization of Soviet agriculture and decline in the number of draft animals, as a component of Stalin's collectivization, released substantial amounts of grain for human consumption (at a saving of about half a ton per horse per year). This was not an option open to China, even if it had been deemed desirable. Lastly, comparative performance of the two countries is best viewed against the background of their vastly different population growth rates mentioned earlier.

In this section, we have broadly ascertained the differences in agricultural policy and performance between Communist China and the Soviet Union during the periods of their respective First Five-Year Plans. Although the extractive part of the Chinese policy was successfully carried out, the development portion of it clearly failed to attain the desired policy objective. To understand this aspect of Chinese policy failures, we turn our attention in the following sections to an analysis of the content of the agrarian program. The purpose is to identify the sources of growth tapped by the Chinese, to gauge their "profitability," and to determine crucial sources of growth either ignored or poorly dealt with by the planners.

III. OUTPUT-INPUT RELATIONS, 1952-1957

THE INPUT INDEX

In Table 5 are given input series for labor, land, livestock, and the principal current production expenses during 1952-57. As explained in detail in the notes to the table, some series are in physical terms, others in values, and still others in index number form. Some are compiled directly or indirectly from official sources while others represent our own estimates. The detailed inputs are then grouped under four headings—labor, land, capital, and current inputs—and converted into index numbers. The manner in which various capital and current items are aggregated is explained in Table 6. The method employed is that of the weighted aggregate of quantity relatives.

The summation of the four components into a single aggregate input index is accomplished by means of the weights presented in Table 7. These weights are in the main in line with Buck's prewar estimates and with Liu and Yeh's summary of several sets of Communist data (Buck, 1930; Liu and Yeh, 1965). They also appear to be quite plausible in relation to the factor weights for a number of selected countries, also shown

Table 5

AGRICULTURAL INPUTS, CHINA, 1952-57

Year	Labor [a] (in millions of workers)	Land [b] (in million mou) Cultivated	Land [b] (in million mou) Sown	Livestock [c] (in million 1952 yuan)	Seed [d] (in million 1952 yuan)	Chemical Fertilizer [e] (in 1000 tons)	Traditional Fertilizer [f] (per cent)	Insecticides [e] (in 1000 tons)	Feed [g] (in billion 1952 yuan)
1952	238	1619	2119	10900	1151	318	100	15	1.10
1953	241	1628	2161	11628	1173	592	102	19	1.17
1954	245	1640	2219	12338	1205	802	105	41	1.25
1955	250	1652	2266	11918	1230	1255	107	67	1.20
1956	255	1677	2388	11808	1297	1608	113	159	1.19
1957	260	1677	2359	11762	1281	1944	111	149	1.32

Notes:

a. Estimated agricultural population from Table 3. These estimates are then multiplied by a factor of 0.9493 to allow for nonagricultural subsidiary work done by farm persons, and further multiplied by 0.615 which is the proportion of the population over 12 years of age but under 65. The first factor $(= 1 - \frac{18.5}{365})$ is based on figures taken from Liu and Yeh, 1965, p. 102. The second is from the reconstructed age distribution by John S. Aird in "The Present and Prospective Population of Mainland China," in *Population Trends in Eastern Europe, The USSR, and Mainland China* (Milbank Memorial Fund, 1960) p. 112.

b. From *TGY*, p. 128.

c. Includes poultry. From Liu and Yeh, 1965, p. 406.

d. Seeds in 1954 amounted in cost to 4.4% of the gross value of plant output of 27.360 million *yuan* (see Liu and Yeh, 1965, pp. 400 and 412). Total seed costs of 1,204 million is divided by the 1954 sown acreage (2,219 million *mou*) to arrive at the cost per *mou* which is then applied to the sown acreage of each year. The index is of course identical to that of sown acreage.

e. From *TGY*, p. 171. These figures are very close to Jung-Chao Liu's estimates (1965a, p. 925; 1965b, p. 38).

f. No data. Consumption assumed to vary with sown acreage whose index is used.

g. From Liu and Yeh, 1965, p. 418.

TABLE 6

AGGREGATE INPUT INDEX
CHINA, 1952-57

Year	Labor [a]	Land [b] Cultivated Acreage	Land [b] Sown Acreage	Capital [c]	Current Inputs [d]	Aggregate Input Index [e] I	Aggregate Input Index [e] II
1952	100%	100.0%	100%	100%	100%	100.0%	100.0%
1953	101	100.6	102	107	115	103.1	103.5
1954	103	101.3	105	113	138	107.3	108.2
1955	105	102.0	107	109	172	112.0	113.2
1956	107	103.6	113	108	243	121.3	123.6
1957	109	103.6	111	120	249	124.2	126.0

Notes:

a. Computed from Col. 1, Table 5.

b. Computed from Cols. 2 and 3, Table 5.

c. Computed from Cols. 4 and 9, Table 5. Index is based on livestock and feed. Machinery as reported in *TGY* (p. 171) was negligible in value even in 1957. Implements are assumed to have grown in value in line with livestock.

d. Index is composite. Seeds, chemical fertilizers, traditional fertilizers, and insecticides series (Table 5) are first converted into index numbers. The latter are summed by means of the following value weights taken from Liu and Yeh (1965, p. 414): 4.4 for seeds, 5.0 for all fertilizers, and 0.9 for insecticides and other miscellaneous items. Converting into relative percentage weights as used in our calculations: 42.7%, 12.2%, 36.4%, and 8.7% for seeds, chemical and traditional fertilizers, and insecticides (and miscellaneous), respectively. It may be noted that the above index for current inputs turns out to be very close to the Communist series on "means of production supplied to agriculture" (*TGY*, p. 170) which shows an index of 231% for 1957 (1952=100).

e. Aggregation of the four major components made on the basis of the weights calculated in Table 7. Aggregate index (I) based on cultivated acreage and (II) on sown acreage.

TABLE 7

RELATIVE INPUT WEIGHTS OF SELECTED COUNTRIES AND CHINA

Country, Year	Relative Input Weights [a] Labor	Land	Capital	Current Inputs
Taiwan, 1952-56	.45	.25	.11	.19
Japan, 1933-37	.52	.26	.08	.14
India, 1945-48	.34	.25	.30	.11
Panajachel (Guat.), 1936	.84	.10	.02	.04
U.S., 1949	.33	.19	.48	[b]
Communist China, 1952-57	.55	.25	.09	.11

Notes:

a. Weights based on factor income shares or value of service flows. International data not strictly comparable.

b. Classification does not permit separation into our capital and current input categories.

Sources:

Taiwan: Yhi-min Ho, *The Agricultural Development of Taiwan 1903-60,* unpublished Ph.D. thesis, Vanderbilt University, 1965, p. 103.

Japan: Anthony M. Tang, "Research and Education in Japanese Agricultural Development, 1880-1938," *The Economic Studies Quarterly* (Riron Keizai Gaku), May 1963, p. 93 (in English).

India and Panajachel: T. W. Schultz, *Transforming Traditional Agriculture,* Yale University Press, 1964, pp. 99-100. India's data pertain to Punjab. Panajachel portrays a primitive agricultural setting among Guatemala's Indians. Professor Schultz, who gave generously of his time to make detailed comments on an earlier draft of this paper, called my attention to Tara Shukla's all-India data in her recent book *(Capital Formation in Indian Agriculture).* Although Shukla does not show the weight for current inputs, her input weights—0.30 for labor, 0.27 for land, and 0.43 for capital—are on the whole close to the figures for the Punjab shown in the table.

U.S.: Zvi Griliches, "Sources of Measured Productivity Growth," *Journal of Political Economy,* Aug. 1963, p. 336.

China: J. L. Buck in his monumental studies of prewar Chinese agriculture shows data (*Chinese Farm Economy,* University of Chicago Press, 1930, pp. 86-87) that suggest the following weights: labor 49%, current inputs 11% and others 40%. The current inputs weight from Buck's farm survey of the 1920's appears to be still current in the light of Liu and Yeh's cost estimates (1965, p. 139): 11% of gross plant output value and 10% of animal product value for 1952-57. The increased labor share over Buck's is deemed plausible in view of Communist China's labor mobilization policy. The land and capital shares, though arbitrarily divided, also appear reasonable in relation to other national statistics; most relevant, those of Taiwan and Japan. The weight for capital is taken to reflect not only the return to livestock investment but also the cost of feed. Current inputs, then, consist of seeds, fertilizers (chemical and traditional), insecticides and other expenses.

in Table 7. Gaps do exist at this and the lower levels of aggregation. These gaps are filled by plausible assumptions. The procedures are of course more or less arbitrary. However, where there are missing weights for some series it is better to assign reasonable, though arbitrary, weights than to discard the series; since to discard is to assign zero weights. (All these procedures are, at any rate, clearly stated in the tables for the reader to make his own judgments.)

As is now widely recognized, the aggregate input index so constructed is really the output index that would have been obtained in the absence of "technical change." As such, the index implies a particular underlying aggregate production function, as well as assumptions about factor markets. When used in conjunction with the observed output index to yield measured productivity changes, it also assumes a particular form of technical change.[22] Such assumptions are highly restrictive, of course; the aggregation procedure and the index number construction are no doubt open to challenge. Following Solow, we make no attempt "to justify what follows by calling on fancy theorems on aggregation and index numbers. Either this kind of aggregate economics appeals or it doesn't" (1957, p. 312).

Two sets of aggregate input indexes are given in Table 6. Set I is based on cultivated acreage as a proxy for land input or service. Set II uses the sown acreage, the increase in which during 1952-57 was more rapid, resulting in upward revisions in the multiple-cropping index. In cultivated acreage terms, the input index shows a 24 per cent increase in total agricultural inputs during the five-year period. The use of the sown acreage figures raises the figure to 26 per cent. With the exception of a discrete jump in 1956, the increases in other years have been gradual, ranging from 3 to 5 per cent a year.

With the obvious exception of current inputs, other resources are measured in stocks rather than in flows. Thus, insofar as the rate of utilization of the stocks changes over time, these changes would be reflected in disparate growths between the output and the input indexes. That is to say, they constitute one of the sources of "productivity growth."

AN APPLICATION OF THE AGGREGATE INPUT INDEX

Before turning to measured productivity change, which is the central concern of this section, it may be of methodological interest to apply the aggregate input index as a check of the consistency of the official output statistics. For a variety of plausible reasons, Chinese Communist agricultural output statistics have been popularly regarded as suspect. Choh-ming Li (1962) cogently argues his case on the basis of his careful study of the Communist statistical system. Liu and Yeh (1965) state their

22. See, for examples, Tang (1963) and Solow (1957). The assumptions are: strictly linear production function, competitive markets, and neutral technical change.

forceful case in terms of discrepancies between reported output and some minimum food consumption standard. Perhaps one of the most direct and damning bits of evidence lies in the apparent impossibility of reconciling the output claims with the reported crop conditions. As Liu and Yeh point out, in anticipation of the possible criticism that their own estimates fail to reflect harvest conditions, the Communist data simply do not make sense in the light of the reported state of the harvest. Thus, " 'bad' years 1954 and 1956 were substantially better than 'average' year 1953; and 'bad' year 1956 was even better than 'good' year 1955" (Liu and Yeh, 1965, p. 54).

The aggregate input index permits a more rigorous kind of check, as is implicit in the following question: Is the reported crop in a "bad" year smaller than that which one would expect on the basis of the inputs employed, modified by the productivity trend? In these terms, the output of a bad year can clearly be greater than that of a good year if the bad year's input index and productivity trend value are sufficiently higher. In Figure 1, we show the computed productivity index for each year, together with a trend line formed by joining the indexes of the two "average" years, 1953 and 1957. The index is obtained by dividing the official output index by our input index. If the output claims are consistent with the reported harvest conditions, the plots for all the "bad" years should be below the trend and those for the "good" years above it. The figure shows that this is the case without exception. Moreover, the least-squares line which does not take the "average" years as reference points (*i.e.,* does not accept the claim of "average") almost precisely coincides with the first line. This supports the inference that the two claimed "average" years were indeed average. A simple sign test also suggests that the natural elements were a random phenomenon.

The above test, of course, does not support the inference that the Communist output data are correct. In fact, the findings are consistent with any of the following possibilities: (1) All output data are wrong, differing from the correct by a constant factor. (2) Underreporting or overreporting of output varies with time, but the variations are matched by similarly underreported or overreported inputs. (3) Errors in reported output change overtime in a manner unrelated to the discrepancies, if any, in the input series, but by coincidence a pattern such as shown in Fig. 1 emerges. (4) Reported harvest conditions themselves are not reliable, hence, the cross-check between these conditions, the claimed output, the computed input index, and productivity change is meaningless.

The first possibility is rejected by scholars who have worked intimately with the data. Foremost among them are Choh-ming Li and T. C. Liu. The second possibility is ruled out because our input series are estimated entirely independent of output consideration. Our computed input index may leave something to be desired, but there is no basis whatever for

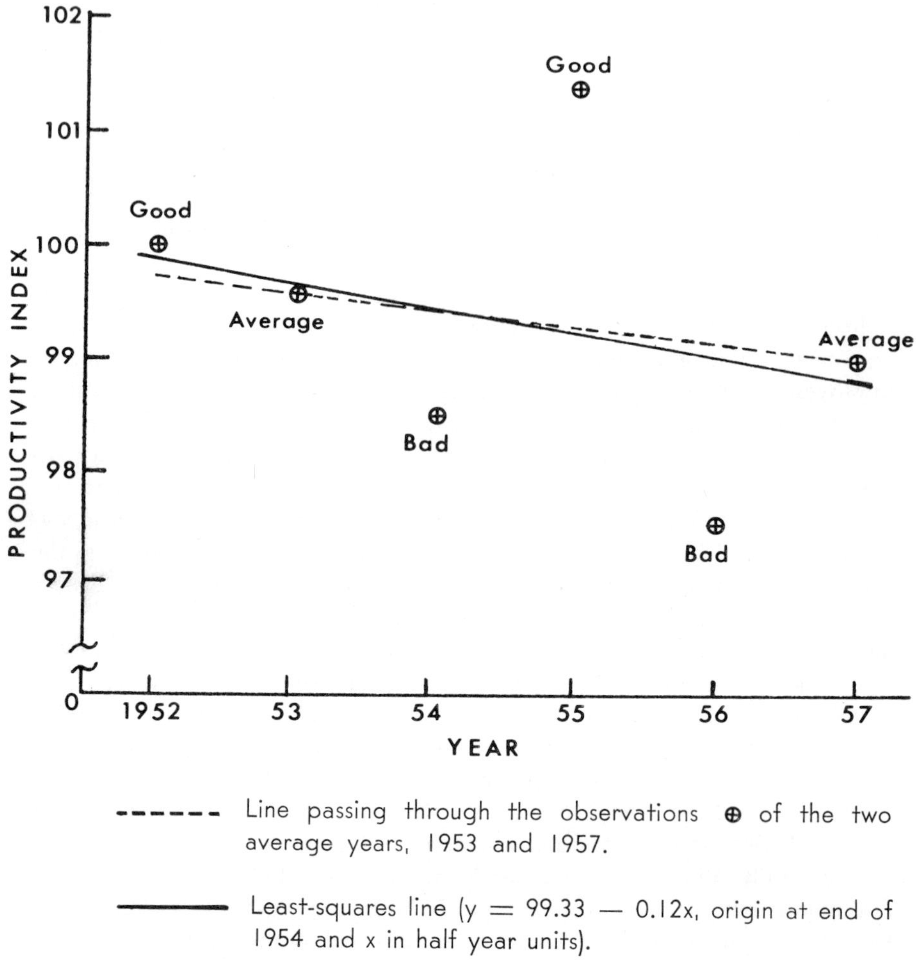

Source: Col. 5, Table 8

FIGURE 1. PRODUCTIVITY INDEX AND HARVEST CONDITIONS

any matching to occur in the discrepancies of the two series. The third possibility cannot be dismissed. If one were to take the computed input series as given and experiment with alternative assumptions about the magnitude and the time profile of the coefficient of output underreporting, one or more profiles will be found that yield configurations consistent with that of Fig. 1. However, such experimentation cannot be very meaningful unless one has a priori grounds for proceeding according to certain particular assumptions. The most plausible conclusion to draw here is that the reporting errors were quite small, so that, whatever assumption one might make regarding their behavior over time, the resulting adjustment to reported output is always overshadowed by the combined influences of weather, the inputs applied, and the productivity trend. The last possibility shown in the list clearly does not merit serious consideration. Our procedure, precisely, is to take the reported output and harvest conditions as "suspect" and to subject them to cross-checks against the independent input series as modified by a trend productivity factor.

From these considerations it would appear reasonable to infer that (1) *in terms of the year-to-year variations,* the Communist agricultural output statistics for 1952-57 are plausible enough; (2) the evidence for initial underreporting as advanced by Li and Liu and Yeh is too strong to ignore; but (3) the initial 1952 underreporting probably was relatively small. Perhaps the order of magnitude suggested by a comparison of Liu and Yeh's independent estimate and their reconstructed Communist figure for 1952 is plausible. The latter is simply official data made to conform to the concept and classification used by Liu and Yeh. Rounding liberally to the nearest billion, the two figures are, respectively, 34 billion *yuan* (in 1952 prices) and 32 billion *yuan* yielding an underreporting coefficient of 6 per cent.[23] In these terms, it can be shown that assuming a straight-line decrease in the coefficient (reaching zero by 1956 as supposed by Liu and Yeh), the resulting adjustment produces an output series that is consistent with the reported weather, inputs and productivity increment. This "adjusted" output series is shown in Table 8, together with the productivity index implied by it.

A SECOND APPLICATION OF THE INPUT INDEX—A DIGRESSION

Earlier in Section II we alluded to the strikingly small fluctuations in Chinese agricultural output compared with those of the Soviet Union. As a matter of fact, the Chinese fluctuations are minor by most national standards. In Japan, it has not been uncommon, especially during 1880-1910, for annual output to fluctuate by 20-30 per cent from one year to the next (Tang, 1963, pp. 93-94). Taiwan, too, falls in the category (Ho, 1965). No doubt China's sheer size and the diversity of its economic areas and climatic regions are responsible for overall yield stability. This need not preclude localized shortfalls in production, famines which in the long history of China have been almost annual occurrences.

What we now want to point up is that when changes in inputs and the increasing or decreasing trend in productivity are accounted for, the output fluctuations become even smaller. This is clear from a comparison

23. From Liu and Yeh, 1965 (p. 312). The reconstructed data are called "adjusted" estimate by Liu and Yeh. It may be noted that the above reconstructed figure comes quite close to Alexander Eckstein's more or less comparable "gross value added" estimate of 31 billion *yuan* for 1952 (1961, p. 92).

of the dispersion of the points about the productivity trend line in Figure 1 and that of the growth rates of annual output. The former is represented by a coefficient of variation of 0.6 per cent and the latter by 6.6 per cent.[24] The coefficient of 0.6 per cent says explicitly that if the period to which the finding pertains is representative of longer time spans,[25] as appears probable, aggregate agricultural output changes in China are almost completely determined by inputs and underlying productivity changes, being only peripherally influenced by harvest conditions. On this basis, it would seem that the Communist attribution of the great production shortfalls during 1959-61 to natural calamities was unwarranted. Only momentous cutbacks in inputs and/or productivity declines (due to organizational and other man-made errors which greatly compounded nature's unkindness) are likely to explain the observed drastic output decline during the Great Leap years.

THE PRODUCTIVITY INDEX

During 1952-57, the official output index shows a 25 per cent increase (Table 8). On the input side, labor increased by 9 per cent, cultivated acreage by 3.6 per cent (sown area by 11 per cent), capital by 20 per cent, and current inputs by 149 per cent. The aggregate input index rose by 24.2 per cent, using cultivated area to reflect land input, or by 26 per cent if sown area is so employed. The substantial increases in current inputs can be attributed to a five-fold rise in chemical fertilizer input and to a thirty-fold increase in the use of insecticides and other modern inputs. By coincidence, our current inputs index turns out to be nearly identical to the Communist index of "means of production supplied to agriculture." The behavior of certain components of the latter series is exceedingly revealing. Insecticide sprayers supplied increased in numbers from 251,000 units in 1952 to a high of 1,308,000 in 1956. One year later, the number dropped to less than half. An even more classic case is the new two-wheeled double-bladed plow. In a single year, 1956, the number supplied reached 1,086,000, only to decline unaccountably to a trickle (95,000 units) the following year (*Ten Great Years,* p. 171). This would suggest "innovation" by ill-conceived and hastily contrived crash programs.

24. The two series are placed on a comparable dimensional footing. The first is expressed in percentages with the trend value equal to 100 per cent; similarly, the second is in percentages with current year output as relatives of the preceding year's output. The coefficient of 6.6 per cent is presented earlier in Section II and calculated from Table 1.

25. Although no attempt is made for data reasons to compute output variations net of inputs and productivity trend for a longer period, it is reassuring to find a coefficient of variation (8 per cent) in annual rates of output change during 1931-40 that is comparable in magnitude to that (6.6 per cent) found for the period under consideration, 1952-57. Output statistics for the 1930's are from Ladejinsky and Rossiter, 1942 (pp. 155-56) and include wheat, rice, and soybean production for all China, including Manchuria. The variability may well be smaller had the data been more comprehensive.

TABLE 8

PRODUCTIVITY INDEX
CHINA, 1952-57
(in per cent)

Year	Output Index: Official	Output Index: Liu and Yeh [a]	Output Index: Adjusted [b]	Productivity Index (Official Output): I	Productivity Index (Official Output): II	Productivity Index (Liu and Yeh): I	Productivity Index (Liu and Yeh): II	Productivity Index (Adjusted): I	Productivity Index (Adjusted): II
1952	100.0	100.0	100.0	100.0	100.0	100.0	100.0	100.0	100.0
1953	103.1	101.8	101.5	100.0	99.6	98.7	98.3	98.4	98.1
1954	106.6	103.8	103.3	99.3	98.5	96.7	95.9	96.3	95.5
1955	114.8	104.8	109.5	102.5	101.4	93.6	92.6	97.8	96.7
1956	120.5	108.1	113.2	99.3	97.5	89.1	87.5	93.3	91.6
1957	124.7	108.7	117.2	100.4	99.0	87.5	86.3	94.4	93.0

Notes:

a. Concept is that of net domestic product originating in agriculture.

b. An initial underreporting of 6% is assumed for 1952 (see text for explanations). It is also assumed that underreporting declined linearly (by 1.5% a year), reaching zero in 1956. Adjusted output index is obtained by revising upward the official data to compensate for underreporting.

Sources:

Official output index: *TGY*, p. 118.

Liu and Yeh, 1965, p. 213.

The widespread character of this Communist affliction is clearly visible elsewhere. Again in terms of the official statistics, irrigated area rose by 218 million *mou* (approximately 36 million acres) or 68 per cent during 1952-57. The percentage of area sown with "improved" seeds jumped from 5 per cent in 1952 to 63 per cent in 1957 for rice; from 5 per cent to 69 per cent for wheat; from 5 per cent to 43 per cent for coarse grains; from zero to 57 per cent for potatoes; from 50 per cent to 94 per cent for cotton; and from 2 per cent to 48 per cent for oil-bearing crops. For all crops, the overall improvement was from 5 per cent to 55 per cent. The year 1956 again stood out as a hectic year of all-out campaigns in these regards. Thus, more than half of the cumulative increase in irrigated acreage during the period 1952-57 occurred in 1956.

Without necessarily taking these statistics seriously, it must be abundantly clear that agricultural policy in China was development-oriented, but that the Party went about it in typical Communist fashion. Without adequate regional experimentation and without the aid of price signals to ensure the appropriate kind of response to the right extent, the Party leadership has had to resort to central directives. The directives have no built-in signal to indicate how far one should go. And to ensure that the directives will not be disregarded, each is duly marked with "top priority" or similar notations. Campaigns via mass media follow. Little wonder, then, that the cadres should wisely toss aside what now must appear to be secondary considerations—output, costs, "profits," etc.—and concentrate on maximizing the object of the new directive. In Communist China, rare is the day when there is not a momentous campaign of some kind in force.

Under these circumstances, it is not surprising to find that even the official output index is completely out of line with the claimed technological triumphs and the reported formation of new as well as traditional capital. Taking the ratio of the (official) output index to the input index to form a productivity index, we find that at best there was no productivity change in the period (Cols. 3 and 4, Table 8). If our "adjusted" output is used, the productivity index falls by 6-7 per cent between 1952-57. Further, if the intensity of factor use increased over time—as is almost certain, especially with labor—the decline in productivity would have been even more pronounced. A 10 per cent rise in the intensity of labor use in current production (by increasing double cropping, for example) would have meant an increase of 6 percentage points in the aggregate input index and a fall of 4 percentage points in the productivity index. Although the bulk of labor mobilization had been for capital formation—an aspect largely reflected in the realized increment in cultivated and sown acreages—part of the increase in the rate of labor force participation and in intensity of use undoubtedly affected current production.

In productivity terms, then, the Chinese experience during 1952-57 was similar to that of the Soviet Union during the early 1930's. In both countries, agricultural productivity fell. But unlike the latter, China managed to raise gross agricultural output by perhaps 3 per cent per year (Col. 3, Table 8) by virtue of its substantial rate of increase of agricultural inputs (a probable minimum of 5 per cent per year).[26]

IV. SOURCES OF AGRICULTURAL GROWTH

COMPONENTS OF OUTPUT GROWTH

As indicated earlier, the construction of the aggregate input index is that of the value-weighted quantity relatives, which is reducible to the price-weighted aggregate method when base year weights are used. Viewed from the standpoint of the underlying production function, the input index gives the relative output expected in the absence of "technical change." The particular construction used here is useful from several standpoints. First, it permits aggregation of dimensionally dissimilar series into the major input categories. Second, it permits the use of more readily obtainable relative service value weights, *i.e.,* relative factor income shares, for the major categories. Third, the direct application of our relative factor share weights to the percentage increase of each input category gives us the contribution of each input to the relative output growth for the period under study, while the productivity index indicates the influence of the shift in the production function.[27]

If we take the official output statistics, the resulting increase of 25 per cent between 1952-57 can be broken down as follows: Increases in labor input have contributed 5 per cent of the output increment, land 3

26. The original plan of this study called for an examination of the gains that may theoretically be had through such programs as land redistribution, consolidation of fragmented holdings, mutual aid teams, and cooperation. Space considerations require us to relegate this aspect to another study. It is sufficient to state here that these sources of productivity increase apparently had not been enough to prevail against diminishing returns and mounting inefficiencies of the sort discussed in the text.

27. In principle, the Cobb-Douglass function is preferable. But as an approximation, our strictly linear, homogeneous production function should do about as well. (Cf. Solow, 1957). Our function is as follows:

$$y_t = A(t)\,(ax_{t,1} + bx_{t,2} + cx_{t,3} + dx_{t,4})$$

where y_t is the output in some year, t; the x's represent the four inputs; A(t) is the shift parameter for "technical change" broadly defined and is equal to one in the base year; the coefficients are marginal value productivities taken to be equal to base year factor prices.
The above equation can be written to accommodate value weights and quantity relatives:

$$y_t = A(t)\left(ax_{0,1}\frac{x_{t,1}}{x_{0,1}} + bx_{0,2}\frac{x_{t,2}}{x_{0,2}} + cx_{0,3}\frac{x_{t,3}}{x_{0,3}} + dx_{0,4}\frac{x_{t,4}}{x_{0,4}}\right);$$

per cent (in sown acreage terms), capital 2 per cent, current inputs 16 per cent, and productivity change a detraction of one per cent. In Communist gross value terms, the output increment has been 12.1 billion (in 1952 prices) with contributions of 2.42 billion from labor, 1.45 from land (in sown acreage), 0.97 from capital, 7.74 from current inputs, and a minus 0.48 from productivity change. These figures, as well as those pertaining to land measured by cultivated area, are shown in Table 9.

TABLE 9

COMPONENTS OF OUTPUT GROWTH [a]
CHINA, 1952-57

Official Output Growth	Contributions From				
	Labor	Land	Capital	Current Inputs	Productivity Change
In Per cent:					
25	5%	3% [b]	2%	16%	—1%
25	5%	1% [c]	2%	16%	1%
In Values (in billions of 1952 prices):					
12.1	2.42	1.45 [b]	0.97	7.74	—0.48
12.1	2.42	0.48 [c]	0.97	7.74	0.49

Notes:

a. Computed from the per cent increases in output and inputs in Tables 6 and 8 and from the relative factor weights in Table 7.

b. Based on sown acreage.

c. Based on cultivated acreage.

It would be tempting to gauge allocative efficiency in agriculture in the light of these estimated factor contributions. However, since the coefficients of the production function have not been estimated, but arrived at through assumptions (for lack of cross-section data on which alternative coefficients could be based), any such exercise is open to serious challenge. As a crude suggestion, however, a return is calculated for investment in land. For this purpose, we use value added by agriculture (31.6 billion)

---

and relative output growth for the period (between year 0 and year t) can be decomposed as follows:

$$\frac{\dot{y}}{y_0} = \dot{A} + \frac{ax_{0,1}}{y_0} \cdot \frac{\dot{x}_1}{x_{0,1}} + \frac{bx_{0,2}}{y_0} \cdot \frac{\dot{x}_2}{x_{0,2}} + \frac{cx_{0,3}}{y_0} \cdot \frac{\dot{x}_3}{x_{0,3}} + \frac{dx_{0,4}}{y_0} \cdot \frac{\dot{x}_4}{x_{0,4}}$$

where the dotted terms refer to absolute changes between the terminal years 0 and t.

in 1952 instead of the Communist gross concept (48.39 billion). The contribution (in value added) from sown acreage increment during 1952-57 comes to 0.937 billion *yuan,* or 0.836 billion after replacement allowance (at one per cent of the cost, as calculated below) to place the return on a perpetual basis.[28] The historical costs of agricultural "capital construction" (both in and out of the state plan), together with projects undertaken by work brigades and the military as well as nonstate budgeted works by cooperatives, are loosely aggregated by means of the data assembled by Liu and Yeh in their monumental study (1965).

It is assumed here that the output effect of water conservation projects, reclamation works, and other "capital construction" in agriculture is reflected in the increased acreage and its more intensive use (*i.e.,* jointly through the incremental sown acreage). Fixed investment within the state plan totaled 3.5 billion *yuan* and that outside the plan 0.6 billion during the five year period 1953-57. Investment by work brigades in conservation projects amounted to 2.3 billion or, say, 3.0 billion including that by the military.[29] The amount of similar investment on acreage and land use by cooperatives or by peasant households is not known. As Liu and Yeh put it, it is doubtful whether the investment that the planners envisioned from this source of six billion *yuan,* was realized. Let us assume it was four billion. In principle, one should cumulate these costs at some compound interest rate and deduct from this sum the net gains already realized during 1953-56, also cumulated at some compound interest rate. The difference between the two provides the relevant capital cost as of 1957, against which a rate of return may then be computed. These procedures are not followed in our calculations. However, since cost compounding and subtraction of net realized returns offset each other, the error incurred by our omission probably is small. At any rate, it is difficult to tell what sort of interest rate may be appropriate for compounding purposes. In these terms, then, the total historical costs of the projects (during 1953-57) with an effect on acreage and land use come to 10.1 billion *yuan* in 1952 prices. Against this cost, the net return in 1957 of 0.836 billion (in 1952 prices) as calculated above yields a rate of return of 8.3 per cent per year.

If we consider the probable underreporting of the output in 1952 and use our "adjusted" production instead (see Table 8 above), total net returns fall from 0.836 billion to 0.785 billion. And the rate of return drops from 8.3 to 7.8 per cent. The rate of return of 8 per cent as calculated

28. The figure of 31.60 billion for value added in 1952 is taken from Liu and Yeh (1965, p. 213). This comes close to Eckstein's estimate, as mentioned earlier. Both figures represent adjusted Communist statistics to conform to the authors' income concept. The above figure of 0.937 is obtained by multiplying 1.45 (Table 9) by (31.6 ÷ 48.39) and further multiplying by the productivity index 0.99 (Table 8).

29. From Liu and Yeh, 1965 (Table 13, p. 74; Table 50, p. 171). For planned construction, see also *First Five-Year Plan* (pp. 21-33).

from a replacement rate of 1 per cent is best thought of as a high estimate. Under a replacement of 5 per cent—which is more reasonable for China, given the prevalence of earthwork construction in its agricultural capital projects—the return falls to less than 4 per cent. This probably comes close to the rate realized during the first plan, a rate which at the margin relevant to 1957 implies a return that could conceivably be close to zero. Also, compulsory labor with little or no compensation may bring down the accounting costs but hardly the real costs. Needless to say, our rough estimate does not reflect such hidden costs. At any rate, even at 8 per cent the return is nothing like the kind of returns that studies have shown to accrue to investments in modern, nontraditional inputs.

Net social returns on investment in the development of hybrid corn have been estimated by Griliches for the U.S., yielding an "external" rate of some 700 per cent per year or an "internal" rate of upwards of 35-40 per cent (Griliches, 1958). Studies of Japan and Taiwan give as internal rates of social return 30-35 per cent per year on investment in rural education, agricultural research, development, and extension (Tang, 1963; Ho, 1965). It is clear that in China during 1952-57 there was some decline in agricultural resource productivity. By contrast, in countries where agricultural development has been proceeding apace, output increased much more rapidly than the aggregate inputs. The United States, Japan, and Taiwan are only some of the outstanding examples. This is true despite the several sources of productivity increases that the Communists were able to realize through their land redistribution and cooperative movement.

The negative effect of share tenancy on output and growth is well known; that of fragmented landholding is equally familiar. Although tenancy in China never reached serious proportions (especially share tenancy), the unusual fragmentation of land is amply documented by Buck's studies. Of the prewar farms he surveyed, the average number of parcels of land per farm was 5.6, while the average number of fields per farm was 11.6, and the average distance of the parcels from the farmstead was about half a mile (Buck, 1937, pp. 181-85). Under such circumstances, the output effect of land consolidation achieved under the Communists must have been substantial. It opened up possibilities for improvement in irrigation, removal of division strips, more efficient use of labor—particularly, in peak labor input seasons that are characterized by "shortages" of workers—and the possible effect of efficient labor use on the multiple-cropping index.[30]

Further, despite the usual supposition that under traditional methods of cultivation there are few, if any, economies of scale, "cooperative" culti-

30. For a well-documented argument concerning the limited scope for further raising the multiple cropping index, under the existing state of technology in Communist China, see chapter 6 in this volume, by Kenneth R. Walker.

vation may benefit production in two ways. First, the resources of family farms may be under-utilized in a given year because of, say, adversities and misfortunes that beset certain families. This is a problem that could be met by the Chinese "mutual aid teams" and, later, by the collective organization. More important, under individual management, the two-acre farm was forced to diversify—even if greater specialization was the more economic alternative—in order to meet the family's own varied needs and to hedge against adverse changes in terms of trade between the farm's most profitable crop and the "dominant" crop needed for payment of rent and taxes in kind. With the enlarged management unit established under the collectivization movement, previous small holdings could be completely specialized while the large unit still had the diversification needed to meet the same purposes.

These considerations of positive sources of productivity growth are speculative and cannot be measured quantitatively. They serve to point up the offsetting negative forces that must have been at work during 1952-57, causing agricultural productivity, on balance, to fall as observed earlier. With the exception of the small private sector and the equally small state farm sector, the agriculture of China and the Soviet Union is, figuratively speaking, a vast, all-embracing system of share tenancy. The share exacted by the state in the Soviet Union (by virtue of the relative constancy of its absolute size) has a family resemblance to the lump sum tax with *relatively* few disincentive effects. In China, on the other hand, the state share fluctuated with current output and was so set as to leave the peasant with a virtually constant remainder per head. This amounts to an extraction policy with characteristics similar to those of a progressive tax on current production with nearly confiscatory marginal rates. The disincentive effect that this implies must be understood against the background of an agricultural policy that was meant to be developmental.

Such then was the dilemma facing the Chinese planner. In contrast, the Soviet planner, blessed with an ample initial agricultural "cushion," not only found it unnecessary to build growth into his agricultural plan (at least for the period under consideration) but was able to meet industrial requirements by means of an extraction policy for agriculture that was relatively neutral in effect.[31] This discussion is no doubt oversimplified.

31. One may get an opposite impression concerning the relative growth orientation of the two countries' agricultural policy from the investment data. Eckstein, for instance, shows a substantially higher share of total investment for agriculture during the first plan period in the Soviet Union than in China (1961, p. 509). However, it should be remembered that much of the Soviet agricultural investment consisted of machine tractors whose purpose was in part to replace the slaughtered workstock and in part to set up a control and extraction mechanism in the form of MTS. Also, insofar as labor-intensive, Nurksian-type capital formation bulked large in Chinese agricultural investment, the valuation problem becomes far more serious in the Chinese case.

The difference between the Chinese and Soviet agricultural policy in this regard is after all one of degree, not of kind. Nonetheless, we believe that the distinction is instructive.

(It may also be noted that even the private sector, long considered to be a source of strength or a saving feature of socialized agriculture, is certain to lead to inefficient resource use when placed alongside the collective sector. An extended discussion of this highly interesting question, however, must be deferred to another occasion.)

The salient features of Chinese agricultural policy appear to have been labor mobilization for current production and, more especially, for capital formation à la Nurkse and for the fuller utilization of other resources.[32] These represent the once-and-for-all type of improvement, although its realization may be spread over several years. They proceed along traditional lines of production possibilities. Once these opportunities are exhausted, all that will have been accomplished is a higher level of output than previously existed. Subsequent growth, if it is to take place, must require the opening up of new production possibilities. The point may not be pathbreaking, but few have stated it as cogently or with as many insights as T. W. Schultz in his *Transforming Traditional Agriculture* (1964). To be sure, on paper the Communist "innovative" activities are quite impressive. But as we indicated earlier, these on the whole amounted to little more than false starts and crash programs without substance, follow-up, or due regard for technical complementarity and regional differences in physical conditions.

Against this background it is clear why Chinese Communist economic policy was at a critical crossroads at the end of 1957. The traditional sources of agricultural growth appeared to be drying up. Moreover, agriculture continued to limit the rate of industrialization. The choice was between (1) pressing ahead in agriculture along the traditional margins through drastic reorganization of production and household activities or

---

Nevertheless, judging by the disparate magnitudes of the several agricultural programs, there can be little question that the Chinese planner placed first emphasis on the cheap sources of growth, *i.e.,* mobilization of "voluntary" labor and exploiting the existing slack in the use of other resources.

32. The statement refers not to the results (in growth terms) attributable to these aspects of the policy but to the emphasis the planner placed on them. As measured earlier in this section, the most important source of agricultural growth during 1952-57 had been the increasing use of current inputs, mainly chemical fertilizers. The fuller utilization of resources had accomplished no more than to hold down the rate of productivity decline, the latter being attributable to the disincentive effects of collectivization and the accompanying "squeeze" policy, to diminishing returns, to the decline in land quality as submarginal acreage was brought under cultivation, to the inherent overstatement of land service given by the sown acreage, as multiple cropping seldom leads to a second crop equal in value to the main crop, etc. Similarly, labor mobilization contributed little to output growth, either directly through its effect on current output or indirectly through Nurksian capital formation.

(2) modernizing the agricultural sector by instituting thoughtful research, development, and information programs, backed up by the sort of intersectoral transformation processes discussed earlier in Section I. The Party opted for the former and coupled it with a bootstrap operation to enable the agrarian sector to meet its own "modernization" needs. Crash programs followed, launching "factories" in rural communes to produce "steel," "fertilizer," and "ball-bearings." Capital formation of the traditional type was pushed to new heights by millions of men and women on conservation and irrigation projects, after household activities had been socialized to free the needed labor. For current production, Mao's "Eight Point Charter," with deep plowing and close planting as its cardinal principles, was suposed to hold the key to China's success in its confrontation with a niggardly nature. These principles were applied indiscriminately by the cadres.

The policy embodied in the Great Leap Forward was in principle consistent with considerations of technical duality in economic processes, and of an abundant agricultural labor supply and its seasonal character, as well as with the elements of the Stalinist model. If agricultural growth can be had without resources of high opportunity cost to industrialization, that is all to the good. The matter, therefore, turns on the practical questions of feasibility, implementation, and results. On these scores, the failure of the Great Leap was monumental.

The Chinese Communist Party up to that time had come a long way equipped with little more than discipline, determination, and an ability to organize. To its members, "socialism shall overcome" was not an empty slogan. Carried away by their own confidence, enthusiasm and visions of unprecedented socialist transformation, the Party and the cadres tended to dismiss such mundane questions as "Will the backyard furnaces produce a useful final product?" They also tended to regard as bourgeois or petty the intricate interrelationships between such factors as irrigation, drainage, seepage, water table level, moisture retention ability, salinization, river flow, water pollution, flood control, etc. During the heady days of 1958 and 1959, it was easy for the Party to overlook the fact that nature is both ingenious and deliberate. To mobilize hundreds of millions of people to build in haste staggering amounts of earthworks may impress other peoples and nations—but not nature.

Possibly, with more thoughtful prior planning and more deliberate implementation, the Great Leap might have produced fairly satisfactory results. But it is clear that without the concurrent introduction of new complementary inputs, the traditional sources of agricultural growth (irrigation, land improvement and reclamation, new land programs, flood control, etc.) are costly and becoming increasingly so. Thus agricultural growth in China, as elsewhere, rests on the country's ability to institutionalize the development and adoption of modern agricultural inputs.

DECOMPOSITION OF YIELD INCREASE

Another meaningful way to analyze agricultural growth is to treat land as the scarce factor and to examine the sources of its increasing (overall) yield. Overall yield increment may arise from increases in the yields of individual crops (with land use constant), or from changes in land use (with individual crop yields unchanged), or from both. Land may also be divided into two parts—land existing at the beginning of the period, and new land—and separate contributions computed for each.

In Tables 10 and 11, we present the breakdown for grain output growth between 1952 and each of the other years in the period. Table 10 shows the contributions of initial and new lands to grain output growth (with potato production calculated in grain equivalent terms), as well as the effects of shifts in land use and of yield increase. Table 11 presents similar results (with potatoes represented in natural weight). The calculations are made on the basis of the equation shown at the end of Table 10, and all data are in physical terms and official in source. Output consists of rice, wheat, coarse grains, and potatoes. We shall limit description of the findings to 1957; those of other years are reported in the tables. In 1957, official grain output with potatoes in grain weight equivalent amounted to 370,000 million catties (or 185 million metric tons). Of this total, 342,334 million catties (92.52 per cent) was produced on the initial (1952) sown acreage. Of this contribution from the initial acreage, 5,725 million catties (1.55 per cent) are due to land use shifts (with individual crop yields held constant at the 1952 levels); 27,809 million (7.51 per cent) to individual crop yield increases (with land use held constant at the 1952 pattern); and 308,800 million (83.46 per cent) to output that would have been obtained had there been no yield changes or use shifts.

Additional sown acreage realized during 1952-57 accounts for 26,172 million catties (7.07 per cent) which can be broken down as follows: 438 (0.12 per cent) from land use shift, 2,126 (0.57 per cent) from yield increases, and 23,608 (6.38 per cent) from the output expected on the basis of 1952 land use and yields. Finally, the residual or interaction effect comes to 1,494 million catties (0.41 per cent).

A quick survey of the temporal changes in the relative importance of these sources of growth shows that during 1953-55 shifts in land use detracted from grain output (with potatoes in grain weight) so that output growth came only from acreage increment and crop yield increases. However, when potatoes are expressed in natural weight, the contribution from land use shifts becomes positive in all three years, while crop yields exert a negative effect in 1953-54. Taken together, these figures are consistent with the following conclusions: (1) Potato yields fell in those years while other crop yields rose. (2) The potato-grain weight conversion ratio of four to one used by the Communists was too high if compared to the yield

TABLE 10

GRAIN OUTPUT I: POTATOES IN GRAIN WEIGHT EQUIVALENT[a]

(in millions of catties)

	Key to Equation	1952	1953	1954	1955	1956	1957
Contribution of Initial Acreage:							
Base output (1952)	A	308,800	308,800	308,800	308,800	308,800	308,800
Output change due to:							
Land use shift	B	......	—1,476	—1,257	—858	6,992	5,725
Yield increase	C	......	1,188	2,017	23,916	13,511	27,809
Total due to initial acreage		308,800	308,512	309,560	331,858	329,303	342,334
Contribution of New Acreage:							
Acreage increase alone	D	......	5,431	11,115	16,768	32,979	23,608
Difference from 1952 in:							
Land use	E	......	—25	—45	—47	747	438
Yield	F	......	18	73	1,299	1,443	2,126
Total due to new acreage		......	5,424	11,143	18,020	35,169	26,172
Interaction	G		—136	197	—278	528	1,494
Grand total or actual output		308,800	313,800	320,900	349,600	365,000	370,000

Source:

Output and sown acreage data are from *TGY*, pp. 119 and 129.

Notes:

Computations are based on the following identities where the subscripts t and o refer to the current and base (1952) years, respectively, and Y, a, and y stand for total output, sown acreage of each crop, and yield of each crop, respectively.

$$Y_t = \Sigma a_t y_t = \underbrace{Y_o}_{A} + \underbrace{\left(\frac{\Sigma a_o}{\Sigma a_t}\Sigma a_t y_o - Yo\right)}_{B} + \underbrace{(\Sigma a_o y_t - Yo)}_{C} + \underbrace{\left(\frac{\Sigma a_t}{\Sigma a_o} - 1\right) Yo}_{D} + \underbrace{\left(\frac{\Sigma a_t}{\Sigma a_o} - 1\right)\left(\frac{\Sigma a_o}{\Sigma a_t}\Sigma a_t y_o - Yo\right)}_{E} +$$

$$\underbrace{\left(\frac{\Sigma a_t}{\Sigma a_o} - 1\right)(\Sigma a_o y_t - Yo)}_{F} + \underbrace{\left\{\Sigma a_t(y_t - y_o) - \frac{\Sigma a_t}{\Sigma a_o}\Sigma a_o (y_t - y_o)\right\}}_{G}$$

TABLE 11

GRAIN OUTPUT II: POTATOES IN NATURAL WEIGHT *
(in millions of catties)

	Key to Equa-tion	1952	1953	1954	1955	1956	1957
Contribution of Initial Acreage:							
Base output (1952)	A	406,900	406,900	406,900	406,900	406,900	406,900
Output change due to:							
Land use shift	B	......	477	7,266	8,727	21,029	17,722
Yield increase	C	......	—645	—5,486	23,808	19,037	38,489
Total due to initial acreage		406,900	406,732	408,680	439,435	446,966	463,111
Contribution of New Acreage:							
Acreage increase alone	D	......	7,157	14,646	22,095	43,456	31,108
Difference from 1952 in:							
Land use	E	......	9	261	474	2,246	1,355
Yield	F	......	—11	—197	1,293	2,033	2,943
Total due to new acreage		......	7,155	14,710	23,862	47,735	35,406
Interaction	G		—187	—490	—297	1,399	2,833
Grand Total or actual output		406,900	413,700	422,900	463,000	496,100	501,400

* See Notes to Table 10.

ratio actually prevailing in 1952; relative potato acreage increased in the meantime.[33] The first finding explains the change in sign in overall yield effect when potatoes are assigned different weights. The second explains the change in sign in land use effect.[34]

A more meaningful percentage distribution of the components of grain output growth (with potatoes in grain weight equivalents) since 1952 is shown in Table 12. It is clear from these data that new acreage

TABLE 12

DISTRIBUTION OF GRAIN OUTPUT GROWTH, CHINA, 1952-57 [a]

	1953	1954	1955	1956	1957
			(in millions of catties)		
Total increase over 1952 (=100%)	5,000	12,100	40,800	56,200	61,200
			(per cent)		
Land use effect [b]	—30.02	—10.76	—2.22	13.77	10.10
Yield effect [b]	24.12	17.27	61.80	26.61	48.86
New land effect [c]	108.62	91.86	41.10	58.68	38.57
Cross effect	—2.72	1.63	—.68	.94	2.47
Total	100.00	100.00	100.00	100.00	100.00

Notes:
a. Computed from Table 10.
b. Total on initial and new acreage.
c. New land effect only, land use and yield held to 1952 pattern and level.

was almost the sole source of output growth during 1953-54. Thereafter, its contribution dropped to about 40 per cent of the output increment. Land use effect accounted for 10-14 per cent of the growth in 1956-57. It was negative in the earlier years due to the dominance of potatoes in land use shift and to the discrepancy between the conversion and yield ratios as noted above. Yield effect showed an upward trend, rising from 24 per cent to nearly 50 per cent between 1952 and 1957. In passing it may be noted that when suitably processed the Communist agricultural

33. In that period, relative acreages of wheat and coarse grains remained virtually unchanged while relative rice acreage declined. Thus, land use substitution was between rice and potatoes. The relevant yield ratio is then between the latter two commodities which was 3.1 to 1 in favor of potatoes in 1952.

34. As Dr. J. L. Buck correctly pointed out in his discussion of this paper, land use shift is a marginal adjustment concept. Thus, if rice acreage goes down in favor of potato acreage—unless the adjustment process is distorted by organizational defects—it is the marginal rice acreage that is displaced. On these acreages, relative rice yield is lower than on the average acreages and relative potato yield higher. In this sense, our use of the 1952 average relative yields leads to errors. In the absence of the relevant marginal rates, all we can do in this connection is to recognize this shortcoming and call it to the reader's attention.

statistics once again prove to be internally consistent. Inasmuch as our computed yield effect represents the "pure" yield effect, one would expect fluctuations in this series to be corroborated by the reported harvest conditions, if consistency is present. Table 12, taken in conjunction with the harvest conditions shown in Figure 1, clearly attests to such a corroboration, especially when some crude allowance is made for the trend factor.

Before concluding, it would be well to stress that the consistency checks made throughout the chapter, and the "sensible" results yielded by the official statistics in the hypothesis testing section, *do not* prove the accuracy of these data. As was shown earlier, internal consistency need not preclude underreporting during 1952-55. Thus, our "adjusted" output data which are corrected for underreporting also pass the consistency check, while the "sensible" testing results merely lend credence to the thesis that the Chinese planner probably acted on the basis of the same official statistics that were subsequently released for public consumption.

What we should like to point out here is that from the standpoint of ascertaining the "hard" component of agricultural growth during 1952-57 it matters little whether one takes the often-criticized Liu and Yeh crop production estimates or accepts the official claims as correct. It seems clear that food crop output for 1952 as reported by the Communists fell short of the level that one would expect on the basis of prewar production experience. In fact, the official 1952 output of 3,088 million *piculs* (in grain-equivalent weights) was below the 1933 output level of 3,456 million *piculs,* despite an acreage increase of 6 per cent.[35]

If it is agreed that the 1952 official output is indeed less than expected from the prewar production record, several possible explanations arise. Of these, weather and agricultural organization must be ruled out, since 1952 was both a "good" crop year and a precollectivization year. Two plausible explanations remain: underreporting or incomplete recovery from the dislocations of prolonged warfare (1937-49). The first is the basis for our adjustment and for that of Liu and Yeh. The latter explanation implies acceptance of the Communist output data as correct. It also implies that growth subsequent to 1952 as calculated from these data contain two elements, the recovery component and the "hard" component. Needless to say, for the purpose of evaluating the success or failure of any agricultural *development* policy it is the "hard" growth that is relevant. One way to abstract from the recovery growth would be to adjust upward the reported output for all the recovery years to the level that would have prevailed had recovery been completed earlier. In this con-

35. The 1933 production and acreage data are from Liu and Yeh, 1965, pp. 128, 135. The data represent estimates by Liu and Yeh, and they fall below Buck's high estimates (generally recognized as too high) but substantially above the estimates of the National Agricultural Research Buerau. The Bureau figures are widely recognized as on the low side. For a discussion of the procedure see Liu and Yeh, 1965 (pp. 126-33).

nection, the adjustment procedure used earlier to correct for underreporting would seem just as applicable here. So applied, the procedure implies the completion of recovery by 1955, an initial "under-recovery" coefficient of 6 per cent, and linear decline in the coefficient during 1952 and 1955. An initial coefficient of 6 per cent is more or less in line with the comparative output and acreage data for 1933 and 1952 shown above. On the basis of these considerations, our "adjusted" agricultural growth of 17 per cent (or roughly 3 per cent per year) and a productivity decline of 7 per cent during 1952-57 (Cols. 3 and 9, Table 8) may be thought of as "firm" estimates of the Chinese agricultural performance under the Communists. The productivity measure is, of course, subject to the usual shortcomings inherent in such a procedure.

V. CONCLUSIONS

The Stalinist model of economic development permits an explicit statement of the performance criterion for agriculture: The role of the agricultural sector is to allow industrialization to proceed at the maximum rate set by forces endogenous to the industrial and trade sectors.

Whether agriculture in a particular setting has been able to fulfill its role is an empirical question. An examination of the Soviet and Chinese experiences during their respective first plan periods turns up some interesting contrasts. The Soviet agricultural policy was essentially extractive at that time. And despite the drastic production shortfalls that followed, the policy succeeded in freeing Soviet industrialization from the restrictive influences of an agriculture that effectively checked its progress in the 1920's. Annual rates of industrial growth (in the priority sector) were unrelated to fluctuations in agricultural output. The state was able to follow a steady procurement policy that put the collectives and their members in a residual claimant position, while allowing industrialization requirements to be met independently of agricultural output.

Communist China also subscribed to the Stalinist strategy of economic development. However, because of China's precarious initial agricultural base, the extractive agricultural policy was accompanied by a developmental orientation from the outset. Nevertheless, industrialization continued to be constrained by the vagaries of agricultural production. Fluctuations in the rate of agricultural growth forced industrial growth rates to move accordingly, even in the high priority industrial sectors. Unlike his Soviet counterpart, the Chinese planner was in the unenviable position of a residual claimant, siphoning off from agriculture all that his enormous extractive power permits, but only after the peasant had claimed his subsistence share. Industrial requirements (as given by the maximum endogenous rate of growth) normally exceeded the extracted agricultural surplus. Agriculture was a source of effective constraint to industrialization.

Consistent with these findings is the fact that Chinese industrial growth rates turn out to be about twice as variable as the Soviet rates. Viewed from the standpoint of our performance criterion, Chinese agricultural policy cannot be said to have been successful. The industrialization program remained just as vulnerable to agricultural uncertainties at the end of the plan period and after as it had been earlier.

Underlying the Chinese difficulties is the plain fact that an agricultural policy that tries to be both extractive and developmental contains inherently conflicting elements. Although the extractive part of the Chinese policy was successfully carried out, the development portion of it clearly failed to attain the desired objective. Further inquiry into the reasons for this aspect of policy failure leads to an analysis of the content of the agrarian program. The purpose is to identify the sources of growth tapped by the Chinese, to measure their output contribution, and to highlight the crucial elements of growth that have been either ignored or poorly dealt with by the planner.

Briefly stated, Chinese development efforts in agriculture bear heavily on the twin concepts of (1) taking up the existing slack in current resource use, and (2) mobilizing labor for capital formation. This means that primary reliance was placed upon exploitation of sources of growth along the traditional margins. These sources, though low in opportunity cost, have limited capacity for generating growth. The usefulness of new inputs and techniques did not go unrecognized. But available evidence shows that the attempt had been to "modernize" cheaply and hastily. Repeated crash programs produced meager results.

At any rate, while some constructive modernization activities no doubt took place (*e.g.,* increased use of chemical fertilizers), their positive impact on productivity was more than offset by the negative influences of declining incentives for producers, and of diminishing returns as both the intensive and extensive margins were progressively exploited under the traditional production possibilities. Thus, even in terms of the official output statistics, which show a 25 per cent growth during 1952-57, the productivity index remained, at best, stable in that period. In terms of our "adjusted" data, agricultural growth comes to 17 per cent or about 3 per cent per year, while productivity falls by 7 per cent during the period of the First Five-Year Plan. Clearly, the true engine of growth—productivity increase—was yet to appear on the Chinese agricultural scene.

A very crude attempt has been made to calculate a rate of return on investment in land—an investment on which mass labor projects bear most particularly. This yields a rate of under 4 per cent realized during the first plan period. At the margin relevant to 1957, the return would have been lower still. This is a far cry from the investment returns that have been and are being realized in many countries through the development and adoption of new inputs and practices.

The China of 1957 was a country at a critical crossroads. The traditional sources of agricultural growth appeared to be drying up. Grain output had increased by only one per cent over the preceding year, and the industrial growth rate was the second lowest under Communist rule so far. Two choices confronted the Party. It could institute a dramatic push along traditional margins by reorganizing agricultural production and household activities, and supplementing this with a bootstrap rural industrialization program to help agriculture meet its own "modernization" needs. Alternatively, it could initiate a serious, thoughtful program of agricultural research, development and information and couple it with a new emphasis on diverting scarce industrial resources to accommodate agricultural modernization. Although such a diversion, properly viewed as the initiation of an intersectoral transformation process, need not mean industrial retrenchment (even in the relative short run), the Party chose the first way. The fiasco that resulted is now well known. To a significant extent, the disaster was perhaps avoidable; the errors were largely those of planning and implementation.

Two things are, however, clear. First, the Communist attribution of production shortfalls to natural calamities in the Great Leap years appears to be unwarranted. Second, the "factories" and ancillary establishments hastily assembled by rural communes are not relevant to a program of agricultural research, development and extension, or to the production of new inputs. Thus, even if the Great Leap Forward had been skillfully implemented, it probably could not have accomplished anything more than extending the useful life of the traditional approach by a few years. Looking ahead, if China is to accelerate its agricultural growth (or even to sustain it) so as to free industrialization from its uncertain pace, Peking will have to turn to new, more promising sources of growth. To do this it must find ways to institutionalize the development and adoption of non-traditional means of production capable of high returns. Here, the crux of the matter rests on agricultural organization and the problem of incentives.

REFERENCES

AIRD, JOHN S., 1960. "The Present and Prospective Population of Mainland China," *Population Trends in Eastern Europe, the USSR, and Mainland China.* Milbank Memorial Fund.

BUCK, J. L., 1930. *Chinese Farm Economy.* Chicago.

BUCK, J. L., 1937. *Land Utilization in China.* Chicago.

CAMPBELL, ROBERT W., 1960. *Soviet Economic Power*. Cambridge, Mass.

CHAPMAN, JANET G., 1963. "Consumption," in A. Bergson and S. Kuznets (eds.), *Economic Trends in the Soviet Union*. Cambridge, Mass.

DOMAR, EVSEY D., 1957. "A Soviet Model of Growth," *Essays in the Theory of Economic Growth*. Oxford.

ECKSTEIN, ALEXANDER, 1961 (a) *The National Income of Communist China*. New York.

ECKSTEIN, ALEXANDER, 1961 (b). "The Strategy of Economic Development in Communist China," *American Economic Review* (May, 1961), *51*, pp. 508–517.

ERLICH, ALEXANDER, 1955. "Stalin's Views on Soviet Economic Development," in E. J. Simmons (ed.), *Continuity and Change in Russian and Soviet Thought*. Cambridge, Mass.

FEI, JOHN, and ALPHA CHIANG, 1965. "Growth under Conditions of Austerity," a paper presented at the Conference on Theory and Design of Economic Development, Center for Agricultural and Economic Development, Iowa State University, Nov. 18–20, 1965 (proceedings forthcoming).

First Five-Year Plan of the People's Republic of China, 1956. Peking: Foreign Language Press.

GRILICHES, ZVI, 1958. "Research Costs and Social Returns: Hybrid Corn and Related Innovation," *Journal of Political Economy* (October, 1958), *66*, pp. 419–431.

GRILICHES, Z., 1963. "Sources of Measured Productivity Growth: U.S. Agriculture, 1940-60," *Journal of Political Economy* (August, 1963), *71*, pp. 331–346.

GROSSMAN, GREGORY, 1960 (Ed.) *Value and Plan*. Berkeley and Los Angeles.

HO, YHI-MIN, 1966. *The Agricultural Development of Taiwan, 1903-60*. Nashville, Tenn.

HODGMAN, D. R., 1954. *Soviet Industrial Production, 1928-51*. Cambridge, Mass.

HOEFFDING, OLEG, 1959. "State Planning and Forced Industrialization," in *Problems of Communism*, Rand Corporation (November-December, 1959), *8*, pp. 38–46.

JASNY, NAUM, 1949. *The Socialized Agriculture of the USSR*. Stanford.

JOHNSON, GALE D., 1963. "Agricultural Production," in A. Bergson and S. Kuznets (eds.), *Economic Trends in the Soviet Union*. Cambridge, Mass.

JOHNSON, GALE D., and ARCADIUS KAHAN, 1959. "Soviet Agriculture: Structure and Growth," in *Comparisons of the United States and Soviet Economies*, Joint Economic Committee, U.S. Congress. Washington, D.C.

KAPLAN, N. M., and R H.. MOORSTEEN, 1960. "An Index of Soviet Industrial Output," *American Economic Review* (June, 1960), *50*, pp. 295–318.

LADEJINSKY, W., and FRED J. ROSSITER, 1942. "Food Situation in Far Eastern and Southeastern Asia," *Foreign Agriculture*, April, 1942. Washington, D.C.

LI, CHOH-MING, 1959. *Economic Development of Communist China*. Berkeley and Los Angeles.

LI, C. M., 1962. *The Statistical System of Communist China.* Berkeley and Los Angeles.

LIU, JUNG-CHAO, 1965 (a). "Fertilizer Application in Communist China," *The China Quarterly,* October-December, 1965, pp. 28–51.

LIU, JUNG-CHAO, 1965 (b). "Fertilizer Supply and Grain Production in Communist China, "*Journal of Farm Economics,* November, 1965, *47,* pp. 915–932.

LIU, T. C., and K. C. YEH, 1965. *The Economy of the Chinese Mainland.* Princeton.

NICHOLLS, WILLIAM H., 1963. "An 'Agricultural Surplus' as a Factor in Economic Development," *Journal of Political Economy* (Feb. 1963), *71,* pp. 1–29.

NICHOLLS, WILLIAM H., 1964. "The Place of Agriculture in Economic Development," reprinted in Carl K. Eicher and Lawrence W. Witt (eds.), *Agriculture in Economic Development.* New York.

NUTTER, WARREN G., 1962. *The Growth of Industrial Production in the Soviet Union.* Princeton.

SCHULTZ, T. W., 1964. *Transforming Traditional Agriculture.* New Haven.

SOLOW, ROBERT M., 1957. "Technical Change and the Aggregate Production Function," *Review of Economics and Statistics* (Aug. 1957), *39,* pp. 312–320.

TANG, ANTHONY M., 1963. "Research and Education in Japanese Agricultural Development, 1880-1938," *The Economic Studies Quarterly,* Part I (Feb. 1963), *13,* pp. 27–41; Part II (May 1963), *13,* pp. 91–99.

TANG, ANTHONY M. (forthcoming). "On Growth under Conditions of Austerity," a discussion paper of Fei and Chang, 1965.

(*TGY*) *Ten Great Years,* 1960. Peking: Foreign Language Press.

T'ung-chi kung-tso, Sept. 29, 1957. Peking.

WALKER, KENNETH R., 1965. *Planning in Chinese Agriculture: Socialization and the Private Sector, 1956-62.* Chicago.

WELLISZ, S., 1964. *The Economies of the Soviet Bloc.* New York.

WILES, P. J. D., 1962. *The Political Economy of Communism.* Cambridge, Mass.

Capital Formation 8

K. C. YEH

THIS CHAPTER EXAMINES the trends in capital formation in Communist China in 1952-59, and discusses some of the implications of the statistical findings. The term "capital formation," or "investment" for short, is used here in the conventional sense, a more precise definition of which is given below. Sections I-III deal with the rate of investment, the structure of investment by types of capital goods, and the pattern of allocation of fixed investment by major economic sectors. To provide a gauge for appraising the data, the results are compared with the corresponding estimates for China in 1931-36 and with selected countries in the postwar period. Section IV discusses some preliminary observations on investment and growth in Communist China in the 1950's.

I. THE RATE OF INVESTMENT

Table 1 presents domestic capital formation, domestic product, and the ratio between them for each year during 1931-36 and 1952-57, gross of capital consumption, given in both 1933 and 1952 constant prices. For comparison between periods, average levels for the prewar and postwar periods are computed. And, to indicate the direction of change in 1958-59, the rates of government fixed investment for these years are also shown.

Before considering the broad trends suggested by these estimates, it will be useful to discuss briefly the conceptual problems, major statistical weaknesses, and the valuation base. Because the income estimates have been explained in detail elsewhere,[1] my remarks will be confined to the nature and limitations of the investment estimates.

By "domestic capital formation," I refer to additions to the stock of reproducible capital within the country, whether they are financed by

I am greatly indebted to Professor T. C. Liu for valuable suggestions, and to Professor Y. C. Yin for stimulating comments.

1. For detailed discussions of the income estimates, see Liu-Yeh, 1965; Yeh, 1964; and Appendix A at the end of the chapter.

domestic savings or investment from abroad. Reproducible capital include structures and buildings, producers' durables, and inventories in the hands of business enterprises and government.[2] Only domestic capital formation is given here because information on net changes in foreign claims is lacking. However, the foreign share during this period was probably small relative to the total volume of domestic investment, so that domestic cap-

TABLE 1

RATE OF INVESTMENT, 1931-1936 AND 1952-1959

	Gross Domestic Capital Formation (in billion yuan)	Gross Domestic Product (in billion yuan)	Rate of Investment (per cent)
In 1933 prices			
1931	1.27	29.58	4.3
1932	1.49	30.67	4.9
1933	1.50	30.45	4.9
1934	1.12	27.82	4.0
1935	1.60	30.13	5.3
1936	1.95	31.90	6.1
1952	5.34	33.83	15.8
1953	6.64	35.25	18.8
1954	7.13	36.83	19.4
1955	7.25	37.96	19.1
1956	7.71	41.14	18.7
1957	7.36	42.29	17.4
Average:			
1931-36	1.49	30.09	5.0
1952-57	6.90	37.88	18.2

2. One hardly needs to point out that this definition has its limitations. In one sense, the conventional concept of investment is too broad for the purpose of studying growth, because it includes some additions to capital that are only remotely related to increases in productive capacity. Examples are construction of military installations and residential buildings. Yet in another sense, it is too narrow, for it excludes expenditures that do not add to the physical items of reproducible capital but that may lead to an increase in productive capacity. Examples are those expenditures generally considered as investment in human capital, agricultural and industrial extension services, and research and development. The problem is further complicated by the extremely low standard of living in Communist China. When per capita consumption is close to, or falls below, the subsistence level (as might have been the case in 1961-62), the conventional demarcation between consumption and investment loses some of its meaning, because under such circumstances an increase in consumption may well enhance the people's ability and willingness to work harder and thus increase the economy's capacity to produce. Unfortunately data on these quasi-consumption and quasi-investment items are incomplete.

In 1952 prices			
1931	4.10	62.34	6.6
1932	4.44	64.11	6.9
1933	4.66	63.91	7.3
1934	4.19	59.53	7.0
1935	5.16	63.55	8.1
1936	6.07	67.56	9.0
1952	14.56	74.67	19.5
1953	18.81	78.99	23.8
1954	20.31	83.31	24.4
1955	21.46	86.57	24.5
1956	26.04	97.28	26.8
1957	23.72	100.82	23.5
1958	26.94[a]	117.71	22.9[a]
1959	32.00[a]	127.98	25.0[a]
Average:			
1931-36	4.77	63.50	7.5
1952-57	20.82	86.94	24.0

Notes:
a. State fixed investment.

Sources:
1931-36 and 1952-57: Yeh, 1964; Liu-Yeh, 1965, p. 66.
1958-59: Appendix A; *TGY,* pp. 55-56; Liu-Yeh, 1965, p. 235. Project-making expenditures in 1958-59 are derived on the assumption that the ratios of such expenditures to state centralized investment in 1958-59 were the same as that in 1957. For the latter ratio see Appendix B. For assumption involved in making adjustment for ancillary expenses, see Yeh, 1964.

ital formation and national capital formation would be nearly the same. For the purpose of studying capital-output relationship, the ratio of net domestic capital formation to net domestic product would have been more appropriate than the gross ratio given in Table 1. However, capital consumption allowances are extremely difficult to estimate, and the gross estimates are, by and large, more reliable than the net; they are therefore used here.[3]

The investment estimates for the prewar period are derived by the commodity flow method.[4] The choice of this method has been dictated largely by the type of data available. The statistics of factory production of producers' durables in 1933, the benchmark year, are taken from the two extensive industry surveys by D. K. Lieu and the South Manchurian Railway, supplemented by two Japanese estimates of production by foreign-owned factories in China proper. Data on imports and exports of pro-

3. For the same reason the ratio of net capital formation to gross domestic product suggested by Norman Kaplan (1953) is not used here.
4. For details, see Yeh, 1964.

ducers' durables are taken from the trade returns of the Chinese Maritime Customs and the Manchurian government. By and large, these basic data are fairly comprehensive in coverage and more reliable than others.

However, there are numerous gaps in information that can be bridged only by making rough approximations. Several limitations should be noted. First, investment in the traditional sector, including military construction, investment in kind, and equipment produced by handicrafts workers, might have been understated.[5] Second, information on the transportation and distribution margin for capital goods is completely lacking. It is assumed that the margin for capital goods was the same as that for all commodities. However, the margin is merely a fraction of the total value of producers' durables, and an even smaller percentage of total investment, so that any error on this score is not likely to be significant. Third, no allowance has been made for changes in inventories other than those in the stock of agricultural products held on the farms and in the number of livestock.

The investment estimates for 1952-57 given in Table 1 are essentially the Communist estimates of capital accumulation, excluding ancillary expenses, but including investment by work brigades, and adjusted for understatement of capital consumption and overstatement of inventory changes (Yeh, 1964, Appendix C). Estimates for 1958-59 and a separate estimate of fixed investment for 1952-57 (discussed in Section III below) are based on Communist estimates of basic construction adjusted to include nonstate fixed investment and major repairs (Appendix B to this chapter).

The reliability of the Communist investment data cannot be easily tested because of the lack of adequate information.[6] However, there are indications that the figures are on the high side. For instance, there have been reports that cadres exaggerated investment results; many construction units inflated the statistics of completed investment by including equipment in storage as installed equipment (*CSYK,* No. 7, 1957, p. 30; *TCKT,* No. 2, 1958, p. 12). Others overstated the volume of work in progress (Ma

5. It should be recalled that in the 1930's China was not a unified national state. Some expenditures on military construction by the provincial governments or local warlords might have escaped observation. Furthermore, the rough estimate of investment in kind may be low because only farm investment in kind is included. This estimate is based on Buck's farm survey, which might be biased because the samples were heavily weighted in favor of the richer and more easily accessible farms. Perhaps farmers with less savings devoted more labor and effort of their own to improving their lower grade land. Finally, major repairs of tools and equipment by the handicraftsmen probably have not been adequately allowed for.

6. According to the Communists' own ranking, the basic construction statistics are generally of lower quality than production statistics, but better than those for agricultural output and trade (*TCKTTH,* No. 1, 1954, p. 2; Hsieh Mu-ch'iao, 1956). By and large, a fairly close correlation between basic construction and the growth of steel, machinery, and construction material output can be observed. However, such correlations are at at best inconclusive, for consistency by itself does not imply reliability.

Nan-fang, 1955). Still others grossly overreported areas of reclaimed land or increase in livestock (*TCKT,* No. 11, 1958, p. 9; *JMJP,* Nov. 25, 1961; April 1, 1962). How extensive such practices were is not clear. But the tremendous pressure on cadres to fulfill or overfulfill investment targets, because of the use of target fulfillment as the major success indicator, tended to encourage overreporting, particularly among the less efficient cadres. Apart from deliberate falsification, the statistics might be biased upwards also because of the inclusion in total basic construction of noninvestment expenditures such as expenses incurred in preparation for production (*TCKTTH,* No. 11, 1955, p. 18); because of double-counting of used equipment transferred from one user to another;[7] or because of the substandard quality of many construction projects and equipment.[8]

To counteract these overstatements, there are probably some shortages. Two such items deserve mention. First, investment by some conscript labor may have been omitted. Second, according to the Communist definition, fixed investment includes only additions to assets with a value of 200 or 500 *yuan* or more. This means that many small tools have been excluded from the Communist figures. But the shortages resulting from both sources are largely limited to the state sector; in all likelihood they are more than offset by the overstatement mentioned above.

Two other complications should be noted. First, there were some changes in the quality of the investment statistics over time. Apparently they became more reliable after 1954, as errors were less frequent, the degree of accuracy higher, and methods of statistical reporting standardized.[9] But the quality clearly deteriorated during the Great Leap period in 1958-59 (Li Choh-ming, 1962). Second, the statistics for the different components are not of the same quality. Those for the state sector are probably better than those for the nonstate sector, and those for fixed investment are perhaps more reliable than those for inventory changes.[10] No doubt these complications distort the statistical picture somewhat, but they are probably not serious enough to change materially the overall trend shown in Table 1.

In calculating the rate of investment, the 1933 and 1952 market prices have been used alternatively as weights. For lack of information, no ad-

7. According to one source, beginning in 1958, the value of such equipment was not to be included as investment, which implies that it had been included prior to 1958 (Cho Ching-hui, 1957).

8. See, for example, *TCKT,* No. 2, 1957 (p. 40); *CSYK,* No. 6, 1956 (pp. 36-37); *JMJP,* July 22, 1956 (p. 3), August 26, 1956 (p. 3).

9. See, for instance, State Statistical Bureau, 1955 and 1957b; Chang Cheng, 1956.

10. Very often inventories of raw materials were under reported by the managers of industrial enterprises to conceal resources at their disposal. *TCKTTH,* No. 7, 1954 (p. 19); *Ta-kung pao,* Feb. 22, 1957 (p. 3); *JMJP,* June 9, 1955 (p. 2); *HHPYK,* No. 5, 1957 (pp. 55-56).

justment has been made for indirect taxes and subsidies, which were probably minuscule during the prewar period but far from negligible during the postwar period. This means that, by and large, the 1933 price weights are closer approximations to factor cost valuation than the 1952 price weights. In the 1950's the indirect taxes were largely levied on consumer goods, and subsidies paid mostly to investment goods industries. Had the adjustments been made, investment would probably be higher than that at established prices.[11]

Several broad findings based on Table 1 can now be stated.

(1) The first is the rather striking contrast between the prewar and postwar rates of investment. It averaged about 18 per cent in 1933 prices in the postwar period, compared to the prewar average of about 5 per cent. The corresponding figures in 1952 prices were 24 and 8 per cent.

This comparison is subject to many qualifications. On the one hand, because of certain statistical biases noted earlier, the spread between the rate of investment might well be narrower than that suggested by Table 1. The prewar rate is probably low because of incomplete coverage of investment in kind, military construction and equipment produced by handicraftsmen, both in the numerator and the denominator; their inclusion in the investment and income estimates would raise the prewar rate of investment. The exaggerations such as overreporting of basic construction in 1952-57 affect both the investment and the income estimates; their corrections would lower the postwar rate of investment.

On the other hand, there are other biases, the allowances for which would widen the gap. For example, if these estimates were valued at factor cost, the difference between the two rates would be wider than that shown in Table 1. The prewar rate of investment at factor cost would be more or less the same as that at established prices, but the postwar rate would probably be higher. Moreover, upward biases in noninvestment component of domestic product tend to understate the postwar rate of investment.

These upward biases include not only the deliberate overreporting in the official statistics, but also two complications arising from making comparisons of income at different times during a period of rapid economic

11. More precisely, this statement holds only if the share of indirect taxes on investment in total indirect taxes is less than, and the share of subsidies to investment in total subsidies exceeds, the share of investment in total output in established prices. So far as indirect taxes is concerned, this condition seems plausible. Investment in kind is not subject to indirect taxes. Although the indirect tax is levied on both manufactured producer goods and consumer goods, a smaller share of the indirect taxes probably came from investment goods, since the tax rates were lower for the producer goods than for the consumer goods, and since the gross value of producer goods output accounted for a smaller percentage of total industrial output than consumer boods during 1952-57. (A. I. Chekhutov, 1962; *Ten Great Years,* p. 90.) It seems also likely that subsidies to the investment activities accounted for more than one-fourth of total subsidies,

transformation. First, the degree of commercialization and urbanization after the war was considerably higher than it had been. Some activities formerly carried on within the household were now performed by commercial organizations; for example, child care, processing of some farm products, and certain services provided by the credit or farm cooperatives. The postwar product is thus biased upwards in relation to the prewar figures because of a broader scope of economic activity. The second bias originated in the changing "netness" of the measure of domestic product. Along with the rather extensive institutional changes and industrialization in the postwar period came several types of expenditures which entered into the final product but which did not actually add to the real stock of goods or services to the consumers or to capital. For example, wage payments to political commissars who were assigned to the joint state-private enterprises, farm cooperatives, schools, and armed forces were in the nature of costs, rather than payments for any ultimate services. There were also the added costs of urban living and of the increased volume of transportation and distribution due to urbanization, rationing and other systems of centralized allocation. In the prewar period, these elements were either negligible or nonexistent. Their inclusion in the postwar estimates thus introduced an upward bias in the national income figures. However, all these distortions together are not enough to invalidate the broad observation that the postwar rate of investment was markedly higher than that in the prewar period.

It is interesting to note that the higher postwar rate of investment was achieved with virtually no capital from abroad.[12] The increase represented largely an increase in the rate of domestic savings. The substantially higher rate of domestic savings is all the more striking if one recalls that the postwar per capita income was only moderately higher, and that the percentage share of government consumption in gross domestic product was considerably larger than in the prewar period (Liu-Yeh, 1965, pp. 80, 82).

(2) Compared with those of other underdeveloped Asian countries during the same period, Communist China's rate of investment was quite high.[13] But, as in the case of the Soviet Union in the late 1920's, what distinguishes Communist China's experience was its steep ascent within a rather short period. The contrast between the prewar and postwar estimates implies that the rate of investment rose from about 5 per cent to a

12. During 1953-57, Communist China actually had a net outflow of resources (United Nations, *Economic Survey, 1957*).

13. The rates of investment for Burma, China (Taiwan), Thailand, India, Ceylon, and Philippines in 1952-57 are, respectively, 24, 20, 17, 16, 14, 11 and 9 per cent. United Nations, *Economic Survey,* 1957 (pp. 216-17); *Economic Survey,* 1960 (p. 129); *Economic Survey,* 1961 (pp. 172-73). See also United Nations, 1964. The underlying totals are in current prices.

level three times that high in a period of two decades or less.[14] Such an abrupt rise is certainly uncommon in the historical record of the developed countries.[15] And even in the underdeveloped countries whose rate of investment rose rapidly during the period from the 1930's to the 1950's, the pace of increase hardly matched that of Communist China.[16] About the only comparable experience is that of the Soviet Union during the short period prior to 1928 (Bergson, 1964, pp. 312-13).

(3) Turning to the changes during 1952-59, one finds some rather pronounced year-to-year fluctuations. The rate of investment rose sharply in 1953, 1956, and 1958-59 over the preceding years, though there was a retrenchment in 1957. Two observations on these changes may be made. First, to some extent, the marked ups and downs reflected changes in the intensity of the Party's effort to quicken the pace of development. Thus, in the years of big push, a substantial part of the increase in investment generally took the form of investment in kind, which could be more readily increased with a sudden spurt of effort. This means, of course, that, at the same time, part of the rise probably represented statistical increase, for at such times the pressure to set and fulfill unrealistically high targets was greater, and the temptation to overreport was particularly strong. For the same reason, the rapid increase in the volume of investment was often achieved at the expense of its quality. Second, except in 1958, each of the ups and downs was preceded by a corresponding good or bad harvest.

(4) Despite the Party's obsession with accumulation, the rate of investment in 1952-59 remained in the neighborhood of 25 per cent, with no markedly rising trend.[17] To provide some rough indicators of what

14. What actually happened to the level of output and investment during 1937-49 is not clear. It may be recalled that this period witnessed prolonged armed conflicts and severe economic disorder. It seems unlikely that the rate of investment had risen much higher, if at all, than that in the 1930's. In any event, the domestic product in 1946 was about the same as that in the 1930's. (Ou Pao-san, 1947.) Because of the relatively large military expenditures, the galloping inflation, the spread of the civil war, and the acute shortage of capital goods, investment during the first few years after the Sino-Japanese War was probably small. This means that the trebling of the rate of investment was probably not a steady rise over the two decades but a rather sharp increase in the course of a few years prior to 1952.

15. For example, in the case of Great Britain, Germany, Sweden, and Japan, the ratio of net investment to net domestic product doubled only after four decades or more (S. Kuznets, 1965, pp. 222-25). It should be noted, however, that the ratios of these countries in their preindustrial stage of development were higher than that of China in the 1930's.

16. For example, the investment rates for Burma and Ceylon in 1950-59 were respectively 60 and 80 per cent higher than those of 1938. (United Nations, *Economic Survey, 1957,* p. 216; and United Nations, 1961, p. 58.) These estimates are in current prices.

17. The figures for 1958-59 are not strictly comparable with those for earlier years. They include only state fixed investment. Allowances for different coverage would probably raise these estimates, and quite possibly the series for 1952-59 may show a slightly rising trend. However, this trend is subject to an upward bias for two reasons. There is probably undercoverage of output in trade and some other traditional sectors during the earlier years; and there is probably a larger degree of overreporting in both investment and output during 1958-59 than in the earlier years.

happened after 1959, the output indexes of 13 key products and imports of machinery during 1959-62 are shown in Table 2. The underlying data

TABLE 2

INDEXES OF OUTPUT OF SELECTED PRODUCTS AND MACHINERY IMPORTS, 1959-1962

	1959	1960	1961	1962
(1) Cement	100	110	65	65
(2) Lumber	100	98	85	72
(3) Steel	100	138	71	75
(4) Machinery imports	100	84	20	6
(5) Grain	100	95	99	106
(6) Cotton	100	78	50	50
(7) Soy beans	100	86	83	81
(8) Peanuts	100	83	74	70
(9) Rapeseed	100	111	67	56
(10) Sesame	100	75	75	75
(11) Electric power	100	132	104	72
(12) Coal	100	121	109	69
(13) Crude oil	100	162	149	162
(14) Salt	100	117	100	90

Sources:

(1) United Nations, 1965, p. 292.

(2) *TGY*, p. 96; Richardson, 1966, p. 166.

(3) Appendix A; *Far Eastern Economic Review*, April 16, 1964, p. 160.

(4) A. Eckstein, 1966, pp. 106-107.

(5) *Current Scene*, Vol. II, No. 27 (Jan. 15, 1964), p. 4.

(6)-(10) Reports of the U.S. Agricultural Officer, American Consulate General's Office, Hong Kong.

(11) Appendix A; *Far Eastern Economic Review*, April 4, 1963, p. 6.

(12) United Nations, 1965, p. 180; *Far Eastern Economic Review*, June 7, 1962, p. 153, April 4, 1963, p. 6.

(13) *JMJP*, Jan. 1, 1960, p. 1; *Far Eastern Economic Review*, April 4, 1963, p. 6.

(14) United Nations, 1965, p. 205.

are rather crude but for the present purpose they seem adequate. Two interesting features may be noted. First, the indexes for all items except grain and other agricultural products show a very steep decline in 1961 and remain quite low in 1962. Second, the indexes closely related to fixed investment (cement, lumber, steel and machinery imports) followed the same pattern but fell more sharply than most other products. One might thus infer that the rate of fixed investment was about the same in 1960 as in 1959, declined precipitously in 1961, and remained fairly low in 1962. No information on investment in working capital is available, but it seems likely that it too fell more sharply than output, because of the sharp reductions both in inventories of grain, other consumer goods, and agricultural raw materials, and in the volume of unfinished construction, after cutbacks in fixed investment. These conjectures suggest that the regime had not been able to sustain the high rate of investment it achieved during the earlier period.

II. STRUCTURE OF INVESTMENT

Table 3 shows the distribution of investment between changes in inventory and fixed investment, and the distribution of gross fixed investment between construction and equipment. Several broad findings from this table can be suggested:

(1) On the average, inventory accumulation constituted about 28 per cent of gross domestic capital formation in the 1950's, much higher than in the 1930's. The contrast between the prewar and postwar shares of inventory accumulation is due partly to the incomplete statistical coverage for the prewar period, and perhaps partly to the upward bias in the Communist statistics of inventory changes. But even if the statistical distortions were adequately accounted for, the difference probably would still be significant.

Several plausible explanations for the higher postwar ratio can be suggested. First, the replenishment of reserves depleted during the Korean War in 1950-53 might account for part of the increase during the earlier years of the First Five-Year Plan period. Second, the launching of an investment program on an increasingly large scale during this period probably resulted in sizable increases in the volume of investment projects under construction. Finally, the difficulties of a centralized distribution system and the lack of experience in managing such a system (particularly during the earlier years) might have resulted in bottlenecks. The period witnessed rapid economic recovery, with a large investment program, and many raw material supplies were short. The plant managers tended to accumulate more raw materials than necessary.

For probably these same reasons, Communist China's share of inventory changes in total investment was also substantially higher than those of other underdeveloped countries.[18] However, there was a discernible downward trend in the inventory ratio in the 1950's, possibly due to better management of inventory holdings and higher efficiency in the transportation system in the latter part of the First Five-Year Plan period.

(2) In gross domestic fixed capital formation, construction was by far the larger component, accounting for about two-thirds of the total in both the 1930's and the 1950's. In the 1950's, though, the volume of construc-

18. The share of changes in inventory accounted for about 10 per cent of gross domestic capital formation in these countries (Kuznets, 1960, p. 33).

TABLE 3

TOTAL AND FIXED INVESTMENT BY TYPES OF CAPITAL GOODS, 1931-1936 AND 1952-1957 [a]
(in per cent)

	Percentage of Total Investment		Percentage of Fixed Investment	
	Change in Inventory	Gross Fixed Investment	Construction	Producers' Durables
1931	...... [b]	......	64.6	35.4
1932	5.0	95.0	65.7	34.3
1933	1.9	98.1	65.8	34.2
1934	8.8	108.8	61.7	38.3
1935	1.6	98.4	61.0	39.0
1936	4.6	95.4	59.8	40.2
1952	47.5	52.5	67.7	32.3
1953	38.7	61.3	67.9	32.1
1954	37.7	62.3	68.6	31.4
1955	31.8	68.2	64.7	35.3
1956	8.0	92.0	63.5	36.5
1957	16.6	83.4	62.4	37.6
Average:				
1931-36	0.9	99.1	62.9	37.1
1952-57	27.8	72.2	65.0	35.0

Notes:
a. Based on totals in 1952 prices.
b. "......" Not available.

Source:
Yeh, 1964. Fixed investments in 1931-36 have been adjusted to include changes in large draft animals on the basis of the proportion of this item in changes in total livestock and the price index for large animals in 1933-52 (given in Liu-Yeh, 1965, p. 398).

tion was substantially higher and expanding much faster than in the 1930's. Furthermore, there was a shift from shorter-lived to longer-lived structures, as suggested by the faster rate of growth in cement production than in construction over the same period. The percentage share of fixed investment in construction for China was almost identical with the ratio for other underdeveloped countries (Kuznets, 1960).

(3) The share of residential construction in total fixed investment in constant prices is not available. However, it was probably fairly low in

the 1950's. In 1952-57 the share of residential construction averaged only about 6 per cent of total state fixed investment in current prices,[19] which is considerably lower than the Soviet Union's 9 per cent for 1928-37, and very much lower than the average share of 19 per cent for non-Communist low-income countries (Kapalan, 1953, p. 61; Kuznets, 1960, p. 33). The contrast is due partly to the narrower coverage of the Chinese statistics. A sizable portion of the nonstate investment consisted of capital repairs of residential houses. Also, the lower share in Communist China might have been due to the prices of equipment and to lower construction cost per unit of floor space and the lower quality of residential houses, compared with the cost and quality of nonresidential buildings. But to a large extent, it reflected the regime's investment policy of deliberately curbing residential construction in order to channel a larger share of resources into buildings and structures more directly related to production.

(4) The average share of equipment in fixed investment in the 1950's was about 35 per cent, close to that for China in the 1930's and for other low-income countries in the 1950's (Kuznets, 1960, p. 33). It increased somewhat toward the latter part of the First Five-Year Plan period. The change was clearly related to the nature of the investment program, which emphasized large capital-intensive projects with long gestation periods. During the first phase of the development in 1953-54, the program consisted largely of erecting the structures and other civil engineering work (*HHYP,* No. 5, 1955, p. 153). From 1955 on, large-scale installation work began, and the percentage share of equipment rose continuously throughout 1955-57.

Imported equipment during 1953-57 accounted for about 45 per cent of total equipment (in current prices) included in state investment (Li Fu-chun, 1959). China's rather high degree of dependence upon foreign equipment indicates the low level of development of its domestic machinery industry relative to its investment requirements. This was true also in the prewar period, but there were notable differences. In the postwar period, imports of complete plants were more important, and the percentage of imported equipment for the heavy industries was probably larger. The sources of supply in the 1930's included many Western countries, but until 1960 the postwar imports came almost exclusively from the Soviet Union.

19. For total state investment see *TGY,* p. 55. For state investment in housing during 1953-57, see Tso Yen-hsing, 1957.

III. ALLOCATION OF INVESTMENT

Table 4 shows the distribution of total gross fixed investment in 1952-57 by four economic sectors: (1) *industry,* which includes manufacturing, mining, electric power generation, construction and surveying; (2) *agriculture,* which includes all farms, machine tractor stations, and such activities as irrigation, flood control, prevention of soil erosion and afforestation; (3) *transportation and communications,* which include railroad, water, land, and air transportation, mail, telephone, telegraph and radio; and (4) *other,* which includes all other sectors. The computations are based on totals in current prices.[20] The findings based on this table can be summarized as follows:

(1) INDUSTRY

Throughout the period, industry's share was consistently higher than those of the other three sectors. It grew continuously from about one-third in 1952 to more than one-half in 1957. Even during the retrenchment in 1957 when all other investments were cut back, investment in industry increased both in absolute and in percentage terms. For the period as a

TABLE 4

DISTRIBUTION OF GROSS FIXED INVESTMENT BY ECONOMIC SECTORS, 1952-1957
(in per cent)

	Industry	Agri-culture	Transportation & Communications	Other	Total
1952	35.5	32.0	13.5	19.0	100.0
1953	39.2	21.1	12.0	27.7	100.0
1954	44.5	16.7	14.5	24.2	100.0
1955	46.1	19.2	16.4	18.2	100.0
1956	47.2	18.8	15.9	18.2	100.0
1957	52.1	17.8	13.8	16.3	100.0
Average:					
1952-57	45.6	19.8	14.6	20.0	100.0

Source:
Table B-1, Appendix B.

20. The underlying totals in Table 4 are not comparable with those in Tables 1 and 3. The former are based on basic construction in current prices, the latter on accumulation in constant 1952 prices. The former includes, while the latter excludes, ancillary expenses. For definition of basic construction, see Appendix B below and Ishikawa, 1965.

whole, it averaged about 46 per cent of the total. Clearly the regime had assigned the highest priority to industrial development in allocating its investable resources.

Several aspects of the industrial investment program not shown in Table 4 should be mentioned. First, of heavy and light industry, heavy industry received the overwhelmingly larger share of total state investment.[21] For the period as a whole, the share of investment in heavy industry amounted to 85 per cent of total state investment in industry.[22] Second, the investment program was primarily oriented toward industrial growth and not to the needs of the agricultural sector. Industries supplying inputs for agricultural production, such as chemical fertilizer and farm equipment, were not among the most-favored ones.[23] Third, in the questions of the scale of the production unit and the choice of technology, the emphasis had been on relatively large and capital-intensive enterprises.[24] Thus, about five-sixths of the total planned industrial investment by the state was for the construction of above-norm enterprises, which were generally large.[25]

(2) AGRICULTURE

The share of agricultural investment averaged 20 per cent of the total, considerably lower than that for industry.[26] In contrast to industry's share, it declined almost continuously throughout the period. However, the

21. Heavy industry includes such industries as electric power, coal mining, petroleum, iron and steel, nonferrous metals, machinery, basic chemicals, construction materials, and lumbering. Light industry includes such industries as textiles, pharmaceuticals, food processing, and manufactures for daily life, educational and cultural activities (State Planning Commission, 1955, p. 1).

22. *TGY*, p. 61. Total industrial investment includes centralized investment only and excludes major repairs.

23. According to the FFYP, 8 major fertilizer plants were to be built or expanded during 1952-57. Upon completion in 1960 these plants would produce 1.1 million tons of nitrous fertilizer (Wang Hsing-fu and Lan Chien-chiao, 1957). However, this would amount to only 6 per cent of the total requirement of 20 million tons given in Liao Lu-yen, 1956. The relative insignificance of farm equipment production is indicated by the small amount of gross value of farm equipment produced during 1953-57 which, according to one report, accounted for only 8 per cent of total gross value of machinery (Wang Kuang-wei, 1958).

24. Sung Shao-wen, 1957. A large enterprise is one that uses mechanical motive power and has 16 or more workers and employees, or does not use mechanical motive power but has 31 or more workers and employees. All power plants with a capacity exceeding 15 Kw are considered as large enterprises, regardless of the number of workers (State Planning Commission, 1955, p. 2).

25. Yang Ying-chieh, 1955. Above-norm projects are those for which the investment cost exceed specified amounts established by the State Planning Commission. For limits of various industries, see State Planning Commission, 1955 (pp. 42-43). According to one report, 78 per cent of the some 490 above-norm projects were enterprises with 500 or more workers (Yi Lin, 1957).

26. The estimates of agricultural investment are subject to a number of reservations. On the one hand, they are probably too high because the estimates of nonstate investment in farm buildings are based on a Communist sample survey which

distinctive feature is not so much the relatively small proportion of agricultural investment as it is the relatively small share of the state's contribution to investment in agriculture (*TGY*, p. 57; Appendix B to this chapter). The small amount of state investment in this sector was due mainly to the regime's heavy reliance upon organizational means of increasing output, and to its anticipation of a sizable volume of investment by the peasants themselves.[27] Of the total state investment in agriculture, about 60 per cent was allocated to water conservation, the rest mainly to state farms, tractor stations, land reclamation, and forestry.

Nonstate farm investment in 1953-57 totaled about 8.6 billion *yuan*, or about two-thirds of total agricultural investment excluding major repairs (Appendix B). Allowing for depreciation in the agricultural sector, net investment amounted to about 4.5 billion *yuan*, somewhat lower than what the planners expected, despite the fact that collectivization proceeded at a much more rapid pace than originally anticipated in the First Five-Year Plan. Of total nonstate farm investment, the purchase of equipment and the construction of irrigation and flood control projects each accounted for about a third of the total. The abrupt increase in these two items in 1956 was apparently the result of the accelerated collectivization program. However, this was offset to some extent by the reduction in the number of draft animals in 1956-57.

(3) TRANSPORTATION AND COMMUNICATIONS

Of all four sectors, the smallest share of investment was in transport and communications. It averaged about 15 per cent, and showed no discernible upward or downward trend. According to the First Five-Year Plan, most of state investment—about 70 per cent of total investment in this sector—was allocated to the railroad department. Of the total investment in railroads, about 75 per cent was for construction, and about 21 per cent for the purchase of rolling stock (*FFYP*, pp. 94, 96). The emphasis was on the construction of new tracks linking the more populous coastal areas with the remote areas in the northwest and with the Soviet Union. Actual investment followed the plan closely.

---

is biased upwards, and because the estimates of nonstate investment in equipment are based on retail sales, which included parts for ordinary maintenance. On the other hand, the statistics for retail sales in the earlier years are in all likelihood underreported, and some investment not requiring purchases from the market might well have been left out. (See Appendix B.) However, these distortions are not likely to have altered the overall distribution appreciably.

27. The regime estimated that during 1953-57 net fixed investment by farm households and collectives would reach a total of 6 billion *yuan*, more than double the planned gross fixed investment in agriculture by the state (*FFYP*, pp. 25-26).

(4) OTHER SECTORS

Investment in all the remaining sectors accounted for about one-fifth of total investment; and it declined continuously after 1953. Several features in the allocation of state investment in this sector may be noted. First, the largest share was put into culture, education and scientific research, indicating the emphasis of the regime on education and training. Second, investment in urban public utilities was the only branch that fell short of planned investment (*FFYP,* p. 24; *TGY,* p. 58). This underfulfillment is significant because the increase in the number of workers and employees during 1952-57 greatly exceeded the increase planned.[28] Third, the miscellaneous item is quite large. Presumably it includes residential construction, but housing construction alone could not account for the sizable volumes in some years such as 1953-54. Possibly some military construction is included in these figures.

Table 5 shows the distribution in the 1950's of state investment by major sectors for Communist China, six non-Communist Asian countries, and seven European Communist countries. The calculations are based on totals in current prices. Although these comparisons are imprecise because of many complications, and the definitions and qualities of statistics and the relative price structures are not uniform in these countries, the following broad findings seem warranted.

By and large, the Chinese allocation pattern is quite similar to those of the other Communist countries. What stands out as the common feature among these countries is the high priority given to industrial investment. Investments in agriculture and transportation in all of them except Bulgaria have been kept relatively low. Agriculture's share in China in particular was lower than in other countries. Communist China's share of investment in transportation was the highest in the group, but its share of investment in other services was among the lowest.

Compared to the non-Communist countries, the Chinese investment pattern is distinguished by (1) a much higher share of industrial investment than those of all countries, (2) a much lower share of agricultural investment, (3) a lower percentage share for transportation and communications, and (4) a larger share for services than most other countries.[29] The contrasts suggest that the regime's industrialization policy had been quite different from those of the low-income countries.

28. For the planned increase, see *FFYP,* p. 128. For the actual increase, see John P. Emerson, 1965, p. 129. Strictly speaking, the two figures are not comparable, but the distortion in no way affects the conclusion here.

29. It should be noted that the fact the share of investment in "other" services is larger in Communist China (and, for that matter, in Communist countries in general) than in the non-Communist countries is misleading. Private investments in the non-Communist countries are mostly investment in services such as residential construction.

TABLE 5

DISTRIBUTION OF GROSS FIXED INVESTMENT BY ECONOMIC SECTORS, SELECTED COUNTRIES[a]
(in per cent)

	Period	Industry	Agri-culture	Trans-portation and Communi-cations	Other
Communist China	1952-57	51.3	8.1	16.5	24.1
Asian countries:					
Burma	1950-59	47.0	15.0	30.0	8.0
Ceylon	1950-59	24.0	35.0	22.0	19.0
China (Taiwan)	1951-62	39.4	20.4	15.1	25.1
India	1950-59	21.0	29.0	32.0	18.0
Philippines	1950-59	9.0	22.0	40.0	29.0
Thailand	1950-59	21.0	19.0	43.0	17.0
Communist countries:					
Bulgaria	1949-57	44.0	21.1	10.0	24.9
Czechoslovakia	1949-57	44.7	11.5	11.7	31.9
East Germany	1950-57	48.5	10.0	11.7	29.8
Hungary	1949-57	42.8	17.0	10.7	29.7
Poland	1950-58	46.3	14.0	11.3	28.5
Rumania	1950-58	55.2	14.6	9.8	20.3
USSR	1951-58	41.8	17.7	8.1	32.3

Note:

a. Based on total state investment in current prices, except for China (Taiwan) for which totals include nonstate investment.

Sources:

Communist China: *TGY*, pp. 57-58.

Other countries: United Nations, *Yearbook, 1958; Yearbook, 1963; World Economic Survey, 1959.*

The contrasts between India and Communist China are especially interesting. First, the spread between the largest and the smallest share is considerably larger in China than in India, indicating a higher degree of concentration of resources in a given sector in Communist China. Second, the policies toward the balance between industry and agriculture were markedly different. Where industry in India obtained less resources than agriculture, China's industry got an overwhelmingly larger share. Third, China placed greater emphasis on investment in the "material production" sectors, *i.e.,* agriculture and industry, than on investment in the two service sectors.

IV. SUMMARY AND CONCLUDING REMARKS

This chapter has tried to describe Communist China's capital formation in a number of dimensions. We have noted that the rate of investment rose very sharply above the prewar level in the postwar period, that it remained at the high level of about 25 per cent during the First Five-Year Plan period, but that it later sank to a rather low level following the collapse of the Great Leap. On the average, the percentage share of inventory changes in total investment in 1952-57 was also higher than the prewar level. There was apparently a shift toward longer lasting capital and more modern technology, even though the ratio of equipment to construction was little different from that before World War II. In the allocation of fixed investment, the regime placed more emphasis on industry than on agriculture; more on the material production sectors than on services; and more on those services related to investment (such as transportation) than on those servicing the consumers (such as residential construction).

The most distinctive feature was perhaps the different treatment of industry and agriculture, not only in the different shares of investment allocated to these sectors but also in the direction of investment within each sector. The new industrial projects adopted the more advanced techniques while the agricultural projects merely extended the use of traditional techniques. Investment in industry, which accounted for the lion's share of total investment, was directed toward those branches that produced inputs primarily for industrial expansion. Meanwhile, agriculture, which provided the bulk of savings, received in return few physical resources from the nonagricultural sector.

What was the relationship between investment and output? No definitive answer to this question can be given because many gaps still remain in our knowledge of the complicated growth process in Communist China. In the next few pages are brief comments on certain aspects of the problem. For the most part, these general remarks are not based on statistical evidence, and therefore should be regarded only as plausible guesses.

Let us first review briefly the growth record of the First Five-Year Plan period. Table 6 shows the average annual rates of increase of gross domestic product and its major components, and the ratio of the increase in each sector's output to the increase in total output in 1952-57.[30] For comparison, estimates for 1931-36 are also presented. The rates of increase

30. It should be noted that other estimates of output and investment in 1952-57 are available, which differ somewhat from the Liu-Yeh estimates used here. See *TGY*, p. 20; W. W. Hollister, 1958 (p. 2); Wu, Hoeber and Rockwell, 1964 (p. 120); Kang Chao, 1965 (p. 88).

TABLE 6

AVERAGE ANNUAL RATES OF INCREASE OF GROSS DOMESTIC PRODUCT, 1931-1936 AND 1952-1957

	Output Increase Per Year (per cent)		Per Cent of Total Increase in Output	
	1931-36	1952-57	1931-36	1952-57
Gross domestic product	1.6	6.2	100.0	100.0
Industry	3.5	15.1	35.3	64.8
Agriculture	1.4	1.7	47.7	11.6
Transportation and communication	1.8	5.8	6.7	6.1
Other services	0.8	4.6	10.3	17.4

Sources:
Liu-Yeh, 1965; Yeh, 1964. The outputs of the individual sectors in 1931-36 and 1952-57 are respectively the net and gross value added in these sectors in 1952 prices.

of output are based on the two totals in the terminal years (1936 and 1957) and therefore are rather sensitive to the conditions in those two years. Despite the crudities, the overall pattern of change is clear. Total output expanded quite rapidly, compared with both the output of prewar China and that of most other underdeveloped countries over the same period.[31]

Industry was the fastest growing of the individual sectors. By contrast, agricultural output rose relatively little; on a per capita basis, there was hardly any increase. Increases in the output of services were substantially higher than in the prewar period, particularly services other than transportation and communications.

However, the distinctive feature of Communist China's economic expansion during this period was not so much that industry grew faster than any other sector. This had also been true in prewar China and in most other underdeveloped Asian countries over the same period.[32] More unusual was the large share of the increase in total output that was contributed by industry. During 1952-57 the rise in industrial output accounted for about two-thirds of the rise in domestic product.

To what extent was the rapid rise in industrial output the result of investment? At a first glance, it would appear that the high rate of industrial expansion was closely related to the large share of fixed invest-

31. For growth rates of other countries, see United Nations, *Economic Survey 1961* (p. 10).

32. For growth of industry and other sectors in Asian countries, see United Nations, *Economic Survey, 1961* (p. 171); *Economic Survey, 1957* (pp. 214-15).

ment allocated to industry during the same period. However, the relationship was neither direct nor close. The large volume of investment in this sector undoubtedly created an enormous demand for industrial products and thus contributed indirectly to the expansion. But the investment program itself made relatively little contribution to the supply of industrial products during this period. An overwhelmingly large proportion of fixed investment was used in the construction of new plants or the expansion of old ones. Major repairs of the existing plants accounted for only a small part. Yet the new and reconstructed plants contributed less than one-third of the increase in industrial output during 1952-57.[33]

The rather small contribution made by the new plants was largely due to the very nature of Communist China's investment program. The pattern of investment was biased toward relatively heavy users of capital, such as heavy industry rather than light; large and capital-intensive projects rather than small and labor-intensive ones; completely new plants rather than extensions of existing ones; and construction sites in cities in the hinterland where social overhead capital was small rather than in the coastal cities. The gestation period of these projects was rather long so that many were still under construction by 1957.[34] And although increased productive capacity in some industries during 1952-57 was considerable compared with the existing capacity in 1952,[35] generally the operating capacity of the new plant could not be raised to a high level within a short period of time.[36]

The rapid rise in industrial output came largely from the fuller use of previously under-utilized capacity in the existing plants. This was possible not only because considerable capacity was unused in 1952, but also because there was excess capacity in the social overhead industries such as power supply and railroads, and a pool of readily available labor in the cities, already urbanized if not yet technically trained. In addition, some technical and organizational improvements also contributed to the better and fuller utilization of the existing plants' equipment.[37]

33. Note that "industry" here includes only the gross value of output of factories and workshops and excludes handicrafts and construction. In 1955 it was estimated that output of the new plants would account for about 30 per cent of the increase in industrial output (Li Fu-chun, 1957). According to Lin I-fu ("Seek All Effective Means to Develop Fully the Productive Potential in Existing Industrial Enterprises," *CHCC,* No. 3, 1958) the new enterprises produced less than 30 per cent of the gross value of industrial output in 1957.

34. The average gestation period was estimated at three to five years (Lo Keng-mo, 1955).

35. See for example the increases in productive capacity of pig iron, steel, coal, electric power, cotton yarn and cotton cloth during 1952-57 and their respective total in 1952 given in SSB, "Communiqué," 1959 (p. 41); Yang Chien-pai, 1955 (p. 194); *FFYP* (p. 50); SSB, 1956 (pp. 70, 154).

36. For example, it took two to three years for a new coal mine with a design capacity of 1.5 million tons to reach its full capacity (*JMJP,* Dec. 1, 1957, p. 3).

37. See, for example, State Planning Commission, 1956, p. 19.

The situation in agriculture was somewhat different. Given the traditional setting, Chinese agriculture was fairly efficient, so that simply increasing the supply of the traditional inputs could not raise production substantially. Any major sustained advance in production must come primarily from the use of new techniques and new inputs as well. The implication of this for investment policy is threefold.

First, investment in research and development, extension services, and technical training might well be more important than investment in the conventional sense. This is because the new techniques must be adapted to the physical and climatic environment of the particular growing area. For an economy striving at the subsistence level and in a society bound to the land with century-old traditions, experimentation and extension services would be all the more necessary to reduce the risk of introducing new cultivation methods and overcome the resistance to them. Second, investment in working capital might well be more important than fixed investment, because new technology in farming, unlike industrial technology, generally takes the form of current inputs such as improved seeds, chemical fertilizers and insecticides. Third, within the fixed investment category itself, some technical knowledge is indispensable in the selection of the type of investment, in its design and construction, and in servicing the new capital.

When we look at the pattern of investment during the 1950's, we find a relatively small amount of expenditure on agricultural research and extension,[38] a negligible supply of such inputs as chemical fertilizers,[39] and a large proportion of fixed investment in agriculture devoted to irrigation projects. The result of these misplaced emphases was compounded by the ineffectiveness of the fixed investment. Many water conservation projects failed to produce results because of errors in design, defects in construction, and inadequate equipment to make effective use of the water supply. Some modern farm tools, such as the double-wheel and shear plows, were unsuitable to the farming conditions in many areas. Others, like tractors, had a low utilization rate mainly because of a shortage of repair services and parts. The heart of the problem seemed to be the lack of proper technical guidance in the supply and the effective use of the new equipment.

38. State noninvestment expenditures on agriculture (excluding dyke repairs) in 1953-57 totalled 3 billion *yuan* (Han Pu, 1958). Included in the amount were subsidies to machine tractor stations, afforestation and other current expenses that did not contribute directly to research and development .After allowing for these items, actual investment in human capital would be considerably less than 3 billion *yuan*. Yet even a total of 3 billion *yuan* amounted to less than one-fourth of fixed investment in agriculture.

39. The average annual consumption of chemical fertilizer during 1952-57 was 1.2 million tons (Liu Jung-chao, 1965, p. 925). This was minuscule compared to the total requirement of 20 million tons of nitrous fertilizer alone (Liao Lu-yen, 1956).

Whatever the cause of the ineffectiveness of agricultural investment, the impact of the agricultural stagnation on the entire economy was profound. This was because government savings, by far the most important source of savings, came largely from the agricultural sector directly or indirectly (Liao Lu-yen, 1960).[40] In addition to its effect on the volume of savings, the slowdown in agricultural growth adversely affected the investment program in two other ways. Because the output of food and clothing, the two most important wage goods, depended heavily on agriculture for raw materials, the only way to meet the rising demand for wage goods brought about by an expanding investment program was to increase agricultural production.[41] Furthermore, at the present stage of its development, Communist China's machinery industry was still in its infancy, and inadequate in size and technological capability to supply the equipment needed. Investment in the modern sector could be accelerated only by expanding machinery imports. Since most foreign exchange earnings came from the exports of agricultural products or goods manufactured from them, the stagnant agricultural production would put a ceiling on Communist China's import capacity unless the exports of other products rose substantially.[42]

In an attempt to solve the problem of lagging agricultural production, the Great Leap policy was adopted in 1958. The essential idea was to convert labor into capital, mainly in the form of water irrigation projects and small industrial plants using indigenous techniques. These investments were to provide the material input necessary to generate rapid and sustained growth in the agricultural sector. The regime could then continue to draw on the agricultural surplus without having to divert resources from industry to agriculture, and thereby maintain a high rate of growth in the modern industrial sector. So far as investment policy was concerned, the only major departure from the pre-1958 policy was the renewed emphasis on investment in kind on an unprecedented scale. As it turned out, the massive investment again failed to bring about any sustained increase in agricultural output.

To recapitulate, during the decade or so after 1949, the Communist Chinese economy went through two phases of development in which investment played somewhat different roles. The first phase, from 1949 to the mid-1950's, was essentially one of rehabilitation. There were considerable slacks in the economy in the form of under-utilized equipment and

40. For this reason the annual state investment plans were primarily based on the harvest conditions of the preceding year (Chou En-lai, 1956, p. 38; Li Chien, 1957).

41. I assume here that an additional supply of food and clothing for the construction workers could not be obtained by cutbacks elsewhere.

42. One might argue that the capacity to import depends not only on the physical volume of exports but also on the terms of trade, so that a decline in agricultural exports need not entail a decline in the import capacity. This is possible but rather unlikely in the present case.

social overhead capital, and underemployed urban labor. In addition, there were certain economies of scale to be exploited as the economy became an integrated whole for the first time in generations. Under these circumstances, the regime was able to increase output rapidly by more fully utilizing the existing resources. This is not to say that investment was unimportant. The replacement of worn equipment and machinery removed by the Russians, and the replenishment of working capital all contributed much to the recovery of production in the existing plants. Investments in the new projects, however, had little to do with the increase in industrial output, for most of them were still under construction. The abrupt rise in the rate of investment during this period was made possible by the increase in output and by the institutional controls that curbed the rise in consumption.

Toward the later part of the First Five-Year Plan period, the sources of growth from more efficient and fuller use of existing resources were more or less exhausted; and the economy entered into the second phase, where further expansion would have to rely mainly on the results of the investments financed by the economic windfalls of the earlier period. The statistical record shows that the regime had failed to sustain a high rate of investment and growth. The causes of this failure are numerous, but the pattern of investment clearly was a major contributing factor.

In at least two respects, the regime's investment policy seems to have been misguided. First, in allocating investment among sectors the regime had underemphasized agriculture, where a greater part of the savings originated. Not only was the volume of investment in agriculture much less than industrial investment, but the larger industrial investment program was primarily oriented toward defense and industrial growth and not agricultural development. Consequently, the expanding investment program and the upsurge in industrial output, together with rapid population growth, created a continuously rising demand for agricultural products, but the new industrial capacity did not provide the material support necessary to raise agricultural output on a sustained basis.

Second, in allocating resources among different uses within the agricultural sector, the regime overemphasized traditional investment to the neglect of investment embodying new techniques. In particular the planners were obsessed with the notion that by organizing unskilled labor, they could expand investment in kind and thereby increase output. This line of reasoning implicitly assumes either that no additional supply of complementary factors was needed because the economy was operating within the range where marginal productivity of labor was positive, or that an unlimited supply of such factors was available, which could always be combined with labor to shift the production function upward. But these conditions hardly existed. The critical element missing was the technical skill required to design and build effective labor-intensive projects. As a result there was an enormous expansion in investment during 1958-59, but these investments were largely abortive.

APPENDIX A
GROSS DOMESTIC PRODUCT, 1958-59

The derivation of gross domestic product in 1958-59, used to calculate rates of investment in Table 1, is explained here with reference to Tables A-1 and A-2. Table A-1 summarizes estimates of gross value added in ten sectors, and Table A-2 presents the output of 38 major products in 1958-59 used in estimating gross value added of certain sectors. For comparison, the corresponding figures for 1957 taken from Liu-Yeh (1965) are also given in these tables.

TABLE A-1

GROSS DOMESTIC PRODUCT, 1957-59
(in billions of yuan in 1952 prices)

	1957	1958	1959
1. Agriculture	38.02	42.21	38.40
2. Manufacturing factories			
Producer goods	12.50	16.16	21.74
Consumer goods	5.81	6.47	7.01
3. Handicrafts	5.86	6.50	7.18
4. Mining	3.29	5.22	7.00
5. Utilities	0.94	1.20	1.65
6. Construction	5.20	7.22	9.09
7. Trade, transportation, communications and finance	19.86	23.55	25.52
8. Government administration	5.08	4.75	5.95
9. Other personal services and residential rent	3.40	3.48	3.55
10. Work brigades	0.85	0.95	0.89
11. Gross domestic product	100.81	117.71	127.98

The sources and methods of calculating the figures in Table A-1 are as follows:

1. *Agriculture.* Gross value added is the sum of values added in the following five product groups: plant, animal, forest, fishery and miscellaneous products, which in turn are obtained by deducting material input from gross value of output for each group. Included in plant products are the 15 crops listed

under agricultural products in Table A-2, along with vegetables and fruits. Gross values of the 15 crops are derived by multiplying their outputs in 1958-59 (given in Table B-2) by the respective prices in 1952 given by Liu-Yeh (1965, p. 136). The gross values of vegetables and fruits are assumed to have increased during 1957-59 at the same rate as that of the 15 crops as a whole over the same period. For gross values of these two crops in 1957, see Liu-Yeh (1965, p. 397).

The gross values of animal products (except hogs), forest products and fishery products are taken from Liu-Yeh (1965, pp. 665-68). The total numbers of hogs at the end of each year during 1957-59 are assumed to have changed in the same proportion as the total gross value of plant products over the same period. The annual slaughter rate is assumed to be 80 per cent of the average of totals at the beginning and end of each year. (For total number in 1957 and the price of hogs, see Liu-Yeh, 1965, pp. 364, 385.) The gross value of hog products is derived as the sum of the annual change in number and the gross value of hogs slaughtered.

For miscellaneous products, gross values in 1958-59 are obtained by extrapolating the estimate for 1957 given in Liu-Yeh (1965, p. 140) on the basis of the index of gross value of the other four product groups for 1957-59. Gross value added by each group is derived by multiplying the gross value of output by the ratio of gross value added to gross value of output calculated from data in Liu-Yeh (1965, p. 140).

2. *Manufacturing factories.* Factory producer goods: Gross values added in 1957-59 are assumed to have increased at the same rate as the total gross value added of those products for which output estimates are available. The outputs of these products in 1957-59 are shown in Table A-2, and gross values added in 1957 are taken from Liu-Yeh (1965, p. 146).

   Factory consumer goods: According to *Jen-min shou-tse, 1958* (*People's Handbook,* Ta-kung-pao-she, Peking, 1958, 445), factories producing 20 per cent of the total output used largely industrial products as raw materials, and the rest consumed largely agricultural products. Gross values added in 1958-59 are calculated by applying the same percentages to gross value added in 1957, and extrapolating the gross values added of these two groups on the basis of the respective indexes of gross values added in factory producer goods and in agriculture.

3. *Handicrafts.* Gross values added by those handicrafts workers producing producer goods and those producing consumers goods in 1957 are first derived from total gross value added in 1957 (given in Liu-Yeh, 1965, p. 153) and the percentage shares of the two groups of products in total gross value of output (given in *Ta-kung pao,* July 17, 1959, p. 3). Gross values added in 1958-59 are derived on the assumption that those of handicraft producer goods increased in 1957-59 in the same proportion as those of factory producers' goods over the same period, and that those of consumer goods increased proportionately with agriculture.
4. *Mining.* Net values added in the production of coal, crude oil, iron ore, manganese ore, limestone, salt and tungsten ore in 1958-59 are based on the estimates for 1957 given by Liu-Yeh (1965, p. 573), and indexes of output for 1957-59 based on data in Table A-2. Net value added for other mineral products is assumed to have changed at the same rate as that of tungsten ore over the same period. The ratio of gross to net value added for all years is assumed to be the same as that for 1957 given in Liu-Yeh.
5. *Utilities.* Gross value added by the electric power industry is derived from the estimate for 1957 given by Liu-Yeh (1965, p. 585) and an index of electric power output in 1957-59 based on data in Table A-2. Estimates for water and gas are based on the estimate for 1957 given by Liu-Yeh (1965, p. 585) and an index of population in 1957-59. Total population in 1957 (637 million is taken from *TGY,* p. 11. Those for 1958-59 (652 and 665 million) are obtained by deducting the population of Taiwan given in United Nations *Statistical Yearbook, 1959* (p. 30); *Statistical Yearbook 1960* (p. 30) from the total population of mainland China and Taiwan given in *Ching-chi tao-pao* (*Economic Bulletin*), Hong Kong, No. 649 (Dec. 14, 1959, p. 11).
6. *Construction.* For estimate of gross value added in 1957, see Liu-Yeh (1965, p. 589). The index used for extrapolation is the combined index of cement, timber, rolled steel and glass consumed by construction in 1957-59. For output of cement, timber and glass, see Table A-2. The outputs of rolled steel in 1957-58 are taken from Kang Chao, 1965 (p. 127). The entire cement and glass output is assumed to have been used for construction. The percentages of timber and rolled steel output used for construction are based on data given in *JMJP,* Feb. 25, 1957 (p. 3), and *TCKT,* No. 13, 1957 (p.

2). Total consumption of rolled steel and glass in 1959 are assumed to have increased over 1958 by the same proportion as cement output. The weights used in obtaining the aggregate index are the gross value of these products consumed by construction. The prices used here are taken from: *HHPYK,* No. 5, 1958 (p. 73); *CHCC,* No. 11, 1957 (p. 24); *HHPYK,* No. 14, 1956 (p. 104); and Liu-Yeh, 1965 (p. 462).

7. *Trade, transportation, communications, and finance.* For gross value added in 1957, see Liu-Yeh, 1965 (pp. 161, 167, 607). Gross value added in 1957-59 is assumed to have changed in the same proportion as gross value added in agriculture, industry, mining, utilities, and construction as a whole over the same period.
8. *Government administration.* For gross value added in 1957, see Liu-Yeh, 1965 (p. 602). The index for 1957-59 is based on government expenditures on administration, defense, and social, cultural and educational expenses given in *TGY* (p. 23) and Li Hsien-nien, 1960. The budget figures are presumably in current prices and have not been deflated.
9. *Other personal services and residential rent.* For gross value added in 1957, see Liu-Yeh, 1965 (pp. 610, 612). The index of total population for 1957-59 cited above is used to derive the estimates for 1958-59.
10. *Work brigades.* For gross value added in 1957, see Liu-Yeh, 1965 (p. 66). I assume that 90 per cent of the total consisted of water conservation work, and the rest road-building and maintenance. The two components for 1957-59 are assumed to have changed at the same rates as gross value added in agriculture and in transportation over the same period respectively.
11. *Gross domestic product.* Sum of lines 1 to 10.

TABLE A-2

OUTPUT OF PRINCIPAL PRODUCTS, 1957-59

	1957	1958	1959
Agricultural products (in million piculs)			
Rice	1,736.0	1,800.0	1,604.0
Wheat	473.0	480.0	486.0
Miscellaneous grain	1,053.0	1,004.0	832.0
Potatoes[a]	438.0	586.0	432.0
Soybean	201.0	210.0	204.0

	1957	1958	1959
Peanuts	51.4	54.4	45.4
Rapeseed	17.8	21.8	19.0
Sesame	6.3	7.3	7.7
Cottonseed	65.6	61.7	58.0
Cotton	32.8	38.6	36.3
Hemp crops	9.9	10.7	10.7
Sugar cane	207.8	270.5	278.6
Sugar beet	30.0	58.0	73.7
Tobacco	13.0	15.4	15.4
Tea	2.2	2.8	3.0
Industrial products[b]			
Steel ingots (1,000) tons	5,350	6,885	8,630
Pig iron (1,000 tons)	5,900	7,530	9,450
Rolled steel (1,000 tons)	4,262	5,485	6,873
Machinery (million 1952 yuan)	6,177	7,710	11,210
Cement (1,000 tons)	6,690	9,300	12,270
Glass (1,000 sq. meters)	46,060	52,670	——[c]
Gunny sacks (1,000 pieces)	78,140	115,000	——
Paper (1,000 tons)	913	1,220	1,700
Ammonium sulfate (1,000 tons)	504	811	1,333
Caustic soda (1,000 tons)	198	270	360
Pure soda (1,000 tons)	506	640	851
Sulfuric acid (1,000 tons)	632	740	1,056
Auto tires (1,000 pieces)	879	1,747	——
Mineral products (1,000 tons)			
Coal	130,700	270,200	347,800
Crude oil	1,460	2,264	3,700
Iron ore	19,370	31,090	66,860
Manganese ore	210	255	300
Limestone	45,120	61,360	80,760
Salt	8,277	10,400	11,040
Tungsten ore	9	9	12
Other products			
Electric power (million kwh)	19,340	27,530	41,500
Timber (1,000 cu. meters)	27,870	35,000	41,200
Fishery products (1,000 piculs)	62,400	81,200	100,360

Notes:

a. In grain equivalent weight
b. Factory output only
c. . . . Not available

The sources and methods of estimating the output of the 38 products in 1958-59 shown in Table A-2 are as follows:

1. *Agricultural products.* Rice, wheat, miscellaneous grain, and potatoes: *Current Scene,* Hong Kong, I: 27, Jan. 15, 1964

(pp. 6-9). Soybean: *TGY* (p. 124), and an index based on data given in USDA, *Foreign Crops and Markets,* March 20, 1961 (p. 23). Peanuts: USDA, *Foreign Agriculture Circular,* July 20, 1960 (p. 1). Rapeseed: USDA, *Foreign Crops and Markets,* Dec. 29, 1960 (p. 9). Sesame: USDA, *Crops and Livestock,* June 28, 1962 (p. 25). Cottonseed: assumed to be twice that of cotton. Cotton: USDA, *Foreign Crops and Markets,* Dec. 27, 1960 (p. 6). Hemp crops: Liu-Yeh, 1965 (p. 662). Sugar cane and sugar beet: *TGY* (p. 124) and *CHYTC,* No. 1, 1960 (p. 27). Tobacco: USDA, *Foreign Crops and Markets,* Aug. 25, 1960 (p. 3). Tea: *TGY* (p. 125) and *CHYTC,* No. 1, 1960 (p. 27).

2. *Industrial products.* Steel ingot: Total productive capacity at the beginning of 1958 was 6.48 million tons and planned increase in capacity was 1.17 million tons (*TCYC,* No. 9, 1958, p. 4; *HHPYK,* No. 5, 1958, p. 16). Actual increase in capacity is assumed to be the same as planned increase. The planned output for 1958 was 6.25 million tons, indicating an average ratio of output to capacity of 83 per cent (*HHPYK,* No. 5, 1958, p. 18). The actual ratio is likely to be higher than 83 per cent because of the emphasis on steel production in the second half of 1958. But it should be somewhat less than 100 per cent because the new plants did not begin operation from the beginning of the year. Total output produced by factories is calculated on the assumption that the utilization rate was 90 per cent. Output in 1959 is obtained by deducting output of medium and small steel plants from total output given in *JMJP,* Jan. 23, 1960 (p. 1).

   Pig iron: Output in 1959 is derived in the same manner as steel output. Output in 1958 is obtained on the assumption that the ratio of pig iron to steel output in 1958 is the same as that in 1959.

   Rolled steel: Outputs in 1958-59 are assumed to have increased over 1957 in the same proportion as steel output over the same period.

   Machinery: For output in 1958, see Liu-Yeh, 1965 (p. 674). Output in 1959 is assumed to have increased over 1958 at the same rate as the total gross value of ten machinery products (lathes, locomotives, freight cars, trucks, merchant vessels, spindles, looms, bicycles, sewing machines and clocks). For output of these products, see Chao, 1965 (pp. 127-29). Prices of all products except those of lathes and trucks are 1952 prices taken from Chao, 1965 (p. 157). Those of lathes and trucks are respectively 1953 and 1960 prices taken from Ma Yin-chu, 1958 (p. 27); and E. Snow, 1961 (p. 204).

Cement and paper: Liu-Yeh, 1965 (p. 674).

Sheet glass, gunny sacks, ammonium sulfate, caustic soda, pure soda, sulfuric acid and auto tires, see Chao, 1965 (pp. 129-130).

3. *Mineral products.* Coal, crude oil and salt: *TGY* (pp. 95, 100), and *JMJP,* Jan. 23, 1960 (p. 1). Iron ore and limestone: Assumed to have increased over 1957 at the same rate as pig iron and cement respectively, given in *TGY* (pp. 95-96), and *JMJP,* Jan. 23, 1960 (p. 1). Maganese ore and tungsten ore: United Nations, *Statistical Yearbook, 1964,* (pp. 186, 196).
4. *Other products. TGY* (pp. 95-96, 100); *JMJP,* Jan. 23, 1960 (p. 1).

APPENDIX B

NOTES TO TABLE B-1

The basic data used to calculate the allocation of capital investment among four economic sectors in 1952-57 are summarized in Table B-1. The sources and methods used to derive the estimates in this table are as follows.

(1) *State Investment*

State investment includes both centralized and noncentralized investment. Centralized investment refers to investment expenditures on projects that come under the state plan, and is generally financed through the state budget. Noncentralized investment includes investment by the workers' union, cooperatives or state enterprises with bonuses and workers' welfare funds (Peng, 1957, p. 30). It is not exactly clear how productive and nonproductive investments are treated in the allocation of total state investment by economic sectors.[43] However, according to one official source, the classifications are "functional and not administrative" (*TGY,* p. 59). I therefore assume that such investments as residential houses built by state enterprises under the Ministries of Industry are listed under "other" investments rather than under "industry."

The data on allocation of state investment are primarily those of basic construction by the state. The Communist concept of basic construction is rather intricate and has not been clearly defined. A brief discussion here seems useful. According to the Communist definition, investment in basic construction ("basic construction" for short) refers to expenditures to increase fixed assets. It includes construction; purchases

43. For definitions of productive and nonproductive investment, see *TGY,* p. 64.

of equipment, tools and instruments; installation costs; and expenditures on engineering survey, design, and scientific experiments and research directly related to the construction project, expenditures to train personnel to operate the new project when completed, and compensation to former residents of the construction site for moving them out, etc. (FFYP, p. 23)

The Communist concept has the following characteristics: (a) Basic construction, often referred to as completed investment, includes new fixed assets (that is, completed plants that are ready to operate and have been inspected) and changes in unfinished construction.[44] But it does not include construction work in progress which has not reached a specified stage of partial completion or which has reached that stage but has not been inspected.[45]

(b) Not all tools and equipment are considered fixed assets. According to the regulation issued by the State Planning Commission in 1955, a fixed asset is one with a minimum serviceable life of one year and a minimum cost of 500 *yuan* for all enterprises except those under the Ministries of Geology and Agriculture, and the educational and cultural departments. The minimum cost standard for equipment purchased by the latter group was 200 *yuan*.[46] Draft animals are also included as fixed assets.[47]

(c) Engineering survey and design expenses were included in basic construction prior to 1955. After that they were considered as current expenses (*CHCC,* No. 8, 1956, p. 32). On the other hand, some ancillary expenses are in the nature of current expenses but have been included in basic construction. For example, expenditures involved in

44. The Chinese term for unfinished construction is *wei-wan kung-cheng*. It is used synonymously with "unfinished basic construction" and "finished construction work in progress." It includes: partially completed construction work that has been inspected, the total value of equipment being installed, the value of equipment and tools that do not require installation but have been shipped to the construction site, and completed plants that are ready to operate but have not yet been inspected. Hsu Chien *et al.,* 1957, pp. 129-30, 134-35; Yang Shih-chuan, 1956; *TCKT,* No. 24, 1957, p. 28.

45. Hsieh Mu-ch'iao, 1956 (p. 9). The Chinese term for construction work in progress is *wei-wan shih-kung. For definition,* see Hsu Chien *et al.,* 1957 and Hung Shih-chun, 1957. The difference between construction work in progress, unfinished construction, and new fixed assets may be illustrated as follows. If a project consists of laying a foundation, putting up walls, and covering the structure with a roof, the value of the unfinished foundation at any given point of time is "construction work in progress." After the foundation is completed and inspected, its value becomes "unfinished construction." After the whole building is completed and inspected, it becomes a "new fixed asset."

46. *TCKTTH,* No. 6, 1955 (p. 42). However, a regulation issued by the Ministry a minimum standard of 500 *yuan* was mentioned in 1957 (Yen Ts 'ui-yu, 1957). of Finance in 1956 set the minimum cost at 200 *yuan.* Hsu Chien *et al.,* 1957, p. 4. But a statement by an official of the Ministry of Machinery in 1956 indicated that the minimum was raised back to 500 *yuan* later (Li Yu, 1956, p. 198). Subsequently

47. Yueh Wei, "The Method of Computing National Income," *CCYC,* No. 3, 1956 (p. 63); *TCKT,* No. 24, 1956 (p. 29).

preparing the plant for production, such as purchases of raw materials and expenditures on trial operations, are included as investment if such expenditures are incurred before the plant is inspected and transferred by the construction unit to the enterprise concerned.[48]

(d) Housing construction under the military departments is included as basic construction.[49] But it is not clear whether other military construction and military equipment are included. Presumably the former is part of basic construction and the latter is listed under stockpiles.

(e) Basic construction does not include major repairs.[50] It is gross of depreciation allowances (*CHCC,* No. 12, 1956, p. 32). The treatment of temporary construction and work done by corvée labor is not clear. Included in the first item are repair shops, roads and dormitories on the construction site, some of which are removed after the project is completed. These expenditures have been referred to as investment and were said to account for about 5 per cent of basic construction (*HHYP,* No. 8, 1955, p. 285). There are references indicating that construction work by conscript labor and military servicemen is included in basic construction.[51] But some construction work is done without compensation to the workers.[52] It is not certain whether such work is also included in construction.

Table B-1 summarizes the estimates of total fixed investment. The sources and methods used to derive the estimates for 1952-57 in current prices are as follows:

1. *Total State Investment.* Included in this item are the centralized and noncentralized state investment. Total state investments in 1952-57 are taken from *TGY* (p. 55). As noted earlier, the figures for 1955-57 do not include project-making expenditures. According to *TCYC,* No. 2, 1958 (p. 36), these expenditures account for 2-3 per cent of total construction expenditures. Construction expenditures in 1955-57 are obtained by deducting investment in equipment from basic construction. Investments in equipment in 1955-56 are derived from data on basic construction in 1955, percentage share of equipment in basic construction

48. *TCKT,* No. 1, 1956 (p. 31); Yang Pang-chieh, "Proper Treatment of Expenses Involved in Production Preparation in Newly Constructed Enterprises," *CHCC,* No. 6, 1957 (p. 24).

49. *CHCC,* No. 12, 1956 (p. 32); Peng Yung-chuan, 1957 (p. 30).

50. Peng Yung-chuan, 1957 (p. 29); *TCKT,* No. 1, 1956 (p. 31).

51. Peng Yung-chuan, 1957 (p. 31); Lung Hua-jung, Chi Hsi-yung, and Chen Ming-kai, "Several Problems Concerning the Computation of Value Added by the Construction Industry," *TCKT,* No. 8, 1957 (p. 16).

52. For example, the labor working on the Huai River was classified into three types: free labor who received no payment for the work done or for the use of their own tools; semi-free labor who received subsidies of about 2 catties of wheat for each cubic meter of earth work done; and paid labor who received about 4 catties per cubic meter of earth work done (*Honan jih-pao* [*Honan Daily*], Kai-feng, January 7, 1951, p. 1). According to a survey of 228 cooperative farms in 1957, unpaid labor contributed by the peasants amounted to 1.5 per cent of their total labor days (SSB, "Data from a Representative Survey of the Distribution of Income in 228 Agricultural Cooperatives in 1957," *TCYC,* No. 8, 1958, p. 8).

TABLE B-1

FIXED INVESTMENT, 1952-57
(in billion of yuan in current prices)

	1952	1953	1954	1955	1956	1957
State investment:	4.36	8.00	9.07	9.46	15.05	14.04
Industry	1.85	3.39	4.48	4.87	7.87	8.00
Agriculture	0.60	0.77	0.42	0.62	1.19	1.19
Water conservation	0.41	0.48	0.22	0.41	0.71	0.73
Transport and communications	0.76	1.07	1.50	1.76	2.61	2.07
Railroad	0.51	0.65	0.95	1.22	1.76	1.34
Other						
Trade	0.12	0.27	0.39	0.35	0.76	0.37
Culture, education and research	0.28	0.62	0.68	0.59	1.00	0.92
Health and welfare	0.06	0.15	0.15	0.11	0.11	0.13
Public utilities	0.17	0.25	0.24	0.22	0.35	0.38
Government bureau	0.02	0.28	0.21	0.14	0.16	0.18
Other	0.50	1.20	1.00	0.64	0.75	0.59
Project-making expenditures	[b]	[b]	[b]	0.16	0.25	0.21
Nonstate investment:						
Farm investment	1.53	1.40	1.50	1.70	2.20	1.77
Equipment	0.34	0.46	0.56	0.63	0.99	0.67
Draft animals	0.42	0.36	0.27	0.12	—0.11	—0.15
Water conservation	0.45	0.25	0.34	0.62	0.96	0.89
Buildings [a]	0.33	0.33	0.34	0.34	0.35	0.35
Nonfarm investment	0.47	0.62	0.49	0.48	0.41	0.36
Factories and workshops	0.21	0.26	0.21	0.16	...... [c]	..... [c]
Handicrafts [a]	0.18	0.24	0.19	0.22	0.28	0.24
Traditional transportation [a]	0.08	0.12	0.09	0.10	0.13	0.12
Major repairs:	0.49	0.54	0.62	0.73	0.84	0.98
National economic sectors	0.34	0.38	0.46	0.56	0.66	0.80
Administrative, educational, social and health organizations	0.02	0.02	0.02	0.02	0.03	0.03
Residential houses	0.13	0.14	0.14	0.14	0.14	0.15
Total fixed investment	6.85	10.55	11.69	12.36	18.49	17.15

Notes:
a. Including major repairs.
b. Included in state investment.
c. . . . Negligible or none.

in 1955, and an index of equipment in 1956 with 1955 as 100, given in *TGY* (p. 55); *TCKT*, No. 18, 1956 (p. 4); *CSYK*, No. 3, 1957 (p. 3). The estimate for 1957 is based on the percentage shares of domestic machinery in total equipment purchases given in *TCKT*, No. 14, 1957 (p. 5) and *CHCC*, No. 2, 1958 (p. 8); and on the assumption that domestic supply of equipment in 1957 increased over 1956 by the same proportion as machinery output, given by Liu-Yeh, 1965 (p. 454).

2. *Nonstate Farm Investment.* Investment in equipment is the sum of farm purchases of: (a) insecticide equipment, (b) irrigation equipment, (c) traditional farm implements, and (d) modern farm implements. The estimates for 1953-56 are obtained by multiplying total retail sales of producer goods to the agricultural sector, given in *TGY* (p. 170), by the percentage share of these five items in the total retail sales, given in Chu Ching, Chu Chung-chien and Wang Chi-ming, 1957 (p. 41). Insecticide is included in the original data for item (a). I assume that one-half of the total represents noninvestment purchases. Estimates for 1952 and 1957 are based on those for 1953 and 1956, and indexes of sales of insecticide sprayers, power machines, total retail sales of producer goods, and two-wheel plows in 1952-53 and 1956-57 given in *TGY* (pp. 170-171). Note that investment derived by this method includes purchases for major repairs but does not include tools made by the peasants themselves.

Increase in large animals is derived by multiplying the increase in the numbers of cattle, horses, mules and donkeys in 1952-57 and their respective prices in 1952 as given by Liu-Yeh (pp. 364, 384). Prices in 1953-57 are lacking, but are assumed to be the same as those in 1952.

Investment in water conservation is derived by multiplying total earth work done in each year by the respective percentage of the total financed by peasants themselves, and by the cost per cubic meter of earth work done. Total volumes of work done in 1952-55 and the total for 1956-57 are taken from Liu-Yeh (p. 616). The annual figures for 1956-57 are derived from the total and an index of increase in irrigated area in 1956-57. The latter is based on increases in irrigated area in 1956-58, from October of a given year to September of the following year, given in *TGY* (p. 130). The figure for 1958 has been adjusted downwards according to a ratio of "effective" to total increase given in *HHPYK*, No. 11, 1958 (p. 15), and all figures have been converted to totals on a calendar year basis. The percentages of total earth work done by peasants for 1952-56 are assumed to be the same as the percentages of total increases in irrigated areas resulting from projects undertaken by the peasants given in *Chung-kuo shui-li* (*China's Water Conservation,* Peking, No. 10, 1956, p. 10). The figure for 1957 is lacking and is assumed to be the same as that for 1956. Since this percentage includes the cost of water wheels, the estimate is on the high side. The unit cost is obtained on the basis of labor cost per cubic meter given in Liu-Yeh (p. 618) and the proportion of total investment accounted for by labor in the peasants' irrigation projects given in *TCYC,* No. 5, 1958 (p. 19).

Investment in houses and other buildings is derived from an estimate for 1957 and an index of extrapolation for 1952-57. The former figure is based on the ratio of such investments to gross value of output computed from data in a survey of 228 cooperative farms in 1957, given in *TCYC,* No. 8, 1958 (pp. 8-12). Total investment in housing and other buildings in 1957 is then calculated by multiplying the average ratio by total gross value of agricultural output given in *TGY* (p. 118). It is assumed that these investments include major repairs of farm houses. The index used to derive investment for 1952-56 is based on the gross value added by agriculture given in Liu-Yeh (p. 140). For lack of data, no adjustment for price changes has been made. However, the effect of such changes is believed to be rather small.

3. *Nonstate Nonfarm Investment.* Factories and workshops: Increase in fixed capital in private, joint state-private enterprises, cooperatives and handicraft workshops during 1952-55 is given at 930 million *yuan* in SSB, 1957a (p. 32). Assuming that retirement of capital was negligible, I take this figure to represent the sum of investment in 1953-55. Assuming further that investment increased during this period at the same rate as the gross value of output of these enterprises over the same period, investment in 1953-55 can be calculated. By the same procedure, the estimate for 1952 is derived. For gross value of output in 1952-55, see *TGY* (p. 16) and SSB, *1956 Abstract* (pp. 26-27). Since investment in the joint state and private enterprises has already been included in state investment, the estimates derived by the procedure above are reduced by a factor equal to the percentage share of output of the joint enterprises in total output. For data on the percentage share, see *TGY* (p. 38).

Handicrafts and traditional transportation: Gross investments in these sectors in the rural area are first derived as follows. Total sales of wheelbarrows and handicraft equipment in 1953-56 are obtained by multiplying total retail sales of producer goods (*TGY,* p. 170) by the percentage shares of wheelbarrows, livestock, and materials for subsidiary work (Chu Ching, *et al.,* 1957.), and by assuming that transportation and handicraft equipment accounted for one-third of these purchases. Purchases in 1952 and 1957 are derived on the assumption that they varied in 1952-53 and 1956-57 in the same proportion as total sales of producer goods in the rural areas over the same period. These purchases are then split into those by handicraftsmen and by transportation workers according to the ratio of value added by these two groups (Liu-Yeh, p. 66).

Purchases by urban handicraftsmen are based on: (a) the assumption that gross investment per worker was the same in rural and urban areas; and (b) the ratio of rural to urban handicraft employment, given in Teng Chieh, 1958 (p. 9). Since retail sales included sales of parts for major repairs, I assume that these estimates also include major repairs. For the same reason, the estimates are probably on the high side because the retail sales included parts for ordinary repairs and maintenance. I assume that investment in all other sectors is negligible.

4. *Major repairs.* National economy: Included here are all the economic sectors except handicrafts and traditional transportation. See SSB, 1957a (p. 31). Total capital stock for the national economy and for the industrial sector in 1952-57 are first derived from data on (a) increases in total fixed assets and industrial fixed assets given in *TGY* (p. 66); (b) capital stock in industry in 1952, given in *TGY* (p. 93); and (c) the percentage share of industrial capital in total capital for the national economy in 1952, given in SSB, *Socialist Industrialization* (p. 59). According to *CHCC,* No. 4, 1958 (p. 28), funds for major repairs, collected presumably from state and semi-state industrial enterprises, amounted to 400 million *yuan* a year on the average. Dividing this total by the average industrial capital stock of these enterprises at the beginning of the year in 1955-57 (based on totals and percentage of totals in these enterprises in 1955, given in SSB, *Socialist Industrialiaztion* (p. 61), I obtain the ratio of major repair funds to capital stock, 1.82 per cent. I apply this percentage to total capital stock for the national economy in 1957 to derive total major repair funds. In general, not all the funds were expended. According to *Tsai-cheng* (*Public Finance*), No. 1, 1957 (pp. 11-12), the amount of unexpended funds was 42 per cent of major repair expenditures, implying that about 70 per cent of major repair funds was spent. I apply this percentage to total major repair funds in 1956-57 to obtain major repair expenditures in 1956-57. Expenditures in 1952-55 are calculated on the basis of the estimate for 1956 and total capital stock in 1952-56. The results are then deflated by the price index taken from Liu-Yeh (p. 235).

Administrative and other non-economic departments: Major repairs consisted largely of repair of buildings. In the absence of a better alternative I assume that major repairs amounted to one-half of depreciation in this sector. The data used in estimating the depreciation are taken from Liu-Yeh (pp. 204, 216, 602).

(c) I assume that major repairs amounted to the same as depreciation given in Liu-Yeh (p. 612). To allow for that part of the major repairs already included in nonstate farm investment in buildings, the estimate is lowered by a factor equal to the ratio of gross rent for rural housing to total gross rent given in Liu-Yeh (p. 610).

REFERENCES

BERGSON, A., 1964. *The Economics of Soviet Planning.* New Haven: Yale Univ. Press.

CHANG CHENG, 1956. "Improve and Apply the Method of Computing Completed Investment," *TCKTTH,* No. 7, p. 5.

CHAO, KANG, 1965. *The Rate and Pattern of Industrial Growth in Communist China.* Ann Arbor: Univ. of Michigan Press.

CHEKHUTOV, A. I., 1962. *Nalogovaya sistema Kitayskoy Narodnoy Respubliki (The Tax System in the People's Republic of China).* Moscow: Oriental Literature Publishing House. (JPRS translation No. 17675, p. 1129.)

CH'U CHING-HUI, 1957. "An Explanation of the Major Changes in the Tabulation Forms for the National Economic Plan," *CHCC,* No. 8, p. 25.

CHOU EN-LAI, 1956. "Report on the Second Five-Year Plan," *HHPYK,* No. 20.

CHU CHING, CHU CHUNG-CHIEN, and WANG CHI-MING, 1957. *Wor-kuo nung-tsun shih-chang ti kai-ch'u (The Reorganization of China's Rural Markets).* Peking.

ECKSTEIN, A., 1966. *Communist China's Economic Growth and Foreign Trade.* New York: McGraw-Hill.

EMERSON, JOHN P., 1965. *Nonagricultural Employment in Mainland China:* 1949-1958. Washington, D.C.: USGPO.

FFYP. Chung-hua jen-min kung-ho-kuo fa-chan kuo-min ching-chi ti ti-yi-ke wu-nien chi-hua. (The First Five-Year Plan for National Economic Development of the People's Republic of China). Peking, 1955

HAN PU, 1958. "Economize Agricultural Current Expenses," *CHCC,* No. 2, p. 18.

HOLLISTER, W. W., 1958. *China's Gross National Product and Social Accounts, 1950-1957.* Glencoe, Ill.: Free Press.

HSIEH MU-CH'IAO, 1956. *"How to Strengthen and Improve Basic Construction Work," TCKTTH,* No. 6, p. 8.

HSU CHIEN, TAI SHIH-KUANG, and YU TAO, 1957. *Ching-chi t'ung-chi-hsueh chian-hua (Lectures on Economic Statistics).* Peking: T'ung-chi chu-pan-she.

HUNG SHIH-CHUN, 1957. "How to Handle Construction in Progress," *TCKT,* No. 19, p. 14.

ISHIKAWA, SHIGERU, 1965. *National Income and Capital Formation in Mainland China.* Tokyo: Institute of Asian Economic Affairs.

KAPLAN, N., 1953. "Capital Formation and Allocation" in A. Bergson (ed.), *Soviet Economic Growth.* New York: Row, Peterson.

KAPLAN, N. *Capital Investments in the Soviet Economy* (unpublished).

KUZNETS, SIMON, 1960. *Quantitative Aspects of the Economic Growth of Nations.* Supplement to *Economic Development and Cultural Change,* Vol. III, No. 4, Part II, July, 1960.

KUZNETS, SIMON, 1965. *Economic Growth and Structure.* New York: Norton.

LI CHIEN, 1957. "Prepare the Investment Plan for 1957 on the Basis of National Financial and Material Resources," *CHCC,* No. 3, p. 4.

LI CHOH-MING, 1962. *The Statistical System of Communist China.* Berkeley and Los Angeles: Univ. of California Press.

LI FU-CHUN, 1957. "Report on the FFYP," *FFYP,* p. 190.

LI FU-CHUN, 1959. "The Great Leap in China's Socialist Construction," *Hung-chi,* No. 19, p. 35.

LI HSIEN-NIEN, 1960. "Report on the 1959 State Budget and the Draft Budget for 1960," *JMJP,* April 1, 1960.

LI YU, 1956. "Basic Construction Work in the First Machinery Ministry and the Tasks Ahead," in *Chi-pen chien-she wen-shuan* (*Selected Papers on Basic Construction*).

LIAO LU-YEN, 1956. "Explanations of the National Agricultural Development Program for 1956-57," *HHPYK,* No. 4, p. 9.

LIAO LU-YEN, 1960. "All Party Members and All People Develop Agriculture the Big Way," *Hung-chi,* No. 17, p. 2.

LIU JUNG-CHAO, 1965. "Fertilized Supply and Grain Production in Communist China," *Journal of Farm Economics,* Vol. 4, No. 4 (November), p. 925.

LIU, T. C., and K. C. YEH, 1965. *The Economy of the Chinese Mainland.* Princeton: Princeton Univ. Press.

LO KENG-MO, 1955. "Practice Economy Is a Major Condition for Successful Implementation of China's FFPY," *Hsueh-hsi,* No. 8, p. 3.

MA NAN-FANG, 1955. "Basic Construction Departments Should Really Economize," *HHYP,* No. 10, p. 173.

MA YIN-CHU, 1958. *Wo-ti ching-chi li-lun tse-hsueh si-hsian ho cheng-chi li-chang* (*My Economic Theory, Philosophy and Political Stand*). Peking.

OU PAO-SAN, 1947. *National Income of China, 1933, 1936, and 1946.* Nanking: Institute of Social Sciences, Academica Sinica.

PENG YUNG-CHUAN, 1957. "Tabulation Forms for Basic Construction Plans," *CHCC,* No. 5,

RICHARDSON, S. D., 1966. *Forestry in Communist China.* Baltimore: Johns Hopkins Press.

SNOW, E., 1961. *The Other Side of the River.* New York: Random House.

State Planning Commission, 1955. *Ti-yi-ke wu-nien-chi-hua ti ming-ts'u chieh-shih* (*Explanation of Terms Used in the First Five-Year Plan*). Peking: Jen-min chu-pan-she.

State Planning Commission, 1956. "Lessons from Drafting the 1956 Plan for Heavy Industry," *CHCC,* No. 7, 1956.

(SSB) State Statistical Bureau, 1955. "Summary Report on the National Basic Construction Statistical Work in 1954 and Basic Tasks for 1955," *HHYP,* No. 2, p. 136.

(SSB) State Statistical Bureau, 1956. *Wo-kuo kang-tieh, tien-li, mei-t'an, chi-hsieh, fang-chih, tsao-chi kung-yeh ti chin-hsi* (*Past and Present of China's Iron and Steel, Electric Power, Coal, Machinery, Textile and Paper Industries*). Peking.

(SSB) State Statistical Bureau, 1957a. "A General Survey of National Industrial Capital," *TCKT,* No. 1.

(SSB) State Statistical Bureau, 1957b. "Several Major Problems Concerning the Computation of Completed Investment in Basic Construction," *TCKT,* No. 10, p. 7.

(SSB) State Statistical Bureau, 1957c. "A General Survey of China's Socialist Industrialization." *HHPYK,* No. 2.

(SSB) State Statistical Bureau, 1959. "Communiqué on the Implementation of the FFYP," *HHPYK,* No. 8, p. 41.

SUNG SHAO-WEN, 1957. "The Policy of Diligence and Economy in Basic Construction," *Hsueh-hsi,* No. 11, p. 22.

(TGY) Ten Great Years, 1960. State Statistical Bureau, Peking: Foreign Language Press.

TENG CHIEH, 1958. *Chung-kuo shou-kung-yeh she-hui tsu-yi kai-tso ti chu-pu chung-chieh* (*A Preliminary Summary of the Socialist Transformation of China's Handicraft Industry*) Peking: Jen-min chu-pan-she.

TSO YEN-HSING, 1957. "Arrange Urban Construction Work According to the Guiding Principle of Building Our Country Industriously and Thriftily," *CHCC,* No. 12, p. 4.

United Nations. *Economic Survey of Asia and the Far East, 1957.* Bangkok, 1958.

United Nations. *Economic Survey of Asia and the Far East, 1960.* Bangkok, 1961.

United Nations. *Economic Survey of Asia and the Far East, 1961.* Bangkok, 1962.

United Nations, 1961. *World Economic Survey 1960.* New York.

United Nations. *Yearbook of National Accounts Statistics, 1958.* New York, 1959.

United Nations. *Yearbook of National Accounts Statistics, 1963.* New York, 1964.

United Nations, 1965. *Statistical Yearbook 1964.* New York.

WANG HSING-FU and LAN CHIEN-CHIAO, 1957. "Develop the Chemical Fertilizer Industry," *CHCC,* No. 10, p. 12.

WANG KUANG-WEI, 1958. "The Problem of Modernizing China's Agriculture," *Hsueh-hsi,* No. 1, p. 19.

WU, Y. L., F. P. HOEBER, and M. M. ROCKWELL, 1964. *The Economic Potential of Communist China,* Vol. 3. Menlo Park, Calif.: Stanford Research Institute.

YANG CHIEN-PAI, 1955. "An Analysis of the Chinese and Soviet FFYP," *HHYP,* No. 9, p. 194.

YANG SHIH-CHUAN, 1956. "Unfinished Construction," *TCKTTH,* No. 1, pp. 29–30.

YANG YING-CHIEH, 1955. "Coordinated Development of Newly Constructed and Eixsting Enterprises," *Hsueh-hsi,* No. 8, p. 8.

YEH, K. C., 1964. *Capital Formation in Mainland China, 1931-36 and 1952-57.* (Unpublished.)

YEN TS'UI-YU, 1957. "The Standard of Fixed Assets and the Authority of the Enterprises," *CHCC,* No. 6, p. 23.

YI LIN, 1957. "Several Problems Concerning the Effectiveness of Investment in Industrial Construction," *CHCC,* No. 6, p. 5.

Policies and Performance in Industry 9

KANG CHAO

I. INTRODUCTION

FROM THE OUTSET of the Communist regime, it has been the cherished desire of the Party leadership to convert the backward agricultural economy of China into an industrial nation on a socialist basis; with all means of production to be eventually owned by the state and all economic activities carried out through centralized planning. Socialization of the private sector was carried out gradually and subtly in the first few years under the so-called "Common Program," but it was greatly accelerated after 1952 when the Communist Party clearly saw that its control over the whole nation had become firmly established. The transitional period ended in 1956-57 when practically all private enterprises in China had been socialized in one form or another.

In economic planning, a regional Financial and Economic Commission was formed in 1949 in the Northeastern provinces (Manchuria), working out the first sketchy plan for that region; but only in 1951 was a national economic plan formulated by the central government in Peking. The economic plans of 1951 and 1952 were confined primarily to production and capital construction of state enterprises. With the establishment of the State Planning Commission and the State Statistical Bureau in 1952, planning in Communist China entered a new stage. The period of rehabilitation officially ended in 1952, and the Peking government announced that the First Five-Year Plan (FFYP) for the development of the national economy would begin in 1953 (*JMJP*, Jan. 1, 1953). The actual work of drawing up this long-term economic plan took considerable time; and all the details, after repeated supplementations and revisions, were not finalized until February, 1955, and were promulgated a few months later. Thus economic planning in the first two years of the plan (1953-54) was actually operated on a year-to-year basis.

One of the reasons given by the Chinese Communist authorities for the delay in formulating the final version of the plan was lack of statistical

The author is indebted to Professors Ta-Chung Liu, Joseph S. Berliner, M. Gardner Clark, and Chu-yuan Cheng for many useful suggestions.

data with which a consistent plan on a national scale could be mapped out (Li Fu-chun, 1955). This, though true, could not have been a decisive factor in view of the fact that the Second Five-Year Plan, drawn up in 1956-57, was much less detailed than the first plan, although by then the planning commission must have had more and better statistical information about the economy. Even the handful of proposed targets in the Second Five-Year Plan underwent frequent readjustment shortly after its publication. This would seem to indicate that the government did not intend the five-year plans, but only the annual ones, to be binding.

The Korean War and negotiations with the Soviet Union in regard to Soviet aid projects were officially cited as the other factors responsible for the delay (Li Fu-chun, 1955). The uncertainty as to whether a truce would be concluded in Korea made it very difficult for the Chinese authorities to decide on the scale of future capital construction and on the locations of new industries. It was not until May, 1953, that any agreement was reached between the Soviet Union and Communist China concerning most of the 156 Soviet aid projects that were supposed to be the core of the First Five-Year Plan.

In this connection there was possibly another important factor which has never been openly mentioned by the Chinese Communists. There is some indication that a strong clique, presumably led by Kao Kang and Yao Shu-shih, existed within the Chinese Communist Party in the early years, favoring regionalism rather than a completely integrated economy. When Kao and Yao were purged the whole issue was described as a purely political one. But it is unlikely that Kao and Yao were so naive as to hope to build "independent kingdoms" within a Communist country only in the political sense, without simultaneously demanding a high degree of autonomy over economic matters in their territories. As Kao and Yao were the administrative heads of the two richest and most industrialized areas in China, the Northeastern provinces and the Eastern provinces, their opposition to complete economic integration would be quite natural. It would inevitably level off the advantages of those two prosperous areas and call for them to subsidize the other relatively backward provinces. Although Yao Shu-shih never openly expressed an attitude favoring economic regionalism, Kao Kang's desire for this had been apparent for some time. Kao even negotiated with the Soviet Union and finally signed a trade agreement in July, 1949, between the Northeast People's Government of China and the Soviet Union (*JMJP,* July 30, 1949), in defiance of the established international tradition that no local or regional government of a country should sign any treaty or agreement with a foreign government. It is very possible, therefore, that the abolition of large administrative regions in 1953 and the liquidation of Kao and Yao in 1954 removed the last major obstacles to nationally integrated economic planning as embodied in the First Five-Year Plan.

So far as industry is concerned, the outcome of the first plan may be considered generally satisfactory. Achievements in heavy industry were very good; the targets set for light industry, though relatively moderate, were reported to have been fulfilled or surpassed. Planning and control of basic construction, material balances and allocation, state budgets, bank credits and industrial administration were all systematized or improved in that period. It was against this background the Second Five-Year Plan was proposed, supposedly for the period 1958-62 (*JMJP,* July 7, 1956; Sept. 19, 1956). The published version of that proposal was stated only in terms of control figures, such as targets for major products and the percentage distribution of basic construction investment. No detailed draft of the plan was ever submitted to the National People's Congress.

The original targets set for the second plan were no more ambitious than those in the first. However, only shortly after the plan was accepted by the State Council it was readjusted (*JMJP,* Dec. 8, 1957), with targets scaled down for some items and raised for others. Even these revisions were temporary, as the Second Five-Year Plan was virtually abandoned in mid-1958 when the nationwide Great Leap Forward and commune movements were launched. A new set of targets, much higher than the original ones, was announced in August, 1959. Yet only a few months later, Peking discovered that even the newly revised targets for some key items had been fulfilled by the end of 1959, or three years ahead of schedule. This led to a "Supplementary Plan for the Last Three Years of the Second Five-Year Plan," which has never been revealed to the public.

The seemingly joyous but actually chaotic situation in the Great Leap years was immediately followed by a rapidly deepening agricultural crisis that soon affected both industrial production and basic construction. The situation was aggravated in July, 1960, by the sudden withdrawal of all Soviet experts from China as a result of the rift in Sino-Soviet relations. To prevent the economy from collapsing, the Communist leadership was forced to announce the policies of "readjustment, consolidation, reinforcement and improvement" at the beginning of 1962. An "Adjusted Plan for the Last Two Years of the Second Five-Year Plan" was mentioned at the National People's Congress in April, 1963 (already a few months after the official termination of the plan), but no detailed information was given.

Practically, one may say that there was no one thing that could be called *the* Second Five-Year Plan in Communist China. What the country had in 1958-60 were several annual plans. And for 1961 and 1962 it is even questionable whether the Peking government really had concrete plans on even an annual basis, because no Chinese Communist newspapers ever mentioned the term "annual production quota" for any item in those two years. It would seem that the approval of the "Adjusted Plan for the Last Two Years of the Second Five-Year Plan" in 1963 was simply an ex post facto recognition of whatever had resulted by the end of 1962. Moreover, Chou En-lai later declared that the Third Five-Year Plan would begin in 1966 (Chou En-lai, 1964). This leaves a three-year lapse (1963-65) unaccounted for by any five-year plan. Presumably, the government was again operating on an annual basis in economic matters during these three years.

II. POLICIES

Although the principal theme of industrializing the economy on a socialist basis has remained constant during the Communist regime in China, specific policies have varied. Sometimes Peking has explicitly articulated its economic policies; on other occasions, especially when drastic reshaping of policies was involved, statements by the Communist leaders have been phrased in a dialectical manner and have been so ambiguous that their real intentions could hardly be understood by unaccustomed readers. Most of the important and interesting policy changes came in a single year, 1958. This section attempts to examine the specific policies adopted by the Communists in China during the various periods in its industrial development.

POLICIES CONCERNING THE DIRECTION OF DEVELOPMENT

The only unmistakably clear and consistent policy of the Communist authorities throughout the whole period has been their intention of developing a "comprehensive and independent industrial system" in China. It was originally hoped that this ultimate goal would be basically accomplished by the end of the Third Five-Year Plan. It has been used by the planners as a guiding principle in formulating economic plans, but it also has had very important international implications. To be consistent with this principle, Communist China must reject any suggestion of international division of labor among the Communist bloc countries. As early as 1955, Li Fu-chun, in his report on the First Five-Year Plan, pointed out:

> Some people say—since our international environment is different from the situation which existed after the revolution of the Soviet Union, and we have the assistance of the Soviet Union and the People's Democracies, why should we make haste over industrialization? We consider this view erroneous. (*JMJP*, July 8, 1955.)

This issue has been elaborated by Tseng Wen-ching, who spends an entire section in his book (1958, pp. 57-66) explaining why China should develop its own comprehensive and independent industrial system and why it should stay outside the scheme of international division of labor among the Communist countries. He gives nine reasons for rejecting the idea that China should follow the pattern of the European "people's democracies," in which a country specializes in those sectors that are relatively advantageous. Some of the reasons, advanced by Tseng and summarized below, are quite plausible on economic grounds:

(1) Unlike the European Communist countries, China has a large population, vast natural resources and a huge domestic market, and these constitute an excellent basis for the development of a comprehensive industrial system.

(2) The much smaller European bloc countries might be unable to supply sufficient quantities of goods needed by China should she decide to join the scheme of international specialization within the bloc.

(3) Since China is so distant from the production centers in the European bloc countries, and, for this matter, in the Soviet Union as well, the high transportation costs permanently involved in shipping large quantities of goods between China and other Communist countries would offset the Ricardian type of economic gain stemming from an international division of labor.

Communist China's insistence on having an independent industrial system is also motivated by political and military considerations. A few years ago it was not clear as to the identity of the "some people" and "some comrades" that Li Fu-chun and Tseng Wen-ching were trying to refute. Now we know this includes the Soviet "comrades" who have opposed the direction of China's industrialization policy. Indeed, this conflict of interests between the Chinese and Soviet Party leaders over the direction of Chinese economic development has been one of the major causes of the current Sino-Soviet rift. A letter from the Chinese Communist Party to the Communist Party of the Soviet Union, published in June, 1963, contains the following passage:

> If, proceeding only from its own partial interest, any socialist country unilaterally demands that other fraternal countries submit to its needs, and uses the pretext of opposing what they call "going it alone" and "nationalism" to prevent other fraternal countries applying the principle of relying mainly on their own efforts in their construction and from developing their economy on the basis of independence, or even goes the length of putting economic pressure on other fraternal countries—then these are pure manifestations of national egoism.
>
> Such economic cooperation [of socialist countries] must be based on the principle of complete equality, mutual benefit and comradely mutual assistance.
>
> It would be great-power chauvinism to deny these basic principles and, in the name of "international division of labor" or "specialization," to impose one's own will on others, infringe on the independence and sovereignty of fraternal countries or harm the interest of their people. (*Peking Review,* 1963)

In another letter the Chinese Communist Party made a stronger and more pointed attack on the Soviet leadership on this issue:

> You constantly accuse us of "going it alone" and claim that you stand for extensive economic ties and divisions of labor among the socialist countries. But what is your actual record in this respect?
>
> You infringe the independence and sovereignty of fraternal countries and oppose their efforts to develop their economy on an independent basis in accordance with their own needs and potentialities.
>
> You bully those fraternal countries whose economies are less advanced and oppose their policy of industrialization and try to force them to remain agricultural countries and serve as your sources of raw materials and as outlets for your goods. (*Peking Review,* 1964)

Until recently we could only surmise [1] without any concrete evidence that Communist China had not formally joined the Council of Mutual Economic Assistance because it feared that participation in this organization, which is designed to promote international division of labor and production specialization among Communist countries, might hinder its pursuit of a comprehensive industrial system. This is again revealed by the publication of the letters just quoted. For instance, the following passage occurs in a letter published in the *Peking Review* in May, 1964:

> Moreover, you have introduced the jungle law of the capitalist world into relations between socialist countries. You openly follow the example of the Common Market which was organized by monopoly capitalist groups.
>
> In the economic, scientific, technical, and cultural spheres, we stand for relations of cooperation of a new type, based on genuine equality and mutual benefit, between China and the Soviet Union and among all the socialist countries.
>
> We hold that it is necessary to transform the present Council of Mutual Economic Assistance of socialist countries to accord with the principle of proletarian internationalism and turn this organization, which is now solely controlled by the leaders of the *CPSU,* into one based on genuine equality and benefit, which the fraternal countries of the socialist camp may join of their own free will.

The outcry about establishing a comprehensive and independent industry has appeared more frequently in Chinese publications and official statements in recent years. It is not that the deteriorating Sino-Soviet relations have forced the Chinese Communists to alter their fundamental developmental policy, but that since the dispute is now public, the Chinese no longer refrain from openly and frankly expressing their real intention. (It is ironical that the result of the dispute is to justify the Chinese position that initiated it.)

Given this ultimate goal of industrialization, it remained to be de-

1. For instance, one East German book says "China is not a member of CMEA because of her peculiar conditions of economic development." See Kohlmey, 1956 (p. 98).

cided by the planners which industry should have highest priority. During the whole First Five-Year Plan period, heavy industry received about 89 per cent of the investment funds earmarked for industrial construction. One reason for this was that though the whole industrial sector in China was extremely backward by any modern standard, heavy industry was the weakest link within the industrial system. The Chinese economy could never be independent in the general sense if industry was to be developed on the old pattern. It was also pointed out that investment in light industry should be kept to the minimum since a very large proportion of its existing capacity was still untapped. Military considerations, such as armament production, were another vital factor underlying their "heavy industry first" policy.

Although this policy was not totally invalid, it was carried to extremes. By 1957, the Communist leaders recognized that the neglected agricultural and light industrial sectors were retarding progress. Some corrective action had to be taken. Reluctant to give up the priority of heavy industry, the Communist authorities began in 1958 to experiment with a new idea by which China could step up the output of agriculture and light industry without a considerable draining of investment funds from heavy industry.

The bumper crop and the seemingly miraculous achievements of the Great Leap Forward in 1958 provided an illusory optimism for the leaders in Peking and they failed to observe the malaise already developing. It was in late 1959 and 1960 that a sharp decline in farm output occurred, because of the combination of widespread natural calamities and adverse human factors such as the effects of communization. This was followed by a drastic setback in production of light industry, 70-80 per cent of which depended on agricultural products as raw materials (*Hung-chi,* 1961, No. 6, p. 9). The shrinking output of agriculture and light industry dried up the sources of investment funds, which in turn reduced the demand for producer goods. It also greatly weakened China's ability to import producer goods and materials needed for economic construction.

During the period from late 1959 to the end of 1961, the policies of Communist China were most confusing. Official documents and semi-official writings related to economic issues were often ambiguous or even contradictory. The uncertainty of the Chinese government in putting forth any new and clear-cut economic policy to cope with the crisis was probably due to the following factors: (1) The extreme chaos in economic statistics, created by the Great Leap movement, was an obstacle to accurate assessment of the severity of the crisis.[2] (2) An understandable

2. For example, the SSB *Communiqué* (*JMJP,* Jan. 23, 1960) claimed that all major crops increased in 1959, resulting in a rise of 16.7 per cent in the gross value of agricultural output over 1958. But all official documents released thereafter insisted that "natural calamities unprecedented in 100 years" began in 1959 and lasted for three consecutive years.

reluctance probably existed among the leaders of the regime to admit their own mistakes and to renounce a policy that had received so much publicity in the past. (3) There was controversy among the leading Communist economists over precisely what new policy should be adopted.[3] The reshaping of economic policy was finalized in late 1961 and made public in early 1962. In Chou En-lai's report of April 17, 1962, the descending order of priority was clearly given as agriculture, light industry and, lastly, heavy industry.

Within the industrial sector itself several noticeable shifts in emphasis among individual branches have taken place since 1957. Until that time production of machinery was of primary importance, but the result was that steel output lagged behind the machine-producing industry (Chi Chung-wei, 1957; *TCKTTH,* 1956b) which used steel as its main material. Instead of decelerating expansion of the machine-producing industry, the Communist leaders launched the fantastic movement of "all people to steel" in 1958-59. It created, among other damaging effects on the economy, new bottlenecks in the industrial system. Thus, more recently, the new economic policy not only called for a general retrenchment in industrial investment and output, but also attached more importance to the extractive industries (Po I-po, 1962), including iron ore, coal and petroleum, which provide the necessary materials and fuel for the processing industries. The extractive industries are indeed a very fundamental bottleneck within China's heavy industry. Unlike manufacturing and processing industries, development of extractive industries depend not only on the planners' will and the availability of investment funds but also, more decisively, on the existence of underground resources and geological knowledge about them. Much of the delay in developing the extractive industries of Communist China has been due to the lack of comprehensive geological surveys of underground resources.

Another change in the last few years can be expressed in the underlying theme of "industry to support agriculture." A great portion of resources within the heavy industry sector has been devoted to the production of tractors, other farm machinery and tools, and chemical fer-

3. One group asserted that the principle of a balanced state budget should not be held as immutable and that during a period of agricultural setback the government should keep on investing, through deficit financing, in those sectors that do not depend on agriculture for raw materials. This argument is, in effect, an adaptation of the Keynesian theory in a Communist economy. Another group of economists held that the investment plan should not be curtailed only because of an anticipated shortage of materials. If the shortage did take place, they argued, budget appropriations for investment purposes would automatically become a budgetary surplus or unspent funds simply because there would be nothing on which the excess funds could be spent. And this would be no more harmful than planned curtailment in investment. This argument has been labelled the "theory of automatic balancing." Both groups have since been criticized by the authorities as erroneous.

tilizers. Consequently, these items have shown a very high rate of increase in the past few years despite general retrenchment in the industrial sector.

Third, Communist planners show a strong desire to reduce the dependence of China's industry on agriculture. This is manifested in their endeavor to build up the synthetic fiber and plastic industries as new sources of raw materials for consumer goods production. They have even attempted, but not very successfully, to grow large quantities of certain wild fibrous plants on land such as the saline area around Tsing-hai Lake, which is unfavorable, or impossible, for ordinary farming. It was hoped that these plants might eventually be used as a substitute for cotton needed in the textile industry.

Fourth, there has been a new drive in recent years to raise the quality and variety of industrial goods. It is partly a measure to correct the deteriorating trend that has existed in this aspect ever since the Great Leap Forward, and partly a means of coping with the mounting difficulties of importing the necessary high-quality producer goods.

In general, during the entire Communist period, the principle of constructing an independent and comprehensive industrial system has remained unchanged. The major problems encountered by the planners have been how to maintain an equilibrium among various branches of industry on the one hand, and between industry and agriculture on the other. In deciding and executing specific policies within this framework, the Communist hierarchy at times miscalculated in one direction or another, and was immediately faced with the problem of how and what corrective measure to take in order to readjust the economic machinery and restore balance.

POLICIES CONCERNING GEOGRAPHICAL DISTRIBUTION OF INDUSTRIES

Modern industry emerged in China in the late nineteenth and early twentieth centuries against a peculiar background. Virtually all foreign firms in China, as well as Chinese firms with some foreign connections, were established in or around the treaty ports. In order to take advantage of external economy and the ease with which skilled labor could be obtained, most Chinese enterprises with native capital were also concentrated in the coastal area. This peculiar pattern of geographical distribution of industry remained the same when the Chinese Communists came to power. According to the official statistics, 73.1 per cent of the total gross value of industrial output in 1952 came from seven coastal provinces, with Shanghai, Tientsin, Tsingtao, Shenyang and Canton as centers. The proportion was particularly high for the major products: 85.5 per cent for steel; 82.6 per cent for cotton yarns; 88.3 per cent for cotton cloth and almost 100 per cent for the machine-producing industry.[4]

Communist planners held this situation to be undesirable on the following grounds. First, most factories in the coastal area were too far away from domestic sources of raw materials. For instance, while more than 80 per cent of the cotton spindles and nearly 90 per cent of the power looms were in the coastal area (SSB, 1958, p. 150), the neighboring provinces supplied only a small portion of the cotton needed. Flour mills were similarly concentrated in a few coastal cities which were far away from the major wheat-growing areas in China. Previously, the mills had depended on imported wheat, but since 1959 they had faced serious shortages of raw material due to the discontinuation of wheat importation. As a result, a considerable portion of the flour-milling facilities in Shanghai and Tientsin were left idle. Furthermore, the unreasonable location of industry imposed a great burden on the transportation system which had to convey raw materials and finished goods for considerable distances between the coastal area and inland China.

Second, since any enemy of Communist China would presumably attack from the sea in case of war, and the Communist Chinese navy was particularly weak, the Party leaders thought the coastal area to be strategically vulnerable. It was feared, therefore, that concentration of industry in that area might someday jeopardize the whole economy. The Sino-Japanese War had already proved this to be a very real threat.

Consequently, in the First Five-Year Plan a policy was enunciated locating new industries in the inland cities close to their sources of raw materials, their fuel supply and their consumption centers. The inland area was also preferable from a military point of view. According to a prospective plan, the schedule would be as follows (Tseng, 1958, pp. 260-62, 266): During the period of the First Five-Year Plan large industrial projects should be rapidly carried out in central China and Inner Mongolia, which were adjacent to, and could conveniently get support from, the old industrial bases in the coastal provinces. In the meantime, preparatory work should begin in the southwest and northwest. The plan entailed the building of two iron and steel production bases in Paotow and Wuhan, several new machine-producing centers in Harbin, Tsitsihar, Changchun and Loyang, and one petroleum-refining center in Lanchow. In the period of the Second Five-Year Plan, construction work was to be moved further inland to the southwest and northwest and around the Sanmen Gorge. By then the new industrial bases in Paotow and Wuhan would be completed, and able to give support from a shorter distance to the new con-

4. For detailed statistics pertaining to geographical distribution of industry in the early years see Tseng, 1958 (pp. 256-57); *TCKTTH,* No. 21, 1956 (pp. 6, 7); and Yang Ching-wen, 1957b.

struction projects in the areas further inland. The next step was to develop the petroleum industry and nonferrous metal industry in Sinkiang on a large scale and to open up industries in Tibet.

Geographically, the whole blueprint is said to be coordinated with the general direction of development in the Soviet Union (Tseng, 1958, pp. 270-71). Taking the Communist bloc as a geographical entity, industrial activities are concentrated in the European region and the Pacific coast, leaving the central section of the Asian continent as an industrial vacuum. The general direction of development in the Soviet Union as manifested in its previous five-year plans has been a gradual moving of construction activities from the west toward the eastern border. In Communist China construction activities would proceed in a reverse direction, *i.e.,* from the east coast to the west. Eventually, the central vacuum would be filled, and the industries of the two countries would be linked up geographically.

In order to implement the policy, 55.3 per cent of industrial investment during the First Five-Year Plan period was in inland China, and 44.7 per cent on the coast. Most of the investment in the coastal area was for reconstruction of existing plants. Considering investment in new industrial enterprises only, 73.9 per cent was for the inland provinces (*TCKTTH,* 1956a). Similarly, of the 694 above-norm industrial projects to be constructed during the period, 472 were distributed inland (Tseng, 1958, p. 260).

Beginning in 1956, the validity of the relocation principle was challenged by a group of people including some responsible planning personnel. It was observed that this policy had been carried to extremes and that existing plants had been neglected; most of those in the coastal area were not yet fully utilized.[5] An extreme case was Shanghai where there was actually disinvestment in 1955.[6] This group also pointed out that virtually all new plants to be built inland had to be accompanied by huge overhead investment in transportation and utilities, whereas expansion of old plants or construction of new ones along the coast did not require much overhead investment because of the utilities and transportation network already existing in that area. Even after the new inland industries were completed, their operation costs would remain high in the foreseeable future. For instance, the wage level in the Tsaidam Basin area (in north-

5. According to a study made in 1956, among the 40 important products surveyed in Shanghai, the utilization rate of production facilities was 40-80 per cent for 19 items and below 40 per cent for 16 items. In Tientsin, among the 38 major products surveyed, the utilization rate was below 40 per cent for 15 items, between 40 per cent and 60 per cent for 17 items, and above 60 per cent for only 6 items. See Tseng, 1958 (p. 264). Statistics of a similar nature were also revealed in *TCKTTH,* 1956b.

6. That is, the gross industrial investment fell short of the depreciation of fixed capital assets in that area. See *TCKTTH,* 1956b.

west China) is almost four times the national average.[7] The high labor costs in those industries tend to offset the advantage of close sources of raw materials. Furthermore, in the early stages of construction the bulk of fuel and building materials had to be transported from the coastal production centers to the sites of new projects. This created serious congestion in the transportation system.[8]

The improved international situation after the truce in Korea made imminent war unlikely. It was also pointed out that in modern warfare the geographical distance from the enemy did not matter too much, and the interior was just as vulnerable as the coast (Sha Ying, 1956). Therefore, the argument of greater inland security had much less validity.

A new policy was adopted in 1956, aiming at a "balanced development" between the two areas. In 1956-57 coastal industries showed a relatively high rate of growth (*TCKTTH,* 1956b), mostly due to expansion of existing plants. At the same time, 73 new projects were added in the coastal area over and above what had been originally planned.[9]

However, this new policy was of short duration. Beginning in 1958, development of the interior was reemphasized. The new argument was that long-run economic advantages stemming from reasonable industrial relocation should outweigh short-run cost considerations. Moreover, careful investigations showed that even the allegedly smaller investment per unit of production capacity in developing coastal industries was illusory. In most new industrial bases in the interior, the investing unit had to bear the capital outlays for construction of the plan itself and overhead items such as water and power supplies. But in the erection of a new plant in a coastal city, the municipal government was held responsible for the overhead investment in additional water and power supply systems. There was very little or no real saving in total investment in further developing coastal industries (Tsao Yen-hsing, 1958). Although some coastal localities had excess capacity in their public utilities that could accommodate new enterprises, this excess had rapidly been absorbed in one or two years under the large-scale expansion of industry. It was certain that by 1958 any new construction on the coast would require accompanying overhead investment.

Another policy adopted in 1958 in regard to geographical distribution of production activities was the dispersal of industries, both coastal and

7. In order to attract enough skilled workers and technicians the government had to pay a substantial "hardship allowance" to employees in the remote area. See *Lao-tung,* No. 7, 1956 (pp. 33-34); and *Shih-yu kan-tan,* No. 4, 1958 (pp. 2-5).

8. The average haul for all building materials rose by 70 per cent in 1953-56. For cement the average haul increased from 537 kilometers in 1953 to 916 kilometers in 1956. See *Chien-chu tsai-liao kung-yeh,* No. 3, 1958 (p. 15). The average haul of coal increased from 323 kilometers in 1952 to 389 kilometers in 1957. See Chin Yu-cheng, 1958.

9. A smaller number (58) of new projects was added to the original plan for the interior; see Yang Ching-wen, 1957b.

inland (Tsao, 1958). Up to 1957, virtually all new plants clustered in cities. Consequently, the number of cities with populations over one million increased from 9 in 1952 to 14 in 1957 (*Ten Great Years,* p. 13). Some of these large cities had already reached the size of increasing diseconomy, and any further expansion ought to be avoided. The policy of dispersing industries was soon reinforced by the "walking with two legs" and communization movements.

POLICIES CONCERNING INDUSTRIAL ADMINISTRATION AND MANAGEMENT

With socialized ownership of the means of production, industrial administration forms a major part of public administration in Communist China. In general, one may label the system before 1958 as "centralized," and that since 1958 as "decentralized." But neither centralization nor decentralization in the two periods has been as extensive as some people have believed.

Before the so-called "socialist transformation" of the private sector in the urban area was completed, the widespread private enterprises and cooperative workshops made complete centralization of planning and administration impossible. Several industrial ministries were set up in the central government to deal with the nationalized sector. In the early years (1949-53), however, due both to lack of experience in industrial administration on the part of the central industrial ministries and to some resistance from the regional governments, Peking had no real control over state enterprises [10] except for those located in the north China region. In the other six large administrative regions, the central government had to "entrust" the People's Government or the Military and Political Committee in each region with complete authority over their own industrial enterprises. Each regional government had its own industrial ministries to exercise the administrative power vested in it.

This arrangement came into being against the special background of the highly autonomous regional Communist authorities during the civil war period. However, having learned from the modern Chinese history about the instability of a weak central government with strong regional or provincial governments, the top leaders in the Party resolved to reduce the military, political and economic powers of the lower-level governments. For economic matters in particular, the highly centralized system of the Soviet Union furnished a good model for China to imitate.

As the first step to overcoming the obstacles of regionalism, the regional People's Governments or the Military and Political Committees were replaced in 1953 by seven regional Administration Committees

10. For the history of industrial administration in the early years of the Communist regime, see Wang Hung-ting and others, "A Great Reform in Our Country's Industrial Administration System," *Tsai-ching yen-chiu,* No. 1, 1958 (pp. 35-37).

which were less powerful than their predecessors (*Jen-min shou-tse,* 1953, p. 182). Industrial ministries under the previous regional governments were reorganized into various less powerful industrial bureaus. All state enterprises were then divided into two categories: central state enterprises, which were to be governed directly by the central government's industrial ministries; and local state enterprises, which were to be subordinate to various industrial bureaus in each regional government. In 1954 these Administrative Committees of the seven large regions were abolished. Jurisdiction over local state enterprises was transferred to provincial or municipal governments.

By 1954 centralized control of industry had been set up, but it was far from complete. In 1954, 57 per cent of the total gross value of industrial output was from local state enterprises, private firms and co-operative industries, while only 43 per cent was accounted for by centrally controlled enterprises (*JMJP* editorial, March 2, 1955). It should be noted, however, that this proportion somewhat understates the relative importance of central state enterprises. Since local state enterprises were generally small in size, with a lower degree of vertical integration than central state enterprises, the gross output value of the former must contain much more double counting than the latter. The true proportions were probably an equal percentage of the total gross value.

The importance of the central state industries gradually increased thereafter. First, according to the First Five-Year Plan, 92.9 per cent of the total industrial investment had been earmarked for the central industries, leaving only 7.1 per cent for local industries.[11] Second, some private industrial enterprises that were previously included in the category of local industries were brought into the ministerial system in the course of the socialist transformation of the private sector.[12] The Peking government even established the Ministry of Local Industry in September, 1954, in an attempt to bring most, if not all, local state enterprises into the centralized system. This idea proved to be impracticable and the ministry was abolished two years later.

On the eve of decentralization, probably 60-70 per cent of industrial

11. See *FFYP,* p. 30. They are the planned magnitudes. The actual distribution of industrial investment funds between central and local industries were:

	Central Industries	Local Industries
1955	82.9%	17.1%
1956	80.7%	19.3%
1957	80.0%	20.0%

See *HHPYK,* No. 14, 1956 (pp. 3, 7); and No. 5, 1958 (p. 7).

12. They were either converted into state-private joint enterprises under the control of the central authorities or directly nationalized by the industrial ministries. See *TCKT,* No. 1, 1957 (p. 31).

activities had been brought into the ministerial administration.[13] The industrial ministries were responsible for the routine "business affairs," planning of production, and investment in central state enterprises, while local governments were in charge of local state enterprises. But the grasp of the central government actually extended beyond this. The drafts of annual production plans for some local state enterprises had to be submitted through proper channels to the State Council for approval. The approved production plans were stated in terms of 12 "mandatory indicators" that local enterprises were required to fulfill. No such indicators, once set as targets, could be altered by individual enterprises or local governments without further approval from the State Council. An equally rigid system of control was exercised over investment plans of individual enterprises. The central government also controlled distribution of important goods and materials for production and construction; the number of goods and materials in this category continued to grow until 1958.

It cannot be denied that centralization contributed to China's socialist economic planning in the early stages, but for certain obvious reasons it became cumbersome toward the end of the First Five-Year Plan. Moreover, in the meantime, decentralization in the Soviet Union inspired the Chinese Communists to reconsider their own administrative system. The Chinese authorities were, however, very cautious on this issue. After numerous discussions and a series of meetings among the top leaders over a period of more than a year, a concrete scheme was formulated toward the end of 1957 and put into effect in 1958. Uncertain about the possible outcome, the Peking government guardedly told the public that readjustment might be necessary after one year's trial (*JMJP,* editorial, Nov. 18, 1957).

A close examination of the programs announced will show that they did not amount to complete decentralization. The publicity given them, however, has created a contrary impression in most outside observers. Even this moderate decentralization, though, caused tremendous economic disorder, as some planners had feared.

Unlike the Soviet Union, which abolished all but two of the industrial ministries at the all-Union level and transferred virtually all enterprises to regional economic commissions under the 1957 decentralization scheme, Communist China retained all its industrial ministries in the new system. The directions governing the Chinese decentralization of industrial administration state that only a small portion of the centrally controlled industries

13. According to Hsieh Mu-chiao's report (*TCKT,* No. 21, 1957, p. 10), there were 60,000 industrial concerns in China in 1956, of which 30,000 were large and medium enterprises whose gross output value accounted for 97 per cent of the total gross output value of the whole industrial sector. And about 5,000-6,000 major enterprises contributed about 70 per cent of the total gross output value in industry.

were to be transferred to lower-level governments. More specifically, most enterprises in the Ministry of Light Industry and the Ministry of Food Industry, plus a few textile enterprises, were to be transferred to local authorities; all large enterprises in heavy industry were to remain under central control (*Jen-min shou-tse,* 1958, p. 461). Judging from the nature of the enterprises to be transferred, the number of units might appear large [14] but their combined weight in terms of output value would be relatively small. Probably at least 40-50 per cent of the whole industrial sector remained in the ministerial system after decentralization.[15]

However, the impact on the economy of the moderate reorganization should not be underestimated. The real significance of the decentralization is that both local governments and individual enterprises were granted more freedom in determining their own production and investment plans, and more sources of funds for financing investment as they wished, without interference from the central government.

In the new system, local governments were also empowered to supervise the enterprises belonging to the industrial ministries. This was the so-called "double-track leadership." Financially, local governments were entitled to a 20 per cent share of profits earned by all newly transferred industries and some central industries; they were asked to balance their own annual budgets for total revenues and expenditures. Although planning for basic construction investment remained a matter for the central government, local authorities were allowed to use their own funds to carry out investment projects outside the state plan (Li Hsien-nien, 1958). In respect to production plans, only four of the original twelve indicators [16]

14. It is even doubtful whether the number of enterprises actually transferred was very large. From the end of 1957 to mid-june, 1958, only 880 enterprises had been transferred. See *HHPYK,* No. 13 (p. 63).

15. One Communist source mentions that the total gross output value of industry rose by 39.3 per cent in 1959, and the rates of increase in the central industries and the local industries in that year were 37 per cent and 40 per cent respectively (*CHYTC,* No. 1, 1960, pp. 24-26). From this information we may calculate the relative shares in 1958 as being roughly 70 per cent for the local industries and 30 per cent for the central industries. However, we know that the figures for local industries include handicraft output, of which the gross value, according to statistics of 1957, was about 20 per cent of the factory output. Furthermore, as we have previously pointed out, the relative shares measured in gross output values always exaggerate the importance of local industries because the gross output value of local industries contains more double counting. This biasing factor is even more serious in 1958 and 1959 due to the mushrooming of tiny indigenous plants and commune industries.

16. The original twelve indicators were:

1. Gross value of output
2. Output of major products
3. Trial manufacture of new products
4. Important technical-ecoonmic norms
5. Cost reduction rate
6. Amount of cost reduction

remained as "mandatory" while the other eight became "non-mandatory"; that is, subject to change at the will of individual enterprises or local governments. Individual enterprises were also allowed to retain profit earnings up to a given percentage,[17] and to dispose of the proceeds of these retained earnings as they saw fit. Previously, all construction projects within the state investment plan had been strictly supervised by the People's Construction Banks on behalf of the central government. Now, under the new system of "self-management of investment" introduced in late 1958 (*Jen-min shou-tse,* 1958, p. 369), the investing enterprise had more flexibility in its use of the investment funds appropriated by the central government, and could make minor changes in the design of the project as long as the four criteria set by the state were met.

All the new measures were meant to promote creativeness and initiative in the local cadres and individual enterprises. But they had the potential to either help or harm the economy, depending on other prevailing political and economic conditions. Unfortunately, the Great Leap Forward, the "walking on two legs" policy, and the "mass line" movement, launched simultaneously, made the Chinese decentralization a fiasco. The combined effect was disastrous. Due to the pressure of the Great Leap, and with an overenthusiastic desire to show "initiative" and "creativeness" in response to decentralization, local cadres repeatedly raised production targets and connived at wholesale falsification of the output reports for enterprises. Since the central government was unwilling to restrain the spontaneous enthusiasm of the local cadres, it did not take any timely action to correct the chaotic situation. As a result, the flow of accurate statistical information was disrupted and rational economic planning was made impossible. At the same time the new sources of funds,[18] the increased freedom of investment for local governments and individual enterprises, the new emphasis by the state on native methods of production, and the shortage of materials created by the Great Leap, all contributed to the widespread establishment of small plants, most of which were unplanned and economically irrational (as will be discussed later). The industrial

---

7. Total number of employees
8. Total number of employees at year end
9. Total wage bill
10. Average wage
11. Labor productivity
12. Profits

After 1958 only Nos. 2, 7, 9, and 12 were retained.

17. Usually no more than 10 per cent of the total profits earned by an enterprise during the year.

18. The extra-budgetary investment funds suddenly increased in 1958 from the previous negligible magnitude to about one-third of the total basic construction investment. See *CHCC,* No. 10, 1958 (p. 31).

sector and, for that matter, the economy as a whole lost their internal balance.

The central planning authorities eventually became fully aware of the gravity of the chaos. But restoring order was by no means an easy task, since the confusion was the net result of so many new policies simultaneously introduced and mutually reinforcing. So far as industrial administration is concerned, there are signs showing that as early as 1959 the Party leaders began to recentralize the system. However, the whole process of recentralization has been gradual, and corrective measures have been adopted piecemeal. Moreover, due to curtailed publication of economic information since 1960, details and effective dates of some reshaped policies are not known to us.

With regard to the distribution of industrial enterprises between the ministerial and local systems, 1958-59 saw a relatively large share go to the latter. Besides those existing plants that had been recently transferred to local jurisdiction, a great number of new small plants were built in this period. Although distribution of budgetary investment funds favored the central system in these two years,[19] local authorities had sizable extra-budgetary funds for investment. Therefore, the local system expanded faster. The relative share of the local system began to decline in the second half of 1959. Small concerns that turned out to be wasteful in production were abandoned; this was, in effect, a kind of disinvestment in local industries.

In the ensuing years, as the economic crisis deepened, total capital investment in industry was drastically reduced. The only exception was the building of large tractor-manufacturing plants and chemical fertilizer plants, most of which were administered by the ministerial system. Thus, the relative share of the centrally controlled industries tended to grow. One of the clear signs pointing to this tendency was the establishment of eight new industrial ministries in the period 1959-65.[20]

Instead of returning outright to the industrial ministries those enterprises which had been transferred to local governments under the decen-

19. The shares were 77.7 per cent for central industries and 22.3 per cent for the local system in 1958; and 57.3 per cent and 42.7 per cent respectively, in 1959. See *HHPYK,* No. 5, 1958 (p. 9) and No. 9, 1959 (p. 16).

20. The following are the new ministries and their dates of establishment:

The Ministry of Agricultural Machine Building Industry, Aug. 26, 1959
The Third Ministry of Machine Building Industry, Sept. 30, 1960
The Fourth Ministry of Machine Building Industry, May 25, 1963
The Fifth Ministry of Machine Building Industry, Sept. 28, 1963
The Sixth Ministry of Machine Building Industry, Jan. 5, 1965

tralization scheme,[21] Peking resorted to other indirect means to weaken the economic power of local governments. Beginning in 1959 the overriding slogan was "the whole country as a single chessboard." Countless articles, newspaper editorials and official reports advocated the necessity of centralized planning for production and investment for the whole country. Other writings, while adhering to the original slogan of "democratic centralization" in economic affairs, put increasingly greater stress on the centralization portion of the slogan. On January 14, 1960, the State Council resolved to strengthen overall financial planning (*CHYTC,* 1960). According to the resolution, all extra-budgetary funds in the hands of local governments and enterprises were to be controlled by the state. When these funds were used for capital investment, the investment plans of the concern had to be approved in advance by the state planning organization. After investment had been carried out, the investing unit had to submit periodic reports to certain supervising offices. Later (but effective from an unknown date), the supervisory power of the People's Construction Banks over construction projects was reinstated. It was in effect an abolition of the system of "self-management of investment." Moreover, the People's Bank was given greater authority to control cash transactions, account transfers and the working capital of all firms.[22]

Recentralization of statistical work was even more noticeable. By 1962, statistical offices at various levels had already reverted from the "double-track leadership" to the old "direct vertical leadership." Interference by local cadres had been reduced to a minimum (Wang Ssu-hua, 1962).

Another mechanism with which Communist China worked out its recentralization was the Party. At the local level, most chief officials in the government are concurrently also the responsible personnel in the local Party. During 1958-59, local cadres gained more freedom in handling local affairs, but they somewhat abused their power by placing regional interest above national interest. This tendency might be attributed either to the fact that the central planning system had been so weakened that it failed to provide local cadres with appropriate and consistent signals about

---

The Seventh Ministry of Machine Building Industry,
Jan. 5, 1965
The Eighth Ministry of Machine Building Industry,
Jan. 5, 1965
The Second Ministry of Light Industry,
Feb. 16, 1965.

21. In fact, there was a suggestion that the central government should take back some of those enterprises, as an effective cure for the chaotic situation. Ironically, this suggestion was made by Wu Hsai, one of the responsible officials in Kiangsu provincial government. See *CHYTC,* No. 6, 1959 (p. 12).

22. For instance, local firms previously could get part of their working capital from local governments, but after late 1959 the People's Bank became the sole source of working capital for all firms. For a fuller description of the new functions of the People's Bank in China see *JMJP,* editorial, May 10, 1962.

national interest; or to the fact that local cadres deliberately ignored the signals when they were counter to regional interest. In seeking a way to arrest this deviation, Communist authorities thought that by consolidating the Party organization and strengthening the subordinative tie between the Party center and local members they would regain centralized control without changing the administrative apparatus. In other words, a local cadre might still have considerable administrative discretion in his capacity as a governmental chief, but as a loyal Party member his freedom in action and decision-making would be greatly restricted by directives issued by the Party central. Based on this reasoning, six "central bureaus" were set up in 1961 within the Party organization (*Hung-chi,* No. 3 and 4, 1961, p. 3), located in the previous "large administrative regions." Each bureau was to represent the Party Central Committee in Peking and to supervise and lead the provincial and municipal Party committees in each region. Through these bridging organs the Party hoped to extend its control more effectively down to the lowest level.

The remaining problem was how to deal with individual enterprises that had gained more power during decentralization. A large number of managers were not Party members; they had been appointed because of their technical competence. Nor was the mass of workers completely trustworthy. As a solution to this problem, in the first half of 1962, the Peking government created the so-called "political departments" in all economic establishments (*JMJP,* March 1, June 7, 1964). It was a highly centralized control mechanism; for instance, an industrial ministry would contain the headquarters of a political department with branch offices extending to all enterprises of that particular industry. Resorting primarily to "political means," the political department could curtail not only the discretionary powers of individual enterprises, but also the authority of local Party committees to formulate economic policies.[23]

Closely related to industrial administration is the problem of management within a state enterprise. The pattern of management has also undergone several changes. In the period 1949-53 the prevailing pattern was one of collective management, with the "factory administrative committee" as the executive body in each enterprise. In addition, there was a workers' representatives conference designed as a consultation organ in each factory. Experience proved that the collective management system was too loose to be suitable for most modern large factories. It usually resulted in a situation where no one was really responsible for anything.

Next, a thoroughgoing reform of the management system in state enterprises was made in 1953. The new pattern was called the "responsibility system" or "general manager system." Specifically, the general manager

23. Under the new system a local enterprise is said to be subject to the double leadership of the local Party committee and the political department. See *JMJP,* June 7, 1964.

was designated as the single head of an enterprise, and was responsible for executing the production plan set forth by the government and for handling the daily work of business administration inside the firm. The chief engineer, who was also the vice general manager in the firm, was in charge of all technical matters. There were then various functional offices, independent of each other but all responsible to the same general manager. The workers' representatives conference, though still in existence, had been relegated to being an instrument to convey the general manager's decisions and orders to workers in the plant.

Although this system worked quite efficiently from a managerial viewpoint, it seemed unsatisfactory to the Party. The common complaint among the Party members associated with industrial enterprises was that general managers tended to dictate on the basis of purely technical considerations, ignoring the Party line. In order to eliminate this "bureaucratic tendency" and to strengthen the Party leadership in production units, the management system was reshuffled in 1956 into the "system of general manager under the guidance of the Party committee." Now, the Party committee, made up of several key Party members in the enterprise, held the major decision-making position. The power of the general manager was further curtailed in 1957 when the government empowered trade unions to organize a "workers' representatives assembly" in each enterprise. It replaced the old "workers' representatives conference" but possessed much broader power. It had the authority to examine and sanction the draft plans made by management, and to review the execution of the plan. It could make suggestions and criticisms to management, and could even demand the removal of the general manager in case of serious dispute.[24]

The principle of mass participation at the enterprise level was carried to its extreme in 1958. Under the "mass line" movement, workers both within and outside the "workers' representatives assembly" began to interfere daily with the managerial works in an enterprise. Although it was only an informal movement without any statutory foundation, its impact on the management system was profound. When industrial administration had been decentralized, enterprises were supposed to have gained a wider range of discretionary power, yet now the general manager and his staff actually became powerless because of the "mass line" movement. Virtually all decisions, large or small, were made by the workers' organization. This dangerous movement soon affected technical matters. Engineers and technicians were downgraded. Technical requirements in production processes and regulations designed for the prevention of accidents were regarded as superstitious, and hence were abandoned. The consequence is now common knowledge. The phenomenon of "no one is responsible for anything" returned to most factories. The workers' discipline collapsed; the frequency

24. For a detailed description of the workers' representatives assembly, see *JMJP,* May 29, 1957.

of industrial accidents rose sharply; engineers and technicians lost their initiative and interest.

Adjustments had to be made if industrial production was to be carried on. Sometime after 1960 the Chinese authorities restored the system of responsibility under the direction of a general manager. The chief engineer was also reestablished in charge of technical matters. Official literature repeatedly urged workers to respect technicians and technical regulations. Even more interesting was the government instruction to local cadres not to equate any disputes made by managerial personnel over technical matters with problems of "political thought."

All these shifts of position merely helped to establish a new balance of power among the management, the Party committee and the workers' organization in an enterprise. But some of the discretionary power vested in the enterprise since the decentralization movement remained intact. This is probably one of the reasons why, in 1962, the political department system was introduced. The Communist leaders hoped that through this new mechanism they might bring individual enterprises back to centralized control.

POLICIES CONCERNING INDUSTRIAL TECHNOLOGY

There have been some drastic changes in technological policies in the Communist era. During the First Five-Year Plan period the guiding principle was the building of large modern plants. The core of the plan itself was the 156 Soviet aid projects. Of these, 145 projects were to be constructed during the five years with an investment of 11,000 million *yuan* (FFYP, p. 39). In addition, an investment of 1,800 million *yuan* was to be made during the same period for the establishment of 143 "large basic construction units" ancillary to the Soviet aid projects (FFYP, p. 39). These two groups of projects accounted for 48.4 per cent of the total planned investment in industry. According to the original First Five-Year Plan, 694 above-norm industrial projects were to be constructed altogether. Subtracting from 694 the 145 Soviet aid projects and the 143 ancillary units, there remained 406 other large projects that would require at least an investment of a few billion *yuan*. Therefore, investment in large plants as a whole could well be over 60 per cent of the planned total investment in industry. The remainder of industrial investment would be spread over about 2,300 below-norm projects. Even the below-norm units in China were not very small, and they were quite modern in their equipment compared with most plants built in 1958.

This general principle was first questioned in 1957 by economists both within and outside the planning commission. They were against so-called "gigantism" in industrialization, and advocated that, for several reasons, more attention be given to small factories. First, due to the generally shorter period of gestation, new projects of a small size could be put into operation quickly. Second, small factories usually have relatively low capital-output ratios, making them suitable for the economic conditions in China, which is short of capital but abundant in labor. Third, a large part of the equipment needed for small plants can be manufactured domestically. Thus the new technological policy could ease the pressure on foreign exchange. Fourth, small plants, when dispersed geographically, can make use of local resources, and supply local markets; consequently, the burden on the transportation system can be greatly relieved.

However, a reading of the literature put out by those economists in 1957 reveals that none of them was really suggesting the use of indigenous methods of industrial production. They all demand certain technological standards and fairly modern equipment for the proposed factories, however small. Only in 1958 was the technical dualism carried out to extremes. The "walking on two legs" policy called for the simultaneous development of "the small and the large" and the simultaneous development of "the modern and the indigenous." Many of the indigenous units built in this period were economically irrational, resulting only in a waste of resources.

According to the final account for the First Five-Year Plan period, about 10,000 industrial projects, above and below norm, were under construction. This figure is much greater than originally planned (SSB *Communiqué,* 1953-57). Of these, 921 were above-norm units, exceeding the planned number by 227. The actual investment in industry made in this period was 25,030 million *yuan* (*Ten Great Years,* p. 57) [25] slightly less than the planned amount. Thus, the actual average investment per project (about 2.5 million *yuan*) [26] was smaller than that in the original plan (about 8.9 million *yuan*). This reflects mainly the changed policy toward the end of the period. In 1958 about 40,000 industrial projects were wholly or partially completed,[27] not counting the numerous backyard furnaces, commune industries, and other tiny indigenous plants. Total industrial investment in 1958 was 17,300 million *yuan* (*Ten Great Years,* p. 57), making the average investment per project only .43 million *yuan.*

The policy difference in the two periods can also be seen from the changes in other indicators. Table 1 shows the remarkable rises from 1952 to 1957 in the average fixed assets per worker, the average capacity of power machinery used per worker, the average amount of electricity used per worker and the number of technical personnel per thousand workers in the industrial sector; these increases reflect the deepening nature of industrial investment in that period. But all these items declined in 1958.

25. It refers to basic construction investment inside and outside the state plan.

26. That is, 25,030 million *yuan* divided by 10,000 projects. It is admittedly not a good measure of the average size of projects because part of the investment funds was spent on those projects which had not been completed by the end of 1957.

27. Compare the relevant figures given in the SSB *Communiqué* (1953-57) and *Ten Great Years* (pp. 46 and 67).

TABLE 1

SELECTED INDICATORS OF THE TECHNOLOGICAL LEVEL OF INDUSTRY IN COMMUNIST CHINA

	Unit	1952	1957	1958
(1) Consumption of Electricity per Worker	kwh	1,430	2,606	942
(2) Capacity of Power Machinery per Worker	hp	1.73	3.01	1.25
(3) Fixed Assets per worker	yuan	3,525	5,168	2,026
(4) Technical Personnel per 1,000 Workers	persons	12	19	11

Sources:

For lines (1), (2) and (3) in 1952 and 1957: *JPRS*, 2059-N, 1960. They are consistent with the rates of change in those indicators given in *Ten Great Years* p. 110.

For line (1) in 1958: these have been calculated from the estimated industrial consumption of electricity in 1958 as given in Wu, 1963 (p. 79), and the estimated number of industrial workers in 1958. Industrial employment excluding that of commune industries is estimated to be 23.4 million in 1958. See John P. Emerson, "Manpower Absorption in the Non-Agricultural Branches of the Economy of Communist China, 1953-58," *China Quarterly*, No. 7, July-September, 1961 (p. 77).

For line (2) in 1958: The estimated total capacity of power machinery existing in 1957 was reached by multiplying the total number of industrial workers in 1957 (*Ten Great Years*, p. 183) by 3.01 hp. The resulting figure was then added to the capacity of power machinery produced in 1958 (*TGY*, p. 97) in order to estimate the total capacity of power machinery existing in 1958. This, of course, understates 1958's capacity somewhat because the net import of power machinery in that year has not been included. The estimated figure of total capacity in 1958 was then divided by the number of industrial workers in 1958.

For line (3) in 1958: These have been calculated from the total value of fixed assets in the industrial sector in 1958 (*Ten Great Years*, p. 93) and the number of industrial workers in that year.

For line (4): the total number of technical personnel in the industrial sector in 1952, 1957 and 1958 are given as 58,000, 175,000 and 260,000 respectively. (See Hsu Kang "The Great Ten Years as Viewed from Three Achievements," *Lao-tung*, 1959, No. 20, p. 12, and Wang Ssu-hua, "The Great Victory of Our Country's Socialist Industrializaiton," *CHYTC*, 1959, No. 12, p. 26). They were then divided respectively by the number of industrial workers in those three years.

The extremes of technical dualism were of short duration. Steps toward readjustment were taken as early as 1959. Most of the two million small blast furnaces erected in 1958 (*CHCC*, No. 12, 1958, p. 21) either melted into piles of mud after a few rains or were discarded because of the prohibitively high costs of operation and the exceedingly low quality of the products. A very small number of them were merged into about 3,000 production units after substantial remolding (*HHPYK*, No. 20, 1960, p. 91). The work of scrapping was extended later to other branches of industry; as generally happens, the economic crisis in those years performed a screening function. Because of the universal shortage of raw materials in the whole industrial sector, raw materials were distributed on a selective basis. All uneconomic and inefficient production units were denied raw materials (*JMJP,* Dec. 27, 1962), and consequently were forced to shut down. As a matter of fact, among the major tasks announced by the Chinese government in the readjustment period were the modernization of the existing industrial establishments, technological reform, more attention to operation costs, and an improvement in the quality of products.

The return to the old policy began in 1959 with the construction of new plants. Under the movement known as "the whole country as a single chessboard," investment funds were concentrated on the high priority large projects instead of scattered small plants. When industrial investment was cut to a very low level in 1961-62, it was allocated to a handful of large or medium projects such as tractor-manufacturing plants, chemical fertilizer plants and synthetic fiber factories.

Another important consideration in the technological aspect was whether new factories should be built along the line of a high degree of specialization. Specialization of production has obvious advantages. First, instead of building numerous workshops of the same kind within various factories, the government can construct one or a small number of specialized plants for the same purpose. Not only is the investment requirement smaller but a certain saving in operation costs can also be achieved because equipment in the specialized plant can be utilized more fully than that in small workshops operated by different factories. Second, management in specialized units is relatively simple. Third, a plant specializing in one product, or in a small number of products, can more easily solve its technical difficulties and ensure higher quality than a factory producing a wide variety of products. By the same token, specialization is conducive to improvement in production techniques. Since a high degree of specialization requires close and stable cooperation among individual factories, theoretically speaking, an economy with centralized planning can gain more from industrial specialization.

During the First Five-Year Plan period, most new factories were designed for industrial specialization (Chi Chung-wei, 1954; Yang Ching-wen, 1957a, 1957b). For example, the Changchun automobile manufacturing factory was not designed to be comprehensive; it had to cooperate with more than 70 specialized plants as suppliers of parts and necessary materials. However, this guiding principle was negated in 1958. The new fashion was "multifarious operation," meaning that each factory should be engaged in the production of a great variety of items.

Of course, diversification can have its own merits if carried out in the right direction. There are two possible types of diversified production.

One type, common in large enterprises in the West, may be called horizontal diversification. A manufacturer may produce several commodities that are the products of the same materials. It may use the waste or scrap from the main product as the raw material for certain by-products. Or, a firm may produce simultaneously different goods that require the same type of machinery, laboratory equipment and technical personnel. In this type of diversification there is some saving in production costs. Furthermore, it may provide some protection for the producer against the risk of sudden decline in the market demand for a single commodity in which he might otherwise have specialized. The other type is vertical diversification, in which a firm produces all the various raw materials required in making its end products. This type of diversification may not render any appreciable cost savings except in industries such as iron and steel works, in which continuous production processes are preferable. And it provides little or no protection for the firm in case of a sudden decline in demand for the end products.

Unfortunately, diversified production in China in 1958 emerged as the second type. To use the Chinese Communist jargon, it followed the idea of building "satellite plants" around the main plant to produce whatever raw materials and goods it needed. A satellite plant might in turn build its own satellite plants (Wang Chen-tsu, 1959; Niu Chung-huang, 1959). Thus, railway bureaus began to run cement plants and steel mills in order to make their own cement and rails; their cement mills in turn established paper mills to supply paper bags; their paper mills erected subsidiary units to produce sulfuric acid and soda. The Changhsintien locomotive manufacturing factory built more than ten satellite plants engaged in activities ranging from steel making down to textiles and the production of alcohol. Since the satellite plants were quite different from the main plant in capital and technical requirements, there was little cost savings. In fact, a great number of satellite plants were built hurriedly to meet exigent needs without any serious consideration being given to the geographical distribution of natural resources or other relevant conditions. Consequently, production costs in those plants were abnormally high, and some even proved to be inoperative after being erected.

It is interesting to note that the changed pattern was not a result of deliberate planning. It was instead a natural by-product of the Great Leap and of administrative decentralization. The Great Leap movement created nationwide shortages of raw materials in almost every field. Under pressure to fulfill production targets that had been set fantastically high, producers scrambled more frantically than ever for raw materials at any expense. Moreover, as previously mentioned, a high degree of industrial specialization depends on satisfactory cooperation between factories, but decentralization had disrupted previously established cooperative relations (Ou Ming, 1959; Wu Hsia, 1959). Some firms that were supposed to supply certain goods to other producers changed their lines of production of their own accord simply because the new lines would result in more profits or gross value of output. A firm that had formerly shipped its products to certain enterprises outside its own area might be ordered by the local authorities to send them to other local manufacturers, because local interest overrode interregional cooperation. Even worse, some local governments forcibly detained goods in transit for their own production purposes. Under the chaotic circumstances, producers were constantly unsure whether they would get enough materials and goods from outside in time for production. It was only natural that enterprises would attempt desperately to be self-sufficient; that is, would build satellite plants to supply the materials and goods needed. Furthermore, decentralization made this development possible, because enterprises and local governments now had their own funds to invest in whatever they wished.

Some planners and economists were aware of the undesirability of the satellite plants at the time they were built.[28] But they did not launch a strong attack against them because Mao Tse-tung on his inspection trip in September, 1958, personally praised the "multifarious operation" as a "heroic struggle" by industrial workers against material shortages (Niu Chung-huang, 1959; Li Fu-chun, 1960). It was only after 1961 that the Communist authorities clearly denounced the pattern of diversified production. A series of directives were issued in which the government instructed production units to observe the principle of specialization and to reestablish stable cooperative relations among themselves. Wasteful satellite plants were to be closed down. Workshops of a similar nature that belonged to different factories were to be merged in order to avoid unnecessary duplication. Diversified production was to be confined to only those industries where cost savings could be achieved by it.

The whole task of readjustment was expected to be accomplished in several stages. In late 1964, several large-scale studies were conducted in selected cities to compare the production costs in specialized factories with those in the so-called comprehensive "almighty" factories (*JMJP*, Oct. 23 and 29, 1964). These studies confirmed all the advantages of industrial specialization, and hence reinforced the government's decision to develop industry according to the principle of inter-enterprise division of labor.

28. For example, see *CHYTC*, No. 1, 1959 (pp. 3-4); No. 4, 1959 (pp. 1-5); No. 6, 1959 (pp. 11-12); No. 9, 1959 (pp. 4-7); and No. 15. 1959.

III. PERFORMANCE

To evaluate performance in Chinese industry it is necessary to divide the whole period into two segments. In the first segment, which covers the years 1949-59, expansion in industry was rather rapid. There are officially published statistics for this period so that appraisals can be made in quantitative terms. The second segment, 1960-66, was characterized by extreme fluctuations in output, major economic crises and subsequent readjustments. Since the general decline in output is unfavorable to the Communist propaganda, very few economic statistics for this period have been released. Consequently, one can only speculate without the strong support of quantitative data.

The discussion in this section will be confined to two major aspects of industrial performance in the country, investment activities and output. To the extent that official statistics are available, investment data and output data differ in reliability. Students of the Chinese economy generally agree that official investment figures, especially investment in fixed capital, are fairly reliable before 1958. The main problems involved here are definitional.[29] As long as the Chinese definition is followed, the official investment data before 1958 can be used without too much risk. The official output data, on the other hand, involve measurement problems. The accuracy of most output series in physical terms varies from period to period, and the aggregate data of gross output value have been suspected to have a strong upward bias.[30]

Furthermore, this discussion will be largely confined to factory production, which, according to the Chinese Communist definition, excludes production by individual and cooperative handicraftsmen but includes that of handicraft factories.

1949-1959

Throughout this period the Chinese Communists rapidly raised the share of current output allocated for investment in fixed capital. In total fixed investment the industrial sector took the lion's share. Moreover, a preponderance of industrial investment was in heavy industry. As shown in Table 2, basic construction investment in industry rose swiftly, even though the extraordinarily large increases in 1958-59 must be received with caution. The percentage of industrial investment in total basic construction also rose from somewhere below 40 per cent in the early 1950's to 64.8 per cent in 1958, only to decline slightly in 1959. From 1953

29. For a detailed discussion of the Chinese definition of various investment items, see Chao, "The Construction Industry . . . ," Appendix.

30. Eleven biasing factors can be identified, see Cho, 1965 (pp. 11-24, and 87); Liu and Yeh, 1965 (pp. 57-63 and 147-52); and C. M. Li, 1959 (pp. 30-35).

TABLE 2

COMMUNIST DATA ON BASIC CONSTRUCTION INVESTMENT[a] IN INDUSTRY, 1950-1959
(at current prices)

	Total Investment in Industry (in million *yuan*) (I)	Percentage of Total Basic Construction Investment (II)	Percentage Distribution between (%) Light Industry (III)	Heavy Industry (IV)	Percentage Distribution between (%) Central Industries (V)	Local Industries (VI)
1950	420	37.1	n.a.	n.a.	n.a.	n.a.
1951	850	36.1	n.a.	n.a.	n.a.	n.a.
1952	1,690	38.8	24.0	76.0	n.a.	n.a.
1953	2,840	35.4	17.6	82.4	n.a.	n.a.
1954	3,830	42.3	17.6	82.4	n.a.	n.a.
1955	4,300	46.2	12.3	87.7	82.9	17.1
1956	6,820	46.1	13.8	86.2	80.7	19.3
1957	7,240	52.3	15.2	84.8	80.0	20.0
1958	17,300	64.8	12.6	87.4	77.7	22.3
1959	20,400	61.0	30.0	70.0	57.3	42.7

Note:
a. The data refer to investment both in and out of the state plan.

Sources:
For 1952-58 in Columns (I), (II), (III) and (IV): *Ten Great Years,* pp. 57, 59, and 61.
For Columns (V) and (VI): 1955 and 1956: *HHPYK,* 1956, No. 14 (pp. 3, 7). 1957 and 1958: *HHPYK,* 1958, No. 5 (pp. 7, 9). 1959: *HHPYK,* 1959, No. 9 (p. 16).
For 1950-51 in Columns (I) and (II): figures have been calculated by the following steps:
a) According to *HHPYK,* 1957, No. 17 (pp. 39-50), basic construction investment in industry within the state plan was 1,550 million *yuan.* The State Statistical Bureau *Communiqué* (1960) states that basic construction investment in industry within the state plan in 1952 was 106% higher than that in 1951. Therefore basic construction investment in industry within the state plan in 1951 was 750 million *yuan.*
b) *Jen-min shou-tse,* 1958, p. 463, states that total basic construction investment in industry within the state plan was 2,700 million *yuan* for the period 1950-52. Therefore the 1950 industrial investment figure can be estimated as 400 million *yuan.*
c) The resultant figures are those within the state plan. Basic construction investment in industry outside the state plan for 1950 and 1951 must be estimated. To do this, we first compute basic construction investment for all sectors outside the state plan for each year in the period 1950-52 by comparing the data given in *Ten Great Years,* pp. 55 and 56. The results are

1950— 90 million *yuan*
1951—470 million *yuan*
1952—650 million *yuan*

d) It is known that basic construction investment in industry outside the state plan in 1952 was

1,690 million *yuan* — 1,550 million = 140 million *yuan* which was 21% of the total outside plan investment in that year.

e) Assuming that the same proportion of outside-plan investment was used in industrial construction in both 1950 and 1951, basic construction in industry outside the state plan can be estimated in these two years as:

1950— 20 million *yuan*
1951—100 million *yuan*

f) The above two figures are added, respectively, to the amounts of industrial investment within the state plan in these two years.

g) From these results and the total basic construction investment inside and outside the state plan in 1950 and 1951, as given in *TGY* (p. 55), the percentages are derived for these two years in Column (II).

For 1959 in Columns (I) and (II): *CHYTC,* No. 1, 1960 (p. 29).

For 1959 in Columns (III) and (IV): the draft economic plan for 1959 (*JMJP,* April 22, 1959). They were the planned figures.

onward, the portion of industrial investment allocated to heavy industry was always above 80 per cent.

Before 1952, most investment was for reconstruction of existing plants that had been partially damaged during the war,[31] but thereafter virtually all investment was devoted to building new units. However, an increase in industrial production capacity was realized only after a gestation period. As can be seen in Table 3, in the early years of this period only a small portion of the current industrial output was attributed to the newly built plants and factories. In 1958, though, about half the gross output value was accounted for by new enterprises. This is true because a great number of large projects undertaken during the First Five-Year Plan period were completed and put into operation in 1958, and because the majority of the current investment for that year was in small plants that could be completed within a year.

It should be noted, however, that some of the investment made in this period was actually fruitless. As has been mentioned earlier, a great number of small plants and mines constructed in 1958 turned out to be extremely uneconomical in production and were later abandoned. A great deal of investment was also wasted on some Soviet aid projects which were carried on for several years, but had to be discontinued before completion because of the sudden withdrawal of Soviet technicians in mid-1960.

Industrial output increased at a remarkably high rate during this period as a result of both the intensive investment program and the fuller utilization of old facilities. It is very difficult, however, to ascertain the precise average rate of growth of industrial output in this period. According to the official gross value index for factory and handicraft production, it was 528.6 in 1959 (with 1952 = 100). The official production index,

31. Only one-third of industrial investment in 1952 was for new construction; see SSB *Communiqué,* 1952.

TABLE 3

INDUSTRIAL INVESTMENT AND INCREASED PRODUCTION CAPACITY IN COMMUNIST CHINA
1953-59

	Large Projects		Small Projects		
	Under construction during the year (in number) (I)	Wholly or partly completed by the end of the year (in number) (II)	Under construction during the year (in number) (II)	Increased production capacity during the year (Index— 1954=100) (IV)	Contribution to current total industrial output of newly increased production capacity (in per cent) (V)
1953	107	36		n.a.	n.a.
1954	411	39		100	26
1955	485	82	9,000	103	25
1956	625	89		184	34
1957	642	178		179	30
1958	1135	700	40,000	449	50
1959	1341	671	75,000	n.a.	n.a.

Sources:
Columns (I) and (II): State Statistical Bureau, *Communiqué,* various years.
Column (III): 1953-57.: SSB, *Communiqué,* 1953-57. 1958: SSB, *Communiqué* 1958. 1959: SSB, *Communiqué,* 1959.
Columns (IV) and (V): C. M. Li, 1964 (p. 19).

however, has been suspected to have a strong upward bias. In another study (Kang Chao, 1965) I have computed an industrial output index covering the period 1949-59. It has, I believe, eliminated some of the identified biasing factors embodied in the official index. Based on my index, industrial production of factories rose to 371.4 (1952 = 100). The average yearly growth rate for the whole period 1949-59 is estimated at 20.6 per cent. The year-to-year variation in growth rate was very great, indicating the uneven tempo of industrial development in the economy. The average rate of growth was lower in the First Five-Year Plan period (14.4 per cent) than in the recovery period (26.0 per cent) or the Great Leap years (32.2 per cent).[32] The highest rate (39.2 per cent) for a single year was in 1958, while 1955 saw the smallest increase in industrial output (3.7 per cent).

32. The estimates for the recovery period and the Great Leap years are less reliable than that for the FFYP period.

A comparison may be made between my index of factory production and the index of net value added in manufacturing factories, mining and utilities estimated by Liu and Yeh for mainland China in the period 1952-59.[33] Table 4 shows that my index numbers are almost identical

TABLE 4

COMPARISON OF CHAO'S INDEX OF FACTORY PRODUCTION WITH LIU-YEH ESTIMATES, 1952-1959
(1952 = 100)

	Chao	Liu-Yeh
1952	100.0	100.0
1953	124.7	122.9
1954	141.6	142.2
1955	146.9	159.0
1956	182.2	210.8
1957	195.9	238.6
1958	272.6	289.2 [a]
1959	371.4	373.5 [a]

Sources:
Chao, 1965 (p. 88) and Liu and Yeh, 1965 (p. 66).
Notes:
a. Considered as conjectural estimates by Liu and Yeh.

with those of Liu and Yeh for 1953, 1954 and 1959; but differ for the remaining years. In general, my index shows a slower rate of growth before 1958 than that suggested by Liu and Yeh's value-added figures, as well as a much greater rate from 1957 to 1959.

The differences between these two series may be attributed largely to (1) the different weights used, and (2) the differences in coverage [34] for

33. See Liu and Yeh, 1965 (p. 66). There are quite a few series of industrial production indexes independently computed by scholars outside Communist China, with different degrees of elaboration. It is impossible to discuss here the different concepts and methods used and the results of all those indexes. Interested readers are referred to Table A-1 in the Appendix, in which all series, including the official one, are tabulated and the original works cited.

34. What I mean by "coverage" is the "identified portion." Both the Liu-Yeh study and the author's have assumed that the unidentified portion increased at a rate equal to that of the identified portion. While this assumption is explicitly made in Liu-Yeh's study (1965, pp. 63, 572), it is only implicit in my study in the sense that any production index based on incomplete output data is automatically assuming that the omitted items, when combined, have increased at the same rate as the items included (for further discussion on the validity of this assumption in the case of Communist China, see Chao, 1965, pp. 82-87). Clearly, the overall growth rate is determined solely by the behavior of the identified portion and the weights applied thereto. The weights, if any, applied to the unidentified portion have no effect whatsoever on the overall growth rate because when one combines two subseries of identical growth rates, the resulting overall growth rate will be the same no matter what weights he uses.

various subgroups of industries. For instance, while I itemized various machinery products, Liu and Yeh accepted the official gross output values of the machine-building industry. On the other hand, they used independent estimates for a number of nonferrous metals in 1952, while I took the official gross output values for that industry.

Industrial growth in this period was also characterized by a pronounced disparity in rate among individual industries. As indicated in Table 5, the average annual rates of growth of industries producing primarily consumer goods lagged far behind those for heavy industry. For instance, in 1953-57 the average growth rate of ferrous metals was almost 4.5 times that of the textile industry. Within heavy industry itself, at least until 1957, coal and timber manifested a slower expansion than processing industries.

TABLE 5

AVERAGE ANNUAL RATE OF INCREASE OF OUTPUT BY INDUSTRY
(in per cent)

Industry	1949-1957	1952-1957
Electricity	20.6	21.6
Coal	19.1	14.6
Petroleum	36.5	27.3
Ferrous metals	53.8	28.7
Nonferrous metals	46.5	29.9
Metal processing	40.3	22.1
Chemical	43.1	25.7
Building materials	30.0	19.3
Timber	18.5	14.8
Textile	13.8	6.5
Paper	28.8	17.1
Food	14.1	9.3
Daily-use commodities	15.0	11.8

Source:
Chao, 1965 (p. 97).

1960-1966 [35]

The economic crisis started in the agricultural sector in 1959 when the crop declined sharply. However, based on the falsified reports submitted by the local cadres, the State Statistical Bureau claimed a 16.7 per

35. The tentative quantitative analysis presented in this section is based on piecemeal Communist information, the reliability of which is difficult to evaluate at present.

cent increase in farm output over 1958. The planners were misled by these data, and accordingly set forth an ambitious program for the industrial sector in 1960, calling for a total investment even larger than that of 1959.

The impact of the agricultural crisis on industry was actually felt in 1960. About 70-80 per cent of light industries were dependent on agriculture for their supplies of raw material and could not fulfill their high production quotas or, in some cases, even maintain the level of 1959. Only those branches of light industry using nonagricultural materials, as well as most of heavy industry, managed to maintain their output level or fulfill the annual quotas. The investment plan for 1960 did not materialize, partly because the Soviet Union cancelled its technical assistance to China and partly because investment funds fell short of the expected level.

The industrial crisis worsened in 1961. It was probably the year in which light industry output fell the most. As the extreme difficulties in agriculture continued in 1960, land formerly devoted to industrial crops was switched to the production of food crops. Thus the supply of raw materials for light industry must have declined in 1961 even more sharply than had the total farm output in the preceding year. Moreover, inventories of industrial crops, which to some extent had acted as a shock-absorber in 1960, had already been exhausted by 1961. All indications seem to suggest that production of light industry reached its nadir in that year.

Aware of the severity of the deterioration in the economy and the necessity of urgent action in order to save the economy from collapsing, the Party Central Committee decided in January, 1961, to institute several corrective measures, including a cut in basic construction investment. This decision led to a reduction in the output of heavy industry simply because the demand for investment goods dropped. It is unlikely, however, that the decline in heavy industry was more pronounced, percentage-wise, than that of light industry. It did not rely on farm output as a source of raw materials. Moreover, under the new policy of support for agriculture, a portion of heavy industry was reoriented in order to produce items such as tractors, farm machinery and chemical fertilizer at an increasing rate.

At the end of 1961 the country was on the verge of making corrections in the economy. In March, 1962, Chou En-lai officially set forth the ten tasks of "readjustment, consolidation, reenforcement and improvement." As far as industry was concerned, the new policy entailed the following major changes:

1) Light industry was to be given priority over heavy industry, with special stress on commodities in everyday use.

2) Basic construction was to be cut down further in order to

spare materials and manpower for strengthening the weak links in industry.

3) The numbers of residents and industrial workers were to be further reduced, beginning with the repatriation of those workers who had recently moved from villages to cities.

Agricultural production in 1962 showed some signs of revival, owing to the moderate weather conditions in that year and to the new supportive measures adopted by the government. However, except in a few branches, there was no significant improvement in industry. In the portion of light industry using farm products as raw materials, output remained at the same low level because of the time lag between the increased agricultural production and the corresponding change in raw material supplies. Only the 20-30 per cent of light industry that used nonagricultural materials was reported to have increased its output by 30 per cent (*Ta-kung pao,* Jan. 3, 1963). In the heavy industry sector, such items as chemical fertilizer and petroleum showed substantial rises in 1962 (*Ta-kung pao,* Jan. 3, 1963). The same may have been true for a few branches that supplied materials to light industry. But this increase was to some extent offset by the continued downward trend in the production of investment goods as the scale of basic construction was further reduced.

A general recovery in industry was reported to have begun in 1963. It probably continued until the Red Guards activities disrupted the economy toward the end of 1966. Increases in production during this period were particularly rapid in a few selected branches.

A great fanfare has been given to the increase in chemical fertilizer production. According to Chou En-lai, the total supply of chemical fertilizer in 1964 was more than three times that in 1957 (Chou En-lai, 1964). The supply in 1957 is known to have been 2,184,000 tons (871,000 tons of domestic production and 1,313,000 tons of imported fertilizer). Thus, the total supply of chemical fertilizer in 1964 should have been approximately 6.6 million tons. Imports of fertilizer in 1964 are estimated at about one million tons; this leaves about 5.6 million tons as domestic output for that year. This figure of 6.6 million tons for the chemical fertilizer supply is very close to the figure of 7 million tons given to a Japanese reporter by Wu Chen, Deputy Minister of Agriculture of Communist China (*Asahi Shinbun,* March 7, 1965). The amount implied by Chou is also consistent with another Chinese report that a total of about 4.6 million tons of chemical fertilizer had been supplied by the state to peasants in the period between January and August, 1964 (*JMJP,* Sept. 26, 1964). Other Chinese Communist sources reported that by the end of November, 1965, chemical fertilizer output for the year already surpassed the total quantity produced in 1964 by 2.79 million tons (*JMJP,* Dec. 8, 1965); and that the quantity produced in the period between

January and November of 1966 was 26 per cent higher than the annual output for 1965 (*JMJP,* Dec. 30, 1966). Again, these figures appear consistent with the progress reports disclosed earlier concerning fertilizer production.[36] After the monthly output of December is imputed for 1965 and 1966, the implied annual outputs would be as follows:

1964	5.6 million tons
1965	9.0 million tons
1966	12.0 million tons

Two major branches of light industry are said to have grown rapidly in the last few years. In response to a new government policy, the total planting area of industrial crops rose after 1963. Moreover, relatively heavy doses of chemical fertilizer, insecticides and farm machines supplied by the state to the land devoted to industrial crops raised the yield per unit of land (*JMJP,* Sept. 22 and 26, 1964). The harvest of sugar cane was unprecedentedly high in 1963 (*Chung-kuo hsin-wen,* May 15, 1964), and it rose further in 1964 and 1965 (*JPRS,* 875-41, January 1966; *JMJP,* April 30, 1966). As a result, in these years, the sugar manufacturing industry in Communist China had to prolong the extraction periods beyond the normal length of time (*Chung-kuo hsin-wen,* Jan. 21, 1965; *JMJP,* March 11, 1965, and April 30, 1966).

A 50 per cent rise in cotton output as compared with the 1962 level was claimed for 1963 (*Ta-kung pao,* March 23, 1964). It further increased by 37 per cent in 1964 (Chou En-lai, 1964). This rising trend of cotton output also continued in 1965 and 1966 (*JMJP,* Jan. 4, 1967; *Chung-kuo hsin-wen,* Feb. 9, 1966). As a result, textile production quickly reached its full capacity production rate in early 1965; and an extensive investment program for that industry was carried out in that year (*JMJP,* Dec. 18 and 25, 1965). The total number of production workers in the textile industry rose to 1.5 million in 1965, an increase of 0.56 million from the 0.94 million in 1956 (*JMJP,* Sept. 21, 1966). This booming situation in the textile industry lasted at least to August, 1966 (*JMJP,* Sept. 21, 1966).

Two other industries in Communist China that claimed relatively rapid growth in recent years are petroleum and electric power. Production in the former expanded primarily because of the discovery of a new oil field in Ta-Ching. It was officially announced that in 1964 China became

36. For instance, it was reported that output of chemical fertilizer in the first half of 1965 exceeded the preceding year's corresponding figure by 1.6 million tons (*JMJP,* Jan. 11, 1965). The total supply of chemical fertilizer was expected to increase by 4 million tons in 1966 (*JMJP,* Sept. 30, 1966); and domestic output for the first nine months of 1966 was 37 per cent above the same period last year (*JMJP,* Oct. 17, 1966).

basically self-sufficient in petroleum products. In the electric power industry, production was probably spurred by the rising need for power to develop the regime's nuclear weapons program and to manufacture more chemical fertilizer.[37]

Another significant aspect of the process of economic readjustment is that the general quality and variety of industrial goods rose considerably. The fact that production reached its physical limits induced the government to spend more manpower, which would otherwise have been left unused, to improve the quality of goods. On the other hand, difficulties in importation forced the Chinese Communists to try to produce a number of articles that they were previously unable to manufacture.

Basic construction activities in the crisis years fluctuated greatly. From the known data it is possible to make an account for the large and medium construction projects carried out in 1953-62.

1) 198 large projects were finished using complete sets of equipment furnished by the Soviet Union (*JMJP,* 1963).

2) 1,400 large projects were completed on the basis of design materials supplied by the Soviet Union (*JMJP,* 1963).

3) 68 projects were built with technical assistance from the Eastern European Communist countries (SSB *Communiqué,* 1953-57).

4) 1,426 large and medium projects were designed by the Chinese themselves and equipped with machinery produced domestically (Li Fu-chun, 1963).

The total number of large and medium projects carried out in the period 1953-62 came to 3,092. An examination of the annual accounts of construction activities in terms of large projects constructed reveals these details:

End of 1957:	
Construction begun	921
Wholly completed	429
Partially completed	109
End of 1958:	
Carried over from 1957	492 (= 921 − 429)
Total number of large projects under construction in the year	1,135

37. One Chinese source mentions that electric power generation has been doubled in recent years; but this source has neither given out the current output level nor specified the time period to which the growth rate refers (*JMJP,* June 7, 1966).

Wholly or partially completed	700	
Wholly completed (estimated)[38]	300	
Partially completed	400	
End of 1959:		
Carried over from 1958	835	(= 1,135 − 300)
Total number of large projects under construction in the year	1,341	
Construction began in 1959	506	(= 1,341 − 835)
Wholly or partially completed	671	
Wholly completed (estimated)	400	
Partially completed	271	

For 1960 only a draft economic plan was published. It gave fewer details than those of the previous years. In this draft plan a total of 989 large projects could be identified in selected industries. Since the planned total investment for basic construction for 1960 was larger than that in 1959, the total number of large projects planned for construction in 1960 must have been more than 1,400. On the other hand, it is known that there were at least 941 (= 1341 − 400) projects left unfinished in 1959, which had to be continued into 1960. Thus, about 500 new large projects had been planned to begin in 1960.

The above account shows that about 1,129 (= 429 + 300 + 400) large projects had been wholly completed by the end of 1959 and about 941 were to be continued into 1960, while construction of another group of 500 large projects was to begin in 1960. They add up to 2,570 large projects. There were probably more than 1,000 medium projects planned or under construction in the period 1953-62. Thus the total number of large and medium projects so counted far exceed the figure of 3,092 as the total number of large and medium projects wholly or partially completed before the end of 1962. This suggests two things. First, a great number of projects that were planned to be under construction in 1960 had been discontinued before their completion. Construction work of some may not have been resumed in later years. Second, the number of large and medium projects actually carried out in 1961 and 1962 was exceedingly small.

In mid-1960 construction was discontinued on 343 projects because of the cancellation of technical assistance contracts by the Soviets (*JMJP*, editorial, Dec. 4, 1963). Presumably a number of other projects also were halted later in the year either because they were ancillary to the Soviet aid projects or because the shortage of building materials grew as the eco-

38. In view of the long construction period for most large projects, we assume that the 492 projects that began before 1958 but were not completed by the end of 1957 would be finished in 1958 and 1959, and that one-third of those begun in 1958 would be completed before the end of 1959.

nomic crisis deepened. The number of projects that were carried on throughout the year may be placed at about 700, and 300 of them may have been completed.

It was announced in early 1961 that basic construction would be scaled down, with major emphasis placed on finishing those projects which were nearing completion (Po I-po, 1961). Therefore, the number of large and medium projects under construction could hardly have exceeded 400 in that year. One Communist source stated that 160 of those projects were carried over from 1961 to 1962 (*JMJP,* July 5, 1963). In view of the fact that Chou En-lai declared a further cut in basic construction activities in 1962 (*JMJP,* April 17, 1962),[39] 160 was probably the total number of large and medium projects under construction in 1962. The number in 1963 may be estimated at about 200 on the basis of the reported increase in the scale of basic construction in that year.[40] The total number of large and medium projects under construction in 1964 was said to be 200 more than in 1963 (*JMJP,* Sept. 30, 1964), which would mean about 400.

Insofar as the number of projects under construction is an indicator, basic construction activities in Communist China would seem to have reached their lowest point in 1962, a level probably comparable to that of 1953.

No statistical information has been released by the Chinese Communist to enable us to make even rough estimates about industrial investment in various years since 1960. However, if only to satisfy intellectual curiosity, we may try a novel way of reaching some hypotheses. The ratio of investment in machinery and equipment to the total basic construction investment has been fairly stable in the industrial sector in the past years.[41] The degree of self-sufficiency in machinery and equipment is known for various years.[42] Fortunately, the value of imported industrial machinery and equipment for each year can be obtained from foreign trade data released by China's trade partners. Using the foreign trade data and the aforementioned relevant ratios we have derived some estimates, shown in Table 6, for industrial investment made in Communist China during the

39. This estimate is quite consistent with another report which mentions that in 1958-62 the machine-building industry supplied complete sets of equipment to more than 1,000 projects in China; see *Peking Review,* No. 50, Dec. 13, 1963 (p. 23).

40. It is said that the construction industry had accomplished 25 per cent more work volume in 1963 than in 1962; see *Chien-chu,* 1963, No. 23 (p. 5); *JMJP,* Dec. 4, 1963; and *Jen-min shou-tse,* 1964 (pp. 6 and 521).

41. It was 38.4 per cent. See *TCKT,* No 4, 1957 (p. 17). Similar ratios can be found in other Chinese Communist sources.

42. The ratio was 60 per cent in 1953-57, 78 per cent in 1958, 80 per cent in 1959-60, 85 per cent in 1961-62, and 90 per cent in 1963. See *HHPYK,* No. 19 (p. 38); *Peking Review,* No. 41, Oct. 11, 1963 (p. 7) and No. 50, Dec. 13, 1963 (p. 22); *China Reconstructs,* May 1964 (p. 27); and *Chung-kuo hsin-wen,* Feb. 26 and Oct. 4, 1964.

crisis years. These estimates are generally consistent with the movement of construction activities mentioned previously.

TABLE 6

ESTIMATION OF FIXED INVESTMENT IN INDUSTRY
1960-1963

	1960	1961	1962	1963
Industrial machinery and equipment imported from the West				
(in million dollars)	61.2	34.2	22.4	12.9
(in million yuan)	160.0	90.0	58.6	34.0
Industrial machinery and equipment imported from USSR				
(in million rubles)	397.2	89.1	12.0	18.4
(in million yuan)	882.6	197.9	26.7	41.0
Total imports of industrial machinery and equipment				
(in million yuan)	1,042.6	287.9	85.3	75.0
Estimated fixed investment in industry				
(in million yuan)	13,505.0	4,972.0	1,473.0	1,943.0

Explanation and sources of data:

The foreign trade data used here exclude transporation equipment, tractors and other agricultural machinery. They are taken from U.S., *Annual Reports* and USSR, *Statischestii Sbornik* for the relevant years. Eastern European countries whose comparable data are inaccessible are not taken into account here. In converting the values in foreign currencies into *yuan* values, the prevailing official exchange rates of Communist China have been used, viz.:

1 ruble = 2,222 *yuan;* 1 dollar = 2,617 *yuan*

During the crisis years there existed considerable idle capacity in many branches of industry. Therefore, there was no need to make new investment in them. Besides, the government had decided to spare as much as possible of the investable funds for agriculture. Only those industrial branches that served to support agriculture had expanded production and received new investment during the readjustment period. It has also been reported that after 1961 a large number of machine-building factories were converted from their original functions into making equipment for the chemical fertilizer industry (*Shin Chugoku Nenken,* 1965, p. 211).

Up to 1964, except for those priority goods, the industrial sector was proceeding more or less along the path of recovery, and output was increased mainly by utilizing the existing capacity more fully. Although a few branches encountered bottlenecks or exhausted their idle capacity as early as mid-1964, most industries arrived at the same stage only in 1965 or early 1966. Therefore, a general upsurge in industrial investment began in 1965 (*Chung-kuo hsin-wen,* Dec. 25, 1965; *JMJP,* Sept. 23, Nov. 29, and Dec. 31, 1966).

Again, investment seems to have been more intensive in some industries than in others during 1965-66. The textile industry was a favored one. A total of 46 major projects were under construction in 1965, including 37 cotton textile mills, 6 printing and dyeing plants and 3 silk mills (*Jen-min shou-tse,* 1965, p. 559). Compared with the corresponding period in 1964, output of textile machinery and equipment in the first half of 1965 nearly doubled (*Peking Review,* Sept. 24, 1965). The total number of new spindles installed in 1965 reached 1.4 million (*JMJP,* Dec. 18 and 25, 1965), which was equal to the amount of new spindles installed in 1959 but exceeded the investment level in the textile industry in any other year. Energy-supplying industries also received concentrated investment. Electric-generating capacity and coal production capacity were reportedly enhanced greatly by new construction after 1965 (*Chung-kuo hsin-wen,* Dec. 25, 1965; *JMJP,* Sept. 23, 1966). The new capacity in petroleum production and refining added in 1966 is said to have exceeded the total amount installed in the whole period of the First Five-Year Plan (*JMJP,* Jan. 6, 1967).

IV. CONCLUDING REMARKS AND PROSPECTS FOR THE FUTURE

Industrialization is the cherished dream of the Chinese Communist leaders. In the process of industrialization, however, they have made numerous mistakes, some disastrous in their effect, others less serious. They have also varied their specific policies in developing industry. However, no matter what changes have been made, they should not be interpreted as the abandonment of the ultimate goal to make China an industrial power in the world. Even the apparent retreat from the industrial front in the last few years is only temporary; in the Communist phraseology, it is merely a preparation for smoother development (Po I-po, 1963; Fang Chung, 1964).

Although data are not sufficient to enable us to make meaningful indexes by which we can measure the overall industrial production of Communist China in recent years, nonquantitative information seems to indicate that most, if not all, branches of industry had already reached their full capacity points by 1965 or early 1966.[43] New investment was needed if industrial production was to be expanded. I am inclined to believe that the timing of the Chinese Communist Third Five-Year Plan was due to this utilization of existing industrial capacity. Otherwise, the Peking government would not have had to postpone the inauguration of the plan to 1966, leaving three years (1963-65) unaccounted for by any five-year plan. As is well known, the core of any Communist five-year plan is the investment plan. The Third Five-Year Plan is unlikely to be an exception. It was scheduled to begin in 1966 probably because the Chinese planners anticipated that by then industrial production in general would have reached its full capacity level and any further expansion would call for new investment.

So far as industry is concerned, Peking announced that the gross value of output increased by more than 20 per cent in 1966, the first year of the Third Five-Year Plan, and the planned target for that year was overfulfilled (*JMJP,* Dec. 31, 1966). Whether the claim of overfulfillment is true or not, it implies that the original target set for industrial production in 1966 must be an increase rate of about or slightly higher than 15 per cent.[44] If we take 15 per cent as the average growth rate projected by the Chinese planners for industry in the whole Third Five-Year Plan period, it is comparable to the 14.7 per cent average growth rate originally projected for that sector in the First Five-Year Plan.

It is hard to predict whether this assumed target for the Third Five-Year Plan can be accomplished. It is true that the original target set for industrial production in the First Five-Year Plan was overfulfilled by a quite large margin, but it would be more difficult for China to attain the same high growth rate in 1966-70. For one thing, the high rate of industrial growth in the First Five-Year Plan was made possible by technical assistance and imports of machinery and equipment from the Soviet Union and, to a lesser extent, from the Eastern European countries. In view of the deepening of the Sino-Soviet dispute, it does not seem very probable that friendly relations will be restored between the two countries in the next few years. The chances of substituting certain Western countries for the Soviet Union as potential large-scale sources of material and technical aid in the immediate future are not bright either.

More important, the future economic development of Communist China is highly contingent on the outcome of the current power struggle

43. This does not necessarily mean that total industrial output was also restored to its previous peak. In view of the fact that a great deal of production facilities in the small and indigenous enterprises built in the Great Leap years were discarded, the full capacity output in 1965-66 may be lower than the full capacity output in 1959-60.

44. Here and in the subsequent discussion we use the Communist definition of industrial growth, *i.e.,* in terms of gross value of output. Our concern here is not to measure Communist China's industrial output in a more meaningful way but to analyze whether the assumed target in the Communist definition can be accomplished.

in that country. First, the disruptive effects of the Red Guards activities on the economy were already felt toward the end of 1966. Should the power struggle continue for a prolonged period of time, it would undoubtedly slow down production, especially in the industrial sector. Second, the policy of economic readjustment was a compromise between two major groups in the Chinese Communist hierarchy, who have quite different visualizations of the basic causes of the economic trouble in China and of the policy prescriptions for the future. The present Third Five-Year Plan was also formulated on this compromise basis. However, this compromise represents an unstable equilibrium that tends to break down when the political situation in Communist China changes. In fact, the basic difference between the two groups concerning economic policy has been one of the important factors underlying the severe power struggle. Therefore, even if the power struggle is quickly brought to an end, the winning group, whoever they are, may contemplate some drastic changes in economic policy. For instance, should the Maoists become victorious, a new Great Leap Forward movement may be attempted and many other economic measures used in 1958-59 may be reinstated.

APPENDIX: TABLE A-1

COMPARISON OF INDUSTRIAL PRODUCTION INDEXES OF COMMUNIST CHINA
(1952 = 100)

	Official: Gross Value, Factory and Handicraft Production	Chao: Factory and Handicraft Production	Chao: Factory Production	Liu-Yeh: Factory Production, Value Added	Liu-Yeh: Factory Production, Estimated Gross Value	Wu-Hung: Gross Value, Modern Industry, Estimated from Power Consumption by Industry, Set I	Wu-Hung: Gross Value, Modern Industry, Estimated from Power Consumption by Industry, Set II	Wu-Hung: Gross Value, Modern Industry, Estimated from Finished Steel Production	Wu-Hung: Modern Industry, Composite Series	Matsuda: With Japanese Value-Added Weights	Matsuda: With Indian Value-Added Weights	Mizoguchi-Matsuda: With Chinese Wage Bill Weights
1949	40.8	50.0	44.3									
1950	55.7	63.3	57.7									
1951	76.8	81.2	77.0									
1952	100.0	100.0	100.0	100.0	100.0	100.0	100.0	100.0	100.0	100.0	100.0	100.0
1953	130.2	122.1	124.7	122.9	120.1	129.3	120.2	128.7	124.1	152.4	146.4	147.6
1954	151.4	139.4	141.6	142.2	138.9	157.7	143.4	140.4	146.0	150.8	155.9	178.1
1955	159.8	149.7	146.9	159.0	151.2	172.6	157.5	164.1	162.5	162.1	175.4	190.7
1956	205.0	179.4	182.2	210.8	202.5	205.1	193.0	208.5	199.6	242.0	252.7	281.0
1957	228.3	189.8	195.9	238.6	219.7	229.3	224.1	216.6	223.2	243.9	266.6	297.5
1958	379.4	251.5	272.6	289.2		278.1	285.5	241.7	272.3	476.6	506.7	625.5
1959	528.6	330.9	371.4	373.5		332.6	393.9	292.4	353.1			

Sources:

For official index and Chao's indexes, 1949-1959, from Chao, 1965 (p. 88).

For Liu-Yeh's series: from Liu-Yeh, 1965 (pp. 66, 146, 157). The figures cited here refer to the sums of manufacturing factories, mining and utilities at 1952 constant *yuan.*

For Wu-Hung's four series: from F. C. Hung and J. L. Wu, "Conceptual Difficulties in Measuring China's Industrial Output", in Li, 1964 (p. 61). Detailed explanation of the estimation procedures are given in Wu *et al.*, 1963 (pp. 199-236). However, except that the series estimated on the basis of finished steel production is identical with the series on p. 209 of Wu, 1963, the other three series differ from what appears in the 1963 publication. Presumably the authors have revised their original series.

For Matsuda's two value-added series: from Yoshiro Matsuda, "Tentative Estimates of Chinese Industrial Production Index" in Ishikawa, 1964 (p. 134).

For Mizoguchi-Matsuda's series: from Toshiyuki Mizoguchi and Yoshiro Matsuda, "Examination of China's Official Industrial Production Indexes," Asian Economic Research Institute, 1960 (p. 164).

REFERENCES

Asian Economic Research Institute, 1960. *Statistical Studies of the Chinese Economic Development,* Vol. II. Tokyo.

CHAO, KANG, 1968. *The Construction Industry in Communist China.* Chicago.

CHAO, KANG, 1965. *The Rate and Pattern of Industrial Growth in Communist China.* Ann Arbor.

CHI CHUNG-WEI, 1954. "Strengthen the Cooperation and Coordination between Light Industry and Other Industries," *HHYP,* No. 6, p. 129.

CHI CHUNG-WEI, 1957. "How to Further Develop Our Industry in a More Balanced Manner," *CHCC,* No. 7, pp. 6–7.

Chi-hsieh kung-yeh (*Machinery Industry*). Peking.

CHCC, various dates. *Chi-hua ching-chi* (*Planned Economy*). Peking.

CHYTC, various dates. *Chi-hua yu tung-chi* (*Planning and Statistics*). Peking.

CHYTC, 1960. "The Resolution of the State Council Concerning the Strengthening of Overall Financial Planning Work," No. 2, p. 1.

Chien-chu (*Construction*). Peking.

Chien-chu tsai-liao kung-yeh (*Building Materials Industry*). Peking.

China Quarterly. London.

China Reconstructs. Peking.

CHIN YU-CHENG, 1958. "Attention Should Be Given to the Regional Balance of

Ching-chi yen-chiu (*Economic Research*). Peking.

Demand and Supply in Constructing New Coal Mines," *CHCC,* No. 6, pp. 10–11.

CHOU EN-LAI, 1964. Report on the Government Works Before the First Session of the Third National People's Congress, in *JMJP,* Dec. 30, 1964.

Chung-kuo hsin-wen (*China News*). Canton.

FANG CHUNG, 1964. "An Economic Policy that Wins," *Peking Review,* No. 11 (March 13, 1964), p. 7.

FFYP *First Five-Year Plan for the Development of the National Economy in 1953-57.* Peking, 1955.

Foreign Trade of the People's Republic of China. Peking.

Hsin chien-she (*New Construction*). Peking.

HHPYK, various dates. *Hsin-hua pan-yueh-kan* (*New China Semi-Monthly*). Peking.

HHYP, various dates. *Hsin-hua yueh-pao* (*New China Monthly*). Peking.

Hung-chi (*Red Flag*). Peking.

ISHIKAWA, SHIGORU, 1964. (Ed.) *Long Run Prospects of the Chinese Economy.* Tokyo.

JMJP, various dates. *Jen-min jih-pao* (*People's Daily*). Peking.

JMJP, 1963. "A Letter from CPSU to CPC," July 20, 1963.

Jen-min shou-tse (*People's Handbook*). Peking.

JPRS Joint Publications and Research Service. Washington, D.C.

KOHLMEY, GUNTHER, 1956. *Der Demokratische Weltmarkt.* Chinese translation, Peking.

Kung-jen jih-pao (*Worker's Daily*). Peking.

Lao-tung (*Labor*). Peking.

LI, CHOH-MING, 1959. *Economic Development of Communist China.* Berkeley.

LI, CHOH-MING, 1964. (Ed.) *Industrial Development in Communist China.* New York.

LI FU-CHUN, 1955. "Report on the First Five-Year Plan for the Development of the National Economy," *JMJP,* July 8, 1955.

LI FU-CHUN, 1960. "Raise High the Red Banner of the General Line and Continue to Leap Forward," *Hung-chi,* No. 16, p. 10.

LI FU-CHUN, 1963. Report in *JMJP,* Dec. 4, 1963.

LI HSIEN-NIEN, 1958. Report in *JMJP,* Feb. 12, 1958.

LIU, TA-CHUNG and K. C. YEH, 1965. *The Economy of the Chinese Mainland: National Income and Economic Development, 1933-1959.* Princeton.

NIU CHUNG-HUANG, 1959. "The Multifarious Operation in Large Factories and Mining Establishments," *Hung-chi,* No. 9, pp. 18–19.

OU MING, 1959. "The Whole Country as a single Chessboard," *CHYTC,* No. 1, p. 3.

Peking Review, various dates. Peking.

Peking Review, 1963. "A Proposal Concerning the General Line of the International Communist Movement" (letter of the CPC in reply to the letter dated March 30, 1963 of the CPSU), No. 25 (June 21, 1963), p. 18.

Peking Review, 1964. "Seven Letters Exchanged between Central Committee of CPC and CPSU," No. 19 (May 8, 1964), p. 15.

PO I-PO, 1961. "Strive for a New Victory in Our Country's Industrial Construction," *Jen-min shou-tse,* pp. 238–240.

PO I-PO, 1962. "Speed up the Development of Extractive Industries, *Jen-min shou-tse,* pp. 236–240.

PO I-PO, 1963. "The Socialist Industrialization of China," *Peking Review,* No. 41 (Oct. 11, 1963), p. 9.

SHA YING, 1956. "The Relations between Coastal and Inland Industries," *JMJP,* Nov. 24, 1956.

Shih-yu kan-tan (*Petroleum Survey*). Peking.

Shin Chugoku Nenken, 1965. Tokyo.

SSB *Communiqué,* various years. State Statistical Bureau of Communist China, *Communiqué of Economic Achievements.* Peking, various years.

SSB, 1958. State Statistical Bureau of Communist China. *Wo-kuo kang-tieh tien-li mei-tan chi-hsieh fang-chih tsao-chi kung-yeh ti chin-hsi* (*The Present and Past Conditions of Our Iron and Steel, Power, Coal, Machinery, Textiles, and Paper Manufacturing Industries*). Peking.

Ta-kung pao (*Impartial Daily*). Peking.

(TGY) Ten Great Years, 1960. State Statistical Bureau of Communist China, Peking.

Tien-chi kung-yeh (*Electric Machinery Industry*). Peking.

Tsai-ching yen-chiu (*Financial and Economic Research*). Shanghai.

TSAO YEN-HSING, 1958. "Industrial Location Is an Important Problem in Socialist Industrial Construction," *CHCC,* No. 12, pp. 13–15.

TSENG WEN-CHING, 1958. *Chung-kuo ti she-hui-chu-i kung-yeh-hua* (*China's Socialist Industrialization*). Peking.

TCKT, various dates. *Tung-chi kung-tso* (*"Statistical Work"*). Peking.

TCKTTH, various dates. *Tung-chi kung-tso tung-hsun ("Statistical Bulletin").* Peking.

TCKTTH (Data Section), 1956a. "The Scope and Development of China's Basic Construction Investment." *TCKTTH,* No. 18, p. 46.

TCKTTH (Data Section), 1956b. "Several Problems Concerning Our Country's Socialist Industrialization." *TCKTTH,* No. 21, pp. 3–7.

U.S. Government. *Annual Reports of the Administrator of the Mutual Defense Assistance Control Act of 1951 to Congress.* Washington, D.C., annually.

USSR Government. *Statischestii Sbornik.* Moscow, annually.

WANG CHEN-TSU, 1959. "Problems of the Economic Effects in Construction of Industrial Enterprises," *CHYTC,* No. 15, p. 12.

WANG SSU-HUA, 1962. "Fully Activate the Functions of Statistical Work in Socialist Construction," *Hung-chi,* No. 18, pp. 13–18.

Wen-hui pao (Wen-hui Daily). Shanghai.

WU-HSIA, 1959. "Strengthen the Organization and Planning for the Economic Cooperation Among Provinces," *CHYTC,* No. 6, p. 12.

WU, YUAN-LI, 1963. *Economic Development and the Use of Energy Resources in Communist China.* New York.

WU, YUAN-LI, F. P. HOEBER and M. M. ROCKWELL, 1963. *The Economic Potential of Communist China.* Stanford Research Institute Technical Report No. 2, Oct. 1963.

YANG CHING-WEN, 1957a. "Concentrated Production of Standardized Parts Is Economical and Rational," *Chi-hsieh kung-yeh,* No. 21, p. 18.

YANG CHING-WEN, 1957b. "Two Problems in Industrial Location," *CHCC,* No. 8, p. 15.

Industrial Planning and Management 10

DWIGHT H. PERKINS

THE CHINESE COMMUNISTS consistently stress the importance of planning to China's economic growth. In one sense or another, of course, nearly every nation plans its economy. But for China and other economies that to some degree follow the Soviet model, "planning," particularly in the industrial sphere, takes on the more specific meaning of control exercised through centrally determined output targets. This chapter will investigate exactly how Peking plans in the industrial sector, why changes in planning techniques have been made over time, and how suitable the alternative methods are for China.

Analytically, planning can be divided into three parts: (1) the determination of broad policy goals (*e.g.,* producer goods versus consumer goods, autarky or reliance on foreign trade, etc.); (2) decisions on specific plan targets for output, costs, etc.; and (3) the implementation of those targets. In practice, the lines between these three parts are not sharply drawn. At times broad policy goals are taken for granted or largely ignored, and planning starts at the specific target level. More important, decisions on what targets are to be and how they are to be implemented are intimately connected. For example, a target may be set higher or lower depending on which will elicit the most effort from the enterprise involved. Or planners may channel resources at their command into one sector or another simply because they are able to control what is going on in that sector, not because to do so is to make the most efficient use of their resources.

All these problems have arisen in China and will be discussed below. In spite of such difficulties, however, the discussion will be carried out in terms of the three suggested phases.

The author wishes to thank the discussants at the Carmel conference, Joseph Berliner, Gardner Clark, Jung-Chao Liu, and Chu-yuan Cheng, for their helpful comments, as well as Abram Bergson and Simon Kuznets, who read an early draft. There were also a number of helpful comments from other conference participants, particularly Gregory Grossman and Ta-Chung Liu.

I. ECONOMIC GOALS

The goal of rapid economic growth has been second only to the security of the Chinese Communist state itself. In fact, economic growth has been considered to be a fundamental guarantee of that security.

Increases in industrial and agricultural output serve national security in a number of ways. They may make possible a rising standard of living for the people as a whole or for major groups within the society, thus promoting domestic political tranquility. Heavy industrial development is the one key prerequisite to an armaments industry. Growth of certain heavy industries may also make possible reduced dependence on foreign trade, not only for the military, but also for further economic development. It should be pointed out that "heavy industry," as the term is used by the Chinese Communists, is not synonymous with producer goods industry. While it includes defense industries, it excludes producer goods industries still operating with relatively primitive technology. Further, heavy industries tend to be large in scale, thus excluding many small-scale producer goods enterprises from the category.

During the first decade of Communist control of the Chinese mainland, it was the advantages of heavy industrialization that held the regime's attention. It was by means of heavy industry and eventually modern weapons that China would achieve great power status. Those same industries, particularly machine-building and steel, would also make possible economic autarky, which at that time, before the deterioration in Sino-Soviet relations, was desired more for its own sake than for its immediate military advantages. With increasing hostility between China and the Soviet Union, autarky has taken on even greater importance for reasons of both security and economic development. Although China has been able to import some needed industrial equipment from the West, the regime undoubtedly considers this a precarious source of assistance at best. In the words of Po I-po, "The socialist industrialization of our country entails building an independent comprehensive and modern industrial system . . ." (1963, p. 22).

Once a decision to promote autarky has been made, emphasis on producer goods industry becomes necessary in order to raise future living standards, whatever the military implications. A given investment in consumer goods industry may yield a higher return than an equivalent expenditure on producer goods,[1] but if one does not want to rely on exporting consumer goods in exchange for imports of producer goods, then economic growth comes to an end. Thus, although producer goods are not

1. There is, of course, no necessity for consumer goods to yield a higher rate of return than producer goods, particularly if prices reflect planners' rather than consumers' preferences.

synonymous with heavy industry, the differences are not great. Even if investment is concentrated in agriculture, the major inputs other than labor are primarily the products of heavy industry (*e.g.,* chemical fertilizer, power machinery, etc.).

Communist China's emphasis on heavy industry, however, has not resulted solely from rational calculations such as these. Heavy industry as the path to economic growth had become a part of the regime's ideology, in effect a goal in itself. Marx had tended to look on economic development and the growth of large-scale heavy industry as one and the same, and the example of the Soviet five-year plans further solidified the place of this model of growth in the regime's ideology. Even if the ideological element had not been present, however, Peking's lack of experience and resulting need to rely on Soviet support would have made it difficult to follow a different path.

As Chinese economic experience grew, this unquestioning reliance on the Soviet model began to wane. Perhaps as early as 1955, the regime began to have doubts about the emphasis on machine-building and supporting industries. The main cause of these doubts was the poor performance of agriculture. As it became increasingly apparent that organizational reforms alone would not raise farm output, Peking was forced to transfer resources to sectors that would directly benefit agriculture.[2] The greatest shifts in resources apparently took place after 1961 or 1962, but there were lesser changes as early as 1956.[3]

This change, given Peking's desire for autarky, did not mean a reallocation of investment funds away from heavy industry so much as a change in direction from one set of heavy industrial products to another. However, this statement must be qualified to the degree that the need to maintain work incentives has caused the regime to lower the rate of investment and thus indirectly transfer resources to consumer goods. In addition, the increasing emphasis on agriculture did involve a transfer of funds from industries producing machines that would produce more machines to machines that would produce end products.

The continued substantial investment in heavy industry can be seen from the fragments of evidence available on industrial performance since 1962. Chemical fertilizer output in the first half of 1964 was 53 per cent above the same period in 1963, and 1963 output was 40 per cent above 1962 (Kao Kuang-chien, 1964, p. 25). Tractor production in the first half of 1963 was 30 per cent above the comparable period in 1962 (Fang Chung, 1963, p. 40). Nor has the shift been toward agricultural supplies only. In weaponry and related fields, the Chinese not only exploded their

2. For a further discussion of these problems, see Perkins, 1966 (Chs. III-IV).

3. In 1956, state investment in agriculture was raised from 6.7 per cent to 8.0 per cent of the total; it reached 8.6 per cent in 1957, and 9.9 per cent in 1958 (SSB, *Ten Great Years,* pp. 59-60).

first nuclear device on October 16, 1964, but are apparently able to produce (not just assemble) MIG-21's (*New York Times,* Dec. 30, 1964). Furthermore, petroleum output in 1963 reached an estimated 6.5 million tons, four and one-half times the level of 1957.

Thus, although the economic content of Chinese Communist goals has changed somewhat over time, the emphasis on autarky and military strength has insured that a large portion of state-controlled investment has gone to heavy industry. This fact, together with a more general understanding of China's economic goals, is fundamental to any appraisal of the effectiveness of Chinese Communist planning technique.

II. DRAWING UP THE PLAN

BALANCE

There are two significantly different problems involved in drawing up an industrial plan. One is deciding how to allocate current production and stocks of goods among individual enterprises so as to maximize current output according to certain criteria, and given existing plant capacity. The other is determining the direction of investment; *i.e.,* where plant capacity is to be expanded and by how much. This section deals with the first of these problems—that of coordinating or balancing inputs and outputs, given existing plant capacity.

At the heart of a typical annual plan, for China as for any Soviet-type economy, are a number of targets set for each industry and enterprise. In China, prior to November, 1957, there were 12 different kinds of targets. After 1957, the number of such targets that were classified as compulsory was reduced to four, but the reasons for this concerned the problem of implementing the plan, not of drawing it up. The other eight targets continued to be computed, but were for advisory purposes only. Five of the original 12 could be classified as physical goals: (1) output of major products, (2) total number of employees, (3) trial manufacture of new varieties of products, (4) total number of employees at year's end, and (5) certain technical-economic norms. If these norms are broken down into their component parts—consumption of raw materials, level of mechanization, and rate of equipment utilization—the number of physical targets increases to seven.

The remaining seven targets involve prices or money: (6) gross value of output, (7) cost reduction rate and (8) cost reduction quota, (9) total wage bill and (10) the average wage, (11) labor productivity, and (12) profits. Except for input targets, targets were the minimum, and an enterprise was expected to exceed the designated figure. In the case of raw material and labor inputs, the targets were set at the maximum.

The major problem in setting the targets for output and material consumption is one of coordination or balance. Many of the outputs of one enterprise are the inputs of another. Any given product, in fact, may be crucial to the manufacture of hundreds of others. The process of achieving coordination in a centrally planned economy is commonly referred to as "material balances planning."

The difficulties involved in attaining balance, however, should not be exaggerated for a country such as China. Because China is underdeveloped, it produces a far fewer number of commodities than a developed economy. In 1957, Chinese central planners dealt with 729 individual items (Hsueh Mu-ch'iao, 1957, p. 24), but it is likely that the number for which coordination was seriously attempted was much fewer. The number of commodities actually distributed by the state in a rationed and "unified" (*i.e.,* coordinated) manner was 28 in 1952; 96 in 1953, the first year in which annual planning was put into operation; and 235 in 1956 (*TCKT,* 1957, p. 26).[4] This compares with the more than 1,500 commodities that were centrally allocated in the Soviet Union in the 1950's.

The fact that China is underdeveloped makes the planners' coordinating task easier in another respect as well. There are fewer interdependencies between industries and sectors in an underdeveloped economy. For example, under the existing plan, textile and cigarette output in China depend almost exclusively on the cotton and tobacco crops of the previous year. The same can be said of most other products of light industry. In China, in particular, substantial unused plan capacity in most such industries makes it possible to expand output greatly before any consideration has to be given to investment in new plants and equipment (Chu Jung-chi, 1956, p. 22). In recent years interdependence has been increased by the regime's policy of expanding those light industrial products that depend on industrial rather than agricultural raw materials. In Shanghai, for example, only 39.5 per cent of total light industrial output in 1962 depended on agricultural raw materials as compared with 63.9 per cent in 1957 (Shih, Yeh, and Ch'en, 1963, p. 9). This change, however, is undoubtedly partly accounted for by a lack of agricultural raw

4. Whether or not formal material balance sheets were drawn up for this number of commodities is not clear. There are statements which indicate that such formal procedures were followed for only a much smaller number of commodities. Nevertheless, if 235 commodities were distributed in a coordinated manner, something approximating the materials balances procedures, by whatever name, must have been followed.

An additional problem in using these numbers arises from uncertainty surrounding the question of whether commodities are defined in the same way in both China and the Soviet Union, and even within China at different times. The differences are probably not great enough to negate the value of such comparisons, but one cannot be certain.

materials due to preceding bad harvests. Most Chinese light industry is still heavily dependent on agriculture.

Unlike the case in heavy industry, most of the products of light industry go directly to the consumer. A reduction in output in this sector, therefore, does not cause a chain reaction through all other sectors. Consumers suffer a decline in consumption, but this is important to overall production only to the extent that it affects incentives. Even consumer tastes in an underdeveloped economy are comparatively easy to predict: they will take virtually any reasonably priced item placed on the market. As per capita incomes rise, questions of style and quality become paramount and make central planning difficult and often very inefficient,[5] but this is a problem not faced in China at present.

Even within heavy industry, the degree of interdependence can be overemphasized. Table 1, showing the Soviet Union's intersectoral balances in 1959, illustrates this point.

The balances for the Soviet Union were selected because its industrial development has followed a pattern that China until recently has attempted to emulate. In fact, as Chenery and Clark (1959) have shown, interindustry relations tend to be similar in all industrialized economies, so that almost any such country's input-output table would probably present essentially the same picture as that of the Soviet Union.[6]

First of all, it is apparent from the table that the heavy industrial sectors (columns [a] to [e]) are almost entirely independent of inputs from outside (except for trade and transport). Furthermore, the degree of interdependence within each sector is limited. Current output of power and fuels depends only on inputs of power and fuels in any quantity. Ferrous metals depend primarily on ferrous ores, nonferrous metals, and fuel and power. Only machinery and metalworking draw heavily from all other heavy industry sectors. This whole picture changes if new investment or expansion of plant capacity is considered, but we are only concerned for the present with the problem of coordinating current output, given existing plant and equipment.

Planning heavy industry, then, becomes increasingly complex as development proceeds not because of increasingly complex patterns of interdependence so much as because of the increasing number of commodities within each sector, which are following already established allocation patterns.[7] Broad sectors thus can be planned individually without regard to what is happening in more than one or two other sectors. Since in

5. An excellent discussion of this problem as it has arisen in Hungary can be found in J. Kornai, 1959. The recent Soviet experimentation with greater emphasis on profits started with consumer goods industries partly for this reason.

6. I am indebted to Herbert S. Levine for a number of observations relevant to the Soviet input-output table.

7. This statement is obviously an oversimplification, but a more precise statement would add much to length and little to clarity.

TABLE 1

SOVIET UNION, INTERSECTORAL BALANCES (1959)
(Gross Output of Each Commodity = 100)
Consuming Sectors

Producing Sectors	(a) Ferrous	(b) Non-ferrous	(c) Fuels	(d) Machi-nery	(e) Chemi-cals	(f) Construc-tion	(g) Trans-port	(h) Trade	(i) Other	(j) Final Demand	(k) Gross Output
(a) Ferrous Ores and Metals (1,2)[a]	16.4	—[b]	—	46.9	—	22.3	—	—	2.8	7.8	100.0
(b) Nonferrous ores and metals (3,4)	11.9	29.0	—	27.9	3.1	—	—	—	—	23.8	100.0
(c) Fuel and power (5,7-11)	8.0	2.7	18.3	5.0	2.7	7.0	10.2	—	21.6	23.7	100.0
(d) Machinery, metal-working, autos, etc. (6,12-20)	—	—	—	14.7	—	9.1	—	—	12.7	58.5	100.0
(e) Chemicals, abra-sives, etc. (21-23)	—	—	2.1	9.5	22.3	4.0	—	—	33.9	25.2	100.0
(f) Construction and construction materi-als (27,33)	—	—	—	—	—	18.4	—	—	—	80.9	100.0
(g) Transport (36)	4.2	—	25.0	8.0	4.9	15.6	—	—	38.8	—	100.0
(h) Trade (37)	2.1	—	7.5	8.8	—	3.9	—	—	81.3	—	100.0
(i) Other (24,26,28-32,34,35,38)	—	—	—	—	—	2.8	—	—	37.1	56.2	100.0

Source:
Joint Economic Committee, *Annual Economic Indicators for the U.S.S.R.*, February, 1964, pp. 202-205.

Notes:
a. The data in the table in the source were aggregated and the percentages of gross output were computed by the author. The row numbers in the original source are included for each row in Table 1.
b. Where the amount was less than 2 per cent of gross output,—were entered in the table rather than the precise figure for purposes of clarity.

China the number of commodities involved in any given sector is comparatively small, the intrasector coordination problem does not appear to be insurmountably difficult.

The underdeveloped nature of China's economy, however, is not an unmixed blessing to those charged with drawing up the material balances. The main problem arises from the fact that Chinese industrial output is produced by a large number of enterprises varying widely in scale, and using techniques that range from the very primitive to the most modern available. This difficulty was accentuated by the emphasis on small-scale industry in 1958 and 1959, though it did not originate then. Approximately one-third of gross industrial output in China was produced in firms that used only the simplest kinds of hand-powered machinery (see Table 2). Altogether there was nearly 170,000 individual industrial firms, 140,000 of which employed fewer than 15 persons (fewer than 30 if no mechanical power was used).

TABLE 2

CHINA'S INDUSTRIAL FIRMS

	Gross Value of Industrial Output in Nonmodern Enterprises		Number of Enterprises		
	(in million yuan)	as per cent of total industrial output)	Total	Large- and medium-scale	Small-scale
	(1)	(2)	(3)	(4)	(5)
1949[a]	6,110	43.6	126,035		
1950	8,230	43.1			
1951	10,440	39.6			
1952	12,280	35.8	167,403	27,527	139,876
1953	15,890	35.5	176,405	31,379	145,026
1954	17,990	34.6	167,626	31,187	136,439
1955	17,790	32.4	125,474		
1956	20,020	28.4			
1957[b]	22,760	29.1			
1958	29,730	25.4			

Source:

See Perkins, 1966 (pp. 108-109). The data on gross value of output in nonmodern enterprises are crude estimates at best, particularly for the years 1949-1951 and 1958.

Notes:

a. Data for 1949 through 1956 are in constant 1952 prices.

b. The 1957 and 1958 data are in constant 1957 prices.

With that many firms operating with such primitive technology, it was impossible to collect statistics of sufficient quality to allow central planners to truly coordinate all industrial inputs and outputs. Within a given industry, for example, consumption of raw materials and other inputs per ton of output was likely to differ considerably. The difference in average cost between a large- and small-scale copper ore-dressing plant was 32 per cent (Secretariat of National Conference, 1959, p. 9). Cost disparities among different plants for 21-count yarn were 70 per cent; wheat flour, 100 per cent; grade "C" cigarettes, 50 per cent; and matches, 150 per cent (*KJJP,* 1956).

In China the problem of achieving balance among so many disparate firms has been accomplished by a number of measures that have considerably reduced the scope of the central material balances. Although the number of commodities subject to centralized allocation has gradually been increased, a portion of each has regularly been set aside and sold on the market. In early years this practice was necessitated by the inability of central authorities to attain the necessary control over allocation. In Shanghai, for example, the state initially controlled only 9.8 per cent of the market supply of metals and machinery, and by the final quarter of 1952 still had only 56.2 per cent (*Shanghai chieh-fang . . . ,* 1958, pp. 380-381, 395). Even in 1956, when the state could have had complete control, 8.6 per cent of all cement, 2.8 per cent of steel products, and 40.9 per cent of coal output were sold in the market (*TCKT,* 1957, p. 26). Much of this (particularly coal) went to consumers and agriculture, but part was presumably bought by small-scale industrial enterprises. The existence of this marketed portion has been one element, although not the most important one, in the Chinese Communist decision not to follow the Soviet practice of setting heavy industrial product prices at 5 per cent above average cost. Instead, partly in order to restrict demand, these prices were held at the high levels prevailing during the Korean War.

More important, Peking has made a number of attempts to remove a large portion of small-scale and consumer goods output entirely from the province of the centrally planned balances. Initially, in 1956, this took the form of allowing various small-scale handicraft-type firms to produce for the market and buy their raw materials from that market without having to deal through state wholesaling agencies or to compete ultimately with large-scale firms for planned allocations (Ch'en Yun, 1956).

In late 1957, the regime ordered a major decentralization of control over production and distribution, placing responsibility at provincial and lower levels (Chinese Communist Party, 1957, pp. 96-99; 100-101). Once the rural communes had been set up, management of many of the smaller firms devolved onto the commune leadership. Although these decentralization measures were shortly to be caught up in the extremes of the "Great Leap Forward," they were not conceived in that atmosphere.

Most of the firms transferred down were either small-scale, consumer-oriented, or both. Generally their raw materials came from the province or region in which they were located, as did their buyers. Local authorities, it was thought, would know local conditions best and could thus achieve the most efficient coordination of activities. A certain amount of general guidance was still to come from the central plan, but basically the central authorities were excused from responsibility for coordinating a significant portion of industrial output and allocation. Unlike the system proposed by Ch'en Yun in 1956, the 1957-58 decentralization did not involve a significant increase in the role of the market. It was more like an attempt to divide the problem of drawing up material balances into several independent parts.

The fact that the system worked badly from the start was not that it was wrong in principle, but that it was implemented in a way that made efficient coordination impossible. (This, however, is the subject of the last half of the chapter.) The basic validity and importance of the principle of decentralized control over these secondary industrial products is testified to by the regime's continuance of the system in one form or another ever since. By 1965, all industrial enterprises were entitled to produce what they liked after they had fulfilled the state plan targets, providing they did not use materials allocated to them under the plan (Ma Wen-kuei, 1964, p. 24). Presumably this provision has had little significance for large-scale heavy industrial establishments, most or all of whose output is centrally planned. It is rather a way of perpetuating decentralization of responsibility away from the central planning authorities to, in this case, the enterprise itself.

Up to this point, the problem of attaining coordination or balance has been treated as a question involving only output targets (in physical or value terms) and input coefficients (items 1, 5, and 6 of the 12 targets listed in Section I.) In practice, these targets, particularly that for gross value of output and later for output of major products, were the heart of the material balances. The other targets were of far less importance, although nominally it was as much a violation of law to slight them as to disregard output targets. Many of the reasons for these priorities concern problems of plan implementation and the kind of men charged with that implementation. In part, however, priority for output targets flows directly from the nature of the balancing problem.

If the profits target is not met in each firm, the national treasury will not be prevented from financing the government budget, for either a number of firms will overfulfill their targets, or taxes can be made to fill the deficit. Similarly, an excess hiring of labor or payment of wages is a problem only for those trying to prevent inflation on the consumer goods market (Perkins, 1966, Ch. VIII). Most unskilled and semiskilled labor is a comparatively homogeneous input and thus can be readily transferred from one occupation to another. With China's surplus of unskilled labor, there is not even any real need, from the point of view of production, to insure that demand for labor by industry as a whole is limited.

On the other hand, an excessive use of steel or petroleum by one firm means that all other firms must either find substitutes (no easy task in the short run) or curtail output. Similarly, if the aluminum industry fails to meet its output target, all aluminum users suffer, as do the consumers of their products in turn. Therefore, given the decision to achieve coordination of inputs and outputs through centralized allocation and material balances planning, the emphasis on output targets follows naturally.

The function of the other targets, of which the profits target is the most important, is in part simply to help enforce the production targets. More important, however, is their role in promoting quality, variety of output, and more efficient use of inputs. In principle, these functions could be carried out by setting production targets so that they could be completed only if inputs were used efficiently, and by establishing a proper pricing policy (so that gross value of output correctly reflected quality). In practice, though, the task of implementing any set of targets is formidable, requiring not only these other kinds of plan targets, but a variety of other measures as well (as will be discussed in later sections).

It has been suggested in some sources that in the early 1960's the profits targets actually replaced the output target in the scale of priorities (Schurmann, 1964). In China during 1961-62 there was a certain amount of debate on this point in economic journals and elsewhere, not unlike the debate surrounding the Liberman proposals in the Soviet Union (and the much more extensive discussion in Eastern Europe). However, there has been no evidence to indicate that Peking has actually put these proposals into operation, as the Soviet Union did for a large number of consumer goods industries in 1964 and 1965. In fact, there is considerable evidence to the contrary.[8]

Such a change in priorities in favor of profits could have taken one of two somewhat different forms. Profits targets could have been set in such a way as to be the main means of enforcing what was still expressed (and drawn up) in the plan in physical output terms. Planners' preferences, ex-

8. The "Seventy Theses for Industry" promulgated in draft form in early 1962, for example, follow earlier directives in calling for obedience to all plan targets, with output targets listed ahead of profits. (These were reproduced in rough form from memory by a refugee for the Union Research Institute. I am indebted to Mr. Chao Yung-ching for making them available to me). See also many articles such as Hsiao Liang, 1962. This article, along with a general discussion of the virtues of imaginatively obeying the state plan, includes the passage:

> "It is necessary, on the basis of a comprehensive balancing to specify concretely what a particular enterprise should produce, how much of the product it should produce, when its product should leave, to which unit it should supply, from where its raw materials should come, and so forth."

pressed in the material balance tables, would still determine what was produced, but the enterprise's only immediate concern would be profits. A much more radical move would be to allow industrial firms to produce directly for the market (consumers' preferences) and judge their performance by the profits they made in that arena. This alternative was in 1965 being tried for certain consumer goods industries in the Soviet Union, and has often been an element in the method of operation of small-scale industrial enterprises in China. From all appearances, however, neither alternative has ever really been tried in China's major industrial enterprises. A more complete understanding of why this has been the case must await the analysis in subsequent sections of this chapter.

INVESTMENT IN NEW CAPACITY

Decisions on where and in what products new investment will be made are quite different, in terms of the demands put on central planners, from drawing up the material balances. Investment plants and the material balances, of course, are not unrelated. Increased output due to increased plant capacity and related inputs must balance out with all other products, new and old, but comparatively large errors in estimating increases in output are reduced in significance when total production is taken into account. The degree to which this simplifies matters, however, should not be exaggerated. Prior to 1960, annual increases in output in sectors where the Chinese Communists concentrated their resources (heavy industry) often loomed large in proportion to total output. Between 1952 and 1959, the output of producer goods factories in China (value added) had increased six-fold (Liu and Yeh, 1965, p. 66).[9]

The more difficult problem for those planning new investment is to decide the direction economic development is to take; *i.e.,* what new products are to be invested in and to what extent. This task, however, is simplified considerably by the nature of Communist China's overall economic goals, particularly the emphasis on autarky and military strength. The alternatives open to Peking were further reduced by the regime's desire to emulate the Soviet economic performance.

The key to both autarky and a modern armaments industry is a machine-tools industry. Machine tools in turn require steel and electric power, which in turn use coal and various ores and metals (see Table 1). Furthermore, these industries (particularly steel and machine tools) make maximum use of modern technology. Although the Chinese Communists had some choice of scale and technology, they had to import modern steel and machine tool plants *in toto* from the Soviet Union. Investment planning, therefore, primarily involved deciding how large total expenditure on new plant and equipment was to be, and then buying the relevant set of

9. Because of the dubious reliability of the 1958-59 data, the Liu and Yeh estimates are intended to be conjectural.

plants from the Soviet Union,[10] at the same time ensuring that supporting industries wholly domestic in origin were not neglected.

At least before 1960, deciding the overall rate of investment was a vitally important, but not very complex decision. It was vitally important not only because of its political impact, but also because the resulting level of consumption, and any changes in it, were a major determinant of individual work incentives and hence of productivity. The relative lack of complexity arose from the low level of output existing when the Communists took power and from the pace with which development proceeded through 1957. In effect, the regime could channel most of the increase in output in these early years into investment, while ensuring that enough was left over to make possible some increase in per capita consumption. As the rate of increase in production began to slow down in 1954 or 1955, particularly in consumer goods, it was no longer possible to push up savings so easily, but by that time China had nearly reached the rate of the Soviet Union in the 1930's and could afford to level off.[11] After output fell off (from 1960 on), investment was cut back sharply, but what principles were used in determining the extent of the reduction are not known.

Once the decision on how much to invest was reached, the questions of which products to invest in and what scale and technology to use remained. As already indicated, this was not as difficult a task as might be supposed, as long as investment was concentrated on an autarkic heavy industrial sector patterned on the Soviet model. The major difficulty, just as in the problem of achieving balance, was how to deal with small-scale traditional industries. Prior to 1958, however, this difficulty was minimized by making such enterprises largely responsible for whatever investment in themselves they were capable of making.

State investment in industry controlled through the central plan was concentrated on a number of key large-scale projects. There were 694 above-norm projects[12] in the First Five-Year Plan (FFYP), published in mid-1955 but meant to cover the years 1953-1957. Of these 694 projects, 455 were to be completed during the First Five-Year Plan, the

10. Approximately one-third of all Soviet exports to China were for "complete plants," generally meaning the import component of the 156 (later 166) projects that the Soviet Union had agreed to help China build.

11. This at least appears to be the implication of Po I-po's remarks in his speech to the Eighth Party Congress (1956), although it is stated in somewhat vaguer returns. Comparison of Soviet and Chinese rates of accumulation is complicated somewhat by valuation problems. The Soviet 1937 rate at current ruble factor cost was 25.9 per cent (Bergson, 1961, p. 237). The Chinese 1957 rate was 23 per cent in 1957 prices, 26 per cent in 1952 prices, and 15 per cent in 1933 prices (Liu and Yeh, 1965, p. 80).

12. "Above-norm" refers to projects in which total investment was above a certain figure, the norm. Above-norm projects were subject to much stricter controls than below-norm projects. The norm for most industries varied between 10 and 30 million *yuan,* depending on what was produced.

remaining during the Second Five-Year Plan. At the heart of the program, however, were the 156 projects for which the Soviet Union had agreed to provide assistance. More than 44 per cent of all investment in industry was to go to these projects, and another 7 per cent to 144 projects designed to directly support them [*FFYP,* p. 39]. By the time the plan was published in 1955, 29 of these Soviet aid projects were wholly or partially completed.

By 1957, the number of above-norm projects had been raised to 921, with 537 already in operation, including 68 of the Soviet aid projects (instead of the 45 in the plan) (Po I-po, 1958, p. 12). By 1958, the number completed had risen to 1,037 (*Ten Great Years,* p. 67) and another 671 were reportedly finished in 1959 (Li Fu-chun, 1960, p. 2), although data for 1958 and 1959 are of dubious quality.

In deciding which above-norm projects to initiate, the state had first to draw up annual (and five-year) output targets for key commodities. To translate these output targets into individual projects, a further decision on what scale and technology to use had to be made. Very little work has been done on how the Chinese made this latter decision.

The impression given by a superficial reading of materials readily available is that Peking never felt that the choices involved were particularly difficult to make. Probably part of the explanation for this apparent lack of concern is that Chinese choices were severely limited by what the Soviet Union was willing and able to offer.

Even as the impact of the Korean War embargo declined and the range of alternatives increased, studies of other underdeveloped countries suggest that the Chinese would not go far wrong by simply selecting the most advanced technology available to them. The most modern steel processes, jet airplanes, and the like are not only labor-saving, a virtue of little benefit to China, but capital-saving as well. A similar line of reasoning is probably not valid for most light industries, but Chinese investment was primarily in heavy industry. It must be reiterated, however, that this issue has yet to be adequately dealt with for China (and for most other underdeveloped countries), and a definitive conclusion must, therefore, await further analysis.

Once a project was approved, its actual rate of output of steel or machinery depended on when the project was allowed to start, how fast it was completed, and how fast the completed project reached capacity output. Given the uncertainties involved at each stage, the number of "tons" of output in any individual year could only be guessed at. Otherwise it would be difficult to explain the widely different rates at which annual output targets were completed. The relevant data are presented in Table 3. Changes in output are used rather than total output, since new investment is related primarily only to changes. In light industry, success in

TABLE 3

ANNUAL PLAN TARGET COMPLETION RECORD

$$\frac{\text{realized output}}{\text{planned output}} = \text{Index}$$

	1953	1954	1955	1956	1957	1958	1959
Steel	143.2	164.9		96.9	169.5	295.1	164.6
Electricity	112.9	134.2		161.4	121.1	231.2	100.0
Cement	210.8	208.7		105.0	112.7	—	75.2
Coal	[a]	197.8		108.1	284.2	671.6	70.7
Petroleum	103.9	163.7		83.8	87.5	—	—
Cotton yarn	148.1	193.5		113.3	97.6[b]	—	111.6
Paper	785.7[c]	185.7		135.3	—	—	—
Sugar	—	38.8		32.3	—	—	—
Cigarettes	—	30.1		36.2	—	—	—

Notes:

a. The plan called for little or no increase in coal output. Actual output rose by over 3 million tons.
b. The plan for cotton yarn called for a decrease in output in 1957.
c. The planned increase was very small.

Sources:

All realized production data (except 1959) are from *Ten Great Years,* pp. 95-100 and Yin and Yin, *Economic Statistics of Mainland China,* pp. 50-51.

1953 plan data: See Wu Yuan-li, *An Economic Survey of Communist China,* pp. 257-258. The 1953 output data in *Ten Great Years* may not be the same as those used in constructing the plan indices, thus causing some error in the figures in the table.

1954 plan data: Derived from data in State Statistical Bureau, "Report on 1954 Development of the National Economy and the Effectiveness of the State Plan," Sept. 21, 1955; *HHPYK,* October 28, 1955, No. 10, p. 166; and Teng Hsiao-p'ing, "Report on the 1954 Draft State Budget," June 18, 1954, in *I-chiu-wu-szu-nien Kuo-chia Yu-suan* (Peking: Financial and Economic Press, 1954), p. 16.

1956 plan data: Jen-min Shou-ts'e, 1957, p. 426.

1957 plan data: Po I-po, "Report on the Results of the 1956 National Economic Plan and the Draft 1957 National Economic Plan," *Fa-kuei hui-pien,* No. 6, pp. 155-157.

1958 plan data: Po I-po, "Report on Proposed 1958 National Plan," Feb. 3, 1958, *HHPYK,* March 10, 1958, No. 5, p. 18.

1959 realized output and plan data: Many 1959 targets apparently were set by looking at the original targets for 1962 in the draft Second Five-Year Plan, except for commodities such as coal, for which 1958 output had already surpassed the 1962 target. Realized output data, of course, have no relation to the true production situation. Li Fu-chun, "Report on the Draft 1958 National Economic Plan," April 21, 1959, *Fa-kuei hui-pien,* No. 9, pp. 45-46; and Li Fu-chun, "Report on the Draft 1960 National Economic Plan," March 30, 1960, *Second Session of the Second National People's Congress of the People's Republic of China,* p. 4.

meeting annual production goals was even more erratic than in heavy industry because of dependence on harvest fluctuations.

With this erratic relationship between planned and actual output, it would appear that annual output targets were intended only as a very rough first approximation used to decide the allocation of key materials. As the months passed and bottlenecks appeared, allocations must have been speeded up in certain cases and slowed down in others in order to overcome the most severe imbalances. It is likely that within a few months of their publication, the annual targets had only very limited operational significance.[13]

It was not so much that China was unable to plan well enough to use more sophisticated procedures. Of course, in early years, planning was at a very rudimentary level. In 1953, the first year for which annual plans in industry had much meaning, production targets were revised three times in the course of the year (Rostow, 1954, p. 274). But, with Soviet assistance, the more conspicuous difficulties were overcome. If a comparison of Soviet and Chinese five-year plan performance is any guide, Chinese planning by 1955 was no worse than that in the Soviet Union in the 1930's (see Table 4). The point is that, given Peking's goals and the underdeveloped state of the economy, more sophisticated planning techniques were, on the whole, not very important. Complex calculations of rates of return and capital-output ratios were of limited use when trade embargos and technologically determined input-output coefficients severely limited the choices of what kind of factories to build. However, when the regime in 1958 turned away from concentration on large-scale heavy industrial plants and from following the Soviet pattern, deciding what plants to put up was no longer so simple a task. More elaborate investment criteria had to be used, particularly in deciding when a small-scale enterprise ought to be built.

As already pointed out, small-scale enterprises played a large role in Chinese industry long before 1958 (see Table 2), but it was not until that year that they achieved relatively high priority status. In the general cutback in investment in late 1956 and 1957, for example, materials and funds for below-norm projects bore the brunt of the reduction (Fang Fa, 1956, p. 41; *CHCC,* 1956, p. 40). Early in 1958 small- and medium-scale enterprises continued to be placed in a low priority position, with only 387 million *yuan* being allocated in the plan for such investment by local authorities (*CHCC,* 1958, p. 40). As the Great Leap Forward got underway, the whole picture changed, and by the end of the year 5,260 million *yuan* had been spent outside the plan, presumably mainly by local

13. It is, of course, true that Soviet-type planning does not call for the exact completion of output plans, but instead for overcompletion. The evidence for "erraticness" in Table 3, however, is not simply that the index numbers are not always 100, but that their departure from 100 differs so much between commodities and between years for each commodity.

Table 4

PLAN COMPLETION RECORD: CHINA AND THE SOVIET UNION

	Soviet Union						China		
	First Five-Year Plan (1927-28—1932-33)			Second Five-Year Plan (1933-1937			First Five-Year Plan [a] (1953-1957)		
	Target [b]	Actual	%	Target	Actual	%	Target	Actual	%
Coal [c]	68	64.4	94.7	152.5	128.0	83.9	113	130	115.0
Oil [c]	19	21.4	112.6	44.3	28.5	64.3	2.01	1.46	73.1
Electric power [d]	17	13.5	79.4	38.0	36.2	95.3	15.9	19.3	121.4
Cement [c]	5.4	3.48	64.4	7.5	5.45	72.7	6.0	6.86	114.3
Steel [c]	8.3	5.93	71.4	17.0	17.73	104.3	4.12	5.35	129.9

Sources:

For Soviet data, see A. Bergson, *The Economics of Soviet Planning,* 1964, Table 5.2, p. 84.

Chinese data are in *First Five-Year Plan,* pp. 48-49; and State Statistical Bureau, "Communique on the Results of Implementing the First Five-Year Plan, 1953-1957," reprinted in *Contemporary China,* vol. iii, p. 205.

Notes:

a. The Chinese First Five-Year Plan was in reality a three-year plan since it was not promulgated until 1955.
b. The target figures for the Soviet Five-Year Plan were expressed in terms of "minimal" and "optimal variants."
c. In million metric tons.
d. In billions of Kilowatt-hours.

authorities on small- and medium-scale plants. In 1959 another 5 billion *yuan* was spent in this way (*Ten Great Years;* Li Fu-chun, 1960).

Although carefully calculated rates of return, or some comparable investment criteria, probably should have been used in deciding whether to build particular small-scale plants, in practice they were not. In fact the only constraint on local authorities was apparently whether or not it was physically possible for them to build the plant with materials obtained locally. The extremes in 1958 and 1959, however, resulted more from the way in which plans were implemented under the Great Leap spirit than from the lack of adequate investment criteria used in drawing them up in the first place.

Even during periods when greater restraint was exercised, it is doubtful that the investment criteria used were adequate to the task of ensuring efficient use of local investment funds. The principal advantages the regime expected from small- and medium-scale enterprises were these (Kao Chen-teh, 1957; Sung Ping, 1957):

(1) A lower amount of investment was required per unit of output, and the time required to build a plant and put it into operation was less.

(2) Quality of output would be raised.

(3) Savings on transport cost could be achieved.

(4) Fewer building materials and machinery would be required.

(5) Employment, particularly employment outside urban areas could be raised more rapidly.

This list presumably also constituted the criteria by which small-scale projects were accepted or rejected. The first four items could be subsumed under a general concept of profitability or rate of return, if China's price structure were meaningful. The employment criterion, to the degree that it was more than a desire to maximize the rate of return by means of capital-saving devices, cannot be so subsumed.

Whether China's price structure was sufficiently meaningful to make possible the effective use of a single profitability measure is too complex a question to deal with in detail here. However, the main point, already mentioned previously, is that Peking has never followed the Soviet practice of pricing producer goods at average cost plus a 5 per cent margin. Instead, these and most other industrial prices were frozen at levels prevailing during the Korean War, with only relatively minor adjustments afterwards. Most such adjustments have been made to overcome particularly irrational prices,[14] but in 1955-56 there was a general lowering of

14. For example, area differentials in petroleum prices had been set prior to completion of rail lines to the northwest oil fields, and had to be revised (Fan Jo-yi, 1957, p. 28).

industrial producer goods prices. At the time, it may have been intended to carry these reductions further, but, if so, the attempt was abandoned.[15] The principal reasons for maintaining prices at these levels involved problems of implementation and control, and will be discussed later. The point here is that China's price structure probably reflected, at least to a degree, the underlying Chinese supply and demand conditions. The further the regime moved from the conditions at the time when prices were frozen, the less this was true. On the other hand, Peking's ability to avoid serious inflation eliminated price distortions arising from this source.[16]

Whether or not the price structure was suitable, rate of return or profitability criteria seem to have played a rather limited role in Chinese investment allocation decisions. They played a part in the decision to emphasize small-scale enterprises in the first place, but evidently had little influence on which small-scale firms were set up. The much higher rate of return on investment in restoring old plants and on construction in well-established industrial centers was a major reason why such areas as Shanghai continued to a significant degree their pre-1949 industrial supremacy (Chu Jung-chi, 1956), but sophisticated criteria were hardly necessary to reach these rather obvious conclusions. The greater profitability of light industry was mentioned in the discussion surrounding the decision in 1956 and 1957 to increase the share of industrial investment funds going to that sector (Ho Cheng, 1956). On the other hand, several writers pointed out that higher returns in light industry were simply the result of the government's high price policy for these commodities, prices which in those authors' eyes did not reflect the commodities' true worth.[17] When, in addition, it became clear that output in this sector could be raised only if raw materials from agriculture were available, the state in 1958 sharply reduced the proportion of light industry investment and shifted it, in part at least, to agriculture (*CHCC,* 1958, pp. 37-41).

Thus, in deciding how to allocate investment in new plant and equipment, the Chinese Communists relied on crude and rather unsystematic criteria. Most decisions were predetermined by the regime's desire to build large-scale plants of Soviet design and to stress heavy industry and autarky. Given these aims, more sophisticated techniques of allocation were largely unnecessary. One can question whether it was proper to emphasize heavy industry, or whether military or other needs required

15. There was considerable debate in the economics literature as to whether China should or should not follow a price policy for producer goods similar to that of the Soviet Union (Fan Jo-yi, 1957; Nan Ping, So Chen, 1957).

16. It will be argued later that plan implementation was partly effected by a policy of overfull utilization of resources (excess demand or inflationary pressure). This pressure made market allocation for many key industrial products impossible even if it had been desired. The degree of pressure did not tend to increase over time and thus did not necessitate raising prices.

17. What these authors meant by the "true worth" or value of a commodity is a subject in itself. See, for example, Wang Tieh-sheng, 1957.

so much investment in the interior, but these were problems related to fundamental aims of the regime. Right or wrong, they did not result primarily from the methods used in planning.

When it was decided to stress small-scale industries, the lack of adequate investment criteria did have a detrimental effect, but it should not be exaggerated. Most of the excesses in small industries during the Great Leap Forward were not caused by the inadequacy of the criteria available to local planners, but by the failure of these lower level cadres to apply any criteria at all. One can also ask whether these decisions might not have been better made if the regime had relied on the market rather than on centralized planning. Such questions, however, cannot be answered without a thorough investigation of the problems of plan implementation, to which we now turn.

III. PLAN IMPLEMENTATION

INTRODUCTION

Most literature on planning in underdeveloped countries deals with problems of investment allocation, but the main barriers to successful growth have far more frequently been failures in implementation.[18] Setting up a system that makes possible effective plan implementation is no easy task. Not only must the regime see to it that enterprises comply with central plan directives, it must also ensure that those directives are carried out flexibly and imaginatively to achieve economic efficiency.

In attaining efficient compliance, a centralized socialist system of planning has both advantages and disadvantages compared with a market-controlled industrial sector under private ownership. On the one hand, the number and strength of control devices available to the centralized, nonmarket system are much greater than in the private market economy. On the other, there are many more activities that must be controlled. State regulations in a market economy are designed primarily to prevent selected forms of "antisocial" behavior or to encourage firms (by subsidies, etc.) to pursue certain particularly desirable activities that the system itself would not automatically promote. Within the broad ranges

18. In actual practice it is not easy to distinguish between failures due to a plan itself and those due to the implementation of that plan. The problems discussed in this section generally would have arisen regardless of what particular numbers appeared in the output plan (unless perhaps there was a radical change in basic priorities); nor could these numbers have been designed so as to overcome implementation problems. It does not follow, however, that any sets of numbers would have done as well as those selected. In fact, if the distinction between planning and implementation is meaningful, and if the plan itself was drawn up properly as was generally argued above, then some arbitrarily chosen set of numbers would have increased the number of bottlenecks, etc.

set down by these regulations, the enterprises may do as they like, co-ordination and efficiency being achieved by allowing the least successful to go out of business.

In an economy centrally planned and controlled by means of targets set for physical output and other factors, however, the state decides in some detail the directions that enterprise activities are expected to take, and so must establish means for checking each aspect. In a private market economy, for example, it does not matter to the state (except for tax purposes) whether the enterprise has an elaborate accounting system that allows it and the state to know exactly how well it performed in every respect. If such a system is necessary to the firm's efficient operation, it will adopt it or go bankrupt. By contrast, in a centrally controlled state economy, the lack of such an accounting system would make central direction of the enterprise virtually impossible.

In the discussion that follows, Chinese Communist efforts to implement the central plan for industry will be dealt with in two parts. The first presents the formal control structure and changes that have been made in it over time. The second analyzes how that formal structure has been undermined by a variety of elements, foremost among which is the need to choose the leaders of enterprises for their political as well as their technical qualifications.

THE FORMAL CONTROL STRUCTURE

The key to control of industrial activities in Communist China (as in the Soviet Union) is the responsibility system in its broadest sense; *i.e.*, the principle that each unit's activities should be clearly defined so that its performance can be properly judged and reward or punishments dealt out accordingly. A unit may be an individual, a workshop, an enterprise or a larger organization; but the key unit is the enterprise.

Each enterprise in China is an independent economic accounting unit responsible for only its own profits and losses.[19] State plans drawn up by the central authorities were broken down into specific targets for each enterprise, but it was the enterprise's own basic responsibility to translate these targets into orders and directives for its subordinate units. The central government judged each enterprise's success or failure in meeting these targets; and the enterprise in turn appraised the performance of its own divisions and individual personnel. When individual units below the central government level dealt with each other, it was usually on an cnter prise-to-enterprise basis. Enterprises, for example, had the right to draw up purchase and sales contracts with each other.

Although the enterprise was an independent unit in the sense described above, its ability to take independent action was, according to the regu-

19. This brief discussion is based largely on Schurmann, "Industrial Management in China."

lations at least, severely limited. Enterprise plan targets were set by the state, and purchase and sales contracts, as well as bank loans, had to be strictly in accordance with the plan. Individual firms could influence the central plan during the period when it was being drawn up. The process of drawing up the plan, in fact, was one of almost continuous negotiation between higher and lower levels. Ultimately, however, authority rested with and was exercised by Peking. Enterprise independence was independence of responsibility, not of authority.

This system, of course, was essentially the same as the Soviet *khozraschet* system and was consciously patterned after it. Other key elements of the structure were one-man management and the production territorial system. One-man management was a key part of what was intended to be a clear-cut vertical command structure. It not only made possible an unimpeded flow of command, but also enabled the regime to attach to individuals the responsibility for success or failure. The production territorial system ordered the chain of command between the enterprise and the central government. In essence, it subordinated all industrial units producing similar types of products and located in the same geographical region to a single superior unit, which in turn was responsible to the national ministry responsible for those particular products.

Even the formal aspects of this system began to undergo changes at least as early as 1956; but before looking at those changes, it will be useful to deal with other formal techniques used to back up the central plans. Several of these measures are either readily understood or have been dealt with earlier in the chapter in other contexts, needing only brief mention here.

Perhaps foremost in importance among these measures is the centralized allocation of key industrial raw materials, machinery and other inputs. Any enterprise that attempts to set out on its own, counter to directions set down in the plan, immediately runs into bottlenecks resulting from shortages of inputs. Furthermore, allocations called for by the plan are backed up in turn by formal contracts between enterprises involved in selling and purchasing these materials.[20] In addition, plan targets are supposed to be set so that unless a firm uses all materials allocated to it efficiently, it will be unable to surpass its targets. Finally, there is generally planning for overfull use of resources; *i.e.,* more inputs are called for in the plan than will be actually allocated, giving, at least in theory, an added incentive to use materials efficiently.

Other key elements in the control process are the various methods set up by the state to ensure the accurate flow of information from the enterprise up to the central authorities. Under the State Statistical Bureau, the

20. Contracts have been used for a number of other purposes as well, including, for example, restricting the activities of private industrial enterprises prior to 1956. For a fuller discussion of industrial contracts, see Pfeffer, 1963.

Chinese Communists have attempted to establish uniform statistical procedures throughout the industrial sector, beginning with a survey of all state and joint industrial and mining enterprises in 1950.[21] Although there was a major setback in statistical collection procedures in 1958 and 1959, industrial statistics in other years, particularly those for large-scale heavy industry, have generally been adequate to the demands put upon them. The major exceptions would appear to be the data for small-scale industry and for items difficult to measure properly (*e.g.*, costs per unit of output; value of fixed capital, etc.) [22] There has also been a problem of getting data early enough to allow central planners to draw up a plan and make the necessary adjustments before the year for which the plan was designed was nearly past. This latter problem, however, was more one of plan formulation than of plan enforcement. Timeliness was somewhat less crucial to those whose job was to reward or punish enterprises for past behavior.

Finally, behind these various types of essentially physical and administrative measures, and the information channels connected with them, there was a complex system of financial controls. Considering both the importance and the complexity of these financial controls, it is desirable to analyze them in some detail.[23]

Financial targets (profits, cost reduction, the wage bill, etc.) appearing in the annual plans, for example, were conceived of partly as devices for backing up the physical output and input targets, and partly as substitutes for an excessive proliferation of physical targets. That is, it was simpler to put a limit on the total wage bill than to specify the number of workers in each salary grade.

The key element of financial control, however, was not financial targets, but controls over sources and uses of enterprise funds. The most important were sales ("industrial and commercial") and profits taxes. These taxes took away a large portion of the funds coming into an individual enterprise and turned them over to the state treasury, where central planners could reissue them or not as they saw fit.

In addition, there were elaborate rules governing how enterprises could obtain funds for their own use and how they could use them once obtained. Enterprise funds for use in meeting everyday expenses (working capital) had to be kept separate from investment funds. The latter were

21. The establishment of a state statistical system is discussed in detail in Li, 1962.

22. The term "adequate" does not imply that there was no falsification or distortion of output and other "relatively good" data by industrial enterprises. To the contrary, *T'ung-chi kung-tso (TCKT)* and *T'ung-chi kung-tso t'ung-hsun (TCKTTH)* are full of examples, but not sufficiently serious examples to negate the statements made in the text. For a much more thorough discussion of these issues, see Yin, "The Reporting of Industrial Statistics in Communist China."

23. The discussion of the role of financial controls in plan implementation is based on Perkins, 1966 (pp. 99-135).

financed out of the budget, and actual payment was handled by a special bank, which closely supervised all expenditures to make sure that they complied with the central plan. Even new investment financed out of profits that an enterprise had been allowed to retain had to be used according to the central plan and under supervision of the construction bank (Ministry of Finance, 1956). Furthermore, only a small portion of retained profits could be used in this way, the remainder being divided among bonuses, welfare funds, and various working capital needs. In any case, total retained profits prior to 1958 were very small. If budget data are an adequate indicator of profit plan overfulfillment (on which calculation of retained profits was based), then enterprise income from this source would have been negligible in 1955 and 1956, less than 3 per cent of total profits in 1957, and less than 9 per cent in 1954.[24]

Sources of working capital were somewhat more complicated. Each enterprise had income from sales of its output, after deductions were made for profits and sales taxes. These deductions were taken out several times a month. Otherwise the very high rates of profit on both consumer and producer goods would have provided firms with so much working capital that serious financial discipline would have been virtually impossible.

Since sales revenue was seldom synchronized with outlays, particularly in rapidly growing firms or ones with wide seasonal fluctuations in activity, funds were required over and above what could be obtained from sales. These needs were met out of a combination of allocations from the budget and loans from the People's Bank. The former were made without interest or need to repay; the latter had to be repaid and carried an interest charge.

Whatever the source of funds, individual firms never had much freedom in using them, at least according to the regulations. Not only was use of working capital for fixed capital investment purposes prohibited, but such funds could not be used to increase the wage bill beyond the target figure. More important, enterprises had to draw up detailed income and outlay plans for approval by higher level authorities. This plan then formed the basis upon which loans were given and budget allocations made. Even the enterprise's own deposits (it was only allowed enough cash for three days' operations) were, according to regulations, not to be used for other than approved purposes (Financial and Economic Committee, 1950).

Still, even in theory the enterprise did retain a limited capacity (and in

24. These estimates are probably somewhat too low since they were obtained by taking 40 per cent of total profits actually paid into the treasury in excess of the planned amount. In fact, many enterprises exceeded the target while others fell below it, but the latter did not have 40 per cent of profits below plan taken away from them.

practice this ability was far from limited) for easing its own financial situation, to the extent that it could readjust the inflow and outflow pattern of its funds. The major areas where this could be done, *i.e.,* through such activities as delaying payment and purchasing on credit, however, were declared illegal from the beginning.

It is clear, then, that financial controls were not conceived of as substitutes for physical or administrative controls, but as backstops to those controls. With such a variety of financial restrictions augmenting equally numerous physical and administrative measures, it is a wonder that industrial enterprises had any room whatsoever for maneuvering. But in fact, they were occasionally able to act as if they were subject to no restrictions at all. Before turning to how the system worked in practice, however, it is desirable to look briefly at the formal measures taken to modify the system of control described above.

FORMAL DECENTRALIZATION MEASURES

The same elements that made drawing up the material balances and investment plans difficult, in particular the existence of a large number of small-scale firms with widely varying techniques, also contributed to the problems of plan implementation. It is doubtful whether many of the firms ever entered into the planning process in a significant way.

Nevertheless, these enterprises had to have materials to work with and money to pay for them. As indicated in a previous section, the materials for such firms were generally obtained locally. The later decentralization (1958) that gave control over the output and inputs of these enterprises to provincial and lower level authorities was probably in part only formal recognition of a situation that had always existed to some degree.

Control over enterprise finances was also partially decentralized, but by price policy rather than by the actual transfer of administrative authority to lower levels. Relatively high prices (see Table 5) for all industrial products (in contrast to the Soviet policy of pricing producer goods at 3-5 per cent above cost) made it unnecessary to provide higher cost (usually small-scale) firms with subsidies or with as large allocations of funds for working capital, tasks that would have created formidable administrative burdens. Local branches of the People's Bank and other local financial units still exercised supervision over an enterprise's use of its own funds, but there was less need to coordinate that control with higher level authorities in order to prevent excessive issuance of funds. Avoiding subsidies, with their attendant administrative burdens, was probably a more important reason for keeping a high price policy than the previously mentioned fact that such a policy also made possible a limited market distribution of certain producer goods.

Closely related to the regime's high price policy was its stress on

TABLE 5

PROFIT RATE ON SELECTED COMMODITIES
(per cent of average cost, including taxes)

Commodity	Rate
All commodities (1957)	50
Consumer Goods	
Cotton cloth (1957)	107
Cotton yarn	43
Cotton cloth	52
Cigarettes	160-335
Sugar	40
Grain	15-20
Average of light industry (including commerce) (1955)	47
Producer Goods	
Electric power (1956)	101
State iron and steel enterprises	25
Average of heavy industry (1955)	43

Source:
See Perkins, 1966 (Table 10). Where the year is not given, it is not known precisely, but is generally 1956 or 1957. These percentages were taken directly from Communist sources or were computed by the author from official price and cost data.

profits taxes over sales taxes.[25] In' the Soviet Union between 1928 and 1940, the sales (turnover) tax provided from three to more than ten times as much revenue as the profits tax (Holzman, 1955, p. 217). This contrasts sharply with China, where profits tax revenue surpassed that received from sales taxes in 1954, and by 1959 was double the sales tax revenue. Both profits taxes and sales taxes served essentially the same function, that of removing most income over cost from enterprise control. If this had been accomplished by a higher uniform sales tax for each industry, however, firms producing at relatively high cost per unit would have had to receive subsidies or go out of business. The Chinese Communists did pay a certain price for this policy. High profits taxes and low sales tax rates lowered a firm's incentive to reduce costs, since there was little danger, whatever the cost, that it would have to ask the state for a subsidy.

These price and tax measures did not allow any great degree of decentralized operation of industry. Control of industry was effected pri-

25. The term generally used by the Chinese Communists is "industrial and commercial taxes." These taxes are expressed as a percentage of price and hence are similar in nature to sales taxes or what in the Soviet Union are called "turnover taxes."

marily by physical means, which were still highly centralized. Beginning with the Eighth Party Congress in 1956, however, the regime began to take steps to reorganize industrial controls generally in the direction of decentralization, although of a very limited kind.

The removal of restrictions on enterprises' dealing directly with each other or with alternative sources of supply in the purchase and sale of non-key commodities has already been discussed. There was also an attempt to upgrade the importance of profits and the profits target. In 1955 the Ministry of Finance issued a directive stating that enterprises could retain 40 per cent of profits made over and above the plan profit target in 1954, and that these funds could be used to meet shortages in circulating capital and for certain very limited basic construction purposes (Ministry of Finance, 1955). In 1956, this regulation was liberalized slightly, in that such funds could be carried over into the next year and bonuses were to be given specifically for exceeding planned profits (Ministry of Finance, 1956). In both directives all enterprise bonus funds were to be taken out of profits in excess of plan before making the 40-60 split.

Major changes in formal financial controls and targets, however, were not made until late 1957 and 1958. The number of compulsory targets, for example, was reduced from 12 to 4 in 1957. Output targets continued to have priority, but the change was probably intended to enhance the importance of the other three targets, particularly profits. In May, 1958, the method of calculating profits retained by the enterprise was changed to a fixed percentage of total profits,[26] usually around 10 per cent, or significantly higher than previously. This change was a further step in enhancing the importance of the profits target.

In addition, in 1957 and 1958 there was the already discussed decentralization of administration, giving authority over many industrial enterprises to provincial and lower level authorities. Along with the basic transfer measure went a number of other measures dealing with related financial and market aspects of this transfer (Sung Hsin-chung, 1961). Unlike the measures dealing with retained profits and the number of targets, however, these transfers of authority did not really enhance the role of the market in controlling industry. Instead, they were primarily designed to enable local authorities to implement plans that they drew up, which were still essentially physical in nature. Even the increased retention of profits itself may have at times only enhanced the independence of the enterprise without increasing its responsiveness to the market.

Although the various measures described above involved decentralization through both the market and administrative measures, both methods were designed to deal with the same problem, that of effectively control-

26. The actual calculation for each firm was based on that firm's expenses in certain areas (on trial of new products, etc.) and so varied between firms (State Council, 1958).

ling many firms using diverse technology without stifling local initiative. In many areas, the formal changes made between 1956 and 1958 have remained intact ever since. Others have been modified by either retightening the reins or relaxing control further. Examples of the former would be the reduction in the size of the portion of profits that the enterprise could retain (Sung Hsin-Chung, 1961), and the apparent rehabilitation of various plan targets other than the four listed in 1957.[27] An example of relaxation would be the regulation allowing enterprises to exchange excess materials with other enterprises (only when it would increase output of producer, not consumer, goods) (Ma Wen-kuei, 1964).

In early 1962, there was also some debate in economic journals over whether decentralization and further use of market controls, especially profits, should be carried further.[28] Although this debate may have led to some enhancement of the role of the profits target, there is no evidence to suggest that it was carried very far, certainly not to the point where the profits target attained first priority and even less near the point where partial consumer sovereignty was restored—as it was for many industrial consumer goods in the Soviet Union in 1964-65.

Formal regulations, however, tell only a very inadequate part of the story of plan implementation in Communist China. Often these regulations were ignored altogether or their original purpose distorted.

PLAN IMPLEMENTATION IN PRACTICE

The major source of difficulty arose out of the nature of the Communist Party control apparatus and the personnel who manned it. The essence of minority Communist control in China is that all key positions, military, political, or economic, be held by Party members of demonstrated loyalty. On occasion high formal titles are bestowed on non-Party personnel, but in all such cases a subordinate Party member exercises real control. Party members of sufficient standing to be appointed factory managers, heads of factory Party committees, and higher positions, however, have usually built their reputations in guerrilla warfare against Japan and the Nationalists. Although thoroughly indoctrinated in Communist ideology, they generally have had little or no formal education.[29] This com-

27. See the "Seventy Theses" (1962) mentioned in footnote 8. The other eight targets were never abolished but only relegated to an advisory role. Regulations (such as No. 24 of the "Seventy Theses") calling firms to comply with several targets other than the basic four may not involve a major change of policy, but only a vaguer working of the directive, but this does not appear as likely as the interpretation in the text. A published source giving essentially the same information, but for a somewhat later date is K'uang Jih-an *et al.*, 1963 (p. 34).

28. The debate, such as it was, began with an article in *Ching-chi yen-chiu* in March, 1962, and was ended by or at the 10th Plenum of the Eighth Party Congress. For a fuller discussion, see CIA, 1963.

29. This discussion is based on refugee interviews and such sources as Hsia Yen, 1959; Ai Wu, 1961; Chandrasekhar, 1961; *TCKTTH*, 1957. For a fuller discussion see Perkins, 1966.

bination of Marxism and lack of sophistication has generated attitudes incompatible with the efficient use of such tools as financial targets and controls and, in fact, with the rational allocation of resources in general.[30] Reality and Russian experience and advice forced modifications in these attitudes, but did not submerge them completely.

Modification of these attitudes was further restricted after 1956 by the shift in the locus of power within factories from the factory manager (one-man management) to factory Party committees (Li Hsueh-feng, 1956). It is not really clear why this shift was made. Part of the explanation may be that the regime did not want to decentralize control even slightly without first guaranteeing the political loyalty of those receiving increased authority. It may also be that the Chinese Communists felt that Party committees, by being closer to the workers, could more effectively mobilize these workers even for purely economic purposes. As events turned out, this shift in power contributed in a major way to the excesses of the Great Leap Forward in 1958 and 1959. Recognizing this fact and its economic consequences, the regime in the early 1960's shifted back to placing primary control over enterprises in the hands of factory managers (Po I-po, 1963, p. 28). In 1964 and 1965, though, this reverse trend was in turn checked by a renewed intensification of ideological education and pressures within enterprises ("learn from the People's Liberation Army," etc.); it, however, was largely confined to attaining political rather than economic objectives.

The attitudes generated by these pressures, and by the backgrounds of the factory leadership personnel involved, manifested themselves first of all in a tendency on the part of factory managers and Party secretaries to ignore all plan targets other than that for the physical output of major products or (pre-1957) the gross value of output. (Such a situation was also in part a result of the nature of material balances planning, as pointed out earlier in Section II.) Nor were the factory managers (or Party secretaries) alone to blame. Similar attitudes were manifested by the central planners themselves (Ishikawa, 1960, pp. 92-93).

A similar emphasis on production targets existed in the Soviet Union, but there it was a result of bonuses being paid primarily on the basis of performance in meeting the production targets only; although the decision to use this basis may itself have been the result of factors similar to those for China. In China, bonuses appear to have been small; in any case they were not supposed to be paid to enterprise leadership cadres.[31]

Equally serious was the tendency on the part of plant managers to

30. Aside from its political implications, resource allocation has little or no place in Marxist ideology (Wiles, 1962, pp. 50-56).

31. This statement is based on refugee interviews, on the fact that bonus laws seem always to be worded so as not to apply to managers, and on criticisms of bonuses given to enterprise cadres. There is also some evidence to the contrary (*JMJP*, 1957).

ignore, whenever possible, not just the financial plan targets, but most financial regulations. However, this lax attitude toward financial controls did not exist because the various financial authorities lacked sufficient legal power to carry out their duties. Final authority for determining whether an enterprise was to receive a particular loan or budget disbursement rested with the People's Bank or the Ministry of Finance and with central and local governments. Industrial firms were never free to demand funds for expenditures above their approved plan, and there was no automatic loophole in the regulations such as existed in the Soviet Union, where enterprises could obtain funds for up to a 10 per cent overpayment of the wage fund in any month following one in which the enterprise had stayed within the authorized amount. Also unlike the Soviet situation, the interests of those with power to grant overpayments were not intertwined with the interests of the individual enterprise.[32]

In spite of the apparently strong position of the authorities, financial control was tight only sporadically. In many cases, enterprise cadres simply disobeyed the regulations. For example, the 1950 regulation setting up many important aspects of financial control specifically stated that state-owned enterprises were not to obtain credit from each other in any form, but could obtain such credit only from the People's Bank (Financial and Economic Committee, 1950). Yet in the second quarter of 1954, this type of credit made up 17.2 per cent of the total working capital of enterprises under the five industrial ministries (People's Bank, 1955, p. 270). In numerous other instances, funds earmarked for one purpose were used for another, and various devices were utilized to inflate costs so that a larger portion of profits could be retained by the enterprise (Pilmin, 1955, p. 37).

More serious than the enterprises' disobedience was the lack of sympathy with tight financial control at even the highest levels within the Party. This attitude toward tight financial control also extended, in many respects, to careful planning in general. It arose out of the same elements that caused factory managers to disregard financial targets and controls, but its effects were more farreaching. How serious they were depended heavily on the prevailing political atmosphere. When Party discipline and Communist ideology were the paramount concerns, careful planning and tight financial control were eschewed. During periods when political controls were more relaxed, technical and economic-minded personnel (both in and out of the Party) were more apt to be listened to.

This can be seen more concretely by reviewing briefly the Chinese

32. For information on the Soviet case, see Holzman, 1955 (p. 37). The independence of the Chinese financial authorities can be seen from the eminence of the Ministers of Finance (Po I-po and Li Hsien-nien) who were among the top echelon in the Communist hierarchy, from the fact that the People's Bank had a position comparable to that of a ministry, and from criticisms of that independence (Chang Ch'uan-shu, 1958).

Communist experience with administrative and financial controls since 1949. From 1949 through 1955 there was slow but steady progress toward tighter administrative control over the availability of funds going to individual enterprises. Faster progress was impossible because of the complexity of problems to be overcome and the limited experience that could be brought to bear. The state began working out basic plan targets in 1951 and 1952, for example, but as already pointed out, the actual introduction of annual plans did not begin until 1953, and the First Five-Year Plan (1953-57) did not come out until 1955. In 1956, following the collectivization of agriculture and the socialization of industry and commerce, an attempt was made to raise the industrial growth rate sharply by increasing investments in basic construction by 59 per cent over the previous year (*Ten Great Years,* p. 55).

The resulting inflationary pressure and depletion of stocks, however, forced the regime to retrench in 1957 (investment declined by 7 per cent). Disregarding the experience of the previous two years, the regime initiated in 1958 a Great Leap Forward in all sectors of the economy, raised investment by 93 per cent, and issued loans to enterprises so freely that deposits in the People's Bank rose in 1958 by an amount equal to the total increase during the previous five years (Ch'en Hsi-ya, 1959, p. 29).

The events of 1958 are worth further analysis because they vividly illustrate forces that have existed during the entire period of Communist rule. Disappointment with economic performance in 1957, and, more important, the avalanche of criticism during the brief "hundred flowers" or free speech campaign, led in the latter half of 1957 to a strong counteractive attempt by the Party to restore Party discipline and the preeminence of Communist ideology. This attempt was so successful that it effectively cowed the voices of caution and restraint, particularly in the economic sphere. It explains, for example, the complete lack of financial discipline in 1958 and 1959. The financial authorities had been intimidated by criticisms that they were ignoring Communist principles and placing too little faith in the masses by maintaining tight financial discipline (Chang Ch'uan-shu, 1958; *JMJP,* 1958).

It was not only the financial authorities who were constrained. The basic idea of the Great Leap was that tremendous economic advances could be achieved if Party cadres in factories and communes were given free reign to exercise initiative. Any constraints on this initiative would simply hamper progress. In the light of this reasoning, even central planning was considered excessively restrictive. Plan targets, therefore, no longer had to balance each other, but merely be set high enough to give the cadres a really "Great Leap" to try for. The process lost all touch with reality when statistics were subjected to similar considerations. They were no longer objective criteria for appraising plan performance, but only an additional means of heaping praise on activities considered desirable by the cadres; *i.e.,* they were grossly falsified to show that any procedure recommended by the cadres had, in fact, achieved the predicted results. The Great Leap, therefore, was not a decentralization through the market, as some of the formal regulations seem to indicate (see preceding section, "Formal Decentralization Measures"), but a decentralization of authority subject to no constraints other than those of Party discipline and ideology. As already indicated, the ideology of the Chinese Communists had little to say about problems of allocation, so that the not-surprising result of this decentralization was economic anarchy. The experience of 1958 and 1959 was, of course, extreme, but it reveals basic forces that have been present since the advent of Communist rule.

The economic costs of the Great Leap Forward were high. They became increasingly apparent through 1959 and into 1960, and were aggravated by the concurrent crisis in agriculture and by the Soviet withdrawal of all Russian technicians in 1960. Yet it was not until the ninth plenary session of the Eighth Party Central Committee in January, 1961, that steps were taken to reinstitute plan discipline by reducing the scale of capital construction and reemphasizing various financial procedures. In fact, tight financial control was not fully achieved until after 1962, if then (*Ta-kung pao,* 1961; *Nan-fang jih-pao,* 1962). One of the key documents upon which reimposition of rigorous controls in industry was based, the "Seventy Theses," was not even promulgated until 1962, and then only in draft form as a basis for further discussion and revision.

Some idea of how heavy the costs of disruption resulting from the Great Leap really were can be seen from the fact that state factories, in the first half of 1961, completed only 15.9 per cent of the planned target for the manufacture of military weapons, equipment, accessories, and parts, the highest priority sector in Chinese industry (*Kung-tso t'ung hsun,* 1961). This same sector was undoubtedly particularly hard hit by the Soviet removal of trade and technical support, but this was certainly not the only reason.

It is even more difficult to isolate the effects of lax administrative and financial discipline in periods when the situation was less extreme than after 1958. For example, one of the most serious problems plaguing the regime from the outset was maintaining quality. The authorities were continually launching drives to get firms to raise the quality of their output; and many changes in the administration of prices were undertaken so that firms would be concerned with quality, but there is no way of measuring the effects of these efforts precisely. The regime has stated, for example, that 99 per cent of the pig iron smelted in early 1963 was up to standard, and 95 per cent of forging and rolled stock were top grade (Ma Wen-Kuei, 1964), but what this means other than that quality undoubtedly improved from the low standards during the Great Leap is difficult to say. However, being unable to make very precise statements about the issue does not mean that it is unimportant. Failure to maintain quality was one of the main sources of disruption during the Great Leap, and has been a major source of inefficiency during all periods of lax control.

Lax administrative and financial control also had a significant effect on costs of production, particularly consumption of raw materials. For example, in 1956 when discipline was weak, coal mine costs (per metric ton) in Liaoning province rose 16 per cent above 1955; costs for 32-count yarn rose nearly 2 per cent in 1956, even though the cotton yarn utilization rate rose from 77 to 94 per cent and raw cotton prices were steady; the amount of wood used in making wood pulp rose in 1956 by 1 or 2 per cent after falling steadily from 1953 through 1955; and raw materials used per unit of output in five types of edible oils, with one exception, increased in 1956 after falling between 1953 and 1955. In the producer goods sector, excess consumption of raw materials was largely responsible for the failure of the Ministry of Heavy Industry to meet its cost reduction and profits targets in the first quarter of 1956.[33] Although it is not possible to make a precise estimate, it is reasonable to assume that this waste in 1956 accounted in part for the slow 1957 rate of growth in industrial output.[34] Unfortunately, data of comparable quality and relevance cannot be found for 1958 and after, but there is little doubt that the effects of lax discipline on costs of production were similar, only more extreme.

It is not going too far, therefore, to say that the nature of Communist Party control in China was such as to make an efficient allocation of resources difficult to achieve. Significant factors encouraged the use of decentralized economic controls, but ideology and lack of sophistication made the most highly developed of all decentralized controls, the market, of only limited use. At times, as during the Great Leap, these same factors undermined all controls, even the most centralized ones, causing high costs of production, low quality of output, and general disorganization. Two possible escapes from these difficulties would have been (1) to turn over more economic authority to non-Party economists and technicians

33. For the sources of these cost data see Perkins, 1966, (pp. 132-33). Rising average cost, of course, does not always indicate inefficiency. In some cases, for example, the long-run average cost curve may be rising for technological reasons completely unconnected with inefficiencies. It is doubtful that an economic justification for the performance described above can be found, however. Even if it were possible, and I doubt that it is, to domonstrate that average costs rose in these industries simply because they were approaching capacity levels of output, and not because of inefficient performance, they still would have been better off (had a greater total output of yarn, oils, etc.) if some of the raw materials had been used in the next year when the more usual condition of excess capacity returned to these industries.

34. The near-stagnation in agricultural output was a more important reason.

(as in 1957 and since 1960) or (2) to emphasize technical and economic training for the cadres themselves. The former, however, endangers the basic political position of the Party and is bound to be resisted. Furthermore, too much relaxation in this direction might weaken the discipline necessary to enforce any plan direction (centralized or decentralized) in state-owned industries. The latter alternative, on the other hand, would eventually transform the Party itself from a revolutionary body to a party of technical bureaucrats, a transformation that has, in fact, progressed quite far in the Soviet Union and for which the Chinese Communists have shown considerable distaste. There is no obvious path out of this dilemma, and one has certainly not been found on the mainland of China.

CONCLUSION

Industrial planning and management in Communist China would have run into fewer difficulties if Soviet economic goals and the Soviet system of centralized planning, emphasizing output targets, had proved as suitable for China as they did for Russia in the 1930's. (This is not to argue that this system was particularly suitable even for the Soviet Union.) In some respects, of course, the system worked quite well for China. The relatively small number of commodities involved, the weak links between different industrial sectors, and the opportunity to rely heavily on importation of complete industrial plants from the Soviet Union, all tended to ease the problem of centralized planning with respect to both the coordination of existing output and the planning of investment in new plant capacity. On the positive side, central planning provided Peking with sufficient authority to bring about a rapid change in the basic structure of Chinese industry.

It can be argued that it was a mistake to try to wrench Chinese industry into the modern world of heavy industry and large-scale plants so quickly, but this decision was based primarily on considerations beyond the narrow purview of economics, principally on the desire for military power and autarky. Beginning in 1961 (and to some extent earlier), there was a shift away from such heavy emphasis on machine tools and steel. However, this did not result from failures of central planning and management, but from the effects of neglect and reorganization on agriculture.

Although failures in central planning and centralized methods of implementation were not the principal cause of the regime's decision to shift emphasis after 1961 toward agriculture and the consumer goods industry, one still cannot conclude that the system had worked very well. As early as 1956, the regime began to realize the shortcomings of overcentralization. The backwardness of Chinese industry, the large number of firms involved, and the desire to develop and exploit more labor-intensive technologies all encouraged the Chinese Communists to give consideration to various decentralized methods of planning and plan implementation. Although central planning remained the most important of the various controls utilized, partial decentralization was carried out both through the market and through administrative reorganizations. The former involved enhancing the profits target and relaxing the rules that prevented firms from dealing directly with each other in the purchase and sale of non-key commodities. Profits, however, were not the principal success criterion, and they never were a major criterion for deciding what products were to be produced and where plant capacity was to be expanded, no matter whether that decision was made by the central planners or by the enterprise itself. Administrative decentralization was usually accomplished by transferring authority down to provincial and lower level authorities; large-scale enterprises generally remained under centralized control.

When decentralization measures were put into effect, however, it was usually in conjunction with a transfer of power to Communist Party units within the enterprise, or, in effect, political centralization. Any alternative would have been considered undesirable because it would have threatened the paramount role of the Party, which is fundamental to the existence of Chinese Communism, at least in its present form. Party influence, however, meant control by cadres inexperienced in economic matters and imbued with an ideology that was, to a degree, incompatible with market forms of decentralization and was not sensitive to problems of allocation in general. When these influences were combined with the bias against financial targets inherent in material balances planning, the cadres' tendency was to ignore or try to evade all varieties of financial constraints on their decisions, even though those constraints would have enhanced the efficiency of the decisions. It was not just financial constraints that were ignored. In fact, during periods of extreme political control, as during the Great Leap Forward, the system degenerated into economic anarchy.

Conceptually, it is possible to divorce the problem of maintaining ideological purity and political reliability from economic rationality. The Chinese Communists' reemphasis on political influence within the enterprise in 1964 and 1965 was apparently not accompanied by a downgrading of economic controls, financial or otherwise. Pressures against long-run maintenance of an effective divorce between politics and economics, however, are great. One cannot get around the problem of giving politically and ideologically reliable personnel the requisite technical training, because that training does itself tend to undermine ideology.

Thus the costs of overcentralization in Chinese industry were high, but the costs of decentralization as it was actually carried out were even higher. The costs of both overcentralization and inappropriate decentralization could be overcome, to a degree, by a higher rate of investment, but events since 1959 have demonstrated that there are strict limitations on how high investment in industry can be without materially affecting incentives and, through incentives, production, particularly in agriculture.

REFERENCES

AI WU, 1961. *Steel and Tempered.* Peking.

BERGSON, A., 1961. *The Real National Income of Soviet Russia Since 1928.* Cambridge, Mass.

CHANDRASEKHAR, S., 1961. *Red China, an Asian View.* New York.

CHANG CH'UAN-SHU, 1958. "The Anshan Financial Office on How to Strengthen Enterprise Financial Overseeing Work," *Ts'ai-cheng* (Jan. 5, 1958), No. 1, pp. 25–27.

CH'EN HSI-YA, 1959. "The 1958 Banking Work and the 1959 Tasks," *Chung-kuo Chin-jung,* May 25, 1959, translated in *Extracts from China Mainland Magazines,* No. 178, pp. 28–39.

CH'EN YUN, 1956. Speech, *Eighth National Congress of the Communist Party of China.* II, pp. 157–176.

CHENERY, H. B., and P. G. CLARK, 1959. *Interindustry Economics.* New York.

CHCC (*Chi-hua ching-chi*), 1956. Editorial, "Prepare Properly the National Economic Plan for 1957," Dec. 23, 1956, translated in *Extracts from China Mainland Magazines.* No. 69, pp. 36–42.

CHCC, 1958. "Problems to Merit Attention in Carrying Out the 1958 Capital Construction Plans," Feb. 9, 1958, translated in *Extracts from China Mainland Magazines.* No. 124, pp. 37–41.

Chinese Communist Party, 1957. Central Committee and State Council, "Regulation Reforming Plan Management Rules." *Fa-kuei hui-pien,* No. 8, pp. 96–99; "Several Regulations for Reforming the Commodity Distribution System," *Fa-kuei hui-pien,* No. 8, pp. 100–101.

CHU JUNG-CHI, 1956. "Full Utilization of Coastal Industry," *Chi-hau ching-chi,* June 23, 1956, translated in *Extracts from China Mainland Magazines,* No. 50, pp. 20–24.

FAN JO-YI, 1957. "More on the Price Policy for Heavy Industry Products," *Ching-chi yen-chiu,* June 17, 1957, translated in *Extracts from China Mainland Magazines,* No. 98, pp. 14–31.

FANG CHUNG, 1963. "All-Round Improvement in China's Economy," *Peking Review* (August 23, 1963), No. 34, pp. 38–43.

FANG FA, 1956. "Some Common Knowledge of the National Economic Plan," *Hsueh-hsi,* Oct. 2, 1956, translated in *Extracts from China Mainland Magazines,* No. 65, pp. 38–41.

Financial and Economic Committee, 1950. "Methods of Enforcing Currency Management and Compiling Currency Income and Outgo Plans," Dec. 25, 1950. Published in *Hsin-hua yueh-pao* (Jan. 25, 1951), No. 15, pp. 610–615.

(*FFYP*) *First Five-Year Plan for Development of the National Economy of the People's Republic of China in 1953-1957.* Peking, 1956.

Ho Cheng, 1956. "What Does Further Development of Light Industry Demand of Agriculture," *Cheng-chih, hsueh-hsi* (Aug. 12, 1956), No. 8.

Holzman, F., 1955. *Soviet Taxation*. Cambridge, Mass.

Hsia Yen, 1959. *K'ao-yen* (*The Test*). Peking.

Hsiao Liang, 1962. "Mindful of the General Good and Strict Execution of Policies and State Plans," *Kung-jen jih-pao,* Feb. 11, 1962, translated in *Survey of China Mainland Press,* No. 2690, pp. 1–4.

Hsueh Mu-ch'iao, 1957. "A Preliminary View of the Current Plan Management System," *Chi-hua Ching-chi,* No. 9, pp. 24–27.

Ishikawa, S., 1960. *Chugoku Ni Okeru Shihon Chikuseki Kiko* ("Capital Formation in China"). Tokyo.

JMJP (*Jen-min jih-pao*), May 5, 1957. (*People's Daily,* Peking.)

JMJP, 1958. Columnist, "The Correct Way of Settling Industrial Circulating Capital Problems," reprinted in *Hsin-hua Pan-yueh-k'an* (Sept. 10, 1958), No. 17, pp. 122–123.

Kao Chen-teh, 1957. "Make Coal Mining Construction More Economical and Rational," *Chien-she yueh-k'an,* July 3, 1957, translated in *Extracts from China Mainland Magazines,* No. 99, pp. 35–37.

Kao Kuang-chien, 1964. "Chemical Fertilized Industry Flourishes," *Peking Review* (Sept. 18, 1964), No. 38, pp. 25–26.

Kornai, J., 1959. *Overcentralization in Industry*. London.

K'uang Jih-an *et al.,* 1963. "Tentative Views on the Question of the Practice of Strict Economic Accounting by State-Owned Industrial Enterprises," *Ching-chi Yen-chiu,* Aug. 17, 1963, translated in *Extracts from China Mainland Magazines*. No. 388, pp. 30–42.

(KJJP) Kung-jen jih-pao, May 9, 1956, translated in *Union Research Institute,* Vol. III, No. 17.

Kung-tso T'ung-hsun, 1961. "Report on Work of the Rear Services Department in the Entire Army" (Aug. 4, 1961), No. 30.

Li, C. M., 1962. *The Statistical System of Communist China.* Berkeley and Los Angeles.

Li Fu-chun, 1960. "Report on the Draft 1960 National Economic Plan," March 30, 1960, *Second Session of the Second National People's Congress of the People's Republic of China,* pp. 1–48.

Li Hsueh-feng, 1956. Speech, *Eighth National Congress of the Communist Party of China.* II, pp. 304–317.

Liu, T. C., and K. C. Yeh, 1965. *The Economy of the Chinese Mainland: National Income and Economic Development, 1933-1959.* Princeton.

Ma Wen-kuei, 1964. "China's State-Owned Industrial Enterprises—Their Nature and Tasks," *Peking Review* (June 26, 1964), No. 26, pp. 23–27.

Ministry of Finance, 1955. "Methods of Dividing and Using Profits of State Enterprises in Excess of the Plan in 1954," *Fa-kuei hui-pien* (Oct. 18, 1955), No. 2, pp. 523–524.

Ministry of Finance, 1956. "Regulation on the Distribution and Use of 1956 State Enterprise Profits in Excess of Plan," *Fa-kuei hui-pien* (Oct. 11, 1956), No. 4, pp. 267–268.

Ministry of Finance, 1958. "Notification of Several Regulations on Dividing

Local Financial Income in 1958," *Fa-kuei hui-pien* (Jan. 23, 1958), No. 7, pp. 221–223.

NAN PING and SO CHEN, 1957. "The Value of the Means of Production and the Function of the Law of Value Under the Socialist System," *Ching-chi yen-chiu* (Feb. 17, 1957), No. 1, pp. 38–51.

New York Times, Dec. 30, 1964, p. 1.

People's Bank of China, 1955. "Report on Eliminating the Use of Commercial Credit Between State Industries and Between State Industries and Other State Enterprises as a Substitute for Bank Balances," *Fa-kuei hui-pien* (March 30, 1955), No. 1, pp. 270–273.

PERKINS, D. H., 1966. *Market Control and Planning in Communist China.* Cambridge, Mass.

PFEFFER, R. M., 1963. "The Institution of Contracts in the Chinese People's Republic," *China Quarterly,* Part I (April-June), pp. 153–177; Part II (July-September), pp. 115–139.

PILMIN, A. M., 1955. "The Role of Public Finance in the Enforcement of the Economy and Austerity Program," *Ching-chi yen-chiu,* Oct. 17, 1955, translated in *Extracts from China Mainland Magazines,* No. 21, pp. 33–42.

PO I-PO, 1956. Speech, *Eighth National Congress of the Chinese Communist Party*. II. 45–62.

PO I-PO, 1958. "Report on the Draft 1958 National Economic Plan," *Hsin-hua Pan-yueh-k'an* (March 10, 1958), No. 5, pp. 12–23.

PO I-PO, 1963. "The Socialist Industrialization of China," *Peking Review* (Oct. 11, 1963), No. 41, in *Extracts from China Mainland Magazines,* No. 388, pp. 20–29.

ROSTOW, W. W., 1954. *The Prospects for Communist China.* Cambridge, Mass.

SCHURMANN, H. F., 1964. "China's 'New Economic Policy'—Transition or Beginning," *China Quarterly,* No. 17 (January-March), pp. 65–91.

SCHURMANN, H. F. "Industrial Management in China" (unpublished manuscript), Chapter II. B.

Secretariat of the National Conference for Small Scale Ore Dressing Plants, 1959. "A Small Copper Dressing Plant Built and Put into Operation in Only 21 Days," *Yu-se chin-shu,* Feb. 18, 1959, translated in *Joint Publications Research Service,* No. 1080D, pp. 1–9.

Shanghai chieh-fang ch'ien-hou wu-chia tzu-liao hui-pien (*A Compilation of Pre- and Post-Liberation Prices in Shanghai*). Shanghai, 1958.

SHIH CHING-HSING, YEH HSIAO-LI, and CH'EN HUI-LI, 1963. "On Aid to Agriculture by Light Industry," *Ching-chi yen chiu,* Nov. 17, 1963, translated in *Extracts from China Mainland Magazines,* No. 396, pp. 1–11.

CIA, 1963. "The Short-lived Liberal Phase in Economic Thinking in Communist China." Washington.

State Council, 1958. "Regulation Putting into Effect the Enterprise Retained Profits System," *Fa-kuei hui-pien* (May 22, 1958), No. 7, pp. 239–242.

State Statistical Bureau, 1960. *Ten Great Years.* Peking.

SUN YEH-FANG, 1957. "A Discussion of 'Gross Value of Output,'" *Tung-chi kung-tso* (July 14, 1957), No. 13, pp. 8–14.

SUNG HSIN-CHUNG, 1961. "The System of Retaining a Percentage of Profits by

Our Enterprises," Peking *Ta-kung pao,* May 12, 1961, translated in *Survey of the China Mainland Press,* No. 2543, pp. 7–8.

SUNG PING, 1957. "The Problem of Employment," *Lao-tung,* Oct. 4, 1957, translated in *Extracts from China Mainland Magazines,* No. 117, pp. 19–23.

Ta-kung pao, 1961. Editorial, "Satisfactorily Control and Use the Circulating Funds of Industry," Peking, June 20, 1961, translated in *Survey of the China Mainland Press,* No. 2543, pp. 5–6.

TCKT (*T'ung-chi kung-tso*), 1957. "A Brief Description of the State Distribution of Commodities During the Past Year," July 14, 1957, translated in *Extracts from China Mainland Magazines,* No. 97, pp. 21–27.

TCKTTH (*T'ung-chi kung-tso t'ung-hsun*), 1957. Data Office, "The Breakdown and Organization of the Number of Workers and Employees in Our Country in 1955," *Hsin-hua pan-yueh-k'an* (Jan. 25, 1957), No. 2, pp. 87–89.

T'ung-chi yen-chiu, 1958. Feb. 23, 1958, No. 2, p. 18.

WANG TIEH-SHENG, 1957. "To Understand Better the Relationship between Light Industry and Capital Accumulation," *Hsueh-hsi,* March 18, 1957, translated in *Extracts from China Mainland Magazines,* No. 86, pp. 20–22.

WILES, P. J. D., 1962. *The Political Economy of Communism.* Cambridge, Mass.

Wo kuo kang-t'ieh, tien-li, mei-tan, chi-chieh, fang-chieh, tsao-chih kung-yeh-te chin-hsi (*Our Country's Iron and Steel, Electric Power, Coal, Machinery, Textile, and Paper Industries*). Peking, 1958.

YIN, H., "The Reporting of Industrial Statistics in Communist China." (Draft, unpublished Ph.D. thesis, Columbia University.)

Labor Productivity in Industry 11

ROBERT MICHAEL FIELD

THE CHINESE COMMUNISTS have claimed that the productivity of labor increased by 61 per cent during the First Five-Year Plan (1953-57). Because the productivity of labor is an important measure of economic performance, the present chapter will try to evaluate this claim and to determine how successful the Chinese have been in their self-imposed task of raising the productivity of labor in industry.

The limitations of the official Chinese Communist productivity statistics will be discussed first. Although these statistics are shown to be consistent with other published data, it is concluded that they are not an adequate measure of the growth of productivity because of defects in the data for gross value of industrial production that have been used in the productivity calculations.

Second, an independently constructed measure of the growth of productivity is presented. This measure, which is derived from an index of value added based directly on physical output data and an index of labor calculated from official data, shows that the value added per worker in Chinese industry grew 40.2 per cent during the First Five-Year Plan, but that the differences from year to year and in various branches of industry were extreme. On the average, the increase in productivity accounted for 45.6 per cent of the increase in output, while the growth of labor inputs accounted for the remaining 54.4 per cent. It is also shown that the shift in the structure of value added toward heavy industry had a negligible effect on the growth of productivity.

Third, some of the factors contributing to the growth of productivity are examined. Data on the aggregate net value of capital and on the aggregate consumption of energy are presented, and it is shown that the substantial increases in the productivity of labor during the First Five-Year Plan were accompanied by a steadily rising capital-labor ratio and by decreases in the productivity of capital. For the individual branches of industry, the average annual rates of growth of output per worker are compared with the rates of growth both in the value of assets per worker and in the consumption of electric power per worker. These comparisons show that the rates of growth in the value of assets per worker and in the consumption of electric power per worker were consistent with the growth of labor productivity. It is tentatively concluded that capacity was not fully utilized in 1952, and that a more intensive use of capacity was an important factor in the growth of productivity during the First Five-Year Plan period.

Although productivity almost certainly declined during the Great Leap Forward (1958-60), and has by now probably recovered to a level equal to or slightly above that of 1957, I have been unable to measure the changes in productivity since 1957 because the necessary data are not available. For a measure of the trend in productivity to have any meaning, it is obvious that the numerator and the denominator of the productivity ratio must refer to the same universe and that the universe must remain constant over time. In 1958, however, the Chinese Communists changed the universe for which industrial statistics are reported to include the employment and output of almost all handicraft cooperatives and all rural commune industries. Official statistics have not yet been reported in sufficient detail to permit the estimation of data comparable to that published for the First Five-Year Plan.

I. THE LIMITATIONS OF CHINESE COMMUNIST PRODUCTIVITY STATISTICS

Chinese Communist economists and statisticians are just as interested in raising the productivity of labor as their comrades in the Soviet Union, and quotations from Lenin such as the following appear as often in Chinese as in Soviet journals (Lenin, 1951, p. 32):

> In the last analysis, productivity of labour is the most important, the principal thing for the victory of the new social system. Capitalism created a productivity of labour unknown under serfdom. Capitalism can be utterly vanquished, and will be utterly vanquished, by the fact that Socialism creates a new and much higher productivity of labour.

But productivity statistics are handled with much less sophistication. Consider, for example, the official handbook on labor statistics, which presents formulas for and discusses various methods of measuring the productivity of labor.[1] In the section of the handbook that discusses measures of productivity based on labor norms, the following formula is given:

$$\frac{\Sigma q_1 t_{no}}{\Sigma q_1 t_1} \bigg/ \frac{\Sigma q_1 t_{no}}{\Sigma q_1 t_o}$$

1. Statistical Work Handbook Editorial Committee (1958, pp. 41-52). An advertisement on the back cover of *TCKT* (1956a) attributes another handbook in this series to the State Statistical Bureau, but most of them were published in the name of the committee.

where q_1 represents output in the given year, t_1 and t_o represent actual labor expended per unit of output in the given and base years, respectively, and t_{no} represents a fixed labor norm per unit of output. Productivity in the given year is expressed as the ratio of the normal expenditure of labor: $\Sigma q_1 t_{no}$ to the actual expenditure: $\Sigma q_1 t_1$, but when the given year is compared with the base year the norms cancel out and the formula is reduced to: $\Sigma q_1 t_o / \Sigma q_1 t_1$. This formula for the productivity of labor appears to be the reciprocal of (and, therefore, the same as) the measure that Strumilin, the dean of Soviet economists, considered to be the only theoretically valid index of labor consumption. Strumilin's index may be represented as follows:

$$\Sigma q_x l_1 \,/\, \Sigma q_x l_o$$

where q_x represents a fixed bundle of commodities, and l_1 and l_o represent unit labor requirements in the given and base years, respectively (Galenson, 1955, p. 11). Because the Chinese version of the index uses given year weights, the Chinese formula is only equivalent to Strumilin's when comparing a given year with the base year. If the index numbers for any two years are compared at random, say, those for years "1" and "2," the comparison may be represented as:

$$\frac{\Sigma q_2 t_o}{\Sigma q_2 t_2} \Big/ \frac{\Sigma q_1 t_o}{\Sigma q_1 t_1}$$

When two years are compared at random, the Chinese formula does not employ a fixed bundle of commodities, although the use of a fixed bundle

TABLE 1

OFFICIAL DATA ON THE GROSS VALUE OF OUTPUT PER WORKER IN CHINESE INDUSTRY 1952-1957

	Value (1952 yuan)	Index (1952 = 100)	Annual Percentage Change
1952	7,506	100	......
1953	8,546	114	14
1954	9,288	124	9
1955	10,274	137	11
1956	12,172	162	18
1957	12,085	161	−1

Sources:

1952-1956: Chung-kuo kung-jen, 1958 (p. 7).

1957: Derived by multiplying the gross value of output per worker in 1952 by the 161 per cent reported in Ma Wen-jui (1959).

of commodities is precisely what Strumilin felt gave his measure its theoretical validity.

This example shows a certain lack of sophistication on the part of the Chinese in handling index numbers, but how sophisticated are the actual statistics on the productivity of labor released by the regime? Table 1 presents the Chinese statistics, both in absolute terms and as index numbers. The table shows that the Chinese claim an increase in productivity of 61 per cent in five years, but can this claim be accepted? Because of the difficulties that Western scholars have experienced in trying to reconstruct Soviet productivity data [2] and because of the confusing array of not clearly identified and seemingly contradictory data that has been published in China,[3] it is necessary to demonstrate that the official series does, in fact, include all sectors of industry and that it is consistent with other published data.

The reported productivity series cannot be compared with a series computed independently from data on the gross value of industrial production and the average number of workers, because the number of workers has not been reported. It is possible, however, to derive the number of

2. An index of Soviet productivity calculated from the official index of industrial production and the official index of employment grows significantly more slowly than the official index of productivity. The reason for the discrepancy appears to be the linking of separate indices that are not comparable in coverage (Schroeder, 1962, pp. 137-162).

3. Consider, for example, the following tabulation from Yuan Fang (1956, p. 19).

	Labor Productivity (percentage increase)
1953	13
1954	15
1955	10

Then compare the data with the following quotations from the annual communiqués of the State Statistical Bureau:

> Productivity of workers in the state-owned and joint state and privately owned large-scale industrial enterprises (comparable section) in 1953 increased by 13 per cent over 1952 (SSB, 1954, p. 8).
>
> In 1954 . . . the productivity of labor of workers in state-owned and joint state-private industrial enterprises rose approximately 15 per cent compared with 1953 (SSB, 1955, p. 9).
>
> In 1955, the productivity of labor of workers in state, cooperative, and joint state-private enterprises increased by 10 per cent as compared with 1954 (SSB, 1956, p. 7).

When the data are clearly identified, as they are in the quotations from the State Statistical Bureau communiqués, it is readily apparent that they are not comparable and should not have been presented as a single series as they were in the article cited above.

workers from the gross value and productivity data, and to compare this derived data on workers with the sum of the number of workers in the socialist and private sectors of industry. These derivations and a comparison of the results are presented in Table 2. It can be seen that the number of workers derived directly and the sum of the number derived for the socialist and private sectors do not differ by more than 0.7 per cent in any

TABLE 2

ALTERNATIVE ESTIMATES OF THE AVERAGE NUMBER OF WORKERS IN CHINESE INDUSTRY 1952-1955

	Unit of Measure	1952	1953	1954	1955
Estimate I					
All industry:					
Gross value [a]	Million yuan	27,014	35,577	41,513	44,748
Productivity [b]	Yuan per worker	7,506	8,546	9,288	10,274
Workers [c]	Thousand persons	3,599	4,163	4,470	4,355
Estimate II					
Socialist sector:					
Gross value [a]	Million yuan	16,488	22,468	31,172	37,482
Productivity [d]	Yuan per worker	8,049	9,016	10,372	11,387
Workers [c]	Thousand persons	2,048	2,492	3,005	3,292
Private sector:					
Gross value [a]	Million yuan	10,526	13,109	10,341	7,266
Productivity [e]	Yuan per worker	6,801	7,848	7,222	6,879
Workers [c]	Thousand persons	1,548	1,670	1,432	1,056
All industry:					
Workers [f]	Thousand persons	3,596	4,162	4,437	4,348
Workers in estimate II as a per cent of workers in estimate I		99.92	99.98	99.26	99.84

Notes:

a. SSB, 1957b (pp. 28-29).

b. *Chung-kuo kung-jen,* 1958 (p. 7).

c. Derived by dividing the gross value of output by the gross value of output per worker.

d. SSB, 1958 (p. 27).

e. *TCKT* Data Section, 1956b (p. 2).

f. Derived as the sum of the number of workers in the socialist and private sectors.

year. It is clear, therefore, that the productivity series does in fact include all industry and that it is consistent with other published data.

Even though the official series on productivity gives complete coverage and is consistent with other published data, it cannot be accepted as a valid measure of the trend in the productivity of labor, because productivity is measured as the gross value of output per worker; and gross value as officially measured is known to be a defective measure of output. Briefly, the defects of the official data for gross value are its sensitivity to organizational changes, and the nature of the prices used.

The official gross value data are particularly sensitive to organizational changes because they are collected by the "factory reporting method." Under this method, each enterprise reports the gross value of its production, and the total gross value of industrial production is simply the sum of the data reported by the separate enterprises. For example, if an enterprise produced one million tons of pig iron and 900,000 tons of steel but consumed 800,000 tons of the pig iron in the process of refining the steel, the gross value of the production of the enterprise would be based on 900,000 tons of steel and 200,000 tons of pig iron (Fang Fa, 1957, p. 29). The value reported, therefore, is neither gross value (price times quantity) nor net value (value added times quantity), but may best be described as the value of enterprise sales.

To explain the sensitivity of the official gross value data, let us consider the Chinese Communist system of record-keeping as it would apply to the production of a commodity that passes through three stages of fabrication, each stage being performed by a different enterprise. Let M be the value of the materials consumed, and V_1, V_2, and V_3 the value added in each successive stage. The gross value reported by each enterprise and the total gross value would be as follows:

	Gross Value
Enterprise 1	$M + V_1$
Enterprise 2	$M + V_1 + V_2$
Enterprise 3	$M + V_1 + V_2 + V_3$
Total	$3\,M + 3\,V_1 + 2\,V_2 + V_3$

If each stage of fabrication were carried out by a number of enterprises, horizontal mergers would not affect the reported gross value. The sole result would be a smaller number of enterprises, each reporting a larger value of production. The effect of vertical integration, however, is quite different. If the enterprises performing the second and third stages of fabrication were integrated, the reported gross value would be as follows:

	Gross Value
Enterprise 1	$M + V_1$
Intergrated Enterprise (Combined Enterprises 2 and 3)	$M + V_1 + V_2 + V_3$
Total	$2M + 2V_1 + V_2 + V_3$

The vertical integration of the enterprises would reduce the total reported gross value by $(M + V_1 + V_2)$.

But how does the factory reporting method work out in practice? In 1956, during the socialist transformation of private industry, the horizontal mergers of large numbers of fairly small enterprises reduced the gross value of their production by less than one per cent. In the same year, however, when the Ministry of Coal Industry shifted primary responsibility for reporting from the control bureau down to the individual mine, the reduction in the degree of vertical integration increased the gross value of its output by about 10 per cent (*TCKT,* 1956b, p. 6). The official gross value data, therefore, are not affected significantly by horizontal mergers but are changed by vertical integration; and the change is inversely related to the change in the degree of vertical integration.

Between 1952 and 1956 the number of industrial enterprises was reduced from 167,000 to 60,000, of which only 40,000 were independent accounting units. Although most of this reduction in the number of enterprises represents horizontal mergers, the degree of vertical integration must also have increased somewhat. This increase must have introduced a downward bias into the official gross value data.

If organizational changes have introduced a downward bias, why do the gross value data have such a strong upward bias? Let us consider the nature of the prices used to value physical output. Physical output is valued in constant 1952 prices, which are defined as the average of prices in use between July and September 1952. Two factors, though, have caused these prices to overweight the faster growing commodities and so impart a strong upward bias to the official gross value data.

The first factor is that the official 1952 prices overstated the value of producer goods in relation to that of consumer goods. (*TCKT,* 1956b, p. 6). Users of small machines, for example, preferred to make their own or to buy them from private enterprises rather than pay the official price to state enterprises (Fan Jo-i, 1957, p. 55). Because the output of producer goods grew faster than that of consumer goods, overpricing of producer goods gave an upward bias to the official data.

The second factor that has distorted the official prices is the overpricing of many of the new commodities that were produced for the first time during the years following 1952. The State Statistical Bureau stated that new products should be priced at "test manufacturing" cost, with some allowance for the expected decline in cost after production has been regularly established. The prices of the new products should then be converted from current to 1952 prices by the same factor used to convert the current price of some similar product on the constant price list. Because of the difficulty in estimating what the actual cost of production would be after the process had been put into operation, this procedure greatly overvalued most of the new products (SSB, 1957a, pp. 11-13). One specific example is that of a 6,000 kilowatt marine engine for which the price was set on the basis of a 1,320,000 *yuan* cost of production in 1955, but which actually cost only 380,000 *yuan* to produce in 1956 (Fan jo-i, 1957, p. 56). In fact, the actual situation was so bad that the prices of some of these new products were far above the actual cost of production even after being converted from current to 1952 prices. Because the production of these new items grew much faster than industrial output as a whole, their overpricing introduced another source of upward bias into the official index.

II. A VALUE-ADDED INDEX OF INDUSTRIAL PRODUCTIVITY

Because of the defects in the official productivity data discussed in the previous section, an independently constructed index must be used to measure the growth of productivity. The index of productivity presented in this section is derived from an index of value added based directly on physical output data and an index of labor calculated from official data. The value added by industry in 1957 was 209.6 per cent of the level of 1952. Labor, which grew by 49.5 per cent between 1952 and 1957, contributed 54.4 per cent of the growth in output, while productivity, which grew by 40.2 per cent, contributed the remaining 45.6 per cent of the growth in output. However, the differences from year to year, and by branch of industry, were extreme. In general, those branches of industry producing industrial materials and machinery not only grew faster than those producing fuels and consumer goods but also had higher increases in productivity. Finally, the shift in the structure of value added toward heavy industry had a negligible effect on the growth of productivity.

The index of industrial production was constructed from Chinese data for the physical output of 32 commodities produced by nine branches of industry.[4] These data were weighted in two stages and then

4. The index of industrial production presented here differs in several respects from the index presented by Kang Chao in Chapter 9 of this book. My index is based on nine branches of industry and is adjusted for coverage, while Professor Chao's is based on 13 branches of industry and is not adjusted for coverage. The

adjusted for coverage. In the first stage the output series were grouped by branch of industry. The indexes for five branches of industry—electric power, coal, ferrous metals, building materials, and paper—are based on a single commodity. For the electric power, coal, and paper industries, production is relatively homogeneous, and a single output series includes the entire production of each branch. For the ferrous metals industry, only the output series for the production of rolled steel was used. Although data were available for the production of iron and manganese ore, pig iron, and crude steel, these commodities were not included because they are intermediate products that are almost entirely consumed within the industry. For the building materials industry, the only commodity for which data were available is cement. The indexes for the remaining branches of industry—metal processing, chemical processing, textiles, and food—were based on a sample of the commodities produced by the branches, weighted by their respective prices.

In the second stage, an index for all nine branches of industry was obtained by aggregating the indexes for the individual branches. The weights employed for the aggregation of the branch indexes were estimates of the values added in 1956, computed from the wage bill paid to workers employed in industry. The wage bill in turn was computed from data on average earnings and average employment. If data on the wage bill had been available in sufficient detail, the value added per unit of output could have been used directly as the weight for each commodity, but these data were available only for branches of industry, not for individual commodities. Finally, the index for the nine branches was adjusted for coverage, on the assumption that the proportion of the value added included in these nine branches was the same as the proportion of the gross value they had contributed.

The indexes for labor were derived from the average number of workers. For industry as a whole, the number of wage workers was estimated by dividing the official gross value of output by the gross value of output per worker. For the individual branches of industry, labor data were reported for the electric power, coal, ferrous metals, paper, and textile industries; they could be derived from data on the consumption of

---

branches of industry included in Professor Chao's index but not in mine are the petroleum, nonferrous metals, timber, and light industries. There are also certain differences within branches of industry. For example, I have adjusted the data on the production of electric power to exclude the power generated at industrial power plants, because the weight assigned to the electric power industry is based on the number of workers employed at public power stations. Or again, for the textile industry I have excluded series for the production of cotton yarn, wool yarn, and raw silk so that the output series included will represent as nearly as possible the final output of the textile industry. Finally, the weight bases are different. We both used wage-bill weights, but Professor Chao's are for 1952 while mine are for 1956. I selected 1956 as the weight base for my index because I felt the quality of the data on average earnings was better for 1956 than for 1952.

electric power in the metal processing, chemical processing, and building material industries. The estimation of the number of workers employed in the food industry, however, was more complicated. The average number of workers in the food industry in 1956 was estimated on the basis of two assumptions—that the proportion of workers among all workers and employees in the food industry was the same as that in industry as a whole, and that the average number of workers and employees was the same as the number reported for the end of 1955. The average number of workers in the food industry in 1952 was estimated by assuming that the number of workers in the food industry as a whole grew at the same rate as the number of workers in those food industry enterprises for which data on the consumption of electric power are available.

The indexes of productivity derived from these indexes of ouput and labor are indexes of output per man-year. Conceptually, output per man-year is the product of the output per man-hour and the average number of hours worked per person per year. That is:

$$\frac{Q}{L} = \frac{Q}{H} \times \frac{H}{L}$$

where Q represents the quantity of output, L represents the average number of workers, and H represents the total number of man-hours worked per year. Thus the movement of an index of output per man-year results from changes in the average number of hours worked per year and from changes in hourly productivity; but specific data that would permit the isolation of the changes due to each of these factors are not available. Because of the physical limitation on the number of hours that can be worked per year, however, it is obvious that long-run increases in output per man-year must come from increases in output per man-hour. In fact, the number of hours worked per year was high in 1952 and remained high throughout the period. The effect of the variation in the number of hours worked per year, therefore, is minor except for year-to-year fluctuations.

The indexes of output, labor, and productivity are presented in Table 3. Between 1952 and 1957, output more than doubled while labor increased by 49.5 per cent and productivity by 40.2 per cent. A gain in productivity of more than 40 per cent in a five-year period is impressive, but the gains from year to year were uneven. In 1953, output increased by 20.7 per cent over the level of 1952, but because of the large increase in the average number of workers, productivity increased by only 4.3 per cent. (Such large increases in the average number of workers occurred annually during the period of economic reconstruction from 1949 to 1952.) In 1954 and 1955 the increases in output declined to 14.8 per cent and 5.5 per cent, respectively, but productivity increased in both years because of a decline in employment in the private sector and

TABLE 3

INDEXES OF OUTPUT, LABOR, AND PRODUCTIVITY IN CHINESE INDUSTRY 1952-1957

	1952	1953	1954	1955	1956	1957
Output						
Index (1952 = 100) [a]	100.0	120.7	138.6	146.2	190.4	209.6
Annual percentage change	......	20.7	14.8	5.5	30.2	10.1
Labor						
Index (1952 = 100) [b]	100.0	115.7	124.2	121.0	133.9	149.5
Annual percentage change	......	15.7	7.3	—2.6	10.7	11.6
Productivity						
Index (1952 = 100) [c]	100.0	104.3	111.5	120.8	142.2	140.2
Annual percentage change	......	4.3	6.9	8.3	17.7	—1.4

Notes:

a. Table A-1 in the Appendix to this chapter.

b. Derived from the number of wage workers in industry. The number of wage workers was estimated by dividing the gross value of output by the gross value of output per worker. The gross value of output is reported in SSB, 1957b (pp. 28-29) and in *Ten Great Years* (1960, p. 16). The gross value of output per worker is from Table 1.

c. Derived by dividing the index of output by the index of labor.

tight control over hiring in the socialist sector. The number of workers increased by only 7.3 per cent in 1954 and actually declined by 2.6 per cent in 1955. In 1956, productivity increased by 17.7 per cent, despite a 10.7 per cent increase in the number of workers, because of the growth of 30.2 per cent in output. In 1957, another large increase occurred in the number of workers, but productivity declined slightly because output grew by only 10.1 per cent.

The data in Table 3 show that output increased by 109.6 per cent between 1952 and 1957, but how much of this increase can be attributed to the growth of productivity? One way in which this question has been answered is by first calculating the amount by which output would have increased if productivity had remained constant, and then attributing all the rest of the growth in output to the growth of productivity.[5] With no increase in productivity, the increase in output for this period would have been the same as the increase in labor, or 49.5 per cent. The proportion of the increase due to the increase in labor, therefore, would be $49.5 \div 109.6 = 45.2$ per cent. And so the proportion due to the increase in productivity would be the residual, or $100.0 - 45.2 = 54.8$ per cent.

But suppose the question had been answered by calculating the amount by which output would have increased if labor had remained constant? With no increase in labor, the increase in output would have been the same as the increase in productivity, or 40.2 per cent, and proportion of the increase in output due to the increase in productivity would be $40.2 \div 109.6 = 36.7$ per cent.

Why are the results of these two attempts to allocate the increment in output between labor and productivity so different? To make the cause of this difference clear, let us consider the relationship that states that output equals productivity times labor, or algebraically:

$$Q = P \times L$$

where Q represents quantity of output, P represents productivity and L represents the average number of workers. If during the period under consideration output, porductivity, and labor increased by $\triangle Q$, $\triangle P$, and $\triangle L$, respectively, then output at the end of the period would be:

$$Q + \triangle Q = (P + \triangle P)\ (L + \triangle L)$$

and the increase in output would be:

$$\triangle Q = P\triangle L + L\triangle P + \triangle P\triangle L$$

$P\triangle L$ is the increment in output associated with the increase in labor, and $L\triangle P$ is the increment associated with the increase in productivity,

5. This is the current practice in China and the Soviet Union. For an example of its use in China, see *TCKT* Data Section, 1957b (pp. 31-32); and for a discussion of its use in the Soviet Union, see Levine, 1960 (pp. 225-228).

while $\triangle L \triangle P$ is the increment associated with the interaction of labor and productivity—that is, the joint product of labor and productivity.

The two attempts to allocate the increase in output between labor and productivity yield different results because the entire joint product was arbitrarily allocated to productivity in the first computation, and equally arbitrarily allocated to labor in the second. Although any method of allocating the joint product of labor and productivity is arbitrary, the method used here is to divide it evenly between labor and productivity (Mills, 1952).[6]

Table 4 presents the annual percentage increases in output from 1952

TABLE 4

ALLOCATION OF THE ANNUAL PERCENTAGE INCREASE IN OUTPUT BETWEEN LABOR AND PRODUCTIVITY 1953-1957

	Annual Percentage Increase in Output [a]	Allocation of the Increase in Output [b]	
		Labor	Productivity
Average, 1953-1957	16.0	54.4	45.6
1953	20.7	77.5	22.5
1954	14.8	51.4	48.6
1955	5.5	−49.1	149.1
1956	30.2	38.4	61.6
1957	10.1	114.4	−14.4

Notes:

a. Table 3.

b. Derived from the annual percentage changes in Table 3 by the method described in the text.

through 1957, dividing them into increments due to the growth of labor and due to the growth of productivity. On the average, the increase in labor accounted for 54.4 per cent of the increase in output, while the increase in productivity accounted for the other 45.6 per cent, but there were extreme differences from year to year.

In 1955, because the average number of workers declined, labor made a negative contribution to the growth of output but it was offset by the growth of productivity. In 1957, because the average number of workers grew faster than output, labor accounted for 114.4 per cent of the increase in output and offset the slight decline in productivity. In 1953, 1954 and

6. This method of decomposition was first used by John T. Dunlop (1944) in his analysis of the cyclical variation of labor's share in national income.

1956, the increase in labor accounted for 77.5 per cent, 51.4 per cent, and 38.4 per cent, respectively, of the increase in output.

Indexes of output, labor, and productivity by branch of industry are presented in Table 5. The growth in productivity averaged 42.2 per cent,

TABLE 5

INDEXES OF OUTPUT, LABOR, AND PRODUCTIVITY BY BRANCH OF INDUSTRY
1956
(1952 =100)

	Output [a]	Labor [b]	Productivity [c]
All industry	190.4	133.9	142.2
Electric power	241.4	200.3	120.5
Coal	166.7	127.0	131.3
Ferrous metals	290.0	155.7	186.3
Metal processing	228.3	145.8	156.6
Chemical processing	262.2	161.8	162.1
Building materials	223.5	138.4	161.5
Paper	196.2	105.8	185.4
Textiles	163.0	121.2	134.5
Food	156.3	117.6	132.9
Other	201.0	150.2	133.8

Notes:
a. Table A-1 in the Appendix to this chapter.
b. Table A-2 in the Appendix.
c. Derived by dividing the indexes of output by the indexes of labor.

but the differences between the rates of growth shown by individual branches of industry are extreme, ranging from only 20.5 per cent for electric power to 86.3 per cent for ferrous metals.

In the fuels industries, the increases in productivity were the lowest among the ten branches presented in Table 5, but for different reasons. The above-average increase of 141.4 per cent in the output of the electric power industry was almost matched by an increase of 100.3 per cent in the number of workers employed; and productivity increased by only 20.5 per cent. In the coal industry the increase in output of 66.7 per cent was below average, but the number of workers increased by only 27.0 per cent, so that the increase in productivity was 31.3 per cent.

In the branches of industries producing industrial materials—the ferrous metals, chemical processing, building materials, and paper industries—the increases in productivity were higher than those for any other group, ranging from 61.5 per cent to 86.3 per cent. The increases in output, which ranged from 96.2 per cent in the paper industry to 190.0 per cent in ferrous metals, were matched by the increases in the electric power, metal processing, and other branches of industry. Increases in the number of workers were all low in relation to these increases in output. In the metal processing industry, the increase in productivity of 56.6 per cent was only slightly lower than in the branches producing industrial materials.

In the branches of industry producing consumer goods, increases in output, labor, and productivity were all below average. In the textile industry, output grew by 63.0 per cent, labor by 21.2 per cent, and productivity by 34.5 per cent; while in the food industry output grew by 56.3 per cent, labor by 17.6 per cent, and productivity by 32.9 per cent.

The category of "other branches of industry" must be treated with caution because the indexes of both output and labor may be subject to a wide range of error. Because the index of output was derived in the process of adjusting the aggregate index for coverage, it is influenced by errors in the indexes estimated for the nine specifically included branches of industry (which may be cumulative), and by errors in the data on the gross value of output used in the adjustment process. The index of labor for the other branches of industry, which was derived from the residual number of workers, is probably more reliable than the index of output, but it too may reflect cumulative errors of estimation. Because the index of output per worker was derived from these indexes of output and labor, it can be taken only as a general indication of the change in productivity.

Has the shift in the structure of industry had any impact on the growth of productivity? Those branches of industry in which output grew faster than average, such as ferrous metals or chemical processing, have increased in relative importance; while those that grew more slowly than average, such as the textile or food processing industries, have decreased in relative importance—but have these changes affected the rate of growth of productivity? To answer this question we must examine the construction of the index of labor productivity. The formula for the index presented in Table 3 is:

$$\frac{\dfrac{\Sigma V_{56}\, Q_i}{\Sigma V_{56}\, Q_{52}}}{\dfrac{\Sigma L_i}{\Sigma L_{52}}}$$

where V represents value added per unit of output, Q represents quantity of output, L represents the average number of workers, and the subscripts 56, 52, and i represent the weight base, the base year, and the given year, respectively. Because this index is derived from an aggregative index of output and an aggregate index of employment, it does not assign fixed weights to the indexes of productivity for the various branches of industry. Changes in aggregate productivity are due not only to changes in productivity within the individual branches of industry, but also to changes in the relative importance of the branches. But an index derived in this manner may be factored into a direct productivity index and an index showing the impact on productivity of the shift in the structure of industry.

The aggregate index of labor productivity may be factored in such a way as to yield a direct index with either value added or labor weights, and the weights may be for the base year or for the given year. One way in which the index may be factored is:

$$\frac{\Sigma L_i \dfrac{\left(\dfrac{V_{56}\,Q_i}{L_i}\right)}{\left(\dfrac{V_{56}\,Q_{52}}{L_{52}}\right)}}{\Sigma L_i} \times \frac{\dfrac{\Sigma V_{56}\,Q_i}{\Sigma V_{56}\,Q_i \left(\dfrac{L_{52}}{V_{56}\,Q_{52}}\right)}}{\dfrac{\Sigma V_{56}\,Q_{52}}{\Sigma V_{56}\,Q_{52} \left(\dfrac{L_{52}}{V_{56}\,Q_{52}}\right)}}$$

The first expression is a direct measure of productivity with given-year labor weights. The second shows the impact of the shift in the industrial structure on the growth of productivity. In particular, the first expression indicates what the growth of productivity would have been if there had been no change in the structure of employment; while the second indicates what the growth would have been if the levels of productivity within the various branches of industry had remained the same.[7]

The direct productivity index cannot be calculated for years other than 1956 (1952=100), because data on the average number of workers by branch of industry are available only for the year 1952 and 1956. However, the index of structural change can be calculated, at least in the form presented here, for each year from 1952 through 1957. The aggregate productivity index, the index of change in productivity due to structural change, and the direct productivity index derived from them are presented in Table 6. An examination of these indexes shows that the change in the structure of industry had very little effect on the growth of productivity, and that almost all the increase in productivity was due to changes within the branches of industry.

7. The meaning of the second expression may not be immediately obvious because the factoring of the aggregate index yields a weighted harmonic mean rather than a weighted arithmetic mean. The numerator is the level of productivity that would have prevailed in the given year if there had been no change in productivity within the branches of industry, and the denominator is the actual level in the base year.

Table 6

INDEXES OF AGGREGATE PRODUCTIVITY, THE CHANGE IN PRODUCTIVITY DUE TO STRUCTURAL CHANGE, AND DIRECT PRODUCTIVITY 1952-1957

(1952 = 100)

	1952	1953	1954	1955	1956	1957
Aggregate productivity [a]	100.0	104.3	111.5	120.8	142.2	140.2
Change in productivity due to structural change [b]	100.0	99.5	99.7	99.8	99.6	99.6
Direct productivity [c]	100.0	104.8	111.8	121.0	142.8	140.8

Notes:

a. Table 3.

b. Calculated from the formula presented in the text. The weights for the index are used for the V_{56}, the index numbers for the Q_i and the average number of workers in 1952 for the L_{52}. The weights and index numbers are presented in Table A-1 and the average number of workers in Table A-2 in the Appendix to this chapter.

c. Derived by dividing the index of aggregate productivity by the index of the change in productivity due to the shift in the structure of value added.

III. FACTORS CONTRIBUTING TO THE GROWTH OF PRODUCTIVITY

The average productivity of labor measures output per worker, but growth in output is due not only to an increase in the number of workers, but also to changes in other inputs—changes in skill, management, plant size, capital, and the like. An attempt to explain the growth of productivity, therefore, should take into account the relationships between productivity and these other economic variables.

One of the most important of these variables is the amount of capital available per worker, but the data on capital, as with other important economic series, are not complete and present conceptual difficulties. The Chinese have reported the following data on the value of fixed capital assets at year end in million *yuan:* [8]

	1949	1952	1955	1957
Gross value	12,800	15,800	26,290	35,200
Net value	......	10,140	18,140	.....

These figures are not suitable for economic analysis because the figures for gross value are the "accumulated total" valued "at original purchase price" (*Ten Great Years,* 1960, pp. xxvi and 93), and the figures for net value are net only in a bookkeeping sense.[9] These figures, therefore, are in neither current nor constant prices, but in mixed prices, each item of capital equipment being valued in terms of the prices prevailing in the year it was purchased.

Although the main purpose of this chapter is not to make estimates of the capital stock in industry, in trying to explain the growth of productivity, a rough measure of the net value of fixed capital assets (in constant prices) was constructed in order to have data on the capital available per worker. The measure was built on the net value of assets reported for

8. The gross value data, except for 1955, are from *Ten Great Years* (1960, p. 93). The net value for 1952 was reported by the New China News Agency on October 1, 1957; see Hollister, 1958 (p. 62); and both the gross and the net value for 1955 are from *TCKT* Data Section, 1957a (p. 32).

9. The rate of depreciation is calculated from the formula:

$$\frac{\text{Original price} - \text{estimated remaining value} + \text{estimated disposal cost}}{\text{estimated number of years of life} \times \text{original price}} \times 100$$

Thus the "net" value of fixed capital assets is simply that portion of the original purchase price which has not yet been written off (*Chung-kuo ch'ing kung-yeh,* 1963, p. 20).

year-end 1952, which was treated as being in constant prices,[10] and extended to other years on the basis of reported data on newly added fixed assets. Because these data are the gross value of additions to capital stock in current prices, with no allowance for depreciation (Hsu Ch'ien *et al.*, 1957, p. 49; Hupeh University, 1960, p. 254), they were converted to constant prices and depreciation was assumed to be 5 per cent of the gross value of assets (see Table A-3).

This index of the net value of capital in Chinese industry is presented in Table 7. It shows that the net value of capital increased 131.9 per cent during a five-year period and that capital growth was accelerating during the period, the percentage increase for each year being larger than that for the previous year.

But how reliable is this index? Before we can answer this question, we must look at another variable that is closely related to the growth of capital—the consumption of energy. There are, however, problems in using the data on energy consumption as a measure of the services of capital. For instance, while the proportion of energy-using equipment tends to rise as industry expands, energy also tends to be used more efficiently, and so these two changes tend to balance each other. Nonetheless, for a country like China, where data on capital are fragmentary, the consumption of energy by industrial enterprises may still be a better indicator of the services of capital than the data on capital themselves.

The data in Table 7 show that the net consumption of electric power, which increased by 192.1 per cent during the First Five-Year Plan, grew significantly faster than capital stock, the consumption of power per unit of capital having grown by 25.9 per cent. Power per unit of capital increased 16.6 per cent in 1953, a further 10.2 per cent in 1954, and then remained fairly constant through 1957. Although the degree of electrification undoubtedly increased during the First Five-Year Plan, this comparison of the data on the consumption of electric power and the growth of capital at least suggests that existing capacity was not fully utilized in 1952, but that it was used more intensively as industrial production expanded, reaching a fairly high level during 1954 and fluctuating thereafter with the year-to-year variations in the rate of growth of industrial production.

These conclusions are based solely on data for electric power, which represented only about one-third of the total amount of energy consumed. If data on the amount of coal consumed per unit of capital were available for years other than 1952 and 1957, the pattern of year-to-year changes in the consumption of energy might be modified, but the trend for the period as a whole would not be changed. The implication that capacity

10. The fixed assets of state-operated enterprises, which accounted for 81 per cent of the gross value of all industrial fixed assets according to *TCKT* Data Section, 1956a (p. 27), were revalued in 1951 and 1952 (*TCKT* Data Section, 1957a, p. 31).

Table 7

NET VALUE OF CAPITAL AND NET CONSUMPTION OF ENERGY IN CHINESE INDUSTRY 1952-1957

	1952	1953	1954	1955	1956	1957
Capital [a]						
Million 1952 yuan	9,942	10,844	12,480	14,718	18,124	23,056
Index (1952 = 100)	100.0	109.1	125.5	148.0	182.3	231.9
Net consumption of electric power [b]						
Million kilowatt-hours	5,100	6,480	8,220	9,300	11,596	14,902
Index (1952 = 100)	100.0	127.0	161.1	182.4	227.3	292.1
Net consumption of coal [c]						
Million metric tons	10.9	......	......	......	......	33.7
Index (1952 = 100)	100.0	......	......	......	......	309.2
Electric power per unit of capital [d]						
Kilowatt-hours per thousand 1952 yuan	513	598	659	632	640	646
Index (1952 = 100)	100.0	116.6	128.5	123.2	124.8	125.9
Coal per unit of capital [e]						
Metric tons per thousand 1952 yuan	1.10	......	......	......	......	1.46
Index (1952 = 100)	100.0	......	......	......	......	132.7

Notes:

a. Table A-3 in the Appendix to this chapter.

b. Excludes consumption of electric power stations and transmission losses. For 1952-1956, see SSB, 1958 (p. 72); for 1957, see Wu, 1963 (p. 79).

c. Excludes consumption of coal by mines and electric power stations. See Bazhenov *et al.*, 1959 (p. 24).

d. Derived by dividing the net consumption of electric power by capital.

e. Derived by dividing the net consumption of coal by capital.

was used more intensively at the end of the period than at the beginning would still stand, too, because the amount of coal consumed between 1952 and 1957 increased even faster than consumption of electric power.

Table 8 presents indexes of output per worker, output per unit of capital, and the capital-labor ratio. A growth of 40.2 per cent in the productivity of labor appears to be reasonable when compared with an increase of 55.1 per cent in the amount of capital per worker. But the trend in the capital-labor ratio may not accurately reflect changes in the amount of capital actually used by each worker, because that ratio is simply the aggregate value of capital stocks divided by the average number of workers employed, and does not reflect changes in the number of shifts worked.

Any change in the number of shifts worked does have a direct impact on the amount of capital actually available to workers on any one shift, because capital is available for use 24 hours a day, while labor ordinarily works only one shift. For example, the effective value of fixed capital assets per worker would be doubled if industry were to change from a single shift to two shifts a day. In the absence of data on the distribution of workers among shifts worked, or some similar measure such as the shift coefficient used in the Soviet Union,[11] the impact of the changes that must have occurred in the number of shifts and in the distribution of persons employed among them cannot be measured. It is likely that the number of shifts increased and that the trend in the capital-labor ratio, therefore, understates the growth in the amount of capital actually available for each person.

A more serious difficulty is that the capital-labor ratio does not reflect the efficiency with which the capital is used, and so a more explicit relationship between output, labor, and capital may be used instead. This relationship is as follows: output per unit of labor = output per unit of capital × capital per unit of labor. Algebraically, the relationship is:

$$\frac{Q}{L} = \frac{Q}{K} \times \frac{K}{L}$$

where Q represents quantity of output, K represents capital, and L represents the average number of workers.

As output increased, the mix of factor inputs changed, and by 1957 considerably more capital was used per worker than had been used in 1952. Real capital stocks not only increased faster than the average number of workers but, after 1953, also increased faster than output. As a re-

11. The Soviet shift coefficient is the ratio of the total number of workers (not including other employees) to the number of workers in the largest shift. For example, the shift coefficient would be 1.54 if 65 per cent of the workers were in the largest shift. The shift coefficient is not affected by the distribution of employment between the second and third shifts.

TABLE 8

INDEXES OF OUTPUT PER WORKER, OUTPUT PER UNIT OF CAPITAL AND THE CAPITAL-LABOR RATIO
1952-1957
(1952 = 100)

	1952	1953	1954	1955	1956	1957
Output per unit of capital	100.0	104.3	111.5	120.8	142.2	140.2
Output per unit of capital	100.0	110.6	110.4	98.8	104.4	90.4
Capital-labor ratio	100.0	94.3	101.0	122.3	136.1	155.1

Sources:
Tables 3 and 7.

sult, the substantial increases in the productivity of labor were accompanied by a steadily rising capital-labor ratio and decreases in the productivity of capital. However, the relationships between output, labor and capital varied considerably among branches of industry.

In Table 9, the average annual rates of growth for output per worker

TABLE 9

AVERAGE ANNUAL RATES OF GROWTH OF OUTPUT PER WORKER, FIXED ASSETS PER WORKER, AND CONSUMPTION OF ELECTRIC POWER PER WORKER, BY BRANCH OF INDUSTRY DURING 1953-1956
(in per cent)

	Output per Worker	Fixed Assets per Worker	Consumption of Electric Power per per Worker
Electric power	4.8	2.3	......
Coal	7.0	2.5	9.8
Ferrous metals	16.8	8.4	17.5
Metal processing	11.9	13.9	14.6
Chemical processing	12.8	11.0	7.8
Building materials	12.7	14.4	9.2
Paper	16.7	9.0	16.6
Textiles	7.7	2.4	8.1
Food	7.4	2.8	7.8

Sources:
Table 5, and Tables A-4 and A-5 in the Appendix to this chapter.

are compared with the growth rates of fixed assets per worker. The data show that, except for the metal processing and the building materials industries, output per worker grew faster than assets per worker. This is the opposite of the relationship shown by the aggregate data in Table 8, where capital per worker grew faster than output per worker.

The principal difference between the relationships shown by these two sets of data lies in the nature of the data on capital. The aggregate data are the net value of fixed capital assets in constant prices, while the data for the branches of industry are gross rather than net, are valued at original purchase price rather than in constant prices, and include only productive fixed assets. However, the exclusion of nonproductive fixed assets from these latter data does not affect the aggregate rates of growth significantly, because the proportion of productive fixed assets in the total fixed assets remained virtually constant, having been 84.2 per cent in 1952 and 83.2 per cent in 1957, (*Ten Great Years,* 1960, p. 93). (Differences for individual branches of industry may have been greater.) Neither does the use of original rather than constant prices have a significant effect, because assets were revalued in 1951 and 1952 (*TCKT* Data Section, 1957a, p. 31) and because prices did not change significantly during the First Five-Year Plan period.[12] The most important difference is that the aggregate data are the net value of capital assets, while the data for branches of industry are the gross value. Because the stock of capital assets was comparatively old in 1952, 36 per cent of its gross value having been written off,[13] the net additions as a percentage of 1952 net value were larger than the gross additions as a percentage of 1952 gross value.

Even though the gross value of assets grew significantly more slowly than the net value, the variations in the average annual growth rates of the gross value of assets are still useful as an explanation of variation in the rates of growth of productivity. When these data are examined, the growth in productivity appears to be reasonable for every branch except the ferrous metals and paper industries, which show a growth in productivity much higher than the growth in the value of assets per worker would have led us to expect.

Table 9 also presents data on the average annual rates of growth in the consumption of electric power per worker. The rates of growth in productivity for the chemical processing and building materials industries are slightly higher, and the rate for the metal processing industry a little lower, than the growth in the consumption of electric power would have led us to expect, but the relationship still appears to be reasonable.

When the data (Table 9) on assets per worker and consumption of electric power per worker are compared, the rates of growth in electric power consumption are higher than the rates of growth in the value of capital for every branch except the chemical processing and the building materials industries. Although this difference is due partly to the fact that the data on the gross value of assets understated the true rate of growth, the pattern of variation in the rates of growth suggests that it is also due to the fact that existing capacity was not fully utilized at the beginning of the First Five-Year Plan, especially in the coal, ferrous metals, and paper industries.

Let us, then, turn to the data on the use of capacity. Table 10 shows the percentage of capacity not used in 1952, compared with the growth of physical output per worker during the First Five-Year Plan. It can be seen that (except for pig iron) the higher the percentage of unused capac-

12. The price index for capital assets (with 1952 = 100) did not rise above 106.5 in 1953 nor fall below 90.4 in 1956 and 1957. See Liu and Yeh, 1965 (p. 235).

13. See the data on the net and gross value of capital assets in Table A-3 in the Appendix to this chapter.

TABLE 10

INDEXES OF PHYSICAL OUTPUT PER WORKER AND CAPACITY PER WORKER, AND THE PER CENT OF CAPACITY NOT USED IN 1952

	Index (1952 = 100) Physical Output per Worker	Index (1952 = 100) Capacity per Worker [a]	Per cent of Capacity Not Used in 1952
1956			
Electric power	120.5[b]	98.6	......
Paper	185.4[b]	123.3	44.1[c]
Cotton yarn	126.0[d]	105.6	16.8[d]
Cotton cloth	104.6[d]	......	13.3[d]
1957			
Coal	145.8[e]	130.9	34.9[f]
Pig iron	238.5[e]	235.4	15.6[d]
Steel	192.9[e]	149.5	41.4[d]
Cement	174.3[e]	184.0	22.3[g]

Notes:

a. Table A-6 in the Appendix to this chapter.

b. Table 5.

c. Derived from data on physical output and capacity reported in SSB, 1958 (pp. 206, 209).

d. SSB, 1958 (pp. 20, 169-170).

e. *Ten Great Years* (1960, p. 110).

f. Derived from data on physical output and capacity reported in SSB, 1957b (pp. 32-33) and *T'ung-chi yen-chiu* Data Section, 1958 (p. 4).

g. Derived from data on physical output and capacity reported in *Ten Great Years* (1960, p. 96) and *T'ung-chi yen-chiu* Data Section, 1958 (p. 4).

ity in 1952, the greater the increase in physical output per worker. Because these data are so fragmentary, referring to only seven commodities, any conclusion must be presented with some caution, but the data at least suggest that putting to work the capacity not used in 1952 is responsible for some of the growth of productivity, particularly for coal, paper, and steel. These are all commodities produced by branches of industry that showed rates of growth of productivity higher than the growth of assets per worker would have led one to expect.

The increase in the output of pig iron per worker, on the other hand, is a great deal higher than one would expect from the 1952 unused capacity; but the more effective use of capacity is only one source of the increases in productivity. Inasmuch as the growth in capacity per worker has also been an important factor, Table 10 presents data on the growth of capacity per unit of labor. The greater the growth in capacity per worker, the greater the growth in physical output per worker, but this relationship does not conflict with that shown between physical output per worker and capacity per worker. Capacity not used in 1952 and the growth of capacity per worker during the First Five-Year Plan are clearly complementary factors in determining the growth of physical output per worker. Those commodities such as electric power, coal, paper, and steel, which showed a higher percentage of unused capacity in 1952 than the growth in output per worker would have led us to expect, all show a lower-than-expected growth in capacity per worker. Conversely, cement and pig iron, which had a less-than-expected percentage of capacity not used in 1952, had a higher-than-expected growth of capacity per worker.

How important was each of these two factors in determining the rate of growth of productivity? One way to answer this question is to examine the relationship which states that output per worker = output per unit of capacity $\times$ capacity per unit of labor, or algebraically:

$$\frac{Q}{L} = \frac{Q}{C} \times \frac{C}{L}$$

where Q represents quantity of output, C represents capacity, and L represents the average number of workers. This relationship can be partitioned to show what percentage of the increase in productivity is due to the increase in output per unit of capacity, and what percentage is due to the increase in capacity per unit of labor. The results of this partition are shown in Table 11.

The picture that emerges is that commodities produced by light industry, such as paper, cotton, yarn, and cotton cloth, enjoyed a very low investment priority and had small increases in capacity per worker; while commodities produced by heavy industry such as coal, pig iron, steel, and cement, had much higher priorities, and with the exception of electric power, greater increases in capacity per worker. So, for light industry, the increase in output per unit of capacity is more important than the increase in capacity per unit of labor; the implication is that the growth of productivity was controlled largely by the extent to which capacity was used in 1952. For heavy industry, on the other hand, the increase in capacity per unit of labor was a much more important factor in the growth of output per worker, even for steel, with only 58.6 per cent of capacity used in 1952.

On the strength of the evidence just presented, it may be tentatively concluded that the more efficient use of capacity was an important factor in the growth of productivity. Once the possible productivity gains due to this factor had been made, further increases would have to come from other factors. Hence the trend in productivity during the First Five-Year Plan period would have been difficult to maintain, even without the irrational policies pursued during the Great Leap Forward.

TABLE 11

ALLOCATION OF THE PERCENTAGE INCREASE IN PHYSICAL OUTPUT PER WORKER BETWEEN OUTPUT PER UNIT OF CAPACITY AND CAPACITY PER WORKER

	Percentage Increase over 1952 in Physical Output per Worker[a]	Allocation of the Increase in Physical Output per Worker[b]	
		Output per Unit of Capacity	Capacity per Worker
1956			
Electric power	20.5	107.6	−7.6
Paper	85.4	65.9	34.1
Cotton yarn	26.0	76.2	23.8
1957			
Coal	45.8	28.6	71.4
Pig iron	138.5	1.6	98.4
Steel	92.9	39.0	61.0
Cement	74.3	−10.1	110.1

Notes:

a. Table 10.

b. Derived from the data in Table 10 by the method described in the text.

APPENDIX: TABLE A-1

INDEXES OF VALUE ADDED IN CHINESE INDUSTRY BY BRANCH OF INDUSTRY [a] 1952-1957

(1956 = 100)

	Weight	1952	1953	1954	1955	1956	1957
All industry	100.00	52.52	63.40	72.78	76.80	100.00	110.08
Electric power	1.46	41.43	52.96	64.68	72.87	100.00	118.84
Coal	10.63	59.98	62.85	75.46	88.37	100.00	117.29
Ferrous metals	5.16	34.48	46.24	54.93	69.07	100.00	133.28
Metal processing	17.30	43.80	51.14	60.88	62.64	100.00	105.53
Chemical processing	2.50	38.14	47.53	63.11	75.96	100.00	119.33
Building materials	8.51	44.75	60.64	71.95	70.44	100.00	107.30
Paper	1.05	50.98	58.56	71.07	78.79	100.00	125.19
Textiles	18.29	61.36	74.88	85.27	77.85	100.00	94.00
Food	15.50	63.98	78.52	85.28	92.97	100.00	115.83
Other	19.60	49.75	60.66	67.27	74.41	100.00	113.13

Note:

a. **The details of the construction of this index are given in the author's doctoral thesis (Field, 1966).**

APPENDIX: TABLE A-2

AVERAGE NUMBER OF WORKERS BY BRANCH OF INDUSTRY
1952 and 1956
(in thousands of persons)

	1952	1956
All industry [a]	3,599.0	4,819.3
Electric power [b]	29.7	59.5
Coal [b]	318.0	404.0
Ferrous metals [b]	134.4	209.2
Metal processing [c]	510.0	743.8
Chemical processing [c]	72.6	117.5
Building materials [c]	275.8	381.8
Paper [b]	53.8	56.9
Textiles [b]	777.5	942.0
Food [d]	732.0	860.6
Other [e]	695.2	1,044.0

Notes:

a. Derived by dividing the gross value of output by the gross value of output per worker. The former is reported in SSB, 1957b (pp. 28-29); and the latter in *Chung-kuo kung-jen,* 1958 (p. 7).

b. SSB, 1958 (pp. 27, 67, 99, 174, 211).

c. Derived by dividing the amount of electric power consumed by the amount consumed per worker (SSB, 1958, pp. 72-73).

d. For 1956, the number of workers was estimated on the assumption that the average number of workers and employees in 1956 was the same as the 1.2 million reported for the end of 1955 in Cheng Ko-huan (1957, p. 7); and on the assumption that the ratio of wage workers to the total number of workers and employees in the food industry was 71.7 per cent, the same as the ratio of workers alone to workers and employees in all industry. For 1952, the number of workers was estimated on the assumption that the number of workers in the food industry as a whole grew at the same rate as the number of workers in enterprises for which data on the consumption of electric power are available. The number of workers in these enterprises was derived in the manner described in note c, above.

e. Residual.

APPENDIX: TABLE A-3

THE DERIVATION OF THE AVERAGE NET VALUE OF FIXED ASSETS IN CHINESE INDUSTRY 1952-1957

	1951	1952	1953	1954	1955	1956	1957
Newly added fixed assets in million current yuan [a]	......	1,130	2,340	2,820	3,530	4,900	6,470
Price index [b] (1952=100)	......	100.0	106.5	102.0	96.7	90.4	90.4
New added fixed assets in million 1952 yuan [c]	......	1,130	2,197	2,765	3,650	5,420	7,157
Gross value of fixed assets at year end in million 1952 yuan [d]	14,670	15,800	17,997	20,762	24,412	29,832	36,989
Depreciation in million 1952 yuan [e]	......	734	790	900	1,038	1,221	1,492
Net value of fixed assets at year end in million 1952 yuan [f]	9,744	10,140	11,547	13,412	16,024	20,223	25,888
Average net value of fixed assets [g]							
Value in million 1952 yuan	......	9,942	10,844	12,480	14,718	18,124	23,056
Index (1952=100)	......	100.0	109.1	125.5	148.0	182.3	231.9

Notes:

a. ***Ten Great Years*** **(1960, p. 66).**

b. **Liu and Yeh, 1965 (p. 235).**

c. Derived as newly added fixed assets in current *yuan* divided by the price index.

d. Derived by adding the value of newly added fixed assets to the gross value of fixed assets at year end 1952. The gross value of fixed assets at year end 1952 is reported in *Ten Great Years* (1960, p. 93).

e. Estimated to be 5 per cent of the gross value of fixed assets at the end of the preceeding year.

f. Derived by subtracting depreciation and adding the value of newly added fixed assets to the net value of fixed assets at year end 1952. The net value of fixed assets at year end 1952 was reported by the New China News Agency on October 1, 1957. See Hollister, 1958 (p. 62).

g. Derived as the mean of the net values of fixed assets at year end.

APPENDIX: TABLE A-4

GROSS VALUE OF PRODUCTIVE FIXED ASSETS PER WORKER, BY BRANCH OF INDUSTRY
1952-1956
(in 1952 yuan per worker)

	1952	1953	1954	1955	1956
Electric power	......	51,197 [a]	58,828 [a]	58,196 [a]	54,784
Coal [a]	5,029	......	......	5,417	......
Ferrous metals [a]	9,251	9,241	11,662	13,302	12,781
Metal processing	2,996	3,139	3,538	4,357	5,037
Chemical processing [a]	8,120	9,066	9,867	11,114	......
Building materials [a]	2,431	2,291	2,531	3,641	......
Paper	5,464	......	......	......	7,712
Textiles	2,856	2,899	3,213	3,452	3,143
Food [a]	......	3,373	3,312	3,566	......

Note:
a. These data apply to state and joint state-privately operated enterprises only.

Sources:
Ma Yin ch'u, 1957; SSB, 1958 (pp. 18, 119, 161, 206, 211); Su Hsing, 1958 (p. 26); and *TCKT* Data Section, 1957c (p. 30).

APPENDIX: TABLE A-5

CONSUMPTION OF ELECTRIC POWER PER WORKER BY BRANCH OF INDUSTRY
1952 and 1956
(kilowatt-hours per worker)

	1952	1956
Coal	2,577	3,747
Ferrous metals	4,174	7,968
Metal processing	751	1,296
Chemical processing	5,665	7,649
Building materials	1,113	1,582
Paper	6,188	11,428
Textiles	1,681	2,299
Food [a]	839	1,135

Note:
a. The data apply only to those enterprises for which information on the consumption of electric power are available.

Source:
SSB, 1958 (p. 73).

APPENDIX: TABLE A-6

THE DERIVATION OF INDEXES OF CAPACITY PER WORKER
(1952 = 100)

	Physical Output	Physical Output per Worker [a]	Average Number of Workers [b]	Capacity	Capacity per Worker [c]
1956					
Electric power	241.4 [d]	120.5	200.3 [d]	197.5 [e]	98.6
Paper	196.2 [d]	185.4	105.8 [d]	130.4 [e]	123.3
Cotton yarn	145.0 [f]	126.0	115.1	121.6 [f]	105.6
Cotton cloth	150.0 [f]	104.6	134.4	......	......
1957					
Coal	195.5 [g]	145.8	134.1	175.6 [h]	130.9
Pig iron	311.7 [i]	238.5	130.7	307.7 [h]	235.4
Steel	396.6 [j]	192.9	205.6	307.3 [h]	149.5
Cement	239.9 [j]	174.3	137.6	253.2 [h]	184.0

Notes:

a. Table 10.

b. Derived by dividing the index of physical output by the index of physical output per worker, except as noted.

c. Derived by dividing the index of capacity by the index of the average number of workers.

d. Table 5.

e. Derived from data on capacity reported in SSB, 1958 (pp. 56, 206).

f. SSB, 1958 (pp. 162, 177).

g. Table A-1.

h. *T'ung-chi yen-chiu* Data Section, 1958 (p. 4).

i. Liu Ch'uang *et al.*, 1958; and SSB, 1958 (p. 30).

j. *Ten Great Years* (1960, pp. 95-96).

REFERENCES

BAZHENOV, I. I., I. A. LEONENKO, and A. K. KHARCHENKO, 1959. *Ugol'naya promyshlennost' Kitayskoy Narodnoy Respubliki* (*The Coal Industry of the Chinese People's Republic*). Moscow.

CHENG KO-HUAN, 1957. "The Significance and Function of the Food Industry in the National Economy," *Shih-p'in kung-yeh* (*Food Industry*), No. 1, pp. 7–8, 10.

Chung-kuo ch'ing kung-yeh (*China's Light Industry*), 1963. "Regulations of the Shanghai Light Industry Bureau on the Management of Fixed Assets," No. 4, pp. 18–21.

Chung-kuo kung-jen (*The Chinese Worker*), 1958. No. 4, p. 7.

DUNLOP, JOHN T., 1944. *Wage Determination Under Trade Unions*. New York.

FAN JO-I, 1957. "More on the Price Policy for Heavy-Industry Products," *Ching-chi yen-chiu (Economic Research),* No. 3, pp. 54–67.

FANG FA, 1957. "Forms for Industrial Production Planning," *Chi-hua ching-chi* (*Planned Economy*), No. 1, pp. 26–31.

FIELD, ROBERT MICHAEL, 1966. *The Growth of Industrial Production and Productivity in Communist China: 1952-1957*. (Doctoral thesis, Harvard University)

GALENSON, WALTER, 1955. *Labor Productivity in Soviet and American Industry*. New York.

HOLLISTER, WILLIAM W., 1958. *China's Gross National Product and Social Accounts, 1950-1957*. Glencoe, Ill.

HSU CH'IEN, TAI SHIH-KUANG, YU T'AO *et al.*, 1957. *Ching-chi t'ung-chi-hsüeh chiang-hua* (*Lectures on the Study of Economic Statistics*). Peking.

Hupeh University, Department of Planning and Statistics, 1960. *Kung-yeh t'ung-chi-hsüeh* (*Industrial Statistics*). Wuhan.

LENIN, V. I., 1951. *A Great Beginning*. Moscow.

LEVINE, HERBERT S., 1960. "A Small Problem in the Analysis of Growth," *The Review of Economics and Statistics,* No. 2, pp. 225–228.

LIU CH'UANG, PAI LI-CH'ANG, and WANG YU-CHUANG, 1958. "Chinese Iron and Steel Production Can Overtake Great Britain in 15 Years," *Ta-kung pao* (*Impartial Daily*), March 2, 1958.

LIU, T. C., and K. C. YEH, 1965. *The Economy of the Chinese Mainland: National Income and Economic Development, 1933-1959*. Princeton.

MA WEN-JUI, 1959. "Ten Year Struggle to Promote the High Speed Development of Productivity and Improvement of Worker's Living Standards," *Jen-min jih-pao* (*People's Daily*), Sept. 25, 1959.

MA YIN-CH'U, 1957. "A New Theory of Population," *Jen-min jih-pao* (*People's Daily*), July 5; translated in U.S. Consulate General, *Current Background,* No. 469, July 25, 1957, pp. 1–18.

MILLS, FREDERICK C., 1952. *Productivity and Economic Progress*. New York.

SCHROEDER, GERTRUDE, 1962. "Soviet Industrial Labor Productivity," Joint Economic Committee of the U.S. Congress, *Dimensions of Soviet Economic Power,* pp. 137–162. Washington, D.C.

(SSB) State Statistical Bureau, 1954. "Communiqué on National Economic Development and Fulfillment of the State Plan in 1953," Sept. 12, 1954; in *People's China,* No. 22, 1954, supplement, pp. 1–9.

SSB, 1955. "Communiqué of the State Statistical Bureau on Fulfillment of 1954 Plans," Sept. 21, 1955; in U.S. Consulate General, Hong Kong, *Current Background,* No. 360, September 29, 1955, pp. 1–10.

SSB, 1956. "Communiqué on Fulfillment of the National Economic Plan in 1955," June 14, 1956; in *People's China,* No. 14, supplement, pp. 1–8.

SSB, 1957a. "Explanations of Certain Problems Arising from the Computation of 1957 Constant Prices for Industrial Products," *T'ung-chi kung-tso* (*Statistical Work*), No. 19, pp. 11–13.

SSB, 1957b. "Kuo-min ching-chi t'ung-chi t'i-yao" ("Statistical Abstract of the National Economy"), appended to the pamphlet *Kuan-yü 1956 nien-tu kuo-min ching-chi chi-hua chih-hsing chieh-kuo ti kung-pao* (*Communiqué on Results of Implementation of the 1956 Economic Plan*), pp. 19–68. Released August 1, 1957, Peking.

SSB, 1958. *Wo-kuo kang-t'ieh tien-li mei-t'an chi-hsieh fang-chih tsao-chih kung-yeh ti chin-hsi* (*Chinese Iron and Steel, Electric Power, Coal, Machinery, Textile, and Paper Industries—Past and Present*). Peking.

Statistical Work Handbook Editorial Committee, 1958. *Lao-tung t'ung-chi kung-tso shou-ts'e* (*Labor Statistical Work Handbook*). Peking.

SU HSING, 1958. "A Critique of an Incorrect View of the Distribution According to Labor," *Hsüeh-hsi* (*Study*), No. 7, pp. 25–26.

Ten Great Years, 1960. State Statistical Bureau. Peking.

(TCKT) T'ung-chi kung-tso (*Statistical Work*), 1956a. No. 12, back cover.

TCKT, 1956b. "Where do the Differences of Opinion Lie? A Discussion of Methodological Problems in Computing the Gross Value of Industrial Production," No. 24, pp. 5–10.

TCKT (*T'ung-chi kung-tso*) Data Section, 1956a. "An Abstract of Socialist Industrialization throughout China," *TCKT,* No. 22, pp. 25–33.

TCKT Data Section, 1956b. "The Development of State Capitalism in China's Industry," *TCKT,* No. 20, pp. 1–4.

TCKT Data Section, 1957a. "An Abstract of Industrial Capital throughout China," *TCKT,* No. 1, pp. 31–33.

TCKT Data Section, 1957b. "The Productive Activities of Building Construction Enterprises During the Past Four Year," *TCKT,* No. 18, pp. 31–32.

TCKT Data Section, 1957c. "The Technical Level of China's Industrial Production," *TCKT,* No. 8, pp. 30–33.

T'ung-chi yen-chiu Data Section, 1958. "The Flying Development of Industrial Construction in China," *T'ung-chi yen-chiu* (*Statistical Research*), No. 9, pp. 4–5.

WU YUAN-LI, 1963. *Economic Development and the Use of Energy Resources in Communist China.* New York.

YUAN FANG, 1956. "The Ratio of Increase Between Labor Productivity and Wages," *Hsin chien-she* (*New Construction*), No. 12, pp. 18–23.

Foreign Trade 12

FENG-HWA MAH

THIS CHAPTER INVESTIGATES the changing trends in Communist China's [1] international trade and balance of international payments for the period 1950-1964. The study of China's foreign trade is important not only because this crucial sector reflects the failures and achievements of the domestic economy, but also because it is indispensable in understanding the country's balance of payments situation. At the same time, even a crude estimate of China's balance of payments during the last fifteen years can be helpful in appraising the country's international economic position and its effect on economic development. The chapter is divided into four parts: (1) a brief account of Communist China's foreign trade system and policy, (2) an analysis of foreign trade trends, (3) a conjectural reconstruction of the balance of payments, and (4) some concluding remarks.

I. COMMUNIST CHINA'S FOREIGN TRADE POLICY AND ORGANIZATION

OBJECTIVES OF COMMUNIST CHINA'S FOREIGN TRADE POLICY

Communist China's foreign trade policy must be viewed within the context of its general politico-economic objectives: internally, to preserve and strengthen the "democratic dictatorship" of the Communist Party by total control; internationally, to safeguard the country's independence and to gain "big power" status by building up its political, economic, and military strength. Within this context, the objectives of China's foreign trade policy can be summarized as follows:

I am indebted to Professors Shun-Hsin Chou, Robert F. Dernberger, Alexander Eckstein, J. Richard Huber, Judith G. Thornton, and Dean A. Worcester for helpful criticisms on an earlier draft. My gratitude goes particularly to Professor Eckstein whose detailed comments and suggestions led to a substantial revision of this paper. I am solely responsible for any remaining errors and for opinions expressed in this paper.

1. For the sake of simplicity, the terms "Communist China" and "China" are used interchangeably in this paper. The prefix "Sino-" refers to "Communist China" for the same reason.

(1) To use the Communists' own words, a major objective of China's foreign trade policy is "strengthening the economic independence and sovereignty of the state, protecting domestic industry and agriculture from the economic aggression of imperialist powers." The argument always refers to China's unhappy experience in its earlier contacts with the West. One Communist writer, for example, says:

> Beginning in the middle of the nineteenth century, the imperialist powers continuously invaded China, depriving her by force of arms of tariff autonomy and customs control. . . . For about a century prior to China's liberation . . . the American and British imperialist elements controlled China's Customs Service and utilized this agency to facilitate, by means of low duty rates and duty exemptions, the dumping on the Chinese market of huge quantities of their surplus stocks and the plundering of China's raw materials at cheap prices. Their cruel economic buccaneering strangled our national commerce and industry, thus rendering China a semicolonial state for a long period of time."

Statements like this have been repeated again and again in Communist documents in spite of the fact that the Chinese national government gained control of tariffs and customs administration from most countries in 1928 and from Japan in 1930, long before the Communist takeover (Liu and Yeh, 1965, p. 8).

(2) Another, and perhaps the most important, objective of Communist China's foreign trade policy is to serve the development of China's industry, particularly heavy industry (Yang Chien-pei, 1956, p. 92). The argument is "without industry, there can be no solid national defense, no people's welfare, and no national prosperity and power." [2] And, in order to guarantee the implementation of the country's industrialization program, it is necessary to export in order to obtain the imported materials and equipment needed for industrial development. In other words, "Export is for import, and import is for the country's socialist industrialization" (Yeh Chi-chuang, 1955).

(3) A third objective is to achieve economic self-reliance. In China's First Five-Year Plan, the Communist planners made the point that the development of the Chinese economy is the responsibility of the Chinese people themselves, that outside help is needed to speed up the industrialization program, and that the purpose of industrialization is to achieve economic and political independence (Li Fu-chun, 1955). The director of the Import Bureau of Peking's Ministry of Foreign Trade has stated that the purpose of importing major industrial equipment from the Soviet Union is to lay the foundation of China's industrial independence, so that in the future China can produce all the producer goods it needs and will

2. This is Mao Tse-tung's statement, quoted in *FFYP* (Chinese ed.), 1955 (p. 15).

not have to rely on imports from outside (Chang Hua-tung, 1955). This objective of self-reliance has been greatly stressed since Sino-Soviet relations deteriorated. The meaning of economic self-reliance has recently been defined by Peking in this way:

> It means that a country should manufacture by itself all the products it needs whenever and wherever possible. . . . It also means that a country should carry on its general economic construction on the basis of its own human, material, and financial resources.[3]

These principles are clearly incompatible with the concept of international division of labor, or with the theory of comparative advantage in foreign trade.

(4) In connection with foreign trade policy, Chinese sources have often stressed the point that for Communist China, foreign trade is also "a weapon for international political struggle" (Kuo Chung-yen, 1956, p. 34). A case in point was Communist China's effort to use foreign trade as a means for establishing de facto diplomatic relations with Japan. A high-ranking Chinese Communist foreign trade official, on a visit to Japan, made this point clear to a group of Japanese businessmen. He declared that in conducting Sino-Japanese trade, Peking would insist on the principle that trade and politics cannot be separated. He elaborated that only by following Peking's "three political principles" could trade between mainland China and Japan be developed.[4] These principles are:

> (1) Japan should not take a hostile attitude toward [Communist] China. (2) Japan should not participate in the American conspiracy of fabricating two Chinas, and (3) there should be no interference in the normalization of relations between [Communist] China and Japan.[5]

Perhaps it is not unreasonable to assume that in Communist China's trade with the developing countries of Asia, Africa, and South America, political considerations may be as important as economic calculations.

However, developments in recent years plainly indicate that political motives have not been the dominant factor in Peking's trade with non-Communist countries. Undoubtedly, in instances where potential political gains may be sizable and foreign trade costs relatively modest, economic considerations may indeed be subordinate to political ones. Such instances are likely to be found in China's trade with the newly independent and

3. Speech by Nan Han-chen, Chairman of the China Committee for the Promotion of International Trade, at the Asian Economic Seminar held in Pyongyang in June, 1964. (Pyongyang Radio broadcast, June 20, 1964.)

4. Report on Nan Han-chen's visit to Japan, *Ta-Kung Pao,* May 10, 1964 (p. 1).

5. These "three principles" were first proposed by Chou En-lai in 1960. See *Kung-shang kwan-cha,* Sept. 7, 1960 (p. 5).

economically backward countries, but it should be kept in mind that such trade constitutes only a very small percentage of Peking's total foreign trade.

In most of China's trade with the free world, imports are primarily directed toward breaking economic bottlenecks, and exports are primarily designed to raise the means of payments for imports. For example, Communist China has been importing large quantities of food grains from Canada and Australia in order to alleviate domestic food shortages, and exporting large quantities of consumer goods to Hong Kong and Malaya-Singapore for the purpose of augmenting foreign exchange earnings. Of these countries, only Hong Kong has diplomatic relations with Peking. Yet no "political principles" have been applied to any of them. Even in the case of Japan, trade has expanded significantly despite uneasy political relations between Peking and Tokyo. In general, it would seem that Communist China simply has not been able to afford to disregard economic realities for the sake of making political gains. Furthermore, since Communist China's foreign trade volume has not been large, even if Peking had indeed followed such a policy, its effectiveness would still be open to serious doubts.

ORGANIZATION OF COMMUNIST CHINA'S FOREIGN TRADE

Foreign trade is a state monopoly in Communist China. The reasons for state control have been given by Peking's Minister of Foreign Trade as follows: (1) to safeguard the absolute leadership of the Communist Party in the foreign trade field, (2) to consolidate the independence of China's foreign trade, and (3) to guarantee the planned development of foreign trade under the policy and guidance of the Party (Yeh Chi-chuang, 1959). Essentially, state monopoly of foreign trade follows from the character of Communist China's whole economic and political system. Table 1 shows the extent of state monopoly, as indicated by the portion of total foreign trade conducted by the state.

TABLE 1

SHARE OF STATE-CONDUCTED FOREIGN TRADE
(percentage of total trade)

1950	1953	1954	1955	1956
61.1	92.0	97.0	99.2	100.0

Sources:
1950, 1954: *JMJP,* February 21, 1955.
1953: State Statistical Bureau, 1954.
1955: Hughes and Luard, 1961.
1956: In this year all private firms were converted into state or joint public-private enterprises.

Communist China's foreign trade system is headed by the Ministry of Foreign Trade. The major functions of this ministry are (1) to draw up national plans for imports and exports and for receipt and payment of foreign exchange, and to supervise the implementation of these plans; (2) to develop trade relations, economic cooperation, and technical cooperation with foreign countries, and to sign agreements and contracts on these matters on behalf of the government; and (3) to lead the state-operated foreign trade corporations and consolidate the leading role played by these corporations in China's foreign trade (*Peking Review,* Sept. 9, 1958). Therefore, the state monopoly of foreign trade extends beyond the mere import and export of commodities, since plans for the receipt and payment of foreign exchange would include many "invisible" items in the balance of payments, while international economic and technical cooperation is a much broader area than trade relations.

Several state foreign trade corporations serve as operating agencies of the Ministry of Foreign Trade.[6] These corporations are described as "independent business enterprises"; each handles certain specified commodities. Their transactions are carried out according to the import and export plans of the state. They engage in domestic purchases for export and domestic distribution of imports.

Foreign trade bureaus, custom houses, and bureaus for inspection of commodities function as administrative units under the ministry. Abroad, Communist China maintains commercial counselor's offices and commercial attachés in its embassies and legations, as well as trade representatives in some countries that do not have diplomatic relations with Peking (*Peking Review,* Sept. 9, 1958, p. 13).

In addition, there is the China Committee for the Promotion of International Trade, which was established in May, 1952, as a result of the Moscow International Economic Conference (Miyashita, 1961). That conference was held in April, 1952, in order to find means to counteract Western restrictions on strategic exports to the Soviet bloc.[7] The committee is a government agency disguised as an "independent legal person," allegedly performing functions similar to a chamber of international commerce. Its regular work includes such matters as establishing contacts with foreign firms, holding exhibitions of Communist Chinese products in foreign countries, and inviting and dispatching "nongovernmental" trade delegations to and from Communist China. Through these contacts, it explores the possibilities of developing trade with countries that do not have

6. The number of these import and export corporations varied slightly over the years. Before 1961, there were 16-18 such corporations. Beginning from January 1, 1961, these were combined into 12. See *Foreign Trade* (Chinese ed.), March, 1961 (p. 56).

7. At the conference, Western businessmen were tempted by offers of billions of dollars of trade with the Soviet bloc if only the strategic trade embargo were disregarded. See Schwartz, 1954 (p. 604).

diplomatic relations with Communist China, and can conclude and sign "nongovernmental" trade and payment agreements with them.[8]

SOME BASIC PRINCIPLES IN COMMUNIST CHINA'S FOREIGN TRADE PLANNING

Communist Chinese sources have listed three basic principles followed in conducting China's centrally planned foreign trade. These are:

(1) *Balance between domestic use and export.* In allocating the total supply of each exportable commodity, a "proper ratio" is supposed to be established between the amount retained for the home market and that set aside for exports. According to official reports, Communist China's total annual exports accounted for an average of approximately 4 per cent of its total gross agricultural and industrial production value. This overall ratio is to "satisfy the basic demand of the domestic market as well as the export trade" (Wen Liang, 1959). As will be pointed out later, the allocations between domestic and export needs are actually determined as part and parcel of the process of planning based on material balances. With the exception of a few crucial items such as food grains and edible oil, for each of which an export quota was supposedly set up in years of shortage, the "proper ratios" for individual commodities are generally flexible and can be determined only through a process of mutual adjustment between import requirements and domestic demand.

(2) *Balance between imports and exports.* In trade with other countries, China, in principle, always seeks to achieve a bilateral balance, at least approximately annually. This balance is usually attained through bilateral barter-trade agreements, in which the values of agreed imports and exports are specified. Annual bilateral balancing is designed both to facilitate economic planning and to alleviate the shortage of foreign exchange. In reality, however, China has frequently reached the end of each trade agreement or contract period with sizable trade deficits or surpluses with individual countries. In Sino-Soviet trade until 1964, large import surpluses were financed by long-term Soviet loans, while substantial export surpluses were used to amortize the Soviet debts. In addition, there have been other arrangements for the settlement of smaller trade balances.

In cases where no direct connections have been established between the central banks of Communist China and its trading partners, the balances are believed to be settled through the accounts kept by the Bank of China with foreign banks, using foreign currencies such as British pounds, Swiss francs, or Hong Kong dollars.[9] In cases where trade and payment

8. Cf. "A Brief Introduction to the China Committee for the Promotion of International Trade," *Foreign Trade* (Chinese ed.), March, 1959 (p. 1).

9. For a discussion of balance between imports and exports, see Wen Liang, 1959. For the use of Western currencies in international settlement, see "The International Clearing Work of the Bank of China," *Foreign Trade* (Chinese ed.), March, 1962 (pp. 4-5).

agreements have been signed, and trade clearing accounts established between Communist China and its trading partners, the balance of trade is usually settled through the Bank of China and the trading partners' central bank. In such cases the balance can be paid, according to agreements, in foreign exchange (including Soviet rubles, U.S. dollars, and British pounds), gold, or specified commodities (Remer, 1961, p. 40). These payments or deliveries by the debtor country must be made during the first quarter of the following year (Bystrov, 1960, p. 57). In many of the trade agreements between Peking and other Communist countries, provisions are also made to permit the carrying over of trade balances to the following year. These arrangements are usually referred to as "technical credits" or "swing credits," and definite limits for them are usually set in the trade agreements. For example, in the 1950 Sino-Soviet trade agreement, the "swing" limit was put at six million old rubles; in the first trade agreement between China and Czechoslovakia (1950) the limit was set at two million old rubles (Remer, 1961, p. 38). According to Communist bloc practice, an interest charge of 2 per cent per annum is charged on the swing credits if they exceed the agreed ceilings (Bystrov, 1960, p. 58). It has been reported that until 1956 China had made extensive use of this provision in trade with the Soviet Union (*Hong Kong Tiger Standard,* Feb. 9, 1964). Thus it seems that the goal of balance between imports and exports with individual countries has seldom been achieved.

(3) *A "policy of fair price"* is also claimed to be one of the basic principles in conducting foreign trade. In reference to non-Communist countries, this "fair price policy" is held up as a concrete expression of Communist China's "principle of equality and mutual benefit" in foreign trade. On the other hand, in Communist China's trade with Asian and African countries, the same policy is always emphatically pointed out as "opposed to the exchange of unequal values" in trade between the capitalist and the developing countries, even though the so-called "fair prices" are actually fixed through negotiations with "capitalist market" prices as the base (Wen Liang, 1959). Occasionally prices are manipulated for political purposes or to reap economic gains. By virtue of its foreign trade monopoly and its control of domestic prices, Communist China is able, in some particular instances, to pay higher prices for imports and to accept lower prices for its exports.[10] The resulting losses can then be directly or indirectly absorbed by the state. However, these practices are severely constrained by Peking's economic capabilities, and probably affect only a very small fraction of Communist China's total foreign

10. For example, statistical evidence shows that in 1957 Communist China offered extremely attractive prices on tin (18 per cent lower than the world market price) at Hong Kong in order to enter the market, but was able to obtain the world price soon thereafter. See Mah, 1963 (pp. 45, 105). Chinese rice was reportedly sold in Malaya in 1956 at prices well below those of both local and imported Thai rice. Communist China was also accused by Hong Kong of having

trade. Nevertheless, in individual cases and for a limited time period, Peking's resources would be sufficient to put individual foreign firms or particular foreign markets into a highly disadvantageous position.

A somewhat different pricing policy is followed in the case of trade between Communist countries. Here again the prices are determined through negotiation, using world market prices as a frame of reference. Once these prices are established, they are maintained throughout the period of the agreement or contract, unless a trade partner requests price adjustments. In that case the contract prices can be adjusted through negotiation (Mah, 1963, pp. 13-14). It is generally true, therefore, that trade between China and other Communist countries is conducted in "practically stable prices" (Wen Liang, 1959, p. 13). This undoubtedly facilitates the work of economic planning in the countries involved. If these fixed prices are kept unchanged for a number of years, as they were in Sino-Soviet trade in the early 1950's, foreign trade prices among Communist nations may diverge substantially at times from world market prices, even though originally based on them (Yeh Chi-chuang, 1957, p. 93).

THE IMPORT AND EXPORT PLANS

Communist China's economic planning mechanism has undergone several important changes during the period of the First and Second Five-Year Plans (Miyashita, 1961, pp. 23-24). As a result, the foreign trade planners have also been groping their way during most of this period. Information on the planning of foreign trade has been very scarce, but presumably Soviet planning methods have been used as a rough guide.[11] Theoretically, the procedure is this:

A general outline of the annual economic plan is drafted on the basis of the overall economic goals and the planned growth of key industries. This plan is then put into more concrete terms in the form of output targets for key industries. It appears that at this stage of planning, foreign trade is not a determining factor in the making of the economic plan. On the basis of the output targets, physical balances of equipment, raw materials, fuel, capital construction, etc., are then formulated. These physical balances are designated to show the desired relations (based on planners'

---

frequently held up shipments of live hogs and other farm products to the colony in order to take advantage of the local inelastic demand for these commodities and so obtain higher prices. *Far Eastern Economic Review,* July 26, 1956 (p. 124); Aug. 23, 1956 (p. 257); and Nov. 15, 1956 (p. 642). For a fuller exposition of this point, see Wu, 1958.

11. "The pattern of material balances (in kind) employed in the practice of national economic planning in the Chinese People's Republic is founded on the experience of the Socialist planning in the Soviet Union." Imports and exports are included in these physical balances. See Maklakov, 1958, and Chen Chieh, 1956 (pp. 11-14). For brief discussions of the Soviet planning process, see Spulber, 1962 (pp. 22-25), and Nove and Donnelly, 1960 (pp. 21-23).

preference) between all available sources (supply) and planned uses (demand) of specific items. At this point, inconsistencies and bottlenecks would appear, as planned demand turns out to be greater than estimated domestic supplies for key items such as machinery, equipment, and raw materials. In this situation, the planners would either have to adjust and revise the output plans, or decide to import the needed items. A list of import requirements would thus be derived.

When the list of import requirements has been drawn up, means of financing them must be estimated. According to Peking's foreign trade minister, the "import requirements for economic construction" are to be adjusted by taking into account such factors as (1) availability of foreign supply, (2) export capacity and identified sources of supply for export goods, and (3) the financial (foreign exchange and credit) situation. The final import targets are the result of a "comprehensive balance" of the relative importance and urgency of the import requirements and these three factors (Yeh Chi-chuang, 1956). To the extent that the availability of free foreign exchange is limited and that credits have to be repaid eventually by export of commodities, export capacity is clearly the most important constraint in the determination of import targets. When the exportable goods are also in great demand for domestic use, the planning authorities must decide whether to trim the import requirements or to curb domestic demand. It is through an iterative process of mutual adjustment that the import and export plans are drawn up and become an integrated part of the national economic plan. It is clear that the role of imports in the planning process is primarily to solve bottlenecks; and, as pointed out earlier, the role of exports is almost exclusively to provide payment for current and past imports. It seems that little consideration is given to relative prices or comparative advantage in the planning of foreign trade.[12]

Because of the ambitious nature of Communist China's industrialization plans, coordination of the export plan with domestic demand has been an ever-present problem for Peking's planners. The First Five-Year Plan stipulates: "Within the scope of plans already drawn up, we must, in case of a conflict between export and domestic demand, guarantee in the first place fulfillment of the export contracts and of the export plan" (*FFYP,* p. 110). This means placing restrictions on domestic consumption for the sake of export. In this connection, the Central Committee of the Chinese Communist Party and the State Council promulgated the following principle in 1954: For such essential commodities as food grain and edible oil, an export quota will be set for each. For most other commodities, the priority is given to export; only after the export targets are met can do-

12. This can be illustrated by Yeh Chi-chuang's (1956) proposal at the Eighth Congress of the Chinese Communist Party that "Commodities which can be produced domestically, or the substitutes of which are available at home, should not be imported."

mestic demand for these goods be taken care of (*Ta-kung Pao,* Tientsin, July 15, 1955).

Fragmentary information indicates that during the period prior to 1957, China's import and export plans were not precise, and that, while import requirements were emphasized, often the export supplies were not assured. Moreover, these plans were changed frequently. To quote the foreign trade minister,

> Sometimes when a temporary surplus was found in certain products in the country, the foreign trade departments were immediately requested to export them. For example, in 1954, the reduced output in agriculture affected certain industrial products and the financial revenue of the state, and capital construction projects were curtailed. So in 1955 there was found some surplus of such items as steel products, cement and pig iron. This was only a temporary phenomenon. But the production departments were afraid lest there be accumulated stocks, and repeatedly requested the foreign trade departments to export the said items in quantity in order to support domestic production. However, by early this year (1956), when the high tide of socialism arrived, the domestic needs for those items greatly increased, and there was a request for the downward revision of the export plans which had already been decided upon. (Yeh Chi-chuang, 1956).

In 1956, because of overinvestment and reduced agricultural production, there was a serious shortage of many important materials in China. As a result, the 1956 annual export plan was only 95 per cent fulfilled. In 1957, the situation was not improved, and less than 90 per cent of the procurement plan for export goods was carried out. As a result, the import plans for 1956 and 1957 also remained unfulfilled. Therefore, in 1957, the State Council decided to make the following modifications in assigning priorities: (1) For most imports, the new principle is to be "export determines import." Evidently this meant that export plans were to be more realistically adjusted to domestic demand, and import requirements more realistically adjusted to export capacity. (2) In cases where key import targets must be fixed independently, and therefore exports have to be adjusted to import requirements, "measures must be taken to guarantee the balance between the foreign exchange payments and receipts of these imports and exports" (Li Pei-fong, 1958). The higher priority given to domestic demand clearly reflects the acute shortage of food grain and many other exportable goods at that time. This priority was restated in 1964 by a high official of Peking's Ministry of Foreign Trade: "The amount of commodities we import will depend on our exports, and the amount of exchange we spend will depend on our income." [13] Although

13. Wilson, 1964. Chen Ming was Director of the Third Bureau of the Ministry of Foreign Trade at the time of the interview.

statements of this kind may reflect a shift in planners' preferences dictated by the circumstances at the time, they do not seem to indicate any basic change in the procedures governing foreign trade planning.

II. TREND IN FOREIGN TRADE [14]

VOLUME

The volume of Communist China's foreign trade can be estimated with reasonable assurance, but not pinpointed with precision. There are next to no foreign trade data from Chinese sources, and what little Peking has published tends to produce a distorted picture, for reasons to be explained briefly below. The alternative to relying on the Chinese data is to derive China's foreign trade volume from its trading partners' statistics. These statistics are relatively abundant, but less than complete. To fill the many small gaps, estimates must be made for some countries' trade with China in certain years. Table 2 presents both the official Chinese series and our derived series based on non-Chinese sources. The nature of each one will be discussed briefly in the following paragraphs. The derived series will be used to represent Communist China's foreign trade value.

The difficulties with the official Chinese series stem in large part from China's use of disequilibrium foreign exchange rates. Peking's Minister of Foreign Trade stated in 1957 that China had insulated its domestic prices from foreign markets. Consequently, in trading with Western countries China as a rule incurred losses in exports and gains in imports, when the foreign trade prices were converted from Western currency units into *yuan* at the official exchange rates (Yeh Chi-chuang, 1957). This means, of course, that the *yuan* is overvalued vis-à-vis Western currencies, making it impossible to compare China's foreign trade data expressed in *yuan* with other *yuan* aggregates reflecting Chinese domestic prices.

This relative overvaluation of the *yuan* also results in the understatement of the volume of China's trade with Western countries, expressed in *yuan*. A hypothetical example will serve to illustrate these relationships (see Table 3). We assume: (1) China's foreign trade statistics are derived from trading partners' data, all converted into U.S. dollars at the prevailing exchange rates. The dollar trade values are then translated into *yuan* at the official *yuan*-dollar rate, and at a certain *yuan*-dollar purchasing power parity rate (PPP rate); (2) the official exchange rate, which overvalues the *yuan*, is 2.36 *yuan* per dollar; and (3) the hypothetical

14. For lack of space, the commodity composition of China's foreign trade is not discussed here. For an analysis of the commodity structure see the author's forthcoming full-length study.

TABLE 2

COMMUNIST CHINA: TOTAL TRADE VALUES, 1950-1964
(in millions)

Year	Chinese Series Value (yuan)	Chinese Series Index	Chinese Series Annual Increase (per cent)	Derived Series Value (US $)	Derived Series Index	Derived Series Annual Increase (per cent)
1950	4,150	100.0	—[a]	1,553	100.0	—
1951	4,950	143.2	43.2	1,968	126.7	26.7
1952	6,460	155.5	8.6	1,929	124.2	-2.0
1953	8,090	194.8	25.2	2,286	147.2	18.5
1954	8,470	203.9	4.7	2,498	160.8	9.3
1955	10,980	264.3	29.6	2,732	175.9	9.4
1956	10,870	261.5	-1.1	3,138	202.1	14.6
1957	10,450	251.5	-3.8	3,057	196.8	-2.6
1958	12,870	309.8	23.2	3,834	246.9	25.4
1959	......[b]	......	......	4,290	276.2	11.9
1960	......	......	......	3,938	253.6	-8.2
1961	......	......	......	2,894	186.3	-26.5
1962	......	......	......	2,601	167.5	-10.1
1963	......	......	......	2,696	173.6	3.7
1964				[3,322][c]	[213.9]	[23.2]

Sources:
Chinese series: *Ten Great Years*, p. 175. No explanation of these figures is given in the original source.
Derived series: See note to Table 4.

Notes:
Symbols used in this and following tables:
a. —: zero or less than half of the final digit shown, or not applicable.
b. ......: not available.
c. [ ]: estimate.

PPP rate is 4 *yuan* to the dollar.[15] The trade figures in Table 3 are also hypothetical.

The distortion effect of an overvalued *yuan* on China's trade volume is clearly shown in the hypothetical example in Table 3. (For a more detailed discussion of the exchange rate problem, see Section III.) The official rate has been pegged at 2.355 *yuan* per dollar since 1955, which is, of course, arbitrary. Neither the changes of domestic prices nor the

15. It should be pointed out that while the overvaluation of the *yuan* at the official *yuan*-dollar rate understates the *yuan* value of China's trade with the West, its undervaluation in the official ruble-*yuan* rate before July, 1959, tended to overstate the *yuan* value of Sino-Soviet trade. For a statistical demonstration of this undervaluation, see Kang Chao and Feng-hwa Mah, 1964 (pp. 192-204).

TABLE 3

HYPOTHETICAL RELATIONSHIP BETWEEN CHINA'S FOREIGN TRADE AND NATIONAL INCOME [a]

	In million U.S. dollars	In million yuan: At official rate	In million yuan: At PPP rate	Yuan value as per cent of national income: At official rate	Yuan value as per cent of national income: At PPP rate
Imports	1,400	3,304	5,600	3.48	5.89
Exports	1,600	3,776	6,400	3.97	6.74
Total trade	3,000	7,080	12,000	7.45	12.63

Note:
a. National income assumed to be 95,000 million yuan.

changes in foreign trade prices of China's export or import goods can affect this official exchange rate. However, since the official exchange rate, however arbitrary, presumably has been used by the Chinese Communists to convert the Western currency values of their foreign transactions into *yuan,*[16] there will be no distortion effect if we use it to convert back the *yuan* values of China's Western transactions into dollar terms.[17]

Moreover, the official *yuan*-dollar rate is inconsistent with both the foreign trade ruble-*yuan* rate and the ruble-dollar rate. They are broken cross rates. The *yuan*-dollar rate overvalued the *yuan,* in effect understating the *yuan* value of Sino-Western trade. The ruble-*yuan* rate undervalued the *yuan* (at least up to July, 1959), with the effect of overstating the *yuan* value of Sino-Soviet trade. Thus the official *yuan* value of China's foreign trade, believed to be the sum of China's trade with the West, converted into *yuan* units at the official *yuan*-dollar rate, and China's trade with the Soviet bloc converted into *yuan* values at the official foreign trade ruble-*yuan* rate, would exaggerate the relative share of Sino-Bloc trade in China's total trade volume. Furthermore, Chinese sources give only total trade figures with no further breakdowns. For all these reasons, the Chinese series in Table 2 will not be used in our analyses.

Our derivation of China's trade volume by major trading areas is pre-

16. Since 1950, the Communist Chinese Maritime Customs has been using U.S. dollars, along with the *yuan,* as one of its two official computing and reporting units. See Chen Chih-shih and Liu Po-Wu, 1958 (p. 174).

17. Similarly, to use the official ruble-dollar rate to convert ruble values of Soviet international transactions into dollar values will not produce distortions. In our later analysis, the official exchange rates will be used to derive dollar values from *yuan* and ruble data.

TABLE 4

COMMUNIST CHINA'S TOTAL TRADE: DERIVED SERIES
1950-1964
(in millions of U.S. dollars)

Year	(1) Trade with Free World	(2) Trade with USSR	(3) Trade with East Europe[a]	(4) Trade with Other Communist Countries[b]	(5) Total Trade[c]
1950	933	580	30	10	1,553
1951	919	809	220	20	1,968
1952	601	968	330	30	1,929
1953	678	1,172	381	55	2,286
1954	636	1,337	435	90	2,498
1955	756	1,392	469	115	2,732
1956	1,012	1,497	504	125	3,138
1957	1,089	1,282	544	142	3,057
1958	1,451	1,515	697	171	3,834
1959	1,286	2,055	676	273	4,290
1960	1,334	1,665	654	285	3,938
1961	1,221	919	328	426	2,894
1962	1,165	750	225	461	2,601
1963	1,400	600	229	467	2,696
1964	2,158	449	226	[489]	3,322

Sources: See Appendix A.

Notes:

a. The countries included are Albania, Bulgaria, Czechoslovakia, East Germany, Hungary, Poland and Rumania.

b. The countries included are North Korea, Outer Mongolia and North Vietnam for all years. Cuba is included for the years 1959-1964.

c. Column (5) = Col. (1) + Col. (2) + Col (3) + Col. (4).

sented in Table 4. The sources and the method of derivation for our series are given in Appendix A. In deriving this series, the only adjustment made was the deduction of estimated freight and insurance charges from the reported values of China's export to free-world countries. This was done because the U.S. Department of Commerce (USDC) data are taken from China's trading partners' statistics. Thus China's exports in the USDC tables are actually its partner countries' import data, valued c.i.f. country of import (with minor exceptions), while China's imports are trading partners' export data, valued f.o.b. If no adjustment were made, the USDC data would exaggerate the values of China's exports by the amount of the freight and insurance costs. These can be roughly estimated as about 10 per cent of the value of China's exports in the USDC tables (based on a comparison of the f.o.b. values of China's imports and exports for 1950-55, with the USDC data for the same years [18]).

The derived series indicates that China's foreign trade expanded rapidly from 1950 through 1959, except that in 1952 and 1957 the total trade turnover declined slightly. In 1952, there was the "five-anti" movement, which severely interrupted domestic industrial and commercial activities, while 1957 was immediately preceded by a year of overinvestment, deficit spending, and serious raw materials shortages on the Chinese mainland. Thus the decline of foreign trade in those two years is largely explained by domestic economic difficulties. It should be recalled that it was in 1957 that Peking modified its export policy concerning many essential consumer goods, to alleviate the pressure of domestic demand for these commodities.[19]

The rapid increase of foreign trade in 1958 and 1959 reflected the rise in agricultural production during the first year of the Great Leap Forward, the sharply increased import demand for producer goods to support the Great Leap, and the need to export more to pay for the imports. At the same time, the stepped-up repayment of Soviet debts also required a greater export. For all of these reasons combined, China's foreign trade reached its peak in 1959, with a total value of over four billion dollars. However, this was followed by three successive years of declining trade, reflecting the Chinese economic crisis of 1960-1962 and the deterioration of Sino-Soviet political and economic relations during these years.

China's economic recovery, beginning in late 1962, was followed by a modest expansion of trade in 1963, and this trend was further strengthened in 1964 as the domestic economy continued to improve. The value of foreign trade in 1963 was close to the 1955 level, while the 1964 trade turnover represented a 23 per cent increase over 1963, and greatly exceeded the 1956 level. The upward recovery trend was unmistakably clear.

DIRECTION

The direction of Communist China's foreign trade has undergone dramatic changes during the past fifteen years. Table 5 provides a brief summary of the direction of China's trade and its change over time. It can be seen that during most of the 1950's, about one-half of the country's total trade was with the Soviet Union, approximately 20 per cent with the other Communist countries, and about 30 per cent with nations of the free world.

18. The f.o.b. values of China's exports and imports for 1950-55 were prepared by Hans Staehle, Director of Research for GATT. For Staehle's figures, see Hoffman, 1957 (p. 261, Table 1). See also C. M. Li, 1959 (p. 190).

19. For example, in 1957, the export of edible oils was 120,000 tons less than the amount exported in 1956. Pork export was 110,000 tons less than in 1956. Food grain export was also reduced in 1957. See *Ta-kuug Pao,* Peking, (May 14, 1957).

TABLE 5

COMMUNIST CHINA: DIRECTION OF FOREIGN TRADE, 1950-1964
(per cent of total trade)

Year	Soviet Union		Other Communist Countries				All Communist Countries		Free World	
	Official	Derived	Official	Derived: Total	Derived: East Europe	Derived: Other	Official	Derived	Official	Derived
1950	30.9	37.3	2.6	2.6	1.9	0.7	33.5	39.9	74.0	60.1
1951	48.7	41.1	14.6	12.2	11.2	1.0	63.3	53.3	39.0	46.7
1952	51.5	50.2	20.5	18.7	17.1	1.6	72.0	68.9	28.0	31.2
1953	56.0	51.3	19.0	19.1	16.7	2.4	75.0	70.4	25.0	29.7
1954	58.0	53.5	22.0	21.0	17.4	3.6	80.0	74.5	20.0	25.5
1955	57.0	51.0	25.0	21.4	17.2	4.2	82.0	72.4	18.0	27.7
1956	53.7	47.7	21.3	20.0	16.0	4.0	75.0	67.7	25.0	32.2
1957	(41.0)	41.9	(24.1)	22.4	17.8	4.6	64.1	64.3	35.9	35.6
1958	(40.0)	39.5	(24.2)	22.6	18.2	4.4	64.2	62.1	35.8	37.8
1959		47.9		22.1	15.7	6.4		70.0		30.0
1960		42.3		23.8	16.6	7.2		66.1		33.9
1961		31.7		26.1	11.4	14.7		57.8		42.2
1962		28.8		26.4	8.7	17.7		55.2		44.8
1963		22.3		25.8	8.5	17.3		48.1		51.9
1964		13.5		21.5	6.8	(14.7)		35.0		65.0

Notes:

(1) The derived percentages may not add to 100 per cent because of rounding errors.

(2) The official percentages for 1950 and 1951 are given in an article by Ma Nai-schu in *Vneshniaia Torgovlia,* May, 1956, quoted in *FEER,* Feb. 14, 1957 (p. 209). The 1950 percentage for all Communist countries, 33.5%, is also confirmed in *JMJP,* Oct. 2, 1956. Official percentages for other years are taken from Eckstein, 1964 p. 139). They are based on Communist Chinese data assembled from Communist Chinese, Russian, West German, and United States publications.

(3) The derived percentages are the author's computations from Table 4.

(4) The discrepancy between the official and our derived percentages is partly due to the distortion effect of the official exchange rates used by the Chinese Communists.

The predominance of the Soviet Union is all the more noteworthy if one recalls that in 1930 only 3 per cent of China's foreign trade was with Russia (Dernberger, 1959, p. 135, Table 2). Because of the complete divorce of domestic and international prices, the ambiguity of cost relationships, and the possibility of nonprofit trade in the Communist countries, this shift of trade toward Russia in the 1950's may not have been due so much to changed "comparative advantage" and changing comparative cost structures in these two Communist countries (even though in reality these factors may have changed in the meantime), as it was to the formation of a Communist political and economic bloc. As further evidence, there has been the sharp decline of Sino-Soviet trade since 1960 when the split between the two countries became obvious.[20] So Communist China's foreign trade dependence on Russia during the 1950's can be explained primarily by (1) its political sympathy for one side and hostility to the other; (2) the advantages of conducting foreign trade (as an integrated part of the national economic plan) between planned economies; (3) the availability of the "market" and the Soviet credit; and (4) to a considerable extent, the Western countries' trade controls.

It is to be noted that Peking's "lean-to-one-side" policy was declared before the Western countries' strategic trade embargo was imposed on Communist China.[21] This orientation governed China's international economic relations until at least 1957, when the Soviet loans were terminated, and when many Western countries began to relax their controls on China trade.[22] But there was no significant change in China's trade pattern until 1960, when agricultural failures forced imports of food grain from the West, and the Soviet Union called back all the Russian experts working in China. Sino-Soviet trade dropped by 20 per cent in 1960, by 45 per cent in 1961, by 18 per cent in 1962, and by 20 per cent in 1963. In an "open letter" published in *Pravda* on July 14, 1963, the Central Committee of the CPSU blamed the Chinese for the deterioration of trade relations, indicating that it was "on the initiative of the Chinese leaders" that

20. This decline was partly due also to Communist China's need for grain import from the West and China's investment cutbacks.

21. The "lean-to-one-side" policy was declared by Mao on July 1, 1949 (see Mao Tse-tung, 1950, pp. 8, 10-11). The United Nations embargo was not imposed until after Peking's active intervention in the Korean War on November 25, 1950. The United States' Mutual Defense Assistance Control Act of 1951 (the Battle Act), which bans American economic aid to foreign countries shipping designated strategic goods to Communist China, did not become fully operative until January 24, 1952 (see U.S. Government, 1952).

22. The British government announced on June 3, 1957, the relaxation of its trade controls against Communist China, and began to apply only one set of strategic controls to trade with all Communist countries (see *1958 Hong Kong Economic Yearbook,* Section IV, p. 15). Japan decided to take similar steps on July 16, 1957 (*Ta-kung Pao,* July 18, 1957). This was followed by most of the other countries that participate in the trade control program. It was also in 1957 that Peking's Finance Minister first declared that "we are now in a better position to rely on our own accumulation to carry on economic construction" (Li Hsien-nien, 1957).

TABLE 6

COMMUNIST CHINA'S TRADE
1950, 1954, 1959 and 1964

Country	1950 China's Export	1950 China's Import	1950 Total	1950 Share of China's Trade (per cent)	1954 China's Import	1954 China's Export	1954 Total	1954 Share of China's Trade (per cent)
Soviet Union [a]	191	389	580	37.3	578	759	1,337	53.5
Hong Kong [a]	150	256	406	26.1	121	68	189	7.6
Japan [a]	39	20	59	3.8	41	19	60	2.4
Australia [a]	5	2	7	0.5	4	3	7	0.3
Canada	5	2	7	0.5	2	—	2	0.1
United Kingdom [a]	29	10	39	2.5	25	19	44	1.8
Malaya and Singapore [a]	31	41	72	4.6	29	6	35	1.4
Indonesia	3	—	3	0.2	4	3	7	0.3
Argentina	—	1	1	0.1	—	6	6	0.2
France	6	3	9	0.6	9	9	18	0.7
West Germany	15	11	26	1.7	36	22	58	2.3
Ceylon [a]	1	—	1	0.1	33	47	80	3.2
Total of above			1,210	78.0			1,843	73.8
China's Total Trade			1,553	100.0			2,498	100.0

Sources:
The author's computations based on USDC, Value Series for relevant years; Table 9 (B), and *China Trade Report,* Hong Kong, 13, November 1965 (p. 2).

"the volume of China's trade with the Soviet Union was cut almost 67 per cent in the last three years [1960-1962]; deliveries of industrial plants dropped 40 times." [23] Why the Communist Chinese leaders took this initiative to reduce China's trade with Russia was not explained in the Soviet open letter. It was, however, answered by the Chinese Communist Party in the following manner:

> You suddenly withdrew all the Soviet experts working for us, thus interrupting the program of construction and production of many of our industrial and mining enterprises. This directly affected our demand for the import of complete plant equipment. May we ask: Under this situation, do you want to force us to buy these things and use them as decorations?
>
> Besides, since 1960 you have pursued a more restrictive and discriminating trade policy towards China. In our economic and trade negotiations, you have deliberately obstructed, delayed, or refused the supply of materials urgently

23. *Tass* English translation of this open letter appeared in *The New York Times,* Western edition, July 16, 1963. The bracketed dates are mine.

WITH MAJOR PARTNERS,
(in millions of U.S. dollars)

1959				1964			
China's Export	China's Import	Total	Share of China's Trade (per cent)	China's Export	China's Import	Total	Share of China's Trade (per cent)
1,100	955	2,055	47.9	314	135	449	13.5
181	20	201	4.7	345	11	356	10.7
19	4	23	0.5	158	153	311	9.4
8	30	38	0.9	23	153	176	5.3
5	2	7	0.2	9	126	135	4.0
55	69	124	2.9	69	50	119	3.6
51	40	91	2.1	99	—	99	3.0
61	53	114	2.7	34[b]	58[b]	92[b]	2.8
—	—	—	—	—	92	92	2.8
16	40	56	1.3	31	50	81	2.4
66	129	195	4.5	52	26	78	2.3
32	16	48	1.1	43	26	69	2.1
		2,952	68.8			2,057	61.9
		4,290	100.0			3,322	100.0

Notes:

a. Figures refer to general trade. That is, these countries' exports to China include domestic exports and re-exports; Their imports from China include imports for consumption and those for re-export.

b. Figure covers January-October trade only.

needed by China, while providing large quantities of materials for which we had no demand or little demand. In reecnt years, you have also utilized the two countries' trade relationships as an instrument of political pressure on China. Why would not this lead to the reduction of trade between the two countries? [24]

The Chinese letter also admitted that during 1959-61, because of "serious natural disasters," China was not able to supply large quantities of agricultural products to the Soviet Union, and this also contributed to the decline of Sino-Soviet trade. This exchange of letters indeed provided a clear account of the trade relationship between the two Communist countries in recent years. Within five years, Sino-Soviet trade dropped from its 1959 peak of over 2 billion U.S. dollars to 450 million in 1964.

As indicated in Table 5, Sino-Soviet trade started with a modest one-third of China's total trade in 1950, went up to over one-half of the total

24. A letter from the Central Committee of the Chinese Communist Party to the Central Committee of CPSU, dated February 29, 1964 (*Ta-kung Pao,* May 9, 1964, p. 3). The translation is mine.

in the mid-1950's, and then within a short period of five years from 1959 to 1964, it dropped from about one-half to a mere 14 per cent. In contrast, before the imposition of controls in 1950, free world trade comprised 60 per cent of China's total foreign trade. It was reduced to about one-quarter in the mid-1950's, and then jumped from less than one-third of the total in 1959 to about two-thirds in 1964. The pendulum seems to have made a full swing. This rapid reorientation of trade away from the Soviet Union, like the swing toward it in the early 1950's, once again demonstrated the great flexibility in the operation of Communist China's foreign trade system. During the same period, China's trade with East European countries more or less followed the same pattern. Its trade with Asian Communist countries and with Cuba increased substantially after the deterioration of Sino-Soviet relations in the late 1950's. This latter trade, however, has been largely in the nature of capital export from China.

Communist China's major trading partners as of 1964 [25] are listed in Table 6 in the order of their share of China's total trade in that year. The table also shows China's trade with these countries in 1954, ten years earlier; in 1950, the year before the embargo; and in 1959, China's peak trade year. It is important to note that in 1964, even after all the ups and downs, the Soviet Union still was Communist China's most important trading partner. Four other countries in the table deserve special mention: Hong Kong and Malaya (together with Singapore), both of which have large Chinese populations and therefore a sizable demand for Chinese consumer goods, are important sources of foreign exchange for Communist China. Australia and Canada, both major suppliers of food grain to China since 1961, are two important absorbers of China's foreign exchange. (To a smaller extent, Argentina belongs also in this category.) The trade balances of these four countries with China are summarized in Tables 7 and 8. These two tables show that for 1961-64, China earned more than enough foreign exchange from Hong Kong and Malaya (and Singapore) to pay for the trade deficit resulting from grain purchases in Australia and Canada.

Among the remaining countries in Table 6, Japan was China's third most important trading partner in 1964, following the USSR and Hong Kong. Japan's advantages in trading with mainland China are these: (1) it is the only advanced industrial country in Asia, as well as being geographically close to China; and (2) it was China's most important trading partner before the Communist period. In the future development of China's foreign trade, Japan is likely to play an increasingly important role. Trade between China and the United Kingdom, France, and West Germany was not large as of 1964, but may be expected to expand. Ceylon probably will continue to hold its present place as a supplier of crude rubber.

25. Arbitrarily defined here as those countries that had a trade turnover with China of over $50 million in 1964.

TABLE 7

COMMUNIST CHINA'S TRADE WITH HONG KONG, MALAYA AND SINGAPORE, 1961-1964
(in millions of U.S. dollars)

	1961	1962	1963	1964	1961-1964
Hong Kong:					
China's import	180	212	260	345	
China's import	17	16	12	11	
Balance	163	196	248	334	941
Malaya and Singapore:					
China's export	56	66	94	99	
China's import	4	1	5	—	
Balance	52	65	89	99	305

Source:
USDC, *Value Series,* 1961-64.

TABLE 8

COMMUNIST CHINA'S TRADE WITH AUSTRALIA AND CANADA, 1961-1964
(in millions of U.S. dollars)

	1961	1962	1963	1964	1961-1964
Australia:					
China's export	7	11	15	23	
China's import	161	98	202	153	
Balance	—154	—87	—187	—130	—558
Canada:					
China's export	3	4	5	9	
China's import	121	137	97	126	
Balance	—118	—133	—92	—117	—460

Source:
USDC, *Value Series,* 1961-1964.

Communist China's overall trade balance, and trade balances by major trading areas, are presented in Table 9 (A and B). As shown in the table, by the end of 1964 China had a cumulative surplus of approximately two billion U.S. dollars in the balance of trade, mostly developed after 1962. However, nearly half of this surplus was due to China's favorable balance with the Asian Communist countries and Cuba, which in

TABLE 9

COMMUNIST CHINA'S TRADE BALANCE, 1950-1964
(in millions of U.S. dollars)

A. Total Trade

Year	Total Trade	Exports	Imports	Balance of Trade Annual	Balance of Trade Cumulative
1950	1,553	699	854	–155	–155
1951	1,968	932	1,035	–103	–258
1952	1,929	940	989	– 49	–307
1953	2,286	1,099	1,188	– 89	–396
1954	2,498	1,197	1,301	–104	–500
1955	2,732	1,425	1,307	118	–382
1956	3,138	1,691	1,446	245	–137
1957	3,057	1,651	1,407	244	107
1958	3,834	1,973	1,861	112	219
1959	4,290	2,253	2,036	217	436
1960	3,938	2,011	1,926	85	521
1961	2,894	1,523	1,370	153	674
1962	2,601	1,525	1,075	450	1,124
1963	2,696	1,557	1,139	418	1,542
1964	3,322	1,930	1,392	538	2,080

B. Trade Balances by Areas

Year	Soviet Union China's Export	Soviet Union China's Import	Soviet Union Balance	Eastern Europe China's Export	Eastern Europe China's Import	Eastern Europe Balance
1950	191	389	—198	22	8	14
1951	331	478	—147	114	106	8
1952	414	554	—140	172	157	15
1953	475	697	—222	188	193	—5
1954	578	759	—181	197	238	—41
1955	644	748	—104	233	237	—4
1956	764	733	31	240	264	—24
1957	738	544	194	249	295	—46
1958	881	634	247	289	408	—119
1959	1100	955	145	351	324	27
1960	848	817	31	316	338	—22
1961	551	367	184	164	164	0
1962	516	233	283	147	78	69
1963	413	187	226	157	73	84
1964	314	135	179	141	85	56
1950-1964			528			12

Year	Other Communist Countries China's Export	China's Import	Balance	Free World China's Export	China's Import	Balance
1950	5	5	0	481	452	29
1951	15	5	10	472	446	26
1952	25	5	20	329	273	56
1953	45	10	35	391	288	103
1954	80	10	70	342	294	48
1955	110	5	105	438	317	121
1956	110	15	95	577	434	143
1957	102	40	62	562	528	34
1958	123	48	75	680	771	—91
1959	185	88	97	617	669	—52
1960	169	115	54	678	656	22
1961	232	194	38	576	645	—69
1962	270	191	79	592	573	19
1963	281	186	95	707	693	14
1964	[294]	[195]	[99]	1,181	977	204
1950-1964			934			607

Sources and Notes:

See Table 4. The computations are the author's; details may not add to the total because of rounding.

turn was largely the result of Peking's economic aid to these smaller Communist countries. (See Table 14 and the discussion of Communist China's foreign aid later in this chapter.)

III. A CONJECTURAL RECONSTRUCTION OF COMMUNIST CHINA'S BALANCE OF PAYMENTS

Having reviewed the trends in Communist China's commodity trade, in the remaining sections of this chapter I will examine China's other major international transactions involving payments or receipts of foreign exchange, and relate them to China's trade balances with a view to drawing up a conjectural balance of payments for an appraisal of Peking's international economic position. In these areas, useful data are extremely scarce. Therefore, what can be done is very limited in scope, and the results can be considered only as tentative. The justification for such an attempt is that some new information on Soviet loans has become available during the last few years, and an effort to compare and analyze these and earlier data seems worthwhile. With the trade and loan data systematically organized, it seems also desirable to attempt estimates of a few other items in the balance of payments that are based on very limited and highly fragmentary information. We shall first examine briefly the available data on Soviet loans and their repayment; and then proceed to the still largely unresolved mystery of Communist China's debts to the Soviet Union.

INTERNATIONAL SETTLEMENT AND EXCHANGE RATES

The general practice in settling the various types of international transactions in the Soviet bloc is for the central bank of each country to employ three types of accounts, each handling the settlement of a different category of transactions, as follows: [26]

(1) The trade clearing accounts. These record the payments and receipts for imports and exports of commodities, for technical assistance, for transportation, and "other operations connected with foreign trade." All ordinary trade payments in the Soviet bloc are made in rubles.

(2) Credit accounts. These are opened to record and to reckon the use of credit and loans, the repayment of debts, and the payment of interest. These accounts are kept in rubles, with a separate account opened for each loan.[27]

(3) Noncommercial payment accounts. These are clearing accounts for the settlement of the various payments not directly connected with trade (such as diplomatic, cultural, and travel expenditures; the payment of royalties; and payments connected with the arrangement of exhibitions, etc.). The noncommercial accounts are also kept in rubles, but these are converted into local currency to cover expenditures in a given Communist country. In the international payment relations between Communist countries, these are the only accounts in which local prices and local currency are used in the settlement.

What are the foreign exchange rates used in the settlement of these three types of Sino-Soviet transaction? As we have pointed out, only in the settlement of noncommercial transactions is the local currency (for example, *yuan*) involved. The trade and credit transactions are settled in rubles. For trade, the ruble-*yuan* exchange rate is used only in do-

26. Unless otherwise noted, the description of the three types of accounts is based on Bystrov, 1960. See particularly p. 57 and p. 64.

27. The settlement of one type of credit transaction is probably not included in the credit account category. This is the case in which "commodity loans" are granted by the Soviet Union to other Communist countries. Such loans are usually made for relatively short periods for the purpose of relieving urgent needs for particular types of raw materials. The repayment of this type of credit and the payment of interest thereon are usually made in the same commodities that were advanced as loans. The valuation of the commodities involved in commodity loans is based on the prices used in transactions concluded under regular trade agreements, not as in the case of long-term loan deliveries, the prices of which are determined by special agreements. In Soviet bookkeeping, commodities shipped under commodity loan arrangements are "regarded as ordinary exports and imports." Thus it is very likely that transactions connected with commodity loans are settled in the trade clearing accounts. See V. Zoloev, 1959.

mestic settlement between the People's Bank of China and the foreign trade corporations. In credit transactions, the ruble-*yuan* exchange rate is again used only when the loan or repayment figures are translated into the *yuan* unit for domestic accounting purposes. Because of the different nature of the two types of transaction, the ruble-*yuan* exchange rates used in trade and noncommercial accounts are different. For the period from 1950 to 1964, these ruble-*yuan* exchange rates are as follows (ruble per *yuan*):

	Foreign Trade Rate	Noncommercial Rate
1950–July, 1959	1 (1.03) old rubles)	—
July, 1959–1960	2 (old rubles)	6 (old rubles)
Jan. 1, 1961–April 1, 1963	0.45 (new ruble)	0.60 (new ruble)
April 1, 1963–1964	0.45 (new ruble)	0.78 (new ruble)

Source: Chao and Mah, 1964, pp. 193, 199; *Foreign Currencies Handbook,* 1963, p. 13.

It is not clear whether identical ruble-*yuan* exchange rates are used in the accounting of trade transactions and of credit transactions. It is true that special accounts have been opened in the state banks of Communist China and the USSR to handle Soviet loans and their repayments.[28] However, because the drawing and repayment of Soviet loans are often made through trade channels, the credit accounts and trade accounts must be closely related (Bystrov, 1960, p. 64). The precise and detailed relationship between these two types of accounts in not clear to us. It may well be that this relationship depends largely on the specifications of each loan. Yet the very fact that trade channels are used for a large part of the credit operations seems to favor the argument that the foreign trade exchange rate between the ruble and the *yuan* is also applicable to credit settlements. However, since the variety, quantity, and pricing of commodities involved in credit transactions are regulated by special agreements, distinguishing them from those under ordinary trade agreements; since U.S. dollars were permitted to be used in repaying at least the 1950 Soviet loan;[29] and since special accounts are opened for the credit transactions, it is conceivable that foreign exchange rates other than the trade rates might have been used in the settlement of credit transactions.

There are indirect indications that in the settlement of Sino-Soviet credit transactions, the U.S. dollar has been used as the unit of account,

28. See, for example, Article 4, "Sino-Soviet Agreement on Soviet Granting Loan to People's Republic of China" (February 14, 1950), *Collected Documents,* Vol. I (p. 80). The 1950 Sino-Soviet loan agreement is the only loan agreement whose full text is published.

29. See Articles 2 and 3, Sino-Soviet Loan Agreement of 1950, *Collected Documents,* Vol. I (p. 80).

with the implied ruble-*yuan* exchange rate being the cross rate derived from the official ruble-dollar and *yuan*-dollar rates. For example: (1) The 1950 Sino-Soviet loan agreement officially used the dollar as the unit of account. (2) Since 1950, the Communist Chinese customs statistics have used the dollar together with the *yuan* as "dual accounting units" (Chen and Liu, 1958, p. 174). (3) Some of the *yuan* figures for Soviet loan receipts, as given in Peking's budget reports, are apaprently converted from rounded dollar figures. Thus, at the then-official *yuan*-dollar rate, the planned Soviet loan receipt of 724 million *yuan* for the First Five-Year Plan period was equivalent to the sum of three unused installments of $60 million each from the 1950 loan, plus the total amount of the 1954 Soviet loan of 520 million rubles or $130 million. Again, the 1956 loan receipt of 117,419,000 *yuan,* and the 1957 loan receipt of 23,320,000 *yuan,* are clearly converted from the round figures of $50 million and $10 million, respectively.[30] (4) Furthermore, it was stipulated in the 1950 Sino-Soviet trade agreement that when U.S. dollars were used for loan repayments, they were to be converted into rubles at the official ruble-dollar rate fixed by the Soviet state bank.[31]

If indeed the U.S. dollar was used as the unit of account in all Sino-Soviet credit transactions, and if consistent cross ruble-*yuan* rates were applied, then the effective rates used by Peking in connection with credit transactions would be these:

	Yuan-dollar rate[32] (yuan per dollar)	Ruble-dollar rate[33] (ruble per dollar)	Cross ruble-yuan rate (ruble per yuan)
1950	2.360	4 (old rubles)	1.70 (old rubles)
1951–1952	2.262	4 (" ")	1.77 (" ")
1953–1954	2.462	4 (" ")	1.63 (" ")
1955–mid-1957	2.355	4 (" ")	1.70 (" ")
Mid-1957–1960	2.355	4 (" ")	1.70 (" ")
	2.617	4 (" ")	1.53 (" ")
Jan. 1, 1961-1964	2.355	0.9 (new ruble)	0.38 (new ruble)
	2.617	0.9 (new ruble)	0.34 (new ruble)

30. For the *yuan* figures, see Li Hsien-nien, 1957; for a more detailed discussion of this point, see Mah, 1959 (pp. 85-86).

31. Art. 7, Sino-Soviet Trade Agreement (April 19, 1950) in *Collection of Treaties,* 1957, Vol. I (p. 47). For an interesting discussion of this and other related points, see Chao, 1964.

32. For 1950-1954, Shanghai telegraphic transfer rates compiled from newspaper daily quotations by Y. L. Wu 1956 (p. 489). The 1950-1952 rates are 12-month averages computed from Wu's monthly data by this author. For 1955-1964, the rate of 2.355 *yuan* per dollar has been maintained. It is the average of the official buying rate of 2.343 and the selling rate of 2.367 for U.S. dollar notes, announced in May 1955. There is no official remittance rate for U.S. dollars during

It will become clear later that in interpreting the Chinese data on Soviet loans and repayments, the use of a foreign trade ruble-*yuan* rate or a consistent cross ruble-*yuan* rate will make a great difference in the dollar or ruble values of the total amounts granted and repaid.

SOVIET LOANS TO COMMUNIST CHINA

From 1950 to 1955, Communist China consistently imported more from the Soviet Union than it exported to that country. During these six years the cumulative import surplus amounted to roughly a billion dollars (US $993 million; see Table 9). This import surplus was financed by Soviet loans to China. But since 1956, China has been running an export surplus every year in its trade with the USSR, which was undoubtedly used for the repayment of Soviet loans and the settlement of other obligations.[34]

Published information is available for only two Soviet loans to Communist China. The first loan agreement, signed on February 14, 1950, provided a five-year Soviet loan of U.S. $300 million, in equal installments of U.S. $60 million a year, from January, 1950, to the end of 1954, at an interest rate of 1 per cent per annum. According to the agreement, the loan was "to be used in payment for deliveries from the USSR of machinery, equipment, and materials including equipment for electric power stations, metallurgical and machine-building plans, mining equipment for extraction of coal and ores, railway and other transport equipment, rails and other materials for the restoration and development of the national economy of China" (*Collected Documents,* Vol. I, pp. 79-80. Thus it may be considered as an "economic loan."

A second Soviet loan to China was announced on October 12, 1954 in a joint Sino-Soviet communiqué. It was reported as a "long-term" credit of 520 million rubles, but no further details were given. At the then-official exchange rate of 4 rubles to the dollar, the amount would have been equivalent to US $130 million. According to a Protocol signed at the same time, the new loan was to be used to finance, first, additional

---

these years. See Li, 1959 (pp. 5, 255); and Wu *et al.,* 1963, Vol. 1 (p. 304). A derived rate of 2.617 *yuan* to the dollar was given in *CHCC,* No. 12, December 9, 1957 (p. 29). But the editor of the journal specially noted that this rate was not an official exchange rate (that is, not a People's Bank quotation), and that it was "computed from relevant data for general reference only." The fact that the average rate of 2.355 *yuan* per dollar is still in force is evidenced by Hong Kong and Chinese publications referring to the above-mentioned buying and selling rates as "current bank quotations of U.S. dollar notes" after 1957 (see, for example, *Kwangtung Traveller's Handbook,* p. 131), and confirmed by informed persons in Hong Kong in 1964.

33. Soviet official rates.

34. Repayments started in 1954, but 1956 marked the year when the Chinese repayment exceeded Soviet loan deliveries. The long-term Soviet loans were exhausted in 1957, as discussed later.

equipment for 141 enterprises that the USSR was to help Communist China build in accordance with the agreements concluded in 1950 and 1953, and second, the construction of 15 additional industrial enterprises. The communiqué specified that the costs of the additional equipment were "over 400 million (old) rubles" (*Communiqué on Negotiations,* 1954).

The purpose of this second loan, as stated in the 1954 Protocol, was again for economic construction. But if the costs of the additional equipment for the Soviet-aid projects were approximately 400 million rubles, as specified in the communiqué, what was the purpose of the remaining 120 million rubles (US $30 million, at the then-official exchange rate)? A Soviet source indicated that, among other things, Peking was to use this loan to pay for Soviet technical and scientific aid and information.[35] It may be surmised that this included salaries and other expenses for Soviet experts in China. The fact that design work for Soviet-aid projects and other kinds of technical assistance rendered to China by the USSR are paid by Peking "through trade procedures" is also explicitly stated in a 1956 Sino-Soviet agreement for the construction of 55 new industrial projects.[36]

The total of the 1950 and 1954 economic loans was U.S. $430 million. No other Soviet loans to China of this nature have been announced. It is not likely that there were unannounced loans of a similar nature, for qualitative information available up to the time of the open split between Peking and Moscow in 1960 seems to indicate that neither China nor Russia attempted to conceal the "generosities" of Soviet economic loans and aid to Mainland China. However, various sources have reported total Soviet loans to Communist China in amounts far exceeding the two published economic loans, though they often give undefined and apparently inconsistent figures. Clarification and reconciliation of the many seeming inconsistencies in the Communist data are important to our understanding of Sino-Soviet economic relations. Yet given the obscurities involved, the available data are naturally susceptible to several alternative interpretations. It ought to be emphasized that the analysis submitted in the next few pages gives only one of these possible interpretations. Nevertheless, it seems to be one that can clarify more obscurities and reconcile more apparent inconsistencies than some of the other explanations.

Of the many different total Soviet loan figures reported by various Communist sources, three official statements of major importance are examined below.

(1) Communist China's Finance Minister, Li Hsien-nien, provided the following relevant figures in his 1957 Budget Report: China's total

35. See V. Holubnychy, "Soviet Economic Aid to China," *Bulletin,* Institute for the Study of the USSR, January, 1956 (p. 7). (Based on *Vneshniaia Torgovlia,* No. 2, February 1955, p. 2).

36. NCNA release, April 7, 1956 (In *SCMP,* No. 1265, April 11, 1956, pp. 30-31).

debts to the USSR during 1950-1957 were 5,294 million *yuan;* of which 2,174 million *yuan* were used before 1953, and 3,120 million *yuan* were used during 1953-1957. The amount received from the USSR in 1956 was 117.42 million *yuan,* and the amount in 1957 was 23.32 million *yuan.* These last two items represent "the balance carried over from foreign loans provided for in agreement(s) concluded previously" (Li Hsien-nien, 1957). The total debt of 5,294 million *yuan* was again referred to by Li in late 1959,[37] indicating that no additional Soviet loan had been granted between 1957 and 1959.

(2) Mikhail A. Suslov, member of the Presidium of the Central Committee of the CPSU, reported on February 14, 1964, that "the Soviet Union supplied the Chinese People's Republic long-term credits for 1,816 million rubles on favorable terms" (*JMJP,* April 27, 1964, p. 5).

(3) Premier Chou En-lai in his report to the National People's Congress in December, 1964, provided some new information on China's debts to the Soviet Union. After reviewing China's economic condition since 1958, Chou stated that "during this period, not only we did not borrow a penny from the outside, but we have repaid almost the whole of our past foreign debts. The total of the various debts and interest that we owed the Soviet Union was 1,406 million new rubles. We have repaid 1,389 million new rubles according to schedule. As to the remaining 17 million new rubles, we have proposed to the Soviet side to pay it off ahead of schedule from a part of this year's favorable balance in our trade with the Soviet Union." [38]

These three sources are equally authoritative. I shall try to show, first, that Li Hsien-nien's total loan figure and Suslov's loan figure are probably equivalents, and second, that Chou En-lai's figure represents only a part of the total Soviet loans, not the whole amount.

Suslov and Li Hsien-nien Figures

First, the Li Hsien-nien figure of 5,294 million *yuan* and the Suslov figure of 1,816 million new rubles can be reconciled by converting both figures into dollars. At the Soviet rate (1 new ruble = US $1.111), 1,816 million new rubles equal US $2,018 million. At the Chinese rate of 2.617 *yuan* to the dollar, 5,294 million *yuan* amount to US $2,023

37. In a 1959 article entitled "Ten Years of Great Achievement in CPR's Public Finance," Li Hsien-nien stated that China's total financial revenue during the period 1950-59 was 265,900 million *yuan,* and that Soviet loans constituted 2 per cent of this total (*JMJP,* Sept. 28, 1959; also in *People's Handbook 1960,* p. 76). The implied total Soviet loan is thus 5,318 million *yuan.* Taking into account the unavoidable rounding errors, this loan figure and Li's 1957 figure of 5,294 million *yuan* appear to be equivalent.

38. *Chou* En-lai (1964), "Report on the Work of the Government" (delivered at the first session of the Third National People's Congress, on Dec. 21-22, 1964). The translation is mine. Notice that Chou apparently did not consider a 1960 Soviet trade credit of US $320 million (to be discussed later) as a debt to the USSR.

million. The two dollar figures are close enough to be considered as equivalents. To show this identity in a different way: Assuming the ruble and *yuan* loan totals given by Suslov and Li are equivalent, the implied ruble-*yuan* rate is 0.34 new ruble per *yuan* (1,816/5,294), which is precisely the cross rate of 0.9 new rubles per dollar (*i.e.*, 1 new ruble = $1.111, as used above) and the Chinese *yuan*-dollar rate of 2.617: 1 (See p. 696 above). These calculations lend strong support to the hypothesis that the American dollar was used as a unit of account in Sino-Soviet credit transactions.[39]

However, this interpretation does not clear up all the mysteries enshrouding Soviet loans to mainland China. While the Li Hsien-nien figure when converted into dollars at the 2.617 rate is more or less identical with the dollar equivalent of the Suslov figure, when converted at the 2.355 rate, it would be $2,247 million, *i.e.*, $229 million larger than the dollar equivalent of Suslov's total. Yet later computations of Soviet loans and their repayments based on Peking's budget data indicate that the appropriate rate [40] for converting the *yuan* figures into dollars is 2.355 *yuan* to the dollar, not 2.617. Which of the two exchange rates should we adhere to in our analysis? Given the inadequacy of available information, it is difficult to judge which *yuan*-dollar rate ought to be applied to which cases. However, since, first, the 2.355 *yuan*-dollar rate has been in effect practically since 1950; [41] second, the 2.617 *yuan*-dollar rate, first reported late in 1957 as a derived rate "computed from relevant data for general reference only," was not on record before that year; and third, almost all long-term Soviet loans to China were used before 1957 (the final balance of long-term Soviet loans received by China in 1957 was only about $10 million), the 2.617:1 rate can hardly be applied to the budget data published before 1957. Therefore, it is assumed that the 2.355 *yuan*-dollar

39. If the trade ruble-*yuan* rate of 0.45 new ruble = 1 *yuan* (*i.e.*, 2.22 *yuan* = 1 new ruble) is used to convert the Suslov loan figure directly into *yuan* values, 1,816 million new rubles would be equal to 4,032 million *yuan*, much smaller than Li Hsien-nien's loan total. (In terms of dollars, it is $482 million smaller than the dollar equivalent of Li's total at the 2.617 *yuan*-dollar rate, or $536 million smaller at the 2.355 *yuan*-dollar rate.) If, on the other hand, the trade rate of 1 old ruble to 1 *yuan* is used to convert Li Hsien-nien's 5,294 million *yuan* directly into old rubles, the total Soviet loan would then be 5,294 million old rubles. At the Soviet rate of 4 old rubles = $1, this amounts to $1,324 million. The Suslov figure is equal to 8,063 million old rubles (1 new ruble = 4.44 old rubles) or $2,016 million (4 old rubles = $1). Now the Suslov loan total is $692 million *larger* than the converted Li Hsien-nien figure. (The trade rate of 1 ruble to 1 *yuan* cannot be used directly to convert either the Suslov figure into *yuan* or the Li figure into new rubles, because it is a conversion rate between the *yuan* and the old ruble, whereas the Suslov figure is in new rubles.) The contradictory results shown here seem to favor the argument that trade ruble-*yuan* rates are probably not used by Peking in reckoning Soviet loans.

40. "Appropriate" in the sense that at this rate more problems can be solved than are created.

41. The 1950-1954 average *yuan*-dollar rate (telegraphic transfer) was 2.36 *yuan* per dollar. See footnote 32.

rate should be used in the analysis of Sino-Soviet credits and repayments.

The remaining unanswered question, then, is how to explain the discrepancy of about $230 million between the dollar equivalents of Suslov's total in rubles and Li Hsien-nien's total in *yuan*. Only a hypothetical interpretation can be offered. It is still assumed that the Sino-Soviet loan transactions are accounted for in dollars. It is further assumed that the total discrepancy of about $230 million is largely the cumulative result of the increasingly greater degree of overvaluation of the *yuan* vis-à-vis the dollar at the 2.355:1 rate, relative to the extent of overvaluation of the ruble vis-à-vis the dollar at the official rate of 4 old rubles per dollar (or 0.9 new ruble per dollar). Thus when a devaluated rate of 2.617 *yuan* per dollar is derived and applied to the *yuan* total in 1957, the calculated discrepancy between the dollar equivalents of Suslov's total ($2,018 million) and Li Hsien-nien's total ($2,247 million at the 2.355 *yuan*-dollar rate) is eliminated. At the same time one should not completely rule out the possibility that "total Soviet loans" as reported by Li Hsien-nien and by Suslov refer to different totals.

Chou En-lai Figure

In interpreting Chou En-lai's loan figures, the time period involved is of key importance. In the earlier part of his report, Chou reviewed Communist China's economic situation since 1958. In the passage on Soviet loans quoted above, he first mentioned that "during this period, not only we did not borrow a penny from the outside. . . ." It is well established that 1957 was the year in which Communist China received the last installment of long-term Soviet loans. My hypothesis, then, is that the "total of the various debts and interest" of 1,406 million new rubles, given by Chou in the same paragraph, is the total amount that Communist China owed the USSR in 1958. To test this hypothesis, we may do the following calculations:

(1) At the official rates of 2.355 *yuan* per dollar and $1.111 per new ruble, Li Hsien-nien's total 5,294 million *yuan* is equal to US $2,248 million, and Chou En-lai's total of 1,406 million new rubles is equal to US $1,561 million. The difference between the two is US $687 million.

(2) My estimate of China's interest payment on the Soviet economic loan during 1950-53 is 7.8 million *yuan*, (see Table 10) or approximately US $3 million at the official exchange rate. China's repayment of Soviet debts and interest payments during 1954-57 as derived from state budget data is 1,605 million *yuan* (see Table 11), or about US $682 million at the official rate. Thus China's total repayment of Soviet debts, and interest payment during 1950-57 is estimated to be approximately US $685 million.

(3) Subtracting the 1950-57 repayment of US $685 million from the dollar equivalent of Li Hsien-nien's total (US $2,248 million), we get US

$1,563 million as the Soviet debts outstanding at the beginning of 1958. This appears to be the same amount that Chou En-lai was referring to (1,406 million new rubles, equivalent to US $1,561 million at the official exchange rate).

Chou En-lai's statement indicates that his total includes "various debts and interest." Because Chou's figure, interpreted as China's debt and interest outstanding in 1958, seems to illuminate China's overall debt position very well, there is a distinct possibility that Li Hsien-nien's total of 5,294 million *yuan* also includes both principal and interest. Until the publication in 1964 of Chou's data, almost all students of Sino-Soviet economic relations took it for granted that interest payments should be added to the Li Hsien-nien or Suslov loan totals. But a careful rereading of Li Hsien-nien's statement (1957) will establish that it neither specifically includes or excludes interest, but it certainly does not preclude the possibility that interest obligations were in fact encompassed in that figure.[42] With the new information from the December, 1964, Chou En-lai report, and in the absence of any evidence to the contrary, we are inclined to interpret Li Hsien-nien's total debt figure of 5,294 million *yuan* as including both the principal and the interest obligations. But there is no question that the announced amounts of the 1950 and 1954 economic loans do not include interest.

On the basis of the above information and interpretation, as well as the relevant information from China's annual budget reports, we tentatively summarize Communist China's debt obligations to the USSR in Table 10.

The separation of economic and other loans for 1950-55 can be at best only rough and rather arbitrary, partly because of lack of data and partly because even conceptually the line of separation is far from clear. To the extent that we accept the known information concerning the two economic loans, it seems reasonable to suppose that the estimated economic loan receipts for 1953-55 in Table 10 represent the upper limits within the framework of the two known loan agreements. As to the estimated economic loans for 1950-52, they are essentially residuals in our estimate. These figures would imply that deliveries of Soviet military supplies to China during the Korean War period forced the curtailment of Soviet industrial equipment deliveries. This conclusion would seem reasonable, given the transportation conditions between the two countries at the time (see Appendix B).

42. A literal translation of the statement is "The funds the Soviet Government credited to our country, converted to people's currency, amounted to a total of 5.294 million *yuan*." See Li Hsien-nien, 1957.

TABLE 10

COMMUNIST CHINA: DEBT OBLIGATIONS TO THE USSR, 1950-1957
(in million yuan)

Year	(1) Economic loans and interest obligations: Loans	(2) Interest	(3) Other loans including interest	(4) Total loans and interest obligations	
1950	(94)	0.47	149	244	
1951	(94)	1.41	530	625	
1952	(94)	2.35	1,209	1,305	
					2,174
1953	(141)	3.53	273	417	
1954	(141)	4.66	738	884	
1955	(305)	9.48	1,343	1,657	
1956	117	11.43	—	128	
1957	23	10.91	—	34	
					3,120
Total	1,012	44.24	4,242		5,294

Source:
See Appendix B.

Note:
The individual columns may not add up because of rounding.

SOME CONJECTURAL EXPLANATIONS OF "OTHER LOANS" (COLUMN [3], TABLE 10)

1. Korean War debts, 1950-1952.

An official Communist Chinese document has made public that:

> Concerning Soviet loans to China, it must be pointed out that the major part of them was used to purchase military materials from the Soviet Union, and a large part of these military materials was used and consumed in the anti-American and assist-Korea War. . . . For a long time, we have been repaying the principal and interest on these debts. They took a considerable portion of our exports to the USSR.[43]

The author believes that the "other loans" in Column (3), Table 10, for 1950-52, are all Korean War debts. The precise amounts and the terms of repayment of these war debts are not known, but it has been hinted that the repayment would take about ten years, presumably from

43. A letter from the Central Committee of the CCP to the Central Committee of the CPSU, dated February 29, 1964 (*Ta-kung Pao,* Hong Kong, May 9, 1964, p. 3).

1954 to 1963.[44] The total amount of "other loans" for 1950-52, according to our estimate, is 1,888 million *yuan,* or US $802 million at the official exchange rate. A Japanese newspaper published in 1963 a Peking source reporting that Korean War debts amounted to 3 billion old rubles (*Mainichi Shimbun,* Dec. 25, 1963). Our estimated $802 million is equivalent to 3.2 billion old rubles at the exchange rate of 4 old rubles to one dollar. The two figures do not seem to be inconsistent.

2. The "other loans" for 1953 (273 million yuan).

At an official exchange rate, these loans amount to US $116 million. Since the Korean War ended in July, 1953, and there had been a lull in the war even before then, we suspect that this amount was not entirely for military supplies. At least a part of it was probably for the rehabilitation of the Chinese economy after the Korean War.

3. The transfer to China of Soviet shares in the joint stock companies, in the form of a Soviet credit in 1954.

A Sino-Soviet joint communiqué, dated October 21, 1954, announced the transfer of four Sino-Soviet joint stock companies to China. The transfer took place before January 1, 1955. The Chinese took over the Soviet shares in these four companies and assumed the obligation in the form of a Soviet credit that they were to repay within "several years" by exporting commodities to the USSR (*Collected Documents,* 1958, Vol. III, p. 180). Corresponding to this announcement, Peking's final budget accounts for 1954 also reported a large increase in Soviet credit (amount not given) which was not anticipated in the planned budget for that year (Li Hsien-nien, 1955). In the absence of any other reported Soviet loans in 1954, we believe the "other loans" of 738 million *yuan* (about US $313 million) roughly indicate the value of these transferred Soviet shares. Although the shares are undeniably "economic" in nature, this credit differs from the 1950 and 1954 economic loans because it is merely the result of transferring to Peking the title to existing assets already in China, not a loan to finance additional imports.

4. The transfer of military materials in Port Arthur to China in the form of a loan in 1955.

Peking's 1955 budget report disclosed a large increase of receipts from foreign loans (again the amount is not given) and provided the following explanation:

> When the Soviet forces withdrew before the end of May 1955 from the naval base of Lushun (Port Arthur) jointly used by the two countries, the Soviet government transferred to us much military materiél in the form of a loan. Li Hsien-nien, 1955)

44. See report on Lung Yun's criticism on Soviet loans and interest charge, in *Kwang-ming jih-pao,* Peking, June 19, 1957 (p. 7) and July 14, 1957 (p. 5).

It is most likely that the 1955 "other loan" of 1,343 million *yuan* (about US $570 million at the official exchange rate) in Table 10 represents the approximate size of this credit (Mah, 1959, pp. 84-86).

Space does not permit a careful evaluation here of the contribution of Soviet loans to China's economic development. It can only be pointed out that in terms of size, Soviet economic loans to China have not been large. As is shown in Table 10, of the total loans of 5,294 million *yuan* (approximately US $2,248 million), only 1,012 million *yuan* (US $430 million), or 19 per cent of the total, were used to finance the import of machinery, equipment, and technical assistance. All the estimated "other loans" (with the possible exception of a part of the 1953 "other loan" of $116 million) did not finance China's imports of additional material and equipment for economic construction. However, all evidence indicates that in terms of the nature of the import mix financed by the economic loans, the Soviet credits, though small in size, played a key role in Communist China's industrialization in the 1950's.

REPAYMENT OF SOVIET LOANS

Very briefly, these were the terms of repayment of the 1950 Soviet loan: (1) Both principal and interest were to be paid in deliveries of raw materials, tea, gold, and U.S. dollars. (2) The prices of these materials were to be based on world market prices and determined by special agreements. (3) The repayment was to be made in ten equal annual installments, to be paid before December 31 of each year, beginning in 1954. (4) The loan carried an interest rate of 1 per cent per annum. Payment of interest was computed from the day of the utilization of the actually drawn part of the credit and was to be made at six-month intervals (*Collected Documents,* Vol. I, p. 80).

The terms of repayment for all other Soviet loans are not known, except that official statements have indicated the following: (1) interest rates on Soviet loans to China are from 1 per cent to 2 per cent per annum (Soong, 1955); and (2) in general, the method of repayment is through the delivery of goods. Major commodities used in repayment of Soviet credit include ferrous metals, handicraft products, wool, jute, rice, pork, tea, tobacco, fruits, etc. (Yang Ying-chieh, 1957). A tentative estimate of China's repayment of Soviet loans has been made. The following is the result.

1. Interest payments on the 1950 Soviet loan: 1950-1953.

These can be computed according to the conditions stipulated in the 1950 loan agreement. (For detailed method and explanations, see Appendix B, section on the estimate of interest on Soviet economic loans.) The computed interest payments for 1950-53 are (in million *yuan*):

1950	1951	1952	1953	Total
0.47	1.41	2.35	3.53	7.76

2. Repayment: 1954-1960

The estimates for these years are based primarily on annual budget data and some assumptions. The basic information relevant to our estimates includes:

(i) The item "total expenditure on debts" in the annual budget report,[45] which comprises: (a) repayment of principal and payment of interest on domestic bonds; (b) "obligations expenditures," interpreted as payment of "fixed interest" to former owners of joint state-private enterprises (Ecklund, 1960, p. 5); and (c) repayment of principal and payment of interest on foreign loans.

(ii) The scheduled redemption of domestic bonds and the interest payments on bonds, which are given in the announced regulations covering each bond issue, and thus can be computed.

(iii) Reports that the Chinese Communist government was paying 120 million *yuan* annually from 1956-62 to the former owners of public-private joint enterprises as "fixed interest" on the private assets of these enterprises (Kuan Ta-tung, 1960, p. 87).

In making the estimates of debt repayment for 1954-1960, our basic calculation is:

[Total budgetary expenditure on loans] — [(scheduled redemption of domestic bonds and interest payments on bonds) + (payment of fixed interest to former owners of joint enterprises)] = repayment of foreign debts (including principal and interest).

Our estimates based on these procedures are presented in Table 11.

3. Repayment: 1961-1965

Communist China stopped publishing detailed budget reports in 1961. Therefore, a different procedure for estimating the repayment of Soviet loans must be used for the years since then. According to Chou En-lai, by the end of 1964 China had repaid all but 17 million new rubles of the debts and interest obligations owed to Russia (Chou, 1964). According to our calculations, China paid 8 million *yuan* in interest to the USSR from 1950 to 1953. Repayment of debts and interest during 1954-60 was 3,072 million *yuan*. Therefore, the Soviet debts and interest obligations

45. The "total debt expenditures" figures used in our computations are the realized amounts as given in or derived from the budget reports, except for the figure for 1960, which is an estimate based on the planned amount.

TABLE 11

COMMUNIST CHINA: REPAYMENT OF SOVIET LOANS AND INTEREST, 1954-1960
(in million yuan)

	1954	1955	1956	1957	1958	1959	1960
State expenditure on debts and obligations [a]	210	666	722	838	904	970	(960)
Less: Expenditure on domestic debts and obligations							
Payment of principal and interest on domestic bonds [b]	63	174	130	224	227	353	377
"Obligation expenditures" [c]	......	......	120	120	120	120	120
Total expenditure on domestic debts and obligations	63	174	250	344	397	473	497
Equals: Payment of Soviet loans and interest	147	492	472	494	507	497	463

Notes:

a) *1954: Tsai Cheng* ("Public Finance"), Aug. 8, 1957. "Statistics on State Receipts and Expenditures During the First Five-Year Plan Period."

1955: Li Hsien-nien, 1956.
1956: Li Hsien-nien, 1957.
1957: Li Hsien-nien, 1958.
1958: Li Hsien-nien, 1959.

1959 and 1960: Li Hsien-nieu, 1960. The 1960 figure is an estimated amount, assuming the realized amount was about 80 per cent of the planned figure of 1,200 million *yuan.* Chinese budget data indicate that the rate of realization of planned debt expenditures was 87.7 per cent in 1958 and 88.2 per cent in 1959.

b) Ecklund, 1960 (App. A. Table 2, p. 8).

c) See text.

left to be repaid during 1961-65 were 5,294 — (3,072 + 8) = 2,214 million *yuan*. The balance China proposed to pay off in 1965, 17 million new rubles, is equivalent to US $18.87 million at the official ruble-dollar rate, which in turn is equal to 44.4 million *yuan* at the official *yuan*-dollar rate. This leaves 2,214 — 44 = 2,170 million *yuan* to be repaid during 1961-64. The amount is approximately $921 million.

In the 1961 Sino-Soviet Communiqué on trade negotiations, it was pointed out that because of the acute economic crisis, China had been unable to fulfill its export obligations. At the end of 1960, Peking was 288 million new rubles (US $320 million at the official exchange rate) in debt to the USSR. Since even in 1960 China still maintained an export surplus in its trade with Russia, the shortfall referred to must have been a large planned repayment of Soviet loans. The Soviet Union agreed to grant China a moratorium on this amount, to be repaid in 1962-65, without interest.[46] The originally agreed-on schedule of repayment was (in million new rubles):

1962	8
1963	50
1964	115
1965	115

However, on the basis of two successive Sino-Soviet accords, China applied its favorable 1962 and 1963 Sino-Soviet trade balances to repay its debt ahead of the moratorium schedule.[47] Assuming that the originally scheduled 1965 repayment of 115 million new rubles was evenly distributed between 1963 and 1964, the revised schedule of repayment under the 1960 moratorium would be (in million new rubles):

1962	8
1963	107
1964	173

Converting these ruble values into *yuan* via the dollar, the repayment would have totaled 754 million *yuan* ($320 million), divided as follows (in million *yuan*):

1962	21
1963	280
1964	453

46. *Vneshniaia Torgovlia,* May, 1961 (p. 18); *JMJP,* April 10, 1961 (p. 3).
47. *Pravda,* April 21, 1962; NCNA, Peking, May 16, 1964.

For the remaining 1,416 million *yuan* (2,174 — 754), it is assumed that China repaid one-fourth of it, or 1,416 ÷ 4 = 354 million *yuan* (about $150 million), each year. Therefore the total annual repayments would be (in million *yuan*):

	1961	1962	1963	1964	1965	1961-65
Repayment according to revised moratorium			280	453	......	754
Plus: regular repayment	......	21				
Equals: total repayment	354	354	354	354	44	1,460
	354	375	634	807	44	2,214

REPAYMENT OF 1961 SUGAR LOAN

In 1961 the Soviet Union granted China a loan in the form of 500,000 tons of raw sugar, to be repaid between 1964 and 1967 with the same quantity of raw sugar.[48] The value of this sugar debt was reported to be about $46.2 million (41.6 million new rubles).[49] There is no interest charge (*JMJP,* April 10, 1961.

According to the International Sugar Council (*Statistical Bulletin,* July, 1965, p. 112), through 1964 China had repaid 162,780 tons, or 32.6 per cent, of this sugar loan. The value of this repayment is estimated to be about $15 million (that is, 32.6 per cent of the total value). The repayment is assumed to have been made in 1964.

Table 12 summarizes the above estimates of repayments of loans and trade debts. It shows that Communist China's repayment to the USSR stayed roughly in the neighborhood of about $200 million a year from 1955 to 1960. The repayment in 1958 was slightly higher, perhaps reflecting the increased availability of agricultural products for export as a result of the Great Leap Forward. The 1960 payment moratorium indicates that China must have planned to speed up the repayment, but was not successful because of its domestic economic difficulties. China's economic crisis in 1959-61, and the resultant 1960 payment moratorium, reduced repayments in 1961 and 1962 to about $150 million a year. The stepped-up repayment in 1963 and 1964, according to our estimate, was due largely to repayment of the postponed debts ahead of schedule. China's total repayment of Soviet debts reached roughly $270 million in 1963, and over $350 million in 1964. Compared with a total Sino-Soviet trade of about $600 million in 1963 and $450 million in 1964, these repayment figures are very high indeed. They must have imposed a heavy burden on the Chinese economy.

48. The scheduled repayment was as follows: 1964 and 1965, 100,000 tons each; 1966 and 1967, 150,000 tons each. *Vneshniaia Torgovlia,* May, 1961 (p. 18).

49. *Vneshniaia Torgovlia SSSR za 1961 god,* p. 185.

TABLE 12

COMMUNIST CHINA: ESTIMATE OF REPAYMENT OF SOVIET LOANS, 1950-1964

Year	(1) Repayment of loans and interest	(2) Repayment of sugar loan	(3) Total repayment of all debts and interest	(4) Total repayment of all debts and interest
	(millions of yuan)			(millions of U.S. dollars)
1950	1 [a]	—	1	0.4
1951	1 [a]	—	1	0.4
1952	2 [a]	—	2	0.8
1953	4 [a]	—	4	1.7
1954	147	—	147	62.4
1955	492	—	492	208.9
1956	472	—	472	200.4
1957	494	—	494	209.8
1958	507	—	507	215.3
1959	497	—	497	211.0
1960	463	—	463	196.6
1961	354	—	354	150.3
1962	375	—	375	159.3
1963	634	—	634	269.2
1964	807	35	842	357.6
Total, 1950-64	5,250 [b]	35	5,285	2,244.1

Notes:

Details may not add to the total because of rounding.

a. The 1950-53 figures are interest payments only.

b. The total of this column, 5,250 million *yuan,* is Li Hsien-nien's total loan figure less the 44 million *yuan* repaid early in 1965. (*JMJP*, Feb. 25, 1956, p. 5). The sum of the 1958-1964 repayments in Column (1), plus the 44 million *yuan* repaid in 1965, equals 3,684 million *yuan* (or $1,563 million, or 1,406 million new rubles), which is the loan figure reported by Chou En-lai in December, 1964.

Sources:

Column (1). See text, Appendix, and Table 11.

Column (2). See text.

Column (3). Column (1) plus Column (2).

Column (4). Converted from Column (3) at the official exchange rate of 2.355 *yuan* per dollar.

By relating the estimated repayment of debts to China's trade balance with the USSR, we may calculate China's net foreign exchange (and/or gold) payments to the USSR during the last 15 years. These are shown in Table 13.

TABLE 13

COMMUNIST CHINA: ESTIMATE OF FOREIGN EXCHANGE PAYMENT TO THE USSR 1950-1964
(in millions of U.S. dollars)

Year	(1) Total repayment of all debts and interest	(2) China's export surplus to USSR	(3) Net foreign exchange payment to USSR
1950	0.4		0.4
1951	0.4		0.4
1952	0.8		0.8
1953	1.7		1.7
1954	62.4		62.4
1955	208.9		208.9
1956	200.4	31.1	169.3
1957	209.8	193.1	16.7
1958	215.3	247.5	−32.2
1959	211.0	145.4	65.6
1960	196.6	31.1	165.5
1961	150.3	184.3	−34.0
1962	159.3	283.1	−123.8
1963	269.2	225.3	43.9
1964	357.6	178.8	178.8
1950-64	2,244.1	1,519.7	724.4

Sources:
Column (1): From Table 12.
Column (2): From Table 9, B.
Column (3): Column (1) minus Column (2).

China's import surplus from the USSR during 1950-55 was about $993 million (Table 9, B); the import surplus was only a part of Soviet aid to Communist China. All Soviet aid to China was to be repaid in either commodity export or foreign exchange (or gold.) According to Table 13, by 1964 China's cumulative foreign exchange payment to the USSR came to approximately U.S. $725 million, about 73 per cent of its total import surplus for 1950-55.

COMMUNIST CHINA'S FOREIGN AID

Given the fact that Peking has had to restrict domestic consumption of many important materials in order to pay for the imported producer goods needed for its own economic development, and that China itself has been heavily in debt during the last fifteen years, there is no good economic reason for Communist China to extend financial aid to other countries. Yet since 1954, Peking has embarked upon a program of foreign aid roughly comparable in extent to the total Soviet credits it received. The recipients of China's economic aid include the smaller Communist countries and politically uncommitted underdeveloped countries in Asia, Africa, and Latin America.[50] Peking's principal motivation in extending economic aid is to acquire political and economic influence in those countries.[51]

Communist China's economic aid often takes the form of free grants or credits either without interest or with very low interest. China's interest rates on foreign aid credits have generally been lower than the 2.5 per cent charged by the Soviet Union. Repayment terms are also generally more liberal than those of the USSR. Repayment is often extended over a long period of time and begins a number of years after the credit has been extended, with a ten-year grace period prior to the final payment (U.S. State Dept., 1964, p. 36). Very little information on actual repayment has been published.

Communist China's total foreign aid commitment during the period 1954-64 is estimated at about US $2,310 million, about the same as the $2,248 million that the Soviets lent to China. Of this total, $1,430 million was extended to Communist states; the remaining $880 million was offered to the other underdeveloped countries. However, available infor-

50. A partial list of recipients of Chinese aid includes:

Communist countries:	North Korea, North Vietnam, Outer Mongolia, Hungary, Albania.
Southeast Asia:	Burma, Ceylon, Cambodia, Indonesia, Nepal, Pakistan.
Middle East:	Yemen, United Arab Republic.
Africa:	Congo (Brazzaville), Ghana, Guinea, Kenya, Tanzania, Central African Republic.
Latin America:	Cuba.

51. This is evidenced by the fact that North Korea, North Vietnam, and Albania have received the lion's share of Peking's aid to the Communist countries, and all three have more or less supported Peking's view in its dispute with the USSR. China's motive of extending aid to the Afro-Asian-Latin-American area can be best explained by this quotation: "The various types of contradictions in the contemporary world are concentrated in the vast areas of Asia, Africa and Latin America; these are the most vulnerable areas under imperialist rule and the storm centers of the world revolution dealing direct blows at imperialism." (See "Apologists of Neo-Colonialism," *Hung-chi,* No. 19, Oct., 1963).

mation indicates that only about $130 million, or 14.7 per cent, of the committed economic aid was actually delivered to non-Communist underdeveloped countries during 1954-64. On the other hand, over 90 per cent of China's economic aid extended to the communist countries seems to have been drawn.[52] An estimate of the annual overpayment of Communist China's foreign aid is presented in Table 14.

TABLE 14

COMMUNIST CHINA: ESTIMATE OF ANNUAL OUTPAYMENT OF FOREIGN AID, 1954-1964
(in millions of U.S. dollars)

Year	(1) Total outpayment of aid	(2) To under-developed countries	(3) To Communist countries
1954	127.4	—	127.4
1955	166.9	—	166.9
1956	171.5	(20)	150.5
1957	192.8	(10)	185.8
1958	116.8	(5)	111.8
1959	148.6	(25)	123.6
1960	(106.2)	(10)	96.2
1961	(106.2)	(10)	98.2
1962	(106.2)	(10)	93.2
1963	(106.2)	(20)	85.2
1964	(106.2)	(20)	87.2
1954-1964	1,455.0	129	1,326.0

Sources:

Column (1) 1954-1959: Derived from annual budget reports.

1960-1964: Our estimates. For details, see Appendix C.

Column (2) Total amount for 1954-1964: Col. (1), last line minus Col. (3), last line.

Annual amounts: Preliminary estimates based on incomplete data and educated guess. All figures are rounded to the nearest $5 million. The details do not add to the total because of rounding.

Column (3) Total amount for 1954-1964: *Ta-kuug Pao,* Hong Kong, February 25, 1965. For details, see Appendix C.

Annual amount: Col. (1) minus Col. (2).

52. The figures referred to in this paragraph are the author's estimates, made on the basis of published data and government sources.

CHINA'S OTHER FOREIGN EXCHANGE PAYMENTS

1. Salary of Soviet experts working in China

From 1950 to 1959, the Soviet Union sent 10,800 experts to work in Communist China (Chou En-Lai, 1959). These Soviet experts stayed in China from three months to more than two years. While in China, most of them received about 520-540 *yuan* a month for their local expenses. In addition, their regular salary in the Soviet Union was continued, paid into their bank accounts in the USSR (Klochko, 1964, pp. 49, 56-57). Communist China was to pay both the *yuan* salary and the ruble salary. For balance-of-payments purposes, only the ruble salary needs to be considered.

In our estimate, we assume that, on the average, each Soviet expert worked in China for one-and-a-half years. We further assume that their average ruble salary was the equivalent of US $500 a month, or $9,000 for the whole period.[53] Thus the total bill would be $9,000 × 10,800 = $97.2 million. We shall use the rounded figure of $100 million as China's total foreign exchange cost for the services of Soviet experts during 1950-60. This total amount is broken down to $10 million a year for 1951-59, and $5 million a year for 1950 and 1960, because a smaller number of Soviet experts arrived in China in 1950, and all Soviet experts were called back to the USSR in the second half of 1960.

2. Expenditures of Chinese students in the USSR

It is reported that between 1951 and 1962, 11,000 Chinese college and postgraduate students studied and finished courses in Soviet higher educational institutes. During the same period, 10,000 Chinese engineers, technicians, and qualified workers, and about 1,000 Chinese scientists, received training in the Soviet Union (*JMJP,* April 27, 1964, p. 5). The Chinese students stayed in Russia for three to six years (Chen, p. 3). In accordance with a Sino-Soviet agreement concluded in 1952, the Soviet government paid the following allowances to students and trainees (*Collection of Treaties,* 1957, Vol. II, p. 179):

College students	500 old rubles per month.
Graduate students	700 old rubles per month.
Professors, teachers	Salary, tuition, dormitory fees, incidental fees, and traveling expenses as required.

53. On the basis of the information given by Klochko, himself a Soviet scientist assigned to China in 1958 and 1960, the assumed average ruble salary of the equivalent of $500 a month is likely to be on the conservative side. See Klochko, 1964 (pp. 56-57).

The 1952 agreement called for China's repayment of 50 per cent of the funds advanced.

We assume that, on the average, each student received 600 old rubles a month, or 7,200 old rubles a year. At the then-official exchange rate, this is equivalent to $1,800 a year. We also assume that for the engineers, scientists, etc., the average allowance was double that of the students—*i.e.*, $3,600 per person per year. The Chinese Communist government was to repay to the Soviet Union one half of these stipends—that is, $900 a year for each student and $1,800 a year for each engineer, etc. We further assume that, on the average, each of the 11,000 Chinese students stayed four years in the USSR, and each of the 11,000 Chinese engineers, etc., stayed for one year. Thus the total bill for Peking would be:

Students:	$\$900 \times 11{,}000 \times 4 = \$39.6$ million
Engineers, etc.:	$\$1{,}800 \times 11{,}000 = \$19.8$ million

The sum of these amounts, $60 million, is then distributed evenly among the 12 years from 1951-62 at $5 million a year, because the exact number of students and trainees in the USSR each year is not known.[54] Since there has been no abrupt withdrawal of Chinese students and other trainees from the USSR comparable to the withdrawal of Soviet experts in China in 1960 (T.H.E. Chen, p. 6), we assume that the payment of $5 million a year for Chinese students and trainees in the USSR continued in 1961 and 1962.

3. Expenditures of Communist China's diplomatic, trade, and other missions abroad

There is no information concerning the expenditures of Communist China's diplomatic missions and trade and cultural delegations sent abroad. We arbitrarily assume that these expenditures are roughly comparable to Chinese expenditures abroad during World War II, which were much higher than in prewar years. These expenditures are thus assumed to be $10 million a year (Wu *et al.,* 1963, Vol. II, p. 31).

4. Freight and insurance on imports

As explained earlier, China's import data are actually its trading partners' export data valued f.o.b. It is estimated that freight and insurance amounted to approximately 10 per cent of the value of China's imports. Since Soviet exports to China are priced f.o.b Sino-Soviet border, there should be no freight and insurance charges over and above the reported

54. René Goldman, who went from Poland to study in China from 1953 to 1958, wrote in 1962 that "China sent an average of 2,000 students yearly to the Soviet Union and a hundred or so to the Eastern European countries." See René Goldman, "The Rectification Campaign at Peking University: May-June 1951," *China Quarterly,* No. 12, Oct.-Dec. 1962 (pp. 147-48).

Soviet export value. This is assumed to be true also in the case of China's imports from North Korea, Outer Mongolia and North Vietnam. Freight and insurance payments are thus estimated to be 10 per cent of the value of China's imports from the free world countries, and 10 per cent of China's imports from Eastern European Communist countries and Cuba.[55] Since China still does not have an ocean-going merchant fleet, it is assumed that all the freight and insurance costs are paid to foreign firms.

CHINA'S OTHER FOREIGN EXCHANGE RECEIPTS

1. Overseas remittances

In the prewar years, remittances sent by overseas Chinese to support their families in China were an important source of foreign exchange for the country. From 1902-30, among the various sources of China's foreign exchange receipts, the importance of overseas remittances ranked below only the proceeds from merchandise exports (Remer, 1933, pp. 220-22). In 1937, the first year of the Sino-Japanese war, overseas remittances to China reached a level of US $132 million (Chang Kia-ngau, 1958, p. 384).

There are indications that after World War II these remittances declined considerably. The decline may be attributed to several reasons. First, the economies of Southeast Asia, where most of the overseas Chinese are concentrated, had suffered severe war damage. Chinese properties in these areas also suffered heavy devastation during the war period, greatly reducing the capacity of the overseas Chinese to remit their savings.

Second, after the war, many countries imposed controls on remittances to mainland China. For example, the United States placed a virtually total ban on all trade and financial transactions with China after the outbreak of the Korean War. As a result, remittances were blocked (*Sing-tao Jih-pao,* Feb. 5, 1951). After March, 1946, Malaya limited Chinese remittances to 45 Malayan dollars (about US $15) per month per family. In 1949 the government of the Philippines closed all Chinese remittance shops and limited remittances to China to US $50 per month per person. Similar restrictions were imposed in Thailand, Vietnam, Indonesia, Burma, Canada, and Cuba at about the same time.[56]

Third, immediately after coming to power, the Chinese Communist government began to take steps to control and to abolish the numerous private remittance shops that in the past had handled the major part of

55. For the values of China's imports from the free world countries, and from the Eastern European Communist countries and Cuba, see Table 9 (B) and Appendix A.

56. For a more detailed discussion of these restrictions, see *Shang-ch'ing hui-pao (Survey of Business Conditions),* Hong Kong, No. 31 (Nov. 2, 1950), pp. 2-3.

overseas Chinese remittances.[57] The Bank of China became the only legal channel for sending funds to the Mainland. This adversely affected remittances because many overseas Chinese were reluctant to transmit large payments through official Communist channels. Finally, the political turmoil, the collectivization measures in China, and fears of government levy or confiscation of the remitted funds further discouraged the flow of remittances. For all these reasons it is to be expected that overseas remittances during the Communist period would be lower than before the war.

According to the latest figures, the total number of overseas Chinese is about 16 million, with over 13 million concentrated in Southeast Asia (*China Yearbook,* 1964, p. 287). Most remittances by overseas Chinese either come from Hong Kong or pass through it, excepting some remittances from Singapore and Malaya. Our estimates are limited to the remittances from or through these two areas only. The results are presented in Table 15.

TABLE 15

OVERSEAS CHINESE REMITTANCES, 1950-1964
(in millions of U.S. dollars)

Year	Hong Kong	Singapore and Malaya	Total
1950	33.3	2.3	35.6
1951	36.0	5.0	41.0
1952	38.7	4.4	43.1
1953	31.8	4.1	35.9
1954	31.7	2.6	34.3
1955	29.0	2.7	31.7
1956	24.7	3.9	28.6
1957	18.9	2.7	21.6
1958	17.4	1.5	18.9
1959	13.3	2.1	15.4
1960	14.9	1.9	16.8
1961	(14.8)	(1.8)	(16.6)
1962	(22.4)	(2.7)	(25.1)
1963	(39.8)	(4.8)	(44.6)
1964	(39.8)	(4.8)	(44.6)
1950-64			453.8

Sources and Notes:
See Appendix D.

57. See, for example, "Provisional Measures for the Control of Overseas Remittance Shops in South China", in *Hsin-chung-kuo Kung-shang-yeh-chia Chi Tao-lu,* p. 260.

Given the uncertainties surrounding all these data for overseas Chinese remittances, we constructed an alternative estimate which is the one actually used in reconstructing the balance of payment totals as given in Table 17 (A and B). A number of sources would suggest that this higher average figure of US $70 per year may be more approximate. For instance, a responsible official of the Hong Kong and Shanghai Banking Corporation, Hong Kong, has indicated that for recent years the overseas Chinese remittances should be put at about US $70-$100 million a year.[58] Another official estimate made at Hong Kong gives a similar range of US $60-$100 million per annum.

2. Narcotics Traffic

In 1955, U.S. Federal Commissioner of Narcotics Harry J. Anslinger estimated that Communist China produced about 6,000 tons of opium annually, and that most of it was smuggled into the free world nations in the form of heroin (U.S. Senate, 1955, p. 3). There are numerous other reports on illicit export of opium or its products from Communist China (including one in *Pravda,* Sept. 13, 1964). However, due to the very character of this trade, all of the figures available concerning tonnage shipped and foreign exchange earned are necessarily subject to large margins of error. Therefore, this item in China's balance of payments could not be estimated.

3. Foreign exchange receipts from food parcels

About 80 per cent of Hong Kong's population of more than 3 million are immigrants from the Chinese Mainland (*Hong Kong Shih-pao,* Feb. 7, 1962). When Communist China's agricultural failure became known toward the end of 1958, the Chinese population in Hong Kong started to send food parcels to their relatives in China. The contents of these food parcels were almost entirely Chinese food products that had been exported to Hong Kong. Roughly one-half of them were sent to China as postal parcels; the others went through Hong Kong food shops with connections in China.

The foreign exchange proceeds collected by Communist China on these food parcels were twofold: first, taxes on the food parcels, usually paid by senders in Hong Kong when purchasing the food in the Chinese stores, in order to relieve the recipients in China of the tax burden. The tax rates ranged from 50 to 100 per cent of the value of the parcels.[59] Second, in early 1960, the Communist Chinese dealers in Hong Kong introduced a new method for collecting hard currency. In this system,

58. Based on an interview at the Bank on March 10, 1964.

59. In some cases the taxes were as high as 300 per cent of the value of the parcel. See *Shih-min Jih-pao, Macao,* Jan. 29, 1961 (p. 4); *Seattle Post-Intelligencer,* March 7, 1962 (p. 8).

often called "food remittance," instead of selling food in Hong Kong, these dealers simply took the orders and payments thereon in Hong Kong dollars. Food parcels were later made up in China and then delivered to the recipients there.

The Hong Kong dollars collected in taxes on food parcels, as well as the proceeds from "food remittances," were all surrendered to the Hong Kong branch of the Bank of China (*Hong Kong Shih-pao,* Dec. 27, 1960, p. 4). In our estimate, we assume that (1) the Chinese taxes on food parcels collected in Hong Kong are on the average 75 per cent of the total value of the food parcels sent to China; and (2) beginning in 1960, food remittances equaled roughly one-half of the value of all food parcels each year. In other words, the Chinese Communists realized approximately 125 per cent, in Hong Kong dollars, of the value of all food parcels sent from Hong Kong to China: 75 per cent of it in the form of taxes, and 50 per cent in the form of food remittances. (See Table 16.)

TABLE 16

COMMUNIST CHINA'S RECEIPTS FROM FOOD PARCELS, 1959-1964
(in millions of U.S. dollars)

	Taxes on food parcels	Food remittances	Total receipts
1959	1.6	—	1.6
1960	6.8	4.6	11.4
1961	24.5	16.4	40.9
1962	25.1	16.7	41.8
1963	16.4	11.0	27.4
1964	10.7	7.1	17.8

Sources and Notes:
See Appendix E.

4. Foreign expenditures in China

There is no information regarding the expenditures of foreign diplomatic missions and other delegations in China. It is arbitrarily assumed here that these foreign expenditures in China are one-half of China's expenditures abroad; that is, $5 million a year for the entire period. In addition, in the early 1950's, considerable sums were sent to the Mainland to finance foreign firms in China. These funds were used to pay fines, punitive taxes, and other overhead costs incurred by these firms, which in most cases were perforce no longer very active. For example, up to early 1953, British firms alone were sending approximately $3 million a year into China for such purposes (Carter, 1954). Foreign religious missions also sent some funds to China during these years. For lack of information, we assume that during 1950-52, roughly $5 million a year was sent into China to support foreign firms and religious organizations. Thus the total of foreign diplomatic, business, and religious expenditures in China is assumed to be $10 million a year for 1950-52, and $5 million a year for 1953-64.

A CONJECTURAL RECONSTRUCTION OF CHINA'S BALANCE OF PAYMENTS

The major items of China's balance of international payments, as discussed and estimated above, are summarized in Table 17 (A and B). It must be emphasized that for some of the items, the estimates are highly conjectural. Therefore the balance of payments presented here should be understood as merely a hypothetical reconstruction. Keeping this in mind, it may be seen that during this fifteen-year period, China had surpluses in its international accounts in the early 1950's and 1960's, and deficits in the late 1950's. The surpluses of the early 1950's were at least in part a function of Soviet credits, while the deficits appeared in the years when repayments of Soviet loans were started.

The cumulative surplus of $501 million for the whole period is rather deceptive as an indication of Peking's foreign exchange position. As shown earlier in Table 9 (A and B), approximately $934 million of China's trade surplus during this period was attributable to its favorable trade balance with the Asian Communist countries and Cuba. Since this part of the export surplus is largely explained by China's economic aid to these smaller Communist countries, it is not likely to yield foreign exchange proceeds for China. If this part of the favorable trade balance were deducted from China's total surplus in the balance of payments, then China would have, instead of a cumulative surplus, a deficit of about $433 million for the whole period. This deficit is roughly equal to the value of China's import of food grains in 1964.[60] It may well reflect the cumulative short-term trade credits since 1961 in China's purchases of food grain and other items from the West.

It is not possible to estimate China's foreign exchange reserves on the basis of available data. However, as of August, 1965, China had purchased 123 tons of gold (equivalent to $138 million) in London (*Hindustan Times,* Aug. 17, 1965). This would suggest that as of mid-1965 China's foreign exchange and/or gold reserves were at least $150-$200 million. They undoubtedly had been higher in earlier years, but were badly depleted between 1960 and 1962. Yet with the shift of Communist China's trade to the Western countries, and without substantial credit accommoda-

60. Since 1961, Communist China has been importing approximately 5 million tons a year of food grain from Australia, Canada, Argentina, France, and other Western countries, costing roughly $400-500 million a year, about 40 per cent of its total import bill. See Dick Wilson, "China's Trading Prospects," *FEER,* Aug. 20, 1964 (pp. 309-10). The value of China's import of food grain in 1964 was between $430-450 million (*Current Scene,* April 15, 1965, p. 4).

tions from the latter, China now needs to maintain a higher reserve of gold and convertible foreign exchange against contingencies than it did in the 1950's. The modest level of China's reserves drives home the hard fact that the improvement of China's balance of payments will primarily depend on the improvement of its domestic production.

The balance of payments estimates are presented in Table 17 (A) for each year and in Table 17(B) in a cumulative form for every five years and for the fifteen-year period as a whole. The aggregate figures are probably more acceptable than the annual ones, since small errors in the annual estimates may offset each other. It is believed that such major items as merchandise imports and exports, and the receipts and repayments of Soviet loans, presented in aggregate form, are not likely to be too far off the mark. The other minor items, on the other hand, are subject to greater margins of error. But since they are relatively small in size, even large differentials in these items are not likely to change substantially the overall picture of the balance of payments.

IV. CONCLUDING REMARKS

During the fifteen years from 1950 to 1964, a major part of China's foreign trade was with the Soviet Union. Trade between these two countries was based on an exchange of Chinese agricultural and mineral products and manufactured consumer goods for Soviet machinery, equipment, and industrial raw materials. Of particular importance were China's imports of complete factory equipment from the USSR, which, together with Soviet technical assistance, were largely responsible for the rapid growth of China's industries in the 1950's.

There is some evidence that in comparison with world market prices the terms of Sino-Soviet trade may have been unfavorable to China.[61] However, it may be argued that in Sino-Soviet trade the gains from trade should not be measured only by the terms of trade. For China, the availability of a ready market for its exports, the existence of a reliable (at least in the 1950's) supplier of the type of producer goods it needed, the availability of Soviet credit arrangements, and the convenience of conducting foreign trade between two planned economies may be considered more important than favorable prices.

When one looks at the whole array of barter ratios in Sino-Soviet trade, one cannot help but think that this type of resource reallocation

61. See Feng-hwa Mah, "The Terms of Sino-Soviet Trade," *China Quarterly,* Jan.-March, 1964 (pp. 174-91). In a letter to the CPSU, dated Feb. 19, 1964, the Central Committee of the Chinese Communist Party made it known that "[The prices of] the materials we imported from the USSR were much higher than the prices of the international markets." (*Ta-kung Pao,* Hong Kong), May 9, 1964, p. 3.)

TABLE 17

CONJECTURAL ESTIMATES OF COMMUNIST CHINA'S BALANCE OF PAYMENTS, 1950-1964
(in millions of U.S. dollars)

	1950	1951	1952	1953	1954	1955	1956	1957
(A) Annual Estimates								
1. China's payments, total	915	1,115	1,058	1,263	1,568	1,763	1,913	1,917
2. Merchandise imports, f.o.b.	854	1,035	989	1,188	1,301	1,307	1,446	1,407
3. Freight and insurance	46	55	43	48	53	55	70	82
4. Salary of Soviet experts	5	10	10	10	10	10	10	10
5. Expenditures of students in USSR	—	5	5	5	5	5	5	5
6. Chinese expenditures abroad	10	10	10	10	10	10	10	10
7. Repayment of Soviet debts	—	—	1	2	62	209	200	210
8. Foreign aid	—	—	—	—	127	167	172	193
9. China's receipts, total	883	1,277	1,574	1,351	1,647	2,204	1,820	1,740
10. Merchandise exports, f.o.b.	699	932	940	1,099	1,197	1,425	1,691	1,651
11. Foreign expenditures in China	10	10	10	5	5	5	5	5
12. Overseas remittances	70	70	70	70	70	70	70	70
13. Receipts from food parcels	—	—	—	—	—	—	—	—
14. Soviet credits	104	265	554	177	375	704	54	14
15. Balance, deficit (—)	–32	162	516	88	79	441	–93	–177

	1958	1959	1960	1961	1962	1963	1964
(A) Annual Estimates (continued)							
1. China's payments, total	2,336	2,520	2,352	1,732	1,429	1,613	1,985
2. Merchandise imports, f.o.b.	1,861	2,036	1,926	1,370	1,075	1,139	1,392
3. Freight and insurance	118	99	103	91	74	84	114
4. Salary of Soviet experts	10	10	5	—	—	—	—
5. Expenditures of students in USSR	5	5	5	5	5	5	5
6. Chinese expenditures abroad	10	10	10	10	10	10	10

7. Repayment of Soviet debts	215	211	197	150	159	269	358
8. Foreign aid	117	149	106	106	106	106	106
9. China's receipts, total	2,048	2,330	2,097	1,685	1,642	1,659	2,023
10. Merchandise exports, f.o.b.	1,973	2,253	2,011	1,523	1,525	1,557	1,930
11. Foreign expenditures in China	5	5	5	5	5	5	5
12. Overseas remittances	70	70	70	70	70	70	70
13. Receipts from food parcels	—	2	11	41	42	27	18
14. Soviet credits	—	—	—	46	—	—	—
15. Balance, deficit (—)	—288	—190	—255	—47	213	46	38

	1950-1954	1955-1959	1960-1964	1950-1964
(B) Five-Year Aggregates				
1. China's payments, total	5,919	10,449	9,111	25,480
2. Merchandise imports, f.o.b.	5,367	8,057	6,902	20,326
3. Freight and insurance	245	424	466	1,135
4. Salary of Soviet experts	45	50	5	100
5. Expenditures of students in USSR	20	25	25	70
6. Chinese expenditures abroad	50	50	50	150
7. Repayment of Soviet debts	65	1,045	1,133	2,244
8. Foreign aid	127	798	530	1,455
9. China's receipts, total	6,732	10,142	9,106	25,981
10. Merchandise exports, f.o.b.	4,867	8,993	8,546	22,406
11. Foreign expenditures in China	40	25	25	90
12. Overseas remittances	350	350	350	1,050
13. Receipts from food parcels	—	2	139	141
14. Soviet credits	1,475	772	46	2,294
15. Balance, deficit (—)	813	—307	—5	501

Note:
Details may not add to the total because of rounding.

Sources:
See text and Appendices.

through foreign trade is clearly to China's advantage as far as its industrialization program is concerned. These barter ratios, as published by the Chinese Communists, include such exchanges as these: one ton of frozen pork for five tons of steel products; 107 tons of shelled peanuts for a set of combine coal-mining machinery; 10,000 tons of cured tobacco for a seamless steel-pipe factory; etc. (Ministry of Foreign Trade, 1955, p. 150). For the Soviet Union, it seems that the gains from trade with China were to a large extent to be measured by the political sympathy and cooperation the USSR received from Peking in the 1950's, regardless of whether the Soviet Union realized any price advantages.

The recent shift of China's trade from the USSR to the West, and China's liquidation of all of its Soviet debts, have created some new problems for Peking. First, China must find other markets for the types of commodities that have been going to the Soviet Union. Secondly, as China's trade with non-Communist countries continues to grow, the task of foreign trade planning is bound to be more complicated. Peking will have to deal with numerous uncoordinated and competitive private businessmen scattered in many different countries. While this will widen Communist China's choices, it will also make the outcome of external transactions less predictable and, therefore, less susceptible to planning. As long as China still depends on the import of capital goods for its industrial development, this may affect the implementation of domestic economic plans.

Payment is also a problem in the expansion of trade between Communist China and the Western countries, for in the final analysis, it takes an outflow of goods and services to pay for an inflow. China's demand for Western commodities may be considerable; it has, for example, been shopping for complete-plant equipment in Western markets.[62] It is estimated that China still needs also to import between 1 and 3 million tons of oil a year, and the demand for food grain, chemical fertilizers, steel products, etc., is also strong (*FEER,* Aug. 20, 1964, p. 310). But with a shortage of foreign exchange and without outside economic aid, China's import capacity depends almost completely on its exports. Deferred payment arrangements do not represent basic solutions to this problem. As far as China's exports are concerned, they, in turn, depend partly on the recovery and expansion of domestic production, and partly on world demand for China's products. These set a limit on the size of the China trade.

The extent of China's trade with the West has not been large. In 1964 it was about $2 billion, roughly the same as Hong Kong's foreign trade in 1963. China's imports from the West are dominated by agricultural prod-

62. By mid-1964, ten complete plants worth over $100 million had been ordered from six Western countries. Orders for ten additional complete industrial plants have been under negotiation. See Alexandra Close, "Compromise for Balance," *FEER,* October 1, 1964 (p. 26). By September, 1965, fifteen contracts for complete factories had been placed by Peking with Western firms. See *China Trade and Economic Newsletter,* No. 119, Sept., 1965 (p. 1).

ucts and raw materials. In 1964, for example, of China's total imports of over $900 million from the West, approximately $450 million was in food grains. Other major import items are: raw cotton, $80-$100 million; chemical fertilizers, $60-$70 million; and crude rubber, $60-$70 million. The import of machinery and equipment from the West amounted to only about $125-150 million (*Current Scene,* April 15, 1965, p. 4). When this limited amount of trade is divided among a number of countries, each trading partner's share must be fairly small.

It is difficult to speculate on the future course of China's foreign trade. But indications are that Sino-Soviet trade may have reached its low point, and that present levels are likely to be maintained. With the gradual recovery and improvement of China's domestic economy, there is reason to believe that China's trade with the West (including Japan) will most certainly continue to increase. But the extent of future expansion would largely depend on, first, the degree to which China can solve the problem of population growth and the resultant increase in domestic consumption; and second, how much the country can widen the range of exportable goods to meet the varying demand of different foreign markets.

APPENDIX A

DERIVATION OF TABLE 4

The total trade values in Table 4 and the import and export values in subsequent tables were derived by this author based on methods outlined below.

(a) Communist China's trade with free world countries:
Based on U.S. Department of Commerce (USDC), *Value Series,* 1947-53, 1954-56, 1957-58, 1959, 1960, 1961, 1962, 1963, and 1964.

In the USDC data, "China" refers to Communist China including Manchuria, Inner Mongolia and Tibet. Minor exceptions occasionally exist in data for an individual country's trade with China. For example, known exceptions for 1964 data are the following: Data for Colombia's trade with China include Taiwan, while data for the China trade of Canada, Ceylon, Hong Kong, Indonesia, Norway, Pakistan, and Senegal include Outer Mongolia. (These minor irregularities differ slightly over the years in the USDC data.) The term "free world countries" covers all non-Communist countries that exported to or imported from Communist China merchandise valued at US $1 million or more in any one year of the period covered, and for which data are available. Yugoslavia is included as a "free world country" in the USDC data. (Sino-Yugoslavian trade was zero or negligible for the years 1950-55 and 1961-64, and very small—about $2 to $10 million a year—for 1956-60.) In this chapter Cuba is classified as a Communist country after January, 1959, when the Castro regime came to power. The USDC *Value Series* included Cuban exports to China in the totals of free world exports to Communist China for 1959-61. These amounts are excluded in our calculations of China's imports from the free world and included in China's trade with "other Communist countries" [Column (4), Table 4]. Cuba's imports from China for 1959-61 are not given in the USDC data, and so no adjustment was necessary in the USDC figures for imports. The USDC data are based on published and unpublished official trade returns of China's trading partners, converted into U.S. dollars at prevailing exchange rates. With a few exceptions, all of these countries value their imports c.i.f., and their exports f.o.b. In my derived series, the c.i.f. values are adjusted to an f.o.b. basis. For a discussion of this problem, see text.

(b) Communist China's trade with the USSR:

1950-1954: *Vneshniaia Torgovlia,* No. 10, 1959 (pp. 2 *ff*); 1955-1964: *Vneshniaia Torgovlia SSSR za 1956 god* and subsequent volumes up to the 1964 issue, published in 1965.

In the Soviet trade returns, both imports and exports are valued at exporting country's delivery price at the border, thus conceptually comparable to f.o.b. values, even though the inland transport costs in Russia and Mainland China must be very high per unit of traded commodity. All Soviet data reported before January 1, 1961, are converted into U.S. dollars at the rate of 4 old rubles to one dollar; those reported after that date are converted into U.S. dollars at the rate of $1.111 per new ruble.

(c) Communist China's trade with East European Communist countries:

Based primarily on China's trading partners' data as reproduced in *Three-monthly Economic Review,* No. 34, June 1961; No. 36, November 1961; No. 41, February 1963; *Quarterly Economic Review,* March, 1965; and *Foreign Trade of European Satellites,* 1963 and 1964. These are supplemented by scattered information from U.S. government sources and other Western publications, all of which, in turn, are based on trading partners' data.

For 1950 and 1951, information for individual countries is incomplete; total figures for these two years from a U.S. government source are used instead. For 1952-54, 1956 and 1964, a number of estimates for individual countries have been made by the author to fill the data gap. The estimates are all in the nature of interpolation or extrapolation. A more detailed documentation and explanation of estimating methods used will be given in the author's forthcoming full-length study of foreign trade of Mainland China.

The valuation systems of East European Communist countries' foreign trade statistics are all assumed to be similar to the Soviet system, that is, comparable to f.o.b. valuation. All figures reported in rubles are converted into dollars at the official exchange rates of 4 old rubles = \$1.00, and 1 new ruble = \$1.111.

(d) Communist China's trade with other Communist countries.

This includes China's trade with North Korea, Outer Mongolia, and North Vietnam for the entire period from 1950-64, and China's trade with Cuba for 1959-64.

Import and export figures for China's trade with the three Asian Communist countries for 1950-56 are estimates based on U.S. government data, obtained through the courtesy of Leon M. Herman of the Library of Congress. Data for China's trade with North Korea and North Vietnam for 1957-63 are taken from U.S. Senate, 1965 (p. 67, Table 2). The 1964 trade value between China and North Korea and North Vietnam is assumed to be the same as in 1963. Values of China's trade with Outer Mongolia for 1957-60 are from *Narodnoye Khozyaystno Mongal' skay Narodnoy Respubliki Za 40 let,* 1961 (by courtesy of Leon M. Herman). For lack of information, values of Sino-Mongolian trade for 1961-64 are assumed to be the same as for 1960.

Communist China's trade with Cuba, 1959-64, can be tabulated as shown in Table A-1.

TABLE A-1

CHINA-CUBA TRADE, 1959-1964

Year	China's export	China's import	Total
1959	—	—	—
1960	12.0	32.0	44.0
1961	75.0	95.6	170.6
1962	(87.6)	87.6	(175.2)
1963	93.3	72.7	166.0
1964	106.3	81.4	187.7

Note: "—" indicates zero or less than one half million dollars.

Sources:

China's exports: 1959-1961: U.S. State Dept., 1962 (p. 37, Table 3). (Estimates). 1962: assume the exports and imports are roughly balanced. 1963-64: *China Trade Report,* May, 1965 (p. 2); Nov., 1965 (p. 2).

China's imports: USDC *Value Series.*

APPENDIX B

DERIVATION OF TABLE 10

For convenience in explaining the steps taken in the derivation of this table, we start with the "hard" statistics in Column (4).
Column (4).

Column (4): Total loans and interest obligations.

The 1950-1952 subtotal, the 1953-1957 subtotal, and the eight-year total are official figures taken from Li Hsien-nien's 1957 Budget Report (Li Hsien-nien, 1957).

The allocation of total loans by year for 1950-52 is based on Ecklund's estimate (1960, p. 3).

The 1956 and 1957 data represent the sum of Soviet credits as given by Li Hsien-nien (117 million *yuan* for 1956, and 23 million *yuan* for 1957) and the estimated interest obligations for these two years (*i.e.,* Col. (4) = Col. (1) + Col. (2) for 1956 and 1957). The figures for 1954 and 1955 are derived from Chinese budget data. The 1953 figure is a residual (3,120 less the 1954-1957 total). For details of the allocation of total loans by year for 1953-57, see Mah, 1959, pp. 76-78.

Column (1): Estimate of annual economic loans.

All the figures in this column are converted from dollar values into *yuan* values at the official exchange rate of 2.355 *yuan* per dollar. The 1953 and 1954 figures are the last two scheduled installments of the 1950 loan, derived on the assumption that there is no discrepancy between the planned and actual loan deliveries in these two years. The 1955 figure is based on the indication given by the 1957 Budget Report that the second (1954) economic loan was used up in one year, *i.e.,* in 1955. The 1956 and 1957 economic loan receipts are given as such in the 1957 Budget Report. It is stated in the report that they are balances carried over from loans provided for in "previous agreements."

The 1957 Budget Report also reveals that credit totals originally scheduled in the comprehensive financial plan were 724 million *yuan* for the First Five-Year Plan period (1953-57). The economic loan totals for 1953-57 as estimated in this column add up to 727 million *yuan*—very close to the 724 million *yuan* originally scheduled for the five-year period. These findings led me to the tentative conclusion that the 1956 and 1957 loan figures given by Li Hsien-nien are most likely to be the unused balance of the 1950-1952 portion of the first (1950) Soviet loan. In view of the established fact that large quantities of Soviet military equipment and supplies were delivered to Communist China during the

Korean War period (see Schwartz, 1954, p. 617), one might surmise that these must have slowed down economic aid shipments as originally scheduled in the 1950 agreements. For these reasons it is assumed that the portion of the 1950 Soviet loan actually used during 1950-52 was 707 million *yuan* (US $300 million) less (1) the scheduled installments for 1953 and 1954 (141 million *yuan,* or US $60 million, for each year); and (2) the loan receipts for 1956 (117 million *yuan*) and 1957 (23 million *yuan*). Thus, the total Soviet credit extensions for 1950-1952 are estimated to be 707 — (141 + 141 + 117 + 23) = 285 million *yuan.* For lack of data it is arbitrarily assumed that this 285 million *yuan* was evenly drawn on during 1950, 1951, and 1952.

Column (2): Estimate of interest on Soviet economic loans.

APPENDIX C

ADDITIONAL NOTES TO TABLE 14

1. China's total foreign aid outpayments for 1954-60 can be derived from Chinese budget data as follows (in millions):

	Planned (yuan)	Realized (yuan)	Realized (dollar)[a]	Realized as per cent of planned (%)
1954	........[b]	300	127.4	....
1955	....	393	166.9	....
1956	440	404	171.5	91.9
1957	508	454	192.8	89.4
1958	414	275	116.8	66.4
1959	600	350	148.6	58.3
1960	500	....	....	....

Notes:

a. Converted from *yuan* values at the official exchange rate of 2.355 *yuan* = $1.

b. .... indicates "not available."

Sources:

1954: *JMJP,* Nov. 21, 1954. North Korea was the only recipient.

1955-56, 1957, 1958, 1959-60: Li Hsien-nien, 1957, 1958, 1959, 1960 (respectively).

2. China's realized total foreign aid, 1960-1964.

The actual amounts of Peking's annual foreign aid outpayments during 1960-64 are not known. However, it is believed that Communist China's capacity to extend foreign aid during these five years must have been more limited than in the late 1950's because of the economic disaster caused by the Great Leap Forward, the withdrawal of Soviet experts in

ESTIMATE OF INTEREST OBLIGATIONS ON SOVIET ECONOMIC LOANS

(in million yuan)

	1950	1951	1952	1953	1954	1955	1956	1957
1. Net economic loan outstanding at end of current year	94	188	282	424	508	756	768	686
2. Repyament of principal	—	—	—	—	57	57	105	105
3. Interest obligations	0.47	1.41	2.35	3.53	4.66	9.48	11.43	10.91

Line 1. Loan outstanding at the end of previous year + current year's loan receipt − current year's repayment of principal = Line 1 figures. The figure for 1950 is current year's receipt only.

Line 2. According to the 1950 loan agreement, the first repayment was to begin in 1954. Each year an equal installment of one-tenth of the total loan was to be repaid before December 31. According to our interpretation, by the end of 1954 only 80 per cent of the 1950 loan had been drawn, and the remaining 20 per cent was used in 1956 and 1957. Therefore we assume that in 1954 and 1955, only one tenth of the actually used portion (*i.e.*, 565/10 = 57 million *yuan*) was repaid. It is also assumed that since 1956 the repayment each year would have been

(total loan − 1954 and 1955 repayment) ÷ 8 = annual repayment amount

or

(705 − 114) ÷ 8 = 74 million *yuan*

so that the total amount of the loan could still have been repaid by the end of 1963, as originally scheduled. The second (1954) economic loan was entirely used up in 1955 (see text). It is assumed here that its repayment was also to be made in 10 equal annual installments of 31 million *yuan* from 1956 to 1965.

Line 3. It is assumed that the interest rate for the period 1950-54 was 1 per cent per annum (as specified in the 1950 loan agreement), and that after 1955 the rate was 1.5 per cent, assuming the 1954 loan carried a slightly higher interest rate.

The items subject to the payment of interest are: (1) the debt outstanding up to December 31 of the previous year, less one-half of the current year's repayment of principal; and (2) one-half the current year's loan receipt.

The computation formula is:

Interest obligation = [(debt outstanding Dec. 31, previous year) + ½ (current year's loan receipt) − ½ (current year's repayment)] × i,

where i is the appropriate interest rate.

Column (3): Other loans including interest

This is the residual, derived from Col. (4) minus [Col. (1) plus Col. (2)].

July, 1960, and the stepped-up repayment of Soviet debts and interest during these years.

As revealed by the above budget data, Communist China's realized foreign aid was 91.9 per cent of the planned amount in 1956, but this percentage decreased every year after that. In 1959 the actual aid was only 58.3 per cent of the planned figure. Taking into consideration the declining trend of this percentage, and based on the reasoning given above, it is assumed that in 1960 only 50 per cent of the planned foreign aid of 500 million *yuan* was realized. This gives us an estimated amount of 250 *yuan,* or about $106.2 million at the official exchange rate, as China's realized total outpayment of foreign aid in 1960. For lack of a better basis in making estimates, this amount for 1960 is also assumed for the years 1961-64 without modification.

3. China's total aid to Communist countries, 1954-64.

Nan Han-chen, Communist China's chief delegate to the 1965 Afro-Asian Economic Seminar held in Algiers, reported that up to the end of 1964, China had spent over 3,124 million *yuan* as economic aid to the Communist countries, (*Ta-kung Pao,* Hong Kong, Feb. 25, 1965). This is equivalent to $1,326.5 million at the official rate of 2.355 *yuan* to the dollar.

APPENDIX D

DERIVATION OF TABLE 15

As pointed out in the text, the bulk of remittances by overseas Chinese either originates in Hong Kong or goes through it. There are some remittances from Singapore and Malaya which do not pass through Hong Kong. Our estimate is limited to the remittances from or through these two areas only.

Hong Kong, 1950-60. Huang Ting-wen, 1961 (in an official publication [*Chiao-wu yueh-pao (CWYP)*] of the Overseas Chinese Affairs Commission, Taipei). Responsible persons of the Commission indicate that these figures were adopted from the Communist Bank of China source in Hong Kong.

Hong Kong, 1961-63. This is the author's estimate based on a comparison of the above *CWYP* series with another series of overseas remittances obtained from interviews with an informed person in Hong Kong in 1964. The interview series covers the period 1950-63. For 1950-60, the two series show remarkably similar trends, but the interview series is substantially lower than the *CWYP* series (and figures from other fragmentary information), particularly for the early 1950's. The two series become closest in 1959, when the *CWYP* series is 30 per cent higher than the interview series.The 1961 to 1963 figures are estimated by adding 30 per cent each to the interview figures for these three years.

Hong Kong, 1964. There are indications that overseas remittances increased in early 1964 as compared with the same period in 1963. (See *South China Morning Post,* Jan. 31, 1964, p. 1.) However, since the general economic situation in China in 1964 was reported to be improved, the need for family remittances may not have been greater than in 1963. Thus the 1964 remittances are assumed to be the same as in 1963.

Singapore and Malaya, 1950-60. Adopted from Tsai Hsuan, 1962; the data are based on official annual reports of the Federation of Malaya government. These figures were converted into U.S. dollars by the author at the exchange rate published by the International Monetary Fund—US $1 = M$ 3.06. The 1951 remittance figure in Tsai's article is not correct, possibly a typographical error. I have changed it to M$ 15.04 million (US $ 4.96 million), taken from *Kung shang Kwan cha,* June 6, 1955 (p. 26), which was also based on official Malaya government reports.

Singapore and Malaya, 1961-64. (Rough estimates.) The Singapore and Malaya remittances during 1950-60 were about 7-16 per cent of Hong Kong remittances in corresponding years, averaging 12 per cent of the Hong Kong figure. For lack of information we arbitrarily assume that the Singapore and Malaya remittances were 12 per cent of the Hong Kong levels between 1961 and 1964.

APPENDIX E

DERIVATION OF TABLE 16
CHINA'S FOREIGN EXCHANGE RECEIPTS FROM FOOD PARCELS DERIVED AS FOLLOWS (in millions of U.S. dollars):

	(1) Postal food parcels (number)	(2) Value of postal food parcels	(3) Value of all food parcels	(4) Tax on all food parcels	(5) Food remittances	(6) Total receipts from food parcels
1959	870,000	1.07	2.14	1.61	—	1.61
1960	3,700,000	4.55	9.10	6.83	4.55	11.38

1961	13,302,500	16.36	32.72	24.54	16.36	40.90
1962	13,600,000	16.73	33.46	25.10	16.73	41.83
1963	8,936,500	10.99	21.98	16.41	10.99	27.40
1964	5,800,000	7.13	14.26	10.70	7.13	17.83

Notes:

Column (1). 1959 and 1960: *Kung sheung Daily News,* Hong Kong, Jan. 1, 1962 (p. 6). 1961: *Hong Kong shih pao,* Feb. 7, 1962 (p. 7). 1962: *Central Daily News,* Taipei, Mar. 1, 1963 (p. 2). 1963, Jan-Nov. figures: *Sing-tao wan pao,* Hong Kong, Dec. 10, 1963 (p. 15). 1963, Dec. figure: *South China Morning Post,* Hong Kong, Jan. 31, 1964 (p. 1). 1964: estimate based on first quarter data.

Column (2). The average value of postal food parcels was HK$ 7 (*Hong Kong shih pao,* Feb. 7, 1962, p. 7). At the official rate of US$ 1 = HK$ 5.71, this would be equivalent to US$ 1.23 per parcel. Thus the figures in Column (2) were derived by multiplying the numbers in Column (1) by this amount.

Column (3). Values of nonpostal food parcels are assumed to be the same as postal food parcels. This is a very conservative assumption.

Column (4). 75 per cent of Column (3).

Column (5). 1960-1964: assumed to be 50 per cent of Column (3). There were no food remittances in 1959.

Column (6). Column (4) plus Column (5).

REFERENCES

Bulletin. Institute for the Study of the USSR, Munich.

BYSTROV, F., 1960. "The Organization of International Settlements Among the Socialist Countries," *Voprosy Ekonomiki,* No. 2. (Translated in *Problems of Economics,* June 1960.)

CARTER, WILLIAM, 1954. "You Can't Do Business with Red China," *Saturday Evening Post,* Dec. 25, 1954, p. 78.

Central Daily News (International edition). Taipei.

CHANG HUA-TUNG, 1955. "The Soviet Assistance to Our Industrialization as Viewed from Import Work," *JMJP,* April 30, 1955.

CHANG KIA-NGAU, 1958. *The Inflationary Spiral.* New York.

CHAO, KANG, 1964. "Pitfalls in the Use of China's Foreign Trade Statistics," *The China Quarterly* (London), July-Sept. 1964, pp. 55–57.

CHAO, KANG, and FENG-HWA MAH, 1964. "A Study of the Ruble-Yuan Exchange Rate," *The China Quarterly* (London), Jan.-Mar. 1964, pp. 192–204.

CHEN CHIEH, 1956. "The Contents and Method of Compilation of Material Balance Report Tables," *TCKTTH,* April 14, 1956, pp. 11–14.

CHEN CHIH-SHIH and LIU PO-WU, 1958. *Textbook of Foreign Trade Statistics.* Peking: Finance and Economics Publishing House. (in Chinese)

CHEN, THEODORE H. E. "Government Encouragement and Control of International Education in Communist China" (typed copy), to be published in a forthcoming issue of *Peabody Journal of Education.*

CHEN TI-PAO, 1963. "Supervision and Control of Imports and Exports by the Chinese Customs Administration," *Foreign Trade of the People's Republic of China* (English ed.). June, 1963.

CHCC. Chi-hua chin-chi (*Planned Economy*). Monthly, Peking.

CHYTC. Chi-hua yu tung-chi (*Planning and Statistics*). Peking.

CSYK. Chien-she yueh-kan (Construction Monthly). Peking.

China Trade and Economic Newsletter. London.

China Trade Report. Hong Kong.

China Yearbook 1963-1964. Taipei, 1964.

CHOU EN-LAI, 1959. "Ten Glorious Years," *JMJP,* Oct. 6, 1959.

CHOU EN-LAI, 1964. "Report on the Work of the Government," *Ta-kung pao,* Dec. 31, 1964, p. 1.

Chung-kuo ching-nien pao (Chinese Youth Daily). Peking.

Chung-kuo hsin-wen (China News). Canton.

Communiqué on Negotiations Between China and the Soviet Union and Other Documents, 1954. Supplement to *People's China,* No. 21, Nov. 1, 1954. Peking.

Communiqué on the Results Of the First Five-Year Plan, 1959. Peking: Statistical Publishing House. (in Chinese)

Collected Documents of the External Relations of the People's Republic of China, 1957, 1958. Vol. I (1949-1950), Peking, 1957; Vol. III (1954-1955), Peking, 1958.

Collection of Treaties of the People's Republic of China, 1957. 2 vols. (in Chinese), Peking.

CB. Current Background. Hong Kong.

Current Scene. Hong Kong.

DERNBERGER, ROBERT F., 1959. "International Trade of Communist China," in C. F. Remer (ed.), *Three Essays on the International Economics of Communist China*. Ann Arbor.

Eastern World. Monthly, London.

ECKLUND, GEORGE, 1960. *Foreign and Domestic Debt in Communist China*. Washington, D.C.

ECKSTEIN, ALEXANDER, 1964. "Sino-Soviet Economic Relations: A Re-appraisal," in C. D. Cowan (ed.), *The Economic Development of China and Japan*. London.

ECMM. Extracts from China Mainland Magazines. Hong Kong.

FEER. Far Eastern Economic Review. Hong Kong.

First Five-Year Plan for the Development of the National Economy in 1953-1957 (Chinese edition). Peking, 1955.

Foreign Currencies Handbook (Ko-kuo ho-pi shou-tse), 1963. Revised edition, Peking.

Foreign Trade of the European Satellites 1963 (CIA/RR ER64-46), Dec. 1964. Washington, D.C.

Foreign Trade of the European Satellites in 1964 (CIA/RR ER65-37), Dec. 1956. Washington, D.C.

Foreign Trade of the People's Republic of China (Chinese edition). Quarterly, Peking.

Foreign Trade of the People's Republic of China (English edition). Quarterly, Peking.

GALENSON, WALTER, 1961. "Economic Relations Between the Soviet Union and Communist China," in Nicholas Spulber (ed.), *Study of the Soviet Economy*. Bloomington, Indiana.

The Hindustan Times. New Delhi.

HOFFMAN, MICHAEL L., 1957. "Problems of East-West Trade," *International Conciliation,* No. 511, Jan. 1957.

1958 Hong Kong Economic Yearbook. Hong Kong, 1958.

Hong Kong shih-pao. Hong Kong.

Hong Kong Tiger Standard. Hong Kong.

Hsin-chung-kuo Kung-shang-yeh-chia Chi Tao-lu (The Path of the Industrialists and Businessmen of New China). Hong Kong, 1950.

HHPYK. Hsinhua pan-yueh-kan (New China Semi-Monthly). Peking.

HUANG TING-WEN, 1961. "An Analysis of the Real Situation of Overseas Chinese Remittances to Communist China," *Chiao-wu yueh-pao (Overseas Chinese Affairs Monthly)* Taipei, No. 107, July 16, 1961, pp. 7–8.

Hung-chi (Red Flag). Peking.

HUGHES, T. J. and D. E. LUARD, 1961. *The Economic Development of Communist China,* 2nd ed. London.

JMJP. Jen-min jih-pao (People's Daily). Peking, various dates.

1960 Jen-min shou-tse (People's Handbook, 1960). Peking.

KLATT, WERNER, 1965. (Ed.) *The Chinese Model.* Hong Kong.

KLOCHKO, MIKHAIL A., 1964. *Soviet Scientist in Red China.* New York.

KUAN TA-TUNG, 1960. *The Socialist Transformation of Capitalist Industry and Commerce in China.* Peking.

Kwang-ming jih-pao (Kwang-ming Daily). Peking.

Kung sheung Daily News. Hong Kong.

Kun-shang kwan-cha. Hong Kong.

KUO CHUNG-YEN, 1956. *The Export Trade of New China's Industrial Products.* Shanghai.

Kwangtung Traveller's Handbook, 1958 (in Chinese). Hong Kong, August, 1958.

LI, CHOH-MING, 1959. *Economic Development of Communist China.* Berkeley and Los Angeles.

LI FU-CHUN, 1955. "Report on the First Five-Year Plan for Development of the National Economy," in FFYP, Chinese edition.

LI HSIEN-NIEN, 1955. "Report on 1954 Final Accounts and 1955 State Budget," *JMJP,* July 10, 1955.

LI HSIEN-NIEN, 1956. "Report on 1955 Final Accounts and 1956 State Budget," *JMJP,* June 16, 1956.

LI HSIEN-NIEN, 1957. "Report on 1956 Final Accounts and 1957 Draft State Budget," *Ta-kung pao,* June 30, 1957.

LI HSIEN-NIEN, 1958. "Report on 1957 Final Accounts and 1958 State Budget," *Tsai Cheng,* No. 2 (Feb. 5, 1958), p. 9.

LI HSIEN-NIEN, 1959. "Report on 1958 Final Accounts and 1959 State Budget," *Tsai Cheng,* No. 9 (May 9, 1959), p. 8.

LI HSIEN-NIEN, 1960. "Report on 1959 Final Accounts and 1960 State Budget," *Tsai Cheng,* No. 7 (April 9, 1960), pp. 2, 6.

LI PEI-FONG, 1958. "Positively Strengthen the Organization of Export Supply," *CHCC,* Feb. 9, 1958, p. 28.

LIU, TA-CHUNG and KUNG-CHIA YEH, 1965. *The Economy of the Chinese Mainland: National Income and Economic Development 1933-1959.* Princeton.

MAH, FENG-HWA, 1959. "The First Five-Year Plan and Its International Aspects," in C. F. Remer (ed.), *Three Essays on the International Economics of Communist China.* Ann Arbor.

MAH, FENG-HWA, 1963. *Communist China's Foreign Trade: Price Structure and Behavior 1955-1959* (RAND RM-3825-RC), Oct. 1963. Santa Monica, Calif.

Mainichi Shimbun (*Daily News*). Tokyo.

MAKLAKOV, A., 1958. "From the History of Socialist Planning in the Economy of the Chinese People's Republic," *Voprosy Ekonomiki,* October, 1958. (Translated in *Problems of Economics,* Feb. 1959, p. 82.)

MAO TSE-TUNG, 1950. *On the People's Democratic Dictatorship* (1950 ed.). Shanghai: Hsin Hua Book Store.

Ministry of Foreign Trade, 1955. *Collected Essays on Foreign Trade.* Peking. (in Chinese)

MIYASHITA, TADAO, 1961. *China's Foreign Trade Machinery.* Tokyo: Institute of Asian Economic Affairs. (in Japanese)

Narodnoye Khozyaystno Mongal'skay Narodnoy Respubliki za 40 let, 1961. Ulan Bator.

NCNA. *New China News Agency.*

The New York Times, Western edition.

NOVE, ALEC, and DESMOND DONNELLY, 1960. *Trade with Communist Countries.* London.

Peking Review. Weekly, Peking.

Peking Review, Sept. 9, 1958. "China's Foreign Trade Organizations," pp. 13–14.

Pravda. Moscow

Problems of Economics (English translations). New York.

Quarterly Economic Review: China, Hong Kong, North Korea. London.

REMER, C. F., 1933. *Foreign Investment in China.* New York.

REMER, C. F., 1961. *The Trade Agreements of Communist China* (RAND P-2208), Feb., 1961. Santa Monica, Calif.

SCHWARTZ, HARRY, 1954. *Russia's Soviet Economy,* 2nd ed. Englewood Cliffs, N.J.

Seattle Post-Intelligencer. Seattle, Wash.

Shang-ch'ing hui-pao (*Survey of Business Conditions*). Hong Kong.

Shih-tai pi-ping (*Modern Critique*). Semi-monthly, Hong Kong.

Shih-min jih-pao, Macao.

Sing tao jih-pao. Hong Kong.

Sing tao wan pao. Hong Kong.

SLADKOVSKIY, M. I., 1959. "Soviet-Chinese Economic Collaboration," in Soong Ching-lin and others, *Ten Years of People's Republic of China* (a collection of articles). Moscow, 1959. (Translated into English by U.S. Joint Publications Research Service [JPRS] Translation no. 2825, Aug. 1960.)

SOONG CHING-LIN, 1955. "A New Type and Higher Type of Relationship," *JMJP,* Feb. 14, 1955.

South China Morning Post. Hong Kong.

SPULBER, NICHOLAS, 1962. *The Soviet Economy.* New York.

State Statistical Bureau, 1954. *Communique on the Results of 1953 National Economic Plan* in *Current Background* No. 292, Sept. 15, 1954, p. 8).

State Statistical Bureau, 1960. *Ten Great Years.* Peking.

SCMP. Survey of China Mainland Press. Hong Kong.

Ta-kung pao (*Impartial Daily*). Peking, Tientsin, Hong Kong.

Ta-lu fei-ching chi-pao (*Chinese Communist Affairs Quarterly*). Taipei.

Three-Monthly Economic Review: China, Hong Kong, North Korea. London.

Tsai Cheng (*Public Finance*). Monthly (changed to semi-monthly in 1958), Peking.

TCKT. Tung-chi kung-tso (*Statistical Work*). Peking.

TCKTTH. Tung-chi kung-tso tung-hsin (*Statistical Work Bulletin*). Peking.

USDC Value Series. U.S. Department of Commerce, *Exports to and Imports from Sino-Soviet Bloc Countries by Free World Countries, Value Series.* Washington, D.C.

USDC (U.S. Department of Commerce). *Summary Tables Showing Exports to and Imports from Soviet Bloc Countries by Free World Countries.* Washington, D.C.

U.S. Department of State, 1962. *The Sino-Soviet Economic Offensive Through June 30, 1962* (Research Memorandum RSB-145), Sept. 18, 1962. Washington, D.C.

U.S. Department of State, 1964. *The Communist Economic Offensive Through 1963* (Research Memorandum RSB-43), June 18, 1964. Washington, D.C.

U.S. Senate, 1955. *Communist China and Illicit Narcotics Traffic,* hearings before the Subcommittee to the Committee of Judiciary, 84th Congress, First Session. Washington, D.C.

U.S. Senate, 1965. Committee on Foreign Relations, *A Background Study on East-West Trade.* Washington, D.C.

Vneshniaia Torgovlia (*Foreign Trade*). Monthly, Moscow.

Vneshniaia Torgovlia SSSR za 1956 god, Moscow 1958; same for 1957, Moscow, 1958; for 1958, Moscow, 1959; for 1959, Moscow, 1960; for 1960, Moscow, 1961; for 1961, Moscow, 1962; for 1962, Moscow, 1963; for 1963, Moscow, 1964; for 1964, Moscow, 1965.

WEN LIANG, 1959. "China's Foreign Trade: Its Growth and Some Basic Principles," *Peking Review,* Sept. 22, 1959, p. 13.

WILSON, DICK, 1964. "Interview with Chen Ming," *FEER,* May 14, 1964.

WU, YUAN-LI, 1956. *An Economic Survey of Communist China.* New York.

WU, YUAN-LI, *et al.,* 1963. *The Economic Potential of Communist China.* Menlo Park, Calif.

WU, Y. L., 1958. "Mainland China's Trade with Other Asian Countries: Its Nature and Design." A paper presented to the 1958 annual meeting of the Association for Asian Studies, New York (mimeo).

YANG CHIEN-PEI, 1956. *China's Achievement in Rehabilitation and Development of the National Economy.* Peking. (in Chinese)

YANG YING-CHIEH, 1957. "The Great Assistance," *CSYK,* No. 11 (Nov. 3, 1957), p. 3.

YEH CHI-CHUANG, 1955. "Speech at the Second Session of the First National People's Congress," *JMJP,* July 30, 1955.

YEH CHI-CHUANG, 1956. "Improve Our Export Work to Assure Industrial Construction," speech delivered at Eighth Congress of the Chinese Communist Party, in *JMJP*, Sept. 28, 1956.

YEH CHI-CHUANG, 1957. "Report on China's Foreign Trade," speech delivered to National People's Congress on July 11, in *HHPYK*, No. 16, p. 93.

YEH CHI-CHUANG, 1959. "Ten Years of China's Foreign Trade," *China News* (Chunk-kuo Hsin-wen) release, Canton, Sept. 2, 1959.

ZOLOEV, V., 1959. "USSR Foreign Trade Indicators," *Vestnik Statistiki* (*Journal of Statistics*), No. 10. (Translated in *Problems of Economics*, Feb. 1960, pp. 46–50.)

Index

Index

Administration Committees, 561, 562
Afforestation projects, 381, 430, 521
Africa, 673, 677, 712
Aggregate product, trends in, 7-12
Agrarian Reform Law, 224
Agriculture, 5-13, 27, 34, 39, 45-46, 64, 70, 75, 95, 98, 147, 159-160, 166, 202-203, 290, 339, 379, 380, 383, 400, 529, 628, 672, 687
  capital in, 427, 450
  centralization, 22, 403, 448-450
  collectivization, 6, 21-23, 397-440, 445, 448, 450, 468, 495-496, 523, 717
    in USSR, 467, 479-380, 627; *see also* Collectives
  decentralization, 434, 439, 446, 452
  double cropping, 21, 23, 37, 399, 405-418, 419-420, 422-423, 425, 427, 432, 435-436, 448
  and industry, 19-21, 154-155, 167, 460-466, 503-504, 551, 555-557, 581-584, 599, 602
    in USSR, 462, 477
  inputs, 17, 21, 24, 459, 462, 477, 480, 482-485, 487-488, 491-492, 494, 497, 504-505, 522, 529, 532-533, 599, 605
  investment in, 16-17, 41, 57, 287, 441, 479, 492, 493, 504, 521-526, 530-531, 541, 598, 615
  labor force; *see* Labor force, agricultural
  land use, 37-38, 78, 93, 427
  mechanization, 22, 399; in USSR, 480
  organization, 21, 445-448
  output, 19-21, 24, 37, 48, 79, 88-89, 92, 99-101, 105, 108, 114, 149, 153, 194, 292, 382, 459, 462, 464, 468, 470, 473-474, 477, 479, 484-485, 487-489, 491-504, 527, 532-533, 535, 543, 555, 581-584, 598-599, 630, 632, 680
    in USSR, 463, 471, 476, 487
  policy, 22, 459-505
  population, 20, 78, 81, 178, 340-347, 375, 467
  private enterprise, 404, 426, 431-432, 434, 437-440, 449, 451, 495, 496
  productivity of, 35, 44, 49, 76, 485, 487-492, 503-504
  products, 3, 37-40, 56, 58, 61-62, 71-73, 78-79, 89, 92-93, 100, 108, 111-114, 116-118, 152-158, 161, 168, 177, 179, 422, 425-426, 466, 490, 498-501, 517, 533, 535-537, 558, 601, 605, 611, 622, 688, 705, 721, 724-725; *see also* Cotton; Grain; Rice; Soybeans; Tea, *and* Wheat
  raw materials, for industry, 104, 154-156, 158, 167, 176, 461, 530, 555, 582, 583, 601, 615
  share in gross domestic product, 532, 535
  share in gross national product, 76, 80, 100
  share in total product, 102, 125-128, 153
  taxes, 230, 330, 340, 341, 402, 495
  in USSR, 368, 399, 460, 462-463, 465-480, 487, 495-496
  wages, 23, 401, 403-404, 430, 443
  yields, 35, 43, 487, 499-501
AIRD, JOHN S., on population, 12-14, 16, 89-92, 183-327, 330-336, 338-339, 344, 370
Allen, G. C., 34, 57, 61
Anhwei Province, 213, 216, 232, 238, 250-251, 372-373, 409-411, 422-423
Animals, draft, 23, 399-400, 402, 405-406, 409, 413-418, 420-422, 424, 432-434, 436, 439, 442, 448, 452, 480, 523, 539, 541
Anslinger, Harry J., 718
Antung, 219

Argentina, 130
trade with, 689-690
Armaments industry, 555, 598, 608
Armies; *see* Defense
Australia, 130, 286
trade with, 674, 689-691
Austria, 123
Autarky, 27-28, 597-600, 608-609, 615, 630

Balance of payments, 155, 671, 675, 693-721, 722
Banks, 3-4, 6, 34, 57-58, 60, 354, 356, 365, 551, 565, 567, 618, 626, 695; *see also* People's Bank of China
Barclay, George W., 269
Beal, E. G., 48
Belgium, 135, 137
Bergson, Abram, on USSR, 120, 128, 130, 132, 460, 478, 516
Birth cohorts, 261-262, 268, 281, 285, 306, 310
Birth control; *see* Fertility control
Blast furnaces, backyard, 354, 381, 443-444, 497, 571
Bogue, D. J., 348
Boxer Rebellion, 59
Brackett, James, 194
British Guiana, 370
Buck, J. Lossing, on agriculture, 15, 35, 42, 44, 75, 78, 79, 82, 89, 377-378, 389, 480, 494,
on birth and death rates, 334, 336-339, 341-343
Budgets, state, 551, 564, 606, 620, 700, 706, 731
Building; *see* Construction
Building materials, 3, 560, 581, 614, 645-646, 659-660, 664-665, 667; *see also* Cement *and* Steel
Bulgaria, 524-525
Bureau of the Census, 194
Burma, 123, 525, 716
Bystrov, F., 677

Cadres, 22-24, 28, 53, 143, 166, 190, 199, 202-204, 207, 210, 221, 223-229, 234, 236-237, 239-241, 244, 382-383, 388, 399-401, 404-405, 413, 418-419, 421, 424-425, 427-431, 433, 435, 438, 440, 445-448, 450-451, 490, 497, 512-513, 565, 567-568, 570, 581, 616, 625-628, 630-631
Canada, 130, 135, 286
trade with, 674, 689-691, 716, 725
Canton, 46, 47, 205, 219, 222, 226-227, 236, 240, 557
Capacity utilization, 26, 155-160
Capital, 7, 26, 31, 119, 136, 170, 194, 290, 379, 380, 427, 450, 510, 512, 515, 517, 529-531, 557, 560, 567, 614, 619-621, 623, 626, 628, 654, 656-657, 659
accumulation, 41
fixed, 132, 135, 576, 619
formation, 16-19, 89, 141, 145-146, 148, 175, 377, 382, 490, 496-497, 504, (Ch. 8) 508-547
proportions, 128-132, 143
goods, 20-21, 29, 64, 98, 462, 469-470, 478, 512, 519, 724
shortages, 52-53, 167
stock, 135, 171, 172, 359, 543-544, 654, 655, 657
Capital-intensive projects, 15, 26, 377, 520, 522, 528
Capital-labor ratio, 637, 657-659
Capital-output ratios, 10, 18, 26, 119, 132, 136, 143-144, 156, 170-171, 382, 511, 612
Communist data on, 133-35
Carter, William, 719
Carters, 361, 388-389
Cement, 3, 19, 63-64, 66, 76-77, 176, 517, 534, 574, 611, 613, 645, 661-663, 668
Censuses, 89, 93-94, 339
of 1910, 186
of 1929-1933, 281
of 1942-1947, 281, 282
of 1953, 12-13, 90-92, 188-189, 191, 198-276, 311, 333, 335, 337, 370
accuracy checks, 239-242
error in, 242-244
fieldwork, 188-192, 195, 198-210, 217, 222-225, 227, 229, 234-236, 238-239, 231-242, 244
household records, 218-222, 226, 228, 230, 235-238, 240, 247
land data, 226
registration, 188, 191, 199-200, 205-207, 209, 218-230, 237-238, 240-241, 247, 260, 268, 275, 278-282, 284, 330, 332, 337
See also Population
Central Committee of Chinese Communist Party, 166, 202-203, 235, 286, 436, 444, 568, 582, 628, 679
Central Handicraft Administration Bureau, 384
Central People's Government Council, 203

Central-South Military-Administrative Committee, 226
Centralization, 28, 145
  in agriculture, 22, 403, 448-450
  in industry, 28, 561-563, 567
Ceylon, 81, 370, 525
  trade with, 689-690, 725
Chandrasekhar, S., 333-334, 383
Chang, C. C., 35, 341, 375
Chang, John, on industrial growth, 1, 64, 65
Chang Chi-hung, 348
Chang Chih-tung, 52
Ch'ang Ch'ing, 428
Chang Ch'uan-shu, 627
Chang Fo-chien, 352, 381
Chang Hua-tung, 673
Chang Kai-fan, 372
Chang Kia-ngau, 58, 716
Changchun, 558, 573
Changhsintien, 574
Chankiang, 426
CHAO, KANG, on domestic product, 534, 537
  on growth rate, 6
  on industry, 24-26, 77, 80, 549-595
  on investment, 16-18
  on national product, 11
  on problems of development, 28-29
Chao Chien, 419
Chao Tzu-yang, 399, 446
Chapman, Janet G., 478
Chekiang Province, 49, 171, 213, 216, 233, 237, 251, 409, 410-412, 414-416, 419, 422-423
Chemicals, 119, 176
  imports, 72
  processing of, 581, 603, 645-646, 650-651, 659-660, 664-665, 667
Chen, D. T., 260, 281-283, 338
Chen, T. H. E., 715
Chen Chang-heng, 257
Ch'en Chih-ho, 339, 347, 350, 352
Chen Chih-shih, 696
Ch'en Hsi-ya, 627
Ch'en Hui-li, 601
Ch'en Ko-chien, 401
Ch'en Man-yuan, 425
Chen Ta, 278, 333-335, 337-338
Ch'en Yun, 605-606
Chenery, H. B., 602
Cheng, Y. K., on foreign trade, 47, 54-56, 69-70, 72-73
Cheng Hsing-yen, 426
Chi Ch'eng, 339
Chi Chung-wei, 556, 573
Chi Nong, 419
Chi Shih-hsun, 428
Chiang-su Province, 1
Ch'iao, C. M., 260, 281-283, 338
Ch'iao Pei-kuo, 436-437
Chile, 372
Chili Province, 251
China Committee for the Promotion of International Trade, 675
China Merchants' Steam Navigation Company, 51, 53
China News Summary, 355
Chinese Eastern Railway, 61
Chinese Maritime Customs, 512
Ch'ing dynasty, 37, 184-187, 191, 198-199, 211-213, 246-255, 258-260, 271
Chou dynasty, 33
Chou En-lai, 166, 231, 235, 334, 335, 379, 401, 556, 582-584, 587, 699, 701-702, 706, 714
Chu Chung-chien, 542, 543
Chu Ching, 542, 543
Chu Jung-chi, 601, 615
Chungking, 219, 221, 242
Circular flow economy, 38, 41
Civil disturbances, 3-5, 43, 59, 60, 74, 91, 256, 261, 265, 266, 285, 561; *see also* Rebellions
Clark, Grover, 62
Clark, P. G., 602
Coal, 2, 3, 19, 56, 60-61, 63, 68, 71-73, 77, 156, 177, 181, 381, 517, 534, 536, 538, 556, 581, 589, 605, 608, 611, 613, 629, 645, 650, 659-665, 667, 668
  consumption by industry, 655-657
  mining, 51, 66, 386
Cole, W. A., 80
Collectives, 23-24, 397-443, 447-452, 465, 495-496
  economic organization, 405-440
  incentives and payments, 400, 403-404, 425-432, 434, 443, 464, 505
  income in, 403, 426, 431, 450-451
  job evaluation in, 426, 428, 451
  production brigades; *see* Work brigades
  production costs, 403
  in USSR, 467, 475, 479-480
  work points, 403-404, 426, 428, 429, 431, 446, 451
  See also Agriculture
Commerce; *see* Trade
Commodities, 119, 581, 601, 602, 604-605, 615, 622, 630-631, 639-640, 642, 645, 677, 685, 693, 695, 726
  exports, 675-676, 679, 694, 705, 712, 724

Commodities (*cont'd*)
imports, 680, 690
shortages, 69
Common Market, 554
"Common Program," 549
Communal services, 136, 138, 140-142, 144, 146-147
Communes, 286, 352, 354, 381, 383, 397, 398, 440-448, 450-451, 497, 505, 551, 555, 571, 605, 627, 638
Communications, 51, 54, 60, 67, 79, 82, 93-95, 102, 104, 106, 116, 156, 171, 177, 354, 364, 527
barriers, 1, 36, 49, 70, 89
investment in, 521, 523-525, 541
share in gross domestic product, 532, 535
share in national product, 76
Compradors, 4, 57
Conservation; *see* Water conservation
Construction, 18, 67, 89, 95, 102, 116, 156, 166-167, 170, 171, 354, 361, 364, 366, 368, 380-381, 429, 442, 493-494, 534-535, 549-551, 555, 558-560, 563, 567, 570, 583, 584-587, 589, 603, 615, 623, 673, 678-679, 688
employment in, 93-94, 104, 106, 339-340
investment in, 18, 513, 518-519, 521, 528, 538, 539, 551, 564-565, 576, 577, 582, 627
military, 512, 514, 524, 540
residential, 520, 524, 526, 540
share in domestic product, 532
share in national product, 76
Consumer goods, 2, 20-21, 27, 60, 81, 99, 119-120, 155, 290, 461, 469, 470, 472-473, 478-479, 532, 581, 597, 599, 607-609, 622, 630, 643-644, 651, 685, 690, 721
exports, 674
investment in, 514, 518, 598
output, 111, 113-114, 471, 605-606
rationing, 139
share in domestic product, 533-534
Consumption, 40, 98, 113, 119, 143, 146, 159, 176-178, 515, 531, 558, 602, 609, 712
capital, 509, 511-512
Communist data on, 138-142, 147-148, 173-174
by factories, 156, 158
of food products, 9, 20, 92, 108, 112, 114, 116-117, 140-142, 153, 464, 465-466, 479, 485
in USSR, 478
government, 141, 157, 175, 515
household, 138, 172-174
per capita, 10, 142, 144-145, 161
private, 109
Cooperatives, 230, 352-353, 538
agricultural, 93, 378-379, 384-386, 388-389, 397, 399-403, 418, 429, 433, 445, 493-494, 515
credit, 391, 515
handicraft, 101, 106, 360, 384, 638
industrial, 561-562
investment in, 543
Cotton, 11, 40, 92, 100, 156, 158, 177-179, 418, 490, 517, 534-537, 557, 584, 601
raw, 629
exports, 73-74
imports, 38, 46-47, 55-56, 72
textiles, 21, 58, 176, 589, 622, 661-662, 668
exports, 73
imports, 38, 46-47, 55-56, 72
yarn, 66, 68, 71, 74, 77, 176, 558, 611, 622, 629, 661-663, 668
exports, 73
imports, 56, 58, 71-72, 74
Council of Mutual Economic Assistance, 554
Cuba, trade with, 689, 691, 716, 725-727
Cultural organizations, 95, 107, 524, 541
Customs, 672, 675, 696
Czechoslovakia, 525, 677

Deane, Phyllis, 80
Decentralization, 27-28, 561-570, 574-575, 605-606, 621-625, 628, 631
Defense, 5, 49, 51-52, 58, 95, 103, 105, 107, 140, 198, 231, 255, 264, 341, 348, 352, 360-361, 443, 493, 515, 555, 558, 598, 600, 608, 615, 628, 630, 672
expenditures, 48, 59
investment in, 531
share in domestic product, 535
Denmark, 125, 135
Depression, 5, 7
Dernberger, Robert F., 687
Directorate General of Budgets, 266
Diseases, 152, 287-288, 291, 334; *see also* Epidemics
Disinvestment, 559, 566
Domar, Evsey D., 461
Domestic product, 10-11, 16-19, 96, 98, 100, 102-103, 106, 114-116, 119, 121, 155-167, 172, 177, 375, 377, 509-511, 515, 526-527, 532-538
Donnithorne, A. G., 34, 57, 61

Dore, R. P., on literacy, 42
Droughts, 79, 114, 152, 162, 265
Durand, John D., 243, 246-248, 252, 254, 255, 257, 258

East Germany, 525
Easton, W. W., 368
Ecklund, George, 706, 728
ECKSTEIN, ALEXANDER, 1-32, 33-85
on economic development, 459, 475
on employment, 105-107, 109
on farm prices, 100
on national product, 8, 76, 96-97, 99-108
Economic development, 3-7, 10, 35-39, 252, 289, 291, 293, 312, 375
Stalinist model, 459-460, 462-463, 467, 475, 478-480, 497, 503, 597, 599, 600, 609, 615
Economic heritage, 1-5, (Ch. 2) 33-85
Economic institutions, 5-6, 36, 67
Education, 43, 95, 443, 515, 624-625
employment in, 365-366
investment in, 524-541
rural, 494
Eggs and egg products, export of, 55, 73
Egypt, 372
"Eight Point Charter," 497
Elections, 90, 199, 202-204, 207-209, 224
Electric power, consumption by industry, 517, 528, 536, 560, 571-572, 581, 584-585, 589, 602, 608, 637-638, 645-646, 655-657, 659-660, 667
generation, 2, 57, 60, 63-64, 66, 76-77, 154, 155, 521, 611, 613, 622, 645, 650-651, 659, 661-665, 667-668, 697
Embargoes, 31, 687, 689
Emerson, John Philip, on Communist statistical system, 89, 94, 99, 104
on employment, 109-110, 126, 350, 353, 357-360, 362, 364-365, 367, 374, 380-381, 384-385, 387-391
on farm prices, 100
on population, 343
Emery, R. F., on food crops output, 152, 180
Employment, 13-16, 66-67, 93-95, 99-101, 104-107, 109-110, 119, 121-123, 126, 132, 143-144, 168-169, 177, 350, 353, 357-365, 367, 374-375, 377, 380-381, 384-385, 386-391
Communist data on, 122, 126
See also Labor force
England; *see* Great Britain
Entrepreneurship, 4, 41, 53
Epidemics, 82, 249, 264, 334
Europe, 552-553
trade with, 54, 684, 686, 692, 716
Expenditures, 99, 143, 148, 175, 564
Communist data on, 136, 139, 141, 146, 147
domestic, 98, 138, 147, 173, 174, 178
government, 136, 138-140, 145-147
Exports, 3, 11, 21, 30-31, 38, 45-47, 54-56, 58, 68-74, 117, 153, 156-157, 159, 163-164, 167, 467, 511, 530, 672-677, 679-681, 683-685, 689-694, 697, 708, 711, 715-716, 720-724, 726-727; *see also names of specific products*

Factories, 4, 24-25, 28, 89, 101-102, 106, 113, 116, 118-120, 156, 158-159, 161, 171, 176-177, 375, 386, 497, 505, 511, 571, 575-576, 578, 579, 592, 608, 612, 624-628, 642-643
investment in, 541, 543
See also Industry
Factors, 36, 95, 98, 101, 514
Fairbank, J. K., 38, 45, 50
Famines, 79, 82, 152, 186, 249, 256-257, 260, 263, 265-266, 287-288, 292, 296-297, 487
Fan Jo-i, 643, 644
Fang Chung, 589, 599
Farms and farmers, 21, 24, 35, 44, 49, 62, 70, 75, 78-79, 100-101, 166, 341, 377-378, 384, 494-495; *see also* Agriculture *and* Peasants
Fel'dman, G. A., 461, 478
Feng Wen-lan, 235
Fertility control, 284, 289, 290-291, 293-296, 312, 315, 383
Fertilizers, 108, 166, 377, 388, 405, 406, 408-410, 413, 421, 422, 437-438, 448, 452
chemical, 17, 21, 24, 43, 287, 430, 451, 481, 488, 497, 504, 522, 529, 556-557, 583, 584, 585, 588, 599, 724, 725
organic, 23, 419, 424, 426, 428, 431, 434, 435, 439, 451, 481
Feudalism, 33, 49
Feuerwerker, A., on industrialization, 51, 53, 58
FIELD, ROBERT, on labor, 6, 17, 26, 637-670
Finance, 1, 3, 27, 67, 103, 114, 116, 156, 157, 391

Finance (*cont'd*)
employment in, 105, 107, 365
share in domestic product, 532, 535
Financial and Economic Commission, 549, 620, 626
Finland, 259
First Five-Year Plan, 2, 6, 8, 10, 15, 20, 26, 28, 29, 32, 80, 94, 125, 130, 132, 145, 277, 284, 310, 313, 314, 353, 372-374, 401, 459, 466, 477, 480, 504, 518, 520, 523, 524, 526, 531, 539, 549, 550-552, 555, 558, 559, 562, 563, 570, 571, 573, 578, 579, 589, 590, 609, 610, 613, 627, 637, 638, 655, 660, 662, 672, 678, 679, 696, 728
Fishing, 354, 356, 380, 381, 387, 412, 536
"Five-anti" campaign against private enterprise, 99, 198, 220, 230, 685
Five-Year Plan; *see* First Five-Year Plan; Second Five-Year Plan, etc.
Floods, 79, 108, 114, 152, 265
control of, 7, 17, 40, 167, 497, 521, 523
Foochow, 51, 222
Food, 6, 11, 13, 43, 61, 81, 92, 117, 178, 289-291, 293, 295, 674
consumption; *see* Consumption, of food products
distribution, 285, 287, 292
parcels, taxes on, 718-719, 722, 723, 732
processing, 3, 21, 66, 167, 645, 646, 650-651, 659, 664-665, 667
shortages, 91, 152, 188, 257, 286-288, 292
See also Agriculture, output; and Agriculture, products
Food and drink industry, 364, 366, 371, 389, 390, 391; *see also* Restaurants
Foreign aid, 450, 712-713, 722, 723, 729, 731
Foreign enterprise, 34-35, 45, 57, 60, 66, 557
Foreign exchange, 54, 674-676, 677, 680, 681, 690, 693-697, 705, 712, 716-721
Foreign trade, 2-5, 27, 38-39, 45, 53, 55-58, 59-61, 69-74, 165, 462, (Ch. 12) 671-738
balance, 47, 69, 676-677, 680, 691-692, 699, 708, 722
costs, 673, 687
credit accounts, 694-695, 701-702, 706
deficits, 30-31, 54, 676, 690, 720
with East Europe, 684, 686, 692, 716
embargoes, 31, 687, 689
"fair price policy," 677
income effects, 46-48
market prices, 677-678, 681, 682-683, 687, 705
organization of, 674-676
payment agreements, 676-677
policy objectives, 29-30, 671-674
surpluses, 30-31, 54, 676, 720
"swing limits," 30, 677
with USSR, 29, 153, 590, 676-678, 683-690, 692, 696, 697-712, 721, 725-729, 731
volume, 681-685
with West, 683-684, 686, 693
Forestry, 105, 231, 380-381, 523
Formosa, 256
France, 125, 133, 135-137, 259
trade with, 689, 690
Fuel, 51, 72, 178, 556, 558, 560, 602, 603, 613, 644, 678; *see also* Petroleum
Fukien Province, 213, 240, 249, 419
Furs, import of, 47

GALENSON, WALTER, 1-32
Gentry, 39, 40
Gold, 38, 54, 677, 705, 712, 720, 721
Government, 6, 30, 38, 45, 51-52, 59, 70-71, 76, 141, 156, 157, 159, 161, 627
administration, 95, 103, 107, 177, 532, 535, 541
control of industry, 563, 618
expenditure, 48, 136, 138-140, 145-147
revenues, 48, 622; *see also* Taxes
services, 48, 75, 105, 107, 116
subsidies, 514, 621-622
See also Central Committee of Chinese Communist Party *and* Peking
Government Administrative Council, 226, 231
Grain, 20, 23, 30, 40, 78, 116, 117, 152, 153-154, 227, 279, 286, 292, 408, 418, 419, 421, 426-429, 432, 435, 437-439, 443-445, 448, 450, 451, 466-467, 473, 476, 477, 480, 490, 498-500, 505, 517, 535, 622, 680
imports, 674, 676, 679, 720, 724-725
Great Britain, 45, 54, 80, 135, 137
trade with, 689, 690, 720
Great Leap Forward, 6-11, 13-16, 19, 21, 25, 32, 80, 94, 144, 148, 149, 152, 153, 165, 167, 168, 179-181, 188, 196, 286, 354, 374, 376, 379, 380-383, 397, 440-445,

Great Leap Forward (*cont'd*)
447, 449, 450, 477, 488, 497, 505, 513, 527, 530, 551, 555, 557, 565, 574, 579, 591, 605, 612, 614, 616, 625, 627, 628-629, 631, 638, 662, 685, 709, 729
Greece, 122
Greenberg, Michael, 45
Griliches, Z., 494
Gross national product, 1, 7, 18, 42, 44, 67, 79-80, 96, 100, 110-111, 116, 155

Handicrafts, 4-5, 38, 40, 46, 55, 58, 67-69, 74, 89, 99, 101-102, 104, 106, 110, 113, 114-116, 118-119, 157, 171, 177-178, 354-356, 360, 384, 386, 532, 534, 576, 605, 638, 705
investment in, 512, 541, 543
output, 104, 578, 592
share in national product, 76
Handicraft workers, 15, 93, 94, 100-101, 104, 384, 386, 514, 576
Hangchow, 60, 219, 222
Harbin, 219, 236, 558
Harbor development, 61, 62
Harvests, 7, 23, 24, 30, 297, 422, 444, 445, 485, 487, 488, 502
Health, 82, 168, 194, 277, 285, 287-289, 291, 293-294
employment in, 365, 366
investment in, 541
See also Medical care
Heilungkiang Province, 240, 436
Heng-yang, 222
Hides, 38, 55, 56, 71, 73
Hinterland, 4-5, 36, 61, 68, 263, 288, 528
Ho, Ping-ti, 37, 40, 41, 49, 61, 62, 246, 247, 253, 254-258, 263, 266, 336
Ho, Yhi-min, 487, 494
Ho Cheng, 615
Hodgman, D. R., 466, 470, 471
Hoeber, F. P., 116
Hoeffding, Oleg, 466
Hollister, William W., 8, 88, 96, 108-110, 120, 149-151
Holzman, F., 622
Honan Province, 209, 213, 224, 409, 415, 416, 417
Hong Kong, 11, 161, 287, 717, 718, 719, 724, 731
trade with, 674, 676, 689-691, 725, 732
Hong Kong and Shanghai Banking Corporation, 34, 57, 718
Hopei (Hopeh) Province, 205, 213, 249, 378, 415, 416-417, 428, 436, 437
Hou Chi-ming, 68
on employment, 14-16, 46, 329-396
Housing, 3, 98, 171, 178
Howard, H. P., 246
Hsiangs (townships), 380, 409, 412, 427, 428, 442, 449
Hsiao Chi, 281, 282
Kan-pu-pao, 420
population of, 224-229, 240, 242
Hsiao Yü, 436
Hsieh Mu-ch'iao, 353
Hsiens (counties), 93, 380, 424, 427, 441, 442, 448
Chang, 337
Cheng Kung, 337, 338
Ch'iung-chou, 336
Fa, 420
Fatshan, 426
Hsiao Chi, 338
Kiangyin, 281
Kükong, 432
Lokchong, 420
Mencheong, 421
Ning-shan-t'ing, 336
Noho, 436
population of, 185, 189, 204, 210, 217, 219, 226, 240, 241, 242, 248, 258, 259, 266, 278
Suikai, 425
Wuan, 428
Wusiang, 425
Yanfa, 421
Hsing Yu-hung, 372
Hsu Ch'ien, 655
Hsu Hsin-hsueh, 357
Hsu Kang, 334, 372
Hsu Li-ch'un, 379
Hsüeh Mu-ch'iao, 94, 601
Hu Huan-yung, 333
Huang Hsiu-chuan, 388
Huang Meng-fan, 339, 379
Huang Ting-wen, 731
Hunan Province, 171, 213, 251, 409-411, 414-416, 421-423
"Hundred Flowers" period, 440, 627
Hung, F. C., 592
Hung Liang-chi, 257
Hungary, 525
Hupeh (Hupei) University, 655
Hupei Province, 213, 229, 232, 233
Hwang Nan-sen, 401
Hyperinflation, 1, 5

Imperial Telegraph Administration, 51
Imperialism, 40, 59, 61

Imports, 3, 11, 21, 29-31, 38, 46-47, 54-56, 58, 64-65, 69-74, 152, 156-157, 159, 511, 517, 520, 530, 598, 672-677, 681, 683, 685, 687, 689-694, 720-721, 723, 724-727
distribution of, 675
freight and insurance charges, 684, 715-716, 722
surplus, 697, 711
targets, 679-680
See also names of specific products
Income, 23-24, 35, 46, 68, 78, 81, 92-94, 99, 291, 340, 602; *see also* National income *and* Peasants, income of
India, 33, 37, 54, 58, 128, 336, 483, 525
trade with, 45-46
Indian life-tables, 269, 282
Indonesia, 370
trade with, 689, 716, 725
Industrial ministries, 384, 538, 564, 566, 626, 629, 643
Industrial planning and management, (Ch. 10) 597-635; *see also* Industry
Industrialization, 5, 25, 34, 46, 50, 52, 69-70, 74, 120, 125, 140, 145, 167, 168, 452, 461, 463-466, 472, 496-497, 503-505, 515, 524, 570, 598, 672, 679, 705, 724
in USSR, 477-478, 554, 589
Industry, 1, 52, 60-61, 65, 81, 88, 92, 95, 105-106, 154, 156, 161, 166-168, 355, 368, 375, 377, 379-380, 382, 386, 399, 468, 472, 473, 597-668, 672
administration and management, 28, 551, 561-570, 617-621, 623, 625-626, 629-630, 654
assets, 654-655, 657, 659-660, 666-667
capacity, 59, 590, 600, 631, 638
capital in, 614, 620-621, 623, 626, 654-657, 659
centralization, 28, 561-563, 567
costs, 27, 619-620, 626, 629, 644
development, 1, 6-7, 19-21, 62-70, 71
equipment, 571, 587, 589-590, 600, 602, 628
financial controls, 619, 621, 627
financial targets, 597, 619-620, 623, 625-626
growth, 6, 27, 68, 80-81, 383, 470, 475, 477, 505, 581, 590
incentives, 599, 602, 609, 618, 622, 632
inputs, 600-601, 608, 619, 654, 657; allocation of, 27, 602, 605, 607, 612, 618, 621, 625, 628, 629, 631
investment in, 16-17, 27, 462, 468, 521-522, 524-526, 528, 530-531, 538, 541, 544-556, 559-560, 562-567, 570-571, 573, 576-579, 582-584, 587-589, 599-601, 608-616, 619-621, 627, 630-632, 662
labor force, 66-67, 80, 94, 100-101, 106, 553-554, 557, 560, 571, 575, 583, 599-600, 606-607, 614, 639
labor productivity, 600, (Ch. 11) 637-670
capacity per worker, 661-662, 668
output per worker, 78, 637, 639, 642, 645, 654, 657, 658-663
location, 28, 550, 557-561
"mass line" movement, 569
material balances, 601, 604-608, 621, 625, 676; in USSR, 603
"multifarious operation," 29, 573, 575
output, 1-3, 5-6, 8, 17, 19, 24-27, 64-66, 75-77, 99, 101, 111, 155, 286, 450, 527-528, 531, 537, 549, 551, 556, 561, 563-564, 567, 574-592, 598, 602, 604, 608-609, 618-621, 624, 637-638, 640, 642, 644-651, 655, 657-659, 688
Communist data on, 11, 89-90, 118-119, 148, 170
quality of, 628-629
targets, 597, 600-601, 606-607, 610-612, 617, 623, 625, 630, 678
planning, 27, 597-616, 624, 627
policy, 27, 549-576
prices, 615, 621-622, 628, 642, 644, 654-655
private enterprise, 6, 15, 93, 549, 561-562, 641, 643, 646
productivity, 24-26, 77, 609, 644-663
profits, 27, 575, 608, 619-620, 622, 624, 626
targets, 27, 607, 619, 623, 629, 631
raw material consumption, 600-601, 605-606, 618, 629
resources, 553, 556-557, 571, 574-575, 618
responsibility system, 27, 568, 617
sales, 618-620
share in gross domestic product, 102, 527, 535
share in national product, 75-76, 99
specialization, 29, 573-575
structure, 2-3, 35-36, 119, 123-128, 143-145, 147
subsidies, 621-622
taxes, 606, 617, 619, 622
technical personnel, 571-572, 574
technology, 29, 570-575, 605, 608-610
trade unions, 569

Industry (*cont'd*)
  wages, 606, 619-620, 626, 645
  See also Agriculture, and industry
Infanticide, 245, 265-266, 268-270, 282-283, 337-338
Inflation, 74, 615, 627
Inner Mongolia, 231-232, 558, 725
Insurance, 3, 365
International Statistical Institute, 278
Inventories, 16, 18, 57, 114, 155, 166, 170, 518
  changes in, 512-513, 519, 526
  investment in, 99, 130
Investment, 4, 19, 45, 52, 113, 139, 145, 147, 155, 174-175, 377, 450-451, 464, 542-543
  allocation of, 521-525
  capital, 10, 538-539, 567
  Communist data on, 16-18, 129-130, 512
  criteria, 27, 614
  domestic, 11, 98, 157, 159, 161-167, 172, 510
  goods industries, 7, 514
  government fixed, 6, 18, 130, 509, 512-513, 520, 525, 538, 540-541, 600
  policy, 529-530
  rate of, 509-518, 532
  share in domestic product, 129
  share in total expenditure, 136, 140, 144
  share in total product, 119, 128, 131-132
  strategy, 10, 17
  structure, 518-520
  See also Agriculture, investment in; Handicrafts, investment in; *and* Industry, investment in
Iron, 26, 51, 64, 66, 76, 381, 558, 574, 622
  ore, 19, 60, 63, 68, 156, 159, 177, 181, 534, 556
  pig iron, 63, 68, 77, 176, 628, 642, 645, 660-663, 668
Irrigation, 7, 17, 40, 108, 167, 354, 380, 402, 406, 409, 413, 415, 419, 452, 490, 494, 497, 521, 523, 530, 543
Ishikawa, S., 625
Israel, 121-123, 143
Italy, 123, 125, 130, 135

Jamaica, 122-123, 143, 370
Japan, 3-4, 10, 33-34, 37, 41-45, 49-50, 54-55, 59, 69, 122-123, 125, 130, 133, 135-137, 140, 143-144, 290, 333, 336, 340, 483, 487, 494, 624, 672-674
  occupation by, 1, 59, 62, 64, 66, 76, 89, 269
  trade with, 673, 689-690, 725
  See also Sino-Japanese war
Jasny, Naum, 467, 475
JMJP (*Jen-ming jih-pao*); *see People's Daily*
Jones, F. C., 61, 62
Jones, P. P., 149, 152
Junks, 60, 355-356, 387

Kaifeng, 209
Kan Min-chung, 401
Kansu Province, 203, 213, 215, 225, 233
Kao Chen-teh, 614
Kao Kang, 550
Kao Kuang-chien, 599
Kaplan, N., 520
Kerosene, import of, 55-56, 58, 72
Kiangnan, 51
Kiangsi Province, 213, 237-238, 378, 409-411, 422-423
Kiangsu Province, 171, 213, 216, 237, 240, 281, 409-411, 415-416, 422-423, 436
Kirin Province, 222, 237, 240, 436
Klochko, Mikhail A., 714
Korean War, 6, 136, 263, 265, 518, 550, 560, 605, 610, 614, 702-705, 716, 729
Krotevich, S. K., 210, 217, 233
Kuan Ta-tung, 706
Kuo Chung-yen, 673
Kuomintang, 268
Kuznets, Simon, on growth rates, 122-123, 125, 128, 130-137, 141, 519-520
  on USSR, 87, 120-121, 126, 139-140
Kwangsi Province, 213, 251, 410-411, 422-423, 425
Kwangtung Province, 205-206, 212-213, 219, 226-229, 240-241, 398, 406-411, 413-414, 416-417, 419, 420-422, 424-426, 429-430, 432, 435-436, 440, 449-447
Kweichow Province, 213

Labor camps; *see* Prisons
Labor force, 10, 16, 41, 119, 124, 127, 135, 144, 148, 166, 329-396, 530-531, 554
  age distribution, 339-340
  agricultural, 15, 21, 24, 78-80, 126, 169, 225, 227, 300, 339-341, 343,

Labor force (*cont'd*)
345-346, 353-354, 377-381, 384, 386-389, 400, 403, 405-406, 409-413, 418-419, 421-422, 424, 426-428, 430, 432-433, 436-437, 441-443, 446, 448-449, 451, 464, 479-481, 490-491, 494, 497, 504
civilian males, 347-350, 376, 380-381
educational level, 353
females, 371, 373, 381, 384, 391
growth, 122-123, 361
industrial (nonagricultural), 14-16, 25-26, 36, 51, 53, 66-67, 80, 105-110, 115-116, 126, 157, 159, 167, 169, 339-340, 342-344, 350-377, 384, 386, 391, 553-554, 557, 560, 571, 575, 583, 599-600, 606-607, 614
mass campaigns, 285, 295, 354
mobilization, 7, 152, 479, 496
policy, 375-383
productivity, 21, 26, 43, 78, 80, 125, 128, 146-147, 359, 377, 464, 600, 637-668
shortages, 1, 378-379, 381, 383
skill, 156, 167, 353, 380
surplus, 167, 267, 378
utilization, 21, 375-383
"workers" and "employees," 350, 352-354, 356, 358, 360, 364-365, 384-386, 389-391
Labor-capital ratios, 14
Labor-intensive projects, 380, 528, 531
Lanchow, 225, 558
Land, 2, 40
consolidation, 494
fragmentation, 78, 494
inputs in, 21, 480-481, 484, 488
investment in, 41, 57, 492, 504
productivity, 38, 43
reclamation, 7, 493, 497, 523
redistribution, 6, 21, 494
reform, 22, 188, 191, 198, 217-218, 220, 223-230, 232, 234-235, 239, 268, 330, 397, 399-400, 404
resources, 41, 49
use, 37-38, 78, 93, 427, 493, 498-501
Land Reform Committee, 227
Landholding, 21, 40, 78, 224-225, 228, 230, 494
Landlords, 224-225, 228-230, 263, 352
Li, Choh-ming, 344, 484-485, 487, 513
on Communist statistical system, 89, 93
on foreign trade, 48, 88
on growth rate, 8
on national income, 120
on national product, 96-97, 110-111
Li Cheng-jui, 340-341
Li Fu-chun, 357, 372, 520, 550, 552-553, 575, 585, 610, 614, 672
Li Hsien-nien, 535, 564, 698-702, 704, 728
Li Hsü-tan, 235
Li Hsueh-feng, 625
Li Hung-chang, 50, 52
Li Pei-fong, 680
Li Shu-teh, 340, 342
Li Yuan-chen, 378-379
Liao Lu-yen (Minister of Agriculture), 418, 444, 530
Liaohsi Province, 242
Liaoning Province, 415, 436, 629
Liaotung Province, 237
Liberman proposals, 607
Lieu, D. K., 58, 511
Life expectancy, 294-297, 306
Life-tables, collected, 194
Indian, 269, 282
model, 193-194
United Nations, 268-270, 282, 313-316, 336
Lin Tse-hsü, 50
Literacy, 43-44
Liu, T. C., 1-32, 86-182
on agricultural output, 8
on domestic product and investment, 10, 18
on growth rate, 6
on input, 485
on investment, 16, 18-19
on national product, 7
on population, 336
See also Liu, T. C., and Yeh, K. C.
Liu, T. C., and Yeh, K. C., 42, 101, 123, 137, 169-181, 480, 484-485, 489, 544, 672
on agricultural output, 88-89, 117-118, 487, 493, 502, 543
on capital-output ratios, 133-135
on consumption, 138-142, 145-146, 515
on domestic product, 96-97, 102-104, 111-116, 129, 160, 532-535, 537-538
on employment, 14-15, 66-67, 105-107, 109-110, 122-123, 143, 353, 359-363, 365, 367, 374-375, 377, 384, 386-391
on expenditures, 136, 140, 147
on factory production, 24-25, 580-581, 592
on farm prices, 100, 542
on growth rate, 9-10, 136, 144
on handicrafts, 118
on industry, 93, 119, 125, 608

Liu, T. C., and Yeh, K. C. (*cont'd*)
  on investment, 18, 131
  on labor force, 126
  on national income, 78, 120, 150-151
  on national product, 8-9, 11, 75-76
  on population, 122, 340-341
  on total product, 121, 124, 128, 130, 132, 148-149
Liu Hsiu-feng, 343
Liu Po-wu, 696
Liuchow, 219
Livestock, 9, 23, 39, 78, 108, 225, 286, 380-381, 412, 421, 433, 438, 479-481, 512, 553; *see also* Animals, draft
Living standard, 39-40, 44, 79, 91, 93-94, 194, 256-258, 262, 271, 290-291, 294-296, 380, 401, 598
Lockwood, W. W., 33
Loyang, 558
Lumber, 100-101, 517, 534, 536, 581
Luo T'ien, 441
Lushun, 704
Luta, 236

Ma Nan-fang, 512-513
Ma Wen-jui (Minister of Labor), 354, 381
Ma Wen-kuei, 606, 624, 628
Ma Yin-chu, 340-342, 538
Machinery, 19, 74, 166, 176, 530, 536-538, 574, 581, 585, 587-588, 598-599, 602-603, 605, 608, 610, 614, 618, 630, 643-644, 679, 697, 705
  imports of, 56, 72, 517, 590, 724-725
  investment in, 521, 523
MAH, FENG-HWA, on foreign trade, 29, 671-738
Malaya, trade with, 674, 689-691, 716-717, 731-732
Malnutrition, 285, 287-288, 296
Manchukuo, 3
Manchuria, 1-4, 34-36, 61-65, 67, 70-71, 74-75, 79, 89, 91, 256, 512, 549, 725
Manpower, employment, and unemployment, (Ch. 5) 329-396; *see also* Employment *and* Unemployment
Manufacturing, 1, 3-4, 36, 40, 52, 64, 67, 100, 158, 380, 521, 532; *see also* Industry
Mao Tse-tung, 235, 397, 401, 404, 497, 575
Markets, 1, 40, 70-71, 79, 101, 379, 553, 624, 629, 631
Marriage Law reforms, 291
Marx, Karl, 461, 599
Matsuda, Yoshiro, 592
Mechanization Bureau, 408-409, 412, 421-423, 436-437
Medical care, 286, 288, 293-295, 364, 391
Meiji period (Japan), 41-44
Meiji Restoration (Japan), 34, 45, 51
Mercantilism, 38-39
Merchants, 4, 40-41, 225, 230
Metals, 47, 56, 72-74, 119, 581, 602-603, 605, 607-608, 645-646, 650-651, 659-660, 664-665, 667, 705; *see also* Iron *and* Steel
Meteorology, 105, 368
Midwives, 364, 391
Migrations, 91, 185, 193, 199, 205-206, 221, 223, 261, 266-267, 280, 332, 343-344, 347, 446
Milbank Memorial Fund, 199, 243
Military; *see* Defense
Military and Political Committees, 561
Mills, Frederick C., 649
Mineral products, 33, 38, 64, 534, 536, 538, 605, 629; *see also* Coal; Iron, ore; *and* Ores
Ming period, 37
Mining, 2, 3, 6, 62, 64, 66-68, 71, 89, 101-102, 104, 156, 158-159, 171, 177, 181, 355, 386, 446, 619, 688, 697
  investment in, 521
  labor force, 80, 100, 106, 380
  share in domestic product, 532, 534-535
Ministry of Agriculture, 231, 234, 384, 418, 539, 583
Ministry of Coal Industry, 643
Ministry of Commerce, 384
Ministry of Finance, 231, 620, 623, 626, 698
Ministry of Food Industry, 564
Ministry of Foreign Trade, 231, 672, 674-675, 680-681, 724
Ministry of Forestry, 231
Ministry of Geology, 539
Ministry of Health, 277-278, 333
Ministry of Heavy Industry, 629
Ministry of Industry, 538
Ministry of Interior, 198, 208-210, 217-218, 232-234, 238, 242-243
Ministry of Internal Affairs, 226, 231
Ministry of Light Industry, 564
Ministry of Local Industry, 384, 562
Ministry of Public Security, 221
Miyashita, Tadao, 675, 678
Mizoguchi, Toshiyuki, 592
Modernization, 5, 34-36, 44-45, 49, 51-53, 504, 573

Mohammedan rebellion, 265
Morse, H. B., 47, 58
Moscow International Economic Conference, 675
Mukden, 209, 236
Murphey, Rhoads, 61
Mutual aid teams, 330, 397, 399-400, 433, 447, 495

Nan Han-chen, 731
Nanking, 59-60, 80
  Treaty of, 38, 45
National Agricultural Research Bureau, 35, 78
National income, 12, 78, 87, 89, 95-110, 119-120, 132, 148, 150-151, 155, 373, 375
National People's Congress, 402, 551, 699
National product, 7-9, 12, 38, 67, 75-76, 87, 89, 95-119, 168, 339; *see also* Gross national product
Nationalist government, 5, 34-35, 624
NCNA; see New China News Agency
Netherlands, 135-137
New China News Agency (*NCNA*), 190, 202-209, 221-222, 231, 235, 242, 287
"New product effect," 8, 9, 99, 111, 113-114, 119
Newchwang, 61
Nien wars, 249, 265
Ninghsia, 278
Niu Chung-huang, 574-575
North Korea, 716, 727
North Vietnam, 716, 727
Northeast People's Government of China, 550
Norway, 130, 135, 137, 725
Notestein, Frank, 200
Nutrition, 194, 277, 286, 287
Nutter, Warren G., 470-471

Ohkawa, K., 44
Oils, 30, 66, 77, 176, 613, 724
  export of, 55-56, 71, 73, 676, 679
Opium, 45, 718
  import of, 46-47, 55-56, 72
Opium War, 45
Ores, 71, 73, 602, 608, 645; *see also* Iron, ore; *and* Mineral products
Organization for agricultural production, (Ch. 6) 397-458; *see also* Agriculture
Ou Ming, 574
Ou Pao-san, 89, 341, 359, 387
  on consumption, 174, 178
Outer Mongolia, 716, 725, 727
Output-capital ratio; *see* Capital-output ratios
Overcentralization, 21-23, 630-631
Overpopulation, 257

Pai Chien-hua, 210, 218, 278, 333
Pakistan, 370, 725
Panajachel, 483
Pao-chia system, 185, 217, 247-255; *see also* Population
Paotow, 558
Paper, 26, 63, 72, 77, 176, 574, 581, 611, 645, 650, 659-668
Peasants, 6, 49, 71, 78, 87, 203, 224-225, 228-230, 237, 274, 288-290, 293, 341, 352, 379-381, 399, 402, 406, 409, 418-422, 433, 435, 438, 440-441, 447, 449, 465, 523, 542-543
  households, 40, 400-401, 493
  incentives, 13, 152, 286, 400, 403-404, 425-432, 434, 437, 439, 443-446, 448, 450-452, 464, 505
  income of, 23-24, 35, 40, 46, 99, 403, 426, 431, 443
  living standards, 39-40, 44, 79
  taxes, 40, 44, 48
Peddlers, 105-106, 157, 177-178, 354, 364, 390
Peking, 5, 27, 49, 189, 196, 198, 204, 208-210, 217-219, 221, 241, 286, 288, 290, 418, 432, 480, 505, 549, 551-552, 555, 561-562, 567-568, 590, 597, 599, 605, 607-608, 610, 612, 614-615, 618, 630, 673-675, 677-681, 685, 687, 693, 696, 698, 700, 704, 708, 712, 715, 720, 724
P'eng Tse-i, 68
Peng Yung-chuan, 538
People's Bank of China, 620-621, 626-627, 676-677, 695, 717, 719
People's Construction Banks, 565, 567
People's Daily (*JMJP*), 190, 202-204, 209, 218, 219, 221, 228, 229, 235-237, 240, 242, 334, 343, 348, 355, 379, 381, 387, 389, 424, 431, 435, 436, 438, 440, 446, 513, 534, 537, 538, 549-552,, 562, 563, 568, 573, 575, 583-587, 589, 590, 627, 699, 709, 714
People's Governments (regional), 561

People's Liberation Army, 198, 231, 287, 625
Perkins, Dwight H., on industry, 27-28, 597-635
Personal services, 89, 95, 103, 105, 107, 110, 116, 157, 177-178, 354, 356, 391, 532, 535
Pestilences, 256
Petroleum, 166, 556, 558-559, 581, 583-585, 600, 607, 611
Philippines, 525, 716
Pilmin, A. M., 626
Plagues, 186, 266
Po I-po, 556, 587, 589, 598, 610, 625
Poland, 525
Poleman, T. T., 149, 152
Police forces, 95, 185, 191, 198, 218-221, 223, 236-237, 279-280
  census registration work, 191, 219, 222
Policies and performance in industry, (Ch. 9) 549-595; *see also* Industry
Policy and performance in agriculture, (Ch. 7) 459-507; *see also* Agriculture
Political Consultative Conference, 231
Population, 10, 12-14, 89-93, 114, 117, 119, 157, 159, 161, 177-178, 188, 553
  adults, 185, 281, 347
  age data, 186, 189, 206-207, 223, 226, 229, 234, 242, 276, 282, 285, 306, 310, 312, 329, 334-336, 338, 344
  age-sex distribution, 189, 193, 198, 243-276, 282, 284-285, 307-309, 314, 316
  agricultural, 20, 78, 81, 178, 340-347, 375, 467
  birth (fertility) rates, 13, 90-91, 185, 192-195, 199-200, 221-222, 243, 245-246, 256-257, 259-262, 268, 270, 272, 275, 277-285, 288, 291, 293-297, 306, 310, 312, 315, 332-334, 336
  children, 185, 281-282
  class status, 224-226, 228
  control, 188, 191, 219, 222
  death (mortality) rates, 13, 82, 90, 185, 192-194, 199-200, 221-223, 245, 248-249, 252, 256-257, 259, 260-264, 266-270, 275, 277-286, 288-289, 291-297, 306, 312, 314-315, 332-334, 336-338
  divorces, 221, 280
  females, 185, 281-282, 306, 336-338
  foreign, 57, 60
  growth, 2-3, 6, 9, 37, 41, 61-62, 68, 82, 122, 144, 152, 168-169, 171, 175, (Ch. 4) 183-327, 329, 450, 531
  infant mortality, 189, 262, 270, 282, 293, 338
  job status, 226, 228-229
  males, 185, 281, 336-338, 347
  marriages, 221, 225, 260, 280, 285, 294, 336
  migration; *see* Migrations
  natural increase, 252-254, 256-260, 268, 270-271, 277-282, 284-285, 288, 293, 297, 306, 333-334, 343-344
  nonagricultural, 340-347
  nonresident, 237
  pressure on land resources, 43, 49, 78-81, 256-257
  projection models, 13-14, 193, 196-198, 245
    age-sex distribution for 1966, 307
    birth, death, natural increase rates for 1953-1965, 303
    birth, death, natural increase rates for 1966-1985, 304-305
    computer use in, 194, 246
    for 1750-1850, 255-261
    for 1851-1953, 261-276
    for 1953-1965, 195, 276-288, 298-299, 303
    for 1966-1986, 300-302, 308-309
  provincial, 199, 231-233, 248-252, 255, 281
  rural, 189, 218, 223-232, 234-236, 277-278, 280, 333, 343, 467
  sex data, 186, 189, 223, 225, 229, 234, 242, 247, 276, 282, 312, 329, 335-339, 347
  totals, 189, 193, 229, 231-232, 235, 242, 248, 253, 256, 259, 264, 312, 331-335, 344
  urban, 189, 218-224, 232-234, 237-241, 276, 278, 280, 287, 331, 343-344, 347
  vital rates, 189, 223, 253, 277-279, 282, 285-286, 293, 312, 333-334, 336, 338
  working age, 339-340
  See also Censuses
Port Arthur, 704
Price weights, 113-114, 128
Primogeniture, 40
Prisons, persons in, 347-348, 352
Private enterprise, 6, 51-52, 99; *see also* Agriculture, private enterprise; *and* Industry, private enterprise

Producer goods, 64, 99, 113-114, 120, 155, 166-167, 178, 555, 557, 597, 608, 614-615, 621-622, 624, 629, 643, 672, 712, 721
share in domestic product, 532-534
Producers' durables, 511-512, 519
Product, 11, 131, 168-169
per capita, 37-38, 44, 121-123, 128, 130, 140, 143, 145-146, 161
per worker, 121-128, 145, 147-148
total, 8, 10, 119, 121-125, 127-128, 130, 132, 143, 145-146, 156, 163, 167
See also Domestic product; Gross national product; *and* National product
"Productivity," 10, 26, 119, 143
and input, 132-137
Professional services, 354, 356, 390
Protocol, 697-698
Provinces, *see the provinces by name*: Anhwei, Chekiang, Chiang-su, Chili, Fukien, Heilungkiang, Honan, Hopei, Hunan, Hupei, Kansu, Kiangsi, Kiangsu, Kirin, Kwangsi, Kwangtung, Kweichow, Liaohsi, Liaoning, Liaotung, Shansi, Shantung, Shensi, Sinkiang, Sungkiang, Szechwan, Yünnan
Public utilities, 3-4, 57, 67, 80, 102, 105-106, 156, 171, 177
employment in, 100-101, 365-366
investment in, 524, 541, 559
share in domestic product, 532, 534-535
Public welfare services, 381, 541
Public works, 40-41, 152

Quantitative trends in the economy, (Ch. 3) 86-182
Quasi-fiefs, 49

Railroads, 2, 5, 44, 51, 58-59, 61-62, 66, 71, 79, 574
investment in, 521, 523, 528, 541
Rationing, 112, 116, 139, 279-280, 284, 515
Raw materials, 21, 30, 60, 114, 158-159, 176, 379, 518, 558, 560, 573-574, 672, 678-679, 705, 725
agricultural, 60, 104, 154-156, 158, 167, 461, 530, 555, 582, 583, 601, 615
shortages of, 1, 6, 128, 156, 685
Rebellions, 5, 186, 211, 256, 265
Red Guards, 583, 591
Reischauer, E. O., 38
Religious orders, persons in, 347-348, 352
Remer, C. F., 46, 54, 58, 677, 716
Rents, 103, 105, 116, 495, 544
incomes from, 99, 156-157, 177
reduction of, 227, 230
share in domestic product, 532, 535
Reparation indemnities, 59
Republic of China period, 122, 184-185, 268
population data, 186-187, 201, 209, 211-213, 217, 223, 226, 231, 233-235, 244, 266
Restaurants, 93, 95, 105-106, 156, 177, 354, 390
Revolutions; *see* Rebellions
Rice, 37, 42-43, 48, 79, 100, 176, 256-257, 399, 405-406, 408-413, 415, 417-418, 420-423, 426, 432, 446, 490, 498, 535, 705
Road building, 354, 361-362, 380-381, 430, 535
Rockhill, W. W., 246, 271
Rockwell, M. M., 116
Rosovsky, Henry, 34, 42, 44
Rostow, W. W., 612
Rumania, 525

Salt, 38, 40, 354, 356, 386, 517, 536, 538
Sanitation, 91, 285, 293, 334
Sanmen Gorge, 558
"Satellite plants," 574-575
Savings, 44, 132, 143, 156, 609
domestic, 510, 515
and domestic product, 160
government, 530
Schools; *see* Education
Schultz, T. W., 496
Schurmann, H. F., 607
Schwartz, Benjamin I., 39
Schwartz, Harry, 729
Scientific research, investment in, 524, 541
Second Five-Year Plan, 6, 20, 550-551, 558, 610, 678
Secretariat of National Conference, 605
Senegal, 725
Servants, domestic, 364, 391
Services, 36, 44, 98, 524, 527
"Seventy Theses," 628
Sha Ch'ien-li, 343
Sha Ying, 560
Shanghai, 36, 54, 57-58, 60-61, 209, 218-219, 221-222, 236, 557-559, 601, 605, 615

Shanghai Gas Company, 57
Shansi Province, 61, 171, 213, 215, 251, 425, 436
Shantung Province, 117, 171, 213, 237, 240, 249, 415-417, 419, 436
Shen, T. H., 35
Shensi Province, 61, 213, 215, 249, 336, 378, 415-416, 436
Shenyang, 222, 557
Shih Ching-hsing, 601
Shimonoseki, Treaty of; *see* Treaty of Shimonoseki
Shipping, 3, 57-60, 71
Shipyards, 51, 57-58
Silk, 3, 54, 68, 176, 589
  export of, 38, 46-47, 55-56, 58, 71, 73
Silver, 38, 46, 48, 54
Singapore, 674, 689-691, 717, 731-732
Sining, 222
Sinkiang Province, 229, 233, 238, 559
Sino-Japanese war, 5, 32, 58-59, 66, 75-76, 80, 89, 91, 170-171, 558, 716
"Sixty articles," 446
Skinner, G. William, on marketing, 40-41, 44
Skins, export of, 55-56, 71, 73
Snow, E., 538
Social conditions, 252, 259, 291, 295
Social institutions, 33, 95
Social overhead facilities, 57, 60, 194
Social services, 107
Soil conditions, 24, 256, 421, 521
Solow, Robert M., 484
Soochow, 60, 219, 222
Soong Ching-lin, 705
South Manchurian Railway, 511
Soviet Union; *see* USSR
Soybeans, 61-62, 71, 79, 100, 517, 535
State Council, 30, 340, 427, 551, 563, 567, 679-680
State Planning Commission, 352, 539, 549
State Statistical Bureau, 77, 90, 93-94, 98, 189-190, 196, 233-234, 243, 277-278, 284, 311, 313, 333, 341, 350, 352-353, 358-359, 400-401, 543-544, 549, 558, 571, 581, 585, 618, 643-644
Statistical system, 89-94
Steamships, 44, 51, 53
Steel, 2, 11, 26, 51, 63-64, 66, 76-77, 154-155, 166, 176, 179-181, 381, 497, 517, 534, 536, 537, 556, 558, 574, 592, 598, 605, 607-608, 610-611, 613, 622, 630, 642, 645, 661-663, 668, 724
Stocks, 627, 704
Storage facilities, 79, 112, 464-465
Students, 347-349, 352, 714-715, 722-723
Suez Canal, 54
Sung Hsin-chung, 623-624
Sung Ping, 614
Sungkiang Province, 242
Surveying, 521
Suslov, Mikhail A., 699-702
Sweden, 125, 130, 135, 259
Szechwan Province, 61, 203, 209, 212-213, 228, 232, 250-251, 265, 333, 336, 378, 413-414, 416-417, 435, 437

Ta-Ching, 584
Taeuber, Irene B., on 1953 census, 13, 199-202, 204, 207-208, 210-217, 238, 246-253, 255
Taiping rebellion, 5, 12, 43, 45, 249, 264-265
  economic consequences, 48-50
Taiwan, 200, 211, 213, 231, 269-270, 290, 334, 483, 487, 494, 525, 534, 725,
Tan Chen-lin, 340-343, 381
TANG, ANTHONY M., on agriculture, 19-21, 459-507
T'ao Chu, 419-420, 422, 427, 447
Tariff autonomy, 4-5, 65, 672
Tawney, R. H., 40
Taxes, 5, 41, 99, 101, 105, 107-108, 185, 263, 348
  agricultural, 230, 330, 340-341, 402, 495
  commercial, 38
  indirect, 8, 60, 95, 103, 514
  industrial, 606, 617, 619, 622
  land, 38, 48-49
  likin, 48
  peasants', 40, 44, 48
  provincial, 255
  sales, 48, 620, 622
Tea, 3, 38, 40, 54, 68, 426
  export of, 45-47, 55-56, 58, 71, 73, 705
Ten Great Years, 372, 375, 400, 418-419, 435, 477, 488, 523-524, 535-536, 538, 540, 542-544, 561, 571, 610, 614, 627, 654, 660
Tenancy, 40, 49, 60, 78, 494-495
Teng, S. Y., 50
Teng Chieh, 386
Teng Hsiao-p'ing, 203
Teng Tzu-hui, 234, 399
Textiles, 3-4, 21, 38, 46, 51, 58, 64, 66, 70-71, 74-76, 167, 473, 557, 564, 574, 581, 584, 589, 601,

Textiles (*cont'd*)
645, 650-651, 659, 664-667; *see also* Cotton *and* Silk
Thailand, 525, 716
Third Five-Year Plan, 552, 590-591
Thompson, W. S., 260, 281-283, 338
"Three-anti" campaign, 220
Tibet, 231-232, 559, 725
T'ien Feng't'ao, 335
Tientsin, 218, 236-237, 557-558
Tihwa; *see* Urumchi
Timber; *see* Lumber
Trade, 1, 30-31, 35, 38, 41, 44-45, 61, 67, 88-89, 92, 94-95, 99, 102, 105-106, 115-116, 171, 389-391, 463, 602-603
investment in, 541
private enterprise in, 6, 93, 358
share in domestic product, 532, 535
share in national product, 76
See also Foreign trade
Trading stores, 105-106, 156, 177, 354
Transport, 35, 44, 51, 60, 67, 72, 79, 82, 89, 92-95, 99, 102, 104-106, 111, 115-116, 156-157, 177-178, 354, 356, 381, 388-389, 436, 515, 527, 558, 560, 571, 602-603
barriers, 1, 4, 36, 49, 61, 70
investment in, 521, 523-525, 541, 543, 559
share in domestic product, 532, 535
share in national product, 76
Treaty of Nanking, 38, 45
Treaty of Shimonoseki, 3, 51, 59, 69
Treaty ports, 1, 3-5, 34-36, 45, 51, 54, 57-61, 66, 557
Trinidad, 370
Tsai Hsuan, 732
Tsaidam Basin, 559
Tsao Yen-hsing, 560-561
Tseng Kuo-fan, 50, 52
Tseng Wen-ching, 552-553, 558-559
Tsinan, 236, 240
Tsing-hai Lake, 557
Tsingtao, 557
Tsitsihar, 558
T'ung-chih Restoration, 49-50
Turkey, 122
"Twelve rules," 446

Ullman, Morris B., 343
Unemployment, 14, 115-116, 167, 329, 339, 352, 362, 376-379, 382
in agriculture, 15, 380
nonagricultural, 350, 370-375, 446
Union of South Africa, 130
United Kingdom; *see* Great Britain
Wang Ming-hsien, 386
United Nations, Department of Economic and Social Affairs, 281
life-tables, 268-270, 282, 313-316, 336, 534
population branch, 198, 283-284, 330, 333-335
United States, 78, 130, 135, 137, 348, 483, 494, 716
Bureau of Mines, 180
Consul General (Hong Kong), 149, 152, 154, 179
Department of Agriculture, 154
Department of Commerce. 98, 684-685
Senate, 718
State Department, 712
trade with, 54-55
Urban facilities, 57, 60
Urbanization, 62, 515
Urumchi, 219, 221
USSR, 27, 74-75, 87, 95, 120-126, 128, 130, 132, 135-137, 139-140, 143, 525
agriculture in, 368, 399, 460, 462-463, 465-480, 487, 495-496
Chinese students in, 714-715, 722-723
five-year plans, 2, 599, 613
Gosplan, 468
industry, 559, 563, 600-603, 607-609, 617-618, 621-622, 624-626, 630, 638-639, 657
investment, 515-516, 520, 523
loans to China, 7, 31, 685, 687, 694-712, 721-724, 728-731
relations with, 28, 31, 551, 553-554, 590, 598, 673, 689, 698, 702
technical aid to China, 7, 26, 31-32, 286, 382-383, 531, 550-554, 570, 578, 582, 585-586, 610, 612, 628, 687, 698, 705, 714-715, 722-723, 729
See also Foreign trade, with USSR
Voter registration, 199, 240, 268; *see also* Elections

Wages, 95, 99, 101, 105, 109-110, 352, 515; *see also* Industry, wages
WALKER, KENNETH, on agriculture, 19-22, 397-458
Wang, Nai-chi, on 1953 census, 13, 199-202, 204, 207-208, 210-217, 238, 247-253, 255
Wang Chen-tsu, 574
Wang Chi-ming, 542-543
Wang Ch'ing-shu, 401
Wang Keng-chin, 384

Wang Shou-tao, 387-389
War mortalities, 264-265, 267, 275, 276, 285
Warlordism, 3, 5, 59-60
Water conservation, 49, 105, 361, 368, 381, 388, 419, 424, 427, 440-441, 493, 529
  investment in, 523, 541-542
Waterways, 44, 60-61, 79
Wellisz, S., 478
Wen Liang, 676-678
West Germany, 10, 122-123, 130, 133, 135-137, 140, 143-144
  trade with, 689-690
Wheat, 42-43, 56, 79, 100, 176, 405-406, 419-420, 422, 435, 490, 498, 535, 558, 605
Willcox, W. F., 246
Wool, 40, 46-47, 56, 73, 176, 705
Work brigades, 103, 106-107, 116, 157, 177-178, 360-361, 403, 418, 425, 427, 430-431, 434, 443, 445, 447, 493, 512, 532, 535
World War I, 65, 69, 71
World War II, 2, 9, 64, 66, 79, 120, 469, 526, 715-716
Wright, Mary C., 48-49
Wu, Yuan-li, 120, 715
  on agriculture, 153
  on domestic product, 150
  on food crops, 118, 154
  on growth rate, 121, 149
  on handicrafts, 118
  on industry, 119, 154-155
  on national product, 96-97, 116-119
Wu Chen (Minister of Agriculture), 583
Wu Hsia, 574
Wuhan, 209, 219, 558

Yang, L. S., 38
Yang Chien-pei, 672
Yang Ching-wen, 573
Yang Ying-chieh, 705
Yangtze River, 49, 60, 79, 265, 414-415
Yao Shu-shih, 550
YEH, K. C.; *see also* Liu, T. C., and Yeh, K. C.
  on agricultural output, 8
  on capital formation and investment, 16-17, 89, 508-547
  on domestic product, 18-19
  on growth rate, 6
  on national product, 89
Yeh Chi-chuang, 672, 674, 678-681
Yeh Fei, 419
Yeh Hsiao-li, 601
Yellow River, 265, 414-415
Yen Chung-p'ing, 66-67, 77
Yen Ling, 430
Yuan Hsing-nan, 386-387
Yueh Wei, 341-342
Yugoslavia, 725
Yünnan Province, 213, 232-233, 251, 337-338, 413, 416